For Lorand,

With my best wishes

Morten,

Free Movement in the European Union

Morten Broberg & Nina Holst-Christensen

Free Movement in the European Union

DJØF Publishing Copenhagen
2016

Morten Broberg & Nina Holst-Christensen
Free Movement in the European Union

5th edition

Cover: Bo Helsted
Print and binding: Toptryk Grafisk, Gråsten

Printed in Denmark 2016
978-87-574-3435-4

Sold and distributed in Scandinavia by:
DJØF Publishing
Copenhagen, Denmark
Email: forlag@djoef.dk
www.djoef-forlag.dk

Sold and distributed in North America by:
International Specialized Book Services (ISBS)
Portland, USA
Email: orders@isbs.com
www.isbs.com

Sold in all other countries by:
The Oxford Publicity Partnership Ltd
Towcester, UK
Email: djof@oppuk.co.uk
www.oppuk.co.uk

Distributed in all other countries by:
Marston Book Services
Abingdon, Oxon, UK
Email: trade.orders@marston.co.uk
www.marston.co.uk

Preface

Since the 4th edition of *Free Movement in the European Union – Cases, Commentaries and Questions* was published in 2014, the Court of Justice of the European Union (CJEU) has given a number of significant new judgments, contributing to the development of Union law. It is therefore now necessary to update the book with this 5th edition. As with updating in connection with previous new editions, we have not merely given commentaries and questions relating to the cases newly included, we have also sought to improve and update a number of the comments and questions that were included in earlier editions. In the text of the commentary and questions which accompany each case report we primarily use the article numbers of the Treaty provisions that have been in use since the Lisbon Treaty entered into force on 1 December 2009. In some of comments and questions we aim to help the reader by giving both the article numbers of the Treaty provisions used in the original judgment and the article numbers that apply today. We are aware that, even with this help, it can be difficult for readers to form a clear picture of what provisions apply. Therefore, for those provisions that are most relevant to this book, we have also compiled a table showing the equivalent article numbers of provisions in the successive versions of the Treaty. This Table of Equivalences is printed at the end of the section titled 'Reading EU case reports'.

In addition to the general updating of the commentaries and questions, we have included 10 new cases. Since the book is primarily aimed at students studying 'Advanced EU law', we have also attempted to restrict the number of cases to a level that is appropriate for such a course. We have therefore deleted six cases that were included in the 4th edition. Altogether, the book now contains 108 cases. Nearly all the new cases relate to the rights of individuals, i.e. Union citizenship and the free movement of workers. This reflects the fact that it is in these areas in particular that Union law has been developing in recent years.

In order to add to the value of the book as a learning tool we have included a short introduction on how to read CJEU judgments. CJEU case reports differ from the case reports of the national courts of the Member States on a number of important points, so we think it appropriate to point out, briefly and clearly, the differences about which there is a particular need to be aware. This introduction to how to read CJEU case reports is placed before the first case report.

Steven Harris has once again carried out the delicate task of translation. The indices have been meticulously prepared by research assistant Venla Manninen. Moreover we have received continuing support for the project from the staff of DJØF Publishing. We are most grateful for their help and support.

We very much hope that the reader will find this work both stimulating and profitable. As with prior editions, a suggestions for improvement will be very welcome.

Morten Broberg and Nina Holst-Christensen
~~Oxford~~ Cambridge and Copenhagen, June 2016

Table of contents

CHAPTER 5. Freedom of Establishment

CHAPTER 6. Free Movement of Services

Reading EU case reports

The writing of a judgment by an international court naturally does not follow the same procedure as the writing of a judgment of a national court of one of the Member States. In order to understand the wider significance of a case report from the Court of Justice of the European Union (CJEU) one must be aware of the following factors in particular:

1. Under Article 251 of the Treaty on the Functioning of the European Union (TFEU), the CJEU sits either in chambers or in a Grand Chamber. According to Article 16 of the Statute of the Court of Justice of the European Union, the CJEU forms chambers consisting of three and five judges, and a Grand Chamber consisting of 15 judges. The CJEU sits as a Grand Chamber either when a Member State or an EU institution is a party to the proceedings and so requests, or if the CJEU itself finds it appropriate, given the nature of the case. The CJEU can also sit as a Full Court, consisting of all 28 judges. This happens if proceedings concern the removal of a member of a European institution (for example, the dismissal of a Commissioner), or if the CJEU decides that a case is of special importance; see e.g. the judgment of 27 November 2012 in Case C-370/12 *Thomas Pringle*, where judgment was given by the Full Court. The case concerned whether the Treaty on European Union (TEU) and the Treaty on the Functioning of the European Union (TFEU) prevented EU Member States whose currency is the euro entering into a Treaty establishing the European Stability Mechanism (ESM Treaty) between Member States outside the EU framework. The ESM Treaty came into being in the light of the financial crisis that started in 2008, and its purpose was to mobilise funding and to provide financial stability support to ESM Members who were experiencing, or were threatened by, severe financing problems. The CJEU ruled that neither the TEU nor the TFEU precludes Member States whose currency is the euro entering into an agreement such as the ESM Treaty.

Judgment given by the CJEU's Grand Chamber or Full Court has greater precedent value (i.e. it has more widespread influence) than a judgment given by a chamber consisting of three or five judges. Thus, when you read one of the case reports printed below you should always note what is written in the first line. If it says 'Judgment of the Court (Full Court)' or 'Judgment of the Court (Grand Chamber)' you will be dealing with an important judgment that can be ascribed decisive importance in similar cases in future. On the other hand, if it says 'Judgment of the Court (X Chamber)', and if the judgment lays down a new and totally different statement of the law than that which has applied hitherto, you should be aware that the judgment does not necessarily express what the majority of the judges would have decided. In other words, even if the judgment expresses what must for the time being be considered the applicable Union law, since the CJEU has stated it in its judgment, the precedent value of the judgment will be more limited.

2. An English language version of a CJEU judgment is a translation from the French. The CJEU's working language is French. Judgments are therefore always drafted in this language and the judges vote on the French draft. This is so even if the language of the written and oral proceedings of the case may have been English, for example. Formally, it is the report of the proceedings (or reports – plural – if the case uses more than one procedural language) that is binding. However, in practice it is sensible to consult the French language version if there are differences between different language versions, or if the language version you are reading is surprising or perhaps does not make sense. When comparing the texts it will sometimes be apparent that the translated version of the judgment is at fault. An example of this is Case 48/75 *Royer* [1976] ECR 497, where the word 'save' was dropped from para. 59 of the English version. The English version was therefore worded: 'Under Article 9 of the procedure of appeal to a competent authority must precede the decision ordering expulsion in cases of emergergency' whilst it should have read '... the procedure of appeal to a competent authority must precede the decision ordering expulsion *save* in cases of emergergency'. By reading the French version of the judgment on this point (which read '..., sauf cas d'urgence, ...'), it is possible to put things back on the right track as it becomes clear that there is simply a mistake in the English translation.

3. The CJEU's style of interpretation is very different from that of an English court. There is nothing surprising in this, as we are dealing with an international court composed of judges from widely differing legal systems in the EU, and where each legal act (treaty, directive, regulation etc.) often exists in 24 official languages, all of which are given equal weight, and where divergences between the different language versions can easily arise. When the CJEU has to interpret a provision in an EU legal act, in addition to having regard to the usual methods of interpretation according to the wording, purpose and context of the act, it will often look at what effect an interpretation of the provision will have (the *effet utile*, in French). This results in judgments which would have been difficult or even impossible to reach according to the normal methods of interpretation of English law. In this connection, one must also be aware that while the *travaux préparatoires* also play a role in Union law, this role is often different from the role which *travaux préparatoires* play in the legal systems of the individual Member States.

4. Another characteristic of the CJEU's judgments is that they never include dissenting opinions. In contrast to the English Supreme Court or the European Court of Human Rights, it is not possible for a judge of the CJEU to give a dissenting view as part of the judgment. This means that, to the outside world, all the judges who have taken part in the proceedings appear to support both the arguments and the conclusions of the judgment. If, for example, a judge agrees with the result supported by a majority of the court, but for different reasons, they may seek to have included in the judgment one or

more of the arguments that support their view. But in this case there will be a risk that the inclusion of such reasoning will mean that, as a whole, the judgment will seem to, simultaneously, point in different directions. It is possible that Case C-341/05 *Laval* [2007] ECR I-11767 (discussed in Chapter 6) is a good example of this. However, we cannot be certain as there is no public access to the CJEU's voting records and the judges have a duty of confidentiality about what happens during voting. For the same reasons, the absence of the possibility of giving a dissenting judgment can mean that the arguments supporting a ruling can be very short, almost merely assertions. A good example of this is Case C-34/09 *Zambrano* [2011] ECR I-0000 (discussed in Chapter 3).

Table of Equivalences – selected provisions

EEC Treaty 1958	EC Treaty 1992	EC Treaty 1999	TFEU 2009
5	5	10	4(3) TEU
7	6	12	18
-	8	17	20
-	8a	18	21
30	30	28	34
34	34	29	35
36	36	30	36
48	48	39	45
52	52	43	49
59	59	49	56
67-73	73b-73g	56-60	63-66

CHAPTER 1

Implementation of EU rules

JUDGMENT OF THE COURT (Second Chamber)
4 October 2012

European Commission v Republic of Austria (Action for failure to fulfil obligations under Article 258 TFEU)

'Failure of a Member State to fulfil obligations – Citizenship of the Union – Right to move and reside freely – Articles 20 TFEU and 21 TFEU – Discrimination on grounds of nationality – Article 18 TFEU – Directive 2004/38/EC – Article 24 – Derogation – Scope – Member State in which reduced fares on public transport are granted only to students whose parents are in receipt of family allowances in that Member State'

Case C-75/11

Judgment

1. By its application, the European Commission asks the Court to declare that, by granting reduced fares on public transport in principle only to students whose parents are in receipt of Austrian family allowances, the Republic of Austria has failed to fulfil its obligations under the combined provisions of Articles 18 TFEU, 20 TFEU and 21 TFEU, and also Article 24 of Directive 2004/38/EC of the European Parliament and of the Council of 29 April 2004 on the right of citizens of the Union and their family members to move and reside freely within the territory of the Member States, amending Regulation (EEC) No 1612/68 and repealing Directives 64/221/EEC, 68/360/EEC, 72/194/EEC, 73/148/EEC, 75/34/EEC, 75/35/EEC, 90/364/EEC, 90/365/EEC and 93/96/EEC (OJ 2004 L 158, p. 77, and corrigendum OJ 2004 L 229, p. 35).

Legal context

European Union law

Regulation (EEC) No 1408/71

2. Article 1(u)(i) of Regulation (EEC) No 1408/71 of the Council of 14 June 1971 on the application of social security schemes to employed persons and their families moving within the Community, as amended and updated by Council Regulation (EC) No 118/97 of 2 December 1996 (OJ 1997 L 28, p. 1), as amended by Regulation (EC) No 592/2008 of the European Parliament and the Council of 17 June 1998 (OJ 2008 L 177, p. 1) ('Regulation No 1408/71') defines 'family benefits' as 'all benefits in kind or in cash intended to meet family expenses under the legislation provided for in Article 4(1)(h) [thereof]'.

3. Article 4(1)(h) of Regulation No 1408/71 provides that that regulation is to apply to all legislation concerning those branches of social security relating to family benefits.

4. The first sentence of Article 13(1) of Regulation No 1408/71 provides that, subject to Articles 14c and 14f, persons to whom that regulation applies are to be subject to the legislation of a single Member State only.

Directive 2004/38

5. Recitals 1 and 10 in the preamble to Directive 2004/38 state as follows:

   '(1) Citizenship of the Union confers on every citizen of the Union a primary and individual right to move and reside freely within the territory of the Member States, subject to the limitations and conditions laid down in the [EC] Treaty and to the measures adopted to give it effect.

   ...

   (10) Persons exercising their right of residence should not, however, become an unreasonable burden on the social assistance system of the host Member State during an initial period of residence. Therefore, the right of residence for Union citizens and their family members for periods in excess of three months should be subject to conditions.'

6. Article 3(1) of Directive 2004/38 provides that that directive is to apply to all Union citizens who move to or reside in a Member State other than that of which they are a national, and to their family members.

7. Article 7(1) of the same directive is worded as follows:

   '1. All Union citizens shall have the right of residence on the territory of another Member State for a period of longer than three months if they:

   ...

   (c) – are enrolled at a private or public establishment, accredited or financed by the host Member State on the basis of its legislation or administrative practice, for the principal purpose of following a course of study, including vocational training; and

   – have comprehensive sickness insurance cover in the host Member State and assure the relevant national authority, by means of a declaration or by such equivalent means as they may choose, that they have sufficient resources for themselves and their family members not to become a burden on the social assistance system of the host Member State during their period of residence; ...'

8. Article 24 of Directive 2004/38, entitled 'equal treatment', reads as follows:

   '1. Subject to such specific provisions as are expressly provided for in the Treaty and secondary law, all Union citizens residing on the basis of this Directive in the territory of the host Member State shall enjoy equal treatment with the nationals of that Member State within the scope of the Treaty. The benefit of this right shall be extended to family members who are not nationals of a Member State and who have the right of residence or permanent residence.

   2. By way of derogation from paragraph 1, the host Member State shall not be obliged to confer entitlement to social assistance during the first three months of residence or, where appropriate, the longer period provided for in Article 14(4)(b), nor shall it be obliged, prior to acquisition of the right of permanent residence, to grant maintenance aid for studies, including vocational training, consisting in student grants or student loans to persons other than workers, self-employed persons, persons who retain such status and members of their families.'

Austrian law

9. There are no federal rules in Austria governing reduced transport fares for students.

10. According to the information provided to the Court, term transport passes at a reduced rate are granted to students on the basis of financing agreements concluded by the Bundesministerium für Verkehr, Innovation und Technologie (Federal Ministry of Transport, Innovation and Technology), the regional municipalities and the relevant transport undertakings. Those agreements not only govern fares, the scope of the reduction and the financial contribution of the federal government, but also establish the categories of beneficiary of the scheme.

11. It is also apparent from the case-file that, in certain Länder, students, as defined in Paragraphs 3 and 4 of the 1992 Law on financial assistance for studies (Studienförderungsgesetz 1992, BGBl. No 305/1992), in the version in force on the date of the dispute ('the 1992 Law'), may be granted the reduced fares only if their registered address or place of study is situated within the area covered by the public transport company in question and if family allowances were received under Paragraph 2 of the 1967 Family Allowance Act (Familienlastenausgleichsgesetz 1967, BGBl. No 376/1967), in the version thereof in force on the date of the dispute ('the FLAG').

12. In other Länder, where the application of the reduced fares is not contingent on the receipt of family allowances, the criteria taken into account, apart from the status of student, are the age and/or residence of the persons concerned.

13. Under Paragraph 2 of the FLAG persons having their registered address or habitual residence in the federal territory are entitled to family allowances for minor chil-

dren and for adult children under the age of 26 who are following vocational training or further training in a specialised educational establishment in relation to the trade they have learned, provided that that training prevents them from working in their trade. As a rule it is the person whose household includes the child who is entitled to family allowances.

14. Paragraph 4 of the 1992 Law provides that the Contracting Parties to the Agreement on the European Economic Area of 2 May 1992 (OJ 1994, L 1, p. 3) or the EC Treaty and nationals of non-member countries are to be equated with Austrian nationals 'in so far as they are so equated as a result of the aforementioned agreements'.

15. Paragraph 52 of the 1992 Law defines transport fare grants as coming under 'other measures for promoting studies'. The objective of the grants is to support the recipients of education allowances by assuming their transport costs. The grants are available only to recipients of education allowances in Austria and differ from reduced transport fares.

Pre-litigation procedure

[Paras 16-35 omitted]

Findings of the Court

36. It should be observed as a preliminary point that Article 20(1) TFEU confers on any person holding the nationality of a Member State the status of citizen of the Union.37. Students from Member States other than the Republic of Austria who follow a course of study in Austria have that status, provided that they hold the nationality of a Member State.

38. As the Court has held on numerous occasions, the status of citizen of the Union is destined to be the fundamental status of nationals of the Member States, enabling those among such nationals who find themselves in the same situation to receive, as regards the material scope of the FEU Treaty, the same treatment in law irrespective of their nationality, subject to such exceptions as are provided for in that regard (see, to that effect, Case C-184/99 *Grzelczyk* [2001] ECR I-6193, paragraph 31, and Case C-224/98 *D'Hoop* [2002] ECR I-6191, paragraph 28).

39. Every citizen of the Union may therefore rely on Article 18 TFEU, which prohibits any discrimination on grounds of nationality, in all situations falling within the scope *ratione materiae* of European Union law, and those situations include the exercise of the freedom conferred by Article 21 TFEU to move and reside within the territory of the Member States (see Case C-85/96 *Martínez Sala* [1998] ECR I-2691, paragraph 63; Case C-209/03 *Bidar* [2005] ECR I-2119, paragraphs 32 and

33; and Case C-158/07 *Förster* [2008] ECR I-8507, paragraphs 36 and 37; and Case C-73/08 *Bressol and Others* [2010] ECR I-2735, paragraph 31).

40. In addition, it is apparent from that case-law that that prohibition also covers situations concerning the conditions of access to vocational training, and that both higher education and university education constitute vocational training (*Bressol and Others*, paragraph 32).

41. It follows that a national of a Member State who is studying in Austria may rely on the right, enshrined in Articles 18 TFEU and 21 TFEU, to move and reside freely within the territory of the host Member State, without being subject to direct or indirect discrimination on grounds of their nationality (*Bressol and Others*, paragraph 33).

42. Regarding the issue whether reduced transport fares such as those granted by certain Länder in Austria come within the scope of the Treaties for the purposes of Article 18(1) TFEU, it should be observed that, in holding that access to training comes within the scope of European Union law, the Court has held previously that national aid granted to students to cover their maintenance costs, social benefits provided for by a national, non-contributory scheme and so-called tideover allowances provided for by national legislation intended for unemployed youth seeking their first employment all come within the scope thereof (see *Bidar*, paragraph 42; *Grzelczyk*, paragraph 46, and *D'Hoop*, paragraphs 34 and 35).

43. It follows that a scheme providing for reduced transport fares for students comes within the scope of the FEU Treaty in so far as it enables them, directly or indirectly, to cover their maintenance costs.

44. As to the Republic of Austria's argument to the effect that the reduced transport fares should be considered a family benefit for the purposes of Regulation No 1408/71, it should be observed that, even if the conflict rules laid down in that regulation do apply to citizens of the Union pursuing their studies in a Member State other than their Member State of origin and whose parents have no link with the host Member State, categorising the reduced fares in this manner still does not justify unequal treatment on grounds of nationality in respect of those citizens.

45. It should be borne in mind, first of all, that certain benefits coming within the specific scope of Regulation No 1408/71 have been held by the Court also to constitute social benefits or advantages subject to the principle of equal treatment on grounds of nationality under other provisions of European Union law relating to the free movement of persons (see, to that effect, *Martínez Sala*, paragraph 27).

46. Second, it must be pointed out that Regulation No 1408/71 does not set up a common scheme of social security, but allows different national social security schemes

to exist. Its sole objective is to ensure the coordination of those schemes (Case C-503/09 *Stewart* [2011] ECR I-0000, paragraph 75 and the case-law cited).

47. Although Member States retain the power to organise their social security schemes, with the result that, in the absence of harmonisation at European Union level, it is for them to determine the conditions concerning the right or duty to be insured with a social security scheme as well as the conditions for entitlement to benefits, in exercising those powers, they must none the less comply with the law of the European Union and, in particular, with the provisions of the FEU Treaty giving every citizen of the Union the right to move and reside within the territory of the Member States (*Stewart*, paragraphs 75 to 77 and the case-law cited).

48. The Republic of Austria's argument relating to the categorisation of reduced transport fares as a family benefit for the purposes of Regulation No 1408/71 does not, therefore, rule out the existence, alleged by the Commission, of discrimination on grounds of nationality against students from other Member States pursuing their studies in Austria.

49. It should be recalled in that regard that the principle of non-discrimination on grounds of nationality, enshrined as a general principle in Article 18 TFEU and laid down specifically in respect of Union citizens coming within the scope of Directive 2004/38 in Article 24 thereof, prohibits not only direct discrimination on grounds of nationality but also all indirect forms of discrimination which, by the application of other criteria of differentiation, lead in fact to the same result (see *Bressol and Others*, paragraph 40).

50. In the present case, making the reduced transport fares subject to the grant of Austrian family allowances, as provided for by certain Länder, gives rise to unequal treatment as between Austrian students pursuing their studies in Austria and students from other Member States pursuing their studies there as well, since such a condition is more easily fulfilled by Austrian students because their parents as a rule receive those allowances.

51. Such inequality of treatment is contrary to the principles which underpin the status of citizen of the Union, referred to in paragraph 38 of this judgment, that is, the guarantee of the same treatment in law in the exercise of the citizen's freedom of movement (*D'Hoop*, paragraph 35).

52. According to settled case-law, indirect discrimination on grounds of nationality can be justified only if it is based on objective considerations independent of the nationality of the persons concerned and is proportionate to the legitimate objective of the national provisions (see *D'Hoop*, paragraph 36; Case C-147/03 *Commission* v *Austria* [2005] ECR I-5969, paragraph 48; and *Bressol and Others*, paragraph 41).

53. In the present case, before even considering whether there is such an objective justification, it is appropriate, in the first place, to examine the Republic of Austria's argument to the effect that reduced transport fares for students come within the scope of the derogation from the principle of equal treatment provided for in Article 24(2) of Directive 2004/38.

54. Since Article 24(2) is a derogation from the principle of equal treatment provided for in Article 18 TFEU, of which Article 24(1) of Directive 2004/38 is merely a specific expression, it must be interpreted narrowly.

55. Although, as evidenced by paragraph 43 of the present judgment, the reduced transport fares granted to the students concerned constitute maintenance aid for them, only maintenance aid for studies 'consisting in student grants or student loans' come within the derogation from the principle of equal treatment provided for in Article 24(2) of Directive 2004/38.

56. Any other interpretation of that provision would run counter to not only its wording but also to the Court's obligation to interpret that derogation in accordance with the provisions of the Treaty, including those relating to Union citizenship (see, to that effect, Joined Cases C-22/08 and C-23/08 *Vatsouras and Koupatantze* [2009] ECR I-4585, paragraph 44).

57. In the second place, regarding the question whether there are objective considerations which might justify the unequal treatment established, as evidenced by paragraph 35 of this judgment, the Republic of Austria argues that the reduced transport fares contribute towards the financing of studies and must therefore not be considered in isolation from other measures which the Member State of origin is required to take in the area of education aid. Some Member States offer education grants which are considerably more generous than those offered in Austria, with the result that students from other Member States can more easily meet the costs of living, including transport costs, than Austrian students. If other Member States have a less generous grants scheme for students than the one in place in Austria, it is not for the host Member State to assist students from those States.

58. It should be noted in that regard that, as observed by the Advocate General in point 62 of her Opinion and according to the information provided to the Court, although the reduced transport fares are no longer granted once the student himself has income over a certain threshold, the granting of the reduced fares does not, as a rule, presuppose insufficient resources. Similarly, if the objective pursued by the Republic of Austria is to prevent a student from another Member State from receiving two sets of financial aid, there is nothing in the information provided by the Austrian Government indicating that, when the reduced fares are granted to students whose parents receive Austrian family allowances, the competent Austrian authorities take into account any benefits received by those students in another Member State.

59. In so far as the Republic of Austria's argument is intended to question whether there is an obligation on a host Member State to finance students who are not integrated there, it should be borne in mind that the Court has held previously, in respect of the provisions relating to Union citizenship, that it is legitimate for a host Member State to wish to ensure that there is a genuine link between a claimant to a benefit and the competent Member State (see, to that effect, *D'Hoop*, paragraph 38; Case C-138/02 *Collins* [2004] ECR I-2703, paragraph 67; *Bidar*, paragraph 57; and *Vatsouras and Koupatantze*, paragraph 38).

60. Although EU law relating to the free movement of persons and, in particular, students, allows for a certain degree of financial solidarity as amongst nationals of the host Member State and nationals of other Member States (see, to that effect, *Grzelczyk*, paragraph 44), as stated in recital 10 in the preamble to Directive 2004/38, persons exercising their right of residence, including students, should not become an unreasonable burden on the social assistance system of the host Member State during an initial period of residence. Therefore, under Article 21 TFEU and the provisions of Directive 2004/38, the right of residence for Union citizens and their family members for periods in excess of three months is subject to conditions.

61. Accordingly a national scheme requiring a student to provide proof of a genuine link with the host Member State could, in principle, reflect a legitimate objective capable of justifying restrictions on the right to move and reside freely in the territory of the Member States provided for in Article 21 TFEU.

62. It should be observed, however, first, that the proof required to demonstrate the genuine link must not be too exclusive in nature or unduly favour an element which is not necessarily representative of the real and effective degree of connection between the claimant to reduced transport fares and the Member State where the claimant pursues his studies, to the exclusion of all other representative elements (see, to that effect, *D'Hoop*, paragraph 39, and *Stewart*, paragraph 95).

63. Second, as the Advocate General has noted in point 76 of her Opinion, the genuine link required between the student claiming a benefit and the host Member State need not be fixed in a uniform manner for all benefits, but should be established according to the constitutive elements of the benefit in question, including its nature and purpose or purposes. The objective of the benefit must be analysed according to its results and not according to its formal structure (see, to that effect, *Vatsouras and Koupatantze*, paragraphs 41 and 42).

64. As regards reduced transport fares for students, the existence of a genuine link between the student pursuing his studies in the host Member State could actually be ascertained for the purposes of the reduced transport fares, inter alia, by checking whether the person in question is enrolled at a private or public establishment, ac-

credited or financed by the host Member State on the basis of its legislation or administrative practice, for the principal purpose of following a course of study, including vocational training, in accordance with the first indent of Article 7(1)(c) of Directive 2004/38.

65. The conclusion must therefore be that the Republic of Austria has not established that the Austrian scheme of reduced transport fares for students applicable in certain Länder is objectively justified.

66. In the light of all the foregoing considerations, the Court finds that, by granting reduced fares on public transport in principle only to students whose parents are in receipt of Austrian family allowances, the Republic of Austria has failed to fulfil its obligations under the combined provisions of Articles 18 TFEU, 20 TFEU and 21 TFEU and also Article 24 of Directive 2004/38.

Costs

[Para. 67 omitted]

On those grounds,

THE COURT (Second Chamber),

hereby rules:

1) **Declares that, by granting reduced fares on public transport in principle only to students whose parents are in receipt of Austrian family allowances, the Republic of Austria has failed to fulfil its obligations under the combined provisions of Articles 18 TFEU, 20 TFEU and 21 TFEU and also Article 24 of Directive 2004/38/EC of the European Parliament and of the Council of 29 April 2004 on the right of citizens of the Union and their family members to move and reside freely within the territory of the Member States, amending Regulation (EEC) No 1612/68 and repealing Directives 64/221/EEC, 68/360/EEC, 72/194/EEC, 73/148/EEC, 75/34/EEC, 75/35/EEC, 90/364/EEC, 90/365/EEC and 93/96/EEC.**

[Para. 2 of the ruling omitted]

Comments and questions

In paragraphs 38-39 and 49-53 of its judgment on reduced transport fares for students, the CJEU gives a short overview of the prohibition of discrimination in Article 18 TFEU. The core of the Union law rules on free movement of goods, persons, services and capital is the prohibition of different treatment on the grounds of origin. For this reason, words like 'hindrance', 'discrimination' and 'restriction' occur frequently in this book. However, they often give rise to confusion, and it is thus appropriate to define them here.

Article 18 TFEU contains a general prohibition of any discrimination on grounds of nationality. Put another way, Article 18 is a special expression of the general principle of equal treatment; see paragraph 14 of Case C-224/00 *Commission* v *Italy* [2002] ECR I-2965. The TFEU also contains a number of special prohibitions. For example, Article 110 prohibits the imposition of internal taxation on goods from other Member States that is higher than internal taxation imposed on equivalent goods of the home Member State. The provisions that ensure the freedom of movement of goods (Article 34 TFEU), the provision of services (Article 56 TFEU), workers (Article 45 TFEU), the right of establishment (Article 49 TFEU) and the free movement of capital (Article 63 TFEU) are of special significance. In accordance with the principle of *lex specialis*, the prohibition of discrimination in Article 18 TFEU does not generally apply where one of these special prohibitions apply. However, the CJEU is not always consistent on this point. See, for example, Case C-147/03 *Commission* v *Austria*, on equal rights to further education in Austria. The CJEU ruled on the Austrian arrangement pursuant to Article 18 TFEU, and not pursuant to Article 56 TFEU. The report of this case is given immediately below.

From the start it has been clear that the special prohibitions covered 'legal discrimination', or as the CJEU often calls it, 'direct discrimination' in which national law or practice favours nationals of the home Member State. This is stated in Articles 45 and 49 TFEU. In other words, this covers situations in which discrimination is expressly based on where goods originate or on a worker's nationality. However, a Member State can introduce rules that do not formally discriminate on the grounds of nationality, but which are nevertheless particularly burdensome for foreign goods or foreign workers. For example, this will be the case if a Member State requires products to comply with a particular standard which only the undertakings in that Member State can fulfil. This will also apply if the sale of a product in Member State X is conditional on obtaining approval on the basis of some specific examination. Producers from Member State X will only be required to submit to an examination by Member State X, while foreign suppliers will often already have been through the approval procedures of their own home Member State so that submitting also to an examination by Member State X will impose an additional burden on them. The same will be the case if there is a requirement for a service provider to be resident in a Member State in order to provide a service there. Such rules are not 'directly discriminatory', but since they have the same effect they can be referred to as being 'indirectly discriminatory', 'discriminatory in fact' or 'covertly discriminatory'.

Article 34 TFEU on the free movement of goods has been covered from the start not only by the prohibition of direct discrimination but also by obstacles that restricted trade by being more burdensome on goods of foreign origin (i.e. indirect discrimination). However, over the years the CJEU has expanded the concept of discrimination so that the prohibition now covers indirect discrimination. The keystone to this construction has been that the CJEU has also applied to prohibition to non-discriminatory requirements that are not particularly burdensome on foreigners but which concern market access. Market access is naturally very important for undertakings that have not yet penetrated a market, which will normally mostly be foreign undertakings. Thus, under normal circumstances it will be foreign undertakings that are restricted by the use of such purely non-discriminatory requirements. On the other hand, domestic undertakings that are already in the market will not be restricted by such requirements. An illustration of this, in the area of the free movement of workers pursuant to Article 45 TFEU is Case C-415/93 *Bosman* [1995] ECR I-4921, which is discussed in Chapter 4. In this case, the CJEU rules that a non-discriminatory requirement, whereby a football club which took on a new player, had to pay a transfer fee to the player's previous club, was covered by the prohibition in Article 45 TFEU. This was so, even though the payment of transfer fees applied to transfers within the same Member State and to cross-border transfers. The CJEU found that there was a regulation that directly affected players' access to the employment market in other Member States. Similarly, in the area of the right of establishment, the CJEU found that a French non-discriminatory prohibition of the payment of remuneration on sight accounts was covered by Article 49 TFEU; see Case C-442/02 *Caixa Bank* [2005] ECR I-7929, printed in Chapter 5). The doctrine was possibly taken even further in the case on Danish company cars (Case C-464/02 *Commission* v *Denmark* [2005] ECR I-7929, printed in Chapter 4) where the CJEU found that there was a hindrance, even though there was unquestionably free access to the market. The hindrance consisted purely of the fact that the Danish tax rules meant that there was a higher tax payable on making a company car available to an employee resident in Denmark than for an employee in another Member State. This judgment does not fit in well with the established line of cases on hindrances. Under the established system, hindrances can broadly be categorised under three headings:

1. Directly discriminatory requirements,
2. Indirectly discriminatory requirements, and
3. Non-discriminatory requirements that concern access to the market.

These distinctions are much more than jurisprudential pedantry. Establishing that a hindrance exists does not in itself mean that there is a breach of the Treaty. A hindrance can be lawful if it pursues a purpose that justifies it. In relation to direct discrimination, the CJEU has established that, in principle, these can only be justified if the Member State concerned pursues a purpose that is expressly referred to in the Treaty. For example, this includes the protection of health and life of humans (as referred to in Article 36 TFEU) or the essential interests of a Member State's security (as referred to in Article 346 TFEU). In contrast, in the case of indirect discrimination or non-discriminatory requirements that concern access to the market, these can also be justified by general considerations that are not listed in the Treaty. However, these considerations may not be of an economic nature. Thus these distinctions can be important.

The concept of discrimination that has been developed by the CJEU has given rise to some justified criticism. Consumer protection and protection of the environment are not listed among the Treaty exceptions to free movement. As a consequence, these considerations can only justify an obstacle if it is an expression of a restriction and not of discrimination. Why should environmental protection be treated differently from, for example, regard for public health? Both considerations are equally important for the State, so why emphasise what the drafters of the Treaty thought important over half a century ago? However, the CJEU has recognised that directly discriminatory measures can be justified by environmental considerations; see Case C-2/90 *Commission* v *Belgium* [1992] ECR I-4431 (the *Walloon Waste* case), Case C-203/96 *Dusseldorp* [1998] ECR I-4075, and Case C-379/98 *Preussen-Elektra* [2001] ECR I-2099, of which the first and last are printed below in Chapter 2. The CJEU has also recognised that 'overriding reasons in the public interest' can justify discriminatory requirements in taxation cases; see e.g. Case C-150/04 *Commission* v *Denmark* [2007] ECR I-1163, which is reproduced in Chapter 6.

The above distinctions can be illustrated as follows:

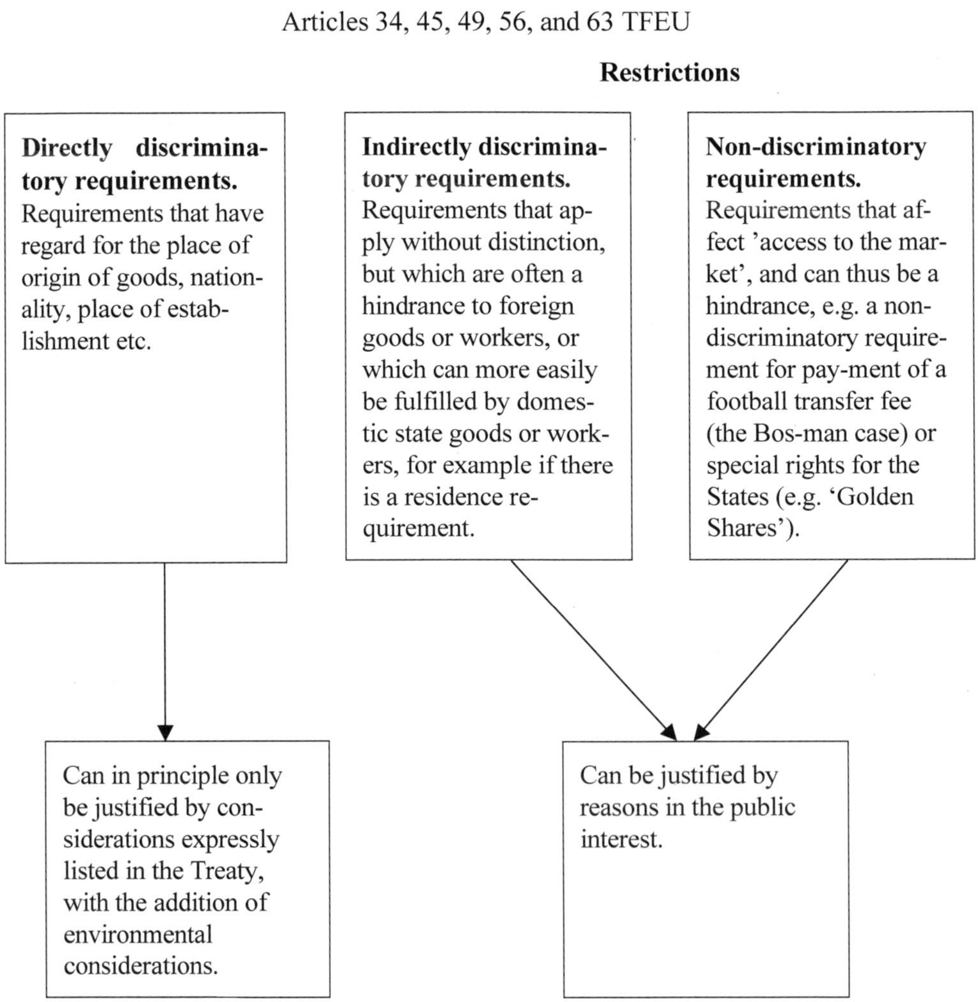

However, in the judgments of the CJEU and in Union law literature in general the use of the terminology referred to above can be far from precise. It is our hope that our choice of terminology can help prevent some of the misunderstandings that can easily arise. There is an example of the prevailing confusion of terms, which can cause problems, in Case C-224/97 *Erich Ciola* v *Land Vorarlberg* [1999] ECR I-2517, which is discussed below in Chapter 6.

To the extent that national legislation affects domestic and foreign undertakings in the same way, and does not affect access to the market, the CJEU will find that the legislation falls outside the scope of the TFEU. See e.g. Joined Cases C-544/03 and C-545/03 *Mobistar* [2005] ECR I-07723, where the CJEU stated as follows in paragraph 31: 'By contrast, measures, the only effect of which is to create additional costs in respect of the service in question and which affect in the same way the provision of services between Member States and that within one Member State, do not fall within the scope of Article 59 [now Article 66] of the Treaty'. See also Case C-190/98 *Volker Graf*, set out in Chapter 4.

The compatibility of national legislation with Union rules on freedom of movement can thus be viewed from two angles. Either one can consider whether there is a hindrance, and if so, whether the hindrance can be justified. Or one can consider whether the legislation at all constitutes different treatment of domestic and foreign undertakings. Where it does not constitute a hindrance, the measure does not fall within the scope of the TFEU.

It is now appropriate to consider the case of reduced transport fares for students in Austria. In this case it was first established that there was discrimination that was prohibited pursuant to Article 18 TFEU if the national legislation or administrative practice (1) constituted unequal treatment that was (2) not properly justified, and (3) which went further than necessary to achieve its goal (paragraph 52 of the judgment). Even though Article 18 TFEU does not contain specific exceptions to the prohibition of discrimination, as in Article 36 and Article 45(3), for example, unequal treatment can be justified if it is proper and proportionate; see Case 287/81 *Anklagemyndigheden* v *Kerr* [1982] ECR 4053. Among other things, Article 18 TFEU has been applied in relation to national rules on payment of compensation to victims of violence which have treated foreigners differently from the Member State's own citizens; see Case 186/87 *Cowan* [1989] ECR 195.

If national legislation distinguishes on the ground of residence, is this directly or indirectly discriminatory according to the CJEU? Would it have made a difference if the Austrian rules had not differentiated on the basis on whether the students' parents received family benefit from the Austrian State, but rather on the ground of whether the students were registered with an Austrian educational institution and were resident in Austria? Discuss what the CJEU understands by 'indirect discrimination'.

According to the Commission's reply to a question from a Dutch member of the European Parliament (Written question E-2930/97, OJ 1998 C 117/29), in imposing traffic fines, the Belgian authorities have required that 'non-resident transport operators in Belgium who do not choose the specified on-the-spot fine but instead opt for their case to be pursued through the courts are obliged to pay a higher amount for each offence'. Is such an arrangement contrary to Article 18 TFEU?

In Case C-45/93 *Commission* v *Spain* [1994] ECR I-911, The CJEU overruled the Spanish legislation under which Spanish citizens resident in Spain had free entrance to Spanish museums while citizens from other member States did not have such free entrance. The CJEU found that this legislation was contrary to Articles 18 and 56 TFEU. Consider whether it would be compatible with Article 18 TFEU if borrowing books free of charge from Danish public libraries were conditional on the borrower being resident in Denmark.

Would it be contrary to Article 18 TFEU to make a provision that, upon application, students pursuing further education courses have a right to discounts when buying tickets for public transport by train, bus or metro, whereby only students entitled to a public student grant would be able to obtain such discounts? In answering this question it will be necessary to take into account that only (1) citizens of the Member State in question and (2) Union citizens who are economically active are entitled to a student grant.

JUDGMENT OF THE COURT (Second Chamber)
7 July 2005

Commission of the European Communities v Republic of Austria
'Failure of a Member State to fulfil obligations – Articles 12 EC, 149 EC and 150 EC – Conditions of access to university education – Discrimination'

Case C-147/03

Judgment

1. By its application, the Commission of the European Communities is seeking a declaration from the Court that, by failing to take the necessary measures to ensure that holders of secondary education diplomas awarded in other Member States can gain access to higher and university education organised by it under the same conditions as holders of secondary education diplomas awarded in Austria, the Republic of Austria has failed to fulfil its obligations under Articles 12 EC, 149 EC and 150 EC.

The legal framework

Community legislation

2. Article 3(1) EC provides:

'For the purposes set out in Article 2, the activities of the Community shall include, as provided in this Treaty and in accordance with the timetable set out therein:
...
(q) a contribution to education and training of quality and to the flowering of the cultures of the Member States'.

3. The first paragraph of Article 12 EC provides:

'Within the scope of application of this Treaty, and without prejudice to any special provisions contained therein, any discrimination on grounds of nationality shall be prohibited.'

4. According to Article 149 EC:

'1. The Community shall contribute to the development of quality education by encouraging cooperation between Member States and, if necessary, by supporting and supplementing their action, while fully respecting the responsibility of the Member States for the content of teaching and the organisation of education systems and their cultural and linguistic diversity.

2. Community action shall be aimed at:

   ...

   – encouraging mobility of students and teachers, inter alia by encouraging the academic recognition of diplomas and periods of study;

   ...

3. The Community and the Member States shall foster cooperation with third countries and the competent international organisations in the field of education, in particular the Council of Europe.

   ...'

5. Finally, under Article 150 EC:

   '1. The Community shall implement a vocational training policy which shall support and supplement the action of the Member States, while fully respecting the responsibility of the Member States for the content and organisation of vocational training.

   2. Community action shall aim to:

   ...

   – facilitate access to vocational training and encourage mobility of instructors and trainees and particularly young people ...'

National legislation

6. Paragraph 36 of the Law on University Studies, (Universitäts-Studiengesetz, 'the UniStG'), entitled 'university entrance qualification' (Besondere Universitätsreife), provides:

   '(1) In addition to possession of a general university entrance qualification, students must demonstrate that they meet the specific entrance requirements for the relevant course of study, including entitlement to immediate admission, applicable in the State which issued the general qualification.

   (2) Where the university entrance qualification was issued in Austria, that means passes in the additional papers prescribed for admission to the relevant course of study in the Universitätsberechtigungsverordnung [University Entrance Regulation].

   (3) If the course of study for which the student is applying in Austria is not offered in the State which issued the qualification, he or she must meet the entrance requirements for a course of study which is offered in that State and which is as closely related as possible to the course applied for in Austria.

(4) The Federal Minister may by regulation designate groups of persons whose university entrance qualification is to be regarded, by reason of their close personal ties with Austria or their activity on behalf of the Republic of Austria, as issued in Austria for the purposes of establishing possession of the specific university entrance requirements.

(5) On the basis of the certificate produced in order to demonstrate possession of a general university entrance qualification, the principal of the university shall determine whether the student meets the specific entrance requirements for the course of study chosen.'

Pre-litigation procedure

[Paras. 7-27 omitted]

Substance

The scope of Community law

Arguments of the parties

28. The Commission is of the opinion that the discrimination contained in Paragraph 36 of the UniStG relates solely to the conditions of access to Austrian higher or university education, a matter which, in its view, falls within the material scope of the Treaty.

29. The Republic of Finland also takes the view, like the Commission, that the action relates solely to the conditions of admission to Austrian higher education of holders of diplomas awarded in another Member State, and that it does not affect the question of the academic recognition of diplomas.

30. The Republic of Austria asserts that Paragraph 36 of the UniStG governs the recognition of secondary education diplomas for the purpose of gaining access to Austrian universities. However, it submits that the academic recognition of diplomas for the purpose of commencing or pursuing higher education or other training does not fall within the scope of the Treaty.

Findings of the Court

31. Under the first paragraph of Article 12 EC, within the scope of application of the Treaty, and without prejudice to any special provisions contained therein, any discrimination on grounds of nationality is to be prohibited.

32. As the Court has already held in paragraph 25 of Case 293/83 *Gravier* [1985] ECR 593, the conditions of access to vocational training fall within the scope of the Treaty (see also Case C-65/03 *Commission* v *Belgium* [2004] ECR I-6427, paragraph 25).

33. It also follows from the case-law that both higher education and university education constitute vocational training (see Case 24/86 *Blaizot* [1988] ECR 379, paragraphs 15 to 20, and Case 42/87 *Commission* v *Belgium* [1988] ECR 5445, paragraphs 7 and 8).

34. In the present case, Paragraph 36 of the UniStG lays down the conditions governing access to higher or university education in Austria. In that connection, it provides that, in addition to satisfying the general requirements for access to higher or university studies, holders of general university entrance qualifications awarded in other Member States must prove that they meet the specific requirements governing access to the chosen course, which are laid down by the State which issued those qualifications and give entitlement to direct admission to those studies.

35. In those circumstances, the provision at issue must be examined in the light of the Treaty and, in particular, in the light of the principle of non-discrimination on the grounds of nationality contained in Article 12 EC.

The plea alleging infringement of Community law

Arguments of the parties

36. The Commission asserts that the right to equal treatment laid down by Article 12 EC necessarily includes the right for holders of diplomas awarded in another Member State, once their diploma is deemed to be equivalent, not to be made subject to conditions which are not imposed on students who have obtained their diploma in Austria for the purpose of gaining access to the same Austrian higher or university education course. Otherwise, that article would be deprived of all useful effect.

37. Pursuant to Paragraph 36 of the UniStG, access by holders of diplomas awarded in another Member State to certain Austrian higher or university education courses is made subject to a condition to which holders of general university entrance qualifications awarded in Austria are not subject.

38. The Commission submits that that condition constitutes indirect discrimination since, although Austrian nationals who have obtained a diploma in another Member State are also subject to that same condition, it affects nationals from other Member States more than Austrian nationals.

39. The Republic of Finland takes the view, like the Commission, that the condition laid down in Paragraph 36 of the UniStG, which does not concern holders of Austrian secondary education diplomas, is contrary to Community law, in particular to Article 12 EC.

40. The Republic of Austria disputes the Commission's analysis according to which access to higher education is subject in Austria to a two-stage procedure consisting of, first, recognition on an equal basis of diplomas awarded on completion of secondary studies and, second, verification of other conditions. Admission to Austrian universities is, in reality, subject to proof of general aptitude and of specific aptitude for university studies and no condition other than academic recognition of the qualification giving access to university studies is required.

Findings of the Court

41. According to settled case-law, the principle of equal treatment prohibits not only overt discrimination based on nationality but also all covert forms of discrimination which, by applying other distinguishing criteria, lead in fact to the same result (see, in particular, Case 152/73 *Sotgiu* [1974] ECR 153, paragraph 11; Case C-65/03 *Commission* v *Belgium*, cited above, paragraph 28, and Case C-209/03 *Bidar* [2005] ECR I-0000, paragraph 51).

42. In the present case, the national legislation in question provides that students who have obtained their secondary education diploma in a Member State other than the Republic of Austria and who wish to pursue their higher or university studies in a given area of Austrian education must not only produce that diploma, but also prove that they fulfil the conditions of access to higher or university studies in the State where they obtained their diploma, such as, in particular, success in an entrance examination or obtaining a sufficient grade to be included in the *numerus clausus*.

43. It appears therefore that Paragraph 36 of the UniStG introduces not only differential treatment to the detriment of students who have obtained their secondary education diplomas in a Member State other than the Republic of Austria, but also between those same students according to the Member State in which they obtained their secondary education diploma.

44. The opportunities offered by the Treaty relating to free movement are not fully effective if a person is penalised merely for using them. That consideration is particularly important in the field of education in view of the aims pursued by Article 3(1)(q) EC and the second indent of Article 149(2) EC, namely encouraging mobility of students and teachers (see Case C-224/98 *D'Hoop* [2002] ECR I-6191, paragraphs 30 to 32).

45. Case-law has moreover established that Union citizenship is destined to be the fundamental status of nationals of the Member States, enabling those who find themselves in the same situation to enjoy the same treatment in law irrespective of their nationality, subject to such exceptions as are expressly provided for (Case C-184/99 *Grzelczyk* [2001] ECR I-6193, paragraph 31, and *D'Hoop*, cited above, paragraph 28).

46. Thus, the legislation in question places holders of secondary education diplomas awarded in a Member State other than the Republic of Austria at a disadvantage, since they cannot gain access to Austrian higher education under the same conditions as holders of the equivalent Austrian diploma.

47. Thus, although Paragraph 36 of the UniStG applies without distinction to all students, it is liable to have a greater effect on nationals of other Member States than on Austrian nationals, and therefore the difference in treatment introduced by that provision results in indirect discrimination.

48. Consequently, the differential treatment in question could be justified only if it were based on objective considerations independent of the nationality of the persons concerned and were proportionate to the legitimate aim of the national provisions (Case C-274/96 *Bickel and Franz* [1998] ECR I-7637, paragraph 27, and *D'Hoop*, cited above, paragraph 36).

Justification of discrimination

Arguments of the parties

– *Justification based on safeguarding the homogeneity of the Austrian higher or university education system*

49. The Republic of Austria submits that justification of unequal treatment falling within the scope of Article 12 EC is not limited to grounds of public policy, public security and public health, and that, according to settled case-law, it is possible to justify discrimination based on nationality in cases of indirect discrimination.

50. The Republic of Austria invokes, in that regard, the safeguarding of the homogeneity of the Austrian education system. Relying by analogy on the case-law of the Court, it submits that, if the rights available in the country of origin are not taken into consideration, it can expect a large number of holders of diplomas awarded in other Member States to try to attend university and higher education courses in Austria and that that situation would cause structural, staffing and financial problems (see Case C-158/96 *Kohll* [1998] ECR I-1931, paragraph 41, and Case C-368/98 *Vanbraekel and Others* [2001] ECR I-5363, paragraph 47).

51. The Commission submits that it follows from the case-law of the Court, in particular from Case 15/69 *Ugliola* [1969] ECR 363 and Case C-484/93 *Svensson and Gustavsson* [1995] ECR I-3955, that a discriminatory measure may be justified only on the exceptional grounds expressly provided for in the Treaty, namely public policy, public security and public health. However, no ground of that type has been put forward by the Republic of Austria.

52. In addition, to concede that the Austrian legislation may be justified by grounds other than those expressly provided for by the Treaty would render meaningless, according to the Commission, the concept of indirect discrimination as it results from *Sotgiu*, cited above, that is discrimination which, although based on an apparently neutral criterion, in fact leads to the same result as discrimination on the grounds of nationality.

53. Moreover, the Commission claims that in any event Paragraph 36 of the UniStG infringes the principle of proportionality.

– *Justification based on preventing abuse of Community law*

54. The Republic of Austria points out that, in Case 115/78 *Knoors* [1979] ECR 399 and Case C-61/89 *Bouchoucha* [1990] ECR I-3551, the Court recognised the legitimate interest that a Member State may have in preventing certain of its nationals, by means of facilities created under the Treaty, from improperly evading the application of their national legislation as regards training for a trade or profession and that Community law does not allow national legislation to be circumvented in that area.

55. In response, the Commission points out that in Case C-436/00 *X and Y* [2002] ECR I-10829, the Court found that whether there is abuse or fraudulent conduct must be examined individually on a case-by-case basis and should be based on objective evidence, and that the mere fact of exercising the right to freedom of movement cannot be regarded as an abuse (Case C-212/97 *Centros* [1999] ECR I-1459).

– *Justification based on international conventions*

56. The Republic of Austria contends that Paragraph 36 of the UniStG complies with conventions concluded within the framework of the Council of Europe, in this case that of 11 December 1953 on the equivalence of diplomas leading to admission to universities (*European Treaties Series*, No 15, 'the 1953 Convention'), and that of 11 April 1997 on the recognition of qualifications concerning higher education in the European Region (*European Treaties Series*, No 165, 'the 1997 Convention').

57. The Commission points out that, under Article 307 EC, the rights and obligations arising from agreements concluded between one or more Member States and one or

more third countries before the accession of a Member State are not affected by the provisions of the Treaty. However, to the extent that such agreements are not compatible with the Treaty, the Member State or States concerned must take all appropriate steps to eliminate the incompatibilities established.

58. It also draws attention to the settled case-law of the Court, according to which whilst Article 307 EC allows Member States to honour obligations owed to non-member States under international agreements preceding the Treaty, it does not authorise them to exercise rights under such agreements in intra-Community relations (Case C-473/93 *Commission* v *Luxembourg* [1996] ECR I-3207, paragraph 40).

59. Consequently, according to the Commission, the Republic of Austria may not rely on the 1953 Convention. Nor may the 1997 Convention be relied on, since it was concluded after the accession of the Republic of Austria.

Findings of the Court

– Justification based on safeguarding the homogeneity of the Austrian higher or university education system

60. It must be borne in mind, as found in paragraph 47 of this judgment, that Paragraph 36 of the UniStG gives rise to indirect discrimination, since it is liable to affect students from other Member States more than Austrian students. Furthermore, it emerged from the hearing before the Court that the Austrian legislation aims to restrict access to Austrian universities for holders of diplomas awarded in other Member States.

61. As the Advocate General points out in point 52 of his Opinion, excessive demand for access to specific courses could be met by the adoption of specific non-discriminatory measures such as the establishment of an entry examination or the requirement of a minimum grade; thus Article 12 EC would be complied with.

62. Furthermore, it must be observed that the risks alleged by the Republic of Austria are not exclusive to its higher or university education system but have been and are suffered by other Member States. Among those Member States is the Kingdom of Belgium, which had introduced similar restrictions, which were held to be incompatible with the requirements of Community law (see Case C-65/03 *Commission* v *Belgium*, cited above).

63. Moreover, it is for the national authorities which invoke a derogation from the fundamental principle of freedom of movement for persons to show in each individual case that their rules are necessary and proportionate to attain the aim pursued. The reasons which may be invoked by a Member State by way of justification must be accompanied by an analysis of the appropriateness and proportionality of the re-

strictive measure adopted by that State and specific evidence substantiating its arguments (see, to that effect, Case C-42/02 *Lindman* [2003] ECR I-13519, paragraph 25, and Case C-8/02 *Leichtle* [2004] ECR I-2641, paragraph 45).

64. In the present case, the Republic of Austria simply maintained at the hearing that the number of students registering for courses in medicine could be five times the number of available places, which would pose a risk to the financial equilibrium of the Austrian higher education system and, consequently, to its very existence.

65. It must be pointed out that no estimates relating to other courses have been submitted to the Court and that the Republic of Austria has conceded that it does not have any figures in that connection. Moreover, the Austrian authorities have accepted that the national legislation in question is essentially preventive in nature.

66. Consequently, it must be held that the Republic of Austria has failed to demonstrate that, in the absence of Paragraph 36 of the UnistG, the existence of the Austrian education system in general and the safeguarding of the homogeneity of higher education in particular would be jeopardised. The legislation in question is therefore incompatible with the objectives of the Treaty.

– *Justification based on preventing abuse of Community law*

67. Second, the Austrian Government has put forward a justification alleging that it is necessary for Member States to prevent abuse of Community law and drawing attention to the legitimate interest that a Member State may have in preventing certain of its nationals, by means of facilities created under the Treaty, from improperly evading the application of their national legislation as regards training for a trade or profession.

68. According to case-law, whether there is abuse or fraudulent conduct must be examined individually on a case-by-case basis and must be based on objective evidence (see *Centros*, paragraphs 24 and 25, and *X and Y*, paragraphs 42 and 43).

69. It must also be borne in mind that Article 149(2) EC, second indent, expressly provides that Community action is to be aimed at encouraging mobility of students and teachers, inter alia by encouraging the academic recognition of diplomas and periods of study. Moreover, Article 150(2) EC, third indent, provides that Community action is to aim to facilitate access to vocational training and encourage mobility of instructors and trainees and particularly young people.

70. In this case, it need merely be observed that the possibility for a student from the European Union, who has obtained his secondary education diploma in a Member State other than Austria, to gain access to Austrian higher or university education under the same conditions as holders of diplomas awarded in Austria constitutes the

very essence of the principle of freedom of movement for students guaranteed by the Treaty, and cannot therefore of itself constitute an abuse of that right.

– *Justification based on international conventions*

71. The Republic of Austria submits, third, that Paragraph 36 of the UniStG complies with the 1953 and 1997 Conventions.

72. In that regard, it must be held that, according to Article 307 EC, the rights and obligations arising from agreements concluded for acceding States, before the date of their accession, between one or more Member States on the one hand, and one or more third countries on the other, are not affected by the provisions of the Treaty. However, and to the extent that such agreements are not compatible with the Treaty, the Member State or States concerned must take all appropriate steps to eliminate the incompatibilities established.

73. It is settled case-law that, whilst Article 307 EC allows Member States to honour obligations owed to non-member States under international agreements preceding the Treaty, it does not authorise them to exercise rights under such agreements in intra-Community relations (see, in particular, *Commission* v *Luxembourg*, cited above, paragraph 40, and Case C-203/03 *Commission* v *Austria* [2005] ECR I-0000, paragraphs 57 to 59).

74. Consequently, the Republic of Austria may not invoke by way of justification either the 1953 Convention or *a fortiori* the 1997 Convention, which was concluded after the Republic of Austria acceded to the Union.

75. Having regard to the foregoing considerations, it must be held that, by failing to take the necessary measures to ensure that holders of secondary education diplomas awarded in other Member States can gain access to higher and university education organised by it under the same conditions as holders of secondary education diplomas awarded in Austria, the Republic of Austria has failed to fulfil its obligations under Articles 12 EC, 149 EC and 150 EC.

Costs

[Para. 76 omitted]

On those grounds,

THE COURT (Second Chamber)

hereby:

1. **Declares that, by failing to take the necessary measures to ensure that holders of secondary education diplomas awarded in other Member States can gain access to higher and university education organised by it under the same conditions as holders of secondary education diplomas awarded in Austria, the Republic of Austria has failed to fulfil its obligations under Articles 12 EC, 149 EC and 150 EC;**

   [Para. 2 of the ruling omitted]

Comments and questions

Austria has a very liberal education system, where it is relatively easy to be accepted at a further education institution or a university. Under Austrian law, a person who wanted to be admitted to a further education institution or a university in Austria, but who had obtained his or her secondary education diplomas for admission in some other Member State had to satisfy two criteria. First, the applicant had to satisfy the ordinary conditions for access to study at a further education institution or a university in Austria. Second, in addition the applicant had to satisfy the special conditions for access to the chosen course which applied in the Member State where the secondary education diplomas were obtained and which gave entitlement to be accepted for this course. Thus, while a student with Austrian secondary education diplomas only had to surmount one barrier, students with foreign secondary education diplomas had to surmount two.

The Commission acknowledged that the Austrian rule did not constitute direct discrimination. Non-Austrian citizens who obtained their secondary education diplomas in Austria only had to satisfy the ordinary admission requirements; i.e. they only had to surmount one barrier. Correspondingly, Austrian citizens who obtained their secondary education diplomas in another Member State would not be better placed than other EU citizens who had obtained their secondary education diplomas in the Member State in question; they both had to surmount two barriers. Nevertheless the Commission believed that the Austrian rule fell foul of the prohibition on discrimination in Article 18 TFEU (formerly Article 12 TEC). The Commission believed that the rule was an expression of indirect discrimination as it affected the citizens of other Member States to a greater extent than Austrian citizens. The CJEU agreed with this assessment. Even though the Austrian rule applied equally to all students, it could affect citizens from other Member States more than citizens from Austria. The rule was therefore covered by the prohibition in Article 18 TFEU. At the same time, the CJEU remarked that it was not merely a question of discrimination between Austrians on the one hand and citizens from other Member States on the other. The rule also involved indirect discrimination between non-Austrian citizens themselves, depending on the Member State in which they had obtained their secondary education diplomas.

Having established that there was indirect discrimination covered by Article 18 TFEU, the CJEU had to decide whether it could be said that the rule pursued a lawful purpose and, if so, whether it was proportionate in relation to that lawful purpose. Austria argued that the discrimination could be justified by legitimate public interests as referred to in the TFEU, as well as other public interests. The Commission was of the view that only the public interests which are expressly referred to in the TFEU could justify discrimination such as that in the case.

In his Opinion, the Advocate General stated that he agreed with the Austrian argument. He added that a distinction should be made between two categories of interests which could be relied upon as justification for measures which would otherwise be found discriminatory. The first category consisted of those interests that are expressly stated in the Treaty. The second non-exhaustive category consisted of considerations that concerned the protection of legitimate national interests which had been added by the practice of the CJEU. Furthermore, he argued that measures which are an expression of direct discrimination could generally only be justified by the interests expressly referred to in the Treaty. In contrast, measures which were an expression of indirect discrimination could be justified by reference to both categories of interests. However, regardless of which category of interests was relied on, they should be interpreted restrictively and satisfy the principle of proportionality.

The proportionality principle in EU law consists of three cumulative conditions. First, the means that are used to attain the claimed lawful purpose must be *suitable*; in other words, the lawful purpose must be achieved by the means used. Second, they must be *necessary*; i.e. they should not go further than is necessary to achieve the lawful purpose. And third, they must be proportionate *stricto sensu* to the lawful purpose pursued. Moreover, where the application of the proportionality principle concerns the rules and practices of the Member States, the CJEU will also require that these rules and practices pursue the purpose that they are held to pursue in a consistent and coherent manner. This means that it is not sufficient that a rule or practice fulfils the three stated conditions if the Member State's full regulatory framework of the matter in question is not sufficiently coherent. See, for example, paragraph 63 in Case C-169/07 *Hartlauer Handelsgesellschaft* [2009] ECR I-1721, which is reproduced in Chapter 5 on freedom of establishment.

However, the CJEU is not always consistent in its practice on this point. Thus, it often limits itself to assessing whether a national measure is 'appropriate', and whether the chosen measure is proportionate; see, e.g. Case C-110/05 *Commission* v *Italy* (Motorcycle trailers) [2009] ECR I-519, which is included in Chapter 2 on the free movement of goods.

In contrast to the Advocate General, the CJEU refrained from directly addressing the question as to what interests could be invoked. Should the judgment be read as supporting the Austrian argument or supporting the Commission's argument? See paragraphs 60-66 of the judgment, and in particular paragraph 63.

The CJEU concluded that the Austrian measure constituted a breach of the prohibition on discrimination. Did the CJEU base this on the grounds that Austria pursued an unlawful purpose, or did it conclude that the measures contravened the proportionality principle?

In paragraphs 64-66 of the judgment the CJEU stated that the Austrian Government had not lifted the burden of proof to show that the Austrian measures were necessary for protecting the Austrian educational system in general, and for ensuring that the coherence of further education in Austria was not put at risk. On this basis, consider whether the CJEU would have reached the same conclusion if the Austrian Government had submitted the following information:

Medical schools in	Total available places 2005	Places taken by Austrians	Places taken by Germans	Increase in German students 2004 to 2005
Vienna	1560	1127	267 (17%)	280%
Graz	300	n/a	n/a	–
Innsbruck	550	258	227 (41%)	550%

The question of whether the homogeneity of the education system can justify a restriction on foreign students being accepted for a place in the educational system of another Member State was also at issue in Case C-73/08 *Bressol and Others* v *Gouvernement de la Communauté française*. This case concerned the fact that universities in the French-speaking part of Belgium received a large number of students for health science courses, particularly from France. The reason for this was that in France there was restricted access to such courses, but this was not the case in Belgium. The Belgian authorities considered this a problem, as it was very expensive to educate these foreign students, as this could create problems for the homogeneity of the further education system, and because it was to be expected that many of the foreign students would return to their home State at the end of their courses. This would mean there would be insufficient scientific personnel to meet the needs of Belgium. The French-speaking community in Belgium therefore decided to limit the number of foreign students on health science courses, and lots were drawn to decide which of the foreign students could be accepted.

As for the argument that the large number of foreign students could undermine the homogeneity of the further education system, the Belgian Government argued that the number of foreign students on the courses in question had reached a level where there was risk that the quality of further education would be harmed because of the limited capacity of higher education institutions and their personnel resources to accept students. With a view to preserving a homogeneous system and ensuring 'wide and democratic access for the population of the French Community to quality higher education', it had proved necessary to treat resident students and foreign students differently and to limit the number of foreign students. Faced with this argument, the CJEU found that it was not impossible that the argument could justify unequal treatment of some students. However, the referring national court had first to examine whether this fear of the Belgian authorities was well-founded. If it was, then the referring national court had to establish whether the Belgian measure fulfilled the principle of proportionality, as explained above in these comments and questions. At the same time, the CJEU added that it was for the Belgian authorities to put forward the necessary analyses to support the Belgian arguments. In her Opinion, the Advocate General had reached the same conclusion as the CJEU. At the same time, she recalled that one of the objectives of the Union is to promote solidarity among the Member States, and that the Member States have a mutual duty of loyal cooperation on the basis of Article 4(3) TEU. She thus proposed that where linguistic patterns and differing national policies on access to higher education encourage particularly high volumes of student mobility that cause real difficulties for the host Member State, it is incumbent on both the host Member State (here Belgium) and the home Member State (here France) to actively seek a negotiated solution that complies with the Treaty.

JUDGMENT OF THE COURT (Sixth Chamber)
11 January 2001

Azienda Agricola Monte Arcosu Srl v Regione Autonoma della Sardegna, and others. (Reference for a preliminary ruling: Tribunale civile e penale di Cagliari – Italy)

'Agriculture – Farmer practising farming as his main occupation – Concept – Private limited company'

Case C-403/98

Judgment

1. By order of 26 March 1998, received at the Court on 13 November 1998, the Tribunale Civile e Penale di Cagliari (Civil and Criminal District Court, Cagliari) referred for a preliminary ruling under Article 177 of the EC Treaty (now Article 234 EC) two questions on the interpretation of Article 2(5) of Council Regulation (EEC) No 797/85 of 12 March 1985 on improving the efficiency of agricultural structures (OJ 1985 L 93, p. 1) and of Article 5(5) of Council Regulation (EEC) No 2328/91 of 15 July 1991 on improving the efficiency of agricultural structures (OJ 1991 L 218, p. 1).

2. Those questions have been raised in proceedings between Azienda Agricola Monte Arcosu Srl ('Monte Arcosu'), on the one hand, and Regione Autonoma della Sardegna (Autonomous Region of Sardinia), Organismo Comprensoriale No 24 della Sardegna (a body responsible for land registration in Sardinia) and Ente Regionale per l'Assistenza Tecnica in Agricoltura (ERSAT; regional authority for technical assistance to agriculture), on the other, concerning the rejection by Organismo Comprensoriale No 24 della Sardegna of Monte Arcosu's application to be entered in the Register of Farmers Practising Farming as their Main Occupation.

Community law

3. Article 2(5) of Regulation No 797/85 provides:

'Member States shall, for the purposes of this regulation, define what is meant by the expression 'farmer practising farming as his main occupation'.'

This definition shall, in the case of a natural person, include at least the condition that the proportion of income derived from the agricultural holding must be 50% or more of the farmer's total income and that the working time devoted to work unconnected with the holding must be less than half of the farmer's total working time.

On the basis of the criteria referred to in the foregoing subparagraph, the Member States shall define what is meant by this same expression in the case of persons other than natural persons.

4. That provision is identical to Article 5(5) of Regulation No 2328/91.

5. Under Article 32(1) of Regulation No 797/85, Member States were required, within six months of 1 April 1985, to bring into force the measures necessary to comply with that regulation.

National law

6. Article 12 of Italian Law No 153 of 9 May 1975, defining what is meant by 'farmer practising farming as his main occupation', laid down the criterion of two-thirds both for the farmer's total income and for the working time devoted to work unconnected with the holding.

7. Under Article 13 of that Law, persons other than natural persons, namely agricultural cooperatives established in accordance with the legislation on cooperation, and farmers' associations, qualify for the measures prescribed in Title III of that Law, provided that, in both cases, 'all the members derive at least 50% of their own income from farming and associated activity and devote at least 50% of their working time to farming and associated activity'.

8. Article 15 of Law No 19 of the Region of Sardinia of 23 March 1979, defining what is meant by 'farmer practising farming as his main occupation', confers that status on those who 'devote not less than two-thirds of their own total working time to farming and derive not less than two-thirds of their own total earned income from farming'.

9. Article 21 of that Law extends the benefits conferred by the Law to farming cooperatives and farmers' associations established in accordance with the legislation in force, 'provided that each member derives at least 50% of his own income from farming and devotes at least 50% of his own working time to farming and associated activity'.

10. Article 2 of the Italian Ministerial Decree of 12 September 1985 provides:

'Beneficiaries

1. The following farmers shall qualify for the intervention measures referred to in Title I of the abovementioned regulation in so far as they satisfy the subjective criteria set out in Article 2(1) of that regulation:
   (a) farmers who cultivate their own land, whether they are owners or tenants, share-croppers and tenant-farmers, whether without the agreement of the lessor or together with the lessor, perpetual lease-holders, family members helping the farmer on a regular and permanent basis;
   (b) owners, usufructuaries and tenants;
   (c) agricultural cooperatives established in accordance with the legislation in force on cooperation;
   (d) associations of farmers who cultivate their own land, perpetual lease-holders, tenant-farmers, family members helping the farmer on a regular and permanent basis, owners, usufructuaries and tenants;
   (e) partnerships which directly manage agricultural holdings which they own or of which they have the use in whatever form. The regions and autonomous provinces shall define, within the limits set in Article 6 of the Regulation, the conditions as to eligibility.
2. The criterion of being a farmer practising farming as his main occupation and that relating to occupational skill and competence, which are laid down in Article 2(1)(a) and (b) of the abovementioned regulation, shall be defined on the basis of the regional legislative provisions adopted pursuant to Directive 72/159/EEC. Failing that, Articles 12 and 13 of Law No 153 of 9 May 1975 shall apply.

3. The cooperatives referred to under (c) above, whose sole object is the management of agricultural holdings, may seek to obtain the investment aid provided for under Title I of the Regulation even if only 20% of their members satisfy the subjective criteria prescribed.'

11. Law No 17 of the Region of Sardinia of 27 September 1992 provided for the creation of a Register of Farmers Practising Farming as their Main Occupation, specifying that the criteria for the management of the Register were to be determined by the Regional Council in accordance with the provisions of Regulation No 2328/91.

The main proceedings

12. Monte Arcosu is a private limited company whose object is to carry on farming activities.

13. Monte Arcosu has acquired several holdings of agricultural land in Uta, Siliqua and Decimomannu. It stipulated in the public deed of sale that it intended to obtain the status of a farmer practising farming as its main occupation and therefore claimed the benefit of registration duties at 8% as provided for in Note 1 to Article 1 of the tariff annexed to Presidential Decree No 131 of 26 April 1986.

14. It is clear from the order for reference that Monte Arcosu subsequently applied to the Organismo Comprensoriale No 24 della Sardegna for entry in the Register of Farmers Practising Farming as their Main Occupation.

15. That application was rejected by decision of 11 September 1991 on the ground that the regional rules did not provide for commercial companies to be entered in that register.

16. Consequently, Monte Arcosu brought proceedings against Regione Autonoma della Sardegna, Organismo Comprensoriale No 24 della Sardegna and Ente Regionale per l'Assistenza Tecnica in Agricoltura in order to obtain its entry in the Register of Farmers Practising Farming as their Main Occupation on the basis of Article 2(5) of Regulation No 797/85 or Article 5(5) of Regulation No 2328/91.

17. Since it took the view that the resolution of the dispute before it depended on the interpretation of the abovementioned provisions, the Tribunale Civile e Penale di Cagliari decided to stay proceedings and to refer the following questions to the Court for a preliminary ruling:

    (1) Despite the silence of the Italian legislature, is it in any event possible to apply the Community provisions in question to persons other than natural persons, and in particular to companies having legal personality?

    (2) If an affirmative answer is given to the first question, what are the necessary and sufficient conditions for conferring the status of farmers practising farming as their main occupation on persons other than natural persons and, in particular, on companies with legal personality?'

Admissibility of the questions referred for a preliminary ruling

[Paras 18-24 omitted]

The questions referred for a preliminary ruling

25. It is clear from the order for reference that, by its first and second questions, which it is appropriate to consider together, the Tribunale Civile e Penale di Cagliari essentially seeks to ascertain whether, and under what conditions, a national court may apply to limited companies the last subparagraph of Article 2(5) of Regulation

No 797/85 and the last subparagraph of Article 5(5) of Regulation No 2328/91 where the legislature of a Member State has not adopted the provisions necessary for their implementation in the national legal system.

26. In this respect, although, by virtue of the very nature of regulations and of their function in the system of sources of Community law, the provisions of those regulations generally have immediate effect in the national legal systems without its being necessary for the national authorities to adopt measures of application, some of their provisions may none the less necessitate, for their implementation, the adoption of measures of application by the Member States.

27. That is true of the last subparagraph of Article 2(5) of Regulation No 797/85 and the last subparagraph of Article 5(5) of Regulation No 2328/91 which provide that, on the basis of the criteria used in respect of natural persons, the Member States are to define what is meant by 'farmer practising farming as his main occupation' in the case of persons other than natural persons.

28. In the light of the discretion enjoyed by the Member States in respect of the implementation of those provisions, it cannot be held that individuals may derive rights from those provisions in the absence of measures of application adopted by the Member States.

29. It follows from the foregoing that the last subparagraph of Article 2(5) of Regulation No 797/85 and the last subparagraph of Article 5(5) of Regulation No 2328/91 may not be relied on before a national court by limited companies seeking to obtain the status of farmers practising farming as their main occupation where the legislature of a Member State has not adopted the provisions necessary for their implementation in the national legal system.

Costs

[Para. 30 omitted]

On those grounds,

THE COURT (Sixth Chamber),

in answer to the questions referred to it by the Tribunale Civile e Penale di Cagliari by order of 26 March 1998, hereby rules:

The last subparagraph of Article 2(5) of Council Regulation (EEC) No 797/85 of 12 March 1985 on improving the efficiency of agricultural structures and the last subparagraph of Article 5(5) of Council Regulation (EEC) No 2328/91 of 15 July 1991 on improving the efficiency of agricultural structures may not

be relied on before a national court by limited companies seeking to obtain the status of farmers practising farming as their main occupation where the legislature of a Member State has not adopted the provisions necessary for their implementation in the national legal system.

Comments and questions

According to Article 288, second paragraph, TFEU (formerly Article 249 TEC), a regulation has general application. It is binding in its entirety and directly applicable in all Member States. A regulation is not to be implemented in national law, but applies in the same way as national law in the legal systems of the Member States. In fact, the CJEU has held that a regulation may not be implemented in national law. Nevertheless, regulations frequently require Member States to implement supplementary rules, which may be necessary for applying the regulation. These will typically be rules identifying the authorities responsible for dealing with cases under the regulation, and rules concerning penalties for infringements of the provisions of the regulation. For example, from time to time Member States will lay down definitions in their national laws which are necessary for the application of a regulation. Case C-403/98 *Azienda Agricola Monte Arcosu Srl* v *Regione Autonoma della Sardegna* [2001] ECR I-103, concerned a regulation which required Member States to introduce a definition in their national laws; this had not been done in Italy.

In its judgment the CJEU found that even though the provisions of a regulation usually have direct effect in national legal regimes, this does not mean that certain provisions do not require implementing measures in the Member States in order to be applicable. In the actual case, the failure of Italy to satisfy the requirements of the regulation in question meant that the plaintiff company could not rely on the regulation when bringing its claim before the Italian courts. The regulation required the Member States to adopt implementing rules (it was not unconditional), and since Italy had not adopted such rules, the disputed provision of the regulation did not have direct effect.

In Union law a distinction is made between 'direct applicability' on the one hand, and 'direct effect' on the other hand.

In principle, regulations are directly applicable. This means that they do not require implementation through national measures. By contrast, directives are not directly applicable, as they always require national implementation. However, it is the well-established practice of the CJEU that a provision of a directive or of the TFEU can nevertheless have direct effect under certain circumstances. Thus, if a Member State has not implemented a directive in due time, a private individual can claim rights under the directive as against public authorities, as long as the provisions of the directive are unconditional and sufficiently precise. The question of the direct effect of provisions in directives is discussed in more detail below in this chapter in connection with Case C-91/92 *Faccini Dori* v *Recreb Srl* [1994] ECR I-3325, and Case C-334/92 *Miret* v *Fondo de Garantía Salarial* [1993] ECR I-6911.

Perhaps it could be argued that the conditions for the direct effect of directive provisions should be carried over to cases, such as the *Monte Arcosu* case, where a regulation exceptionally has a requirement for national provisions for its implementation. The idea would be that a provision of a regulation which has not been implemented in due time, but which is sufficiently precise and unconditional, should be given direct effect. Even the fact that the provisions of a regulation require the implementation of national measures does not of itself mean that the provision fails to satisfy the requirement of being unconditional. This requirement merely corresponds to the general requirements for implementation which applies to all directives. Only if the provisions of a regulation were to impose special requirements, for example, setting up national administrative bodies, would the requirement for unconditionality not be satisfied. On the other hand, it must be assumed that the requirement that the non-implemented provision should be sufficiently precise, will often not be satisfied. It is natural to assume that a regulation will only require national provisions for its implementation in situations where it is not possible to lay down unambiguous and precise provisions. If the provisions were unambiguous and precise, there would be no reason to require them to be implemented by the Member States.

Should the situation nevertheless arise where a Member State has failed to implement national provisions, in contravention of a regulation, and where the regulation's provisions are sufficiently unconditional and precise, it is natural to assume that the CJEU would make the provisions of the regulation have direct effect, so that private citizens could assert their rights under the regulation against the Member State in question.

If a private citizen wishes to rely on a provision in a regulation in a case against a Member State, but is prevented from doing so because the Member State has not carried out the necessary implementation, then in effect the Member State could hide behind its own infringement of Union law, unless the provision in question can be given direct effect against the Member State, as discussed above. This would lead to a risk that Member States would have an advantage by failing to implement measures. There is a corresponding risk in relation to the failure to implement directives in due time. Because of this, the CJEU has established a number of rules *in relation to directives* which reduce this risk, as follows:

The principle of 'harmonious interpretation'. This means that, following the expiry of the deadline for implementing a directive within the framework of national law, the authorities of the Member State are required to adopt an interpretation of national law which is as far as possible in accordance with the directive which should have been implemented.

Direct effect. A directive provision which has not been implemented in due time and where the directive contains provisions that are unconditional and sufficiently precise that give individuals rights as against the public authorities, can be relied upon by private citizens as against the public authorities of the Member State.

> *Claims for damages*. Where certain conditions are met, citizens can claim compensation from the Member State. The question of the liability of a Member State to pay compensation for its failure to implement a directive was first established in Joined Cases C-6/90 and C-9/90 *Francovich* [1991] ECR I-5357, which is discussed below in the comments on the Joined Cases C-46/93 and C-48/93 *Brasserie du Pêcheur* v *Germany* [1996] ECR I-1029.

In the *Monte Arcosu* case, the Italian court referred the case to the CJEU for a preliminary ruling on whether the rules which apply to the direct effect of provisions of directives can also be applied to the provisions of a regulation. Since the regulation allowed the Member States a certain margin of discretion over the implementation of the disputed provisions, the CJEU held that they could not have direct effect.

The Italian authorities had subsequently adopted national implementation measures, albeit after the implementation deadline had expired. In his Opinion, the Advocate General proposed that the referring court should apply these implementing provisions to the case before it. In other words, he proposed that the implementing provisions should be given retrospective effect. In proposing this the Advocate General referred to the principle of the interpretation of national law in conformity with directives. Do you think that the Advocate General's comparison is a fair one, and is his view reflected in the judgment of the CJEU?

JUDGMENT OF THE COURT
14 July 1994

Paola Faccini Dori v Recreb Srl (Reference to the Court for a preliminary ruling by the Giudice Conciliatore di Firenze: Judge-Conciliator, Florence – Italy)

'Consumer protection in the case of contracts negotiated away from business premises – Availability in disputes between private individuals'

Case C-91/92

Judgment

1. By order of 24 January 1992, received at the Court on 18 March 1992, the Giudice Conciliatore di Firenze (Judge-Conciliator, Florence), Italy, referred to the Court for a preliminary ruling under Article 177 of the EEC Treaty a question on the interpretation of Council Directive 85/577/EEC, concerning protection of the consumer in respect of contracts negotiated away from business premises (OJ 1985 L 372, p. 31, hereinafter 'the directive'), and on the possibility of relying on that directive in proceedings between a trader and a consumer.

2. The question was raised in proceedings between Paola Faccini Dori, of Monza, Italy, and Recreb Srl ('Recreb').

3. It appears from the order for reference that on 19 January 1989, without having been previously approached by her, Interdiffusion Srl concluded a contract with Miss Faccini Dori at Milan Central Railway Station for an English language correspondence course. Thus the contract was concluded away from Interdiffusion's business premises.

4. Some days later, by registered letter of 23 January 1989, Miss Faccini Dori informed that company that she was cancelling her order. The company replied on 3 June 1989 that it had assigned its claim to Recreb. On 24 June 1989, Miss Faccini Dori wrote to Recreb confirming that she had cancelled her subscription to the course, indicating *inter alia* that she relied on the right of cancellation provided for by the directive.

5. As is apparent from its preamble, the directive is intended to improve consumer protection and eliminate discrepancies between national laws providing such protection, which may affect the functioning of the common market. According to the fourth recital in the preamble, where contracts are concluded away from the business premises of the trader, it is as a rule the trader who initiates the negotiations, for which the consumer is wholly unprepared and is therefore often taken by sur-

prise. In most cases, the consumer is not in a position to compare the quality and price of the offer with other offers. According to the same recital, that surprise element generally exists not only in contracts made on the doorstep but also in other forms of contract for which the trader takes the initiative away from his business premises. The purpose of the directive is thus, as indicated by the fifth recital in its preamble, to grant the consumer a right of cancellation for a period of at least seven days in order to enable him to assess the obligations arising under the contract.

6. On 30 June 1989, Recreb asked the Giudice Conciliatore di Firenze to order Miss Faccini Dori to pay it the agreed sum with interest and costs.

7. By order of 20 November 1989, the judge ordered Miss Faccini Dori to pay the sums in question. She lodged an objection to that order with the same judge. She again stated that she had withdrawn from the contract under the conditions laid down by the directive.

8. However, it is common ground that at the material time Italy had not taken any steps to transpose the directive into national law, although the period set for transposition had expired on 23 December 1987. It was not until the adoption of Decreto Legislativo No 50 of 15 January 1992 (GURI, ordinary supplement to No 27 of 3 February 1992, p. 24), which entered into force on 3 March 1992, that Italy transposed the directive.

9. The national court was uncertain whether, even though the directive had not been transposed at the material time, it could nevertheless apply its provisions.

10. It therefore referred the following question to the Court for a preliminary ruling:

    'Is Community Directive 85/577/EEC of 20 December 1985 to be regarded as sufficiently precise and detailed and, if so, was it capable, in the period between the expiry of the 24-month time-limit given to the Member States to comply with the directive and the date on which the Italian State did comply with it, of taking effect as between individuals and the Italian State and as between individuals themselves?'

11. The directive requires the Member States to adopt certain rules intended to govern legal relations between traders and consumers. In view of the nature of the dispute, which is between a consumer and a trader, the question submitted by the national court raises two issues, which should be considered separately. The first is whether the provisions of the directive concerning the right of cancellation are unconditional and sufficiently precise. The second is whether a directive which requires the Member States to adopt certain rules specifically intended to govern relations between private individuals may be relied on in proceedings between such persons in the absence of measures to transpose the directive into national law.

Whether the provisions of the directive concerning the right of cancellation are unconditional and sufficiently precise

12. Article 1(1) of the directive provides that the directive is to apply to contracts concluded between a trader supplying goods and services and a consumer, either during an excursion organized by the trader away from his business premises or during a visit by him to the consumer's home or place of work, where the visit does not take place at the express request of the consumer.

13. Article 2 states that 'consumer' means a natural person who, in transactions covered by the directive, is acting for purposes which can be regarded as outside his trade or profession and that 'trader' means a natural or legal person who, for the transaction in question, acts in his commercial or professional capacity.

14. Those provisions are sufficiently precise to enable the national court to determine upon whom, and for whose benefit, the obligations are imposed. No specific implementing measure is needed in that regard. The national court may confine itself to verifying whether the contract was concluded in the circumstances described by the directive and whether it was concluded between a trader and a consumer as defined by the directive.

15. In order to protect consumers who have concluded contracts in such circumstances, Article 4 of the directive provides that traders are to be required to give consumers written notice of their right of cancellation, together with the name and address of a person against whom that right may be exercised. It adds that, in the case of Article 1(1), that information must be given to the consumer at the time of conclusion of the contract. Finally, it provides that Member States are to ensure that their national legislation lays down appropriate consumer protection measures for cases where the information in question is not supplied.

16. Furthermore, pursuant to Article 5(1) of the directive, the consumer is to have the right to renounce the effects of his undertaking by sending notice within a period of not less than seven days from the time at which the trader informed him of his rights in accordance with the terms and conditions laid down by national law. Article 5(2) provides that the giving of such notice is to have the effect of releasing the consumer from any obligations under the contract.

17. Admittedly, Articles 4 and 5 allow the Member States some latitude regarding consumer protection when information is not provided by the trader and in determining the time-limit and conditions for cancellation. That does not, however, affect the precise and unconditional nature of the provisions of the directive at issue in this case. The latitude allowed does not make it impossible to determine minimum rights. Article 5 provides that the cancellation must be notified within a period of not less than seven days after the time at which the consumer received the pre-

scribed information from the trader. It is therefore possible to determine the minimum protection which must on any view be provided.

18. As regards the first issue therefore, the answer to be given to the national court must be that Article 1(1), Article 2 and Article 5 of the directive are unconditional and sufficiently precise as regards determination of the persons for whose benefit they were adopted and the minimum period within which notice of cancellation must be given.

Whether the provisions of the directive concerning the right of cancellation may be invoked in proceedings between a consumer and a trader

19. The second issue raised by the national court relates more particularly to the question whether, in the absence of measures transposing the directive within the prescribed time-limit, consumers may derive from the directive itself a right of cancellation against traders with whom they have concluded contracts and enforce that right before a national court.

20. As the Court has consistently held since its judgment in Case 152/84 *Marshall* v *Southampton and South-West Hampshire Health Authority* [1986] ECR 723, paragraph 48, a directive cannot of itself impose obligations on an individual and cannot therefore be relied upon as such against an individual.

21. The national court observes that if the effects of unconditional and sufficiently precise but untransposed directives were to be limited to relations between State entities and individuals, this would mean that a legislative measure would operate as such only as between certain legal subjects, whereas, under Italian law as under the laws of all modern States founded on the rule of law, the State is subject to the law like any other person. If the directive could be relied on only as against the State, that would be tantamount to a penalty for failure to adopt legislative measures of transposition as if the relationship were a purely private one.

22. It need merely be noted here that, as is clear from the judgment in *Marshall*, cited above (paragraphs 48 and 49), the case-law on the possibility of relying on directives against State entities is based on the fact that under Article 189 a directive is binding only in relation to 'each Member State to which it is addressed'. That case-law seeks to prevent 'the State from taking advantage of its own failure to comply with Community law'.

23. It would be unacceptable if a State, when required by the Community legislature to adopt certain rules intended to govern the State's relations – or those of State entities – with individuals and to confer certain rights on individuals, were able to rely on its own failure to discharge its obligations so as to deprive individuals of the benefits of those rights. Thus the Court has recognized that certain provisions of di-

rectives on conclusion of public works contracts and of directives on harmonization of turnover taxes may be relied on against the State (or State entities) (see the judgment in Case 103/88 *Fratelli Costanzo* v *Comune di Milano* [1989] ECR 1839 and the judgment in Case 8/81 *Becker* v *Finanzamt Münster-Innenstadt* [1982] ECR 53).

24. The effect of extending that case-law to the sphere of relations between individuals would be to recognize a power in the Community to enact obligations for individuals with immediate effect, whereas it has competence to do so only where it is empowered to adopt regulations.

25. It follows that, in the absence of measures transposing the directive within the prescribed time-limit, consumers cannot derive from the directive itself a right of cancellation as against traders with whom they have concluded a contract or enforce such a right in a national court.

26. It must also be borne in mind that, as the Court has consistently held since its judgment in Case 14/83 *Von Colson and Kamann* v *Land Nordrhein-Westfalen* [1984] ECR 1891, paragraph 26, the Member States' obligation arising from a directive to achieve the result envisaged by the directive and their duty under Article 5 of the Treaty to take all appropriate measures, whether general or particular, is binding on all the authorities of Member States, including, for matters within their jurisdiction, the courts. The judgments of the Court in Case C-106/89 *Marleasing* v *La Comercial Internacional de Alimentación* [1990] ECR I-4135, paragraph 8, and Case C-334/92 *Wagner Miret* v *Fondo de Garantía Salarial* [1993] ECR I-6911, paragraph 20, make it clear that, when applying national law, whether adopted before or after the directive, the national court that has to interpret that law must do so, as far as possible, in the light of the wording and the purpose of the directive so as to achieve the result it has in view and thereby comply with the third paragraph of Article 189 of the Treaty.

27. If the result prescribed by the directive cannot be achieved by way of interpretation, it should also be borne in mind that, in terms of the judgment in Joined Cases C-6/90 and C-9/90 *Francovich and Others* v *Italy* [1991] ECR I-5357, paragraph 39, Community law requires the Member States to make good damage caused to individuals through failure to transpose a directive, provided that three conditions are fulfilled. First, the purpose of the directive must be to grant rights to individuals. Second, it must be possible to identify the content of those rights on the basis of the provisions of the directive. Finally, there must be a causal link between the breach of the State's obligation and the damage suffered.

28. The directive on contracts negotiated away from business premises is undeniably intended to confer rights on individuals and it is equally certain that the minimum

content of those rights can be identified by reference to the provisions of the directive alone (see paragraph 17 above).

29. Where damage has been suffered and that damage is due to a breach by the State of its obligation, it is for the national court to uphold the right of aggrieved consumers to obtain reparation in accordance with national law on liability.

30. So, as regards the second issue raised by the national court, the answer must be that in the absence of measures transposing the directive within the prescribed time-limit consumers cannot derive from the directive itself a right of cancellation as against traders with whom they have concluded a contract or enforce such a right in a national court. However, when applying provisions of national law, whether adopted before or after the directive, the national court must interpret them as far as possible in the light of the wording and purpose of the directive.

Costs

[Para. 31 omitted]

On those grounds,

THE COURT,

in answer to the question referred to it by the Giudice Conciliatore di Firenze, by order of 24 January 1992, hereby rules:

1) **Article 1(1), Article 2 and Article 5 of Council Directive 85/577/EEC of 20 December 1985, concerning protection of the consumer in respect of contracts negotiated away from business premises, are unconditional and sufficiently precise as regards determination of the persons for whose benefit they were adopted and the minimum period within which notice of cancellation must be given.**

2) **In the absence of measures transposing Directive 85/577 within the prescribed time-limit, consumers cannot derive from the directive itself a right of cancellation as against traders with whom they have concluded a contract or enforce such a right in a national court. However, when applying provisions of national law, whether adopted before or after the directive, the national court must interpret them as far as possible in the light of the wording and purpose of the directive.**

Comments and questions

In paragraph 24 of the judgment in Case C-91/92 *Faccini Dori* v *Recreb Srl* [1994] ECR I-3325, the CJEU held that if it extended the principle of giving direct effect to directives to cover relations between individuals as well, this would be tantamount to giving the European Union powers to enact rules creating obligations for private citizens, whereas the Union only has powers to adopt such rules in the form of regulations. Consider the CJEU's respect for the principle that the Union can only act within the powers conferred on it by the Treaty in the Joined Cases C-46/93 and C-48/93 *Brasserie du Pêcheur* v *Germany* [1996] ECR I-1029 reproduced below in this chapter.

Consider whether, by reference to Article 20 TFEU (formerly Article 17 TEC) on Union citizenship, a citizen could argue that a directive should always be given direct effect, also horizontally (i.e. between two private parties), since a citizen of the Union is entitled to the same legal status throughout the Union. A citizen should thus not suffer from the fact that he has the misfortune to live in a Member State which has not implemented a directive in due time. Compare this argument with the judgment in Case C-194/94 *CIA Security International SA* v *Signalson et al* [1996] ECR I-2201, where the CJEU construed Directive 83/189 as laying down a procedure for the provision of information in the field of technical standards and regulations (the Technical Standards and Regulations Directive) in such a way that in the view of some observers, *in reality* the Directive was given effect between two citizens (direct horizontal effect). This judgment is included in Chapter 2. According to the *CIA* judgment, the Technical Standards and Regulations Directive meant that two private undertakings were prevented from asserting a national law against a third private undertaking. In litigation between the parties, this third undertaking was effectively given a right on the basis of the Technical Standards and Regulations Directive.

Where a directive does not have direct effect, the Member States' public authorities have a duty to interpret national laws *as far as possible* in accordance with a directive, cf. paragraph 26 of the judgment in the *Dori* case. Note that this does not mean that there is a duty to interpret national laws in a way which would be contrary to their wording and contents (*contra legem* interpretation). This duty to interpret national law in conformity with a directive only applies to the extent that it is possible, cf. the CJEU's use of the words 'as far as possible'. The CJEU has maintained this approach in more recent cases, but it has tightened up on the language used. See Joined Cases C-397/01 to C-403/01 *Bernhard Pfeiffer and others* v *Deutsches Rotes Kreuz, Kreisverband Waldshut eV* [2004] ECR I-8835, where in paragraph 119 the CJEU said as follows: '... a national court is required, when applying the provisions of domestic law adopted for the purpose of transposing obligations laid down by a directive, to consider the whole body of rules of national law and to interpret them, so far as possible, in the light of the wording and purpose of the directive in order to achieve an outcome consistent with the objective pursued by the directive. *In the main proceedings, the national court must thus do whatever lies within its jurisdiction to ensure that the maximum period of weekly working time, which is set at 48 hours* by Article 6(2) of Directive 93/104, is not exceeded' (emphasis added). In this connection, reference can also be made to Case C-144/04 *Werner Mangold* v *Rüdiger Helm* [2005] ECR I-9981, where for the first time the CJEU stated that the principle of the prohibition of discrimination on the grounds of age should be regarded as a general principle of Union law. The CJEU held that Union law, and in particular Article 6 of Directive 2000/78 establishing a general framework for equal treatment in employment and occupation, should be interpreted as preventing national legislation, such as the German legislation referred before the CJEU, which allowed an unlimited right to enter into employment contracts for a limited period, expiring when the employee reached 52. However, Union law would not prevent entering into such contracts where there is a close connection with an earlier contract of employment of indefinite duration concluded with the same employer. At the same time, in paragraph 78 the CJEU established that 'It is the responsibility of the national court to guarantee the full effectiveness of the general principle of non-discrimination in respect of age, setting aside any provision of national law which may conflict with Community law, even where the period prescribed for transposition of that directive has not yet expired.' This finding means that the Union law principle prohibiting discrimination on the grounds of age also applies in parallel circumstances. The principle should therefore be applied in the actual dispute between the employee Mangold and the private employer. The case shows that the distinction between, on the one hand, the direct effect of the Directive which does not apply to parallel circumstances and, on the other hand, the direct effect of the Treaty provisions and principles of Union law, which do apply in parallel circumstances, is finely balanced. In the *Mangold* case, by elevating a right in a directive to a principle of Union law, the CJEU seems to have given this right direct horizontal effect without having thereby changed the well-established practice that directives cannot be given direct horizontal effect.

Where it is not possible to interpret national law in accordance with the directive, which was the situation in the *Dori* case, since the Italian law did not allow consumers the right of reconsidering doorstep purchases, the question arises of the State's duty to compensate private parties for any loss which they may have suffered through the State's failure to implement the directive. This special Union law liability was laid down for the first time in Joined Cases C-6/90 and C-9/90 *Francovich* [1991] ECR I-5357. This case is discussed below in the comments on the *Brasserie du Pêcheur* case.

JUDGMENT OF THE COURT (Fifth Chamber)
16 December 1993

Teodoro Wagner Miret and Fondo de Garantía Salarial. (Reference to the Court for a preliminary ruling by the Tribunal Superior de Justicia, Catalonia – Spain)

'Directive on the protection of employees in the event of the insolvency of their employer – Scope of application – Guarantee institution'

Case C-334/92

Judgment

1. By order of 31 July 1992, registered at the Court Registry on 4 August 1992, the Tribunal Superior de Justicia (High Court of Justice), Catalonia (Spain), referred to the Court pursuant to Article 177 of the EEC Treaty certain questions for a preliminary ruling on the interpretation of Council Directive 80/987/EEC of 20 October 1980 on the approximation of the laws of the Member States relating to the protection of employees in the event of the insolvency of their employer (OJ 1980 L 283, p. 23, 'directive on the insolvency of employers'), as amended by Council Directive 87/164/EEC of 2 March 1987 (OJ 1987 L 66, p. 11).

2. Those questions arose in proceedings in which Mr Wagner Miret, a member of the higher management staff of an undertaking which became insolvent, claims the payment of arrears of remuneration from the Fondo de Garantía Salarial.

3. The directive on the insolvency of employers requires the Member States to adopt the measures necessary to ensure that guarantee institutions guarantee the payment of employees' outstanding claims in the event of their employer's insolvency.

4. Under Spanish law a guarantee fund was established by Article 33 of Law 8/80, Employees' Statute, of 10 March 1980 ('Employees' Statute'), that is to say, before the adoption of the directive on the insolvency of employers.

5. On its accession to the European Communities the Kingdom of Spain did not consider it necessary to amend its national law in order to bring it into line with that directive.

6. It is apparent from the documents before the Court that the Spanish courts took the view that the protection established by Article 33 of the Employees' Statute does not apply to higher management staff. Article 15 of Royal Decree No 1382/85 of 1 August 1985, relating to guarantees for higher management staff, makes no reference to that provision. On the other hand, the judgments of Spanish courts differ as

to whether higher management staff may claim such protection on the basis of the directive on the insolvency of employers.

7. Mr Wagner Miret, a member of the higher management staff of CEP Catalana SA, was dismissed under a 'redundancy' procedure authorized on 24 November 1989 by the head of the Local Labour Department of the Labour Department of the Autonomous Community of Catalonia. After the company was declared insolvent, he brought an action before the Juzgado de lo Social No 27, Barcelona, to recover the unpaid salary for October and November 1989 and for the appropriate severance payments. These amounts totalled PTA 434 880. By judgment of 18 December 1991 his application was dismissed on the ground that he had been a member of the higher management staff.

8. The plaintiff then appealed against this judgment to the Tribunal Superior de Justicia, Catalonia, which referred the following questions to the Court:
   (a) Does Directive 80/987/EEC of 20 October 1980 apply to all employees, to the exclusion of those listed in the Annex to the said Directive (87/164/EEC of 11 March 1987)?
   (b) In view of the fact that Spain has not included in the Annex to Directive 87/164/EEC of 11 March 1987, which supplements the original Annex following Spain's accession to the Community, the specific exception concerning higher management staff, may such persons be excluded from the general application of the guarantees provided for in Directive 80/987/EEC?
   (c) In the event that the guarantees under Directive 80/987/EEC apply to higher management staff in Spain, should the specific implementation thereof be carried out by the ordinary body envisaged for all other employees (Fondo de Garantía Salarial) or by means of compensation payable directly by the State?

The first two questions

9. By the first two questions the national court is asking in essence whether members of the higher management staff may be excluded from the scope of the directive on the insolvency of employers as they are not included in Section I of the Annex to that directive.

10. The directive on the insolvency of employers applies, according to Article 1(1) thereof, to employees' claims arising from contracts of employment or employment relationships and existing against employers who are in a state of insolvency. However, Article 1(2) authorizes the Member States to exclude 'claims by certain categories of employee from the scope of this Directive by virtue of the special nature of the employee's contract of employment or employment relationship or of the existence of other forms of guarantee offering the employee protection equivalent to that resulting from this Directive'. A list of the excluded categories of employee is given in Section I of the Annex to the directive.

11. However, under Article 2(2) of the directive the definition of 'employee' is a matter of national law.

12. It follows that the directive on the insolvency of employers is intended to apply to all categories of employee defined as such by the national law of a Member State, with the exception of those listed in the Annex to the directive.

13. Exercising the option provided for by Article 1(2) of the directive, the Kingdom of Spain requested the exclusion of domestic servants employed by a natural person. This exclusion appears in Section I of the Annex to the directive on the insolvency of employers, as amended, by reason of the accession of the Kingdom of Spain, by Directive 87/164 of 2 March 1987. In contrast, the Kingdom of Spain did not request the inclusion of the category of higher management staff in Section I of the Annex.

14. The reply to the first two questions must therefore be that higher management staff may not be excluded from the scope of Council Directive 80/987/EEC on the approximation of the laws of the Member States relating to the protection of employees in the event of the insolvency of their employer, as amended by Council Directive 87/164/EEC of 2 March 1987, where they are classified under national law as employees and they are not listed in section I of the Annex to the directive.

Third question

15. By the third question, the national court in essence asks whether higher management staff are entitled, by virtue of the directive on the insolvency of employers, to request the payment of amounts owing to them by way of salary from the guarantee body established by national law for the other categories of employee or, if this is not the case, whether they are entitled to request the Member State concerned to make good the loss and damage sustained as a result of the failure to implement the directive in their respect.

16. It should first be observed that the Kingdom of Spain has established no guarantee institution other than the Fondo de Garantía Salarial.

17. Secondly, in its judgment of 19 November 1991, Cases C-6/90 and C-9/90 *Francovich and Others* [1991] ECR I-5357, the Court held (paragraph 25) that under Article 5 of the directive on the insolvency of employers, the Member States have a broad discretion with regard to the organization, operation and financing of the guarantee institutions. The Court concluded (paragraph 26) that even though the provisions of the directive are sufficiently precise and unconditional as regards the determination of the persons entitled to the guarantee and as regards the content of that guarantee, those elements are not sufficient to enable individuals to rely, as against the State, on those provisions before the national courts.

18. With regard, more particularly, to the problem raised by the national court, it should be pointed out that the directive on the insolvency of employers does not oblige the Member States to set up a single guarantee institution for all categories of employee, and consequently to bring higher management staff within the ambit of the guarantee institution established for the other categories of employee. Article 3(1) leaves it to the Member States to adopt the measures necessary to ensure that guarantee institutions guarantee payment of employees' outstanding claims.

19. From the discretion thus given to the Member States it must therefore be concluded that higher management staff cannot rely on the directive in order to request the payment of amounts owing by way of salary from the guarantee institution established for the other categories of employee.

20. Thirdly, it should be borne in mind that when it interprets and applies national law, every national court must presume that the State had the intention of fulfilling entirely the obligations arising from the directive concerned. As the Court held in its judgment in Case 106/89 *Marleasing* v *La Comercial Internacional de Alimentación* [1990] ECR I-4135, paragraph 8, in applying national law, whether the provisions in question were adopted before or after the directive, the national court called upon to interpret it is required to do so, so far as possible, in the light of the wording and the purpose of the directive in order to achieve the result pursued by the latter and thereby comply with the third paragraph of Article 189 of the Treaty.

21. The principle of interpretation in conformity with directives must be followed in particular where a national court considers, as in the present case, that the pre-existing provisions of its national law satisfy the requirements of the directive concerned.

22. It would appear from the order for reference that the national provisions cannot be interpreted in a way which conforms with the directive on the insolvency of employers and therefore do not permit higher management staff to obtain the benefit of the guarantees for which it provides. If that is the case, it follows from the *Francovich* judgment, cited above, that the Member State concerned is obliged to make good the loss and damage sustained as a result of the failure to implement the directive in their respect.

23. The reply to the third question must therefore be that (a) higher management staff are not entitled, under Directive 80/987, to request payment of amounts owing to them by way of salary from the guarantee institution established by national law for the other categories of employee, and (b) in the event that, even when interpreted in the light of that directive, national law does not enable higher management staff to obtain the benefit of the guarantees for which it provides, such staff are entitled to request the State concerned to make good the loss and damage sustained as a result of the failure to implement the directive in their respect.

Costs

[Para. 24 omitted]

On those grounds,

THE COURT (Fifth Chamber),

in answer to the questions referred to it by the Tribunal Superior de Justicia, Catalonia, by order of 31 July 1992, hereby rules:

1. **Higher management staff may not be excluded from the scope of Council Directive 80/987/EEC of 20 October 1980 on the approximation of the laws of the Member States relating to the protection of employees in the event of the insolvency of their employer, as amended by Council Directive 87/164/EEC of 2 March 1987, where they are classified under national law as employees and they are not listed in Section I of the Annex to the directive;**

2. **(a) Under Directive 80/987, higher management staff are not entitled to request payment of amounts owing to them by way of salary from the guarantee institution established by national law for the other categories of employee.**
   (b) In the event that, even when interpreted in the light of that directive, national law does not enable higher management staff to obtain the benefit of the guarantees for which it provides, such staff are entitled to request the State concerned to make good the loss and damage sustained as a result of the failure to implement the directive in their respect.

Comments and questions

What conditions did the CJEU lay down in the Case C-334/92 *Miret* v *Fondo de Garantía Salarial* [1993] ECR I-6911, for Directive 80/987/EEC on the approximation of the laws of the Member States relating to the protection of employees in the event of the insolvency of their employer, to have direct effect? If the CJEU had held that the Directive should satisfy these conditions in all respects in order to have direct effect, would Miret have been able to rely on the Directive in its claim against Fondo de Garantía Salarial? Or would the situation have been the same as in Case C-91/92 *Faccini Dori* v *Recreb Srl* [1994] ECR I-3325? Would the situation have been different if the Directive made clear that local government authorities were obliged to pay unpaid salary, and if it were shown that the Directive had not been implemented in Spanish law at all? In this connection, consider the concept of the State in EU law.

Consider whether it would be possible for the referring Spanish court to interpret the Spanish law in conformity with the Directive. If this was not possible, what conditions should have been satisfied so that Miret could have obtained compensation from the Spanish State? In this connection, refer to Joined Cases C-6/90 and C-9/90 *Francovich* v *Italy* [1991] ECR I-5357, which is discussed below in the comments on the *Brasserie du Pêcheur* case. Must such compensation be decided by the national courts or by the CJEU (General Court of the European Union)?

What is the legal distinction between a directive's direct effect and the duty to interpret national laws as far as possible in conformity with the directive? Does the duty to interpret national laws in conformity with directives also apply horizontally, i.e., between private citizens? Does the duty also apply in relations between the State and the citizens where the interpretation will lead to placing a greater burden on citizens (see Joined Cases C-74/95 and C-129/95 *Criminal proceedings against X* [1996] ECR I-6609 (printed below)?

JUDGMENT OF THE COURT (Fifth Chamber)
12 December 1996

Criminal proceedings against X. (References to the Court for a preliminary ruling by the Procura della Repubblica presso la Pretura Circondariale di Torino, Italy, and by the Pretura Circondariale di Torino, Italy)

'Directive 90/270/EEC on the minimum safety and health requirements for work with display screen equipment – Definition of worker – Eye and eyesight tests – Definition of workstation for the purposes of Articles 4 and 5 – Extent of the obligations laid down in Articles 4 and 5'

Joined Cases C-74/95 and C-129/95

Judgment

1. By orders of 10 March and 18 April 1995 respectively, received at the Court on 13 March and 20 April 1995, the Procura della Repubblica (Office of the Public Prosecutor) to the Pretura Circondariale di Torino (District Magistrate's Court, Turin) in Case C-74/95 and the Pretura Circondariale itself in Case C-129/95 referred to the Court for a preliminary ruling under Article 177 of the EC Treaty a number of questions on the interpretation of Council Directive 90/270/EEC of 29 May 1990 on the minimum safety and health requirements for work with display screen equipment (fifth individual Directive within the meaning of Article 16(1) of Directive 89/391/EEC) (OJ 1990 L 156, p. 14, hereinafter 'the Directive').

2. Those questions were raised in criminal proceedings against persons unknown for a presumed breach of Legislative Decree No 626 of 19 September 1994 (*Gazzetta Ufficiale della Repubblica Italiana* No 265, 12 November 1994, hereinafter 'the Decree'), in particular Title VI thereof ('Use of display screen equipment'), which implements the provisions of the Directive in Italian law.

3. In the context of those proceedings, inspectors from the Unità Sanitaria Locale (Local Health Authority), Turin, had collated information at the request of the Procura della Repubblica on the use of display screens at the headquarters of Telecom Italia in Turin. It transpired that certain workers used such screens more than four hours per day for fewer than the full number of days per working week, whereas others used a display screen less than four hours per day every day of the working week.

4. In its reference, the Procura della Repubblica observes that, in order to decide whether it should, in this case, take measures falling within its competence, such as a summons to appear or a precautionary sequestration in order to prevent the exacerbation or prolongation of the effects of any possible offences, it must ascertain

whether the constitutive elements of an offence are present and in particular whether Articles 50 to 59 of the Decree have been infringed.

5. Article 51 of the Decree defines a worker for the purposes of Title VI as one who 'systematically and habitually uses display screen equipment for at least four consecutive hours daily, discounting the breaks referred to in Article 54, every day of the working week'. The other provisions of Title VI concern employers' obligations, the organization of work, daily working conditions, arrangements for medical checks, information and training for workers, consultation of workers and worker participation. Title IX of the Decree provides for a system of criminal penalties.

6. The Procura della Repubblica considers that in order to interpret the relevant provisions of the Decree it is first necessary to ascertain the precise scope of the definition of 'worker' given in Article 2(c) of the Directive. For the purposes of the Directive, that provision gives the following definition: '(c) *worker*: any worker as defined in Article 3(a) of Directive 89/391/EEC who habitually uses display screen equipment as a significant part of his normal work'.

7. The Procura della Repubblica wishes to know in particular whether that definition excludes workers who use display screens every day of the working week but not necessarily for four consecutive hours every day or those who use such screens for at least four consecutive hours on every day but one of the working week.

8. It points out that Article 51 of the Decree implementing the Directive defines a worker as one who 'systematically and habitually uses display screen equipment for at least four consecutive hours daily, discounting the breaks referred to in Article 54, every day of the working week' and that Articles 54 and 55 of the Decree require breaks or changes of activity to provide relief from display screen work and impose health monitoring for those who 'work for at least four consecutive hours'.

9. The Procura della Repubblica then seeks further enlightenment on the scope of Article 9(1) and (2) of the Directive, according to which:

'1. Workers shall be entitled to an appropriate eye and eyesight test carried out by a person with the necessary capabilities:
   - before commencing display screen work,
   - at regular intervals thereafter, and
   - if they experience visual difficulties which may be due to display screen work.

2. Workers shall be entitled to an ophthalmological examination if the results of the test referred to in paragraph 1 show that this is necessary.'

10. The Procura della Repubblica wishes to know in particular whether Article 9(1) provides for regular eye and eyesight tests for all workers or whether such tests are confined to specific categories of workers, and also whether Article 9(2) requires ophthalmological examinations following the regular medical examinations as well as after the initial medical examination. It points out that, under Article 55 of the Decree, regular medical examinations concern only workers who have been classified as fit subject to certain reservations and those who have reached the age of 45; furthermore, it appears to require specialist checks only after the initial medical examination, and an ophthalmological examination only at a worker's request, whenever he or she suspects, and a doctor confirms, that there has been a deterioration in eyesight.

11. Finally, the Procura della Repubblica raises questions regarding the extent of the employer's obligation to bring workstations into conformity with the minimum requirements laid down in the Annex to the Directive, since the investigation in the present case has revealed possible infringements of Section 2 thereof ('Environment'). Those questions relate to Articles 4 and 5 of the Directive.

12. Article 4 provides: 'Employers must take the appropriate steps to ensure that workstations first put into service after 31 December 1992 meet the minimum requirements laid down in the Annex'; while Article 5 provides: 'Employers must take the appropriate steps to ensure that workstations already put into service on or before 31 December 1992 are adapted to comply with the minimum requirements laid down in the Annex not later than four years after that date'.

13. The Procura della Repubblica asks, first, whether the abovementioned provisions apply only where the 'workstation' as defined in Article 2 of the Directive is actually used by a 'worker' as also defined therein. Secondly, it wishes to know whether Articles 4 and 5 of the Directive require workstations to be adapted to comply only with the minimum requirements laid down in Section 1 of the Annex ('Equipment') or whether they must also meet the requirements in Sections 2 ('Environment') and 3 ('Operator/computer interface'). It points out that under Article 58 of the Decree workstations must comply with the minimum requirements laid down in Annex VII thereto, which concerns only equipment.

14. The Procura della Repubblica therefore decided, by decision of 10 March 1995, to refer those questions to the Court of Justice.

15. By decision of 18 April 1995, anticipating the possibility that the Court might consider that the Procura della Repubblica was not entitled to request a preliminary ruling under Article 177 of the EC Treaty, the Pretura Circondariale referred the same questions to the Court for a preliminary ruling.

16. The Pretura Circondariale considers that the request for a preliminary ruling concerns questions to which it needs an answer in order to be able to decide whether the application made to it by the Procura della Repubblica – for an order requiring an expert opinion for the purpose of determining whether the breaks accorded to the workers in question are sufficient, whether the medical tests are appropriate and whether the workstations comply with the minimum requirements – is well founded. The national court observes that, before making such an order, it must determine in particular whether the presumed infringements of the Decree have been committed. The interpretation of the Decree, which implements the Directive, depends on the answer to the questions referred for a preliminary ruling.

Case C-74/95

[Paras. 17-20 omitted]

Case C-129/95

21. It must first be noted that the Court cannot, in proceedings under Article 177 of the Treaty, rule whether a measure of national law is valid from the point of view of Community law, as it might in proceedings under Article 169 (see, for example, Case 6/64 *Costa* v *ENEL* [1964] ECR 585). It is, however, competent to provide the national court with all criteria for the interpretation of Community law which may enable that court to determine the issue of compatibility for the purposes of the decision in the case before it (see, for example, Case 223/78 *Grosoli* [1979] ECR 2621, paragraph 3).

22. In the present case, however, it is clear from the order for reference that the national court does not rule out the possibility that the effect of taking the provisions of the Directive into account might be to determine or aggravate the liability in criminal law of persons who act in contravention of those provisions, although no such liability would arise out of the interpretation of the legislation specifically adopted to implement the Directive.

23. It has consistently been held (see, for example, Case C-168/95 *Arcaro* [1996] ECR I-0000, paragraph 36) that a directive may not of itself create obligations for an individual and that a provision of a directive may not therefore, as such, be relied upon against such a person.

24. It is true that the national court must apply its domestic law as far as possible in the light of the wording and the purpose of the Directive so as to achieve the result it seeks to achieve and thereby comply with the third paragraph of Article 189 of the Treaty (see, for example, Case C-91/92 *Faccini Dori* v *Recreb* [1994] ECR I-3325, paragraph 26). However, that obligation on the national court to refer to the content of the Directive when interpreting the relevant rules of its national law is not unlim-

ited, particularly where such interpretation would have the effect, on the basis of the Directive and independently of legislation adopted for its implementation, of determining or aggravating the liability in criminal law of persons who act in contravention of its provisions (see, in particular, Case 80/86 *Kolpinghuis Nijmegen* [1987] ECR 3969, paragraph 13).

25. More specifically, in a case such as that in the main proceedings, which concerns the extent of liability in criminal law arising under legislation adopted for the specific purpose of implementing a directive, the principle that a provision of the criminal law may not be applied extensively to the detriment of the defendant, which is the corollary of the principle of legality in relation to crime and punishment and more generally of the principle of legal certainty, precludes bringing criminal proceedings in respect of conduct not clearly defined as culpable by law. That principle, which is one of the general legal principles underlying the constitutional traditions common to the Member States, has also been enshrined in various international treaties, in particular in Article 7 of the Convention for the Protection of Human Rights and Fundamental Freedoms (see, *inter alia*, the judgments of the European Court of Human Rights in *Kokkinakis* v *Greece*, 25 May 1993, Series A, No 260-A, paragraph 52, and in *S.W.* v *United Kingdom* and *C.R.* v *United Kingdom*, 22 November 1995, Series A, No 335-B, paragraph 35, and No 335-C, paragraph 33).

26. The national court must therefore ensure that that principle is observed when interpreting, in the light of the wording and the purpose of the Directive, the national legislation adopted in order to implement it.

27. Subject to those observations, an answer must be given to the questions raised by the national court.

Interpretation of Article 2(c) of the Directive

[Paras. 28-42 omitted]

On those grounds,

THE COURT (Fifth Chamber)

hereby:

Declares that the questions referred to it by the Procura della Repubblica presso la Pretura Circondariale di Torino are inadmissible;

and, in answer to the questions referred to it by the Pretura Circondariale di Torino, by order of 18 April 1995, rules:

1) **Article 9(1) of Council Directive 90/270/EEC of 29 May 1990 on the minimum safety and health requirements for work with display screen equipment (fifth individual Directive within the meaning of Article 16(1) of Directive 89/391/EEC) must be interpreted as meaning that the regular eye tests for which it provides are to be carried out on all workers to whom the Directive applies and Article 9(2) is to be interpreted as meaning that workers are entitled to an ophthalmological examination in all cases where the eye and eyesight test carried out pursuant to Article 9(1) shows that this is necessary.**

2) **On a proper construction of Articles 4 and 5 of Directive 90/270, the obligations they impose apply to all workstations as defined in Article 2(b), even if they are not used by workers as defined in Article 2(c), and workstations must be adapted to comply with all the minimum requirements laid down in the Annex.**

Comments and questions

In Joined Cases C-74/95 and C-129/95 *Criminal proceedings against X* [1996] ECR I-6609, the Italian court had to consider liability to punishment for infringements of Italian laws which *implemented* certain provisions of a directive. The Italian court was of the view that taking account of the provisions of the directive could lead to establishing or aggravating liability in criminal law, which was not a consequence of the national laws which were intended to implement the directive in Italian law.

In paragraph 24 of its judgment, the CJEU confirmed that the national court must apply its domestic law as far as possible in the light of the wording and purpose of the Directive so as to achieve its aims. However, the CJEU added that this obligation is not unlimited, particularly where such an interpretation would have the effect of establishing or aggravating the criminal liability of those who contravene its provisions. The CJEU referred in particular to the principle that a provision of criminal law may not be applied extensively to the detriment of the defendant, and to the general principle of legal certainty, which precludes bringing criminal proceedings for conduct which has not clearly been defined as criminal.

In his Opinion, the Advocate General pointed out that the CJEU had already established that directives cannot create or intensify criminal liability when liability has not been implemented in national laws. The Advocate General argued that the same should apply in cases of incomplete implementation, i.e., in cases where national implementation has taken place in principle, but where the implementation is defective.

In paragraph 23 of its judgment, the CJEU confirmed that a directive may not, of itself, create obligations for an individual. Thus, a provision of a directive may not, as such, be relied upon against private individuals. Compare this with the CJEU's decision in Case C-194/94 *CIA Security International SA* v *Signalson SA and Securitel SPRL* [1996] ECR I-2201, printed in Chapter 2 below, where in a case between two citizens one party was able to assert against the other party the State's failure to comply with the provisions of a directive. However, it must still be assumed that neither in public law nor in civil law can a directive provision have direct effect against private citizens. In this respect, see the 'Comments and questions' on Case C-91/92 *Paola Faccini Dori* v *Recreb Srl* (printed above).

In a recent case, the Danish High Court had to decide a dispute which concerned a difference between a national VAT rule and the 6th VAT Directive. The facts of the case were centred on the question of how far some bowling centres, which were operated as profit-making businesses, were liable to VAT on their activities. According to the then wording of the exemption provision of the Danish VAT Act, there was no requirement for an undertaking not to operate with the aim of making a profit in order to be exempt from the duty to pay VAT. On the other hand, Article 13 of the 6th VAT Directive states that exemption from liability to pay VAT can only be given to non-profit-making organizations. In its judgment, the High Court held that, under the Danish VAT Act, the bowling centres were exempt from liability to pay VAT under the Danish VAT Act. Which Union law principle did the High Court apply in this case?

JUDGMENT OF THE COURT
5 March 1996

Brasserie du Pêcheur SA v Bundesrepublik Deutschland and The Queen v Secretary of State for Transport, ex parte: Factortame Ltd and others. (References for a preliminary ruling: Bundesgerichtshof – Germany and High Court of justice, Queen's Bench Division, Divisional court – United Kingdom)

'Principle of Member State liability for damage caused to individuals by breaches of Community law attributable to the State – Breaches attributable to the national legislature – Conditions for State liability – Extent of reparation'

Joined Cases C-46/93 and C-48/93

Judgment

1. By orders of 28 January 1993 and 18 November 1992, received at the Court on 17 February 1993 and 18 February 1993, respectively, the Bundesgerichtshof (Federal Court of Justice) (Case C-46/93) and the High Court of Justice, Queen's Bench Division, Divisional Court (Case C-48/93) referred to the Court for a preliminary ruling under Article 177 of the EEC Treaty questions concerning the conditions under which a Member State may incur liability for damage caused to individuals by breaches of Community law attributable to that State.

2. The questions were raised in two sets of proceedings between, on the one hand, Brasserie du Pêcheur SA and the Federal Republic of Germany and, on the other, Factortame Ltd and others (hereinafter 'Factortame') and the United Kingdom of Great Britain and Northern Ireland.

C-46/93

3. Before the national court, Brasserie du Pêcheur, a French company based at Schiltigheim (Alsace), claims that it was forced to discontinue exports of beer to Germany in late 1981 because the competent German authorities considered that the beer it produced did not comply with the Reinheitsgebot (purity requirement) laid down in Paragraphs 9 and 10 of the Biersteuergesetz of 14 March 1952 (Law on Beer Duty, BGBl. I, p. 149), in the version dated 14 December 1976 (BGBl. I, p. 3341, hereinafter 'the BStG').

4. The Commission took the view that those provisions were contrary to Article 30 of the EEC Treaty and brought infringement proceedings against the Federal Republic of Germany on two grounds, namely the prohibition on marketing under the designation 'Bier' (beer) beers lawfully manufactured by different methods in other

Member States and the prohibition on importing beers containing additives. By judgment of 12 March 1987 in Case 178/84 *Commission* v *Germany* [1987] ECR 1227, the Court held that the prohibition on marketing beers imported from other Member States which did not comply with the provisions in question was incompatible with Article 30 of the Treaty.

5. Brasserie du Pêcheur consequently brought an action against the Federal Republic of Germany for reparation of the loss suffered by it as a result of that import restriction between 1981 and 1987, seeking damages in the sum of DM 1 800 000, representing a fraction of the loss actually incurred.

6. The Bundesgerichtshof refers to Paragraph 839 of the Bürgerliches Gesetzbuch (German Civil Code, 'the BGB') and Article 34 of the Grundgesetz (Basic Law, 'the GG'). According to the first sentence of Paragraph 839 of the BGB, 'If an official wilfully or negligently commits a breach of official duty incumbent upon him as against a third party, he shall compensate the third party for any damage arising therefrom.' Article 34 of the GG provides that 'If a person infringes, in the exercise of a public office entrusted to him, the obligations incumbent upon him as against a third party, liability therefor shall attach in principle to the State or to the body in whose service he is engaged.'

7. If those provisions are read together, it appears that, in order for the State to be liable, the third party must be capable of being regarded as beneficiary of the obligation breached, which means that the State is liable for breach only of obligations conceived in favour of a third party. However, as the Bundesgerichtshof points out, in the case of the BStG the task assumed by the national legislature concerns only the public at large and is not directed towards any particular person or class of persons who could be regarded as 'third parties' within the meaning of the provisions mentioned above.

8. In this context, the Bundesgerichtshof has referred the following questions to the Court for a preliminary ruling:

'1. Does the principle of Community law according to which Member States are obliged to pay compensation for damage suffered by an individual as a result of breaches of Community law attributable to those States also apply where such a breach consists of a failure to adapt a national parliamentary statute to the higher-ranking rules of Community law (this case concerning a failure to adapt Paragraphs 9 and 10 of the German Biersteuergesetz to Article 30 of the EEC Treaty)?

2. May the national legal system provide that any entitlement to compensation is to be subject to the same limitations as those applying where a national statute

breaches higher-ranking national law, for example where an ordinary Federal law breaches the Grundgesetz of the Federal Republic of Germany?

3. May the national legal system provide that entitlement to compensation is to be conditional on fault (intent or negligence) on the part of the organs of the State responsible for the failure to adapt the legislation?

4. If Question 1 is to be answered in the affirmative and Question 2 in the negative:
   (a) May liability to pay compensation under the national legal system be limited to the reparation of damage done to specific individual legal interests, for example property, or does it require full compensation for all financial losses, including lost profits?
   (b Does the obligation to pay compensation also require reparation of the damage already incurred before it was held in the judgment of the European Court of Justice of 12 March 1987 in Case 178/84 *Commission* v *Germany* [1987] ECR 1227 that Paragraph 10 of the German Biersteuergesetz infringed higher-ranking Community law?'

Case C-48/93

9. On 16 December 1988 Factortame and others, being individuals and companies incorporated under the laws of the United Kingdom, together with the directors and shareholders of those companies, brought an action before the High Court of Justice, Queen's Bench Division, Divisional Court (hereinafter 'the Divisional Court'), in which they challenged the compatibility of Part II of the Merchant Shipping Act 1988 with Community law, in particular Article 52 of the EEC Treaty. That act entered into force on 1 December 1988, subject to a transitional period expiring on 31 March 1989. It provided for the introduction of a new register for British fishing boats and made registration of such vessels, including those already registered in the former register, subject to certain conditions relating to the nationality, residence and domicile of the owners. Fishing boats ineligible for registration in the new register were deprived of the right to fish.

10. In answer to questions referred by the Divisional Court, the Court held by judgment of 25 July 1991 in Case C-221/89 *Factortame II* [1991] ECR I-3905 that conditions relating to the nationality, residence and domicile of vessel owners and operators as laid down by the registration system introduced by the United Kingdom were contrary to Community law, but that it was not contrary to Community law to stipulate as a condition for registration that the vessels in question must be managed and their operations directed and controlled from within the United Kingdom.

11. On 4 August 1989 the Commission brought infringement proceedings against the United Kingdom. In parallel, it applied for interim measures ordering the suspension of the abovementioned nationality conditions on the ground that they were

contrary to Articles 7, 52 and 221 of the EEC Treaty. By order of 10 October 1989 in Case 246/89 R *Commission* v *United Kingdom* [1989] ECR 3125, the President of the Court granted that application. Pursuant to that order, the United Kingdom adopted provisions amending the new registration system with effect from 2 November 1989. By judgment of 4 October 1991 in Case C-246/89 *Commission* v *United Kingdom* [1991] ECR I-4585, the Court confirmed that the registration conditions challenged in the infringement proceedings were contrary to Community law.

12. Meanwhile, on 2 October 1991, the Divisional Court made an order designed to give effect to this Court's judgment of 25 July 1991 in *Factortame II* and, at the same time, directed the claimants to give detailed particulars of their claims for damages. Subsequently, the claimants provided the national court with a detailed statement of their various heads of claim, covering expenses and losses incurred between 1 April 1989, when the legislation at issue entered into force, and 2 November 1989, when it was repealed.

13. Lastly, by order of 18 November 1992, the Divisional Court gave Rawlings (Trawling) Ltd, the 37th claimant in Case C-48/93, leave to amend its claim to include a claim for exemplary damages for unconstitutional behaviour on the part of the public authorities.

14. In that context, the Divisional Court referred the following questions to the Court for a preliminary ruling:

'1. In all the circumstances of this case, where:
(a) a Member State's legislation laid down conditions relating to the nationality, domicile and residence of the owners and managers of fishing vessels, and of the shareholders and directors in vessel-owning and managing companies, and
(b) such conditions were held by the Court of Justice in Cases C-221/89 and C-246/89 to infringe Articles 5, 7, 52 and 221 of the EEC Treaty, are those persons who were owners or managers of such vessels, or directors and/or shareholders in vessel-owning and managing companies, entitled as a matter of Community law to compensation by that Member State for losses which they have suffered as a result of all or any of the above infringements of the EEC Treaty?

2. If Question 1 is answered in the affirmative, what considerations, if any, does Community law require the national court to apply in determining claims for damages and interest relating to:
(a) expenses and/or loss of profit and/or loss of income during the period subsequent to the entry into force of the said conditions, during which the vessels were forced to lay up, to make alternative arrangements for fishing and/or to seek registration elsewhere;

(b) losses consequent on sales at an undervalue of the vessels, or of shares therein, or of shares in vessel-owning companies;
(c) losses consequent on the need to provide bonds, fines and legal expenses for alleged offences connected with the exclusion of vessels from the national register;
(d) losses consequent on the inability of such persons to own and operate further vessels;
(e) loss of management fees;
(f) expenses incurred in an attempt to mitigate the above losses;
(g) exemplary damages as claimed?'

15. Reference is made to the Report for the Hearing for a fuller account of the facts of the main proceedings, the procedure and the observations submitted to the Court, which are mentioned or discussed hereinafter only in so far as is necessary for the reasoning of the Court.

State liability for acts and omissions of the national legislature contrary to Community law (first question in both Case C-46/93 and Case C-48/93)

16. By their first questions, each of the two national courts essentially seeks to establish whether the principle that Member States are obliged to make good damage caused to individuals by breaches of Community law attributable to the State is applicable where the national legislature was responsible for the infringement in question.

17. In Joined Cases C-6/90 and C-9/90 *Francovich and Others* [1991] ECR I-5357, paragraph 37, the Court held that it is a principle of Community law that Member States are obliged to make good loss and damage caused to individuals by breaches of Community law for which they can be held responsible.

18. The German, Irish and Netherlands Governments contend that Member States are required to make good loss or damage caused to individuals only where the provisions breached are not directly effective: in *Francovich and Others* the Court simply sought to fill a lacuna in the system for safeguarding rights of individuals. In so far as national law affords individuals a right of action enabling them to assert their rights under directly effective provisions of Community law, it is unnecessary, where such provisions are breached, also to grant them a right to reparation founded directly on Community law.

19. That argument cannot be accepted.

20. The Court has consistently held that the right of individuals to rely on the directly effective provisions of the Treaty before national courts is only a minimum guarantee and is not sufficient in itself to ensure the full and complete implementation of the Treaty (see, in particular, Case 168/85 *Commission* v *Italy* [1986] ECR 2945,

paragraph 11, Case C-120/88 *Commission* v *Italy* [1991] ECR I-621, paragraph 10, and C-119/89 *Commission* v *Spain* [1991] ECR I-641, paragraph 9). The purpose of that right is to ensure that provisions of Community law prevail over national provisions. It cannot, in every case, secure for individuals the benefit of the rights conferred on them by Community law and, in particular, avoid their sustaining damage as a result of a breach of Community law attributable to a Member State. As appears from paragraph 33 of the judgment in *Francovich and Others*, the full effectiveness of Community law would be impaired if individuals were unable to obtain redress when their rights were infringed by a breach of Community law.

21. This will be so where an individual who is a victim of the non-transposition of a directive and is precluded from relying on certain of its provisions directly before the national court because they are insufficiently precise and unconditional, brings an action for damages against the defaulting Member State for breach of the third paragraph of Article 189 of the Treaty. In such circumstances, which obtained in the case of *Francovich and Others*, the purpose of reparation is to redress the injurious consequences of a Member State's failure to transpose a directive as far as beneficiaries of that directive are concerned.

22. It is all the more so in the event of infringement of a right directly conferred by a Community provision upon which individuals are entitled to rely before the national courts. In that event, the right to reparation is the necessary corollary of the direct effect of the Community provision whose breach caused the damage sustained.

23. In this case, it is undisputed that the Community provisions at issue, namely Article 30 of the Treaty in Case C-46/93 and Article 52 in Case C-48/93, have direct effect in the sense that they confer on individuals rights upon which they are entitled to rely directly before the national courts. Breach of such provisions may give rise to reparation.

24. The German Government further submits that a general right to reparation for individuals could be created only by legislation and that for such a right to be recognized by judicial decision would be incompatible with the allocation of powers as between the Community institutions and the Member States and with the institutional balance established by the Treaty.

25. It must, however, be stressed that the existence and extent of State liability for damage ensuing as a result of a breach of obligations incumbent on the State by virtue of Community law are questions of Treaty interpretation which fall within the jurisdiction of the Court.

26. In this case, as in *Francovich and Others*, those questions of interpretation have been referred to the Court by national courts pursuant to Article 177 of the Treaty.

27. Since the Treaty contains no provision expressly and specifically governing the consequences of breaches of Community law by Member States, it is for the Court, in pursuance of the task conferred on it by Article 164 of the Treaty of ensuring that in the interpretation and application of the Treaty the law is observed, to rule on such a question in accordance with generally accepted methods of interpretation, in particular by reference to the fundamental principles of the Community legal system and, where necessary, general principles common to the legal systems of the Member States.

28. Indeed, it is to the general principles common to the laws of the Member States that the second paragraph of Article 215 of the Treaty refers as the basis of the non-contractual liability of the Community for damage caused by its institutions or by its servants in the performance of their duties.

29. The principle of the non-contractual liability of the Community expressly laid down in Article 215 of the Treaty is simply an expression of the general principle familiar to the legal systems of the Member States that an unlawful act or omission gives rise to an obligation to make good the damage caused. That provision also reflects the obligation on public authorities to make good damage caused in the performance of their duties.

30. In any event, in many national legal systems the essentials of the legal rules governing State liability have been developed by the courts.

31. In view of the foregoing considerations, the Court held in *Francovich and Others*, at paragraph 35, that the principle of State liability for loss and damage caused to individuals as a result of breaches of Community law for which it can be held responsible is inherent in the system of the Treaty.

32. It follows that that principle holds good for any case in which a Member State breaches Community law, whatever be the organ of the State whose act or omission was responsible for the breach.

33. In addition, in view of the fundamental requirement of the Community legal order that Community law be uniformly applied (see, in particular, Joined Cases C-143/88 and C-92/89 *Zuckerfabrik Süderdithmarschen and Zuckerfabrik Soest* [1991] ECR I-415, paragraph 26), the obligation to make good damage caused to individuals by breaches of Community law cannot depend on domestic rules as to the division of powers between constitutional authorities.

34. As the Advocate General points out in paragraph 38 of his Opinion, in international law a State whose liability for breach of an international commitment is in issue will be viewed as a single entity, irrespective of whether the breach which gave rise to the damage is attributable to the legislature, the judiciary or the executive. This

must apply *a fortiori* in the Community legal order since all State authorities, including the legislature, are bound in performing their tasks to comply with the rules laid down by Community law directly governing the situation of individuals.

35. The fact that, according to national rules, the breach complained of is attributable to the legislature cannot affect the requirements inherent in the protection of the rights of individuals who rely on Community law and, in this instance, the right to obtain redress in the national courts for damage caused by that breach.

36. Consequently, the reply to the national courts must be that the principle that Member States are obliged to make good damage caused to individuals by breaches of Community law attributable to the State is applicable where the national legislature was responsible for the breach in question.

Conditions under which the State may incur liability for acts and omissions of the national legislature contrary to Community law (second question in Case C-46/93 and first question in Case C-48/93)

37. By these questions, the national courts ask the Court to specify the conditions under which a right to reparation of loss or damage caused to individuals by breaches of Community law attributable to a Member State is, in the particular circumstances, guaranteed by Community law.

38. Although Community law imposes State liability, the conditions under which that liability gives rise to a right to reparation depend on the nature of the breach of Community law giving rise to the loss and damage (*Francovich and Others*, paragraph 38).

39. In order to determine those conditions, account should first be taken of the principles inherent in the Community legal order which form the basis for State liability, namely, first, the full effectiveness of Community rules and the effective protection of the rights which they confer and, second, the obligation to cooperate imposed on Member States by Article 5 of the Treaty (*Francovich and Others*, paragraphs 31 to 36).

40. In addition, as the Commission and the several governments which submitted observations have emphasized, it is pertinent to refer to the Court's case-law on non-contractual liability on the part of the Community.

41. First, the second paragraph of Article 215 of the Treaty refers, as regards the non-contractual liability of the Community, to the general principles common to the laws of the Member States, from which, in the absence of written rules, the Court also draws inspiration in other areas of Community law.

42. Second, the conditions under which the State may incur liability for damage caused to individuals by a breach of Community law cannot, in the absence of particular justification, differ from those governing the liability of the Community in like circumstances. The protection of the rights which individuals derive from Community law cannot vary depending on whether a national authority or a Community authority is responsible for the damage.

43. The system of rules which the Court has worked out with regard to Article 215 of the Treaty, particularly in relation to liability for legislative measures, takes into account, *inter alia*, the complexity of the situations to be regulated, difficulties in the application or interpretation of the texts and, more particularly, the margin of discretion available to the author of the act in question.

44. Thus, in developing its case-law on the non-contractual liability of the Community, in particular as regards legislative measures involving choices of economic policy, the Court has had regard to the wide discretion available to the institutions in implementing Community policies.

45. The strict approach taken towards the liability of the Community in the exercise of its legislative activities is due to two considerations. First, even where the legality of measures is subject to judicial review, exercise of the legislative function must not be hindered by the prospect of actions for damages whenever the general interest of the Community requires legislative measures to be adopted which may adversely affect individual interests. Second, in a legislative context characterized by the exercise of a wide discretion, which is essential for implementing a Community policy, the Community cannot incur liability unless the institution concerned has manifestly and gravely disregarded the limits on the exercise of its powers (Joined Cases 83/76, 94/76, 4/77, 15/77 and 40/77 *HNL and Others* v *Council and Commission* [1978] ECR 1209, paragraphs 5 and 6).

46. That said, the national legislature – like the Community institutions – does not systematically have a wide discretion when it acts in a field governed by Community law. Community law may impose upon it obligations to achieve a particular result or obligations to act or refrain from acting which reduce its margin of discretion, sometimes to a considerable degree. This is so, for instance, where, as in the circumstances to which the judgment in *Francovich and Others* relates, Article 189 of the Treaty places the Member State under an obligation to take, within a given period, all the measures needed in order to achieve the result required by a directive. In such a case, the fact that it is for the national legislature to take the necessary measures has no bearing on the Member State's liability for failing to transpose the directive.

47. In contrast, where a Member State acts in a field where it has a wide discretion, comparable to that of the Community institutions in implementing Community pol-

icies, the conditions under which it may incur liability must, in principle, be the same as those under which the Community institutions incur liability in a comparable situation.

48. In the case which gave rise to the reference in Case C-46/93, the German legislature had legislated in the field of foodstuffs, specifically beer. In the absence of Community harmonization, the national legislature had a wide discretion in that sphere in laying down rules on the quality of beer put on the market.

49. As regards the facts of Case C-48/93, the United Kingdom legislature also had a wide discretion. The legislation at issue was concerned, first, with the registration of vessels, a field which, in view of the state of development of Community law, falls within the jurisdiction of the Member States and, secondly, with regulating fishing, a sector in which implementation of the common fisheries policy leaves a margin of discretion to the Member States.

50. Consequently, in each case the German and United Kingdom legislatures were faced with situations involving choices comparable to those made by the Community institutions when they adopt legislative measures pursuant to a Community policy.

51. In such circumstances, Community law confers a right to reparation where three conditions are met: the rule of law infringed must be intended to confer rights on individuals; the breach must be sufficiently serious; and there must be a direct causal link between the breach of the obligation resting on the State and the damage sustained by the injured parties.

52. Firstly, those conditions satisfy the requirements of the full effectiveness of the rules of Community law and of the effective protection of the rights which those rules confer.

53. Secondly, those conditions correspond in substance to those defined by the Court in relation to Article 215 in its case-law on liability of the Community for damage caused to individuals by unlawful legislative measures adopted by its institutions.

54. The first condition is manifestly satisfied in the case of Article 30 of the Treaty, the relevant provision in Case C-46/93, and in the case of Article 52, the relevant provision in Case C-48/93. Whilst Article 30 imposes a prohibition on Member States, it nevertheless gives rise to rights for individuals which the national courts must protect (Case 74/76 *Iannelli & Volpi* v *Meroni* [1977] ECR 557, paragraph 13). Likewise, the essence of Article 52 is to confer rights on individuals (Case 2/74 *Reyners* [1974] ECR 631, paragraph 25).

55. As to the second condition, as regards both Community liability under Article 215 and Member State liability for breaches of Community law, the decisive test for

finding that a breach of Community law is sufficiently serious is whether the Member State or the Community institution concerned manifestly and gravely disregarded the limits on its discretion.

56. The factors which the competent court may take into consideration include the clarity and precision of the rule breached, the measure of discretion left by that rule to the national or Community authorities, whether the infringement and the damage caused was intentional or involuntary, whether any error of law was excusable or inexcusable, the fact that the position taken by a Community institution may have contributed towards the omission, and the adoption or retention of national measures or practices contrary to Community law.

57. On any view, a breach of Community law will clearly be sufficiently serious if it has persisted despite a judgment finding the infringement in question to be established, or a preliminary ruling or settled case-law of the Court on the matter from which it is clear that the conduct in question constituted an infringement.

58. While, in the present cases, the Court cannot substitute its assessment for that of the national courts, which have sole jurisdiction to find the facts in the main proceedings and decide how to characterize the breaches of Community law at issue, it will be helpful to indicate a number of circumstances which the national courts might take into account.

59. In Case C-46/93 a distinction should be drawn between the question of the German legislature's having maintained in force provisions of the Biersteuergesetz concerning the purity of beer prohibiting the marketing under the designation 'Bier' of beers imported from other Member States which were lawfully produced in conformity with different rules, and the question of the retention of the provisions of that same law prohibiting the import of beers containing additives. As regards the provisions of the German legislation relating to the designation of the product marketed, it would be difficult to regard the breach of Article 30 by that legislation as an excusable error, since the incompatibility of such rules with Article 30 was manifest in the light of earlier decisions of the Court, in particular Case 120/78 *Rewe-Zentral* [1979] ECR 649 ('Cassis de Dijon') and Case 193/80 *Commission* v *Italy* [1981] ECR 3019 ('vinegar'). In contrast, having regard to the relevant case-law, the criteria available to the national legislature to determine whether the prohibition of the use of additives was contrary to Community law were significantly less conclusive until the Court's judgment of 12 March 1987 in *Commission* v *Germany*, cited above, in which the Court held that prohibition to be incompatible with Article 30.

60. A number of observations may likewise be made about the national legislation at issue in Case C-48/93.

61. The decision of the United Kingdom legislature to introduce in the Merchant Shipping Act 1988 provisions relating to the conditions for the registration of fishing vessels has to be assessed differently in the case of the provisions making registration subject to a nationality condition, which constitute direct discrimination manifestly contrary to Community law, and in the case of the provisions laying down residence and domicile conditions for vessel owners and operators.

62. The latter conditions are prima facie incompatible with Article 52 of the Treaty in particular, but the United Kingdom sought to justify them in terms of the objectives of the common fisheries policy. In the judgment in *Factortame II*, cited above, the Court rejected that justification.

63. In order to determine whether the breach of Article 52 thus committed by the United Kingdom was sufficiently serious, the national court might take into account, *inter alia*, the legal disputes relating to particular features of the common fisheries policy, the attitude of the Commission, which made its position known to the United Kingdom in good time, and the assessments as to the state of certainty of Community law made by the national courts in the interim proceedings brought by individuals affected by the Merchant Shipping Act.

64. Lastly, consideration should be given to the assertion made by Rawlings (Trawling) Ltd, the 37th claimant in Case C-48/93, that the United Kingdom failed to adopt immediately the measures needed to comply with the Order of the President of the Court of 10 October 1989 in *Commission* v *United Kingdom,* cited above, and that this needlessly increased the loss it sustained. If this allegation – which was certainly contested by the United Kingdom at the hearing – should prove correct, it should be regarded by the national court as constituting in itself a manifest and, therefore, sufficiently serious breach of Community law.

65. As for the third condition, it is for the national courts to determine whether there is a direct causal link between the breach of the obligation borne by the State and the damage sustained by the injured parties.

66. The aforementioned three conditions are necessary and sufficient to found a right in individuals to obtain redress, although this does not mean that the State cannot incur liability under less strict conditions on the basis of national law.

67. As appears from paragraphs 41, 42 and 43 of *Francovich and Others*, cited above, subject to the right to reparation which flows directly from Community law where the conditions referred to in the preceding paragraph are satisfied, the State must make reparation for the consequences of the loss and damage caused in accordance with the domestic rules on liability, provided that the conditions for reparation of loss and damage laid down by national law must not be less favourable than those relating to similar domestic claims and must not be such as in practice to make it

impossible or excessively difficult to obtain reparation (see also Case 199/82 *Amministrazione delle Finanze dello Stato* v *San Giorgio* [1983] ECR 3595).

68. In that regard, restrictions that exist in domestic legal systems as to the non-contractual liability of the State in the exercise of its legislative function may be such as to make it impossible in practice or excessively difficult for individuals to exercise their right to reparation, as guaranteed by Community law, of loss or damage resulting from the breach of Community law.

69. In Case C-46/93 the national court asks in particular whether national law may subject any right to compensation to the same restrictions as apply where a law is in breach of higher-ranking national provisions, for instance, where an ordinary Federal law infringes the Grundgesetz of the Federal Republic of Germany.

70. While the imposition of such restrictions may be consistent with the requirement that the conditions laid down should not be less favourable than those relating to similar domestic claims, it is still to be considered whether such restrictions are not such as in practice to make it impossible or excessively difficult to obtain reparation.

71. The condition imposed by German law where a law is in breach of higher-ranking national provisions, which makes reparation dependent upon the legislature's act or omission being referable to an individual situation, would in practice make it impossible or extremely difficult to obtain effective reparation for loss or damage resulting from a breach of Community law, since the tasks falling to the national legislature relate, in principle, to the public at large and not to identifiable persons or classes of person.

72. Since such a condition stands in the way of the obligation on national courts to ensure the full effectiveness of Community law by guaranteeing effective protection for the rights of individuals, it must be set aside where an infringement of Community law is attributable to the national legislature.

73. Likewise, any condition that may be imposed by English law on State liability requiring proof of misfeasance in public office, such an abuse of power being inconceivable in the case of the legislature, is also such as in practice to make it impossible or extremely difficult to obtain effective reparation for loss or damage resulting from a breach of Community law where the breach is attributable to the national legislature.

74. Accordingly, the reply to the questions from the national courts must be that, where a breach of Community law by a Member State is attributable to the national legislature acting in a field in which it has a wide discretion to make legislative choices, individuals suffering loss or injury thereby are entitled to reparation where the rule

of Community law breached is intended to confer rights upon them, the breach is sufficiently serious and there is a direct causal link between the breach and the damage sustained by the individuals. Subject to that reservation, the State must make good the consequences of the loss or damage caused by the breach of Community law attributable to it, in accordance with its national law on liability. However, the conditions laid down by the applicable national laws must not be less favourable than those relating to similar domestic claims or framed in such a way as in practice to make it impossible or excessively difficult to obtain reparation.

The possibility of making reparation conditional upon the existence of fault (third question in Case C-46/93)

75. By its third question, the Bundesgerichtshof essentially seeks to establish whether, pursuant to the national legislation which it applies, the national court is entitled to make reparation conditional upon the existence of fault (whether intentional or negligent) on the part of the organ of the State to which the infringement is attributable.

76. As is clear from the case-file, the concept of fault does not have the same content in the various legal systems.

77. Next, it follows from the reply to the preceding question that, where a breach of Community law is attributable to a Member State acting in a field in which it has a wide discretion to make legislative choices, a finding of a right to reparation on the basis of Community law will be conditional, *inter alia*, upon the breach having been sufficiently serious.

78. So, certain objective and subjective factors connected with the concept of fault under a national legal system may well be relevant for the purpose of determining whether or not a given breach of Community law is serious (see the factors mentioned in paragraphs 56 and 57 above).

79. The obligation to make reparation for loss or damage caused to individuals cannot, however, depend upon a condition based on any concept of fault going beyond that of a sufficiently serious breach of Community law. Imposition of such a supplementary condition would be tantamount to calling in question the right to reparation founded on the Community legal order.

80. Accordingly, the reply to the question from the national court must be that, pursuant to the national legislation which it applies, reparation of loss or damage cannot be made conditional upon fault (intentional or negligent) on the part of the organ of the State responsible for the breach, going beyond that of a sufficiently serious breach of Community law.

The actual extent of the reparation (question 4(a) in Case C-46/93 and the second question in Case C-48/93)

81. By these questions, the national courts essentially ask the Court to identify the criteria for determination of the extent of the reparation due by the Member State responsible for the breach.

82. Reparation for loss or damage caused to individuals as a result of breaches of Community law must be commensurate with the loss or damage sustained so as to ensure the effective protection for their rights.

83. In the absence of relevant Community provisions, it is for the domestic legal system of each Member State to set the criteria for determining the extent of reparation. However, those criteria must not be less favourable than those applying to similar claims based on domestic law and must not be such as in practice to make it impossible or excessively difficult to obtain reparation.

84. In particular, in order to determine the loss or damage for which reparation may be granted, the national court may inquire whether the injured person showed reasonable diligence in order to avoid the loss or damage or limit its extent and whether, in particular, he availed himself in time of all the legal remedies available to him.

85. Indeed, it is a general principle common to the legal systems of the Member States that the injured party must show reasonable diligence in limiting the extent of the loss or damage, or risk having to bear the damage himself (Joined Cases C-104/89 and C-37/90 *Mulder and Others* v *Council and Commission* [1992] ECR I-3061, paragraph 33).

86. The Bundesgerichtshof asks whether national legislation may generally limit the obligation to make reparation to damage done to certain, specifically protected individual interests, for example property, or whether it should also cover loss of profit by the claimants. It states that the opportunity to market products from other Member States is not regarded in German law as forming part of the protected assets of the undertaking.

87. Total exclusion of loss of profit as a head of damage for which reparation may be awarded in the case of a breach of Community law cannot be accepted. Especially in the context of economic or commercial litigation, such a total exclusion of loss of profit would be such as to make reparation of damage practically impossible.

88. As for the various heads of damage referred to in the Divisional Court's second question, Community law imposes no specific criteria. It is for the national court to rule on those heads of damage in accordance with the domestic law which it applies, subject to the requirements set out in paragraph 83 above.

89. As regards in particular the award of exemplary damages, such damages are based under domestic law, as the Divisional Court explains, on the finding that the public authorities concerned acted oppressively, arbitrarily or unconstitutionally. In so far as such conduct may constitute or aggravate a breach of Community law, an award of exemplary damages pursuant to a claim or an action founded on Community law cannot be ruled out if such damages could be awarded pursuant to a similar claim or action founded on domestic law.

90. Accordingly, the reply to the national courts must be that reparation by Member States of loss or damage which they have caused to individuals as a result of breaches of Community law must be commensurate with the loss or damage sustained. In the absence of relevant Community provisions, it is for the domestic legal system of each Member State to set the criteria for determining the extent of reparation. However, those criteria must not be less favourable than those applying to similar claims or actions based on domestic law and must not be such as in practice to make it impossible or excessively difficult to obtain reparation. National legislation which generally limits the damage for which reparation may be granted to damage done to certain, specifically protected individual interests not including loss of profit by individuals is not compatible with Community law. Moreover, it must be possible to award specific damages, such as the exemplary damages provided for by English law, pursuant to claims or actions founded on Community law, if such damages may be awarded pursuant to similar claims or actions founded on domestic law.

Extent of the period covered by reparation (question 4(b) in Case C-46/93)

91. By this question, the Bundesgerichtshof asks whether the damage for which reparation may be awarded extends to harm sustained before a judgment is delivered by the Court finding that an infringement has been committed.

92. Following from the reply to the second question, the right to reparation under Community law exists where the conditions set out in paragraph 51 above are satisfied.

93. One of those conditions is that the breach of Community law must have been sufficiently serious. The fact that there is a prior judgment of the Court finding an infringement will certainly be determinative, but it is not essential in order for that condition to be satisfied (see paragraphs 55, 56 and 57 of this judgment).

94. Were the obligation of the Member State concerned to make reparation to be confined to loss or damage sustained after delivery of a judgment of the Court finding the infringement in question, that would amount to calling in question the right to reparation conferred by the Community legal order.

95. In addition, to make the reparation of loss or damage conditional upon the requirement that there must have been a prior finding by the Court of an infringement of Community law attributable to a Member State would be contrary to the principle of the effectiveness of Community law, since it would preclude any right to reparation so long as the presumed infringement had not been the subject of an action brought by the Commission under Article 169 of the Treaty and of a finding of an infringement by the Court. Rights arising for individuals out of Community provisions having direct effect in the domestic legal systems of the Member States cannot depend on the Commission's assessment of the expediency of taking action against a Member State pursuant to Article 169 of the Treaty or on the delivery by the Court of any judgment finding an infringement (see, to this effect, Joined Cases 314/81, 315/81, 316/81 and 83/82 *Waterkeyn and Others* [1982] ECR 4337, paragraph 16).

96. Accordingly, the reply to the national court's question must be that the obligation for Member States to make good loss or damage caused to individuals by breaches of Community law attributable to the State cannot be limited to damage sustained after the delivery of a judgment of the Court finding the infringement in question.

The request that the temporal effects of the judgment should be limited

97. The German Government requests the Court to limit any damage to be made good by the Federal Republic of Germany to loss or damage sustained after delivery of judgment in this case, in so far as the victims did not bring legal proceedings or make an equivalent claim before. It considers that such a temporal limitation of the effects of this judgment is necessary owing to the scale of its financial consequences for the Federal Republic of Germany.

98. It must be borne in mind that, were the national court to find that the conditions for liability of the Federal Republic of Germany are satisfied in this case, the State would have to make good the consequences of the damage caused within the framework of its domestic law on liability. Substantive and procedural conditions laid down by national law on reparation of damage are able to take account of the requirements of the principle of legal certainty.

99. However, those conditions may not be less favourable than those relating to similar domestic claims and must not be such as in practice to make it impossible or excessively difficult to obtain reparation (*Francovich and Others*, paragraph 43).

100. In view of the foregoing, there is no need for the Court to limit the temporal effects of this judgment.

Costs

[Para. 101 omitted]

On those grounds,

THE COURT,

in answer to the questions referred to it by the Bundesgerichtshof, by order of 28 January 1993, and by the High Court of Justice, Queen's Bench Division, Divisional Court, by order of 18 November 1992, hereby rules:

1) **The principle that Member States are obliged to make good damage caused to individuals by breaches of Community law attributable to the State is applicable where the national legislature was responsible for the breach in question.**

2) **Where a breach of Community law by a Member State is attributable to the national legislature acting in a field in which it has a wide discretion to make legislative choices, individuals suffering loss or injury thereby are entitled to reparation where the rule of Community law breached is intended to confer rights upon them, the breach is sufficiently serious and there is a direct causal link between the breach and the damage sustained by the individuals. Subject to that reservation, the state must make good the consequences of the loss or damage caused by the breach of Community law attributable to it, in accordance with its national law on liability. However, the conditions laid down by the applicable national laws must not be less favourable than those relating to similar domstic claims or framed in such a way as in practice to make it impossible or excessively difficult to obtain reparation.**

3) **Pursuant to the national legislation which it applies, reparation of loss or damage cannot be made conditional upon fault (intentional or negligent) on the part of the organ of the State responsible for the breach, going beyond that of a sufficiently serious breach of Community law.**

4) **Reparation by Member States of loss or damage which they have caused to individuals as a result of breaches of Community law must be commensurate with the loss or damage sustained. In the absence of relevant Community provisions, it is for the domestic legal system of each Member State to set the criteria for determining the extent of reparation. However, those criteria must not be less favourable than those applying to similar claims or actions based on domestic law and must not be such as in practice to make it impossible or excessively difficult to obtain reparation. National**

legislation which generally limits the damage for which reparation may be granted to damage done to certain, specifically protected individual interests not including loss of profit by individuals is not compatible with Community law. Moreover, it must be possible to award specific damages, such as the exemplary damages provided for by English law, pursuant to claims or actions founded on Community law, if such damages may be awarded pursuant to similar claims or actions founded on domestic law.

5) **The obligation for Member States to make good loss or damage caused to individuals by breaches of Community law attributable to the State cannot be limited to damage sustained after the delivery of a judgment of the Court finding the infringement in question.**

Comments and questions

The judgment in Joined Cases C-46/93 and C-48/93 *Brasserie du Pêcheur* v *Germany* [1996] ECR I-1029, laid down the conditions for the liability of Member States to pay compensation under Union law. The three conditions which must be met (see paragraph 51 of the judgment) are:

1. The rule or law infringed must be intended to confer rights on individuals.
2. The breach must be sufficiently serious.
3. There must be a direct causal link between the breach of its obligation by the State and the damage suffered by the injured party.

The conditions for compensation apply regardless of whether the Member State has failed to implement a directive, whether it has implemented a directive inadequately, or whether a Member State has contravened the substantive provisions of the TFEU. Furthermore, the same conditions apply even though the Union rules allow some discretion to the Member States. See paragraph 28 of the judgment in Case C-5/94 *The Queen* v *Ministry of Agriculture, ex parte Lomas* [1996] ECR I-4845.

The assessment of whether an infringement should be regarded as sufficiently serious is not the usual standard of assessment of culpability. What is decisive is whether the infringement is manifest and grave. As examples of the circumstances which the national court can take into consideration, the CJEU listed the following in paragraphs 56 and 57 of its judgment in Joined Cases C-46/93 and C-48/93 *Brasserie du Pêcheur* v *Germany* [1996] ECR I-1029.

i. The clarity and precision of the rule breached.
ii. The measure of discretion left to the national authorities.
iii. Whether the infringement or the damage caused was intentional or involuntary.
iv. Whether any error of law was excusable or not.

v. The fact that the position taken by a Union institution may have contributed towards the omission, adoption or retention of national measures or practices contrary to Union law.
vi. Whether a breach of Union law has persisted, despite a judgment by the CJEU which makes it clear that the infringement in question has been established.

In the judgment of the Bundesgericht of 24th October 1996 (*Entscheidungen des Bundesgerichthofes in Zivilsachen* Vol. 134, p. 30) it is stated, among other things, that: 'In zusammenfassender Würdigung dieses Sachverhalts sieht der Senat – den Vorgaben des Europäischen Gerichtshofs folgend – den Verstoss, soweit er für den Schaden unmittelbar ursächlich geworden ist, insgesamt als nicht hinreichend qualifiziert an.' In other words, the German court held that even if there had been a direct causal connection between the loss claimed and the actions of the German authorities, these actions were not sufficiently serious to establish liability to pay compensation in accordance with the guidelines of the CJEU. Is this the outcome which the CJEU would have expected from its preliminary ruling? Do you think the German State should have been liable to pay compensation under the Union rules on liability because it maintained the *Reinheitsgebot* rules (on the 'purity' of beer), so that the French brewer could not sell its French brewed beer in Germany?

It is worth noting that in the *Factortame* case, the English court found that the British government's infringement of Union law was sufficiently serious to justify awarding compensation to the owners of fishing vessels, cf. the judgment of the House of Lords of 28th October 1999 (All England Law Reports, 1999 p. 906).

A little over six months after giving its judgment in the *Brasserie du Pêcheur* case, the CJEU gave judgment in Case C-178/94 *Dillenkofer et al* [1996] ECR I-4845. In this case the CJEU summarised its practice on the liability of Member States to pay compensation in such a way that the rules are now presented as a coherent system. In particular, a problem had arisen from the fact that in its judgment in Joined Cases C-6/90 and C-9/90 *Francovich* [1991] ECR 5357, (in which the CJEU laid down for the first time that a Member State is liable under Union law to pay compensation if it implements a directive either inadequately or late), the CJEU did not appear to have required the infringement to have been 'sufficiently serious'. In the *Dillenkofer* judgment, the CJEU got round this problem by merely stating in paragraph 23 that 'the conditions laid down in that group of judgments are the same, since the condition that there should be a sufficiently serious breach, although not expressly mentioned in *Francovich*, was nevertheless evident from the circumstances of that case.' In other words, the CJEU held that the conditions under which a Member State can be liable to pay compensation depend on the nature of the breach of Union law causing the damage (cf. paragraph 24 of the *Dillenkofer* judgment).

The CJEU laid down that a breach is sufficiently serious where, in the exercise of its powers to issue general laws, a Member State manifestly and gravely exceeds its powers. Furthermore, the mere fact that there has been a breach of Union law can be sufficient to establish the existence of a sufficiently serious breach, if, when it committed the infringement, the Member State in question was not called upon to make any legislative choices and had only very limited discretion or none at all. Put in another way, there will be a sufficiently serious breach even if a Member State only has very narrow scope for action and it has acted outside this scope (cf. paragraph 25 of the *Dillenkofer* judgment). This will be the case where, for example, a Member State does not adopt any of the measures necessary for attaining the objectives of a directive within the deadline set in the directive (cf. paragraph 26 of the *Dillenkofer* judgment). Compensation for loss cannot be made conditional on the CJEU making a prior finding that a breach of Union law exists which can be ascribed to the State (cf. paragraphs 94-96 of the *Brasserie du Pêcheur* judgment), or that there should be culpability, whether intentional or negligent, of the body whose breach is in question (cf. paragraphs 75-80 of the *Brasserie du Pêcheur* judgment).

Consider whether, when assessing liability under Union law, there are differences between the following three situations:

1. The Member State has implemented a directive within the deadline set, but it later becomes apparent that the implementation was inadequate.
2. The Member State has completely failed to implement a directive in its national law.
3. The Member State has implemented a directive, but not before the deadline for doing so. (See the *Dillenkofer* judgment).

Consider whether the following circumstances are relevant for the assessment of liability to pay compensation, and if so, describe the relevance:

I. The Commission has refrained from bringing a case before the CJEU for failure to fulfil an obligation under the Treaty, in accordance with Article 258 TFEU.
II. The Union provision which has been contravened allows Member States very broad discretion, or alternatively, very narrow discretion.
III. The Union provision which has been contravened is very clear and precise, or alternatively, it is unclear and imprecise.

Under Union law, the liability to pay compensation for failures in the implementation of Union law is the liability of the Member States as such. However, this does not mean that municipal and regional authorities and other public authorities cannot be liable to pay compensation. In Case C-424/97 *Haim* v *Kassenzahnärztliche Vereinigung Nordrhein* [2000] ECR I-5123, the CJEU held that, in addition to the Member State itself, a public body, such as the Association of Dental Practitioners in Social Security Schemes in Nordrhein, could be liable to pay compensation for loss caused to individuals as a result of measures taken in breach of Union law.

Similarly, in Case C-470/03 *Lehtinen* [2007] ECR I-2749, the CJEU ruled that statements of State officials can be attributable to a Member State if, by reason of their form and circumstances, they give the persons to whom they are addressed the impression that they are official positions taken by the State, and not the personal opinion of the official. This means that a Member State can be liable to pay compensation for losses that are suffered, for example by a foreign producer, as a consequence of an incorrect statement by a State official concerning the producer's products. This applies even if the ruling is contrary to the directions of the Member State

Correspondingly, national courts which take decisions which are in conflict with Union law, so that a citizen or an undertaking suffers a loss, may be liable to pay compensation under Union law. This also applies to the supreme courts of the Member States. The question whether a Member State's supreme court has incurred a liability to pay compensation under Union law can be established by the Member State's lower courts, cf. Case C-224/01 *Gerhard Köbler* v *Austria* [2003] ECR I-10239, where in paragraph 36 the CJEU stated that: 'it follows from the requirements inherent in the protection of the rights of individuals relying on [Union] law that they must have the possibility of obtaining redress in the national courts for the damage caused by the infringement of those rights owing to a decision of a court adjudicating at last instance.' Some of the governments that made submissions in the case argued that such an outcome would be contrary to the principle of legal certainty and the authority of the courts. To this the CJEU replied in paragraph 39 that: 'recognition of the principle of State liability for a decision of a court adjudicating at last instance does not in itself have the consequence of calling in question that decision as *res judicata*. Proceedings seeking to render the State liable do not have the same purpose and do not necessarily involve the same parties as the proceedings resulting in the decision which has acquired the status of *res judicata*. The applicant in an action to establish the liability of the State will, if successful, secure an order against it for reparation of the damage incurred but not necessarily a declaration invalidating the status of *res judicata* of the judicial decision which was responsible for the damage. In any event, the principle of State liability inherent in the Union legal order requires such reparation, but not revision of the judicial decision which was responsible for the damage.' In the specific case the CJEU did not find that it constituted a sufficiently serious infringement that the Austrian administrative court had withdrawn a reference to the CJEU for a preliminary ruling after the Registrar of the CJEU drew the attention of the administrative court to the CJEU's decision in Case C-15/96 *Kalliope Schöning-Kougebetopoulou* v *Freie und Hansestadt Hamburg* [1998] ECR I-47 (Greek doctors).

CHAPTER 2

Free movement of goods

JUDGMENT OF THE COURT
23 November 1978

Regina v Ernest George Thompson, Brian Albert Johnson and Colin Alex Norman Woodiwiss. (Reference for a preliminary ruling: Court of Appeal (England) – United Kingdom)

'Means of payment and movements of capital'

Case 7/78

Judgment

1. The Court of Appeal of England and Wales (Criminal Division), by an order of 15 December 1977 received at the Court on 16 January 1978 referred to the Court under article 177 of the EEC Treaty several questions on the interpretation of Articles 30 to 37 and Articles 67 to 73 of the Treaty.

2. These questions were raised in a criminal appeal by three British nationals (hereinafter referred to as 'the appellants') who had been found guilty by the Crown Court at Canterbury of being knowingly concerned in a fraudulent evasion of the prohibition on importation of gold coins into the United Kingdom and on the export of silver alloy coins minted before 1947 from the United Kingdom.

3. The importation of gold coins into the United Kingdom is prohibited by the Import of Goods (Control) Order 1954 made by the Board of Trade in exercise of its powers under the Import, Export and Customs Powers (Defence) Act 1939.

4. By virtue of an Open General Licence granted by the Secretary of State for Trade and Industry and dated 5 July 1973 the importation of all goods was authorized with certain exceptions not including gold coins. However, pursuant to an amendment to the said licence entitled 'Amendment No 10' dated 15 April 1975, which came into operation on 16 April 1975, gold coins were included among the goods the importation of which was prohibited except under the authority of a licence granted by the Board of Trade.

5. By virtue of the Export of Goods (Control) Order 1970, made in exercise of powers under the said Act of 1939, the export from the United Kingdom, except under licence, of silver alloy coins minted before 1947 in a quantity exceeding ten in number and not more than 100 years old at the date of exportation is prohibited.

6. The export of such coins to another Member State of the EEC was authorized by an Open General Licence dated 20 December 1972 which was granted by the Secre-

tary of State and which, as far as such coins are concerned, was revoked and replaced by another Open General Licence dated 25 June 1973.

7. This second Open General Licence was revoked by another Open General Licence dated 5 July 1974 which came into operation on 15 july 1974 and had the effect of taking such coins out of the ambit of the Open General Licence with the result that as from 15 July 1974 they could not be exported except under licence.

8. The appellants arranged for 3 400 South African Krugerrands which came from the Agosi firm in Pforzheim in the Federal Republic of Germany to be brought into the United Kingdom between 24 April 1975 and 30 June 1975.

9. They also exported between 7 August 1974 and 26 May 1975 for the same German firm 40.39 tonnes of silver alloy coins minted in the United Kingdom before 1947, namely sixpences, shillings, florins and half-crowns.

10. The appellants, having pleaded guilty before the court of first instance, appealed to the Court of Appeal (Criminal Division) before which they submitted that the provisions of British law prohibiting the imports and exports in question infringe articles 30 and 34 of the Treaty.

11. Article 30, as complemented by Article 42 of the act of accession, prohibits, as from 1 January 1975 at the latest, in the case of the United Kingdom, any measure having an effect equivalent to a quantitative restriction on imports from other member states.

12. Article 34, as complemented by the said Article 42, prohibits, as from 1 January 1975 at the latest, in the case of the United Kingdom, any measure having an effect equivalent to a quantitative restriction on exports to other Member States.

13. The appellants also submitted that the restrictions on exports and imports contained in British legislation cannot be justified on grounds of public policy on the basis of Article 36 of the Treaty.

14. On the other hand the British Government has maintained that the coins imported and those exported are 'capital' within the meaning of Article 67 *et seq.* of the Treaty and that the provisions of Articles 30 and 34 are consequently inapplicable.

15. Even if the coins in question were to be regarded as goods falling within the scope of Article 30 *et seq.* of the Treaty the restrictions on imports and exports would be authorized under Article 36 of the Treaty, since they could be justified on grounds of public policy.

16. As far as concerns the restrictions on imports the ban on the importation of certain gold coins into the United Kingdom was, according to the British Government, enacted in order:
    (i) to prevent the drain on its balance of payments and
    (ii) to prevent the speculation and hoarding of unproductive assets.

17. As far as concerns the restrictions on exports the ban on exports from the United Kingdom of silver coins minted before 1947 was enacted in order:

    (i) to ensure that there is no shortage of current coins for use of the public;
    (ii) to ensure that any profit resulting from any increase in the value of metal content of the coin accrues to the Member State rather than to an individual and
    (iii) to prevent the destruction of these United Kingdom coins – which if it occurred within its jurisdiction would be a criminal offence – from occurring outside its jurisdiction.

18. In these circumstances the Court of Appeal has asked the following questions:

    1. Are the following coins in principle 'capital' within the meaning of Part Two, title III, Chapter 4 of the Treaty of Rome:
       (a) gold coins which are produced in a third country such as Krugerrands, but which circulate freely within a Member State;
       (b) silver alloy coins, which are legal tender in a Member State;
       (c) silver alloy coins of a Member State, which have been, and which, although no longer legal tender in that State are protected as coin from destruction in that State?

    2. If so, can the quantity and manner in which and the purposes for which such coins are traded result in such coins ceasing to be within the term 'capital' in Part Two, Title III, Chapter 4?

    3. Do the provisions of Part Two, Title III, Chapter 4 of the Treaty of Rome apply to such of the aforesaid coins as are 'capital' to the exclusion of the provisions of Part Two, Title I, Chapter 2 of the Treaty?

    4. If the answers to all or any of the above questions are such as to determine that the Articles in this case fall within Part Two, Title I, Chapter 2, does the term 'public policy' in Article 36 of the Treaty of Rome mean that a Member State may seek to justify restrictions on:
       (a) The import of gold coins on either or both of the following grounds:
       (i) to prevent the drain on its balance of payments,
       (ii) to prevent the speculation and hoarding of unproductive assets,
       (b) the export of its own silver alloy coinage on any or all of the following grounds:

(i) to ensure that there is no shortage of current coins for use of the public,
(ii) to ensure that any profit resulting from any increase in the value of metal content of the coin accrues to the Member State rather than to an individual,
(iii) to prevent the destruction of its coins occurring outside its jurisdiction, which if it occurred within its jurisdiction would be a criminal offence?

19. An examination of the questions asked shows that, even if these questions have been formulated so as to lay emphasis on the description of the coins in question as 'capital', their actual purpose is to find out whether these coins are goods falling within the provisions of Articles 30 to 37 of the Treaty or constitute a means of payment falling within the scope of other provisions.

20. Understood in this way, these questions must be considered in the context of the general system of the Treaty.

21. An analysis of this system shows that the rules relating to the free movement of goods and, in particular, Articles 30 *et seq.* concerning the elimination of quantitative restrictions and measures having equivalent effect, must be considered not only with reference to the specific rules relating to transfers of capital but with reference to all the provisions of the Treaty relating to monetary transfers, which can be effected for a great variety of purposes, of which capital transfers only comprise one specific category.

22. Although Articles 67 to 73 of the Treaty, which are concerned with the liberalization of movements of capital, assume special importance as far as one of the aims set out in Article 3 of the Treaty is concerned, namely the abolition of obstacles to freedom of movement for capital, the provisions of Articles 104 to 109, which are concerned with the overall balance of payments and which for this reason relate to all monetary movements, must be considered as essential for the purpose of attaining the free movement of goods, services or capital which is of fundamental importance for the attainment of the Common Market.

23. In particular, Article 106 provides that 'Each Member State undertakes to authorize, in the currency of the Member State in which the creditor or the beneficiary resides, any payments connected with the movement of goods, services or capital, and any transfers of capital and earnings, to the extent that the movement of goods, services, capital and persons between Member States has been liberalized pursuant to this Treaty'.

24. The aim of this provision is to ensure that the necessary monetary transfers may be made both for the liberalization of movements of capital and for the free movement of goods, services and persons.

25. It must be inferred from this that under the system of the Treaty means of payment are not to be regarded as goods falling within the purview of Articles 30 to 37 of the Treaty.

26. Silver alloy coins which are legal tender in a Member State are, by their very nature, to be regarded as means of payment and it follows that their transfer does not fall within the provisions of Articles 30 to 37 of the Treaty.

27. Although doubts may be entertained on the question whether Krugerrands are to be regarded as means of legal payment it can nevertheless be noted that on the money markets of those Member States which permit dealings in these coins they are treated as being equivalent to currency.

28. Their transfer must consequently be designated as a monetary transfer which does not fall within the provisions of the said Articles 30 to 37.

29. Having regard to the above-mentioned considerations it is unnecessary to deal with the question under what circumstances the transfer of these two categories of coins might possibly be designated either as a movement of capital or as a current payment.

30. Question 1 (c) refers to silver alloy coins of a Member State, which have been legal tender in that State and which, although no longer legal tender, are protected as coinage from destruction.

31. Such coins cannot be regarded as means of payment within the meaning stated above, with the result that they can be designated as goods falling within the system of Articles 30 to 37 of the Treaty.

32. It is for the Member States to mint their own coinage and to protect it from destruction.

33. The court's file shows that in the United Kingdom the melting down or destruction of national coins is prohibited, even if they are no longer legal tender.

34. A ban on exporting such coins with a view to preventing their being melted down or destroyed in another Member State is justified on grounds of public policy within the meaning of Article 36 of the Treaty, because it stems from the need to protect the right to mint coinage which is traditionally regarded as involving the fundamental interests of the State.

Costs

[Paras 35 and 36 omitted]

THE COURT

in answer to the questions referred to it by the Court of Appeal (Criminal Division) by order of 15 December 1977, hereby rules:

1. **The provisions of Articles 30 to 37 of the Treaty do not apply to**
   (a) silver alloy coins which are legal tender in a Member State,
   (b) gold coins such as Krugerrands which are produced in a non- member country but which circulate freely within a Member State.

2. **A ban on the export from a Member State of silver alloy coins, which have been but are no longer legal tender in that State and the melting down or destruction whereof on national territory is forbidden, which has been adopted with a view to preventing such melting down or destruction in another Member State, is justified on grounds of public policy within the meaning of Article 36 of the Treaty.**

Comments and questions

The TFEU contains provisions for the free movement of goods, workers, services and capital. Even though there is a high degree of similarity between the different sets of rules for these different freedoms, there are nevertheless differences, so that deciding which set of rules applies can be important for the outcome of a case. This only occasionally gives rise to problems. It frequently happens that one transaction concerns more than one of the fundamental freedoms, but it will normally be obvious that one of these takes primacy over the other, and the subsidiary aspects of the transaction are linked to the primary aspect. For example, if a motor trader sells a car to a customer, and in connection with this offers to wash the car, then it is clear that the sale of the car (supply of goods) is more important than the washing of the car (provision of service). If the car owner subsequently wants the car to be polished, then the task of polishing (provision of service) will be the prime object of the transaction, while the provision of cleaning materials and polish used (supply of goods) will be secondary.

It is the practice of the CJEU only to judge a dispute on the basis of the rules which apply to its primary aspects. However, it is sometimes not possible to establish which aspect of a dispute is the primary one. This applies not least in the area of telecommunications. In such cases it can be necessary to investigate the facts in relation to more than one set of rules; cf. Case C-390/99 *Canal Satélite Digital SL* v *Adminstración General del Estado* [2002] ECR I-607.

Certain types of goods cause special problems. Coins are an example of this. In the Case 7/78 *R* v *Thompson and others* [1978] ECR 2247, the question was whether British rules which restricted the free exchange of certain coins should be judged under the TFEU provisions on the free movement of capital or according to the rules on the free movement of goods. How did the CJEU distinguish the two sets of rules from each other? Could there be situations in which this distinction could lead to unintended consequences?

Are postage stamps goods or capital? Will the answer to this question depend on whether the stamp is a collector's item with a value which is many times higher than its face value?

Energy is regarded as being a type of good. In Case 72/83 *Campus Oil Limited et al* v *Minister for Industry and Energy* [1984] ECR 2727, the Irish Government argued that oil should not be covered by the TFEU provisions on the free movement of goods because it was of such great importance for the economy. The CJEU rejected this argument and stated that 'the Treaty applies the principle of free movement to all goods, subject only to the exceptions expressly provided for in the Treaty itself. Goods cannot therefore be considered exempt from the application of that fundamental principle merely because they are of particular importance for the life or the economy of a Member State.' Thereafter, it seems obvious that coal, oil and gas, for example, constitute goods within the meaning of the TFEU. This also applies to electricity; cf. Case C-379 *PreussenElektra AG* v *Schleswag AG* [2001] ECR I-2099, discussed in more detail below.

In Case 7/68 *Commission* v *Italy* [1968] ECR 423 (in the English special edition), the CJEU defined 'goods' within the meaning of the TFEU as being 'products which can be valued in money and which are capable, as such, of forming the subject of commercial transactions.' The definition was given in response to a claim that articles of artistic, historical, archaeological or ethnographic interest were not covered by the Treaty provisions. For example, would a rhinoceros horn, which cannot legally be imported to or sold in the EU, be a good covered by Article 34 TFEU (formerly Article 28 TEC)? Does opium constitute a good? Consider whether the answer to this depends on whether a case concerns opium which can legally sold for medicinal purposes, or illegal sales of opium on the black market. In this connection see Case C-324/93 *R* v *Home Secretary, ex parte Evans Medical* [1995] ECR I-563, printed below.

The CJEU has classified intellectual property (patents, copyright, trademarks etc.) as *sui generis*, which cannot obviously be placed in the customary categories of goods, services etc. Because of the effects which these rights can have on trade in goods and services, they are subject to a general prohibition on discrimination under the authority of Article 18 TFEU (formerly Article 12 TEC); cf. Joined Cases C-92/92 and C-326/92, *Phil Collins* v *Imtrat Handelsgesellschaft* [1993] ECR I-5145.

Article 346 TFEU gives Member States the right to protect their essential security interests, including the production of or trade in arms, munitions and war material. Would a modern rifle, which could be used both for hunting and for military purposes be exempt from the TFEU provisions on the freedom of movement of goods? How would the answer differ if the weapon concerned was a fully functioning muzzle-loader from the early 18th century?

Consider whether each of the following would be classified as a good or as a service: (1) a cheap DVD with an off-the-shelf computer game for a children's computer, or (2) an expensive and specially developed computer programme for a business.

Is a car which has been totally wrecked and is transported from Germany to a scrap dealer in France covered by Article 34 TFEU? Does your answer vary, depending on whether the wreck is totally valueless or whether it has some scrap value? In this connection see Case C-2/90 *Commission* v *Belgium* (the Walloon waste disposal case) [1992] ECR I-4413.

JUDGMENT OF THE COURT
9 July 1992

Commission of the European Communities v Kingdom of Belgium

'Failure to fulfil obligations – Prohibition of tipping waste originating in another Member State'

Case C-2/90

Judgment

1. By application lodged at the Court Registry on 3 January 1990, the Commission of the European Communities brought an action under Article 169 of the EEC Treaty for a declaration that by prohibiting the storage, tipping or dumping or causing the storage, tipping or dumping in Wallonia of waste originating in another Member State or in a region of Belgium other than Wallonia, the Kingdom of Belgium had failed to fulfil its obligations under Council Directive 75/442/EEC of 15 July 1975 on waste (OJ 1975 L 194, p. 39), Council Directive 84/631/EEC of 6 December 1984 on the supervision and control within the European Community of the transfrontier shipment of hazardous waste (OJ 1984 L 326, p. 31), and Articles 30 and 36 of the EEC Treaty.

2. It is apparent from the case-file that the basic measure dealing with waste management in Wallonia is the Decree of the Walloon Regional Council of 5 July 1985 on waste (*Moniteur Belge*, 14 December 1985), whose objective is to prevent waste accruing, encourage recycling and recovery of energy and materials, and make arrangements for waste disposal (Article 1).

3. Pursuant to Article 19(6) of that decree, which gave the Walloon Regional Executive power to make special rules governing the use of authorized tips, depots and treatment installations for waste originating in foreign countries or other regions of Belgium, the executive adopted the Decree of 19 March 1987 on the dumping of certain waste products in Wallonia (*Moniteur Belge*, 28 March 1987, p. 4671).

4. Under Article 1 of that decree, as amended by the Decrees of 9 and 23 July 1987, The storage, tipping or dumping, or causing the storage, tipping or dumping of waste from a foreign State in waste depots, stores and tips which require authorization ... except in depots annexed to an installation for the destruction, neutralization and disposal of toxic waste, shall be prohibited. Operators of the installations referred to in the first paragraph shall be prohibited from permitting or tolerating the tipping or dumping of waste from a foreign State in the installations operated by them.'

5. Article 2 of the decree provides that derogations from Article 1 may be granted on request by a foreign public authority. However, a derogation can be granted only for a specified period and must be justified by serious and exceptional circumstances.

6. Under Article 3, the prohibition in Article 1 applies also to waste originating in a region of Belgium other than Wallonia. Exceptions may be made in accordance with agreements between Wallonia and the other regions of Belgium.

7. Article 5 of the decree reads as follows:
   'Waste not produced in Wallonia shall be deemed to be waste from a foreign State or a region of Belgium other than Wallonia. If the waste results from a process in which two or more States or regions have taken part, it originates in the State or region where the last substantial processing, carried out for economic reasons in an undertaking equipped for that purpose, takes place ...'

8. The Commission took the view that the Belgian legislation was contrary to Community law, in so far as it prohibited the dumping in Wallonia of waste from other Member States and the effect of Article 3 in conjunction with Article 5 of the Decree of 19 March 1987 was to prohibit the dumping in Wallonia of waste from other Member States which had undergone substantial processing for economic reasons in another region of Belgium. It therefore initiated the procedure under Article 169 of the Treaty against the Kingdom of Belgium.

9. Reference is made to the Report for the Hearing for a fuller account of the facts of the case, the procedure and the pleas in law and arguments of the parties, which are mentioned or discussed hereinafter only in so far as is necessary for the reasoning of the Court.

10. The Commission contends that the Belgian rules are contrary to Directives 75/442/EEC and 84/631/EEC and Articles 30 and 36 of the Treaty.

Directive 75/442/EEC

[Paras. 11-21 omitted]

Articles 30 and 36 of the Treaty

22. It remains to consider the Belgian rules in question from the point of view of Articles 30 and 36 of the Treaty, in so far as those rules relate to waste which is not covered by Directive 84/631/EEC.

23. It is not disputed that recyclable and reusable waste has an intrinsic commercial value, possibly after being treated, constitutes 'goods' for the purposes of the Treaty, and consequently comes under Article 30 et seq. of the Treaty.

24. With respect to non-recyclable and non-reusable waste, the Court heard argument as to whether such waste also comes under Article 30 et seq.

25. The Belgian Government argued that waste which was not recyclable and not reusable could not be regarded as 'goods' within the meaning of Article 30 et seq. of the Treaty. It had no intrinsic commercial value and thus could not be the subject of a sale. Operations for the disposal or tipping of such waste came under the Treaty provisions on the freedom to provide services.

26. In response to that argument, suffice it to note that objects which are shipped across a frontier for the purposes of commercial transactions are subject to Article 30, whatever the nature of those transactions.

27. As was explained to the Court, moreover, the distinction between recyclable and non-recyclable waste is particularly difficult to apply in practice, especially with respect to controls at frontiers. That distinction is based on factors which are uncertain and liable to change in the course of time according to technical progress. Furthermore, whether waste is recyclable or not also depends on the cost of the recycling process and consequently on whether its proposed reutlization is viable, with the result that classification of waste is necessarily subjective and depends on variable factors.

28. It must therefore be concluded that waste, whether recyclable or not, is to be regarded as 'goods' the movement of which, in accordance with Article 30 of the Treaty, must in principle not be prevented.

29. To justify the restrictions placed on the movement of waste, the defendant State argues that the contested legislation meets imperative requirements relating to environmental protection and the objective of protection of health, which takes precedence over the objective of freedom of movement for goods, and constitutes an exceptional and temporary protective measure to counter the inflow into Wallonia of waste from neighbouring countries.

30. With respect to the environment, it is important to note that waste is matter of a special kind. Accumulation of waste, even before it becomes a health hazard, constitutes a danger to the environment, regard being had in particular to the limited capacity of each region or locality for waste reception.

31. In the instant case the Belgian Government argued, without being contradicted by the Commission, that in view of the abnormal large-scale inflow of waste from oth-

er regions for tipping in Wallonia, there was a real danger to the environment, having regard to the limited capacity of that region.

32. It follows that the argument that the contested measures were justified by imperative requirements of environmental protection must be considered to be well founded.

33. The Commission argues, however, that those imperative requirements cannot be relied upon in the present case, given that the measures in question discriminate against waste originating in other Member States, which is no more harmful than waste produced in Wallonia.

34. Imperative requirements can indeed be taken into account only in the case of measures which apply without distinction to both domestic and imported products (see *inter alia* the judgment in Joined Cases C-1/90 and C-176/90 *Aragonesa de Publicidad Exterior and Publivía* [1991] ECR I-4151). However, in assessing whether or not the barrier in question is discriminatory, account must be taken of the particular nature of waste. The principle that environmental damage should as a matter of priority be remedied at source, laid down by Article 130r (2) of the Treaty as a basis for action by the Community relating to the environment, entails that it is for each region, municipality or other local authority to take appropriate steps to ensure that its own waste is collected, treated and disposed of; it must accordingly be disposed of as close as possible to the place where it is produced, in order to limit as far as possible the transport of waste.

35. Moreover, that principle is consistent with the principles of self-sufficiency and proximity set out in the Basel Convention of 22 March 1989 on the control of transboundary movements of hazardous wastes and their disposal, to which the Community is a signatory (see *International Environmental Law*, Kluwer, Deventer and Boston, 1991, p. 546).

36. It follows that having regard to the differences between waste produced in different places and to the connection of the waste with its place of production, the contested measures cannot be regarded as discriminatory.

37. The application must therefore be dismissed to the extent that it relates to waste which is not covered by Directive 84/631/EEC.

Costs

[Para. 38 omitted]

On those grounds,

THE COURT

hereby:

1. **Declares that by imposing an absolute prohibition on the storage, tipping or dumping in Wallonia of hazardous waste originating in another Member State and thereby precluding the application of the procedure laid down in Council Directive 84/631/EEC of 6 December 1984 on the supervision and control within the European Community of the transfrontier shipment of hazardous waste, the Kingdom of Belgium has failed to fulfil its obligations under that directive;**

2. **Dismisses the remainder of the application;**

[Para. 3 of the ruling omitted]

Comments and questions

In Case C-2/90 *Commission* v *Belgium* [1992] ECR I-4413 (the Walloon waste disposal case), the CJEU laid down general rules as to what should be considered as goods covered by Article 34 TFEU (formerly Article 30 EEC Treaty). Paragraph 26 of the judgment states as follows: '... objects which are shipped across a frontier for the purposes of commercial transactions are subject to Article 30 [now Article 34 TFEU], whatever the nature of those transactions.' The classification of goods is not linked to whether the object in question has an economic value in itself. On this basis, waste was regarded as goods covered by Article 34 TFEU, regardless of its recyclable value, when it was transported across a national border as part of a commercial transaction. The CJEU considered that the contested measures of the Walloon Government were justified by imperative requirements of environmental protection; cf. paragraph 32 of the judgment.

However, the CJEU ran into a problem, as according to its own established practice, only national measures which are applied without distinction between domestic and foreign goods can be justified on grounds other than those listed in Article 36 TFEU (formerly Article 36 EEC Treaty); cf. the '*Cassis de Dijon*' doctrine discussed below in this chapter. Environmental protection is not one of the considerations referred to in Article 36 TFEU. Thus on the face of it the Walloon measures had to be held to be discriminatory. The CJEU got round this problem by finding that waste is of a particular nature (paragraph 34 of the judgment), *since there are differences with regard to waste, depending on where it is produced and its connection with its place of production, the contested measures could not be regarded as discriminatory* (paragraph 36). In other words, there is a relative concept of discrimination, where the assessment of whether discrimination exists depends on the goods which are the object of the national regulations. Does the CJEU's interpretation and application of the concept of discrimination in this case correspond with its normal practice, and do you find this solution satisfactory?

Would it make any difference to evaluating this case if it had been the Belgian State which had prohibited the importation of waste from another EU Member State? On this, see Case C-360/89 *Commission* v *Italy* [1992] ECR I-3401, at paragraphs 8 and 9, according to which discrimination was found to exist, even though the discriminatory measures only regulated the conditions of one region within a Member State.

Consider whether it would be possible to prohibit the export of waste on the basis of the fact that national waste is used as fuel for national power stations for generating heat and electricity, and that it is most economic for the power stations to have continual production, without interruption, for which they are dependent on a continuous supply of combustible material. Compare this with the decision of the CJEU in Case C-277/02 *EU-Wood-Trading GmbH* v *Sonderabfall-Management-Gesellschaft Rheinland-Pfalz mbH* [2004] ECR I-11957.

JUDGMENT OF THE COURT (Second Chamber)
16 December 2010

Marc Michel Josemans v Burgemeester van Maastricht. (Reference for a preliminary ruling from the Raad van State – Netherlands)

'Freedom to provide services – Free movement of goods – Principle of non-discrimination – Measure adopted by a local public authority which restricts access to coffee-shops to Netherlands residents – Marketing of 'soft' drugs – Marketing of non-alcoholic beverages and of food – Objective of combating drug tourism and the accompanying public nuisance – Public order – Protection of public health – Coherence – Proportionality'

Case C-137/09

Judgment

1. This reference for a preliminary ruling concerns the interpretation of Articles 12 EC, 18 EC, 29 EC and 49 EC.

2. The reference has been made in proceedings between Mr Josemans, who runs the 'Easy Going' coffee-shop, and the Burgemeester van Maastricht (the Mayor of the municipality of Maastricht) on the ground that the latter declared the establishment in question temporarily closed following two reports attesting that persons who are not resident in the Netherlands had been admitted to it contrary to the provisions in force in that municipality.

Legal context

European Union legislation

3. The necessity of combating drugs, inter alia by punishing the illegal trafficking in those drugs and by preventing the consumption of narcotic drugs and drug addiction, has been acknowledged by a number of measures and instruments of the European Union.

4. Recital 1 in the preamble to Council Framework Decision 2004/757/JHA of 25 October 2004 laying down minimum provisions on the constituent elements of criminal acts and penalties in the field of illicit drug trafficking (OJ 2004 L 335, p. 8) states that illicit drug trafficking poses a threat to health, safety and the quality of life of citizens of the European Union, and to the legal economy, stability and security of the Member States.

5. Article 2(1)(a) of Framework Decision 2004/757 states that each Member State is to take the necessary measures to ensure that the following intentional conduct when committed without right is punishable: the production, manufacture, extraction, preparation, offering, offering for sale, distribution, sale, delivery on any terms whatsoever, brokerage, dispatch, dispatch in transit, transport, importation or exportation of drugs. Article 2(2) states that the conduct described in paragraph 1 is not included in the scope of that framework decision when it is committed by its perpetrators exclusively for their own personal consumption as defined by national law.

   1. Under Article 1 of the Protocol integrating the Schengen acquis into the framework of the European Union, annexed to the Treaty on European Union and to the Treaty establishing the European Community by the Treaty of Amsterdam, 13 Member States of the European Union, amongst them the Kingdom of the Netherlands, are authorised to establish, within the institutional and legal framework of the European Union and the EU and EC Treaties, closer cooperation among themselves within the scope of the Schengen acquis as set out in the annex to that protocol.

6. The Convention implementing the Schengen Agreement, of 14 June 1985, between the Governments of the States of the Benelux Economic Union, the Federal Republic of Germany and the French Republic on the gradual abolition of checks at their common borders (OJ 2000 L 239, p. 19), signed at Schengen (Luxembourg) on 19 June 1990 is part of the Schengen acquis so set out.

7. Article 71(1) of that convention provides that the Contracting Parties undertake as regards the direct or indirect sale of narcotic drugs and psychotropic substances of whatever type, including cannabis, and the possession of such products and substances for sale or export, to adopt in accordance with the existing United Nations Conventions, all necessary measures to prevent and punish the illicit trafficking in narcotic drugs and psychotropic substances.

8. Article 71(2) to (4) specifies the various measures which the Parties undertake to adopt in connection with the prevention and punishment inter alia of the illegal export and import of narcotic drugs and psychotropic substances, including cannabis, and in connection with the sale, supply and handing over of such products and substances. Article 71(5) states that the Parties are to do their utmost to prevent and combat the negative effects arising from the illicit demand for narcotic drugs and psychotropic substances.

9. Certain instruments of the European Union, such as the Council Resolution of 29 November 1996 on measures to address the drug tourism problem within the European Union (OJ 1996 C 375, p. 3) and the Joint Action of 17 December 1996 adopted by the Council on the basis of Article K.3 of the Treaty on European Un-

ion concerning the approximation of the laws and practices of the Member States of the European Union to combat drug addiction and to prevent and combat illegal drug trafficking (OJ 1996 L 342, p. 6), relate expressly to the fight against drug tourism.

10. The European Union is a party to the United Nations Convention against illicit traffic in narcotic drugs and psychotropic substances, concluded in Vienna on 20 December 1988 (United Nations Treaty Series, Vol. 1582, No 1-27627). According to the declaration annexed to Council Decision 90/611/EEC of 22 October 1990 concerning the conclusion, on behalf of the European Economic Community, of the United Nations Convention against Illicit Traffic in Narcotic Drugs and Psychotropic Substances (OJ 1990 L 326, p. 56), the Community is competent for questions of commercial policy relating to the substances frequently used in the illicit manufacture of narcotic drugs and psychotropic substances.

National legislation

11. Under the 1976 Law on opium (Opiumwet 1976), the possession, dealing, cultivation, transportation, production, import and export of narcotic drugs, including cannabis and its derivatives, are prohibited. Those acts are subject to criminal sanctions unless the substance or product in question is used for medical, scientific or educational purposes and prior authorisation has been given.

12. The Kingdom of the Netherlands applies a policy of tolerance with regard to the sale and consumption of cannabis. That policy is based on a distinction between 'hard' drugs, which present an unacceptable risk to health, and 'soft' drugs, which although deemed to be 'risky' do not give rise to the same concerns.

13. The policy of tolerance has been implemented within the framework of the directives issued by the College van procureurs-general (College of public prosecutors). The competent authorities have relied on the principle of discretionary prosecution to pursue a policy of selective punishment. In the interest of the effectiveness of criminal prosecutions, the sale of cannabis, in strictly limited quantities and in controlled conditions, is tolerated, priority thus being given to the punishment of other offences which are considered to be more dangerous.

14. That policy of tolerance is reflected inter alia in the establishment of coffee-shops. In such establishments, which are classified as catering establishments, cannabis is sold and consumed in the same way as food and non-alcoholic beverages. The sale of alcoholic beverages is, however, prohibited.

15. The local authorities may authorise coffee-shops in compliance with certain criteria. Such establishments need an operating licence and must satisfy the same condi-

tions relating to management and hygiene as are applicable to other catering establishments.

16. The conditions under which the marketing of cannabis in coffee-shops may be tolerated are defined, at national level, by the directives of the Openbaar Ministerie (the Public Prosecutor's Office). Those criteria, commonly known as 'the AHOJG criteria', are the following:

17. 'A ('affichering') drugs may not be advertised; H ('harddrugs') no hard drugs may be sold; O ('overlast') the coffee-shop must not cause any nuisance; J ('jeugdigen') no drugs may be sold to minors (under the age of 18) nor may minors be admitted to the premises; G ('grote hoeveelheden') no more than five grams per person may be sold in any one transaction. Furthermore, the commercial stock ('handelsvoorraad' of a tolerated coffee shop must not exceed 500 grams.'

18. The municipality of Maastricht adopted a policy on cannabis by defining, inter alia, certain strict conditions in which a limited number of coffee-shops are tolerated. At the material time in the main proceedings, that number was set at 14.

19. In an effort to reduce drug tourism, indeed to prevent it, the Gemeenteraad (Municipal Council) of that municipality, by decision of 20 December 2005, inserted a residence criterion in the 2006 version of the General Maastricht Municipal Regulation (Algemene plaatselijke verordening Maastricht) ('the APV'). That amendment entered into force on 13 January 2006.

20. Pursuant to Article 2.3.1.3e(1) of the APV, the proprietor of an establishment as referred to in Article 2.3.1.1(1)(a)(3) of that regulation is forbidden to admit persons other than residents to the establishment or to permit them to remain in or at the establishment. The term 'establishment' is defined by the latter provision as a space to which the public has access and where food and/or non-alcoholic beverages are provided commercially, whether or not by means of vending machines, for consumption on the premises. Under Article 2.3.1.1(1)(d), 'residents' means persons who have their actual place of residence in the Netherlands.

21. Article 2.3.1.3e(2) of the APV provides that the Burgemeester van Maastricht may specify that the rule laid down in subparagraph (1) does not apply to one or more types of establishment referred to in that ordinance throughout the municipality or in one or more parts of the municipality designated therein. By decision of 13 July 2006, the Burgemeester von Maastricht exempted, throughout the municipality of Maastricht, certain categories of establishment from the obligation to refuse access to non-residents, namely all the establishments referred to in Article 2.3.1.1(1)(a)(3) of the APV, with the exception of coffee-shops, tearooms and the like, by whatever designation they might be known.

22. Pursuant to Article 2.3.1.5a(f) of the APV, the Burgemeester van Maastricht may declare an establishment as referred to in Article 2.3.1.1(1)(a)(3) of that ordinance closed for a specified or unspecified period if the proprietor of the establishment acts contrary to Article 2.3.1.3e(1).

The facts which gave rise to the dispute in the main proceedings and the questions referred for a preliminary ruling

23. Mr Josemans runs the 'Easy Going' coffee-shop in the municipality of Maastricht, an establishment in which 'soft' drugs, non-alcoholic beverages and food are sold and consumed.

24. The 'Easy Going' coffee-shop falls within the scope of the policy of tolerance applied by the Kingdom of the Netherlands with regard to the marketing of cannabis. The sale of cannabis, although illegal, does not give rise to criminal proceedings if it takes place in a recognised coffee-shop and if a certain number of conditions, inter alia 'the AHOJG criteria', are complied with.

25. Following two reports attesting that persons who are not resident in the Netherlands had been admitted to the coffee-shop in question contrary to Article 2.3.1.3e(1) of the APV, which establishes a criterion of residence, the Burgemeester van Maastricht, by decision of 7 September 2006, declared that establishment temporarily closed.

26. Mr Josemans lodged an objection against that decision. As that objection was dismissed by the Burgemeester van Maastricht by decision of 28 March 2007, Mr Josemans brought an action before the Rechtbank Maastricht (Maastricht Court). By judgment of 1 April 2008, that court annulled that decision and revoked the decision of 7 September 2006. According to that court, the prohibition set out in the APV of admitting persons who are not resident in the Netherlands to coffee-shops constitutes indirect discrimination on grounds of nationality, which is contrary to Article 1 of the Netherlands Constitution. By contrast, there is no infringement of European Union law. It considers that it is apparent from Case 289/86 *Vereniging Happy Family Rustenburgerstraat* [1988] ECR 3655 and Case C-158/98 *Coffeeshop 'Siberië'* [1999] ECR I-3971 that the trade in narcotic drugs is not covered by the EC Treaty.

27. Mr Josemans and the Burgemeester van Maastricht, on 5 and 8 May 2008 respectively, appealed against that judgment to the Raad van State (Council of State). The Burgemeester van Maastricht disputes the interpretation of the Netherlands Constitution. Mr Josemans submits that the legislation at issue in the main proceedings constitutes unjustified unequal treatment of citizens of the European Union and that, more specifically, people who are not resident in the Netherlands are denied

the possibility of buying legal products in coffee-shops, which is contrary to European Union law.

28. In those circumstances, the Raad van State decided to stay the proceedings and to refer the following questions to the Court of Justice for a preliminary ruling:

    '1. Does a regulation, such as that at issue in the main proceedings, concerning the access of non-residents to coffee-shops, fall wholly or partly within the scope of the EC Treaty, with particular reference to the free movement of goods and/or services, or of the prohibition of discrimination laid down in Article 12 [EC] in conjunction with Article 18 [EC]?

    2. In so far as the provisions of the EC Treaty concerning the free movement of goods and/or services are applicable, does a prohibition of the admission of non-residents to coffee-shops form a suitable and proportionate means of reducing drug tourism and the public nuisance which accompanies it?

    3. Is the prohibition of discrimination against citizens on grounds of nationality, as laid down in Article 12 [EC] in conjunction with Article 18 [EC], applicable to the rules on the access of non-residents to coffee-shops if and in so far as the provisions of the EC Treaty concerning the free movement of goods and services are not applicable?

    4. If so, is the resulting indirect distinction between residents and non-residents justified, and is the prohibition of the admission of non-residents to coffee-shops a suitable and proportionate means of reducing drug tourism and the public nuisance which accompanies it?'

Consideration of the questions referred

Initial observations

29. By its reference for a preliminary ruling the national court seeks to ascertain whether European Union law precludes municipal rules, such as those forming the subject-matter of the dispute in the main proceedings, which prohibit the admission of persons who are non-resident in the Netherlands to coffee-shops situated in the municipality in question. It refers more specifically to the free movement of goods under Article 28 EC et seq., the free movement of services under Article 49 EC et seq., and the principle of non-discrimination on grounds of nationality under Article 12 EC in conjunction with Article 18 EC, which relates to citizenship of the Union.

30. At the outset, it must be borne in mind that, as is apparent from paragraphs 15 to 17 of this judgment, coffee-shops constitute establishments covered by the category of

catering establishments in which cannabis is marketed to consumers of at least 18 years of age. Such an establishment must have an operating licence and must, moreover, satisfy all of 'the AHOJG criteria'.

31. It is common ground that the cannabis sold in coffee-shops is not distributed through channels strictly controlled by the competent authorities with a view to use for medical or scientific purposes.

32. Although, according to the Netherlands Government, there are such establishments whose sole activity is the marketing of cannabis, the fact remains that in a number of coffee-shops non-alcoholic beverages and food are also sold and consumed. According to the order for reference, that is the case as regards the 'Easy Going' coffee-shop.

33. In such circumstances, it is necessary to assess, in the light of the provisions referred to by the reference for a preliminary ruling, first, the marketing of cannabis in coffee-shops and, secondly, the question of whether the sale of non-alcoholic beverages and food in such establishments may have an effect on the answer to be given to the national court.

The first question

34. By its first question the national court asks, in essence, whether a coffee-shop proprietor may, when marketing, first, narcotic drugs which are not distributed through channels strictly controlled by the competent authorities with a view to use for medical or scientific purposes and, secondly, non-alcoholic beverages and food, rely on Articles 29 EC, 49 EC and/or 12 EC, the latter in conjunction with Article 18 EC, to object to municipal rules such as those at issue in the main proceedings.

35. As regards the marketing of cannabis, Mr Josemans submits that that activity falls within the scope of European Union law and that the rules at issue in the main proceedings are contrary to the principle of non-discrimination on grounds of nationality. The Burgemeester van Maastricht and the Netherlands, Belgian, German and French Governments submit, by contrast, that the activity in question does not fall within the scope either of the freedoms of movement or of the principle of non-discrimination, in view of the existence of a prohibition on the offering for sale of narcotic drugs. The European Commission takes the view that it is not necessary, in order to give a decision on the reference for a preliminary ruling, to rule on the marketing of cannabis.

36. In that connection it is important to bear in mind that, since the harmfulness of narcotic drugs, including those derived from hemp, such as cannabis, is generally recognised, there is a prohibition in all the Member States on marketing them, with the exception of strictly controlled trade for use for medical and scientific purposes

(see, to that effect, Case 50/80 Horvath [1981] ECR 385, paragraph 10; Case 221/81 Wolf [1982] ECR 3681, paragraph 8; Case 240/81 Einberger [1982] ECR 3699, paragraph 8; Case 294/82 Einberger [1984] ECR 1177, paragraph 15; Case 269/86 Mol [1988] ECR 3627, paragraph 15; and Vereniging Happy Family Rustenburgerstraat, paragraph 17).

37. That legal position complies with various international instruments which the Member States have cooperated on or acceded to, such as the United Nations Single Convention on Narcotic Drugs, concluded at New York on 30 March 1961, amended by the 1972 Protocol amending the Single Convention of 1961 (United Nations Treaty Series, Vol. 520, No 7515) ('the Single Convention') and the United Nations Convention on Psychotropic Substances, concluded at Vienna on 21 February 1971 (United Nations Treaty Series, Vol. 1019, No 14956). The measures provided for by those conventions were subsequently strengthened and supplemented by the Convention concluded at Vienna on 20 December 1988, to which all the Member States of the European Union are parties. Cannabis is among the substances and products referred to in those conventions.

38. In the preamble to the Single Convention the parties declare themselves conscious of their duty to prevent and combat addiction to narcotic drugs, whilst recognising that the medical use of narcotic drugs continues to be indispensable for the relief of pain and suffering and that adequate provision must be made to ensure the availability of narcotic drugs for such purposes. Under Article 4 of that convention, the parties are to take all the measures necessary to limit exclusively to medical and scientific purposes the production, manufacture, export, import, distribution of, trade in, use and possession of drugs (see Wolf, paragraph 9, and Case 240/81 Einberger, paragraph 9).

39. As regards more specifically European Union law, Framework Decision 2004/757 provides, in Article 2(1)(a), that each Member State is to take the necessary measures to ensure that, inter alia, the following intentional conduct when committed without right is punishable: offering, offering for sale, distribution, sale, delivery on any terms whatsoever and brokerage of drugs. Under Article 2(2) the conduct described in paragraph 1 is not to be included in the scope of that Framework Decision when it is committed by its perpetrators exclusively for their own personal consumption as defined by national law. It is stated in Article 1(1) of that act that the term 'drugs' includes any of the substances covered by the Single Convention and by the United Nations Convention on Pyschotropic Substances, concluded at Vienna on 21 February 1971.

40. Furthermore, pursuant to Article 71(1) of the Convention implementing the Schengen Agreement, of 14 June 1985, the States who are parties to that convention undertook, as regards both the direct or indirect sale of narcotic drugs and psychotropic substances of whatever type, including cannabis, and the possession of

such products and substances for sale or export, to adopt in accordance with the existing United Nations Conventions all necessary measures to prevent and punish the illicit trafficking in narcotic drugs and psychotropic substances.

41. It follows that narcotic drugs which are not distributed through channels which are strictly controlled by the competent authorities to be used for medical and scientific purposes are, because of their very nature, subject to a prohibition on importation and offering for sale in all the Member States (see, to that effect, Wolf, paragraph 10; Case 240/81 Einberger, paragraph 10; Case 294/82 Einberger, paragraph 15; Mol, paragraphs 15 and 18; Vereniging Happy Family Rustenburgerstraat, paragraphs 17 and 20; and Coffeeshop 'Siberië', paragraph 14). The fact that some Member States describe a narcotic drug as a 'soft' drug is not capable of calling that finding into question (see, to that effect, Vereniging Happy Family Rustenburgerstraat, paragraph 25).

42. As narcotic drugs which are not distributed through such strictly controlled channels are prohibited from being released into the economic and commercial channels of the European Union, a coffee-shop proprietor cannot rely on the freedoms of movement or the principle of non-discrimination, in so far as concerns the marketing of cannabis, to object to municipal rules such as those at issue in the main proceedings.

43. That finding cannot be impugned by the fact that, as is apparent from paragraphs 12 to 14 of the present judgment, the Kingdom of the Netherlands applies a policy of tolerance to the sale of cannabis, even though trade in narcotic drugs is prohibited in that Member State. It is apparent from the case-law of the Court that such a prohibition is not affected by the mere fact that, in view in particular of their limited manpower and means, the national authorities responsible for implementing that prohibition give lower priority to bringing proceedings against a certain type of trade in drugs, because they consider other types to be more dangerous. Above all, such an approach cannot put illegal drugs dealing on the same footing as economic channels which are strictly controlled by the competent authorities in the medical and scientific field. The latter trade is actually legalised whereas illegal dealings, albeit tolerated, remain prohibited (see, to that effect, Vereniging Happy Family Rustenburgerstraat, paragraph 29).

44. As regards the marketing of non-alcoholic beverages and food in coffee-shops, Mr Josemans, the German Government and the Commission submit that the Court should assess the effects of the rules at issue in the main proceedings on the exercise of that activity. The German Government stresses that those goods are to be consumed on the premises. The Commission doubts that non-residents buy them with the intention of exporting them to their States of residence. Therefore, the provisions to be applied are those governing the freedom to provide services within the

meaning of Article 49 EC and not those relating to the free movement of goods under Article 29 EC.

45. The Burgemeester van Maastricht and the Netherlands, Belgian, German and French Governments submit that the marketing of non-alcoholic beverages and food in such establishments is altogether secondary to the marketing of cannabis and cannot have any bearing on the outcome of the main proceedings.

46. That latter argument cannot be accepted. Although coffee-shops are primarily dedicated to the sale and consumption of cannabis, the fact remains that the marketing, in such establishments, of non-alcoholic beverages and food generally constitutes a not inconsiderable economic activity. In reply to a question asked by the Court, the Netherlands Government stated, at the hearing, that that activity generally represents between 2.5% and 7.1% of the turnover of coffee-shops in the municipality of Maastricht. As regards more specifically the economic situation of the 'Easy Going' coffee-shop, according to the information provided by Mr Josemans, the proportion of its turnover from the sale of such goods is in that bracket.

47. Consequently, it is necessary to examine whether, and, if so, to what extent, the rules at issue in the main proceedings are capable of affecting, in so far as concerns the marketing of non-alcoholic beverages and food, the exercise of the freedoms of movement governed by Articles 29 EC and 49 EC or of undermining the principle of non-discrimination 'on grounds of nationality' within the meaning of Article 12 EC in conjunction with Article 18 EC.

48. In order to ascertain whether such an activity concerns the free movement of goods or the freedom to provide services, it must be borne in mind that an establishment is defined in Article 2.3.1.1(1)(a)(3) of the APV as a space to which the public has access and where food and/or non-alcoholic beverages are provided commercially, whether or not by means of vending machines, for consumption on the premises.

49. In such circumstances, as the Advocate General pointed out at point 76 of his Opinion, the marketing of non-alcoholic beverages and food in coffee-shops appears to constitute a catering activity characterised by an array of features and acts in which services predominate as opposed to the supply of the product itself (see, by analogy, Case C-491/03 Hermann [2005] ECR I-2025, paragraph 27).

50. Since the free movement of goods aspect is entirely secondary to that of the freedom to provide services and may be considered together with it, the Court will examine the rules at issue in the main proceedings only in the light of the latter fundamental freedom (see, to that effect, Case C-275/92 Schindler [1994] ECR I-1039, paragraph 22; Case C-71/02 Karner [2004] ECR I-3025, paragraph 46; Case C-36/02 Omega [2004] ECR I-9609, paragraph 26; Case C-452/04 Fidium Fi-

nanz [2006] ECR I-9521, paragraph 34; and Case C-233/09 Dijkman and Dijkman-Laveleije [2010] ECR I-0000, paragraph 33).

51. As regards the applicability of Article 12 EC, which lays down a general prohibition of all discrimination on grounds of nationality, it should be noted that that provision applies independently only to situations governed by European Union law for which the EC Treaty lays down no specific rules of non-discrimination (see, inter alia, Case 305/87 Commission v Greece [1989] ECR 1461, paragraphs 12 and 13; Case C-443/06 Hollmann [2007] ECR I-8491, paragraph 28; and Case C-269/07 Commission v Germany [2009] ECR I-7811, paragraph 98).

52. As the principle of non-discrimination has been implemented, in the area of the freedom to provide services, by Article 49 EC, Article 12 EC does not apply in circumstances such as those in the main proceedings.

53. As regards the applicability of Article 18 EC, that provision, which lays down generally the right for every citizen of the Union to move and reside freely within the territory of the Member States, finds specific expression in the provisions guaranteeing the freedom to provide services (see, inter alia, Case C-92/01 Stylianakis [2003] ECR I-1291, paragraph 18; Case C-76/05 Schwarz and Gootjes-Schwarz [2007] ECR I-6849, paragraph 34; and Case C-56/09 Zanotti [2010] ECR I-0000, paragraph 24). As citizens of the European Union who do not reside in the Netherlands and wish to go into coffee-shops in the municipality of Maastricht to consume lawful goods there are to be regarded as 'persons for whom' services 'are intended' within the meaning of Article 49 EC, it is not necessary for the Court to rule on the interpretation of Article 18 EC.

54. Consequently, the answer to the first question is that, in the course of marketing narcotic drugs which are not distributed through channels strictly controlled by the competent authorities with a view to use for medical or scientific purposes, a coffee-shop proprietor may not rely on Articles 12 EC, 18 EC, 29 EC or 49 EC to object to municipal rules such as those at issue in the main proceedings, which prohibit the admission of persons who are non-resident in the Netherlands to such establishments. As regards the marketing of non-alcoholic beverages and food in those establishments, Article 49 EC et seq. may be relied on by such a proprietor.

The second question

55. The second question was asked in the event that the provisions governing the free movement of goods or those relating to the freedom to provide services apply in the circumstances of the dispute in the main proceedings. It relates, in essence, to whether municipal rules, such as those at issue in the main proceedings, constitute a restriction on the exercise of one of those freedoms and, if so, whether that measure may be justified by the objective of combating drug tourism and the accompanying

public nuisance and, lastly, whether it constitutes a proportionate measure in relation to that objective.

56. Having regard to the answer to the first question, that question must be assessed solely in the light of Article 49 EC et seq. and limited to an examination of the effects of those rules on the marketing, in coffee-shops, of non-alcoholic beverages and food.

57. It is common ground that, under the rules at issue in the main proceedings, only 'residents' are admitted to coffee-shops. That term covers, under Article 2.3.1.1(1)(d) of the APV, any person who has his actual place of residence in the Netherlands. Consequently, the proprietors of such establishments are not entitled to provide catering services to persons residing in other Member States and those persons are precluded from enjoying such services.

58. It is clear from the Court's case-law that the principle of equal treatment, of which Article 49 EC embodies a specific instance, prohibits not only overt discrimination by reason of nationality but also all covert forms of discrimination which, by the application of other criteria of differentiation, lead in fact to the same result (see, inter alia, Case C-3/88 Commission v Italy [1989] ECR 4035, paragraph 8; Case C-388/01 Commission v Italy [2003] ECR I-721, paragraph 13; Case C-28/04 Tod's and Tod's France [2005] ECR I-5781, paragraph 19; and Case C-147/03 Commission v Austria [2005] ECR I-5969, paragraph 41).

59. That is true, in particular, of a measure under which a distinction is drawn on the basis of residence, in that that requirement is liable to operate mainly to the detriment of nationals of other Member States, since non-residents are in the majority of cases foreigners (see, inter alia, Case C-224/97 Ciola [1999] ECR I-2517, paragraph 14; Case C-388/01 Commission v Italy, paragraph 14; Case C-103/08 Gottwald [2009] ECR I-9117, paragraph 28; and Case C-73/08 Bressol and Others [2010] ECR I-0000, paragraph 45).

60. It must, however, be examined whether such a restriction may be justified by legitimate interests which European Union law recognises.

61. The German Government takes the view that the rules at issue in the main proceedings are justified by the derogating provisions set out in Article 46(1) EC in conjunction with Article 55 EC, namely grounds of public policy, public security or public health. The Burgemeester van Maastricht and the Belgian Government rely, in the alternative, on grounds of public policy and public security. According to the Netherlands Government, the need to combat drug tourism constitutes a public-interest objective for the purposes of the line of case-law initiated in 'Cassis de Dijon' (Case 120/78 Rewe-Zentral [1979] ECR 649).

62. While acknowledging the importance of the fight against drug tourism, the Commission submits that, as they are discriminatory, those rules can be compatible with European Union law only if they are covered by an express derogating provision, namely Article 46 EC in conjunction with Article 55 EC. The derogations provided for by those provisions should be interpreted restrictively. As regards more specifically grounds of public policy, they may be relied on only if there is a genuine and sufficiently serious threat to a fundamental interest of society (see, inter alia, Case 30/77 Bouchereau [1977] ECR 1999, paragraph 35).

63. In the present case, it is common ground that the rules at issue in the main proceedings are intended to put an end to the public nuisance caused by the large number of tourists wanting to purchase or consume cannabis in the coffee-shops in the municipality of Maastricht. According to the information provided by the Burgemeester van Maastricht at the hearing, the 14 coffee-shops in the municipality attract around 10 000 visitors per day and a little more than 3.9 million visitors per year, 70% of which are not resident in the Netherlands.

64. The Burgemeester van Maastricht and the Netherlands Government state that the problems associated with the sale of 'soft' drugs which arise in that commune, such as the various forms of public nuisance and crime and the increasing number of illegal points of sale of drugs, including 'hard' drugs, have been exacerbated by drug tourism. The Belgian, German and French Governments refer to the public order problems to which that phenomenon, including the illegal export of cannabis, gives rise in Member States other than the Kingdom of the Netherlands, in particular in neighbouring States.

65. It must be pointed out that combating drug tourism and the accompanying public nuisance is part of combating drugs. It concerns both the maintenance of public order and the protection of the health of citizens, at the level of the Member States and also of the European Union.

66. Given the commitments entered into by the European Union and its Member Sates, there is no doubt that the abovementioned objectives constitute a legitimate interest which, in principle, justifies a restriction of the obligations imposed by European Union law, even under a fundamental freedom such as the freedom to provide services.

67. In that connection, it is important to bear in mind, as is apparent from paragraphs 11, 37 and 38 of this judgment, that the need to combat drugs has been recognised by various international conventions which the Member States, and even the European Union, have cooperated on or acceded to. The preambles to those instruments mention the danger to the health and well-being of individuals constituted, in particular, by demand for and the illicit traffic in narcotic drugs and psychotropic sub-

stances, as well as their harmful effects on the economic, cultural and political bases of society.

68. Furthermore, the need to fight drugs, in particular by preventing drug addiction and punishing the illicit trafficking in such products or substances, has been set out in Article 152(1) EC and in Articles 29 EU and 31 EU. As regards provisions of secondary law, the first recital in the preamble to Framework Decision 2004/757 states that illicit drug trafficking poses a threat to health, safety and the quality of life of citizens of the European Union, and to the legal economy, stability and security of the Member States. Furthermore, as is apparent from paragraph 10 of this judgment, certain instruments of the European Union relate expressly to the prevention of drug tourism.

69. However, measures which restrict the freedom to provide services may be justified by the objective of combating drug tourism and the accompanying public nuisance only if they are suitable for securing the attainment of that objective and do not go beyond what is necessary in order to attain it (see, to that effect, Omega, paragraph 36; Case C-438/05 International Transport Workers' Federation and Finnish Seamen's Union [2007] ECR I-10779, paragraph 75; and Case C-244/06 Dynamic Medien [2008] ECR I-505, paragraph 42).

70. In that connection it is important to bear in mind that a restrictive measure can be considered to be suitable for securing the attainment of the objective pursued only if it genuinely reflects a concern to attain that objective in a consistent and systematic manner (see, to that effect, Case C-169/07 Hartlauer [2009] ECR I-1721, paragraph 55; Joined Cases C-171/07 and C-172/07 Apothekerkammer des Saarlandes and Others [2009] ECR I-4171, paragraph 42; and Case C-42/07 Liga Portuguesa de Futebol Profissional and Bwin International [2009] ECR I-7633, paragraphs 59 to 61).

71. Mr Josemans calls into question the suitability and proportionality of the rules at issue in the main proceedings. They relate exclusively to coffee-shops. Under 'the AHOJG criteria', those establishments are required, unlike the illegal premises selling drugs in the municipality of Maastricht, to fight against the public nuisance caused by their customers. Furthermore, those rules are liable to drive drug tourists to use illegal channels.

72. The Commission expresses doubts as to the necessity of the rules at issue in the main proceedings and as to their consistency. It states that the national measures to combat the public nuisance caused by the consumption of drugs should be based on objective and non-discriminatory criteria. It refers, in that connection, to the judgment in Joined Cases 115/81 and 116/81 Adoui and Cornuaille [1982] ECR 1665, concerning the right of residence or establishment of prostitutes, and to the case-law deriving from it.

73. The Burgemeester van Maastricht and the Netherlands, Belgian and German Governments take the view, by contrast, that the rules at issue in the main proceedings constitute an appropriate and proportionate means of combating drug tourism and the accompanying public nuisance. The Burgemeester van Maastricht and the Netherlands Government state that the various measures adopted by municipalities applying a policy of tolerance with regard to coffee-shops in order to deal with that phenomenon have not achieved the objective pursued.

74. In the present case, it cannot be denied that the policy of tolerance applied by the Kingdom of the Netherlands with regard to the sale of cannabis encourages persons who are resident in other Member States to travel to that State, and more specifically to the municipalities in which coffee-shops are tolerated, in particular in border regions, in order to buy and consume that drug. Furthermore, according to the information in the case-file, some of those persons purchase cannabis in such establishments in order to export it illegally to other Member States.

75. It is indisputable that a prohibition on admitting non-residents to coffee-shops, such as that which is the subject-matter of the dispute in the main proceedings, constitutes a measure capable of substantially limiting drug tourism and, consequently, of reducing the problems it causes.

76. In that connection, it is important to point out that the discriminatory nature of the rules at issue in the main proceedings does not, on its own, mean that the way in which they pursue the intended objective is inconsistent. Although the Court took the view in Adoui and Cornuaille that a Member State cannot validly rely on grounds of public policy with regard to the behaviour of a non-national inasmuch as it does not adopt repressive measures or other genuine and effective measures with respect to the same conduct on the part of its own nationals, the fact remains that the dispute in the main proceedings is part of a different legal context.

77. As was pointed out in paragraph 36 of this judgment, there is, under international law and European Union law, a prohibition in all the Member States on marketing narcotic drugs, with the exception of strictly controlled trade for use for medical and scientific purposes. By contrast, prostitution, the behaviour referred to in Adoui and Cornuaille, aside from trafficking in human beings, is tolerated or regulated in a number of Member States (see, to that effect, Case C-268/99 Jany and Others [2001] ECR I-8615, paragraph 57).

78. It cannot be held to be inconsistent for a Member State to adopt appropriate measures to deal with a large influx of residents from other Member States who wish to benefit from the marketing – tolerated in that Member State – of products which are, by their very nature, prohibited in all Member States from being offered for sale.

79. As regards the scope of rules such as those at issue in the main proceedings, it is important to bear in mind that they apply only to establishments the main activity of which is the marketing of cannabis. They do not preclude a person who is not resident in the Netherlands from going, in the municipality of Maastricht, into other catering establishments in order to consume non-alcoholic beverages and food. According to the Netherlands Government, there are more than 500 such establishments.

80. As regards the possibility of adopting measures which are less restrictive of the freedom to provide services, according to the case-file, in the municipalities which apply a policy of tolerance with regard to coffee-shops, various measures relating to combating drug tourism and the accompanying public nuisance have been implemented, such as a restriction on the number of coffee-shops or their opening hours, the implementation of a card system which allows customers access to them or even a reduction in the amount of cannabis per person which may be bought. According to the information provided by the Burgemeester van Maastricht and the Netherlands Government, those measures have nevertheless proved to be insufficient and ineffective in the light of the objective pursued.

81. As regards more specifically the possibility of granting non-residents access to coffee-shops whilst refusing to sell cannabis to them, it must be pointed out that it is not easy to control and monitor with accuracy that that product is not served to or consumed by non-residents. Furthermore, there is a danger that such an approach would encourage the illegal trade in or the resale of cannabis by residents to non-residents inside coffee-shops.

82. Member States cannot be denied the possibility of pursuing the objective of combating drug tourism and the accompanying public nuisance by the introduction of general rules which are easily managed and supervised by the national authorities (see, by analogy, Case C-110/05Commission v Italy [2009] ECR I-519, paragraph 67, and Case C-142/05 Mickelsson and Roos [2009] ECR I-4273, paragraph 36). In the present case, nothing in the case-file gives grounds to assume that the objective pursued could be achieved to the extent envisaged by the rules at issue in the main proceedings by granting non-residents access to coffee-shops whilst refusing to sell them cannabis.

83. In such circumstances, it must be stated that rules such as those at issue in the main proceedings are suitable for attaining the objective of combating drug tourism and the accompanying public nuisance and do not go beyond what is necessary in order to attain it.

84. Having regard to all of the foregoing considerations, the answer to the second question is that Article 49 EC must be interpreted as meaning that rules such as those at issue in the main proceedings constitute a restriction on the freedom to provide ser-

vices laid down by the EC Treaty. That restriction is, however, justified by the objective of combating drug tourism and the accompanying public nuisance.

The third and fourth questions

85. The third and fourth questions were asked in the alternative and relate to the application of the principle of non-discrimination on grounds of nationality laid down in Article 12 EC in conjunction with Article 18 EC, which governs the free movement of citizens of the European Union.

86. Having regard to the answer given to the first question, there is no need to answer those questions.

Costs

[Para. 87 omitted]

On those grounds,

THE COURT (Second Chamber),

hereby rules:

1. **In the course of marketing narcotic drugs which are not distributed through channels strictly controlled by the competent authorities with a view to use for medical or scientific purposes, a coffee-shop proprietor may not rely on Articles 12 EC, 18 EC, 29 EC or 49 EC to object to municipal rules, such as those at issue in the main proceedings, which prohibit the admission of persons who are non-resident in the Netherlands to such establishments. As regards the activity of marketing non-alcoholic beverages and food in those establishments, Article 49 EC et seq. may be relied on by such a proprietor.**

2. **Article 49 EC must be interpreted as meaning that rules such as those at issue in the main proceedings constitute a restriction on the freedom to provide services laid down by the EC Treaty. That restriction is, however, justified by the objective of combating drug tourism and the accompanying public nuisance.**

Comments and questions

The great majority of goods that are sold within the EU can be lawfully sold in all Member States – from mineral water, to garden hoses to mobile telephones and so on.

However, for some products the situation is different. This applies, for example to narcotics. Most Member States prohibit the sale of narcotics for recreational use. The Netherlands is a clear exception in this respect as the authorities 'tolerate' the sale and use of cannabis to a limited extent. Cannabis can only be sold in 'coffee shops' that are licensed to sell it. And sales can only be made to persons who are resident in the Netherlands, which is to prevent 'narco-tourism'. However, in principle such a restriction will constitute indirect discrimination as in practice it mainly prevents Union citizens who are not Dutch from buying the goods.

In the *Josemans* case a coffee shop in Maastricht was closed down by the local authorities because the owner had breached the prohibition by admitting people to the shop who were not resident in the Netherlands. When the case cane before the Dutch court, the question arose as to whether this was contrary to Union law. A key question was whether cannabis in fact falls within the concept of 'goods' as referred to in the TFEU. On the one hand there is no doubt that cannabis was a physical object which was lawfully traded in the Netherlands. On the other hand the sale of cannabis was prohibited outside the Netherlands, and international agreements had been entered into to prevent the sale of cannabis and other narcotics. The CJEU stated in paragraph 42 of its judgment that, as narcotic drugs that are not distributed through strictly controlled channels are prohibited from being released into economic and commercial channels in the EU, a Dutch coffee shop proprietor cannot rely on the freedoms of movement or the principle of non-discrimination, in so far as concerns the marketing of cannabis, with a view to challenging the prohibition of admitting persons who are not resident in the Netherlands to the shop. In other words, narcotics are not a 'good' that is protected by the Union rules on free movement.

Consider the extent to which the following kinds of goods may be assumed to fall outside the scope of the Union concept of 'goods':

- Modern military equipment – such as tanks, frigates, assault rifles and hand grenades; and such as night vision binoculars, camouflage clothing, and rifles that can also be used for hunting;
- Medicines – including products that are usually used for recreational use;
- Pornographic materials;
- Religious objects;
- Counterfeit money;
- Tobacco, including snuff; and
- Alcohol.

JUDGMENT OF THE COURT (First Chamber)
9 December 2010

Humanplasma GmbH v Republik Österreich. (Reference for a preliminary ruling from the Landesgericht für Zivilrechtssachen Wien – Austria)

'Articles 28 EC and 30 EC – National rules prohibiting the importation of blood products provided from donations which were not entirely unpaid'

Case C-421/09

Judgment

1. This reference for a preliminary ruling concerns the interpretation of Articles 28 EC and 30 EC.

2. The reference has been made in proceedings between Humanplasma GmbH ('Humanplasma'), a company established under Austrian law, and the Republik Österreich (Republic of Austria) concerning the legislative prohibition on the importation of erythrocyte concentrates provided from blood donations which were not entirely unpaid.

Legal context

European Union legislation

3. Recitals 22 and 23 in the preamble to Directive 2002/98/EC of the European Parliament and of the Council of 27 January 2003 setting standards of quality and safety for the collection, testing, processing, storage and distribution of human blood and blood components and amending Directive 2001/83/EC (OJ 2003 L 33, p. 30), read as follows:

'(22) According to Article 152(5) of the Treaty, the provisions of this Directive cannot affect national provisions on the donations of blood. Article 152(4)(a) of the Treaty states that Member States cannot be prevented from maintaining or introducing more stringent protective measures as regards standards of quality and safety of blood and blood components.

(23) Voluntary and unpaid blood donations are a factor which can contribute to high safety standards for blood and blood components and therefore to the protection of human health. The efforts of the Council of Europe in this area should be supported and all necessary measures should be taken to encourage voluntary and unpaid donations through appropriate measures and

initiatives and through ensuring that donors gain greater public recognition, thereby also increasing self-sufficiency. The definition of voluntary and unpaid donation of the Council of Europe should be taken into account.'

4. Article 4(2) of Directive 2002/98 provides:

'This Directive shall not prevent a Member State from maintaining or introducing in its territory more stringent protective measures which comply with the provisions of the Treaty.
In particular, a Member State may introduce requirements for voluntary and unpaid donations, which include the prohibition or restriction of imports of blood and blood components, to ensure a high level of health protection and to achieve the objective set out in Article 20(1), provided that the conditions of the Treaty are met.'

5. Article 20(1) of Directive 2002/98 provides:

'Member States shall take the necessary measures to encourage voluntary and unpaid blood donations with a view to ensuring that blood and blood components are in so far as possible provided from such donations.'

6. Article 21 of Directive 2002/98 provides:

'Blood establishments shall ensure that each donation of blood and blood components is tested in conformity with requirements listed in Annex IV.
Member States shall ensure that blood and blood components imported into the Community are tested in conformity with requirements listed in Annex IV.'

International rules

7. Under Article 2 of Recommendation No R (95) 14 of the Committee of Ministers to the Member States of the Council of Europe on the protection of health of donors and recipients in the area of blood transfusion, adopted on 12 October 1995, '[d]onation is considered voluntary and unpaid if the person gives blood, plasma or cellular components of his or her own free will and receives no payment for it, either in the form of cash or in kind which could be considered a substitute for money. This would include time off work other than that reasonably needed for the donation and travel. Small tokens, refreshments and reimbursements of direct travel costs are compatible with voluntary, non-remunerated donation.'

National legislation

8. Paragraph 7(1) of the Law of 2002 on medicinal imports (Arzneiwareneinfuhrgesetz 2002), in the version published in BGBl. I, 153/2005 ('the Law on medicinal imports'), provided that products covered by that law could be imported only if the

authority responsible for safety in the health sector concerned had confirmed that they could be placed on the market.

9. Article 7(3) of the Law on medicinal imports laid down the precise information to be provided by, inter alia, importers of blood products at the request of the competent authorities. That information included the donor's identity, proof that the donor had been chosen in accordance with the relevant international criteria and that he was not suffering from certain viral infections.

10. Following a legislative amendment published in BGBl. I, 41/2006, a subparagraph 1a was inserted into Paragraph 7 of the Law on medicinal imports, with effect from 29 March 2006. That provision states as follows:

    'When blood products are imported for direct transfusion they may in any case not be placed on the market unless the blood was donated without any payment whatsoever having been made, except in cases in which the donor was asked by the blood establishment to make an immediate donation because of an urgent need in an acute emergency. That does not apply where the importation is necessary in order to secure supplies for particularly rare blood groups.'

11. In addition, pursuant to that same amendment, a subparagraph 2a was inserted into Paragraph 7(3) of the Law on medicinal imports, which provides that the importers must in all cases establish that, with regard to 'blood products for direct transfusion, the blood was donated without any payment whatsoever having been made, or in cases in which the donor was asked by the blood establishment to make an immediate donation because of an urgent need in an acute emergency, only expenses were covered ...'.

12. Paragraph 8(4) of the Law of 1999 on Blood Safety (Blutsicherheitsgesetz 1999), in the version published in BGBl. I, 63/2005, provides:

    'Donors of blood or of blood components or third parties may not be paid or promised payment for a donation. If the blood (whole blood) is donated for direct transfusion, it must be given without payment being made. Coverage of expenses in such cases is permitted only where a donor was asked by the blood establishment to make an immediate donation because of an urgent need in an acute emergency.'

The main proceedings and the question referred for a preliminary ruling

13. On 1 November 2005, a contract notice was published for the supply, to the Wiener Krankenanstaltenverbund (Vienna Hospital Association), of blood products, in the instant case leukocyte-depleted erythrocyte concentrates. Those erythrocyte concentrates are sold as medicines.

14. It was laid down that the period for submission of tenders would expire on 1 March 2006. The supply contract was divided into five separate lots, and tenders could be made separately for individual lots. The framework contracts put out to tender were to run for three years with the possibility of being extended once only for a further three years.

15. According to paragraph 2.2 of the contractual conditions:

'The product supplied must ... comply with the Austrian Law concerning the importation of medicines (Law on medicinal imports) in the version currently applicable, ... be provided from unpaid donations and be in conformity with the current state of scientific knowledge.'

16. Paragraph 6 of the special contractual provisions, headed 'Failure to supply', provides in particular:

'The contractor is obliged to guarantee supplies. Should there however be a delay in or failure to supply, the Wiener Krankenanstaltenverbund (on account of its obligation to maintain supplies) is entitled to obtain the required leukocyte-depleted erythrocyte concentrates by means not provided for under the framework contract, with the additional or consequential costs arising in that connection being borne by the contractor.'

17. Two tenderers participated in the procedure, that is to say Humanplasma and the Österreichisches Rotes Kreuz (Austrian Red Cross). It was established that Humanplasma had submitted the cheaper tender for two of the five lots.

18. In a letter accompanying its tender, Humanplasma confirmed that it had all the authorisations necessary to carry out the service in question. It therefore guaranteed that the product supplied complied with the requirements laid down in point 2.2 of the contractual conditions when it submitted its tender. It pointed out however that it could not give any warranty or guarantee with regard to the future legal position and that if, following a legislative amendment and in particular an amendment to the Law on medicinal imports, it should become impossible for it to comply with the obligation to supply the products concerned, it would not accept liability of any kind for possible additional or consequential costs within the meaning of point 6 of the special contractual provisions.

19. According to the order for reference, since, after the end of the period for submission of tenders, the Law on medicinal imports was amended so that blood products imported for transfusion could no longer be placed on the market – subject to two special cases – unless the blood had been donated without any payment whatsoever having been made, the products offered by Humanplasma, which were not provid-

ed predominantly from such donations, were no longer in conformity with the provisions of that law.

20. When the tender was being assessed, the contracting authority requested clarification from Humanplasma whether it could nevertheless guarantee that the conditions of supply referred to in the call for tender would be met. As it could not give those guarantees, the contracting authority informed it that its tender would be excluded pursuant to the provisions of national law concerning public contracts.

21. The objection brought by Humanplasma before the Vergabekontrollsenat für Wien (Public Procurement Review Tribunal, Vienna) against the decision excluding its tender was rejected on the ground, inter alia, that, since Humanplasma could not guarantee that it could provide the services to which the conditions in the specification applied, its tender was non-compliant, for the purposes of the national provisions, and therefore could not be ruled upon. According to the Vergabekontrollsenat für Wien, the contracting authority was therefore correct to reject Humanplasma's tender.

22. In its action against that decision of the Vergabekontrollsenat für Wien, Humanplasma claimed damages from the defendant amounting to EUR 840 000, including the refund of costs incurred, on the ground of State liability for the breach of Community law. In support of its action, it argues that Paragraph 7(1a) of the Law on medicinal imports constitutes a measure of equivalent effect to a quantitative restriction prohibited under Article 28 EC. Since it did not obtain its products predominantly from completely unpaid donations, it had been obliged to express a proviso and to assert that it might be impossible to comply with the conditions of supply. Had the Law on medicinal imports not been amended it would not have had to issue the proviso and its tender could not have been excluded from the public procurement procedure.

23. The case having been brought before it, the Landesgericht für Zivilrechtssachen Wien (Regional Civil Court, Vienna) decided to stay the proceedings and to refer the following question to the Court for a preliminary ruling:

    'Does Article 28 EC (in conjunction with Article 30 EC) preclude the application of a national provision under which the importation of erythrocyte concentrates from Germany is permitted only where the blood was donated without any payment having been made (with not even expenses being covered), that being a condition which is also applicable to the obtaining of erythrocyte concentrates within Austria?'

The question referred for a preliminary ruling

24. By its question, the referring court asks, in essence, whether Article 28 EC, read in conjunction with Article 30 EC, must be interpreted as precluding national legislation which provides that the importation of blood or blood components from another Member State is permitted only on the condition, which is also applicable to national products, that the donations of blood on which those products are based were made without any payment being made to the donors, even in terms of the coverage of costs.

25. The free movement of goods is a fundamental principle of the EC Treaty which is expressed in the prohibition, set out in Article 28 EC, of quantitative restrictions on imports between Member States and all measures having equivalent effect (Case C-170/04 Rosengren and Others [2007] ECR I-4071, paragraph 31).

26. According to settled case-law, the prohibition of measures having an effect equivalent to a quantitative restriction, laid down in Article 28 EC, applies to all legislation of the Member States that is capable of hindering, directly or indirectly, actually or potentially, intra-Community trade (see, inter alia, Case 8/74 Dassonville [1974] ECR 837, paragraph 5; Rosengren and Others, paragraph 32; C-297/05 Commission v Netherlands [2007] ECR I-7467, paragraph 53; and Case C-143/06 Ludwigs-Apotheke [2007] ECR I-9623, paragraph 26).

27. In the present case, according to the order for reference, the national legislation at issue in the main proceedings prohibits the importation and the placing on the market, in principle, of blood and blood components obtained from donations of blood for which payment has been made, it being understood that the reimbursement of costs incurred by the donor in order to carry out the blood donation is also considered, under that legislation, as constituting payment.

28. It must be added that the prohibition of marketing in the main proceedings applies without distinction to donations of blood made on Austrian territory and blood obtained in other Member States.

29. Since, in certain other Member States, donations of blood give rise, in accordance with the provisions of Directive 2002/98, to the reimbursement of costs, blood and blood components lawfully obtained and marketed in those Member States cannot be imported and marketed in Austria.

30. Therefore, it must be held, as the Austrian Government also expressly accepts, that national legislation such as that at issue in the main proceedings is capable of hindering intra-Community trade and therefore constitutes a measure of equivalent effect to a quantitative restriction on imports within the meaning of Article 28 EC.

31. In order to determine whether that legislation constitutes a restriction which is prohibited under Article 28 EC, it must therefore also be examined whether, as inter alia the Austrian Government and the European Commission claim, it can be justified on grounds of the protection of human health.

32. In that regard, it must be noted that human health ranks foremost among the assets or interests protected by Article 30 EC and it is for the Member States, within the limits imposed by the Treaty, to decide on the degree of protection which they wish to afford to human health and on the way in which that protection is to be achieved (Case C-322/01 Deutscher Apothekerverband [2003] ECR I-14887, paragraph 103; Case C-262/Commission v France [2004] ECR I-6569, paragraph 24; Rosengren and Others, paragraph 39: and Ludwigs-Apotheke, paragraph 27).

33. In the present case, it is common ground that the legislation at issue in the main proceedings, which, according to the Austrian Government, has the aim, first, of ensuring that blood and blood components marketed in Austria satisfy the criteria of high quality and safety and, second, of attaining the objective enshrined in Article 20(1) of Directive 2002/98, that is, encouraging voluntary and unpaid blood donations, addresses human health concerns such as those acknowledged in Article 30 EC. Therefore, those objectives are in principle capable of justifying a restriction on the free movement of goods.

34. However, according to the case-law, a provision which is capable of restricting a fundamental freedom guaranteed by the Treaty, such as the free movement of goods, can be properly justified only if it is appropriate for securing the attainment of that objective and does not go beyond what is necessary in order to attain it (see, inter alia, Case C-14/02 ATRAL [2003] ECR I-4431, paragraph 64; Case C-254/05 Commission v Belgium [2007] ECR I-4269, paragraph 33; judgment of 13 March 2008 in Case C-227/06 Commission v Belgium, paragraph 61; and Case C-141/07 Commission v Germany [2008] ECR I-6935, paragraph 48).

35. With regard, first, to whether the legislation at issue in the main proceedings is appropriate, it should be noted that, according to recital 23 in the preamble to Directive 2002/98, voluntary and unpaid blood donations are a factor which can contribute to high safety standards for blood and blood components and therefore to the protection of human health.

36. In so far as legislation such as that at issue in the main proceedings precludes blood donors from obtaining any financial benefit from their donation, such legislation can meet those concerns, improve the quality and safety of blood and blood components and protect human health.

37. By contrast, it is not apparent from the observations lodged with the Court that, as claimed by the Austrian Government, legislation such as that at issue in the main

proceedings, which prohibits donors from receiving any reimbursement, for example, of the travel costs incurred in attending the blood establishment nearest their home or place of work, is such as to encourage the persons concerned to donate their blood. In those circumstances, it must be held that such legislation does not make it possible to attain the second objective allegedly pursued by that national legislation.

38. With regard, second, to the assessment of whether legislation such as that at issue in the main proceedings is proportionate, it must be noted that it follows from the case-law of the Court that since Article 30 EC constitutes an exception, which is to be strictly interpreted, to the rule of the free movement of goods within the Community, it is for the national authorities to demonstrate that their rules are necessary in order to achieve the declared purpose and that that objective could not be achieved by less extensive prohibitions or restrictions, or by prohibitions or restrictions having less effect on intra-Community trade (see, to that effect, Case C-17/93 van der Veldt [1994] ECR I-3537, paragraph 15; Case C-189/95 Franzén [1997] ECR I-5909, paragraphs 75 and 76; Case C-434/04 Ahokainen and Leppik [2006] ECR I-9171, paragraph 31; andRosengren and Others, paragraph 50).

39. Admittedly, according to the settled case-law of the Court, noted in paragraph 32 of the present judgment, when assessing whether the principle of proportionality has been observed in the field of human health, account must be taken of the fact that a Member State has the power to determine the degree of protection which it wishes to afford to human health and the way in which that degree of protection is to be achieved. Since that degree of protection may vary from one Member State to another, Member States must be allowed discretion (Commission v Germany, paragraph 51).

40. Also, the mere fact that one Member State imposes less strict rules than those applicable in another Member State does not mean that the latter's rules are incompatible with Articles 28 EC and 30 EC (see, in particular, Commission v Germany, paragraph 51).

41. However, the fact that a number of other Member States reimburse blood donors' costs may be relevant when assessing the objective justification put forward in relation to the Austrian legislation, and, particularly, concerning the assessment of its proportionality (see, in that regard, Case C-333/08 Commission v France [2010] ECR I-0000, paragraph 105).

42. In that regard, it should be pointed out that, as is apparent inter alia from Article 21 of Directive 2002/98, in order to ensure the quality and safety of blood and blood components, each donation of blood must be tested in conformity with the requirements listed in Annex IV to that directive, it being understood that those requirements will evolve in line with scientific and technical progress.

43. It follows that, considered in isolation, the obligation that the blood donation must have been made without any of the costs incurred by the donor having been reimbursed is, in any case, not necessary in order to ensure the quality and safety of the blood and the blood components.

44. That conclusion is supported by the fact that, although Directive 2002/98 and Recommendation No R (95) 14, to which that directive refers, aim to improve the health of donors or recipients of blood by laying down rules and principles with which voluntary and unpaid blood donations must comply, they do not require that donations be completely unpaid but provide that small tokens, refreshments and reimbursements of travel costs connected with the donation are compatible with voluntary, non-remunerated donation, with the result that those elements cannot be considered as liable to compromise the quality and safety of those donations or the protection of human health.

45. In the light of those considerations, it must be concluded that legislation such as that at issue in the main proceedings goes beyond what is necessary to attain the objective pursued, that is, to ensure the quality and safety of the blood and of the blood components.

46. In the light of all of the foregoing, the answer to the question referred is that Article 28 EC, read in conjunction with Article 30 EC, must be interpreted as precluding national legislation which provides that the importation of blood or blood components from another Member State is permitted only on the condition, which is also applicable to national products, that the donations of blood on which those products are based were made not only without any payment being made to the donors but also without any reimbursement of the costs incurred by them in connection with those donations.

Costs

[Para. 47 omitted]

On those grounds,

THE COURT (First Chamber),

hereby rules:

Article 28 EC, read in conjunction with Article 30 EC, must be interpreted as precluding national legislation which provides that the importation of blood or blood components from another Member State is permitted only on the condition, which is also applicable to national products, that the donations of blood on which those products are based were made not only without any payment

being made to the donors but also without any reimbursement of the costs incurred by them in connection with those donations.

Comments and questions

Blood and products made from blood are frequently used in the treatment of illness. Obtaining sufficient quantities of healthy blood is thus of major importance to the operation of the health sectors of the Member States. Blood is largely obtained from the donations of volunteers who receive no payment for their contributions. In some Member States, such as Austria, blood donors have not received any form of financial support in connection with their donations. In other Member States blood donors have received compensation for the expenses they incur in connection with their donations, for example reimbursement of travel costs.

Blood is a physical product which can be subject to sale. If a Member State requires that blood that is sold to its health sector must be obtained without any form of compensation to the donors, this effectively means that there is a prohibition of the sale of blood from Member States in which the blood donors receive compensation for their donations in some form or other.

Consider whether blood, that is given voluntarily and without any consideration by a group of voluntary donors, ought unconditionally to be categorised as a good pursuant to Article 34 TFEU (formerly Article 28 TEC). Scientists are working to produce 'artificial blood'. Should such artificial blood be treated as equivalent to blood given by voluntary blood donors? In some cases people donate other parts of their bodies. This is the case with kidneys, bone marrow, semen and eggs, for example. Should such donations be treated in the same way as blood donations – what are the arguments for and against?

If a person has made a living will with regard to organ donation and, for example, has donated their liver, lungs, heart and other organs to help others or for the benefit of science, will the transfer of such organs be covered by the rules on the free movement of goods? In this connection, see Case C-203/99 *Veedfald* [2001] ECR I-2569, where the Danish Supreme Court referred a question to the CJEU for a preliminary ruling on the application of Directive 85/374/EEC concerning liability for defective products in connection with a patient's kidney transplant. Unfortunately, the hospital treated the kidney with fluid that was defective. This damaged the kidney which became unusable. The question was whether the Directive on product liability (which was aimed to promote the free movement of goods in the EU) applied to this case. The CJEU ruled that the defective fluid must be regarded as having been traded when used for an actual medical procedure. At the same time, the CJEU ruled that the medical procedure was wholly financed by public means for which the patient did not have to pay and therefore could not make the hospital liable.

In the *Humanplasma* case, the CJEU decided that blood is covered by the TFEU rules on the free movement of goods. The CJEU ruled that the Austrian rules prevented the free movement of the goods, but that they pursued a lawful purpose – public health.

Thus the question was whether there was proportionality between the measures of the Austrian authorities and the purpose pursued. The CJEU found that there was not. Which part of the proportionality principle was it that the Austrian rules failed to satisfy? Consider how the Austrian authorities can adapt the practice followed hitherto so as both to conform with Union law and to make as little change as possible.

JUDGMENT OF THE COURT
14 December 1979

Regina v Maurice Donald Henn and John Frederick Ernest Darby.
(Preliminary ruling requested by the House of Lords)

'Prohibition on imports – Justification on grounds of public morality – Art. 36 of the Treaty – Pornographic articles'

Case 34/79

Judgment

1. By order of 22 February 1979, received at the Court of Justice on 1 March 1979, the House of Lords, pursuant to Article 177 of the EEC Treaty, referred to the Court a number of questions concerning the interpretation of Articles 30, 36 and 234 of the Treaty. These questions have arisen in the context of criminal proceedings against the appellants who, on 14 July 1977, were convicted at Ipswich Crown Court of a number of offences. Only one of the charges brought against the appellants is relevant to the present reference – that of being knowingly concerned in the fraudulent evasion of the prohibition of the importation of indecent or obscene articles, contrary to section 42 of the Customs Consolidation Act, 1876, and section 304 of the Customs and Excise Act, 1952.

2. The articles involved in the charge against the appellants formed part of a consignment of several boxes of obscene films and magazines which had been brought into the United Kingdom on 14 October 1975 by a lorry which arrived at Felixstowe by ferry from Rotterdam. The charge related to six films and seven magazines, all of Danish origin.

3. The appellants appealed against their conviction to the Court of Appeal of England and Wales. That court dismissed their appeals by judgment of 13 July 1978. On 9 November 1978 the House of Lords granted both appellants leave to appeal. On 29 January 1979, after hearing the appellants, the House of Lords decided that it was necessary to refer to the Court of Justice, in accordance with Article 177 of the Treaty, the questions set forth in the order seeking a preliminary ruling.

4. The appellants contended that the United Kingdom had no consistent policy of public morality in regard to indecent or obscene articles. In that respect they pointed to differences in the law applied in the different constituent parts of the United Kingdom. They contended furthermore that a complete prohibition of the importation of indecent or obscene articles resulted in the application to importation of stricter

rules than those which applied internally and constituted arbitrary discrimination within the meaning of Article 36 of the Treaty.

5. According to the Agreed Statement of Law accompanying the order seeking the preliminary ruling, it is true that, in this field, the laws of the different parts of the United Kingdom, that is to say, England and Wales, Scotland, Northern Ireland and the Isle of Man, differ from each other and that each is derived from a number of different sources, some of which are to be found in the common law and others in statute.

6. According to the same statement, the various laws of the United Kingdom recognize and apply two different and distinct criteria. The first, referred to in the statement as Standard A, relates to the words indecent or obscene which appear in the customs legislation and in certain other legislation and are also used to indicate the ambit of the English common law offence of outraging public decency. These words convey, according to the statement, a single idea, that of offending against recognized standards of propriety, indecent being at the lower end of the scale, and obscene at the upper end.

7. The second criterion, referred to in the statement as Standard B, relates to the word obscene as used alone in the Obscene Publications Acts, 1959 and 1964, (which apply to England and Wales only) and in describing the ambit of certain common law offences in England and Wales, Scotland and Northern Ireland. According to the statement, this word applies to a more restricted class of material, namely that which tends to deprave and corrupt those exposed to the material.

8. The Obscene Publications Acts, 1959 and 1964, create certain offences in regard to the publication of obscene articles but exclude from their field of application obscene articles, as defined therein, if their publication is justified on the ground that it is in the interests of science, literature, art or learning or other objects of general concern.

9. The mere possession, for non-commercial purposes, of articles which offend against either Standard A or Standard B is not a criminal offence in any part of the United Kingdom.

10. The relevant provisions concerning the importation of pornographic articles are section 42 of the Customs Consolidation Act, 1876, and section 304 of the Customs and Excise Act, 1952. They apply throughout the United Kingdom. Put shortly, they provide that indecent or obscene articles are liable for forfeiture and destruction upon arrival in the United Kingdom and that whoever attempts fraudulently to bring such articles into the United Kingdom shall be guilty of an offence. The seventh schedule to the Customs and Excise Act, 1952, provides a procedure for testing before a court the liability of goods to forfeiture.

First question

11. The first question asks whether a law of a Member State which prohibits the import into that State of pornographic articles is a measure having equivalent effect to a quantitative restriction on imports within the meaning of Article 30 of the Treaty.

12. That article provides that quantitative restrictions on imports and all measures having equivalent effect shall be prohibited between Member States. It is clear that this provision includes a prohibition on imports inasmuch as this is the most extreme form of restriction. The expression used in Article 30 must therefore be understood as being the equivalent of the expression prohibitions or restrictions on imports occurring in Article 36.

13. The answer to the first question is therefore that a law such as that referred to in this case constitutes a quantitative restriction on imports within the meaning of Article 30 of the Treaty.

Second and third questions

14. The second and third questions are framed in the following terms:

    2. If the answer to Question 1 is in the affirmative, does the first sentence of Article 36 upon its true construction mean that a Member State may lawfully impose prohibitions on the importation of goods from another Member State which are of an indecent or obscene character as understood by the laws of that Member State?

    3. In particular:
       (i) is the Member State entitled to maintain such prohibitions in order to prevent, to guard against or to reduce the likelihood of breaches of the domestic law of all constituent parts of the customs territory of the State?
       (ii) is the Member State entitled to maintain such prohibitions having regard to the national standards and characteristics of that State as demonstrated by the domestic laws of the constituent parts of the customs territory of that State including the law imposing the prohibition, notwithstanding variations between the laws of the constituent parts?

    It is convenient to consider these questions together.

15. Under the terms of Article 36 of the Treaty the provisions relating to the free movement of goods within the Community are not to preclude prohibitions on imports which are justified inter alia on grounds of public morality. In principle, it is for each Member State to determine in accordance with its own scale of values and in the form selected by it the requirements of public morality in its territory. In any

event, it cannot be disputed that the statutory provisions applied by the United Kingdom in regard to the importation of articles having an indecent or obscene character come within the powers reserved to the Member States by the first sentence of Article 36.

16. Each Member State is entitled to impose prohibitions on imports justified on grounds of public morality for the whole of its territory, as defined in Article 227 of the Treaty, whatever the structure of its constitution may be and however the powers of legislating in regard to the subject in question may be distributed. The fact that certain differences exist between the laws enforced in the different constituent parts of a Member State does not thereby prevent that State from applying a unitary concept in regard to prohibitions on imports imposed, on grounds of public morality, on trade with other Member States.

17. The answer to the second and third questions must therefore be that the first sentence of Article 36 upon its true construction means that a Member State may, in principle, lawfully impose prohibitions on the importation from any other Member State of articles which are of an indecent or obscene character as understood by its domestic laws and that such prohibitions may lawfully be applied to the whole of its national territory even if, in regard to the field in question, variations exist between the laws in force in the different constituent parts of the Member State concerned.

Fourth, fifth and sixth questions

18. The fourth, fifth and sixth questions are framed in the following terms:

    4. If a prohibition on the importation of goods is justifiable on grounds of public morality or public policy, and imposed with that purpose, can that prohibition nevertheless amount to a means of arbitrary discrimination or a disguised restriction on trade contrary to Article 36?

    5. If the answer to Question 4 is in the affirmative, does the fact that the prohibition imposed on the importation of such goods is different in scope from that imposed by the criminal law upon the possession and publication of such goods within the Member State or any part of it necessarily constitute a means of arbitrary discrimination or a disguised restriction on trade between Member States so as to conflict with the requirements of the second sentence of Article 36?

    6. If it be the fact that the prohibition imposed upon importation is, and a prohibition such as is imposed upon possession and publication is not, capable as a matter of administration of being applied by customs officials responsible for examining goods at the point of importation, would that fact have any bearing upon the answer to Question 5?

19. In these questions the House of Lords takes account of the appellants submissions based upon certain differences between, on the one hand, the prohibition on importing the goods in question, which is absolute, and, on the other, the laws in force in the various constituent parts of the United Kingdom, which appear to be less strict in the sense that the mere possession of obscene articles for non-commercial purposes does not constitute a criminal offence anywhere in the United Kingdom and that, even if it is generally forbidden, trade in such articles is subject to certain exceptions, notably those in favour of articles having scientific, literary, artistic or educational interest. Having regard to those differences the question has been raised whether the prohibition on imports might not come within the second sentence of Article 36.

20. According to the second sentence of Article 36 the restrictions on imports referred to in the first sentence may not constitute a means of arbitrary discrimination or a disguised restriction on trade between Member States.

21. In order to answer the questions which have been referred to the Court it is appropriate to have regard to the function of this provision, which is designed to prevent restrictions on trade based on the grounds mentioned in the first sentence of Article 36 from being diverted from their proper purpose and used in such a way as either to create discrimination in respect of goods originating in other Member States or indirectly to protect certain national products. That is not the purport of a prohibition, such as that in force in the United Kingdom, on the importation of articles which are of an indecent or obscene character. Whatever may be the differences between the laws on this subject in force in the different constituent parts of the United Kingdom, and notwithstanding the fact that they contain certain exceptions of limited scope, these laws, taken as a whole, have as their purpose the prohibition, or at least, the restraining, of the manufacture and marketing of publications or articles of an indecent or obscene character. In these circumstances it is permissible to conclude, on a comprehensive view, that there is no lawful trade in such goods in the United Kingdom. A prohibition on imports which may in certain respects be more strict than some of the laws applied within the United Kingdom cannot therefore be regarded as amounting to a measure designed to give indirect protection to some national product or aimed at creating arbitrary discrimination between goods of this type depending on whether they are produced within the national territory or another Member State.

22. The answer to the fourth question must therefore be that if a prohibition on the importation of goods is justifiable on grounds of public morality and if it is imposed with that purpose the enforcement of that prohibition cannot, in the absence within the Member State concerned of a lawful trade in the same goods, constitute a means of arbitrary discrimination or a disguised restriction on trade contrary to Article 36.

23. In these circumstances it is not necessary to answer the fifth and sixth questions.

Seventh question

24. The seventh question asks whether, independently of the questions posed above, a Member State may lawfully impose prohibitions on the importation of such goods from another Member State by reference to obligations arising from the Geneva Convention, 1923, for the suppression of traffic in obscene publications and the Universal Postal Convention (renewed at Lausanne in 1974, which came into force on 1 January 1976), bearing in mind the provisions of Article 234 of the Treaty.

25. Article 234 provides that the rights and obligations arising from agreements concluded before the entry into force of the Treaty between one or more Member States on the one hand, and one or more third countries on the other, are not to be affected by the provisions of the Treaty. However, to the extent to which such agreements are not compatible with the Treaty, the Member State concerned is to take all appropriate steps to eliminate the incompatibilities established.

26. It appears from a comparison of the foregoing considerations with the provisions of the Conventions to which the House of Lords refers that the observance by the United Kingdom of those international Conventions is not likely to result in a conflict with the provisions relating to the free movement of goods if account is taken of the exception made by Article 36 in regard to any prohibitions on imports based on grounds of public morality.

27. The answer to the seventh question should therefore be that, in so far as a Member State avails itself of the reservation relating to the protection of public morality provided for in Article 36 of the Treaty, the provisions of Article 234 do not preclude that State from fulfilling the obligations arising from the Geneva Convention, 1923, for the suppression of traffic in obscene publications and from the Universal Postal Convention (renewed at Lausanne in 1974, which came into force on 1 January 1976).

Costs

[Paras 28 and 29 omitted]

On those grounds,

THE COURT,

in answer to the questions referred to it by the House of Lords by order of 22 February 1979, hereby rules:

1. **A law of a Member State prohibiting any importation of pornographic articles into that State constitutes a quantitative restriction on imports within the meaning of Article 30 of the Treaty.**

2. **The first sentence of Article 36 upon its true construction means that a Member State may, in principle, lawfully impose prohibitions on the importation from any other Member State of articles which are of an indecent or obscene character as understood by its domestic laws and that such prohibitions may lawfully be applied to the whole of its national territory even if, in regard to the field in question, variations exist between the laws in force in the different constituent parts of the Member State concerned.**

3. **If prohibition on the importation of goods is justifiable on grounds of public morality and if it is imposed with that purpose the enforcement of that prohibition cannot, in the absence within the Member State concerned of a lawful trade in the same goods, constitute a means of arbitrary discrimination or a disguised restriction on trade contrary to Article 36.**

4. **In so far as a Member State avails itself of the reservation relating to the protection of public morality provided for in Article 36 of the Treaty, the provisions of Article 234 do not preclude that State from fulfilling the obligations arising from the Geneva Convention, 1923, for the suppression of traffic in obscene publications and from the Universal Postal Convention (renewed at Lausanne in 1974, which came into force on 1 January 1976).**

Comments and questions

In paragraph 12 of its judgment in Case 34/79 *R* v *Henn and Darby* [1979] ECR 3795, the CJEU stated that a prohibition on imports is a quantitative restriction on imports within the terms of Article 34 TFEU (formerly Article 30 EEC Treaty). A total prohibition on imports is thus not equivalent to a quantitative restriction, but is in itself a quantitative restriction on imports.

The case is interesting because the CJEU leaves it up to each Member State to determine, in accordance with the respective Member State's own values and in the form selected by it, the requirements of public morality in its territory; cf. paragraph 15 of the judgment. This is surprising, since the CJEU usually closely examines how far national regulations really do serve the purposes which Member States allege are the motivation of their regulations, see for example the decision in Case C-362/88 *GB-INNO-BM* v *Confédération du commerce luxembourgeois* [1990] ECR I-667, discussed below. In the *GB-INNO* case the Luxembourg Government argued that the prohibition against displaying 'before' and 'after' prices was for the protection of consumers. The CJEU dismissed this argument after investigating the claim closely.

It is possible that the *Henn and Darby* case can be seen as expressing the view that the intensity of the CJEU's investigation will depend on the motive which lies behind the national regulation (consideration for public morality, health, security, protection of consumers, environmental considerations etc.).

In principle, the CJEU did not accept that a Member State can have one set of (less strict) moral rules in relation to products or services which originate in the Member State itself, and another (stricter) set of moral rules for products and services which originate in other Member States; cf. for example Joined Cases 115 and 116/81 *Adoui* v *Belgium & Liège and Cornuaille* v *Belgium* [1982] ECR 1665, and Case C-100/01 *Ministre de l'Intérieur* v *Olazabal* [2002] ECR I-10981, the latter referred to below in Chapter 3. The judgment in *Henn and Darby* can perhaps be interpreted as the CJEU accepting that the prohibition on imports was in some respects stricter than certain national rules which applied within the UK; cf. paragraph 21 of the judgment. However, it is important to be aware that in this paragraph, the CJEU expressly reasoned that there was not a legal market for obscene publications in the UK. In other words, at the material time there was no legal domestic market for the goods in question.

JUDGMENT OF THE COURT
28 March 1995

The Queen v Secretary of State for Home Department, ex parte Evans Medical Ltd and Macfarlan Smith Ltd. (Reference for a preliminary ruling: High Court of Justice, Queen's Bench Division – United Kingdom)

'Free movement of goods – Importation of a narcotic drug (diamorphine)'

Case C-324/93

Judgment

1. By order of 23 June 1993, received at the Court on 25 June 1993, the High Court of Justice (Queen's Bench Division) referred for a preliminary ruling under Article 177 of the EEC Treaty two questions on the interpretation of Articles 30, 36 and 234 of the EEC Treaty and of Council Directive 77/62/EEC of 21 December 1976 coordinating procedures for the award of public supply contracts (OJ 1977 L 13, p. 1), as amended by Council Directive 88/295/EEC of 22 March 1988 (OJ 1988 L 127, p. 1) ('the directive').

2. Those questions have arisen in proceedings brought by Evans Medical Ltd ('Evans') and Macfarlan Smith Ltd ('Macfarlan') against the Secretary of State for the Home Department ('the Secretary of State'), supported by Generics (UK) Ltd ('Generics'), in connection with Generics' importation into the United Kingdom of a consignment of diamorphine originating in the Netherlands.

3. Under the Misuse of Drugs Act 1971 the importation of diamorphine is prohibited unless licensed by the Secretary of State under section 3(2)(b).

4. Diamorphine, which is an opium derivative, is occasionally used as an analgesic in medical treatment. This is particularly so in the United Kingdom since, according to information provided by the national court, 238 of the 241 kilograms of diamorphine used world-wide for medical purposes in 1990 were used in that State.

5. Diamorphine is covered by the 1961 Single Convention on Narcotic Drugs (United Nations Treaty Series, 520, p. 204) ('the Convention'), which entered into force in the United Kingdom in 1964 and which is also applicable in the other Member States.

6. The Convention provides in particular that the Contracting States are to: 'take such legislative and administrative measures as may be necessary: ... to limit exclusively to medical and scientific purposes the production, manufacture, export, import, dis-

tribution of, trade in, use and possession of drugs' (Article 4(c)); 'require that the trade in and distribution of drugs be under licence except where such trade or distribution is carried out by a State enterprise or State enterprises' (Article 30(1)(a)); and 'control under licence the import and export of drugs except where such import or export is carried out by a State enterprise or State enterprises' (Article 31(3)(a)).

7. Until 1992, under the policy prevailing at that time in the United Kingdom, the Secretary of State prohibited importation of diamorphine and allowed Macfarlan to have the exclusive right to manufacture the product in powder form from concentrated poppy straw imported from non-member States and Evans to have the exclusive right to process the product (by freezing, dehydration and packaging) for medical use and marketing within the United Kingdom.

8. According to the Secretary of State, this practice was justified by the need to avoid the risk of diamorphine being diverted to illicit trade and to ensure that supplies were reliably maintained in the United Kingdom.

9. In September 1990 the Secretary of State rejected an application by Generics for a licence to import a consignment of diamorphine from the Netherlands. After obtaining leave, Generics brought an action for judicial review of the decision refusing a licence in which it sought a declaration that the decision was contrary to Article 30 of the Treaty and could not be justified under Article 36. In the course of those proceedings the Secretary of State acknowledged that the refusal to grant a licence to Generics was not justified and stated that his decision was being reviewed.

10. By two letters of 17 August 1992 the Secretary of State informed Evans and Macfarlan that he was authorizing Generics to import the consignment of diamorphine as he considered that the policy then in force impeded intra-Community trade and that reliability of supplies could be satisfactorily guaranteed, in full compliance with Community law, through the introduction of a tendering scheme.

11. The applicants in the main proceedings then brought an action before the High Court in which they seek a declaration that the legal reasoning in those letters supporting the grant of a licence and therefore abandonment of the previous policy is vitiated by an error of law so that those decisions must be set aside.

12. They contend that the requirements of the Convention are incompatible with Articles 30 and 36 of the Treaty. They accordingly submit, first, that those Treaty articles are not applicable to trade in narcotic drugs by virtue of Article 234 of the Treaty on the ground that the Convention was concluded prior to the United Kingdom's accession to the Communities, given that Article 234 of the Treaty provides that: 'The rights and obligations arising from agreements concluded before the entry into force of this Treaty between one or more Member States on the one hand, and one or more third countries on the other, shall not be affected by the provisions

of this Treaty.' Thus, according to the applicants, the Convention requires that the previous arrangements be maintained.

13. Second, the applicants contend that, even if Article 30 of the Treaty were applicable, the Secretary of State could, on the one hand, have relied on Article 36 to justify the refusal to grant an import licence to Generics and, on the other hand, ought to have satisfied himself beforehand that the tendering scheme could be implemented, that it was compatible with the Convention and that it made it possible to ensure continuity of supplies of diamorphine for the National Health Service.

14. Those are the circumstances in which the national court has referred the following questions to the Court of Justice for a preliminary ruling:

'1. Upon the true construction of Articles 30, 36 and 234 of the EEC Treaty, is a Member State entitled to refuse to issue a licence, required by the law of that Member State, to import from another Member State narcotic drugs either originating in or in free circulation in the second Member State on the ground that

(a) the provisions of Articles 30 to 36 are inapplicable to trade in narcotic drugs within the meaning or ambit of the Single Convention on Narcotic Drugs concluded at New York on 30 March 1961; and/or

(b) compliance with the Convention would in practice require the arbitrary allocation of quotas between imports and local manufacturers; and/or that the system of controls laid down by the Convention would otherwise be less effective;

and/or

(c) (in the circumstances that the Community has failed to adopt any directive or other regime on trade in narcotic drugs such as would enable it to declare itself a 'single territory' under Article 43 of the Single Convention and several Member States that manufacture narcotic drugs prohibit their importation) the importation of narcotic drugs from another Member State would threaten the viability of a sole licensed manufacturer of those drugs in the Member State, and that the reliability of supply of those drugs for essential medical purposes in that Member State would be jeopardized?

2. On the proper interpretation of Council Directive 77/62 of 21 December 1976, OJ 1977 L 13, p. 1, as amended, is a public authority, when charged with the task of purchasing essential pain-relieving drugs for medical use, entitled to take into account the need for reliability and continuity of supply when awarding contracts for the supply of such drugs?'

Appositeness of the questions submitted

15. The Commission submits first that there is no need to reply to the questions submitted since the first question concerns the compatibility with Community law of a practice which has now been discontinued and which consisted in prohibiting imports of diamorphine from other Member States, and since the second question seeks from the Court an interpretation of Community law in relation to a purely hypothetical situation, namely where there is a procedure for obtaining diamorphine within the framework of the directive.

16. It need only be observed here that the Secretary of State reached the view that the national practice of prohibiting imports of diamorphine was contrary to Community law since reliability of supplies to the United Kingdom market could be ensured, in conformity with Community law, within the framework of the directive. The preliminary questions have therefore been submitted in order to enable the national court to determine whether the change in national practice was indeed necessary in order to ensure compliance with Community law. The High Court of Justice will then have to determine, on the basis of the replies to its questions, whether under its own national law the decisions of the Secretary of State must be set aside for error of law.

17. Consequently, the questions submitted by the national court should be answered.

Question 1(a)

18. By this question the national court wishes to know whether Article 30 of the Treaty applies to a national practice prohibiting importation of narcotic drugs covered by the Convention and marketable under it.

19. As the Court found in its judgments in Case 221/81 Wolf v Hauptzollamt Duesseldorf [1982] ECR 3681 and Case 240/81 Einberger v Hauptzollamt Freiburg [1982] ECR 3699, the drugs covered by the Convention are subject, in all the Member States, to a range of measures strictly regulating their importation and marketing so as to ensure that they are used in the Member States only for pharmaceutical or medical purposes, in accordance with the Convention.

20. According to the Court's case-law, goods taken across a frontier for the purposes of commercial transactions are subject to Article 30 of the Treaty, whatever the nature of those transactions (judgment in Case C-2/90 Commission v Belgium [1992] ECR I-4431, paragraph 26). Since they have those characteristics, the drugs covered by the Convention and marketable under it are subject to Article 30.

21. It is also settled case-law that all measures capable of hindering, directly or indirectly, actually or potentially, intra-Community trade constitute a barrier to trade (judgment in Case 8/74 Procureur du Roi v Dassonville [1974] ECR 837).

22. Under that case-law, a national practice prohibiting imports of drugs is caught by Article 30 of the Treaty since it affects trade in the way described above.

23. The fact that such a measure may have been adopted under an international agreement predating the Treaty or accession by a Member State and that the Member State maintains the measure pursuant to Article 234, despite the fact that it constitutes a barrier, does not remove it from the scope of Article 30, since Article 234 takes effect only if the agreement imposes on a Member State an obligation that is incompatible with the Treaty.

24. The answer to this question must therefore be that Article 30 of the Treaty applies to a national practice prohibiting importation of narcotic drugs covered by the Convention and marketable under it.

Question 1(b)

[Paras 25-33 omitted]

Question 1(c)

34. By this question the national court asks whether a Member State is entitled to refuse a licence for importation of narcotic drugs from another Member State on the ground that importation of such drugs from another Member State threatens the viability of the sole licensed manufacturer in the first State and jeopardizes reliability of supply of diamorphine for medical purposes.

35. Article 36 of the Treaty allows a Member State to maintain or introduce measures prohibiting or restricting trade if those measures are justified on, inter alia, grounds of public morality, public policy, public security or the protection of health and life of humans, and provided that they do not constitute a means of arbitrary discrimination or a disguised restriction on intra-Community trade.

36. It is clear from the Court's case-law that Article 36 relates to measures of a non-economic nature (judgment in Case 238/82 Duphar and Others v Netherlands [1984] ECR 523). A measure which restricts intra-Community trade cannot therefore be justified by a Member State's wish to safeguard the survival of an undertaking.

37. On the other hand, the need to ensure that a country has reliable supplies for essential medical purposes may, under Article 36 of the Treaty, justify a barrier to intra-Community trade if that objective is one of protecting the health and life of humans.

38. It must, however, be borne in mind that the derogation provided for in Article 36 cannot apply to national rules or practices if the health and life of humans can be as

effectively protected by measures less restrictive of intra-Community trade (see, in particular, the judgment in Case 104/75 De Peijper [1976] ECR 613, paragraph 17).

39. The answer to this question must therefore be that a national practice of refusing licences for importation of drugs from another Member State is not covered by the derogation provided for in Article 36 of the Treaty if it is based on the need to safeguard an undertaking's survival but that derogation may apply to it if protection of the health and life of humans requires a reliable supply of drugs for essential medical purposes to be safeguarded and that objective cannot be achieved as effectively by measures less restrictive of intra-Community trade.

Question 2

Costs

[Paras 40-51 omitted]

On those grounds,

THE COURT,

in answer to the questions referred to it by the High Court of Justice (Queen's Bench Division) by order of 23 June 1993, hereby rules:

1. **Article 30 of the EEC Treaty applies to a national practice prohibiting importation of narcotic drugs covered by the 1961 Single Convention on Narcotic Drugs and marketable under that Convention.**

2. **Article 30 of the EEC Treaty is to be interpreted as requiring a Member State to ensure that this provision is fully effective by disapplying a national practice contrary to it unless that practice is necessary in order for the Member State concerned to comply with obligations towards non-member States laid down in an agreement concluded prior to entry into force of the Treaty or to accession by that Member State.**

3. **A national practice of refusing licences for importation of drugs from another Member State is not covered by the derogation provided for in Article 36 of the EEC Treaty if it is based on the need to safeguard an undertaking's survival but that derogation may apply to it if protection of the health and life of humans requires a reliable supply of drugs for essential medical purposes to be safeguarded and that objective cannot be achieved as effectively by measures less restrictive of intra-Community trade.**

4. **Council Directive 77/62/EEC of 21 December 1976 coordinating procedures for the award of public supply contracts, as amended by Council Directive 88/295/EEC of 22 March 1988, is to be interpreted as authorizing the bodies covered by that directive which wish to obtain diamorphine to award the contract on the basis of the tendering undertakings' ability to provide reliable and continuous supplies to the Member State concerned.**

Comments and questions

In paragraph 20 of the judgment in Case C-324/93 *R* v *Home Secretary, ex parte Evans Medical* [1995] ECR I-563, it is stated that drugs are products covered by Article 34 TFEU (formerly Article 30 EEC Treaty), since they are products which are taken across a frontier for the purposes of commercial transactions. This means that the same definition of the concept of goods is used as in Case C-2/90 *Commission* v *Belgium* (the Walloon waste disposal case) [1992] ECR I-4413, dealt with above in this chapter.

In paragraph 22 of the judgment it is stated that a national prohibition of the import of drugs is caught by Article 34 TFEU. See also the judgment in Case 34/79 *R* v *Henn and Darby* [1979] ECR 3795. Note that when national rules prohibit the import of certain goods, then according to the practice of the CJEU, this will always be treated as a quantitative restriction on imports, as referred to in Article 34 TFEU, see paragraphs 21 and 22 of the judgment. The CJEU's subsequent *Keck* doctrine is in line with this. See too the decision of the CJEU in Case C-189/95 *Franzén* [1997] ECR I-5909.

In Case C-324/93 *R* v *The Home Secretary, ex parte Evans Medical and another* [1995] ECR I-563, the British authorities had given one British company the exclusive right to produce a drug and another British company the exclusive right to process the product for medical use and marketing within the United Kingdom. This meant that it was illegal to import the drug from other Member States. Against this background, the CJEU assessed how far the national provisions could be justified under Article 36 TFEU (formerly Article 36 EEC Treaty). In paragraph 36 of its judgment, the CJEU held that, according to its practice, it is clear that Article 36 TFEU only relates to measures of a non-economic nature. It is therefore not possible to justify a measure by reference to a need to ensure the survival of an undertaking. On the other hand, the CJEU did expressly recognise that it is possible to justify a national measure under Article 36 TFEU if this is necessary for ensuring security of supply; cf. paragraph 37: 'the need to ensure that a country has reliable supplies for essential medical purposes'. However, the national measures must be proportionate. In paragraph 44 of the judgment it is stated that reliability of supplies is one of the criteria which may be taken into account in determining the most economically advantageous tender for a contract of supply.

Is there proportionality between the permitted aim (security of supply) and the means adopted for attaining that aim (granting exclusive rights to two British companies)?

JUDGMENT OF THE COURT
5 November 2002

Commission of the European Communities v Federal Republic of Germany

'Free movement of goods – Measures having equivalent effect – Label of origin and quality'

Case C-325/00

Judgment

1. By application lodged at the Court Registry on 4 September 2000, the Commission of the European Communities brought an action under Article 226 EC for a declaration that by awarding the quality label 'Markenqualität aus deutschen Landen' (quality label for produce made in Germany) to finished products of a certain quality produced in Germany, the Federal Republic of Germany has failed to fulfil its obligations under Article 30 of the EC Treaty (now, after amendment, Article 28 EC).

Background to the dispute

2. The Gesetz über die Errichtung eines zentralen Fonds zur Absatzförderung der deutschen Land- und Ernährungswirtschaft (Absatzfondsgesetz) (Law establishing a central fund for the promotion of German agriculture and the German food industry of 26 June 1969 (BGBl. 1969 I, p. 653), in its consolidated version of 21 June 1993 (BGBl. 1993 I, p. 998, the 'AFG') set up a fund called the 'Absatzförderungsfonds der deutschen Land- und Ernärungswirtschaft (Absatzfonds)' (the 'Fund'). Under Paragraph 2(1) of the AFG, the Fund has, *inter alia*, the object of promoting, at central level, the marketing and development of agricultural products and the German food industry by researching and developing markets inside and outside Germany.

3. In accordance with Paragraph 4 of the AFG, the Fund is run by a Management Board of three members, chosen by a Supervisory Board and appointed by the president of the Supervisory Board, that appointment being subject to the approval of the competent federal minister. Under Paragraph 5 of the AFG, the Supervisory Board is composed of 21 members who are appointed by the federal minister, five on the proposal of parties represented in the Bundestag, thirteen on the proposal of the German agriculture and food sectors and three on the proposal of the governing organs of the central body responsible for the implementation of the Fund's objectives, referred to in paragraph 5 of this judgment.

4. Under Paragraph 10 of the AFG, the Fund's tasks are financed by compulsory contributions paid by undertakings in the German agriculture and food sector. The obligation to contribute to the Fund applies to all undertakings in the relevant sectors. The Fund is an economic body based on principles of mutual aid. Its income, consisting of those compulsory contributions, is used exclusively for purposes in the interest of mutual aid.

5. Paragraph 2(2) of the AFG provides that the Fund is to carry out its task through a central body ('einer zentralen Einrichtung der Wirtschaft'). That central body is the Centrale Marketing-Gesellschaft der deutschen Agrarwirtschaft mbH (the 'CMA'). It is a limited company (GmbH) which, in accordance with Paragraph 2(2) and (4) of the AFG is responsible for promoting the distribution and exploitation of products in the sectors of the German economy in question with resources which are granted to it through the Fund.

6. The CMA's Articles of Association – which were originally approved by the competent Federal minister – provide in Article 9, for the setting up of a Supervisory Board composed of 26 members appointed by the general meeting of the members of the company. The members are professional associations from the German food and agriculture sectors having shares in the company. Three of the members of that Board are appointed, under Paragraph 2(2) of the AFG, on the proposal of the Fund, the 23 others being proposed, in accordance with Article 9 of the CMA's Articles of Association, by the professional associations concerned.

7. Article 2 of the CMA's Articles of Association provides:

'(1) The company is to assist the Fund for the promotion of agriculture and the German food sector and its purpose is the promotion, at central level, of the marketing and exploitation of German agricultural and food products.

(2) To achieve that objective, the company must use all appropriate means to research and develop markets, inside and outside the country, in particular:
...
(d) the promotion of indications of origin and quality labels
...

(3) The company is bound to observe the Fund's rules and additionally to be guided, particularly in relation to the commitment of its financial resources, by the general interest of the German agricultural and food sector.

(4) The company is not authorised to provide, for pecuniary gain, goods or services on its own account. Without prejudice to the obligation to manage its activities according to commercial principles, the company is non-profit-making

and confines itself to the promotion of the German agricultural and food sector.'

8. Under Article 2(2)(d) of its Articles of Association, the CMA awards a quality label ('Gütezeichen'), which enables the mark 'Markenqualität aus deutschen Landen' 'CMA label') to be affixed to the products concerned. That label is awarded, on the application of an agricultural or food company, to products satisfying certain quality requirements set by the CMA. The latter constantly verifies, with the help of independent laboratories, that the products authorised to carry its label satisfy the corresponding quality requirements. The CMA reserves the use of its label for products made in Germany, whether they are made from raw materials produced in Germany or imported.

9. When the CMA has verified that an undertaking's products fulfil the conditions for the grant of its label, it concludes a licence contract with the undertaking.

10. The CMA label has existed since the beginning of the 1970s and is, according to the file before the Court, used by 2 538 undertakings for 11 633 different products across 23 sectors of production.

Pre-litigation procedure

11. Following an investigation carried out in 1992 in order to list the quality labels existing in the Member States for agricultural products and food, the Commission, by letters of 6 July 1994 and 18 October 1995, informed the German Government that the award of the CMA label in the circumstances set out in paragraphs 2 to 9 of this judgment ('the contested scheme') constituted a breach of the principle of the free movement of goods enshrined in Article 30 of the Treaty.

12. On 22 January 1998, the Commission sent a formal notice to the German Government concerning the CMA label, to which it replied on 3 June 1998. As the Commission was not satisfied by that reply, on 11 December 1998 it sent a reasoned opinion to the Federal Republic of Germany calling on it to comply with its obligations under Article 30 of the Treaty within two months of the notification of that opinion. The German Government replied on 16 March 1999 that the award of the CMA label was compatible with Community law.

13. In those circumstances, the Commission decided to bring the present action.

The action

Whether the contested scheme can be classified as a public measure attributable to the State

14. The German Government argues that the CMA's activities do not fall within the competence of the public authorities and are therefore outside the scope of Article 30 of the Treaty. It argues that unlike the position in Case 249/81 *Commission* v *Ireland* ([1982] ECR 4005), the CMA does not merely have the legal form of a private capital company, but also its organs were set up in accordance with private law rules and its resources are supplied by economic operators.

15. Additionally, the German Government points out that CMA label is not used on the basis of a law or other official act but on the basis of contracts concluded between the CMA and the undertakings. The CMA concludes licence contracts with the undertakings on its own responsibility and no licensee is obliged, by act of state or for other reasons, to conclude such a contract. In addition, the CMA's financial resources come exclusively from contributions from undertakings and the amounts constituting those contributions are used exclusively for purposes which are in the interest of mutual aid.

16. Finally, the German Government argues that, although the Fund is effectively a public law body, its only influence on the CMA's organs is to the extent that three members of the CMA's Supervisory Board, which number 26, are appointed by the Fund. The activity and influence of the State on the CMA is limited to the collection and supervision of the contributions paid to the CMA which come exclusively from the private sector.

17. In that regard, it must be recalled that the CMA, although set up as a private company is
    - established on the basis of a law, the AFG, is characterised by that law as a central economic body and has, among the objects assigned to it by that law, the promotion, at central level, of the marketing and exploitation of German agricultural and food products;
    - is bound, according to its Articles of Association, originally approved by the competent federal minister, to observe the rules of the Fund, itself a public body, and additionally to be guided, in particular in relation to the commitment of its financial resources, by the general interest of the German agricultural and food sector;
    - is financed, according to the rules laid down by the AFG, by a compulsory contribution by all the undertakings in the sectors concerned.

18. Such a body, which is set up by a national law of a Member State and which is financed by a contribution imposed on producers, cannot, under Community law, en-

joy the same freedom as regards the promotion of national production as that enjoyed by producers themselves or producers' associations of a voluntary character (see Case 222/82 *Apple and Pear Development Council* [1983] ECR 4083, paragraph 17). Thus it is obliged to respect the basic rules of the Treaty on the free movement of goods when it sets up a scheme, open to all undertakings of the sectors concerned, which can have effects on intra-Community trade similar to those arising under the scheme adopted by the public authorities.

19. Furthermore, it must be observed that:
    - the Fund is a public law body;
    - the CMA is required to respect the Fund's guidelines;
    - the financing of the CMA's activities, under legislation, comes from resources which are granted to it through the Fund, and
    - the Fund supervises the CMA's activities and the proper management of the finances which are granted to it by the Fund.

20. In those circumstances, it must be held that the Commission could rightly take the view that the contested scheme is ascribable to the State.

21. Thus it follows that the contested scheme must be considered to be a public measure for the purpose of Article 30 ascribable to the State.

Restriction on trade

22. The Court has consistently held that Article 30 of the Treaty aims to prohibit all trading rules enacted by Member States which are capable of hindering, directly or indirectly, actually or potentially, intra-Community trade (see, in particular, Case 8/74 *Dassonville* [1974] ECR 837, paragraph 5).

23. The contested scheme has, at least potentially, restrictive effects on the free movement of goods between Member States. Such a scheme, set up in order to promote the distribution of agricultural and food products made in Germany and for which the advertising message underlines the German origin of the relevant products, may encourage consumers to buy the products with the CMA label to the exclusion of imported products (see, in that respect, *Commission* v *Ireland*, paragraph 25, and *Apple and Pear Development Council*, paragraph 18, cited above).

24. The fact that the use of that quality label is optional does not mean that it ceases to be an unjustified obstacle to trade if the use of that designation promotes or is likely to promote the marketing of the product concerned as compared with products which do not benefit from its use (see, in that regard, Case 13/78 *Eggers* [1978] ECR 1935, paragraph 26).

25. In the same way, the argument that the fact that the contested scheme pursues a quality policy takes it outside the scope of Article 30 of the Treaty must be dismissed. The existence of a restriction for the purposes of Article 30 of the Treaty must be determined by reference to the effect on trade of the measure concerned.

Justification on the basis of the protection of industrial and commercial property

26. Finally, the argument that the contested scheme is justified by Article 36 of the EC Treaty (now, after amendment, Article 30 EC), as coming within the derogation for the protection of industrial and commercial property in so far as the CMA label constitutes simply a geographical indication of provenance, must be dismissed.

27. While it is true, as the German Government points out, that the Court acknowledges in its judgment in Case C-3/91 *Exportur* [1992] ECR 5529, that the protection of geographical indications may, under certain conditions, fall within the protection of industrial and commercial property for the purposes of Article 36 of the Treaty, a scheme such as that at issue in the present proceedings, defining the area of provenance as the extent of German territory and applying to all agricultural and food products fulfilling certain quality requirements, cannot in any case be considered as a geographic indication capable of justification under Article 36 of the Treaty.

28. In the light of the preceding considerations, it must be held that by awarding the quality label CMA to finished products of a certain quality made in Germany, the Federal Republic of Germany has failed to fulfil its obligations under Article 30 of the Treaty.

Costs

[Para. 29 omitted]

On those grounds,

THE COURT

hereby:

1. **Declares that, by awarding the quality label 'Marenqualität aus deutschen Landen' (quality label for produce made in Germany) to finished products of a certain quality made in Germany, the Federal Republic of Germany has failed to fulfil its obligations under Article 30 of the EC Treaty (now, after amendment, Article 28 EC);**

[Para. 2 of the ruling omitted]

Comments and questions

It has been clearly established that, in principle, only Member States have responsibilities under Article 34 TFEU (formerly Article 30 TEC). However, the CJEU has adopted a broad definition of what constitutes the Member State. In Case C-325/00 *Commission* v *Germany* (the *Markenqualität* case) [2002] ECR I-9977, the question arose as to whether a private company, which had been set up primarily to promote the sale and consumption of the products of the German agricultural and food industry, was subject to the terms of Article 28.

The CJEU found that, even though the disputed scheme was administered by a body set up as a private company, a number of factors meant that the scheme should nevertheless be seen as a measure which was covered by Article 34 TFEU. Thus, in paragraphs 17-19, the CJEU referred to the following circumstances which all indicated that the actions of the private company (the body) should be considered as being the actions of the German State:

1. The body was established on the basis of a law.
2. According to that law, the body was characterised as a central economic body which had the aim of promoting, at a central level, the marketing and exploitation of certain German products.
3. In carrying out its activities, the body was guided by the general interest of the German agricultural and food sector.
4. The articles of association of the body were approved by the competent federal minister.
5. According to its articles of association, the body had to observe the rules of a Fund, which was itself a public body.
6. The financing of the body, which was regulated by law, was by payments from the public Fund.
7. The Fund supervised the activities of the body and the proper management of the finances granted to the body by the Fund.

Compare the CJEU's reasoning in this case with its reasoning in Case 249/81 *Commission* v *Ireland* (the *Buy Irish* case) [1982] ECR 4005, (paragraphs 11-15 of the judgment), printed below, and in this connection, see the arguments of the German government in the *Markenqualität* case, which are reproduced in paragraphs 14-15 of the judgment. Is there a difference between the CJEU's reasoning (listing of the relevant factors) in the two cases? In which of the two cases does the CJEU most stretch the limits of legal responsibility?

Consider the extent to which a genuinely private body can be subject to Article 34 TFEU. Where do you think that the boundary should be drawn between undertakings etc. which ought to be subject to Article 34 TFEU, and undertakings etc. which ought not to be subject to it? Compare the limits of the concept of the State in this case with that in Case C-415/93 *Union royale belge des sociétés de football association* v *Bosman*

[1995] ECR I-4921, and Case 71/76 *Thieffry* v *Conseil des avocats* [1977] ECR 765. These cases are discussed in detail in Chapters 4 and 5 respectively.

It seems natural to assume that the distinction in the TFEU, between the rules on the freedom of movement of goods in Article 34 and the rules on competition in Articles 101 and 102, is based on the premise that Article 34 regulates the Member States, while the provisions on competition are aimed at undertakings. In paragraph 30 of the judgment in Case 311/85 *Vlaamse Reisbureaus* v *Sociale Dienst* [1987] ECR 3801, the CJEU held that '... Articles 30 [now Article 34] and 34 [now Article 36] of the Treaty [TFEU] concern only *public measures* and not the *conduct of undertakings*' (italics added). Do you think that the CJEU applied this distinction in the *Markenqualität* case? See paragraph 18 in the judgment in the *Markenqualität* case.

The question has been raised whether the judgment in Case C-281/98 *Angonese* v *Cassa di Risparmio di Bolzano* [2000] ECR I-4139, (printed below) means that the Treaty provisions on the free movement of goods now apply in general to private persons. In the *Angonese* case, the CJEU held that Article 45 TFEU on the free movement of workers has horizontal effect, applying to private persons as well as Member States; in other words, Article 45 TFEU contains a horizontal prohibition of discrimination. Given the way the *Angonese* judgment is phrased, there is nothing to stop its arguments being equally applicable to Article 34 TFEU. Does the fact that, in the *Markenqualität* case, the CJEU discussed the degree to which the German State was behind the body mean that the CJEU considered the extent to which Article 34 TFEU does or does not contain a horizontal prohibition of discrimination? On this point, compare the case with Case 249/81 *Commission* v *Ireland* (the *Buy Irish* case) [1982] ECR 4005, and Case C-265/95 *Commission* v *France* (the *Strawberry* case) [1997] ECR I-6959, both printed below.

In evaluating the *Markenqualität* case, is it relevant to emphasise that the use of the certification mark in the case was not regulated by law or by any other public regulation, but was merely granted on the basis of a licence agreement between the certifying company (the CMA) and individual undertakings?

Case C-448/98 *Guimont* [2000] ECR I-10663, printed below, referred to the generic name 'Emmenthal', which ought in principle to be available for use on all products which satisfy certain quality standards, regardless of their origin. On the other hand, the *Markenqualität* case concerned products which carry the certification mark, are made in Germany and have a certain quality. As the Advocate General said in his Opinion, such branding cannot logically be considered as a generic product description. He therefore argued that, in order to decide whether the arrangement contravened Article 34 TFEU, it was necessary to investigate whether it restricted trade within the Union. Referring to Case 8/74 *Procureur du Roi* v *Dassonville* [1974] ECR 837, and to the *Buy Irish* case, both printed below, the CJEU (paragraphs 22-24 of the judgment) and the Advocate General concluded that it did restrict trade. Do you agree that the German scheme involved a restriction on trade within the Union, as defined in the *Dassonville* case? Consider whether the case concerned direct discrimination or whether it concerns a restriction. Does the CJEU state a view on this in its judgment?

JUDGMENT OF THE COURT (Fourth Chamber)
12 July 2012

Fra.bo SpA. V Deutsche Vereinigung des Gas – und Wasserfaches eV (DVGW) – Technisch-Wissenschaftlicher Verein. (Reference for a preliminary ruling from the Oberlandesgericht Düsseldorf – Germany)

'Free movement of goods – Measures having equivalent effect to a quantitative restriction – National certification procedure – Presumption of compliance with national law – Applicability of Article 28 EC to a private-law certification body'

Case C-171/11

Judgment

1. This reference for a preliminary ruling concerns the interpretation of Articles 28 EC, 81 and 86(2) EC.

2. That reference was made in the context of proceedings between Fra.bo SpA ('Fra.bo'), a company governed by Italian law specialised in the production and distribution of copper fittings intended in particular for piping for water or gas, and the German certification body, the Deutsche Vereinigung des Gas- und Wasserfaches eV (DVGW) – Technisch-Wissenschaftlicher Verein ('DVGW') concerning the latter's decision to withdraw or refuse to extend the certificate for copper fittings produced and distributed by Fra.bo.

German legal context

3. It is apparent from the order for reference and the observations of the parties concerned that the Regulation on General Conditions for Water Supply (Verordnung über Allgemeine Bedingungen für die Versorgung mit Wasser) of 20 June 1980 (BGBl. 1980 I, p. 750) ('the AVBWasserV'), lays down the general sales conditions for water supply undertakings and their customers, from which the parties are free to depart.

4. On the date of the facts in the main proceedings, Paragraph 12(4) of the AVBWasserV was worded as follows:

   'Only materials and devices which comply with the recognised rules of technology may be used. The mark of a recognised inspection body (such as the DIN-DVGW, DVGW or GS mark) shall testify to the fulfilment of those requirements.'

5. The Regulation of 13 January 2010 (BGBl. 2010 I, p. 10) amended Paragraph 12(4) of the ABVWasserV as follows:

   'Only products and devices supplied in accordance with the recognised rules of technology may be used. Compliance with the conditions laid down in the first sentence shall be assumed if they have specific CE marking for drinking water use. Where such CE marking is not stipulated, it shall also be assumed if the product or device bears the mark of an accredited certifying body for the industry, in particular the DIN-DVGW or DVGW mark. Products and devices which

   1. were lawfully manufactured in another contracting state of the Agreement on the European Economic Area or

   2. were lawfully manufactured or marketed in another Member State of the European Union or in Turkey

   and do not meet the technical specifications for the mark referred to in the third sentence shall be treated as equivalent, inclusive of the inspections and surveillance carried out in the aforementioned States, if the same level of protection as required in Germany is thereby permanently ensured.'

The dispute in the main proceedings and the questions referred for a preliminary ruling

6. It is apparent from the order for reference and the observations of the parties concerned that Fra.bo is an undertaking established in Italy which manufactures and sells copper fittings. Copper fittings are connections between two pieces of piping for water or gas, with sealing rings made of malleable material at the ends to make them watertight.

7. The DVGW is a non-profit body governed by private law, set up in 1859, the object of which, according to its articles of association, is to promote the gas and water sector. The DVGW is recognised in Germany as a 'public benefit' body, a status conferred under Paragraph 51 et seq. of the Regulations on Taxes (Abgabenordnung) on bodies whose activity is dedicated to the altruistic advancement of the general public in material, spiritual or moral respects. Under Paragraph 2(2) of its articles of association, the DVGW does not defend the interests of the manufacturers in that sector.

8. For the water sector, there are approximately 350 standards drawn up by the DVGW. Technical standard W 534 is relevant to the dispute in the main proceedings. It serves as the basis for certification, on a voluntary basis, of products which come into contact with drinking water.

9. In late 1999 Fra.bo applied to the DVGW for certification of the copper fittings at issue in the main proceedings. The DVGW instructed the Materialprüfungsanstalt Darmstadt to carry out the necessary tests. These were in turn sub-contracted to the firm Cerisie Laboratorio, established in Italy, which is approved by the relevant Italian authorities, though not by the DVGW. In November 2000, the DVGW then granted the claimant a water industry certificate for a period of five years.

10. After complaints by third parties, the DVGW instituted a re-assessment procedure in which Materialprüfungsanstalt Darmstadt was again commissioned to carry out the testing. An ozone test to establish the ozone resistance of the copper fitting's elastomeric waterproof joint was conducted on a sample of material provided by the Italian manufacturer. In June 2005 the DVGW informed Fra.bo that its fitting had not passed the ozone test but it could, as provided for in the DGVW's rules, produce a positive test report within three months. However, the DGVW did not recognise the test report drawn up subsequently by Cerisie Laboratorio, on the ground that it was not one of its approved testing laboratories. In the dispute in the main proceedings, the DGVW also challenges that test report on the ground that the content is insufficient, in that it did not indicate the test specifications or the material-testing conditions.

11. In the meantime, in a formalised procedure in which Fra.bo was not involved, the DGVW amended technical standard W 534 by introducing the 3 000-hour test, aimed at ensuring longer life for certified products. The DGVW's reply to a written question from the Court indicates that the 3 000-hour test consists in exposing the copper fitting's elastomeric waterproof joint to a temperature of 110 degrees Celsius in boiling water for 3 000 hours. According to the DGVW's rules, certificate holders are required to obtain additional certification within three months of the entry into effect of the amendment to the technical standard, as evidence of compliance with the amended conditions. Fra.bo did not make such an application and did not subject its copper fittings to the 3 000-hour test.

12. In June 2005 the DVGW cancelled Fra.bo's certificate for copper fittings on the ground that it had not submitted a positive test report on the 3 000-hour test. The DVGW also rejected an application for extension of the certificate on the ground that compliance certificates could no longer be extended.

13. Fra.bo brought an action against the DVGW before the Landgericht Köln (Regional Court, Cologne), arguing that the cancellation and/or the refusal to extend the certificate are contrary to European Union law. In Fra.bo's submission, the DVGW is bound by the provisions governing the free movement of goods, namely Article 28 EC et seq., and the cancellation and the refusal to extend the certificate both restrict considerably its access to the German market. Due to the presumption of compliance conferred on products certified by the DVGW under Paragraph 12(4) of the ABVWasserV, it is virtually impossible for Fra.bo to distribute its products

in Germany without that certificate. The 3000-hour test has no objective justification and the DVGW is not entitled to reject outright test reports from laboratories which are accredited by the competent authorities in Member States other than the Federal Republic of Germany, but not by the DGVW. The DVGW ought to be regarded as an association of undertakings which, in drawing up the contested technical standards, also infringes Article 81 EC.

14. As a private-law association, the DVGW considers that it is not bound by the provisions governing the free movement of goods and that only the Federal Republic of Germany is required to answer for any infringements of Article 28 EC in connection with the adoption of Paragraph 12(4) of the ABVWasserV. Consequently, there is nothing preventing the DVGW from drawing up technical standards which go beyond those in place in Member States other than the Federal Republic of Germany and to apply them to its certification activities. It is also free, on quality-related grounds, to take account only of laboratories accredited by it. Moreover, as a standard-setting body, it does not pursue economic activities for the purpose of agreements, with the result that Article 81 EC does not apply in the present case.

15. The Landgericht Köln dismissed Fra.bo's action, holding that the DVGW was free to set out the conditions under which it would issue a compliance certificate. Fra.bo appealed against that decision before the referring court in order to have, on the same grounds, the DVGW ordered to extend the compliance certificate for the fittings in question and to pay EUR 1 000 000 in damages plus interest.

16. As it had doubts as to the applicability of the provisions governing the free movement of goods and agreements between undertakings to the DVGW's activities, the Oberlandesgericht Düsseldorf decided to stay the proceedings and to refer the following questions to the Court for a preliminary ruling:

'1. Is Article 28 EC ..., if appropriate in conjunction with Article [86(2)] EC ..., to be interpreted as meaning that private-law bodies which have been set up for the purpose of drawing up technical standards in a particular field and certifying products on the basis of those technical standards are bound by the aforementioned provisions when drawing up technical standards and in the certification process where the national legislature expressly regards the products in respect of which certificates have been issued as lawful, thus making it at least considerably more difficult in practice to distribute products in respect of which certificates have not been issued?

2. If the answer to the first question is in the negative:
Is Article 81 EC ... to be interpreted as meaning that the activity pursued by a private-law body in the field of drawing up technical standards and certifying products on the basis of those technical standards, as described in question 1, is to be regarded as 'economic' where the body is controlled by those undertakings?

If the first part of this question is answered in the affirmative:
Is Article 81 EC ... to be interpreted as meaning that the drawing-up of technical standards and the certification of products on the basis of those technical standards by an association of undertakings is capable of impeding trade between the Member States if a product lawfully manufactured and distributed in another Member State cannot be distributed in the importing Member State, or can be distributed there only with considerable difficulty, because it does not meet the requirements of the technical standard and, in the light of the predominance of the technical standard on the market and of a legal provision adopted by the national legislature to the effect that a certificate from the association of undertakings must indicate compliance with the requirements laid down by law, distribution without such a certificate is virtually impossible, and if the technical standard would not be applicable if it had been adopted directly by the national legislature because it infringes the principle of the free movement of goods?'

The questions referred for a preliminary ruling

The first question

17. By its first question, the referring court asks, in essence, whether Article 28 EC must be interpreted as meaning that it applies to standardisation and certification activities of a private-law body, where the national legislation considers the products certified by that body to be compliant with national law and that has the effect of restricting the marketing of products which are not certified by that body.

18. As a preliminary point, it is common ground that the copper fittings at issue in the main proceedings are a 'construction product' within the meaning of Council Directive 89/106/EEC of 21 December 1988 on the approximation of laws, regulations and administrative provisions of the Member States relating to construction products (OJ 1989 L 40, p. 12), as amended by Regulation (EC) No 1882/2003 of the European Parliament and of the Council of 29 September 2003 (OJ 2003 L 284, p. 1) ('Directive 89/106'), which are not subject to a harmonised standard, a European technical approval or a national technical specification recognised at European Union level, as referred to in Article 4(2) of that directive.

19. In respect of construction products not covered by Article 4(2) of Directive 89/106, Article 6(2) of that directive provides that the Member States are to allow such products to be placed on the market in their territory if they satisfy national provisions consistent with the EC Treaty until the European technical specifications provide otherwise.

20. Thus, national provisions governing the placing on the market of a construction product not covered by technical specifications harmonised or recognised at Euro-

pean Union level must, as provided for by Directive 89/106, comply with obligations under the Treaty, in particular with the principle of the free movement of goods as set out in Articles 28 EC and 30 EC (see, to that effect, judgment of 13 March 2008 in Case C-227/06 Commission v Belgium, paragraph 34).

21. It must be ascertained, first, whether Article 28 EC must be interpreted as meaning that it applies to standardisation and certification activities of a private-law body in circumstances such as those in the main proceedings, as the applicant in the main proceedings claims that it does.

22. According to settled case-law, all rules enacted by Member States which are capable of hindering, directly or indirectly, actually or potentially, intra-Community trade are to be considered as measures having an effect equivalent to quantitative restrictions, prohibited by Article 28 EC (Case 8/74 Dassonville [1974] ECR 837, paragraph 5; Case C-270/02 Commission v Italy [2004] ECR I-1559, paragraph 18; and Commission v Belgium, paragraph 40). Thus, the mere fact that an importer might be dissuaded from introducing or marketing the products in question in the Member State concerned constitutes a restriction on the free movement of goods for the importer (judgment of 24 April 2008 in Case C-286/07 Commission v Luxembourg, paragraph 27).

23. Similarly, the Court has held that a Member State fails to fulfil its obligations under Articles 28 EC and 30 EC when, without valid justification, it encourages economic operators wishing to market in its territory construction products lawfully manufactured and/or marketed in another Member State to obtain national marks of conformity (see, to that effect, Commission v Belgium, paragraph 69) or when it refuses to recognise the equivalence of approval certificates issued by another Member State (see, to that effect, Case C-432/03 Commission v Portugal [2005] ECR I-9665, paragraphs 41, 49 and 52).

24. It is common ground that the DVGW is a non-profit, private-law body whose activities are not financed by the Federal Republic of Germany. It is, moreover, uncontested that that Member State has no decisive influence over the DVGW's standardisation and certification activities, although some of its members are public bodies.

25. The DVGW contends that, accordingly, Article 28 EC is not applicable to it, as it is a private body. The other parties concerned consider that private-law bodies are, in certain circumstances, bound to observe the free movement of goods as guaranteed by Article 28 EC.

26. It must therefore be determined whether, in the light of inter alia the legislative and regulatory context in which it operates, the activities of a private-law body such as the DVGW has the effect of giving rise to restrictions on the free movement of goods in the same manner as do measures imposed by the State.

27. In the present case, it should be observed, firstly, that the German legislature has established, in Paragraph 12(4) of the ABVWasserV, that products certified by the DVGW are compliant with national legislation.

28. Secondly, it is not disputed by the parties to the main proceedings that the DVGW is the only body able to certify the copper fittings at issue in the main proceedings for the purposes of Paragraph 12(4) of the ABVWasserV. In other words, the DVGW offers the only possibility for obtaining a compliance certificate for such products.

29. The DVGW and the German Government have referred to there being a procedure other than certification by the DVGW, which consists in entrusting an expert with the task of verifying a product's compliance with the recognised rules of technology within the meaning of Paragraph 12(4) of the ABVWasserV. It is apparent, however, from the answers to the written and oral questions put by the Court that the administrative difficulties associated with the absence of specific rules of procedure governing the work of such experts, on the one hand, combined with the additional costs incurred by having an individual expert report drawn up, on the other, make that other procedure of little or no practical use.

30. Thirdly, the referring court takes the view that, in practice, the lack of certification by the DVGW places a considerable restriction on the marketing of the products concerned on the German market. Although the ABVWasserV merely lays down the general sales conditions as between water supply undertakings and their customers, from which the parties are free to depart, it is apparent from the case-file that, in practice, almost all German consumers purchase copper fittings certified by the DVGW.

31. In such circumstances, it is clear that a body such as the DVGW, by virtue of its authority to certify the products, in reality holds the power to regulate the entry into the German market of products such as the copper fittings at issue in the main proceedings.

32. Accordingly, the answer to the first question is that Article 28 EC must be interpreted as meaning that it applies to standardisation and certification activities of a private-law body, where the national legislation considers the products certified by that body to be compliant with national law and that has the effect of restricting the marketing of products which are not certified by that body.

The second question

33. Since the second question was asked by the referring court only in the event of the first question being answered in the negative, there is no need to answer it.

Costs

[Para. 34 omitted]

On those grounds,

THE COURT (Fourth Chamber),

hereby rules:

> **Article 28 EC must be interpreted as meaning that it applies to standardisation and certification activities of a private-law body, where the national legislation considers the products certified by that body to be compliant with national law and that has the effect of restricting the marketing of products which are not certified by that body.**

Comments and questions

In the *Fra.bo* case, the CJEU applied the rules on the free movement of goods in Article 34 TFEU (formerly Article 28 TEC) to a non-commercial German body whose activities were not financed by the German State and over which the German State did not have a decisive influence in relation to the matter that was at issue in the case. On the face of it, the CJEU thus applied the free movement rules to a private body. However, on closer examination of the judgment it can be seen that such an understanding would be wrong.

It is clear from the judgment that the CJEU was very careful to emphasise that the private German body had been given important public law powers over the matter at issue. Thus, in paragraph 32 of the judgment it was stated that Article 34 TFEU must be interpreted as meaning that it applies to standardisation and certification activities of a private-law body, where the national legislation considers the products certified by that body to be compliant with national law, with the effect of restricting the marketing of products which are not certified by that body. Even though there were other means for obtaining such certification, it was in practice very difficult to obtain certification by these other means, so that producers who wanted such certification effectively had to apply to the body that was the subject of dispute.

In other words, the CJEU found that the case concerned a private body which had been given certain responsibilities by the German State. This was why Article 34 TFEU applied in this case.

Consider whether there are private bodies in your State that have been given competences corresponding to those in the situation in the Fra.bo case, and which could thus, in principle, be covered by the TFEU rules on free movement.

JUDGMENT OF THE COURT
11 July 1974

Procureur du Roi (Public Prosecutor) v Benoit and Gustave Dassonville
(Reference to the Court by the Tribunal de Première Instance of Brussels for a preliminary ruling)

'Quantitative Restrictions – abolition – measures having equivalent effect – designation of origin of a product – protective measures – admissibility – comditions competition – agreements – exclusive dealing agreement – prohibition – application – criteria – economic and legal context'

Case 8/74

Judgment

1. By judgment of 11 January 1974, received at the Registry of the Court on 8 February 1974, the Tribunal de Première Instance of Brussels referred, under Article 177 of the EEC Treaty, two questions on the interpretation of Articles 30, 31, 32, 33, 36 and 85 of the EEC Treaty, relating to the requirement of an official document issued by the government of the exporting country for products bearing a designation of origin.

2. By the first question it is asked whether a national provision prohibiting the import of goods bearing a designation of origin where such goods are not accompanied by an official document issued by the government of the exporting country certifying their right to such designation constitutes a measure having an effect equivalent to a quantitative restriction within the meaning of Article 30 of the Treaty.

3. This question was raised within the context of criminal proceedings instituted in Belgium against traders who duly acquired a consignment of Scotch whisky in free circulation in France and imported it into Belgium without being in possession of a certificate of origin from the British customs authorities, thereby infringing Belgian rules.

4. It emerges from the file and from the oral proceedings that a trader, wishing to import into Belgium Scotch whisky which is already in free circulation in France, can obtain such a certificate only with great difficulty, unlike the importer who imports directly from the producer country.

5. All trading rules enacted by Member States which are capable of hindering, directly or indirectly, actually or potentially, intra-Community trade are to be considered as measures having an effect equivalent to quantitative restrictions.

6. In the absence of a Community system guaranteeing for consumers the authenticity of a product's designation of origin, if a Member State takes measures to prevent unfair practices in this connexion, it is however subject to the condition that these measures should be reasonable and that the means of proof required should not act as a hindrance to trade between Member States and should, in consequence, be accessible to all Community nationals.

7. Even without having to examine whether or not such measures are covered by Article 36, they must not, in any case, by virtue of the principle expressed in the second sentence of that Article, constitute a means of arbitrary discrimination or a disguised restriction on trade between Member States.

8. That may be the case with formalities, required by a Member State for the purpose of proving the origin of a product, which only direct importers are really in a position to satisfy without facing serious difficulties.

9. Consequently, the requirement by a Member State of a certificate of authenticity which is less easily obtainable by importers of an authentic product which has been put into free circulation in a regular manner in another Member State than by importers of the same product coming directly from the country of origin constitutes a measure having an effect equivalent to a quantitative restriction as prohibited by the Treaty.

10. By the second question it is asked whether an agreement the effect of which is to restrict competition and adversely to affect trade between Member States when taken in conjunction with a national rule with regard to certificates of origin is void when that agreement merely authorizes the exclusive importer to exploit that rule for the purpose of preventing parallel imports or does not prohibit him from doing so.

11. An exclusive dealing agreement falls within the prohibition of Article 85 when it impedes, in law or in fact, the importation of the products in question from other Member States into the protected territory by persons other than the exclusive importer.

12. More particularly, an exclusive dealing agreement may adversely affect trade between Member States and can have the effect of hindering competition if the concessionaire is able to prevent parallel imports from other Member States into the territory covered by the concession by means of the combined effects of the agreement and a national law requiring the exclusive use of a certain means of proof of authenticity.

13. For the purpose of judging whether this is the case, account must be taken not only of the rights and obligations flowing from the provisions of the agreement, but also

of the legal and economic context in which it is situated and, in particular, the possible existence of similar agreements concluded between the same producer and concessionaires established in other Member States.

14. In this connexion, the maintenance within a Member State of prices appreciably higher than those in force in another Member State may prompt an examination as to whether the exclusive dealing agreement is being used for the purpose of preventing importers from obtaining the means of proof of authenticity of the product in question, required by national rules of the type envisaged by the question.

15. However, the fact that an agreement merely authorizes the concessionaire to exploit such a national rule or does not prohibit him from doing so, does not suffice, in itself, to render the agreement null and void.

Costs

[Paras 16 and 17 omitted]

On those grounds,

THE COURT

in answer to the questions referred to it by the Tribunal de Première Instance of Brussels by Judgment of 11 January 1974, hereby rules:

1. **The requirement of a Member State of a certificate of authenticity which is less easily obtainable by importers of an authentic product which has been put into free circulation in a regular manner in another Member State than by importers of the same product coming directly from the country of origin constitutes a measure having an effect equivalent to a quantitative restriction as prohibited by the Treaty.**

2. **The fact that an agreement merely authorizes the concessionaire to exploit such a national rule or does not prohibit him from doing so does not suffice, in itself, to render the agreement null and void.**

Comments and questions

The judgment in Case 8/74 *Procureur du Roi* v *Dassonville* [1974] ECR 837), is one of the key decisions of the CJEU. It was in this case that the CJEU established, for the first time, what it considers to be a measure having equivalent effect to a quantitative restriction on imports, as laid down in Article 34 TFEU (formerly Article 30 EEC Treaty). In paragraph 5 of the judgment it is stated that: 'All trading rules enacted by Member States which are capable of hindering, directly or indirectly, actually or potentially, intra-[EU] trade are to be considered as measures having an effect equivalent to quantitative restrictions.'

The *Dassonville* case concerned a trade-related rule, since under Belgian law it was only permitted to sell imported goods with a designation of their origin if they were accompanied by an official document issued by the authorities of the exporting country certifying the right to such designation.

Consider whether the definition of a restriction on trade, which was borrowed from the area of competition (first used in Case 56/65 *Société La Technique Minière* v *Machinbau Ulm* [1966] ECR 235), is appropriate for cases dealt with under Article 34 TFEU. Consider too, whether it is important to this assessment that competition law concerns the regulation of conduct between undertakings, while Article 34 TFEU concerns the laws of Member States on trade related issues, and was introduced to deal with the frequently conflicting interests of society.

Note that in paragraph 6 of the judgment it is stated that a Member State can take measures for the prevention of 'unfair practices', if such measures are reasonable, non-discriminatory (open to all), and do not act as a hindrance to trade. Are such considerations covered by Article 36 TFEU (formerly Article 36 EEC Treaty)? Consider whether the CJEU has laid down the same conditions in the later Case 120/78 *Rewe-Central AG* v *Bundesmonopol für Branntwein* (*Cassis de Dijon* case) [1979] ECR 649, which is discussed in detail below.

Several of the parties in this case argued that the hindrance was lawful, since the rule was intended to protect intellectual property rights, specifically the right of the producers of Scotch whisky to use the designation 'Scotch whisky'. The CJEU itself did not consider this argument, but the Advocate General argued that a Member State's right to restrict the free movement of goods cannot be justified on the basis of the protection of intellectual property rights of people in other Member States. (Likewise, the Advocate General argued that a Member State cannot restrict the free movement of goods on the basis of protecting public health in another Member State). Another argument put forward in favour of the legality of the restriction was that it was aimed at protecting public health in Belgium. The Advocate General rejected this argument, pointing out that the Belgian rules did not prohibit the import of whisky, but merely put difficulties in the way of its import when it was designated 'Scotch whisky'. If the same product had been sold simply under the designation of 'whisky', the Belgian rules would not have hindered its import.

JUDGMENT OF THE COURT
20 February 1979

Rewe-Zentral AG v Bundesmonopolverwaltung für Branntwein.
(Preliminary ruling requested by the Hessisches Finanzgericht)

'Measures having an effect equivalent to quantitative restrictions'

Case 120/78

Judgment

1. By order of 28 April 1978, which was received at the Court on 22 May, the Hessisches Finanzgericht referred two questions to the Court under Article 177 of the EEC Treaty for a preliminary ruling on the interpretation of Articles 30 and 37 of the EEC Treaty, for the purpose of assessing the compatibility with Community law of a provision of the German rules relating to the marketing of alcoholic beverages fixing a minimum alcoholic strength for various categories of alcoholic products.

2. It appears from the order making the reference that the plaintiff in the main action intends to import a consignment of Cassis de Dijon originating in France for the purpose of marketing it in the Federal Republic of Germany. The plaintiff applied to the Bundesmonopolverwaltung (Federal Monopoly Administration for Spirits) for authorization to import the product in question and the monopoly administration informed it that because of its insufficient alcoholic strength the said product does not have the characteristics required in order to be marketed within the Federal Republic of Germany.

3. The monopoly administration's attitude is based on Article 100 of the Branntweinmonopolgesetz and on the rules drawn up by the monopoly administration pursuant to that provision, the effect of which is to fix the minimum alcohol content of specified categories of liqueurs and other potable spirits (Verordnung über den Mindestweingeistgehalt von Trinkbranntweinen of 28 February 1958, Bundesanzeiger No 48 of 11 March 1958). Those provisions lay down that the marketing of fruit liqueurs, such as Cassis de Dijon, is conditional upon a minimum alcohol content of 25%, whereas the alcohol content of the product in question, which is freely marketed as such in France, is between 15 and 20%.

4. The plaintiff takes the view that the fixing by the German rules of a minimum alcohol content leads to the result that well-known spirits products from other Member States of the Community cannot be sold in the Federal Republic of Germany and that the said provision therefore constitutes a restriction on the free movement of goods between Member States which exceeds the bounds of the trade rules reserved

to the latter. In its view it is a measure having an effect equivalent to a quantitative restriction on imports contrary to Article 30 of the EEC Treaty. Since, furthermore, it is a measure adopted within the context of the management of the spirits monopoly, the plaintiff considers that there is also an infringement of Article 37, according to which the Member States shall progressively adjust any State monopolies of a commercial character so as to ensure that when the transitional period has ended no discrimination regarding the conditions under which goods are procured or marketed exists between nationals of Member States.

5. In order to reach a decision on this dispute the Hessisches Finanzgericht has referred two questions to the Court, worded as follows:

   1. Must the concept of measures having an effect equivalent to quantitative restrictions on imports contained in Article 30 of the EEC Treaty be understood as meaning that the fixing of a minimum wine-spirit content for potable spirits laid down in the German Branntweinmonopolgesetz, the result of which is that traditional products of other Member States whose wine-spirit content is below the fixed limit cannot be put into circulation in the Federal Republic of Germany, also comes within this concept?

   2. May the fixing of such a minimum wine-spirit content come within the concept of discrimination regarding the conditions under which goods are procured and marketed ... between nationals of Member States contained in Article 37 of the EEC Treaty?

6. The national court is thereby asking for assistance in the matter of interpretation in order to enable it to assess whether the requirement of a minimum alcohol content may be covered either by the prohibition on all measures having an effect equivalent to quantitative restrictions in trade between Member States contained in Article 30 of the Treaty or by the prohibition on all discrimination regarding the conditions under which goods are procured and marketed between nationals of Member States within the meaning of Article 37.

7. It should be noted in this connexion that Article 37 relates specifically to State monopolies of a commercial character. That provision is therefore irrelevant with regard to national provisions which do not concern the exercise by a public monopoly of its specific function – namely, its exclusive right – but apply in a general manner to the production and marketing of alcoholic beverages, whether or not the latter are covered by the monopoly in question. That being the case, the effect on intra-Community trade of the measure referred to by the national court must be examined solely in relation to the requirements under Article 30, as referred to by the first question.

8. In the absence of common rules relating to the production and marketing of alcohol – a proposal for a regulation submitted to the Council by the Commission on 7 December 1976 (Official Journal C 309, p. 2) not yet having received the Council's approval – it is for the Member States to regulate all matters relating to the production and marketing of alcohol and alcoholic beverages on their own territory. Obstacles to movement within the Community resulting from disparities between the national laws relating to the marketing of the products in question must be accepted in so far as those provisions may be recognized as being necessary in order to satisfy mandatory requirements relating in particular to the effectiveness of fiscal supervision, the protection of public health, the fairness of commercial transactions and the defence of the consumer.

9. The Government of the Federal Republic of Germany, intervening in the proceedings, put forward various arguments which, in its view, justify the application of provisions relating to the minimum alcohol content of alcoholic beverages, adducing considerations relating on the one hand to the protection of public health and on the other to the protection of the consumer against unfair commercial practices.

10. As regards the protection of public health the German Government states that the purpose of the fixing of minimum alcohol contents by national legislation is to avoid the proliferation of alcoholic beverages on the national market, in particular alcoholic beverages with a low alcohol content, since, in its view, such products may more easily induce a tolerance towards alcohol than more highly alcoholic beverages.

11. Such considerations are not decisive since the consumer can obtain on the market an extremely wide range of weakly or moderately alcoholic products and furthermore a large proportion of alcoholic beverages with a high alcohol content freely sold on the German market is generally consumed in a diluted form.

12. The German Government also claims that the fixing of a lower limit for the alcohol content of certain liqueurs is designed to protect the consumer against unfair practices on the part of producers and distributors of alcoholic beverages. This argument is based on the consideration that the lowering of the alcohol content secures a competitive advantage in relation to beverages with a higher alcohol content, since alcohol constitutes by far the most expensive constituent of beverages by reason of the high rate of tax to which it is subject. Furthermore, according to the German Government, to allow alcoholic products into free circulation wherever, as regards their alcohol content, they comply with the rules laid down in the country of production would have the effect of imposing as a common standard within the Community the lowest alcohol content permitted in any of the Member States, and even of rendering any requirements in this field inoperative since a lower limit of this nature is foreign to the rules of several Member States.

13. As the Commission rightly observed, the fixing of limits in relation to the alcohol content of beverages may lead to the standardization of products placed on the market and of their designations, in the interests of a greater transparency of commercial transactions and offers for sale to the public. However, this line of argument cannot be taken so far as to regard the mandatory fixing of minimum alcohol contents as being an essential guarantee of the fairness of commercial transactions, since it is a simple matter to ensure that suitable information is conveyed to the purchaser by requiring the display of an indication of origin and of the alcohol content on the packaging of products.

14. It is clear from the foregoing that the requirements relating to the minimum alcohol content of alcoholic beverages do not serve a purpose which is in the general interest and such as to take precedence over the requirements of the free movement of goods, which constitutes one of the fundamental rules of the Community. In practice, the principle effect of requirements of this nature is to promote alcoholic beverages having a high alcohol content by excluding from the national market products of other Member States which do not answer that description. It therefore appears that the unilateral requirement imposed by the rules of a Member State of a minimum alcohol content for the purposes of the sale of alcoholic beverages constitutes an obstacle to trade which is incompatible with the provisions of Article 30 of the Treaty. There is therefore no valid reason why, provided that they have been lawfully produced and marketed in one of the Member States, alcoholic beverages should not be introduced into any other Member State; the sale of such products may not be subject to a legal prohibition on the marketing of beverages with an alcohol content lower than the limit set by the national rules.

15. Consequently, the first question should be answered to the effect that the concept of measures having an effect equivalent to quantitative restrictions on imports contained in Article 30 of the Treaty is to be understood to mean that the fixing of a minimum alcohol content for alcoholic beverages intended for human consumption by the legislation of a Member State also falls within the prohibition laid down in that provision where the importation of alcoholic beverages lawfully produced and marketed in another Member State is concerned.

Costs

[Para. 16 omitted]

On those grounds,

THE COURT,

in answer to the questions referred to it by the Hessisches Finanzgericht by order of 28 April 1978, hereby rules:

The concept of measures having an effect equivalent to quantitative restrictions on imports contained in Article 30 of the EEC Treaty is to be understood to mean that the fixing of a minimum alcohol content for alcoholic beverages intended for human consumption by the legislation of a Member State also falls within the prohibition laid down in that provision where the importation of alcoholic beverages lawfully produced and marketed in another Member State is concerned.

Comments and questions

In Case 120/78 *Rewe-Central AG* v *Bundesmonopol für Branntwein* (the *Cassis de Dijon* case) [1979] ECR 649, the CJEU gives a rather different definition of restrictions on trade in Article 34 TFEU (formerly Article 30 EEC Treaty), and measures having equivalent effect, than is given in Case 8/74 *Dassonville* [1974] ECR 837. In paragraph 14 of the judgment it is stated, even if indirectly, that a restriction on trade will exist if a product which is lawfully produced and sold in one Member State, cannot be lawfully sold in another Member State (the condition of reciprocity). This definition was given without reference to the definition in the *Dassonville* case.

Which of the concepts of restrictions on trade in the two judgments do you believe is wider?

Where in the judgment is it recognised that effective tax controls and the protection of consumers can justify a restriction on trade? On what basis can the CJEU allow these considerations to influence its decisions?

Note that the judgment concerned national laws which applied without distinction to both German and foreign fruit liqueurs. The case therefore concerned non-discriminatory trade related laws, i.e., a restriction. In paragraph 8 of the judgment the CJEU presented the 2nd *Cassis* principle or the 'Rule of reason' for the first time. According to this, a restriction on trade can be justified on grounds other than those listed in Article 36 TFEU (formerly ex Article 36), provided that the national laws apply equally to domestic and foreign products. Moreover, the national laws must satisfy the requirement of proportionality. This latter was important, because consideration for the maintenance of good trade practice could have been achieved in a less interventionist way than by requiring a minimum alcohol content for fruit liqueurs, since Germany could simply have introduced a requirement for the declaration of alcoholic content instead; cf. paragraph 13 of the judgment.

In Case 261/81 *Walter Rau Lebensmittelwerke* v *De Smedt PVBA*,[1982] ECR 3961, the CJEU was required to consider a Belgian law which required that margarine should be sold in conical packaging and butter in rectangular packaging, so that consumers could tell the difference between butter and margarine. This requirement affected a German producer who produced margarine in rectangular packaging. How do you think the CJEU decided this case?

Assume that the German government identified a sharp increase in alcohol consumption among the very young. The principal cause of the increase was due to the consumption of 'alcopops', sometimes known as 'RTD' (ready-to-drink). These are drinks which are similar to ordinary soft drinks (fizzy drinks), with the addition of alcohol. The German government wanted to protect public health and believed that there was good support for its measures in the Advocate General's Opinion in Case C-405/98 *Konsumentombudsmannen* v *Gourmet International Products* [2001] ECR I-1795, (this case is discussed in detail below), in which he stated that there can be good reasons to prohibit advertising for products such as alcopops since, as he pointed out, these are clearly designed to appeal to young people and even to children. However, the German government was convinced that a ban on advertising would not have a material effect, so it considered imposing a total ban on the sale of alcopops, or at least a ban on their sale to people under the age of 15. Would there be a difference in the assessment of these alternative prohibitions under Union law?

JUDGMENT OF THE COURT (Sixth Chamber)
7 March 1990

GB-INNO-BM v Confédération du commerce luxembourgeois.
(Reference to the Court by the Cour de cassation of the Grand Duchy of Luxembourg for a preliminary ruling)

'Free movement of goods – National prohibition on publication of the duration of a special offer or the price previously charged'

Case C-362/88

Judgment

1. By judgment of 8 December 1988, which was received at the Court on 14 December 1988, the Cour de cassation of the Grand Duchy of Luxembourg referred to the Court for a preliminary ruling under Article 177 of the EEC Treaty a question on the interpretation of Article 30, the first paragraph of Article 31 and Article 36 of the EEC Treaty in order to enable it to assess the compatibility with those provisions of national legislation on advertising.

2. The question was raised in proceedings between the Confédération du commerce luxembourgeois (hereinafter referred to as CCL), a non-profit-making association which claims to represent the interests of Luxembourg traders, and GB-INNO-BM, which operates supermarkets in Belgian territory, inter alia in Arlon, near the Belgian-Luxembourg border. The Belgian company had distributed advertising leaflets on Luxembourg territory as well as on Belgian territory and CCL applied to the Luxembourg courts for an injunction against the company to stop the distribution of those advertising leaflets. CCL claimed that the advertising contained in the leaflets was contrary to the Grand-Ducal Regulation of 23 December 1974 on unfair competition (Mémorial A 1974, p. 2392), according to which sales offers involving a temporary price reduction may not state the duration of the offer or refer to previous prices.

3. The presiding judge of the tribunal d'arrondissement (District Court), Luxembourg, competent for commercial matters granted the injunction, taking the view that the distribution of the leaflets in question constituted a sales offer prohibited by the Grand-Ducal Regulation of 1974 and an unfair practice prohibited by the same regulation. The cour d'appel upheld the injunction, whereupon GB-INNO-BM appealed to the Cour de cassation. It argued that the advertising contained in the leaflets complied with the Belgian provisions on unfair competition and that it would thus be contrary to Article 30 of the EEC Treaty to apply to it the prohibitions laid down in the Luxembourg legislation.

4. The Cour de cassation stayed proceedings and submitted the following question to the Court of Justice for a preliminary ruling:

   Is a legislative provision of a Member State whereby the offering of goods for retail sale at a temporarily reduced price, other than in special sales or clearance sales, is permitted only on condition that the offers may not state their duration and that there may be no reference to previous prices contrary to Article 30, the first paragraph of Article 31 and Article 36 of the EEC Treaty, properly construed?

5. Reference is made to the Report for the Hearing for a fuller account of the facts of the case, the course of the procedure and the observations submitted to the Court, which are mentioned or discussed hereinafter only in so far as is necessary for the reasoning of the Court.

6. As a preliminary point, an argument that was raised by CCL and the German and Luxembourg Governments calls for examination. That argument is to the effect that the provisions of Articles 30, 31 and 36 of the Treaty have no relevance to the subject-matter of the main proceedings, which solely concern advertising, not the movement of goods between Member States. Moreover, it is said, GB-INNO-BM sells its wares only on Belgian territory.

7. That argument cannot be accepted. The Court has already held, in its judgment of 15 December 1982 in Case 286/81 Oosthoek's Uitgeversmaatschappij [1982] ECR 4575, that legislation which restricts or prohibits certain forms of advertising and certain means of sales promotion may, although it does not directly affect trade, be such as to restrict the volume of trade because it affects marketing opportunities.

8. Free movement of goods concerns not only traders but also individuals. It requires, particularly in frontier areas, that consumers resident in one Member State may travel freely to the territory of another Member State to shop under the same conditions as the local population. That freedom for consumers is compromised if they are deprived of access to advertising available in the country where purchases are made. Consequently a prohibition against distributing such advertising must be examined in the light of Articles 30, 31 and 36 of the Treaty.

9. It is therefore clear that the question referred to the Court for a preliminary ruling concerns the compatibility with Article 30 of the Treaty of an obstacle to the free movement of goods resulting from disparities between the applicable national legislation. It is apparent from the documents before the Court that the advertising of sales offers involving a price reduction and stating the duration of the offer and the prices previously charged is prohibited by the Luxembourg legislation but permitted by the provisions in force in Belgium.

10. The Court has consistently held that in the absence of common rules relating to marketing, obstacles to the free movement of goods within the Community resulting from disparities between national laws must be accepted in so far as such rules, applicable to domestic and imported products without distinction, may be justified as being necessary in order to satisfy mandatory requirements relating inter alia to consumer protection or the fairness of commercial transactions (see, in particular, the judgments of 20 February 1979 in Case 120/78 Rewe [1979] ECR 649, and of 26 June 1980 in Case 788/79 Gilli and Andres [1980] ECR 2071).

11. According to CCL and the Luxembourg Government, the two prohibitions in question – against stating the duration of a special offer and against specifying the previous price – are justified on the grounds of consumer protection. The purpose of the prohibition concerning the duration of the special offer is to avoid the risk of confusion between special sales and half-yearly clearance sales the timing and duration of which is restricted under Luxembourg legislation. The prohibition against allowing the previous price to appear in the offer is justified, they say, by the fact that the consumer is not normally in a position to check that a previous reference price is genuine. In addition, the marking of a previous price might exert excessive psychological pressure on the consumer. In substance the German Government shares that point of view.

12. That view is contested by GB-INNO-BM and the Commission, who point out that any normally aware consumer knows that annual sales take place only twice a year. As regards comparison of prices, the Commission has submitted an overview of the relevant legislation in various Member States and concludes that, with the exception of the Luxembourg and German provisions, they all allow both prices to be indicated if the reference price is genuine.

13. The question thus arises whether national legislation which prevents the consumer from having access to certain information may be justified in the interest of consumer protection.

14. It should be observed first of all that Community policy on the subject establishes a close link between protecting the consumer and providing the consumer with information. Thus the preliminary programme adopted by the Council in 1975 (Official Journal 1975, C 92, p. 1) provides for the implementation of a consumer protection and information policy. By a Resolution of 19 May 1981 (Official Journal 1981, C 133, p. 1), the Council approved a second programme of the European Economic Community for a consumer protection and information policy the objectives of which were confirmed by the Council Resolution of 23 June 1986 concerning the future orientation of the policy of the Community for the protection and promotion of consumer interests (Official Journal 1986, C 167, p. 1).

15. The existence of a link between protection and information for consumers is explained in the introduction to the second programme. There it is stressed that measures taken or scheduled in accordance with the preliminary programme contribute towards improving the consumer's situation by protecting his health, his safety and his economic interest, by providing him with appropriate information and education, and by giving him a voice in decisions which involve him. It is stated that often those same measures have also resulted in harmonizing the rules of competition by which manufacturers and retailers must abide.

16. The introduction goes on to specify that the purpose of the second programme is to continue and intensify the measures in this field and to help establish conditions for improved consultation between consumers on the one hand and manufacturers and retailers on the other. To that end the programme sets out five basic rights to be enjoyed by the consumer, amongst which appears the right to information and education. One of the measures proposed in the programme is the improvement of consumer education and information (paragraph 9D). The part of the programme which lays down the principles which must govern the protection of the economic interests of consumers includes passages which aim to ensure the accuracy of information provided to the consumer, but without refusing him access to certain information. Thus, according to one of the principles (Paragraph 28(4)), no form of advertising should mislead the buyer; an advertiser must be able to justify, by appropriate means, the validity of any claims he makes.

17. As the Court has held, a prohibition against importing certain products into a Member State is contrary to Article 30 where the aim of such a prohibition may be attained by appropriate labelling of the products concerned which would provide the consumer with the information he needs and enable him to make his choice in full knowledge of the facts (judgments of 9 December 1981 in Case 193/80 Commission v Italy [1981] ECR 3019, and of 12 March 1987 in Case 178/84 Commission v Germany [1987] ECR 1227).

18. It follows from the foregoing that under Community law concerning consumer protection the provision of information to the consumer is considered one of the principal requirements. Thus Article 30 cannot be interpreted as meaning that national legislation which denies the consumer access to certain kinds of information may be justified by mandatory requirements concerning consumer protection.

19. In consequence, obstacles to intra-Community trade resulting from national rules of the type at issue in the main proceedings may not be justified by reasons relating to consumer protection. They thus fall under the prohibition laid down in Article 30 of the Treaty. The exceptions to the application of that provision contained in Article 36 are not applicable; indeed, no reliance was placed on them during the proceedings before the Court.

20. Since Article 30 is applicable, there is no need to interpret Article 31 of the Treaty, which was also mentioned in the reference for a preliminary ruling.

21. The reply to the question posed must therefore be that under Articles 30 and 36 of the EEC Treaty, properly interpreted, advertising lawfully distributed in another Member State cannot be made subject to national legislation prohibiting the inclusion, in advertisements relating to a special purchase offer, of a statement showing the duration of the offer or the previous price.

Costs

[Para. 22 omitted]

On those grounds,

THE COURT (Sixth Chamber),

in answer to the question submitted to it by the Cour de cassation of the Grand Duchy of Luxembourg, by order of 8 December 1988, hereby rules:

> **Under Articles 30 and 36 of the EEC Treaty, properly interpreted, advertising lawfully distributed in another Member State cannot be made subject to national legislation prohibiting the inclusion, in advertisements relating to a special purchase offer, of a statement showing the duration of the offer or the previous price.**

Comments and questions

Case C-362/88 *GB-INNO-BM* v *Confédération du commerce luxembourgeois* [1990] ECR I-667, concerned a Luxembourg law under which sales offers involving a temporary price reduction may not state the duration of the offer nor refer to previous prices. There was thus a non-discriminatory marketing regulation which was justified on the grounds of consumer protection; cf. paragraph 11 of the judgment.

In paragraph 7 of the judgment, it was stated that, although it does not directly affect trade, legislation which restricts or prohibits certain forms of advertising or sales promotion may restrict the volume of trade because it affects marketing opportunities.

The CJEU recognised that consideration for the protection of consumers can justify national laws which restrict trade. However, the CJEU rejected the argument that the law in question, which prevented consumers from being given certain information, was justified on consumer protection grounds. The CJEU reached this conclusion by including, among other things, non-binding EU provisions, so-called 'soft laws'; cf. paragraph 14 of the judgment which refers to the Union's 'consumer protection and information policy'.

Compare the intensity of the examination of the arguments in this case with the examination in the *Henn and Darby* case. Can it be that the difference between the two cases is based on the considerations which the Member States claim as justifying their legislation?

JUDGMENT OF THE COURT (Sixth Chamber)
11 July 1989

Quietlynn Limited and Brian James Richards v Southend Borough Council.
(Reference for a preliminary ruling: Crown Court, Chelmsford – United Kingdom)

'Free movement of goods – Interpretation of Articles 30 and 36 of the EEC Treaty – National legislation prohibiting the sale of lawful sex articles from unlicensed sex establishments'

Case C-23/89

Judgment

1. By order dated 7 September 1988 which was received at the Court on 30 January 1989, Chelmsford Crown Court referred to the Court for a preliminary ruling under Article 177 of the EEC Treaty three questions on the interpretation of Articles 30 and 36 of the EEC Treaty in order to determine whether national legislation prohibiting the sale of lawful sex articles from unlicensed sex establishments was compatible with those provisions.

2. Those questions were raised in proceedings brought against Quietlynn Ltd and Brian James Richards, its Managing Director, who operate retail shop premises selling inter alia sex articles, by Southend Borough Council.

3. Section 2 of the Local Government (Miscellaneous Provisions) Act 1982 (hereinafter referred to as the Act) provides local authorities in England and Wales with the power to control sex shops in their area. In particular, it empowers them to resolve that Schedule 3 to the Act, which provides for the sale of such articles to be subject to licensing, is to apply to their area.

4. Southend Borough Council exercised that power, with effect from 23 June 1983. It subsequently brought a prosecution against Quietlynn Ltd and Mr Richards for using their premises without a licence on 13 March and 11 April 1985. They were found guilty of two offences by Southend Magistrates Court on 11 February 1986, fined UKL 1 000 in respect of each offence, and ordered to pay costs.

5. Quietlynn Ltd and Mr Richards appealed to Chelmsford Crown Court against the convictions, their sole defence being that the provisions of the Act relating to the licensing system for sex establishments were incompatible with Article 30 of the EEC Treaty inasmuch as they constituted a measure having an effect equivalent to a quantitative restriction on imports from other Member States and fell neither within one of the exceptions provided for in Article 36 nor under any other derogation.

6. Chelmsford Crown Court considered that the dispute raised questions relating to the interpretation of Community law and has therefore asked the Court for a preliminary ruling on the following questions:

Question 1

Where a Member State (once a Local Authority has resolved that the legislation is to apply to their area subject to the requirement for premises which are sex establishments to be licensed) prohibits the sale (inter alia) of lawful sex articles from unlicensed sex establishments, and where the effect of such a prohibition is to enable the Local Authority to exercise control over sex establishments within their area, and where the effect is to have restricted the appellants from selling goods from other Member States since they have been attempting not to contravene the Act by their stocking policy and in doing so have been selling less imported material from Member States than would otherwise have been the case and thus to restrict the availability of sex articles manufactured in other Member States; is such a prohibition a measure having equivalent effect to a quantitative restriction on imports within the meaning of Article 30 of the Treaty?

Question 2

If the answer to Question 1 is in the affirmative, does such a measure benefit from the justification set out in Article 36?

Question 3

If the prohibition referred to in Question 1 contravenes Article 30 and is not justified under Article 36, is it totally unenforceable against a trader in the Member State or only unenforceable to the extent that it prohibits transactions involving goods manufactured in or imported from other Member States?

7. Reference is made to the Report for the Hearing for a fuller account of the relevant provisions, the facts of the case in the main proceedings, the course of the procedure and the written observations submitted to the Court, which are referred to hereinafter only in so far as is necessary for the reasoning of the Court.

Question 1

8. By its first question, the national court seeks to ascertain whether provisions prohibiting the sale of lawful sex articles from unlicensed sex establishments constitute a measure having an effect equivalent to a quantitative restriction within the meaning of Article 30 of the Treaty.

9. First, it must be noted that national legislation prohibiting the sale of sex articles from unlicensed sex establishments applies without distinction to imported and domestic products. It thus does not constitute an absolute prohibition on the sale of the products in question, but merely a rule regarding their distribution, regulating the outlets through which the products may be marketed. In principle, therefore, the marketing of products imported from other Member States is not rendered any more difficult than that of domestic products.

10. It must be pointed out that in similar cases concerning rules governing the marketing of certain products the Court has held Article 30 of the Treaty not to be applicable. In its judgment in Case 155/80 Oebel [1981] ECR 1993, the Court held that national rules governing working hours in bakeries and the hours of delivery and sale of baker's wares were compatible with Article 30 of the Treaty since trade within the Community remained possible at all times. Likewise, in its judgment in Case 75/81 Blesgen v Belgium [1982] ECR 1211, the Court considered that a legislative provision that concerned only the sale of strong spirits for consumption on the premises in all places open to the public and did not concern other forms of marketing the same drinks had in fact no connection with the importation of the products and for that reason was not of such a nature as to impede trade between Member States.

11. It must also be pointed out that the provisions prohibiting the sale of sex articles from unlicensed sex establishments have in fact no connection with intra-Community trade, since the products covered by the Act may be marketed through licensed sex establishments and other channels, that is to say through shops in which sex articles account for only an insignificant proportion of sales and which are therefore not required to be licensed, or by mail order. Moreover, those provisions are not intended to regulate trade in goods within the Community and they are therefore not of such a nature as to impede trade between Member States.

12. The answer to the first question must therefore be that Article 30 of the Treaty should be construed as meaning that national provisions prohibiting the sale of lawful sex articles from unlicensed sex establishments do not constitute a measure having an effect equivalent to a quantitative restriction on imports.

Questions 2 and 3

13. In view of the answer to the first question, the second and third questions do not require an answer.

Costs

[Para. 14 omitted]

On those grounds,

THE COURT (Sixth Chamber),

in answer to the questions referred to it by Chelmsford Crown Court, by order of 7 September 1988, hereby rules:

> **Article 30 of the Treaty should be construed as meaning that national provisions prohibiting the sale of lawful sex articles from unlicensed sex establishments do not constitute a measure having an effect equivalent to a quantitative restriction on imports.**

Comments and questions

In his Opinion in Case C-23/89 *Quietlynn* v *Southend Borough Council* [1990] I-3059, Advocate General Lenz argued that there could be little doubt that the provisions at issue in the case were capable of hindering, directly or indirectly, actually or potentially intra-Union trade, so they were covered by the *Dassonville* criteria. The Advocate General went on to argue that, without the Act and the local authority resolutions adopted under it, sales of pornographic articles would be more extensive and imports therefore greater.

The Advocate General went further by stating that a distinction should be made between an outright prohibition on the sale of certain products and marketing rules such as those under discussion. He emphasised that the case concerned non-discriminatory marketing rules, unrelated to trade between Member States, as the pornographic products in question could be sold on the English market through outlets other than those prohibited by the law in question (i.e., through other channels than sex shops).

To what extent is the Advocate General's argument reflected in the judgment of the CJEU? Consider whether the disputed British law contained trade related requirements. Is there a difference between the trade restrictive effect in Case C-362/88 *GB-INNO-BM* [1990] ECR I-667, and the *Quietlynn* case? Discuss why the CJEU came to different results.

JUDGMENT OF THE COURT
24 November 1993

Criminal proceedings against Bernard Keck and Daniel Mithouard. (Reference to the Court by the Tribunal de Grande Instance (Regional Court), Strasbourg (France))

'Free movement of goods – Prohibition of resale at a loss'

Joined Cases C-267/91 and C-268/91

Judgment

1. By two judgments of 27 June 1991, received at the Court on 16 October 1991, the Tribunal de Grande Instance, Strasbourg, referred to the Court for a preliminary ruling under Article 177 of the EEC Treaty two questions on the interpretation of the rules of the Treaty concerning competition and freedom of movement within the Community.

2. Those questions were raised in connection with criminal proceedings brought against Mr Keck and Mr Mithouard, who are being prosecuted for reselling products in an unaltered state at prices lower than their actual purchase price ('resale at a loss'), contrary to Article 1 of French Law No 63-628 of 2 July 1963, as amended by Article 32 of Order No 86-1243 of 1December 1986.

3. In their defence Mr Keck and Mr Mithouard contended that a general prohibition on resale at a loss, as laid down by those provisions, is incompatible with Article 30 of the Treaty and with the principles of the free movement of persons, services, capital and free competition within the Community.

4. The Tribunal de Grande Instance, taking the view that it required an interpretation of certain provisions of Community law, stayed both sets of proceedings and referred the following question to the Court for a preliminary ruling:

   'Is the prohibition in France of resale at a loss under Article 32 of Order No 86-1243 of 1 December 1986 compatible with the principles of the free movement of goods, services and capital, free competition in the Common Market and non-discrimination on grounds of nationality laid down in the Treaty of 25 March 1957 establishing the EEC, and more particularly in Articles 3 and 7 thereof, since the French legislation is liable to distort competition:

   (a) firstly, because it makes only resale at a loss an offence and exempts from the scope of the prohibition the manufacturer, who is free to sell on the market the product which he manufactures, processes or improves, even very slightly, at a price lower than his cost price;

(b) secondly, in that it distorts competition, especially in frontier zones, between the various traders on the basis of their nationality and place of establishment?'

5. Reference is made to the Report for the Hearing for a fuller account of the facts of the case, the procedure and the written observations submitted to the Court, which are mentioned or discussed hereinafter only in so far as is necessary for the reasoning of the Court.

6. It should be noted at the outset that the provisions of the Treaty relating to free movement of persons, services and capital within the Community have no bearing on a general prohibition of resale at a loss, which is concerned with the marketing of goods. Those provisions are therefore of no relevance to the issue in the main proceedings.

7. Next, as regards the principle of non-discrimination laid down in Article 7 of the Treaty, it appears from the orders for reference that the national court questions the compatibility with that provision of the prohibition of resale at a loss, in that undertakings subject to it may be placed at a disadvantage vis-à-vis competitors in Member States where resale at a loss is permitted.

8. However, the fact that undertakings selling in different Member States are subject to different legislative provisions, some prohibiting and some permitting resale at a loss, does not constitute discrimination for the purposes of Article 7 of the Treaty. The national legislation at issue in the main proceedings applies to any sales activity carried out within the national territory, regardless of the nationality of those engaged in it (see the judgment in Case 308/86 *Ministère Public* v *Lambert* [1988] ECR 4369).

9. Finally, it appears from the question submitted for a preliminary ruling that the national court seeks guidance as to the possible anti-competitive effects of the rules in question by reference exclusively to the foundations of the Community set out in Article 3 of the Treaty, without however making specific reference to any of the implementing rules of the Treaty in the field of competition.

10. In these circumstances, having regard to the written and oral argument presented to the Court, and with a view to giving a useful reply to the referring court, the appropriate course is to look at the prohibition of resale at a loss from the perspective of the free movement of goods.

11. By virtue of Article 30, quantitative restrictions on imports and all measures having equivalent effect are prohibited between Member States. The Court has consistently

held that any measure which is capable of directly or indirectly, actually or potentially, hindering intra-Community trade constitutes a measure having equivalent effect to a quantitative restriction.

12. National legislation imposing a general prohibition on resale at a loss is not designed to regulate trade in goods between Member States.

13. Such legislation may, admittedly, restrict the volume of sales, and hence the volume of sales of products from other Member States, in so far as it deprives traders of a method of sales promotion. But the question remains whether such a possibility is sufficient to characterize the legislation in question as a measure having equivalent effect to a quantitative restriction on imports.

14. In view of the increasing tendency of traders to invoke Article 30 of the Treaty as a means of challenging any rules whose effect is to limit their commercial freedom even where such rules are not aimed at products from other Member States, the Court considers it necessary to re-examine and clarify its case-law on this matter.

15. It is established by the case-law beginning with 'Cassis de Dijon' (Case 120/78 *Rewe-Zentral* v *Bundesmonopolverwaltung für Branntwein* [1979] ECR 649) that, in the absence of harmonization of legislation, obstacles to free movement of goods which are the consequence of applying, to goods coming from other Member States where they are lawfully manufactured and marketed, rules that lay down requirements to be met by such goods (such as those relating to designation, form, size, weight, composition, presentation, labelling, packaging) constitute measures of equivalent effect prohibited by Article 30. This is so even if those rules apply without distinction to all products unless their application can be justified by a public-interest objective taking precedence over the free movement of goods.

16. By contrast, contrary to what has previously been decided, the application to products from other Member States of national provisions restricting or prohibiting certain selling arrangements is not such as to hinder directly or indirectly, actually or potentially, trade between Member States within the meaning of the *Dassonville* judgment (Case 8/74 [1974] ECR 837), so long as those provisions apply to all relevant traders operating within the national territory and so long as they affect in the same manner, in law and in fact, the marketing of domestic products and of those from other Member States.

17. Provided that those conditions are fulfilled, the application of such rules to the sale of products from another Member State meeting the requirements laid down by that State is not by nature such as to prevent their access to the market or to impede access any more than it impedes the access of domestic products. Such rules therefore fall outside the scope of Article 30 of the Treaty.

18. Accordingly, the reply to be given to the national court is that Article 30 of the EEC Treaty is to be interpreted as not applying to legislation of a Member State imposing a general prohibition on resale at a loss.

Costs

[Para. 19 omitted]

On those grounds,

THE COURT,

in answer to the questions referred to it by the Tribunal de Grande Instance, Strasbourg, by two judgments of 27 June 1991, hereby rules:

> **Article 30 of the EEC Treaty is to be interpreted as not applying to legislation of a Member State imposing a general prohibition on resale at a loss.**

Comments and questions

In Joined Cases C-267/91 and C-268/91 *Keck and Mithouard* [1993] ECR I-6097, the CJEU made a review of its previous practice. Following the *Keck* case, there is now an *assumption* that, in general, non-discriminatory marketing rules ('national provisions restricting or prohibiting certain selling arrangements') fall outside the scope of Article 34 TFEU (formerly Article 30 EEC Treaty). This is laid down in paragraph 16 of the judgment. According to the wording of the judgment, there is merely an assumption which can either be confirmed or invalidated by the presentation of evidence before national courts. However, where national measures do not hinder access to the market, the CJEU has hitherto rejected the invalidation of the assumption, even in cases where the court in question has found that the sale of foreign goods has been affected; cf. Joined Cases C-418/93 et al. *Semeraro Casa Uno Srl* v *Sindaco del Comune di Erbusco et al* [1996] I-2975. In reality, non-discriminatory marketing rules fall outside the scope of Article 34 TFEU.

However, it is important to be aware that, in cases where marketing rules effectively exclude new goods from access to markets, the *Keck* doctrine will not apply; cf. the conditions laid down in paragraph 17 of the *Keck* judgment. See also the judgment in Case C-405/98 *Konsumentombudsmannen* v *Gourmet International Products* [2001] I-1795, and Case C-316/95 *Generics BV* v *Smith, Kline & French* [1997] I-3129.

Prior to the CJEU's ruling in the *Keck* case there had been general criticism that Article 34 TFEU had been interpreted unreasonably broadly, undermining the principle of legal certainty. With its judgment in the *Keck* case, the CJEU addressed this criticism, but the judgment has since been criticised for being too inflexible and limiting the scope of application of Article 34 TFEU too much. However, not least the CJEU's decision in the *Gourmet International* case shows that, through the 'access to the market' criteria, the CJEU does interpret the *Keck* doctrine flexibly.

Where in its judgment does the CJEU define the concept of a restriction on trade, and which kind of restriction of trade was under consideration in the *Keck* case? Does the CJEU follow the precedent of the *Dassonville* case or of the *Cassis de Dijon* case?

The *Keck* doctrine means that non-discriminatory 'national provisions restricting or prohibiting certain selling arrangements' fall outside the scope of Article 34 TFEU. In a number of cases since the *Keck* case the CJEU has filled out the detail of what are considered as 'certain selling arrangements'. In Case C-292/92 *Hünermund et al* v *Landesapotheker-kammer Baden-Württemberg* [1993] I-6787, which concerned a non-discriminatory prohibition against pharmacists advertising outside pharmacies for goods which are normally sold in pharmacies, the CJEU found that there were 'certain selling arrangements', as understood in the *Keck* case. Correspondingly, a French prohibition against television advertising for certain goods was regarded as being covered by the *Keck* doctrine; cf. Case C-412/93 *Société d'Importation Edouard Leclerc-Siplec* v *TF1 Publicité* [1995] I-179. Joined Cases C-401/92 and C-402/92 *Tankstation 't Heukske* [1994] I-2199, concerned the Dutch shop opening hours applying to petrol stations, among others. In its judgment in this case, at the suggestion of the Advocate General, the CJEU introduced two new parameters for assessing when 'certain selling arrangements' can be said to exist. In paragraph 14 of the judgment, conditions relating to the *time* and *place* of sales are covered by the *Keck* doctrine.

In paragraph 61 of her Opinion in Case C-322/01 *Deutscher Apothekerverband eV* v *0800 DocMorris NV and Jacques Waterval* [2003] ECR I-14887, Advocate General Stix-Hackl listed a number of national measures which the CJEU has considered as being covered by the *Keck* doctrine. She referred to the following:

- Time restrictions, such as a ban on Sunday trading,
- Restrictions on those who offer goods for sale and on those from whom they may be obtained, such as the prohibition on the marketing of processed milk for infants other than by pharmacies,
- The prohibition on the sale of tobacco products other than by specially authorised retailers,
- The prohibition on obtaining beverages from anyone other than a holder of a production or wholesale licence,
- A prohibition on pharmacists advertising products usually sold in pharmacies outside the pharmacy,
- A prohibition on televised advertising in the distribution sector,
- Provisions on advertising which is not physically connected to the product, and
- Provisions on sales yielding low profit margins.

However, there can still be doubt about what constitutes a restriction on trade and what falls outside the concept. In Case C-254/98 *Schutzverband gegen unlauteren Wettbewerb* v *TK-Heimdienst Sass GmbH* [2000] I-151, the CJEU had to decide on an Austrian rule under which butchers, bakers and other retailers selling food were only permitted to sell goods outside their shops (e.g. from door-to-door) in a given administrative district if they carried on business from a permanent establishment in that given district. The rule applied without discrimination between domestic and foreign goods, was not product related, and applied to all undertakings in Austria. The rule restricted *who* could sell from a mobile shop, market stall, door-to-door sales etc., and should therefore concern 'certain selling arrangements' under the *Keck* doctrine. In paragraph 24 of the judgment, the CJEU acknowledged that the Austrian law related to 'selling arrangements', but found that it did not affect domestically produced goods and goods from other Member States in the same way, in other words the rule was indirectly discriminatory. This was because butchers, bakers and other retailers, who already had a permanent establishment in another Member State, and who wished to sell their goods in a specific administrative district in Austria, were forced to open a new permanent establishment in the administrative district in question; this did not apply to the local traders who were already established there; cf. paragraphs 27 and 28 of the judgment. This meant that the Austrian rule constituted a measure having equivalent effect to a quantitative restriction on imports, and the CJEU found that it could not be justified, so it was illegal. It is difficult to reconcile the decision of the CJEU in this case with its practice in relation to the *Keck* doctrine; cf. for example, Case C-391/92 *Commission* v *Greece* [1995] I-1621, referred to in detail below, and in reality the decision should be seen as a return to the pre-*Keck* times.

It is remarkable to think that, if the CJEU had found that the Austrian rule in the case of *Schutzverband gegen unlauteren Wettbewerb* v *TK-Heimdienst Sass GmbH* was covered by the *Keck* doctrine, the law could not have been challenged under Article 34 TFEU, and would therefore have been legal under the TFEU. The judgment is also interesting in that Article 34 TFEU was applied in a case which did not have any specific cross-border element. It is also worth noting that that CJEU was sitting as a chamber, and not in plenary session, so that the precedent value of the judgment may be more limited. Subsequently the CJEU gave a ruling which seems to have overruled the *Schutzverband gegen unlauteren Wettbewerb* judgment. This was in Case C-20/03 *Criminal proceedings against Marcel Burmanjer and others* [2005] ECR I-4133, where it was held that Article 34 TFEU does not, in principle, prevent national measures under which a Member State, in this case Belgium, imposes penalties for the itinerant sale of subscriptions for periodicals without prior authorisation. However, the CJEU left it to the referring Belgian court to examine 'whether the application of national law is such as to ensure that those rules affect in the same manner, in law and in fact, the marketing of domestic products and that of products from other Member States'.

What decision do you think the CJEU would have reached in Case C-362/88 *GB-INNO-BM* [1990] ECR I-667, referred to above, if it had been decided after the *Keck* case?

Note that, in the *Keck* case, the CJEU gave decisive emphasis to the fact that non-discriminatory marketing rules cannot, by their nature, be considered as preventing the *access* of goods to the market. The CJEU presumably applied a related consideration in its decision in Case C-190/98 *Volker Graf* v *Filzmoser Maschinenbau GmbH* [2000] ECR I-493, which is considered in Chapter 4. In paragraph 23 of the judgment in this case, it is stated that there will only be an obstacle to the free movement of workers according to Article 45 TFEU, if the non-discriminatory hindrance affects the *access* of workers to the labour market. In a later judgment in Case C-464/02 *Commission* v *Denmark* [2005] ECR I-7929, which is also printed in Chapter 4 below, the CJEU seems to have narrowed the scope of application of the Keck doctrine, at least in relation to Article 45 TFEU on freedom of movement of persons. Here the CJEU held that, even in a situation where there was a non-discriminatory rule which did not restrict access to the market, there was nevertheless an unlawful restriction as the rule imposed a cost on undertakings in other Member States when taking on employees resident in Denmark and providing them with a company car. In connection with this it is noted that in Joined Cases C-544/03 and C-545/03 *Mobistar SA* v *Commune de Fléron* [2005] ECR I-7723, the CJEU held that Article 56 TFEU does not cover measures the 'only effect of which is to create additional costs in respect of the service in question and which affect in the same way the provision of services between Member States and that within one Member State'.

Consider what national measures are covered by the concept of 'certain selling arrangements'. For example, would a condition that taxi business in London could only be carried on by using the traditional 'black cabs', and not by other vehicles, constitute a measure that only concerned 'certain selling arrangements'? Would a prohibition of the use of an app such as Uber, for ordering a personal transport service, constitute a 'certain selling arrangement'? Would a requirement that only authorised opticians should be allowed to sell glasses be covered by the concept of 'certain selling arrangements'? Are there 'certain selling arrangements', without distinction between domestic and foreign products, if there is a rule in Austria that the retail price of books in the German language from Austrian publishers must be the price set by the publisher (the retail price maintenance system), and that books in German imported from publishers in other countries may only be sold at the prices that the non-Austrian publishers have set or recommended in their home State? The consequence of such an Austrian rule would be that an Austrian book importer who buys books in German at a favourable price from a German publisher would not be able to sell these books at a lower price than the price set for their sale in Germany. See Case C-531/07 *Fachverband* [2009] ECR I-3717. In this case the CJEU ruled that the objective of the Austrian pricing rule, namely the protection of books as cultural goods, could be achieved by measures that were less intrusive for the Austrian importer, for example, by giving the importer or the foreign publisher the right to set a retail price for the Austrian market that takes account of the special characteristics of the market.

JUDGMENT OF THE COURT (Fifth Chamber)
10 November 1994

Lucien Ortscheit GmbH v Eurim-Pharm Arzneimittel GmbH.
(Reference to the Court by the Landgericht Saarbrücken (Germany))

'Imported medicinal products not authorized in the State of import – Prohibition of advertising – Articles 30 and 36 of the Treaty'

Case C-320/93

Judgment

1. By order of 24 March 1993, received at the Court on 21 June 1993, the Landgericht Saarbrücken (Saarbrücken Regional Court) referred to the Court for a preliminary ruling under Article 177 of the EEC Treaty two questions on the compatibility with Articles 30 and 36 of the EEC Treaty of a rule of national law prohibiting advertising for foreign medicinal products which are not authorized in Germany but which can be imported into that country under certain conditions.

2. Those questions arose in proceedings between two companies importing medicinal products, Lucien Ortscheit GmbH and Eurim-Pharm Arzneimittel GmbH. Lucien Ortscheit seeks an order that Eurim-Pharm cease all advertising for foreign medicinal products not authorized by the German authorities.

3. Under Paragraph 21(1) of the Arzneimittelgesetz (Law on medicinal products, 'the AMG'), medicinal products may not be marketed in the Federal Republic of Germany unless they have been authorized by the competent federal authorities. That rule also applies in principle to imported medicinal products (Paragraph 73(1) of the AMG).

4. However, under Paragraph 73(3) of the AMG, foreign medicinal products which have not been authorized in Germany may be imported if they have been authorized in their country of origin, provided they have been ordered by pharmacies in limited quantities on the basis of a prescription from a doctor, dentist or veterinary surgeon.

5. Article 8(2) of the Heilmittelwerbegesetz (Law on advertising in the health sector, 'the HWG') provides, however, with reference to those medicinal products: 'Advertisements containing an offer to obtain specified medicinal products by individual importation under ... Paragraph 73(3) shall ... be prohibited.'

6. Making use of the opportunity afforded by Paragraph 73(3) of the AMG, Eurim-Pharm imports into Germany medicinal products which have not been authorized

by the German authorities. Since April 1992 it has published advertisements in German publications aimed at professionals in the health sector, indicating which non-authorized products it imports and the address from which they can be obtained.

7. On 14 October 1992 Lucien Ortscheit, a competitor of Eurim-Pharm, applied to the Landgericht Saarbrücken for an order that Eurim-Pharm desist from those acts, on the ground that they were prohibited by Paragraph 8(2) of the HWG.

8. The Landgericht Saarbrücken considered that the advertisements published by Eurim-Pharm were advertisements within the meaning of Paragraph 8(2) of the HWG and that the question arose whether that provision was compatible with Community law; it therefore referred to the Court for a preliminary ruling two questions on the interpretation of Articles 30 and 36 of the Treaty:

   1. Is the national prohibition of advertising for medicinal products which despite the requirement of authorization are not authorized in Germany, but may lawfully be imported from another Member State of the European Communities in response to an individual order if they have already been lawfully put into circulation in that Member State, a measure having equivalent effect to a quantitative restriction within the meaning of Article 30 of the EEC Treaty?

   2. If the prohibition of advertising described above is a measure having equivalent effect within the meaning of Article 30 of the EEC Treaty, in what circumstances can it be permitted by way of exception under Article 36 of the EEC Treaty for the protection of health and life of humans?'

The first question (Article 30 of the Treaty)

9. It must be observed first that the prohibition of advertising under Paragraph 8(2) of the HWG applies solely to foreign medicinal products. Since it thus does not have the same effect on the marketing of medicinal products from other Member States as on the marketing of national medicinal products, it must fall within the scope of Article 30 of the Treaty (see the judgment in Joined Cases C-267/91 and C-268/91 *Keck and Mithouard* [1993] ECR I-6097, paragraph 16).

10. Secondly, the prohibition of advertising at issue may restrict the volume of imports of medicinal products not authorized in Germany, since it deprives pharmacists and doctors, whose participation is essential for the import of those medicinal products under Paragraph 73(3) of the AMG, of a source of information on the existence and availability of such products.

11. A provision such as that in Paragraph 8(2) of the HWG is therefore a measure having equivalent effect to a quantitative restriction within the meaning of Article 30 of the Treaty.

12. The answer to the first question must therefore be that the national prohibition of advertising for medicinal products which despite the general requirement of authorization are not authorized in a country, but may be imported from another Member State of the European Communities in response to an individual order if they have already been lawfully put into circulation in that Member State, is a measure having equivalent effect to a quantitative restriction within the meaning of Article 30 of the Treaty.

The second question (Article 36 of the Treaty)

13. By its second question the national court asks essentially whether the prohibition of advertising at issue is justified under Article 36 of the Treaty on grounds relating to the protection of health and life of humans.

14. It must be observed that Article 36 of the Treaty remains applicable as regards the manufacture and marketing of proprietary medicinal products as long as harmonization of national rules has not been fully achieved in that field (see the judgments in Case 215/87 *Schumacher* [1989] ECR 617, paragraph 15; Case C-369/88 *Delattre* [1991] ECR I-1487, paragraph 48; Case C-347/89 *Eurim-Pharm* [1991] ECR I-1747, paragraph 26; Case C-62/90 *Commission* v *Germany* [1992] ECR I-2575, paragraph 10; and Case C-317/92 *Commission* v *Germany* [1994] ECR I-2039, paragraph 14).

15. It must be emphasized that Council Directive 92/28/EEC of 31 March 1992 on the advertising of medicinal products for human use (OJ 1992 L 113, p. 13), which *inter alia* imposes on the Member States an obligation to subject the advertising of medicinal products to health professionals to strict conditions and effective monitoring (see the sixth recital in the preamble and Articles 6 to 14), does not apply to the main proceedings. The events giving rise to those proceedings occurred in the period from April to October 1992, whereas in accordance with Article 15(1) the directive was to be transposed by the Member States by 1 January 1993 at the latest.

16. That being so, it should be noted that it is also settled law that the health and life of humans rank foremost among the property or interests protected by Article 36 of the Treaty and that it is for the Member States, within the limits imposed by the Treaty, to decide what degree of protection they intend to ensure.

17. However, national rules or practices having, or likely to have, a restrictive effect on the importation of pharmaceutical products are compatible with the Treaty only to the extent that they are necessary for the effective protection of health and life of

humans. A national rule or practice cannot benefit from the derogation provided for in Article 36 if the health and life of humans may be protected just as effectively by measures which are less restrictive of intra-Community trade (see the judgments, cited above, in Case C-62/90 *Commission* v *Germany*, paragraphs 10 and 11; *Schumacher*, paragraphs 17 and 18; *Delattre*, paragraph 53; and *Eurim-Pharm*, paragraph 27).

18. In this case it must be noted that Member States are entitled, at the present stage of harmonization and in the absence of a procedure for Community authorization or mutual recognition of national authorizations, to prohibit entirely the marketing in their territory of medicinal products which have not been authorized by the competent national authorities. Under Article 3 of Council Directive 65/65/EEC of 26 January 1965 on the approximation of provisions laid down by law, regulation or administrative action relating to proprietary medicinal products (OJ, English Special Edition 1965-1966, p. 20), as amended by Council Directive 89/341/EEC of 3 May 1989 (OJ 1989 L 142, p. 11), 'no proprietary medicinal product may be placed on the market in a Member State unless an authorization has been issued by the competent authority of that Member State'.

19. As the Advocate General has rightly stated in paragraph 23 of his Opinion, the prohibition of advertising in Paragraph 8(2) of the HWG has the purpose of ensuring that the individual importation of medicinal products which have not been authorized remains an exception, in order to prevent the general requirement of national authorization under German law from being systematically circumvented. If medicinal products which were not authorized in Germany could be advertised there, there would be a danger that manufacturers would obtain authorization for their medicinal products in a Member State imposing fewer requirements and then import them into Germany on the basis of individual orders which they would have encouraged by advertising campaigns.

20. The prohibition of advertising imposed by Paragraph 8(2) of the HWG is therefore necessary for the effectiveness of the national authorization scheme. Consequently, it is justified on public health grounds under Article 36 of the Treaty.

21. The answer to the second question must therefore be that the prohibition of advertising at issue is justified under Article 36 of the Treaty on grounds pertaining to the protection of the health and life of humans.

Costs

[Para. 22 omitted]

On those grounds,

THE COURT (Fifth Chamber),

in answer to the questions referred to it by the Landgericht Saarbrücken by order of 24 March 1993, hereby rules:

1. **The national prohibition of advertising for medicinal products which despite the general requirement of authorization are not authorized in a country, but may be imported from another Member State of the European Communities in response to an individual order if they have been lawfully put into circulation in that Member State, is a measure having equivalent effect to a quantitative restriction within the meaning of Article 30 of the EEC Treaty.**

2. **That prohibition of advertising is justified however under Article 36 of the EEC Treaty on grounds pertaining to the protection of the health and life of humans.**

Comments and questions

In Case C-320/93 *Lucien Ortscheit GmbH* v *Eurim-Pharm Arzneimittel GmbH* [1994] ECR I-5243, the CJEU had to consider a discriminatory marketing rule for the first time following the *Keck* case; the rule concerned the prohibition of advertising for non-approved medicines, which could be sold in Germany subject to certain conditions even though they were not approved. In accordance with its ruling in the *Keck* case, in paragraph 9 of the judgment the Court stated that, since the prohibition of advertising only applied to foreign medicines, the measure must fall within the scope of Article 34 TFEU (formerly Article 30 EEC Treaty).

What concept of restriction on trade did the Court use in its judgment?

Note that in paragraph 14 of the judgment it was stated that Article 36 TFEU (formerly Article 36 EEC Treaty) remains applicable as long as national rules have not been fully harmonised. In paragraph 16 it is emphasised that the protection of the health and life of humans ranks foremost among the interests protected by Article 36 TFEU, and that it is for Member States to decide the degree of protection they want to ensure. Consider the significance of this finding for the right of Member States to regulate trade with a view to protecting public health, compared with the protection of other concerns such as consumer protection.

Did the German rule comply with the principle of proportionality?

If the German government found that Germans as a whole were so overweight as to constitute a health risk for the population, would it be allowed to introduce a prohibition against advertising for *pâté de foie gras* which is very fattening, though usually eaten in small portions, and is virtually only produced in France?

The purpose of Article 267 TFEU is that the CJEU should interpret Union law for the national courts. However, it is for the national courts to apply the law to concrete cases. Consider whether Point 2 of the Operative part of the judgment in this case is restricted to the interpretation of Union law, or whether it goes further to express a view on the concrete case.

In paragraph 33 in Case C-434/04 *Criminal proceedings against Jan-Erik Anders Ahokainen and Mati Leppik* [2006] ECR I-9171, the CJEU referred to paragraph 16 in Case C-320/93 *Lucien Ortscheit GmbH* v *Eurim-Pharm Arzneimittel GmbH* [1994] ECR I-5243, and stated that it is for the Member States, in compliance with Union law and, in particular, with the principle of proportionality, to decide what degree of protection they wish to ensure, and the manner in which this can be achieved. In accordance with this, the CJEU left it to the referring court to decide whether a requirement in the Finnish legislation on alcohol, that the import of non-denatured ethanol with an alcohol content of over 80% constituted an effective measure against the abuse of alcohol.

JUDGMENT OF THE COURT
29 June 1995

Commission of the European Communities v Hellenic Republic

'Free movement of goods – Processed milk for infants
– Prohibition of marketing other than by pharmacies'

Case C-391/92

Judgment

1. By application lodged at the Court Registry on 6 November 1992, the Commission of the European Communities brought an action under Article 169 of the EEC Treaty for a declaration that, by requiring that processed milk for infants should be sold exclusively by pharmacies under Article 10 of Ministerial Decision No A2/οικ.361 of 29 January 1988, the Hellenic Republic has failed to fulfil its obligations under Article 30 of the Treaty.

2. Article 10 of Ministerial Decision No A2/οικ.361 of 29 January 1988 on the sale of infant formulae and follow-on formulae provides that, in the Hellenic Republic, processed milk for infants may be sold only in pharmacists' shops except in municipalities possessing no pharmacists' shop, in which case that product may be marketed in other shops.

3. Following a complaint brought in April 1988 by the Greek Association of Infant Formulae, the Commission took the view that the Greek legislation constituted a measure having equivalent effect to a quantitative restriction on imports, prohibited by Article 30 of the Treaty, and exceeded what was necessary to achieve the aims of protecting the health of infants and promoting breast feeding. Accordingly, by letter of 10 August 1989, the Commission, in accordance with Article 169 of the Treaty, gave the Greek Government notice to submit within one month its observations on the alleged failure to fulfil its obligations.

4. The Greek Government replied, in a letter of 5 March 1990, that the exclusive sale in pharmacies of milk for infants did not affect importation of that product from other Member States and therefore did not constitute a measure having equivalent effect within the meaning of Article 30 of the Treaty. Moreover, it considered that measure to be justified under Article 36 of the EEC Treaty, inasmuch as it was necessary and appropriate in order to protect the health and life of infants during the critical first five months of life.

5. Since it considered that the Greek legislation constituted a serious restriction on the free movement of goods within the Community and was not justified by protection of health in accordance with Article 36 of the Treaty, the Commission, on 28 October 1991, issued a reasoned opinion pursuant to Article 169 of the Treaty. In that opinion, the Commission considered that the Hellenic Republic, by prohibiting the sale other than in pharmacists' shops of processed milk for infants, had failed to fulfil its obligations under Article 30 of the Treaty and requested it to take the necessary steps within two months in order to comply with that opinion.

6. Since the Hellenic Republic neither replied to the reasoned opinion nor amended the legislation of which the Commission complained, the Commission brought the present action.

7. In support of its action, the Commission maintains that national legislation which reserves the sale of a certain category of product in principle solely to pharmacies constitutes a measure having equivalent effect prohibited by Article 30 of the Treaty on the ground that the prohibition of certain forms of marketing channels sales and is consequently likely to hinder, albeit indirectly, intra-Community trade in the product concerned. In reply to a question put to it by the Court, the Commission stated that the legislation at issue did not constitute a mere restriction of certain selling arrangements within the meaning of the judgment in Joined Cases C-267/91 and C-268/91 *Keck and Mithouard* [1993] ECR I-6097 but entailed a restrictive effect on trade by making the importation of the product concerned from the other Member States more difficult and more onerous: if that product could be sold in large stores their price would drop, which would lead to an increase in demand and therefore in the volume of imports.

8. The Greek Government denies that its legislation constitutes a measure having equivalent effect within the meaning of Article 30 of the Treaty. According to the Greek Government, the only effect of the measure called in question by the Commission is to restrict the commercial freedom of traders and fulfils the conditions which the Court in *Keck and Mithouard*, cited above, stated as having to be satisfied for a measure to fall outside the scope of Article 30. It points out, moreover, that the measure has entailed neither a fall in the consumption of infant milk during the year in which the measure was introduced by comparison with the preceding year, nor an increase in the price of the product concerned, nor problems of supply for consumers.

9. Under Article 30 of the Treaty, quantitative restrictions on imports and all measures having equivalent effect are prohibited between Member States.

10. The Court has consistently held that any measure which is capable of, directly or indirectly, actually or potentially, hindering intra-Community trade constitutes a

measure having an effect equivalent to a quantitative restriction (judgment in Case 8/74 *Dassonville* [1974] ECR 837, paragraph 5).

11. National legislation which reserves the sale of processed milk for infants solely to pharmacies is not designed to regulate trade in goods between Member States.

12. Such legislation may, admittedly, restrict the volume of sales and hence the volume of sales of processed milk for infants originating in other Member States inasmuch as it deprives traders other than pharmacists of the possibility of marketing that product. But the question remains whether such a possibility is sufficient to characterize the legislation in question as a measure having equivalent effect to a quantitative restriction on imports, within the meaning of Article 30 of the Treaty.

13. In that respect it should be observed that the application to products from other Member States of national provisions restricting or prohibiting certain selling arrangements is not such as to hinder directly or indirectly, actually or potentially, trade between Member States within the meaning of the *Dassonville* judgment, cited above, so long as those provisions apply to all relevant traders operating within the national territory and so long as they affect in the same manner, in law and in fact, the marketing of domestic products and of those from other Member States. Provided that those conditions are fulfilled, the application of such rules to the sale of products from another Member State meeting the requirements laid down by that State is not by nature such as to prevent their access to the market or to impede access any more than it impedes the access of domestic products. Such rules therefore fall outside the scope of Article 30 of the Treaty (see, in particular, the judgments in *Keck and Mithouard*, cited above, paragraphs 16 and 17, in Case C-292/92 *Hünermund and Others* [1993] ECR I-6787, paragraph 21, and in Case C-412/93 *Société d'Importation Édouard Leclerc-Siplec* [1995] ECR I-0000, paragraph 21).

14. So far as concerns the Greek legislation called in question in this case by the Commission, those conditions are fulfilled.

15. Thus, that legislation, the effect of which is to limit the commercial freedom of traders irrespective of the actual characteristics of the product referred to, concerns the selling arrangements of certain goods, inasmuch as it prohibits the sale, other than exclusively by pharmacies, of processed milk for infants and thus generally determines the points of sale where they may be distributed.

16. Moreover, the legislation objected to by the Commission, which applies, without distinction according to the origin of the products in question, to all of the traders operating within the national territory, does not affect the sale of products originating in other Member States any differently from that of domestic products.

17. The fact, invoked by the Commission, that the Hellenic Republic does not itself produce processed milk for infants does not undermine those findings. The applicability of Article 30 of the Treaty to a national measure for the general regulation of commerce, which concerns all the products concerned without distinction according to their origin, cannot depend on such a purely fortuitous factual circumstance, which may, moreover, change with the passage of time. If it did, this would have the illogical consequence that the same legislation would fall under Article 30 in certain Member States but fall outside the scope of that provision in other Member States.

18. The situation would be different only if it was apparent that the legislation at issue protected domestic products which were similar to processed milk for infants from other Member States or which were in competition with milk of that type.

19. In this instance, the Commission has not shown that that was the case.

20. It follows from the foregoing considerations that the Greek legislation called in question by the Commission is confined to limiting the places where the product concerned may be distributed by regulating the marketing of that product, without thereby preventing access to the market of products from other Member States or specifically placing them at a disadvantage.

21. That being so, the Greek legislation reserving the sale of processed milk for infants in principle exclusively to pharmacies falls outside the scope of Article 30 of the Treaty. The Commission's application must therefore be dismissed.

Costs

[Para. 22 omitted]

On those grounds,

THE COURT

hereby:

1. **Dismisses the application;**

[Para. 2 of the ruling omitted]

Comments and questions

In the judgment in Case C-391/92 *Commission* v *Greece* [1995] I-1621 (the *Infant milk formula* case), the CJEU held that the Greek laws which only allowed pharmacies to sell infant milk formula constituted a 'selling arrangement'; cf. paragraph 15 of the judgment. The law merely determined the *point of sale* where the product could be sold. Since the law applied without distinction to where the product originated, it did not affect the sales of foreign products differently from the sales of domestic products, and it was therefore a non-discriminatory marketing rule; cf. paragraph 16.

The fact that there was no production of infant milk formula in Greece did not affect the finding under the *Keck* doctrine. Thus the CJEU held that the applicability of Article 34 TFEU (formerly Article 30 EEC Treaty) to a national measure for the general regulation of commerce, which concerns *all* the products concerned regardless of their origin, cannot depend on whether or not there is domestic production. If such factors were taken into account, this could lead to the unreasonable consequence that the same legislation would fall within Article 34 TFEU in some Member States but outside it in other Member States; cf. paragraph 17 of the judgment.

Would it make a difference to the judgment if Greece produced a good which could be substituted for infant milk formula, and which according to Greek law was permitted to be sold freely, including in supermarkets?

By contrast, in Case C-323/93 *La Crespelle* v *Coopérative d'Elevage* [1994] I-5077, the CJEU held that French rules requiring bulls' semen to be stored at approved bovine insemination centres was covered by the concept of a measure having equivalent effect to a quantitative restriction on imports, as laid down in Article 34 TFEU. The CJEU referred to the fact that the requirement applied to the step in the distribution chain immediately after importation, and that it laid a financial burden on importers, and could restrict imports. The French rules could not be said to be 'certain selling arrangements' nor 'product related'. In a way, the CJEU set up an extra category of trade restrictions covered by the concept of measures having equivalent effect to quantitative restrictions in Article 34 TFEU, which concerns the importing link in the distribution chain and the link immediately after importation. The *La Crespelle* case is in line with Case C-189/95 *Franzén* [1997] I-5909 and Case 104/75 *de Peijper* [1976] ECR 613, since a national law which leads to imports being channelled so that only some undertakings are permitted to import certain goods, while others are excluded from doing so, will be a measure having equivalent effect to a quantitative restriction on imports, as laid down in Article 34 TFEU. The situation is judged differently when there is a national non-discriminatory regulation at the *retail level*, after the imported goods have obtained access to the market, as in the case of the Greek laws on the sale of infant milk formula, for example, where the law was covered by the *Keck* doctrine and therefore falls outside the scope of Article 34 TFEU.

JUDGMENT OF THE COURT (Sixth Chamber)
8 March 2001

Konsumentombudsmannen (KO) v Gourmet International Products AB (GIP).
(Reference for a preliminary ruling: Stockholms tingsrätt – Sweden)

'Free movement of goods – Articles 30 and 36 of the EC Treaty
(now, after amendment, Articles 28 EC and 30 EC) – Freedom to provide services – Articles 56 and 59 of the EC Treaty (now, after amendment, Articles 46 EC and 49 EC) – Swedish legislation on the advertising of alcoholic beverages – Selling arrangements – Measure having an effect equivalent to a quantitative restriction – Justification in the interest of the protection of health'

Case C-405/98

Judgment

1. By order of 18 September 1998, received at the Court on 16 November 1998, the Stockholms Tingsrätt (Stockholm District Court) referred to the Court for a preliminary ruling under Article 177 of the EC Treaty (now Article 234 EC) two questions on the interpretation of Articles 30, 36, 56 and 59 of the EC treaty (now, after amendment, Articles 28 EC, 30 EC, 46 EC and 49 EC).

2. The two questions have been raised in the context of an application made by the Konsumentombudsman (the Swedish ombudsman responsible for consumer protection, hereinafter 'the Consumer Ombudsman') for an injunction restraining Gourmet International Products AB (hereinafter 'GIP') from placing advertisements for alcoholic beverages in magazines.

National legislation

3. Lagen 1978:763 med vissa bestämmelser om marknadsföring av alkoholdrycker (Swedish Law 1978:763 laying down provisions on the Marketing of Alcoholic Beverages, as amended, hereinafter 'the Alkoholreklamlagen'), which entered into force on 1 July 1979, is, according to Article 1, applicable to the promotion of alcoholic beverages to consumers by manufacturers and retailers. Pursuant to the Alkohollagen 1994:738 (Swedish Law on Alcohol), alcoholic beverages are beverages containing more than 2.25% of alcohol by volume. Those beverages comprise spirits, wines, 'strong beer' (containing more than 3.5% of alcohol by volume) and 'beer' (containing between 2.25% and 3.5% of alcohol by volume).

4. Article 2 of the Alkoholreklamlagen provides:

   'In view of the health risks involved in alcohol consumption, alcoholic beverages should be marketed with particular moderation. In particular, advertisements or other marketing measures must not be insistent, involve unsolicited approaches or encourage alcohol consumption.

   Advertising may not be used to market alcoholic beverages on radio or television. The same prohibition applies to satellite broadcasts subject to Law 1996:844 on Radio and Television.

   Advertising may not be used to market spirits, wines or strong beers either in periodicals or in other publications subject to the Regulation on Press Freedom and comparable to periodicals by reason of their publication schedule. That prohibition does not however apply to publications distributed solely at the point of sale of such beverages. Law 1996:851.'

5. It is apparent from the order for reference that, owing to the object of the Alkoholreklamlagen, which is to restrict the possibilities of marketing alcoholic beverages to consumers, the prohibition on advertisements in periodicals does not apply to advertisements in the specialist press, meaning the press aimed essentially at traders, that is to say, in particular, at manufacturers and restaurateurs.

6. It is also apparent from the order for reference that advertising on the public highway and the direct mailing of advertising material to individuals, in particular, are regarded as contrary to the obligation to exercise moderation laid down by the Alkoholreklamlagen.

Main proceedings

7. GIP publishes a magazine entitled *Gourmet*. Issue No 4 (August-October 1997) of the edition intended for subscribers contained three pages of advertisements for alcoholic beverages, one for red wine and two for whisky. Those pages did not appear in the edition sold in shops. According to the order for reference, 90% of the magazine's 9 300 subscribers are traders, manufacturers or retailers, and 10% are private individuals.

8. The Consumer Ombudsman applied to the Stockholms Tingsrätt for an injunction, and imposition of a fine in the event of failure to comply therewith, restraining GIP from contributing to the marketing of alcoholic beverages to consumers by means of such advertisements, which were contrary to Article 2 of the Alkoholreklamlagen.

9. GIP contended that the application should be dismissed. It argued, in particular, that the proceedings brought against it were based on legislation that was contrary to Community law.

10. When examining the application, the Tingsrätt was unsure, in particular, whether national rules imposing an absolute prohibition on certain advertisements might be regarded as having an effect equivalent to a quantitative restriction within the meaning of Article 30 of the Treaty and, if so, whether, in view of their object, they might be regarded as lawful under Article 36 of the Treaty. It was also unsure whether such national rules were compatible with the freedom to provide services.

11. The Stockholms Tingsrätt considered that an interpretation of the relevant provisions of the Treaty seemed necessary. It therefore decided to stay proceedings and to refer the following questions to the Court for a preliminary ruling:

   '1. Is Article 30 or Article 59 of the EC Treaty to be interpreted as precluding national legislation entailing a general prohibition of alcohol advertising, such as the prohibition laid down in Article 2 of Alkoholreklamlagen?

   2. If so, can such a prohibition be regarded as justified and proportionate for the protection of life and health of humans?'

12. The Consumer Ombudsman lodged an appeal against the order for reference before the Marknadsdomstolen, Sweden, which dismissed the appeal by decision of 11 March 1999.

Free movement of goods

13. By the questions referred to the Court, which can be considered together, the national court is asking essentially, first, whether the provisions of the Treaty on the free movement of goods preclude a prohibition on advertisements for alcoholic beverages such as that laid down in Article 2 of the Alkoholreklamlagen.

14. The Consumer Ombudsman and the intervening Governments accept that the prohibition on advertising in Sweden affects sales of alcoholic beverages there, including those imported from other Member States, since the specific purpose of the Swedish legislation is to reduce the consumption of alcohol.

15. However, observing that the Court held in paragraph 16 of its judgment in Joined Cases C-267/91 and C-268/91 *Keck and Mithouard* [1993] ECR I-6097 that national provisions restricting or prohibiting certain selling arrangements are not liable to hinder intra-Community trade, so long as they apply to all relevant traders operating within the national territory and so long as they affect in the same manner, in law and in fact, the marketing of domestic products and of those from other Member

States, the Consumer Ombudsman and the intervening Governments contend that the prohibition on advertising in issue in the main proceedings does not constitute an obstacle to trade between Member States, since it satisfies the criteria laid down by the Court in that judgment.

16. GIP contends that an outright prohibition such as that at issue in the main proceedings does not satisfy those criteria. It argues that such a prohibition is, in particular, liable to have a greater effect on imported goods than on those produced in the Member State concerned.

17. Although the Commission takes the view that the decision as to whether, on the facts of the case, the prohibition does or does not constitute an obstacle to intra-Community trade is a matter for the national court, the Commission expresses similar doubts as to the application in the present case of the criteria referred to in paragraph 15 above.

18. It should be pointed out that, according to paragraph 17 of its judgment in *Keck and Mithouard*, if national provisions restricting or prohibiting certain selling arrangements are to avoid being caught by Article 30 of the Treaty, they must not be of such a kind as to prevent access to the market by products from another Member State or to impede access any more than they impede the access of domestic products.

19. The Court has also held, in paragraph 42 of its judgment in Joined Cases C-34/95 to C-36/95 *De Agostini and TV-Shop* [1997] ECR I-3843, that it cannot be excluded that an outright prohibition, applying in one Member State, of a type of promotion for a product which is lawfully sold there might have a greater impact on products from other Member States.

20. It is apparent that a prohibition on advertising such as that at issue in the main proceedings not only prohibits a form of marketing a product but in reality prohibits producers and importers from directing any advertising messages at consumers, with a few insignificant exceptions.

21. Even without its being necessary to carry out a precise analysis of the facts characteristic of the Swedish situation, which it is for the national court to do, the Court is able to conclude that, in the case of products like alcoholic beverages, the consumption of which is linked to traditional social practices and to local habits and customs, a prohibition of all advertising directed at consumers in the form of advertisements in the press, on the radio and on television, the direct mailing of unsolicited material or the placing of posters on the public highway is liable to impede access to the market by products from other Member States more than it impedes access by domestic products, with which consumers are instantly more familiar.

22. The information provided by the Consumer Ombudsman and the Swedish Government concerning the relative increase in Sweden in the consumption of wine and whisky, which are mainly imported, in comparison with other products such as vodka, which is mainly of Swedish origin, does not alter that conclusion. First, it cannot be precluded that, in the absence of the legislation at issue in the main proceedings, the change indicated would have been greater; second, that information takes into account only some alcoholic beverages and ignores, in particular, beer consumption.

23. Furthermore, although publications containing advertisements may be distributed at points of sale, Systembolaget AB, the company wholly owned by the Swedish State which has a monopoly of retail sales in Sweden, in fact only distributes its own magazine at those points of sale.

24. Last, Swedish legislation does not prohibit 'editorial advertising', that is to say, the promotion, in articles forming part of the editorial content of the publication, of products in relation to which the insertion of direct advertisements is prohibited. The Commission correctly observes that, for various, principally cultural, reasons, domestic producers have easier access to that means of advertising than their competitors established in other Member States. That circumstance is liable to increase the imbalance inherent in the absolute prohibition on direct advertising.

25. A prohibition on advertising such as that at issue in the main proceedings must therefore be regarded as affecting the marketing of products from other Member States more heavily than the marketing of domestic products and as therefore constituting an obstacle to trade between Member States caught by Article 30 of the Treaty.

26. However, such an obstacle may be justified by the protection of public health, a general interest ground recognised by Article 36 of the Treaty.

27. In that regard, it is accepted that rules restricting the advertising of alcoholic beverages in order to combat alcohol abuse reflects public health concerns (Case 152/78 *Commission* v *France* [1980] ECR 2299, paragraph 17, and Joined Cases C-1/90 and C-176/90 *Aragonesa de Publicidad Exterior and Publivía* [1991] ECR I-4151, paragraph 15).

28. In order for public health concerns to be capable of justifying an obstacle to trade such as that inherent in the prohibition on advertising at issue in the main proceedings, the measure concerned must also be proportionate to the objective to be achieved and must not constitute either a means of arbitrary discrimination or a disguised restriction on trade between Member States.

29. The Consumer Ombudsman and the intervening Governments claim that the derogation provided for in Article 36 of the Treaty can cover the prohibition on advertising at issue in the main proceedings. The Consumer Ombudsman and the Swedish Government emphasise in particular that the prohibition is not absolute and does not prevent members of the public from obtaining information, if they wish, in particular in restaurants, on the Internet, in an 'editorial context' or by asking the producer or importer to send advertising material. Furthermore, the Swedish Government observes that the Court of Justice has acknowledged that, in the present state of Community law, Member States are at liberty, within the limits set by the Treaty, to decide on the degree of protection which they wish to afford to public health and on the way in which that protection is to be achieved (*Aragonesa de Publicidad Exterior and Publivía*, cited above, paragraph 16). The Swedish Government maintains that the legislation at issue in the main proceedings constitutes an essential component of its alcohol policy.

30. GIP claims that the outright prohibition on advertising laid down by the legislation at issue in the main proceedings is disproportionate, since the protection sought could be obtained by prohibitions of a more limited nature, concerning, for example, certain public places or the press aimed at children and adolescents. It must be borne in mind that the Swedish policy on alcoholism is already catered for by the existence of the monopoly on retail sales, by the prohibition on sales to persons under the age of 20 years and by information campaigns.

31. The Commission submits that the decision as to whether the prohibition on advertising at issue in the main proceedings is or is not proportionate is a matter for the national court. However, it also states that the prohibition does not appear to be particularly effective, owing in particular to the existence of 'editorial' publicity and the abundance of indirect advertising on the Internet, and that requirements as to the form of advertising, such as the obligation to exercise moderation already found in the Alkoholreklamlagen, may suffice to protect the interest in question.

32. It should be pointed out, first, that there is no evidence before the Court to suggest that the public health grounds on which the Swedish authorities rely have been diverted from their purpose and used in such a way as to discriminate against goods originating in other Member States or to protect certain national products indirectly (Case 34/79 *Regina* v *Henn and Darby* [1979] ECR 3795, paragraph 21, and *Aragonesa de Publicidad Exterior and Publivía*, cited above, paragraph 20).

33. Second, the decision as to whether the prohibition on advertising at issue in the main proceedings is proportionate, and in particular as to whether the objective sought might be achieved by less extensive prohibitions or restrictions or by prohibitions or restrictions having less effect on intra-Community trade, calls for an analysis of the circumstances of law and of fact which characterise the situation in

the Member State concerned, which the national court is in a better position than the Court of Justice to carry out.

34. The answer to the question must therefore be that, as regards the free movement of goods, Articles 30 and 36 of the Treaty do not preclude a prohibition on the advertising of alcoholic beverages such as that laid down in Article 2 of the Alkoholreklamlagen, unless it is apparent that, in the circumstances of law and of fact which characterise the situation in the Member State concerned, the protection of public health against the harmful effects of alcohol can be ensured by measures having less effect on intra-Community trade.

Freedom to provide services

35. By the questions it has referred to the Court, the national court is essentially asking, second, whether the Treaty provisions on freedom to provide services preclude a prohibition on the advertising of alcoholic beverages such as that laid down in Article 2 of the Alkoholreklamlagen.

36. The Consumer Ombudsman, GIP, the Swedish Government and the Commission agree that provision of advertising space may constitute a provision of cross-border services falling within the scope of Article 59 of the Treaty. The other intervening Governments, on the other hand, contend that Article 59 does not apply in the main proceedings.

37. In that regard, as the Court has frequently held, the right to provide services may be relied on by an undertaking as against the Member State in which it is established if the services are provided to persons established in another Member State (see, in particular, Case C-18/93 *Corsica Ferries Italia* v *Corpo dei Piloti del Porto di Genova* [1994] ECR I-1783, paragraph 30, and Case C-384/93 *Alpine Investments* [1995] ECR I-1141, paragraph 30).

38. That is particularly so where, as in the case before the referring court, the legislation of a Member State restricts the right of press undertakings established in the territory of that Member State to offer advertising space in their publications to potential advertisers established in other Member States.

39. A measure such as the prohibition on advertising at issue in the proceedings before that court, even if it is non-discriminatory, has a particular effect on the cross-border supply of advertising space, given the international nature of the advertising market in the category of products to which the prohibition relates, and thereby constitutes a restriction on the freedom to provide services within the meaning of Article 59 of the Treaty (see, in that regard, *Alpine Investments*, cited above, paragraph 35).

40. However, such a restriction may be justified by the protection of public health, which is a ground of general interest recognised by Article 56 of the EC Treaty, which is applicable to the provision of services in accordance with Article 66 of the EC Treaty (now Article 55 EC).

41. As observed in paragraph 33 above, in relation to obstacles to the free movement of goods, it is for the national court to determine whether, in the circumstances of law and of fact which characterise the situation in the Member State concerned, the prohibition on advertising at issue in the main proceedings meets the condition of proportionality required in order for the derogation from the freedom to provide services to be justified.

42. The answer to be given must therefore be that, as regards freedom to provide services, Articles 56 and 59 of the Treaty do not preclude a prohibition on the advertising of alcoholic beverages such as that laid down in Article 2 of the Alkoholreklamlagen, unless it is apparent that, in the circumstances of law and of fact which characterise the situation in the Member State concerned, the protection of public health against the harmful effects of alcohol can be ensured by measures having less effect on intra-Community trade.

Costs

[Para. 43 omitted]

On those grounds,

THE COURT (Sixth Chamber),

in answer to the questions referred to it by the Stockholms Tingsrätt by order of 18 September 1998, hereby rules:

> **Articles 30 and 36 of the EC Treaty (now, after amendment, Articles 28 EC and 30 EC) and Articles 56 and 59 of the EC Treaty (now, after amendment, Articles 46 EC and 49 EC) do not preclude a prohibition on the advertising of alcoholic beverages such as that laid down in Article 2 of Lagen 1978:763 med vissa bestämmelser om marknadsföring av alkoholdrycker (Swedish Law laying down provisions on the Marketing of Alcoholic Beverages), as amended, unless it is apparent that, in the circumstances of law and of fact which characterise the situation in the Member State concerned, the protection of public health against the harmful effects of alcohol can be ensured by measures having less effect on intra-Community trade.**

Comments and questions

In Joined Cases C-267/91 and C-268/91 *Keck and Mithouard* [1993] ECR I-6097, referred to above, the CJEU reviewed its earlier interpretation of what is today Article 34 TFEU (formerly Article 30 EEC Treaty). Thus, in paragraph 16 of the *Keck* judgment the CJEU stated that national measures which prohibit certain selling arrangements are not covered by Article 34 TFEU, so long as the measures apply to all relevant traders operating within the national territory and so long as they affect the marketing of domestic products and those from other Member States in the same manner, in law and in fact. In paragraph 17 the CJEU stated that such provisions may be assumed not to prevent or impede access to the market, so that such provisions fall outside the scope of Article 34 TFEU.

The *Keck* case has given rise to considerable debate, and many have argued that the CJEU has constructed a rule which is too inflexible, and which excludes the application of Article 34 TFEU to cases which ought properly to be covered by its provisions. Advocate General Francis Jacobs has made a particularly important contribution to this debate in his Opinion in Case C-412/93 *Société d'Importation Edouard Leclerc-Siplec* v *TF1 Publicité* [1995] I-179.

In the *Leclerc-Siplec* case a French supermarket chain was prevented from broadcasting advertisements about its sale of petrol, because France had a prohibition against the distribution sector using television advertising. The French supermarket chain challenged this prohibition, among other things, on the basis of Article 34 TFEU. In his proposal to the CJEU, Advocate General Jacobs noted that, in Case C-292/92 *Hünermund et al* v *Landesapotheker-kammer Baden-Württemberg* [1993] I-6787, the CJEU applied the *Keck* doctrine to a restriction on advertising. He added that advertising restrictions may pose a particularly serious threat to the integration of markets. The Advocate General was in no doubt that the test laid down in the *Keck* case was satisfied in the *Leclerc-Siplec* case. However, he made a strong criticism of the criteria. In his view the appropriate test for the CJEU to consider was whether a measure involved a substantial restriction on access to the market. If it does so, the measure should be regarded as being covered by Article 34 TFEU, so it can only be lawful if it can be justified on recognised grounds and if it satisfies the principle of proportionality. Advocate General Jacobs argued that the *Keck* doctrine could perhaps be best understood as excluding from the scope of Article 34 TFEU a number of measures which ought not properly to be regarded as being covered by it. However, the doctrine ought to be supplemented by a rule that measures can be caught by Article 34 TFEU if they involve a substantial restriction on access to the market. As an example of measures which, in principle, fulfil the conditions laid down in the *Keck* case, but which ought nevertheless to be considered as being prohibited under Article 34 TFEU, the Advocate General referred to 'a total ban on the advertising of a product which may lawfully be sold in the Member State where the ban is imposed and in other Member States.' The effect of such a ban would be that 'manufacturers in other Member States would find it virtually impossible to penetrate the market in which the ban was imposed, if their products were not already known to consumers in that country.'

In the *Leclerc-Siplec* case the CJEU merely stated that the disputed measure was covered by the principle laid down in the *Keck* case. The criticisms of the Advocate General were passed over without comment.

Case C-405/98 *Konsumentombudsmannen* v *Gourmet International Products* [2001] ECR I-1795, dealt with a Swedish ban on advertising for alcoholic drinks. The Gourmet company referred to the ban as 'total', which was not entirely correct. The Swedish rules contained a number of exemptions, so it was more correct to refer to them, in the words of Advocate General Jacobs as being 'total as regards advertising material devised by or on behalf of a producer, importer, wholesaler or retailer and addressed to (potential) consumers in general, as opposed to those who have specifically requested it or are already in an alcohol-purchasing situation.' There was no doubt that the ban restricted the sale of these products; this was the purpose of the measure and there was agreement that it had effect.

In assessing whether the Swedish ban formally fulfilled the criteria of the *Keck* doctrine, the Advocate General said that this was not so. The ban on advertising meant that products which were already well known by consumers would have a significant advantage over new and unknown products. Since it was more likely that new products would come from another Member State than Sweden, the ban did not affect domestic and imported products equally. Do you agree with this reasoning? Would any restriction on the right to advertise not primarily affect new and unknown products, regardless of their origin, compared with well-established brands? Would it not be more reasonable to compare new and unknown foreign products and new and unknown domestic products?

In its judgment the CJEU largely accepted the argument of the Advocate General. However, while affirming that the Swedish ban would put imported products at a disadvantage; cf. paragraphs 24-25, the CJEU simultaneously seemed to attach particular importance to the fact that the ban involved a restriction on access to the market for foreign goods; cf. paragraphs 18 and 21 of the judgment. In other words, to a fair extent the CJEU seemed to be pointing to the interpretation which Advocate General Jacobs argued for in his Opinion on the *Leclerc-Siplec* case.

The decision of the CJEU is very short. On the basis of the CJEU's reasoning, can it be said that a ban on advertising to a certain category of consumers, for example children under the age of 12, would be covered by the *Keck* doctrine and so fall outside the scope of Article 34 TFEU?

In your opinion, is the Swedish ban an expression of direct discrimination, indirect discrimination or non-discriminatory regulation of access to the Swedish market? On this point see paragraph 25 of the judgment.

The *Gourmet International* case was dealt with not only under the rules on the free movement of goods (alcoholic beverages), but also under the rules on the freedom to provide services. What was the service which the case concerned?

The Swedish prohibition on the advertising of alcoholic beverages did not apply to advertising in the specialist press, meaning the press aimed essentially at the trade. The *Gourmet* periodical was sold both in shops and by subscription. Only the edition sold by subscription contained the advertisements which were the subject of the dispute. 10% of the subscribers were private individuals, while 90% of the subscribers were commercial customers, so that one could argue that the subscription edition should be regarded as a trade periodical in which it was permitted to advertise for alcoholic drinks. It appears from the Opinion of the Advocate General that this question was not clarified, and it is surprising that the CJEU did not require it to be clarified prior to giving its preliminary ruling. One could have expected that the whole case would have lapsed if it had been established that the periodical in question was a trade publication, since the advertising would then have been allowed under Swedish law.

In paragraph 21 the CJEU expressly stated that it is for the referring national courts to carry out an analysis of the facts in the case; cf. the allocation of responsibilities in Article 267 TFEU (formerly Article 177 EEC Treaty). Does the CJEU respect this allocation of responsibilities? Compare this with the CJEU's finding on proportionality; cf. in particular paragraph 33 of the judgment.

JUDGMENT OF THE COURT (Third Chamber)
2 December 2010

Ker-Optika bt v ÀNTSZ Dél-dunántúli Regionális Intézete. (Reference for a preliminary ruling from the Baranya megyei bíróság – Hungary)

'Free movement of goods – Public health – Selling of contact lenses via the Internet – National legislation authorising the sale of contact lenses solely in medical supply shops – Directive 2000/31/EC – Information society – Electronic commerce'

Case C-108/09

Judgment

1. This reference for a preliminary ruling concerns the interpretation of Directive 2000/31/EC of the European Parliament and of the Council of 8 June 2000 on certain legal aspects of information society services, in particular electronic commerce, in the Internal Market ('Directive on electronic commerce') (OJ 2000 L 178, p. 1) and of Articles 34 TFEU and 36 TFEU.

2. The reference has been made in proceedings between Ker-Optika bt ('Ker-Optika') and ÀNTSZ Dél-dunántúli Regionális Intézete (South Transdanubian Regional Directorate of the national public health and medical services; 'ÀNTSZ') concerning an administrative decision whereby ÀNTSZ prohibited Ker-Optika from selling contact lenses via the Internet.

Legal context

European Union ('EU') legislation

[Paras. 3-9 omitted]

National legislation

10. Under Article 3(1) of Law CVIII of 2001 on electronic commerce and information society services (a elektronikus kereskedelmi szolgáltatások, valamint az információs társadalommal összefüggő szolgáltatásokról szóló 2001. évi CVIII. Törvény; 'the Law on electronic commerce'):

'No prior authorisation or official decision having equivalent effect shall be required in order to take up or pursue the activity of an information society services provider.'

11. Under Article 3(1) of Order 7/2004 (XI. 23.) of the Ministry of Health on the technical requirements relating to the sale, repair and hiring of medical devices (a gyógyászati segédeszközök forgalmazásának, javításának, kölcsönzésének szakmai követelményeiről szóló 7/2004 (XI. 23.) Egészségügyi Minisztériumi rendelet) ('the Ministry of Health Order'):

    'Medical devices may be sold, repaired and hired ... in a specialist shop, provided that it has an operating licence under a separate provision and that it satisfies the conditions laid down in Points I.1 and I.2 of Annex 2 to this order.'

12. Under Annex 1 of that Order:

    'The following medical devices are excluded from the scope of this order:
    ...
    – mass-produced optical products, with the exception of contact lenses;
    ...'

13. It is apparent from Point I.1(d) of Annex 2 to that Order that, in order to sell contact lenses and custom-made spectacles, a shop with a minimum area of 18 m2 or premises separated from the workshop is required. One of the conditions relating to staff, in point I.2(c) of that Annex, is the requirement that the services of an optometrist or an ophthalmologist qualified in the field of contact lenses must be used.

The dispute in the main proceedings and the questions referred for a preliminary ruling

14. Ker-Optika sells contact lenses via its Internet site. By a decision of 29 August 2008, ÀNTSZ Pécsi, Sellyei, Siklósi Kistérségi Intézete (the local ÀNTSZ office for the districts of Pécs, Sellye and Siklós), prohibited that activity.

15. Following a complaint made by Ker-Optika against that decision, ÀNTSZ confirmed that prohibition by a decision of 14 November 2008.

16. ÀNTSZ relied, in particular, on the provisions of the Ministry of Health Order, under which the only ways in which contact lenses can be sold are either in a shop which specialises in the sale of medical devices or by home delivery for final consumption. Neither the name nor the content of the latter concept covers selling via the Internet.

17. Ker-Optika brought an action against that decision claiming, in particular, that the sale of contact lenses via the Internet cannot be subject to restrictions in the light of Article 3(1) of the Law on electronic commerce, which safeguards the right of an information society service provider to pursue that activity freely.

18. In that regard, ÀNTSZ relied on Recital 18 of Directive 2000/31 which makes it clear that the scope of the Law on electronic commerce cannot encompass the sale of contact lenses via the Internet. According to Recital 18, activities which, by their very nature, cannot be carried out at a distance or by electronic means, such as medical advice requiring the physical examination of a patient, are not information society services. The selling of contact lenses requires such an examination.

19. In those circumstances, the Baranya megyei bíróság decided to stay proceedings and to refer to the Court of Justice the following questions for a preliminary ruling:

 '1. Does the sale of contact lenses constitute medical advice requiring the physical examination of a patient and thus not fall within the scope of Directive [2000/31]?

 2. If the sale of contact lenses does not constitute medical advice requiring the physical examination of a patient, must Article 30 EC be interpreted as precluding legislation of a Member State under which contact lenses may be sold only in shops which specialise in the supply of medical devices?

 3. Does the principle of the free movement of goods laid down in Article 28 EC preclude the provision of Hungarian law which authorises the selling of contact lenses solely in shops which specialise in the supply of medical devices?'

Consideration of the questions referred for a preliminary ruling

20. By its questions, which should be examined together, the referring court asks, in essence, whether EU law precludes national legislation, such as that at issue in the main proceedings, which authorises the sale of contact lenses only in shops which specialise in the sale of medical devices and which prohibits, consequently, the sale of contact lenses via the Internet.

21. To answer the questions raised, the Court must identify the provisions of EU law applicable to the sale of contact lenses via the Internet and then decide whether those provisions preclude national rules such as those at issue in the main proceedings.

22. First, in relation to Internet sales, the following features can, inter alia, be identified. Such sales comprise, initially, the act of selling per se which consists in the making of a contractual offer on-line and the conclusion of a contract by electronic means. Next, such sales involve the delivery of the product sold, generally to the customer's home. Furthermore, in certain individual cases, the customer obtains medical advice before the sale or the supply takes place.

Directive 2000/31

[Paras 23-40 omitted]

Primary law

41. Given that the rules relating to the conditions of the supply of contact lenses are not covered by Directive 2000/31, those rules must be assessed under primary law, namely the FEU Treaty.

42. As a preliminary point, the Court must consider whether those rules fall to be examined in relation to the freedom to provide services, as maintained by the Hungarian Government, or in relation to the free movement of goods, as suggested by the referring court.

43. In that regard, it is settled case-law that, where a national measure relates to both the free movement of goods and another fundamental freedom, the Court will in principle examine it in relation to one only of those two fundamental freedoms, if it appears that one of them is entirely secondary in relation to the other and may be considered together with it (see, to that effect, Case C-275/92 Schindler [1994] ECR I-1039, paragraph 22, and Case C-20/03 Burmanjer and Others [2005] ECR I-4133, paragraph 35).

44. Further, it follows from Case C-322/01 Deutscher Apothekerverband [2003] ECR I-14887, paragraphs 65, 76 and 124, that a national measure concerning an arrangement characterised by the sale of goods via the Internet and the delivery of those goods to the customer's home is to be examined only with regard to the rules relating to the free movement of goods and, consequently, with regard to Articles 34 TFEU and 36 TFEU.

45. In the present case, the national legislation prohibiting the selling of contact lenses via the Internet concerns a selling arrangement characterised by the delivery of such lenses to the customer's home.

46. Consequently, that legislation must be examined with regard to Articles 34 TFEU and 36 TFEU.

Whether there is a restriction on the free movement of goods

47. According to settled case-law, all trading rules enacted by Member States which are capable of hindering, directly or indirectly, actually or potentially, trade within the European Union are to be considered as measures having an effect equivalent to quantitative restrictions and are, on that basis, prohibited by Article 34 TFEU (see,

inter alia, Case 8/74 Dassonville [1974] ECR 837, paragraph 5, and Case C-110/05 Commission v Italy [2009] ECR I-519, paragraph 33).

48. It is also apparent from settled case-law that Article 34 TFEU reflects the obligation to comply with the principles of non-discrimination and of mutual recognition of products lawfully manufactured and marketed in other Member States, as well as the principle of ensuring free access of EU products to national markets (see Commission v Italy, paragraph 34 and the case-law cited).

49. Accordingly, measures adopted by a Member State the object or effect of which is to treat products coming from other Member States less favourably are to be regarded as measures having an effect equivalent to quantitative restrictions, as are rules that lay down requirements to be met by such goods, even if those rules apply to all products alike (see Commission v Italy, paragraphs 35 and 37).

50. Any other measure which hinders access of products originating in other Member States to the market of a Member State is also covered by that concept (Commission v Italy, paragraph 37).

51. For that reason, the application to products from other Member States of national provisions restricting or prohibiting certain selling arrangements is such as to hinder directly or indirectly, actually or potentially, trade between Member States for the purposes of the case-law flowing from Dassonville, unless those provisions apply to all relevant traders operating within the national territory and affect in the same manner, in law and in fact, the selling of domestic products and of those from other Member States. The application of such rules to the sale of products from another Member State meeting the requirements laid down by that State is by nature such as to prevent their access to the market or to impede such access more than it impedes the access of domestic products (see, to that effect, Joined Cases C-267/91 and C-268/91 Keck and Mithouard [1993] ECR I-6097, paragraphs 16 and 17, and Commission v Italy, paragraph 36).

52. Accordingly, it is necessary to examine whether the national legislation at issue in the main proceedings meets the two conditions stated in the preceding paragraph of this judgment, in other words, whether it applies to all relevant traders operating within the national territory and whether it affects in the same manner, in law and in fact, the selling of domestic products and the selling of those from other Member States.

53. As regards the first condition, it is clear that the legislation applies to all relevant traders involved in selling contact lenses, which means that that condition is satisfied.

54. As regards the second condition, it is undisputed that the prohibition on the selling of contact lenses via the Internet applies to contact lenses from other Member States which are sold by mail order and delivered to the home of customers resident in Hungary. It is clear that the prohibition on selling contact lenses by mail order deprives traders from other Member States of a particularly effective means of selling those products and thus significantly impedes access of those traders to the market of the Member State concerned (see, by analogy, in relation to medicinal products, Deutscher Apothekerverband, paragraph 74).

55. In those circumstances, that legislation does not affect in the same manner the selling of contact lenses by Hungarian traders and such selling as carried out by traders from other Member States.

56. It follows that that legislation constitutes a measure having an effect equivalent to a quantitative restriction, as prohibited by Article 34 TFEU, unless that legislation can be objectively justified.

Whether the restriction on the free movement of goods is justified

57. According to settled case-law, an obstacle to the free movement of goods may be justified on one of the public interest grounds set out in Article 36 TFEU or in order to meet overriding requirements. In either case, the national provision must be appropriate for securing the attainment of the objective pursued and must not go beyond what is necessary in order to attain it (see, inter alia, Commission v Italy, paragraph 59 and the case-law cited).

58. In that regard, if that measure is within the field of public health, account must be taken of the fact that the health and life of humans rank foremost among the assets and interests protected by the Treaty and that it is for the Member States to determine the level of protection which they wish to afford to public health and the way in which that level is to be achieved. Since the level may vary from one Member State to another, Member States should be allowed a measure of discretion (see Joined Cases C-570/07 and C-571/07 Blanco Pérez and Chao Gómez [2010] ECR I-0000, paragraph 44 and the case-law cited).

59. In the present case, the justification relied on by the Hungarian Government concerns the need to ensure protection of the health of contact lens users. That justification corresponds, therefore, to the public health concerns acknowledged in Article 36 TFEU which may justify an obstacle to the free movement of goods.

60. Accordingly, it is necessary to examine whether the legislation at issue in the main proceedings is appropriate for securing the attainment of the objective pursued.

61. In that regard, the Hungarian and Spanish Governments maintain that it is necessary to require customers to take delivery of contact lenses in specialist shops, because they must have access to an optician who can carry out the necessary physical examinations, undertake checks and give those customers instructions on the wearing of the lenses.

62. On that point, it should be recalled, as was stated in paragraph 35 of this judgment, that the mere wearing of contact lenses may, in individual cases, cause eye ailments, and even lasting visual impairment.

63. Given the risks to public health which thus exist, a Member State may impose a requirement that contact lenses are to be supplied by qualified staff who are to alert the customer to those risks, carry out an examination of the customer and recommend or advise against the wearing of lenses, while inviting the person concerned, where necessary, to obtain the advice of an ophthalmologist. Because of those risks, a Member State may also impose a requirement that, where the wearing of lenses is not advised against, qualified staff are to determine the most appropriate type of lenses, check the positioning of the lenses on the eyes and provide the customer with information on the correct use and care of the lenses (see, to that effect, Case C-271/92 LPO [1993] ECR I-2899, paragraph 11).

64. While not entirely eliminating the risks incurred by users of lenses, the establishment of a link to a qualified optician and the services provided by such an optician are likely to reduce those risks. Accordingly, by reserving the supply of contact lenses to the opticians' shops which offer the services of such an optician, the legislation at issue in the main proceedings is appropriate for securing the attainment of the objective of ensuring protection of the health of those users.

65. It is also necessary, however, that that legislation does not go beyond what is necessary in order to attain that objective, in other words that there are not other measures less restrictive of the free movement of goods by means of which that objective could be achieved.

66. First, as regards the requirement that the customer must be physically present to have his eyes examined by an optician at the sales outlet, it must be observed, first, that precautionary examinations, carried out for investigative purposes, can be undertaken by ophthalmologists in places other than opticians' shops.

67. Also, there is nothing in the documents submitted to the Court to suggest that it is a requirement of the legislation at issue in the main proceedings either that an optician must make every supply of lenses dependent on a precautionary examination or on medical advice having first been obtained or that those conditions are imposed, in particular, on each occasion when there is a series of supplies of lenses to the same customer.

68. Accordingly, undergoing such examinations and obtaining such advice must be held to be optional, and consequently it is primarily the responsibility of each contact lens user to make use of them, while the task of the optician in that regard is to give advice to the users.

69. However, customers can be advised, in the same way, before the supply of contact lenses, as part of the process of selling the lenses via the Internet, by means of the interactive features on the Internet site concerned, the use of which by the customer must be mandatory before he can proceed to purchase the lenses (see, to that effect, as regards the selling of medicinal products via the Internet, *Deutscher Apothekerverband*, paragraph 114).

70. Second, it is true that the Member State can require – as was stated in paragraph 63 of this judgment – that the determination of which type of contact lenses is the most appropriate should be undertaken by a optician, who is under an obligation, at that time, to check the positioning of the lenses on the customer's eyes and to make available to the customer advice on the correct use and care of the lenses.

71. However, it should be observed that those services are required, as a general rule, only when contact lenses are first supplied. At the time of subsequent supplies, there is, as a general rule, no need to provide the customer with such services. It is sufficient that the customer advise the seller of the type of lenses which were provided when lenses were first supplied, the specifications of those lenses having been adjusted, where necessary, by an ophthalmologist who has issued a new prescription which takes into account any change in the customer's vision.

72. Third, while the extended use of contact lenses must be accompanied by supplementary information and advice, those can be given to the customer by means of the interactive features to be found on the supplier's Internet site.

73. Moreover, the Member State may require the economic operators concerned to make available to the customer a qualified optician whose task is to give to the customer, at a distance, individualised information and advice on the use and care of the contact lenses. The provision of such information and advice at a distance may, moreover, offer advantages, since the lens user is enabled to submit questions which are well thought out and pertinent, and without the need to go out (see, to that effect, as regards the selling of medicinal products via the Internet, *Deutscher Apothekerverband*, paragraph 113).

74. It follows from the foregoing that the objective of ensuring protection of the health of users of contact lenses can be achieved by measures which are less restrictive than those provided for under the legislation at issue in the main proceedings, namely measures which subject to certain restrictions only the first supply of lenses

and which require the economic operators concerned to make available a qualified optician to the customer.

75. Consequently, where a Member State adopts legislation such as that at issue in the main proceedings, it exceeds the limits of the discretion referred to in paragraph 58 of this judgment, and that legislation must therefore be held to go beyond what is necessary to attain the objective the Member State claims to pursue.

76. For the same reasons, since it contains a prohibition on selling contact lenses via the Internet, that legislation cannot be held to be proportionate to the objective of ensuring the protection of public health, for the purposes of Article 3(4) of Directive 2000/31.

77. In the light of the foregoing, the answer to the questions submitted by the referring court is that the national rules relating to the selling of contact lenses fall within the scope of Directive 2000/31 since they concern the act of selling such lenses via the Internet; on the other hand, the national rules relating to the supply of contact lenses are not covered by that directive.

78. Articles 34 TFEU and 36 TFEU, and Directive 2000/31, must be interpreted as precluding national legislation which authorises the selling of contact lenses only in shops which specialise in medical devices.

Costs

[Para. 79 omitted]

On those grounds,

THE COURT (Third Chamber),

hereby rules:

1) **The national rules relating to the selling of contact lenses fall within the scope of Directive 2000/31/EC of the European Parliament and the Council of 8 June 2000 on certain legal aspects of information society services, in particular electronic commerce, in the Internal market ('Directive on electronic commerce'), since they concern the act of selling such lenses via the Internet. On the other hand, the national rules relating to the supply of contact lenses are not covered by that directive.**

2) **Articles 34 TFEU and 36 TFEU, and Directive 2000/31, must be interpreted as precluding national legislation which authorises the selling of contact lenses only in shops which specialise in medical devices.**

Comments and questions

Ker-Optika was an undertaking that sold contact lenses via the internet. However the Hungarian authorities prohibited such sales on the grounds that they constituted a threat to public health. Ker-Optika sought to have this prohibition overturned by a Hungarian court, arguing that it was contrary to Union law. The Hungarian court referred this question to the CJEU.

Before the CJEU could decide on the question referred, it had first to determine which rules applied. The area in question was governed by a directive. In Union law, where there has been exhaustive harmonisation at Union level of the law governing an area, the harmonising provisions (secondary Union legislation) apply instead of the TFEU (primary Union legislation). However, this does not mean that the TFEU is redundant. When the Member States implement the harmonisation rules of a directive they must comply with the Treaty rules. Thus, even though the area of sales via the internet was harmonised, it was relevant to examine whether the Hungarian prohibition was compatible with Articles 34 and 36 TFEU. As long as an area has not been subject to full harmonisation, Article 36 TFEU still applies.

The CJEU then went on to examine whether the Hungarian prohibition constituted a measure having equivalent effect to a prohibition. In connection with this, in paragraphs 47-51 of its judgment, the CJEU made a 'pedagogic review' of the situation. First the CJEU repeated the well established definition from the *Dassonville* case, according to which: 'all trading rules enacted by Member States which are capable of hindering, directly or indirectly, actually or potentially, trade within the European Union are to be considered as measures having an effect equivalent to quantitative restrictions and are, on that basis, prohibited by Article 34 TFEU' (paragraph 47). Thereafter the CJEU noted that Article 34 TFEU reflects the obligation to comply with the principles of non-discrimination and mutual recognition of products lawfully manufactured and marketed in other Member States, as well as the principle of ensuring free access of EU products to national markets. From this it follows that measures adopted by a Member State, the object or effect of which is to treat products coming from other Member States less favourably, are to be regarded as measures having an effect equivalent to quantitative restrictions. The same applies to rules that lay down requirements to be met by such goods, even if those rules apply to all products alike. Likewise, any other measure which hinders access of products originating in other Member States to the market of a Member State is also covered by the same concept. Thus, national provisions that limit or prohibit certain selling arrangements hinder, directly or indirectly, actually or potentially, trade between Member States under the doctrine laid down in the *Dassonville* case. However, the CJEU added that this does not apply if the national provisions fulfil two criteria laid down in the *Keck* case:

> *First*, whether the provisions apply to all relevant traders operating within the national territory (the universality condition); and

> *Second*, whether the provisions affect in the same manner, in law and in fact, the selling of domestic products and the selling of those from other Member States (the neutrality condition).

The first condition was unquestionably satisfied (see paragraph 53). However, the second condition was not satisfied. According to the CJEU, while the prohibition of internet selling applied to Hungarian sellers of contact lenses as well as to others, it had a significantly different effect as in practice it prevented foreign undertakings from selling to Hungarian customers. It is presumably implicit that Hungarian undertakings will still have the possibility of selling via their physical shops. This meant that the second condition was not fulfilled.

The Hungarian prohibition of internet sales of contact lenses thus meant that a citizen situated in Hungary who wanted to buy some specific contact lenses could not buy the lenses via the internet from Ker-Optika, but instead had to buy them from the local optician. Regardless of whether the lenses were bought via the internet or from the local optician, the lenses would be the same product, produced in the same factory. Thus the different treatment did not concern the origin of the product, but who supplied it. Why was this hindrance covered by Article 34 TFEU?

Having established that the Hungarian prohibition of the sale of contact lenses constituted a hindrance contrary to Article 34 TFEU, the CJEU considered whether the prohibition could be justified out of regard for the protection of health and life of humans, as expressly referred to in Article 36 TFEU. The CJEU ruled first, that the Hungarian prohibition was appropriate for achieving the aim of ensuring the protection of the health of users. However, the Hungarian rule should not go beyond what was necessary for achieving the lawful aim; i.e. there must not be other appropriate measures for achieving the aim that caused less hindrance to the free movement of goods. Following a very thorough review of this question, the CJEU concluded that the aim of protecting the health of users of contact lenses could be achieved by measures that were less intrusive than those pursuant to the legislation at issue. The Hungarian legislation thus meant that Hungary had exceeded the limits of the discretion allowed Member States by adopting rules such as those in the case. In other words, the Hungarian prohibition was contrary to Union law.

Consider the extent to which the CJEU's decision actually was a decision on the case which had been brought before the Hungarian court and which was the basis for the reference for a preliminary ruling.

JUDGMENT OF THE COURT (Grand Chamber)
10 February 2009

Commission of the European Communities v Italian Republic

'Failure of a Member State to fulfil obligations – Article 28 EC – Concept of 'measures having equivalent effect to quantitative restrictions on imports' – Prohibition on mopeds, motorcycles, motor tricycles and quadricycles towing a trailer in the territory of a Member State – Road safety – Market access – Obstacle – Proportionality'

Case C-110/05

Judgment

1. In its application, the Commission of the European Communities asks the Court to find that, by maintaining rules which prohibit mopeds, motorcycles, tricycles and quadricycles ('motoveicoli', hereinafter 'motorcycles') from towing a trailer, the Italian Republic has failed to fulfil its obligations under Article 28 EC.

Legal context

Community rules

2. Council Directive 92/61/EEC of 30 June 1992 relating to the type-approval of two or three-wheel motor vehicles (OJ 1992 L 225, p. 72) laid down uniform definitions and the procedure for granting Community type-approval or component type-approval in respect of certain types of vehicle covered by the directive. Article 1(1) and (2) thereof provide as follows:

'1. This Directive applies to all two or three-wheel motor vehicles, twin-wheeled or otherwise, intended to travel on the road, and to the components or separate technical units of such vehicles.

...

2. The vehicles referred to in paragraph 1 shall be subdivided into:
   - moped[s], i.e. two or three-wheel vehicles fitted with an engine having a cylinder capacity not exceeding 50 cm^3 if of the internal combustion type and a maximum design speed of not more than 45 km/h,
   - motorcycles, i.e. two-wheel vehicles with or without sidecar, fitted with an engine having a cylinder capacity of more than 50 cm^3 if of the internal combustion type and/or having a maximum design speed of more than 45 km/h,

- motor tricycles, i.e. vehicles with three symmetrically arranged wheels fitted with an engine having a cylinder capacity of more than 50 cm^3 if of the internal combustion type and/or a maximum design speed of more than 45 km/h.'

3. It is apparent from Article 1(3) that Directive 92/61 also applied to motor vehicles with four wheels, namely 'quadricycles', which were to be considered to be mopeds or motor tricycles depending on their technical characteristics.

4. The sixth recital in Council Directive 93/93/EEC of 29 October 1993 on the masses and dimensions of two or three-wheel motor vehicles (OJ 1993 L 311, p. 76), which is intended to harmonise imperative technical requirements in order to enable the type-approval and component type-approval procedures laid down in Directive 92/61 to be applied, states the following:
'Whereas the provisions of this Directive should not oblige those Member States which do not allow two-wheel motor vehicles on their territory to tow a trailer to amend their rules'.

5. The purpose of Directive 97/24/EC of the European Parliament and of the Council of 17 June 1997 on certain components and characteristics of two or three-wheel motor vehicles (OJ 1997 L 226, p. 1) is to further harmonise certain technical requirements of such vehicles, including coupling devices and attachments. The 12th recital in this directive states as follows:
'Whereas ... the object of the requirements of this Directive should not be to oblige those Member States which do not allow two or three-wheel motor vehicles in their territory to tow a trailer to amend their rules'.

National legislation

6. In Italy, Article 53 of Legislative Decree No 285 of 30 April 1992 (GURI, ordinary supplement, No 114 of 18 May 1992, 'the Highway Code') defines motorcycles as motor vehicles with two, three or four wheels. Only four-wheeled vehicles may be called 'motor quadricycles'.

7. Pursuant to Article 54 of the Highway Code, automobiles ('autoveicoli') are motor vehicles with at least four wheels, excluding the vehicles defined in Article 53 of the Code.

8. Pursuant to Article 56 of the Highway Code, only automobiles, trolleybuses (vehicles with an electric motor not travelling on rails which take their energy from an overhead contact line) and automobile tractors (three wheeled motor vehicles intended to tow semi-trailers) are allowed to tow trailers.

II – The pre-litigation procedure

9. As a result of a complaint lodged by an individual concerning the Italian Republic and an informal inquiry by the Commission, the latter, on 3 April 2003, sent a formal notice to the Member State in which it argued that the prohibition on motorcycles towing trailers constituted a failure to fulfil obligations under Article 28 EC.

10. In a letter of 13 June 2003, the Italian Republic gave a commitment to make the requisite changes to the national rules and to remove the obstacle to imports raised in the formal notice mentioned above.

11. Since it received no further communication concerning the making of such changes, the Commission, on 19 December 2003, sent a reasoned opinion to the Italian Republic calling on it to submit its observations within a period of two months as from receipt of that notice.

12. Having received no reply to that notice, the Commission decided to institute the present proceedings.

Procedure before the Court

13. By decision of 11 July 2006, the Court assigned the case to the Third Chamber. Since none of the parties applied to submit oral arguments, the Court decided to rule without holding a hearing. Advocate General Léger delivered his Opinion on 5 October 2006, after which the oral procedure was closed.

14. Pursuant to Article 44(4) of the Rules of Procedure, the Third Chamber, on 9 November 2006, decided to refer the case back to the Court in order that it might be reassigned to a formation composed of a greater number of judges.

15. By order of 7 March 2007, the Court ordered the re-opening of the oral procedure and the holding of a hearing. The parties to the case and, pursuant to the second paragraph of Article 24 of the Statute of the Court of Justice, the Member States other than the Italian Republic were invited to answer the question of the extent to which and the conditions under which national provisions which govern not the characteristics of goods but their use, and which apply without distinction to domestic and imported goods, are to be regarded as measures having equivalent effect to quantitative restrictions on imports within the meaning of Article 28 EC.

The action

Observations submitted on the Court's question

16. The parties to the case as well as the Czech Republic, the Kingdom of Denmark, the Federal Republic of Germany, the Hellenic Republic, the French Republic, the Republic of Cyprus, the Kingdom of the Netherlands and the Kingdom of Sweden submitted written or oral observations to the Court on the question.

17. In the Commission's view, it is possible to identify two categories of rules concerning the use of a product, namely, first, those which make use of the product subject to compliance with certain conditions specific to the product or which limit that use in space or time and, second, those which lay down absolute, or almost absolute, prohibitions of the use of the product.

18. The Commission proposes to apply to the first category of rules the criteria set out in paragraph 5 of the judgment in Case 8/74 *Dassonville* [1974] ECR 837 and to consider each case separately. With regard to the second category of rules, once they impose an absolute prohibition on the use of a certain product or a prohibition which permits only limited or exceptional use of it, they constitute, by definition, measures having equivalent effect to quantitative restrictions on imports within the meaning of Article 28 EC. The Commission considers that it is neither appropriate nor necessary to extend the criteria set out in paragraphs 16 and 17 of the judgment in Joined Cases C-267/91 and C-268/91 *Keck and Mithouard* [1993] ECR I-6097 to rules concerning the use of a product and thereby create an additional category of measures which are not within the scope of Article 28 EC.

19. The Italian Republic argues that a rule concerning use is covered by Article 28 EC only if it prohibits all uses of a product or its only use, if the product only has one. On the other hand, if there is a discretion as to the possible uses of the product, the situation no longer falls under Article 28 EC.

20. The Czech Republic argues that it is inappropriate to draw rigid distinctions between different categories of measures and to apply different legal criteria depending on the category into which they fall because the introduction of any new category of measures inevitably implies difficulties in regard to its definition.

21. Like the Commission, that Member State points out that the criteria introduced by *Keck and Mithouard*, for selling arrangements for products should not be extended to rules concerning the use of products because the application of those criteria has not been without difficulty in the Court's case-law and they have not really been necessary. Indeed, the provisions declared to govern selling arrangements could have been defended by the national authorities even in the absence of the criteria laid down in that judgment.

22. On the other hand, the Kingdom of Denmark, the Federal Republic of Germany, the Hellenic Republic, the French Republic, the Republic of Cyprus and the Kingdom of Sweden consider that the case-law commencing with *Keck and Mithouard*, should be applied by analogy to a national provision which restricts or prohibits certain forms of use of a product. They therefore propose that a national provision should not fall under Article 28 EC in so far as it is not connected with the product, it applies to all economic operators concerned who pursue their activities in the national territory and it affects in the same manner, in law and in fact, national products and those coming from other Member States.

23. By contrast, those same Member States point out that a derogation from those criteria would be necessary if it was established that restrictive national provisions simply prohibited the use of a particular product or permitted only a limited use thereof, thereby restricting its access to the market.

24. In the view of the Kingdom of Denmark, it is important to note that national rules which limit the freedom of action of an individual or an undertaking in regard to a particular product are not all prohibited. With regard to the criterion that a national rule may not prevent a product's access to the market, it considers that it is difficult to determine from what point a restriction on the use of a product may be regarded as so restrictive that it hinders such access. It is of the opinion that it is for the national courts to decide to what extent the person who challenges such a rule has established that access to the market has been hindered by the application thereof.

25. The Federal Republic of Germany considers that rules concerning the use of a product constitute the other side of those concerning selling arrangements in the sense that some of the forms of use may be regarded as selling arrangements and vice versa. In it's view, the principles flowing from *Keck and Mithouard*, should apply in the same fashion to rules concerning the use of a product in so far as those rules do not involve discrimination, ensure equal opportunity in regard to competition between products manufactured in the Member State having laid down such rules and those coming from other Member States and not hinder, completely or almost completely, access to the market of the said Member State for those products.

26. The Hellenic Republic considers that the use of a product is not, in itself, apt to hinder intra-Community trade. If, however, use is a relevant factor inherent in placing the product in circulation, a matter which must be considered in each individual case, the obstacle to its use would fall within the scope of Article 28 EC.

27. The French Republic considers that national rules concerning the use of a product and those concerning selling arrangements for that product are comparable in regard to both the nature and the degree of their effect on intra-Community trade inasmuch as those rules give rise to effects, in principle, only after the importation of

the product and by way of consumer behaviour. The same criteria must therefore apply to both types of provision.

28. The Republic of Cyprus, although sharing the reserves expressed by other Member States concerning the introduction of a new, essentially economic, criterion, argues that if the case-law flowing from *Keck and Mithouard*, is not extended to measures governing the use of a product, any measure concerning use could be assimilated to a prohibition under the rule laid down in *Dassonville*. In it's view, the Court's analysis should concentrate on the question whether the measure at issue is likely to preclude, in whole or in part, access of goods to the national market.

29. The Kingdom of Sweden considers that a national measure which prohibits a form of use of a product comes within the scope of Article 28 EC if the measure is drawn up in such a way as to prevent, in practice, the product's access to the market.

30. The Kingdom of the Netherlands argues that national measures must be examined first in regard to the question whether their repercussions on the free movement of goods are not too uncertain and too indirect. In other words, it must be asked whether there is a causal link between the measures and the effect on intra-Community trade. Many rules concerning the use of a product could be upheld under this first test, which constitutes a filter permitting them to avoid the scope of Article 28 EC.

31. With regard to the extension of the case-law commencing with *Keck and Mithouard*, to rules concerning the use of a product, the Kingdom of the Netherlands puts forward arguments both for and against such an extension. On the positive side, such an approach would first of all allow all rules intended to protect interests of a non-economic nature to fall outside the scope of Article 28 EC. Secondly, such an approach would follow the Court's earlier case-law and permit the national courts to make a reasonably abstract application which would increase legal certainty and promote consistency in the case-law. Finally, it would prevent misuse of the exception flowing from *Keck and Mithouard* in the case of rules which lead to a prohibition of the use of a product or permit it only to a limited extent.

32. With regard to arguments against extension of the said case-law to rules concerning the use of a product, it considers, first, that it is difficult to define forms of use of a product clearly as a category. It also considers that a new category of exceptions could create confusion for the national courts because different criteria apply depending on the category into which a given provision falls. Finally, it argues that there are still exceptions among rules concerning the use of a product, namely the cases in which a measure fulfils the criteria for the exception even though it will have serious repercussions on trade between the Member States.

Preliminary observations

33. It should be recalled that, according to settled case-law, all trading rules enacted by Member States which are capable of hindering, directly or indirectly, actually or potentially, intra-Community trade are to be considered as measures having an effect equivalent to quantitative restrictions and are, on that basis, prohibited by Article 28 EC (see, in particular, *Dassonville*, paragraph 5).

34. It is also apparent from settled case-law that Article 28 EC reflects the obligation to respect the principles of non-discrimination and of mutual recognition of products lawfully manufactured and marketed in other Member States, as well as the principle of ensuring free access of Community products to national markets (see, to that effect, Case 174/82 *Sandoz* [1983] ECR 2445, paragraph 26; Case 120/78 *Rewe-Zentral* ('*Cassis de Dijon*') [1979] ECR 649, paragraphs 6, 14 and 15; and *Keck and Mithouard*, paragraphs 16 and 17).

35. Hence, in the absence of harmonisation of national legislation, obstacles to the free movement of goods which are the consequence of applying, to goods coming from other Member States where they are lawfully manufactured and marketed, rules that lay down requirements to be met by such goods constitute measures of equivalent effect to quantitative restrictions even if those rules apply to all products alike (see, to that effect, '*Cassis de Dijon*', paragraphs 6, 14 and 15; Case C-368/95 *Familiapress* [1997] ECR I-3689, paragraph 8; and Case C-322/01 *Deutscher Apothekerverband* [2003] ECR I-14887, paragraph 67).

36. By contrast, the application to products from other Member States of national provisions restricting or prohibiting certain selling arrangements is not such as to hinder directly or indirectly, actually or potentially, trade between Member States for the purposes of the case-law flowing from *Dassonville*, on condition that those provisions apply to all relevant traders operating within the national territory and that they affect in the same manner, in law and in fact, the marketing of domestic products and of those from other Member States. Provided that those conditions are fulfilled, the application of such rules to the sale of products from another Member State meeting the requirements laid down by that State is not by nature such as to prevent their access to the market or to impede access any more than it impedes the access of domestic products (see *Keck and Mithouard*, paragraphs 16 and 17).

37. Consequently, measures adopted by a Member State the object or effect of which is to treat products coming from other Member States less favourably are to be regarded as measures having equivalent effect to quantitative restrictions on imports within the meaning of Article 28 EC, as are the measures referred to in paragraph 35 of the present judgment. Any other measure which hinders access of products originating in other Member States to the market of a Member State is also covered by that concept.

The failure to fulfil obligations

38. The Commission's complaints concerning Article 56 of the Highway Code must be considered in the light of the principles set out in paragraphs 33 to 37 of the present judgment.

Arguments of the parties

39. In support of its action, the Commission claims that the effect of the prohibition laid down in Article 56 of the Highway Code is to prevent the use of trailers lawfully produced and marketed in the Member States where there is no such prohibition and to hinder their importation into, and sale in, Italy.

40. Therefore, that prohibition constitutes, in the Commission's view, an obstacle to imports within the meaning of Article 28 EC and may be regarded as compatible with the EC Treaty only if justified under Article 30 EC or by an overriding reason relating to the public interest. However, the Italian Republic put forward no justification nor any overriding reason relating to the public interest during the pre-litigation procedure. On the contrary, the Member State admitted the existence of the prohibition and the obstacle to imports which flowed from it and undertook to remove it.

41. The Italian Republic points out, in regard to the alleged obstacle to imports, that the infringement complained of refers to a prohibition on motorcycles registered in Italy towing a trailer and not the refusal to register such a vehicle or a trailer manufactured in another Member State and intended to be marketed in Italy. It considers that the Commission is confusing the legal conditions for circulation, in Italy, of a vehicle specifically type-approved in another Member State or in a non-member country with the marketing of the same vehicle in Italy.

42. The Italian Republic also contends that the Commission's conclusion is based on an erroneous premise. Article 56 of the Highway Code is a means of exercising a power of derogation expressly granted to the Member States in the sixth recital in Directive 93/93. Until there has been harmonisation at Community level both of the technical requirements for type-approval of trailers and the rules concerning registration and circulation of them on the road, mutual recognition of such trailers remains at the discretion of the Member States.

43. In its reply, the Commission submits that the recitals in a directive are not binding and that it is neither the purpose nor the effect of the sixth recital in Directive 93/93 to declare compatible with Community law national provisions such as those in Article 56 of the Highway Code. That recital determines the scope of Directive 93/93 by excluding therefrom rules concerning trailers intended to be towed by two-wheeled vehicles, without stating whether or not any prohibition which might be

laid down is compatible with the rules in the Treaty. The Commission also draws attention to the principle of the primacy of the provisions of the Treaty over secondary legislation, which the Court has recognised on several occasions.

44. In addition, the Commission observes that the absence of harmonised rules in no way justifies the infringement of a fundamental freedom guaranteed by the Treaty.

45. In its rejoinder, the Italian Republic contends that, given the possibilities for using motorcycles and trailers, which may be used separately, those products cannot be regarded as the subject of quantitative restrictions on imports within the meaning of Article 28 EC.

46. Moreover, the prohibition at issue affects only the product as such, irrespective of the place of production and the nationality of the manufacturer, and does not therefore constitute a means of protecting Italian products or rules which discriminate against products manufactured in the other Member States. In Italy, no motorcycle can obtain type-approval to tow a trailer and no trailer to be towed by a motorcycle. Since the consequence of the prohibition on using such vehicles and trailers together is that Italian undertakings have no interest in manufacturing motorcycles equipped to tow trailers or trailers intended solely to be towed by such vehicles, the effect of the prohibition is to exclude products with such characteristics from the Italian market.

47. The Italian Republic refers to the Convention on Road Traffic, concluded in Vienna on 8 November 1968, which provides, in point 3(a) of Annex I thereto, that 'Contracting Parties may refuse to admit to their territories in international traffic the following combinations of vehicles in so far as the use of such combinations is prohibited by their domestic legislations: ... Motor cycles with trailers'. However, it makes clear that it did not avail itself of that possibility and that motorcycles that are registered in other Member States are allowed to tow a trailer in Italian territory since they are considered to be in international traffic within the meaning of the said Convention.

48. The Italian Republic also refers to the 12th recital in Directive 97/24, which has essentially the same content as the 6th recital in Directive 93/93. It points out that the reservation granted to the Member States in that recital corresponds to the fact that, by reason of the different contours of the national territories, the technical characteristics of vehicles are important from the point of view of road safety. In the Member State's view, in the absence of rules for type-approval of the two products used together (towing vehicle and trailer), there are no safety conditions necessary for road traffic.

Findings of the Court

49. In order to assess whether the Commission's complaint is well founded, it should be pointed out that, although Article 56 of the Highway Code concerns a prohibition on using a motorcycle and a trailer together in Italy, the national provision must be considered, in particular, from the angle of the restriction that it could represent for free movement of trailers. Although it is not disputed that motorcycles can easily be used without a trailer, the fact remains that the latter is of little use without a motor vehicle that may tow it.

50. It is common ground that Article 56 of the Highway Code applies without regard to the origin of trailers.

51. The Commission has not specified whether its action concerns solely trailers which are specially designed for motorcycles or if it also covers other types of trailers. Those two types of trailers must therefore be distinguished when assessing the alleged failure to fulfil obligations.

52. With regard, first, to trailers not specially designed for motorcycles but intended to be towed by automobiles or other types of vehicle, it should be noted that the Commission has not established that the prohibition laid down in Article 56 of the Highway Code hinders access to the market for that type of trailer.

53. The Commission's action must therefore be dismissed in so far as it concerns trailers which are not specially designed to be towed by motorcycles and are legally produced and marketed in Member States other than the Italian Republic.

54. Secondly, the failure to fulfil obligations alleged by the Commission in regard to trailers which are specially designed to be towed by motorcycles and are legally produced and marketed in Member States other than the Italian Republic remains to be examined.

55. In its reply to the Court's written question, the Commission claimed, without being contradicted by the Italian Republic, that, in the case of trailers specially designed for motorcycles, the possibilities for their use other than with motorcycles are very limited. It considers that, although it is not inconceivable that they could, in certain circumstances, be towed by other vehicles, in particular, by automobiles, such use is inappropriate and remains at least insignificant, if not hypothetical.

56. It should be noted in that regard that a prohibition on the use of a product in the territory of a Member State has a considerable influence on the behaviour of consumers, which, in its turn, affects the access of that product to the market of that Member State.

57. Consumers, knowing that they are not permitted to use their motorcycle with a trailer specially designed for it, have practically no interest in buying such a trailer (see, by analogy, Case C-265/06 *Commission* v *Portugal* [2008] ECR I-0000, paragraph 33, concerning the affixing of tinted film to the windows of motor vehicles). Thus, Article 56 of the Highway Code prevents a demand from existing in the market at issue for such trailers and therefore hinders their importation.

58. It follows that the prohibition laid down in Article 56 of the Highway Code, to the extent that its effect is to hinder access to the Italian market for trailers which are specially designed for motorcycles and are lawfully produced and marketed in Member States other than the Italian Republic, constitutes a measure having equivalent effect to quantitative restrictions on imports within the meaning of Article 28 EC, unless it can be justified objectively.

59. Such a prohibition may be justified on one of the public interest grounds set out in Article 30 EC or in order to meet imperative requirements (see, in particular Case C-420/01 *Commission* v *Italy* [2003] ECR I-6445, paragraph 29, and Case C-270/02 *Commission* v *Italy* [2004] ECR I-1559, paragraph 21). In either case, the national provision must be appropriate for securing the attainment of the objective pursued and not go beyond what is necessary in order to attain it (Case C-54/05 *Commission* v *Finland* [2007] ECR I-2473, paragraph 38, and Case C-297/05 *Commission* v *Netherlands* [2007] ECR I-7467, paragraph 75).

60. In the present case, the justification put forward by the Italian Republic relates to the need to ensure road safety, which, according to the case-law, constitutes an overriding reason relating to the public interest capable of justifying a hindrance to the free movement of goods (see, in particular, Case C-55/93 *van Schaik* [1994] ECR I-4837, paragraph 19; Case C-314/98 *Snellers* [2000] ECR I-8633, paragraph 55; *Commission* v *Finland*, paragraph 40, *Commission* v *Netherlands*, paragraph 77, *Commission* v *Portugal*, paragraph 38; and C-170/07 *Commission* v *Poland* [2008] ECR I-0000, paragraph 49).

61. In the absence of fully harmonising provisions at Community level, it is for the Member States to decide upon the level at which they wish to ensure road safety in their territory, whilst taking account of the requirements of the free movement of goods within the European Community (see, to that effect, Case 50/83 *Commission* v *Italy* [1984] ECR 1633, paragraph 12, and, by analogy, Case C-131/93 *Commission* v *Germany* [1994] ECR I-3303, paragraph 16).

62. According to settled case-law, it is for the competent national authorities to show that their rules fulfil the criteria set out in paragraph 59 of the present judgment (see, to that effect, *Commission* v *Netherlands*, paragraph 76, *Commission* v *Portugal*, paragraph 39, and Case C-286/07 *Commission* v *Luxembourg* [2008] ECR I-0000, paragraph 37).

63. With regard, first, to whether the prohibition laid down in Article 56 of the Highway Code is appropriate, the Italian Republic contends that it introduced the measure because there were no type-approval rules, whether at Community level or national level, to ensure that use of a motorcycle with a trailer was not dangerous. In the absence of such a prohibition, circulation of a combination composed of a motorcycle and an unapproved trailer could be dangerous both for the driver of the vehicle and for other vehicles on the road, because the stability of the combination and its braking capacity would be affected.

64. In that regard, it must be held that the prohibition in question is appropriate for the purpose of ensuring road safety.

65. With regard, second, to whether the said prohibition is necessary, account must be taken of the fact that, in accordance with the case-law of the Court referred to in paragraph 61 of the present judgment, in the field of road safety a Member State may determine the degree of protection which it wishes to apply in regard to such safety and the way in which that degree of protection is to be achieved. Since that degree of protection may vary from one Member State to the other, Member States must be allowed a margin of appreciation and, consequently, the fact that one Member State imposes less strict rules than another Member State does not mean that the latter's rules are disproportionate (see, by analogy, Case C-262/02 *Commission* v *France* [2004] ECR I-6569, paragraph 37, and Case C-141/07 *Commission* v *Germany* [2008] ECR I-0000, paragraph 51).

66. In the present case, the Italian Republic contends, without being contradicted on this point by the Commission, that the circulation of a combination composed of a motorcycle and a trailer is a danger to road safety. Whilst it is true that it is for a Member State which invokes an imperative requirement as justification for the hindrance to free movement of goods to demonstrate that its rules are appropriate and necessary to attain the legitimate objective being pursued, that burden of proof cannot be so extensive as to require the Member State to prove, positively, that no other conceivable measure could enable that objective to be attained under the same conditions (see, by analogy, Case C-157/94 *Commission* v *Netherlands* [1997] ECR I-5699, paragraph 58).

67. Although it is possible, in the present case, to envisage that measures other than the prohibition laid down in Article 56 of the Highway Code could guarantee a certain level of road safety for the circulation of a combination composed of a motorcycle and a trailer, such as those mentioned in point 170 of the Advocate General's Opinion, the fact remains that Member States cannot be denied the possibility of attaining an objective such as road safety by the introduction of general and simple rules which will be easily understood and applied by drivers and easily managed and supervised by the competent authorities.

68. Moreover, it should be noted that neither the terms of the International Convention on Road Traffic nor those of the recitals in Directives 93/93 and 97/24, referred to by the Italian Republic, allow the presumption that road safety could be ensured at the same level as envisaged by the Italian Republic by a partial prohibition of the circulation of such a combination or by a road traffic authorisation issued subject to compliance with certain conditions.

69. In the light of those factors, it must be held that the prohibition on motorcycles towing trailers specially designed for them and lawfully produced and marketed in Member States other than the Italian Republic must be regarded as justified by reasons relating to the protection of road safety.

70. The Commission's action must therefore be dismissed.

Costs

[Para. 71 omitted]

On those grounds, the Court (Grand Chamber) hereby:

1. Dismisses the action;

[Para. 2 of the ruling omitted]

Comments and questions

The *Italian motorcycle trailer* case concern the question of whether a Member State's prohibition of the use of a certain good was covered by the concept of restrictions on imports in Article 34 TFEU (formerly Article 28 TEC), or whether such a prohibition falls outside the scope of Article 34 TFEU in the same way as national rules on 'certain selling arrangements' that fulfil the criteria laid down in the *Keck and Mithouard* case discussed above. As set out in the judgment, the Italian road traffic law prohibits motorcycles from pulling trailers.

Before the CJEU decided on the question of whether the rule in the Italian road traffic law constituted a breach of the TFEU, it made some important comments on when there would be considered to be measures having equivalent effect to quantitative restrictions within the meaning of Article 34 TFEU. Having reviewed its decisions in the *Dassonville, Cassis de Dijon* and *Keck and Mithouard* cases in paragraphs 33-36, in paragraph 37 the CJEU stated that there would be a prohibited restriction on trade pursuant to Article 34 TFEU if a Member State frames its national laws etc. in such a way as to be covered by one or more of the following three criteria:

1. The legislation etc. has the object of treating products coming from other Member States less favourably than domestic products, or it has this effect even if this is not intended (direct or indirect discrimination).
2. The legislation etc. sets aside the principle of reciprocity, i.e. the principle that a product must be allowed to be sold in a Member State if that product is lawfully produced and sold in other Member States.
3. The legislation etc. restricts access to the market in a Member State for goods from other Member States.

What is notable is that, by laying down the third criterion, the CJEU ruled for the first time that the general criterion on 'access to the market' applies to restrictions on trade covered by Article 34 TFEU. Hitherto, the CJEU had only used the criterion on access to the market as a negative criterion in cases on sales conditions in relation to Article 34 TFEU, so that if a national measure fulfil the conditions of the *Keck* doctrine, then according to the view of the CJEU this would not restrict access to the market for the imported goods and such a measure would not fall foul of Article 34 TFEU. On the other hand the CJEU has used the market access criterion as a general criterion in relation to the assessment of whether national legislation etc. constitutes an obstacle under the other rights of free movement in the TFEU, in Article 45 TFEU on the free movement of workers, Article 49 TFEU on the right of establishment, Article 56 TFEU on the freedom to provide services, and Article 63 TFEU on the free movement of capital. By introducing the market access criterion as a general criterion under Article 34 TFEU, the CJEU followed the Opinion of the Advocate General, that any judicial review of national rules under Article 34 TFEU should be based on the market access criterion (point 108 et seq. of the Advocate General's Opinion).

The CJEU then considered the specific question of breach of the TFEU. It found, first, that the disputed provision in the Italian road traffic law applied without discrimination, regardless of the origin of the trailer. It then found that, with regard to trailers not specially designed for motorcycles but intended to be towed by cars and other types of vehicle, it had not established that the prohibition restricted access to the market for 'that type of trailer'. Italy was thus not found to be in breach of the TFEU on that point. The CJEU then found that there was a restriction on trade under the market access criterion in relation to trailers specially designed to be towed by motorcycles and legally produced and marketed in other Member States; see paragraphs 56-58 of the judgment. Thus, in the view of the CJEU the prohibition of use is a restriction on trade pursuant to Article 34 TFEU, and thus a breach of the TFEU, unless a Member State can rely on one of the grounds referred to in Article 36 TFEU (formerly Article 30 TEC), or other compelling considerations. In either case the national measure must satisfy the requirements of proportionality; see paragraph 59.

After having found that the Italian rule was justified by regard for road safety, and appropriate for that purpose (see paragraphs 60-64), the CJEU turned to the question of whether the prohibition was necessary. What did the CJEU decide in this connection on a Member State's right to determine for itself the level of road safety in its territory? What did the CJEU rule on the burden of proof for a Member State to show that a national measure is necessary for satisfying an imperative requirement (see paragraph 66)?

This decision clearly established that a non-discriminatory **prohibition of the use** of a specific product that is lawfully produced and sold in other Member States is covered by the concept of a restriction of trade in Article 34 TFEU. Such a prohibition affects a product's 'access to the market' in the Member State in question. There is an illustrative example of this in Case C-265/06 *Commission* v *Portugal* [2008] ECR I-2245, where the Commission brought Portugal before the CJEU, because Portugal had prohibited the affixing of tinted film to car windows. The CJEU found that this prohibition affected the sale of nearly all tinted film which was lawfully produced and sold in other Member States with a view to it being affixed to car windows. Portugal argued that the prohibition was intended to promote the fight against crime and road safety. The CJEU acknowledged that the prohibition could contribute to these lawful purposes, but it also found that the measure was excessive in relation to its purpose. Portugal was thus found to have infringed Article 34 TFEU.

Even though it is clear that a non-discriminatory prohibition of the use of a particular product that is lawfully produced and sold in other Member States is covered by the concept of a restriction of trade in Article 34 TFEU, the judgment in the *Italian Motorcycle trailer* case did not consider whether a non-discriminatory **regulation of use**, that does not amount to an actual prohibition of use, should also be considered as being covered by the concept of a restriction on trade. However, this question was referred to the CJEU in the Swedish *Jet-ski* case (Case C-142/05 *Åklagaren* v *Mickelsson and Roos* [2009] ECR I-4273). In contrast to the *Italian Motorcycle trailer* case, in the Swedish *Jet-ski* case there was not a prohibition of the use of the product (jet-skis), merely that the use of jet-skis was only allowed within certain defined areas. There was thus only a **restriction on use**. The CJEU stated that a significant restriction on the use of a product, such as that in the *Jet-ski* case, could have a material influence on the demand for jet-skis and could therefore affect market access in Sweden. There was thus a measure having an equivalent effect to a quantitative restriction which was thereby covered by Article 34 TFEU. In this connection it is interesting to note that the CJEU applied the new definition of the concept of an obstacle to trade which it laid down in paragraph 37 of the *Italian Motorcycle trailer* case; see paragraph 24 of the Swedish *Jet-ski* case. The Swedish restriction on the use of jet-skis was therefore only permissible if it pursued a lawful purpose and as long as the requirements of the proportionality principle were fulfilled.

Consider whether Denmark would be in breach of its obligations under Article 34 TFEU if the Danish Parliament were to adopt a law prohibiting the driving of goods vehicles with a total weight of more than 7.5 tons carrying specific goods on part of the motorway between the borders to Sweden and Germany respectively (see Case C-28/09 *Commission* v *Austria* [2001] ECR 0000). In this connection, assume that the measure is intended to improve the air quality on this stretch of motorway. Would a rule governing use that sets the speed limit on Danish motorways at 110 kph constitute a measure having equivalent effect according to the CJEU's latest definition of the concept of a restriction on trade, so that the Danish state would be required to justify such a rule?

It must be assumed that the judgment in the *Italian Motorcycle trailer* case is an important precedent, as the CJEU frequently refers to paragraph 34 of the judgment in its subsequent cases on whether a measure constitutes a hindrance to the free movement of goods. See, for example Case C-385/10 *Elenca Srl.* judgment of 18 October 2012, which concerned an Italian requirement that, regardless of whether they were manufactured in Italy or imported, inflatable liners for flues and chimney pipes should carry CE marking pursuant to Italian law, which it would not be possible for imported goods to comply with since there was no corresponding EU harmonised standard. This meant that in practice the Italian requirement hindered the import and sale of such goods even though they were lawfully manufactured and sold in other EU Member States. In paragraph 23 of its judgment, the CJEU stated: 'According to settled case-law, all trading rules enacted by Member States which are capable of hindering, directly or indirectly, actually or potentially, trade within the European Union are to be considered as measures having an effect equivalent to quantitative restrictions and are, on that basis, prohibited by Article 34 TFEU ... the mere fact that an importer might be dissuaded from introducing or marketing the products in question in the Member State concerned constitutes a restriction on the free movement of goods'. What decision do you think the CJEU reached?

JUDGMENT OF THE COURT
26 June 1997

Vereinigte Familiapress Zeitungsverlags- und vertriebs GmbH v Heinrich Bauer Verlag. (Reference to the Court by the Handelsgericht Wien (Austria))

'Measure having equivalent effect – Distribution of periodicals – Prize competitions – National prohibition'

Case C-368/95

Judgment

1. By order of 15 September 1995, received at the Court on 29 November 1995, the Handelsgericht Wien (Commercial Court, Vienna), referred to the Court for a preliminary ruling under Article 177 of the EC Treaty a question on the interpretation of Article 30 of that Treaty.

2. That question was raised in proceedings brought by Vereinigte Familiapress Zeitungsverlags- und vertriebs GmbH ('Familiapress'), an Austrian newspaper publisher, against Heinrich Bauer Verlag, a newspaper publisher established in Germany, for an order that the latter should cease to sell in Austria publications offering readers the chance to take part in games for prizes, in breach of the Gesetz über unlauteren Wettbewerb 1992 (Austrian Law on Unfair Competition; 'the UWG').

3. Heinrich Bauer Verlag publishes the weekly magazine 'Laura' in Germany, which it also distributes in Austria. The 22 February 1995 issue contained a crossword puzzle. Readers sending in the correct solution were entitled to be entered in a draw for two prizes of DM 500. There were two other puzzles in the same issue, for prizes of DM 1 000 and DM 5 000 respectively, which were also to be awarded by drawing lots among the persons sending in the correct answers. The following issues invited readers to play similar games. Each issue indicated that there would be more puzzles the following week.

4. According to the order for reference, that practice is contrary to Austrian law. Paragraph 9a(1)(1) of the UWG contains a general prohibition on offering consumers free gifts linked to the sale of goods or the supply of services. Paragraph 9a(2)(8) of the UWG authorizes prize competitions and draws for which 'the value of the potential individual entries, obtained by dividing the total number of prizes at stake by the number of entry vouchers (lots) distributed, does not exceed 5 schillings and the total value of the prizes competed for does not exceed 300 000 schillings', this, however, was declared inapplicable to the press by an amending law of 1993. Con-

sequently, there has, since then, no longer been any exception to the prohibition on publishers of periodicals inviting consumers to take part in draws.

5. Since there is no provision to the same effect in the German Gesetz gegen den unlauteren Wettbewerb (Law against Unfair Competition), the Handelsgericht Wien took the view that the prohibition of the sale of periodicals under the UWG potentially affected intra-Community trade. It therefore stayed proceedings and referred the following question to the Court for a preliminary ruling:

   'Is Article 30 of the EC Treaty to be interpreted as precluding application of legislation of Member State A prohibiting an undertaking established in Member State B from selling in Member State A a periodical produced in Member State B, where that periodical contains prize puzzle competitions or games which are lawfully organized in Member State B?'

6. Under Article 30 of the Treaty, quantitative restrictions on imports and all measures having equivalent effect are prohibited between Member States.

7. The Court has consistently held that any measure capable of hindering, directly or indirectly, actually or potentially, intra-Community trade constitutes a measure having an effect equivalent to a quantitative restriction (Case 8/74 *Procureur du Roi* v *Dassonville* [1974] ECR 837, paragraph 5).

8. It should also be borne in mind that, in accordance with the case-law beginning with *Cassis de Dijon* (Case 120/78 *Rewe-Zentral* v *Bundesmonopolverwaltung für Branntwein* [1979] ECR 649), in the absence of harmonization of legislation, obstacles to free movement of goods which are the consequence of applying, to goods coming from other Member States where they are lawfully manufactured and marketed, rules that lay down requirements to be met by such goods (such as those relating to designation, form, size, weight, composition, presentation, labelling, packaging) constitute measures of equivalent effect prohibited by Article 30, even if those rules apply without distinction to all products, unless their application can be justified by a public-interest objective taking precedence over the free movement of goods (Joined Cases C-267/91 and C-268/91 *Keck and Mithouard* [1993] ECR I-6097, paragraph 15).

9. By contrast, the application to products from other Member States of national provisions restricting or prohibiting certain selling arrangements is not such as to hinder directly or indirectly, actually or potentially, trade between Member States within the meaning of the *Dassonville* judgment, so long as those provisions apply to all relevant traders operating within the national territory and so long as they affect in the same manner, in law and in fact, the marketing of domestic products and of those from other Member States (*Keck and Mithouard*, paragraph 16).

10. The Austrian Government maintains that the prohibition at issue falls outside Article 30 of the Treaty. In its view, the possibility of offering readers of a periodical the chance to take part in prize competitions is merely a method of promoting sales and hence a selling arrangement within the meaning of the judgment in *Keck and Mithouard*.

11. The Court finds that, even though the relevant national legislation is directed against a method of sales promotion, in this case it bears on the actual content of the products, in so far as the competitions in question form an integral part of the magazine in which they appear. As a result, the national legislation in question as applied to the facts of the case is not concerned with a selling arrangement within the meaning of the judgment in *Keck and Mithouard*.

12. Moreover, since it requires traders established in other Member States to alter the contents of the periodical, the prohibition at issue impairs access of the product concerned to the market of the Member State of importation and consequently hinders free movement of goods. It therefore constitutes in principle a measure having equivalent effect within the meaning of Article 30 of the Treaty.

13. The Austrian Government and the Commission argue, however, that the aim of the national legislation in question is to maintain press diversity, which is capable of constituting an overriding requirement for the purposes of Article 30.

14. They point out that shortly after the Gesetz über die Deregulierung des Wettbewerbs (Law on the Deregulation of Competition) entered into force in Austria in 1992 and liberalized *inter alia* the organization of prize competitions, fierce competition set in between periodicals publishers, as a result of their offering larger and larger gifts, in particular the chance to take part in prize competitions.

15. Fearing that small publishers might not be able to resist that cut-throat competition in the long term, in 1993 the Austrian legislature excluded the press from the application of Paragraph 9a(2)(8) of the UWG which, as mentioned in paragraph 4 of this judgment, authorizes to a certain extent the organization of prize competitions and draws linked to the sale of products or the supply of services.

16. In the explanatory memorandum of the relevant bill, the Austrian Government pointed out in particular that, given the relatively low selling price of periodicals, especially of daily newspapers, there was a risk, in spite of the limits to prizes set by Article 9a(2)(8) of the UWG, that consumers would attach more importance to the chance of winning than to the quality of the publication (explanatory memorandum of the Government bill, *RV* 365 Blg No 18. GP).

17. The Austrian Government and the Commission also point to the very high degree of concentration of the press in Austria. The Austrian Government states that in the

early 1990s the market share of the largest press group was 54.5% in Austria, as compared with only 34.7% in the United Kingdom and 23.9% in Germany.

18. Maintenance of press diversity may constitute an overriding requirement justifying a restriction on free movement of goods. Such diversity helps to safeguard freedom of expression, as protected by Article 10 of the European Convention on Human Rights and Fundamental Freedoms, which is one of the fundamental rights guaranteed by the Community legal order (see Case C-353/89 *Commission* v *Netherlands* [1991] ECR I-4069, paragraph 30, and Case C-148/91 *Vereiniging Veronica Omroep Organisatie* v *Commissariaat voor de Media* [1993] ECR I-487, paragraph 10).

19. However, the Court has also consistently held (*Cassis de Dijon*, cited above; Case C-238/89 *Pall* [1990] ECR I-4827, paragraph 12, and Case C-470/93 *Mars* [1995] ECR I-1923, paragraph 15) that the provisions of national law in question must be proportionate to the objective pursued and that objective must not be capable of being achieved by measures which are less restrictive of intra-Community trade.

20. Admittedly, in Case C-275/92 *Schindler* [1994] ECR I-1039, paragraph 61, concerning freedom to provide services, the Court held that the special features of lotteries justify allowing national authorities a sufficient degree of latitude to determine what is required to protect the players and, more generally, in the light of the specific social and cultural features of each Member State, to maintain order in society, as regards the manner in which lotteries are operated, the size of the stakes and the allocation of the profits they yield. The Court therefore considered that it was for the national authorities to assess not only whether it is necessary to restrict the activities of lotteries but also whether they should be prohibited, provided that those restrictions are not discriminatory.

21. Games such as those at issue in the main proceedings are not, however, comparable to the lotteries the features of which were considered in *Schindler*.

22. The facts on which that judgment was based were concerned exclusively, as the Court expressly pointed out, with large-scale lotteries in respect of which the discretion enjoyed by national authorities was justified because of the high risk of crime or fraud, given the amounts which could be staked and the winnings which could be held out to players (paragraphs 50, 51 and 60).

23. By contrast, such concerns for the maintenance of order in society are not present in this case. The draws in question are organized on a small scale and less is at stake; they do not constitute an economic activity in their own right but are merely one aspect of the editorial content of a magazine; and under Austrian legislation, draws are prohibited only in the press.

24. Furthermore, it is to be noted that where a Member State relies on overriding requirements to justify rules which are likely to obstruct the exercise of free movement of goods, such justification must also be interpreted in the light of the general principles of law and in particular of fundamental rights (see Case C-260/89 *ERT* [1991] ECR I-2925, paragraph 43).

25. Those fundamental rights include freedom of expression, as enshrined in Article 10 of the European Convention for the Protection of Human Rights and Fundamental Freedoms (*ERT*, paragraph 44).

26. A prohibition on selling publications which offer the chance to take part in prize games competitions may detract from freedom of expression. Article 10 of the European Convention for the Protection of Human Rights and Fundamental Freedoms does, however, permit derogations from that freedom for the purposes of maintaining press diversity, in so far as they are prescribed by law and are necessary in a democratic society (see the judgment of the European Court of Human Rights of 24 November 1993 in *Informationsverein Lentia and Others* v *Austria* Series A No 276).

27. In the light of the considerations set out in paragraphs 19 to 26 of this judgment, it must therefore be determined whether a national prohibition such as that in issue in the main proceedings is proportionate to the aim of maintaining press diversity and whether that objective might not be attained by measures less restrictive of both intra-Community trade and freedom of expression.

28. To that end, it should be determined, first, whether newspapers which offer the chance of winning a prize in games, puzzles or competitions are in competition with those small press publishers who are deemed to be unable to offer comparable prizes and whom the contested legislation is intended to protect and, second, whether such a prospect of winning constitutes an incentive to purchase capable of bringing about a shift in demand.

29. It is for the national court to determine whether those conditions are satisfied on the basis of a study of the Austrian press market.

30. In carrying out that study, it will have to define the market for the product in question and to have regard to the market shares of individual publishers or press groups and the trend thereof.

31. Moreover, the national court will also have to assess the extent to which, from the consumer's standpoint, the product concerned can be replaced by papers which do not offer prizes, taking into account all the circumstances which may influence the decision to purchase, such as the presence of advertising on the title page referring to the chance of winning a prize, the likelihood of winning, the value of the prize or

the extent to which winning depends on a test calling for a measure of ingenuity, skill or knowledge.

32. The Belgian and Netherlands Governments consider that the Austrian legislature could have adopted measures less restrictive of free movement of goods than an outright prohibition on the distribution of newspapers which afford the chance of winning a prize, such as blacking out or removing the page on which the prize competition appears in copies intended for Austria or a statement that readers in Austria do not qualify for the chance to win a prize.

33. The documents before the Court suggest that the prohibition in question would not constitute a barrier to the marketing of newspapers where one of the above measures had been taken. If the national court were nevertheless to find that this was the case, the prohibition would be disproportionate.

34. In the light of the foregoing considerations, the answer to be given to the national court's question must be that Article 30 of the EC Treaty is to be interpreted as not precluding application of legislation of a Member State the effect of which is to prohibit the distribution on its territory by an undertaking established in another Member State of a periodical produced in that latter State containing prize puzzles or competitions which are lawfully organized in that State, provided that that prohibition is proportionate to maintenance of press diversity and that that objective cannot be achieved by less restrictive means. This assumes, *inter alia*, that the newspapers offering the chance of winning a prize in games, puzzles or competitions are in competition with small newspaper publishers who are deemed to be unable to offer comparable prizes and the prospect of winning is liable to bring about a shift in demand. Furthermore, the national prohibition must not constitute an obstacle to the marketing of newspapers which, albeit containing prize games, puzzles or competitions, do not give readers residing in the Member State concerned the opportunity to win a prize. It is for the national court to determine whether those conditions are satisfied on the basis of a study of the national press market concerned.

Costs

[Para. 35]

On those grounds,

THE COURT,

in answer to the question referred to it by the Handelsgericht Wien, by order of 15 September 1995, hereby rules:

Article 30 of the EC Treaty is to be interpreted as not precluding application of legislation of a Member State the effect of which is to prohibit the distribution on its territory by an undertaking established in another Member State of a periodical produced in that latter State containing prize puzzles or competitions which are lawfully organized in that State, provided that that prohibition is proportionate to maintenance of press diversity and that that objective cannot be achieved by less restrictive means. This assumes, *inter alia*, that the newspapers offering the chance of winning a prize in games, puzzles or competitions are in competition with small newspaper publishers who are deemed to be unable to offer comparable prizes and the prospect of winning is liable to bring about a shift in demand. Furthermore, the national prohibition must not constitute an obstacle to the marketing of newspapers which, albeit containing prize games, puzzles or competitions, do not give readers residing in the Member State concerned the opportunity to win a prize. It is for the national court to determine whether those conditions are satisfied on the basis of a study of the national press market concerned.

Comments and questions

In paragraph 11 of Case C-368/95 *Vereinigte Familiapress* v *Heinrich Bauer Verlag* [1997] ECR I-3689, the CJEU found that national laws which prohibit readers' competitions in magazines have a bearing on the content of the product, and therefore fall within the scope of Article 34 TFEU (formerly Article 30 EEC Treaty). This means that the *Keck* doctrine does not apply to such cases. The CJEU's reasons for regarding the requirements of the Austrian law as being related to the goods are given in paragraph 12 of the judgment, where it is stated that the law requires publishers to publish a special edition for Austria.

In the *Familiapress* case the Austrian government claimed that the 'maintenance of press diversity' justified a restriction on free movement of goods. The CJEU accepted that such a consideration could justify restrictions, since it can help to safeguard freedom of expression; cf. paragraph 18 of the judgment.

In the view of the CJEU, is freedom of expression a general legal principle, amounting to a fundamental right? How does the CJEU draw freedom of expression into its judgment? What decision should the referring court reach?

In Case C-244/06 *Dynamic Medien Vertrieb* [2008] ECR I-505, a question was referred to the CJEU on the lawfulness of a German prohibition of mail-order sales of DVDs and video cassettes that did not carry a statement that they had been subject to a German assessment of their suitability for young persons. The actual case concerned mail-order sales from the UK to Germany. The DVDs sold did carry certification from the British censorship authorities, stating whether their content was such that it may be viewed only by adolescents aged 15 years or older. It was clear that the German rules were not intended to regulate the trade in goods between the Member States. Among other things, the German government was of the view that the German rules concerned 'certain selling arrangements', in line with the *Keck* doctrine. It pointed out that the rules were applied without discrimination to all goods and that in law and in practice they affected the sales of domestic and imported goods in the same way. Against this, the British government argued that the German rules constituted a measure having equivalent effect to a quantitative restriction, so that the rules in question were covered by the prohibition in Article 34 TFEU. Do you think the CJEU found that the German rules were covered by the *Keck* doctrine or that they were covered by the prohibition in Article 34 TFEU?

In Case C-470/93 *Verein gegen Unwesen in Handel und Gewerbe Köln* v *Mars GmbH* [1995] ECR I-1923, a German association for combating unfair competition brought proceedings against Mars GmbH. What prompted the action was that Mars had run an advertising campaign for ice cream products which covered the whole of Europe. As part of this campaign the ice cream packaging was flashed with '+ 10%'.

The plaintiff argued first, that consumers would expect the additional quantity indicated by the '+10%' to be provided without a price increase, since any price increase would reduce or eliminate the advantage which was advertised. However, it was contrary to German competition law for Mars to fix retailers' prices to consumers. This meant that neither the consumers nor Mars could be sure that consumers really did get 10% more ice cream for the same price.

The plaintiffs also claimed that the '+ 10%' flash on the Mars bar packaging itself covered much more than 10% of the packaging. The consumers must consequently get the impression that the increase was much larger than the actual 10% increase. The plaintiff was therefore of the opinion that this was misleading for consumers and contrary to German law.

The CJEU dismissed the idea that the case concerned a non-discriminatory marketing rule covered by the *Keck* doctrine. It thus stated that, even though the German prohibition applied to all goods, regardless of their origin, the case nevertheless concerned a prohibition against the marketing of goods in one Member State which carried an advertising claim which could lawfully be used in other Member States. Such a prohibition would constitute a restriction on trade within the Union and require importers to use different packaging for their products, depending on where they were to be sold, which would lead to increased costs for packaging and advertising.

It follows from this that, where marketing activities are so closely linked to the goods, any restriction on marketing which would require some change to the product would not be covered by the *Keck* doctrine. In the *Mars* case the German government also referred to considerations for consumer protection. However, the CJEU denied that the prohibition was proportionate.

JUDGMENT OF THE COURT
9 December 1997

Commission of the European Communities v French Republic

'Free movement of goods – Agricultural products – Trade barriers resulting from actions by private individuals – Obligations of the Member States'

Case C-265/95

Judgment

1. By application lodged at the Court Registry on 4 August 1995, the Commission of the European Communities brought an action under Article 169 of the EC Treaty for a declaration that, by failing to take all necessary and proportionate measures in order to prevent the free movement of fruit and vegetables from being obstructed by actions by private individuals, the French Republic has failed to fulfil its obligations under the common organization of the markets in agricultural products and Article 30 of the EC Treaty, in conjunction with Article 5 of that Treaty.

2. The Commission states that for more than a decade it has regularly received complaints concerning the passivity of the French authorities in face of violent acts committed by private individuals and by protest movements of French farmers directed against agricultural products from other Member States. Those acts consist, *inter alia*, in the interception of lorries transporting such products in France and the destruction of their loads, violence against lorry drivers, threats against French supermarkets selling agricultural products originating in other Member States, and the damaging of those goods when on display in shops in France.

3. The Commission has noted that as from 1993 certain groupings of French farmers, including an organization known as 'Coordination Rurale', launched a systematic campaign to restrict the supply of agricultural products from other Member States, which takes the form in particular of threats to wholesalers and retailers in order to induce them to stock exclusively French products, the imposition of a minimum selling price for the products concerned, and the organization of checks to verify whether those traders are complying with the instructions given.

4. Thus, from April to July 1993 that campaign was directed particularly at strawberries originating in Spain. In August and September 1993 tomatoes from Belgium were treated in the same way.

5. In 1994 the same type of action, involving threats against shopping centres and destruction of goods and means of transport, was directed against Spanish strawber-

ries in particular. Violent incidents took place on two occasions at the same place within a period of two weeks but the police who were present took no action to provide effective protection for the lorries and their loads.

6. The Commission also refers to other cases of vandalism which have hindered the free movement in France of agricultural products originating in Italy and Denmark.

7. After the Commission had raised the matter on several occasions with the French authorities, it took the view that, by failing to take all necessary and proportionate measures in order to prevent the free movement of agricultural products from being obstructed by criminal acts of private individuals, the French Republic had failed to fulfil its obligations under the common organizations of the markets in agricultural products and Article 30 of the EC Treaty, in conjunction with Article 5 of that Treaty. Consequently, by letter of 19 July 1994, the Commission gave the French Government formal notice under Article 169 of the Treaty to submit its observations within a period of two months on the failure to fulfil obligations with which it was charged.

8. In a letter dated 10 October 1994 the French Government replied that it had always strongly condemned the acts of vandalism committed by French farmers. It stated that the preventive measures which it had taken by way of surveillance, protection and the gathering of information had brought about a notable reduction in incidents between 1993 and 1994. Moreover, the fact that public prosecutors had systematically conducted criminal investigations showed the French authorities' determination to bring prosecutions in respect of all criminal conduct aimed at obstructing imports of agricultural products from other Member States. However, unpredictable commando-type operations conducted by small, highly mobile groups made it extremely difficult for the police to intervene and explained the often unsuccessful nature of the criminal proceedings initiated. Lastly, the practices of 'Coordination Rurale' that aimed to regulate the market for agricultural products through threats and destruction were the subject of proceedings before the Conseil de la Concurrence (Competition Council).

9. None the less, on 20 April 1995 further serious incidents occurred in the south west of France, in the course of which agricultural products from Spain were destroyed.

10. On 5 May 1995 the Commission therefore delivered a reasoned opinion under the first paragraph of Article 169 of the Treaty. In that opinion it stated that, by failing to take all necessary and proportionate measures in order to prevent the free movement of fruit and vegetables from being obstructed by actions by private individuals, the French Republic had failed to fulfil its obligations under the common organizations of the markets in agricultural products and Article 30 of the EC Treaty, in conjunction with Article 5 of that Treaty. Pursuant to the second paragraph of Article 169 of the Treaty, the Commission called upon the French Republic to adopt the

measures necessary in order to comply with that opinion within a period of one month from the date thereof.

11. On 16 June 1995 the French Government stressed that it had adopted all the measures open to it in order to ensure the free movement of goods on its territory and that the means of deterrence introduced had substantially contained the number of acts of violence committed in 1995. At national level, joint action to combat the recurrence of acts of vandalism had been agreed between the ministries concerned. This included, in particular, increased surveillance and instructions to prefects and the police to take firm action. Moreover, at the local level, an early-warning scheme consisting of a system of close surveillance of premises at risk had enabled a number of incidents to be prevented. Although it was impossible to prevent all risk of destruction, since the actions concerned were unforeseeable, isolated acts, whose perpetrators were very difficult to identify, in 1994 the Tribunal Correctionnel de Nîmes (Criminal Court, Nîmes) had convicted 24 farmers on charges of damage to property. Since the entry into force on 1 March 1994 of Article 322-13 of the new Criminal Code, prosecution and punishment for threats of damage to property had been made more effective. Finally, responsibility for the damage caused was assumed by the State and instructions had been given to expedite settlement of compensation for the loss or damage sustained by the economic operators concerned.

12. According to the Commission, however, in 1995 the French Minister for Agriculture stated that, although he disapproved of and condemned the violence by the farmers, he in no way contemplated any intervention by the police in order to put a stop to it.

13. On 3 June 1995 three lorries transporting fruit and vegetables from Spain were the subject of acts of violence in the south of France, without any intervention by the police. At the beginning of July 1995 Italian and Spanish fruit were once again destroyed by French farmers.

14. The Commission therefore brought the present action.

15. By orders of 14 and 27 February 1996 respectively, the Court granted the United Kingdom of Great Britain and Northern Ireland and the Kingdom of Spain leave to intervene in support of the form of order sought by the Commission.

16. In support of its application the Commission claims that Article 30 of the Treaty and the common organizations of the markets in fruit and vegetables, which are based on the same principle of the elimination of obstacles to trade, prohibit quantitative restrictions on imports between the Member States and any measures having equivalent effect. Furthermore, in accordance with Article 5 of the Treaty, the Member States are required to take all appropriate measures to ensure fulfilment of their obligations arising out of that Treaty.

17. Consequently, the interception of means of transport and the damaging of agricultural products originating in other Member States, and also the climate of insecurity caused by the threats made by various farmers' organizations against distributors of fruit and vegetables from those States, which have been found to have taken place in France, constitute an obstacle to intra-Community trade in those products, which the Member States are required to prevent by adopting appropriate measures, including measures against private individuals who imperil the free movement of goods.

18. In the present case, the fact that, year after year, serious incidents continued to hinder the importation and transit in France of fruit and vegetables originating in other Member States shows that the preventive and penal measures to which the French Government refers in defence are in practice neither adequate nor proportionate for the purpose of deterring the perpetrators of such offences from committing and repeating them. Moreover, it is clear from the factual evidence before the Commission that the French authorities have persistently abstained from taking effective action to prevent violent acts by farmers in France or to prosecute and punish them for the commission of such acts.

19. The United Kingdom Government and the Spanish Government support the form of order sought by the Commission.

20. On the other hand, the French Government contends that there is no foundation for the Commission's action.

21. Thus, it claims that it put into effect, under conditions similar to those applicable to comparable breaches of domestic law, all necessary and appropriate means to prevent actions by private individuals that impeded the free movement of agricultural products and to prosecute and punish them for such actions. The surveillance measures implemented in 1993 enabled the number of acts of violence committed during subsequent years to be contained to a substantial degree.

22. However, in view of the large number of lorries transporting agricultural products in France and the wide variety of their destinations, on the one hand, and the unforeseeable nature of actions by farmers acting in small, commando-type groups, on the other, it is not possible to eliminate all risk of destruction. The latter reason also explains why it is very difficult to identify the perpetrators and to prove their individual participation in the acts of violence so as systematically to prosecute and punish such persons. Six more persons have, however, been convicted or placed under investigation since 1994. Moreover, the police must be allowed a discretion in deciding whether they should intervene in order to safeguard public order. In any event, the State compensates the victims of the offences on the basis of liability without fault on the part of the public authorities. Thus, a sum in excess of

FF 17 million was paid by way of damages in respect of the years 1993, 1994 and 1995.

23. The French Government adds that the dissatisfaction of French farmers is due to the considerable increase in exports of Spanish products since the accession of the Kingdom of Spain, which has led to a substantial fall in prices magnified by the competitive devaluation of the peseta and the dumping prices charged by Spanish producers. The French market for fruit and vegetables was seriously disrupted by the fact that the transitional period provided for on that accession had not been accompanied by any mechanism for monitoring the export prices charged by Spanish producers. The French Government also states that, far from having adopted a protectionist attitude, in this case it had demonstrated its constructive approach by taking steps in the Council to resolve the difficulties on the market for fruit and vegetables and in conferring with the Spanish authorities.

24. In order to determine whether the Commission's action is well founded, it should be stressed from the outset that the free movement of goods is one of the fundamental principles of the Treaty.

25. Article 3(c) of the EC Treaty provides that, for the purposes set out in Article 2, the activities of the Community are to include an internal market characterized by the abolition, as between Member States, of, *inter alia*, obstacles to the free movement of goods.

26. Pursuant to the second paragraph of Article 7a of the EC Treaty, the internal market is to comprise an area without internal frontiers in which the free movement of goods is ensured in accordance with the provisions of the Treaty.

27. That fundamental principle is implemented by Article 30 et seq. of the Treaty.

28. In particular, Article 30 provides that quantitative restrictions on imports and all measures having equivalent effect are prohibited between Member States.

29. That provision, taken in its context, must be understood as being intended to eliminate all barriers, whether direct or indirect, actual or potential, to flows of imports in intra-Community trade.

30. As an indispensable instrument for the realization of a market without internal frontiers, Article 30 therefore does not prohibit solely measures emanating from the State which, in themselves, create restrictions on trade between Member States. It also applies where a Member State abstains from adopting the measures required in order to deal with obstacles to the free movement of goods which are not caused by the State.

31. The fact that a Member State abstains from taking action or, as the case may be, fails to adopt adequate measures to prevent obstacles to the free movement of goods that are created, in particular, by actions by private individuals on its territory aimed at products originating in other Member States is just as likely to obstruct intra-Community trade as is a positive act.

32. Article 30 therefore requires the Member States not merely themselves to abstain from adopting measures or engaging in conduct liable to constitute an obstacle to trade but also, when read with Article 5 of the Treaty, to take all necessary and appropriate measures to ensure that that fundamental freedom is respected on their territory.

33. In the latter context, the Member States, which retain exclusive competence as regards the maintenance of public order and the safeguarding of internal security, unquestionably enjoy a margin of discretion in determining what measures are most appropriate to eliminate barriers to the importation of products in a given situation.

34. It is therefore not for the Community institutions to act in place of the Member States and to prescribe for them the measures which they must adopt and effectively apply in order to safeguard the free movement of goods on their territories.

35. However, it falls to the Court, taking due account of the discretion referred to above, to verify, in cases brought before it, whether the Member State concerned has adopted appropriate measures for ensuring the free movement of goods.

36. It should be added that, by virtue of the combined provisions of Articles 38 to 46 and Article 7(7) of the EC Treaty, the foregoing considerations apply also to Council regulations on the common organization of the markets for the various agricultural products (see Joined Cases 3/76, 4/76 and 6/76 *Kramer and Others* [1976] ECR 1279, paragraphs 53 and 54, and Case C-228/91 *Commission* v *Italy* [1993] ECR I-2701, paragraph 11, relating to regulations on the common organization of the markets in fishery products).

37. As regards more specifically the present case, the facts which gave rise to the action brought by the Commission against the French Republic for failure to fulfil obligations are not in dispute.

38. The acts of violence committed in France and directed against agricultural products originating in other Member States, such as the interception of lorries transporting those products, the destruction of their loads and violence towards drivers, as well as threats to wholesalers and retailers and the damaging of goods on display, unquestionably create obstacles to intra-Community trade in those products.

39. It is therefore necessary to consider whether in the present case the French Government complied with its obligations under Article 30, in conjunction with Article 5, of the Treaty, by adopting adequate and appropriate measures to deal with actions by private individuals which create obstacles to the free movement of certain agricultural products.

40. It should be stressed that the Commission's written pleadings show that the incidents to which it objects in the present proceedings have taken place regularly for more than 10 years.

41. It was as long ago as 8 May 1985 that the Commission first sent a formal letter to the French Republic calling on it to adopt the preventive and penal measures necessary to put an end to acts of that kind.

42. Moreover, in the present case the Commission reminded the French Government on numerous occasions that Community law imposes an obligation to ensure *de facto* compliance with the principle of the free movement of goods by eliminating all restrictions on the freedom to trade in agricultural products from other Member States.

43. In the present case the French authorities therefore had ample time to adopt the measures necessary to ensure compliance with their obligations under Community law.

44. Moreover, notwithstanding the explanations given by the French Government, which claims that all possible measures were adopted in order to prevent the continuation of the violence and to prosecute and punish those responsible, it is a fact that, year after year, serious incidents have gravely jeopardized trade in agricultural products in France.

45. According to the summary of the facts submitted by the Commission, which is not contested by the French Government, there are particular periods of the year which are primarily concerned and there are places which are particularly vulnerable where incidents have occurred on several occasions during one and the same year.

46. Since 1993 acts of violence and vandalism have not been directed solely at the means of transport of agricultural products but have extended to the wholesale and retail sector for those products.

47. Further serious incidents of the same type also occurred in 1996 and 1997.

48. Moreover, it is not denied that when such incidents occurred the French police were either not present on the spot, despite the fact that in certain cases the competent authorities had been warned of the imminence of demonstrations by farmers, or did

not intervene, even where they far outnumbered the perpetrators of the disturbances. Furthermore, the actions in question were not always rapid, surprise actions by demonstrators who then immediately took flight, since in certain cases the disruption continued for several hours.

49. Furthermore, it is undisputed that a number of acts of vandalism were filmed by television cameras, that the demonstrators' faces were often not covered and that the groups of farmers responsible for the violent demonstrations are known to the police.

50. Notwithstanding this, it is common ground that only a very small number of the persons who participated in those serious breaches of public order has been identified and prosecuted.

51. Thus, as regards the numerous acts of vandalism committed between April and August 1993, the French authorities have been able to cite only a single case of criminal prosecution.

52. In the light of all the foregoing factors, the Court, while not discounting the difficulties faced by the competent authorities in dealing with situations of the type in question in this case, cannot but find that, having regard to the frequency and seriousness of the incidents cited by the Commission, the measures adopted by the French Government were manifestly inadequate to ensure freedom of intra-Community trade in agricultural products on its territory by preventing and effectively dissuading the perpetrators of the offences in question from committing and repeating them.

53. That finding is all the more compelling since the damage and threats to which the Commission refers not only affect the importation into or transit in France of the products directly affected by the violent acts, but are also such as to create a climate of insecurity which has a deterrent effect on trade flows as a whole.

54. The above finding is in no way affected by the French Government's argument that the situation of French farmers was so difficult that there were reasonable grounds for fearing that more determined action by the competent authorities might provoke violent reactions by those concerned, which would lead to still more serious breaches of public order or even to social conflict.

55. Apprehension of internal difficulties cannot justify a failure by a Member State to apply Community law correctly (see, to that effect, Case C-52/95 *Commission* v *France* [1995] ECR I-4443, paragraph 38).

56. It is for the Member State concerned, unless it can show that action on its part would have consequences for public order with which it could not cope by using

the means at its disposal, to adopt all appropriate measures to guarantee the full scope and effect of Community law so as to ensure its proper implementation in the interests of all economic operators.

57. In the present case the French Government has adduced no concrete evidence proving the existence of a danger to public order with which it could not cope.

58. Moreover, although it is not impossible that the threat of serious disruption to public order may, in appropriate cases, justify non-intervention by the police, that argument can, on any view, be put forward only with respect to a specific incident and not, as in this case, in a general way covering all the incidents cited by the Commission.

59. As regards the fact that the French Republic has assumed responsibility for the losses caused to the victims, this cannot be put forward as an argument by the French Government in order to escape its obligations under Community law.

60. Even though compensation can provide reparation for at least part of the loss or damage sustained by the economic operators concerned, the provision of such compensation does not mean that the Member State has fulfilled its obligations.

61. Nor is it possible to accept the arguments based on the very difficult socio-economic context of the French market in fruit and vegetables after the accession of the Kingdom of Spain.

62. It is settled case-law that economic grounds can never serve as justification for barriers prohibited by Article 30 of the Treaty (see, *inter alia*, Case 288/83 *Commission* v *Ireland* [1985] ECR 1761, paragraph 28).

63. As regards the suggestion by the French Government, in support of those arguments, that the destabilization of the French market for fruit and vegetables was brought about by unfair practices, and even infringements of Community law, by Spanish producers, it must be remembered that a Member State may not unilaterally adopt protective measures or conduct itself in such a way as to obviate any breach by another Member State of rules of Community law (see, to that effect, Case C-5/94 *R* v *MAFF, ex parte Hedley Lomas* [1996] ECR I-2553, paragraph 20).

64. This must be so *a fortiori* in the sphere of the common agricultural policy, where it is for the Community alone to adopt, if necessary, the measures required in order to deal with difficulties which some economic operators may be experiencing, in particular following a new accession.

65. Having regard to all the foregoing considerations, it must be concluded that in the present case the French Government has manifestly and persistently abstained from

adopting appropriate and adequate measures to put an end to the acts of vandalism which jeopardize the free movement on its territory of certain agricultural products originating in other Member States and to prevent the recurrence of such acts.

66. Consequently, it must be held that, by failing to adopt all necessary and proportionate measures in order to prevent the free movement of fruit and vegetables from being obstructed by actions by private individuals, the French Government has failed to fulfil its obligations under Article 30, in conjunction with Article 5, of the Treaty and under the common organizations of the markets in agricultural products.

Costs

[Para. 67 omitted]

On those grounds,

THE COURT

hereby:

1. **Declares that, by failing to adopt all necessary and proportionate measures in order to prevent the free movement of fruit and vegetables from being obstructed by actions by private individuals, the French Republic has failed to fulfil its obligations under Article 30 of the EC Treaty, in conjunction with Article 5 of that Treaty, and under the common organizations of the markets in agricultural products;**

[Paras 2 and 3 of the ruling omitted]

Comments and questions

In paragraph 30 of the judgment in Case C-265/95 *Commission* v *France* (the *Strawberry* case) [1997] ECR I-6959, the CJEU established for the first time that Article 34 TFEU (formerly Article 30 EEC Treaty) not only prohibits measures emanating from States which restrict trade between Member States, but the Treaty provision 'also applies where a Member State abstains from adopting the measures required in order to deal with obstacles to the free movement of goods which are not caused by the State.' In other words, the CJEU interprets Article 34 TFEU as making Member States liable for a failure to act, or alternatively as imposing a positive duty to act. Thus, under Article 28, the failure of a Member State to take action is treated as equivalent to its positive acts; cf. paragraph 31 of the judgment. The CJEU reached this result by including a reference to the principle of cooperation set out in Article 4(3) TEU (formerly Article 5 EEC Treaty).

Will any failure by a Member State to act against private individuals who cause restrictions on trade make that State liable under Article 34 TFEU together with Article 4(3) TEU? In this connection, consider whether the United Kingdom could be found to be in breach of its Treaty obligations if the British authorities failed to take action against Sainsbury's supermarket chain if Sainsbury's chose to sell only British beef in its stores. Also, consider Case C-325/00 *Commission* v *Germany* (the *Markenqualität* case) [2002] ECR I-9977, referred to above. The Advocate General also considered this question in his Opinion on the *Strawberry* case. In the view of the Advocate General, a Member State could not be required to guarantee the absolute protection of the free movement of goods against the actions of individuals; cf. paragraphs 45 and 66 of the Advocate General's Opinion. In the view of the Advocate General, a Member State is not responsible for the actions of individuals, and it cannot be a requirement that Member States should use unlimited means to secure the freedom of movement of goods. However, a Member State is required to adopt necessary, appropriate and adequate measures to do so.

Note that the CJEU did not accept that 'apprehension of internal difficulties' could justify the failure by a Member State to apply Union law correctly; cf. paragraph 55 of the judgment. Internal difficulties can only be used as a justification where a Member State can show that action on its part would have consequences for public order; cf. paragraph 56 of the judgment.

It appeared from the case that the French government had offered compensation to the victims of the violent demonstrations. Did this have any bearing on the assessment of whether France was in breach of the TFEU?

According to paragraph 61, the CJEU did not accept the arguments based on the difficult socio-economic context of the French market in fruit and vegetables as justifying trade restrictions. Was this in line with the usual practice of the CJEU?

Consider whether the decision in this case can affect the right to strike.

The question, about the responsibility of Member States under Article 34 TFEU for the actions of private individuals which affect the freedom of movement of goods, was also considered in Case C-112/00 *Eugen Schmidberger, Internationale Transporte und Planzüge* v *Austria* [2003] ECR I-5659. An association with the aim of protecting the Alpine environment had given notice to the Austrian authorities of its intention to hold a demonstration. According to the notice given, the demonstration was to take place on the Brenner motorway from 11 a.m. on Friday, 12th June until 3 p.m. on Saturday, 13th June 1998. This amounted to a 30 hour blockade. The Brenner motorway goes over the Brenner Pass and is one of the main routes between northern Europe and northern Italy. All traffic on the motorway would be stopped by the demonstration. The Austrian authorities decided not to ban the demonstration, as it was lawful under Austrian law. The demonstration, which took place as planned, meant that five lorries owned by a German haulage firm could not use the Brenner motorway. In the view of the German haulage firm, the Brenner motorway was the only practicable route between Germany and Italy.

In paragraph 64 of its judgment the CJEU stated that the fact that the Austrian authorities had not banned the demonstration, leading to the 30 hour long blockade, was capable of restricting intra-Union trade in goods. There was therefore a measure having equivalent effect to a quantitative restriction on imports, which was incompatible with Articles 34 and 35 TFEU, taken together with Article 4(3) TEU, unless the failure to ban the demonstration could be objectively justified. The CJEU also held that the obligation of each Member State to ensure the free movement of products in its territory applies to the acts of individuals which affect the flow of imports, exports or merely the transit of goods; cf. paragraph 60 of the judgment.

In its judgment in the *Brenner Pass* case, has the CJEU departed from what it established in the *Strawberry* case? Or do you think that the CJEU merely applied established principles? Do you think that the decision of the CJEU would have been different if the demonstration had instead taken place on one of the main roads into Vienna?

The *Brenner Pass* case required the CJEU to reconcile the conflict between, on the one hand, the protection of fundamental rights, freedom of expression and freedom of assembly and, on the other hand, the right of the free movement of goods; cf. paragraph 77 of the judgment. Having referred to the fact that freedom of expression and freedom of assembly can be restricted under Articles 10(2) and 11(2) of the European Convention of Human Rights (cf. the judgment of 23rd September 1998 of the European Court of Human Rights in the case of *Steel and Others* v *the United Kingdom*), and are thus not absolute rights, the CJEU noted that this case was clearly distinguished from the *Strawberry* case. As distinct from the *Strawberry* case, this case concerned a previously notified demonstration, and there was only a single event. The restriction on the free movement of goods was thus limited both in its geographical extent and the seriousness of the action. The aim of the demonstration was not to restrict a particular type of goods or goods of foreign origin. The Austrian authorities had taken steps to reduce the interruption of traffic as far as possible. Several alternative routes were made available. Therefore, considering the wide discretion allowed to Member States in this area, the CJEU found that the fact that the Austrian authorities did not ban the demonstration did not contravene Articles 34 and 35 TFEU, taken together with Article 4(3) TEU.

JUDGMENT OF THE COURT
17 June 2003

De Danske Bilimportører v Skatteministeriet, Told- og Skattestyrelsen.
(Reference for a preliminary ruling: Østre Landsret – Denmark)

'Free movement of goods – Charge on the registration of new motor vehicles – Internal taxation – Measure having an equivalent effect to a quantitative restriction'

Case C-383/01

Judgment

1. By order of 26 September 2001, received at the Court on 5 October 2001, the Østre Landsret (Eastern Regional Court) referred to the Court for a preliminary ruling under Article 234 EC two questions on the interpretation of Articles 28 EC and 30 EC.

2. The questions were raised in the context of proceedings between De Danske Bilimportører ('DBI'), a professional association of car importers, and the Skatteministeriet (Danish Ministry of Fiscal Affairs) concerning the levy of a charge on the registration of new motor vehicles.

Legal background

Community provisions

3. Articles 23 EC to 31 EC, which form Title I, entitled 'Free movement of goods', of the EC Treaty, introduce a customs union and prohibit quantitative restrictions on trade between Member States.

4. In particular, Article 25 EC states:

   'Customs duties on imports and exports and charges having equivalent effect shall be prohibited between Member States. This prohibition shall also apply to customs duties of a fiscal nature.'

5. Furthermore, under Article 28 EC, '[q]uantitative restrictions on imports and all measures having equivalent effect shall be prohibited between Member States'. Article 29 EC contains an identical prohibition in respect of exports.

6. However, under Article 30 EC:

   'The provisions of Articles 28 and 29 shall not preclude prohibitions or restrictions on imports, exports or goods in transit justified on grounds of public morality, public policy or public security; the protection of health and life of humans, animals or plants ... Such prohibitions or restrictions shall not, however, constitute a means of arbitrary discrimination or a disguised restriction on trade between Member States.'

7. Articles 90 EC to 93 EC form Chapter 2, entitled 'Tax provisions', of Title VI, entitled 'Common rules on competition, taxation and approximation of laws', of the Treaty.

8. Article 90 EC states:

   'No Member State shall impose, directly or indirectly, on the products of other Member States any internal taxation of any kind in excess of that imposed directly or indirectly on similar domestic products.

   Furthermore, no Member State shall impose on the products of other Member States any internal taxation of such a nature as to afford indirect protection to other products.'

National legislation

9. The lov om registreringsafgift af motorkøretøjer (Law on registration duty on motor vehicles), in the version resulting from Consolidating Law No 222 of 14 April 1999, which was applicable at the material time, provides for the levy of a charge, known as 'registration duty', on new motor vehicles. That charge, levied upon first registration of the vehicle in the national territory, is based on the purchase price. The rate of the charge is 105% on the first portion, which is fixed annually, and 180% on the remainder of the price. In 1999, the first portion was DKK 52 800.

10. Furthermore, the price taken as the tax base already includes 25% value added tax and a flat-rate mark-up of 9% to take account of dealer margin, regardless of the margin actually taken by the dealer.

11. It is apparent from the documents before the Court that the principal purpose of the registration duty is to raise tax revenue, although other considerations such as environmental protection and road safety may also account for the levy.

12. Since the duty is levied upon first registration of the vehicle in Denmark, but not upon any subsequent resale, it is also levied when a used vehicle is imported into Denmark.

13. Before 1990, the registration duty was applied to imported used vehicles in a way which did not adequately reflect depreciation in their value. Therefore, in Case C-47/88 *Commission* v *Denmark* [1990] ECR I-4509, the Court held that, by imposing a registration duty on imported used motor vehicles generally based on an estimated value which is higher than the real value of the vehicle, with the result that imported used motor vehicles were taxed more heavily than used motor vehicles sold on the domestic market after being registered in Denmark, the Kingdom of Denmark had failed to fulfil its obligations under Article 95 of the EEC Treaty (which became Article 95 of the EC Treaty and is now, after amendment, Article 90 EC).

14. In the infringement proceedings which resulted in that judgment, the Commission also contested the compatibility of the registration duty on new motor vehicles with Article 95 of the Treaty, having regard in particular to the very high level of the duty.

15. The Court however rejected that claim of infringement after having found that Article 95 of the Treaty could not be invoked against internal taxation imposed on imported products where there is no similar or competing domestic production, and that, in particular, that article did not provide a basis for censuring the excessiveness of the level of taxation which the Member States might adopt for particular products, in the absence of any discriminatory or protective effect (*Commission* v *Denmark*, paragraph 10).

16. In paragraph 12 of *Commission* v *Denmark*, the Court admittedly noted that, as it had held in Case 31/67 *Stier* [1968] ECR 235, it is not permissible for the Member States to impose on products which, in the absence of comparable domestic production, escape the application of the prohibitions contained in Article 95 of the Treaty charges of such an amount that the free movement of goods within the common market would be impeded as far as those goods were concerned. It added, however, in paragraph 13 of *Commission* v *Denmark*, that the only possibility of appraising an adverse effect of that kind on the free movement of goods is by reference to Article 30 of the EEC Treaty (which became Article 30 of the EC Treaty and is now, after amendment, Article 28 EC) et seq. The Commission's action in that case was not however based on those articles.

The main proceedings and the questions referred for a preliminary ruling

17. It should be stated at the outset that, as is apparent from the documents before the Court, there is no production of motor vehicles in Denmark. During the period from 1985 to 2000, the total number of registered vehicles in Denmark rose from 1 501 000 to 1 854 000 and the number of new registrations varied between 78 453 and 169 492 per year.

18. In January 1999, DBI purchased a new Audi vehicle for the use of its director for a total price (including delivery costs) of DKK 498 546, including DKK 297 456 in registration duty.

19. Since DBI took the view that that charge had been levied in breach, *inter alia*, of Article 28 EC, it requested its repayment from the tax authorities, relying in particular on paragraphs 12 and 13 of *Commission* v *Denmark*. In its submission, the excessive level of the registration duty made it impossible to import motor vehicles to Denmark under normal commercial conditions, to the benefit of domestic purchases of previously registered used vehicles, which were to be regarded as Danish products, in accordance with the case-law of the Court (*Commission* v *Denmark*, paragraph 17, and Case C-228/98 *Dounias* [2000] ECR I-577, paragraph 42).

20. The Skatteministeriet responded that, according to the case-law of the Court (see, *inter alia, Dounias*, paragraph 39), fiscal contributions cannot be caught by Article 28 EC, since the lawfulness of domestic taxation may be assessed only in the light of Article 90 EC. It stated further that, in Case C-132/88 *Commission* v *Greece* [1990] ECR I-1567, paragraph 17, the Court found that, as Community law stands at present, the Member States are at liberty to make products such as cars subject to a system of tax which increases progressively in amount according to an objective criterion and that Article 95 of the Treaty does not provide a basis for censuring the excessiveness of the level of taxation which the Member States might adopt for particular products in the light of considerations of social policy.

21. According to the Skatteministeriet, the proviso adopted by the Court in paragraphs 12 and 13 of *Commission* v *Denmark* relates only to cases in which, as a result of internal taxation, trade in the product in question ceases or is insignificant in volume. The registration duty on motor vehicles, however, is not prohibitive and the total number of motor vehicles in Denmark is comparable to that in other Member States.

22. In those circumstances the Østre Landsret decided to stay proceedings and to refer the following two questions to the Court for a preliminary ruling:

   '1) Can an indirect duty (registration duty) charged by a Member State, which in the case of new cars amounts to 105% of DKK 52 800 and 180% of the remainder of the taxable value, be a measure having an effect equivalent to a quantitative restriction on imports and for that reason prohibited under Article 28 EC (reference is made in this connection to the Court's judgment in Case C-47/88 *Commission* v *Denmark* [1990] ECR I-4509, paragraph 13)?

   2) If the answer to Question 1 is yes: can that registration duty be justified on the grounds that are mentioned in Article 30 EC or follow from the Court's case-

law on Article 28 EC (reference is made to Case 120/78 *Rewe-Zentral* (Cassis de Dijon) [1979] ECR 649)?'

The first question referred for a preliminary ruling

23. By its first question, the national court is essentially asking the Court whether Article 28 EC must be interpreted as precluding, as a rule, the levy of a charge on the registration of new motor vehicles, such as the registration duty at issue in the main proceedings.

Observations submitted to the Court

24. DBI claims, in substance, that the Danish registration duty impedes the free movement of new vehicles since, because of its excessive level, it prevents the importation of those goods to Denmark under normal commercial conditions, whilst benefiting domestic purchases of used vehicles previously registered in Denmark, which must be regarded as Danish products. That duty thus amounts to a quantitative restriction on imports contrary to Article 28 EC.

25. The applicant in the main proceedings bases its analysis on paragraphs 12 and 13 of *Commission* v *Denmark*, from which it is apparent that charges of an amount such that they impede the free movement of goods may be assessed in the light of Article 28 EC.

26. The Danish Government submits that the registration duty cannot be regarded as a quantitative restriction on imports prohibited under Article 28 EC. It argues that the assertion in paragraph 13 of *Commission* v *Denmark* has never been reiterated by the Court in subsequent judgments. On the contrary, it follows from settled case-law that barriers of a fiscal nature to the free movement of goods must be assessed in the light of Articles 23 EC to 25 EC or Articles 90 EC to 93 EC. In the main proceedings, however, the registration duty on new motor vehicles, which is internal taxation, neither discriminates against imported products nor protects domestic production, with the result that it is not prohibited by Article 90 EC.

27. As to the remainder, if the Commission were to consider that the registration duty is excessively high, it would be for it to draw up a proposal for a measure on the basis of Article 93 EC with a view to harmonising national legislation.

28. In the alternative, the Danish Government contends that paragraph 13 of *Commission* v *Denmark* must be interpreted as meaning that the prohibition on quantitative restrictions on imports, laid down in Article 28 EC, relates only to fiscal provisions which have such an impact on intra-Community trade that, as far as the taxed product is concerned, that trade is reduced to nothing or becomes insignificant. Howev-

er, that is not the case in the main proceedings since the number of motor vehicles per inhabitant in Denmark is comparable to that in other Member States.

29. The observations of the Italian and Finnish Governments are to the same effect.

30. The Commission considers that barriers of a fiscal nature which do not have an effect equivalent to a customs duty fall, as a rule, under Article 90 EC, which is a *lex specialis* as opposed to the general prohibition on barriers to trade, laid down in Article 28 EC. Barriers of a fiscal nature which are not covered by Article 90 EC – or by Articles 23 EC to 25 EC – may therefore be caught by Article 28 EC where they impede the free movement of goods. By contrast, according to the case-law of the Court, a barrier of a fiscal nature cannot fall at the same time under the two provisions.

31. As a consequence, it is for the national court to assess, in the light of the facts in the main proceedings, whether the registration duty on new motor vehicles is of a level such that it impedes the free movement of goods. The Commission notes, in that regard, that it is apparent from the order for reference that a considerable number of motor vehicles are registered each year in Denmark, that the variations in the number of registrations appear to be purely short-term and that the number of motor vehicles per inhabitant is at the same level as in other countries of the Organisation for Economic Cooperation and Development (OECD). It is therefore not established that the Danish legislation at issue in the main proceedings impedes the free movement of goods.

Reply of the Court

32. The scope of Article 28 EC does not extend to the obstacles to trade covered by other specific provisions of the Treaty and obstacles of a fiscal nature or having an effect equivalent to customs duties, which are covered by Articles 23 EC, 25 EC and 90 EC, do not fall within the prohibition laid down in Article 28 EC (see Joined Cases C-78/90 to C-83/90 *Compagnie Commerciale de l'Ouest and Others* [1992] ECR I-1847, paragraph 20, and *Dounias*, paragraph 39).

33. Furthermore, as regards the scope of Articles 25 EC and 90 EC, it is settled case-law that provisions relating to charges having equivalent effect and those relating to discriminatory internal taxation cannot be applied together, with the result that, under the system established by the Treaty, the same charge cannot belong to both categories at the same time (see Case C-234/99 *Nygård* [2002] ECR I-3657, paragraph 17).

34. In the present case, since a charge on the registration of new motor vehicles, such as the Danish registration duty at issue in the main proceedings, is manifestly of a fiscal nature and is charged not by reason of the vehicle crossing the frontier of the

Member State which introduced the charge, but upon first registration of the vehicle in the territory of that State, the charge must be regarded as part of a general system of internal dues on goods and thus examined in the light of Article 90 EC.

35. The fact that a charge of that sort is in fact imposed solely on imported new vehicles, because there is no domestic production, is not such as to cause it to be characterised as a charge having equivalent effect, for the purposes of Article 25 EC, rather than internal taxation, within the meaning of Article 90 EC, since it is part of a general system of internal dues applied systematically to categories of vehicles in accordance with objective criteria irrespective of the origin of the products (see, to that effect, Case 90/79 *Commission* v *France* [1981] ECR 283, paragraph 14).

36. Since the applicability of Article 90 EC in the main proceedings is thus established, it should be noted that that article expressly prohibits the imposition on products from other Member States of internal taxation in excess of that imposed on similar domestic products or internal taxation of such a nature as to afford indirect protection to other products (see *Commission* v *Denmark*, paragraph 8).

37. It should also be noted that, as paragraph 9 of *Commission* v *Denmark* shows, the aim of Article 90 EC as a whole is to ensure the free movement of goods between the Member States in normal conditions of competition by the elimination of all forms of protection which may result from the application of internal taxation that discriminates against products from other Member States. Thus Article 90 EC must guarantee the complete neutrality of internal taxation as regards competition between domestic products and imported products.

38. On the other hand, Article 90 EC cannot be invoked against internal taxation imposed on imported products where there is no similar or competing domestic production. In particular, it does not provide a basis for censuring the excessiveness of the level of taxation which the Member States might adopt for particular products, in the absence of any discriminatory or protective effect (see *Commission* v *Denmark*, paragraph 10).

39. At present there is no domestic production of cars in Denmark, as has already been noted in paragraph 17 above, nor indeed of any products liable to compete with cars. In those circumstances, it must be concluded that the Danish registration duty imposed on new motor vehicles is not covered by the prohibitions laid down in Article 90 EC.

40. It is true, as DBI pointed out, that the Court held, in paragraph 12 of *Commission* v *Denmark*, that it is not permissible for the Member States to impose on products which, in the absence of comparable domestic production, escape the application of the prohibitions contained in Article 90 EC charges of such an amount that the free

movement of goods within the common market would be impeded as far as those goods were concerned.

41. It is however sufficient in that regard to state that, in any event, the figures communicated by the national court as to the number of new vehicles registered in Denmark, and thus imported into that Member State, do not in any way show that the free movement of that type of goods between Denmark and the other Member States is impeded.

42. In those circumstances, it cannot be considered that a charge such as the Danish registration duty has ceased to be internal taxation, within the meaning of Article 90 EC, and should be classified as a measure having equivalent effect to a quantitative restriction, for the purposes of Article 28 EC, nor is it appropriate to examine the scope of the proviso adopted by the Court in paragraphs 12 and 13 of *Commission* v *Denmark*.

43. In conclusion, the answer to the first question referred for a preliminary ruling must be that:

– a charge on the registration of new motor vehicles established by a Member State which does not have any domestic production of vehicles, such as that laid down by the lov om registreringsafgift af motorkøretøjer (Law on registration duty on motor vehicles), in the version resulting from Consolidating Law No 222 of 14 April 1999, constitutes internal taxation whose compatibility with Community law must be examined in the light not of Article 28 EC, but of Article 90 EC;

– Article 90 EC must be interpreted as not precluding such a charge.

The second question referred for a preliminary ruling

44. Having regard to the considerations set out in connection with the first question, it is not necessary to examine the justifications put forward in the alternative by the Danish Government in support of the compatibility of the Danish registration duty with Community law, with the result that the second question becomes devoid of purpose.

Costs

[Para. 45 omitted]

On those grounds,

THE COURT,

in answer to the question referred to it by the Østre Landsret by order of 26 September 2001, hereby rules:

1. **A charge on the registration of new motor vehicles established by a Member State which does not have any domestic production of vehicles, such as that laid down by the lov om registreringsafgift af motorkøretøjer (Law on registration duty on motor vehicles), in the version resulting from Consolidating Law No 222 of 14 April 1999, constitutes internal taxation whose compatibility with Community law must be examined in the light not of Article 28 EC, but of Article 90 EC.**

2. **Article 90 EC must be interpreted as not precluding such a charge.**

Comments and questions

The TFEU contains three different sets of provisions which prohibit restrictions on the free movement of goods within the Union. Articles 28 and 30 TFEU (formerly Articles 23 and 25 TEC) prohibit the imposition of customs duties and all charges having equivalent effect on the import and export of goods between Member States. Articles 34-37 TFEU (formerly Articles 28-31 TEC) prohibit Member States from imposing quantitative restrictions on imports or exports as well as measures having an equivalent effect. And Article 110 TFEU (formerly Article 90 TEC) prohibits the imposition by Member States of discriminatory internal taxes.

The prohibition against customs duties in Article 30 TFEU covers every kind of charge which is imposed as a result of crossing a border. The prohibition is absolute; it is thus irrelevant whether the measure does in fact restrict the free movement of goods. The prohibition in Article 110 TFEU seeks to remove all forms of protection resulting from discriminatory internal taxes. Where Article 30 TFEU is directed against the imposition of customs duties, Article 110 TFEU is solely directed at the discriminatory effect of internal taxes. This means that non-discriminatory internal taxes do not contravene Article 110 TFEU. For both the prohibition in Article 30 TFEU and the prohibition in Article 110 TFEU, there is in principle no possibility of justifying taxes which are covered by these prohibitions.

Article 34 TFEU prohibits all quantitative restrictions and measures having equivalent effect to quantitative restrictions. As distinct from Articles 30 and 110 TFEU, it is possible to justify measures covered by Article 34 TFEU on the grounds of one of the considerations listed in Article 36 TFEU or on the basis of protecting an important public interest (the *Cassis de Dijon* doctrine). Article 34 TFEU has a very wide scope of application, and it is generally assumed that it covers all measures which can restrict imports and which are not specifically covered by other provisions in the TFEU. Article 34 TFEU is thus a kind of residual provision, compared with Articles 30 and 110 TFEU.

The different consequences which flow from the three provisions mean that it is very important to clarify which of them is relevant to the evaluation of a concrete situation. According to the practice of the CJEU, a measure can only be subject to one of the three provisions. However, the CJEU has previously considered the legality of tax measures in relation to Article 34 TFEU in both Case 18/84 *Commission* v *France* [1985] ECR I-1339, and in Case C-189/95 *Franzén* [1997] I-5909. If there is doubt about which heading a case falls under, the CJEU first examines whether the case is covered by Article 30 or Article 90 TFEU, and only if neither of these provisions apply will the CJEU consider whether the measure in question falls within the scope of Article 34 TFEU.

In Case C-383/01 *Danske Bilimportører* v *Skatteministeriet* [2003] ECR I-6065, the CJEU had to consider which of the three provisions applied to the high registration duty on cars in Denmark. The registration duty was first applied when cars were registered. The duty was thus not linked to the import of a car to Denmark (i.e., it did not relate to the crossing of the border), so it was not a customs duty. Since there was also no question of the duty being discriminatory, as Denmark does not produce cars itself, it was natural to conclude that the case concerned a non-discriminatory (i.e., lawful) internal tax according to Article 110 TFEU. Since the duty fell within the scope of Article 110 TFEU, it ought, in principle, to fall outside the scope of Article 34 TFEU.

However, the case was not as straightforward as one might think. The CJEU had already, in 1990, had the opportunity to consider the compatibility of the Danish registration duty with Union law, (Case C-47/88 *Commission* v *Denmark* [1990] ECR I-4509), and in paragraphs 12 and 13 the CJEU had stated as follows:

> '12. It is true that, as the Court held in its judgment in Case 31/67, *Stier* v *Hauptzollamt Hamburg-Ericus* [1968] ECR 235, it is not permissible for the Member States to impose on products which, in the absence of comparable domestic production, escape the application of the prohibitions contained in Article 95 [now Article 110 TFEU] charges of such an amount that the free movement of goods within the common market [i.e. within the EU] would be impeded as far as those goods were concerned.
>
> 13. Nevertheless, the only possibility of appraising an adverse effect of that kind on the free movement of goods is by reference to the general rules contained in Article 30 et seq. [now Article 34 TFEU et seq.] of the Treaty, and the Commission's action is based exclusively on infringement of Article 95 [now Article 110 TFEU].'

In other words, the CJEU held that an internal tax, which was permitted under Article 110 TFEU because there was no domestic production, could nevertheless be contrary to Article 34 TFEU, because it risked causing a restriction on the free movement of goods. It is this statement which the plaintiff, *De Danske Bilimportører* (the Danish Society of

Motor Car Importers), seized upon when they argued that the Danish registration duty constituted a non-discriminatory internal tax of such a dimension that it became impossible to import cars on normal trade terms.

In assessing the legality of the car registration duty, the CJEU started from the basis that Articles 30, 110 and 34 TFEU cannot be applied together (paragraphs 32-33 of the judgment). Just as in the previous case on the Danish registration duty, the CJEU held that a non-discriminatory internal tax can lose its character as an internal tax within the terms of Article 110 TFEU, and can instead become a measure having an equivalent effect to quantitative restrictions within the scope of Article 34 TFEU (paragraphs 40-42). However, the CJEU noted that the number of registered vehicles in Denmark was at the same level as in other OECD countries, so there was no evidence to show that the free movement of cars between Denmark and the other Member States had been endangered (paragraphs 31 and 41). For this reason the CJEU dismissed the claim that the Danish registration duty could constitute a measure having an equivalent effect to quantitative restrictions (paragraph 42).

In his Opinion on the case, the Advocate General recommended that the CJEU should maintain the original distinction between Articles 30, 110 and 34 TFEU, according to which the provisions are mutually exclusive. According to the Advocate General, an extraordinarily high internal tax should not be regarded as a measure having equivalent effect to a quantitative restriction, covered by Article 34 TFEU. The Advocate General based his argument partly on the requirements of legal certainty, and partly on the structure of Article 34 TFEU. Consider why the CJEU did not accept the argument of the Advocate General on this point. When the CJEU does not exclude the possibility that extraordinarily high internal taxes could fall within the scope of Article 34 TFEU, this necessarily raises the key question of when a tax can be regarded as being 'extraordinarily high'. Will this be the case with the imposition of a tax of 80%, 100%, 150%, 180% or 390%? If a tax is considered as being covered by Article 34 TFEU, it then becomes necessary to ask whether such a tax can be justified under the CJEU's *Cassis de Dijon* doctrine. According to this doctrine, only overriding public concerns of a non-financial nature can justify restrictions on the free movement of goods. However, the problem is that a tax will presumably always also be fiscally based and it is therefore unlikely that it will ever be possible to say that it is merely of a non-financial nature.

Do you agree with the CJEU that the number of registered cars in Denmark is appropriate for showing that the free movement of cars between Denmark and the other Member States is not at risk? For example, is it likely that a lower registration duty (and thus a lower price) on cars in Denmark would have affected the number of cars sold, or at least influenced which cars are sold (make, model, specification)? Consider whether it is likely that the CJEU intended that a non-discriminatory internal tax should only be seen as a measure having equivalent effect to a quantitative restriction covered by Article 34 TFEU if the tax is in fact prohibitive, so that the tax effectively excludes the taxed goods from the country.

If the CJEU had regarded the Danish car registration duty as a measure having equivalent effect to a quantitative restriction covered by Article 34 TFEU, would the tax have been lawful (justified) taking into account that 'the principal purpose of the registration duty is to raise tax revenue'?

Both the Danish government (paragraph 27) and the Advocate General were of the view that a restructuring and approximation of the registration duties on cars in the Member States ought to take place via Union legislation, and not on the basis of a decision by the CJEU. Does the CJEU express a view on this in its judgment? Do you think that the CJEU is normally careful in refraining from expressing a view on matters which would generally be regarded as falling within the scope of legislative responsibility?

De Danske Bilimportører (the Danish Society of Motor Car Importers) did not succeed in its attack on the Danish registration duty on new cars from a Union law perspective in Case C-383/01. Subsequently, in Case C-464/02 *Commission* v *Denmark* [2005] ECR I-7929 (the *Company car* case), which is printed below in Chapter 4, the Commission disputed the legality of the registration duty under Union law. The Commission only had modest success; cf. the comments on the case printed below. The third attempt to overturn the car registration duty took the form of Case C-98/05 *De Danske Bilimportører* v *Skatteministeriet* (ii) [2006] ECR I-4945. In this case the Danish Eastern High Court made a new referral – in the same case as that which formed the basis for Case C-383/01 – for a preliminary ruling as to whether it was contrary to Article 11(A)(3)(c) of Sixth Council Directive 77/388/EEC on the harmonization of the laws of the Member States relating to turnover taxes, that the VAT on the purchase of a car should be included in the calculation of the registration duty. De Danske Bilimportører argued that the registration duty should not be included in the calculation of the VAT. De Danske Bilimportører's argument was not accepted by the CJEU.

JUDGMENT OF THE COURT
5 December 2000

Criminal proceedings against Jean-Pierre Guimont.
(Reference for a preliminary ruling: Tribunal de police de Belley – France)

'Measures having equivalent effect to a quantitative restriction – Purely internal situation – Manufacture and marketing of Emmenthal cheese without rind'

Case C-448/98

Judgment

1. By judgment of 24 November 1998, received at the Court on 9 December 1998, the Tribunal de Police (Local Criminal Court), Belley, referred to the Court for a preliminary ruling under Article 177 of the EC Treaty (now Article 234 EC) a question on the interpretation of Articles 3(a) and 30 et seq. of the EC Treaty (now, after amendment, Articles 3(1)(a) EC 28 EC et seq.).

2. That question was raised in the context of criminal proceedings against Jean-Pierre Guimont for holding for sale, selling or offering a foodstuff, in this case Emmenthal, with deceptive labelling.

The national rules in question

3. The first paragraph of Article 3 of French Decree No 84-1147 of 7 September 1984 applying the Law of 1 August 1905 on frauds and falsifications relating to products or services ('the 1984 Decree') provides:

   'The labels and labelling methods used must not be such as to give rise to confusion in the mind of the purchaser or the consumer, particularly as to the characteristics of the foodstuff and, specifically, as to its nature, identity, properties, composition, quantity, durability, method of conservation, origin or provenance, method of manufacture or production.'

4. The 'characteristics of the foodstuff' bearing the designation 'Emmenthal' within the meaning of the French legislation are defined by Article 6 of, and the Annex to, Decree No 88-1206 of 30 December 1988 applying the Law of 1 August 1905 on frauds and falsifications relating to products or services and the Law of 2 July 1935 on the organisation and restructuring of the milk market as regards cheeses (JORF (Official Journal of the French Republic) of 31 December 1988, p. 16753, hereinafter 'the 1988 Decree '). Article 6 of the 1988 Decree provides that 'the designations listed in the Annex are reserved for cheeses meeting the requirements relating to

manufacture and composition which are described in the said Annex '. In that Annex, Emmenthal is described as a product with the following characteristics: 'a firm cheese produced by curing, pressing and salting on the surface or in brine; of a colour between ivory and pale yellow, with holes of a size between a cherry and a walnut; hard, dry rind, of a colour between golden yellow and light brown'.

Facts and procedure before the national court

5. By order of 6 January 1998, Mr Guimont was sentenced to 260 fines of FRF 20 each for holding for sale, selling or offering a foodstuff with deceptive labelling, in this case Emmenthal, which is an offence punishable under the first paragraph of Article 3 of the 1984 Decree.

6. At a hearing in which the Tribunal de Police, Belley, examined Mr Guimont's formal objection to that order, it was stated that an inspection had been carried out on 5 March 1996 by the Directorate for Competition, Consumer Affairs and Prevention of Fraud of the Department of Vaucluse at the premises of a company specialising in the cutting and packaging of portions of cheese prepacked in plastic film intended particularly for sale in supermarkets. During that inspection, 260 whole Emmenthal cheeses were discovered from the 'Laiterie d'Argis', of which Mr Guimont is the technical manager.

7. In its inspection, referred to in the paragraph above, the Departmental Directorate noted the total lack of rind on the cheeses examined, contrary to Article 6 of, and the Annex to, the 1988 Decree.

8. In his defence before the national court, Mr Guimont has argued in particular that Article 6 of the 1988 Decree is incompatible with the provisions of Articles 3(a) and 30 et seq. of the Treaty.

9. He has pointed out before the referring court that the name 'Emmenthal' is generic and widely used in a number of countries of the European Union without any requirement as to the existence of a rind. He has argued that, by reserving the designation 'Emmenthal' for cheeses with 'a hard, dry rind, of a colour between golden yellow and light brown', the 1988 Decree introduces a quantitative restriction on intra-Community trade or a measure having equivalent effect.

10. In its judgment making the reference, the Tribunal de Police, Belley, has made, *inter alia*, the following observations:

   - The charge against the accused can be maintained only in so far as the 1988 Decree is not contrary to supranational norms;
   - Mr Guimont has shown by the evidence adduced that Emmenthal without rind is manufactured or marketed in other countries of the European Community;

- The *Codex Alimentarius* of the UN Food and Agriculture Organisation and the World Health Organisation contains a norm which refers to the consumption of Emmenthal without rind;
- The variation between different national rules and, in particular, the restrictive position adopted in the French regulations as compared with those of other European countries is capable of hindering, directly or indirectly, actually or potentially, intra-Community trade, while no right to protection of the generic name 'Emmenthal' is recognised by Community legislation;
- Such discrimination does not seem justified on any of the grounds allowed under Article 36 of the Treaty.

11. In those circumstances, the national court decided to stay the proceedings and refer the following question to the Court of Justice for a preliminary ruling:

    'On a proper construction of Articles 3(a) and 30 et seq. of the Treaty establishing the European Community, must the French rules enacted by Decree No 88-1206 of 30 December 1988, which prohibit the manufacture and marketing in France of a cheese without rind under the designation 'Emmenthal', be regarded as constituting a quantitative restriction or a measure having equivalent effect on intra-Community trade?'

Preliminary observations

12. It should be noted first that Article 3 of the Treaty determines the fields and objectives to which the activities of the Community are to relate. It thus lays down the general principles of the internal market, which are to be applied in conjunction with the respective chapters of the Treaty devoted to their implementation (Case C-341/95 *Bettati* v *Safety Hi-Tech* [1998] ECR I-4355, paragraph 75). The general objective laid down in Article 3(a) of the Treaty is explained by the provisions of Article 30 et seq. In those circumstances, the reference in the question to Article 3(a) of the Treaty does not call for an answer distinct from that to be given on the interpretation of Article 30 et seq. of the Treaty.

13. Second, it is necessary to examine the argument of the French Government that Article 30 of the Treaty does not apply to a case such as that at issue in the main proceedings.

14. On the one hand, the French Government argues that the inapplicability of Article 30 follows from the simple fact that the rule which Mr Guimont is accused of infringing is not, in practice, applied to imported products. It maintains that that rule was designed to create obligations solely for national producers and does not therefore concern intra-Community trade in any way. In its submission, the case-law of the Court of Justice, and particularly the judgment in Case 98/86 *Mathot* [1987]

ECR 809, paragraphs 8 and 9, demonstrates that Article 30 of the Treaty is designed to protect only intra-Community trade.

15. In response to that argument, it should be observed that Article 30 of the Treaty covers any measure of the Member States which is capable, directly or indirectly, actually or potentially, of hindering intra-Community trade (Case 8/74 *Procureur du Roi* v *Dassonville* [1974] ECR 837, paragraph 5). However, that article is not designed to ensure that goods of national origin enjoy the same treatment as imported goods in every case, and a difference in treatment as between goods which is not capable of restricting imports or of prejudicing the marketing of imported goods does not fall within the prohibition contained in that article (*Mathot*, paragraphs 7 and 8).

16. However, as regards the national rule at issue in the main proceedings, the French Government does not deny that, according to its wording, it is applicable without distinction to both French and imported products.

17. This argument of the French Government cannot therefore be accepted. The mere fact that a rule is not applied to imported products in practice does not exclude the possibility of it having effects which indirectly or potentially hinder intra-Community trade (see Case C-184/96 *Commission* v *France* [1998] ECR I-6197, paragraph 17).

18. On the other hand, the French Government, supported on this point by the Danish Government, argues that, in the particular case before the national court, the rule at issue does not constitute a hindrance, even an indirect or a potential hindrance, to intra-Community trade within the meaning of the Court's case-law. According to those governments, the facts underlying the reference to the Court relate to a purely internal situation, the accused being of French nationality and the product in question being manufactured entirely in French territory.

19. Mr Guimont, the German, Netherlands and Austrian Governments and the Commission argue that, according to the Court's case-law, Article 30 cannot be considered inapplicable simply because all the facts of the specific case before the national court are confined to a single Member State (Joined Cases C-321/94 to C-324/94 *Pistre and Others* [1997] ECR I-2343, paragraph 44).

20. In regard to that argument, it should be noted that the *Pistre* judgment concerned a situation where the national rule in question was not applicable without distinction but created direct discrimination against goods imported from other Member States.

21. As for a rule such as that at issue in the main proceedings, which, according to its wording, applies without distinction to national and imported products and is designed to impose certain production conditions on producers in order to permit them

to market their products under a certain designation, it is clear from the Court's case-law that such a rule falls under Article 30 of the Treaty only in so far as it applies to situations that are linked to the importation of goods in intra-Community trade (Case 286/81 *Oosthoek's Uitgeversmaatschappij* [1982] ECR 4575, paragraph 9; *Mathot*, paragraphs 3 and 7 to 9).

22. However, that finding does not mean that there is no need to reply to the question referred to the Court for a preliminary ruling in this case. In principle, it is for the national courts alone to determine, having regard to the particular features of each case, both the need for a preliminary ruling in order to enable them to give their judgment and the relevance of the questions which they refer to the Court. A reference for a preliminary ruling from a national court may be rejected only if it is quite obvious that the interpretation of Community law sought by that court bears no relation to the actual nature of the case or the subject-matter of the main action (Case C-281/98 *Angonese* v *Cassa di Risparmio di Bolzano* [2000] ECR I-4139, paragraph 18).

23. In this case, it is not obvious that the interpretation of Community law requested is not necessary for the national court. Such a reply might be useful to it if its national law were to require, in proceedings such as those in this case, that a national producer must be allowed to enjoy the same rights as those which a producer of another Member State would derive from Community law in the same situation.

24. In those circumstances, it needs to be examined whether a national rule such as that at issue in the main proceedings might, in so far as applied to imported products, constitute a measure having equivalent effect to a quantitative restriction contrary to Article 30 of the Treaty.

The interpretation of Article 30 of the Treaty

25. As a preliminary observation, it should be noted that, as is undisputed in these proceedings, a national rule such as that at issue in the main proceedings constitutes a measure having equivalent effect to a quantitative restriction on imports within the meaning of Article 30 of the Treaty, in so far as it is applied to imported products.

26. National legislation which subjects goods from other Member States, where they are lawfully manufactured and marketed, to certain conditions in order to be able to use the generic designation commonly used for that product, and which thus in certain cases requires producers to use designations which are unknown to, or less highly regarded by, consumers, does not, it is true, absolutely preclude the importation into the Member State concerned of products originating in other Member States. It is, however, likely to make their marketing more difficult and thus impede trade between Member States (Case 298/87 *Smanor* [1988] ECR 4489, paragraph 12).

27. As for the question whether such a rule may still be in conformity with Community law, it should be remembered that, according to the Court's case-law, national rules adopted in the absence of common or harmonised rules and applicable without distinction to national products and to products imported from other Member States may be compatible with the Treaty in so far as they are necessary in order to satisfy overriding requirements relating, *inter alia*, to fair trading and consumer protection (Case C-39/90 *Denkavit* v *Land Baden-Württemberg* [1991] ECR I-3069, paragraph 18), where they are proportionate to the objective pursued and that objective is not capable of being achieved by measures which are less restrictive of intra-Community trade (Case C-368/95 *Familiapress* v *Bauer Verlag* [1997] ECR I-3689, paragraph 19).

28. In this context, it is necessary to refer, as the Commission has done, to Council Directive 79/112/EEC of 18 December 1978 on the approximation of the laws of the Member States relating to the labelling, presentation and advertising of foodstuffs for sale to the ultimate consumer (OJ 1979 L 33, p. 1), as amended by Council Directive 89/395/EEC of 14 June 1989 (OJ 1989 L 186, p. 17), which, at the time of the facts at issue in the main proceedings, provided in Article 5(1):

    'The name under which a foodstuff is sold shall be the name laid down by whatever laws, regulations or administrative provisions apply to the foodstuff in question or, in the absence of any such name, the name customary in the Member State where the product is sold to the ultimate consumer and to mass caterers, or a description of the foodstuff and, if necessary, of its use, that is sufficiently precise to inform the purchaser of its true nature and to enable it to be distinguished from products with which it could be confused.'

29. Whilst that provision demonstrates the importance of a correct use of foodstuff designations for the protection of consumers, it does not authorise Member States to adopt in the matter of designations rules which restrict the importation of goods lawfully manufactured and marketed in another Member State where those rules are not proportionate to that purpose or where that protection could have been achieved by measures less restrictive of intra-Community trade.

30. It is true that, according to the case-law of the Court, Member States may, for the purpose of ensuring fair trading and the protection of consumers, require the persons concerned to alter the description of a foodstuff where a product offered for sale under a particular name is so different, in terms of its composition or production, from the products generally understood as falling within that description within the Community that it cannot be regarded as falling within the same category (Case C-366/98 *Geffroy* [2000] ECR I-6579, paragraph 22).

31. However, where the difference is of minor importance, appropriate labelling should be sufficient to provide the purchaser or consumer with the necessary information (*Geffroy*, paragraph 23).

32. In the case at issue in the main proceedings, it should be noted that, according to the *Codex alimentarius* referred to in paragraph 10 of this judgment, which provides indications allowing the characteristics of the product concerned to be defined, a cheese manufactured without rind may be given the name 'Emmenthal' since it is made from ingredients and in accordance with a method of manufacture identical to those used for Emmenthal with rind, save for a difference in treatment at the maturing stage. Moreover, it is undisputed that such an 'Emmenthal' cheese variant is lawfully manufactured and marketed in Member States other than the French Republic.

33. Therefore, even if the difference in the maturing method between Emmenthal with rind and Emmenthal without rind were capable of constituting a factor likely to mislead consumers, it would be sufficient, whilst maintaining the designation 'Emmenthal', for that designation to be accompanied by appropriate information concerning that difference.

34. In those circumstances, the absence of rind cannot be regarded as a characteristic justifying refusal of the use of the 'Emmenthal' designation for goods from other Member States where they are lawfully manufactured and marketed under that designation.

35. The answer to the question referred for a preliminary ruling must therefore be that Article 30 of the Treaty precludes a Member State from applying to products imported from another Member State, where they are lawfully produced and marketed, a national rule prohibiting the marketing of a cheese without rind under the designation 'Emmenthal' in that Member State.

Costs

[Para. 36 omitted]

On those grounds,

THE COURT,

in answer to the question referred to it by the Tribunal de Police, Belley, by judgment of 24 November 1998, hereby rules:

Article 30 of the EC Treaty (now, after amendment, Article 28 EC) precludes a Member State from applying to products imported from another Member

State, where they are lawfully produced and marketed, a national rule prohibiting the marketing of a cheese without rind under the designation 'Emmenthal' in that Member State.

Comments and questions

According to its wording, Article 34 TFEU (formerly Article 30 of TEC) concerns imports of goods between Member States. In other words, the provision only applies to situations which have a cross-border element, so that purely internal situations are not covered by Article 34 TFEU. However, the practice of the CJEU in relation to 'purely internal situations' has not been entirely clear. In Case C-448/98 *Guimont* [2000] ECR I-10663, the CJEU went far in clearing up uncertainties.

The *Guimont* case concerned a French undertaking's production and sale of cheese under the designation 'Emmenthal'. The cheese was produced without rind. Under French rules, the designation 'Emmenthal' could only be used on certain cheeses which had rind. The undertaking had infringed this rule, and criminal proceedings were taken against the director of the undertaking. It was noted that the designation 'Emmenthal' was lawfully used in other Member States on cheeses without rind. This gave rise to the question of whether the French rules conflicted with Article 34 TFEU, and, if so, whether the defendant could rely on this in his defence against the criminal prosecution.

First, the CJEU made it clear that Article 34 TFEU prohibits any measure of the Member States which is capable of hindering intra-Union trade, as defined in Case 8/74 *Procureur du Roi* v *Dassonville* [1974] ECR 837, printed above. On the other hand, Article 34 TFEU does not require domestically produced and foreign produced goods to be treated in the same way. The provision does not prevent a Member State subjecting domestically produced goods for the domestic market to stricter requirements than those which apply to imported goods. Such 'reverse discrimination' is allowed, as long as it does not restrict imports or prejudice the marketing of imported goods. It is different if the restrictive national rules affect the export of the goods in question. Compare this with the practice of the CJEU in relation to persons who exercise the right to freedom of movement (for example, Joined Cases C-224/98 *Prinz and Seeberger*, printed below in Chapter 3).

The French Government argued that, in practice, the prohibition against the use of the designation 'Emmenthal' on cheese without a rind only applied to domestic production. Cheese produced abroad was not required to comply with this rule. However, the prohibition was expressed generally so that it could not be understood from the wording of the provision that foreign produced cheese could be called 'Emmenthal', even if it had no rind. Thus, a foreign cheese manufacturer would not have been able to see that he could sell his rindless cheese in France under the name 'Emmenthal'. Even if the foreign producer had known that the French authorities did not normally enforce the prohibition against foreign producers, the provision could have caused reasonable doubt among foreign producers about the legality of using the name 'Emmenthal'. The CJEU therefore held that a provision which, according to its wording, appeared to infringe against Article 34 TFEU, would not be presumed to be lawful, merely because it was not enforced in practice.

In other words, the French prohibition could not *generally* be regarded as concerning a purely internal situation, and could not thus be excluded from the scope of Article 34 TFEU. However, the French Government argued further that, even though the French measure might fall within the Article 34 TFEU prohibition, it was not a restriction on trade in the *actual case*. The accused was a French national, and the goods in question had been produced and sold in France. The CJEU agreed with this. The particular case concerned a purely internal situation, so Article 34 TFEU did not apply; cf. paragraph 21 of the judgment. However, under French law, a French producer must enjoy the same rights as those which a producer of another Member State would derive from Union law in the same situation; cf. paragraph 23. In other words, a purely national law basis for equal treatment applied, which made the preliminary ruling important. On this basis, the CJEU considered the question in relation to Article 34 TFEU. See likewise Case C-300/01 *Salzmann II* [2003] ECR I-4899, paragraph 33.

The situation would have been different if the prohibition had involved direct discrimination to the disadvantage of imported goods. In this connection the CJEU expressly referred to the judgment in Joined Cases C-321/94 to C-324/94 *Pistre and Others* [1997] ECR I-2343, in which all the facts of the case, as in the *Guimont* case, concerned a single Member State, France. As distinct from the *Guimont* case, the *Pistre* case concerned a French rule that the designation '*montagne*' could only be applied to foods produced in specific mountain regions in France. According to its wording, goods which were imported from other Member States could not use this designation, so the rule was regarded as introducing a directly discriminating provision.

In both the *Guimont* and the *Pistre* cases, there were national provisions which fell within the scope of Article 34 TFEU, but where the facts of both cases only concerned a single Member State. The only difference was that the disputed provision in the *Pistre* case concerned different treatment of domestic and imported goods, which was not the case in the *Guimont* case. Do you agree with the CJEU that the fact that a national rule discriminates as in the *Pistre* case means that the CJEU can consider a referral for a preliminary ruling on the interpretation of Article 34 TFEU, even though the actual case does not contain a cross-border element? In this connection, take into consideration the *Dassonville* doctrine according to which potential restrictions on trade are also covered by Article 34 TFEU.

The fact that the *Guimont* case concerned a purely internal situation means that, under Union law, the case is not covered by Article 34 TFEU. In principle, there is no reason for the CJEU to give judgment on the question, unless national law requires it; cf. the French principle of equivalent treatment referred to above. In his Opinion, Advocate General Saggio stated that the purely internal character of the case must mean it was not necessary for the CJEU to consider the question of national law. However the CJEU did not follow the view of the Advocate General, and chose to consider the question. What reasons does the CJEU give for this (see paragraphs 22 and 23)? Are you persuaded by this reasoning?

In his Opinion, the Advocate General argued that in the *Pistre* case, the CJEU gave Article 34 TFEU a different content than that normally applied by the CJEU to the freedom of movement of persons. For example, see Joined Cases C-64/96 and C-65/96 *Land Nordrhein-Westfalen* v *Uecker and Jacquet* v *Land Nordrhein-Westfalen* [1997] ECR I-3171, which is printed in Chapter 4. See also Case C-281/98 *Roman Angonese* v *Cassa di Risparmio di Bolzano SpA* [2000] ECR I-4139 on Article 45 TFEU, and Joined Cases C-515/99 and others *Hans Reisch and others* v *Bürgermeister der Landeshauptstadt Salzburg and others* [2002] ECR I-2157 (on Article 63 TFEU), both printed below in Chapters 4 and 7 respectively. In these cases, as in the *Guimont* case, the CJEU emphasised the importance of the fact that the cases concerned purely national law bases for equal treatment, which can therefore explain the difference from the *Jacquet* case on this point. What limits to the concept of restriction on trade does the CJEU use in the *Guimont* case?

If a national rule involves non-discriminatory regulation of a product, will it be possible to refer to Article 34 TFEU in national proceedings where all the circumstances of the case concern a single Member State?

JUDGMENT OF THE COURT
17 June 1981

Commission of the European Communities v Ireland

'Failure to fulfil obligations – Measures having an effect equivalent to quantitative restrictions'

Case 113/80

Judgment

1. By an application lodged at the Court Registry on 28 April 1980, the Commission instituted proceedings under Article 169 of the EEC Treaty, for a declaration that Ireland had failed to fulfil its obligations under Article 30 of the EEC Treaty by requiring that the imported goods falling within the scope of the Merchandise Marks (Restriction on Sale of Imported Jewellery) Order 1971 (S. I. No 306, Iris Oifigiúil of 21 November 1971) and the Merchandise Marks (Restriction on Importation of Jewellery) Order 1971 (S. I. No 307, Iris Oifigiúil of 21 November 1971) bear an indication of origin or the word foreign.

2. According to the explanatory notes thereto, Statutory Instrument No 306 (hereinafter referred to as the Sale Order) prohibits the sale or exposure for sale of imported articles of jewellery depicting motifs or possessing characteristics which suggest that they are souvenirs of Ireland, for example an Irish character, event or scene, wolfhound, round tower, shamrock etc. and Statutory Instrument No 307 (hereinafter referred to as the Importation Order) prohibits the importation of such articles unless, in either case, they bear an indication of their country of origin or the word foreign.

3. The articles concerned are listed in a schedule to each order. However, in order to come within the scope of the orders the article must be made of precious metal or rolled precious metal or of base metal, including polished or plated articles suitable for setting.

4. In the Commission's opinion, the restrictions on the free movement of the goods covered by the two orders constitute measures having an effect equivalent to quantitative restrictions on imports, contrary to the provisions of Article 30 of the EEC Treaty; it also observes that according to Article 2 (3) (f) of Directive 70/50/EEC of 22 December 1969, based on the provisions of Article 33 (7) of the Treaty, on the abolition of measures which have an effect equivalent to quantitative restrictions on imports and are not covered by other provisions adopted in pursuance of the EEC Treaty (Official Journal, English Special Edition 1970 (I), p. 17) measures which

lower the value of an imported product, in particular by causing a reduction in its intrinsic value, or increase its costs must be regarded as measures having an effect equivalent to quantitative restrictions, contrary to Article 30 of the EEC Treaty.

5. The Irish Government does not dispute the restrictive effects of these orders on the free movement of goods. However, it contends that the disputed measures are justified in the interests of consumer protection and of fairness in commercial transactions between producers. In this regard, it relies upon Article 36 of the Treaty which provides that Articles 30 to 34 shall not preclude prohibitions or restrictions on imports justified on grounds of public policy or the protection of industrial and commercial property.

6. The defendant is, however, mistaken in placing reliance on Article 36 of the Treaty as the legal basis for its contention.

7. In fact, since the Court stated in its judgment of 25 January 1977 in Case 46/76 Bauhuis [1977] ECR 5 that Article 36 of the Treaty constitutes a derogation from the basic rule that all obstacles to the free movement of goods between Member States shall be eliminated and must be interpreted strictly, the exceptions listed therein cannot be extended to cases other than those specifically laid down.

8. In view of the fact that neither the protection of consumers nor the fairness of commercial transactions is included amongst the exceptions set out in Article 36, those grounds cannot be relied upon as such in connexion with that article.

9. However, since the Irish Government describes its recourse to these concepts as the central issue in the case, it is necessary to study this argument in connexion with Article 30 and to consider whether it is possible, in reliance on those concepts, to say that the Irish orders are not measures having an effect equivalent to quantitative restrictions on imports within the meaning of that article, bearing in mind that, according to the established case-law of the Court, such measures include all trading rules enacted by Member States which are capable of hindering, directly or indirectly, actually or potentially, intra-Community trade (judgment of 11 July 1974 in Case 8/74 Dassonville [1974] ECR 837).

10. In this respect, the Court has repeatedly affirmed (in the judgments of 20 February 1979 in Case 120/78 REWE [1979] ECR 649, 26 June 1980 in Case 788/79 Gilli and Andres [1980] ECR 2071, 19 February 1981 in Case 130/80 Kelderman [1981] ECR) that in the absence of common rules relating to the production and marketing of the product in question it is for Member States to regulate all matters relating to its production, distribution and consumption on their own territory subject, however, to the condition that those rules do not present an obstacle ... to intra-Community trade and that it is only where national rules, which apply without discrimination to both domestic and imported products, may be justified as being necessary in order

to satisfy imperative requirements relating in particular to ... the fairness of commercial transactions and the defence of the consumer that they may constitute an exception to the requirements arising under Article 30.

11. The orders concerned in the present case are not measures which are applicable to domestic products and to imported products without distinction but rather a set of rules which apply only to imported products and are therefore discriminatory in nature, with the result that the measures in issue are not covered by the decisions cited above which relate exclusively to provisions that regulate in a uniform manner the marketing of domestic products and imported products.

12. The Irish Government recognizes that the contested measures apply solely to imported articles and render their importation and sale more difficult than the sale of domestic products. However, it maintains that this difference in the treatment awarded to home-produced articles and to imported articles does not constitute discrimination on the ground that the articles referred to in the contested orders consist mainly of souvenirs; the appeal of such articles lies essentially in the fact of their being manufactured in the place where they are purchased and they bear in themselves an implied indication of their Irish origin, with the result that the purchaser would be misled if the souvenir bought in Ireland was manufactured elsewhere. Consequently, the requirement that all imported souvenirs covered by the two orders must bear an indication of origin is justified and in no way constitutes discrimination because the articles concerned are different on account of the differences between their essential characteristics.

13. The Commission rejects this reasoning. In reliance on the judgment of 20 February 1975 in Case 12/74 Commission v Federal Republic of Germany [1975] ECR 191, it submits that it is unnecessary for a purchaser to know whether or not a product is of a particular origin, unless such origin implies a certain quality, basic materials or process of manufacture or a particular place in the folklore or tradition of the region in question; since none of the articles referred to in the orders display these features, the measures in question cannot be justified and are therefore overtly discriminatory.

14. It is therefore necessary to consider whether the contested measures are indeed discriminatory or whether they constitute discrimination in appearance only.

15. The souvenirs referred to in the Sale Order and in the Importation Order are generally articles of ornamentation of little commercial value representing or incorporating a motif or emblem which is reminiscent of an Irish place, object, character or historical event or suggestive of an Irish symbol and their value stems from the fact that the purchaser, more often than not a tourist, buys them on the spot. The essential characteristic of the souvenirs in question is that they constitute a pictorial re-

minder of the place visited, which does not by itself mean that a souvenir, as defined in the orders, must necessarily be manufactured in the country of origin.

16. Furthermore, leaving aside the point argued by the Commission – with regard to the articles covered by the contested orders – that it would not be enough to require a statement of origin to be affixed to domestic products also, it is important to note that the interests of consumers and fair trading would be adequately safeguarded if it were left to domestic manufacturers to take appropriate steps such as affixing, if they so wished, their mark of origin to their own products or packaging.

17. Thus by granting souvenirs imported from other Member States access to the domestic market solely on condition that they bear a statement of origin, whilst no such statement is required in the case of domestic products, the provisions contained in the Sale Order and the Importation Order indisputably constitute a discriminatory measure.

18. The conclusion to be drawn therefore is that by requiring all souvenirs and articles of jewellery imported from other Member States which are covered by the Sale Order and the Importation Order to bear an indication of origin or the word foreign, the Irish rules constitute a measure having equivalent effect within the meaning of Article 30 of the EEC Treaty. Ireland has consequently failed to fulfil its obligations under the article.

Costs

[Paras 19 and 20 omitted]

On those grounds,

THE COURT

hereby:

1. **Declares that by requiring all articles imported from other Member States which are covered by the Merchandise Marks (Restriction on Sale of Imported Jewellery) Order 1971 and by the Merchandise Marks (Restriction on Importation of Jewellery) Order 1971 to bear an indication of origin or the word foreign, Ireland has failed to fulfil its obligations under Article 30 of the EEC Treaty;**

[Para. 2 of the ruling omitted]

Comments and questions

In Case 113/80 *Commission* v *Ireland* (the *Irish Souvenirs* case) [1981] ECR 1625, the CJEU held that the relevant Irish legislation only applied to imported goods, since it was only these which had to be marked with an indication of origin. The question was whether this amounted to discrimination. It was the view of the Irish Government that the different treatment of souvenirs produced in Ireland and those produced abroad did not amount to discrimination, since souvenirs produced in Ireland were not comparable with souvenirs produced elsewhere. Irish souvenirs had particular characteristics (produced there where they are bought, and thus a true souvenir of Ireland); cf. paragraph 12 of the judgment. The CJEU held that there was discrimination; cf. paragraph 15.

Define when a measure is directly discriminatory, and when it is indirectly discriminatory. Could Article 34 TFEU (formerly Article 30 EEC Treaty) apply if the CJEU agreed with the Irish Government that there was not discrimination?

Consider whether there is discrimination in the following cases – and if so, whether the discrimination is direct or indirect:

- A Member State has a requirement that cinemas may only show films if the producer is listed on the Member State's register of film producers.
- A Member State has a requirement that cinemas may only show films where at least 50% of a film's total financing is derived from that Member State.
- A Member State has a requirement that cinemas may only show films if the actors are citizens of the Member State in question.
- A Member State has a requirement that cinemas may only show films if Swedish actors do not play some of the principal roles.
- A Member State has a requirement that at least 50% of all films shown in the country's cinemas must be films in which the original language is the Member State's official language. The other films must be dubbed in the Member State's official language.
- A Member State prohibits the showing of Danish films in cinemas or on television, because these 'all too often' contain scenes which offend against public morality.
- A Member State requires of cinemas that the prime viewing slots should be reserved for films where the producer, director or principal actors are resident in that Member State.
- A Member State has a requirement that films may only be shown in cinemas if the film itself (the medium which carried the images) is manufactured in the Member State. There are otherwise no requirements as to the origin of the film

Why was it so important for the Irish Government in the *Irish Souvenirs* case to have the CJEU rule that the provision was not discriminatory?

It is stated in paragraph 7 of the judgment that Article 36 TFEU (formerly Article 36 EEC Treaty) is a derogation from the basic rule, and so must be interpreted strictly. The exemptions listed in Article 30 are therefore exhaustive. Is the CJEU's 'Rule of reason' practice (set out in the *Cassis de Dijon* case) applicable to the Irish legislation, so that consideration for the protection of consumers or good business practice could justify the legislation; see paragraph 11?

Note, that Article 34 TFEU does not preclude having stricter requirements for domestically produced goods, since Article 34 TFEU is not concerned with regulating domestic markets, but only trade between Member States; cf. paragraph 16. The Irish Government could thus have required Irish produced souvenirs to be marked with an indication of origin. However, the requirements for such indications of origin may not mean that domestic products thereby receive some special recommendation, as that situation would correspond to that which existed in the *Irish Souvenirs* case.

JUDGMENT OF THE COURT
24 November 1982

Commission of the European Communities v Ireland

'Measures having equivalent effect – Promotion of domestic products'

Case 249/81

Judgment

1. By an application lodged at the Court Registry on 15 September 1981 the Commission of the European Communities brought an action before the Court under Article 169 of the EEC Treaty for a declaration that by organizing a campaign to promote the sale and purchase of Irish products in its territory Ireland has failed to fulfil its obligations under the Treaty.

I – The subject-matter of the application

2. In a reasoned opinion addressed to Ireland on 25 February 1981 concerning the Buy Irish campaign, the Commission noted that in January 1978 the Irish Government had introduced a three-year programme to help to promote Irish products. The campaign was launched on 18 January 1978 in a speech delivered by the Irish Minister for Industry, Commerce and Energy. The Minister declared on that occasion that the aim of the campaign was to achieve a switch from imports to Irish products equivalent to 3% of total consumer spending and that the campaign was a carefully thought out set of initiatives that add up to an integrated programme for promoting Irish goods, with specific proposals to involve the producer, distributor and consumer.

3. The Irish Government, it was said, had taken and was continuing to take a series of measures designed to promote Irish products in accordance with the terms of that speech. The reasoned opinion cited the following measures:

   (a) The organization of a free information service for consumers wishing to know which products in a particular category of goods are made in Ireland and where they may be obtained (the Shoplink Service);
   (b) The provision of exhibition facilities, exclusively for exhibiting Irish products, in a large exhibition centre in Dublin run by the Irish Goods Council, which is, it is claimed, a public authority;
   (c) The encouragement of the use of the Guaranteed Irish symbol for products made in Ireland together with the organization by the Irish Goods Council of a special system for investigating complaints about products bearing that symbol;

(d) The organization of a big publicity campaign by the Irish Goods Council in favour of Irish products, involving in particular the publication and distribution by that institution of literature encouraging consumers to buy only domestic products.

4. The Commission notes in the application that the activities connected with the Shoplink Service and the exhibition facilities in Dublin have now been abandoned by the Irish Government. However, the other two activities have continued, even after the expiry of the three-year period for which the campaign was to last. Moreover, the publicity campaign has been gradually extended, in particular by means of widespread advertising in favour of Irish products in the press and on television.

5. The Irish Government admits that there was a three-year programme in favour of buying Irish products in Ireland. It says that since the Shoplink Service and the exhibition facilities in Dublin were abandoned at the request of the Commission the programme consists merely of an advertising campaign, by means of the press and television, the publication of posters and pamphlets and the use of the Guaranteed Irish symbol, designed to make Irish consumers better acquainted with products made in Ireland and to stimulate awareness in the Irish public of the link between the marketing of such products in Ireland and the unemployment problem in that country.

6. As far as the advertising campaign is concerned, the Irish Government confirms that it forms part of the activities of the Irish Goods Council. However, that institution cannot be regarded as a public authority; it is merely an arrangement whereby the various industries in Ireland may cooperate for their common good. The activities of the Irish Goods Council are not based on any official enactment and the involvement of the Government consists exclusively of financial aid and moral support.

7. The Commission maintains that the actions of the Irish Goods Council are unquestionably attributable to the Irish Government. It points out, in particular, that the members of the Management Committee of the Council are appointed, under the Articles of Association of that body, by the Minister for Industry, Commerce and Energy.

8. The Commission is of the opinion that the campaign to promote the sale and purchase of Irish products in Ireland must be regarded as a measure having an effect equivalent to a quantitative restriction on imports. Ireland contends, first, that the Irish Government has never adopted measures within the meaning of Article 30 of the Treaty and, secondly, that the financial aid given to the Irish Goods Council must be judged in the light of Articles 92 and 93 of the Treaty, and not Article 30.

9. Before assessing the merits of those arguments the position of the Irish Goods Council must be considered.

II – The Irish Goods Council

10. The Irish Goods Council was created on 25 August 1978, a few months after the disputed campaign was launched, in the form of a company limited by guarantee and not having a share capital; it was registered in accordance with Irish company law (Companies Act 1963). The Council is in fact the result of the amalgamation of two bodies, the National Development Council, a company limited by guarantee and registered under the Companies Act, and the Working Group on the Promotion and Sale of Irish Goods.

11. The Irish Government maintains that the Irish Goods Council was created under the sponsorship of the government in order to encourage Irish industry to overcome its own difficulties. The Council was established for the purpose of creating a framework within which the various industries could come together in order to cooperate for their common good.

12. The Management Committee of the Irish Goods Council consists, according to the Articles of Association of that institution, of 10 persons appointed in their individual capacities by the Minister for Industry, Commerce and Energy; the same Minister appoints the chairman from among the members of the Management Committee. The members and the chairman are appointed for a period of three years, and their appointments may be renewed. In practice, the members of the Management Committee are selected by the Minister in such a manner as to represent the appropriate sectors of the Irish economy.

13. It appears from the information supplied by the Irish Government at the request of the Court that the activities of the Irish Goods Council are financed by subsidies paid by the Irish Government and by private industry. The subsidies from the State and from the private sector amounted, respectively to IRL 1 005 000 and IRL 175 000 for the period between August 1978 and December 1979; IRL 940 000 and IRL 194 000 for 1980; and IRL 922 000 and IRL 238 000 for 1981.

14. The Irish Government has not denied that the activities of the Irish Goods Council consist in particular, after the abandonment of the Shoplink Service and the exhibition facilities offered to Irish manufacturers in Dublin, in the organization of an advertising campaign in favour of the sale and purchase of Irish products, and in promoting the use of the Guaranteed Irish symbol.

15. It is thus apparent that the Irish Government appoints the members of the Management Committee of the Irish Goods Council, grants it public subsidies which cover the greater part of its expenses and, finally, defines the aims and the broad outline

of the campaign conducted by that institution to promote the sale and purchase of Irish products. In the circumstances the Irish Government cannot rely on the fact that the campaign was conducted by a private company in order to escape any liability it may have under the provisions of the Treaty.

III – The applicability of Articles 92 and 93 of the Treaty

16. The Irish Government maintains that, even if the purpose or the effect of the campaign was to discourage imports from other Member States, it must be judged on the basis of Articles 92 and 93 of the Treaty, which deal with State aids. The applicability of those provisions excludes the applicability of Article 30 of the Treaty, upon which the Commission has based its case.

17. The Irish Government states that the campaign has in fact been conducted by the Irish Goods Council and that the role of the government has been restricted to moral support and financial assistance. If, as the Commission maintains, the campaign was liable to hinder the free movement of goods within the Community by promoting domestic products at the expense of imported ones that circumstance is attributable solely to a single government decision, namely the decision to subsidize the Irish Goods Council.

18. It must be observed, however, that the fact that a substantial part of the campaign is financed by the Irish Government, and that Articles 92 and 93 of the Treaty may be applicable to financing of that kind, does not mean that the campaign itself may escape the prohibitions laid down in Article 30.

19. In any case, if the Irish Government considered that such financing amounted to aid within the meaning of Articles 92 and 93 it ought to have notified the aid to the Commission in accordance with Article 93 (3).

IV – The application of Article 30 of the Treaty

20. The Commission maintains that the Buy Irish campaign and the measures taken to prosecute the campaign must be regarded, as a whole, as measures encouraging the purchase of domestic products only. Such measures are said to be contrary to the obligations imposed on the Member States by Article 30. The Commission refers to Article 2 (3) (k) of Commission Directive No 70/50/EEC of 22 December 1969, based on the provisions of Article 33 (7), on the abolition of measures which have an effect equivalent to quantitative restrictions on imports and are not covered by other provisions adopted in pursuance of the EEC Treaty (Official Journal, English Special Edition 1970 (I), p. 17). According to Article 2 (3) (k), measures which encourage the purchase of domestic products only must be regarded as contrary to the prohibitions contained in the Treaty.

21. The Irish Government maintains that the prohibition against measures having an effect equivalent to quantitative restrictions in Article 30 is concerned only with measures, that is to say, binding provisions emanating from a public authority. However, no such provision has been adopted by the Irish Government, which has confined itself to giving moral support and financial aid to the activities pursued by the Irish industries.

22. The Irish Government goes on to emphasize that the campaign has had no restrictive effect on imports since the proportion of Irish goods to all goods sold on the Irish market fell from 49.2% in 1977 to 43.4% in 1980.

23. The first observation to be made is that the campaign cannot be likened to advertising by private or public undertakings, or by a group of undertakings, to encourage people to buy goods produced by those undertakings. Regardless of the means used to implement it, the campaign is a reflection of the Irish Government's considered intention to substitute domestic products for imported products on the Irish market and thereby to check the flow of imports from other Member States.

24. It must be remembered here that a representative of the Irish Government stated when the campaign was launched that it was a carefully thought-out set of initiatives constituting an integrated programme for promoting domestic products; that the Irish Goods Council was set up at the initiative of the Irish Government a few months later; and that the task of implementing the integrated programme as it was envisaged by the government was entrusted, or left, to that Council.

25. Whilst it may be true that the two elements of the programme which have continued in effect, namely the advertising campaign and the use of the Guaranteed Irish symbol, have not had any significant success in winning over the Irish market to domestic products, it is not possible to overlook the fact that, regardless of their efficacity, those two activities form part of a government programme which is designed to achieve the substitution of domestic products for imported products and is liable to affect the volume of trade between Member States.

26. The advertising campaign to encourage the sale and purchase of Irish products cannot be divorced from its origin as part of the government programme, or from its connection with the introduction of the Guaranteed Irish symbol and with the organization of a special system for investigating complaints about products bearing that symbol. The establishment of the system for investigating complaints about Irish products provides adequate confirmation of the degree of organization surrounding the Buy Irish campaign and of the discriminatory nature of the campaign.

27. In the circumstances the two activities in question amount to the establishment of a national practice, introduced by the Irish Government and prosecuted with its assis-

tance, the potential effect of which on imports from other Member States is comparable to that resulting from government measures of a binding nature.

28. Such a practice cannot escape the prohibition laid down by Article 30 of the Treaty solely because it is not based on decisions which are binding upon undertakings. Even measures adopted by the government of a Member State which do not have binding effect may be capable of influencing the conduct of traders and consumers in that State and thus of frustrating the aims of the Community as set out in Article 2 and enlarged upon in Article 3 of the Treaty.

29. That is the case where, as in this instance, such a restrictive practice represents the implementation of a programme defined by the government which affects the national economy as a whole and which is intended to check the flow of trade between Member States by encouraging the purchase of domestic products, by means of an advertising campaign on a national scale and the organization of special procedures applicable solely to domestic products, and where those activities are attributable as a whole to the government and are pursued in an organized fashion throughout the national territory.

30. Ireland has therefore failed to fulfil its obligations under the Treaty by organizing a campaign to promote the sale and purchase of Irish goods within its territory.

Costs

[Para. 31 omitted]

On those grounds,

THE COURT

hereby:

1. **Declares that by organizing a campaign to promote the sale and purchase of Irish products within its territory Ireland has failed to fulfil its obligations under the Treaty;**

[Para. 2 of the ruling omitted]

Comments and questions

Note that in Case 249/81 *Commission* v *Ireland* (the *Buy Irish* case) [1982] ECR 4005, the CJEU stated, in paragraph 15 of the judgment, that it is the Irish Government which appoints the members of the management committee of the Irish Goods Council, grants it public subsidies which cover the greater part of its expenses and, finally, defines the aims and the broad outline of the campaign conducted by that institution to promote the sale and purchase of Irish products. It was also clear from paragraph 11 that it was the Irish Government which took the initiative for setting up the Irish Goods Council. On this basis, the CJEU held that the Irish Government was responsible for the company, even if only indirectly; cf. paragraph 15. Compare the reasoning of the CJEU in the *Buy Irish* case with its reasoning in Case 325/00 *Commission* v *Germany* (the *Markenqualität* case) [2002] ECR I-9977.

Do you find that in the *Buy Irish* case the CJEU applies a general or an expanded interpretation of the term 'measures having equivalent effect'?

The fact that a measure is covered by Article 107 TFEU (formerly Article 92 EEC Treaty) (on State aid) does not mean that the measure cannot also be considered in relation to other Treaty provisions, e.g. Article 34 TFEU (formerly Article 30 EEC Treaty); cf. paragraph 18 of the judgment. Similarly, in both Case C-47/88 *Commission* v *Denmark* (on car registration taxes) [1990] ECR I-4509, and Case C-383/01 *Danske Bilimportører* v *Skatteministeriet* (on car imports) [2003] ECR I-6065, the latter of which is printed above, the CJEU stated that in special cases it is possible to consider an internal tax both under Article 110 TFEU (formerly Article 95 EEC Treaty), which contains a prohibition of discriminatory internal taxation, and under Article 34 TFEU. However, it remains the view of the CJEU that Article 34 TFEU does not cover measures which can be dealt with under other provisions of the TFEU.

Under Article 34 TFEU, it is *not* a requirement that the measure in the actual case should constitute an *appreciable* restriction on trade; cf. paragraph 25 of the judgment. Even where the sales of foreign goods have not fallen, and may even have increased following the introduction of a measure, it may be covered by Article 34 TFEU, if it is *capable* of affecting trade. It was sufficient that the campaign was potentially restrictive on trade; cf. Case 8/74 *Procureur du Roi* v *Dassonville* [1974] ECR 837, and the comments below on Case C-67/97 *Bluhme (Brown Bees)* [1998] ECR I-8033, on the absence of a *de minimis* rule in Article 28.

The judgment also shows that *non-binding state measures*, which are capable of having an effect on trade, are covered by Article 34 TFEU; cf. paragraph 28. In contrast, in point 6 of his Opinion on this case, the Advocate General argued that the encouragement to 'buy Irish' was not covered by Article 34 TFEU. He argued that the Irish initiative did not constitute a 'measure' within the meaning of Article 34 TFEU.

The *Buy Irish* case concerned certain marketing measures. Would the case have been covered by the *Keck* doctrine today?

Under the headline 'Food label rules tightened to promote best of British', *The Guardian* reported on 25th October 1999, that the British Government 'will spend an extra £15m on promoting British-produced food.' The background to this government initiative was that, in particular, French farm animals had been fed on human and animal excrement. According to the article, the existing British rules allowed for using the designation 'Produced in the UK'. However, it was possible to use this designation, even though the product in question was not 100% British. The article also reported that the 'new regulations would force producers to declare when meat does not come from Britain – and give this disclosure as much prominence as the claim that the item is 'British''. Consider the extent to which such rules are in accordance with the TFEU rules on the free movement of goods.

In the spring of 2000, the British Ministry of Agriculture and the Meat and Livestock Commission conducted an advertising campaign which accused non-British pig production of cannibalism, because in a number of other countries pigs were fed on bone-meal manufactured from other pigs. The British Ministry of Agriculture contributed about £5m to the campaign, about half its cost. Does the campaign comply with the TFEU rules on the free movement of goods? Is it important for your assessment whether, before running the campaign, the British Government knew that it was aimed at promoting British pig meat at the expense of pig meat produced in other Member States?

In June 2000, Ritt Bjerregaard, the then Danish Minister for Food and former European Commissioner, let it be known that she was dissatisfied with the steps taken by the EU on salmonella in poultry, which is a health hazard. Research showed that there were salmonella bacteria in 20% of the poultry imported into Denmark, while the equivalent figure for Danish produced poultry was 3%. The Danish Minister for Food therefore wanted to stop imports of foreign poultry which was not guaranteed free from salmonella, but did not wish to risk infringing the EU rules. She therefore expressed her views to a Danish newspaper: 'We are up against EU rules which mean that, every time we want to do something about importing poultry with salmonella, we can't prevent imports, but if we make a general agreement with the retail industry, then it isn't Denmark which is discriminating against imports.' Do you think that a general and non-binding agreement to keep foreign poultry out of the Danish market would fall under the prohibition in Article 34 TFEU? Consider whether, under the heading of the protection of public health, the Danish authorities could set up a general requirement that all poultry (both domestic and foreign) sold in Denmark should be guaranteed free from salmonella (in other words that there should be a prohibition of the sale of salmonella infected poultry)?

In June 2009 one third of Swedish local government authorities stated that they would boycott the purchase of Danish pig meat for their care homes, schools and day care centres, because a documentary film that had just been broadcast on Swedish television had shown that Danish pigs do not have enough room in their pens, they have pressure sores etc. Is such a boycott compatible with Article 34 TFEU?

In connection with the procurement of military equipment, such as fighter aircraft, would a Member State be able to impose a condition requiring the manufacturer of such equipment to make purchases in the procuring Member State corresponding to over 50% of the value of the military equipment bought, on the basis that the purchasing Member State wishes to maintain its domestic defence industry? In this connection, see Article 346 TFEU.

JUDGMENT OF THE COURT (Fifth Chamber)
3 December 1998

Criminal proceedings against Ditlev Bluhme.
(Reference for a preliminary ruling: Kriminalretten i Frederikshavn – Denmark)

'Free movement of goods – Prohibition of quantitative restrictions and measures having equivalent effect between Member States – Derogations – Protection of the health and life of animals – Bees of the subspecies Apis mellifera mellifera (Læsø brown bee)'

Case C-67/97

Judgment

1. By order of 3 July 1995, received at the Court on 17 February 1997, the Kriminalret i Frederikshavn (Criminal Court, Frederikshavn) referred to the Court for a preliminary ruling under Article 177 of the EC Treaty a number of questions on the interpretation of Article 30 of the EC Treaty and Article 2 of Council Directive 91/174/EEC of 25 March 1991 laying down zootechnical and pedigree requirements for the marketing of pure-bred animals and amending Directives 77/504/EEC and 90/425/EEC (OJ 1991 L 85, p. 37, hereinafter 'the Directive').

2. The questions have been raised in criminal proceedings brought against Ditlev Bluhme for infringement of Danish legislation prohibiting the keeping on the island of Læsø of bees other than those of the subspecies Apis mellifera mellifera (Læsø brown bee).

3. Article 1 of the Directive provides:

   'For the purposes of this Directive 'pure-bred animal' shall mean any animal for breeding covered by Annex II to the Treaty the trade in which has not yet been the subject of more specific Community zootechnical legislation and which is entered or registered in a register or pedigree record kept by a recognised breeders' organisation or association.'

4. Article 2 of the Directive provides:

   'Member States shall ensure that:

   – the marketing of pure-bred animals and of the semen, ova and embryos thereof is not prohibited, restricted or impeded on zootechnical or pedigree grounds,
   – in order to ensure that the requirement provided for in the first indent is satisfied, the criteria for approval and recognition of breeders' organisations or as-

sociations, the criteria for entry or registration in pedigree records or registers, the criteria for approval for reproduction of pure-bred animals and for the use of their semen, ova and embryos, and the certificate to be required for their marketing should be established in a non-discriminatory manner, with due regard for the principles laid down by the organisation or association which maintains the register or pedigree record of the breed in question. Pending the implementation of detailed rules for application as provided for in Article 6, national laws shall remain applicable with due regard for the general provisions of the Treaty.'

5. Article 6 of the Directive provides that the detailed rules for application of the Directive are to be adopted in accordance with the so-called 'committee' procedure. No such rules have been adopted in relation to bees.

6. In Denmark, Article 14a of Law No 115 of 31 March 1982 on beekeeping (lov om biavl), introduced by Law No 267 of 6 May 1993, authorises the Minister for Agriculture to enact provisions to protect certain species of bee in certain areas defined by him, and in particular provisions concerning the removal or destruction of swarms of bees regarded as undesirable for protection reasons. Article 1 of Decision No 528 of 24 June 1993 on the keeping of bees on the island of Læsø (Bekendtgørelse om biavl på Laesø, hereinafter 'the Decision'), which was adopted pursuant to that enabling provision, prohibits the keeping on Læsø and certain neighbouring islands of nectar-gathering bees other than those of the subspecies Apis mellifera mellifera (Læsø brown bee).

7. The Decision also provides, in Article 2, for the removal or destruction of those other swarms or the replacement of their queen by one of the Læsø brown bee subspecies. Article 6 prohibits the introduction onto Læsø or neighbouring islands of living domestic bees, whatever their stage of development, or of reproductive material for domestic bees. Finally, Article 7 of the Decision provides for full State compensation in respect of any loss duly proved to have resulted from the destruction of a swarm pursuant to the Decision.

8. Mr Bluhme, who is being prosecuted for keeping on Læsø bees other than those of the subspecies Apis mellifera mellifera (Læsø brown bee), in breach of the Decision, argues inter alia that Article 30 of the Treaty precludes the national legislation.

9. Taking the view that resolution of the dispute before it depended on the interpretation of Community law, the Kriminalret decided to stay the proceedings and to refer the following questions to the Court:

'I Concerning the interpretation of Article 30 of the EC Treaty:

1) Can Article 30 be interpreted as meaning that a Member State may, under certain circumstances, introduce rules prohibiting the keeping – and consequently the importation – of all bees other than bees belonging to the species Apis mellifera mellifera (Læsø brown bee) with regard to a specific island in the country in question, for example, an island of 114 km2, one half of which consists of country villages and small ports, and is used for purposes of tourism or agriculture, while the other half consists of uncultivated land, that is to say, plantations, moorland, meadows, tidal meadows, beaches and dunes, which had on 1 January 1997 a population of 2 365, and which is an island on which opportunities for gainful activity are in general limited but where beekeeping constitutes one of the few forms of gainful activity by reason of the island's special flora and high proportion of uncultivated and extensively used land?

2) If a Member State can introduce such rules, the Court is requested to describe in general the conditions governing those rules and in particular to answer the following questions:

   (a) Can a Member State introduce such rules as described in (1) on the ground that the rules concern solely such an island as described and that the effect of the rules is therefore geographically limited?

   (b) Can a Member State introduce such rules as described in (1) if the reason for those rules lies in the desire to protect the bee strain Apis mellifera mellifera against eradication, an objective which, in the Member State's opinion, can be attained by excluding all other bee strains from the island in question?

   In the criminal proceedings underlying this order for reference, the accused:

   - disputes that there is at all any such bee strain as Apis mellifera mellifera and submits that the bees at present to be found on Læsø are a mixture of different bee strains;
   - submits that the brown bees to be found on Læsø are not unique but are found in many parts of the world; and

   submits that those bees are not threatened with eradication.

   In its response, the Court is therefore requested to indicate whether it is sufficient that the Member State in question considers it appropriate or necessary to introduce the rules as a step in preserving the bee population in question, or whether it must be regarded as a further condition that the bee strain exists, and/or that it is unique, and/or that it is threatened with eradication if the import ban is not valid or cannot be enforced.

(c) If the grounds set out in (a) or in (b) cannot make it lawful to introduce such rules, can a combination of those grounds make it so lawful?

II Concerning Council Directive 91/174/EEC of 25 March 1991 laying down zootechnical and pedigree requirements for the marketing of pure-bred animals and amending Directives 77/504/EEC and 90/425/EEC:

1) Under what circumstances can a bee be a pure-bred animal within the meaning attached to those words by Article 2 of Directive 91/174? Is a golden bee, for example, a pure-bred animal?

2) What constitutes a zootechnical ground (Article 2)?

3) What constitutes a pedigree ground (Article 2)?

4) Must Directive 91/174 be understood as meaning that a Member State may, notwithstanding the Directive, ban the importation onto an island such as that described in Question 1 of Part I and the existence there of all bees other than bees belonging to the strain Apis mellifera mellifera?

If a Member State can do so under certain conditions, the Court is requested to set out those conditions.'

Part II of the questions

10. By its questions the national court is essentially asking the Court to give an interpretation of Article 1 and the first paragraph of Article 2 of the Directive.

11. It should however be pointed out that, as the Danish Government and the Commission have rightly observed, no detailed rules for applying the Directive in relation to bees have been adopted under the procedure provided for by Article 6 of the Directive.

12. Therefore, pursuant to the second paragraph of Article 2 of the Directive, national laws remain applicable, subject, however, to due regard for the general provisions of the Treaty.

13. It is therefore in relation to Articles 30 and 36 of the EC Treaty that legislation such as that at issue in the main proceedings must be examined.

Part I of the questions

14. By its questions the national court is essentially asking whether national legislation prohibiting the keeping of any species of bee on an island such as Læsø other than

the subspecies Apis mellifera mellifera (Læsø brown bee) constitutes a measure having equivalent effect to a quantitative restriction within the meaning of Article 30 of the Treaty and whether, if that is the case, such legislation may be justified on the ground of the protection of the health and life of animals.

Existence of a measure having equivalent effect

15. Mr Bluhme and the Commission consider that a prohibition on the keeping on the island of Læsø of bees other than those belonging to the Læsø brown species involves a prohibition on importation, and thus constitutes a measure having equivalent effect contrary to Article 30 of the Treaty. Mr Bluhme considers that the legislation at issue in the main proceedings effectively precludes the importation onto the island of Læsø of bees from Member States. The Commission adds in that respect that Article 30 also applies to measures that concern only part of the territory of a Member State.

16. The Danish, Italian and Norwegian Governments, on the other hand, maintain that the establishment of pure breeding areas for a given species in a delimited geographical area within a Member State does not affect trade between Member States. The Danish and Norwegian Governments further maintain that the prohibition on importing onto the island of Læsø bees other than Læsø brown bees does not constitute discrimination in respect of bees originating in other Member States, is not intended to regulate trade between Member States, and has effects on trade that are too hypothetical and uncertain to be regarded as a measure likely to obstruct it.

17. The Danish Government also argues that, since the national legislation does not concern the access of bees as goods to the Danish market, but merely regulates the conditions under which bees may be kept within that Member State, it falls outside the scope of Article 30 of the Treaty.

18. On that point, the Court observes that its case-law has long established that all measures capable of hindering intra-Community trade, whether directly or indirectly, actually or potentially, constitute measures having an effect equivalent to quantitative restrictions (Case 8/74 Procureur du Roi v Dassonville [1974] ECR 837, paragraph 5).

19. In so far as Article 6 of the legislative measure at issue in the main proceedings involves a general prohibition on the importation onto Læsø and neighbouring islands of living bees and reproductive material for domestic bees, it also prohibits their importation from other Member States, so that it is capable of hindering intra-Community trade. It therefore constitutes a measure having an effect equivalent to a quantitative restriction.

20. That conclusion is not altered by the fact that the measure in question applies to only part of the national territory (on this point, see Joined Cases C-1/90 and C-176/90 Aragonesa de Publicidad and Publivíía v Departamento de Sanidad [1991] ECR I-4151, paragraph 24; Joined Cases C-277/91, C-318/91 and C-319/91 Ligur Carni and Others [1993] ECR I-6621, paragraph 37).

21. Moreover, contrary to the Danish Government's argument that the prohibition on keeping certain bees on the island of Læsø must be regarded as a regulation on selling arrangements within the meaning of the judgment in Joined Cases C-267/91 and C-268/91 Keck and Mithouard [1993] ECR I-6097, this Court finds, on the contrary, that the legislation in question concerns the intrinsic characteristics of the bees. In those circumstances, its application to the facts of the case cannot be a matter of a selling arrangement within the meaning of the judgment in Keck and Mithouard (Case C-368/95 Familiapress v Heinrich Bauer Verlag [1997] ECR I-3689, paragraph 11).

22. Finally, as the Advocate General points out at point 19 of his Opinion, since the Decision prohibits the importation of bees from other Member States onto a part of Danish territory, it has a direct and immediate impact on trade, and not effects too uncertain and too indirect for the obligation which it lays down not to be capable of being regarded as being of such a kind as to hinder trade between Member States.

23. It follows that a legislative measure prohibiting the keeping on an island such as Læsø of any species of bee other than the subspecies Apis mellifera mellifera (Læsø brown bee) constitutes a measure having an effect equivalent to a quantitative restriction within the meaning of Article 30 of the Treaty.

Justification for legislation such as that at issue in the main proceedings

24. Mr Bluhme argues that the legislation in question cannot be justified on any ground, especially since, in his submission, there is no subspecies Apis mellifera mellifera (Læsø brown bee) that is genetically distinct and unique to the island of Læsø. Moreover, since such legislation does not fall within the scope of health policy, he submits that it cannot be justified under Council Directive 92/65/EEC of 13 July 1992 laying down animal health requirements governing trade in and imports into the Community of animals, semen, ova and embryos not subject to animal health requirements laid down in specific Community rules referred to in Annex A (I) to Directive 90/425/EEC (OJ 1992 L 268, p. 54).

25. The Danish Government considers that, should the Court regard the prohibition laid down by the Decision as a measure having an effect equivalent to a quantitative restriction, it is a measure applying to bees indiscriminately whatever their State of provenance which is justified by the aim of protecting biological diversity, such aim being recognised, inter alia, by Council Directive 92/43/EEC of 21 May 1992 on

the conservation of natural habitats and of wild fauna and flora (OJ 1992 L 206, p. 7) and by the Convention on Biological Diversity signed at Rio de Janeiro on 5 June 1992, approved on behalf of the European Community by Council Decision 93/626/EEC of 25 October 1993 (OJ 1993 L 309, p. 1; hereinafter 'the Rio Convention'). The Danish Government goes on to explain that the subspecies Apis mellifera mellifera (Læsø brown bee) is disappearing and can be preserved only on the island of Læsø, so that the measure adopted is necessary to prevent the disappearance of the species and is proportionate to the aim pursued. Moreover, the Decision does not affect the possibility of carrying on bee-keeping on the island but merely regulates the species of bee which may be used.

26. The Danish Government concludes by referring to numerous scientific studies establishing the particular nature of that subspecies of bee in relation to others.

27. As its main argument, the Norwegian Government submits that the Danish legislation is justified on environmental protection grounds in accordance with Article 30 of the Treaty and the judgment in Case 120/78 REWE-Zentral v Bundesmonopolverwaltung füür Branntwein [1979] ECR 649 ('Cassis de Dijon'), paragraph 8.

28. In the alternative, like the Italian Government and the Commission, it considers that the preservation of a rare and threatened species falls within the protection of the health and life of animals referred to in Article 36 of the Treaty.

29. In the Norwegian Government's submission, the establishment of pure breeding areas is the only means of preserving the Læsø brown bee.

30. The Commission maintains that the same ground of justification should be upheld if the species were not rare and threatened, but it was desirable on scientific grounds to breed a pure strain.

31. On the question of the existence of a disappearing subspecies Apis mellifera mellifera (Læsø brown bee), the Commission considers that this is an evidential matter which is therefore one for the national court to determine. It maintains that the prohibition should not extend to the keeping of brown bees of the species Apis mellifera mellifera from other Member States or from non-member countries in the absence of a valid reason to justify such a restriction, and points out that such a prohibition must not constitute a means of arbitrary discrimination or be aimed at protecting certain occupational interests.

32. The Italian Government states that there are several subspecies of Apis mellifera mellifera, identifiable as strains and within the latter as ecotypes, representing the result of a natural process of adaptation to environmental conditions and various territories.

33. On this question, the Court considers that measures to preserve an indigenous animal population with distinct characteristics contribute to the maintenance of biodiversity by ensuring the survival of the population concerned. By so doing, they are aimed at protecting the life of those animals and are capable of being justified under Article 36 of the Treaty.

34. From the point of view of such conservation of biodiversity, it is immaterial whether the object of protection is a separate subspecies, a distinct strain within any given species or merely a local colony, so long as the populations in question have characteristics distinguishing them from others and are therefore judged worthy of protection either to shelter them from a risk of extinction that is more or less imminent, or, even in the absence of such risk, on account of a scientific or other interest in preserving the pure population at the location concerned.

35. It does, however, have to be determined whether the national legislation was necessary and proportionate in relation to its aim of protection, or whether it would have been possible to achieve the same result by less stringent measures (Case 124/81 Commission v United Kingdom [1983] ECR 203, paragraph 16).

36. Conservation of biodiversity through the establishment of areas in which a population enjoys special protection, which is a method recognised in the Rio Convention, especially Article 8a thereof, is already put into practice in Community law [in particular, by means of the special protection areas provided for in Council Directive 79/409/EEC of 2 April 1979 on the conservation of wild birds (OJ 1979 L 103, p. 1), or the special conservation areas provided for in Directive 92/43].

37. As for the threat of the disappearance of the Læsø brown bee, it is undoubtedly genuine in the event of mating with golden bees by reason of the recessive nature of the genes of the brown bee. The establishment by the national legislation of a protection area within which the keeping of bees other than Læsø brown bees is prohibited, for the purpose of ensuring the survival of the latter, therefore constitutes an appropriate measure in relation to the aim pursued.

38. The answer to be given must therefore be that a national legislative measure prohibiting the keeping on an island such as Læsø of any species of bee other than the subspecies Apis mellifera mellifera (Læsø brown bee) must be regarded as justified, under Article 36 of the Treaty, on the ground of the protection of the health and life of animals.

Costs

[Para. 39 omitted]

On those grounds,

THE COURT (Fifth Chamber),

in answer to the questions referred to it by the Kriminalret i Frederikshavn by order of 3 July 1995, hereby rules:

1. **A national legislative measure prohibiting the keeping on an island such as Læsø of any species of bee other than the subspecies Apis mellifera mellifera (Læsø brown bee) constitutes a measure having an effect equivalent to a quantitative restriction within the meaning of Article 30 of the EC Treaty.**

2. **A national legislative measure prohibiting the keeping on an island such as Læsø of any species of bee other than the subspecies Apis mellifera mellifera (Læsø brown bee) must be regarded as justified, under Article 36 of the Treaty, on the ground of the protection of the health and life of animals.**

Comments and questions

Article 34 TFEU (formerly Article 30 EEC Treaty) concerns the free movement of goods. The concept of 'goods' is very wide, and can cover all products to which a value can be attached and which can be the subject of trading. Even goods which have a negative value (waste) are covered by Article 34 TFEU; cf. the judgment in Case C-2/90 *Commission* v *Belgium* [1992] ECR I-4413, printed below, (the *Walloon waste disposal* case). Insects, such as bees, fall within the concept of 'goods' in Article 34 TFEU and are also be covered.

In Case C-67/97 *Bluhme* [1998] ECR 8033, the Danish Government put forward four reasons in support of its argument for why an Executive Order concerning Læsø brown bees was not covered by Article 34 TFEU. *First,* the Danish Government argued that the effect of the Executive Order on trade was negligible, if measurable at all, since the prohibition of the keeping bees other than the Læsø brown bee only concerned the very small island of Læsø. The CJEU rejected this argument in paragraphs 18 and 19 of the judgment, since it stated that the case involved a general prohibition which constituted a measure having an effect equivalent to a quantitative restriction according to the *Dassonville* doctrine.

Second, it was the view of the Danish Government that the prohibition would, in any case, have too hypothetical and uncertain an effect on trade to be regarded as being capable of being a restriction. The CJEU also rejected this argument; cf. paragraph 22, in which it was stated that since the Executive Order prohibits the importation of bees from other Member States to a part of Danish territory, it has a direct and immediate impact on trade. Consider whether the CJEU's reasoning means that a prohibition on imports can never fall outside the scope of the TFEU, regardless of how insignificant the area covered may be. Does the CJEU accept that there could be situations in which a measure can have such uncertain and indirect effects on trade that the measure could fall outside the scope of the TFEU (see Case C-69/88 *H. Krantz GmbH & Co* v *Ontvanger der Directe Belastingen and the Netherlands* [1990] ECR I-583)? In European competition law it is accepted that there is a *de minimis* threshold, so that certain measures may have such limited effect (on competition or on trade between Member States), that they are not covered by the Treaty prohibition. Does this *de minimis* threshold apply to the rules on the free movement of goods?

The *third* argument of the Danish Government was that the prohibition of the use of bees, other than the Læsø brown bee, was a measure to regulate the manner in which honey was produced on Læsø. On the question of the regulation of use, see the judgments in Case C-110/05 *Commission* v *Italy* (Motorcycle trailers) [2009] ECR I-519, reproduced above, and Case C-142/05 *Åklagaren* v *Mickelsson and Roos* (Jet-skis), [2009] ECR I-4273, referred to above. The Danish Government therefore believed that the prohibition was covered by the *Keck* doctrine, and was thus lawful. The counter-argument to this was that the prohibition against other bees concerned the intrinsic characteristics of the product (i.e., the bees), and there was therefore a 'product requirement' within the meaning of the *Keck* doctrine. Do you agree that the principles of the *Keck* case are applicable to the facts of this case?

In his Opinion on the case, Advocate General Fennelly discussed whether the prohibition was discriminatory. He argued that the answer depends on the point of view. If one looks upon the measure as a prohibition, it is a prohibition against the import of both Danish and foreign golden bees. The prohibition thus applied, regardless of the origin of the bees. On the other hand, if one looks at the measure as an order only to keep brown bees on Læsø, this means that only one particular kind of Danish bee could be allowed on the island, while all foreign bees, both brown and golden, were excluded. The Advocate General argued that, if the measure is viewed from this angle, it was discriminatory. Do you agree with the Advocate General that the measure can be seen as discriminatory?

The fact that an import prohibition has a very limited territorial scope, applying to only part of a national territory, does not mean that there is not discrimination. For such an import prohibition to be regarded as discriminatory or protective, it is not necessary to show that *all* domestically produced goods are advantaged, or that only foreign and no domestic goods are disadvantaged; cf. for example, paragraph 24 in Joined Cases C-1/90 and C-176/90 *Aragonesa de Publicidad Exterior* v *Departamento de Sanidad de Cataluña* [1991] ECR I-4151. The CJEU also established, even if indirectly in paragraph 20, that there was discrimination in the *Bluhme* case. Compare this point with the definition of discrimination in the judgment in Case C-2/90 *Commission* v *Belgium* [1992] ECR I-4413 (the *Walloon waste disposal* case). However, there is not necessarily discrimination in all cases where, for example, there is a requirement for residence in a given area in order to obtain certain rights. See the Advocate General's Opinion in Case C-452/01 *Margarethe Ospelt and Schlössle Weissenberg Familienstiftung* [2003] ECR I-9743, paragraph 124 et seq. (the case is printed below in Chapter 7).

As for the *fourth* argument of the Danish Government, the CJEU refrained from expressing a view on it. In the view of the Danish Government, the criminal case concerned purely internal circumstances, so the accused could not claim rights under Article 34 TFEU. The fact was that Ditlev Bluhme was a Danish national who kept Danish golden bees on Læsø, in contravention of a Danish Executive Order. Thus, in the view of the Danish Government, there was no cross-border element in the case. The Advocate General disagreed with this, referring to the fact that Bluhme was permitted, by the Danish authorities, to import and export bees. This meant, said the Advocate General, that there was a possibility that the Executive Order could prevent Bluhme importing foreign bees to Læsø; cf. paragraph 21 of the Advocate General's Opinion. However, it is questionable whether this view is in accordance with the practice of the CJEU. Until judgment was given in Joined Cases C-321/94 to C-324/94 *Pistre and Others* [1997] ECR I-2343 referred to above, it was the established practice of the CJEU that Article 34 TFEU was only applicable to proceedings before national courts *if* the case in question *actually* contained cross-border elements. This applied even if the national law was in conflict with Article 34 TFEU, and could therefore be challenged by an importer or a foreign producer. In the *Pistre* case the CJEU considered a national rule which was discriminatory, but in a case which did not in fact have any cross-border elements. See Case C-448/98 *Guimont* [2000] ECR I-10663, printed above. Do you think that the *Bluhme* case involves a *purely internal situation*, and should Article 34 TFEU apply?

The *Bluhme* case concerned a Danish rule that prohibited the importation of all bees (with one exception) into a limited area of Denmark. Such a prohibition is normally classified as a quantitative restriction, but in the judgment Mr Bluhme and the Commission (in paragraph 15) as well as the CJEU itself (paragraphs 18-20 and 23) classified it as a measure having an equivalent effect. Is it possible to provide a convincing explanation for this?

Article 267 TFEU is intended to give national courts the possibility of referring questions to the CJEU with a view to obtaining an authoritative interpretation of Union law. However, it is national courts which apply that interpretation to the actual case and which therefore determine the result of the case. Read again paragraphs 9 and 38, as well as 31. How much room for manoeuvre does the referring court have, to decide whether the Danish prohibition is permitted under Union law?

JUDGMENT OF THE COURT
13 March 2001

PreussenElektra AG v Schhleswag AG, in the presence of
Windpark Reußenköge III GmbH and Land Schleswig-Holstein.
(Reference for a preliminary ruling: Landgericht Kiel – Germany)

'Electricity – Renewable sources of energy – National legislation requiring electricity supply undertakings to purchase electricity at minimum prices and apportioning the resulting costs between those undertakings and upstream network operators – State aid – Compatibility with the free movement of goods'

Case C-379/98

Judgment

1. By order of 13 October 1998, received at the Court on 23 October 1998, the Landgericht Kiel (Regional Court, Kiel) referred to the Court for a preliminary ruling under Article 177 of the EC Treaty (now Article 234 EC) three questions on the interpretation of Article 30 of the EC Treaty (now, after amendment, Article 28 EC), Article 92 of the EC Treaty (now, after amendment, Article 87 EC) and Article 93(3) of the EC Treaty (now Article 88(3) EC).

2. The questions were raised in proceedings between PreussenElektra AG ('PreussenElektra') and Schleswag AG ('Schleswag') concerning the repayment of sums paid by the former to the latter pursuant to Paragraph 4(1) of the Gesetz über die Einspeisung von Strom aus erneuerbaren Energien in das öffentliche Netz (Law on feeding electricity from renewable energy sources into the public grid) of 7 December 1990 (BGBl. 1990 I, p. 2633; 'the Stromeinspeisungsgesetz'), as amended by Paragraph 3(2) of the Gesetz zur Neuregelung des Energiewirtschaftsrechts (New law for the energy industry) of 24 April 1998 (BGBl. 1998 I, p. 730; 'the 1998 Law).

Legislative background

[Paras 3-16 omitted]

The main proceedings and the questions referred

17. PreussenElektra operates more than 20 conventional and nuclear power stations in Germany as well as a maximum-voltage and high-voltage electricity distribution network, through which it feeds electricity to regional electricity suppliers, medium-scale local undertakings and industry.

18. Schleswag is a regional electricity supplier which buys electricity to supply to its customers in Schleswig-Holstein almost exclusively from PreussenElektra.

19. PreussenElektra owns 65.3% of Schleswag's shares. The remaining 34.7% are held by various municipal authorities in Schleswig-Holstein.

20. By virtue of Paragraph 2 of the Stromeinspeisungsgesetz, Schleswag is obliged to purchase electricity from renewable sources produced within its area of supply, including wind-generated electricity. The order for reference shows that the proportion of wind-generated electricity in Schleswag's total turnover in electricity sales, which was 0.77% in 1991, has increased continuously to an estimated 15% in 1998. In consequence, the additional costs accruing to Schleswag on account of the obligation to purchase at the minimum price laid down by the Stromeinspeisungsgesetz rose from DEM 5.8 million in 1991 to an estimated DEM 111.5 million in 1998, of which only DEM 38 million remained the responsibility of Schleswag, taking into account the application of the compensation mechanism introduced into Paragraph 4(1) of the Stromeinspeisungsgesetz by the 1998 Law.

21. At the end of April 1998 Schleswag's purchases of electricity produced from renewable energy sources reached 5% of the total volume of electricity it had sold over the previous year. Schleswag therefore invoiced PreussenElektra, pursuant to Paragraph 4(1) of the Stromeinspeisungsgesetz, as amended by the 1998 law ('the amended Stromeinspeisungsgesetz'), for the additional costs entailed by the purchase of electricity from renewable energy sources, initially claiming from it monthly instalments of DEM 10 million.

22. PreussenElektra transferred the instalment for May 1998, reserving the right to claim the money back at any time. That is what it did by making an application to the Landgericht Kiel for the repayment of DEM 500 000, representing the part of the sum paid to Schleswag in compensation for the additional costs entailed by the latter's purchase of wind-generated electricity. The Landgericht states, in its order for reference, that those additional costs cannot be passed on to Schleswag's customers since the Minister for Energy of Land Schleswig Holstein refused to approve an application by Schleswag to amend its tariffs.

23. Before the Landgericht, PreussenElektra argued that the sum claimed had been paid to Schleswag without a valid legal reason and should be recoverable, since Paragraph 4 of the Stromeinspeisungsgesetz, as amended, on which that payment was based, was contrary to the directly applicable provisions of the Treaty on State aid and could not therefore be applied. The plaintiff argued that prior to the entry into force of the 1998 Law it would have been necessary, in order to amend the scope of the Stromeinspeisungsgesetz and introduce a rule for sharing additional costs, as the 1998 Law did, to have recourse to the procedure laid down by Article 93 of the Treaty; this the Federal Republic of Germany had omitted to do. PreussenElektra

therefore requested that Schleswag be ordered to repay to it the sum of DEM 500 000, together with interest at 5% as from 15 July 1998.

24. Schleswag contended that that claim should be dismissed. Whilst recognising that the Stromeinspeisungsgesetz, as amended, contained a modified aid scheme, it maintained that Paragraph 4 was merely a redistribution rule, intended to mitigate the consequences which electricity supply undertakings suffered by reason of Paragraphs 2 and 3 of the amended Stromeinspeisungsgesetz, and, taken on its own, was not therefore in the nature of aid within the meaning of Article 92 of the Treaty. In the first place, Paragraphs 2 and 3 of the amended Stromeinspeisungsgesetz did not affect the legal relationship between PreussenElektra and Schleswag, with the result that the Landgericht could not disapply them in the main proceedings. Secondly, the non-application of Paragraph 4 of the amended Stromeinspeisungsgesetz left intact the obligation of Schleswag to purchase electricity produced from renewable energy sources at fixed minimum prices. The penalty effect of the direct application of the third sentence of Article 93(3) of the Treaty did not, therefore, enable the unlawful aid constituted by Paragraphs 2 and 3 of the amended Stromeinspeisungsgesetz to be penalised or prevent the application of Paragraph 4 of the amended Stromeinspeisungsgesetz, so that the payment in question must be regarded as having been made on a sound legal basis.

25. The Landgericht found, first that the Commission had not been informed, in accordance with Article 93(3) of the Treaty, of the amendments made to the Stromeinspeisungsgesetz by the 1998 Law, and considered that the question whether the new version of the latter represented in whole or in part constituted State aid within the meaning of Article 92 of the Treaty remained relevant, even if the German Government and the Commission had already classified the original content of the Stromeinspeisungsgesetz as aid in the context of the notification made in 1990. The Landgericht considered that even if the amendments to the Stromeinspeisungsgesetz by the 1998 Law were to be regarded as modifying the original scheme, the procedure under Article 93(3) of the Treaty did not have to be applied to the modified scheme unless the latter itself constituted a system of aid within the meaning of Article 92 of the Treaty.

26. The Landgericht found, secondly, that the obligation to purchase electricity produced in Germany from renewable energy sources on conditions which could not be obtained on the open market might depress demand for electricity produced in other Member States, which might constitute an obstacle to trade between Member States prohibited by Article 30 of the Treaty.

27. In those circumstances, considering that interpretation of Articles 30, 92 and 93(3) of the Treaty was necessary to enable it to resolve the dispute before it, the Landgericht Kiel decided to stay the proceedings and refer the following questions to the Court of Justice for a preliminary ruling:

'1. Do the rules on payment and compensation for supplies of electricity, laid down in Paragraph 2 or 3 or 4 or in Paragraphs 2 to 4 of the Gesetz über die Einspeisung von Strom aus erneuerbaren Energien in das öffentliche Netz of 7 December 1990 (BGBl. 1990 I, p. 2633), as amended by Article 3(2) of the Gesetz zur Neuregelung des Energiewirtschaftsrechts of 24 April 1998 (BGBl. 1998 I, p. 730 (734-736] constitute State aid for the purposes of Article 92 of the EC Treaty?

Is Article 92 of the EC Treaty to be interpreted as meaning that the underlying concept of aid also covers national rules for the benefit of the recipient of the payment, under which the costs entailed are not met, either directly or indirectly, from the public budget but are borne by individual undertakings in a sector, which have a statutory obligation to purchase at fixed minimum prices, and which are precluded by law and circumstance from passing those costs on to the final consumer?

Is Article 92 of the EC Treaty to be interpreted as meaning that the underlying concept of aid also covers national rules which merely govern the apportionment of the costs between undertakings at the various production levels which have arisen through purchasing obligations and minimum prices, where the legislature's approach creates in practice a permanent burden for which the undertakings affected obtain no consideration?

In the event that the [first] question is answered in the negative in respect of Paragraph 4 of the [amended] Stromeinspeisungsgesetz:

Is Article 93(3) of the EC Treaty to be interpreted as meaning that its restrictive effects apply not only to the benefit itself but also to implementing rules such as Paragraph 4 of the [amended] Stromeinspeisungsgesetz?

3. In the event that the first and second questions are answered in the negative:

Is Article 30 of the EC Treaty to be interpreted as meaning that a quantitative restriction on imports – and/or a measure having equivalent effect as between Member States for the purposes of the aforementioned provision – arises where a provision of national law places undertakings under an obligation to purchase electricity produced from renewable energy sources at minimum prices and requires grid operators to meet the costs entailed for no consideration? '

Admissibility

[Paras 28-53 omitted]

The interpretation of Article 92 of the Treaty

[Paras 54-67 omitted]

Interpretation of Article 30 of the Treaty

68. In its third question, the referring court asks in substance whether the rules concerned are compatible with Article 30 of the Treaty.

69. In that respect, it must first be borne in mind that, according to the case-law of the Court, Article 30 of the Treaty, in prohibiting all measures having equivalent effect to quantitative restrictions on imports, covers any national measure which is capable of hindering, directly or indirectly, actually or potentially, intra-Community trade (Case 8/74 *Dassonville* [1974] ECR 837, paragraph 5).

70. Secondly, the case-law of the Court also shows that an obligation placed on traders in a Member State to obtain a certain percentage of their supplies of a given product from a national supplier limits to that extent the possibility of importing the same product by preventing those traders from obtaining supplies in respect of part of their needs from traders situated in other Member States (see, to that effect, Case 72/83 *Campus Oil* [1984] ECR 2727, paragraph 16; Case C-21/88 *Du Pont de Nemours Italiana* [1990] ECR I-889, paragraph 11).

71. In this case, Paragraphs 1 and 2 of the amended Stromeinspeisungsgesetz expressly state that the purchase obligation imposed on electricity supply undertakings applies only to electricity produced from renewable energy sources within the scope of that statute and within the respective supply area of each undertaking concerned, and is therefore capable, at least potentially, of hindering intra-Community trade.

72. However, in order to determine whether such a purchase obligation is nevertheless compatible with Article 30 of the Treaty, account must be taken, first, of the aim of the provision in question, and, second, of the particular features of the electricity market.

73. The use of renewable energy sources for producing electricity, which a statute such as the amended Stromeinspeisungsgesetz is intended to promote, is useful for protecting the environment in so far as it contributes to the reduction in emissions of greenhouse gases which are amongst the main causes of climate change which the European Community and its Member States have pledged to combat.

74. Growth in that use is amongst the priority objectives which the Community and its Member States intend to pursue in implementing the obligations which they contracted by virtue of the United Nations Framework Convention on Climate Change, approved on behalf of the Community by Council Decision 94/69/EC of 15 De-

cember 1993 (OJ 1994 L 33, p. 11), and by virtue of the Protocol of the third conference of the parties to that Convention, done in Kyoto on 11 December 1997, signed by the European Community and its Member States on 29 April 1998 (see *inter alia* Council Resolution 98/C 198/01 of 8 June 1998 on renewable sources of energy (OJ 1998 C 198, p. 1), and Decision No 646/2000/EC of the European Parliament and of the Council of 28 February 2000 adopting a multiannual programme for the promotion of renewable energy sources in the Community (Altener) (1998 to 2002) (OJ 2000 L 79, p. 1].

75. It should be noted that that policy is also designed to protect the health and life of humans, animals and plants.

76. Moreover, as stated in the third sentence of the first subparagraph of Article 130r(2) of the EC Treaty, environmental protection requirements must be integrated into the definition and implementation of other Community policies. The Treaty of Amsterdam transferred that provision, in a slightly modified form, to Article 6 of the Treaty, which appears in Part One, headed 'Principles '.

77. In addition, the 28th recital in the preamble to Directive 96/92 expressly states that it is 'for reasons of environmental protection' that the latter authorises Member States in Articles 8(3) and 11(3) to give priority to the production of electricity from renewable sources.

78. It should also be noted that, as stated in the 39th recital in its preamble, the directive constitutes only a further phase in the liberalisation of the electricity market and leaves some obstacles to trade in electricity between Member States in place.

79. Moreover, the nature of electricity is such that, once it has been allowed into the transmission or distribution system, it is difficult to determine its origin and in particular the source of energy from which it was produced.

80. In that respect, the Commission took the view, in its Proposal for a Directive 2000/C 311 E/22 of the European Parliament and of the Council on the promotion of electricity from renewable energy sources in the internal electricity market (OJ 2000 C 311 E, p. 320), submitted on 10 May 2000, that the implementation in each Member State of a system of certificates of origin for electricity produced from renewable sources, capable of being the subject of mutual recognition, was essential in order to make trade in that type of electricity both reliable and possible in practice.

81. Having regard to all the above considerations, the answer to the third question must be that, in the current state of Community law concerning the electricity market, legislation such as the amended Stromeinspeisungsgesetz is not incompatible with Article 30 of the Treaty.

Costs

[Para. 82 omitted]

On those grounds,

THE COURT,

in answer to the questions referred to it by the Landgericht Kiel by order of 13 October 1998, hereby rules:

1. **Statutory provisions of a Member State which, first, require private electricity supply undertakings to purchase electricity produced in their area of supply from renewable energy sources at minimum prices higher than the real economic value of that type of electricity, and, second, distribute the financial burden resulting from that obligation between those electricity supply undertakings and upstream private electricity network operators do not constitute State aid within the meaning of Article 92(1) of the EC Treaty (now, after amendment, Article 87(1) EC).**

2. **In the current state of Community law concerning the electricity market, such provisions are not incompatible with Article 30 of the EC Treaty (now, after amendment, Article 28 EC).**

Comments and questions

Case C-379/98 *PreussenElektra AG* v *Schleswag AG* [2001] ECR I-2099, concerned a situation in which the German authorities required German electricity suppliers to purchase electricity produced in their area of supply from renewable energy sources. This geographical limitation meant that electricity suppliers were required to buy electricity from renewable energy sources in Germany. This naturally meant that the electricity suppliers were restricted from buying corresponding amounts of electricity from foreign producers. This requirement was therefore directly discriminatory.

Was it relevant to the decision, as to whether the buying restriction was covered by the prohibition in Article 34 TFEU (formerly Article 30 EEC Treaty), whether the German electricity suppliers were privately owned or state owned?

The German buying restriction was a measure having an equivalent effect to a quantitative restriction, and was therefore covered by Article 34 TFEU. In this case it was argued that the measure did not have an appreciable effect on the trade in electricity between Member States. How far will this be relevant for determining whether or not there was a measure having an equivalent effect to a quantitative restriction under Article 34 TFEU?

In determining whether the purchasing requirement obligation was compatible with the TFEU, the CJEU took account of the aim of imposing this requirement on the electricity supply companies, and the 'particular features' of the electricity market; cf. paragraph 72 of the judgment.

The aim of the purchasing requirement was to protect the environment against the release of greenhouse gases. The protection of the environment is not one of the grounds for exemption listed in Article 36 TFEU (formerly Article 36 EEC Treaty). This means that there is not an assumption that protection of the environment can justify a directly discriminatory prohibition covered by Article 34 TFEU. The CJEU nevertheless reached the conclusion that the measure could be justified on environmental grounds. Compare the reasoning of the CJEU in paragraphs 73-78 in this case with its reasoning in paragraphs 30-35 in Case C-2/90 *Commission* v *Belgium* [1992] ECR I-4413 (the *Walloon waste disposal* case) printed above. In both the *Walloon waste disposal* case and in *PreussenElektra*, the nature of the goods was said to be significant. Consider the extent to which these two cases support the view that environmental protection can generally be regarded as one of the considerations which can justify discriminatory measures.

As for the particular features of the electricity market, the CJEU stated that once electricity has been introduced into the electricity grid, it is impossible in practice to determine whether it has been produced conventionally or from renewable energy sources. It was effectively possible to promote 'environmentally-friendly' electricity by setting up a system with certificates of origin, so that supply and demand determine the price of environmentally-friendly electricity. However, such a system was not set up. The CJEU seems implicitly to have acknowledged that the German authorities could not have attained their aim of promoting environmentally-friendly electricity by other means. Consider whether, through direct subsidies to the producers of electricity from renewable sources, the authorities could equally well have promoted environmentally-friendly electricity generation, without partially preventing electricity suppliers from buying electricity generated in other Member States. In his Opinion, the Advocate General admitted that he found it difficult to understand how the aim of the German measure (a reduction in the release of greenhouse gases through electricity generation) could not equally well have been achieved by the direct purchase of electricity generated by environmentally-friendly means from other Member States.

In its judgment of 1 July 2014 in Case C-573/12, *Ålands Vindkraft* (Grand Chamber), the CJEU ruled on a similar problem concerning Swedish legislation on the allocation of green certificates promoting the production of electricity from renewable energy sources. In this case the Swedish authorities had refused to grant green certificates to Ålands Vindkraft on the grounds that the renewable energy in question had been produced in Finland (Ålandsøerne), even though the company supplied the Swedish clectricity grid. Among other things, the question was whether the Swedish rules constituted a restriction of trade covered by Article 34 TFEU. Since the granting of green certificates put domestic producers of renewable energy in a more advantageous position than foreign producers who did not have green certificates, the CJEU concluded that the Swedish rules, at least indirectly and potentially, hindered imports of electricity, especially green electricity, from other Member States. There was thus a trade restriction, but was it directly discriminatory? And if so, could environmental considerations justify the trade restriction? In his Opinion on the case, Advocate General Bot recommended that the CJEU should change the practice it had had hitherto and accept that environmental considerations could justify discriminatory restrictions on trade. However, the CJEU did not follow the recommendation of the Advocate General and ruled instead that the Swedish rules could be justified pursuant to Article 36 TFEU. The CJEU thus stated that according to settled case-law, national measures that are capable of hindering intra-Union trade may *inter alia* be justified by overriding requirements relating to protection of the environment and the use of renewable energy sources for the production of electricity. The CJEU stated that legislation such as that at issue in the main proceedings is useful for the protection of the environment inasmuch as it contributes to the reduction in greenhouse gas emissions, which are among the main causes of climate change that the European Union and its Member States have pledged to combat. The CJEU also noted that the increased use of renewable energy sources constituted an important component of the package of measures needed to reduce greenhouse gas emissions and to comply with the Union's international obligations to reduce these emissions. Such an increase was also designed to protect the health and life of humans, animals and plants, which are among the public interest grounds listed in Article 36 TFEU.

See also Case C-206/06, *Essent* [2008] ECR I-5497, which concerned whether Dutch rules on a price surcharge for the transmission of electricity were contrary to Union law. The CJEU found that rules such as those disputed in the main case could be contrary to [now] Article 30 TFEU and [now] Article 110 TFEU. Note, however, that the *Essent* judgment was given by a chamber consisting of five judges, which means that the precedent value of the judgment is limited.

JUDGMENT OF THE COURT
23 May 1996

The Queen v Ministry of Agriculture, Fisheries and Food, ex parte Hedley Lomas (Ireland) Ltd. (Reference to the Court by the High Court of Justice, Queen's Bench Division (England and Wales) – United Kingdom)

'Free movement of goods – Protection of animals – Harmonizing directive – Article 36 of the EC Treaty – Non-contractual liability of a Member State for breach of Community law'

Case C-5/94

Judgment

1. By order of 6 December 1993, received at the Court on 10 January 1993, the High Court of Justice of England and Wales, Queen's Bench Division, referred to the Court for a preliminary ruling under Article 177 of the EC Treaty a number of questions on the interpretation of Articles 34 and 36 of that Treaty and the principle of non-contractual State liability for breach of Community law.

2. Those questions have been raised in proceedings between Hedley Lomas (Ireland) Ltd (hereinafter 'Hedley Lomas') and the Ministry of Agriculture, Fisheries and Food for England and Wales following that Ministry's refusal to issue a licence for the export of live sheep to Spain requested by Hedley Lomas on 7 October 1992.

3. Between April 1990 and 1 January 1993 the Ministry of Agriculture, Fisheries and Food systematically refused to issue licences for the export to Spain of live animals for slaughter on the ground that their treatment in Spanish slaughterhouses was contrary to Council Directive 74/577/EEC of 18 November 1974 on stunning of animals before slaughter (OJ 1974 L 316, p. 10, hereinafter 'the Directive').

4. As is clear from its preamble, the Directive, which is based on Articles 43 and 100 of the EEC Treaty, is intended to remove the disparities between the legislation of Member States in the field of protection of animals which directly affect the functioning of the common market. It also seeks, in general, to avoid all forms of cruelty to animals and, as a first step, to avoid all unnecessary suffering on the part of animals when being slaughtered. Articles 1 and 2 of the Directive require Member States to ensure the stunning, by appropriate approved methods, of animals for slaughter of the following species: bovine animals, swine, sheep, goats and solipeds. The Directive does not harmonize procedures for monitoring compliance with its provisions.

5. The Kingdom of Spain had to comply with the Directive as from the date of its accession to the Community on 1 January 1986.

6. The Directive was transposed in Spain by Royal Decree of 18 December 1987 (Boletin Oficial del Estado No 312 of 30 December 1987) which reproduces in particular the provisions of Articles 1 and 2 of the Directive and specifies, as approved methods of stunning, the use of a captive-bolt gun or pistol, electric shock or carbon dioxide. It does not lay down any penalty for breach of its provisions.

7. Despite the adoption of that decree, the Ministry of Agriculture, Fisheries and Food became convinced, in particular on the basis of information obtained from the Spanish Society for the Protection of Animals, that a number of Spanish slaughterhouses were not complying with the rules contained in the Directive, either because they did not have the necessary equipment for stunning animals or because the equipment was not being used correctly or at all. Although it did not have sufficient evidence as to the overall position in Spanish slaughterhouses, the Ministry formed the view that the information in its possession indicated a degree of non-compliance with the Directive such as to create a substantial risk that animals exported to Spain for slaughter would suffer treatment contrary to the Directive.

8. Following complaints in 1990 by animal welfare groups in the United Kingdom and Spain, the Commission contacted the Spanish authorities and held several meetings with them to discuss the situation in Spain, in particular the absence of punitive measures for non-compliance with the Spanish provisions implementing the Directive. In view of assurances given by the national and regional authorities in Spain regarding the application of the Directive, the Commission decided, in 1992, not to take any action under Article 169 of the EEC Treaty. The Commission informed the United Kingdom authorities that it considered the United Kingdom's general ban on exports of live animals to Spain to be contrary to Article 34 of the EEC Treaty and not capable of justification under Article 36 of that Treaty.

9. That general ban was lifted, with effect from 1 January 1993, following a meeting between the United Kingdom's Chief Veterinary Officer and his Spanish counterpart to review the progress achieved by Spain in giving effect to the Directive and to examine means of ensuring in future that all animals exported from the United Kingdom would be treated in accordance with the Directive. Following those exchanges of views, the two Governments drew up measures to ensure that animals sent from the United Kingdom for immediate slaughter in Spain would be sent only to slaughterhouses which the Spanish authorities had confirmed as meeting Community requirements on animal welfare.

10. On 7 October 1992 Hedley Lomas applied for an export licence for a quantity of live sheep intended for slaughter in a specified Spanish slaughterhouse. The licence was not issued, even though, according to the information obtained by Hedley Lo-

mas, the slaughterhouse in question had been approved since 1986 and was complying with Community directives on animal welfare and the United Kingdom authorities did not have any evidence to the contrary.

11. Hedley Lomas brought proceedings before the High Court of Justice in which it seeks, first, a declaration that the refusal by the Ministry of Agriculture, Fisheries and Food to grant it an export licence is contrary to Article 34 of the Treaty and, second, damages.

12. The Ministry does not deny that the refusal to issue the export licence constitutes a quantitative restriction on exports but argues that it was justified under Article 36 of the Treaty and was consequently compatible with Community law.

13. Taking the view that the case before it necessitated the interpretation of Community law, the High Court of Justice decided to stay proceedings and to refer the following questions to the Court for a preliminary ruling:

‘1) Does the existence of a harmonizing directive (Directive 74/577/EEC), which does not contain any sanctions or procedures for non-compliance, prevent a Member State (Member State A) from relying on Article 36 of the EEC Treaty to justify measures restrictive of exports in circumstances where an interest specified in that article is threatened by the failure of another Member State (Member State B), as a matter of fact, to secure the results required by the directive?

If the answer to Question 1 is in the negative,

2) In the circumstances described in Question 1, does Article 36 entitle Member State A to prohibit the export of live sheep to Member State B for slaughter
(i) generally; or
(ii) in a case where the stated destination of the sheep is a slaughterhouse in Member State B in respect of which Member state A does not have evidence that the provisions of the Directive are not complied with?
If the answer to Question 1 is in the affirmative, or if the answer to Question 2 is in the negative, and in the circumstances of this case:

3) Is Member State A liable as a matter of Community law to compensate a trader in damages for any loss caused to the trader by the failure to grant an export licence in breach of Article 34 and, if so, under what conditions does such liability arise and how is such compensation to be calculated?’

The first and second questions

14. The first question must be understood as asking whether Community law precludes a Member State from invoking Article 36 of the Treaty to justify a limitation of exports of goods to another Member State on the sole ground that, according to the first State, the second State is not complying with the requirements of a Community harmonizing directive which pursues an objective which Article 36 is intended to protect, but does not lay down either any procedure for monitoring their application or any penalties in the event of their breach.

15. Before the substance of the question is addressed, it must be observed, as is clear from the order for reference, that in the present case the United Kingdom authorities' general refusal to grant export licences for Spain was based solely on the conviction that a certain number of Spanish slaughterhouses were not complying with the requirements of the Directive itself and that there was at least a significant risk that animals exported to Spain would undergo, upon slaughter, treatment contrary to the Directive.

16. It is against that factual background that the first question asked by the national court must be answered.

17. The refusal by a Member State to issue export licences constitutes a quantitative restriction on exports, contrary to Article 34 of the Treaty.

18. Article 36 of the Treaty allows the maintenance of restrictions on the free movement of goods, justified on grounds of the protection of the health and life of animals, which constitutes a fundamental requirement recognized by Community law. However, recourse to Article 36 is no longer possible where Community directives provide for harmonization of the measures necessary to achieve the specific objective which would be furthered by reliance upon this provision.

19. This exclusion of recourse to Article 36 cannot be affected by the fact that, in the present case, the Directive does not lay down any Community procedure for monitoring compliance nor any penalties in the event of breach of its provisions. The fact that the Directive lays down no monitoring procedure or penalties simply means that the Member States are obliged, in accordance with the first paragraph of Article 5 and the third paragraph of Article 189 of the Treaty, to take all measures necessary to guarantee the application and effectiveness of Community law (see, in particular, the judgment in Case 68/88 Commission v Greece [1989] ECR 2965, paragraph 23). In this regard, the Member States must rely on trust in each other to carry out inspections on their respective territories (see also the judgment in Case 46/76 Bauhuis v Netherlands [1977] ECR 5, paragraph 22).

20. A Member State may not unilaterally adopt, on its own authority, corrective or protective measures designed to obviate any breach by another Member State of rules of Community law (judgment in Joined Cases 90/63 and 91/63 Commission v Luxembourg and Belgium [1964] ECR 625 and judgment in Case 232/78 Commission v France [1979] ECR 2729, paragraph 9).

21. The answer to the first question must accordingly be that Community law precludes a Member State from invoking Article 36 of the Treaty to justify a limitation of exports of goods to another Member State on the sole ground that, according to the first State, the second State is not complying with the requirements of a Community harmonizing directive which pursues the objective which Article 36 is intended to protect but does not lay down either any procedure for monitoring their application or any penalties in the event of their breach.

22. In view of the reply given to the first question, it is unnecessary to reply to the second question.

The third question

23. By its third question the national court asks the Court to state the conditions under which a Member State is obliged to make good damage caused to an individual by its refusal to issue an export licence in breach of Article 34 of the Treaty.

24. The principle of State liability for loss and damage caused to individuals as a result of breaches of Community law for which the State can be held responsible is inherent in the system of the Treaty (judgment in Joined Cases C-6/90 and C-9/90 Francovich and Others [1991] ECR I-5357, paragraph 35, and judgment in Joined Cases C-46/93 and C-48/93 Brasserie du Pêcheur and Factortame, not yet published in the ECR, paragraph 31). Furthermore, the conditions under which State liability gives rise to a right to reparation depend on the nature of the breach of Community law giving rise to the loss or damage (judgment in Francovich and Others, cited above, paragraph 38; judgment in Brasserie du Pêcheur and Factortame, cited above, paragraph 38).

25. In the case of a breach of Community law attributable to a Member State acting in a field in which it has a wide discretion to make legislative choices the Court has held, at paragraph 51 of its judgment in Brasserie du Pêcheur and Factortame, cited above, that such a right to reparation must be recognized where three conditions are met: the rule of law infringed must be intended to confer rights on individuals; the breach must be sufficiently serious; and there must be a direct causal link between the breach of the obligation resting on the State and the damage sustained by the injured parties.

26. Those three conditions are also applicable in the circumstances of this case.

27. As regards the first condition, as is clear from the answer given to the first question, the United Kingdom's refusal to issue an export licence to Hedley Lomas constituted a quantitative restriction on exports contrary to Article 34 of the Treaty which could not be justified under Article 36. Whilst Article 34 imposes a prohibition on Member States, it also creates rights for individuals which the national courts must protect (judgment in Case 83/78 Pigs Marketing Board v Redmond [1978] ECR 2347, paragraphs 66 and 67).

28. As regards the second condition, where, at the time when it committed the infringement, the Member State in question was not called upon to make any legislative choices and had only considerably reduced, or even no, discretion, the mere infringement of Community law may be sufficient to establish the existence of a sufficiently serious breach.

29. In that respect, in this particular case, the United Kingdom was not even in a position to produce any proof of non-compliance with the Directive by the slaughterhouse to which the animals for which the export licence was sought were destined.

30. As regards the third condition, it is for the national court to determine whether there is a direct causal link between the breach of the obligation resting on the State and the damage sustained by the applicant in the main proceedings.

31. As appears from paragraphs 41, 42 and 43 of Francovich and Others, cited above, subject to the right to reparation which flows directly from Community law where the three conditions referred to above are satisfied, the State must make reparation in accordance with its domestic law on liability for the consequences of the loss and damage caused. However, the conditions for reparation of loss and damage laid down by domestic law must not be less favourable than those relating to similar domestic claims and must not be such as in practice to make it impossible or excessively difficult to obtain reparation (see also the judgment in Brasserie du Pêcheur and Factortame, cited above, paragraph 67).

32. The answer to the third question must therefore be that a Member State has an obligation to make reparation for the damage caused to an individual by a refusal to issue an export licence in breach of Article 34 of the Treaty where the rule of Community law infringed is intended to confer rights on individuals, the breach is sufficiently serious and there is a direct causal link between the breach and the damage sustained by the individuals. Subject to that reservation, the State must make good the consequences of the loss or damage caused by a breach of Community law attributable to it, in accordance with its domestic law on liability. However, the conditions laid down by the applicable domestic laws must not be less favourable than those relating to similar domestic claims or framed in such a way as in practice to make it impossible or excessively difficult to obtain reparation.

Costs

[Para. 33 omitted]

On those grounds,

THE COURT

in answer to the questions referred to it by the High Court of Justice, Queen's Bench Division, by order of 6 December 1993, hereby rules:

1. **Community law precludes a Member State from invoking Article 36 of the EC Treaty to justify a limitation of exports of goods to another Member State on the sole ground that, according to the first State, the second State is not complying with the requirements of a Community harmonizing directive which pursues the objective which Article 36 is intended to protect but does not lay down either any procedure for monitoring their application or any penalties in the event of their breach.**

2. **A Member State has an obligation to make reparation for the damage caused to an individual by a refusal to issue an export licence in breach of Article 34 of the Treaty where the rule of Community law infringed is intended to confer rights on individuals, the breach is sufficiently serious and there is a direct causal link between the breach and the damage sustained by the individuals. Subject to that reservation, the State must make good the consequences of the loss or damage caused by a breach of Community law attributable to it, in accordance with its domestic law on liability. However, the conditions laid down by the applicable domestic laws must not be less favourable than those relating to similar domestic claims or framed in such a way as in practice to make it impossible or excessively difficult to obtain reparation.**

Comments and questions

Note that in paragraph 17 of the judgment in Case C-5/94 *R* v *Ministry of Agriculture, ex parte Lomas* [1996] ECR I-2553, it was stated that the refusal by a Member State to issue export licences constituted a quantitative restriction on exports. Indeed a Member State's denial of an export licence in reality constitutes a total prohibition on exports, see Case C-324/93 *R* v *Home Secretary, ex parte Evans Medical* [1995] ECR I-563, printed above.

In the *Lomas* case, it was the British government which instituted the ban on exports. Would the decision of the CJEU have been different if it had been an animal welfare organisation which had imposed a physical blockade on the exports? If so, would the decision have been influenced by whether the British Government had actively sought to prevent the blockade? In this connection, see Case C-265/95 *Commission* v *France* (the *Strawberry* case) [1997] ECR I-6959, printed above and Case C-112/00 *Eugen Schmidberger, Internationale Transporte und Planzüge* v *Austria* [2003] ECR I-5659. Assume that pig producers and producers of veal calves in a Member State consider the possibility of setting a limit of eight hours from the animals leaving the farm to their arriving at an abattoir. This would not totally prevent exports, but it would restrict them significantly. Would such a private agreement be in breach of Article 34 TFEU (formerly Article 30 EEC Treaty)? Assume also that the parliament of a Member State considers introducing a substantial tariff on the transport of pigs to slaughter in order to remove the economic incentive for farmers to send their animals on long journeys. Such an arrangement would increase the probability that animals would be slaughtered close to where they are produced, to the advantage of animal welfare. Would such an arrangement be in accordance with the TFEU rules on the free movement of goods?

Paragraph 18 of the *Lomas* case states the well-known principle that recourse to Article 36 TFEU (formerly Article 36 EEC Treaty) is no longer possible where EU directives provide for harmonisation of the measures necessary to achieve the specific objective which would be furthered by reliance on Article 36 TFEU. This also applies even if a directive does not contain Union law procedures for monitoring compliance with its terms, and even if the directive does not provide for sanctions for the infringement of its terms. If a directive does not contain provisions on controls and sanctions, then pursuant to the duty of loyalty in Article 4 TEU, the Member States have a duty to implement such sanctions in their national laws when enacting the directive.

In addition to this, the CJEU stated that a Member State may not unilaterally adopt, on its own authority, corrective or protective measures designed to obviate any breach of Union rules by another Member State; cf. paragraph 20. This is the direct opposite of the normal principles of international law, where a state can quite legally impose a trade boycott on another state which contravenes the principles of international law.

Consider whether, under Article 34 TFEU, the United Kingdom could prohibit the import of French quails on the grounds that the quails are captured in a way which offends against animal welfare. Consider too whether it would be against Union law if the British Government had introduced a prohibition against the breeding of fur animals in the United Kingdom, for ethical reasons. In this connection, note that Denmark and Finland, among others, export juvenile mink with a view to breeding fur animals in the importing countries. Compare this with Case C-384/93 *Alpine Investment* [1995] ECR I-1141, printed in Chapter 6.

JUDGMENT OF THE COURT (Grand Chamber)
16 December 2008

Lodewijk Gysbrechts and Santurel Inter BVBA. (Reference for a preliminary ruling from the Hof van Beroep te Gent – Belgium)

'Articles 28 EC to 30 EC – Directive 97/7/EC – Consumer protection in distance contracts – Period for withdrawal – Prohibition on requiring from a consumer a deposit or payment before the end of the period for withdrawal'

Case C-205/07

Judgment

1. This reference for a preliminary ruling relates to the interpretation of Articles 28 EC to 30 EC.

2. The reference was made within criminal proceedings brought against Mr Gysbrechts and Santurel Inter BVBA ('Santurel') for contraventions of the Belgian law on distance selling.

Legal context

Community law

3. Article 6 of Directive 97/7/EC of the European Parliament and of the Council of 20 May 1997 on the protection of consumers in respect of distance contracts (OJ 1997 L 144, p. 19) provides:

'1. For any distance contract the consumer shall have a period of at least seven working days in which to withdraw from the contract without penalty and without giving any reason. The only charge that may be made to the consumer because of the exercise of his right of withdrawal is the direct cost of returning the goods.

The period for exercise of this right shall begin:
– in the case of goods, from the day of receipt by the consumer where the obligations laid down in Article 5 have been fulfilled,

...

2. Where the right of withdrawal has been exercised by the consumer pursuant to this Article, the supplier shall be obliged to reimburse the sums paid by the consumer free of charge. The only charge that may be made to the consumer be-

cause of the exercise of his right of withdrawal is the direct cost of returning the goods. Such reimbursement must be carried out as soon as possible and in any case within 30 days.

...'

4. Article 14 of Directive 97/7 is worded as follows:

   'Member States may introduce or maintain, in the area covered by this Directive, more stringent provisions compatible with the [EC] Treaty, to ensure a higher level of consumer protection. Such provisions shall, where appropriate, include a ban, in the general interest, on the marketing of certain goods or services, particularly medicinal products, within their territory by means of distance contracts, with due regard for the Treaty.'

National law

5. The consumer's right to withdraw is governed by Article 80 of the [Belgian] Law of 14 July 1991 on commercial practices and consumer information and protection, as amended ('the Law on consumer protection').

6. Article 80(3) of the Law on consumer protection provides:

   'Without prejudice to the application of Article 45(1) of the Law of 12 June 1991 on consumer credit, no deposit or any form of payment may be required from the consumer before the end of the withdrawal period of seven working days referred to in paragraph 1.

   If the right of withdrawal provided for in paragraphs 1 and 2 is exercised, the vendor shall repay the amounts paid by the consumer, without costs. This repayment shall be made within 30 days of the withdrawal.

   The prohibition referred to in the first paragraph shall be waived if the vendor is able to prove that he complies with the rules laid down by the Crown on the repayment of amounts paid by the consumer.'

7. The royal decree referred to in the last paragraph of that provision has not yet been adopted.

The main proceedings and the question referred for a preliminary ruling

8. Santurel is an undertaking which specialises in the wholesale and retail sale of food supplements. The greater part of its sales are made online by means of the company's internet site, and goods ordered are then sent to the purchasers by post.

9. Mr Gysbrechts is the founder and manager of that undertaking.

10. In 2001, Santurel brought an action against one of its customers, Mr Delahaye, who resided in France, for failure to pay the price of a number of products which had been delivered to him. The outcome of that action was that the judge in Dendermonde (Belgium) who heard the case gave judgment in default against Mr Delahaye.

11. Mr Delahaye then lodged a complaint and stated, though he produced no evidence of the fact, that he had returned the products concerned to Santurel. The Belgian Economic Inspection Board then carried out an investigation which established that there had been failures to fulfil the obligations to provide information on the right of withdrawal provided for by the Law on consumer protection. Those failures were brought to Santurel's attention and a request was made that the situation be corrected.

12. Santurel therefore altered the information provided on its internet site to state, inter alia, that payment for goods must be made within a week of receipt of the goods. In respect of goods delivered in Belgium, the price may be paid by bank transfer, postal order or by credit card. In respect of other countries, the only acceptable means of payment is credit card. In all cases, when a payment is to be made by credit card, the customer must state on the order form the number and validity period of the card.

13. The Belgian Economic Inspection Board considered that that amendment was inadequate and brought charges against Santurel and Mr Gysbrechts as its manager, to the effect that they had committed offences under the provisions on distance selling in the Law on consumer protection. In particular, it was alleged that they had disregarded the prohibition, laid down in Article 80(3) of that law, on requiring that the consumer provide a deposit or any form of payment before expiry of the period of seven working days within which withdrawal from the contract is permitted. According to the Economic Inspection Board, the statement of the credit card number on the order form for goods enables Santurel to collect the price of those goods before expiry of the period for withdrawal of seven working days, which contravenes the requirements laid down by law.

14. The Court of First Instance of Dendermonde found Santurel and Mr Gysbrechts guilty and imposed on each party a fine of EUR 1 250. All parties to the main proceedings brought an appeal against that judgment before the Hof van Beroep te Gent (Court of Appeal, Ghent).

15. The Hof van Beroep te Gent held that the prohibition laid down in Article 80(3) of the Law on consumer protection creates a risk that a Belgian trader will have difficulty in obtaining payment for his goods when they have been delivered to customers established in another Member State, that risk being all the more acute when, as in the main proceedings, the sums involved are relatively small.

16. In those circumstances, that court considers that Santurel and Mr Gysbrechts have an arguable case that the prohibition concerned is an unjustified obstacle to the free movement of goods within the European Community. The court consequently decided to stay the proceedings and referred the following question to the Court for a preliminary ruling:

 'Does the Belgian Law of 14 July 1991 on commercial practices and consumer information and protection constitute a measure having equivalent effect, as prohibited in Articles 28 EC to 30 EC, inasmuch as Article 80(3) of that national law prohibits demands for an advance or payment from the consumer during the compulsory period for withdrawal, as a result of which the actual effect of the Law of 14 July 1991 on the trading of goods in the trader's own country differs from its effect on trading with nationals of another Member State, and does this give rise in fact to an obstacle to the free movement of goods, a principle enshrined in Article 23 EC?'

The question referred for a preliminary ruling

Observations of the parties

[Pars 17-37 omitted]

A measure having equivalent effect to a quantitative restriction on exports within the meaning of Article 29 EC

38. To answer the question put by the referring court, it must therefore be determined whether the prohibition laid down by the provision at issue in the main proceedings constitutes a measure having equivalent effect to a quantitative restriction on exports.

39. The compatibility of a provision such as that at issue in the main proceedings with Article 29 EC must be examined by taking into account also the national authorities' interpretation of it, namely that suppliers are not allowed to require that consumers provide their payment card number, even though the suppliers undertake not to use it before expiry of the period for withdrawal.

40. In that regard, the Court has classified as measures having equivalent effect to quantitative restrictions on exports national measures which have as their specific object or effect the restriction of patterns of exports and thereby the establishment of a difference in treatment between the domestic trade of a Member State and its export trade in such a way as to provide a particular advantage for national production or for the domestic market of the State in question, at the expense of the production or of the trade of other Member States (Case 15/79 *Groenveld* [1979] ECR 3409, paragraph 7).

41. In the main proceedings, it is clear, as the Belgian Government has moreover noted in its written observations, that the prohibition on requiring an advance payment deprives the traders concerned of an efficient tool with which to guard against the risk of non-payment. That is even more the case when the national provision at issue is interpreted as prohibiting suppliers from requesting that consumers provide their payment card number even if they undertake not to use it to collect payment before expiry of the period for withdrawal.

42. As is clear from the order for reference, the consequences of such a prohibition are generally more significant in cross-border sales made directly to consumers, in particular, in sales made by means of the internet, by reason, inter alia, of the obstacles to bringing any legal proceedings in another Member State against consumers who default, especially when the sales involve relatively small sums.

43. Consequently, even if a prohibition such as that at issue in the main proceedings is applicable to all traders active in the national territory, its actual effect is none the less greater on goods leaving the market of the exporting Member State than on the marketing of goods in the domestic market of that Member State.

44. It must therefore be held that a national measure, such as that at issue in the main proceedings, prohibiting a supplier in a distance sale from requiring an advance or any payment before expiry of the period for withdrawal constitutes a measure having equivalent effect to a quantitative restriction on exports. The same is true of a measure prohibiting a supplier from requiring that consumers provide their payment card number, even if the supplier undertakes not to use it to collect payment before expiry of the period for withdrawal.

The possible justification of the measure having equivalent effect

45. A national measure contrary to Article 29 EC may be justified on one of the grounds stated in Article 30 EC, and by overriding requirements of public interest, provided that the measure is proportionate to the legitimate objective pursued.

46. In that regard, none of the grounds referred to in Article 30 EC has any relevance in the circumstances of the main proceedings.

47. It must however be added that, in accordance with settled case-law, consumer protection may constitute a legitimate objective in the public interest capable of justifying a restriction on the free movement of goods (see Case 120/78 *Rewe-Zentral* [1979] ECR 649, paragraph 8, and Case C-441/04 *A-Punkt Schmuckhandel* [2006] ECR I-2093, paragraph 27).

48. In the main proceedings, it is not disputed that the provision at issue was introduced with the aim of ensuring the protection of the consumer and, in particular, the effectiveness of the right of withdrawal guaranteed to him by Article 6 of Directive 97/7.

49. Pursuant to the discretion accorded to Member States by Article 14 of Directive 97/7 to introduce, in the area governed by it, more stringent provisions, the Kingdom of Belgium chose to give greater protection to the consumer by prohibiting suppliers not only from imposing a penalty upon the exercise of the right to withdraw, but also from requiring an advance or any payment before expiry of the period for withdrawal. The provision at issue in the main proceedings is intended to increase in that way the consumer's freedom to terminate a contractual relationship, without his having to worry about repayment of monies which he has paid in advance.

50. It remains to be determined whether that provision, as it is interpreted by the national authorities, is proportionate to the objective pursued.

51. In that regard, according to settled case-law, in order for national rules to comply with the principle of proportionality, it must be ascertained not only whether the means which they employ are suitable for the purpose of ensuring the attainment of the objectives pursued but also whether those means do not go beyond what is necessary to attain those objectives (see Joined Cases C-158/04 and C-159/04 *Alfa Vita Vassilopoulos and Carrefour-Marinopoulos* [2006] ECR I-8135, paragraph 22).

52. The prohibition on requiring an advance or any payment before expiry of the period for withdrawal and the prohibition on requesting that purchasers provide their payment card number are capable of ensuring a high level of consumer protection in distance selling, in particular in relation to the exercise of the right to withdraw.

53. It is however necessary to examine whether the national measure at issue in the main proceedings does not go beyond what is necessary to attain the proposed objective and, in particular, whether measures which would have been equally effective in protecting consumers but with a less restrictive effect on intra-Community trade could have been considered.

54. It must be borne in mind that one of the features of distance-selling contracts is the fact that there is often a gap between the performance by each party of his contractual obligations. Thus, the consumer may be induced to pay for the goods before he has received them or, on the contrary, the supplier may be led to deliver the goods without having received the price for them. That gap exposes the contracting parties to a specific risk of non-performance.

55. It falls to the Member States to determine, in compliance with Community law, first, how that risk of non-performance ought to be allocated between supplier and

consumer and, secondly, what means should be made available to the contracting parties to protect themselves.

56. Even if the prohibition on requiring a payment during the period for withdrawal increases the uncertainty of suppliers as to whether the price for the delivered goods will be paid, that prohibition is clearly necessary to ensure the level of protection intended by the provision at issue in the main proceedings. In fact, a consumer who has made an advance payment to a supplier will be less inclined to exercise his right of withdrawal, even if he finds the delivered goods to be not entirely in accordance with his requirements.

57. As regards more specifically the prohibition on a supplier requiring a consumer's payment card number, it is clear that that prohibition is inseparable from the prohibition laid down in Article 80(3) of the Law on consumer protection.

58. First, that prohibition is the consequence of the application, by the competent Belgian authorities, of the prohibition laid down by the provision at issue in the main proceedings and, secondly, it pursues the same objective, namely the effective exercise of the right to withdraw.

59. Just like the prohibition laid down by the provision at issue in the main proceedings, the prohibition on a supplier requiring a consumer's payment card number is capable of ensuring the attainment of the objective pursued, as is clear from paragraph 52 of this judgment.

60. However, as is made clear in point 85 of the Opinion of the Advocate General, the value of the prohibition on a supplier requiring a consumer's payment card number resides only in the fact that it eliminates the risk that the supplier may collect the price before expiry of the period for withdrawal.

61. If, however, that risk materialises, the supplier's action is, in itself, a contravention of the prohibition laid down by the provision at issue in the main proceedings, a prohibition which must be regarded as an appropriate and proportionate measure to attain the objective pursued, as is made clear in paragraphs 54 to 57 of this judgment.

62. It must therefore be held that the imposition on a supplier of a prohibition on requiring that a consumer provide his payment card number goes beyond what is necessary to attain the objective pursued.

63. The answer to the question put by the referring court is therefore that Article 29 EC does not preclude national rules which prohibit a supplier, in cross-border distance selling, from requiring an advance or any payment from a consumer before expiry of the withdrawal period, but Article 29 EC does preclude a prohibition, under

those rules, on requesting, before expiry of that period, the number of the consumer's payment card.

Costs

[Para. 64 omitted]

On those grounds

THE COURT (Grand Chamber)

hereby rules:

Article 29 EC does not preclude national rules which prohibit a supplier, in cross-border distance selling, from requiring an advance or any payment from a consumer before expiry of the withdrawal period, but Article 29 EC does preclude a prohibition, under those rules, on requesting, before expiry of that period, the number of the consumer's payment card.

Comments and questions

Prior to the CJEU's judgment in the *Gysbrechts* case, the so-called *Groenveld* test was used when it was necessary to determine whether a measure was covered by the prohibition of export restrictions in Article 35 TFEU (formerly Article 29 TEC). The *Groenveld* test had three interdependent conditions:

1. The measure's object or effect must be the restriction, specifically, of export trade.
2. The measure must give rise to a difference in treatment between the Member State's domestic trade and its export trade.
3. By virtue of the measure, a particular advantage must be provided for national production or for the domestic market of the State in question, at the expense of the trade or production of other Member States.

These conditions were not fulfilled in the *Gysbrechts* case. The Belgian rule on payment did not concern specific exports, but a general prohibition on demanding payment and the impossibility of requiring a credit card number before the expiry of the period for repudiation of the transaction. On the basis of the established practice of the CJEU, the Belgian rule would thus not infringe Article 35 TFEU.

In this case the Commission recommended that the CJEU should revise the *Groenveld* test so as to give greater consistency between Article 35 and Article 34 TFEU (formerly Article 28 TEC). The Commission proposed that the CJEU should modify the definition of measures having an equivalent effect to quantitative restrictions on exports and should define them as measures 'which have the effect of restricting exports and which give rise to a difference in treatment between the internal trade of a Member State and exports'. In other words, the Commission proposed that the CJEU should give up the requirement that a measure should specifically have the object or effect of restricting export trade.

The CJEU decided to follow the recommendation of the Commission to revise the *Groenveld* test, though without expressly drawing attention to the fact that the test that had applied hitherto was abandoned. Thus the CJEU commented that the Belgian rule, which was intended to protect consumers, would generally have a greater impact on cross-border sales made directly to consumers in other Member States – for example by sales via the internet. Since the rule had a greater impact on sales of goods exported from Belgium than on sales of goods within Belgium, it constituted a measure having an equivalent effect to a quantitative restriction on exports. The CJEU thereafter examined whether the rule could be justified by one of the reasons referred to in Article 36 TFEU (formerly Article 30 TEC) or on general grounds of overriding public interest, and whether there was proportionality between the rule and its purpose.

By the ruling in the *Gysbrechts* case the CJEU has created greater consistency between Articles 34 and 35 TFEU. Prior to the *Gysbrechts* case the CJEU's practice in relation to Article 35 TFEU was much more cautious than its practice in relation to Article 34 TFEU. In her Opinion, the Advocate General pointed out that a change to the *Groenveld* test could be made in two ways. Either the CJEU could establish fully parallel definitions of 'measures having equivalent effect' for both Articles 34 and 35 TFEU, or the CJEU could establish a new definition which was not as restrictive as the definition in the *Groenveld* test, but was nevertheless more restrictive than the definition known from Article 34 TFEU. To what extent do you think the CJEU chose the first or the second of these two possibilities pointed out by the Advocate General? To what extent (and where) is there a statement in the judgment that supports your conclusion? Consider whether the decision in the *Gysbrechts* case means that there is a restriction on the right of Member States to regulate business enterprises – in particular to what extent will the Member States be restricted in future in adopting consumer protection measures?

Note that the Belgian rule concerned distance selling, i.e. 'certain selling arrangements', but the rule imposed greater burdens on export sales than on sales within Belgium. This meant that the *Keck* doctrine did not apply in this case.

Consider whether it would be contrary to Article 35 TFEU if Denmark were to introduce a requirement for freight companies to pay a charge of DKK 500 per live pig exported from Denmark for slaughter abroad, if the reason for the charge was a desire to restrict long journeys for live animals so as to improve animal welfare?

JUDGMENT OF THE COURT
12 March 1987

Commission of the European Communities v Federal Republic of Germany

'Failure of a State to fulfil its obligations – Purity requirement for beer'

Case 178/84

Judgment

1. By an application lodged at the Court Registry on 6 July 1984, the Commission of the European Communities has brought an action under Article 169 of the EEC Treaty for a declaration that, by prohibiting the marketing of beers lawfully manufactured and marketed in another Member State if they do not comply with Articles 9 and 10 of the Biersteuergesetz (Law on beer duty) (Law of 14 March 1952, Bundesgesetzblatt I, p. 149), the Federal Republic of Germany has failed to fulfil its obligations under Article 30 of the EEC Treaty.

2. Reference is made to the Report for the Hearing for the facts of the case, the course of the procedure and the arguments of the parties, which are mentioned or discussed hereinafter only in so far as is necessary for the reasoning of the Court.

The applicable national law

3. In the course of the proceedings before the Court, the German Government gave the following account of its legislation on beer, which was not contested by the Commission and is to be accepted for the purposes of these proceedings.

4. As far as the present proceedings are concerned, the Biersteuergesetz comprises, on the one hand, manufacturing rules which apply as such only to breweries in the Federal Republic of Germany and, on the other, rules on the utilization of the designation Bier (beer), which apply both to beer brewed in the Federal Republic of Germany and to imported beer.

5. The rules governing the manufacture of beer are set out in Article 9 of the Biersteuergesetz. Article 9 (1) provides that bottom-fermented beers may be manufactured only from malted barley, hops, yeast and water. Article 9 (2) lays down the same requirements with regard to the manufacture of top-fermented beer but authorizes the use of other malts, technically pure cane sugar, beet sugar or invert sugar and glucose and colourants obtained from those sugars. Article 9 (3) states that malt means any cereal artificially germinated. It must be noted in that connection that under Article 17 (4) of the Durchführungsbestimmungen zum Bier-

steuergesetz (Implementing provisions to the Biersteuergesetz) of 14 March 1952 (Bundesgesetzblatt I, p. 153) rice, maize and sorghum are not treated as cereals for the purposes of Article 9 (3) of the Biersteuergesetz. Under Article 9 (7) of the Biersteuergesetz, derogations from the manufacturing rules laid down in Article 9 (1) and (2) may be granted on application in specific cases in respect of the manufacture of special beers, beer intended for export or beer intended for scientific experiments. In addition, under Article 9 (8), Article 9 (1) and (2) do not apply to breweries making beer for consumption on their premises (Hausbrauer). Under Article 18 (1) (1) of the Biersteuergesetz fines may be imposed for contraventions of the manufacturing rules set out in Article 9.

6. The rules on the commercial utilization of the designation Bier are set out in Article 10 of the Biersteuergesetz. Under that provision only fermented beverages satisfying the requirements set out in Article 9 (1), (2), (4), (5) and (6) of the Biersteuergesetz may be marketed under the designation Bier -- standing alone or as part of a compound designation -- or under other designations, or with pictorial representations, giving the impression that the beverage in question is beer. Article 10 of the Biersteuergesetz entails merely a partial prohibition on marketing in so far as beverages not manufactured in conformity with the aforementioned manufacturing rules may be sold under other designations, provided that those designations do not offend against the restrictions laid down in that provision. Contraventions of the rules on designation may give rise to a fine under Article 18 (1) (4) of the Biersteuergesetz.

7. Imports into the Federal Republic of Germany of beers containing additives will also be confronted by the absolute prohibition on marketing in Article 11 (1) (2) of the Gesetz über den Verkehr mit Lebensmitteln, Tabakerzeugnissen, kosmetischen Mitteln und sonstigen Bedarfsgegenständen (Law on foodstuffs, tobacco products, cosmetics and other consumer goods), hereinafter referred to as the Foodstuffs Law, of 15 August 1974 (Bundesgesetzblatt I, p. 1945).

8. Under the Foodstuffs Law, which is based on considerations of preventive health protection, all additives are in principle prohibited, unless they have been authorized. Article 2 of the Law defines additives as substances which are intended to be added to foodstuffs in order to alter their characteristics or to give them specific properties or produce specific effects. It does not cover substances which are of natural origin or are chemically identical to natural substances and which, according to general trade usage, are mainly used on account of their nutritional, olfactory or gustatory value or as stimulants, and drinking and table water.

9. Article 11 (1) (1) of the Foodstuffs Law prohibits the use of unauthorized additives, whether pure or mixed with other substances, for the manufacture or processing by way of trade of foodstuffs intended to be marketed. Article 11 (2) (1) and Article 11 (3) provide that that prohibition does not cover processing aids or enzymes. Article

11 (2) (1) defines processing aids as additives which are eliminated from the foodstuff altogether or to such an extent that they ... are present in the product for sale to the consumer ... only as technically unavoidable and technologically insignificant residues in amounts which are negligible from the point of view of health, odour and taste.

10. Article 11 (1) (2) of the Foodstuffs Law prohibits the marketing by way of trade of products manufactured or processed in contravention of Article 11 (1) (1) or not conforming with a regulation issued pursuant to Article 12 (1). Under Article 12 (1) a ministerial regulation approved by the Bundesrat may authorize the use of certain additives for general use, for use in specific foodstuffs or for specific applications provided that it is compatible with consumer protection from the point of view of technological, nutritional and dietary requirements. The relevant authorizations are set out in the annexes to the Verordnung über die Zulassung von Zusatzstoffen zu Lebensmitteln (Regulation on the authorization of additives in foodstuffs) of 22 December 1981 (Bundesgesetzblatt I, p. 1633), hereinafter referred to as the Regulation on Additives).

11. As a foodstuff, beer is subject to the legislation on additives, but it is governed by special rules. The rules on manufacture in Article 9 of the Biersteuergesetz preclude the use of any substances, including additives, other than those listed therein. As a result, those rules constitute specific provisions on additives within the meaning of Article 1 (3) of the Regulation on Additives. That paragraph provides that the Regulation on Additives is to be without prejudice to any contrary provisions prohibiting, restricting or authorizing the use of additives in particular foodstuffs. In this way, additives authorized for general use or for specific uses in the annexes to the Regulation on Additives may not be used in the manufacture of beer. However, that exception applies only to substances which are additives within the meaning of the Law on Foodstuffs and whose use is not covered by an exception laid down in the Foodstuffs Law itself, which was enacted after the Biersteuergesetz. Consequently, the prohibition on the use of additives in beer does not cover processing aids or enzymes.

12. As a result, Article 11 (1) (2) of the Foodstuffs Law, in conjunction with Article 9 of the Biersteuergesetz, has the effect of prohibiting the importation into the Federal Republic of Germany of beers containing substances covered by the ban on the use of additives laid down by Article 11 (1) (1) of the Foodstuffs Law.

The subject-matter of the proceedings

13. It must first be established whether the proceedings are limited to the prohibition of the marketing under the designation Bier of beer manufactured in other Member States in accordance with rules inconsistent with Article 9 of the Biersteuergesetz or whether they extend to the ban on the importation of beer containing additives

which are authorized in the Member State of origin but prohibited in the Federal Republic of Germany.

14. In its letter giving the Federal Republic of Germany formal notice, the Commission's objections were directed against Articles 9 and 10 of the Biersteuergesetz in so far as they precluded the importation into the Federal Republic of Germany of beers which, although lawfully manufactured in other Member States, had not been brewed in conformity with the rules applicable in the Federal Republic of Germany. The Commission took the view that that marketing prohibition could not be justified on grounds of the public interest relating to the protection of consumers or the safeguarding of public health.

15. In its reply to that letter the German Government argued that the Reinheitsgebot was vital in order to safeguard public health: if beer was manufactured using only the raw materials listed in Article 9 of the Biersteuergesetz the use of additives could be avoided. In a supplementary letter dated 15 December 1982 to a Member of the Commission, the German Government repeated that argument and made it clear that the requirement to use only the raw materials listed in Article 9 of the Biersteuergesetz included the prohibition of the use of additives, which was designed to protect public health.

16. In its reasoned opinion the Commission adhered to its point of view. It considered that the fact that beer brewed according to the German tradition of the Reinheitsgebot could be manufactured without additives did not signify generally that there was no technological necessity for the use of additives in beer brewed according to other traditions or using other raw materials. The question of the technological necessity for the use of additives could be decided only in the light of the manufacturing methods employed and in relation to specific additives.

17. In its reply to the reasoned opinion the German Government reiterated its arguments relating to preventive health protection which, in its view, justified the provisions in Articles 9 and 10 of the Biersteuergesetz. However, it did not elucidate the exact scope of that legislation or its relationship with the rules on additives.

18. In the statement of the grounds it relies on in its application, the Commission complains of the barriers to imports resulting from the application of the Biersteuergesetz to beers manufactured in other Member States from other raw materials or using additives authorized in those States.

19. It was only when it submitted its defence that the German Government stated that the rules on the purity of beer were contained in two separate but complementary pieces of legislation, and provided the description of its legislation which is given above.

20. In its reply the Commission set out its separate objections to the rules on designation in Article 10 of the Biersteuergesetz and to the absolute ban on additives in beer. In the Commission's view, the German Government's comprehensive description of the applicable law does not fundamentally alter the facts underlying this case. The Commission stresses that its application is not aimed exclusively at Articles 9 and 10 of the Biersteuergesetz but generally at the prohibition on the marketing of beer from other Member States which does not satisfy the manufacturing criteria set out in those provisions. In its opinion, the precise statutory basis for that prohibition is of no importance.

21. In those circumstances there are two reasons why it must be considered that the application is directed both against the prohibition on the marketing under the designation Bier of beers manufactured in other Member States in accordance with rules not corresponding to those in Article 9 of the Biersteuergesetz, and against the prohibition on the importation of beers containing additives whose use is authorized in the Member State of origin but forbidden in the Federal Republic of Germany.

22. In the first place, the Commission identified the substance of the infringement from the outset in so far as from the beginning of the pre-litigation procedure it challenged the prohibition on marketing beer imported into the Federal Republic of Germany from other Member States which is not brewed in accordance with the rules in force in the Federal Republic of Germany. It referred to Article 9 of the Biersteuergesetz only in order to specify those rules more precisely. As the German Government stated, the scope of Article 9 is not restricted to raw materials but also covers additives. Besides, the arguments developed by the Commission during the pre-litigation procedure to the effect that an absolute ban on additives is inappropriate show that it intended its action to cover that prohibition.

23. In the second place, it must be observed that, from the start of the procedure, the German Government itself raised in its defence mainly arguments concerning additives and the protection of public health, which shows that it understood and acknowledged that the subject-matter of the proceedings also covered the absolute ban on the use of additives and makes it clear that it has not been denied the right to a fair hearing in that respect.

The prohibition on the marketing under the designation Bier of beers not complying with the requirements of Article 9 of the Biersteuergesetz

24. It must be noted in the first place that the provision on the manufacture of beer set out in Article 9 of the Biersteuergesetz cannot in itself constitute a measure having an effect equivalent to a quantitative restriction on imports contrary to Article 30 of the EEC Treaty, since it applies only to breweries in the Federal Republic of Germany. Article 9 of the Biersteuergesetz is at issue in this case only in so far as Article 10 of that law, which covers both products imported from other Member States

and products manufactured in Germany, refers thereto in order to determine the beverages which may be marketed under the designation Bier.

25. As far as those rules on designation are concerned, the Commission concedes that as long as harmonization has not been achieved at Community level the Member States have the power in principle to lay down rules governing the manufacture, the composition and the marketing of beverages. It stresses, however, that rules which, like Article 10 of the Biersteuergesetz, prohibit the use of a generic designation for the marketing of products manufactured partly from raw materials, such as rice and maize, other than those whose use is prescribed in the national territory are contrary to Community law. In any event, such rules go beyond what is necessary in order to protect the German consumer, since that could be done simply by means of labelling or notices. Those rules therefore constitute an impediment to trade contrary to Article 30 of the EEC Treaty.

26. The German Government has first sought to justify its rules on public-health grounds. It maintains that the use of raw materials other than those permitted by Article 9 of the Biersteuergesetz would inevitably entail the use of additives. However, at the hearing the German Government conceded that Article 10 of the Biersteuergesetz, which is merely a rule on designation, was exclusively intended to protect consumers. In its view, consumers associate the designation Bier with a beverage manufactured from only the raw materials listed in Article 9 of the Biersteuergesetz. Consequently, it is necessary to prevent them from being misled as to the nature of the product by being led to believe that a beverage called Bier complies with the Reinheitsgebot when that is not the case. The German Government maintains that its rules are not protectionist in aim. It stresses in that regard that the raw materials whose use is specified in Article 9 (1) and (2) of the Biersteuergesetz are not necessarily of national origin. Any trader marketing products satisfying the prescribed rules is free to use the designation Bier and those rules can readily be complied with outside the Federal Republic of Germany.

27. According to a consistent line of decisions of the Court (above all, the judgment of 11 July 1974 in Case 8/74 Procureur du Roi v Dassonville [1974] ECR 837) the prohibition of measures having an effect equivalent to quantitative restrictions under Article 30 of the EEC Treaty covers all trading rules enacted by Member States which are capable of hindering, directly or indirectly, actually or potentially, intra-Community trade.

28. The Court has also consistently held (in particular in the judgment of 20 February 1979 in Case 120/78 REWE-Zentral AG v Bundesmonopolverwaltung [1979] ECR 649, and the judgment of 10 November 1982 in Case 261/81 Walter Rau Lebensmittelwerke v De Smedt [1982] ECR 3961) that in the absence of common rules relating to the marketing of the products concerned, obstacles to free movement within the Community resulting from disparities between the national laws must be ac-

cepted in so far as such rules, applicable to domestic and to imported products without distinction, may be recognized as being necessary in order to satisfy mandatory requirements relating inter alia to consumer protection. It is also necessary for such rules to be proportionate to the aim in view. If a Member State has a choice between various measures to attain the same objective it should choose the means which least restricts the free movement of goods.

29. It is not contested that the application of Article 10 of the Biersteuergesetz to beers from other Member States in whose manufacture raw materials other than malted barley have been lawfully used, in particular rice and maize, is liable to constitute an obstacle to their importation into the Federal Republic of Germany.

30. Accordingly, it must be established whether the application of that provision may be justified by imperative requirements relating to consumer protection.

31. The German Government's argument that Article 10 of the Biersteuergesetz is essential in order to protect German consumers because, in their minds, the designation Bier is inseparably linked to the beverage manufactured solely from the ingredients laid down in Article 9 of the Biersteuergesetz must be rejected.

32. Firstly, consumers' conceptions which vary from one Member State to the other are also likely to evolve in the course of time within a Member State. The establishment of the common market is, it should be added, one of the factors that may play a major contributory role in that development. Whereas rules protecting consumers against misleading practices enable such a development to be taken into account, legislation of the kind contained in Article 10 of the Biersteuergesetz prevents it from taking place. As the Court has already held in another context (judgment of 27 February 1980 in Case 170/78 Commission v United Kingdom [1980] ECR 417), the legislation of a Member State must not crystallize given consumer habits so as to consolidate an advantage acquired by national industries concerned to comply with them.

33. Secondly, in the other Member States of the Community the designations corresponding to the German designation Bier are generic designations for a fermented beverage manufactured from malted barley, whether malted barley on its own or with the addition of rice or maize. The same approach is taken in Community law as an be seen from heading No 22.03 of the Common Customs Tariff. The German legislature itself utilizes the designation Bier in that way in Article 9 (7) and (8) of the Biersteuergesetz in order to refer to beverages not complying with the manufacturing rules laid down in Article 9 (1) and (2).

34. The German designation Bier and its equivalents in the languages of the other Member States of the Community may therefore not be restricted to beers manufactured in accordance with the rules in force in the Federal Republic of Germany.

35. It is admittedly legitimate to seek to enable consumers who attribute specific qualities to beers manufactured from particular raw materials to make their choice in the light of that consideration. However, as the Court has already emphasized (judgment of 9 December 1981 in Case 193/80 Commission v Italy [1981] ECR 3019), that possibility may be ensured by means which do not prevent the importation of products which have been lawfully manufactured and marketed in other Member States and, in particular, by the compulsory affixing of suitable labels giving the nature of the product sold. By indicating the raw materials utilized in the manufacture of beer such a course would enable the consumer to make his choice in full knowledge of the facts and would guarantee transparency in trading and in offers to the public. It must be added that such a system of mandatory consumer information must not entail negative assessments for beers not complying with the requirements of Article 9 of the Biersteuergesetz.

36. Contrary to the German Government's view, such a system of consumer information may operate perfectly well even in the case of a product which, like beer, is not necessarily supplied to consumers in bottles or in cans capable of bearing the appropriate details. That is borne out, once again, by the German legislation itself. Article 26 (1) and (2) of the aforementioned regulation implementing the Biersteuergesetz provides for a system of consumer information in respect of certain beers, even where those beers are sold on draught, when the requisite information must appear on the casks or the beer taps.

37. It follows from the foregoing that by applying the rules on designation in Article 10 of the Biersteuergesetz to beers imported from other Member States which were manufactured and marketed lawfully in those States the Federal Republic of Germany has failed to fulfil its obligations under Article 30 of the EEC Treaty.

The absolute ban on the marketing of beers containing additives

38. In the Commission's opinion the absolute ban on the marketing of beers containing additives cannot be justified on public-health grounds. It maintains that the other Member States control very strictly the utilization of additives in foodstuffs and do not authorize the use of any given additive until thorough tests have established that it is harmless. In the Commission's view, there should be a presumption that beers manufactured in other Member States which contain additives authorized there represent no danger to public health. The Commission argues that if the Federal Republic of Germany wishes to oppose the importation of such beers then it bears the onus of proving that such beers are a danger to public health. The Commission considers that in this case that burden of proof has not been discharged. In any event, the rules on additives applying to beer in the Federal Republic of Germany are disproportionate in so far as they completely preclude the use of additives whereas the rules for other beverages, such as soft drinks, are much more flexible.

39. For its part, the German Government considers that in view of the dangers resulting from the utilization of additives whose long-term effects are not yet known and in particular of the risks resulting from the accumulation of additives in the organism and their interaction with other substances, such as alcohol, it is necessary to minimize the quantity of additives ingested. Since beer is a foodstuff of which large quantities are consumed in Germany, the German Government considers that it is particularly desirable to prohibit the use of any additive in its manufacture, especially in so far as the use of additives is not technologically necessary and can be avoided if only the ingredients laid down in the Biersteuergesetz are used. In those circumstances, the German rules on additives in beer are fully justified by the need to safeguard public health and do not infringe the principle of proportionality.

40. It is not contested that the prohibition on the marketing of beers containing additives constitutes a barrier to the importation from other Member States of beers containing additives authorized in those States, and is to that extent covered by Article 30 of the EEC Treaty. However, it must be ascertained whether it is possible to justify that prohibition under Article 36 of the Treaty on grounds of the protection of human health.

41. The Court has consistently held (in particular in the judgment of 14 July 1983 in Case 174/82 Sandoz BV [1983] ECR 2445) that in so far as there are uncertainties at the present state of scientific research it is for the Member States, in the absence of harmonization, to decide what degree of protection of the health and life of humans they intend to assure, having regard however to the requirements of the free movement of goods within the Community.

42. As may also be seen from the decisions of the Court (and especially the judgment of 14 July 1983 in the Sandoz case, cited above, the judgment of 10 December 1985 in Case 247/84 Motte [1985] ECR 3887, and the judgment of 6 May 1986 in Case 304/84 Ministère public v Muller and Others [1986] ECR 1511), in such circumstances Community law does not preclude the adoption by the Member States of legislation whereby the use of additives is subjected to prior authorization granted by a measure of general application for specific additives, in respect of all products, for certain products only or for certain uses. Such legislation meets a genuine need of health policy, namely that of restricting the uncontrolled consumption of food additives.

43. However, the application to imported products of prohibitions on marketing products containing additives which are authorized in the Member State of production but prohibited in the Member State of importation is permissible only in so far as it complies with the requirements of Article 36 of the Treaty as it has been interpreted by the Court.

44. It must be borne in mind, in the first place, that in its judgments in the Sandoz, Motte and Muller cases, cited above, the Court inferred from the principle of proportionality underlying the last sentence of Article 36 of the Treaty that prohibitions on the marketing of products containing additives authorized in the Member State of production but prohibited in the Member State of importation must be restricted to what is actually necessary to secure the protection of public health. The Court also concluded that the use of a specific additive which is authorized in another Member State must be authorized in the case of a product imported from that Member State where, in view, on the one hand, of the findings of international scientific research, and in particular of the work of the Community's Scientific Committee for Food, the Codex Alimentarius Committee of the Food and Agriculture Organization of the United Nations (FAO) and the World Health Organization, and, on the other hand, of the eating habits prevailing in the importing Member State, the additive in question does not present a risk to public health and meets a real need, especially a technical one.

45. Secondly, it should be remembered that, as the Court held in its judgment of 6 May 1986 in the Muller case, cited above, by virtue of the principle of proportionality, traders must also be able to apply, under a procedure which is easily accessible to them and can be concluded within a reasonable time, for the use of specific additives to be authorized by a measure of general application.

46. It should be pointed out that it must be open to traders to challenge before the courts an unjustified failure to grant authorization. Without prejudice to the right of the competent national authorities of the importing Member State to ask traders to produce the information in their possession which may be useful for the purpose of assessing the facts, it is for those authorities to demonstrate, as the Court held in its judgment of 6 May 1986 in the Muller case, cited above, that the prohibition is justified on grounds relating to the protection of the health of its population.

47. It must be observed that the German rules on additives applicable to beer result in the exclusion of all the additives authorized in the other Member States and not the exclusion of just some of them for which there is concrete justification by reason of the risks which they involve in view of the eating habits of the German population; moreover those rules do not lay down any procedure whereby traders can obtain authorization for the use of a specific additive in the manufacture of beer by means of a measure of general application.

48. As regards more specifically the harmfulness of additives, the German Government, citing experts' reports, has referred to the risks inherent in the ingestion of additives in general. It maintains that it is important, for reasons of general preventive health protection, to minimize the quantity of additives ingested, and that it is particularly advisable to prohibit altogether their use in the manufacture of beer, a foodstuff consumed in considerable quantities by the German population.

49. However, it appears from the tables of additives authorized for use in the various foodstuffs submitted by the German Government itself that some of the additives authorized in other Member States for use in the manufacture of beer are also authorized under the German rules, in particular the Regulation on Additives, for use in the manufacture of all, or virtually all, beverages. Mere reference to the potential risks of the ingestion of additives in general and to the fact that beer is a foodstuff consumed in large quantities does not suffice to justify the imposition of stricter rules in the case of beer.

50. As regards the need, and in particular the technological need, for additives, the German Government argues that there is no need for additives if beer is manufactured in accordance with the requirements of Article 9 of the Biersteuergesetz.

51. It must be emphasized that mere reference to the fact that beer can be manufactured without additives if it is made from only the raw materials prescribed in the Federal Republic of Germany does not suffice to preclude the possibility that some additives may meet a technological need. Such an interpretation of the concept of technological need, which results in favouring national production methods, constitutes a disguised means of restricting trade between Member States.

52. The concept of technological need must be assessed in the light of the raw materials utilized and bearing in mind the assessment made by the authorities of the Member State where the product was lawfully manufactured and marketed. Account must also be taken of the findings of international scientific research and in particular the work of the Community's Scientific Committee for Food, the Codex Alimentarius Committee of the FAO and the World Health Organization.

53. Consequently, in so far as the German rules on additives in beer entail a general ban on additives, their application to beers imported from other Member States is contrary to the requirements of Community law as laid down in the case-law of the Court, since that prohibition is contrary to the principle of proportionality and is therefore not covered by the exception provided for in Article 36 of the EEC Treaty.

54. In view of the foregoing considerations it must be held that by prohibiting the marketing of beers lawfully manufactured and marketed in another Member State if they do not comply with Articles 9 and 10 of the Biersteuergesetz, the Federal Republic of Germany has failed to fulfil its obligations under Article 30 of the EEC Treaty.

Costs

[Para. 55 omitted]

On those grounds,

THE COURT

hereby:

1. **Declares that, by prohibiting the marketing of beers lawfully manufactured and marketed in another Member State if they do not comply with Articles 9 and 10 of the Biersteuergesetz, the Federal Republic of Germany has failed to fulfil its obligations under Article 30 of the EEC Treaty;**

[Para. 2 of the ruling omitted]

Comments and questions

Note that in paragraph 29 of the judgment in Case 178/84 *Commission* v *Germany* (*German Beer* or *Reinheitsgebot*) [1987] ECR 1227, the CJEU used the same definition of a restriction on imports as had been used in the *Cassis de Dijon* case (beer that was lawfully manufactured in another Member State using ingredients other than malted barley could not lawfully be sold in Germany). The CJEU considered that the German law on beer was a restriction on imports.

It was clear from paragraph 30 that the CJEU examined whether the provision could be justified by imperative requirements for consumer protection. As previously noted, this can only apply if the national legislation is non-discriminatory; cf. the 'Rule of reason'.

The CJEU used a formal criterion for discrimination, since the CJEU takes the view that deciding whether or not discrimination exists depends on whether the national legislation emphasises the place where the goods are produced. If national legislation applies regardless of whether the goods are produced domestically or abroad but which nevertheless constitutes a restriction on foreign goods, there will be a restriction. The German rules, under which beer which did not satisfy the *Reinheitsgebot* (purity conditions) may not be sold under the designation '*Bier*' constituted a restriction, since the rules applied without distinction between foreign and domestic ale; cf. paragraph 24.

The CJEU rejected the argument that consumer protection could justify the requirement. The CJEU held that the legislation of a Member State should not 'crystallise given consumer habits' so as to consolidate an advantage acquired by national industries in complying with them; cf. paragraph 32. Furthermore, 'beer' is a generic designation used in the Union's own legislation (such as the Common Customs Tariff). The CJEU also noted that consumer concerns could have been protected less radically (the principle of proportionality), simply by making suitable provisions for labelling. It was emphasised that the labelling requirement should not lead to the disparagement of beers which do not meet the German requirements; cf. paragraph 35; compare this point with

Case 113/80 *Commission* v *Ireland* (the *Souvenirs* case) [1981] ECR 1625, printed above.

As for the prohibition of the use of additives in beer, the CJEU stated that, under the principle of proportionality, Member States should have an arrangement whereby manufacturers can apply for the authorisation of the use of specific additives; cf. paragraph 45. When processing such applications the Member States shall take account of the *international standards* laid down by the FAO and WHO; cf. paragraphs 44 and 52, and the question of technological need must be assessed on this basis. Note too that the CJEU in paragraph 41 stated the principle that insofar as there are uncertainties at the present state of scientific research it is for the Member States, in the absence of harmonization, to decide what degree of protection of the health and life of humans they intend to assure, having regard, however to the requirements of the free movement of goods within the Union. In other words, in *case of any reasonable doubt, the law should err on the side of the protection of public health.* Subsequently, in paragraph 45 of the judgment in Case C-473/98 *Kemikalieinspektionen* v *Toolex Alpha AB* [2000] ECR I-5681, the CJEU held that a measure which restricted trade was lawful, given the difficulty of establishing the threshold above which exposure to the substance in question posed a serious health risk to humans, in the current state of the research.

What was the most decisive factor for the result of the *German Beer* case? On which party does the burden of proof lie for justifying a restriction on trade?

After judgment had been given in the case, the German authorities proposed to introduce a requirement that imported beer should state whether it has been produced in accordance with the *Reinheitsgebot.* Would such a proposal be permissible under Article 34 TFEU (formerly Article 30 EEC Treaty)? Today, the German rules require German-produced beer to state whether or not it has been produced in accordance with the terms of the *Reinheitsgebot.* Is this requirement compatible with Article 34 TFEU? Compare this with the judgment in Case 113/80 *Commission* v *Ireland* (the *Souvenirs* case) [1981] ECR 1625, printed above.

Note that, in paragraph 45 of the judgment in the *Reinheitsgebot* case the CJEU stated that, under the principle of proportionality, the administrative authorities must enable traders to apply for authorisation for the use of specific additives under a procedure which is easily accessible to them and can be concluded within a reasonable time. In other words, on the basis of the rules on the free movement of goods, the CJEU has laid down procedural requirements for national administrative authorities.

JUDGMENT OF THE COURT
20 September 1988

Commission of the European Communities v Kingdom of Denmark

'Free movement of goods – Containers for beer and soft drinks'

Case 302/86

Judgment

1. By an application lodged at the Court Registry on 1 December 1986, the Commission of the European Communities brought an action under Article 169 of the EEC Treaty for a declaration that by introducing and applying by Order No 397 of 2 July 1981 a system under which all containers for beer and soft drinks must be returnable, the Kingdom of Denmark had failed to fulfil its obligations under Article 30 of the EEC Treaty.

2. The main feature of the system which the Commission challenges as incompatible with Community law is that manufacturers must market beer and soft drinks only in re-usable containers. The containers must be approved by the National Agency for the Protection of the Environment, which may refuse approval of new kinds of container, especially if it considers that a container is not technically suitable for a system for returning containers or that the return system envisaged does not ensure that a sufficient proportion of containers are actually re-used or if a container of equal capacity, which is both available and suitable for the same use, has already been approved.

3. Order No 95 of 16 March 1984 amended the aforementioned rules in such a way that, provided that a deposit-and-return system is established, non-approved containers, except for any form of metal container, may be used for quantities not exceeding 3 000 hectolitres a year per producer and for drinks which are sold by foreign producers in order to test the market.

4. By order of 8 May 1987 the United Kingdom was granted leave to intervene in the case in support of the Commission's conclusions.

5. Reference is made to the Report for the Hearing for a fuller account of the facts of the case, the course of the procedure and the submissions and arguments of the parties, which are mentioned or discussed hereinafter only in so far as is necessary for the reasoning of the Court.

6. The first point which must be made in resolving this dispute is that, according to an established body of case-law of the Court (judgment of 20 February 1979 in Case 120/78 Rewe-Zentral AG v Bundesmonopolverwaltung für Branntwein [1979] ECR 649; judgment of 10 November 1982 in Case 261/81 Walter Rau Lebensmittelwerke v De Smedt PvbA [1982] ECR 3961), in the absence of common rules relating to the marketing of the products in question, obstacles to free movement within the Community resulting from disparities between the national laws must be accepted in so far as such rules, applicable to domestic and imported products without distinction, may be recognized as being necessary in order to satisfy mandatory requirements recognized by Community law. Such rules must also be proportionate to the aim in view. If a Member State has a choice between various measures for achieving the same aim, it should choose the means which least restricts the free movement of goods.

7. In the present case the Danish Government contends that the mandatory collection system for containers of beer and soft drinks applied in Denmark is justified by a mandatory requirement related to the protection of the environment.

8. The Court has already held in its judgment of 7 February 1985 in Case 240/83 Procureur de la République v Association de défense des brûleurs d'huiles usagées [1985] ECR 531 that the protection of the environment is one of the Community's essential objectives, which may as such justify certain limitations of the principle of the free movement of goods. That view is moreover confirmed by the Single European Act.

9. In view of the foregoing, it must therefore be stated that the protection of the environment is a mandatory requirement which may limit the application of Article 30 of the Treaty.

10. The Commission submits that the Danish rules are contrary to the principle of proportionality in so far as the aim of the protection of the environment may be achieved by means less restrictive of intra-Community trade.

11. In that regard, it must be pointed out that in its aforementioned judgment of 7 February 1985 the Court stated that measures adopted to protect the environment must not go beyond the inevitable restrictions which are justified by the pursuit of the objective of environmental protection.

12. It is therefore necessary to examine whether all the restrictions which the contested rules impose on the free movement of goods are necessary to achieve the objectives pursued by those rules.

13. First of all, as regards the obligation to establish a deposit-and-return system for empty containers, it must be observed that this requirement is an indispensable ele-

ment of a system intended to ensure the re-use of containers and therefore appears necessary to achieve the aims pursued by the contested rules. That being so, the restrictions which it imposes on the free movement of goods cannot be regarded as disproportionate.

14. Next, it is necessary to consider the requirement that producers and importers must use only containers approved by the National Agency for the Protection of the Environment.

15. The Danish Government stated in the proceedings before the Court that the present deposit-and-return system would not work if the number of approved containers were to exceed 30 or so, since the retailers taking part in the system would not be prepared to accept too many types of bottles owing to the higher handling costs and the need for more storage space. For that reason the Agency has hitherto followed the practice of ensuring that fresh approvals are normally accompanied by the withdrawal of existing approvals.

16. Even though there is some force in that argument, it must nevertheless be observed that under the system at present in force in Denmark the Danish authorities may refuse approval to a foreign producer even if he is prepared to ensure that returned containers are re-used.

17. In those circumstances, a foreign producer who still wished to sell his products in Denmark would be obliged to manufacture or purchase containers of a type already approved, which would involve substantial additional costs for that producer and therefore make the importation of his products into Denmark very difficult.

18. To overcome that obstacle the Danish Government altered its rules by the aforementioned Order No 95 of 16 March 1984, which allows a producer to market up to 3 000 hectolitres of beer and soft drinks a year in non-approved containers, provided that a deposit-and-return system is established.

19. The provision in Order No 95 restricting the quantity of beer and soft drinks which may be marketed by a producer in non-approved containers to 3 000 hectolitres a year is challenged by the Commission on the ground that it is unnecessary to achieve the objectives pursued by the system.

20. It is undoubtedly true that the existing system for returning approved containers ensures a maximum rate of re-use and therefore a very considerable degree of protection of the environment since empty containers can be returned to any retailer of beverages. Non-approved containers, on the other hand, can be returned only to the retailer who sold the beverages, since it is impossible to set up such a comprehensive system for those containers as well.

21. Nevertheless, the system for returning non-approved containers is capable of protecting the environment and, as far as imports are concerned, affects only limited quantities of beverages compared with the quantity of beverages consumed in Denmark owing to the restrictive effect which the requirement that containers should be returnable has on imports. In those circumstances, a restriction of the quantity of products which may be marketed by importers is disproportionate to the objective pursued.

22. It must therefore be held that by restricting, by Order No 95 of 16 March 1984, the quantity of beer and soft drinks which may be marketed by a single producer in non-approved containers to 3 000 hectolitres a year, the Kingdom of Denmark has failed, as regards imports of those products from other Member States, to fulfil its obligations under Article 30 of the EEC Treaty.

23. The remainder of the application must be dismissed.

Costs

[Para. 24 omitted]

On those grounds,

THE COURT

hereby:

1. **Declares that by restricting, by Order No 95 of 16 March 1984, the quantity of beer and soft drinks which may be marketed by a single producer in non-approved containers to 3 000 hectolitres a year, the Kingdom of Denmark has failed, as regards imports of those products from other Member States, to fulfil its obligations under Article 30 of the EEC Treaty;**

2. **Dismisses the remainder of the application;**

[Para. 3 of the ruling omitted]

Comments and questions

For many years a system has been used in Denmark whereby a returnable deposit is taken on bottles when selling beer or other drinks. Originally the system was voluntary, and it worked well. In the mid 1970s Danish brewers began to use cans and bottles of varying shapes. In order to ensure that the deposit-and-return scheme could continue to work effectively, a law was brought in which made the scheme obligatory. This scheme covered carbonated mineral water and non-alcoholic drinks in general as well as beer. The scheme meant that, as a general rule, such drinks could only be sold in Denmark if their packaging had been approved by the Danish authorities. A number of drinks manufacturers and bottle manufacturers etc. complained to the Commission about the Danish scheme. The Commission found that the deposit-and-return scheme contravened Article 34 TFEU (formerly Article 30 EEC Treaty), and since the Danish Government refused to abandon the scheme, and was only willing to allow very limited exceptions to it, the Commission brought a case against Denmark before the CJEU, Case 302/86, *Commission* v *Denmark* [1988] ECR 4607.

The Danish Government stated, in the proceedings before the Court, that the deposit-and-return system would not work if there were more than about 30 different types of container, if the scheme was to be effective. It also appeared that the authorities had in fact never refused to approve a form of package. Thus, there were no foreign bottle types which had in fact been refused access to the Danish market. In these circumstances, can the scheme constitute a restriction on imports, covered by Article 34 TFEU?

The Commission and the foreign producers claimed that the Danish scheme constituted an indirectly discriminatory measure. In his Opinion, the Advocate General took the same view. He argued that, 'Even though on the face of it the system is indiscriminately applicable to Danish and to non-Danish brewers ... the system as it presently operates does have greater disadvantages for the non-Danish brewer.' Do you agree that this constitutes indirect discrimination? Does the Court express a view on the question?

In Paragraph 9 of the judgment, the Court stated that the protection of the environment is a mandatory requirement which may limit the application of Article 34 TFEU of the Treaty. Why could the Danish Government claim consideration for the environment as a justification (see Paragraph 6)?

Could Denmark maintain the deposit-and-return scheme after the judgment?

Denmark has since permitted the sale of the drinks in question in metal cans. The cans are also covered by a deposit-and-return scheme. Was the earlier prohibition of the sale of beers and non-alcoholic drinks in cans compatible with Article 34 TFEU?

It may cause some surprise that Article 36 TFEU (formerly Article 36 EEC Treaty) has not been amended in the light of the practice of the Court, so as to include environmental protection as a possible justification for a discriminatory national measure. Compare the Court's decision in this case with Case C-2/90 *Commission* v *Belgium* [1992] ECR I-4413 (the *Walloon waste disposal* case); and Case C-379/98 *PreussenElektra AG* v *Schleswag AG* [2001] ECR I-2099, both of which are printed above. In the *PreussenElektra* case the Court recognised that environmental considerations could, in some circumstances, justify discriminatory restriction on imports or exports. See also the CJEU's judgment in Case C-573/12 *Ålands Vindkraft*, referred to above in the comments and questions on the *PreussenElektra* case.

The decision in the Danish deposit-and-return scheme case is fundamentally based on an assessment of proportionality, cf. Paragraph 12 of the judgment. The question was whether the Danish scheme (obligatory deposit-and-return system) was proportionate to its aim (protection of the environment). The Advocate General's view was that: 'Although the conservation of resources is an important objective, it does not seem to me in the present state of [Union] legislation that an obligatory re-utilisation should be accepted if its effect is seriously to inhibit the free movement of goods.' In accordance with this, he suggested to the Court that it should disallow the Danish deposit-and-return scheme. What was the proportionality assessment used by the Court?

Among other things, the Danish deposit-and-return scheme did not cover wine bottles. Consider whether this is an argument for or against the legality of the scheme. On one hand it could be argued that the costs of the scheme primarily falls on Danish producers of beer and non-alcoholic drinks, so it benefits the sellers of (foreign) wine. On the other hand, it could be argued that the scheme was introduced in two areas in which there was substantial Danish production, so the scheme was only a hindrance for those foreign products which competed most directly with corresponding Danish products. Consider whether a country such as France or Italy could legally introduce a deposit-and-return scheme like the Danish one, in which the scheme only affected beer and non-alcoholic drinks (which are substantially produced by foreign manufacturers), without covering wine and mineral water (which are substantially produced by domestic undertakings).

Many Swedes travel to Denmark to buy beer because Danish beer prices are considerably lower than Swedish beer prices. However, Danish beer sales to Swedish customers are somewhat discouraged by the requirement to pay a deposit on bottles and crates. In practice the deposit has the effect of increasing the price of Danish beer paid by Swedes who do not immediately return to Denmark in order to reclaim their deposits on the empty bottles and crates (typically throwing them away and thus losing their deposits). As a result, those Swedish consumers who expect to be able to reclaim their deposits will not be deterred from buying beer in Denmark, while Swedish consumers who will merely throw away the empties, and thus impose a burden on the environment, will to some extent be deterred from buying beer in Denmark. This is entirely in line with the aim of the deposit system to promote environmental protection. Consider whether it would be in breach of the rules on free movement if the Danish Government allowed Danish supermarkets to sell beer to Swedes without demanding a deposit, on the grounds that the Government wished to support the competitiveness of Danish supermarkets vis-à-vis Swedish supermarkets – the Danish Government pointing out in this connection that increased sales of beer by Danish supermarkets would create Danish jobs and secure tax revenues for Denmark.

JUDGMENT OF THE COURT (Fifth Chamber)
14 July 1994

Criminal proceedings against J.J.J. Van der Veldt.
(Reference to the Court by the Rechtbank van Eerste Aanleg, Ghent – Belgium)

'Prohibition of the sale of bread and other bakery products whose salt content is higher than 2% – Obligation to set out certain information on the labelling Articles 30 and 36 of the Treaty and Council Directive 79/112/EEC'

Case C-17/93

Judgment

1. By judgment of 15 January 1993, received at the Court on 20 January 1993, the Rechtbank van Eerste Aanleg (Court of First Instance) Ghent, referred to the Court for a preliminary ruling under Article 177 of the EEC Treaty three questions on the interpretation of Articles 30 and 36 of that Treaty and of Council Directive 79/112/EEC of 18 December 1978 on the approximation of the laws of the Member States relating to the labelling, presentation and advertising of foodstuffs for sale to the ultimate consumer (OJ 1979 L 33, p. 1, hereinafter 'Directive 79/112').

2. Those questions were raised in criminal proceedings against Mr Van der Veldt, who was charged with having sold on the Belgian market bread whose salt content did not comply with Belgian law and with having failed to fulfil his obligation to set out on the labels of bakery products the specific name or the EEC number of the preservative used.

3. It emerges from the written observations submitted by Mr Van der Veldt to the Court that Hema-Belgique, the company for which he manages a shop in Ghent, imports practically all its products, including bread and other bakery products, from the Netherlands.

4. Checks carried out on 8 September and 29 November 1988 by food inspectors on samples of products sold in the Ghent shop disclosed that the bread contained between 2.11% and 2.17% salt, whereas the Belgian Royal Decree of 2 September 1985 concerning bread and other bakery products (*Belgisch Staatsblad* of 7 November 1985), adopted pursuant to the Law of 24 January 1977 on the protection of consumer health with respect to foodstuffs and other products (*Belgisch Staatsblad* of 8 April 1977), permits no more than 2%. Furthermore, although the word 'preservative' appeared on the packaging of the products in dispute, neither the specific name of the ingredient used, namely 'propionic acid', nor its EEC number, 'E 280', was stated, contrary to the requirements of the Belgian Royal Decree of 13 Novem-

ber 1986 (*Belgisch Staatsblad* of 2 December 1986), which also gives effect to the Law of 24 January 1977.

5. That provision transposes into Belgian law the second indent of Article 6(5)(b) of Directive 79/112, according to which: '... ingredients belonging to one of the categories listed in Annex II must be designated by the name of that category, followed by their specific name or EEC number'. One of the categories expressly listed in Annex II of Directive 79/112 is that of preservatives.

6. According to the second indent of Article 22(1) of Directive 79/112, Member States were required, no later than four years after notification of the directive, to make such amendments to their laws as were necessary to prohibit trade in those products which did not comply with the directive's provisions. However, by way of derogation from that rule, Article 23(1)(a) allowed Member States to make implementation of the second indent of Article 6(5)(b) optional, that is to say, they were not obliged to require the designation of the specific name or EEC number of the ingredients belonging to one of the categories listed in Annex II. The Netherlands exercised that option.

7. Subsequent to the events which gave rise to the main proceedings, the option was removed with effect from 20 June 1992 by Article 2 of Council Directive 89/395/EEC of 14 June 1989 amending Directive 79/112/EEC (OJ 1989 L 186, p. 17, hereinafter 'Directive 89/395').

8. In view of the fact that the products at issue were lawfully manufactured and marketed in the Netherlands, where the maximum salt content for bread is 2.5% and where additives may simply be designated by the term 'preservative', that is to say, by the name of the general category given in Annex II to the Algemeen Aanduidungsbesluit (Warenwet) (Decree on the Labelling of Goods (Law on Goods], the Rechtbank van Eerste Aanleg, Ghent, considered it necessary, to enable it to give judgment, to submit the following questions to the Court of Justice:

   '1. Must national legislation prohibiting the sale of bread whose maximum salt content by reference to the dry matter is higher than 2% be regarded as a quantitative restriction or a measure having equivalent effect within the meaning of Article 30 of the EEC Treaty, if, by reason thereof, bread which has been lawfully marketed in another Member State and whose salt content by reference to the dry matter is higher than 2.5% cannot, when imported into the first Member State mentioned, be sold, on the ground that its salt content exceeds the maximum limit of 2% which the law there permits?

   2. If the answer to the first question is in the affirmative and if the legal provision referred to infringes Article 30 of the EEC Treaty, may the first Member State mentioned, in the circumstances set out above, rely on the derogation provided

for in Article 36 of the EEC Treaty for the purposes of protecting public health in order to maintain the measure in dispute notwithstanding the prohibition contained in Article 30 of the EEC Treaty?

3. Pursuant to Article 23(1)(a) of Council Directive 79/112/EEC of 18 December 1978 on the approximation of the laws of the Member States relating to the labelling, presentation and advertising of foodstuffs for sale to the ultimate consumer (OJ 1979 L 33, p. 1), Member States need not require compliance with the provisions concerning the designation, provided for in the second indent of Article 6(5)(b), of the specific name or EEC number of the ingredients belonging to one of the categories listed in Annex II to that directive (particularly preservatives), reference to the general category thus being sufficient.

   (a) May a Member State which has nevertheless made the designations provided for in the second indent of Article 6(5)(b) compulsory prohibit the sale of products which have been lawfully marketed in another Member State where, pursuant to Article 23(1)(a), those designations are not compulsory, but on which the designations required by the first Member State are not provided? In other words, does the first State have the right to exclude the products in question from the free movement of goods as defined by Article 30 of the EEC Treaty?

   (b) If Article 30 continues to apply in every respect to a product that is not in conformity with its legislation, may the first-mentioned Member State, by relying on Article 36 of the EEC Treaty, exclude the application of Article 30 thereof on the ground that the designations referred to in the second indent of Article 6(5)(b) are not set out on the packaging of the product, even though they are compulsory in that Member State, which is not the case in the Member State where the product is lawfully marketed?'

The first question

9. The first question put by the national court is whether national legislation prohibiting the marketing of bread and other bakery products whose salt content by reference to the dry matter is higher than 2% constitutes a measure having equivalent effect to a quantitative restriction within the meaning of Article 30 of the Treaty, if it is also applied to imports of products which have been lawfully manufactured and marketed in another Member State.

10. As the Court has consistently held, in the absence of common or harmonized rules on the making and marketing of bread and other bakery products, it is for Member States to regulate all matters relating to the composition, making and marketing of those foodstuffs on their own territory, provided that they do not thereby discriminate against imported products or hinder the importation of products from other

Member States (see Case 130/80 *Kelderman* [1981] ECR 527 and Case 237/82 *Jongeneel Kaas* v *Netherlands* [1984] ECR 483).

11. The extension to imported products of a requirement that they contain no more than a specific amount of salt, calculated by reference to the dry matter, may prevent bread and other bakery products originating in other Member States from being marketed in the State concerned. It may make it necessary, if identical manufacturing standards are not prescribed in those States, to vary the method of manufacture according to the place where the bread or bakery product in question is to be sold and thus impede the movement of products lawfully produced and marketed in the Member States of origin.

12. Accordingly, it should be stated in reply to the first question that national legislation prohibiting the marketing of bread and other bakery products whose salt content by reference to the dry matter exceeds the maximum permitted level of 2%, when applied to products which have been lawfully manufactured and marketed in another Member State, constitutes a measure having equivalent effect to a quantitative restriction within the meaning of Article 30 of the Treaty.

The second question

13. The second question is whether a rule such as that at issue in the main proceedings is to be regarded as justified under Article 36 of the Treaty on public health grounds.

14. The Belgian rule in dispute was adopted in pursuance of the Law of 24 January 1977, mentioned above, whose purpose, as its title indicates, is to protect consumer health.

15. Since it concerns an exception to the principle of the free movement of goods, it is for the national authorities to demonstrate that their rules are consistent with the principle of proportionality, that is to say, that they are necessary in order to achieve the declared purpose, which in the present case is the protection of public health.

16. In that regard, the Belgian Ministry of Health, in its letter of 6 August 1990 to the Ghent Openbaar Ministerie (Public Prosecutor's Office), which is repeated word for word in the written observations submitted by Mr Van der Veldt, confines itself to the statement that 'the Belgian authorities with responsibility for public health are of the opinion that the levels permitted in the Netherlands are too high'. The Ministry points out that, 'if the level permissible in the Netherlands were retained, the daily intake would amount to 3.1 g, which represents – not counting those who eat bread in large quantities – a daily increase of 0.6 g of salt for the average person'.

17. General conjecture of that nature does not prove that increasing salt intake by such an amount poses a risk for public health. It is true that, as the Court has already held (see Case 97/83 *Melkunie* [1984] ECR 2367), the fact that there is a risk to consumers is sufficient to make legislation of the kind at issue compatible with the requirements of Article 36. However, the risk must be measured, not according to the yardstick of general conjecture, but on the basis of relevant scientific research (see, in particular, Case 178/84 *Commission* v *Germany* [1987] ECR 1227).

18. In neglecting to produce scientific data on the basis of which the Belgian legislature would have been justified in enacting and retaining the measures at issue, the Belgian authorities have failed to demonstrate the risk to public health of a salt content in excess of 2%.

19. Furthermore, instead of prohibiting and penalizing the marketing of bread and other bakery products whose salt content is higher than 2%, the Belgian legislature could have prescribed suitable labelling to give consumers the desired information regarding the composition of the product. The protection of public health would thus have been ensured without such serious restrictions on the free movement of goods.

20. It follows from all the foregoing considerations that the Belgian authorities have failed to prove that the legislation at issue is necessary in order to protect consumer health and that it goes no further than is necessary in order to achieve that aim. The legislation in dispute is therefore incompatible with the principle of proportionality.

21. Accordingly it should be stated in reply to the second question that rules such as those at issue in the main proceedings are likely to hinder trade between Member States and cannot be regarded as justified under Article 36 of the Treaty on the ground of protecting public health.

The third question

22. The third question is, in essence, whether in the context of Directive 79/112 a Member State which had made it compulsory to designate – as provided for by the second indent of Article 6(5)(b) – the specific name or EEC number of the ingredients listed in Annex II to the directive, was entitled to rely on the imperative requirement of protecting consumers or on one of the grounds listed in Article 36 of the Treaty in order to prohibit the marketing of a product from another Member State which, by exercising the option allowed for in Article 23(1)(a) of that directive, required merely designation of the general category 'preservative'.

23. It should first of all be noted that the obligation to mark on the packaging of products sold the specific name or EEC number of the preservative makes it more difficult to import products from other Member States where no such obligation is imposed. Consequently, as has been consistently held (see, in particular, Case 8/74

Procureur du Roi v *Dassonville* [1974] ECR 837 and Case 120/78 *Rewe* v *Bundesmonopolverwaltung für Branntwein* [1979] ECR 649), an obligation of that sort is in principle caught by the prohibition in Article 30 of the Treaty.

24. Secondly, according to the Court's decision in Case 76/86 (*Commission* v *Germany* [1989] ECR 1021), it follows from Article 30 et seq. of the Treaty that national legislation, adopted in the absence of common or harmonized rules, applicable to both domestic products and to products imported from other Member States where they are lawfully manufactured and marketed, is compatible with the Treaty only in so far as it is necessary on grounds of public interest listed in Article 36 or in order to satisfy imperative requirements relating, in particular, to the protection of consumers.

25. Lastly, it is clear from the judgment in Case 5/77 (*Tedeschi* v *Denkavit* [1977] ECR 1555) that recourse to Article 36 ceases to be justified only where, in application of Article 100 of the Treaty, Community directives provide for the complete harmonization of national laws. It must therefore be conceded that, so long as the laws of Member States relating to a particular field have not been harmonized, the corresponding national legislation may restrict the principle of free movement to the extent that those restrictions are justified on one of the grounds listed in Article 36 of the Treaty or by imperative requirements.

26. In the present case, Directive 79/112 represents, as follows specifically from its first and eighth recitals, only the initial stage of a harmonization process which is designed progressively to eliminate all obstacles to the free movement of foodstuffs resulting from the differences which exist between the laws, regulations and administrative provisions of the Member States with respect to the labelling of those products.

27. Moreover, since the rule in dispute in the main proceedings is applicable to domestic and imported products alike, it must be considered whether it may be justified by imperative requirements – in this case, protecting consumers – or on one of the grounds referred to in Article 36 of the Treaty.

28. As is apparent from the sixth recital in the preamble to Directive 79/112 and from the second recital in Directive 89/395, which makes it compulsory to mark on the packaging of foodstuffs either the specific name or the EEC number of the ingredients, the prime consideration for any rules on the labelling of foodstuffs should be the need to inform and to protect the consumer. That implies that the latter should be able to know the exact nature of all the ingredients used.

29. As a reflection of those concerns, the purpose of the obligation to designate on the packaging of bread and other bakery products either the specific name or the EEC number of the preservatives is, therefore, to ensure the protection of consum-

ers, which is recognized by the case-law of the Court as being an imperative requirement.

30. Nevertheless, an obligation of that kind must be fulfilled by means which are not out of proportion to the desired result and which hinder as little as possible the importation of products which have been lawfully manufactured and marketed in other Member States.

31. Those requirements are satisfied by the obligatory designation of either the specific name or the EEC number of the preservative: to designate only the general category 'preservative' would be inadequate, particularly in view of the multiplicity of preserving agents which the products in question may contain. Furthermore, the Court has already observed (see Case C-39/90 *Denkavit Futtermittel* v *Land Baden-Württemberg* [1991] ECR I-3069, at paragraph 24) that labelling is one of the means that least restricts the free movement of products within the Community.

32. Accordingly, it should be stated in reply to the third question that, in the context of Directive 79/112, a Member State which had made it obligatory to designate, as provided by the second indent of Article 6(5)(b), either the specific name or the EEC number of the ingredients listed in Annex II to the directive, was entitled to rely on the imperative requirement of protecting consumers in order to prohibit the marketing of a product from another Member State which had chosen to exercise the option allowed by Article 23(1)(a) of that directive and to require only designation of the general category 'preservative'.

Costs

[Para. 33 omitted]

On those grounds,

THE COURT (Fifth Chamber),

in answer to the questions referred to it by the Rechtbank van Eerste Aanleg, Ghent, by judgment of 15 January 1993, hereby rules:

1. **National legislation prohibiting the marketing of bread and other bakery products whose salt content by reference to the dry matter exceeds the maximum permitted level of 2%, when applied to products which have been lawfully manufactured and marketed in another Member State, constitutes a measure having equivalent effect to a quantitative restriction within the meaning of Article 30 of the EEC Treaty.**

2. **Rules such as those at issue in the main proceedings are likely to hinder trade between Member States and cannot be regarded as justified under Article 36 of the EEC Treaty on the ground of protecting public health.**

3. **In the context of Council Directive 79/112/EEC of 18 December 1978 on the approximation of the laws of the Member States relating to the labelling, presentation and advertising of foodstuffs for sale to the ultimate consumer, a Member State which had made it obligatory to designate, as provided by the second indent of Article 6(5)(b), either the specific name or the EEC number of the ingredients listed in Annex II to that directive, was entitled to rely on the imperative requirement of protecting consumers in order to prohibit the marketing of a product from another Member State which had chosen to exercise the option allowed by Article 23(1)(a) of that directive and to require only designation of the general category 'preservative'.**

Comments and questions

What definition of a restriction on trade does the CJEU use in Case C-17/93 *Van der Veldt* [1994] ECR I-3537, with regard to the requirement that bread may not contain more than 2% salt, and where in the judgment is this to be found? Were the Belgian rules (as to salt content and labelling) a product requirement or a selling arrangement, as defined in the *Keck* case?

According to paragraph 16 of the judgment, it was the view of the Belgian Ministry of Health that the permitted Dutch levels were too high. Compared with the permitted Belgian levels, the Dutch levels would lead to an increase in the daily intake of salt from 2.5g to 3.1g for the average person. The CJEU dismissed the argument that such general observations could be used to show that the national measures were justified on the grounds of protecting public health. The CJEU accepted that Member States cannot be required to prove absolutely that there is a risk to public health. On the basis of the precautionary principle, it is enough to satisfy the requirements of Article 36 TFEU (formerly Article 36 EEC Treaty) that there is a *risk* to consumers. However, this risk must be *supported by relevant scientific research*; cf. paragraph 17. Compare this with paragraph 41 in Case 178/84 *Commission* v *Germany* (*German Beer*) [1987] ECR 1227, printed above.

Several times the CJEU emphasised that the Belgian rules should be consistent with the principle of proportionality (see paragraphs 15 and 30). Who has the burden of proof that national rules fulfil this requirement?

There is a close correlation between the precautionary principle and the principle of proportionality. An increased salt content in bread is hardly an acute and serious danger to public health. This means that there will be a high requirement for scientific validation to support the claim of a health risk. On the other hand, if there had been a suspicion that some food preservative could, in certain circumstances, have constituted an acute risk to consumer health, there would not be the same high demand for proof from the Member States to support a prohibition.

The rules on maximum salt content were based on consideration for public health. On the other hand, the rules on declarations of food preservatives or labelling with E numbers are based on consumer considerations in general. Why did the CJEU arrive at different conclusions? With a reference for a preliminary ruling is it principally the CJEU or the referring national court which determines whether a concrete measure is necessary and proportionate?

In the *Van der Veldt* case, Belgium had stricter requirements than the Netherlands, both as regards the permitted level of salt and the labelling of preservatives. Assume that, instead, Belgium had stricter requirements for labelling, but less strict rules on salt content, while the Netherlands had stricter requirements for the permitted level of salt but less strict requirements for labelling. In such a case, the bread sold by Van der Veldt would infringe the Belgian labelling requirements and the Netherlands provisions on salt content. In other words, the bread could not legally be sold in the country where it was produced. In such a situation, could Van der Veldt rely on the rules on the free movement of goods against the Belgian authorities?

Denmark introduced a prohibition on the addition of industrially produced trans fatty acids to foodstuffs above a very limited level (2%). The advantage of trans fatty acids is that by using an industrial process it is possible to give cheap fats certain characteristics which are highly suitable for use in the production of biscuits and cakes, for example. The disadvantage of trans fatty acids is that a number of scientific studies have shown that they cause heart and vascular diseases. This means that if one eats too much trans fatty acid there is presumed to be a greatly increased risk of dying from a heart attack. Is the Danish prohibition of the use of trans fatty acids a trade barrier? If it is a trade barrier, how should it be decided whether the prohibition is lawful when Denmark is, so far, the only EU Member State to introduce such a limit (and when the content of naturally occurring trans fatty acids can be up to 6%)?

The Commission has issued an important interpretative communication on Facilitating the access of products to the markets of other Member States: the practical application of mutual recognition (OJ 2003 C 265/2). See also Regulation (EC) No 764/2008 of the European Parliament and of the Council of 9 July 2008 laying down procedures relating to the application of certain national technical rules to products lawfully marketed in another Member State. Among other things, the Regulation means that economic operators have a right to be heard and to submit comments within 20 working days from the receipt of written notice in which a national authority states that it intends to prohibit the sale or refrain from granting a licence for the sale of a product, where that product is lawfully produced and sold in another Member State.

JUDGMENT OF THE COURT
23 September 2003

Commission of the European Communities v Kingdom of Denmark

'Failure of a Member State to fulfil obligations – Articles 28 EC and 30 EC – Prohibition on marketing of foodstuffs to which vitamins and minerals have been added – Justification – Public health – Nutritional need'

Case C-192/01

Judgment

1. By an application lodged at the Court Registry on 4 May 2001, the Commission of the European Communities brought an action under Article 226 EC for a declaration that, by applying an administrative practice which entails that enriched foodstuffs lawfully produced or marketed in other Member States may be marketed in Denmark only if it is shown that such enrichment with nutrients meets a need in the Danish population, the Kingdom of Denmark has failed to fulfil its obligations under Article 28 EC.

2. It is common ground that, at the date relevant to this action, there were no provisions of Community legislation laying down the conditions under which nutrients, such as vitamins and minerals, could be added to foodstuffs for daily consumption.

3. As regards foodstuffs intended for particular nutritional uses, certain of them have been the subject of directives adopted by the Commission under Council Directive 89/398/EEC of 3 May 1989 on the approximation of the laws of the Member States relating to foodstuffs intended for particular nutritional uses (OJ 1989 L 186, p. 27).

National legislation

4. Article 14 of lov n° 471 om fødevarer m.m. (Law No 471 on Foodstuffs) of 1 July 1998 (Lovtidende A 1998, p. 2826), which replaced Law No 310 of 6 June 1973, leaving the law on additives unchanged, provides that: For the purposes of this law, a food additive is any substance which, without itself being a food or a usual ingredient of compound foods, is intended to be added to foods in order to modify their nutritional value, their shelf-life, colour, flavour, taste or for technical or other purposes.

5. Under Article 15(1) of Law No 471, only substances authorised by the Minister for Food (hereinafter the Minister) may be used or sold as additives.

6. According to Article 15(2) of that law, the Minister may draw up rules relating to the conditions of use of additives, *inter alia* the aim, the quantities and the products with which they are associated, as well as rules relating to the identity and purity of additives.

7. Bekendtgørelse n° 282 om tilsætningsstoffer til fødevarer (Decree No 282 on Food Additives) of 19 April 2000 (Lovtidende A 2000, p. 1861), imposes the obligation to declare additives to the Food and Veterinary Office (hereinafter the Office) six months before their use.

8. Under Article 20 of Decree No 282:

    1. The following additives may be used six months after their declaration to the Food and Veterinary Office: bacterial cultures,moulds and yeasts,enzymes, andnutrients.

    2. The use of an additive under paragraph 1 is always subject to the condition that the Office has not previously prohibited the declared additive.

    3. The Office may authorise the use of the additive prior to the expiry of the time-limit of six months from the date of the declaration.

9. Before the entry into force of Decree No 282, such declaration was made to the Minister in accordance with the provisions of Article 16(2) of Law No 471.

10. As regards the addition of vitamins and minerals to foodstuffs, the functioning of the Danish system of prior authorisation is characterised by the existence of an administrative practice, based on the provisions of Law No 471 and of Decree No 282 mentioned in paragraphs 4 to 9 of this judgment, which makes authorisation of the addition of such ingredients subject to one or more of the criteria laid down in accordance with the general principles for the addition of essential nutrients to foods, taken from the Codex Alimentarius, established in 1963 by the FAO (United Nations Food and Agriculture Organisation) and the WHO (World Health Organisation) (hereinafter the Danish administrative practice).

11. By virtue of the Danish administrative practice additives such as vitamins and minerals may be lawfully added only in the following cases:

    – the addition of the additive is required to correct (or prevent) a situation where a large part of the population has an insufficient intake of the nutrient in question (for example, the addition of iodine to salt); the addition of the additive is required to correct (or prevent) a situation where a large part of the population has an insufficient intake of the nutrient in question (for example, the addition of iodine to salt);

- the addition of the additive must have the purpose of restoring any loss of a product's nutritional value during industrial processing (for example, the addition of vitamin C to fruit juices); the addition of the additive must have the purpose of restoring any loss of a product's nutritional value during industrial processing (for example, the addition of vitamin C to fruit juices);
- the addition relates to new foodstuffs, or similar products, which may be used in place of and in the same way as a traditional product (for example, the addition of vitamin A to margarine, which is a butter substitute); the addition relates to new foodstuffs, or similar products, which may be used in place of and in the same way as a traditional product (for example, the addition of vitamin A to margarine, which is a butter substitute);
- the addition relates to foodstuffs that constitute a meal in themselves or are intended as special-purpose foods (for example, breast milk substitutes, baby foods or slimming products). the addition relates to foodstuffs that constitute a meal in themselves or are intended as special-purpose foods (for example, breast milk substitutes, baby foods or slimming products).

Pre-litigation procedure

12. In 1998, a complaint casting doubt on the compliance of the Danish administrative practice with the provisions of Articles 28 EC and 30 EC was made to the Commission by an economic operator because of obstacles to the marketing of a foodstuff lawfully marketed in other Member States.

13. On 4 November 1999, the Commission sent a letter of formal notice to the Kingdom of Denmark, in which it drew the attention of that Member State to the fact that the Danish administrative practice constitutes an unjustified obstacle to trade for the purposes of Articles 28 EC to 30 EC, since the Office applies the said practice in such a way as to prohibit the marketing in Denmark of foodstuffs to which nutrients, in particular vitamins and minerals, have been added, unless there is a nutritional need for those elements in the Danish population.

14. In their answer of 22 December 1999, the Danish authorities maintained that, in light of the fact that the degree of harmfulness of vitamins and of minerals cannot be determined with sufficient certainty and in accordance with the judgment in Case 174/82 *Sandoz* [1983] ECR 2445, Member States have only to show that the enrichment of the foodstuffs with vitamins and minerals does not meet a real need, in order to found their reliance on Article 30 EC.

15. Since it was not satisfied by that reply, the Commission, on 12 September 2000, issued a reasoned opinion requesting the Kingdom of Denmark to comply with its obligations under Articles 28 EC and 30 EC within two months of the date of notification of that opinion. The Commission claimed, in particular, that a prohibition on marketing by virtue of the Danish administrative practice on the ground that the addition of

vitamins and minerals does not meet any nutritional need constitutes an unjustified interference with trade for the purposes of those provisions. For such interference to be justified under Article 30 EC, the Danish authorities would have to show that the product to which the nutrients were added constitutes a real threat to public health if it was marketed and consumed on the Danish market. According to the Commission, that means that those authorities would have to outline the scientific data upon which they based their refusal of authorisation, as well as the reasons why the vitamin and mineral content of the relevant products represents a threat to public health.

16. By letter of 6 November 2000, the Danish authorities replied to the reasoned opinion. They claimed that the Court had clearly indicated in its judgment in *Sandoz*, cited above, that Member States, when they apply a prohibition on addition of vitamins, are not required to establish a real risk associated with the relevant product, a task which is impossible under existing circumstances. According to those authorities, in order to ensure observance of the principle of proportionality, Member States have only to establish that the addition of the nutrient in question does not meet a real need.

17. Since it was not convinced by the Danish authorities' reply to the reasoned opinion, the Commission brought this action.

The action

Arguments of the parties

18. The Commission submits that the Danish administrative practice constitutes an obstacle to the free movement of goods.

19. The Danish Government does not dispute the fact that its practice constitutes an obstacle to the free movement of goods, but it contends that it is justified under Article 30 EC.

20. The Commission submits that the general prohibition, in the absence of a nutritional need in the Danish population, of the marketing of food products to which vitamins or minerals have been added is not justified by any of the grounds set out in Article 30 EC and, in particular, the protection of human life and health. The absence of nutritional need is not, according to the Commission, a justification under Article 30 EC.

21. Whilst fully recognising the necessity for the Member States to establish a food policy intended to improve the state of the population's general health, the Commission maintains, none the less, that general preoccupations relating to the desired composition of the nutritional regime of the population of those States cannot constitute a lawful justification for obstacles to trade between them.

22. As regards the judgment in *Sandoz*, cited above, the Commission maintains that the prohibition on marketing at issue in the proceedings which gave rise to that judgment was justified not by the absence of a nutritional need, but by the fact that the presence of two particular vitamins in the products in question in those proceedings posed a risk to public health.

23. The Commission submits that the interpretation by the Danish authorities of the judgment in *Sandoz* is based on an erroneous *a contrario* deduction from paragraph 20 thereof. It maintains that that paragraph establishes only that a prohibition on marketing of foodstuffs to which vitamins have been added is contrary to the principle of proportionality when the addition meets a nutritional need. Conversely, that judgment cannot be validly relied upon to support the argument that, in all cases where there is no nutritional need in the relevant population, the addition of vitamins to foodstuffs poses a risk to public health.

24. The Commission points out that a Member State which seeks to justify, by relying on Article 30 EC, a prohibition on marketing a product lawfully manufactured and/or marketed in other Member States, such as that in issue in this case, must, in accordance with that provision, show that such prohibition is necessary for the protection of public health.

25. Referring to paragraph 28 of the judgment of the EFTA Court of 5 April 2001 in Case E-3/00 *EFTA Surveillance Authority* v *Norway* (EFTA Court Report 2000/01, p. 73), the Commission submits that the mere finding of the absence of a nutritional need is not enough to justify a general prohibition on foodstuffs enriched with vitamins or minerals. Such a prohibition should at the very least be made subject to the condition that the risks to public health posed by the addition of such vitamins be proved by a detailed analysis of those risks.

26. According to the Commission, the Member State must show, in each case, by referring to the scientific data justifying the refusal of authorisation, the reasons why the vitamin and mineral content of the foodstuffs in question is a threat to public health.

27. As regards this case, the Commission claims, first, that general considerations such as those invoked by the Danish authorities with regard to the potential risk from excessive consumption of vitamins do not constitute sufficient proof of the existence of a risk to public health in relation to the addition of vitamins to foodstuffs. Secondly, it argues that the fact that there is a specific risk associated with the ingestion of certain vitamins, such as vitamins A or D, does not justify a general or systematic prohibition on the enrichment of foodstuffs in all cases other than those covered by the Codex Alimentarius.

28. For its part, the Danish Government maintains that the Court has already observed in the judgment in *Sandoz* that, where Member States apply a prohibition on addi-

tion of vitamins, they do not have to show an actual risk associated with each foodstuff, such a task being impossible in the current state of scientific knowledge. According to that government, in order to comply with the principle of proportionality, it is sufficient to establish that the enrichment of foodstuffs does not meet a nutritional need in the population concerned.

29. As regards the establishment of a risk to public health, the Danish Government submits that it is also clear from the judgment in *Sandoz* that it is sufficient to determine that the ingestion of high doses of vitamins and minerals can have harmful effects, that scientific research is not yet in a position to lay down with certainty the critical limits or to determine the precise effects of such ingestion and that, therefore, the existence of a danger to human health cannot be excluded, since the consumer ingests additional quantities which it is not possible to foresee or monitor.

30. According to it, a specific evaluation of the danger on a case-by-case basis finds no support in the Court's case-law and would not be possible in practice. The Danish Government claims that, in order to maintain a genuine view of the overall quantities of vitamins and minerals absorbed by the population through the consumption of foodstuffs, it is necessary to implement an overall policy of prevention, which takes into consideration the fact that the sources of absorption of such nutrients are many and which takes account of the complex interaction occurring in the course of the ingestion thereof and in the course of absorption of other substances important for the organism.

31. In that regard, the Danish Government refers to various scientific studies on vitamins and minerals which, according to it, show the harmful effect of the ingestion of those nutrients not only in large doses, but also in relatively low doses because of the way in which those nutrients combine.

32. Thus, with regard to vitamins A, D and B 6, the Danish Government claims that, even in relatively low doses, it can be established that they have a toxic effect.

33. As regards the judgment in *EFTA Surveillance Authority* v *Norway*, cited above, to which the Commission refers, the Danish Government submits that it can be explained by the specific circumstances surrounding the treatment of the originating application submitted by the Kellogg's company in that case.

34. According to the Danish Government, for a prohibition on marketing to be justified on the basis of Article 30 EC, it is not necessary to prove that the quantities of nutrients added to a given product are so large as to constitute a risk to public health.

35. It maintains, in addition, that the Court has already accepted, in particular in *Sandoz* and in Case C-473/98 *Toolex* [2000] ECR I-5681, that the scientific uncertainty,

which underlies the precautionary principle, can justify a prudent approach of Member States in relation to the existence of potential dangers.

36. The Danish Government adds that its administrative practice is directly inspired by the Codex Alimentarius to which the Court's case-law frequently refers.

37. In short, that government claims that its administrative practice is justified by the fact that there is a potential risk to public health inasmuch as vitamins and minerals are added to foodstuffs although, in Denmark, there is no nutritional need.

Findings of the Court

38. The free movement of goods between Member States is a fundamental principle of the EC Treaty which finds its expression in the prohibition, set out in Article 28 EC, of quantitative restrictions on imports between Member States and all measures having equivalent effect.

39. The prohibition on measures having an effect equivalent to restrictions set out in Article 28 EC covers all commercial rules enacted by the Member States which are capable of hindering, directly or indirectly, actually or potentially, intra-Community trade (see, in particular, Case 8/74 *Dassonville* [1974] ECR 837, paragraph 5; Case 178/84 *Commission* v *Germany* [1987) ECR 1227 (*Beer purity law*), paragraph 27; and Case C-12/00 *Commission* v *Spain* [2003] ECR I-459, paragraph 71).

40. It is not disputed that the Danish administrative practice is a measure having equivalent effect to quantitative restrictions within the meaning of Article 28 EC.

41. Indeed, that practice, which requires that the marketing of foodstuffs enriched with vitamins and minerals coming from other Member States where they are lawfully manufactured or marketed be made subject to proof of a nutritional need in the Danish population, makes the marketing of such foodstuffs more difficult, if not impossible, and, consequently, hinders trade between the Member States.

42. As regards the question whether that administrative practice may none the less be justified on the basis of Article 30 EC, it is for the Member States, in default of harmonisation and to the extent that uncertainties continue to exist in the current state of scientific research, to decide on their intended level of protection of human health and life and on whether to require prior authorisation for the marketing of foodstuffs, always taking into account the requirements of the free movement of goods within the Community (see *Sandoz*, paragraph 16; Case C-42/90 *Bellon* [1990] ECR I-4863, paragraph 11; and Case C-400/96 *Harpegnies* [1998] ECR I-5121, paragraph 33).

43. That discretion relating to the protection of public health is particularly wide where it is shown that uncertainties continue to exist in the current state of scientific research as to certain substances, such as vitamins, which are not as a general rule harmful in themselves but may have special harmful effects solely if taken to excess as part of the general nutrition, the composition of which cannot be foreseen or monitored (see *Sandoz*, paragraph 17).

44. Community law does not therefore, in principle, preclude a Member State from prohibiting, save for prior authorisation, the marketing of foodstuffs incorporating nutrients, such as vitamins or minerals other than those whose use is lawful under Community legislation.

45. However, in exercising their discretion relating to the protection of public health, the Member States must comply with the principle of proportionality. The means which they choose must therefore be confined to what is actually necessary to ensure the safeguarding of public health; they must be proportional to the objective thus pursued, which could not have been attained by measures which are less restrictive of intra-Community trade (see *Sandoz*, paragraph 18; *Bellon*, paragraph 14; and *Harpegnies*, paragraph 34).

46. Furthermore, since Article 30 EC provides for an exception, to be interpreted strictly, to the rule of free movement of goods within the Community, it is for the national authorities which invoke it to show in each case, in the light of national nutritional habits and in the light of the results of international scientific research, that their rules are necessary to give effective protection to the interests referred to in that provision and, in particular, that the marketing of the products in question poses a real risk to public health (see, to that effect, *Sandoz*, paragraph 22; Case 227/82 *Van Bennekom* [1983] ECR 3883, paragraph 40; *Beer purity law*, cited above, paragraph 46; and Case C-228/91 *Commission* v *Italy* [1993] ECR I-2701, paragraph 27).

47. A prohibition on the marketing of foodstuffs to which nutrients have been added must therefore be based on a detailed assessment of the risk alleged by the Member State invoking Article 30 EC (see, to that effect, *EFTA Surveillance Authority* v *Norway*, cited above, paragraph 30).

48. A decision to prohibit marketing, which indeed constitutes the most restrictive obstacle to trade in products lawfully manufactured and marketed in other Member States, can only be adopted if the real risk alleged for public health appears sufficiently established on the basis of the latest scientific data available at the date of the adoption of such decision. In such a context, the object of the risk assessment to be carried out by the Member State is to appraise the degree of probability of harmful effects on human health from the addition of certain nutrients to foodstuffs and the seriousness of those potential effects.

49. It is clear that such an assessment of the risk could reveal that scientific uncertainty persists as regards the existence or extent of real risks to human health. In such circumstances, it must be accepted that a Member State may, in accordance with the precautionary principle, take protective measures without having to wait until the reality and seriousness of those risks are fully demonstrated (see, to that effect, Case C-157/96 *National Farmers' Union and* Others [1998] ECR I-2211, paragraph 63). However, the risk assessment cannot be based on purely hypothetical considerations (see, to that effect, *EFTA Surveillance Authority* v *Norway*, paragraph 29, and Case C-236/01 *Monsanto Agricoltura Italia and Others* [2003] ECR I-8105, paragraph 106).

50. In assessing the risk in question, it is not only the particular effects of the marketing of an individual product containing a definite quantity of nutrients which are relevant. It could be appropriate to take into consideration the cumulative effect of the presence on the market of several sources, natural or artificial, of a particular nutrient and of the possible existence in the future of additional sources which can reasonably be foreseen (see *EFTA Surveillance Authority* v *Norway*, paragraph 29).

51. In many cases, the assessment of those factors will demonstrate that there is a high degree of scientific and practical uncertainty in that regard. A proper application of the precautionary principle presupposes, in the first place, the identification of the potentially negative consequences for health of the proposed addition of nutrients, and, secondly, a comprehensive assessment of the risk to health based on the most reliable scientific data available and the most recent results of international research (see, to that effect, *EFTA Surveillance Authority* v *Norway*, paragraph 30, and *Monsanto Agricoltura Italia and Others*, paragraph 113).

52. Where it proves to be impossible to determine with certainty the existence or extent of the alleged risk because of the insufficiency, inconclusiveness or imprecision of the results of studies conducted, but the likelihood of real harm to public health persists should the risk materialise, the precautionary principle justifies the adoption of restrictive measures (see, to that effect, *EFTA Surveillance Authority* v *Norway*, paragraph 31).

53. Such measures must not be allowed unless they are non-discriminatory and objective (see, to that effect, *EFTA Surveillance Authority* v *Norway*, paragraph 32).

54. It must be added that, in such a context, the criterion of the nutritional need of the population of a Member State can play a role in its detailed assessment of the risk which the addition of nutrients to foodstuffs may pose for public health. However, contrary to the interpretation of the *Sandoz* judgment suggested by the Danish Government, the absence of such a need cannot, by itself, justify a total prohibition, on the basis of Article 30 EC, of the marketing of foodstuffs lawfully manufactured and/or marketed in other Member States.

55. In the present case, the Danish administrative practice is disproportionate since, apart from the four restrictively defined cases of what is considered to constitute a nutritional need and which are mentioned in paragraph 11 of this judgment, it systematically prohibits the marketing of all foodstuffs to which vitamins and minerals have been added, without distinguishing according to the different vitamins and minerals added or according to the level of risk which their addition may possibly pose to public health.

56. Indeed, the systematic prohibition under the Danish administrative practice on the marketing of enriched products which do not meet a nutritional need of the population does not enable Community law to be observed in regard to the identification and assessment of a real risk to public health, which requires a detailed assessment, case-by-case, of the effects which the addition of the minerals and vitamins in question could entail.

57. In light of the foregoing, it must be declared that, by applying an administrative practice which entails that enriched foodstuffs lawfully produced or marketed in other Member States can be marketed in Denmark only if it is shown that such enrichment with nutrients meets a need in the Danish population, the Kingdom of Denmark has failed to fulfil its obligations under Article 28 EC.

Costs

[Para. 58 omitted]

On those grounds,

THE COURT

hereby:

1. **Declares that by applying an administrative practice which entails that enriched foodstuffs lawfully produced or marketed in other Member States can be marketed in Denmark only if it is shown that such enrichment with nutrients meets a need in the Danish population, the Kingdom of Denmark has failed to fulfil its obligations under Article 28 EC;**

[Para. 2 of the ruling omitted]

Comments and questions

In Denmark there was in principle a prohibition on the use of additives, including vitamins and minerals. However, there were four exceptions to this prohibition. The basis for the exceptions was that enriched foodstuffs could be marketed if, in the Danish population in general, there was a nutritional need for the additives. The consequence of the Danish rules was that enriched foodstuffs which could be lawfully produced and marketed in other Member States could not be lawfully marketed in Denmark, unless they were covered by one of the exceptions. Even though Danish goods were not put in a better position than foreign goods, there was nevertheless agreement that the Danish rules constituted a restriction on trade, contrary to Article 34 TFEU (formerly Article 28 TEC). What was the type of restriction (see in particular paragraph 41 of the judgment)?

The Danish Government was of the view that the Danish rules could be justified in accordance with Article 36 TFEU (formerly Article 30 TEC), because it was not possible to establish the harmful effects of the vitamins and minerals with sufficient certainty. The Commission did not agree with this. It held that a general prohibition on the marketing of products, unless there was a nutritional need for the additives in the population, could not be justified by reference to Article 36 TFEU. In the view of the Commission, the application of Article 36 TFEU by a Member State must require that the enrichment of a specific product should constitute a real threat, and evidence must be provided in support of this.

The CJEU agreed that, in principle, a Member State may prohibit the marketing, without prior authorisation, of foodstuffs incorporating added vitamins or minerals. However, such prohibition must comply with the principle of proportionality. Therefore, there could not be a general prohibition on the basis that the population did not need added vitamins and minerals. On the contrary, a Member State wishing to introduce such a prohibition must show that there was a real risk in each specific case. This meant, among other things, that the Danish authorities could not eliminate all vitamins and minerals with one broad sweep of the hand; it was necessary to explain what risks each of the additives were assumed to give rise to. The CJEU also stated that a purely hypothetical assumption that there was a risk would be insufficient. The risk had to be established by scientific *evidence*. On the other hand, there could not be a requirement for the risk to be scientifically *proven*; in principle it would be sufficient to prohibit use of the additive if the scientific evidence showed that the addition of a vitamin or mineral caused a risk. The CJEU's judgment meant that Denmark could still maintain its requirement that enriched foodstuffs should be approved, but in assessing whether approval should be granted, the Danish authorities had to make a concrete evaluation in each case.

Several Member States have requirements that certain products must be enriched. For example, there can be a requirement that table salt must have iodine added to it. The aim is that the population thereby gets important elements which it might otherwise lack (for example iodine). Another substance that is relevant to health is folic acid. This is important because a child which does not receive sufficient folic acid in the womb risks being born with a handicap. If a Member State had a requirement that all products containing flour must have added folic acid, in order to combat this risk, would this constitute a trade barrier? If it were a trade barrier, would it be lawful?

JUDGMENT OF THE COURT
30 April 1996

CIA Security International SA v Signalson SA and Securitel SPRL.
(Reference for a preliminary ruling: Tribunal de commerce de Liège – Belgium)

'Interpretation of Article 30 of the EC Treaty and of Directive 83/189/EEC laying down a procedure for the provision of information in the field of technical standards and regulations – National legislation on the marketing of alarm systems and networks – Prior administrative approval'

Case C-194/94

Judgment

1. By judgment of 20 June 1994, received at the Court on 4 July 1994, the Tribunal de Commerce (Commercial Court), Liège, referred to the Court for a preliminary ruling under Article 177 of the EC Treaty six questions on the interpretation of Article 30 of that Treaty and of Council Directive 83/189/EEC of 28 March 1983 laying down a procedure for the provision of information in the field of technical standards and regulations (OJ 1983 L 109, p. 8, hereinafter 'Directive 83/189'), as amended by Council Directive 88/182/EEC of 22 March 1988 (OJ 1988 L 81, p. 75).

2. Those questions have been raised in two sets of proceedings between (i) CIA Security International SA (hereinafter 'CIA Security') and Signalson SA (hereinafter 'Signalson') and (ii) CIA Security and Securitel SPRL (hereinafter 'Securitel'), those three companies being security firms within the meaning of the Belgian Law of 10 April 1990 on caretaking firms, security firms and internal caretaking services (hereinafter 'the 1990 Law').

3. Article 1(3) of the 1990 Law provides: 'Any legal or natural person pursuing an activity consisting in supplying to third parties, on a permanent or occasional basis, design, installation and maintenance services for alarm systems and networks shall be considered to be a security firm for the purposes of this Law.'

4. Article 1(4) of the 1990 Law provides: 'The alarm systems and networks referred to in this article are those intended to prevent or record crimes against persons or property'.

5. Article 4 of the 1990 Law provides: 'Only persons with prior authorization from the Home Affairs Ministry may operate a security firm. Authorization shall be granted only if the firm meets the requirements laid down in this Law and the conditions concerning financial means and technical equipment prescribed by royal decree ...'.

6. Article 12 of the 1990 Law provides: 'The alarm systems and networks referred to in Article 1(4) and their components may be marketed or otherwise made available to users only after prior approval has been granted under a procedure to be laid down by royal decree ...'.

7. That procedure was laid down by Royal Decree of 14 May 1991 laying down the procedure for approval of the alarm systems and networks referred to in the 1990 Law (hereinafter 'the 1991 Decree').

8. Article 2(1) of the 1991 Decree provides: 'No manufacturer, importer, wholesaler or any other natural or legal person may market new equipment or otherwise make it available to users in Belgium if it has not been previously approved by a committee established for that purpose (the 'equipment committee').'

9. Articles 4 to 7 of the 1991 Decree provide for equipment to be examined and tested before it can be approved.

10. According to Article 5, that examination is to consist of identifying the equipment, checking electrical circuits against the documents submitted by the manufacturer and checking the minimum required functions. The tests carried out on the equipment, provided for by Article 6 of the 1991 Decree, concern functional adequacy, mechanical aspects, mechanical and/or electronic reliability, sensitivity to false alarms, and protection against fraud or attempts to neutralize the equipment. For that purpose, equipment is subjected to the tests prescribed in Annexes 3 and 4 to the 1991 Decree.

11. Article 8 of the 1991 Decree provides that: 'If the applicant establishes by means of the necessary documents that his equipment has already undergone tests which are at least equivalent to those described in Article 7 in an authorized laboratory in another Member State of the EEC according to EEC rules and that it has been approved at most three years before the date of the current application, a body referred to in Article 4(1) shall carry out on the equipment only such tests as have not yet been carried out in the other Member State of the EEC.'

12. The case-file also shows that the 1991 Decree was not notified to the Commission in accordance with the procedure for the provision of information on technical regulations laid down in Directive 83/189 and that, in February 1993, following delivery of a reasoned opinion by the Commission pursuant to Article 169 of the EEC Treaty, the Belgian Government notified a new draft royal decree laying down the procedure for approval of alarm systems and networks. That draft, adopted on 31 March 1994, is substantially identical to the 1991 Decree which it repealed, Article 8 of the 1991 Decree having, however, been amended in accordance with suggestions made by the Commission.

13. The three companies involved in the main proceedings are competitors whose business is, in particular, the manufacture and sale of alarm systems and networks.

14. On 21 January 1994 CIA Security applied to the Liège Commercial Court for orders requiring Signalson and Securitel to cease alleged unfair trading practices pursued in January 1994. It based its claims on Articles 93 and 95 of the Belgian Law of 14 July 1991 on Commercial Practices which prohibits unfair trading practices. CIA Security claims that Signalson and Securitel have libelled it by claiming in particular that the *Andromède* alarm system which it markets did not fulfil the requirements laid down by Belgian legislation on security systems.

15. Signalson and Securitel have lodged counterclaims, the main one being for an order restraining CIA Security from continuing to carry on business on the ground that it is not authorized as a security firm and that it is marketing an alarm system which has not been approved.

16. In an interim judgment the Liège Commercial Court held that, although the main claims and counterclaims seek orders restraining unfair practices prohibited by the Law on Commercial Practices, those practices must still be assessed by reference to the provisions of the 1990 Law and the 1991 Decree.

17. It then found that if CIA Security has infringed the 1990 Law and the 1991 Decree, the actions which it has brought could be declared inadmissible for lack of *locus standi* or sufficient legal interest in bringing proceedings whilst if the 1990 Law and the 1991 Decree are incompatible with Community law, Signalson and Securitel will not be able to base their counterclaims for restraining orders on breach of those legal provisions.

18. Unsure whether the Belgian provisions in question are compatible with Article 30 of the Treaty and having found that those provisions had not been previously notified to the Commission in accordance with Directive 83/189, the Liège Commercial Court decided to stay proceedings and to refer the following questions to the Court for a preliminary ruling:

‘1) Does the Law of 10 April 1990 on caretaking firms, security firms and internal caretaking services and, more particularly, Articles 4 and 12 thereof, create quantitative restrictions on imports or does it contain measures having an effect equivalent to a quantitative restriction prohibited by Article 30 of the EEC Treaty?

2) Is the Royal Decree of 14 May 1991 laying down the procedure for approving alarm systems and networks, which is referred to in the Law of 10 April 1990, and in particular Articles 2 and 8 thereof, compatible with Article 30 of the

Treaty which prohibits quantitative restrictions on imports and all measures having an effect equivalent to a quantitative restriction?

3) Does the abovementioned Law of 10 April 1990, in particular Articles 4 and 12 therefore, contain technical regulations which should have been communicated to the Commission beforehand in accordance with Article 8 of Directive 83/189/EEC?

4) Does the Royal Decree of 14 May 1991, in particular Articles 2 and 8 thereof, contain technical regulations which should have been communicated to the Commission beforehand in accordance with Article 8 of Directive 83/189/EEC?

5) Are the provisions of Council Directive 83/189/EEC laying down a procedure for the provision of information in the field of technical standards and regulations, in particular Articles 8 and 9 thereof, unconditional and sufficiently precise to be relied upon by individuals in proceedings before national courts?

6) Do Community law and the protection which it affords to individuals require a national court to refuse to apply a national technical regulation which has not been communicated to the Commission by the Member State which adopted it, in accordance with the obligation laid down in Article 8 of Council Directive 83/189/EEC?'

Preliminary observations

19. According to the Belgian Government, Signalson and Securitel, any question as to the compatibility of the 1991 Decree with Community law is now redundant since in the type of case before it the national court must apply the law in force at the time when it gives its ruling and that, since the time when proceedings were commenced, the 1991 Decree has been replaced by the Royal Decree of 31 March 1994, which, according to the Commission, is in accordance with Community law.

20. That argument cannot be accepted. According to the case-law of the Court, it is for the national court to assess the scope of the national provisions and the manner in which they must be applied (see, in particular, the judgment in Case C-45/94 *Ayuntamiento de Ceuta* [1995] ECR I-4385, paragraph 26). Since the national court is best placed to assess, in view of the particularities of the case, the need for a preliminary ruling in order to give its judgment, the preliminary questions cannot be regarded as having become redundant as a result of the Decree of 14 May 1991 being replaced by the Royal Decree of 31 March 1994.

21. That being so, the third, fourth, fifth and sixth questions should be answered first.

The third and fourth questions

22. By its third and fourth questions the national court asks in substance whether provisions such as Articles 4 and 12 of the 1990 Law and the 1991 Decree constitute technical regulations which should have been notified to the Commission prior to their adoption, in accordance with Article 8 of Directive 83/189.

23. 'Technical regulation' is defined in point (5) of Article 1 of Directive 83/189 as 'technical specifications, including the relevant administrative provisions, the observance of which is compulsory, *de jure* or *de facto*, in the case of marketing or use in a Member State or a major part thereof, except those laid down by local authorities'. 'Technical specification' is defined in point (1) of that article as 'a specification contained in a document which lays down the characteristics required of a product such as levels of quality, performance, safety or dimensions, including the requirements applicable to the product as regards terminology, symbols, testing and test methods, packaging, marking or labelling ...'.

24. The first point which must be examined is whether a provision such as Article 4 of the 1990 Law constitutes a technical regulation within the meaning of Directive 83/189.

25. The answer to that question must be negative since according to Directive 83/189 technical regulations are specifications defining the characteristics of products and Article 4 is confined to laying down conditions governing the establishment of security firms.

26. As regards the 1991 Decree, it contains detailed rules defining, in particular, the conditions concerning the quality tests and function tests which must be fulfilled in order for an alarm system or network to be approved and marketed in Belgium. Those rules therefore constitute technical regulations within the meaning of Directive 83/189.

27. As regards Article 12 of the 1990 Law, it is to be recalled that it provides that the products in question may be marketed only after having been previously approved according to a procedure to be laid down by royal decree, which was laid down by the 1991 Decree.

28. According to the Commission and CIA Security, Article 12 of the 1990 Law constitutes a technical regulation within the meaning of Directive 83/189 whilst Signalson, the United Kingdom and the Belgian Government, in their written observations, submit that this article is merely a framework law not comprising any technical regulation within the meaning of Directive 83/189.

29. A rule is classified as a technical regulation for the purposes of Directive 83/189 if it has legal effects of its own. If, under domestic law, the rule merely serves as a basis for enabling administrative regulations containing rules binding on interested parties to be adopted, so that by itself it has no legal effect for individuals, the rule does not constitute a technical regulation within the meaning of the directive (see the judgment in Case C-317/92 *Commission* v *Germany* [1994] ECR I-2039, paragraph 26). It should be recalled here that, according to the first subparagraph of Article 8(1) of Directive 83/189, the Member States must communicate, at the same time as the draft technical regulation, the enabling instrument on the basis of which it was adopted, should knowledge of such text be necessary to assess the implications of the draft technical regulation.

30. However, a rule must be classified as a technical regulation within the meaning of Directive 83/189 if, as the Belgian Government submitted at the hearing, it requires the undertakings concerned to apply for prior approval of their equipment, even if the administrative rules envisaged have not been adopted.

31. The reply to be given to the third and fourth questions must therefore be that a rule such as Article 4 of the 1990 Law does not constitute a technical regulation within the meaning of Directive 83/189 whereas provisions such as those contained in the 1991 Decree do constitute technical regulations and that classification of a rule such as Article 12 of the 1990 Law depends on the legal effects which it has under domestic law.

The fifth and sixth questions

32. By its fifth and sixth questions the national court asks in substance whether the provisions of Directive 83/189, and particularly Articles 8 and 9 thereof, are unconditional and sufficiently precise for individuals to be able to rely on them before a national court which must decline to apply a national technical regulation which has not been notified in accordance with the directive.

33. Article 8(1) and (2) of Directive 83/189 provides:

'1. Member States shall immediately communicate to the Commission any draft technical regulation, except where such technical regulation merely transposes the full text of an international or European standard, in which case information regarding the relevant standard shall suffice; they shall also let the Commission have a brief statement of the grounds which make the enactment of such a technical regulation necessary, where these are not already made clear in the draft. Where appropriate, Member States shall simultaneously communicate the text of the basic legislative or regulatory provisions principally and directly concerned, should knowledge of such text be necessary to assess the implications of the draft technical regulation.

The Commission shall immediately notify the other Member States of any draft it has received; it may also refer this draft to the Committee referred to in Article 5 and, if appropriate, to the Committee responsible for the field in question for its opinion.

2. The Commission and the Member States may make comments to the Member State which has forwarded a draft technical regulation; that Member State shall take such comments into account as far as possible in the subsequent preparation of the technical regulation.'

34. Article 9 of Directive 83/189 provides:

'1. Without prejudice to paragraphs 2 and 2a, Member States shall postpone the adoption of a draft technical regulation for six months from the date of notification referred to in Article 8(1) if the Commission or another Member State delivers a detailed opinion, within three months of that date, to the effect that the measure envisaged must be amended in order to eliminate or reduce any barriers which it might create to the free movement of goods. The Member State concerned shall report to the Commission on the action it proposes to take on such detailed opinions. The Commission shall comment on this reaction.

2. The period in paragraph 1 shall be 12 months if, within three months following the notification referred to in Article 8(1), the Commission gives notice of its intention of proposing or adopting a Directive on the subject.

2a. If the Commission ascertains that a communication pursuant to Article 8(1) relates to a subject covered by a proposal for a directive or regulation submitted to the Council, it shall inform the Member State concerned of this fact within three months of receiving the communication. Member States shall refrain from adopting technical regulations on a subject covered by a proposal for a directive or regulation submitted by the Commission to the Council before the communication provided for in Article 8(1) for a period of 12 months from the date of its submission. Recourse to paragraphs 1, 2 and 2a of this Article cannot be accumulative.

3. Paragraphs 1, 2 and 2a shall not apply in those cases where, for urgent reasons relating to the protection of public health or safety, the protection of health and life of animals or plants, a Member State is obliged to prepare technical regulations in a very short space of time in order to enact and introduce them immediately without any consultations being possible. The Member State shall give, in the communication referred to in Article 8, the reasons which warrant the urgency of the measures taken. The Commission shall take appropriate action in cases where improper use is made of this procedure.'

35. Article 10 of Directive 83/189 provides that: 'Articles 8 and 9 shall not apply where the Member States fulfil their obligations as arising out of Community directives and regulations; the same shall apply in the case of obligations arising out of international agreements which result in the adoption of uniform technical specifications in the Community.'

36. In 1986, in Communication 86/C 245/05 (OJ 1986 C 245, p. 4) the Commission defined its position on the point raised by the Liège Commercial Court in its last two questions. In that communication the Commission stated that Directive 83/189 enabled it, as well as the Member States, to play an important role in preventing the creation of new technical barriers to trade and that the obligations of the Member States created by the directive are clear and unequivocal in that:

- the Member States must notify all draft technical regulations falling under the Directive;
- they must suspend the adoption of the draft technical regulations automatically for three months, other than in the special cases covered by Article 9(3) of the Directive;
- they must suspend the adoption of the draft technical regulation for a further period of three or nine months depending on whether objections have been raised or whether Community legislation is envisaged.

Finally, the Commission stated that failure by Member States to respect the obligations arising under the directive would lead to the creation of serious loopholes in the internal market, with potentially damaging trade effects.

37. In the communication the Commission deduces from the points made therein that 'when a Member State enacts a technical regulation falling within the scope of Directive 83/189/EEC without notifying the draft to the Commission and respecting the standstill obligation, the regulation thus adopted is unenforceable against third parties in the legal system of the Member State in question. The Commission therefore considers that litigants have a right to expect national courts to refuse to enforce national technical regulations which have not been notified as required by Community law'.

38. In the present case the Commission has maintained that interpretation of Directive 83/189, which CIA Security has endorsed.

39. The German and Netherlands Governments and the United Kingdom do not agree with that interpretation. They consider that technical regulations within the meaning of Directive 83/189 may be enforced against individuals even if they were adopted in breach of the obligations which the directive entails. The arguments on which that interpretation is based are examined below.

40. The first point which must be made is that Directive 83/189 is designed to protect, by means of preventive control, freedom of movement for goods, which is one of the foundations of the Community. This control serves a useful purpose in that technical regulations covered by the directive may constitute obstacles to trade in goods between Member States, such obstacles being permissible only if they are necessary to satisfy compelling public interest requirements. The control is also effective in that all draft technical regulations covered by the directive must be notified and, except in the case of those regulations whose urgency justifies an exception, their adoption or entry into force must be suspended during the periods laid down by Article 9.

41. The notification and the period of suspension therefore afford the Commission and the other Member States an opportunity to examine whether the draft regulations in question create obstacles to trade contrary to the EC Treaty or obstacles which are to be avoided through the adoption of common or harmonized measures and also to propose amendments to the national measures envisaged. This procedure also enables the Commission to propose or adopt Community rules regulating the matter dealt with by the envisaged measure.

42. It is settled law that, wherever provisions of a directive appear to be, from the point of view of their content, unconditional and sufficiently precise, they may be relied on against any national provision which is not in accordance with the directive (see the judgment in Case 8/81 *Becker* [1982] ECR 53 and the judgment in Joined Cases C-6/90 and C-9/90 *Francovich and Others* [1991] ECR I-5357.

43. The United Kingdom considers that the provisions of Directive 83/189 do not satisfy those criteria on the ground, in particular, that the notification procedure contains a number of elements that are imprecise.

44. That view cannot be adopted. Articles 8 and 9 of Directive 83/189 lay down a precise obligation on Member States to notify draft technical regulations to the Commission before they are adopted. Being, accordingly, unconditional and sufficiently precise in terms of their content, those articles may be relied on by individuals before national courts.

45. It remains to examine the legal consequences to be drawn from a breach by Member States of their obligation to notify and, more precisely, whether Directive 83/189 is to be interpreted as meaning that a breach of the obligation to notify, constituting a procedural defect in the adoption of the technical regulations concerned, renders such technical regulations inapplicable so that they may not be enforced against individuals.

46. The German and Netherlands Governments and the United Kingdom consider that Directive 83/189 is solely concerned with relations between the Member States and

the Commission, that it merely creates procedural obligations which the Member States must observe when adopting technical regulations, their competence to adopt the regulations in question after expiry of the suspension period being, however, unaffected, and, finally, that it contains no express provision relating to any effects attaching to non-compliance with those procedural obligations.

47. The Court observes first of all in this context that none of those factors prevents non-compliance with Directive 83/189 from rendering the technical regulations in question inapplicable.

48. For such a consequence to arise from a breach of the obligations laid down by Directive 83/189, an express provision to this effect is not required. As pointed out above, it is undisputed that the aim of the directive is to protect freedom of movement for goods by means of preventive control and that the obligation to notify is essential for achieving such Community control. The effectiveness of Community control will be that much greater if the directive is interpreted as meaning that breach of the obligation to notify constitutes a substantial procedural defect such as to render the technical regulations in question inapplicable to individuals.

49. That interpretation of the directive is in accordance with the judgment given in Case 380/87 *Enichem Base and Others* v *Comune di Cinisello Balsamo* [1989] ECR 2491, paragraphs 19 to 24. In that judgment, in which the Court ruled on the obligation for Member States to communicate to the Commission national draft rules falling within the scope of an article of Council Directive 75/442/EEC of 15 July 1975 on waste (OJ 1975 L 194, p. 39), the Court held that neither the wording nor the purpose of the provision in question provided any support for the view that failure by the Member States to observe their obligation to give notice in itself rendered unlawful the rules thus adopted. In this regard, the Court expressly considered that the provision in question was confined to imposing an obligation to give prior notice which did not make entry into force of the envisaged rules subject to the Commission's agreement or lack of opposition and which did not lay down the procedure for Community control of the drafts in question. The Court therefore concluded that the provision under examination concerned relations between the Member States and the Commission but that it did not afford individuals any right capable of being infringed in the event of breach by a Member State of its obligation to give prior notice of its draft regulations to the Commission.

50. In the present case, however, the aim of the directive is not simply to inform the Commission. As already found in paragraph 41 of this judgment, the directive has, precisely, a more general aim of eliminating or restricting obstacles to trade, to inform other States of technical regulations envisaged by a State, to give the Commission and the other Member States time to react and to propose amendments for lessening restrictions to the free movement of goods arising from the envisaged measure and to afford the Commission time to propose a harmonizing directive.

Moreover, the wording of Articles 8 and 9 of Directive 83/189 is clear in that those articles provide for a procedure for Community control of draft national regulations and the date of their entry into force is made subject to the Commission's agreement or lack of opposition.

51. Finally, it must be examined whether, as the United Kingdom in particular observes, there are reasons specific to Directive 83/189 which preclude it from being interpreted as rendering technical regulations adopted in breach of the directive inapplicable to third parties.

52. In this regard, it has already been observed that if such regulations were not enforceable against third parties, this would create a legislative vacuum in the national legal system in question and could therefore entail serious drawbacks, particularly where safety regulations were concerned.

53. This argument cannot be accepted. A Member State may use the urgent-case procedure provided for in Article 9(3) of Directive 83/189 where, for reasons defined by that provision, it considers it necessary to prepare technical regulations in a very short space of time which must be enacted and brought into force immediately without any consultations being possible.

54. In view of the foregoing considerations, it must be concluded that Directive 83/189 is to be interpreted as meaning that breach of the obligation to notify renders the technical regulations concerned inapplicable, so that they are unenforceable against individuals.

55. The answer to the fifth and sixth questions must therefore be that Articles 8 and 9 of Directive 83/189 are to be interpreted as meaning that individuals may rely on them before the national court which must decline to apply a national technical regulation which has not been notified in accordance with the directive.

The first two questions

56. By its first and second questions the national court asks in substance whether Article 30 of the Treaty precludes national provisions such as Articles 4 and 12 of the 1990 Law and the 1991 Decree.

57. In view of the answers given to the third, fourth, fifth and sixth questions, it is not necessary to reply to the first two questions in so far as they relate to Article 12 of the 1990 Law and the 1991 Decree since those provisions are not enforceable against individuals. Therefore, only the part of the first question that inquires whether a provision such as Article 4 of the 1990 Law, which provides that no one may run a security firm without approval from the Home Affairs Ministry, is compatible with Article 30 of the Treaty need be answered.

58. Since such a provision imposes a condition for the establishment and carrying on of business as a security firm, it does not fall directly within the scope of Article 30 of the Treaty which concerns the free movement of goods between Member States. Furthermore, the case-file does not contain the slightest indication that such a provision has restrictive effects on the free movement of goods or is otherwise contrary to Community law.

59. The answer to the first preliminary question must therefore be that Article 30 of the Treaty does not preclude a national provision such as Article 4 of the 1990 Law.

Costs

[Para. 60 omitted]

On those grounds,

THE COURT

in answer to the questions referred to it by the Tribunal de Commerce, Liège, by judgment of 20 June 1994, hereby rules:

1. **A rule such as Article 4 of the Belgian Law of 10 April 1990 on caretaking firms, security firms and internal caretaking services does not constitute a technical regulation within the meaning of Council Directive 83/189/EEC of 28 March 1983 laying down a procedure for the provision of information in the field of technical standards and regulations, as amended by Council Directive 88/182/EEC of 22 March 1988, whereas provisions such as those contained in the Belgian Royal Decree of 14 May 1991 laying down the procedure for approval of the alarm systems and networks referred to in the Law of 10 April 1990 do constitute technical regulations and classification of a rule such as Article 12 of the Law of 10 April 1990 depends on the legal effects which it has under domestic law.**

2. **Articles 8 and 9 of Directive 83/189, as amended by Directive 88/182, are to be interpreted as meaning that individuals may rely on them before the national court which must decline to apply a national technical regulation which has not been notified in accordance with the directive.**

3. **Article 30 of the EC Treaty does not preclude a national provision such a Article 4 of the Law of 10 April 1990.**

Comments and questions

In paragraph 44 of Case C-194/94 *CIA Security International SA* v *Signalson SA and Securitel SPRL* [1996] ECR I-2201, the CJEU stated that Articles 8 and 9 of the Technical Standards and Regulations Directive (a Directive laying down a procedure for the provision of information in the field of technical standards and regulations, then Directive 83/189, now Directive (EU) 2015/1535 lay down a precise obligation on Member States to notify draft technical regulations to the Commission before they are adopted. Since these Articles are unconditional and sufficiently precise, the CJEU held that they have direct effect, and can be relied on by individuals before national courts. The question then arises as to the legal consequences of insufficient notification. The CJEU answered this in paragraph 54 of its judgment by stating that a failure to notify would mean that the technical regulations in question would be inapplicable and unenforceable against individuals.

It is important to note that the case concerned the legal relations between two private individuals before a national court. The consequence of the CJEU's preliminary ruling was therefore that, by invoking Articles 5 and 6 of the Technical Standards and Regulations Directive (insufficient notification by the Member State), one party could prevent the other party from relying on the national technical standards.

The *CIA* case has provoked considerable discussion on whether the CJEU departed from its usual practice, that directives should not be given direct horizontal effect. The reality of the *CIA* case was that the Technical Standards and Regulations Directive was of decisive importance for the dispute in the case between Signalson and Securitel on the one hand and CIA Security on the other hand. A more detailed examination of the case will, however, show that the effect of the Directive was only indirect.

In the *CIA* case the CJEU held that Member States must comply with the requirements laid down in the Technical Standards and Regulations Directive when issuing technical standards. Compliance with this requirement is a precondition for implementing the standards. If a Member State does not comply with the requirements of the Directive when issuing technical standards, these standards will not be applicable, and neither the Member State nor private individuals will be able to rely on them against private individuals. In other words, the Technical Standards and Regulations Directive is addressed to the Member States, but in cases where the Member States infringe the provisions of the Directive, the legal consequences will also affect private individuals. This has been referred to as the 'triangular effect', and can be illustrated as follows:

On the face of it, it seems as if the private undertaking, CIA Security, could successfully base its claim against the private counterparty on the direct effect of the Technical Standards and Regulations Directive (see the dotted line). However, the reality is that the Directive only imposes obligations on Member States. If a Member States infringes the Directive in the issuing of technical standards, this could influence cases which only involve private individuals, since private individuals will be prevented from relying on the standards in disputes between them. Thus, the Technical Standards and Regulations Directive does not in itself create obligations on private individuals, but it does prevent Member States from imposing obligations on them in certain cases.

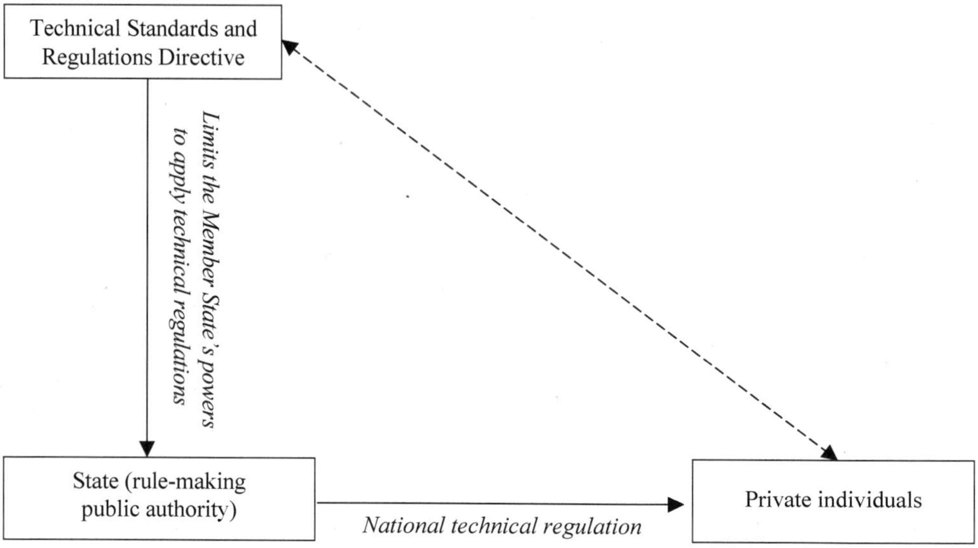

Compare the CJEU's decision in the *CIA* case with its decision in Case C-91/92 *Dori* v *Recreb Srl* [1994] ECR I-3325, printed in Chapter 1, especially paragraphs 24 and 25. Do you think that the two decisions accord with one another? Consider whether the CJEU's interpretation of the Technical Standards and Regulations Directive creates any problems of legal certainty.

According to Article 7(4) of the Technical Standards and Regulations Directive, no postponement period applies under Article 6 to national standards which are linked to taxation or financial measures which affect the use of products; cf. Article 1(1)(f), second paragraph, No iii. With reference to paragraph 49 of the *CIA* judgment, consider whether the lack of notification of such national measures would also mean that the judicial authorities would also be prevented from applying this measure.

In the *CIA* case the CJEU did not express a view on all the questions which arise when setting aside the requirements of the Technical Standards and Regulations Directive. For example, in a civil case which concerns a contract, should a national court disregard national technical standards which, even though they have been notified to the Commission in accordance with the Technical Standards and Regulations Directive, have been adopted and published in the national Legal Gazette within the three months suspension period? In Case C-443/98 *Unilever Italia SpA* v *Central Food SpA* [2000] ECR I-7535, the CJEU held that, not only the failure to notify a technical standard in accordance with Article 5 of the Directive, but also the failure to comply with the requirement for a period of suspension in accordance with Article 6 of the Directive meant that national technical standards were not applicable.

Consider whether a private undertaking could make a claim for compensation on the basis of Union law where its business suffered loss as a result of a Member State's non-compliance with the Technical Standards and Regulations Directive (see Chapter 1)?

JUDGMENT OF THE COURT
16 June 1998

Criminal proceedings against Johannes Martinus Lemmens.
(Reference for a preliminary ruling: Arrondissementsrechtbank Maastricht – Netherlands)

'Directive 83/189/EEC – Procedure for the provision of information in the field of technical standards and regulations – Direct effect of the directive'

Case C-226/97

Judgment

1. By order of 13 June 1997, received at the Court on 18 June 1997, the Arrondissementsrechtbank, Maastricht, referred to the Court for a preliminary ruling under Article 177 of the EC Treaty two questions concerning the interpretation of Council Directive 83/189/EEC of 28 March 1983 laying down a procedure for the provision of information in the field of technical standards and regulations (OJ 1983 L 109, p. 8, hereinafter 'the Directive').

2. Those questions were raised in criminal proceedings instituted against Mr Lemmens, who was charged with driving a vehicle while under the influence of alcohol.

3. Article 8(2)(a) of the Wegenverkeerswet 1994 (Road Traffic Law, Stb. 1995, 475) makes it an offence for any person to drive or ride a vehicle after consuming intoxicating liquor so that, upon testing, the alcohol content of his breath is shown to be higher than 220 micrograms of alcohol per litre of expelled breath.

4. Article 163(1) and (2) of that Law is worded as follows:

   '1. If he suspects the driver of a vehicle of infringing Article 8, the police officer may order him to undergo a test within the meaning of Article 8(2)(a).

   2. The driver to whom the order referred to in paragraph 1 is addressed is required to exhale his breath in an apparatus used for the test and to comply with all the instructions given to him by the police officer in order to ensure that the test is properly carried out'.

5. Article 163(10) provides that the Minister for Justice is to lay down, by an administrative regulation, further rules for the application of those provisions.

6. The Besluit Alcoholonderzoeken (Decree on the conduct of tests to determine the alcohol level) of 24 September 1987 (Stb. 432), as frequently amended (hereinafter 'the 1987 Decree'), provides in Article 3 that in order to carry out a breathalyser test, breath-analysis apparatus must be used of a type designated by the Minister for Justice, which presupposes that the apparatus has been approved following a test carried out by the control body designated by the Minister for Justice. Article 5 of the 1987 Decree further provides that the Minister for Justice is to lay down the requirements for breath-analysis apparatus and the rules for testing such apparatus.

7. The rules referred to in Article 5 of the 1987 Decree were laid down by the Regeling Ademanalyse (Regulation on breath analysis) of 25 September 1987 (Stcrt. 1987), as frequently amended (hereinafter 'the 1987 Regulation'). That Regulation provides, in Article 2(1), that in order to be capable of being used by the police for measuring alcohol content, breath-analysis apparatus must be of a type approved in a test carried out by the control body on the basis of paragraph 4.3 of Annex 1 thereto and, in Article 3(1), that the breath-analysis apparatus must also have been approved in a test carried out by the control body on the basis of paragraph 4.4 or 4.5 of that annex.

8. Annex 1 to the 1987 Regulation sets out the characteristics which breath-analysis apparatus must exhibit, in particular so far as concerns quality, performance, testing and test methods as well as the procedures for assessing conformity.

9. Articles 8 and 9 of the Directive, in the version initially in force at the time when the 1987 Decree and the 1987 Regulation were adopted, require Member States to communicate to the Commission any draft technical regulation falling within the scope of the Directive, and to postpone the adoption of such draft regulations for three months, except in specific cases where urgent reasons are involved, which are described in Article 9(3). In certain circumstances, described in Article 9(1) and (2), that period is to be extended by three or by nine months.

10. In its judgment of 30 April 1996 in Case C-194/94 *CIA Security International* [1996] ECR I-2201, paragraph 54, the Court interpreted the Directive as meaning that breach of the obligation to notify, imposed by Articles 8 and 9 thereof, renders the technical regulations concerned inapplicable, so that they are unenforceable against individuals. The Court therefore held that individuals may rely on the aforesaid provisions in proceedings before the national court which must decline to apply a national technical regulation which has not been notified in accordance with the Directive.

11. Following that judgment, the Netherlands Government drew up a list of national measures which should possibly have been notified to the Commission in accordance with the Directive and which included both the 1987 Decree and the 1987 Regulation. In an attempt to make up for lost time, the Netherlands Government no-

tified the Commission of the 1997 Decree on the conduct of tests to determine the alcohol level and the 1997 Regulation on breath analysis, which are identical to their predecessors from 1987.

12. It is apparent from the order for reference that, in the course of the criminal proceedings instituted against him, Mr Lemmens said 'I understand from the press that there are difficulties regarding the breath-analysis apparatus. I maintain that this apparatus has not been notified to Brussels and wonder what the consequences of this could be for my case'.

13. In those circumstances, the national court decided to stay proceedings and to refer the following questions to the Court for a preliminary ruling:

    '1) Can a defendant in criminal proceedings instituted for an offence contrary to Article 8(2)(a) of the Wegenverkeerswet (Road Traffic Law) 1994 successfully rely on the application of the Regeling Ademanalyse (Regulation on breath analysis) ..., as amended, laying down further rules concerning the requirements for breath-analysis apparatus and the tests which such apparatus must undergo, being set aside – where, for the purposes of the investigation referred to in Article 8(2)(a) of the Wegenverkeerswet 1994, that Regulation is based, pursuant to Article 65 of the Invoeringswet Wegenverkeerswet (Law implementing the Road Traffic Law) 1994, on Article 163 of the Wegenverkeerswet viewed in conjunction with Article 5 of the Besluit Alcoholonderzoeken (Decree on the conduct of tests to determine alcohol level) ..., as amended – in view of the failure to notify the Regulation to the European Commission, as required by Article 8 of Directive 83/189/EEC?

    2) Should a court in criminal proceedings of the kind referred to above disapply that Regulation of its own motion on account of the failure to notify it as required?'

14. As the Netherlands and French Governments contend that the 1987 Regulation is not a technical regulation within the meaning of the Directive, it is appropriate to examine this point at the outset.

15. In that regard, it should be noted that the term 'technical regulation' is defined in Article 1(5) of the Directive as 'technical specifications, including the relevant administrative provisions, the observance which is compulsory, *de jure* or *de facto*, in the case of marketing or use in a Member State or a major part thereof, except those laid down by local authorities'. According to Article 1(1), the term 'technical specification' is to be interpreted as meaning 'a specification contained in a document which lays down the characteristics required of a product such as levels of quality, performance, safety or dimensions, including the requirements applicable to the

product as regards terminology, symbols, testing and test methods, packaging, marking or labelling'.

16. The Netherlands and French Governments submit that, although the 1987 Regulation sets out the characteristics for breath-analysis apparatus and the police is required to use approved apparatus in order to establish that an infringement has actually been committed, the Regulation does not fall within the scope of the Directive for two reasons.

17. To begin with, the Netherlands Government submits that the 1987 Regulation applies in the field of criminal law, which falls outside the sphere of Community law.

18. The French Government, for its part, contends that the Directive does not apply to products which, like those in this case, are intended to be used in connection with the exercise of public authority and *a fortiori* in criminal proceedings instituted by the Member States.

19. Those arguments cannot be accepted. Although in principle criminal legislation and the rules of criminal procedure are matters for which the Member States are responsible, it does not follow that this branch of the law cannot be affected by Community law (see, to that effect, Case 186/87 *Cowan* [1989] ECR 195, paragraph 19, and Case 203/80 *Casati* [1981] ECR 2595, paragraph 27).

20. In this case, there is nothing in the Directive to suggest that technical regulations within the meaning of Article 1 thereof are excluded from the notification requirement because they fall within the scope of criminal law, or that the scope of the Directive is limited to products intended to be used otherwise than in connection with the exercise of public authority. As the Court has already stated in Case C-13/96 *Bic Benelux* [1997] ECR I-1753, paragraph 19, a directive applies to technical regulations irrespective of the grounds on which they were adopted.

21. Secondly, the Netherlands Government submits that the regulations in question apply not to persons manufacturing or marketing breath-analysis apparatus, but only to a certain type of purchaser, namely the police. Breath-analysis apparatus not in conformity with the 1987 Regulation can be marketed and used without any restrictions on the part of the market in such apparatus which is not concerned.

22. Furthermore, according to the Netherlands Government, the instructions contained in the 1987 Regulation are addressed to police officers and are designed to ensure that breath-analysis apparatus is reliable inasmuch as it provides evidence that a driver is under the influence of alcohol, but they do not specify the conditions for marketing such apparatus.

23. The French Government states, along the same lines, that, in order to be classified as technical regulations within the meaning of the Directive, the regulations concerned must apply to products intended for everyday use.

24. Those arguments cannot be accepted. Admittedly, certain measures may impose, in respect of a product intended for a particular group of users, technical specifications whose content depends on the specific objective pursued by that group and which are too remote in terms of their relationship with the production and marketing of the product to be classified as technical regulations within the meaning of the Directive. However, that is not the case here.

25. Even on the assumption that in the Netherlands there is a market for breath-analysis apparatus that is not in conformity with the 1987 Regulation, the fact remains that the rules laid down by that regulation must be complied with by those who sell such apparatus to the police, which is a major user of that product on the Netherlands market.

26. The 1987 Regulation therefore constitutes a technical regulation which should, prior to its adoption, have been notified to the Commission in accordance with Article 8 of the Directive.

27. In its first question, the national court essentially asks whether the Directive is to be interpreted as meaning that, if the obligation imposed by Article 8 thereof to notify a technical regulation on breath-analysis apparatus has been infringed, the effect is that evidence obtained by means of such apparatus, authorised in accordance with that regulation, cannot be relied upon against an individual charged with driving while under the influence of alcohol.

28. The Commission and the Governments which have submitted observations to the Court consider that this question calls for a negative answer.

29. The Netherlands Government submits, in particular, that, in this case, the accused has no interest worthy of protection in pleading that the technical regulation is inapplicable. Since the aim of the Directive is to guarantee the free movement of goods, only individuals who manufacture or import goods have a direct interest in the technical rules contained in the 1987 Regulation having been verified on the basis of the Directive.

30. According to the United Kingdom Government, it follows from the *CIA Security International* judgment, cited above, that it is the technical regulation itself, which has not been notified, that cannot be enforced against an individual. The Directive, which is aimed merely at removing obstacles to trade, does not have as its purpose to render unlawful the use of a product marketed in accordance with a technical regulation which has not been notified.

31. The Commission and the French Government submit that, while the conditions for Article 8 of the Directive to have direct effect and the penalty for breach of that provision, namely that a regulation which has not been notified may not be enforced against individuals, are laid down in mandatory terms by Community law, it is for national law to determine the content and specific consequences of that penalty, on the understanding, first, that the conditions in which an individual may rely on the breach of Community law cannot be less favourable to him than those which he must comply with in the event of a comparable breach of national law and, secondly, that the effectiveness of Community law must remain intact. The Commission therefore considers that Community law does not preclude the application of a principle of national law to the effect that breach of the obligation to notify technical regulations does not render inapplicable the legislation on driving while under the influence of alcohol, provided the accused is also precluded from relying on breach of a similar obligation under national law.

32. In that regard, it should be noted that, in paragraph 40 of its judgment in *CIA Security International*, cited above, the Court emphasised that the Directive is designed to protect, by means of preventive control, freedom of movement for goods, which is one of the foundations of the Community. This control serves a useful purpose in that technical regulations covered by the Directive may constitute obstacles to trade in goods between Member States, such obstacles being permissible only if they are necessary to satisfy compelling requirements relating to the public interest.

33. In paragraphs 48 and 54 of that judgment, the Court pointed out that the obligation to notify is essential for achieving such Community control and went on to state that the effectiveness of such control will be that much greater if the Directive is interpreted as meaning that breach of the obligation to notify constitutes a substantial procedural defect such as to render the technical regulations in question inapplicable, and thus unenforceable against individuals.

34. In criminal proceedings such as those in the main action, the regulations applied to the accused are those which, on the one hand, prohibit and penalise driving while under the influence of alcohol and, on the other, require a driver to exhale his breath into an apparatus designed to measure the alcohol content, the result of that test constituting evidence in criminal proceedings. Such regulations differ from those which, not having been notified to the Commission in accordance with the Directive, are unenforceable against individuals.

35. While failure to notify technical regulations, which constitutes a procedural defect in their adoption, renders such regulations inapplicable inasmuch as they hinder the use or marketing of a product which is not in conformity therewith, it does not have the effect of rendering unlawful any use of a product which is in conformity with regulations which have not been notified.

36. The use of the product by the public authorities, in a case such as this, is not liable to create an obstacle to trade which could have been avoided if the notification procedure had been followed.

37. The answer to the first question must therefore be that the Directive is to be interpreted as meaning that breach of the obligation imposed by Article 8 thereof to notify a technical regulation on breath-analysis apparatus does not have the effect of making it impossible for evidence obtained by means of such apparatus, authorised in accordance with regulations which have not been notified, to be relied upon against an individual charged with driving while under the influence of alcohol.

38. In the light of the answer to the first question, there is no need to answer the second question.

Costs

[Para. 39 omitted]

On those grounds,

THE COURT,

in answer to the questions referred to it by the Arrondissementsrechtbank, Maastricht, by order of 13 June 1997, hereby rules:

> **Council Directive 83/189/EEC of 28 March 1983 laying down a procedure for the provision of information in the field of technical standards and regulations is to be interpreted as meaning that breach of the obligation imposed by Article 8 thereof to notify a technical regulation on breath-analysis apparatus does not have the effect of making it impossible for evidence obtained by means of such apparatus, authorised in accordance with regulations which have not been notified, to be relied upon against an individual charged with driving while under the influence of alcohol.**

Comments and questions

In Case C-226/97 *Lemmens* [1998] ECR I-3711, the CJEU restricted the scope of the judgment in Case C-194/94 *CIA Security International SA* v *Signalson SA and Securitel SPRL* [1996] ECR I-2201, printed above, so that the failure to notify technical regulations in accordance with the Technical Standards and Regulations Directive will only lead to the inapplicability of a national regulation where the national regulations prevent the use of or marketing of a product which does not comply with them; cf. paragraph 35 of the judgment. Thus, it is not all usage of a product which is in accordance with non-notified technical regulations which will be unlawful. The use by public authorities (in this case, the police) of a product (in this case, an apparatus for analysing the alcohol content of breath, or breathalyser) was not capable of constituting a hindrance to trade, which could have been avoided if the notification procedure had been followed in accordance with national technical regulations (in this case, the technical requirements for breathalysers).

Can a Danish fish farmer who is accused of infringing a non-notified national executive order, which contains certain requirements as to the methods to be used in fish farming, claim that the order is not applicable? In Case C-67/97 *Bluhme* [1998] ECR 8033 (the *Brown Bee* case) there was an order that only brown bees were permitted to be kept in a specified area in Denmark, and it was prohibited to introduce and keep golden bees in that area. Was this requirement a notifiable technical specification? If the Government of a Member State enters into a voluntary agreement with the association of local government authorities of that Member State not to use weedkiller on publicly owned land, will this agreement be notifiable to the Commission under the Technical Standards and Regulations Directive? Should rules that poultry meat may not contain salmonella be notified?

In Case C-13/96 *Bic Benelux SA* v *Belgium* [1997] ECR I-1753, the CJEU had to consider whether was a 'technical regulation', which was covered by the notification requirements of the Technical Standards and Regulations Directive, in a case in which there was a requirement for marking products as evidence that a special environmental tax had been levied. The CJEU answered this question in the affirmative. The CJEU also held that such a marking requirement does not constitute a requirement linked to a fiscal measure for the purposes of the third indent of the second subparagraph of Article 1(9) of Directive 83/189; cf. paragraph 25 of the judgment.

Would a reduction of car registration tax for cars with a minimum of four airbags be covered by the notification requirements of the Technical Standards and Regulations Directive?

The scope of the notification requirements is not always clear. Could a Dutch pig breeder rely on the Technical Standards and Regulations Directive if he were prosecuted because he had failed to have a disinfectant bath for rubber boots standing outside his pigsty, as required by Dutch regulations? The Dutch rule had not been notified to the Commission, but should it have been? This question came up in Case C-37/99 *Donkersteeg* [2000] ECR I-10223. In paragraph 20 of the judgment, the CJEU pointed out that a 'technical specification' should be understood as 'a specification contained in a document which lays down the characteristics required of a product and also, in the case of agricultural products, production methods and procedures.' A requirement for a disinfectant bath for rubber boots outside a pigsty did not amount to a technical regulation which lays down product characteristics or, in the case of agricultural products, production methods and procedures. The CJEU concluded that the requirement did not amount to a technical regulation within the meaning of the Technical Standards and Regulations Directive.

CHAPTER 3

EU Citizenship

JUDGMENT OF THE COURT
20 September 2001

Rudy Grzelczyk v Centre public d'aide sociale d'Ottignies-Louvain-la-Neuve.
(Reference for a preliminary ruling: Tribunal du travail de Nivelles – Belgium)

'Articles 6, 8 and 8a of the EC Treaty (now, after amendment, Articles 12 EC, 17 EC and 18 EC) – Council Directive 93/96/EEC – Right of residence for students – National legislation which guarantees a minimum subsistence allowance only for nationals, persons covered by Regulation (EEC) No 1612/68 and stateless persons and refugees – Foreign student who has met his own living expenses during the first years of his studies'

Case C-184/99

Judgment

1. By judgment of 7 May 1999, received at the Court on 19 May 1999, the Tribunal du travail de Nivelles (Industrial Tribunal, Nivelles) referred to the Court for a preliminary ruling under Article 234 EC two questions on the interpretation of Articles 6, 8 and 8a of the EC Treaty (now, after amendment, Articles 12 EC, 17 EC and 18 EC) and Council Directive 93/96/EEC of 29 October 1993 on the right of residence for students (OJ 1993 L 317, p. 59).

2. Those questions were raised in proceedings between Mr Rudy Grzelczyk and the Centre public d'aide sociale d'Ottignies-Louvain-la-Neuve (Public Social Assistance Centre for Ottignies-Louvain-la-Neuve, hereinafter the CPAS) concerning the CPAS's decision to stop payment of the minimex, the minimum subsistence allowance (hereinafter referred to as the minimex).

Relevant Community legislation

3. The first paragraph of Article 6 of the Treaty provides:

   Within the scope of application of this Treaty, and without prejudice to any special provisions contained therein, any discrimination on grounds of nationality shall be prohibited.

4. Article 8 of the Treaty provides:

   1. Citizenship of the Union is hereby established. Every person holding the nationality of a Member State shall be a citizen of the Union.

2. Citizens of the Union shall enjoy the rights conferred by this Treaty and shall be subject to the duties imposed thereby.

5. Article 8a of the Treaty is worded as follows:

   1. Every citizen of the Union shall have the right to move and reside freely within the territory of the Member States, subject to the limitations and conditions laid down in this Treaty and by the measures adopted to give it effect.

   2. The Council may adopt provisions with a view to facilitating the exercise of the rights referred to in paragraph 1; save as otherwise provided in this Treaty, the Council shall act unanimously on a proposal from the Commission and after obtaining the assent of the European Parliament.

6. The fourth recital in the preamble to both Council Directive 90/364/EEC of 28 June 1990 on the right of residence (OJ 1990 L 180, p. 26) and Council Directive 90/365/EEC of 28 June 1990 on the right of residence for employees and self-employed persons who have ceased their occupational activity (OJ 1990 L 180, p. 28) and the sixth recital in the preamble to Directive 93/96 – which essentially replaced Council Directive 90/366/EEC of 28 June 1990 on the right of residence for students (OJ 1990 L 180, p. 30) after it was annulled by the Court of Justice (Case C-295/90 *Parliament* v *Council* [1992] ECR I-4193) – state that beneficiaries of those directives must not become an unreasonable burden on the public finances of the host Member State.

7. According to Article 1 of Directive 93/96,

   In order to lay down conditions to facilitate the exercise of the right of residence and with a view to guaranteeing access to vocational training in a non-discriminatory manner for a national of a Member State who has been accepted to attend a vocational training course in another Member State, the Member States shall recognise the right of residence for any student who is a national of a Member State and who does not enjoy that right under other provisions of Community law, and for the student's spouse and their dependent children, where the student assures the relevant national authority, by means of a declaration or by such alternative means as the student may choose that are at least equivalent, that he has sufficient resources to avoid becoming a burden on the social assistance system of the host Member State during their period of residence, provided that the student is enrolled in a recognised educational establishment for the principal purpose of following a vocational training course there and that he is covered by sickness insurance in respect of all risks in the host Member State.

Relevant national legislation

8. Article 1 of the Law of 7 August 1974 establishing the right to a minimum subsistence allowance (Moniteur belge of 18 September 1974, p. 11363) provides:

   1. Any Belgian having reached the age of majority, who is actually resident in Belgium and who does not have adequate resources and is not able to obtain them either by his own efforts or from other sources, shall be entitled to a minimum subsistence allowance. The King shall determine the meaning of the words 'actually resident'.

   The same entitlement is granted to minors treated as being of full age on account of marriage, and also to single persons who are responsible for one or more children.

   2. The King may, by decree deliberated by the Council of Ministers, extend the application of this law, subject to such conditions as he shall set, to other categories of minors, and also to persons not possessing Belgian nationality.

9. According to Article 1 of the Royal Decree of 27 March 1987 (Moniteur belge of 7 April 1987, p. 5068), which extends application of the Law of 7 August 1974 to persons not possessing Belgian nationality:

   The scope of the Law of 7 August 1974 establishing a right to a minimum subsistence allowance shall be extended to the following persons:
   (i) those to whom Regulation (EEC) No 1612/68 of the Council of the European Communities of 15 October 1968 on the freedom of movement for workers within the Community applies;
   (ii) stateless persons to whom the Convention on the Status of Stateless Persons, signed in new York on 28 September 1954 and approved by the Law of 12 May 1960 applies;
   (iii) refugees within the meaning of Article 49 of the Law of 15 December 1980 on entry to Belgian territory, residence, establishment and the expulsion of foreigners.

The main proceedings and the questions referred for a preliminary ruling

10. In 1995 Mr Grzelczyk, a French national, began a course of university studies in physical education at the Catholic University of Louvain-la-Neuve and for that purpose took up residence in Belgium. During the first three years of his studies, he defrayed his own costs of maintenance, accommodation and studies by taking on various minor jobs and by obtaining credit facilities.

11. At the beginning of his fourth and final year of study, he applied to the CPAS for payment of the minimex. In its report, the CPAS observed that Mr Grzelczyk had

worked hard to finance his studies, but that his final academic year, involving the writing of a dissertation and the completion of a qualifying period of practical training, would be more demanding than the previous years. For those reasons, by decision of 16 October 1998, the CPAS granted Mr Grzelczyk the minimex, calculated at the single rate, for the period from 5 October 1998 to 30 June 1999.

12. The CPAS applied to the Belgian State authorities for reimbursement of the minimex paid to Mr Grzelczyk. The competent federal minister, however, refused to reimburse the CPAS on the ground that the legal requirements for the grant of the minimex, and in particular the nationality requirement, had not been satisfied, whereupon the CPAS withdrew the minimex from Mr Grzelczyk with effect from 1 January 1999, for the stated reason that the person concerned is an EEC national enrolled as a student.

13. Mr Grzelczyk challenged that decision before the Labour Tribunal, Nivelles. The tribunal observed that, according to the case-law of the Court of Justice, the minimex is a social advantage within the meaning of Article 7(2) of Regulation (EEC) No 1612/68 of the Council of 15 October 1968 on freedom of movement for workers within the Community (OJ, English Special Edition, 1968 (II), p. 47) and that, under Belgian law, entitlement to the minimex had been extended to persons to whom Regulation No 1612/68 applies. It pointed out, however, that Mr Grzelczyk did not, in the CPAS's view, satisfy all the requirements for claiming the minimex under its extended scope since his student status prevented him from being regarded as a worker and his residence in Belgium was not attributable to operation of the principle of free movement of workers. The Labour Tribunal also referred to the judgment of the Court of Justice in Case C-85/96 *Martiínez Sala* [1998] ECR I-2691 and queried whether the principles of European citizenship and non-discrimination precluded application of the national legislation at issue in the main proceedings.

14. In those circumstances, the Labour Tribunal, Nivelles, recognising the urgency of Mr Grzelczyk's situation, granted him a flat-rate allowance of BEF 20 000 per month for the period from 1 January 1999 to 30 June 1999 and stayed the proceedings in order to refer the following questions to the Court of Justice for a preliminary ruling:

    1. Is it contrary to Community law – more particularly the principles of European citizenship and of non-discrimination enshrined in Article 6 and 8 of the Treaty establishing the European Community – for entitlement to a non-contributory social benefit, such as that introduced by the Belgian Law of 7 August 1974 on the minimum subsistence allowance, to be granted only to nationals of the Member States to whom Regulation (EEC) No 1612/68 of 15 October 1968 applies and not to all citizens of the Union?

2. In the alternative, are Articles 6 and 8a of the Treaty and Directive 93/96 of 29 October 1993 on the right of residence for students to be interpreted to the effect that, after a student's right of residence has been acknowledged, he may subsequently be barred from entitlement to non-contributory social benefits, such as the minimum subsistence allowance, payable by the host country, and, if so, is that exclusion general and definitive in nature?

Preliminary remarks

15. The parties to the main proceedings, the Member States which have submitted observations and the Commission have all devoted a substantial part of their observations, both written and oral, to the question whether the fact that during the first three years of his studies Mr Grzelczyk took various paid jobs brings him within the scope of the Royal Decree of 27 March 1987 as a worker within the meaning of Community law.

16. However, it is clear from the national court's order for reference that it adopted the analysis of the CPAS that Mr Grzelczyk did not fulfil the criteria for treatment as a worker within the meaning of Community law. Against that factual and legal background the national court raises the question of the compatibility of the relevant Belgian legislation with Community law, and in particular with Articles 6, 8 and 8a of the Treaty.

17. That being so, the Court must answer its questions as they have been framed and within the limits set by the national court.

18. It is for the national court to determine, in the light, in particular, of the Opinion of the Advocate General, whether or not the facts and circumstances of the case are such as to permit Mr Grzelczyk to be regarded as a worker for the purposes of Community law.

The first question referred for a preliminary ruling

19. By its first question, the Belgian court asks essentially whether Articles 6 and 8 of the Treaty preclude entitlement to a non-contributory social benefit, such as the minimex, from being made conditional, in the case of nationals of Member States other than the host State where they are legally resident, on their falling within the scope of Regulation No 1612/68 when no such condition applies to nationals of the host Member State.

Observations submitted to the Court

20. The CPAS argues that, as Community law stands at present, it would be wrong to regard all citizens of the European Union as being entitled to claim non-

contributory social benefits, such as the minimex. It is clear from the wording of the provision itself that Article 8a(1) of the Treaty does not have direct effect and that its implementation must always have due regard for the limits laid down in the Treaty and defined in secondary legislation. This includes, in particular, Directives 90/364, 90/365 and 93/96, which subject exercise of the freedom of movement to a requirement to demonstrate that the person concerned possesses sufficient resources and social security cover.

21. The Belgian and Danish Governments submit that the entry into force of the Treaty on European Union and the Treaty of Amsterdam does not affect that interpretation. Citizenship of the Union does not mean that Union citizens obtain rights that are new and more extensive than those already deriving from the EC Treaty and secondary legislation. The principle of citizenship of the Union has no autonomous content, but is merely linked to the other provisions of the Treaty.

22. The French Government submits that the idea that the principle of equal treatment in the matter of social advantages should be extended to all citizens of the Union when at present it applies only to workers and members of their families would amount to establishing total equality between citizens of the Union established in a Member State and nationals of that State, which would be difficult to reconcile with rights attaching to nationality.

23. The Portuguese Government points out that, since the entry into force of the Treaty on European Union, nationals of the Member States are no longer regarded in Community law as being primarily economic factors in an essentially economic community. One consequence of the introduction of Union citizenship is that the limits and conditions which Community law imposes on the exercise of the right to freedom of movement and residence within the territory of the Member States should no longer be construed as envisaging a purely economic right arising from the EC Treaty but as being concerned only with those exceptions that are based on reasons of public policy, public security or public health. Furthermore, if from the time when the Treaty on European Union entered into force, nationals of the Member States acquired the status of citizen of the Union and ceased to be regarded as purely economic agents, it follows that the application of Regulation No 1612/68 ought also to be extended to all citizens of the Union, whether or not they are workers within the meaning of that regulation.

24. The United Kingdom Government, referring to the judgment in Martíinez Sala, cited above, argues that, whilst Mr Grzelczyk is suffering discrimination on the grounds of his nationality, Article 6 of the EC Treaty does not apply to his situation because any discrimination against him falls outside the scope of the Treaty. Article 6 cannot have the effect of striking down limitations upon the scope of Regulation No 1612/68, whether read alone or together with Article 8 of the Treaty.

25. The Belgian Government adds that the applicant in the main proceedings is claiming the minimex whereas this type of funding falls outside the scope of Article 6 of the Treaty, of Article 126 of the EC Treaty (now Article 149 EC) and of Article 127 of the EC Treaty (now, after amendment, Article 150 EC). Funding such as the minimex is an instrument of social policy with no particular link with vocational training. As Community law stands at present, it is not within Community competence.

26. The Commission takes the view that Articles 6 and 8 of the Treaty must be interpreted as granting to every citizen of the Union the right not to suffer discrimination by a Member State on grounds of nationality, within the scope of application ratione materiae of the Treaty, provided that the Union citizen's situation has some relevant connection with the Member State concerned.

Findings of the Court

27. In order to place the legal problem raised by this case in its context, it should be recalled that, in Case 249/83 *Hoeckx* [1985] ECR 973, concerning an unemployed Dutch national returning to Belgium where she made a fresh application for the minimex, the Court held that a social benefit providing a general guarantee of a minimum subsistence allowance, such as that provided for by the Belgian Law of 7 August 1974, constitutes a social advantage within the meaning of Regulation No 1612/68.

28. At the time of the facts giving rise to Hoeckx, all Community nationals were entitled to the minimex, although nationals of Member States other than Belgium had to satisfy the additional requirement of having actually resided in Belgium for at least five years immediately preceding the date on which the minimex was granted (see Article 1 of the Royal Decree of 8 January 1976, Moniteur belge of 13 January 1976, p. 311). It was the Royal Decree of 27 March 1987, which repealed the Royal Decree of 8 January 1976, which restricted entitlement to the minimex, in the case of nationals of other Member States, to persons to whom Regulation No 1612/68 applied. The residence condition, which had been amended in the meantime, was finally removed after infringement proceedings were brought by the Commission against the Kingdom of Belgium (Case C-326/90 *Commission* v *Belgium* [1992] ECR I-5517).

29. It is clear from the documents before the Court that a student of Belgian nationality, though not a worker within the meaning of Regulation No 1612/68, who found himself in exactly the same circumstances as Mr Grzelczyk would satisfy the conditions for obtaining the minimex. The fact that Mr Grzelczyk is not of Belgian nationality is the only bar to its being granted to him. It is not therefore in dispute that the case is one of discrimination solely on the ground of nationality.

30. Within the sphere of application of the Treaty, such discrimination is, in principle, prohibited by Article 6. In the present case, Article 6 must be read in conjunction with the provisions of the Treaty concerning citizenship of the Union in order to determine its sphere of application.

31. Union citizenship is destined to be the fundamental status of nationals of the Member States, enabling those who find themselves in the same situation to enjoy the same treatment in law irrespective of their nationality, subject to such exceptions as are expressly provided for.

32. As the Court held in paragraph 63 of its judgment in Martíínez Sala, cited above, a citizen of the European Union, lawfully resident in the territory of a host Member State, can rely on Article 6 of the Treaty in all situations which fall within the scope ratione materiae of Community law.

33. Those situations include those involving the exercise of the fundamental freedoms guaranteed by the Treaty and those involving the exercise of the right to move and reside freely in another Member State, as conferred by Article 8a of the Treaty (see Case C-274/96 *Bickel and Franz* [1998] ECR I-7637, paragraphs 15 and 16).

34. It is true that, in paragraph 18 of its judgment in Case 197/86 *Brown* [1988] ECR 3205, the Court held that, at that stage in the development of Community law, assistance given to students for maintenance and training fell in principle outside the scope of the EEC Treaty for the purposes of Article 7 thereof (later Article 6 of the EC Treaty).

35. However, since Brown, the Treaty on European Union has introduced citizenship of the European Union into the EC Treaty and added to Title VIII of Part Three a new chapter 3 devoted to education and vocational training. There is nothing in the amended text of the Treaty to suggest that students who are citizens of the Union, when they move to another Member State to study there, lose the rights which the Treaty confers on citizens of the Union. Furthermore, since Brown, the Council has also adopted Directive 93/96, which provides that the Member States must grant right of residence to student nationals of a Member State who satisfy certain requirements.

36. The fact that a Union citizen pursues university studies in a Member State other than the State of which he is a national cannot, of itself, deprive him of the possibility of relying on the prohibition of all discrimination on grounds of nationality laid down in Article 6 of the Treaty.

37. As pointed out in paragraph 30 above, in the present case that prohibition must be read in conjunction with Article 8a(1) of the Treaty, which proclaims the right to move and reside freely within the territory of the Member States, subject to the

limitations and conditions laid down in this Treaty and by the measures adopted to give it effect.

38. As regards those limitations and conditions, it is clear from Article 1 of Directive 93/96 that Member States may require of students who are nationals of a different Member State and who wish to exercise the right of residence on their territory, first, that they satisfy the relevant national authority that they have sufficient resources to avoid becoming a burden on the social assistance system of the host Member State during their period of residence, next, that they be enrolled in a recognised educational establishment for the principal purpose of following a vocational training course there and, lastly, that they be covered by sickness insurance in respect of all risks in the host Member State.

39. Article 3 of Directive 93/96 makes clear that the directive does not establish any right to payment of maintenance grants by the host Member State for students who benefit from the right of residence. On the other hand, there are no provisions in the directive that preclude those to whom it applies from receiving social security benefits.

40. As regards more specifically the question of resources, Article 1 of Directive 93/96 does not require resources of any specific amount, nor that they be evidenced by specific documents. The article refers merely to a declaration, or such alternative means as are at least equivalent, which enables the student to satisfy the national authority concerned that he has, for himself and, in relevant cases, for his spouse and dependent children, sufficient resources to avoid becoming a burden on the social assistance system of the host Member State during their stay (see paragraph 44 of the judgment in Case C-424/98 *Commission* v *Italy* [2000] ECR I-4001).

41. In merely requiring such a declaration, Directive 93/96 differs from Directives 90/364 and 90/365, which do indicate the minimum level of income that persons wishing to avail themselves of those directives must have. That difference is explained by the special characteristics of student residence in comparison with that of persons to whom Directives 90/364 and 90/365 apply (see paragraph 45 of the judgment in Commission v Italy, cited above).

42. That interpretation does not, however, prevent a Member State from taking the view that a student who has recourse to social assistance no longer fulfils the conditions of his right of residence or from taking measures, within the limits imposed by Community law, either to withdraw his residence permit or not to renew it.

43. Nevertheless, in no case may such measures become the automatic consequence of a student who is a national of another Member State having recourse to the host Member State's social assistance system.

44. Whilst Article 4 of Directive 93/96 does indeed provide that the right of residence is to exist for as long as beneficiaries of that right fulfil the conditions laid down in Article 1, the sixth recital in the directive's preamble envisages that beneficiaries of the right of residence must not become an unreasonable burden on the public finances of the host Member State. Directive 93/96, like Directives 90/364 and 90/365, thus accepts a certain degree of financial solidarity between nationals of a host Member State and nationals of other Member States, particularly if the difficulties which a beneficiary of the right of residence encounters are temporary.

45. Furthermore, a student's financial position may change with the passage of time for reasons beyond his control. The truthfulness of a student's declaration is therefore to be assessed only as at the time when it is made.

46. It follows from the foregoing that Articles 6 and 8 of the Treaty preclude entitlement to a non-contributory social benefit, such as the minimex, from being made conditional, in the case of nationals of Member States other than the host State where they are legally resident, on their falling within the scope of Regulation No 1612/68 when no such condition applies to nationals of the host Member State.

The second question referred for a preliminary ruling

47. In view of the answer given to the first question, and since the second question was put in the alternative, it is not necessary to reply to that question.

The temporal effects of the present judgment

[Paras 48-55 omitted]

Costs

[Para. 56 omitted]

On those grounds,

THE COURT,

in answer to the questions referred to it by the Tribunal du travail de Nivelles by judgment of 7 May 1999, hereby rules:

> **Articles 6 and 8 of the EC Treaty (now, after amendment, Articles 12 EC and 17 EC) preclude entitlement to a non-contributory social benefit, such as the minimex, from being made conditional, in the case of nationals of Member States other than the host State where they are legally resident, on their falling within the scope of Regulation No 1612/68 of the Council of 15 October 1968**

on the freedom of movement for workers within the Community when no such condition applies to nationals of the host Member State.

Comments and questions

'Citizenship' of the European Union was introduced in the Maastricht Treaty in 1993, by the inclusion of Articles 17 and 18 in the EC Treaty; these were formerly Articles 8 and 8A TEC and are now Articles 20 and 21 TFEU. In 1999, Article 17 TEC was clarified so that now the third sentence in Article 17(1) expressly states that citizenship of the Union shall complement and not replace national citizenship.

The question whether and if so what rights are derived from EU citizenship under Articles 20 and 21 TFEU has been referred to the CJEU in a number of cases. In deciding these cases the CJEU has held that the introduction of EU citizenship in (now) the TFEU has significance in its own right. First, in the view of the CJEU, Union citizenship implies a requirement that a Member State shall give treatment to Union citizens of another Member State, which is *equal to the treatment of its own citizens*. For example, this is expressed in paragraph 31 of the judgment in Case C-184/99 *Grzelczyk* v *Centre public d'aide sociale d'Ottignies-Louvain-la-Neuve* [2001] ECR I-6193, and was first laid down in Case C-85/96 *Sala* v *Freistaat Bayern* [1998] ECR I-2691. In the *Sala* case the CJEU held that Union citizens, who are nationals of one Member State and lawfully resident in another Member State, may not be discriminated against compared with the host Member State's own nationals with regard to the payment of social benefits which fall within the scope of the TFEU. This applies regardless of the basis for the Union citizen's lawful residence. Sala was a Spanish national who lived on German social security benefits, and therefore had a right to be paid child-raising allowance on the same terms as German nationals. However, in the case of non-economically active citizens such as Sala, this statement of the law on the right of Union citizens to equal treatment when they are lawfully resident pursuant to national law but not pursuant to Union law (under the Free Movement Directive) has subsequently been changed by the CJEU Grand Chamber in Case C-333/13 *Dano*, which is reproduced below in this chapter.

In the *Grzelczyk* case, the CJEU had to consider a similar case in relation to a French national who was studying in Belgium. After studying in Belgium for three years, Grzelczyk applied to the Belgian authorities for the minimum subsistence allowance (known as the 'minimex'), paid as a support to Belgian students. The Belgian authorities rejected the application on the grounds that the payment was restricted to students who were Belgian nationals.

The CJEU had previously held that student support payments were, in principle, not covered by the EC Treaty; cf. Case 197/86 *Brown* v *The Secretary of State for Scotland* [1988] ECR 3205. Referring to the fact that, since the *Brown* case, Union citizenship and a new chapter devoted to education and vocational training had been included in the EC Treaty, the CJEU held, in paragraphs 34-35 of the *Grzelczyk* case, that it must thereafter be assumed that students who are lawfully resident in another Member State have the same rights as other Union citizens to claim rights under the Treaty, including the right to rely on what is now Article 18 TFEU (originally Article 7 of the EEC Treaty, then Article 6 TEC, and then Article 12 TEC) with its general prohibition of discrimination on the grounds of nationality. The CJEU added that this prohibition should be read in conjunction with Article 21 TFEU (formerly Article 18 TEC), under which Union citizens 'have the right to move and reside freely within the territory of the Member States, subject to the limitations and conditions laid down in the Treaties and by the measures adopted to give it effect.' Do you agree that such a change in the practice of the CJEU can be based on Article 21 TFEU? Do you think the Member States wanted the insertion of Article 18 in the EC Treaty (now Article 21 TFEU) to lead to such a change in practice?

The right of residence of students is subject to the restrictions laid down in Article 7(1)(s) of Directive 2004/38 on the right of citizens of the Union and their family members to move and reside freely within the territory of the Member States (the 'Free Movement Directive') (which has replaced, among others, Directive 93/96). According to its provisions, any Union citizen has a right to reside in another Member State's territory for more than three months, if such persons 'are enrolled at a private or public establishment, accredited or financed by the host Member State on the basis of its legislation or administrative practice, for the principal purpose of following a course of study, including vocational training; and have comprehensive sickness insurance cover in the host Member State and assure the relevant national authority, by means of a declaration or by such equivalent means as they may choose, that they have sufficient resources for themselves and their family members not to become a burden on the social assistance system of the host Member State during their period of residence'. The provision only calls for a declaration to be made to this effect.

In the *Grzelczyk* case, the CJEU held that the Directive means that the host Member State can revoke a student's residence permit if the student no longer has sufficient resources. In paragraph 43, the CJEU also said that 'in *no case may such measures become the automatic consequence* of a student who is a national of another Member State having recourse to the host Member State's social assistance system' (emphasis added).

In accordance with the sixth recital in the preamble to Directive 93/96/EEC, then in force, the CJEU stated in paragraph 44 of the judgment, that where a student from another Member State receives social security benefits and perhaps other social support, the host Member State can only revoke the student's residence permit if the student constitutes an unreasonable burden on the public finances of the host Member State. Without going into the reasons for it, in paragraph 44 the CJEU also stated that Directive 93/96 then in force (as with the earlier Directives 90/364 on the right of residence and 90/365 on the right of residence for employees and self-employed persons who have ceased their occupational activity) expresses 'a certain degree of financial solidarity between nationals of a host Member State and nationals of other Member States, particularly if the difficulties which a beneficiary of the right of residence encounters are temporary.' Under Articles 12 and 18 TEC (now Articles 18 and 21 TFEU), Grzelczyk had a right to social security benefits on an equal footing with Belgian nationals. It is worth noting that the Directive 93/96 contained two different formulations of the requirement that a student may not be a burden on the social security system of the host Member State. According to Article 1 of the Directive, a student must not become 'a burden on the social assistance system of the host Member State', whereas according to the sixth recital of the preamble, a student must not become 'become an unreasonable burden on the public finances of the host Member State.' The CJEU could therefore justifiably use the criterion of an 'unreasonable burden', which is more favourable for the Union citizen. However, the criterion involves a major problem of interpretation since neither the practice of the CJEU nor Union law in general make it possible to define the circumstances under which a student would be considered as imposing an 'unreasonable burden' on public finances. The CJEU has merely established that the first that a student seeks and receives social security benefit it is not an unreasonable burden on the state. But what if a student seeks and receives help a fifth or sixth time? Or a fifteenth time?

The requirement that a student must not become an unreasonable burden on the public finances is in reality merely an expression of the principle of proportionality; cf. Case C-413/99 *Baumbast and R* v *The Home Secretary* [2002] ECR I-7091, printed below, in which the CJEU applied the principle of proportionality to Article 21 TFEU. How should Member States attempt to establish the limits for what may be regarded as being an 'unreasonable burden' in relation to students from other Member States who seek cash benefits?

As stated above, the CJEU changed its previous practice on the equal treatment of non-economically active Union citizens in the *Dano* case, which is reproduced below. Consider whether the *Dano* case has thereby also changed the legal situation as laid down in the *Grzelczyk* case. In answering this question, assume that the facts are the same as in the *Grzelczyk* case.

JUDGMENT OF THE COURT
17 September 2002

Baumbast and R v Secretary of State for the Home Department. (Reference for a preliminary ruling: Immigration Appeal Tribunal – United Kingdom)

'Freedom of movement for persons – Migrant worker – Rights of residence of members of the migrant worker's family – Rights of the children to pursue their studies in the host Member State – Articles 10 and 12 of Regulation (EEC) No 1612/68 – Citizenship of the European Union – Right of residence – Directive 90/364/EEC – Limitations and conditions'

Case C-413/99

Judgment

1. By order of 28 May 1999, received at the Court on 28 October 1999, the Immigration Appeal Tribunal referred to the Court for a preliminary ruling under Article 234 EC four questions on the interpretation of Article 18 EC and Article 12 of Regulation (EEC) No 1612/68 of the Council of 15 October 1968 on freedom of movement for workers within the Community (OJ, English Special Edition 1968 (II), p. 475).

2. Those questions were raised in proceedings between, first, Mr and Mrs Baumbast, Maria Fernanda Sarmiento and Idanella Baumbast (together 'the Baumbast family') and, second, R, on the one hand, and the Secretary of State for the Home Department ('the Secretary of State'), on the other, concerning the latter's refusal to grant them leave to remain within the territory of the United Kingdom.

Legal background

Community legislation

3. Under Article 17 EC:

> '1. Citizenship of the Union is hereby established. Every person holding the nationality of a Member State shall be a citizen of the Union. Citizenship of the Union shall complement and not replace national citizenship.
>
> 2. Citizens of the Union shall enjoy the rights conferred by this Treaty and shall be subject to the duties imposed thereby.'

4. Article 18(1) EC provides that every citizen of the Union is to have the right to move and reside freely within the territory of the Member States, subject to the limitations and conditions laid down in the EC Treaty and by the measures adopted to give it effect.

5. Articles 10 to 12 of Regulation No 1612/68 provide as follows:

'Article 10

1. The following shall, irrespective of their nationality, have the right to install themselves with a worker who is a national of one Member State and who is employed in the territory of another Member State:
   (a) his spouse and their descendants who are under the age of 21 years or are dependants;
   (b) dependent relatives in the ascending line of the worker and his spouse.

2. Member States shall facilitate the admission of any member of the family not coming within the provisions of paragraph 1 if dependent on the worker referred to above or living under his roof in the country whence he comes.

3. For the purposes of paragraphs 1 and 2, the worker must have available for his family housing considered as normal for national workers in the region where he is employed; this provision, however, must not give rise to discrimination between national workers and workers from the other Member States.

Article 11

Where a national of a Member State is pursuing an activity as an employed or self-employed person in the territory of another Member State, his spouse and those of the children who are under the age of 21 years or dependent on him shall have the right to take up any activity as an employed person throughout the territory of that same State, even if they are not nationals of any Member State.

Article 12

The children of a national of a Member State who is or has been employed in the territory of another Member State shall be admitted to that State's general educational, apprenticeship and vocational training courses under the same conditions as the nationals of that State, if such children are residing in its territory. Member States shall encourage all efforts to enable such children to attend these courses under the best possible conditions.'

6. Under the first subparagraph of Article 1(1) of Council Directive 90/364/EEC of 28 June 1990 on the right of residence (OJ 1990 L 180, p. 26), Member States are to

grant the right of residence to nationals of Member States who do not enjoy that right under other provisions of Community law and to members of their families as defined in Article 1(2) of that directive, provided that they themselves and the members of their families are covered by sickness insurance in respect of all risks in the host Member State and have sufficient resources to avoid becoming a burden on the social assistance system of the host Member State during their period of residence.

7. The second subparagraph of Article 1(1) of Directive 90/364 provides that the resources referred to in the first subparagraph of that paragraph are to be deemed sufficient where they are higher than the level of resources below which the host Member State may grant social assistance to its nationals, taking into account the personal circumstances of the applicant and, where appropriate, the personal circumstances of persons admitted pursuant to Article 1(2) of that directive.

8. The third subparagraph of Article 1(1) of Directive 90/364 provides that, where the second subparagraph of that paragraph cannot be applied, the resources of the applicant are to be deemed sufficient if they are higher than the level of the minimum social security pension paid by the host Member State.

9. Under Article 1(2) of Directive 90/364:

   'The following shall, irrespective of their nationality, have the right to install themselves in another Member State with the holder of the right of residence:
   (a) his or her spouse and their descendants who are dependants;
   (b) dependent relatives in the ascending line of the holder of the right of residence and of his or her spouse.'

10. Article 3 of Directive 90/364 provides that the right of residence is to remain for as long as beneficiaries of that right fulfil the conditions laid down in Article 1 of that directive.

National legislation

11. Section 7(1) of the Immigration Act 1988 provides:

    'A person shall not under the [Immigration Act 1971] require leave to enter or remain in the United Kingdom in any case in which he is entitled to do so by virtue of an enforceable Community right or of any provision made under section 2(2) of the European Communities Act 1972.'

12. Article 3 of the Immigration (European Economic Area) Order 1994 (SI 1994, No 1895; 'the EEA Order') lays down the general principle that nationals of a State which is a contracting party to the Agreement on the European Economic Area of 2

May 1992 (OJ 1994 L 1, p. 3; 'the EEA Agreement') and the members of their families are to be admitted to the United Kingdom on production of a valid national identity card or passport.

13. Under Article 4(1) of the EEA Order, a 'qualified person' is to be entitled to reside in the United Kingdom for as long as he remains a qualified person. That right is extended to family members including spouses by Article 4(2) of the EEA Order.

14. According to Article 6 of the EEA Order, a 'qualified person' means, inter alia, a national of a State which is a contracting party to the EEA Agreement who undertakes in the United Kingdom the activities of a worker.

15. Paragraph 255 of the United Kingdom Immigration Rules (House of Commons Paper 395) 1994 ('the Immigration Rules') provides:

    'An EEA national (other than a student) and the family member of such a person who has been issued with a residence permit or residence document valid for five years and who has remained in the United Kingdom in accordance with the provisions of the 1994 EEA Order for four years and continues to do so may, on application, have his residence permit or residence document (as the case may be) endorsed to show permission to remain in the United Kingdom indefinitely.'

The main proceedings

Baumbast

16. Mrs Baumbast, a Colombian national, married Mr Baumbast, a German national, in the United Kingdom in May 1990. Their family consists of two daughters, the elder, Maria Fernanda Sarmiento, Mrs Baumbast's natural daughter, who is a Colombian national and the younger, Idanella Baumbast, who has dual German and Colombian nationality.

17. According to the order for reference, for the purposes of the reference for a preliminary ruling, the parties to the main proceedings have agreed that, as regards questions of Community law, Maria Fernanda Sarmiento is to be treated as a member of Mr Baumbast's family. She is therefore referred to in the order for reference as one of the two children of that family.

18. In June 1990, the members of the Baumbast family were granted residence permits/documents valid for five years. Between 1990 and 1993, Mr Baumbast pursued an economic activity in the United Kingdom, initially as an employed person and then as head of his own company. However, since that company failed and he was unable to obtain a sufficiently well-paid job in the United Kingdom, he has been employed since 1993 by German companies in China and Lesotho. Although

Mr Baumbast has from time to time sought work in the United Kingdom since that date, his employment situation had not changed at the time of the order for reference.

19. During the material period, Mr and Mrs Baumbast owned a house in the United Kingdom and their daughters went to school there. They did not receive any social benefits and, having comprehensive medical insurance in Germany, they travelled there, when necessary, for medical treatment.

20. In May 1995, Mrs Baumbast applied for indefinite leave to remain in the United Kingdom for herself and for the other members of her family. In January 1996, the Secretary of State refused to renew Mr Baumbast's residence permit and the residence documents of Mrs Baumbast and her children.

21. On 12 January 1998, that refusal was brought before the Immigration Adjudicator (United Kingdom). He found that Mr Baumbast was neither a worker nor a person having a general right of residence under Directive 90/364. As regards the children, the Adjudicator decided that they enjoyed an independent right of residence under Article 12 of Regulation No 1612/68. Moreover, he held that Mrs Baumbast enjoyed a right of residence for a period co-terminous with that during which her children exercised rights under Article 12 of that regulation. According to the Adjudicator, Mrs Baumbast's rights flowed from the obligation on Member States under that provision to encourage all efforts to enable children to attend courses in the host Member State under the best possible conditions.

22. Mr Baumbast appealed to the Immigration Appeal Tribunal against the Adjudicator's decision in his regard. The Secretary of State lodged a cross-appeal before that tribunal against the Adjudicator's decision regarding Mrs Baumbast and her two children.

R

23. R a United States citizen has, as a result of her first marriage to a French national, two children who have dual French and United States nationality. In 1990, she moved to the United Kingdom in her capacity as the spouse of a Community national exercising rights conferred by the EC Treaty and was granted leave to remain in the United Kingdom until October 1995.

24. R and her first husband were divorced in September 1992 but, as no measures were taken at that time by the Secretary of State affecting R's immigration status, she continued to reside in the United Kingdom. The divorce settlement provided that the children were to reside with their mother in England and Wales for a period of at least five years after the date of the divorce or until such other time as agreed by the parties. After the divorce, the children had regular contact with their father, who

still resides and works in the United Kingdom and who shares responsibility with their mother for their upbringing from both an emotional and financial point of view.

25. The file in the main proceedings also shows that, during her residence in the United Kingdom, R purchased a house and established a business as an interior designer in which she has invested substantial sums of money. She married a United Kingdom national in 1997.

26. In October 1995, an application for indefinite leave to remain in the United Kingdom was made under domestic law on behalf of R and her two daughters. On 3 December 1996, the children were granted indefinite leave to remain in the United Kingdom as members of the family of a migrant worker. Mrs R's application was refused, however, on the ground that the Secretary of State was not satisfied that the family situation was so exceptional as to justify the exercise of his discretion. In his view, the children were young enough to adapt to life in the United States if they had to accompany their mother there.

27. One of the issues raised in the action brought before the Adjudicator against the Secretary of State's refusal to grant R indefinite leave to remain was whether that refusal would interfere with her children's Community law rights to be educated and to reside in the United Kingdom and with the right to family life. The Adjudicator dismissed that application by a decision against which R appealed to the Immigration Appeal Tribunal.

The questions referred for preliminary ruling

28. Taking the view that the cases before it depended on the interpretation of Article 18 EC and Regulation No 1612/68, the Immigration Appeal Tribunal decided to stay proceedings and to refer the following questions to the Court for a preliminary ruling:

'The questions in common

Question 1

(a) Are children of a citizen of the European Union who are themselves such citizens and who have installed themselves in primary education during the exercise by their father (or parent) of rights of residence as a worker in another Member State of which he is not a national ('the host State') entitled to reside in the host State in order to undergo general educational courses there, pursuant to Article 12 of Council Regulation No 1612/68?

(b) In so far as the answer to the preceding question may vary in circumstances where:
   (i) their parents are divorced;
   (ii) only one parent is a citizen of the European Union and that parent has ceased to be a worker within the host State;
   (iii) the children are not themselves citizens of the European Union; what criteria are to be applied by the national authorities?

Question 2

Where children have the right to reside in a host State in order to undergo general education[al] courses pursuant to Article 12 of Council Regulation No 1612/68, is the obligation of the host State to 'encourage all efforts to enable such children to attend these courses under the best possible conditions' to be interpreted as entitling their primary carer, whether or not a citizen of the Union, to reside with them in order to facilitate such a right notwithstanding:
(i) their parents are divorced; or
(ii) the father who is a citizen of the European Union ceases to be a worker within the host State?

The questions exclusive to the *Baumbast* case

Question 3

(a) On the facts of Mr Baumbast's case, does he, as an EU citizen, enjoy a directly effective right of residence in another EU Member State pursuant to Article 18 (ex Article 8a) of the Treaty of Rome in circumstances where he no longer enjoys rights of residence as a worker under Article 39 (ex Article 48) of the Treaty of Rome, and does not qualify for residence in the host State under any other provision of EU law?
(b) If so, are his wife and children consequently able to enjoy derivative residence, employment and other rights?
(c) If so, do they do so on the basis of Articles 11 and 12 of Regulation No 1612/68 or some other (and if so, which) provision of EU law?

Question 4

(a) Assuming that the preceding question is answered in the EU citizen's disfavour, do that person's family members retain the derivative rights that they, as such members, originally acquired upon being installed in the UK with a worker?
(b) If so, what are the conditions that apply?'

Admissibility of the first two questions

29. As a preliminary point, it must be noted that, according to the observations submitted to the Court, between the commencement of the main proceedings and the reference for a preliminary ruling both Mrs Baumbast and her two children and R have been granted indefinite leave to remain in the United Kingdom. In the case of R, that leave was granted probably because of her marriage to a United Kingdom national, although no details in that regard have been provided by the national tribunal. Consequently, only Mr Baumbast has been denied indefinite leave to remain.

30. In those circumstances, it is necessary to determine whether the first two questions referred by the national tribunal for a preliminary ruling are admissible.

31. The procedure provided for in Article 234 EC is an instrument of cooperation between the Court of Justice and national courts by means of which the former provides the latter with interpretation of such Community law as is necessary for them to give judgment in cases upon which they are called to adjudicate (see Case C-231/89 *Gmurzynska-Bscher* [1990] ECR I-4003, paragraph 18).

32. It follows that it is for the national courts alone which are seised of the case and are responsible for the judgment to be delivered to determine, in view of the special features of each case, both the need for a preliminary ruling in order to enable them to give their judgment and the relevance of the questions which they put to the Court. Consequently, where the questions put by national courts concern the interpretation of a provision of Community law, the Court is, in principle, bound to give a ruling (see, inter alia, Gmurzynska-Bscher, paragraphs 19 and 20).

33. Thus in the division of functions in the administration of justice between national courts and the Court of Justice provided for by Article 234 EC the Court of Justice gives preliminary rulings without, in principle, having to examine the circumstances in which the national courts have been led to refer questions and propose to apply the provision of Community law which they have asked the Court to interpret (see Gmurzynska-Bscher, paragraph 22).

34. It would be otherwise only in cases where either it appears that the procedure of Article 234 EC has been misused and been resorted to, in fact, in order to elicit a ruling from the Court in the absence of a real dispute or it is obvious that the provisions of Community law submitted for the interpretation of the Court cannot apply, either directly or indirectly, to the circumstances of the case (see, to that effect, *Gmurzynska-Bscher*, paragraph 23, and Case C-130/95 *Giloy* [1997] ECR I-4291, paragraph 22).

35. Admittedly, indefinite leave to remain in the United Kingdom was granted to Mrs Baumbast and her children on 23 June 1998, that is, before even the national tribunal's decision of 28 May 1999, and to R at a later, unspecified date.

36. However, it is apparent from the observations submitted at the hearing that that leave was granted under English law and that the question of the rights conferred under Community law on the persons concerned has not been resolved definitively.

37. Equally, these questions were raised in the context of a real dispute and the national tribunal has provided the Court with a statement of their factual and legal context as well as of the reasons which led it to take the view that an answer to those questions was necessary for it to make its decision.

38. It follows from the foregoing that the first two questions raised by the national tribunal are admissible.

The first question

39. By its first question, the national tribunal seeks essentially to ascertain whether children of a citizen of the European Union who have installed themselves in a Member State during the exercise by their parent of rights of residence as a migrant worker in that Member State are entitled to reside there in order to attend general educational courses there, pursuant to Article 12 of Regulation No 1612/68. Further, it queries whether those rights are affected by the fact that the parents have meanwhile divorced, that only one parent is a citizen of the Union and that parent has ceased to be a migrant worker in the host Member State or that the children are not themselves citizens of the Union.

Observations submitted to the Court

40. Even though they accept that the right of residence and the right to be admitted to the educational system of the host Member State under Articles 10 and 12 of Regulation No 1612/68 are not absolute, R and the Baumbast family submit that the conditions laid down for the enjoyment of the rights under Article 12 of that regulation are satisfied in the main proceedings. In fact, in the R case, there are no grounds for suggesting that the children ceased to be members of the family of their father, who continues to work in the host Member State. In the Baumbast case, the only basis for considering that the children ceased to qualify under Article 12 of that regulation is that their father no longer works in that State. However, in accordance with Joined Cases 389/87 and 390/87 *Echternach and Moritz* [1989] ECR 723, that fact is irrelevant to the continued existence of their rights.

41. The United Kingdom and German Governments also submit that the rights acquired by the child of a migrant worker under Article 12 of Regulation No 1612/68 continue in principle to subsist even where the parents leave the host Member State.

42. The German Government argues, however, that, in accordance with Echternach and Moritz, it is only where education cannot be continued in the Member State of origin that Article 12 of Regulation No 1612/68 grants the child an independent right of residence.

43. As regards, in particular, the R case, the United Kingdom Government claims that R's children enjoy rights to reside in the United Kingdom under Article 12 of Regulation No 1612/68 on the ground that, although R and their father are divorced, he continues to exercise rights as a migrant worker in the United Kingdom.

44. As regards the R case, the Commission submits that, even though the parents are divorced, as long as one of them retains the status of a migrant worker in the host State the children continue to enjoy a right of residence under Article 10 of Regulation No 1612/68 and a right of access to education under Article 12 of that regulation.

45. In respect of the Baumbast case, the Commission submits that, according to Echternach and Moritz, the child of a migrant worker retains the status of member of that worker's family for the purposes of Regulation No 1612/68 where the child's family returns to the Member State of origin and the child remains in the host Member State in order to continue studies which he could not pursue in the Member State of origin.

46. According to the Commission, even though the facts of Echternach and Moritz were particular, in that the child was not able to pursue his studies in the Member State of origin, the Court adopted a broad interpretation of Article 12 of Regulation No 1612/68. The situation of the children of the Baumbast family is not so very far removed from that in Echternach and Moritz and there is thus no prima facie reason to reach a different result. The Commission concludes that if the Court maintains the interpretation adopted in that case, the children of the Baumbast family may continue to reside in the United Kingdom in order to exercise their rights under Article 12 of Regulation No 1612/68.

Findings of the Court

47. In order to give a helpful answer to the first question, a distinction must be drawn between the two situations which form the basis of the national tribunal's question.

48. First of all, it must be recalled that Article 1(1) of Regulation No 1612/68, relating to the status of migrant worker, provides that any national of a Member State, irre-

spective of his place of residence, is to have the right to take up an activity as an employed person, and to pursue such activity, within the territory of another Member State.

49. As regards, first, the Baumbast case, it is apparent from the documents before the Court that this case is different from the R case in that Mr Baumbast, a German national who pursued an activity both as an employed person and as a self-employed person in the United Kingdom for several years and continues to reside there, no longer works in the United Kingdom. Under those circumstances, the national tribunal seeks to ascertain whether his children can continue their education in the United Kingdom under the provisions of Article 12 of Regulation No 1612/68.

50. In that respect, it must be borne in mind that the aim of Regulation No 1612/68, namely freedom of movement for workers, requires, for such freedom to be guaranteed in compliance with the principles of liberty and dignity, the best possible conditions for the integration of the Community worker's family in the society of the host Member State (see Case C-308/89 *Di Leo* [1990] ECR I-4185, paragraph 13).

51. As the Court pointed out in paragraph 21 of Echternach and Moritz, for such integration to come about, a child of a Community worker must have the possibility of going to school and pursuing further education in the host Member State, as is expressly provided in Article 12 of Regulation No 1612/68, in order to be able to complete that education successfully.

52. In circumstances such as those in the Baumbast case, to prevent a child of a citizen of the Union from continuing his education in the host Member State by refusing him permission to remain might dissuade that citizen from exercising the rights to freedom of movement laid down in Article 39 EC and would therefore create an obstacle to the effective exercise of the freedom thus guaranteed by the EC Treaty.

53. Although the Court found in Echternach and Moritz that the child concerned could not, after his father's return to his Member State of origin, continue his studies there because there is no coordination of school diplomas, it is none the less the case that the Court's reasoning sought essentially to ensure, in accordance with the aim of integration of members of the families of migrant workers pursued by Regulation No 1612/68, that a child of one of those workers could go to school and pursue further education in the host Member State, under conditions which do not constitute discrimination, in order to be able to complete that education successfully (see, also, Case 42/87 *Commission* v *Belgium* [1988] ECR 5445, paragraph 10).

54. In fact, to permit children of a citizen of the Union who are in a situation such as that of Mr Baumbast's children to continue their education in the host Member State only where they cannot do so in their Member State of origin would offend not only the letter of Article 12 of Regulation No 1612/68, which provides a right of access

to educational courses for the children of a national of a Member State 'who is or has been employed' in the territory of another Member State, but also its spirit.

55. Consequently, the restrictive interpretation of that provision proposed by the German Government cannot be accepted.

56. As to whether the fact that the children are not themselves citizens of the Union can affect the answer to the first question, suffice it to state that, under Article 10 of Regulation No 1612/68, the descendants of a Community worker who are under the age of 21 or are dependants, irrespective of their nationality, are to be regarded as members of his family and have the right to install themselves with that worker and that, accordingly, they have the right to be admitted to the school system in accordance with Article 12 of that regulation.

57. Furthermore, the right of 'his spouse and their descendants who are under the age of 21 years or are dependants' to install themselves with the migrant worker must be interpreted as meaning that it is granted both to the descendants of that worker and to those of his spouse. To give a restrictive interpretation to that provision to the effect that only the children common to the migrant worker and his spouse have the right to install themselves with them would run counter to the aim of Regulation No 1612/68 noted above.

58. As regards, second, the R case, the children concerned enjoy, as members of the family of a worker who is a national of one Member State and who is employed in the territory of another Member State, a right of residence and a right to pursue their education under Articles 10 and 12 of Regulation No 1612/68.

59. As is apparent from paragraph 50 above, those provisions seek to facilitate the integration of the migrant worker and his family in the host Member State in order to attain the objective of Regulation No 1612/68, namely freedom of movement for workers, in compliance with the principles of liberty and dignity.

60. Even though R and her first husband have meanwhile divorced, it is apparent from the file that he continues to pursue an activity as an employed person in the United Kingdom and therefore enjoys the status of a worker who is a national of one Member State and who is employed in the territory of another Member State for the purposes of Articles 1 and 10 of Regulation No 1612/68.

61. Under those circumstances, it follows clearly from the provisions of Regulation No 1612/68, in particular Articles 10 and 12 thereof, that the children of R's first husband continue to enjoy a right to reside in the host Member State as well as the right to pursue their education there under the same conditions as the nationals of that State.

62. The fact that the children of R's first husband do not live permanently with him does not affect the rights which they derive from Articles 10 and 12 of Regulation No 1612/68. In providing that a member of a migrant worker's family has the right to install himself with the worker, Article 10 of that regulation does not require that the member of the family in question must live permanently with the worker, but, as is clear from Article 10(3), only that the accommodation which the worker has available must be such as may be considered normal for the purpose of accommodating his family (see Case 267/83 *Diatta* [1985] ECR 567, paragraph 18).

63. In the light of the foregoing, the answer to the first question must be that children of a citizen of the European Union who have installed themselves in a Member State during the exercise by their parent of rights of residence as a migrant worker in that Member State are entitled to reside there in order to attend general educational courses there, pursuant to Article 12 of Regulation No 1612/68. The fact that the parents of the children concerned have meanwhile divorced, the fact that only one parent is a citizen of the Union and that parent has ceased to be a migrant worker in the host Member State and the fact that the children are not themselves citizens of the Union are irrelevant in this regard.

The second question

64. By its second question, the national tribunal seeks essentially to ascertain whether, where children have the right to reside in a host Member State in order to attend general educational courses pursuant to Article 12 of Regulation No 1612/68, that provision must be interpreted as entitling the parent who is the primary carer of those children, irrespective of his nationality, to reside with them in order to facilitate the exercise of that right notwithstanding the fact that the parents have meanwhile divorced or that the parent who has the status of citizen of the European Union has ceased to be a migrant worker in the host Member State.

Observations submitted to the Court

65. According to R and the Baumbast family, the provisions of Community law must be interpreted broadly so that the rights granted are effective, particularly where a right as fundamental as the right to family life is concerned. They thus submit that, in the case of minor children who have spent all their life living with their mother and continue to do so, the refusal to afford her a right of residence during the continuation of the children's education is an interference with their rights which impairs the exercise of those rights. They also submit that such a refusal is a disproportionate interference with family life, contrary to Article 8 of the European Convention for the Protection of Human Rights and Fundamental Freedoms ('the European Convention').

66. The United Kingdom and German Governments as well as the Commission propose that the Court answer the second question in the negative. They submit that it is not possible to deduce from Article 12 of Regulation No 1612/68 a right of residence in favour of parents who are nationals of a non-member country. Their rights are determined by the criteria which directly govern the exercise of freedom of movement. Following divorce or termination by the spouse who is a Community national of his activity as a migrant worker in the host Member State, Community law does not confer on the spouse who is a national of a non-member country a right of residence derived from the children's right to be educated.

67. According to the United Kingdom Government, in circumstances where the host Member State is obliged to allow children to reside there in order to attend general educational courses under Article 12 of Regulation No 1612/68, its duty to encourage all efforts to enable such children to attend those courses under the best possible conditions is not to be interpreted as requiring that State to allow the person who is their carer to reside with them. The United Kingdom Government states that if and in so far as it is established that refusal of such a right of residence would unjustifiably interfere with family life as protected by Article 8 of the European Convention, the Home Office may grant exceptional leave to remain to the carer parent in derogation from the Immigration Rules.

Findings of the Court

68. First, Article 12 of Regulation No 1612/68 and the rights which flow from it must be interpreted in the context of the structure and purpose of that regulation. It is apparent from the provisions of the regulation, taken as a whole, that in order to facilitate the movement of members of workers' families the Council took into account, first, the importance for the worker, from a human point of view, of having his entire family with him and, secondly, the importance, from all points of view, of the integration of the worker and his family into the host Member State without any difference in treatment in relation to nationals of that State (see, to that effect, Case 249/86 *Commission* v *Germany* [1989] ECR 1263, paragraph 11).

69. As is clear from the answer to the first question, Article 12 of Regulation No 1612/68 seeks in particular to ensure that children of a Community worker can, even if he has ceased to pursue the activity of an employed person in the host Member State, undertake and, where appropriate, complete their education in that Member State.

70. Second, according to the case-law of the Court, just like the status of migrant worker itself, the rights enjoyed by members of a Community worker's family under Regulation No 1612/68 can, in certain circumstances, continue to exist even after the employment relationship has ended (see, to that effect, Echternach and Moritz, paragraph 21, and Case C-85/96 *Martiínez Sala* [1998] ECR I-2691, paragraph 32).

71. In circumstances such as those of the main proceedings, where the children enjoy, under Article 12 of Regulation No 1612/68, the right to continue their education in the host Member State although the parents who are their carers are at risk of losing their rights of residence as a result, in one case, of a divorce from the migrant worker and, in the other case, of the fact that the parent who pursued the activity of an employed person in the host Member State as a migrant worker has ceased to work there, it is clear that if those parents were refused the right to remain in the host Member State during the period of their children's education that might deprive those children of a right which is granted to them by the Community legislature.

72. Moreover, in accordance with the case-law of the Court, Regulation No 1612/68 must be interpreted in the light of the requirement of respect for family life laid down in Article 8 of the European Convention. That requirement is one of the fundamental rights which, according to settled case-law, are recognised by Community law (see Commission v Germany, cited above, paragraph 10).

73. The right conferred by Article 12 of Regulation No 1612/68 on the child of a migrant worker to pursue, under the best possible conditions, his education in the host Member State necessarily implies that that child has the right to be accompanied by the person who is his primary carer and, accordingly, that that person is able to reside with him in that Member State during his studies. To refuse to grant permission to remain to a parent who is the primary carer of the child exercising his right to pursue his studies in the host Member State infringes that right.

74. As to the Commission's argument to the effect that a right of residence cannot be derived from Article 12 of Regulation No 1612/68 in favour of a person who is not the child of a migrant worker, on the ground that possession of that status is a sine qua non of any right under that provision, having regard to its context and the objectives pursued by Regulation No 1612/68 and in particular Article 12 thereof, that provision cannot be interpreted restrictively (see, to that effect, Diatta, paragraph 17) and must not, under any circumstances, be rendered ineffective.

75. In the light of the foregoing, the answer to the second question must be that where children have the right to reside in a host Member State in order to attend general educational courses pursuant to Article 12 of Regulation No 1612/68, that provision must be interpreted as entitling the parent who is the primary carer of those children, irrespective of his nationality, to reside with them in order to facilitate the exercise of that right notwithstanding the fact that the parents have meanwhile divorced or that the parent who has the status of citizen of the European Union has ceased to be a migrant worker in the host Member State.

The third question

76. By the first part of its third question, the national tribunal seeks essentially to ascertain whether a citizen of the European Union who no longer enjoys a right of residence as a migrant worker in the host Member State can, as a citizen of the European Union, enjoy there a right of residence by direct application of Article 18(1) EC.

Observations submitted to the Court

77. According to Mr Baumbast, the fact that the right to reside freely within the territory of the Member States under Article 18 EC is subject to restrictions and is laid down in the EC Treaty does not deprive the right of direct effect. That provision should be interpreted to mean that Mr Baumbast continues to exercise a right of residence in the United Kingdom while he is working outside the European Union. Such an application of Article 18 EC would enable the right of freedom of movement laid down in the EC Treaty to be exercised simply on proof of nationality, but is consistent with pre-existing legislation on the subject.

78. The United Kingdom and German Governments argue that a right of residence cannot be derived directly from Article 18(1) EC. The limitations and conditions referred to in that paragraph show that it is not intended to be a free-standing provision.

79. Whilst underlining the political and legal importance of Article 18 EC, the Commission submits that the very wording of that provision, and in particular its first paragraph, shows its limitations. As Community law stands at present, the right to move and reside established by that article is conditioned by the pre-existing rules, both primary and secondary, which define the categories of persons eligible for it. Those rights are still linked either to an economic activity or to sufficient resources. Since the point of departure for the third question is that Mr Baumbast has no other Community law foundation for his right to reside in the United Kingdom, the Commission concludes that Article 18 EC cannot, as the law stands at present and in such circumstances, be of any use to him.

Findings of the Court

80. According to settled case-law, the right of nationals of one Member State to enter the territory of another Member State and to reside there constitutes a right conferred directly by the EC Treaty or, depending on the case, by the provisions adopted to implement it (see, inter alia, Case 48/75 *Royer* [1976] ECR 497, paragraph 31).

81. Although, before the Treaty on European Union entered into force, the Court had held that that right of residence, conferred directly by the EC Treaty, was subject to

the condition that the person concerned was carrying on an economic activity within the meaning of Articles 48, 52 or 59 of the EC Treaty (now, after amendment, Articles 39 EC, 43 EC and 49 EC) (see Case C-363/89 *Roux* [1991] ECR I-273, paragraph 9), it is none the less the case that, since then, Union citizenship has been introduced into the EC Treaty and Article 18(1) EC has conferred a right, for every citizen, to move and reside freely within the territory of the Member States.

82. Under Article 17(1) EC, every person holding the nationality of a Member State is to be a citizen of the Union. Union citizenship is destined to be the fundamental status of nationals of the Member States (see, to that effect, Case C-184/99 *Grzelczyk* [2001] ECR I-6193, paragraph 31).

83. Moreover, the Treaty on European Union does not require that citizens of the Union pursue a professional or trade activity, whether as an employed or self-employed person, in order to enjoy the rights provided in Part Two of the EC Treaty, on citizenship of the Union. Furthermore, there is nothing in the text of that Treaty to permit the conclusion that citizens of the Union who have established themselves in another Member State in order to carry on an activity as an employed person there are deprived, where that activity comes to an end, of the rights which are conferred on them by the EC Treaty by virtue of that citizenship.

84. As regards, in particular, the right to reside within the territory of the Member States under Article 18(1) EC, that right is conferred directly on every citizen of the Union by a clear and precise provision of the EC Treaty. Purely as a national of a Member State, and consequently a citizen of the Union, Mr Baumbast therefore has the right to rely on Article 18(1) EC.

85. Admittedly, that right for citizens of the Union to reside within the territory of another Member State is conferred subject to the limitations and conditions laid down by the EC Treaty and by the measures adopted to give it effect.

86. However, the application of the limitations and conditions acknowledged in Article 18(1) EC in respect of the exercise of that right of residence is subject to judicial review. Consequently, any limitations and conditions imposed on that right do not prevent the provisions of Article 18(1) EC from conferring on individuals rights which are enforceable by them and which the national courts must protect (see, to that effect, Case 41/74 *Van Duyn* [1974] ECR 1337, paragraph 7).

87. As regards the limitations and conditions resulting from the provisions of secondary legislation, Article 1(1) of Directive 90/364 provides that Member States can require of the nationals of a Member State who wish to enjoy the right to reside within their territory that they themselves and the members of their families be covered by sickness insurance in respect of all risks in the host Member State and have suf-

ficient resources to avoid becoming a burden on the social assistance system of the host Member State during their period of residence.

88. As to the application of those conditions for the purposes of the Baumbast case, it is clear from the file that Mr Baumbast pursues an activity as an employed person in non-member countries for German companies and that neither he nor his family has used the social assistance system in the host Member State. In those circumstances, it has not been denied that Mr Baumbast satisfies the condition relating to sufficient resources imposed by Directive 90/364.

89. As to the condition relating to sickness insurance, the file shows that both Mr Baumbast and the members of his family are covered by comprehensive sickness insurance in Germany. The Adjudicator seems to have found that that sickness insurance could not cover emergency treatment given in the United Kingdom. It is for the national tribunal to determine whether that finding is correct in the light of Regulation (EEC) No 1408/71 of the Council of 14 June 1971 on the application of social security schemes to employed persons and their families moving within the Community (OJ, English Special Edition 1971 (II), p. 416). Particular reference should be made to Article 19(1)(a) of that regulation which ensures, at the expense of the competent Member State, the right for an employed or self-employed person residing in the territory of another Member State other than the competent State whose condition requires treatment in the territory of the Member State of residence to receive sickness benefits in kind provided by the institution of the latter State.

90. In any event, the limitations and conditions which are referred to in Article 18 EC and laid down by Directive 90/364 are based on the idea that the exercise of the right of residence of citizens of the Union can be subordinated to the legitimate interests of the Member States. In that regard, according to the fourth recital in the preamble to Directive 90/364 beneficiaries of the right of residence must not become an 'unreasonable' burden on the public finances of the host Member State.

91. However, those limitations and conditions must be applied in compliance with the limits imposed by Community law and in accordance with the general principles of that law, in particular the principle of proportionality. That means that national measures adopted on that subject must be necessary and appropriate to attain the objective pursued (see, to that effect, Joined Cases C-259/91, C-331/91 and C-332/91 Alluè and Others [1993] ECR I-4309, paragraph 15).

92. In respect of the application of the principle of proportionality to the facts of the Baumbast case, it must be recalled, first, that it has not been denied that Mr Baumbast has sufficient resources within the meaning of Directive 90/364; second, that he worked and therefore lawfully resided in the host Member State for several years, initially as an employed person and subsequently as a self-employed person; third, that during that period his family also resided in the host Member State and

remained there even after his activities as an employed and self-employed person in that State came to an end; fourth, that neither Mr Baumbast nor the members of his family have become burdens on the public finances of the host Member State and, fifth, that both Mr Baumbast and his family have comprehensive sickness insurance in another Member State of the Union.

93. Under those circumstances, to refuse to allow Mr Baumbast to exercise the right of residence which is conferred on him by Article 18(1) EC by virtue of the application of the provisions of Directive 90/364 on the ground that his sickness insurance does not cover the emergency treatment given in the host Member State would amount to a disproportionate interference with the exercise of that right.

94. The answer to the first part of the third question must therefore be that a citizen of the European Union who no longer enjoys a right of residence as a migrant worker in the host Member State can, as a citizen of the Union, enjoy there a right of residence by direct application of Article 18(1) EC. The exercise of that right is subject to the limitations and conditions referred to in that provision, but the competent authorities and, where necessary, the national courts must ensure that those limitations and conditions are applied in compliance with the general principles of Community law and, in particular, the principle of proportionality.

95. By the second and third parts of the third question, the national tribunal seeks to ascertain whether, if Mr Baumbast enjoys a right of residence on the basis of Article 18(1) EC, the members of his family enjoy rights of residence on the same basis. In the light of the answers given to the first two questions, it is not necessary to answer those parts of the third question.

96. In the light of the answer given to the first part of the third question, nor is it necessary to answer the fourth question.

Costs

[Para. 97 omitted]

On those grounds,

THE COURT,

in answer to the questions referred to it by the Immigration Appeal Tribunal by order of 28 May 1999, hereby rules:

1. **Children of a citizen of the European Union who have installed themselves in a Member State during the exercise by their parent of rights of residence as a migrant worker in that Member State are entitled to reside**

there in order to attend general educational courses there, pursuant to Article 12 of Regulation (EEC) No 1612/68 of the Council of 15 October 1968 on freedom of movement for workers within the Community. The fact that the parents of the children concerned have meanwhile divorced, the fact that only one parent is a citizen of the Union and that parent has ceased to be a migrant worker in the host Member State and the fact that the children are not themselves citizens of the Union are irrelevant in this regard.

2. **Where children have the right to reside in a host Member State in order to attend general educational courses pursuant to Article 12 of Regulation No 1612/68, that provision must be interpreted as entitling the parent who is the primary carer of those children, irrespective of his nationality, to reside with them in order to facilitate the exercise of that right notwithstanding the fact that the parents have meanwhile divorced or that the parent who has the status of citizen of the European Union has ceased to be a migrant worker in the host Member State.**

3. **A citizen of the European Union who no longer enjoys a right of residence as a migrant worker in the host Member State can, as a citizen of the Union, enjoy there a right of residence by direct application of Article 18(1) EC. The exercise of that right is subject to the limitations and conditions referred to in that provision, but the competent authorities and, where necessary, the national courts must ensure that those limitations and conditions are applied in compliance with the general principles of Community law and, in particular, the principle of proportionality.**

Comments and questions

Case C-413/99 *Baumbast and R* v *The Home Secretary* [2002] ECR I-7091, in which judgment was given by the plenary Court of the CJEU, is an important case in which the CJEU further developed the legal effect of Article 21 TFEU (formerly Article 18 TEC) on Union citizenship. In this judgment the CJEU held, for the first time, that Article 21 TFEU has *direct effect*. The CJEU stated that Article 21(1) TFEU introduced a right for every citizen of the Union to move and reside freely within the territory of the Member States. This differs from the situation prior to the Maastricht Treaty coming into force in 1993, where the right of residence, conferred directly by the then applicable EC Treaty, was subject to the condition that the person concerned exercised a right under what are now Articles 45, 49 or 56 TFEU. In other words, the CJEU established that it is not a requirement for a Union citizen to be an employee or to carry on business as a self-employed person in order to acquire the rights contained in Part II of the TFEU, on citizenship of the EU; cf. paragraph 81 of the judgment. However, the CJEU refrained from drawing any more general conclusions from the fact that the right to move freely and take up residence under Article 21 TFEU has direct effect.

Having established that Article 21 TFEU has direct effect, the CJEU considered whether Baumbast, who was a German national, satisfied the conditions of the right of residence laid down in the earlier Directive 90/364 on the right of residence for citizens who do not qualify for a right of residence under the other provisions of Union law (sometimes known as the 'Playboy Directive') now replaced by Directive 2004/38 (the 'Free Movement Directive'). It was established that Baumbast, who lived in the United Kingdom with his family, was employed in third countries by German companies, and that neither he nor others of his family made use of the social security system in the United Kingdom. The CJEU therefore found that Baumbast fulfilled the requirement of the then Directive 90/364 of having had sufficient resources.

As for the second condition of Directive 90/364, that a citizen should be covered by sickness insurance in the host Member State, the CJEU found that Baumbast and his family were covered by such full health insurance in Germany. While it was found that the sickness insurance did not cover emergency treatment given in the United Kingdom, the CJEU nevertheless found that this, by itself, could not justify the United Kingdom refusing Baumbast the right of residence as granted in Article 21(1) TFEU. Which basic principle of Union law did the CJEU use to arrive at its decision (see paragraphs 90-93 of the judgment)? Do you agree with the decision of the CJEU?

The CJEU thus applied Article 21(1) TFEU using the principle of proportionality. The limitations and conditions referred to in Article 21(1) TFEU shall be applied in accordance with the general principles of Union law, in particular the principle of proportionality. National measures in this area must be necessary and appropriate to attain the objective pursued; cf. paragraph 91 of the judgment.

According to Article 21(1) TFEU, all Union citizens have a right to move freely and to reside in other Member States. There cannot be a requirement for a person to be employed in order to acquire a right of residence in the host Member State. Article 21 TFEU has direct effect. However, the right of residence is not unconditional, since the limitations and conditions laid down in the TFEU, and measures adopted to give it effect, will apply. This is the basis on which, in both Case C-184/99 *Grzelczyk* [2001] ECR I-6193, and in the *Baumbast* case, having first established that the circumstances were covered by the provisions on Union citizenship in Article 21 TFEU, the CJEU went on to consider which conditions applied to Union citizens, other than the right of residence. In the *Grzelczyk* case the right was exercised by a student on the basis of the earlier Directive 93/96 on the right of residence for students. In the *Baumbast* case the right was exercised on the basis of Directive 90/364 on the right of residence. However, the limitations and conditions laid down in these directives should be applied in accordance with the general principles of Union law, and in particular the principle of proportionality. This means that if a Member State applies the conditions too inflexibly, this would normally contravene the principle of proportionality.

When deciding whether a Union citizen has a right, under Union law, to reside in another Member State, it is relevant whether the period of residence is longer or shorter than three months. The Free Movement Directive (Directive 2004/38) distinguishes between residences of less than or more than three months. Thus, under Article 6 of the Free Movement Directive, Union citizens have a right to reside in the territory of another Member State for a period of up to three months without any conditions or formalities other than the requirement to hold a valid identity card or passport. During this three month period the host Member State is not obliged to give social assistance to those who are not in active employment, i.e. those who are not employed or self-employed and their family members; see Article 24(2) of the Directive. Under the Directive, cash payments are regarded as social assistance. At the end of the three month period a non-economically active Union citizen only has a right to stay in another Member States only subject to the conditions set out in Article 7 of the Directive, in particular they must 'have sufficient resources'. If a Union citizen has a right to take up residence, under Article 24(1) of the Directive they must be treated equally with the Member State's own citizens with regard to the payment of social assistance such as cash payments. After five years residence in the host Member State, a Union citizen obtains an unlimited right of residence according to the Directive. Thus, after five years the host Member State cannot lay down any conditions relating to self-maintenance or suchlike.

In Case C-148/02 *Carlos Garcia Avello* [2003] ECR I-11613, the Belgian Supreme Administrative Court referred a case to the CJEU for preliminary rulings on the interpretation of Articles 20 and 21 TFEU. The question was whether the Belgian authorities had a duty to allow a change of name under Spanish law when the person in question had dual Spanish and Belgian nationality and was resident in Belgium. Garcia Avello and his wife Weber, with parental responsibility over their two children who were minors, had requested the Belgian authorities to change their children's surnames from 'Garcia Avello' to 'Garcia Weber' in accordance with Spanish practice. Both children had dual nationality, as they were born in Belgium of Spanish parents working in Belgium. The Belgian authorities rejected the application, because children in Belgium carry their father's surname. Garcia Avello argued that this constituted different treatment, since persons with dual nationality were treated in the same way as people with purely Belgian nationality. In his Opinion, Advocate General Jacobs proposed that the CJEU should respond to the Belgian court that the refusal to recognise the change of name is contrary to Articles 18 and 20 TFEU read together. It was Advocate General Jacobs's view that the different treatment could not be justified. In its decision, the CJEU followed the proposal of the Advocate General. Do you agree that it is possible to derive from Articles 20 and 21 TFEU a right to have a change of name recognised which is lawful under Spanish law? In your view, does the case concern purely internal Belgian circumstances? Consider the issue both in relation to the parents and in relation to the children.

Subsequently, in its decision in Case C-353/06 *Grunkin and Paul* [2008] ECR I-7639, the CJEU had to decide on a different question, concerning names. The case concerned the recognition of the surname of a child of German nationality who had been born in and was resident in Denmark and who, at birth, had been registered with a double-barrelled name, consisting of the father's and mother's names (Grunkin-Paul). The child's parents applied to have this surname registered in the family register in Germany, but this was refused on the grounds that the surnames of German nationals are regulated by German law, according to which a child may not have a double-barrelled surname. The CJEU ruled that, even though the rules on a person's surname falls within the competence of the Member States, the Member States must nevertheless comply with Union law when exercising that competence. The CJEU also stated that a Union citizen who is required to bear a different name in the Member State of which he is a national than the name he has already been given and which is registered in the Member State where he was born and is resident can be an obstacle to the Union citizen's freedom of movement. A situation in which a person uses different surnames in various German and Danish documents can cause serious problems for the person concerned, both as a private person and in their work. Since the restrictive German provisions were not sufficiently justified, the CJEU concluded that the Union citizens' right to move freely and take up residence in the territories of other Member States should restrict the German law in question. The question of names can be an emotional one, and there are considerable differences in the laws of the different Member States on names and the determination of surnames, including the extent of freedom of choice in this area. In particular, surnames that combine the surnames of both parents are prohibited in some Member States but permitted in others, while in yet other Member States this combining of names is traditional. The present case was therefore a matter of great importance for a number of Member States, and this is reflected in the fact that eight Member States submitted observations on it. From the point of view of the Member States, the decision in the *Grunkin and Paul* case could be regarded as yet another irritating example of the CJEU intervening in sensitive matters of national law, where it ought to tread with care. On the other hand, seen from the point of view of the citizen, the decision is a good example of where EU law can be used as a battering ram to cut down bothersome and outdated national rules.

In the *Baumbast* case, the CJEU held that a child of a Union citizen had a right to reside in another Member State in order to complete his or her school attendance, as long as the child in question had taken up residence in the Member State at a time when the Union citizen exercised his or her right of residence as a worker in that Member State; cf. Article 12 of the then applicable Regulation No 1612/68 on freedom of movement for workers within the Union (now Article 10 of Regulation 492/2011). This is a right of the child, regardless of whether the parents may have been divorced in the meantime, even if only one of the parents is a Union citizen, and even if the parent who is a Union citizen is no longer a worker in the Member State. The right applies even if the child is not a Union citizen. Further, the CJEU held that where, under Article 12 of Regulation 1612/68, a child has a right of residence in order to attend school, it follows that the parent who is responsible for the child's care has a right to reside in the same Member State. This also applies if the parent in question is not a Union citizen. Any other conclusion would infringe the rights of the child given in Article 12 of Regulation 1612/68. In other words, situations can arise in which a person from a third country has right of residence at second remove, where it is based on his or her third country child's right of residence which in turn is based on the other parent's former right of residence in their capacity as a Union citizen who has exercised the right to be a migrant worker. Do you agree that the right of residence should be stretched as far as the CJEU stretches it in the *Baumbast* case?

Does it follow from the *Baumbast* decision that two third country citizens, who had had their applications for asylum rejected, but who had two children born in Belgium while their asylum applications were being processed by the Belgian aliens authority, the children receiving Belgian nationality under the Belgian nationality law then in force, can derive a right of residence in Belgium as parents of the children, as long as the children are minors and Union citizens? Does the case concern purely internal matters? See Case C-34/09 *Zambrano* [2011] ECR I-1177 and Case C-86/12 *Alokpa*, judgment of 10 October 2013, both printed below.

JUDGMENT OF THE COURT (Grand Chamber)
18 November 2008

Jacqueline Förster v Hoofddirectie van de Informatie Beheer Groep.
(Reference for a preliminary ruling
from the Centrale Raad van Beroep – Netherlands)

'Freedom of movement for persons – Student who is a national of one Member State and goes to another Member State to follow a training course – Student maintenance grant – Citizenship of the Union – Article 12 EC – Legal certainty'

Case C-158/07

Judgment

1. This reference for a preliminary ruling concerns the interpretation of Article 12 EC, Article 18 EC, Article 7 of Regulation (EEC) No 1251/70 of the Commission of 29 June 1970 on the right of workers to remain in the territory of a Member State after having been employed in that State (OJ, English Special Edition 1970 (II), p. 402), and Article 3 of Council Directive 93/96/EEC of 29 October 1993 on the right of residence for students (OJ 1993 L 317, p. 59).

2. The reference was made in the course of proceedings between Ms Förster and the Hoofddirectie van de Informatie Beheer Groep (the administrative body charged with the enforcement of Netherlands legislation relating to the financing of studies; 'the IB-Groep') concerning the partial annulment of a maintenance grant which Ms Förster had received under the Law of 2000 on the financing of studies (Wet studiefinanciering 2000, 'the WSF 2000').

Legal context

Community legislation

3. Article 7(2) of Regulation (EEC) No 1612/68 of the Council of 15 October 1968 on freedom of movement for workers within the Community (OJ, English Special Edition 1968 (II), p. 475), as amended by Council Regulation (EEC) No 2434/92 of 27 July 1992 (OJ 1992 L 245, p. 1), ('Regulation No 1612/68') provides that a worker who is a national of a Member State is to enjoy in the territory of another Member State 'the same social and tax advantages as national workers'.

4. Article 2 of Regulation No 1251/70 provides, inter alia:

'1. The following shall have the right to remain permanently in the territory of a Member State:
   (a) a worker who, at the time of termination of his activity, has reached the age laid down by the law of that Member State for entitlement to an old-age pension and who has been employed in that State for at least the last twelve months and has resided there continuously for more than three years;
   (b) a worker who, having resided continuously in the territory of that State for more than two years, ceases to work there as an employed person as a result of permanent incapacity to work. ...
   (c) a worker who, after three years' continuous employment and residence in the territory of that State, works as an employed person in the territory of another Member State, while retaining his residence in the territory of the first State, to which he returns, as a rule, each day or at least once a week.

...'

5. Pursuant to Article 7 of Regulation No 1251/70:
'The right to equality of treatment, established by Council Regulation (EEC) No 1612/68, shall apply also to persons coming under the provisions of this Regulation.'

6. Article 1 of Directive 93/96 provides:
'In order to lay down conditions to facilitate the exercise of the right of residence and with a view to guaranteeing access to vocational training in a non-discriminatory manner for a national of a Member State who has been accepted to attend a vocational training course in another Member State, the Member States shall recognise the right of residence for any student who is a national of a Member State and who does not enjoy that right under other provisions of Community law, and for the student's spouse and their dependent children, where the student assures the relevant national authority, by means of a declaration or by such alternative means as the student may choose that are at least equivalent, that he has sufficient resources to avoid becoming a burden on the social assistance system of the host Member State during their period of residence, provided that the student is enrolled in a recognised educational establishment for the principal purpose of following a vocational training course there and that he is covered by sickness insurance in respect of all risks in the host Member State.'

7. Article 3 of Directive 93/96 states:
'This Directive shall not establish any entitlement to the payment of maintenance grants by the host Member State on the part of students benefiting from the right of residence.'

8. Directive 93/96 was repealed, with effect from 30 April 2006, by Directive 2004/38/EC of the European Parliament and of the Council of 29 April 2004 (OJ 2004 L 158, p. 77, and corrigendum OJ 2004 L 229, p. 35), which should, pursuant to Article 40, have been transposed by the Member States before 30 April 2006.

National legislation

9. From 1 September 2000 to 21 November 2003, Article 2.2 of the WSF 2000 was worded as follows:

   '1. Study finance may be granted to:
   (a) students who possess Netherlands nationality,
   (b) students who do not possess Netherlands nationality but are resident in the Netherlands and are treated as Netherlands nationals in respect of the financing of studies by virtue of a treaty or a decision of an organisation of public international law, or
   (c) students who do not have Netherlands nationality but are resident in the Netherlands and belong to a group of persons who, by administrative order, are treated as Netherlands nationals in respect of the financing of studies.'

10. With effect from 21 November 2003 a second paragraph was added to Article 2.2 of the WSF 2000. It reads as follows:
    'In derogation from Article 2.2(1)(b), the requirement that a student be resident in the Netherlands shall not apply to a student on whom that requirement may not be imposed because of a Treaty or a decision of an organisation of public international law. By or pursuant to an administrative order, rules may be laid down in connection with the satisfactory implementation of this paragraph.'

11. On 4 March 2005, the IB-Groep adopted the Policy rule on the monitoring of migrant workers (Beleidsregel controlebeleid migrerend werknemerschap, AG/OCW/MT 05.11). That Policy rule entered into force on 23 March 2005 and concerns the monitoring of periods for which maintenance grants have been awarded from the 2003 calendar year. It provides that any student who has worked for an average of 32 hours or more per month in the period subject to monitoring automatically enjoys the status of Community worker. If a student does not satisfy the 32-hour criterion, the IB-Groep undertakes a more detailed investigation into the specific circumstances of that student.

12. Following the judgment in Case C-209/03 *Bidar* [2005] ECR I-2119, the IB-Groep adopted on 9 May 2005 the Policy rule on the adaptation of applications for study finance for students from the European Union, European Economic Area and Switzerland (Beleidsregel aanpassing aanvraag studiefinanciering voor studenten uit EU, EER en Zwitserland, 'the Policy rule of 9 May 2005'), which was published on 18 May 2005.

13. Article 2(1) of that Policy rule provides:

    '1. A student who is a national of a Member State of the European Union ... may, on application, be eligible for study finance pursuant to the WSF 2000 ... if, prior to the application, he has been lawfully resident in the Netherlands for an uninterrupted period of at least five years. The other provisions of the WSF 2000 ... shall apply without qualification.'

14. Article 5 of the Policy rule of 9 May 2005 is worded as follows:
'This Policy rule will enter into force on its publication with retroactive effect from 15 March 2005.'

The dispute in the main proceedings and the questions referred for a preliminary ruling

15. On 5 March 2000, Ms Förster, a German national aged 20, settled in the Netherlands, where she enrolled for training as a primary school teacher and, from 1 September 2001, for a course in educational theory leading to a bachelor's degree at the Hogeschool van Amsterdam (the College of Amsterdam).

16. During her studies, Ms Förster had various kinds of paid employment.

17. From October 2002 until June 2003, Ms Förster completed a paid work placement in a Dutch special school providing secondary education to pupils with behavioural and/or psychiatric problems.

18. After that placement, Ms Förster did not undertake any further employment.

19. Having passed the final examination for the bachelor's degree in educational theory in the middle of 2004, Ms Förster accepted a post as a social worker in an institution for people with psychiatric problems on 15 June 2004.

20. From September 2000, the IB-Groep granted Ms Förster a maintenance grant. That grant was periodically renewed by the IB-Groep. It took the view that Ms Förster was to be regarded as a 'worker' within the meaning of Article 39 EC and, consequently, should be treated in the same way as a student of Netherlands nationality as regards maintenance grants, under Article 7(2) of Regulation No 1612/68.

21. Following a check, the IB-Groep ascertained that between July 2003 and December 2003 Ms Förster had not been gainfully employed. It therefore held, by decision of 3 March 2005, that she could no longer be regarded as a worker. As a result, the decision concerning the maintenance grant paid in respect of the period from July to December 2003 was annulled and Ms Förster was requested to repay the excess sums.

22. By judgment of 12 September 2005, the action brought by Ms Förster before the Rechtbank Alkmaar (Alkmaar District Court) was held to be unfounded on two grounds. First, that court held that, since Ms Förster had not had any real and genu-

ine employment in the second half of 2003, she could no longer be regarded as a Community worker during that period. Second, that court held that Ms Förster could not claim entitlement to a maintenance grant pursuant to *Bidar* because, before her degree in educational theory, she had not been in any way integrated into Dutch society.

23. Ms Förster appealed against that judgment before the Centrale Raad van Beroep (Higher Social Security Court), claiming primarily that, during the period at issue, she was already sufficiently integrated into Dutch society to be able to claim a maintenance grant for the second half of 2003 under Community law. In the alternative, Ms Förster submitted that she should be regarded as a Community worker for the whole of 2003.

24. Accordingly, the Centrale Raad van Beroep decided to stay the proceedings and to refer the following questions to the Court of Justice for a preliminary ruling:

‘1. Does Article 7 of Regulation (EEC) No 1251/70 also apply to students who came to the Netherlands principally to study and initially worked as employed persons on a limited scale while continuing to study but have meanwhile ceased to work?

2. Does Directive 93/96/EEC preclude students as referred to in the first question from successfully relying on Article 12 EC to claim [a maintenance grant]?

3. (a) Does the rule that citizens of the Union who are not economically active can rely on Article 12 EC only if they have resided lawfully in the host Member State for a certain period or are in possession of a residence permit also apply to assistance to cover the maintenance costs of students?
(b) If so, is it permissible to impose during that period a residence duration requirement only on nationals of Member States other than the host Member State?
(c) If so, is the application of a five-year residence duration requirement consistent with Article 12 EC?
(d) If not, what residence duration may be required?

4. Should a shorter period of lawful residence be required in individual cases if factors other than the duration of residence indicate a substantial degree of integration into the society of the host Member State?

5. If, as is evident from a judgment of the Court of Justice with retroactive effect, persons are able to derive from Article 12 EC more rights than was previously assumed, may justified requirements connected therewith be imposed in respect of periods in the past if those requirements were published shortly after the publication of the judgment?’

On the questions referred for a preliminary ruling

The first question

25. By that question, the referring court is essentially enquiring whether a student in the situation of the applicant in the main proceedings may rely on Article 7 of Regulation No 1251/70 in order to obtain a maintenance grant.

26. Regulation No 1251/70 entitles a worker who has ceased his or her employment activity to remain permanently in the territory of a Member State after having worked there as an employed person and to continue to be entitled to equality of treatment with nationals, as laid down in Regulation No 1612/68. Those rights are extended to the members of the worker's family who reside with him or her in the territory of that Member State.

27. The conditions of entitlement to the worker's right to remain in the host Member State are set out exhaustively in Article 2 of Regulation No 1251/70 (see Case C-257/00 *Givane and Others* [2003] ECR I-345, paragraph 29).

28. In addition to complying with the conditions linked to the duration of employment and residence, a worker who has been employed in a host Member State has the right to remain there in three cases. First, where that worker, when he or she terminates his or her activity, has reached the age laid down in that Member State to claim an old-age pension. Second, where the termination of the employment is due to a permanent incapacity to work. Third, where that worker is employed in another Member State, while retaining his or her residence in the territory of the first State, to which he or she returns, as a rule, each day or at least once a week.

29. As the order for reference shows, the applicant's situation does not fall within any of the cases set out in Article 2 of Regulation No 1251/70.

30. It must be added that Ms Förster ceased all employment during the period at issue in order to pursue her studies, without however having abandoned her plan to continue her career in the Netherlands, where she maintained her residence.

31. In those circumstances, Ms Förster cannot be regarded as a '[national] of a Member State who [has] worked as [an employed person] in the territory of another Member State' within the meaning of Article 1 of Regulation No 1251/70.

32. Regulation No 1251/70 is thus not applicable in the present case.

33. Therefore, the answer to the first question must be that a student in the situation of the applicant in the main proceedings cannot rely on Article 7 of Regulation No 1251/70 in order to obtain a maintenance grant.

The second to fourth questions

34. By these questions, which should be examined together, the referring court is essentially enquiring whether, and in what conditions, a student who is a national of a Member State and travels to another Member State in order to study there can rely on the first paragraph of Article 12 EC in order to obtain a maintenance grant. The referring court also asks whether the application to nationals of other Member States of a prior residence requirement of five years may be regarded as compatible with the first paragraph of Article 12 and, if so, if it is necessary, in individual cases, to take into account other criteria pointing to a substantial degree of integration into the society of the host Member State.

35. The first paragraph of Article 12 EC prohibits, within the scope of application of the EC Treaty and without prejudice to any special provisions contained therein, any discrimination on grounds of nationality.

36. It is settled case-law that a citizen of the European Union lawfully resident in the territory of the host Member State can rely on Article 12 EC in all situations which fall within the scope *ratione materiae* of Community law (Case C-85/96 *Martínez Sala* [1998] ECR I-2691, paragraph 63, and *Bidar*, paragraph 32).

37. Those situations include those involving the exercise of the fundamental freedoms guaranteed by the Treaty and those involving the exercise of the right to move and reside within the territory of the Member States conferred by Article 18 EC (see Case C-148/02 *Garcia Avello* [2003] ECR I-11613, paragraph 24, and Case C-403/03 *Schempp* [2005] ECR I-6421, paragraph 18).

38. In this connection, the Court has already held that a national of a Member State who goes to another Member State and pursues secondary education there exercises the freedom to move guaranteed by Article 18 EC (see Case C-224/98 *D'Hoop* [2002] ECR I-6191, paragraphs 29 to 34, and *Bidar*, paragraph 35).

39. With regard to social assistance benefits, the Court has held that a citizen of the Union who is not economically active may rely on the first paragraph of Article 12 EC where he or she has been lawfully resident in the host Member State for a certain time (*Bidar*, paragraph 37).

40. A student who travels to another Member State to start or pursue education can benefit from a right of residence on the basis of Article 18 EC and Directive 93/96 when he or she fulfils the conditions set out in Article 1 of that directive as regards having sufficient resources and sickness insurance and being enrolled in a recognised educational establishment for the principal purpose of following a vocational training course.

41. The situation of a student who is lawfully resident in another Member State thereby falls within the scope of application of the Treaty within the meaning of the first paragraph of Article 12 EC for the purposes of obtaining a maintenance grant (see *Bidar*, paragraph 42).

42. Admittedly, in accordance with Article 3 of Directive 93/96, that does not establish any entitlement to the payment of maintenance grants by the host Member State on the part of students benefiting from the right of residence.

43. However, that provision does not preclude a national of a Member State who, by virtue of Article 18 EC and the provisions adopted to implement that article, is lawfully resident in the territory of another Member State where he or she intends to start or pursue education from relying during that residence on the fundamental principle of equal treatment enshrined in the first paragraph of Article 12 EC (see, to that effect, *Bidar*, paragraph 46).

44. For that purpose, the fact that Ms Förster came to the Netherlands principally in order to study there is irrelevant.

45. Moreover, pursuant to the Policy rule of 9 May 2005, a student who is a national of a Member State of the European Union may be eligible for a maintenance grant if, prior to the application, he or she has been lawfully resident in the Netherlands for an uninterrupted period of at least five years. Since that requirement concerning the duration of residence is not applicable to students of Netherlands nationality, the issue is raised of what restrictions may be imposed on the right of students who are nationals of other Member States to a maintenance grant without the different treatment of those students in comparison to national students which may result being considered discriminatory and, consequently, prohibited under the first paragraph of Article 12 EC.

46. That issue was examined by the Court in *Bidar*.

47. Unlike the present case, the *Bidar* case concerned national legislation which, in addition to imposing a residence requirement, required students from other Member States claiming assistance to cover their maintenance expenses to be established in the host Member State. In so far as the legislation at issue in the main proceedings in that case made it impossible for a national of another Member State to acquire, as a student, the status of established person, that legislation placed such nationals, whatever their actual degree of integration into the society of the host Member State, in a position in which they could not satisfy that condition, and consequently could not enjoy the right to assistance to cover their maintenance costs.

48. In *Bidar*, the Court observed that, although the Member States must, in the organisation and application of their social assistance systems, show a certain degree of

financial solidarity with nationals of other Member States, it is permissible for a Member State to ensure that the grant of assistance to cover the maintenance costs of students from other Member States does not become an unreasonable burden which could have consequences for the overall level of assistance which may be granted by that State (see *Bidar*, paragraph 56).

49. The Court also pointed out that it is legitimate for a Member State to grant assistance covering maintenance costs only to students who have demonstrated a certain degree of integration into the society of that State (*Bidar*, paragraph 57).

50. On the basis of those considerations, the Court held that the existence of a certain degree of integration may be regarded as established by a finding that the student in question has resided in the host Member State for a certain length of time (*Bidar*, paragraph 59).

51. As regards, specifically, the compatibility with Community law of a condition of five years' uninterrupted residence, as required by the national legislation at issue in the main proceedings, it is necessary to examine whether such a requirement can be justified by the objective, for the host Member State, of ensuring that students who are nationals of other Member States have to a certain degree integrated into its society.

52. In the present case, such a condition of five years' uninterrupted residence is appropriate for the purpose of guaranteeing that the applicant for the maintenance grant at issue is integrated into the society of the host Member State.

53. That requirement must also be proportionate to the legitimate objective pursued by the national law in order to be justified in the light of Community law. It may not go beyond what is necessary in order to attain that objective.

54. A condition of five years' continuous residence cannot be held to be excessive having regard, inter alia, to the requirements put forward with respect to the degree of integration of non-nationals in the host Member State.

55. In that connection, Directive 2004/38, although not applicable to the facts in the main proceedings, provides in Article 24(2) that, in the case of persons other than workers, self-employed persons, persons who retain such status and members of their families, the host Member State is not obliged to grant maintenance assistance for studies, including vocational training, consisting in student grants or student loans, to students who have not acquired the right of permanent residence, while also providing, in Article 16(1), that Union citizens will have a right of permanent residence in the territory of a host Member State where they have resided legally for a continuous period of five years.

56. The Court has also stated that, in order to be proportionate, a residence requirement must be applied by the national authorities on the basis of clear criteria known in advance (see Case C-138/02 *Collins* [2004] ECR I-2703, paragraph 72).

57. By enabling those concerned to know, without any ambiguity, what their rights and obligations are, the residence requirement laid down by the Policy rule of 9 May 2005 is, by its very existence, such as to guarantee a significant level of legal certainty and transparency in the context of the award of maintenance grants to students.

58. It must therefore be stated that a residence requirement of five years, such as that laid down in the national legislation at issue in the main proceedings, does not go beyond what is necessary to attain the objective of ensuring that students from other Member States are to a certain degree integrated into the society of the host Member State.

59. That finding is without prejudice to the option for Member States to award maintenance grants to students from other Member States who do not fulfil the five year residence requirement should they wish to do so.

60. In the light of the foregoing, the response to the second to fourth questions must be that a student who is a national of a Member State and travels to another Member State to study there can rely on the first paragraph of Article 12 EC in order to obtain a maintenance grant where he or she has resided for a certain duration in the host Member State. The first paragraph of Article 12 EC does not preclude the application to nationals of other Member States of a requirement of five years' prior residence.

The fifth question

61. By this question, the Centrale Raad van Beroep is essentially enquiring whether Community law, in particular the principle of legal certainty, precludes the retroactive application of a residence requirement which, at the time of the facts in the main proceedings, could not have been known to the applicant.

62. It must be pointed out in this connection that the Policy rule of 9 May 2005 entered into force on its publication, with retroactive effect from 15 March 2005, that is, after the facts in the main proceedings took place.

63. The referring court, however, takes the view that the Policy rule of 9 May 2005 is relevant to the outcome of the dispute in the main proceedings, since it reflects the way in which the IB-Groep decided to implement the judgment in *Bidar*, and the effects of that judgment were not temporally limited.

64. The referring court states that its doubt on that issue originates from the judgment in *Collins*, inasmuch as the Court held, in that judgment, that a residence requirement could not be imposed on an applicant for social assistance unless that applicant could have already known of the existence of that requirement during the reference period.

65. As is apparent from paragraph 56 above, the Court held in *Collins* that, in order to be proportionate, a residence requirement must be applied by the national authorities on the basis of clear criteria known in advance.

66. With a view to answering the question, it should be recalled that, since the effects of *Bidar* were not temporally limited, the interpretation of Article 12 EC which follows from that judgment may, and must, be applied by the national courts to legal relationships arising and established before that judgment, provided that in other respects the conditions enabling an action relating to the application of that rule to be brought before the courts having jurisdiction are satisfied (see, to that effect, Case 61/79 *Denkavit italiana* [1980] ECR 1205, paragraph 16, and *Bidar*, paragraph 66).

67. According to settled case-law, the principle of legal certainty – which is one of the general principles of Community law – requires, particularly, that rules of law be clear, precise and predictable in their effects, in particular where they may have negative consequences on individuals and undertakings (see, to that effect, Case C-143/93 *Van Es Douane Agenten* [1996] ECR I-431, paragraph 27, and Case C-347/06 *ASM Brescia* [2008] ECR I-0000, paragraph 69).

68. The file shows that the residence requirement laid down in the Policy rule of 9 May 2005 was introduced in order to cover the transitional period between the judgment in *Bidar* and the transposition of Directive 2004/38. That option is said to have been chosen in order to satisfy the requirements of Articles 24(2) and 16 of that directive.

69. It therefore seems that, in a situation such as that at issue in the main proceedings, making the right of students from other Member States to a maintenance grant subject to a residence requirement, as an essential element of that right, does not have any negative consequences for the students concerned.

70. Likewise, since the Policy rule of 9 May 2005 gives greater rights to the students concerned than those to which they were entitled under the former national rules, the requirement set out in *Collins* is not applicable to the present case.

71. The answer to the question referred must therefore be that, in circumstances such as those of the main proceedings, Community law, in particular the principle of legal certainty, does not preclude the application of a residence requirement which makes the right of students from other Member States to a maintenance grant subject to the

completion of periods of residence which occurred prior to the introduction of that requirement.

Costs

[Para. 72 omitted]

On those grounds,

THE COURT (Grand Chamber)

hereby rules:

1. **A student in the situation of the applicant in the main proceedings cannot rely on Article 7 of Regulation (EEC) No 1251/70 of the Commission of 29 June 1970 on the right of workers to remain in the territory of a Member State after having been employed in that State in order to obtain a maintenance grant.**

2. **A student who is a national of a Member State and travels to another Member State to study there can rely on the first paragraph of Article 12 EC in order to obtain a maintenance grant where he or she has resided for a certain duration in the host Member State. The first paragraph of Article 12 EC does not preclude the application to nationals of other Member States of a requirement of five years' prior residence.**

3. **In circumstances such as those of the main proceedings, Community law, in particular the principle of legal certainty, does not preclude the application of a residence requirement which makes the right of students from other Member States to a maintenance grant subject to the completion of periods of residence which occurred prior to the introduction of that requirement.**

Comments and questions

According to the CJEU's case law, the inclusion of Union citizenship in the TFEU, including in Article 21, has had a number of legal consequences which a Union citizen can assert against a host Member State, i.e. a Member State other than their own.

First, Article 21 TFEU means that Union citizens have a direct right of residence pursuant to the provision. However, there can be restrictions on this right pursuant to other provisions in the TFEU and Directive 2004/38 on the right of citizens of the Union and their family members to move and reside freely within the territory of the Member States. Directive 2004/38 (the 'Free Movement Directive') replaces Directive

93/96 and Articles 10 and 11 of the previous Regulation 1612/68 (now Regulation 492/2011). However, according to the case law, restrictions on the right of residence must be interpreted narrowly and must comply with the principle of proportionality; see the *Baumbast* case printed above. Among other things, the CJEU has ruled that a small child of Irish nationality had a right of permanent residence in the UK pursuant to (now) Article 21 TFEU and the then Directive 90/364 (now Article 7(1)(b) of the Free Movement Directive 2004/38), since the child was covered by health insurance and was cared for by a parent (a Chinese citizen) with sufficient means so that the child would not become a burden on the State in the UK; see Case C-200/02 *Chen* [2004] ECR I-9925.

Second, the CJEU has ruled that a Union citizen has a right to social assistance on an equal footing with the host Member State's own citizens if the Union citizen has a right of residence pursuant to the Free Movement Directive and fulfils the condition of that Directive. From their first day in the host Member State, economically active Union citizens have a right to equal treatment with regard to social assistance. However, in the case of cross-border workers, the host Member State can require there to be special links to it; see Case C-20/12 *Giersch* and Case C-212/05 *Hartmann*, which are reproduced in Chapter 4 below. In the case of non-economically active Union citizens, the host Member State is not obliged to give social assistance in the first three months, nor is it obliged to pay student maintenance aid in the first five years of residence; see Article 24(2) of the Free Movement Directive. After the first three months of residence, the host Member State is only obliged to pay social assistance if the non-economically active Union citizen has sufficient resources; see Case C-333/13, *Dano*, printed below.

Third, the CJEU's case law means that the requirement for equal treatment laid down in Article 21 TFEU, cf. Article 18 TFEU, must be considered a prohibition of restrictions, so the host Member State must be able to justify national law or practice in respect of a Union citizen on the grounds of overriding necessity, and among other things its legislation must comply with the principle of proportionality; see for example Case C-224/02 *Pusa* [2004] ECR I-5763, where the CJEU ruled on a Finnish rule on the deduction of national tax when calculating the net pension that could form the basis for the maximum attachment by creditors. The Finnish law did not take account of any obligations to pay tax in another Member State in which the Union citizen had become resident, which meant that the Union citizen received a lesser amount from their Finnish pension after deduction of payments to creditors. The CJEU ruled that such an arrangement was in breach of Article 21 TFEU. Similarly, the CJEU has ruled that Article 21 TFEU prohibits a Member State measure under which the right to reduce taxable income by deducting health insurance premiums was conditional on the premiums being paid in that Member State in accordance with national rules, which meant that such a tax advantage was not allowed when the premiums were paid pursuant to an obligatory health insurance scheme in another Member State; Case C-544/07 *Rüffler* [2009] ECR I-3389. The CJEU also had the opportunity to rule on the relationship between Articles 18 and 21 TFEU on the one hand, and on the other hand national rules on tax deductions for maintenance payments to a divorced spouse who was resident in another Member State; see Case C-403/03 *Egon Schempp* [2005] ECR I-6421. In this case the CJEU stated that the payment of maintenance to a recipient resident in the same Member State cannot be compared to the payment of maintenance to a recipient resident in another Member State. In each of these cases the recipient is subject to a different tax system as regards the taxation of maintenance payments; see paragraph 35. The fact that a taxable person who was resident in Germany could not deduct maintenance payments made to his divorced wife who was resident in Austria was therefore not unequal treatment according to Article 18 TFEU. Moreover, the German tax rule did not breach Article 21 TFEU, as the less generous tax treatment of the husband was not due to the fact that he had exercised his right to freedom of movement, but due the fact that his former wife had taken up residence in another Member State.

Fourth, the CJEU uses Article 21 TFEU to make expansive interpretations of the TFEU's rights provision.

In the *Förster* case important questions of principle were referred to the CJEU for a preliminary ruling on whether Article 18 TFEU (formerly Article 12 TEC) is an obstacle to Member State A establishing requirements that a national from Member State B, who has gone to Member State A to complete her studies, must have been resident in Member State A for five years as a condition for obtaining student maintenance to cover her living costs. The importance of the case is illustrated by the fact that eight Member States submitted observations on the submission for a preliminary ruling. Prior to the *Förster* case the CJEU had ruled in Case C-209/03 *Bidar* [2005] ECR I-2119 that it was not incompatible with Article 18 TFEU for a Member State only to provide maintenance for students' living costs to students who could show that they were, *to a certain degree, integrated* in the society of the Member State in question. In the *Bidar* case the CJEU thus recognised a requirement for three years prior residence in that Member State. However, in the *Bidar* case Member State A also required that the student should be established, and this was a condition which it was impossible for a student from another Member State to fulfil, so the CJEU found that the national provisions infringed Article 18 TFEU.

Union legislators have also established time limits for when a national from another Member State is entitled to obtain student maintenance to cover their living costs. Under Article 24(2) of Directive 2004/38/EC (the Free Movement Directive), a host Member State is not obliged to provide student maintenance, including vocational training, consisting of student grants or student loans to persons other than workers, self-employed persons, persons who retain such status and members of their families, i.e. following five years residence in the host Member State.

The background to the *Förster* case was that in March 2000 a German national, Jacqueline Förster, had taken up residence in the Netherlands where she applied to train as a teacher and from 1 September 2001 for a course for a Bachelor's degree in pedagogy at the Hogeschool van Amsterdam. In parallel with pursuing these studies Jacqueline Förster had various forms of paid work. In mid 2004 Jacqueline Förster passed the final exam of the course for a Bachelor's degree in pedagogy and on 5 June in that year she accepted an offer of a job as a social worker in an institution for persons with psychiatric problems. From September 2000 the Dutch authorities gave Jacqueline Förster student maintenance to cover her living costs. The student maintenance was regularly extended. The Dutch authorities granted this student maintenance by reference to the fact that Jacqueline Förster must be regarded as being a 'worker' within the meaning of Article 45 TFEU (formerly Article 39 TEC), and therefore according to Article 7(2) of Regulation (EEC) No 1612/68 on freedom of movement for workers within the Union, she must be treated equally with Dutch nationals with regard to student maintenance to cover living costs. However, when carrying out a control, the Dutch authorities found that Jacqueline Förster had not had paid work between July and December 2003. By a decision of 3 March 2005 they therefore decided that she should no longer be regarded as a worker. The decision to grant her maintenance to cover living costs for the period between July and December 2003 was therefore rescinded and she was encouraged to repay the incorrectly obtained amount. Jacqueline Förster appealed to the Dutch courts against this decision.

The first question on which the CJEU was requested to give a preliminary ruling was whether a student who found herself in the same situation as Jacqueline Förster could rely on the then applicable Article 7 of Regulation (EEC) No 1251/70 on the right of workers to remain in the territory of a Member State after having been employed in that State in order to obtain student maintenance to cover living costs in the Netherlands. The CJEU rejected this.

The next question was whether a student who is a national of one Member State and goes to another Member State to complete her education can rely on Article 18(1) TFEU in order to obtain student maintenance to cover her living costs. The CJEU ruled that a student who is lawfully resident in another Member State is covered by the TFEU with regard to the grant of student maintenance to cover living costs. The CJEU added that even though Article 3 of the since repealed Directive 93/96/EEC on the right of residence for students did not give students who had a right of residence a right to be paid student support in the host Member State, this provision did not mean that a national of one Member State who, by virtue of Article 21 TFEU (formerly Article 18 TEC) and provisions adopted to implement that Article, is lawfully resident in the territory of another Member State where he or she intends to start or pursue education, is prevented from relying, during that residence, on the fundamental principle of equal treatment provided for in Article 18(1) TFEU; see paragraphs 40-43 of the judgment. In this connection the CJEU noted that it was irrelevant that Jacqueline Förster had gone to the Netherlands principally to finish her education there.

After having ruled that Jacqueline Förster could rely on Article 18 TFEU against the Dutch authorities, the question arose as to whether a condition of uninterrupted prior residence of five years, as required under the Dutch rules, was compatible with Union law. This meant that the CJEU had to decide whether such a condition could be justified by the host Member State's desire to ensure that students who are national of other Member States were, *to a certain degree, integrated* in the society of the host Member State. Since the CJEU had, in the *Bidar* case discussed above, already established that it was justified for a Member State only to give support to cover the living costs of such students as could show that they were, to a certain extent, integrated in the society of that Member State, in paragraph 52 the CJEU stated very briefly: 'In the present case, such a condition of five years' uninterrupted residence is *appropriate* for the purpose of guaranteeing that the applicant for the maintenance grant at issue is integrated into the society of the host Member State' (emphasis added). In paragraph 53 the CJEU added that the: 'requirement must also be *proportionate to the legitimate objective pursued* by the national law in order to be justified in the light of Union law. *It may not go beyond what is necessary* in order to attain that objective' (emphasis added). Without giving any more detailed reasons, in paragraph 54 the CJEU decided that a condition of five years continuous residence cannot be held to be excessive having regard to the requirement on the degree of integration of non-nationals in the host Member State – a finding that was most welcome to the Member States that finance student maintenance from tax revenues. Moreover, the CJEU found that the residence requirement laid down in the Dutch policy rule enabled those concerned to know, without any ambiguity, what their rights and obligations are, such as to guarantee a significant level of legal certainty and transparency in the context of the award of maintenance grants to students. The CJEU could thus also hold that the residence requirement of five years in the Dutch guidelines did not go beyond what was necessary to attain the objective of ensuring that students from other Member States were to a certain degree integrated into the society of the host Member State. The requirements of the proportionality principle were thus fulfilled.

The decision in the *Förster* case established that it is not contrary to Article 18 TFEU, including the principle of proportionality, for a Member State to lay down requirements in its national laws with respect to students from other Member States requiring them to have had prior residence in the host Member States for five years, as a condition for obtaining student maintenance to cover their living costs. In relation to Article 24(2) of the Free Movement Directive, in paragraph 55 the CJEU recognised, even albeit indirectly, the five year period which the Union legislator has laid down in the Free Movement Directive as a condition for obtaining student maintenance in the host Member State for persons who are not economically active in the host Member State. See also Joined Cases C-11/06 and C-12/06 *Morgan* [2007] ECR I-9161, where the CJEU held that it was contrary to Article 21 TFEU for Germany to have laid down a condition that students could only receive German student maintenance for studies in another Member State if the student had completed at least one year's study in Germany, and the same study in the other Member State, if there would not be a corresponding requirement for students who continue their studies in Germany.

In contrast to the above, the CJEU has found that a German rule, under which support for the construction of owner-occupied homes which was granted to persons who were fully liable to tax in Germany and was conditional on the home being built in Germany, was not compatible with Articles 21, 45 and 49 TFEU; see Case C-152/05 *Commission* v *Germany* [2008] ECR I-39, included in Chapter 4 below. The CJEU stated that such a measure had a deterrent effect and therefore constituted an obstacle to the free movement of workers and the right of establishment. The German government had justified the measure on the grounds of the aim of encouraging the construction of homes in German territory, but the CJEU found that the German measure did not comply with the proportionality principle, as it went beyond what was necessary to attain the objective. In the view of the CJEU, the aim of satisfying the demand for homes could just as well have been achieved if a person who was fully liable to pay tax in

Germany chose to take up residence in the territory of another Member State than Germany; see paragraph 28. Moreover, the CJEU stated that, for persons who were fully liable to tax in Germany and who were not economically active, the same reasons would lead to the same conclusion. Similarly, the CJEU has found that it was in breach of Articles 21, 45 and 56 TFEU that under a German tax provision it was not generally possible to make tax deductions for school fees for attendance at schools in another Member State; see Case C-318/05 *Commission* v *Germany* [2007] ECR I-6957.

JUDGMENT OF THE COURT (Grand Chamber)
11 November 2014

Elisabeta Dano, Florin Dano v Jobcenter Leipzig. (Request for a preliminary ruling: Sozialgericht Leipzig – Germany)

'Reference for a preliminary ruling – Free movement of persons – Citizenship of the Union – Equal treatment – Economically inactive nationals of a Member State residing in the territory of another Member State – Exclusion of those persons from special non-contributory cash benefits under Regulation (EC) No 883/2004 – Directive 2004/38/EC – Right of residence for more than three months – Articles 7(1)(b) and 24 – Condition requiring sufficient resources'

Case C-333/13

Judgment

1. This request for a preliminary ruling concerns the interpretation of Article 18 TFEU, of point (a) of the first subparagraph, and the second subparagraph, of Article 20(2) TFEU, of Articles 1, 20 and 51 of the Charter of Fundamental Rights of the European Union ('the Charter'), of Articles 4 and 70 of Regulation (EC) No 883/2004 of the European Parliament and of the Council of 29 April 2004 on the coordination of social security systems (OJ 2004 L 166, p. 1, and corrigendum at OJ 2004 L 200, p. 1), as amended by Commission Regulation (EU) No 1244/2010 of 9 December 2010 (OJ 2010 L 338, p. 35) ('Regulation No 883/2004), and of Article 24(2) of Directive 2004/38/EC of the European Parliament and of the Council of 29 April 2004 on the right of citizens of the Union and their family members to move and reside freely within the territory of the Member States amending Regulation (EEC) No 1612/68 and repealing Directives 64/221/EEC, 68/360/EEC, 72/194/EEC, 73/148/EEC, 75/34/EEC, 75/35/EEC, 90/364/EEC, 90/365/EEC and 93/96/EEC (OJ 2004 L 158, p. 77).

2. The request has been made in proceedings brought by Ms Dano and her son Florin against Jobcenter Leipzig concerning the latter's refusal to grant them benefits by way of basic provision ('Grundsicherung') that are envisaged by German legislation, namely, for Ms Dano, subsistence benefit ('existenzsichernde Regelleistung') and, for her son, social allowance ('Sozialgeld'), as well as a contribution to accommodation and heating costs.

[Paras 3-34 omitted]

The dispute in the main proceedings and the questions referred for a preliminary ruling

35. Ms Dano, who was born in 1989, and her son Florin, who was born on 2 July 2009 in Saarbrücken (Germany), are both Romanian nationals. According to the findings of the referring court, Ms Dano last entered Germany on 10 November 2010.

36. On 19 July 2011, the city of Leipzig issued Ms Dano with a residence certificate of unlimited duration ('unbefristete Freizügigkeitsbescheinigung') for EU nationals, establishing 27 June 2011 as the date of entry into German territory. On 28 January 2013 it also issued her with a duplicate certificate.

37. Since their arrival in Leipzig, Ms Dano and her son have been living in the apartment of Ms Dano's sister, who provides for them materially.

38. Ms Dano receives child benefit ('Kindergeld') for her son Florin, which is paid by the Leipzig family benefits office on behalf of the Federal Employment Agency and amounts to EUR 184 per month. The Leipzig social assistance service for children and young people also pays an advance on maintenance payments of EUR 133 per month for that child, whose father's identity is not known.

39. Ms Dano attended school for three years in Romania, but did not obtain any leaving certificate. She understands German orally and can express herself simply in German. On the other hand, she cannot write in German and her ability to read texts in that language is only limited. She has not been trained in a profession and, to date, has not worked in Germany or Romania. Although her ability to work is not in dispute, there is nothing to indicate that she has looked for a job.

40. The first application that Ms Dano and her son submitted for the grant of benefits by way of basic provision under SGB II was refused by Jobcenter Leipzig by decision of 28 September 2011, on the basis of point 2 of the second sentence of Paragraph 7(1) of SGB II. Since that decision was not contested, it became final.

41. A fresh application for the same benefits, submitted on 25 January 2012, was also refused, by decision of Jobcenter Leipzig of 23 February 2012. Ms Dano and her son lodged an administrative objection against that refusal, relying on Articles 18 TFEU and 45 TFEU and on the judgment in *Vatsouras and Koupatantze* (C-22/08 and C-23/08, EU:C:2009:344). That objection was dismissed by decision of 1 June 2012.

42. On 1 July 2012, Ms Dano and her son brought an action challenging that decision before the Sozialgericht Leipzig (Social Court, Leipzig), by which they again sought the grant of benefits by way of basic provision for jobseekers under SGB II in respect of the period commencing on 25 January 2012.

43. The Sozialgericht Leipzig considers that, by virtue of point 2 of the second sentence of Paragraph 7(1) of SGB II and Paragraph 23(3) of SGB XII, Ms Dano and her son are not entitled to benefits granted by way of basic provision. However, it expresses doubts as to whether provisions of EU law, in particular Article 4 of Regulation No 883/2004, the general principle of non-discrimination resulting from Article 18 TFEU and the general right of residence resulting from Article 20 TFEU, preclude those provisions of German law.

44. According to the findings of the referring court, the main proceedings concern persons who cannot claim a right of residence in the host State by virtue of Directive 2004/38.

45. In those circumstances, the Sozialgericht Leipzig decided to stay the proceedings and to refer the following questions to the Court for a preliminary ruling:

‘1) Do persons who do not wish to claim payment of any benefits of social security law or family benefits under Article 3(1) of Regulation No 883/2004 but rather special non-contributory benefits under Article 3(3) and Article 70 of the regulation fall within the scope *ratione personae* of Article 4 of the regulation?

2) If Question 1 is answered in the affirmative: are the Member States precluded by Article 4 of Regulation No 883/2004, in order to prevent an unreasonable recourse to non-contributory social security benefits under Article 70 of the regulation which guarantee a level of subsistence, from excluding in full or in part Union citizens in need from accessing those benefits, which are provided to their own nationals who are in the same situation?

3) If Question 1 or Question 2 is answered in the negative: are the Member States precluded by (a) Article 18 TFEU and/or (b) [point (a) of the first subparagraph of Article 20(2)] TFEU in conjunction with the [second subparagraph] of Article 20(2) TFEU and Article 24(2) of Directive 2004/38/EC, in order to prevent an unreasonable recourse to non-contributory social security benefits under Article 70 of Regulation No 883/2004 which guarantee a level of subsistence, from excluding in full or in part Union citizens in need from accessing those benefits, which are provided to their own nationals who are in the same situation?

4) If, according to the answers to the abovementioned questions, the partial exclusion of benefits which guarantee a level of subsistence complies with EU law: may the provision of non-contributory benefits which guarantee a level of subsistence for Union citizens, outside acute emergencies, be limited to the provision of the necessary funds for return to the home State or do Articles 1, 20 and 51 of the Charter … require more extensive payments which enable permanent residence?’

Consideration of the questions referred

Question 1

46. By its first question, the referring court asks, in essence, whether Article 4 of Regulation No 883/2004 must be interpreted as meaning that 'special non-contributory benefits' for the purposes of Articles 3(3) and 70 of the regulation fall within its scope.

47. A preliminary point to note is that the referring court has classified the benefits at issue in the main proceedings as 'special non-contributory cash benefits' within the meaning of Article 70(2) of Regulation No 883/2004.

48. It must be pointed out, first, that Article 3 of Regulation No 883/2004 defines the matters covered by the regulation, expressly stating in Article 3(3) that the regulation 'shall also apply to the special non-contributory cash benefits covered by Article 70 [of the regulation]'.

49. Accordingly, it is clear from the wording of Article 3 of Regulation No 883/2004 that the regulation applies to special non-contributory cash benefits.

50. Second, Article 70(3) of Regulation No 883/2004 provides that Article 7 of the regulation, which governs the waiving of residence rules, and the other chapters of Title III thereof, which is devoted to the various categories of benefits, are not to apply to special non-contributory cash benefits.

51. Whilst Article 70(3) of Regulation No 883/2004 therefore, by way of exception, renders certain of the regulation's provisions inapplicable to special non-contributory cash benefits, Article 4 is not among those provisions.

52. Finally, the interpretation that Article 4 of Regulation No 883/2004 applies to special non-contributory cash benefits corresponds to the intention of the EU legislature, as is apparent from the third recital in the preamble to Regulation No 1247/92 which amended Regulation No 1408/71, inserting provisions relating to benefits of this type in order to take account of the case-law in that regard.

53. In accordance with the seventh recital, such benefits should be granted solely in accordance with the legislation of the Member State of residence of the person concerned or of the members of his or her family, with such aggregation of periods of residence completed in any other Member State as is necessary and without discrimination on grounds of nationality.

54. The specific provision which the EU legislature thus inserted into Regulation No 1408/71 by means of Regulation No 1247/92 is thus characterised by

non-exportability of special non-contributory cash benefits as the counterpart of equal treatment in the State of residence.

55. In the light of all the foregoing considerations, the answer to the first question is that Regulation No 883/2004 must be interpreted as meaning that 'special non-contributory cash benefits' as referred to in Articles 3(3) and 70 of the regulation fall within the scope of Article 4 of the regulation.

Questions 2 and 3

56. By its second and third questions, which it is appropriate to examine together, the referring court asks, in essence, whether Article 18 TFEU, Article 20(2) TFEU, Article 24(2) of Directive 2004/38 and Article 4 of Regulation No 883/2004 must be interpreted as precluding legislation of a Member State under which nationals of other Member States who are not economically active are excluded, in full or in part, from entitlement to certain 'special non-contributory cash benefits' within the meaning of Regulation No 883/2004 although those benefits are granted to nationals of the Member State concerned who are in the same situation.

57. It should be observed first of all that Article 20(1) TFEU confers on any person holding the nationality of a Member State the status of citizen of the Union (judgment in *N.*, C-46/12, EU:C:2013:9725, paragraph 25).

58. As the Court has held on numerous occasions, the status of citizen of the Union is destined to be the fundamental status of nationals of the Member States, enabling those among such nationals who find themselves in the same situation to enjoy within the scope *ratione materiae* of the FEU Treaty the same treatment in law irrespective of their nationality, subject to such exceptions as are expressly provided for in that regard (judgments in *Grzelczyk*, C-184/99, EU:C:2001:458, paragraph 31; *D'Hoop*, C-224/98, EU:C:2002:432, paragraph 28; and *N.*, EU:C:2013:9725, paragraph 27).

59. Every Union citizen may therefore rely on the prohibition of discrimination on grounds of nationality laid down in Article 18 TFEU in all situations falling within the scope *ratione materiae* of EU law. These situations include those relating to the exercise of the right to move and reside within the territory of the Member States conferred by point (a) of the first subparagraph of Article 20(2) TFEU and Article 21 TFEU (see judgment in *N.*, EU:C:2013:97, paragraph 28 and the case-law cited).

60. In this connection, it is to be noted that Article 18(1) TFEU prohibits any discrimination on grounds of nationality '[w]ithin the scope of application of the Treaties, and without prejudice to any special provisions contained therein'. The second subparagraph of Article 20(2) TFEU expressly states that the rights conferred on Union citizens by that article are to be exercised 'in accordance with the conditions and

limits defined by the Treaties and by the measures adopted thereunder'. Furthermore, under Article 21(1) TFEU too the right of Union citizens to move and reside freely within the territory of the Member States is subject to compliance with the 'limitations and conditions laid down in the Treaties and by the measures adopted to give them effect' (see judgment in *Brey*, C-140/12, EU:C:2013:565, paragraph 46 and the case-law cited).

61. Thus, the principle of non-discrimination, laid down generally in Article 18 TFEU, is given more specific expression in Article 24 of Directive 2004/38 in relation to Union citizens who, like the applicants in the main proceedings, exercise their right to move and reside within the territory of the Member States. That principle is also given more specific expression in Article 4 of Regulation No 883/2004 in relation to Union citizens, such as the applicants in the main proceedings, who invoke in the host Member State the benefits referred to in Article 70(2) of the regulation.

62. Accordingly, the Court should interpret Article 24 of Directive 2004/38 and Article 4 of Regulation No 883/2004.

63. It must be stated first of all that 'special non-contributory cash benefits' as referred to in Article 70(2) of Regulation No 883/2004 do fall within the concept of 'social assistance' within the meaning of Article 24(2) of Directive 2004/38. That concept refers to all assistance schemes established by the public authorities, whether at national, regional or local level, to which recourse may be had by an individual who does not have resources sufficient to meet his own basic needs and those of his family and who by reason of that fact may, during his period of residence, become a burden on the public finances of the host Member State which could have consequences for the overall level of assistance which may be granted by that State (judgment in *Brey*, EU:C:2013:565, paragraph 61).

64. That having been said, it must be pointed out that, whilst Article 24(1) of Directive 2004/38 and Article 4 of Regulation No 883/2004 reiterate the prohibition of discrimination on grounds of nationality, Article 24(2) of that directive contains a derogation from the principle of non-discrimination.

65. Under Article 24(2) of Directive 2004/38, the host Member State is not obliged to confer entitlement to social assistance during the first three months of residence or, where appropriate, the period of seeking employment, referred to in Article 14(4)(b) of the directive, that extends beyond that first period, nor is it obliged, prior to acquisition of the right of permanent residence, to grant maintenance aid for studies to persons other than workers, self-employed persons, persons who retain such status and members of their families.

66. It is apparent from the documents before the Court that Ms Dano has been residing in Germany for more than three months, that she is not seeking employment and

that she did not enter Germany in order to work. She therefore does not fall within the scope *ratione personae* of Article 24(2) of Directive 2004/38.

67. In those circumstances, it must be established whether Article 24(1) of Directive 2004/38 and Article 4 of Regulation No 883/2004 preclude refusal to grant social benefits in a situation such as that at issue in the main proceedings.

68. Article 24(1) of Directive 2004/38 provides that all Union citizens residing on the basis of the directive in the territory of the host Member State are to enjoy equal treatment with the nationals of that Member State within the scope of the Treaty.

69. It follows that, so far as concerns access to social benefits, such as those at issue in the main proceedings, a Union citizen can claim equal treatment with nationals of the host Member State only if his residence in the territory of the host Member State complies with the conditions of Directive 2004/38.

70. First, in the case of periods of residence of up to three months, Article 6 of Directive 2004/38 limits the conditions and formalities for the right of residence to the requirement to hold a valid identity card or passport and, under Article 14(1) of the directive, that right is retained as long as the Union citizen and his family members do not become an unreasonable burden on the social assistance system of the host Member State (judgment in *Ziolkowski and Szeja*, C-424/10 and C-425/10, EU:C:2011:866, paragraph 39). In accordance with Article 24(2) of Directive 2004/38, the host Member State is thus not obliged to confer entitlement to social benefits on a national of another Member State or his family members during that period.

71. Second, for periods of residence longer than three months, the right of residence is subject to the conditions set out in Article 7(1) of Directive 2004/38 and, under Article 14(2) that right is retained only if the Union citizen and his family members satisfy those conditions. It is apparent from recital 10 in the preamble to the directive in particular that those conditions are intended, inter alia, to prevent such persons from becoming an unreasonable burden on the social assistance system of the host Member State (judgment in *Ziolkowski and Szeja*, EU:C:2011:866, paragraph 40).

72. Third, it is apparent from Article 16(1) of Directive 2004/38 that Union citizens acquire the right of permanent residence after residing legally for a continuous period of five years in the host Member State and that that right is not subject to the conditions referred to in the preceding paragraph. As stated in recital 18 in the preamble to the directive, once obtained, the right of permanent residence is not to be subject to any conditions, with the aim of it being a genuine vehicle for integration into the society of that State (judgment in *Ziolkowski and Szeja*, EU:C:2011:866, paragraph 41).

73. In order to determine whether economically inactive Union citizens, in the situation of the applicants in the main proceedings, whose period of residence in the host Member State has been longer than three months but shorter than five years, can claim equal treatment with nationals of that Member State so far as concerns entitlement to social benefits, it must therefore be examined whether the residence of those citizens complies with the conditions in Article 7(1)(b) of Directive 2004/38. Those conditions include the requirement that the economically inactive Union citizen must have sufficient resources for himself and his family members.

74. To accept that persons who do not have a right of residence under Directive 2004/38 may claim entitlement to social benefits under the same conditions as those applicable to nationals of the host Member State would run counter to an objective of the directive, set out in recital 10 in its preamble, namely preventing Union citizens who are nationals of other Member States from becoming an unreasonable burden on the social assistance system of the host Member State.

75. It should be added that, as regards the condition requiring possession of sufficient resources, Directive 2004/38 distinguishes between (i) persons who are working and (ii) those who are not. Under Article 7(1)(a) of Directive 2004/38, the first group of Union citizens in the host Member State have the right of residence without having to fulfil any other condition. On the other hand, persons who are economically inactive are required by Article 7(1)(b) of the directive to meet the condition that they have sufficient resources of their own.

76. Therefore, Article 7(1)(b) of Directive 2004/38 seeks to prevent economically inactive Union citizens from using the host Member State's welfare system to fund their means of subsistence.

77. As the Advocate General has observed in points 93 and 96 of his Opinion, any unequal treatment between Union citizens who have made use of their freedom of movement and residence and nationals of the host Member State with regard to the grant of social benefits is an inevitable consequence of Directive 2004/38. Such potential unequal treatment is founded on the link established by the Union legislature in Article 7 of the directive between the requirement to have sufficient resources as a condition for residence and the concern not to create a burden on the social assistance systems of the Member States.

78. A Member State must therefore have the possibility, pursuant to Article 7 of Directive 2004/38, of refusing to grant social benefits to economically inactive Union citizens who exercise their right to freedom of movement solely in order to obtain another Member State's social assistance although they do not have sufficient resources to claim a right of residence.

79. To deny the Member State concerned that possibility would, as the Advocate General has stated in point 106 of his Opinion, thus have the consequence that persons who, upon arriving in the territory of another Member State, do not have sufficient resources to provide for themselves would have them automatically, through the grant of a special non-contributory cash benefit which is intended to cover the beneficiary's subsistence costs.

80. Therefore, the financial situation of each person concerned should be examined specifically, without taking account of the social benefits claimed, in order to determine whether he meets the condition of having sufficient resources to qualify for a right of residence under Article 7(1)(b) of Directive 2004/38.

81. In the main proceedings, according to the findings of the referring court the applicants do not have sufficient resources and thus cannot claim a right of residence in the host Member State under Directive 2004/38. Therefore, as has been stated in paragraph 69 of the present judgment, they cannot invoke the principle of non-discrimination in Article 24(1) of the directive.

82. Accordingly, Article 24(1) of Directive 2004/38, read in conjunction with Article 7(1)(b) thereof, does not preclude national legislation such as that at issue in the main proceedings in so far as it excludes nationals of other Member States who do not have a right of residence under Directive 2004/38 in the host Member State from entitlement to certain 'special non-contributory cash benefits' within the meaning of Article 70(2) of Regulation No 883/2004.

83. The same conclusion must be reached in respect of the interpretation of Article 4 of Regulation No 883/2004. The benefits at issue in the main proceedings, which constitute 'special non-contributory cash benefits' within the meaning of Article 70(2) of the regulation, are, under Article 70(4), to be provided exclusively in the Member State in which the persons concerned reside, in accordance with its legislation. It follows that there is nothing to prevent the grant of such benefits to Union citizens who are not economically active from being made subject to the requirement that those citizens fulfil the conditions for obtaining a right of residence under Directive 2004/38 in the host Member State (see, to this effect, judgment in *Brey*, EU:C:2013:965, paragraph 44).

84. In the light of the foregoing, the answer to the second and third questions is that Article 24(1) of Directive 2004/38, read in conjunction with Article 7(1)(b) thereof, and Article 4 of Regulation No 883/2004 must be interpreted as not precluding legislation of a Member State under which nationals of other Member States are excluded from entitlement to certain 'special non-contributory cash benefits' within the meaning of Article 70(2) of Regulation No 883/2004, although those benefits are granted to nationals of the host Member State who are in the same situation, in

so far as those nationals of other Member States do not have a right of residence under Directive 2004/38 in the host Member State.

Question 4

85. By its fourth question, the referring court asks, in essence, whether Articles 1, 20 and 51 of the Charter must be interpreted as requiring the Member States to grant Union citizens non-contributory cash benefits by way of basic provision such as to enable permanent residence or whether those States may limit their grant to the provision of funds necessary for return to the home State.

86. It should be recalled that, in the context of a reference for a preliminary ruling under Article 267 TFEU, the Court is called upon to interpret EU law only within the limits of the powers conferred on the European Union (see, inter alia, judgment in *Betriu Montull*, C-5/12, EU:C:2013:571, paragraph 68 and the case-law cited).

87. Article 51(1) of the Charter states that the provisions of the Charter are addressed 'to the Member States only when they are implementing Union law'.

88. According to Article 6(1) TEU, the provisions of the Charter are not to extend in any way the competences of the European Union as defined in the Treaties. Likewise, the Charter, pursuant to Article 51(2) thereof, does not extend the field of application of EU law beyond the powers of the European Union or establish any new power or task for the European Union, or modify powers and tasks as defined in the Treaties (see judgment in *Åkerberg Fransson*, C-617/10, EU:C:2013:105, paragraphs 17 and 23, and order in *Nagy and Others*, C-488/12 to C-491/12 and C-526/12, EU:C:2013:703, paragraph 15).

89. In paragraph 41 of the judgment in *Brey* (EU:C:2013:565), the Court confirmed that Article 70 of Regulation No 883/2004, which defines the term 'special non-contributory cash benefits', is not intended to lay down the conditions creating the right to those benefits. It is thus for the legislature of each Member State to lay down those conditions.

90. Accordingly, since those conditions result neither from Regulation No 883/2004 nor from Directive 2004/38 or other secondary EU legislation, and the Member States thus have competence to determine the conditions for the grant of such benefits, they also have competence, as the Advocate General has observed in point 146 of his Opinion, to define the extent of the social cover provided by that type of benefit.

91. Consequently, when the Member States lay down the conditions for the grant of special non-contributory cash benefits and the extent of such benefits, they are not implementing EU law.

92. It follows that the Court does not have jurisdiction to answer the fourth question.

Costs

[Para. 93 omitted]

On those grounds,

THE COURT (Grand Chamber),

hereby rules:

1. **Regulation (EC) No 883/2004 of the European Parliament and of the Council of 29 April 2004 on the coordination of social security systems, as amended by Commission Regulation (EU) No 1244/2010 of 9 December 2010, must be interpreted as meaning that 'special non-contributory cash benefits' as referred to in Articles 3(3) and 70 of the regulation fall within the scope of Article 4 of the regulation.**

2. **Article 24(1) of Directive 2004/38/EC of the European Parliament and of the Council of 29 April 2004 on the right of citizens of the Union and their family members to move and reside freely within the territory of the Member States amending Regulation (EEC) No 1612/68 and repealing Directives 64/221/EEC, 68/360/EEC, 72/194/EEC, 73/148/EEC, 75/34/EEC, 75/35/EEC, 90/364/EEC, 90/365/EEC and 93/96/EEC, read in conjunction with Article 7(1)(b) thereof, and Article 4 of Regulation No 883/2004, as amended by Regulation No 1244/2010, must be interpreted as not precluding legislation of a Member State under which nationals of other Member States are excluded from entitlement to certain 'special non-contributory cash benefits' within the meaning of Article 70(2) of Regulation No 883/2004, although those benefits are granted to nationals of the host Member State who are in the same situation, in so far as those nationals of other Member States do not have a right of residence under Directive 2004/38 in the host Member State.**

3. **The Court of Justice of the European Union does not have jurisdiction to answer the fourth question.**

Comments and questions

The *Dano* case concerned a situation in which a Romanian citizen and her young son, who was also a Romanian citizen, had taken up residence in Germany. As Romanian citizens, both mother and son were Union citizens. The mother had the capacity to work, but there was nothing to indicate that she was seeking work. When the mother applied to the German authorities for payment of basic social assistance this was refused, and the case was referred to the German courts.

The principal issue in the case was whether Union law prevents a Member State from being able to refuse to pay non-contributory social assistance to non-economically active citizens from other Member States to provide a minimum subsistence income, as referred to in Regulation 883/2004. The interest of host Member States in not making such payments to non-economically active Union citizens from other Member States is that such payments can be an unreasonable burden on the host Member State, even if such payments are made to its own citizens who are in an equivalent situation. To answer this, the CJEU had to examine the relation between Regulation 883/2004 and the Free Movement Directive (Directive 2004/38)

Under German law job-seekers were entitled to two different forms of basic social assistance:

1. Assistance aimed at ensuring integration in the labour market.
2. Assistance aimed at ensuring a minimum subsistence income.

However, under German law these benefits should not be given to: 'foreign nationals who are not workers or self-employed persons in the Federal Republic of Germany and do not enjoy the right of freedom of movement under the [German] Law on freedom of movement of Union citizens ... and their family members, for the first three months of their residence', or to 'foreign nationals whose right of residence arises solely out of the search for employment and their family members'. Thus under German law a Union citizen was not entitled to the basic social assistance if they entered Germany solely for the purpose of seeking work or obtaining a social benefit.

The CJEU ruled that Regulation 883/2004 should be interpreted so that 'special non-contributory cash benefits', as referred to in Article 70(2) of Regulation No 883/2004 fall within the concept of 'social assistance' within the meaning of Article 4 of the Regulation.

Thereafter the CJEU turned its attention to the second and third questions in the reference for a preliminary ruling, which concerned the relation between Article 4 of Regulation 883/2004 and Article 24(2) of the Free Movement Directive (Directive 2004/38). The CJEU started by noting that the principle of the prohibition of discrimination, which is generally ensured under Article 18 TFEU, is given more specific expression in Article 24 of Directive 2004/38 in relation to Union citizens who exercise their right to move and reside within the territory of the Member States. That principle is also given more specific expression in Article 4 of Regulation 883/2004 in relation to Union citizens who claim the benefits referred to in Article 4 of the Regulation in the host Member State. The CJEU then stated, in paragraph 63 of the judgment:

It must be stated first of all that 'special non-contributory cash benefits' as referred to in Article 70(2) of Regulation No 883/2004 do fall within the concept of 'social assistance' within the meaning of Article 24(2) of Directive 2004/38. That concept refers to all assistance schemes established by the public authorities, whether at national, regional or local level, to which recourse may be had by an individual who does not have resources sufficient to meet his own basic needs and those of his family and who by reason of that fact may, during his period of residence, become a burden on the public finances of the host Member State which could have consequences for the overall level of assistance which may be granted by that State ... [paragraph 64] That having been said, it must be pointed out that, whilst Article 24(1) of Directive 2004/38 and Article 4 of Regulation 883/2004 reiterate the prohibition of discrimination on grounds of nationality, Article 24(2) of that directive contains a derogation from the principle of non-discrimination. [paragraph 65] Under Article 24(2) of Directive 2004/38, the host Member State is not obliged to confer entitlement to social assistance during the first three months of residence or, where appropriate, the period of seeking employment, referred to in Article 14(4)(b) of the directive, that extends beyond that first period, nor is it obliged, prior to acquisition of the right of permanent residence, to grant maintenance aid for studies to persons other than workers, self-employed persons, persons who retain such status and members of their families.

The CJEU then found that the Romanian citizen had lived in Germany for more than three months, that she had not sought work and that she had not entered Germany with a view to obtaining work. Accordingly, she was not covered by the provisions in Article 24(2) of the Free Movement Directive. The next question was whether, in these circumstances, Article 24(1) of the Directive and Article 4 of Regulation 883/2004 prohibited the refusal to pay social assistance. According to Article 24(1) of the Directive, the provisions of the TFEU apply without discrimination to all Union citizens residing in the territory of a host Member State. The CJEU found that 'It follows that, so far as concerns access to social benefits, such as those at issue in the main proceedings, a Union citizen can claim equal treatment with nationals of the host Member State only if his residence in the territory of the host Member State complies with the conditions of [the Free Movement] Directive'. Against this background the CJEU reviewed the three forms of rights of residence enjoyed by Union citizens pursuant to the Free Movement Directive.

First, in the case of periods of residence of up to three months, Article 6 of the Free Movement Directive limits the conditions and formalities for the right of residence to the requirement to hold a valid identity card or passport, as long as the Union citizen and their family members do not become an unreasonable burden on the social assistance system of the host Member State. In accordance with Article 24(2) of the Free Movement Directive, the host Member State is not obliged to give social benefits to a national of another Member State or their family members during that period.

Second, for periods of residence longer than three months, the right of residence is subject to the conditions set out in Article 7(1) of the Free Movement Directive. It is apparent from recital 10 in the preamble to the Directive that, among other things, those conditions are intended to prevent such persons becoming an unreasonable burden on the social assistance system of the host Member State.

Third, it is apparent from Article 16(1) of the Free Movement Directive that Union citizens acquire the right of permanent residence after residing legally for a continuous period of five years in the host Member State and that this right is not subject to the condition that such persons should not become an unreasonable burden on the social assistance system of the host Member State.

The CJEU then found that a Union citizen who is not economically active but who has been resident in another Member State for longer than three months but less than five years could claim the same treatment as the host Member State's own citizens with regard to social assistance. In this connection the CJEU examined whether such a Union citizen's residence fulfilled the conditions of Article 7(1)(b) of the Free Movement Directive, including the obligation that a non-economically active citizen should have sufficient resources for themselves and their family members. In Paragraphs 74-76 of the judgment the CJEU made the following important statements:

> 74. To accept that persons who do not have a right of residence under Directive 2004/38 may claim entitlement to social benefits under the same conditions as those applicable to nationals of the host Member State would run counter to an objective of the directive, set out in recital 10 in its preamble, namely preventing Union citizens who are nationals of other Member States from becoming an unreasonable burden on the social assistance system of the host Member State.
>
> 75. It should be added that, as regards the condition requiring possession of sufficient resources, Directive 2004/38 distinguishes between (i) persons who are working and (ii) those who are not. Under Article 7(1)(a) of Directive 2004/38, the first group of Union citizens in the host Member State have the right of residence without having to fulfil any other condition. On the other hand, persons who are economically inactive are required by Article 7(1)(b) of the directive to meet the condition that they have sufficient resources of their own.
>
> 76. Therefore, Article 7(1)(b) of Directive 2004/38 seeks to prevent economically inactive Union citizens from using the host Member State's welfare system to fund their means of subsistence.

Like the Advocate General in his Opinion, the CJEU attached decisive importance to the intentions of the Union legislator by including the conditions in the Free Movement Directive. Thus the CJEU pointed out that any unequal treatment between Union citizens who have made use of their freedom of movement with regard to the grant of social benefits 'is an inevitable consequence of [the Free Movement Directive]. Such potential unequal treatment is founded on the link established by the Union legislature in Article 7 of the Directive between the requirement to have sufficient resources as a condition for residence and the concern not to create a burden on the social assistance systems of the Member States'. On this basis the CJEU concluded that: 'A Member State must therefore have the possibility, pursuant to Article 7 of Directive 2004/38, of refusing to grant social benefits to economically inactive Union citizens who exercise their right to freedom of movement solely in order to obtain another Member State's social assistance although they do not have sufficient resources to claim a right of residence ... Therefore, the financial situation of each person concerned should be examined specifically, without taking account of the social benefits claimed, in order to determine whether he meets the condition of having sufficient resources to qualify for a right of residence under Article 7(1)(b) of [the Free Movement Directive]'.'

Thereafter the CJEU turned to consider the circumstances of the actual case, and found that neither the Romanian citizen nor her son had sufficient resources. This meant that they did not have a right to take up residence in Germany pursuant to the Free Movement Directive and thus could not invoke the principle of non-discrimination in Article 24(1) of the Directive, nor claim non-contributory cash benefits by way of basic provision . The CJEU reached the same conclusion in its interpretation of Article 4 of the Regulation, stating: 'The benefits at issue in the main proceedings, which constitute "special non-contributory cash benefits" within the meaning of Article 70(2) of the regulation, are, under Article 70(4), to be provided exclusively in the Member State in which the persons concerned reside, in accordance with its legislation. It follows that there is nothing to prevent the grant of such benefits to Union citizens who are not economically active from being made subject to the requirement that those citizens fulfil the conditions for obtaining a right of residence under [the Free Movement Directive] in the host Member State.'

The fourth question referred for a preliminary ruling concerned whether Articles 1, 20 and 51 of the Charter of Fundamental Rights of the European Union must be interpreted as requiring the Member States to grant Union citizens non-contributory cash benefits by way of basic provision such as to enable permanent residence or whether Member States may limit their grant to the provision of funds necessary for returning to the home State. The CJEU refused to answer this question. What was the reason for the CJEU's refusal?

By its judgment in the *Dano* case the CJEU established that Union law does not admit a right to social assistance for non-economically active Union citizens who exercise their right of freedom of movement without an intention of becoming economically active if they do not have sufficient resources to make good a claim to a right of residence of more than three months pursuant to Article 7(1)(b) of the Free Movement Directive. Thus the welfare system of a host Member State is not required to finance the maintenance of non-economically active Union citizens. Where Union citizens take up residence in another Member State in order to obtain social assistance, this is referred to as 'welfare tourism'. In particular, the more wealthy Member States in north-west Europe have been increasingly concerned about welfare tourism. It is natural so see the decision of the CJEU in the *Dano* case as an expression of the CJEU's awareness that Union rules do not exist in a vacuum, but have to function in the real world.

In the *Dano* case the Romanian citizen and her son referred to the CJEU's 2009 ruling in the *Vatsouras* case. In this case two Union citizens from Greece, who had sought work in Germany, applied to the German authorities for benefits by way of basic provision for job-seekers. This had been refused. On that occasion the CJEU stated that: 'Benefits of a financial nature which, independently of their status under national law, are intended to facilitate access to the labour market cannot be regarded as constituting "social assistance" within the meaning of Article 24(2) of [the Free Movement Directive].' In the *Vatsouras* case the CJEU interpreted the terms 'social assistance' in Article 24(2) of the Free Movement Directive very narrowly. Thus, after the *Vatsouras* judgment a Member State could not refuse payment of social assistance intended to facilitate access to the labour market to Union citizens from another Member State seeking work in the host Member State. This was so even though Article 24(2) of the Free Movement Directive expressly states that a Member State shall not be obliged to confer entitlement to social assistance to such first-time job-seekers in the Member State.

Consider whether, by attaching special importance to the Union legislator's intentions in the Free Movement Directive in the *Dano* case, the CJEU effectively circumvented the interpretation established in the *Vatsouras* case. See also Case C-67/14 *Alimanovic*, included in Chapter 4 below, where the German Federal Social Court (*Bundessozialgericht*) among other things asked the CJEU whether job-seeking Union citizens and their family members had a right to German social assistance, including the social assistance intended to ensure the provision of basic needs and to facilitate access to the labour market.

See also Case C-299/14 *Garcia-Nieto*, judgment of 25 February 2016 in which the CJEU rules out that Germany in relation to the same German benefit was not obliged to grant it to a national of another Member State who was non-economically active during the period of residence of up to three months, cf. Article 6 of the Free Movement Directive. See also Case C-308/14 *Commission* v *UK*, judgment of 14 June 2016 regarding the right of non-economically Union Citizens to get British child benefits and child tax credits even if their residence did not comply with the conditions of the Free Movement Directive. The CJEU found again – as it did in the Dano Case – that a Member State have the possibility to refusing to grant social benefits to economically inactive Union Citizens who do not meet the conditions under the Free Movement Directive for a right of residence.

JUDGMENT OF THE COURT (Grand Chamber)
16 October 2012

Hungary v Slovak Republic
(Action under Article 259 TFEU for failure to fulfil obligations)

'Failure of a Member State to fulfil obligations – Article 259 TFEU – Citizenship of the European Union – Article 21 TFEU – Directive 2004/38/EC – Right to move within the territory of the Member States – President of Hungary – Prohibition on entering the territory of the Slovak Republic – Diplomatic relations between Member States'

Case C-364/10

Judgment

1. By its application, Hungary asks the Court to:

- find that the Slovak Republic failed to fulfil its obligations under Directive 2004/38/EC of the European Parliament and of the Council of 29 April 2004 on the right of citizens of the Union and their family members to move and reside freely within the territory of the Member States, amending Regulation (EEC) No 1612/68 and repealing Directives 64/221/EEC, 68/360/EEC, 72/194/EEC, 73/148/EEC, 75/34/EEC, 75/35/EEC, 90/364/EEC, 90/365/EEC and 93/96/EEC (OJ 2004 L 158, p. 77), and Article 21(1) TFEU in that, on 21 August 2009, relying on that directive, but failing to respect its provisions, it did not allow the President of Hungary, Mr Sólyom, to enter its territory;
- declare that the position of the Slovak Republic, which it was still maintaining at the time when the present action was brought, namely, that it is entitled under Directive 2004/38 to prohibit the entry to the territory of the Slovak Republic of a representative of Hungary, such as the President of that State, thereby confirming that such an unlawful attitude may recur, conflicts with the law of the European Union, in particular Article 3(2) TEU and Article 21(1) TFEU;
- declare that the Slovak Republic applied European Union ('EU') law wrongfully in that its authorities did not allow President Sólyom access to its territory on 21 August 2009; and
- in the event that a specific provision of international law may limit the personal scope of Directive 2004/38, define the extent and scope of such derogations.

Legal context

2. Article 5(1) of Directive 2004/38 states:

'Without prejudice to the provisions on travel documents applicable to national border controls, Member States shall grant Union citizens leave to enter their territory with a valid identity card or passport and shall grant family members who are not nationals of a Member State leave to enter their territory with a valid passport.

No entry visa or equivalent formality may be imposed on Union citizens.'

3. Chapter VI of that directive, entitled 'Restrictions on the right of entry and the right of residence on grounds of public policy, public security or public health', contains Article 27, paragraphs 1 and 2 of which provide as follows:

'1. Subject to the provisions of this Chapter, Member States may restrict the freedom of movement and residence of Union citizens and their family members, irrespective of nationality, on grounds of public policy, public security or public health. These grounds shall not be invoked to serve economic ends.

2. Measures taken on grounds of public policy or public security shall comply with the principle of proportionality and shall be based exclusively on the personal conduct of the individual concerned. Previous criminal convictions shall not in themselves constitute grounds for taking such measures.

3. The personal conduct of the individual concerned must represent a genuine, present and sufficiently serious threat affecting one of the fundamental interests of society. Justifications that are isolated from the particulars of the case or that rely on considerations of general prevention shall not be accepted.'

4. Finally, Article 30 of that directive provides:

'1. The persons concerned shall be notified in writing of any decision taken under Article 27(1), in such a way that they are able to comprehend its content and the implications for them.

2. The persons concerned shall be informed, precisely and in full, of the public policy, public security or public health grounds on which the decision taken in their case is based, unless this is contrary to the interests of State security.

3. The notification shall specify the court or administrative authority with which the person concerned may lodge an appeal, the time-limit for the appeal and, where applicable, the time allowed for the person to leave the territory of the Member State. Save in duly substantiated cases of urgency, the time allowed to leave the territory shall be not less than one month from the date of notification.'

The facts of the dispute, the pre-litigation procedure and the proceedings before the Court

5. On the invitation of an association based in Slovakia, Mr Sólyom, the President of Hungary, was scheduled to go to the Slovak town of Komárno on 21 August 2009 to take part in the ceremony inaugurating a statute of Saint Stephen.

6. It is apparent from the documents before the Court, first, that 20 August is a national holiday in Hungary, in commemoration of Saint Stephen, the founder and first king of the Hungarian State. Second, 21 August is considered to be a sensitive date in Slovakia, since on 21 August 1968 the armed forces of five Warsaw Pact countries, which included Hungarian troops, invaded the Czechoslovak Socialist Republic.

7. After several diplomatic exchanges between the embassies of the two Member States regarding the President of Hungary's planned visit, the Ministry of Foreign Affairs of the Slovak Republic finally sent, on 21 August 2009, a *note verbale* to the Ambassador of Hungary in the Slovak Republic in which it prohibited the President of Hungary from entering Slovak territory. As justification for that prohibition, that note relied on Directive 2004/38 as well as on provisions of domestic law governing, first, the stay of foreign nationals and, second, the national police force.

8. President Sólyom was informed of the terms of that note while on his way to the Slovak Republic. He acknowledged receipt of that note at the border and refrained from entering the territory of that Member State.

9. By note of 24 August 2009, the Hungarian authorities argued, in particular, that Directive 2004/38 could not form a valid legal basis to justify the refusal of the Slovak Republic to allow the President of Hungary to enter its territory. They also expressed the view that insufficient reasons had been given for that decision to refuse access. For those reasons, they considered that the Slovak Republic had adopted that measure in breach of European Union (EU) law.

10. At a meeting held on 10 September 2009 in Szécsény (Hungary), the Hungarian and Slovak Prime Ministers adopted a joint declaration maintaining their respective positions in regard to the legal aspects of the contested decision, while regretting the circumstances surrounding President Sólyom's trip. On that same occasion, a memorandum was adopted with a view to clarifying certain practical arrangements for future official and unofficial visits to the two States at issue.

11. By a note of 17 September 2009, the Slovak authorities replied to the note of 24 August 2009, stating that, in view of the circumstances of the incident, the application of Directive 2004/38 had been the 'last chance' to stop the President of

Hungary from entering the territory of the Slovak Republic, and that they had not acted in any way contrary to EU law.

12. Meanwhile, on 3 September 2009, the Hungarian Minister for Foreign Affairs sent a letter to the Vice-President of the Commission of the European Communities seeking the Commission's opinion on the possible breach of EU law by the Slovak Republic.

13. In his reply dated 10 September 2009, the Vice-President of the Commission acknowledged that, in accordance with Directive 2004/38, any restriction of the right to free movement must observe the principle of proportionality, that, under Article 27(2) of that directive, it must be based on the personal conduct of the individual concerned, and that the person concerned must be notified, in the manner prescribed in Article 30, of that restriction and be given a full and precise explanation of the reasons. He also expressed the view that it was for the national courts in the first place to consider whether the rules of that directive had been properly applied. He emphasised that everything possible had to be undertaken in order to avoid any repetition of such situations and stated that he was confident that a constructive bilateral dialogue between the two Member States could resolve the dispute.

14. On 12 October 2009, the Hungarian Minister for Foreign Affairs, acting on behalf of the Hungarian Government, addressed a complaint to the President of the Commission, requesting that the Commission examine whether it was appropriate to initiate infringement proceedings against the Slovak Republic under Article 258 TFEU for breach of Article 21 TFEU and Directive 2004/38.

15. In a letter of 11 December 2009, the Commission expressed the view that 'Union citizens are entitled to move and reside freely within the territory of the Member States pursuant to Article [21 TFEU] and Directive 2004/38'. However, the Commission pointed out that 'under international law, the Member States reserve the right to control the access of a foreign Head of State to their territory, regardless of whether that Head of State is a Union citizen'.

16. The Member States, according to the Commission, continue to arrange official visits through bilateral political channels, with the result that this is not a sphere in which EU law applies. In the Commission's opinion, while a Head of State may indeed decide to visit another Member State as a private individual under Article 21 TFEU and Directive 2004/38, it is evident from the documents attached to the complaint lodged by the Hungarian Minister for Foreign Affairs that Hungary and the Slovak Republic are in disagreement as to the nature of the proposed visit.

17. The Commission concluded, therefore, that it was not in a position to find that the Slovak Republic had failed to observe the provisions of EU law on the free move-

ment of Union citizens, even though that Member State had been wrong, in its *note verbale* of 21 August 2009, to rely on Directive 2004/38 and on the legislation adopted for its implementation in national law.

18. On 30 March 2010, Hungary brought the matter before the Commission in accordance with Article 259 TFEU. On 30 April 2010, the Slovak Republic submitted its observations. Finally, on 12 May 2010, the two Member States presented their oral observations at a hearing arranged by the Commission.

19. In its reasoned opinion dated 24 June 2010, the Commission expressed the view that Article 21(1) TFEU and Directive 2004/38 do not apply to visits made by the head of one Member State to the territory of another Member State and that, in those circumstances, the alleged infringement was unfounded.

20. On 8 July 2010 Hungary brought the present action. The Slovak Republic contends that the Court should dismiss the action and order Hungary to pay the costs.

21. By order of the President of the Court of 28 January 2011, the Commission was granted leave to intervene in support of the form of order sought by the Slovak Republic.

The action

[Paras 22-39 omitted]

Findings of the Court

40. In order to rule on the first head of complaint, it should be stated from the outset that citizenship of the Union is intended to be the fundamental status of nationals of the Member States (see, inter alia, Case C-184/99 *Grzelczyk* [2001] ECR I-6193, paragraph 31; Case C-135/08 *Rottmann* [2010] ECR I-1449, paragraph 43; and Case C-256/11 *Dereci and Others* [2011] ECR I-0000, paragraph 62).

41. To that end, Article 20 TFEU confers the status of citizen of the Union on every person holding the nationality of a Member State (see, inter alia, Case C-224/98 *D'Hoop* [2002] ECR I-6191, paragraph 27; Case C-148/02 *Garcia Avello* [2003] ECR I-11613, paragraph 21; and Case C-34/09*Ruiz Zambrano* [2011] ECR I-0000, paragraph 40).

42. It follows that, since Mr Sólyom is of Hungarian nationality, he unquestionably enjoys that status.

43. It is true, first, that, in accordance with Article 21 TFEU, citizenship of the Union confers on each Union citizen a primary and individual right to move and reside

freely within the territory of the Member States, subject to the limitations and restrictions laid down by the Treaties and the measures adopted for their implementation (Case C-162/09 *Lassal* [2010] ECR I-9217, paragraph 29, and Case C-434/09 *McCarthy* [2011] ECR I-0000, paragraph 27).

44. Second, it is necessary to note that EU law must be interpreted in the light of the relevant rules of international law, since international law is part of the European Union legal order and is binding on the institutions (see, to that effect, *Racke*, paragraphs 45 and 46, and Joined Cases C-402/05 P and C-415/05 P *Kadi and Al Barakaat International Foundation* v *Council and Commission* [2008] ECR I-6351, paragraph 291).

45. In the present case, it is therefore necessary to establish whether, as the Slovak Republic claims, the fact that Mr Sólyom, while a Union citizen, was carrying out, at the material time, the duties of the Hungarian Head of State is liable to constitute a limitation, on the basis of international law, on the application of the right of free movement conferred on him by Article 21 TFEU.

46. To that end, it should be noted that, on the basis of customary rules of general international law and those of multilateral agreements, the Head of State enjoys a particular status in international relations which entails, inter alia, privileges and immunities.

47. In particular, Article 1 of the New York Convention of 14 December 1973 on the Prevention and Punishment of Crimes against Internationally Protected Persons, including Diplomatic Agents, states, inter alia, that every Head of State, while on the territory of a foreign State, enjoys that protection.

48. Thus, the presence of a Head of State on the territory of another State imposes on that latter State the obligation to guarantee the protection of the person who carries out that duty, irrespective of the capacity in which his stay is effected.

49. The status of Head of State therefore has a specific character, resulting from the fact that it is governed by international law, with the consequence that the conduct of such a person internationally, such as that person's presence in another State, comes under that law, in particular the law governing diplomatic relations.

50. Such a specific character is capable of distinguishing the person who enjoys that status from all other Union citizens, with the result that that person's access to the territory of another Member State is not governed by the same conditions as those applicable to other citizens.

51. Accordingly, the fact that a Union citizen performs the duties of a Head of State is such as to justify a limitation, based on international law, on the exercise of the right of free movement conferred on that person by Article 21 TFEU.

52. In the light of all of the foregoing, it must be held that, in the circumstances of the present case, neither Article 21 TFEU nor, *a fortiori*, Directive 2004/38 obliged the Slovak Republic to guarantee access to its territory to the President of Hungary and that, therefore, the first head of complaint must be rejected as unfounded.

The third head of complaint

[Paras 53-61 omitted]

The second and fourth heads of complaint

[Paras 62-71 omitted]

72. As none of the heads of complaint raised by Hungary has been upheld, the action must be dismissed in its entirety.

Costs

[Paras 73 and 74 omitted]

On those grounds,

THE COURT (Grand Chamber),

hereby:

1. Dismisses the action;

[Paras 2 and 3 of the ruling omitted]

Comments and questions

The case of the refusal of the Slovak Republic to allow the President of Hungary to enter its territory is unusual, but it illustrates that the EU is a gathering of many different states that have far from always lived peaceably together. In this case the President of Hungary wanted to take part in an arrangement in Slovakia. However, the Slovak Government did not want the President of Hungary to enter Slovakia, and it thus sent a *note verbale* (a diplomatic communication) to the Hungarian Government with a view to excluding the Hungarian President from Slovakia. The Hungarian President thereupon cancelled his visit to Slovakia. Hungary then criticised Slovakia for having breached Union rules, and the Hungarian Government sought the Commission's support for its criticism. The Commission did not support Hungary so that, quite exceptionally, Hungary brought proceedings against Slovakia before the CJEU, with a view to deciding a conflict that was primarily of a political nature.

The Hungarian Government based its claim on the fact that, as a Union citizen, the Hungarian President had free access to Union territory, and thus his exclusion from Slovakia was a breach of Union law. Against this, the Slovak Government (supported by the Commission) argued that Heads of State are in a different position to that of Union citizens, they are not covered by Union law and cannot claim protection under Union law. This argument gave rise to a different and fundamental problem: if the CJEU can only decide on matters of Union law, how could it decide on a matter that falls outside its jurisdiction? If the CJEU were to undertake a thorough examination of the case and then conclude that it does not fall within Union law, would the CJEU have exceeded its jurisdiction? On this, see in particular paragraphs 22-26.

As for the substantive issue in the case, the CJEU ruled that, even though the Hungarian President, as a Hungarian citizen, was unquestionably a Union citizen pursuant to Article 20 TFEU, which would under normal circumstances have given him a right to move and reside freely in the Union territory (see Article 21 TFEU), the President was prevented from claiming the freedom of movement of Union citizens. The CJEU's reasons for reaching this conclusion are not entirely clear. What do you think was the central argument of the CJEU? On this, see the Opinion of Advocate General Bot, who stated in points 53 and 54:

53. I do not agree with the idea put forward by Hungary that the status of citizen of the Union and the resulting rights and obligations should prevail over the status enjoyed by Heads of State of the Member States, so that the latter must always enjoy freedom of movement within the Union. Such an extensive interpretation of what is meant by citizenship of the Union would ultimately extend the competences of the Union in a manner incompatible with the principle of the conferral of competences.

54. Moreover, that is a view that ignores the specific character of the position of Heads of State, which lies essentially in their capacity as the supreme organ of the State, representing, personifying and committing the State at international level. (13) In other words, that special position implies that, when a Head of State travels on a public visit, he can never do so on an entirely personal basis in so far as it is primarily the community he represents that is welcomed by the State receiving him.

Would it have made any difference if the Hungarian President had been invited not in his capacity as Head of State but in a private capacity to a family wedding in Slovakia?

JUDGMENT OF THE COURT (Third Chamber)
18 July 2013

Laurence Prinz v Region Hannover (C-523/11), and Philipp Seeberger v Studentenwerk Heidelberg (C-585/11). (Request for a preliminary ruling made by the Verwaltungsgericht Hannover – Germany and the Verwaltungsgericht Karlsruhe – Germany)

'Citizenship of the Union – Articles 20 TFEU and 21 TFEU – Right of freedom of movement and residence – Education or training grant awarded to nationals of a Member State in order to pursue their studies in another Member State – Requirement of residence in the home Member State for at least three years prior to the commencement of studies'

Joined Cases C-523/11 and C-585/11

Judgment

1. The requests for a preliminary ruling concern the interpretation of Articles 20 TFEU and 21 TFEU.

2. Those requests have been made in proceedings between Ms Prinz, a German national and Region Hannover (Hanover Region, Department for Education and Training Grants) and Mr Seeberger, also a German national and Studentenwerk Heidelberg, Amt für Ausbildungsförderung (Student Administration, Heidelberg, Office for Education and Training Assistance; 'Studentenwerk') concerning the right to a grant for studies in educational establishments in Member States other than the Federal Republic of Germany.

Legal context

3. Under the heading 'Education and training abroad', Paragraph 5 of the Federal Law on assistance for education and training [Bundesgesetz über individuelle Förderung der Ausbildung (Bundesausbildungsförderungsgesetz)], as amended on 1 January 2008, by the twenty-second law amending the Federal Law on assistance for education and training (BGBl. I, p. 3254; 'the BAföG'), states:

   '1. Permanent residence for the purposes of this Law shall be established in the place where, in a manner which is not merely temporary, the person concerned has his centre of family interests, without any requirement that he intends to be permanently established there. A person who resides in a place solely for the purposes of education or training has not established his permanent residence there.

2. Students who have their permanent residence in Germany shall be awarded an education or training grant for attending an education or training establishment abroad if:

...

3. the student commences or continues his education or training in an educational establishment in a Member State of the European Union or in Switzerland.

...'

4. Paragraph 6 of the BAföG, entitled 'Grants for education or training for German citizens abroad' provides that German nationals whose permanent residence is situated in a foreign State and who attend an educational institution there or who attend an establishment situated in a neighbouring State from that residence may receive an education or training grant where the particular circumstances of a specific case justify one.

5. Paragraph 16 of the BAföG, entitled 'Duration of the grant for education or training abroad' is worded as follows:

'1. For education or training abroad within the meaning of Paragraph 5(2)(1) or (5), the education or training grant shall be paid for a maximum period of one year ...

...

2. In the cases referred to in Paragraph 5(2)(2) and 5(2)(3) receipt of the education or training grant is not subject to the time limit laid down in Paragraph 5(1) and (2). However, as regards the cases referred to in Paragraph 5(2)(3), the grant shall be paid for more than one year only if, when the student commenced his residence abroad after 31 December 2007, his permanent residence was situated in Germany for a minimum of 3 years.'

Background to the disputes in the main proceedings and the questions referred for a preliminary ruling

Case C-523/11

6. Ms Prinz, who was born in Germany in 1991, lived with her family for 10 years in Tunisia where her father was employed by a German company. On her return to Germany, in January 2007, Ms Prinz finished her studies in Frankfurt (Germany) where she obtained the baccalaureat (Abitur) in June 2009. She commenced her studies at the Erasmus University in Rotterdam (Netherlands) on 1 September 2009.

7. In response to an application for an education grant for the academic year 2009/2010 made by Ms Prinz on 18 August 2009, the Region Hannover, by decision of 30 April 2010, awarded that grant for the period from September 2009 to August 2010.

8. However, the grant application submitted by Ms Prinz for the academic year 2010/2011 was rejected, by decision of 4 May 2010, on the ground that since she did not fulfil the condition of residence laid down by the BAföG she could not claim an education grant for an unlimited period, her rights being limited, in accordance with Paragraph 16(3) of that law to a period of one year.

9. On 1 June 2010, Ms Prinz brought an action against that decision. She argued that she fulfilled the condition in question as she had resided in Germany from September 1993 until April 1994 and from January 2007 until August 2009, that is, for three years and four months. She also argued that the residence condition laid down by the BAföG is contrary to Article 21 TFEU and relied on the connections she had maintained with the Member State concerned, explaining that she was born there, has German nationality, that she left that Member State only because of her father's work transfer and that she had always maintained links with her country of origin. According to Ms Prinz, residence of a further four months would not have significantly strengthened those links.

10. The Region Hannover submits that the minimum period of three years laid down in Paragraph 16(3) of the BAföG necessarily corresponds to a continuous period. That law does not infringe European law on freedom of movement and residence in any way since that right does not impose any obligation on Member States to award grants to its own nationals without limits.

11. The national court queries the compatibility with European Union law of a residence condition such as that at issue in the main proceedings. It takes the view that, like the condition applicable before the entry into force of the twenty-second law amending the Federal Law on assistance for education and training, which was the obligation to have attended a German educational establishment for at least one year, the condition at issue in the main proceedings might dissuade a citizen of the European Union from commencing his studies in another Member State, since, after one year, he would no longer receive an education or training grant. According to that court, although it may be legitimate for a Member State to award education or training grants only to students who have shown a certain degree of integration into the society of that State, the criterion based on continuous residence of three years in Germany prior to the start of the residence abroad is not of such a nature as to establish the existence of such integration.

12. In those circumstances, the Verwaltungsgericht Hannover decided to stay proceedings and to refer the following question to the Court for a preliminary ruling:

'Does it constitute a restriction of the right to freedom of movement and residence conferred on citizens of the European Union by Articles 20 and 21 TFEU, which is not justified under [EU] law, if pursuant to the [BAföG], a German national, who has her permanent residence in Germany and attends an education establishment in a Member State of the European Union, is awarded an education grant for attending that education establishment abroad for only one year because when she commenced her stay abroad she had not already had her permanent residence in Germany for at least three years?'

Case C-585/11

13. Mr Seeberger, who was born in Germany in 1983, lived there until 1994 with his parents who are also German nationals. He attended primary and then secondary school in Munich (Germany) from 1989 to 1994. From 1994 until December 2005 he lived with his parents in Majorca (Spain), where his father worked as a self-employed business consultant.

14. In January 2006, Mr Seeberger's parents settled in Cologne (Germany). Although Mr Seeberger was registered in the Munich population register only from 26 October 2006, he maintains that from January 2006 his permanent residence was in Germany.

15. In September 2009, Mr Seeberger began a course in Economics at the University of the Balearics in Palma de Majorca (Spain) and submitted an application for an educational grant to the Studentenwerk.

16. The Studentenwerk rejected that application on the ground that the fact that Mr Seeberger did not fulfill the residence condition laid down in Paragraph 16(3) of the BAföG precluded him from receiving that grant pursuant to Paragraph 5(2), first sentence, point three thereof.

17. Relying on his rights to freedom of movement as a citizen of the European Union, Mr Seeberger brought an action against that decision which was rejected by the Studentenwerk by decision of 14 June 2010.

18. In an action brought before the Verwaltungsgericht Karlsruhe, Mr Seeberger argued that the residence condition laid down by Paragraph 16(3) of the BAföG infringed his right to freedom of movement, since it obliged him either to give up his permanent residence in another Member State or to transfer in time his permanent residence back to Germany, failing which he would risk the award of the education grant for his studies in Spain. In that connection, he submits that his right to be admitted to higher education is recognised only in Spain and that he wishes to pursue all his studies in that Member State.

19. The Studentenwerk contends that since the residence requirement laid down by the BAföG applies in the same way to all nationals, it may apply to citizens of the European Union from other Member States who have the right to freedom of movement. That obligation merely gives concrete expression to the legitimate interest of the Member State which pays social benefits that those benefits, paid from public funds financed by taxes, are reserved to categories of persons who are able to demonstrate a minimum level of integration into the Member State paying those benefits.

20. In its order for reference, the Verwaltungsgericht Karlsruhe states that the residence requirement at issue in the main proceedings does not apply to a grant for education or training in Germany. It observes that such a residence condition, on account of the personal disadvantages, additional costs and possible delays that it involves, may dissuade citizens of the European Union from leaving Germany in order to study in another Member State. That court expresses doubts as to whether the requirement that the applicant for the grant must have established his residence in Germany for at least three years when he starts the education or training is justified and asks whether a certain degree of integration in the society of that Member State that the latter may legitimately require should not be recognised in the case in the main proceedings on the ground that the applicant, a German national, was raised by his parents in Germany and had completed his schooling until the 'sixth' class when he moved with his family, at 12 years of age, because his father had exercised his rights under Articles 45 TFEU and 49 TFEU. According to that court, a criterion based on a specific date and a period of three years prior to the commencement of education or training abroad appears prima facie inappropriate as a means of demonstrating the required integration.

21. Accordingly, the Verwaltungsgericht Karlsruhe decided to stay proceedings and to refer the following question to the Court for a preliminary ruling:

'Does European Union law preclude national legislation which denies an education or training grant for studies in another Member State solely on the ground that the student, who has exercised the right to freedom of movement, has not, at the commencement of the studies, had his permanent residence in his Member State of origin for at least three years?'

Consideration of the questions referred

22. By these questions, which it is appropriate to examine together, the referring courts ask essentially whether Articles 20 TFEU and 21 TFEU must be interpreted as meaning that they preclude the legislation of a Member State which makes the award of an education grant for studies in another Member State for a period of more than one year subject to a sole condition, such as that laid down in Paragraph 16(3) of the BAföG, that requires the applicant to have a permanent residence,

within the meaning of that law, in national territory for at least three years prior to commencing those studies.

23. First of all, it must be recalled that, as German nationals, Ms Prinz and Mr Seeberger enjoy the status of citizens of the Union under Article 20(1) TFEU and may therefore rely on the rights conferred on those having that status, including against their Member State of origin (see, Case C-192/05 *Tas-Hagen and Tas* [2006] ECR I-10451, paragraph 19, and Joined Cases C-11/06 and C-12/06 *Morgan and Bucher* [2007] ECR I-9161, paragraph 22).

24. As the Court has repeatedly held, Union citizenship is destined to be the fundamental status of nationals of the Member States, enabling those who find themselves in the same situation to enjoy within the scope *ratione materiae* of the TFEU the same treatment in law irrespective of their nationality, subject to such exceptions as are expressly provided for (Case C-184/99 *Grzelczyk* [2001] ECR I-6193, paragraph 31; Case C-224/98 *D'Hoop* [2002] ECR I-6191, paragraph 28; and Case C-46/12 *N.* [2013] ECR I-0000, paragraph 27).

25. The situations falling within the scope of European Union law include those involving the exercise of the fundamental freedoms guaranteed by the Treaty, in particular those involving the freedom to move and reside within the territory of the Member States, as conferred by Article 21 TFEU (*Tas-Hagen and Tas*, paragraph 22; Case C-76/05 *Schwarz and Gootjes-Schwarz* [2007] ECR I-6849, paragraph 87 and the case-law cited; and *Morgan and Bucher*, paragraph 23).

26. In that connection, it must be recalled, as the German Government and the Commission have observed, that although the Member States are competent, under Article 165(1) TFEU as regards the content of teaching and the organisation of their respective education systems, it is none the less the case that that competence must be exercised in compliance with European Union law and, in particular, in compliance with the Treaty provisions on the freedom to move and reside within the territory of the Member States, as conferred by Article 21(1) TFEU (see, *Morgan and Bucher*, paragraph 24 and the case-law cited).

27. National legislation which places at a disadvantage certain of the nationals of the Member State concerned simply because they have exercised their freedom to move and to reside in another Member State is a restriction on the freedoms conferred by Article 18(1) EC on every citizen of the Union (see Case C-406/04 *De Cuyper* [2006] ECR I-6497, paragraph 39; *Tas-Hagen and Tas*, paragraph 31; and *Morgan and Bucher*, paragraph 25).

28. Indeed, the opportunities offered by the Treaty in relation to freedom of movement for citizens of the Union cannot be fully effective if a national of a Member State can be deterred from availing himself of them by obstacles placed in the way of his

stay in another Member State by legislation of his State of origin penalising the mere fact that he has used those opportunities (see, to that effect, *D'Hoop*, paragraph 31; Case C-224/02 *Pusa* [2004] ECR I-5763, paragraph 19; and *Morgan and Bucher*, paragraph 26).

29. That consideration is particularly important in the field of education in view of the aims pursued by Article 6(e) TFEU and the second indent of Article 165(2) TFEU, namely, inter alia, encouraging mobility of students and teachers (see *D'Hoop*, paragraph 32; Case C-147/03 *Commission* v*Austria* [2005] ECR I-5969, paragraph 44; and *Morgan and Bucher*, paragraph 27).

30. Consequently, where a Member State provides for a system of education or training grants which enables students to receive such grants if they pursue studies in another Member State, it must ensure that the detailed rules for the award of those grants do not create an unjustified restriction of the right to move and reside within the territory of the Member States laid down in Article 21 TFEU (see *Morgan and Bucher*, paragraph 28).

31. It must be stated that a condition of uninterrupted residence of three years, like that laid down in Article 16(3) of the BAföG, even though it applies without distinction to German nationals and other citizens of the European Union, constitutes a restriction on the right to freedom of movement and residence enjoyed by all citizens of the Union pursuant to Article 21 TFEU.

32. Such a condition is likely to dissuade nationals, such as the applicants in the main proceedings, from exercising their right to freedom of movement and residence in another Member State, given the impact that exercising that freedom is likely to have on the right to the education or training grant.

33. According to settled case-law, legislation which is likely to restrict a fundamental freedom guaranteed by the Treaty can be justified in the light of European Union law only if it is based on objective considerations of public interest independent of the nationality of the persons concerned and if it is proportionate to the legitimate objective pursued by the provisions of national law (see *De Cuyper*, paragraph 40; *Tas-Hagen and Tas*, paragraph 33; and *Morgan and Bucher*, paragraph 33) It also follows from the case-law that a measure is proportionate when, while appropriate for securing the attainment of the objective pursued, it does not go beyond what is necessary in order to attain it (*De Cuyper*, paragraph 42; *Morgan and Bucher*, paragraph 33; and Case C-379/11 *Caves Krier Frères* [2012] ECR I-0000, paragraph 48 and the case-law cited).

34. In the present cases, the German Government contends that the BAföG is based on objective considerations of public interest. Paragraph 16(3) of that law guarantees that an education grant for a full course of studies abroad is paid only to students

able to demonstrate a sufficient degree of integration into German society. The requirement of a minimum level of integration thus preserves the national scheme for education grants for studies abroad by protecting the State paying the grant from an unreasonable financial burden.

35. According to that government, it is therefore legitimate to provide financial support for their entire course of studies abroad only to students who demonstrate a sufficient level of integration in Germany, that evidence being invariably produced by a student in a position to fulfil the condition of three years' continuous residence.

36. In that connection, it is true that the Court has recognised that it may be legitimate for a Member State, in order to ensure that the grant of assistance to cover the maintenance costs of students from other Member States does not become an unreasonable burden which could have consequences for the overall level of assistance which may be granted by that State, to grant such assistance only to students who have demonstrated a certain degree of integration into the society of that State, and that if a risk exists that a Member State may have to bear such an unreasonable burden, similar considerations may apply as regards the award by that State of education or training grants to students wishing to study in other Member States (*Morgan and Bucher*, paragraphs 43 and 44 and the case-law cited).

37. However, according to settled case-law, the proof required to demonstrate the genuine link must not be too exclusive in nature or unduly favour one element which is not necessarily representative of the real and effective degree of connection between the claimant and this Member State, to the exclusion of all other representative elements (see, to that effect, *D'Hoop*, paragraph 39; Case C-503/09 *Stewart* [2011] ECR I-0000, paragraph 95; and Case C-75/11 *Commission* v *Austria* [2012] ECR I-0000, paragraph 62).

38. Although the existence of a certain level of integration may be regarded as established by the finding that a student has resided in the Member State where he may apply for an education or training grant for a certain period, a sole condition of residence, such as that at issue in the main proceedings, risks, as the Advocate General observes in point 95 of her Opinion, excluding from funding students who, despite not having resided for an uninterrupted period of three years in Germany immediately prior to studying abroad, are nevertheless sufficiently connected to German society. That may be the case where the student is a national of the State concerned and was educated there for a significant period or on account of other factors such as, in particular, his family, employment, language skills or the existence of other social and economic factors. Furthermore, other provisions of the legislation at issue in the main proceedings themselves permit factors distinct from the place of residence of the applicant for the grant to be relevant, both in order to establish the centre of family interests of the person concerned and to determine whether the

conditions for the award of the grant are fulfilled in the case of home-country nationals who have established their permanent residence abroad.

39. Taking account of the foregoing, it is for the national court to carry out the necessary checks in order to determine whether the persons concerned can prove a sufficient level of connection with German society capable of demonstrating their integration into that society.

40. It follows that a sole condition of uninterrupted residence of three years, such as that at issue in the main proceedings, is too general and exclusive, and goes beyond what is necessary to achieve the objectives pursued and cannot, therefore, be regarded as proportionate.

41. Having regard to all of the foregoing considerations, the answer to the questions referred is that Articles 20 TFEU and 21 TFEU must be interpreted as meaning that they preclude legislation of a Member State which makes the award of an education grant for studies in another Member State for a period of more than one year subject to a sole condition, such as that laid down in Paragraph 16(3) of the BAföG, requiring the applicant to have had a permanent residence, within the meaning of that law, in national territory for at least three years before commencing those studies.

Costs

[Para. 42 omitted]

On those grounds,

THE COURT (Third Chamber),

hereby rules:

Articles 20 TFEU and 21 TFEU must be interpreted as meaning that they preclude legislation of a Member State which makes the award of an education grant for studies in another Member State for a period of more than one year subject to a sole condition, such as that laid down in Paragraph 16(3) of the Federal Law on assistance for education and training [Bundesgesetz über individuelle Förderung der Ausbildung (Bundesausbildungsförderungsgesetz)], as amended on 1 January 2008, by the twenty-second law amending the Federal Law on assistance for education and training, requiring the applicant to have had a permanent residence, within the meaning of that law, in national territory for at least three years before commencing those studies.

Comments and questions

The *Prinz and Seeberger* case concerned a situation in which Union citizens were subject to restrictions under measures adopted by their own Member State, specifically a requirement for three years residence in order to be entitled to an educational grant from Germany to study in other Member States. The case is one of several in which the CJEU has had to consider whether a Member State's legislation on the right to student support has been compatible with Union law. However, what was unusual about the *Prinz and Seeberger* case was that it concerned the right of non-economically active Union citizens to receive educational grants for study abroad, pursuant to Article 20 TFEU on Union citizenship and Article 21 TFEU on the right to move and reside freely within EU territory and to receive educational grants to study abroad.

For both Laurence Prinz and Philipp Seeberger the problem was that they did not fulfil the requirement of three years residence in Germany at the moment when they left Germany to study abroad. The CJEU started by noting that the two students were Union citizens pursuant to Article 20(1) TFEU by virtue of their being German citizens, and as a consequence of this they could claim the rights attached to such status. This applied also with regard to their Member State of origin. While, the Member States are competent, under Article 165(1) TFEU as regards the content of teaching and the organisation of their respective education systems, that competence must be exercised in compliance with Union law and, in particular, in compliance with the TFEU provisions on the freedom to move and reside within the territory of the Member States, as conferred by Article 21(1) TFEU.

The CJEU also noted that national legislation which places at a disadvantage certain of the nationals of the Member State concerned simply because they have exercised their freedom to move and to reside in another Member State is a restriction on the freedoms conferred by Article 21(1) TFEU on every citizen of the Union. Moreover, the CJEU observed that the opportunities offered by the TFEU 'in relation to freedom of movement for citizens of the Union cannot be fully effective if a national of a Member State can be deterred from availing himself of them by obstacles placed in the way of his stay in another Member State by legislation of his State of origin penalising the mere fact that he has used those opportunities'. On this basis the CJEU ruled that a requirement for three years uninterrupted residence, as laid down in the German legislation, was a restriction on the right of movement and residence which all Union citizens enjoy pursuant to Article 21 TFEU, even though it applied without distinction between German citizens and citizens of other Member States. The CJEU found that such a requirement was 'likely to dissuade nationals, such as the applicants in the main proceedings, from exercising their right to freedom of movement and residence in another Member State, given the impact that exercising that freedom is likely to have on the right to the education or training grant'. There was thus found to be a restriction that could only be compatible with Article 21 TFEU if it were based on objective considerations of public interest independent of the nationality of the persons concerned, if it were appropriate for the attainment of the objective pursued, and if it did not go beyond what was necessary in order to attain it.

In the case the German Government argued that the requirement for residence in Germany was based on objective considerations of public interest as the law guaranteed that an education grant for a full course of studies abroad was paid only to students able to demonstrate a sufficient degree of integration into German society. How did the CJEU assess this argument – see especially paragraphs 36-41? By its ruling in *Prinz and Seeberger*, has the CJEU ruled against Member States requiring a sufficient degree of integration in the Member State's society as a condition for providing a grant for study abroad?

It must be assumed that, in its ruling in the *Prinz and Seeberger* case, the CJEU has not invalidated Article 24(2) of Directive 2004/38 on the right of Union citizens and their family members to move and reside freely within the territory of the Member States, according to which a host Member State is not obliged to provide student grants in the first five years of residence other than to employed persons, self-employed persons, persons who have maintained such status and their family members (see Case C-158/07 *Förster* [2008] ECR I-8507, paragraph 54 ff.). This means that, in relation to Union citizens other than its own nationals, a Member State can still retain the five years residence requirement in relation to the right of those who are not economically active to receive educational grants for studies in that Member State or in another Member State. From this perspective it must be expected that the CJEU's ruling will have a more limited impact, because it concerns the rights of a Member State's own nationals to receive educational grants to study in another Member State.

Subsequently, in Case C-220/12 *Meneses* judgment of 24 October 2013 and Case C-275/12 *Elrick* judgment of 24 October 2013, the CJEU has given judgments on the right to German educational support for studies abroad. In the *Meneses* case, in line with the *Prinz and Seeberger* case, the CJEU concluded that a residence requirement alone is too one-sided. In the *Elrick* case, Articles 20 and 21 TFEU were found to be incompatible with the German rule at issue. Under the German rule, in order to receive an educational grant abroad there was a requirement that the foreign studies should lead to a vocational qualification following a course of study of two years. However, there was not a corresponding requirement in relation to studies in Germany. The objective of the German rule was to subsidise only those courses abroad which improve students' chances on the labour market. However, the CJEU found that rule appeared to be inconsistent and could not be regarded as proportionate to its objective when corresponding conditions that a study should be of at least two years did not apply in Germany.

In its judgment of 26 February 2015 in Case C-359/13 *Babette Martens*, the CJEU ruled on Dutch legislation on the right to receive student financial support abroad. Under the Dutch legislation, applicants for student finance outside the Netherlands should both be entitled to student finance in the Netherlands and have been lawfully resident in that country for at least three of the six years immediately prior to admission to the course of study in question (the 'three-out-of-six' rule). In this case the Dutch authorities rejected an application for student financial support from Babette Martens, a Dutch citizen. The financial support was to be used in connection with further education on the West Indian island Curaçao, which is part of the Dutch realm and which is classified by the EU as one of the group of overseas countries and territories. This means that, as a matter of principle, Curaçao is outside of the EU. Babette Martens's father, who was also a Dutch citizen, was resident in Belgium but had had part-time work in the Netherlands. The refusal of student financial support to the Dutch citizen was made after the Dutch citizen's father, who was also a Dutch citizen though resident in Belgium, had ceased to be a cross-border worker in the Netherlands. According to the Dutch authorities, Babette Martens could no longer claim student financial support on the ground that her father was a cross-border worker, and she did not fulfil the three-out-of-six criterion.

The CJEU rejected the arguments of the Dutch authorities. It found that the Dutch rule did not satisfy the proportionality principle as it was both too exclusive and too arbitrary an element that did not necessarily represent the degree of integration of the applicant in the Member State concerned and was given undue priority to the exclusion of all other representative elements. Thus the Dutch three-out-of-six rule could not be regarded as proportionate in relation to the aim of integration.

The Dutch Government argued that there was no restriction on Babette Martens's right to freedom of movement, as she had exercised her right, granted in Article 20(2)(a) TFEU, to move and reside freely within the territory of the Member States. The CJEU rejected this argument and stated in paragraphs 30-32 of the judgment that: 'as it fails to take account of the fact that the appellant in the main proceedings exercised her rights to move freely by moving from the Netherlands to Belgium with her family in 1993 and continued to exercise those rights throughout the period during which she lived in Belgium ... By making the continued grant of funding for studies abroad subject to the three-out-of-six-years rule, the legislation at issue in the main proceedings is liable to penalise an applicant merely because he has exercised his right to freedom of movement and residence in another Member State, given the effect that exercising that freedom is likely to have on the possibility of receiving funding for higher education ... it is, in that regard, irrelevant that considerable time has elapsed since the appellant in the main proceedings exercised her free movement rights'.

In the *Babette Martens* case the CJEU did not decide on the territorial application, outside the EU, of the rights linked to Union citizenship pursuant to Article 20 TFEU. The CJEU gave weight to the fact that Babette Martens had exercised her right of free movement between two Member States before travelling to Curaçao, namely between the Netherlands and Belgium. Thus it remains unclear whether Union law applies in a situation where a Union citizen moves directly from their home Member State to an area outside the EU in order to pursue their education. In the *Prinz and Seeberger* case the CJEU appeared to overlook this territorial aspect, as it was not considered important that Laurence Prinz had lived in Tunisia for 10 years; see paragraph 6 of that judgment.

JUDGMENT OF THE COURT
23 September 2003

Secretary of State for the Home Department v Hacene Akrich.
(Reference for a preliminary ruling from the Immigration Appeal Tribunal – United Kingdom)

'Freedom of movement for workers – National of a non-Member State who is the spouse of a national of a Member State – Spouse under a prohibition on entering and remaining in that Member State – Temporary establishment of the couple in another Member State – Establishment with a view to acquisition by spouse of a right under Community law to enter and remain in the first Member State – Abuse'

Case C-109/01

Judgment

[Paras 1-28 omitted]

The dispute in the main proceedings

29. In February 1989, Mr Akrich, a Moroccan citizen born in 1967, was granted leave to enter the United Kingdom on a one month's tourist visa. His application for leave to remain as a student was refused in July 1989 and his subsequent appeal was dismissed in August 1990.

30. In June 1990, he was convicted of attempted theft and use of a stolen identity card. On the basis of a deportation order by the Secretary of State, he was deported to Algeria on 2 January 1991.

31. In January 1992, he returned to the United Kingdom by using a false French identity card. He was arrested and again deported in June 1992. He clandestinely returned to the United Kingdom, having remained outside the United Kingdom for less than a month.

32. On 8 June 1996, whilst he was residing unlawfully in the United Kingdom, he married Mrs Helina Jazdzewska, a British citizen, and, at the end of that month, he applied for leave to remain as the spouse of a British citizen.

33. Mr Akrich was detained under the Immigration Act 1971 at the beginning of 1997 and deported in August 1997, in accordance with his wishes, to Dublin (Ireland) where his spouse had been established since June 1997.

34. In January 1998, Mr Akrich applied for revocation of the deportation order and, the following month, for entry clearance as the spouse of a person settled in the United Kingdom.

35. At the time of that application, Mr and Mrs Akrich were interviewed by a British official at the embassy in Dublin about their stay in Ireland and their intentions. It appeared, first, that Mr Akrich's wife had worked in Dublin since August 1997, and full-time in a bank since January 1998, initially being asked to work until May or June 1998 but with the possibility of an extension. Mr Akrich himself worked as a catering assistant through an agency, doing whatever work was available. Mrs Akrich's brother made an offer of accommodation for them in the United Kingdom if they returned and Mrs Akrich was offered employment in the United Kingdom commencing in August 1998.

36. Second, it appears from those interviews that Mr and Mrs Akrich were applying for entry clearance on the basis of the decision of the Court in *Singh*. Thus, in reply to one question, Mrs Akrich said that they intended to return to the United Kingdom because we had heard about EU rights, staying six months and then going back to the UK. She said that she had been given that information by solicitors and others in same situation.

37. On 21 September 1998, the Secretary of State refused to revoke the deportation order. On the instructions of the Secretary of State the application for entry clearance on the basis of *Singh* was also refused, on 29 September 1998. The Secretary of State considered that Mr and Mrs Akrich's move to Ireland was no more than a temporary absence deliberately designed to manufacture a right of residence for Mr Akrich on his return to the United Kingdom and thereby to evade the provisions of the United Kingdom's national legislation, and that Mrs Akrich had not been genuinely exercising rights under the EC Treaty as a worker in another Member State.

38. In October 1998, Mr Akrich appealed against those two decisions to an Immigration Adjudicator (United Kingdom), who allowed the appeal in November 1999.

39. Having found as a fact, *inter alia*, that Mr and Mrs Akrich had moved to Ireland for the express purpose of subsequently exercising Community rights to enable them to return to the United Kingdom, the Immigration Adjudicator nevertheless concluded that, as a matter of law, there had been an effective exercise by Mrs Akrich of Community rights which had not been tainted by the intentions of the spouses, and that they had therefore not relied on Community law to evade the provisions of the United Kingdom's national legislation. He also found that Mr Akrich did not constitute such a genuine and sufficiently serious threat to public policy as to justify the continuation of the deportation order.

40. The Secretary of State appealed to the Immigration Appeal Tribunal against that determination.

Order for reference and questions referred

41. In its order for reference the Immigration Appeal Tribunal pointed out that, at paragraph 24 of the *Singh* judgment, cited above, the Court had formulated a proviso in the following terms: As regards the risk of fraud referred to by the United Kingdom, it is sufficient to note that, as the Court has consistently held ..., the facilities created by the Treaty cannot have the effect of allowing persons who benefit from them to evade the application of national legislation and of prohibiting Member States from taking measures necessary to prevent such abuse.

42. The Immigration Appeal Tribunal questions whether, in accepting Mr Akrich's submission that any measure taken to prevent abuse by a Member State must be compatible with EC law, the Immigration Adjudicator applied the proviso correctly.

43. The Secretary of State takes the view that the proviso must be taken into account at both stages of Mr Akrich's argument, so that it is not possible to determine whether Mr and Mrs Akrich are entitled to the rights conferred on workers, or the scope of the public policy exemption permitting the exclusion of the spouse of a worker from a Member State, without giving due weight to the fact that the purpose of the putative exercise of Community law rights was precisely to avoid the ordinary operation of United Kingdom immigration law.

44. The referring tribunal considered that this was a matter not clearly resolved by the *Singh* judgment and that it was therefore appropriate for the Court to be asked to give further guidance on the issue.

45. In light of those considerations the Immigration Appeal Tribunal decided to stay the proceedings and to refer to the Court the following questions for a preliminary ruling: Where a national of a Member State is married to a third-country national who does not qualify under national legislation to enter or reside in that Member State, and moves to another Member State with the non-national spouse, intending to exercise Community law rights by working there for only a limited period of time in order thereafter to claim the benefit of Community law rights when returning to the Member State of nationality together with the non-national spouse:

(1) is the Member State of nationality entitled to regard the intention of the couple, when moving to the other Member State, to claim the benefit of Community law rights when returning to the Member State of nationality, notwithstanding the non-national spouse's lack of qualification under national legislation, as a reliance on Community law in order to evade the application of national legislation; and

(2) if so, is the Member State of nationality entitled to refuse:
   (a) to revoke any preliminary obstacle to the entry of the non-national spouse into that Member State (on the facts of this case an outstanding deportation order); and
   (b) to accord the non-national spouse a right of entry into its territory?

The questions referred

46. By its questions, which it is appropriate to examine together, the referring tribunal is essentially seeking to ascertain the scope of the judgment in *Singh* in regard to a situation such as that at issue in the main proceedings.

47. In that judgment the Court held that Article 52 of the EEC Treaty (which became Article 52 of the EC Treaty and is now, after amendment, Article 43 EC) and Council Directive 73/148 must be interpreted as requiring a Member State to grant leave to enter and remain in its territory to the spouse, of whatever nationality, of a national of that State who has gone, with that spouse, to another Member State in order to work there as an employed person as envisaged by Article 48 of the EEC Treaty (which became Article 48 of the EC Treaty and is now, after amendment, Article 39 EC) and returns to establish himself or herself as envisaged by Article 52 of the Treaty in the State of which he or she is a national. Under the operative part of that judgment, the spouse must enjoy at least the same rights as would be granted to him or her under Community law if his or her spouse entered and remained in another Member State.

48. The same consequences flow from Article 39 EC if the national of the Member State concerned envisages a return to that Member State in order to work there as an employed person. Consequently, where the spouse is a national of a non-Member State he must enjoy at least the same rights as would be granted to him by Article 10 of Regulation No 1612/68 if his or her spouse entered and resided in another Member State.

49. However, Regulation No 1612/68 covers only freedom of movement within the Community. It is silent as to the rights of a national of a non-Member State, who is the spouse of a citizen of the Union, in regard to access to the territory of the Community.

50. In order to benefit in a situation such as that at issue in the main proceedings from the rights provided for in Article 10 of Regulation No 1612/68, the national of a non-Member State, who is the spouse of a citizen of the Union, must be lawfully resident in a Member State when he moves to another Member State to which the citizen of the Union is migrating or has migrated.

51. That interpretation is consistent with the structure of the Community provisions seeking to secure freedom of movement for workers within the Community, whose exercise must not penalise the migrant worker and his family.

52. Where a citizen of the Union, established in a Member State and married to a national of a non-Member State with a right to remain in that Member State, moves to another Member State in order to work there as an employed person, that move must not result in the loss of the opportunity lawfully to live together, which is the reason why Article 10 of Regulation No 1612/68 confers on such spouse the right to install himself in that other Member State.

53. Conversely, where a citizen of the Union, established in a Member State and married to a national of a non-Member State without the right to remain in that Member State, moves to another Member State in order to work there as an employed person, the fact that that person's spouse has no right under Article 10 of Regulation No 1612/68 to install himself with that person in the other Member State cannot constitute less favourable treatment than that which they enjoyed before the citizen made use of the opportunities afforded by the Treaty as regards movement of persons. Accordingly, the absence of such a right is not such as to deter the citizen of the Union from exercising the rights in regard to freedom of movement conferred by Article 39 EC.

54. The same applies where a citizen of the Union married to a national of a non-Member State returns to the Member State of which he or she is a national in order to work there as an employed person. If the citizen's spouse has a valid right to remain in another Member State, Article 10 of Regulation No 1612/68 applies so that the citizen of the Union is not deterred from exercising his or her right to freedom of movement on returning to the Member State of which he or she is a national. If, conversely, that citizen's spouse does not already have a valid right to remain in another Member State, the absence of any right of the spouse under Article 10 aforesaid to install himself or herself with the citizen of the Union does not have a dissuasive effect in that regard.

55. As regards the question of abuse mentioned at paragraph 24 of the *Singh* judgment, cited above, it should be mentioned that the motives which may have prompted a worker of a Member State to seek employment in another Member State are of no account as regards his right to enter and reside in the territory of the latter State provided that he there pursues or wishes to pursue an effective and genuine activity (Case 53/81 *Levin* [1982] ECR 1035, paragraph 23).

56. Nor are such motives relevant in assessing the legal situation of the couple at the time of their return to the Member State of which the worker is a national. Such conduct cannot constitute an abuse within the meaning of paragraph 24 of the *Singh* judgment even if the spouse did not, at the time when the couple installed itself in

another Member State, have a right to remain in the Member State of which the worker is a national.

57. Conversely, there would be an abuse if the facilities afforded by Community law in favour of migrant workers and their spouses were invoked in the context of marriages of convenience entered into in order to circumvent the provisions relating to entry and residence of nationals of non-Member States.

58. That said, where the marriage is genuine and where, on the return of the citizen of the Union to the Member State of which he is a national, his spouse, who is a national of a non-Member State and with whom he was living in the Member State which he is leaving, is not lawfully resident on the territory of a Member State, regard must be had to respect for family life under Article 8 of the European Convention for the Protection of Human Rights and Fundamental Freedoms, signed at Rome on 4 November 1950 (hereinafter the Convention). That right is among the fundamental rights which, according to the Court's settled case-law, restated by the preamble to the Single European Act and by Article 6(2) EU, are protected in the Community legal order.

59. Even though the Convention does not as such guarantee the right of an alien to enter or to reside in a particular country, the removal of a person from a country where close members of his family are living may amount to an infringement of the right to respect for family life as guaranteed by Article 8(1) of the Convention. Such an interference will infringe the Convention if it does not meet the requirements of paragraph 2 of that article, that is unless it is in accordance with the law, motivated by one or more of the legitimate aims under that paragraph and necessary in a democratic society, that is to say justified by a pressing social need and, in particular, proportionate to the legitimate aim pursued (Case C-60/00 *Carpenter* [2002] ECR I-6279, paragraph 42).

60. The limits of what is necessary in a democratic society where the spouse has committed an offence have been highlighted by the European Court of Human Rights in *Boultif* v *Switzerland*, judgment of 2 August 2001, *Reports of Judgments and Decisions* 2001-IX §§ 46 to 56, and *Amrollahi* v *Denmark*, judgment of 11 July 2002, not yet published in the Reports of Judgments and Decisions, §§ 33 to 44.

61. In light of all the foregoing considerations, the reply to the questions raised should be that:

   – In order to be able to benefit in a situation such as that at issue in the main proceedings from the rights provided for in Article 10 of Regulation No 1612/68, a national of a non-Member State married to a citizen of the Union must be lawfully resident in a Member State when he moves to another Member State to which the citizen of the Union is migrating or has migrated.

In order to be able to benefit in a situation such as that at issue in the main proceedings from the rights provided for in Article 10 of Regulation No 1612/68, a national of a non-Member State married to a citizen of the Union must be lawfully resident in a Member State when he moves to another Member State to which the citizen of the Union is migrating or has migrated.

– Article 10 of Regulation No 1612/68 is not applicable where the national of a Member State and the national of a non-Member State have entered into a marriage of convenience in order to circumvent the provisions relating to entry and residence of nationals of non-Member States.

Article 10 of Regulation No 1612/68 is not applicable where the national of a Member State and the national of a non-Member State have entered into a marriage of convenience in order to circumvent the provisions relating to entry and residence of nationals of non-Member States.

– Where the marriage between a national of a Member State and a national of a non-Member State is genuine, the fact that the spouses installed themselves in another Member State in order, on their return to the Member State of which the former is a national, to obtain the benefit of rights conferred by Community law is not relevant to an assessment of their legal situation by the competent authorities of the latter State.

Where the marriage between a national of a Member State and a national of a non-Member State is genuine, the fact that the spouses installed themselves in another Member State in order, on their return to the Member State of which the former is a national, to obtain the benefit of rights conferred by Community law is not relevant to an assessment of their legal situation by the competent authorities of the latter State.

– Where a national of a Member State married to a national of a non-Member State with whom she is living in another Member State returns to the Member State of which she is a national in order to work there as an employed person and, at the time of her return, her spouse does not enjoy the rights provided for in Article 10 of Regulation No 1612/68 because he has not resided lawfully on the territory of a Member State, the competent authorities of the first-mentioned Member State, in assessing the application by the spouse to enter and remain in that Member State, must none the less have regard to the right to respect for family life under Article 8 of the Convention, provided that the marriage is genuine.

– Where a national of a Member State married to a national of a non-Member State with whom she is living in another Member State returns to the Member State of which she is a national in order to work there as an employed person and, at the time of her return, her spouse does not enjoy the rights provided for in Article 10 of Regulation No 1612/68 because he has not resided lawfully on the territory of a Member State, the competent authorities of the first-mentioned Member State, in assessing the application by the spouse to enter and remain in that Member State, must none the less have regard to the right to respect for family life under Article 8 of the Convention, provided that the marriage is genuine.

Costs

[Para. 62 omitted]

On those grounds,

THE COURT,

in answer to the questions referred to it by the Immigration Appeal Tribunal by order of 3 October 2000, hereby rules:

1. **In order to be able to benefit in a situation such as that at issue in the main proceedings from the rights provided for in Article 10 of Regulation (EEC) No 1612/68 of the Council of 15 October 1968 on freedom of movement for workers within the Community, a national of a non-Member State married to a citizen of the Union must be lawfully resident in a Member State when he moves to another Member State to which the citizen of the Union is migrating or has migrated.**

2. **Article 10 of Regulation No 1612/68 is not applicable where the national of a Member State and the national of a non-Member State have entered into a marriage of convenience in order to circumvent the provisions relating to entry and residence of nationals of non-Member States.**

3. **Where the marriage between a national of a Member State and a national of a non-Member State is genuine, the fact that the spouses installed themselves in another Member State in order, on their return to the Member State of which the former is a national, to obtain the benefit of rights conferred by Community law is not relevant to an assessment of their legal situation by the competent authorities of the latter State.**

4. **Where a national of a Member State married to a national of a non-Member State with whom she is living in another Member State returns to the Member State of which she is a national in order to work there as an employed person and, at the time of her return, her spouse does not enjoy the rights provided for in Article 10 of Regulation No 1612/68 because he has not resided lawfully on the territory of a Member State, the competent authorities of the first-mentioned Member State, in assessing the application by the spouse to enter and remain in that Member State, must none the less have regard to the right to respect for family life under Article 8 of the European Convention for the Protection of Human Rights and Fun-**

damental Freedoms, signed at Rome on 4 November 1950, provided that the marriage is genuine.

Comments and questions

In Case C-370/90 *Singh* [1992] ECR I-4265, the CJEU established a Union citizen's right of residence under Article 49 TFEU (formerly Article 43 TEC), together with their spouse from a third country, where the married couple had carried out paid employment in another Member State, and had returned to the Union citizen's home state in order to establish a commercial undertaking. The judgment in the *Akrich* case concerns the interpretation of the *Singh* judgment where a Union citizen married a citizen of a third country after that third country citizen has been illegally resident in the Union citizen's home Member State, whereupon the married couple travelled to another Member State and took up paid employment, and then returned to the home Member State to take up paid employment there. In such a case, is the married couple entitled to reside in the home Member State as a family, according to Union law? If the answer to this is in the affirmative, does this mean that Union law restricts the scope of the home Member State's immigration laws where they are more restrictive?

In his Opinion, the Advocate General followed a similar line of thought on Union law's restriction of national immigration laws. He noted the opposition between, on the one hand, more restrictive immigration laws, including rules on the right to live together as a family, and on the other hand the more liberal rules on residence in Union law. He therefore proposed that where a third country citizen had not originally had permission to enter the European Union, the home Member State could deny that party admission, by reference to overriding national interests, after having undertaken a prior individual investigation in accordance with the criteria of the national immigration laws.

In response to this, in paragraph 54 of the *Akrich* judgment the CJEU stated that, if the citizen's spouse (a citizen of a third country) has a valid right to remain in another Member State, Article 10 of Regulation (EEC) No 1612/68 on freedom of movement for workers within the Union (then in force) applies so that the Union citizen is not deterred from exercising their right to freedom of movement on returning to the Member State of which they are a national to take up paid employment. If that citizen's spouse does not have a valid right to remain in another Member State, the CJEU took the view that the Union citizen could be prevented from exercising their freedom of movement. On the other hand, if the spouse does not already have a valid right to remain in another Member State, the married couple does not have a right, under Union law, to return as a family to the Union citizen's home Member State. In the case in question this meant that if Akrich had had a right of residence under Irish immigration laws while the couple was working in Ireland, then as a British citizen under Article 45 TFEU (formerly Article 39 TEC) and Article 10 of Regulation (EEC) No 1612/68 Akrich's wife would have been entitled to live together with him as a family in the UK, by virtue of her professional occupation in the UK. This applied regardless of whether the British immigration law recognised such a right and regardless of whether Akrich had previously been resident illegally in the UK. Do you agree that, if the CJEU had reached the opposite conclusion, British citizens might not have been able to exercise their right of freedom of movement to work by moving back to the UK?

The CJEU refused to allow that the reasons that had led the married couple to take work in Ireland had any significance for the British citizen's right under Union law to live with his spouse as a family in the UK; cf. paragraphs 55-56 of the judgment. This meant that the British immigration authorities could not assert the question of abuse of the law against the couple. The CJEU would only recognise the objection of abuse in the context of marriages of convenience; cf. paragraph 57.

Article 10 of Regulation No 1612/68 on freedom of movement for workers within the Union has now been replaced by Article 7(1)(d) of Directive 2004/38/EC on the right of citizens of the Union and their family members to move and reside freely within the territory of the Member States.

It is important to emphasise that the *Akrich* case concerned a case where a citizen from a third country had, under British law, been resident illegally in the UK, so the question was whether the Union rules on freedom of movement for workers limited the UK's right to enforce its immigration laws against Akrich. In the view of the CJEU, Akrich and his British wife could only rely on the Union rules against the British authorities if, prior to this, Akrich had been lawfully resident in Ireland under the Irish immigration laws. In Case C-1/05 *Yunying Jia* v *Migrationsverket* [2007] ECR I-9607, a Swedish immigration board referred a question for a preliminary ruling on whether the decision in the *Akrich* case required that, when deciding whether to grant a residence permit to a third country citizen who is a member of the family of a Union citizen who has exercised their right to freedom of movement, a Member State must (always) make it conditional on the family member having previously had lawful residence in another Member State.

The case concerned a German-Chinese married couple and the German spouse's Chinese mother-in-law. The couple had lived in Sweden since 1995, where the German spouse (the Union citizen) was self-employed. The mother-in-law, who had been given a 90 day visa to visit Sweden issued by the Swedish Embassy in China, and the father-in-law who had subsequently been granted a 180 day visa to visit Sweden, also issued by the Swedish Embassy in China, applied for Swedish residence permits but were refused (the reference for a preliminary ruling only concerned the mother-in-law). As the mother-in-law had come directly from China to the Member State where she sought a residence permit, the question was whether Union law applied to the case at all. In paragraphs 31-32 of the judgment the CJEU stated that, in contrast to *Akrich*, the mother-in-law was legally present in Sweden at the time when she sought a residence permit. The CJEU therefore held that '[i]t follows that the condition of previous lawful residence in another Member State, as formulated in the judgment in *Akrich*, cannot be transposed to the present case and thus cannot apply to such a situation.' On this basis, the CJEU found that Union law does not *impose* on Member States a requirement to make the grant of a residence permit to a national of a third country, who is a family member of a Union citizen who has exercised their right of free movement, conditional on the family member already being lawfully resident in another Member State. As can be seen, the CJEU did not thereby decide whether Union law *entitles* Member States to make a residence permit conditional on a national of a third country having had prior lawful residence in another Member State. This question was decided by the CJEU in Case C-127/08 *Metock* [2008] ECR I-6241, discussed above. In this case the CJEU rejected the argument that the Free Movement Directive (Directive 2004/38/EC) allows such a requirement to be imposed.

As the German citizen was self-employed in a Member State other than his own, the rules then in force of Directive 73/148 on the abolition of restrictions on movement and residence within the Union for nationals of Member States with regard to establishment and the provision of services applied. It followed from Article 1(1)(d) of the Directive that Member States should repeal travel and residence restrictions on 'the relatives in the ascending and descending lines of such nationals and of the spouse of such nationals, which relatives are dependent on them, irrespective of their nationality'. The CJEU had to determine more specifically what this condition of dependence consisted of. The CJEU referred to the fact that, according to its practice, the status of a family member who is dependent arises from a situation which is characterised by the fact that the family member's material needs are provided for by a Union citizen who has exercised the right of freedom of movement, or by the Union citizen's spouse. The material needs must exist in the relative's home country or the country where he/she has come from at the time when he/she seeks to join the Union citizen in question. The CJEU thereafter stated that 'evidence may be adduced by any appropriate means' to show that the relative in question is provided for by the Union citizen or by the Union citizen's spouse. This may be by a document issued by the competent authority in the relative's home country. On the other hand, 'a mere undertaking from the [Union] national or his or her spouse to support the family members concerned need not be regarded as establishing the existence of the family members' situation of real dependence'; cf. paragraph 43 of the judgment.

Consider whether the right which, following the *Akrich* case, a Union citizen has to live together with his/her third country spouse upon returning to the Union citizen's home Member State, in accordance with Article 45 TFEU and Article 7(1)(d) of Directive 2004/38, will also apply where a married couple moves to another Member State without carrying out any form of work there, but where the third-country national is granted a residence permit in accordance with that other Member State's immigration laws, and where, after a period, the married couple move back to the Union citizen's home Member State where the Union citizen takes up paid employment? What are the arguments for and against the right in the *Akrich* case applying in this situation? Would it make any difference to this assessment if the married couple merely moved back to the Union citizen's home Member State, without the Union citizen taking up any paid employment there? On these issues, see judgment of the CJEU in Case C-456/12 O, reproduced below.

JUDGMENT OF THE COURT (Grand Chamber)
25 July 2008

Blaise Baheten Metock and others v Minister for Justice, Equality and Law Reform.
(Reference for a preliminary ruling from the High Court – Ireland)

'Directive 2004/38/EC – Right of Union citizens and their family members to move and reside freely in the territory of a Member State – Family members who are nationals of non-member countries – Nationals of non-member countries who entered the host Member State before becoming spouses of Union citizens'

Case C-127/08

Judgment

1. This reference for a preliminary ruling concerns the interpretation of Directive 2004/38/EC of the European Parliament and of the Council of 29 April 2004 on the right of citizens of the Union and their family members to move and reside freely within the territory of the Member States amending Regulation (EEC) No 1612/68 and repealing Directives 64/221/EEC, 68/360/EEC, 72/194/EEC, 73/148/EEC, 75/34/EEC, 75/35/EEC, 90/364/EEC, 90/365/EEC and 93/96/EEC (OJ 2004 L 158, p. 77, and corrigenda (OJ 2004 L 229, p. 35, OJ 2005 L 30, p. 27, OJ 2005 L 197, p. 34, and OJ 2007 L 204, p. 28)).

2. The reference was made in the course of four applications for judicial review before the High Court, each seeking inter alia an order of certiorari quashing the decision of the Minister for Justice, Equality and Law Reform ('the Minister for Justice') refusing to grant a residence card to a national of a non-member country married to a Union citizen residing in Ireland.

Legal context

Community legislation

3. Directive 2004/38 was adopted on the basis of Articles 12 EC, 18 EC, 40 EC, 44 EC and 52 EC.

4. Recitals 1 to 5, 11, 14 and 31 in the preamble to that directive read as follows:

   '(1) Citizenship of the Union confers on every citizen of the Union a primary and individual right to move and reside freely within the territory of the Member States, subject to the limitations and conditions laid down in the Treaty and to the measures adopted to give it effect.

(2) The free movement of persons constitutes one of the fundamental freedoms of the internal market, which comprises an area without internal frontiers, in which freedom is ensured in accordance with the provisions of the Treaty.

(3) Union citizenship should be the fundamental status of nationals of the Member States when they exercise their right of free movement and residence. It is therefore necessary to codify and review the existing Community instruments dealing separately with workers, self-employed persons, as well as students and other inactive persons in order to simplify and strengthen the right of free movement and residence of all Union citizens.

(4) With a view to remedying this sector-by-sector, piecemeal approach to the right of free movement and residence and facilitating the exercise of this right, there needs to be a single legislative act ...

(5) The right of all Union citizens to move and reside freely within the territory of the Member States should, if it is to be exercised under objective conditions of freedom and dignity, be also granted to their family members, irrespective of nationality ...

...

(11) The fundamental and personal right of residence in another Member State is conferred directly on Union citizens by the Treaty and is not dependent upon their having fulfilled administrative procedures.

...

(14) The supporting documents required by the competent authorities for the issuing of a registration certificate or of a residence card should be comprehensively specified in order to avoid divergent administrative practices or interpretations constituting an undue obstacle to the exercise of the right of residence by Union citizens and their family members.

...

(31) This Directive respects the fundamental rights and freedoms and observes the principles recognised in particular by the Charter of Fundamental Rights of the European Union. In accordance with the prohibition of discrimination contained in the Charter, Member States should implement this Directive without discrimination between the beneficiaries of this Directive on grounds such as sex, race, colour, ethnic or social origin, genetic characteristics, language, religion or beliefs, political or other opinion, membership of an ethnic minority, property, birth, disability, age or sexual orientation'.

5. According to Article 1(a) of Directive 2004/38, the directive concerns inter alia 'the conditions governing the exercise of the right of free movement and residence within the territory of the Member States by Union citizens and their family members'.

6. According to Article 2(2)(a) of Directive 2004/38, for the purposes of the directive, 'family member' means inter alia the spouse.

7. Article 3 of Directive 2004/38, 'Beneficiaries', provides in paragraph 1:

   'This Directive shall apply to all Union citizens who move to or reside in a Member State other than that of which they are a national, and to their family members as defined in point 2 of Article 2 who accompany or join them.'

8. Article 5 of Directive 2004/38, 'Right of entry', states:

   '1. Without prejudice to the provisions on travel documents applicable to national border controls, Member States shall grant Union citizens leave to enter their territory with a valid identity card or passport and shall grant family members who are not nationals of a Member State leave to enter their territory with a valid passport.

   ...

   2. Family members who are not nationals of a Member State shall only be required to have an entry visa in accordance with Regulation (EC) No 539/2001 or, where appropriate, with national law. For the purposes of this Directive, possession of the valid residence card referred to in Article 10 shall exempt such family members from the visa requirement.

   ...

   5. The Member State may require the person concerned to report his/her presence within its territory within a reasonable and non-discriminatory period of time. Failure to comply with this requirement may make the person concerned liable to proportionate and non-discriminatory sanctions.'

9. Article 7 of Directive 2004/38, 'Right of residence for more than three months', states:

   '1. All Union citizens shall have the right of residence on the territory of another Member State for a period of longer than three months if they:
   (a) are workers or self-employed persons in the host Member State; or

   (b) have sufficient resources for themselves and their family members not to become a burden on the social assistance system of the host Member State during their period of residence and have comprehensive sickness insurance cover in the host Member State; or

(c) – are enrolled at a private or public establishment, accredited or financed by the host Member State on the basis of its legislation or administrative practice, for the principal purpose of following a course of study, including vocational training; and
– have comprehensive sickness insurance cover in the host Member State and assure the relevant national authority, by means of a declaration or by such equivalent means as they may choose, that they have sufficient resources for themselves and their family members not to become a burden on the social assistance system of the host Member State during their period of residence; ...

...

2. The right of residence provided for in paragraph 1 shall extend to family members who are not nationals of a Member State, accompanying or joining the Union citizen in the host Member State, provided that such Union citizen satisfies the conditions referred to in paragraph 1(a), (b) or (c).

...'

10. Article 9 of Directive 2004/38, 'Administrative formalities for family members who are not nationals of a Member State', provides:

'1. Member States shall issue a residence card to family members of a Union citizen who are not nationals of a Member State, where the planned period of residence is for more than three months.

2. The deadline for submitting the residence card application may not be less than three months from the date of arrival.

3. Failure to comply with the requirement to apply for a residence card may make the person concerned liable to proportionate and non-discriminatory sanctions.'

11. Article 10 of Directive 2004/38, 'Issue of residence cards', provides:

'1. The right of residence of family members of a Union citizen who are not nationals of a Member State shall be evidenced by the issuing of a document called 'Residence card of a family member of a Union citizen' no later than six months from the date on which they submit the application. A certificate of application for the residence card shall be issued immediately.

2. For the residence card to be issued, Member States shall require presentation of the following documents:

(a) a valid passport;
(b) a document attesting to the existence of a family relationship or of a registered partnership;
(c) the registration certificate or, in the absence of a registration system, any other proof of residence in the host Member State of the Union citizen whom they are accompanying or joining;
(d) in cases falling under points (c) and (d) of Article 2(2), documentary evidence that the conditions laid down therein are met;

...'

12. Article 27 of Directive 2004/38, which appears in Chapter VI of the directive, 'Restrictions on the right of entry and the right of residence on grounds of public policy, public security or public health', provides in paragraphs 1 and 2:

'1. Subject to the provisions of this Chapter, Member States may restrict the freedom of movement and residence of Union citizens and their family members, irrespective of nationality, on grounds of public policy, public security or public health. These grounds shall not be invoked to serve economic ends.

2. Measures taken on grounds of public policy or public security shall comply with the principle of proportionality and shall be based exclusively on the personal conduct of the individual concerned. Previous criminal convictions shall not in themselves constitute grounds for taking such measures.

The personal conduct of the individual concerned must represent a genuine, present and sufficiently serious threat affecting one of the fundamental interests of society. Justifications that are isolated from the particulars of the case or that rely on considerations of general prevention shall not be accepted.'

13. Article 35 of Directive 2004/38, 'Abuse of rights', provides:

'Member States may adopt the necessary measures to refuse, terminate or withdraw any right conferred by this Directive in the case of abuse of rights or fraud, such as marriages of convenience. Any such measure shall be proportionate and subject to the procedural safeguards provided for in Articles 30 and 31.'

14. As stated in Article 38 of Directive 2004/38, it repealed inter alia Articles 10 and 11 of Regulation (EEC) No 1612/68 of the Council of 15 October 1968 on freedom of movement for workers within the Community (OJ, English Special Edition 1968 (II), p. 475), as amended by Council Regulation (EEC) No 2434/92 of 27 July 1992 (OJ 1992 L 245, p. 1) ('Regulation No 1612/68').

National legislation

15. At the material time, Directive 2004/38 was transposed into Irish law by the European Communities (Free Movement of Persons) (No 2) Regulations 2006, which were made on 18 December 2006 and entered into force on 1 January 2007 ('the 2006 Regulations').

16. Regulation 3(1) and (2) of the 2006 Regulations provides:

'(1) These Regulations shall apply to –
(a) Union citizens,
(b) subject to paragraph (2), qualifying family members of Union citizens who are not themselves Union citizens, and
(c) subject to paragraph (2), permitted family members of Union citizens.

(2) These Regulations shall not apply to a family member unless the family member is lawfully resident in another Member State and is –
(a) seeking to enter the State in the company of a Union citizen in respect of whom he or she is a family member, or
(b) seeking to join a Union citizen, in respect of whom he or she is a family member, who is lawfully present in the State.'

17. 'Qualifying family members of Union citizens' within the meaning of Regulation 3 of the 2006 Regulations include spouses of Union citizens.

The main proceedings

The Metock case

18. Mr Metock, a national of Cameroon, arrived in Ireland on 23 June 2006 and applied for asylum. His application was definitively refused on 28 February 2007.

19. Ms Ngo Ikeng, born a national of Cameroon, has acquired United Kingdom nationality. She has resided and worked in Ireland since late 2006.

20. Mr Metock and Ms Ngo Ikeng met in Cameroon in 1994 and have been in a relationship since then. They have two children, one born in 1998 and the other in 2006. They were married in Ireland on 12 October 2006.

21. On 6 November 2006 Mr Metock applied for a residence card as the spouse of a Union citizen working and residing in Ireland. The application was refused by decision of the Minister for Justice of 28 June 2007, on the ground that Mr Metock did not satisfy the condition of prior lawful residence in another Member State required by Regulation 3(2) of the 2006 Regulations.

22. Mr Metock, Ms Ngo Ikeng and their children brought proceedings against that decision.

The Ikogho case

23. Mr Ikogho, a national of a non-member country, arrived in Ireland in November 2004 and applied for asylum. His application was definitively refused and the Minister for Justice made a deportation order against him on 15 September 2005. A challenge to the deportation order was dismissed by order of the High Court of 19 June 2007.

24. Mrs Ikogho, who is a United Kingdom national and a Union citizen, has resided and worked in Ireland since 1996.

25. Mr and Mrs Ikogho met in Ireland in December 2004 and were married there on 7 June 2006.

26. On 6 July 2006 Mr Ikogho applied for a residence card as the spouse of a Union citizen residing and working in Ireland. His application was refused by decision of the Minister for Justice of 12 January 2007, on the ground that, by reason of the deportation order of 15 September 2005, Mr Ikogho was staying in Ireland illegally at the time of his marriage.

27. Mr and Mrs Ikogho brought proceedings against that decision.

The Chinedu case

28. Mr Chinedu, a Nigerian national, arrived in Ireland in December 2005 and applied for asylum. His application was definitively refused on 8 August 2006. Ms Babucke, of German nationality, is lawfully resident in Ireland.

29. Mr Chinedu and Ms Babucke were married in Ireland on 3 July 2006.

30. By application received by the Minister for Justice on 1 August 2006, Mr Chinedu applied for a residence card as the spouse of a Union citizen. The application was refused by decision of the Minister for Justice of 17 April 2007, on the ground that Mr Chinedu did not satisfy the condition of prior lawful residence in another Member State required by Regulation 3(2) of the 2006 Regulations.

31. Mr Chinedu and Ms Babucke brought proceedings against that decision.

The Igboanusi case

32. Mr Igboanusi, a Nigerian national, arrived in Ireland on 2 April 2004 and applied for asylum. His application was refused on 31 May 2005 and the Minister for Justice made a deportation order against him on 15 September 2005.

33. Ms Batkowska, a Polish national, has resided and worked in Ireland since April 2006.

34. Mr Igboanusi and Ms Batkowska met in Ireland and were married there on 24 November 2006.

35. On 27 February 2007 Mr Igboanusi applied for a residence card as the spouse of a Union citizen. His application was refused by decision of the Minister for Justice of 27 August 2007, on the ground that Mr Igboanusi did not satisfy the condition of prior lawful residence in another Member State required by Regulation 3(2) of the 2006 Regulations.

36. Mr Igboanusi and Ms Batkowska brought proceedings against that decision.

37. On 16 November 2007 Mr Igboanusi was arrested and detained pursuant to the deportation order against him. He was deported to Nigeria in December 2007.

The main proceedings and the order for reference

38. The four cases were heard together before the national court.

39. All the applicants in the main proceedings submitted essentially that Regulation 3(2) of the 2006 Regulations is not compatible with Directive 2004/38.

40. They argued that nationals of non-member countries who are spouses of Union citizens have a right, consequential to and dependent on that of the Union citizen, to move and reside in a Member State other than that of which the Union citizen is a national, a right which derives from the family relationship alone.

41. They submitted that Directive 2004/38 governs exhaustively the conditions of entry into and residence in a Member State for a Union citizen who is a national of another Member State and his family members, so that the Member States are not entitled to impose additional conditions. Since the directive makes no provision for a condition of prior lawful residence in another Member State, such as that imposed by the Irish legislation, that legislation is not consistent with Community law.

42. The applicants in the main proceedings further submitted that a national of a non-member country who becomes a family member of a Union citizen while that citi-

zen is resident in a Member State other than that of which he is a national accompanies that citizen within the meaning of Articles 3(1) and 7(2) of Directive 2004/38.

43. The Minister for Justice replied essentially that Directive 2004/38 does not preclude the condition of prior lawful residence in another Member State laid down in Regulation 3(2) of the 2006 Regulations.

44. He submitted that there is a division of competences between the Member States and the Community, under which the Member States have competence in relation to the admission into a Member State of nationals of non-member countries coming from outside Community territory, while the Community has competence to regulate the movement of Union citizens and their family members within the Union.

45. He argued that Directive 2004/38 therefore leaves Member States discretion to impose on nationals of non-member countries who are spouses of Union citizens a condition of prior lawful residence in another Member State. Moreover, that such a condition is consistent with Community law follows from Case C-109/01 *Akrich* [2003] ECR I-9607 and Case C-1/05 *Jia* [2007] ECR I-1.

46. The national court points out that none of the marriages in question is a marriage of convenience.

47. Since it considered that an interpretation of Directive 2004/38 was necessary for it to give judgment in the main proceedings, the High Court decided to stay the proceedings and refer the following questions to the Court for a preliminary ruling:

‘(1) Does Directive 2004/38/EC permit a Member State to have a general requirement that a non-EU national spouse of a Union citizen must have been lawfully resident in another Member State prior to coming to the host Member State in order that he or she be entitled to benefit from the provisions of Directive 2004/38/EC?

(2) Does Article 3(1) of Directive 2004/38/EC include within its scope of application a non-EU national who is:

- a spouse of a Union citizen who resides in the host Member State and satisfies a condition in Article 7(1)(a), (b) or (c) and
- is then residing in the host Member State with the Union citizen as his/her spouse

irrespective of when or where their marriage took place or when or how the non-EU national entered the host Member State?

(3) If the answer to the preceding question is in the negative does Article 3(1) of Directive 2004/38/EC include within its scope of application a non-EU national spouse of a Union citizen who is:

- a spouse of a Union citizen who resides in the host Member State and satisfies a condition in Article 7(1)(a), (b) or (c) and
- resides in the host Member State with the Union citizen as his/her spouse
- has entered the host Member State independently of the Union citizen and
- subsequently married the Union citizen in the host Member State?'

The first question

48. By its first question the referring court asks whether Directive 2004/38 precludes legislation of a Member State which requires a national of a non-member country who is the spouse of a Union citizen residing in that Member State but not possessing its nationality to have previously been lawfully resident in another Member State before arriving in the host Member State, in order to benefit from the provisions of that directive.

49. In the first place, it must be stated that, as regards family members of a Union citizen, no provision of Directive 2004/38 makes the application of the directive conditional on their having previously resided in a Member State.

50. As Article 3(1) of Directive 2004/38 states, the directive applies to all Union citizens who move to or reside in a Member State other than that of which they are a national, and to their family members as defined in point 2 of Article 2 of the directive who accompany them or join them in that Member State. The definition of family members in point 2 of Article 2 of Directive 2004/38 does not distinguish according to whether or not they have already resided lawfully in another Member State.

51. It must also be pointed out that Articles 5, 6(2) and 7(2) of Directive 2004/38 confer the rights of entry, of residence for up to three months, and of residence for more than three months in the host Member State on nationals of non-member countries who are family members of a Union citizen whom they accompany or join in that Member State, without any reference to the place or conditions of residence they had before arriving in that Member State.

52. In particular, the first subparagraph of Article 5(2) of Directive 2004/38 provides that nationals of non-member countries who are family members of a Union citizen are required to have an entry visa, unless they are in possession of the valid residence card referred to in Article 10 of that directive. In that, as follows from Articles 9(1) and 10(1) of Directive 2004/38, the residence card is the document that evidences the right of residence for more than three months in a Member State of

the family members of a Union citizen who are not nationals of a Member State, the fact that Article 5(2) provides for the entry into the host Member State of family members of a Union citizen who do not have a residence card shows that Directive 2004/38 is capable of applying also to family members who were not already lawfully resident in another Member State.

53. Similarly, Article 10(2) of Directive 2004/38, which lists exhaustively the documents which nationals of non-member countries who are family members of a Union citizen may have to present to the host Member State in order to have a residence card issued, does not provide for the possibility of the host Member State asking for documents to demonstrate any prior lawful residence in another Member State.

54. In those circumstances, Directive 2004/38 must be interpreted as applying to all nationals of non-member countries who are family members of a Union citizen within the meaning of point 2 of Article 2 of that directive and accompany or join the Union citizen in a Member State other than that of which he is a national, and as conferring on them rights of entry and residence in that Member State, without distinguishing according to whether or not the national of a non-member country has already resided lawfully in another Member State.

55. That interpretation is supported by the Court's case-law on the instruments of secondary law concerning freedom of movement for persons adopted before Directive 2004/38.

56. Even before the adoption of Directive 2004/38, the Community legislature recognised the importance of ensuring the protection of the family life of nationals of the Member States in order to eliminate obstacles to the exercise of the fundamental freedoms guaranteed by the EC Treaty (Case C-60/00 *Carpenter* [2002] ECR I-6279, paragraph 38; Case C-459/99 *MRAX* [2002] ECR I-6591, paragraph 53; Case C-157/03 *Commission* v *Spain* [2005] ECR I-2911, paragraph 26; Case C-503/03 *Commission* v *Spain* [2006] ECR I-1097, paragraph 41; Case C-441/02 *Commission* v *Germany* [2006] ECR I-3449, paragraph 109; and Case C-291/05 *Eind* [2007] ECR I-0000, paragraph 44).

57. To that end, the Community legislature has considerably expanded, in Regulation No 1612/68 and in the directives on freedom of movement for persons adopted before Directive 2004/38, the application of Community law on entry into and residence in the territory of the Member States to nationals of non-member countries who are spouses of nationals of Member States (see, to that effect, Case C-503/03 *Commission* v *Spain*, paragraph 41).

58. It is true that the Court held in paragraphs 50 and 51 of *Akrich* that, in order to benefit from the rights provided for in Article 10 of Regulation No 1612/68, the nation-

al of a non-member country who is the spouse of a Union citizen must be lawfully resident in a Member State when he moves to another Member State to which the citizen of the Union is migrating or has migrated. However, that conclusion must be reconsidered. The benefit of such rights cannot depend on the prior lawful residence of such a spouse in another Member State (see, to that effect, *MRAX*, paragraph 59, and Case C-157/03 *Commission* v *Spain*, paragraph 28).

59. The same interpretation must be adopted a fortiori with respect to Directive 2004/38, which amended Regulation No 1612/68 and repealed the earlier directives on freedom of movement for persons. As is apparent from recital 3 in the preamble to Directive 2004/38, it aims in particular to 'strengthen the right of free movement and residence of all Union citizens', so that Union citizens cannot derive less rights from that directive than from the instruments of secondary legislation which it amends or repeals.

60. In the second place, the above interpretation of Directive 2004/38 is consistent with the division of competences between the Member States and the Community.

61. It is common ground that the Community derives from Articles 18(2) EC, 40 EC, 44 EC and 52 EC – on the basis of which Directive 2004/38 inter alia was adopted – competence to enact the necessary measures to bring about freedom of movement for Union citizens.

62. As already pointed out in paragraph 56 above, if Union citizens were not allowed to lead a normal family life in the host Member State, the exercise of the freedoms they are guaranteed by the Treaty would be seriously obstructed.

63. Consequently, within the competence conferred on it by those articles of the Treaty, the Community legislature can regulate the conditions of entry and residence of the family members of a Union citizen in the territory of the Member States, where the fact that it is impossible for the Union citizen to be accompanied or joined by his family in the host Member State would be such as to interfere with his freedom of movement by discouraging him from exercising his rights of entry into and residence in that Member State.

64. The refusal of the host Member State to grant rights of entry and residence to the family members of a Union citizen is such as to discourage that citizen from moving to or residing in that Member State, even if his family members are not already lawfully resident in the territory of another Member State.

65. It follows that the Community legislature has competence to regulate, as it did by Directive 2004/38, the entry and residence of nationals of non-member countries who are family members of a Union citizen in the Member State in which that citi-

zen has exercised his right of freedom of movement, including where the family members were not already lawfully resident in another Member State.

66. Consequently, the interpretation put forward by the Minister for Justice and by several of the governments that have submitted observations that the Member States retain exclusive competence, subject to Title IV of Part Three of the Treaty, to regulate the first access to Community territory of family members of a Union citizen who are nationals of non-member countries must be rejected.

67. Indeed, to allow the Member States exclusive competence to grant or refuse entry into and residence in their territory to nationals of non-member countries who are family members of Union citizens and have not already resided lawfully in another Member State would have the effect that the freedom of movement of Union citizens in a Member State whose nationality they do not possess would vary from one Member State to another, according to the provisions of national law concerning immigration, with some Member States permitting entry and residence of family members of a Union citizen and other Member States refusing them.

68. That would not be compatible with the objective set out in Article 3(1)(c) EC of an internal market characterised by the abolition, as between Member States, of obstacles to the free movement of persons. Establishing an internal market implies that the conditions of entry and residence of a Union citizen in a Member State whose nationality he does not possess are the same in all the Member States. Freedom of movement for Union citizens must therefore be interpreted as the right to leave any Member State, in particular the Member State whose nationality the Union citizen possesses, in order to become established under the same conditions in any Member State other than the Member State whose nationality the Union citizen possesses.

69. Furthermore, the interpretation mentioned in paragraph 66 above would lead to the paradoxical outcome that a Member State would be obliged, under Council Directive 2003/86/EC of 22 September 2003 on the right to family reunification (OJ 2003 L 251, p. 12), to authorise the entry and residence of the spouse of a national of a non-member country lawfully resident in its territory where the spouse is not already lawfully resident in another Member State, but would be free to refuse the entry and residence of the spouse of a Union citizen in the same circumstances.

70. Consequently, Directive 2004/38 confers on all nationals of non-member countries who are family members of a Union citizen within the meaning of point 2 of Article 2 of that directive, and accompany or join the Union citizen in a Member State other than that of which he is a national, rights of entry into and residence in the host Member State, regardless of whether the national of a non-member country has already been lawfully resident in another Member State.

71. The Minister for Justice and several of the governments that have submitted observations contend, however, that, in a context typified by strong pressure of migration, it is necessary to control immigration at the external borders of the Community, which presupposes an individual examination of all the circumstances surrounding a first entry into Community territory. An interpretation of Directive 2004/38 prohibiting a host Member State from requiring prior lawful residence in another Member State would undermine the ability of the Member States to control immigration at their external frontiers.

72. The Minister for Justice submits in particular that that interpretation would have serious consequences for the Member States by bringing about a great increase in the number of persons able to benefit from a right of residence in the Community.

73. On this point, the answer must be, first, that it is not all nationals of non-member countries who derive rights of entry into and residence in a Member State from Directive 2004/38, but only those who are family members, within the meaning of point 2 of Article 2 of that directive, of a Union citizen who has exercised his right of freedom of movement by becoming established in a Member State other than the Member State of which he is a national.

74. Second, Directive 2004/38 does not deprive the Member States of all possibility of controlling the entry into their territory of family members of Union citizens. Under Chapter VI of that directive, Member States may, where this is justified, refuse entry and residence on grounds of public policy, public security or public health. Such a refusal will be based on an individual examination of the particular case.

75. Moreover, in accordance with Article 35 of Directive 2004/38, Member States may adopt the necessary measures to refuse, terminate or withdraw any right conferred by that directive in the case of abuse of rights or fraud, such as marriages of convenience, it being understood that any such measure must be proportionate and subject to the procedural safeguards provided for in the directive.

76. Those governments further submit that that interpretation of Directive 2004/38 would lead to unjustified reverse discrimination, in so far as nationals of the host Member State who have never exercised their right of freedom of movement would not derive rights of entry and residence from Community law for their family members who are nationals of non-member countries.

77. In that regard, it is settled case-law that the Treaty rules governing freedom of movement for persons and the measures adopted to implement them cannot be applied to activities which have no factor linking them with any of the situations governed by Community law and which are confined in all relevant respects within a single Member State (Case C-212/06 *Government of the French Community and Walloon Government* [2008] ECR I-0000, paragraph 33).

78. Any difference in treatment between those Union citizens and those who have exercised their right of freedom of movement, as regards the entry and residence of their family members, does not therefore fall within the scope of Community law.

79. Moreover, it should be recalled that all the Member States are parties to the European Convention for the Protection of Human Rights and Fundamental Freedoms signed in Rome on 4 November 1950, which enshrines in Article 8 the right to respect for private and family life.

80. The answer to the first question must therefore be that Directive 2004/38 precludes legislation of a Member State which requires a national of a non-member country who is the spouse of a Union citizen residing in that Member State but not possessing its nationality to have previously been lawfully resident in another Member State before arriving in the host Member State, in order to benefit from the provisions of that directive.

The second question

81. By its second question the referring court asks essentially whether the spouse of a Union citizen who has exercised his right of freedom of movement by becoming established in a Member State whose nationality he does not possess accompanies or joins that citizen within the meaning of Article 3(1) of Directive 2004/38, and consequently benefits from the provisions of that directive, irrespective of when and where the marriage took place and of the circumstances in which he entered the host Member State.

82. It should be noted at the outset that, as may be seen from recitals 1, 4 and 11 in the preamble, Directive 2004/38 aims to facilitate the exercise of the primary and individual right to move and reside freely within the territory of the Member States that is conferred directly on Union citizens by the Treaty.

83. Moreover, as recital 5 in the preamble to Directive 2004/38 points out, the right of all Union citizens to move and reside freely within the territory of the Member States should, if it is to be exercised under objective conditions of dignity, be also granted to their family members, irrespective of nationality.

84. Having regard to the context and objectives of Directive 2004/38, the provisions of that directive cannot be interpreted restrictively, and must not in any event be deprived of their effectiveness (see, to that effect, *Eind*, paragraph 43).

85. Article 3(1) of Directive 2004/38 provides that the directive is to apply to all Union citizens who move to or reside in a Member State other than that of which they are a national, and to their family members as defined in point 2 of Article 2 of the directive who accompany or join them.

86. Articles 6 and 7 of Directive 2004/38, relating respectively to the right of residence for up to three months and the right of residence for more than three months, likewise require that the family members of a Union citizen who are not nationals of a Member State 'accompany' or 'join' him in the host Member State in order to enjoy a right of residence there.

87. First, none of those provisions requires that the Union citizen must already have founded a family at the time when he moves to the host Member State in order for his family members who are nationals of non-member countries to be able to enjoy the rights established by that directive.

88. By providing that the family members of the Union citizen can join him in the host Member State, the Community legislature, on the contrary, accepted the possibility of the Union citizen not founding a family until after exercising his right of freedom of movement.

89. That interpretation is consistent with the purpose of Directive 2004/38, which aims to facilitate the exercise of the fundamental right of residence of Union citizens in a Member State other than that of which they are a national. Where a Union citizen founds a family after becoming established in the host Member State, the refusal of that Member State to authorise his family members who are nationals of non-member countries to join him there would be such as to discourage him from continuing to reside there and encourage him to leave in order to be able to lead a family life in another Member State or in a non-member country.

90. It must therefore be held that nationals of non-member countries who are family members of a Union citizen derive from Directive 2004/38 the right to join that Union citizen in the host Member State, whether he has become established there before or after founding a family.

91. Second, it must be determined whether, where the national of a non-member country has entered a Member State before becoming a family member of a Union citizen who resides in that Member State, he accompanies or joins that Union citizen within the meaning of Article 3(1) of Directive 2004/38.

92. It makes no difference whether nationals of non-member countries who are family members of a Union citizen have entered the host Member State before or after becoming family members of that Union citizen, since the refusal of the host Member State to grant them a right of residence is equally liable to discourage that Union citizen from continuing to reside in that Member State.

93. Therefore, in the light of the necessity of not interpreting the provisions of Directive 2004/38 restrictively and not depriving them of their effectiveness, the words 'family members [of Union citizens] who accompany ... them' in Article 3(1) of that di-

rective must be interpreted as referring both to the family members of a Union citizen who entered the host Member State with him and to those who reside with him in that Member State, without it being necessary, in the latter case, to distinguish according to whether the nationals of non-member countries entered that Member State before or after the Union citizen or before or after becoming his family members.

94. Application of Directive 2004/38 solely to the family members of a Union citizen who 'accompany' or 'join' him is thus equivalent to limiting the rights of entry and residence of family members of a Union citizen to the Member State in which that citizen resides.

95. From the time when the national of a non-member country who is a family member of a Union citizen derives rights of entry and residence in the host Member State from Directive 2004/38, that State may restrict that right only in compliance with Articles 27 and 35 of that directive.

96. Compliance with Article 27 is required in particular where the Member State wishes to penalise the national of a non-member country for entering into and/or residing in its territory in breach of the national rules on immigration before becoming a family member of a Union citizen.

97. However, even if the personal conduct of the person concerned does not justify the adoption of measures of public policy or public security within the meaning of Article 27 of Directive 2004/38, the Member State remains entitled to impose other penalties on him which do not interfere with freedom of movement and residence, such as a fine, provided that they are proportionate (see, to that effect, *MRAX*, paragraph 77 and the case-law cited).

98. Third, neither Article 3(1) nor any other provision of Directive 2004/38 contains requirements as to the place where the marriage of the Union citizen and the national of a non-member country is solemnised.

99. The answer to the second question must therefore be that Article 3(1) of Directive 2004/38 must be interpreted as meaning that a national of a non-member country who is the spouse of a Union citizen residing in a Member State whose nationality he does not possess and who accompanies or joins that Union citizen benefits from the provisions of that directive, irrespective of when and where their marriage took place and of how the national of a non-member country entered the host Member State.

The third question

100. In view of the answer to the second question, there is no need to answer the third question.

Costs

[Para. 101 omitted]

On those grounds,

THE COURT (Grand Chamber)

hereby rules:

1. **Directive 2004/38/EC of the European Parliament and of the Council of 29 April 2004 on the right of citizens of the Union and their family members to move and reside freely within the territory of the Member States amending Regulation (EEC) No 1612/68 and repealing Directives 64/221/EEC, 68/360/EEC, 72/194/EEC, 73/148/EEC, 75/34/EEC, 75/35/EEC, 90/364/EEC, 90/365/EEC and 93/96/EEC precludes legislation of a Member State which requires a national of a non-member country who is the spouse of a Union citizen residing in that Member State but not possessing its nationality to have previously been lawfully resident in another Member State before arriving in the host Member State, in order to benefit from the provisions of that directive.**

2. **Article 3(1) of Directive 2004/38 must be interpreted as meaning that a national of a non-member country who is the spouse of a Union citizen residing in a Member State whose nationality he does not possess and who accompanies or joins that Union citizen benefits from the provisions of that directive, irrespective of when and where their marriage took place and of how the national of a non-member country entered the host Member State.**

Comments and question

In the *Metock* case a number of important questions were referred to the CJEU on whether Directive 2004/38/EC on the right of citizens of the Union and their family members to move and reside freely within the territory of the Member States (the Free Movement Directive) prevented a Member State's legislation which laid down a requirement that a national from a third country, who was married to a Union citizen who was resident in a Member State of which he was not a citizen, should have had *prior lawful residence in another Member State* before coming to the host Member State in order to benefit from the provisions of the Directive. The case effectively concerned the allocation of powers between the Member States and the EU. To the extent that access to a Member State by a national of a third country, who arrives from outside the EU, is not yet regulated by Union rules in accordance with Title IV of the then EC Treaty (see now Title V TFEU) on visas, asylum, immigration and other policies related to free movement of persons, should such questions be determined by (1) the Member States' national immigration rules, or (2) the Union rules on the freedom of movement of Union citizens and their family members within the EU?

The CJEU has previously had such problems referred to it in a number of references for preliminary rulings, where the decisions clearly have reflected that the CJEU seems to have been aware that the answer to the question requires an evaluation of whether the Member States have retained their sovereignty in the area of immigration from countries outside the EU, or whether authority in this area has been transferred to the EU. For example, in paragraph 33 of Case 1/05 *Yunying Jia* [2007] ECR I-1, which is commented on above in the comments and questions on the *Akrich* case, the CJEU stated that Union law *does not require* Member States to make the grant of a residence permit to nationals of a third country, who are members of the family of a Union citizen who has exercised his or her right of free movement, subject to the condition that those family members must previously have been lawfully resident in another Member State. As is clear from the quotation from the judgment which is reproduced in the comments on the *Akrich* case, the CJEU has merely held that under Union law a Member State is *not required* to impose requirements that such a third-country national should have had *prior lawful residence in another Member State*. By using such a formulation, the CJEU cleverly avoided deciding whether, under Union law, a Member State is *entitled* to impose such a requirement. Previously, in the *Akrich* case the CJEU had stated that the Union rules, namely Article 10 of Regulation (EEC) No 1612/68 on freedom of movement for workers within the Union, then in force, did not apply in a situation where a national of a third country who is married to a Union citizen and who did not have prior lawful residence in another Member State. However, on this point the *Akrich* case was not in line with what the CJEU had ruled in Case C-459/99 *MRAX* [2002] ECR I-6591.

The clear statements of the CJEU in the *Metock* case have finally settled that, under Union law, a Member State is not entitled to impose requirements on a national of a third country that they must have had prior lawful residence in another Member State as a condition for being allowed family reunification with regard to a Union citizen.

The background to the case was that Ireland had implemented the Free Movement Directive in such a way that the implementing measure included a provision that a third-country national who was a family member of a Union citizen could only be granted Irish residence if the third-country national had already been lawfully resident in another Member State. As a result of this requirement, four third-country nationals, who has been refused asylum in Ireland, and who were married to citizens of other Member States (Union citizens), had their applications for residence permits, as a spouse of a Union citizen, rejected. In three of these four cases the Union citizen lived and worked in Ireland. In the fourth case the Union citizen lived in Ireland without apparently working there. It was not disputed that these were *not* pro-forma marriages.

Purely on the basis of a textual interpretation of the Free Movement Directive, the CJEU reached the conclusion that the Directive does not allow a Member State to include a requirement that a third-country national must have had prior lawful residence in another Member State in order to obtain a right of residence under Union law. It is the responsibility of the Member States in the Council – as joint legislator together with the European Parliament – that it has not expressly included this requirement in the Free Movement Directive. Even though the CJEU had in fact given its answer to the question in paragraph 54 of the judgment, it nevertheless found cause to refer to other aspects of the case which strengthened its interpretation. Thus, in paragraph 55 the CJEU noted that its 'interpretation is supported by the CJEU's case law on the instruments of secondary law concerning freedom of movement for persons adopted before [the Free Movement Directive].' However, this statement seems somewhat surprising in the light of the judgment in the *Akrich* case; see below. Moreover, the CJEU pointed out that prior to the adoption of the Free Movement Directive in 2004 the Union legislator recognised the importance of ensuring the protection of Union citizens' family life; see paragraphs 56 and 57.

In addition, the CJEU had to reconcile its previous decisions. The Irish requirement was not just conjured up out of thin air, as in the *Akrich* case in 2003 the CJEU had expressly stated that Article 10 of the applicable Regulation (EEC) No 1612/68 did not apply in a situation where a third-country national who is married to a Union citizen has not had prior lawful residence in another Member State. The application of such a requirement did not give less favourable treatment than that which the couple received before the Union citizen exercised the right of free movement; see paragraphs 50-51 and 53-54 of the *Akrich* judgment. The CJEU dealt with its previous decisions by clearly distancing itself from the *Akrich* judgment in paragraph 58 of the *Metock* judgment. The CJEU then found there were even stronger grounds for adopting this – new – approach pursuant to the Free Movement Directive as it is 'apparent from recital 3 in the preamble to Directive 2004/38, it aims in particular to 'strengthen the right of free movement and residence of all Union citizens', so that Union citizens cannot derive less rights from that directive than from the instruments of secondary legislation which it amends or repeals'; see paragraph 59.

Moreover, the CJEU found that this interpretation of the Directive was consistent with the division of competences between the Member States and the Union; see paragraph 60. In paragraph 61, the CJEU found that it was not disputed that the Union has competence, under (now) Articles 21(2), 46, 50 and 59 TFEU, which was the basis on which the Free Movement Directive was adopted, to enact the necessary measures to bring about freedom of movement for Union citizens. In this connection the CJEU noted that if Union citizens were not allowed to lead a normal family life in the host Member State, the exercise of the freedoms guaranteed by the TFEU would be seriously obstructed. The CJEU went on to state that: 'The refusal of the host Member State to grant rights of entry and residence to the family members of a Union citizen is such as to discourage that citizen from moving to or residing in that Member State, even if his family members are not already lawfully resident in the territory of another Member State'; see paragraphs 62-64 of the judgment.

Member States argued before the CJEU that, among other things, in a situation where there is strong immigration pressure it is necessary to control immigration at the EU's outer borders. This requires individual examination of all the circumstances relating to the first entry into EU territory. If it were not permitted for a Member State to establish a requirement for prior lawful residence in another Member State, this would undermine the Member States' possibility of controlling immigration at their outer borders. It was also argued that if such requirements could not be established, the result would be an enormous increase in the number of people who would be able to obtain rights of residence in the EU. To this the CJEU stated in paragraph 73 that: 'it is not all nationals of non-member countries who derive rights of entry into and residence in a Member State from Directive 2004/38, but only those who are family members, within the meaning of point 2 of Article 2 of that directive, of a Union citizen who has exercised his right of freedom of movement by *becoming established* in a Member State other than the Member State of which he is a national' (emphasis added). The CJEU continued in paragraph 74: 'Second, Directive 2004/38 does not deprive the Member States of all possibility of controlling the entry into their territory of family members of Union citizens. Under Chapter VI of that directive, Member States may, where this is justified, refuse entry and residence on grounds of public policy, public security or public health. Such a refusal will be based on an individual examination of the particular case.' Furthermore, in relation to Article 35 of the Free Movement Directive, the CJEU noted that the Member States 'may adopt the necessary measures to refuse, terminate or withdraw any right conferred by that directive in the case of abuse of rights or fraud, such as marriages of convenience, it being understood that any such measure must be proportionate and subject to the procedural safeguards provided for in the directive'; see paragraph 75.

At the same time, the CJEU emphasised in paragraph 78 that the Free Movement Directive can only be relied upon by Union citizens who have exercised their right of freedom of movement and who therefore fall within the scope of Union law. Without going into more detail on the extent of the obligations under Article 8 of the European Convention on Human Rights, on the right to respect for private and family life, in paragraph 79 the CJEU stated that 'all the Member States are parties to the European Convention for the Protection of Human Rights and Fundamental Freedoms signed in Rome on 4 November 1950, which enshrines in Article 8 the right to respect for private and family life.'

In addition to this, the CJEU was asked whether there could be requirements as to when and where the marriage between the third-country national and the Union citizen was entered into, and to how the third-country national had entered the host Member State. This was rejected by the CJEU. Thus, the Free Movement Directive contains no requirements with regard to where the marriage between the Union citizen and the third-country national is entered into.

The CJEU dealt with the *Metock* case under the accelerated procedure. The time for dealing with the *Metock* case was thereby limited to only four months. The Advocate General's Opinion in the *Metock* case, which was first published subsequently, corresponds with the decision of the CJEU. In this connection it is interesting to note that the

Advocate General stated that the (then new) Free Movement Directive (2004/38) gives a Union citizen a right freely to reside in the territory of any Member State, so that it is no longer only the mobility but also the stability and permanence of residence in another Member State that is intended to be secured. From this new standpoint, it was the Advocate General's view that it is easy to see how requiring nationals of third countries to have had prior lawful residence in another Member State in order to benefit from the right to family reunification under the Free Movement Directive might affect the continued residence in the Member State in which a Union citizen has chosen to reside and which has established such a requirement. If a Union citizen's family life changes and a family member is unable to rely on Union law in order to join him because he has not been lawfully resident in another Member State, the Union citizen will be obliged to leave the territory of the Member State in question and reside in another Member State or a third country in which he will be able to achieve family reunification. The requirement for prior lawful residence, that is an obstacle to the possibility of leading a normal family life, affects the effective exercise of the right of residence granted to Union citizens by the Union rules; see point 13 of the Advocate General's Opinion.

Special problems arise when a third-country national derives their right to reside in a host Member State from their marriage to a Union citizen and where the married couple are separated or divorced. In its judgment of 16 July 2015 in Case C-218/14 *Kuldip Singh*, the CJEU ruled for the first time that a third-country national does not have a right, under Article 13(2) of the Free Movement Directive, to continue to reside in the host Member State if the Union citizen from whom the third-country national derives their right of residence has terminated their residence in the host Member State prior to the start of the divorce proceedings. This applies even if the marriage has lasted for at least three years before the start of divorce proceedings, of which at least one year of the marriage has been spent in the host Member State.

In its judgment of 10 July 2014 in Case C-244/13 *Ogieriakhi*, the CJEU established that, despite its wording, Article 16(2) of Directive 2004/38 (the Free Movement Directive) must be interpreted as meaning that a third-country national who, for a continuous period of five years before the transposition date for that Directive, has resided in a Member State as the spouse of a Union citizen working in that Member State, must be regarded as having acquired a right of permanent residence under that provision, even though, during that period, the spouses decided to separate and lived with other partners. It must thus be a condition that the Union citizen from whom the third-country national derives their right of residence works or resides in the host Member State in the five years in question; see the judgment of 16 July 2015 in Case C-218/14 *Kuldip Singh*. The *Ogieriakhi* contrasts with the judgment of 16 January in Case C-378/12 *Nnamdi Onuekwerede*, in which the same Second Chamber of the CJEU found that Article 16(2) and (3) of the Free Movement Directive must be interpreted as meaning that periods of imprisonment in the host Member State of a third-country national, who is a family member of a Union citizen who has acquired the right of permanent residence in that Member State during those periods, cannot be taken into consideration in the context of the acquisition by that national of the right of permanent residence for the purposes of that provision. Thus, the assessment of the continuous nature of the cohabitation is relative; see Article 16(3) of the Free Movement Directive which qualifies the nature of continuous residence. According to this provision, continuity of residence is not affected by temporary absences which do not together exceed a total of six months per year, or by absences of a longer duration caused by compulsory military service or by one absence of a maximum of twelve consecutive months for reasons such as pregnancy or childbirth, serious illness, study or vocational training or posting in another Member State or third country.

JUDGMENT OF THE COURT (Grand Chamber)
12 March 2014

O. v Minister voor Immigratie, Integratie en Asiel, and Minister voor Immigratie, Integratie en Asiel v B. (Request for a preliminary ruling: Raad van State – Netherlands)

'Directive 2004/38/EC – Article 21(1) TFEU – Right to move and reside freely within the territory of the Member States – Beneficiaries – Right of residence of a third-country national who is a family member of a Union citizen in the Member State of which that citizen is a national – Return of the Union citizen to that Member State after short periods of residence spent in another Member State'

Case C-456/12

Judgment

1. This request for a preliminary ruling concerns the interpretation of Directive 2004/38/EC of the European Parliament and of the Council of 29 April 2004 on the right of citizens of the Union and their family members to move and reside freely within the territory of the Member States amending Regulation (EEC) No 1612/68 and repealing Directives 64/221/EEC, 68/360/EEC, 72/194/EEC, 73/148/EEC, 75/34/EEC, 75/35/EEC, 90/364/EEC, 90/365/EEC and 93/96/EEC (OJ 2004 L 158, p. 77, and corrigenda at OJ 2004 L 229, p. 35, and OJ 2005 L 197, p. 34), and Article 21(1) TFEU.

2. The request has been made in proceedings between Mr O. and the Minister voor Immigratie, Integratie en Asiel (Minister for Immigration, Integration and Asylum) ('the Minister'), on the one hand, and between the Minister and Mr B., on the other, concerning the decisions refusing to grant them a certificate of lawful residence as a family member of a European Union citizen in the Netherlands.

Legal context

Directive 2004/38

3. Article 1 of Directive 2004/38, which is entitled 'Subject', provides:

'This Directive lays down:

(a) the conditions governing the exercise of the right of free movement and residence within the territory of the Member States by Union citizens and their family members;

...'

4. Under the heading 'Definitions', Article 2 of that directive provides:

   'For the purposes of this Directive:

   1. "Union citizen" means any person having the nationality of a Member State;
   2. "family member" means:
      (a) the spouse;
      ...
   3. "host Member State" means the Member State to which a Union citizen moves in order to exercise his/her right of free movement and residence.'

5. Article 3 of that directive, which is entitled 'Beneficiaries', provides in paragraph 1 thereof:

   'This Directive shall apply to all Union citizens who move to or reside in a Member State other than that of which they are a national, and to their family members as defined in [Article 2(2)] who accompany or join them.'

6. Article 6 of Directive 2004/38 states:

   '1. Union citizens shall have the right of residence on the territory of another Member State for a period of up to three months ...
   2. The provisions of paragraph 1 shall also apply to family members in possession of a valid passport who are not nationals of a Member State, accompanying or joining the Union citizen.'

7. Article 7(1) and (2) of that directive is worded as follows:

   '1. All Union citizens shall have the right of residence on the territory of another Member State for a period of longer than three months if they:
      (a) are workers or self-employed persons in the host Member State; or
      (b) have sufficient resources for themselves and their family members not to become a burden on the social assistance system of the host Member State during their period of residence and have comprehensive sickness insurance cover in the host Member State; or
      (c) – are enrolled at a private or public establishment, accredited or financed by the host Member State on the basis of its legislation or administrative practice, for the principal purpose of following a course of study, including vocational training; and
      – have comprehensive sickness insurance cover in the host Member State and assure the relevant national authority, by means of a declaration or by such equivalent means as they may choose, that they have sufficient re-

sources for themselves and their family members not to become a burden on the social assistance system of the host Member State during their period of residence; or

(d) are family members accompanying or joining a Union citizen who satisfies the conditions referred to in points (a), (b) or (c).

2. The right of residence provided for in paragraph 1 shall extend to family members who are not nationals of a Member State, accompanying or joining the Union citizen in the host Member State, provided that such Union citizen satisfies the conditions referred to in paragraph 1(a), (b) or (c).'

8. Article 10(1) of that directive provides:

'The right of residence of family members of a Union citizen who are not nationals of a Member State shall be evidenced by the issuing of a document called "Residence card of a family member of a Union citizen" no later than six months from the date on which they submit the application. A certificate of application for the residence card shall be issued immediately.'

9. Under Article 16(1), first sentence, of Directive 2004/38, 'Union citizens who have resided legally for a continuous period of five years in the host Member State shall have the right of permanent residence there'. Article 16(2) provides that '[p]aragraph 1 shall apply also to family members who are not nationals of a Member State and have legally resided with the Union citizen in the host Member State for a continuous period of five years'.

Netherlands law

10. The Law on Foreign Nationals (Vreemdelingenwet) of 23 November 2000 (Stb. 2000, No 495) and the Decree on Foreign Nationals of 2000 (Vreemdelingenbesluit 2000, Stb. 2000, No 497) implemented Directive 2004/38 into Netherlands law.

11. Article 1 of the Law on Foreign Nationals provides:

'Within the meaning of the present Law and of the provisions adopted on the basis thereof:

...

(e) Community nationals shall mean:

1. nationals of the Member States of the European Union who, under the Treaty establishing the European Community, have the right to enter and reside on the territory of another Member State;
2. the family members of those persons referred to in paragraph 1 who are nationals of a third State and who, on the basis of a decision taken in applica-

tion of the EC Treaty, are entitled to enter and reside on the territory of a Member State;

...'

12. Article 8 of that law provides:

'Foreign nationals are not lawfully resident in the Netherlands:

...

(e) as Community nationals, except where their residence in the Netherlands is based on a rule adopted under the EC Treaty or the Treaty on the European Economic Area;

...'

13. Under Article 9(1) of that law, the Minister is required to provide the foreign national who is lawfully resident on the territory of the Netherlands on the basis of Union law with a document or written statement evidencing the lawful residence ('the residence document').

The disputes in the main proceedings and the questions referred for a preliminary ruling

Mr O.'s situation

14. In 2006, Mr O., a Nigerian national, married a Netherlands national ('sponsor O'). Mr O. stated that from 2007 to April 2010 he lived in Spain. According to the documents submitted by the Spanish municipality of Malaga, Mr O. and sponsor O have been registered at the same address in that municipality since 7 August 2009. Mr O. also submitted a residence document, valid until 20 September 2014, from which it appears that he resided in Spain as a family member of a Union citizen.

15. According to sponsor O, she resided for two months with Mr O. in Spain between 2007 and April 2010 but she returned to the Netherlands because she could not find work in Spain. During that time, however, sponsor O regularly spent time with Mr O. in the form of holidays in Spain.

16. Since 1 July 2010, Mr O. has been registered in the Netherlands Personal Records Database as residing at the same address as sponsor O.

17. By decision of 15 November 2010, the Minister rejected Mr O.'s request for the residence document referred to in Article 9(1) of the Law on Foreign Nationals. By decision of 21 March 2011, the Minister rejected Mr O.'s objection to that decision as unfounded.

18. By judgment of 7 July 2011, the Rechtbank 's-Gravenhage (District Court, The Hague) rejected the action brought by Mr O. against the decision of 21 March 2011 as unfounded.

19. Mr O. lodged an appeal against that judgment before the referring court.

Mr B.'s situation

20. Mr B., a Moroccan national, stated that from December 2002 he had lived for several years in the Netherlands with his partner ('sponsor B') who has Netherlands nationality.

21. By decision of 14 October 2005, the Minister declared Mr B. to be undesirable within the territory of the Netherlands as a result of a prison sentence of two months for using a false passport. Mr B. then moved to Retie (Belgium) and lived in an apartment rented by sponsor B from October 2005 to May 2007. Sponsor B stated that, during that period, she resided there every weekend.

22. In April 2007, Mr B. returned to Morocco because he was denied residence in Belgium on the basis of the decision of 14 October 2005.

23. On 31 July 2007, Mr B. and sponsor B were married. On 30 December 2008, Mr B. applied to have his declaration of undesirability lifted. By decision of 16 March 2009, the Minister lifted that declaration.

24. In June 2009, Mr B. moved to the Netherlands to reside there with sponsor B.

25. By decision of 30 October 2009, the Staatssecretaris van Justitie (State Secretary for Justice) rejected Mr B.'s application for a residence document. By decision of 19 March 2010, the Minister held Mr B.'s challenge to the decision rejecting his application to be unfounded.

26. By judgment of 11 November 2010, the Rechtbank 's-Gravenhage upheld the action brought by Mr B. against the decision of 19 March 2010, annulled that decision and ordered the Minister to adopt a new decision taking into account the considerations set out in that judgment.

27. The Minister lodged an appeal against that judgment before the referring court.

The questions referred for a preliminary ruling

28. As Mr O. and Mr B. were family members of Union citizens, within the meaning of Article 2(2) of Directive 2004/38, on the dates on which the decisions rejecting their respective applications for a residence document were taken, the referring

court is unsure, first of all, whether that directive grants them a right of residence in the Member State of which those citizens are nationals.

29, According to the referring court, it is conceivable that the term 'move to' within the meaning of Article 3(1) of Directive 2004/38 means travelling to and from, without moving to, a Member State other than the Member State of which those citizens are nationals. Likewise, it is conceivable that the term 'join them' within the meaning of Article 3(1) of that directive could be construed to mean joining the Union citizens in the Member State of which they are nationals. However, the referring court states that other provisions of that directive, in particular Article 6(1) and Article 7(1) and (2), seem to rule out such an interpretation, in so far as they expressly mention 'another Member State' and 'the host Member State' as the Member State to which the right of residence applies. The judgment in Case C-434/09 *McCarthy* [2011] ECR I-3375 confirms that Articles 6 and 7 govern the legal situation of a Union citizen in a Member State of which he is not a national.

30. Next, the referring court points out that it is apparent from Case C-370/90 *Singh* [1992] ECR I-4265 and Case C-291/05 *Eind* [2007] ECR I-10719 that when a national of a Member State who has availed himself or herself of the right to freedom of movement returns to his or her State of origin, his or her spouse must enjoy at least the same rights of entry and residence as would be granted to him or her under Union law if the Union citizen chose to enter and reside in another Member State. However, the referring court expresses doubts as to whether that case-law may be applied to situations such as those at issue in the main proceedings. It states in that regard that, unlike in the cases which gave rise to the judgments in *Singh* and *Eind*, the Union citizens in question in the main proceedings resided in the host Member State not as workers but as Union citizens pursuant to Article 21(1) TFEU, and as recipients of services within the meaning of Article 56 TFEU.

31. Lastly, if the case-law in *Singh* and *Eind* were to apply to situations such as those at issue in the main proceedings, the referring court asks to what extent it is a requirement that the residence of the Union citizen in a Member State other than that of which he is a national must have been of a certain minimum duration if, after the return of the Union citizen to the Member State of which he is a national, the member of his family who is a third-country national wishes to gain a right of residence in that Member State. In the case concerning Mr B. the referring court is also uncertain whether Mr B.'s right of residence in the Netherlands under Directive 2004/38 is affected by the fact that he only joined sponsor B in the Member State of which she is a national more than two years after her return to that Member State.

32. In those circumstances the Raad van State decided to stay the proceedings and to refer the following questions to the Court of Justice for a preliminary ruling, the first three of which are formulated in the same terms in the cases of Mr O. and Mr B., with only the fourth question specific to the case of Mr B.:

'(1) Should Directive 2004/38 ..., as regards the conditions governing the right of residence of members of the family of a Union citizen who have third-country nationality, be applied by analogy, as in the judgments of the Court of Justice of the European Communities in [*Singh* and in *Eind*], where a Union citizen returns to the Member State of which he is a national after having resided in another Member State in the context of Article 21(1) [TFEU], and as the recipient of services within the meaning of Article 56 [TFEU]?

(2) [If the first question is answered in the affirmative], is there a requirement that the residence of the Union citizen in another Member State must have been of a certain minimum duration if, after the return of the Union citizen to the Member State of which he is a national, the member of his family who is a third-country national wishes to gain a right of residence in that Member State?

(3) [If the second question is answered in the affirmative], can that requirement then also be met if there was no question of continuous residence, but rather of a certain frequency of residence, such as during weekly residence at weekends or during regular visits?

(4) As a result of the time which elapsed between the return of the Union citizen to the Member State of which he is a national and the arrival of the family member from a third country in that Member State, in circumstances such as those of the ... case [concerning Mr B.], has there been a lapse of possible entitlement of the family member with third-country nationality to a right of residence derived from Union law?'

Consideration of the questions referred

The first, second and third questions

33. By its first, second and third questions, which should be examined together, the referring court asks, in essence, whether Directive 2004/38 and Article 21(1) TFEU must be interpreted as precluding a Member State from refusing a right of residence to a third-country national who is the family member of a Union citizen holding the nationality of that Member State, following the return of that citizen to that Member State, in circumstances where that citizen, before his return, had exercised his right of freedom of movement under Article 21(1) TFEU by residing in another Member State with the family member in question, solely by virtue of his being a Union citizen, and, if that question is answered in the affirmative, what are the conditions under which such a right of residence is granted?

34. In that regard, it should be borne in mind that under Article 21(1) TFEU, '[e]very citizen of the Union shall have the right to move and reside freely within the territory of the Member States, subject to the limitations and conditions laid down in the Treaties and by the measures adopted to give them effect'.

35. The Court has already had occasion to point out that Directive 2004/38 aims to facilitate the exercise of the primary and individual right to move and reside freely within the territory of the Member States that is conferred directly on Union citizens by Article 21(1) TFEU and that it aims in particular to strengthen that right (see, to that effect, Case C-127/08 *Metock and Others* [2008] ECR I-6241, paragraphs 59 and 82; Case C-162/09 *Lassal* [2010] ECR I-9217, paragraph 30; and *McCarthy*, paragraph 28).

36. Article 21(1) TFEU and Directive 2004/38 do not confer any autonomous right on third-country nationals (see, to that effect, Case C-40/11 *Iida* [2012] ECR, paragraph 66, and Case C-87/12 *Ymeraga and Ymeraga-Tafarshiku* [2013] ECR, paragraph 34). Any rights conferred on third-country nationals by provisions of EU law on Union citizenship are rights derived from the exercise of freedom of movement by a Union citizen (see *Iida*, paragraph 67; *Ymeraga and Ymeraga-Tafarshiku*, paragraph 35; and Case C-86/12 *Alokpa and Others* [2013] ECR, paragraph 22).

37. It follows from a literal, systematic and teleological interpretation of Directive 2004/38 that it does not establish a derived right of residence for third-country nationals who are family members of a Union citizen in the Member State of which that citizen is a national.

38. Article 3(1) of Directive 2004/38, defines the 'beneficiaries' of the rights conferred by it as 'all Union citizens who move to or reside in a Member State other than that of which they are a national, and ... their family members as defined in [Article 2(2)] who accompany or join them'.

39. Accordingly, Directive 2004/38 establishes a derived right of residence for third-country nationals who are family members of a Union citizen, within the meaning of Article 2(2) of that directive, only where that citizen has exercised his right of freedom of movement by becoming established in a Member State other than the Member State of which he is a national (see, to that effect, *Metock and Others*, paragraph 73; Case C-256/11 *Dereci and Others* [2011] ECR I-11315, paragraph 56; *Iida*, paragraph 51; and Joined Cases C-356/11 and C-357/11 *O. and Others* [2012] ECR, paragraph 41).

40. Other provisions of Directive 2004/38, in particular Article 6, Article 7(1) and (2) and Article 16(1) and (2), refer to the right of residence of a Union citizen and to the derived right of residence conferred on the family members of that citizen either in 'another Member State' or in 'the host Member State' and thus confirm that a third-country national who is a family member of a Union citizen cannot invoke, on the basis of that directive, a derived right of residence in the Member State of which that citizen is a national (see *McCarthy*, paragraph 37, and *Iida*, paragraph 64).

41. As regards the teleological interpretation of Directive 2004/38, it should be borne in mind that whilst it is true that Directive 2004/38 aims to facilitate and strengthen the exercise of the primary and individual right to move and reside freely within the territory of the Member States that is conferred directly on each citizen of the Union, the fact remains that the subject of the directive concerns, as is apparent from Article 1(a), the conditions governing the exercise of that right (*McCarthy*, paragraph 33).

42. Since, under a principle of international law, a State cannot refuse its own nationals the right to enter its territory and remain there, Directive 2004/38 is intended only to govern the conditions of entry and residence of a Union citizen in a Member State other than the Member State of which he is a national (see *McCarthy*, paragraph 29).

43. In those circumstances and having regard to what is said in paragraph 36 above, Directive 2004/38 is therefore also not intended to confer a derived right of residence on third-country nationals who are family members of a Union citizen residing in the Member State of which the latter is a national.

44. Since third-country nationals in situations such as those of Mr O. and Mr B. are not entitled, on the basis of Directive 2004/38, to a derived right of residence in the Member State of which their sponsors are nationals, it must be examined whether a derived right of residence may, in some circumstances, be based on Article 21(1) TFEU.

45 In that regard, it should be borne in mind that the purpose and justification of that derived right of residence is based on the fact that a refusal to allow such a right would be such as to interfere with the Union citizen's freedom of movement by discouraging him from exercising his rights of entry into and residence in the host Member State (see *Iida*, paragraph 68; *Ymeraga and Ymeraga-Tafarshiku*, paragraph 35; and *Alokpa and Others*, paragraph 22).

46. The Court has accordingly held that where a Union citizen has resided with a family member who is a third-country national in a Member State other than the Member State of which he is a national for a period exceeding two and a half years and one and half years respectively, and was employed there, that third-country national must, when the Union citizen returns to the Member State of which he is a national, be entitled, under Union law, to a derived right of residence in the latter State (see *Singh*, paragraph 25, and *Eind*, paragraph 45). If that third-country national did not have such a right, a worker who is a Union citizen could be discouraged from leaving the Member State of which he is a national in order to pursue gainful employment in another Member State simply because of the prospect for that worker of not being able to continue, on returning to his Member State of origin, a way of family life which may have come into being in the host Member State as a result of marriage or family reunification (see *Eind*, paragraphs 35 and 36, and *Iida*, paragraph 70).

47. Therefore, an obstacle to leaving the Member State of which the worker is a national, as mentioned in *Singh* and *Eind*, is created by the refusal to confer, when that worker returns to his Member State of origin, a derived right of residence on the family members of that worker who are third-country nationals, where that worker resided with his family members in the host Member State pursuant to, and in conformity with, Union law.

48. It is therefore necessary to determine whether the case-law resulting from *Singh* and *Eind* is capable of being applied generally to family members of Union citizens who, having availed themselves of the rights conferred on them by Article 21(1) TFEU, resided in a Member State other than that of which they are nationals, before returning to the Member State of origin.

49. That is indeed the case. The grant, when a Union citizen returns to the Member State of which he is a national, of a derived right of residence to a third-country national who is a family member of that Union citizen and with whom that citizen has resided, solely by virtue of his being a Union citizen, pursuant to and in conformity with Union law in the host Member State, seeks to remove the same type of obstacle on leaving the Member State of origin as that referred to in paragraph 47 above, by guaranteeing that that citizen will be able, in his Member State of origin, to continue the family life which he created or strengthened in the host Member State.

50. So far as concerns the conditions for granting, when a Union citizen returns to the Member State of which he is a national, a derived right of residence, based on Article 21(1) TFEU, to a third-country national who is a family member of that Union citizen with whom that citizen has resided, solely by virtue of his being a Union citizen, in the host Member State, those conditions should not, in principle, be more strict than those provided for by Directive 2004/38 for the grant of such a right of residence to a third-country national who is a family member of a Union citizen in a case where that citizen has exercised his right of freedom of movement by becoming established in a Member State other than the Member State of which he is a national. Even though Directive 2004/38 does not cover such a return, it should be applied by analogy to the conditions for the residence of a Union citizen in a Member State other than that of which he is a national, given that in both cases it is the Union citizen who is the sponsor for the grant of a derived right of residence to a third-country national who is a member of his family.

51. An obstacle such as that referred to in paragraph 47 above will arise only where the residence of the Union citizen in the host Member State has been sufficiently genuine so as to enable that citizen to create or strengthen family life in that Member State. Article 21(1) TFEU does not therefore require that every residence in the host Member State by a Union citizen accompanied by a family member who is a third-country national necessarily confers a derived right of residence on that family

member in the Member State of which that citizen is a national upon the citizen's return to that Member State.

52. In that regard, it should be observed that a Union citizen who exercises his rights under Article 6(1) of Directive 2004/38 does not intend to settle in the host Member State in a way which would be such as to create or strengthen family life in that Member State. Accordingly, the refusal to confer, when that citizen returns to his Member State of origin, a derived right of residence on members of his family who are third-country nationals will not deter such a citizen from exercising his rights under Article 6.

53. On the other hand, an obstacle such as that referred to in paragraph 47 above may be created where the Union citizen intends to exercise his rights under Article 7(1) of Directive 2004/38. Residence in the host Member State pursuant to and in conformity with the conditions set out in Article 7(1) of that directive is, in principle, evidence of settling there and therefore of the Union citizen's genuine residence in the host Member State and goes hand in hand with creating and strengthening family life in that Member State.

54. Where, during the genuine residence of the Union citizen in the host Member State, pursuant to and in conformity with the conditions set out in Article 7(1) and (2) of Directive 2004/38, family life is created or strengthened in that Member State, the effectiveness of the rights conferred on the Union citizen by Article 21(1) TFEU requires that the citizen's family life in the host Member State may continue on returning to the Member of State of which he is a national, through the grant of a derived right of residence to the family member who is a third-country national. If no such derived right of residence were granted, that Union citizen could be discouraged from leaving the Member State of which he is a national in order to exercise his right of residence under Article 21(1) TFEU in another Member State because he is uncertain whether he will be able to continue in his Member State of origin a family life with his immediate family members which has been created or strengthened in the host Member State (see, to that effect, *Eind*, paragraphs 35 and 36, and *Iida*, paragraph 70).

55. *A fortiori*, the effectiveness of Article 21(1) TFEU requires that the Union citizen may continue, on returning to the Member State of which he is a national, the family life which he led in the host Member State, if he and the family member concerned who is a third-country national have been granted a permanent right of residence in the host Member State pursuant to Article 16(1) and (2) of Directive 2004/38 respectively.

56. Accordingly, it is genuine residence in the host Member State of the Union citizen and of the family member who is a third-country national, pursuant to and in conformity with the conditions set out in Article 7(1) and (2) and Article 16(1) and (2)

of Directive 2004/38 respectively, which creates, on the Union citizen's return to his Member State of origin, a derived right of residence, on the basis of Article 21(1) TFEU, for the third-country national with whom that citizen lived as a family in the host Member State.

57. It is for the referring court to determine whether sponsor O and sponsor B, who are both Union citizens, settled and, therefore, genuinely resided in the host Member State and whether, on account of living as a family during that period of genuine residence, Mr O. and Mr B. enjoyed a derived right of residence in the host Member State pursuant to and in conformity with Article 7(2) or Article 16(2) of Directive 2004/38.

58. It should be added that the scope of Union law cannot be extended to cover abuses (see, to that effect, Case C-110/99 *Emsland-Stärke* [2000] ECR I-11569, paragraph 51, and Case C-303/08 *Bozkurt* [2010] ECR I-13445, paragraph 47). Proof of such an abuse requires, first, a combination of objective circumstances in which, despite formal observance of the conditions laid down by the European Union rules, the purpose of those rules has not been achieved, and, secondly, a subjective element consisting in the intention to obtain an advantage from the European Union rules by artificially creating the conditions laid down for obtaining it (Case C-364/10 *Hungary* v *Slovakia* [2012] ECR, paragraph 58).

59. As regards the question whether the cumulative effect of various short periods of residence in the host Member State may create a derived right of residence for a family member of a Union citizen who is a third-country national on the citizen's return to the Member State of which he is a national, it should be borne in mind that only a period of residence satisfying the conditions set out in Article 7(1) and (2) and Article 16(1) and (2) of Directive 2004/38 will give rise to such a right of residence. In that regard, short periods of residence such as weekends or holidays spent in a Member State other than that of which the citizen in question is a national, even when considered together, fall within the scope of Article 6 of Directive 2004/38 and do not satisfy those conditions.

60. So far as concerns Mr O., who, according to the order for reference, holds a residence card as a family member of a Union citizen pursuant to Article 10 of Directive 2004/38, it should be borne in mind that Union law does not require the authorities of the Member State of which the Union citizen in question is a national to grant a derived right of residence to a third-country national who is a member of that citizen's family because of the mere fact that, in the host Member State, that third-country national held a valid residence permit (see *Eind*, paragraph 26). A residence card issued on the basis of Article 10 of Directive 2004/38 has a declaratory, as opposed to a constitutive, character (see Case C-325/09 *Dias* [2011] ECR I-6387, paragraph 49).

61. In the light of all the foregoing considerations, the answer to the first, second and third questions is that Article 21(1) TFEU must be interpreted as meaning that where a Union citizen has created or strengthened a family life with a third-country national during genuine residence, pursuant to and in conformity with the conditions set out in Article 7(1) and (2) and Article 16(1) and (2) of Directive 2004/38, in a Member State other than that of which he is a national, the provisions of that directive apply by analogy where that Union citizen returns, with the family member in question, to his Member State of origin. Therefore, the conditions for granting a derived right of residence to a third-country national who is a family member of that Union citizen, in the latter's Member State of origin, should not, in principle, be more strict than those provided for by that directive for the grant of a derived right of residence to a third-country national who is a family member of a Union citizen who has exercised his right of freedom of movement by becoming established in a Member State other than the Member State of which he is a national.

The fourth question

62. As is apparent from paragraphs 21 to 23 above, Mr B. acquired the status of family member, within the meaning of Article 2(2) of Directive 2004/38, of a Union citizen after sponsor B's residence in the host Member State.

63. A third-country national, who has not had, at least during part of his residence in the host Member State, the status of family member, within the meaning of Article 2(2) of Directive 2004/38, is not entitled to a derived right of residence in that Member State pursuant to Article 7(2) or Article 16(2) of Directive 2004/38. Accordingly, that third-country national is also unable to rely on Article 21(1) TFEU for the grant of a derived right of residence on the return of the Union citizen in question to the Member State of which he is a national.

64. There is therefore no need to answer the fourth question.

Costs

[Para. 65 omitted]

On those grounds,

THE COURT (Grand Chamber),

hereby rules:

Article 21(1) TFEU must be interpreted as meaning that where a Union citizen has created or strengthened a family life with a third-country national during genuine residence, pursuant to and in conformity with the conditions set out in

Article 7(1) and (2) and Article 16(1) and (2) of Directive 2004/38/EC of the European Parliament and of the Council of 29 April 2004 on the right of citizens of the Union and their family members to move and reside freely within the territory of the Member States amending Regulation (EEC) No 1612/68 and repealing Directives 64/221/EEC, 68/360/EEC, 72/194/EEC, 73/148/EEC, 75/34/EEC, 75/35/EEC, 90/364/EEC, 90/365/EEC and 93/96/EEC, in a Member State other than that of which he is a national, the provisions of that directive apply by analogy where that Union citizen returns, with the family member in question, to his Member State of origin. Therefore, the conditions for granting a derived right of residence to a third-country national who is a family member of that Union citizen, in the latter's Member State of origin, should not, in principle, be more strict than those provided for by that directive for the grant of a derived right of residence to a third-country national who is a family member of a Union citizen who has exercised his right of freedom of movement by becoming established in a Member State other than the Member State of which he is a national.

Comments and questions

The CJEU's ruling in the *O* case, Case C-456/12, concerned two cases pending before the Dutch Raad van State between O and B, on the one hand, and the Minister for Immigration, Integration and Asylum (*Minister voor Immigratie, Integratie en Asiel*) on the other hand, in which the Minister had refused to issue a document attesting that O and B were lawfully resident in the Netherlands as family members of a Union citizen.

Mr O, who was a Nigerian citizen, entered into a marriage with a Dutch citizen in October 2006. He lived in Spain from 2007 until April 2010. During this period his wife lived with him in Spain for a two-month period, but since she had been unable to find work in Spain, she returned to the Netherlands. However, during this period she regularly took holidays with O in Spain. Since July 2010 O had been registered in the Netherlands Personal Records Database as residing at the same address as his wife. In November 2010 the Dutch authorities refused an application to unite their family pursuant to Union law on the ground that the parties had not given sufficient evidence of their residence in Spain and thus that it could not be accepted that they had genuinely and effectively exercised their right of free movement in Spain.

From December 2002 Mr B, who was a Moroccan citizen, had lived in the Netherlands for some years together with his partner, who was a Dutch citizen. After B had been sentenced to two months imprisonment for using a false passport, he had been declared an undesirable alien in the Netherlands by the Dutch authorities in October 2005. Mr B then moved into a flat in Brussels which his partner rented from October 2005 until May 2007. His partner visited Mr B in Belgium every week until April 2007, when he returned to Morocco as he had been refused residence in Belgium. The couple were married in July 2007.The status of Mr B as an undesirable alien in the Netherlands was terminated in March 2009, after which Mr B moved in with his wife in the Netherlands.

In October 2010 the Dutch authorities refused an application from Mr B to issue a residence permit.

The background to the Raad van State's reference for a preliminary ruling was the CJEU's earlier rulings on 'secondary movement', i.e. cases where a third-country national derives a right to reside in a Member State where the Union citizen from whom the third-country national derives their right of residence is a national. This is in contrast to 'primary movement' where a Union citizen moves to another Member State in order to unite their family.

The CJEU first ruled on this secondary movement in the *Singh* case (Case C-370/90), where it stated that Article 49 TFEU on freedom of establishment requires a Member State to grant leave to enter and reside in its territory to the spouse, of whatever nationality, of a national of that State who has gone, with that spouse, to another Member State in order to work there as an employed person (pursuant to Article 45 TFEU) and returns to establish him- or herself in the territory of the State of which they are a national. Thus it is possible to deduce a special Union EU law rule on family unification from Article 49 TFEU. Similarly in the *Akrich* case printed above, under Article 45 TFEU a spouse from a third country can derive a right of residence if their spouse is a Union citizen returning to their home Member State in order to take up paid employment. However, the CJEU added that the third-country national spouse could derive a right of residence in the Union citizen's home State if the couple had previously been lawfully resident in another Member State. In both the *Singh* and the *Akrich* cases the CJEU made the right, under Union law, to unite a family with a third-country national family member dependent on the Union law status of the Union citizen in their home State. If the Union citizen exercised the right of establishment in their home State after returning there, the right to unite the family was governed by Article 49 TFEU. If the Union citizen took up paid employment in their home State after returning there, the right to unite their family was governed by Article 45 TFEU.

The third time the CJEU ruled on the extent of the right, under Union law, to unite a family with a third-country national family member, after the married couple had been resident in another Member State, was in the *Eind* case (Case C-291/05). In this case a Union citizen had lived and worked in another Member State and there, pursuant to Article 10 of Regulation (EEC) No 1612/68 on freedom of movement for workers within the Community then in force (now Regulation (EU) No 429/2011), had been united with his daughter who was a citizen of a third country. Subsequently the Union citizen and his daughter returned to the Union citizen's home Member State where the Union citizen was not employed and received social assistance. In the *Eind* case the CJEU ruled that the daughter could derive a right of residence pursuant to Article 10 of Regulation (EEC) No 1612/68, which applied analogously. In contrast to the situations in the *Singh* and *Akrich* cases, in the *Eind* case the CJEU focused on the status of the Union citizen in the other Member State, before returning to their home State, since this determined the Union law provision under which the third-country national could derive a right. However, the CJEU did not explain its changed approach in the *Eind* case.

Thus it was partly on the basis of the *Singh* case and partly on the basis of the *Eind* case that the Dutch Raad van State referred four questions to the CJEU for preliminary rulings. In its first question the Raad van State asked whether, as regards the conditions governing the right of residence of members of the family of a Union citizen who have third-country nationality, the Free Movement Directive (Directive 2004/38) should be applied by analogy, as in the *Singh* and *Eind* cases, where a Union citizen returns to the Member State of which they are a national, after having resided in another Member State in the context of Article 21(1) TFEU, and as the provider of services within the meaning of Article 56 TFEU?

In its answer the CJEU first noted that neither Article 21(1) TFEU nor the Free Movement Directive confer any autonomous right on third-country nationals. Any rights conferred on third-country nationals by EU law on Union citizenship are rights derived from the exercise of freedom of movement by a Union citizen. The CJEU went on to say that a literal, systematic and teleological (i.e. purpose-oriented) interpretation of the Directive does not establish a derived right of residence for third-country nationals who are family members of a Union citizen in the Member State of which that citizen is a national. Accordingly, the Free Movement Directive only establishes a derived right of residence for third-country nationals who are family members of a Union citizen, within the meaning of its Article 2(2) where that citizen has exercised their right of freedom of movement by becoming established in a Member State other than the Member State of which they are a national; see paragraphs 36-39.

The CJEU then examined whether Article 21(1) TFEU could give a basis for a derived right of residence for third-country nationals who find themselves in a situation corresponding to that of O and B. What did the CJEU determine in this respect (see in particular paragraphs 45-47)?

The CJEU found that, in the case before it, it was possible to remove the same type of obstacle on leaving the Member State of origin as that referred to in the earlier *Singh* and *Eind* cases if, when a Union citizen returns to the Member State of which they are a national, a derived right of residence is granted to a third-country national who is a family member of that Union citizen and with whom that citizen has resided, solely by virtue of his being a Union citizen, pursuant to and in conformity with Union law in the host Member State,

Next, the CJEU found that the conditions for granting (pursuant to Article 21(1) TFEU) a derived right of residence to a third-country national who is a family member of a Union citizen with whom they have resided, when that Union citizen returns to the Member State of which they are a national, should not be stricter than the condition provided for by Directive 2004/38 for the grant of such a right of residence to a third-country national who is a family member of a Union citizen, when that citizen has exercised their right of freedom of movement by becoming established in a Member State other than their home Member State. While the Free Movement Directive does not cover such a right, it should be applied by analogy.

In the view of the CJEU, an obstacle to a Union citizen moving from their home Member State could only arise where the residence of the Union citizen in the host Member State has been sufficiently genuine to enable them to create or strengthen family life in that Member State. Therefore, Article 21(1) TFEU does not require that every residence in the host Member State of a Union citizen accompanied by a family member who is a third-country national should necessarily confer on that family member a derived right of residence in the Union citizen's home State upon the Union citizen's return to that Member State.

Again, in the view of the CJEU, a Union citizen who has exercised their right of freedom of movement to reside in another Member State for less than three months, under Article 6(1) of the Free Movement Directive, does not intend to settle in the host Member State in such a way as would create or strengthen family life in that Member State. The situation would be otherwise if a Union citizen intended to exercise their rights under Article 7(1) of the Free Movement Directive (i.e. to take up residence for more than three months), since such a residence in the host Member State would, in principle, be evidence of settling there and of the Union citizen's genuine residence in the host Member State, which would be compatible with creating and strengthening family life in that Member State.

If family life has been established or strengthened in a host Member State in connection with a Union citizen's genuine residence in that State, in compliance with the conditions in Article 7(1) and (2) of the Free Movement Directive, the effective exercise of the Union citizen's rights under Article 21(1) TFEU would require that the Union citizen's family life could continue after the Union citizen has returned to their home State. From this it follows that family members who are third-country nationals should be allowed a derived right of residence. If such a derived right of residence were not allowed, Union citizens would be deterred from leaving their home States to exercise their right of free movement in another Member State, as provided for in Article 21(1) TFEU, as such a Union citizen could not be sure that they would be able to continue in their Member State of origin the family life with their close family members which they will have established or strengthened in the host Member State. The CJEU was of the view that the effectiveness of Article 21(1) TFEU requires that, on returning to the Member State of which they are a national, Union citizens must be able to continue the family life which they have led in the host Member State, and this is even more the case if the Union citizen has a family member who is a third-country national who has been granted a permanent right of residence in the host Member State pursuant to Article 16(1) and (2) of Free Movement Directive.

The CJEU also ruled that short periods of residence, such as weekends or holidays, spent in a Member State other than that of which the citizen in question is a national, do not satisfy the conditions for constituting residence which may form the basis for a derived right of residence under Union law. On the contrary, such periods of residence fall within the scope of Article 6 of the Free Movement Directive, even if they are considered collectively.

The CJEU noted that Union law does not require the Member State of which a Union citizen is a national to grant a derived right of residence to a third-country national who is a member of that citizen's family merely because that third-country national held a valid residence permit in the host Member State. Why did the CJEU rule that a residence permit issued pursuant to Article 10 of the Free Movement Directive could not form the basis of such a derived right of residence?

As can be seen, in the O case the CJEU ruled that it follows from Article 21(1) TFEU that, where a Union citizen has established or strengthened family life with a third-country national during a genuine residence (in accordance and compliance with the conditions in Article 7(1) and (2) or Article 16(1) and (2) of the Free Movement Directive), in a Member State other than that of which the Union citizen is a national, the provisions of the Directive apply by analogy if the Union citizen returns to their home State together with the family member in question.

The CJEU declined to answer the fourth question referred for a preliminary ruling. In its fourth question the referring court asked, with reference to the situation of B, whether a family member who is a third-country national loses a right of residence on the basis of Union law as a result of the time which has elapsed between the return of the Union citizen to the Member State of which they are a national and the arrival of the family member from a third country in that Member State. Why did the CJEU decline to answer this question?

In certain Member States a practice has developed with regard to secondary movement under which it is a condition for being allowed to unite a family under Union law that the Member State's citizen has had a genuine and actual residence in another Member State. Among other things on the basis of the judgment in the Metock case, printed immediately above, national authorities demand evidence of a genuine and actual residence in another Member State where there is doubt about whether the Member State's own citizen has met this condition. Does the CJEU's ruling in the *O* case mean that this practice must be changed in this respect?

JUDGMENT OF THE COURT (Grand Chamber)
8 March 2011

Gerardo Ruiz Zambrano, v Office national de l'emploi (ONEm).
(Reference for a preliminary ruling from the Tribunal du travail de Bruxelles – Belgium)

'Citizenship of the Union – Article 20 TFEU – Grant of right of residence under European Union law to a minor child on the territory of the Member State of which that child is a national, irrespective of the previous exercise by him of his right of free movement in the territory of the Member States – Grant, in the same circumstances, of a derived right of residence, to an ascendant relative, a third-country national, upon whom the minor child is dependent – Consequences of the right of residence of the minor child on the employment law requirements to be fulfilled by the third-country national ascendant relative of that minor'

Case C-34/09

Judgment

1. The reference for a preliminary ruling concerns the interpretation of Articles 12 EC, 17 EC and 18 EC, and also Articles 21, 24 and 34 of the Charter of Fundamental Rights of the European Union ('the Charter of Fundamental Rights').

2. That reference was made in the context of proceedings between Mr Ruiz Zambrano, a Columbian national, and the Office national de l'emploi (National Employment Office) ('ONEm') concerning the refusal by the latter to grant him unemployment benefits under Belgian legislation.

Legal context

European Union law

3. Article 3(1) of Directive 2004/38/EC of the European Parliament and of the Council of 29 April 2004 on the right of citizens of the Union and their family members to move and reside freely within the territory of the Member States, amending Regulation (EEC) No 1612/68 and repealing Directives 64/221/EEC, 68/360/EEC, 72/194/EEC, 73/148/EEC, 75/34/EEC, 75/35/EEC, 90/364/EEC, 90/365/EEC and 93/96/EEC (OJ 2004 L 158, p. 77, and corrigenda OJ 2004 L 229, p. 35, and OJ 2005 L 197, p. 34), provides:

‘ This Directive shall apply to all Union citizens who move to or reside in a Member State other than that of which they are a national, and to their family members as defined in point 2 of Article 2 who accompany or join them.’

National law

The Belgian Nationality Code

4. Under Article 10(1) of the Belgian Nationality Code (*Moniteur belge*, 12 July 1984, p. 10095), in the version applicable at the time of the facts in the main proceedings (‘the Belgian Nationality Code’):

   ‘Any child born in Belgium who, at any time before reaching the age of 18 or being declared of full age, would be stateless if he or she did not have Belgian nationality, shall be Belgian.’

The Royal Decree of 25 November 1991

5. Article 30 of the Royal Decree of 25 November 1991 (*Moniteur belge* of 31 December 1991, p. 29888) concerning rules on unemployment provides as follows:

   ‘In order to be eligible for unemployment benefit, a full-time worker must have completed a qualifying period comprising the following number of working days:
   ...

   2. 468 during the 27 months preceding the claim [for unemployment benefit], if the worker is more than 36 and less than 50 years of age,

   ...’

6. Article 43(1) of the Royal Decree states:

   ‘Without prejudice to the previous provisions, a foreign or stateless worker is entitled to unemployment benefit if he or she complies with the legislation relating to aliens and to the employment of foreign workers.

   Work undertaken in Belgium is not taken into account unless it complies with the legislation relating to the employment of foreign workers.
   ...’

7. Under Article 69(1) of the Royal Decree:

   ‘In order to receive benefits, foreign and stateless unemployed persons must satisfy the legislation concerning aliens and that relating to the employment of foreign labour.’

The Decree-Law of 28 December 1944

8. Article 7(14) of the Decree-Law of 28 December 1944 on social security for workers (*Moniteur belge* of 30 December 1944), inserted by the Framework Law of 2 August 2002 (*Moniteur belge* of 29 August 2002, p. 38408), is worded as follows:

   'Foreign and stateless workers shall be eligible to receive benefits only if, at the time of applying for benefits, they satisfy the legislation concerning residency and that relating to the employment of foreign labour.

   Work done in Belgium by a foreign or stateless worker shall be taken into account for the purpose of the qualifying period only if it was carried out in accordance with the legislation on the employment of foreign labour.
   ...'

The Law of 30 April 1999

9. Article 4(1) of the Law of 30 April 1999 on the employment of foreign workers (*Moniteur belge* of 21 May 1999, p. 17800) provides:

   'An employer wishing to employ a foreign worker must obtain prior employment authorisation from the competent authority.

   The employer may use the services of that worker only as provided for in that authorisation.

   The King may provide for exceptions to the first paragraph herein, as He deems appropriate.'

10. Under Article 7 of that law:

   'The King may, by a decree debated in the Council of Ministers, exempt such categories of foreign workers as He shall determine from the requirement to obtain a work permit.

   Employers of foreign workers referred to in the preceding paragraph shall be exempted from the obligation to obtain a work permit.'

The Royal Decree of 9 June 1999

11. Article 2(2) of the Royal Decree of 9 June 1999 implementing the Law of 30 April 1999 on the employment of foreign workers (*Moniteur belge* of 26 June 1999, p. 24162) provides:

'The following shall not be required to obtain a work permit:

...

2. The spouse of a Belgian national, provided that s/he comes in order to settle, or does settle, with that national;
   (a) descendants under 21 years of age or dependants of the Belgian national or his spouse;
   (b) dependent ascendants of the Belgian national or his/her spouse;
   (c) the spouse of the persons referred to in (a) or (b);

...'

The Law of 15 December 1980

12. Article 9 of the Law of 15 December 1980 on access to Belgian territory, residence, establishment and expulsion of foreign nationals (*Moniteur belge* du 31 December 1980, p. 14584), in the version thereof applicable to the main proceedings ('the Law of 15 December 1980'), provides:

'In order to be able to reside in the Kingdom beyond the term fixed in Article 6, a foreigner who is not covered by one of the cases provided for in Article 10 must be authorised by the Minister or his representative.

Save for exceptions provided for by international treaty, a law or royal decree, the foreigner must request that authorisation from the competent diplomatic mission or Belgian consul in his place of residence or stay abroad.

In exceptional circumstances, the foreigner may request that authorisation from the mayor of the municipality where he is residing, who will forward to the Minister or his representative. It will, in that case, be issued in Belgium.'

13. Article 40 of the same law provides:

'1. Without prejudice to the provisions in the regulations of the Council [of the European Union] and the Commission of the European Communities and more favourable ones on which an EC foreign national might rely, the following provisions shall apply to him.

2. For the purposes of this Law, 'EC foreign national' shall mean any national of a Member State of the European Communities who resides in or travels to the Kingdom and who:
   (i) pursues or intends to pursue there an activity as an employed or self-employed person;
   (ii) receives or intends to receive services there:
   (iii) enjoys or intends to enjoy there a right to remain;

(iv) enjoys or intends to enjoy there a right of residence after ceasing a professional activity or occupation pursued in the Community;
(v) undergoes or intends to undergo there, as a principal pursuit, vocational training in an approved educational establishment; or
(vi) belongs to none of the categories under (i) to (v) above.

3. Subject to any contrary provisions of this Law, the following persons shall, whatever their nationality, be treated in the same way as an EC foreign national covered by paragraph 2(i), (ii) and (iii) above, provided that they come in order to settle, or do settle, with him:
   (i) the spouse of that national;
   (ii) the national's descendants or those of his spouse who are under 21 years of age and dependent on them;
   (ii) the national's ascendants or those of his spouse who are dependent on them;
   (iv) the spouse of the persons referred to in (ii) or (iii).

4. Subject to any contrary provisions of this Law, the following persons shall, whatever their nationality, be treated in the same way as an EC foreign national covered by paragraph 2(iv) and (vi) above, provided that they come in order to settle, or do settle, with him:
   (i) the spouse of that national;
   (ii) the national's descendants or those of his spouse who are dependent on them;
   (iii) the national's ascendants or those of his spouse who are dependent on them;
   (iv) the spouse of the persons referred to in (ii) or (iii).

5. Subject to any contrary provisions of this Law, the spouse of an EC foreign national covered by paragraph 2(v) above and his children or those of his spouse who are dependent on them shall, whatever their nationality, be treated in the same way as the EC foreign national provided that they come in order to settle, or do settle, with him.

6. The spouse of a Belgian who comes in order to settle, or does settle, with him, and also their descendants who are under 21 years of age or dependent on them, their ascendants who are dependent on them and any spouse of those descendants or ascendants, who come to settle, or do settle, with them, shall also be treated in the same way as an EC foreign national.'

The dispute in the main proceedings and the questions referred for a preliminary ruling

14. On 14 April 1999, Mr Ruiz Zambrano, who was in possession of a visa issued by the Belgian embassy in Bogotá (Colombia), applied for asylum in Belgium. In February 2000, his wife, also a Columbian national, likewise applied for refugee status in Belgium.

15. By decision of 11 September 2000, the Belgian authorities refused their applications and ordered them to leave Belgium. However, the order notified to them included a *non-refoulement* clause stating that they should not be sent back to Colombia in view of the civil war in that country.

16. On 20 October 2000, Mr Ruiz Zambrano applied to have his situation regularised pursuant to the third paragraph of Article 9 of the Law of 15 December 1980. In his application, he referred to the absolute impossibility of returning to Colombia and the severe deterioration of the situation there, whilst emphasising his efforts to integrate into Belgian society, his learning of French and his child's attendance at pre-school, in addition to the risk, in the event of a return to Columbia, of a worsening of the significant post-traumatic syndrome he had suffered in 1999 as a result of his son, then aged 3, being abducted for a week.

17. By decision of 8 August 2001, that application was rejected. An action was brought for annulment and suspension of that decision before the Conseil d'État, which rejected the action for suspension by a judgment of 22 May 2003.

18. Since 18 April 2001, Mr Ruiz Zambrano and his wife have been registered in the municipality of Schaerbeek (Belgium). On 2 October 2001, although he did not hold a work permit, Mr Ruiz Zambrano signed an employment contract for an unlimited period to work full-time with the Plastoria company, with effect from 1 October 2001.

19. On 1 September 2003, Mr Ruiz Zambrano's wife gave birth to a second child, Diego, who acquired Belgian nationality pursuant to Article 10(1) of the Belgian Nationality Code, since Columbian law does not recognise Colombian nationality for children born outside the territory of Colombia where the parents do not take specific steps to have them so recognised.

20. The order for reference further indicates that, at the time of his second child's birth, Mr Ruiz Zambrano had sufficient resources from his working activities to provide for his family. His work was paid according to the various applicable scales, with statutory deductions made for social security and the payment of employer contributions.

21. On 9 April 2004, Mr and Mrs Ruiz Zambrano again applied to have their situation regularised pursuant to the third paragraph of Article 9 of the Law of 15 December 1980, putting forward as a new factor the birth of their second child and relying on Article 3 of Protocol 4 to the European Convention for the Protection of Human Rights and Fundamental Freedoms, signed at Rome on 4 November 1950 ('ECHR'), which prevents that child from being required to leave the territory of the State of which he is a national.

22. Following the birth of their third child, Jessica, on 26 August 2005, who, like her brother Diego, acquired Belgian nationality, on 2 September 2005 Mr and Mrs Ruiz Zambrano lodged an application to take up residence pursuant to Article 40 of the Law of 15 December 1980, in their capacity as ascendants of a Belgian national. On 13 September 2005, a registration certificate was issued to them provisionally covering their residence until 13 February 2006.

23. Mr Ruiz Zambrano's application to take up residence was rejected on 8 November 2005, on the ground that he '[could] not rely on Article 40 of the Law of 15 December 1980 because he had disregarded the laws of his country by not registering his child with the diplomatic or consular authorities, but had correctly followed the procedures available to him for acquiring Belgian nationality [for his child] and then trying on that basis to legalise his own residence'. On 26 January 2006, his wife's application to take up residence was rejected on the same ground.

24. Since the introduction of his action for review of the decision rejecting his application for residence in March 2006, Mr Ruiz Zambrano has held a special residence permit valid for the entire duration of that action.

25. In the meantime, on 10 October 2005, Mr Ruiz Zambrano's employment contract was temporarily suspended on economic grounds, which led him to lodge a first application for unemployment benefit, which was rejected by a decision notified to him on 20 February 2006. That decision was challenged before the referring court by application of 12 April 2006.

26. In the course of the inquiries in the action brought against that decision, the Office des Étrangers (Aliens' Office) confirmed that 'the applicant and his wife cannot pursue any employment, but no expulsion measure can be taken against them because their application for legalising their situation is still under consideration'.

27. In the course of an inspection carried out on 11 October 2006 by the Direction générale du contrôle des lois sociales (Directorate General, Supervision of Social Legislation) at the registered office of Mr Ruiz Zambrano's employer, he was found to be at work. He had to stop working immediately. The next day, Mr Ruiz Zambrano's employer terminated his contract of employment with immediate effect and without compensation.

28. The application lodged by Mr Ruiz Zambrano for full-time unemployment benefits as from 12 October 2006 was rejected by a decision of the ONEm (National Employment Office), which was notified on 20 November 2006. On 20 December 2006 an action was also brought against that decision before the referring court.

29. On 23 July 2007, Mr Ruiz Zambrano was notified of the decision of the Office des Étrangers rejecting his application of 9 April 2004 to regularise his situation. The action brought against that decision before the Conseil du contentieux des étrangers (Council for asylum and immigration proceedings) was declared to be devoid of purpose by a judgment of 8 January 2008, as the Office des Étrangers had withdrawn that decision.

30. By letter of 25 October 2007, the Office des Étrangers informed Mr Ruiz Zambrano that the action for review he had brought in March 2006 against the decision rejecting his application to take up residence of 2 September 2005 had to be reintroduced within 30 days of the notification of that letter, in the form of an action for annulment before the Conseil du contentieux des étrangers.

31. On 19 November 2007, Mr Ruiz Zambrano brought such an action for annulment, based, first, on the inexistence of the 'legal engineering' of which he had been charged in that decision, since the acquisition of Belgian nationality by his minor children was not the result of any steps taken by him, but rather of the application of the relevant Belgian legislation. Mr Ruiz Zambrano also alleges infringement of Articles 2 and 7 of Directive 2004/38, as well as infringement of Article 8 of the ECHR, and of Article 3(1) of Protocol No 4 thereto.

32. In its written observations lodged before the Court, the Belgian Government states that, since 30 April 2009, Mr Ruiz Zambrano has had a provisional and renewable residence permit, and should have a type C work permit, pursuant to the instructions of 26 March 2009 of the Minister for immigration and asylum policy relating to the application of the former third paragraph of Article 9 and Article 9a of the Law of 15 December 1980.

33. It is apparent from the order for reference that the two decisions which are the subject-matter of the main proceedings, by which the ONEm refused to recognise Mr Ruiz Zambrano's entitlement to unemployment benefit, first, during the periods of temporary unemployment from 10 October 2005 and then 12 October 2006, following the loss of his job, are based solely on the finding that the working days on which he relies for the purpose of completing the qualifying period for his age category, that is, 468 working days during the 27 months preceding his claim for unemployment benefit, were not completed as required by the legislation governing foreigners' residence and employment of foreign workers.

34. Mr Ruiz Zambrano challenges that argument before the referring court, stating inter alia that he enjoys a right of residence directly by virtue of the EC Treaty or, at the very least, that he enjoys the derived right of residence, recognised in Case C-200/02 *Zhu and Chen* [2004] ECR I-9925 for the ascendants of a minor child who is a national of a Member State and that, therefore, he is exempt from the obligation to hold a work permit.

35. In those circumstances, the Tribunal du travail de Bruxelles (Employment Tribunal, Brussels) (Belgium) decided to stay proceedings and to refer the following questions to the Court of Justice for a preliminary ruling:

'1. Do Articles 12 [EC], 17 [EC] and 18 [EC], or one or more of them when read separately or in conjunction, confer a right of residence upon a citizen of the Union in the territory of the Member State of which that citizen is a national, irrespective of whether he has previously exercised his right to move within the territory of the Member States?

2. Must Articles 12 [EC], 17 [EC] and 18 [EC], in conjunction with the provisions of Articles 21, 24 and 34 of the Charter of Fundamental Rights, be interpreted as meaning that the right which they recognise, without discrimination on the grounds of nationality, in favour of any citizen of the Union to move and reside freely in the territory of the Member States means that, where that citizen is an infant dependent on a relative in the ascending line who is a national of a non-member State, the infant's enjoyment of the right of residence in the Member State in which he resides and of which he is a national must be safeguarded, irrespective of whether the right to move freely has been previously exercised by the child or through his legal representative, by coupling that right of residence with the useful effect whose necessity is recognised by Community case-law [*Zhu and Chen*], and granting the relative in the ascending line who is a national of a non-member State, upon whom the child is dependent and who has sufficient resources and sickness insurance, the secondary right of residence which that same national of a non-member State would have if the child who is dependent upon him were a Union citizen who is not a national of the Member State in which he resides?

3. Must Articles 12 [EC], 17 [EC] and 18 [EC], in conjunction with the provisions of Articles 21, 24 and 34 of the Charter of Fundamental Rights, be interpreted as meaning that the right of a minor child who is a national of a Member State to reside in the territory of the State in which he resides must entail the grant of an exemption from the requirement to hold a work permit to the relative in the ascending line who is a national of a non-member State, upon whom the child is dependent and who, were it not for the requirement to hold a work permit under the national law of the Member State in which he resides, fulfils the condition of sufficient resources and the possession of sickness insurance by virtue

of paid employment making him subject to the social security system of that State, so that the child's right of residence is coupled with the useful effect recognised by Community case-law [*Zhu and Chen*] in favour of a minor child who is a European citizen with a nationality other than that of the Member State in which he resides and is dependent upon a relative in the ascending line who is a national of a non-member State?'

The questions referred for a preliminary ruling

36. By its questions, which it is appropriate to consider together, the referring court asks, essentially, whether the provisions of the TFEU on European Union citizenship are to be interpreted as meaning that they confer on a relative in the ascending line who is a third-country national, upon whom his minor children, who are European Union citizens, are dependent, a right of residence in the Member State of which they are nationals and in which they reside, and also exempt him from having to obtain a work permit in that Member State.

37. All governments which submitted observations to the Court and the European Commission argue that a situation such as that of Mr Ruiz Zambrano's second and third children, where those children reside in the Member State of which they are nationals and have never left the territory of that Member State, does not come within the situations envisaged by the freedoms of movement and residence guaranteed under European Union law. Therefore, the provisions of European Union law referred to by the national court are not applicable to the dispute in the main proceedings.

38. Mr Ruiz Zambrano argues in response that the reliance by his children Diego and Jessica on the provisions relating to European Union citizenship does not presuppose that they must move outside the Member State in question and that he, in his capacity as a family member, is entitled to a right of residence and is exempt from having to obtain a work permit in that Member State.

39. It should be observed at the outset that, under Article 3(1) of Directive 2004/38, entitled '[b]eneficiaries', that directive applies to 'all Union citizens who move to or reside in a Member State other than that of which they are a national and to their family members ...'. Therefore, that directive does not apply to a situation such as that at issue in the main proceedings.

40. Article 20 TFEU confers the status of citizen of the Union on every person holding the nationality of a Member State (see, inter alia, Case C-224/98 *D'Hoop* [2002] ECR I-6191, paragraph 27, and Case C-148/02 *Garcia Avello* [2003] ECR I-11613, paragraph 21). Since Mr Ruiz Zambrano's second and third children possess Belgian nationality, the conditions for the acquisition of which it is for the Member State in question to lay down (see, to that effect, inter alia, Case C-135/08 *Rott-*

mann [2010] ECR I-0000, paragraph 39), they undeniably enjoy that status (see, to that effect, *Garcia Avello*, paragraph 21, and *Zhu and Chen*, paragraph 20).

41. As the Court has stated several times, citizenship of the Union is intended to be the fundamental status of nationals of the Member States (see, inter alia, Case C-184/99 *Grzelczyk* [2001] ECR I-6193, paragraph 31; Case C-413/99 *Baumbast and R* [2002] ECR I-7091, paragraph 82;*Garcia Avello*, paragraph 22; *Zhu and Chen*, paragraph 25; and *Rottmann*, paragraph 43).

42. In those circumstances, Article 20 TFEU precludes national measures which have the effect of depriving citizens of the Union of the genuine enjoyment of the substance of the rights conferred by virtue of their status as citizens of the Union (see, to that effect, *Rottmann*, paragraph 42).

43. A refusal to grant a right of residence to a third-country national with dependent minor children in the Member State where those children are nationals and reside, and also a refusal to grant such a person a work permit, has such an effect.

44. It must be assumed that such a refusal would lead to a situation where those children, citizens of the Union, would have to leave the territory of the Union in order to accompany their parents. Similarly, if a work permit were not granted to such a person, he would risk not having sufficient resources to provide for himself and his family, which would also result in the children, citizens of the Union, having to leave the territory of the Union. In those circumstances, those citizens of the Union would, in fact, be unable to exercise the substance of the rights conferred on them by virtue of their status as citizens of the Union.

45. Accordingly, the answer to the questions referred is that Article 20 TFEU is to be interpreted as meaning that it precludes a Member State from refusing a third-country national upon whom his minor children, who are European Union citizens, are dependent, a right of residence in the Member State of residence and nationality of those children, and from refusing to grant a work permit to that third-country national, in so far as such decisions deprive those children of the genuine enjoyment of the substance of the rights attaching to the status of European Union citizen.

Costs

[Para. 46 omitted]

On those grounds,

THE COURT (Grand Chamber),

hereby rules:

Article 20 TFEU is to be interpreted as meaning that it precludes a Member State from refusing a third-country national upon whom his minor children, who are European Union citizens, are dependent, a right of residence in the Member State of residence and nationality of those children, and from refusing to grant a work permit to that third-country national, in so far as such decisions deprive those children of the genuine enjoyment of the substance of the rights attaching to the status of European Union citizen.

Comments and questions

The *Zambrano* case concerned two minors who had been born while their parents, who were Columbian nationals, were resident in Belgium. The children had solely Belgian nationality, and there was no doubt that they were Union citizens. At the same time it was clear that the case had no cross-border aspects within the EU. The case gave rise to two important questions: first, could there be a law governing Union citizenship when there was no cross-border aspect; and second, could the children's parents derive a right of residence – and possibly a right to work – from their children's Union citizenship?

Prior to the Zambrano case the CJEU had not directly applied the TFEU provisions on Union citizenship to a case in which there was no cross-border aspect. However, in her Opinion, Advocate General Sharpston argued that, according to the Practice of the CJEU, in assessing whether Article 20 TFEU on Union citizenship applies to a case, the focus should not be on whether a person has hitherto exercised the right of free movement, but rather on whether the Member State's treatment of the case would affect the future status of a person as a Union citizen. The CJEU chose to follow the Advocate General on this point. However, the CJEU stated that Directive 2004/38, on the right of citizens of the Union and their family members to move and reside freely within the territory of the Member States, did not apply to a situation such at issue in the main proceedings (see Article 3(1) of the Directive). At the same time, the CJEU ruled that Article 20 TFEU 'precludes national measures which have the effect of depriving citizens of the Union of the genuine enjoyment of the substance of the rights conferred by virtue of their status as citizens of the Union', and that 'A refusal to grant a right of residence to a third-country national with dependent minor children in the Member State where those children are nationals and reside, and also a refusal to grant such a person a work permit, has such an effect'. In other words, the CJEU established that parents can derive a right both to reside and to work in a Member State if the parents have dependent children who are Union citizens and if these children would otherwise have to leave Union territory. The CJEU did not establish that there is a requirement for there to be a prior cross-border element.

On the one hand the *Zambrano* unquestionably breaks new ground. But on the other hand the judgment leaves many unanswered questions. First, it is unclear whether the judgment means that there is no longer a general requirement for there to be a cross-border element in order for the TFEU provisions on Union citizenship to apply. Consider whether the judgment should be understood as meaning that Article 20 TFEU must now also apply generally in a situation in which a Union citizen has never left their Member State. Or does the judgment merely mean that Article 20 TFEU only applies to cases that have no cross-border element where a requirement for a cross-border element would mean that the Union citizen would be prevented from taking up residence in the EU where they might wish, for example because the Union citizen is a minor and must therefore follow their parents (who are not Union citizens) if they are required to leave the Union territory? Consider whether the judgment means, for example, that a Spanish national can rely on Article 21 TFEU in proceedings against the Spanish authorities to challenge a Spanish legal act, even though there are no cross-border elements in the case. Also, consider whether the CJEU's case law hitherto, requiring a case to have a cross-border element before the provisions on a person's freedom of movement in Articles 45, 49 and 56 TFEU can apply, is still applicable following the decision in the *Zambrano* case.

What is the significance of the CJEU's reference to the children being dependent on Mr Zambrano for the wider significance of the judgment? Does the reference mean that the children's mother, Mrs Zambrano, cannot also derive a right to remain in Belgium from the children's Union citizenship if she does not take part in providing for the children (i.e. that she has paid work)? On this, see Case C-127/08 *Metock*, paragraph 62 (printed above). Note that the mother's right of residence could also be based on the right to family life as laid down in Article 8 of the European Convention on Human Rights and in Article 7 of the Charter of fundamental rights of the European Union. However, the CJEU did not decide on the application of these provisions to the *Zambrano* case.

As can be seen, the *Zambrano* case left several questions unanswered. In the subsequent judgment in Joined Cases C-356/11 and C-357/11 *O and S* v *Maahanmuuttovirasto* judgment of 6 December 2012, the CJEU was asked to clarify the *Zambrano* judgment on some significant points. In this case a third-country national was a member of a reunited family. The third-country national did not have parental or financial responsibility for a minor who was a Union citizen. In other words, the question was whether, under Union law, a third-country national can derive a right of residence from a stepchild who is a Union citizen.

The situation in each of the two joined cases (O and S) was similar to the key points of the *Zambrano* case, as there were small children who had Union citizenship, and neither the children nor their family members had exercised their right of freedom of movement, but had always been resident in the Member State where they were citizens. As in the *Zambrano* case, neither the children who were Union citizens nor their family members came under the heading of 'beneficiaries' within the meaning of Directive 2004/38 on the right of citizens of the Union and their family members to move and reside freely within the territory of the Member States. The question was thus whether Article 20 TFEU on Union citizenship applied to this situation. In answering this, the CJEU first repeated its ruling in the *Zambrano* case, that Article 20 TFEU precludes national measures which have the effect of denying Union citizens the genuine enjoyment of the substance of the rights conferred by their status. Such national measures can include refusals to grant rights of residence to family members of a Union citizen.

However, at the same time the CJEU stated that this that criterion is 'specific in character inasmuch as it relates to situations in which a right of residence, exceptionally, may not be refused to a third-country national who is a family member of a national of a Member State, as the effectiveness of the Union citizenship enjoyed by that national would otherwise be undermined'. The CJEU also said that the principles laid down in the *Zambrano* case 'apply only in exceptional circumstances'. In other words, the CJEU made it clear that the *Zambrano* case was 'exceptional'.

The CJEU then laid out the principles which it had originally set in the *Zambrano* case, noting that these are not limited to cases in which there is a blood relationship between the third-country national for whom a right of residence is sought and a Union citizen who is a minor. Thus, the principles can be extended to other dependent relationships between a child who is a Union citizen and a national of a third country. What is decisive is whether the Member State's actions would mean that a Union citizen who is a minor would be prevented from exercising the substance of the rights conferred by their Union citizenship. It is thus the dependent relationship between the Union citizen who is a minor and the third-country national who is refused a right of residence that must be established with a view to deciding whether this dependent relationship would lead to the Union citizen being obliged to leave not only the territory of the Member State of which they are a national, but also that of the European Union as a whole, as a consequence of such a refusal. In deciding whether a refusal of a residence permit to a third-country national can mean that a Union citizen who is a minor and a stepchild of a third-country national would be denied the genuine enjoyment of the substance of the rights conferred by their status, a number of factors must be considered. Among these factors is that the mere fact that it might appear desirable, for economic reasons or in order to preserve the family unit in the territory of the Union, for members of a family consisting of third-country nationals and a Union citizen who is a minor to be able to reside with that citizen in the territory of the Union in the Member State of which the citizen is a national is not sufficient in itself to support the view that the Union citizen would be forced to leave the territory of the Union if such a right of residence were not granted.

In other words, the CJEU found that Article 20 TFEU did not prevent a Member State refusing to grant a third-country national a residence permit on the basis of family reunification, where that national seeks to reside with his spouse who is also a third-country national and resides lawfully in that Member State and is the mother of a child from a previous marriage who is a Union citizen. This applied even though the two spouses (third-country nationals) had a child of their own marriage who was also a third-country national. In this connection it was decisive that the refusal of a residence permit to the third-country national who was a step-parent to the Union citizen would not mean that the Union citizen concerned would be deprived of the effective enjoyment of the substance of the rights conferred by the status of citizen of the Union.

If an Irish national were married to a third-country national, and they have a child together who is a minor and who only has Irish nationality, would the Irish authorities be able to expel the third-country national if the Irish spouse falls ill and is therefore unable to provide for the family and care for their child? Will it affect the answer if their child has to leave with the parent who is a third-country national in the event that that parent is forced to leave Ireland (and the EU)? Is it relevant that the parent who is denied residence is the financial provider for the child, or is it sufficient that this parent is of decisive importance for the child in other ways (including emotionally)?

See also Case C-40/11 *Iida* judgment of 8 November 2012 which concerned the situation where a third-country national who was the father of a child who was a Union citizen, could derive a right of residence from the child in a situation where the father and the child (together with the mother) were residing in different Member States. The CJEU denied that the father could derive a right of residence from the child, partly because the father had a right of residence which could be extended pursuant to the national law on third-country nationals, and partly because the father could in principle be granted the status of a long-term resident pursuant to Directive 2003/109 on the status of third-country nationals who are long-term residents. However, the *Iida* case says nothing about how the CJEU will assess the situation under Union law if the third country parent does not already have a right of residence in the Member State of origin of the child who is a Union citizen and the parents live separately, in each their own Member State, with shared parental responsibility for the child. If in this situation the third country parent has to exercise the shared parental responsibility from a great distance (for example from Japan), this can raise the question of whether in such a situation the CJEU would find that the third country parent could derive a right of residence from the child who is a Union citizen, even if that child does not live permanently with that parent, but lives with the other parent in another Member State.

At the time of writing (Autumn 2015) the CJEU is dealing with Case C-165/14 *Marín*, which is a reference for a preliminary ruling on the scope of the *Zambrano* judgment. In reality, this case concerns whether third-country parents' right of residence derived from a child who is a Union citizen is absolute. A Spanish court has referred the following question:

> 'Is national legislation which excludes the possibility of granting a residence permit to the parent of a European Union citizen who is a child and dependent on that parent, because the parent has a criminal record in the country in which the request is made, compatible with Article 20 of the Treaty on the Functioning of the European Union, interpreted in the light of the decisions of 19 October 2004 (Case C-200/02 *Zhu-Chen*) and 8 March 2011 (Case C-34/09 *Ruiz Zambrano*), even if this results in the removal of the child from the territory of the European Union, as that child has to follow the parent?'

What answer do you think the CJEU will give? See also Case C-304/14 *CS*, which at the time of writing equally is pending.

JUDGMENT OF THE COURT (Third Chamber)
5 May 2011

Shirley McCarthy v Secretary of State for the Home Department. (Reference for a preliminary ruling from the Supreme Court of the United Kingdom, formerly the House of Lords – United Kingdom)

'Freedom of movement for persons – Article 21 TFEU – Directive 2004/38/EC – 'Beneficiary' – Article 3(1) – National who has never made use of his right of free movement and has always resided in the Member State of his nationality – Effect of being a national of another Member State – Purely internal situation'

Case C-434/09

Judgment

1. This reference for a preliminary ruling concerns the interpretation of Article 3(1) and Article 16 of Directive 2004/38/EC of the European Parliament and of the Council of 29 April 2004 on the right of citizens of the Union and their family members to move and reside freely within the territory of the Member States amending Regulation (EEC) No 1612/68 and repealing Directives 64/221/EEC, 68/360/EEC, 72/194/EEC, 73/148/EEC, 75/34/EEC, 75/35/EEC, 90/364/EEC, 90/365/EEC and 93/96/EEC (OJ 2004 L 158, p. 77, and corrigendum OJ 2004 L 229, p. 35).

2. The reference was made in the course of proceedings between Mrs McCarthy and the Secretary of State for the Home Department ('the Secretary of State') concerning an application for a residence permit made by Mrs McCarthy.

Legal context

European Union law

3. According to recitals 1 to 3 in the preamble to Directive 2004/38:

'(1) Citizenship of the Union confers on every citizen of the Union a primary and individual right to move and reside freely within the territory of the Member States, subject to the limitations and conditions laid down in the Treaty and to the measures adopted to give it effect.

(2) The free movement of persons constitutes one of the fundamental freedoms of the internal market, which comprises an area without internal frontiers, in which freedom is ensured in accordance with the provisions of the Treaty.

(3) Union citizenship should be the fundamental status of nationals of the Member States when they exercise their right of free movement and residence. It is therefore necessary to codify and review the existing Community instruments dealing separately with workers, self-employed persons, as well as students and other inactive persons in order to simplify and strengthen the right of free movement and residence of all Union citizens.'

4. Chapter I of Directive 2004/38, entitled 'General provisions', comprises Articles 1 to 3 of the directive.

5. Article 1, entitled 'Subject', states:

'This Directive lays down:
(a) the conditions governing the exercise of the right of free movement and residence within the territory of the Member States by Union citizens and their family members;
(b) the right of permanent residence in the territory of the Member States for Union citizens and their family members;
(c) the limits placed on the rights set out in (a) and (b) on grounds of public policy, public security or public health.'

6. Article 2 of Directive 2004/38, entitled 'Definitions', provides:

'For the purposes of this Directive:

1. 'Union citizen' means any person having the nationality of a Member State;
2. 'family member' means:
   (a) the spouse;
   (b) the partner with whom the Union citizen has contracted a registered partnership, on the basis of the legislation of a Member State, if the legislation of the host Member State treats registered partnerships as equivalent to marriage and in accordance with the conditions laid down in the relevant legislation of the host Member State;
   (c) the direct descendants who are under the age of 21 or are dependants and those of the spouse or partner as defined in point (b);
   (d) the dependent direct relatives in the ascending line and those of the spouse or partner as defined in point (b);

'host Member State' means the Member State to which a Union citizen moves in order to exercise his/her right of free movement and residence.'

7. Article 3 of Directive 2004/38, entitled 'Beneficiaries', provides in paragraph 1:

   'This Directive shall apply to all Union citizens who move to or reside in a Member State other than that of which they are a national, and to their family members as defined in point 2 of Article 2 who accompany or join them.'

8. Chapter III of that directive, entitled 'Right of residence', comprises Articles 6 to 15 of the directive.

9. Article 6 provides:

   '1. Union citizens shall have the right of residence on the territory of another Member State for a period of up to three months without any conditions or any formalities other than the requirement to hold a valid identity card or passport.

   2. The provisions of paragraph 1 shall also apply to family members in possession of a valid passport who are not nationals of a Member State, accompanying or joining the Union citizen.'

10. Article 7 of Directive 2004/38 states:

   '1. All Union citizens shall have the right of residence on the territory of another Member State for a period of longer than three months if they:
   (a) are workers or self-employed persons in the host Member State; or
   (b) have sufficient resources for themselves and their family members not to become a burden on the social assistance system of the host Member State during their period of residence and have comprehensive sickness insurance cover in the host Member State; or
   (c) – are enrolled at a private or public establishment, accredited or financed by the host Member State on the basis of its legislation or administrative practice, for the principal purpose of following a course of study, including vocational training; and
   – have comprehensive sickness insurance cover in the host Member State and assure the relevant national authority, by means of a declaration or by such equivalent means as they may choose, that they have sufficient resources for themselves and their family members not to become a burden on the social assistance system of the host Member State during their period of residence; or
   (d) are family members accompanying or joining a Union citizen who satisfies the conditions referred to in points (a), (b) or (c).

   2. The right of residence provided for in paragraph 1 shall extend to family members who are not nationals of a Member State, accompanying or joining the Un-

ion citizen in the host Member State, provided that such Union citizen satisfies the conditions referred to in paragraph 1(a), (b) or (c).

3. For the purposes of paragraph 1(a), a Union citizen who is no longer a worker or self-employed person shall retain the status of worker or self-employed person in the following circumstances:

...

4. By way of derogation from paragraphs 1(d) and 2 above, only the spouse, the registered partner provided for in Article 2(2)(b) and dependent children shall have the right of residence as family members of a Union citizen meeting the conditions under 1(c) above. Article 3(2) shall apply to his/her dependent direct relatives in the ascending lines and those of his/her spouse or registered partner.'

11. Under Chapter IV, headed 'Right of permanent residence', Article 16 of Directive 2004/38, entitled 'General rule for Union citizens and their family members', provides:

'1. Union citizens who have resided legally for a continuous period of five years in the host Member State shall have the right of permanent residence there. This right shall not be subject to the conditions provided for in Chapter III.

2. Paragraph 1 shall apply also to family members who are not nationals of a Member State and have legally resided with the Union citizen in the host Member State for a continuous period of five years.

...

4. Once acquired, the right of permanent residence shall be lost only through absence from the host Member State for a period exceeding two consecutive years.'

12. Chapter V of that directive, entitled 'Provisions common to the right of residence and the right of permanent residence', includes Article 22 which, under the heading 'Territorial scope', provides:

The right of residence and the right of permanent residence shall cover the whole territory of the host Member State. Member States may impose territorial restrictions on the right of residence and the right of permanent residence only where the same restrictions apply to their own nationals.'

National law

13. Under the United Kingdom Immigration Rules, nationals of third countries who do not have leave to remain in the United Kingdom thereunder also do not meet the requirements to be granted leave to remain under those Rules as the spouse of a person settled in the United Kingdom.

The dispute in the main proceedings and the questions referred for a preliminary ruling

14. Mrs McCarthy, a national of the United Kingdom, is also an Irish national. She was born and has always lived in the United Kingdom, and has never argued that she is or has been a worker, self-employed person or self-sufficient person. She is in receipt of State benefits.

15. On 15 November 2002, Mrs McCarthy married a Jamaican national who lacks leave to remain in the United Kingdom under the Immigration Rules of that Member State.

16. Following her marriage, Mrs McCarthy applied for an Irish passport for the first time and obtained it.

17. On 23 July 2004, Mrs McCarthy and her husband applied to the Secretary of State for a residence permit and residence document under European Union law as, respectively, a Union citizen and the spouse of a Union citizen. The Secretary of State refused their applications on the ground that Mrs McCarthy was not 'a qualified person' (essentially, a worker, self-employed person or self-sufficient person) and, accordingly, that Mr McCarthy was not the spouse of 'a qualified person'.

18. Mrs McCarthy appealed against the decision that had been made in relation to her by the Secretary of State before the Asylum and Immigration Tribunal ('the Tribunal'), which dismissed the appeal on 17 October 2006. The High Court of Justice of England and Wales ordered the Tribunal to reconsider the appeal, and on 16 August 2007 the Tribunal upheld the decision to dismiss it.

19. The appeal brought by Mrs McCarthy against the decision of the Tribunal was dismissed by the Court of Appeal (Civil Division) (England and Wales). Mrs McCarthy brought an appeal against the decision of that court before the referring court.

20. For his part, Mr McCarthy did not appeal against the decision of the Secretary of State in relation to him, but nevertheless made a further application which was also refused. Mr McCarthy then appealed against that second decision to the Tribunal, which adjourned the appeal to await the final outcome of Mrs McCarthy's appeal.

21. In that context, the Supreme Court of the United Kingdom decided to stay the proceedings and to refer the following questions to the Court of Justice for a preliminary ruling:

‘1. Is a person of dual Irish and United Kingdom nationality who has resided in the United Kingdom for her entire life a ‘beneficiary’ within the meaning of Article 3 of Directive 2004/38 ...?

2. Has such a person ‘resided legally’ within the host Member State for the purpose of Article 16 of [that] directive in circumstances where she was unable to satisfy the requirements of Article 7 of [that directive]?’

Consideration of the questions referred

22. As is apparent from paragraphs 14 to 19 of this judgment, the main proceedings concern an application for a right of residence under European Union law brought by Mrs McCarthy, a Union citizen, to a Member State of which she is a national and where she has always resided.

23. That application is in fact intended to confer on Mr McCarthy, a national of a third country, a right of residence under Directive 2004/38, as a member of Mrs McCarthy’s family, given that a comparable right of residence does not arise under the Immigration Rules of the United Kingdom.

The first question

24. At the outset, it should be noted that, even though, formally, the national court has limited its questions to the interpretation of Articles 3(1) and 16 of Directive 2004/38, such a situation does not prevent the Court from providing the national court with all the elements of interpretation of European Union law which may be of assistance in adjudicating on the case before it, whether or not that court has specifically referred to them in the questions (see Case C-251/06 *ING. AUER* [2007] ECR I-9689, paragraph 38 and the case-law cited).

25. There is no indication in the order for reference, in the case-file or in the observations submitted to the Court that Mrs McCarthy has ever exercised her right of free movement within the territory of the Member States, either individually or as a family member of a Union citizen who has exercised such a right. Likewise, Mrs McCarthy is applying for a right of residence under European Union law even though she does not argue that she is or has been a worker, self-employed person or self-sufficient person.

26. Thus, the first question from the national court must be understood as asking, in essence, whether Article 3(1) of Directive 2004/38 or Article 21 TFEU is applicable

to the situation of a Union citizen who has never exercised his right of free movement, who has always resided in a Member State of which he is a national and who is also a national of another Member State.

Preliminary observations

27. As a preliminary point, it should be observed that citizenship of the Union confers on each Union citizen a primary and individual right to move and reside freely within the territory of the Member States, subject to the limitations and restrictions laid down by the Treaties and the measures adopted for their implementation, freedom of movement for persons being, moreover, one of the fundamental freedoms of the internal market, which was also reaffirmed in Article 45 of the Charter of Fundamental Rights of the European Union (Case C-162/09 *Lassal* [2010] ECR I-0000, paragraph 29).

28. With regard to Directive 2004/38, the Court has already had occasion to point out that it aims to facilitate the exercise of the primary and individual right to move and reside freely within the territory of the Member States that is conferred directly on Union citizens by the Treaty and that it aims in particular to strengthen that right (see Case C-127/08 *Metock and Others* [2008] ECR I-6241, paragraphs 82 and 59, and *Lassal*, paragraph 30).

29. Likewise, the Court has also held that a principle of international law, reaffirmed in Article 3 of Protocol No 4 to the European Convention for the Protection of Human Rights and Fundamental Freedoms, signed in Rome on 4 November 1950, that European Union law cannot be assumed to disregard in the context of relations between Member States, precludes a Member State from refusing its own nationals the right to enter its territory and remain there for any reason (see Case 41/74 *van Duyn* [1974] ECR 1337, paragraph 22, and Case C-257/99 *Barkoci and Malik* [2001] ECR I-6557, paragraph 81); that principle also precludes that Member State from expelling its own nationals from its territory or refusing their right to reside in that territory or making such right conditional (see Cases C-370/90 *Singh* [1992] ECR I-4265, paragraph 22 and C-291/05 *Eind* [2007] ECR I-10719, paragraph 31).

The applicability of Directive 2004/38

30. The first part of the first question, as reformulated by the Court, concerns whether Article 3(1) of Directive 2004/38 is to be interpreted as meaning that that directive applies to a citizen in a situation such as that of Mrs McCarthy, who has never exercised his right of free movement, who has always resided in a Member State of which he is a national and who is also a national of another Member State.

31. A literal, teleological and contextual interpretation of that provision leads to a negative reply to that question.

32. First, according to Article 3(1) of Directive 2004/38, all Union citizens who 'move to' or reside in a Member State 'other' than that of which they are a national are beneficiaries of that directive.

33. Secondly, whilst it is true that, as stated in paragraph 28 of this judgment, Directive 2004/38 aims to facilitate and strengthen the exercise of the primary and individual right to move and reside freely within the territory of the Member States that is conferred directly on each citizen of the Union, the fact remains that the subject of the directive concerns, as is apparent from Article 1(a), the conditions governing the exercise of that right.

34. Since, as stated in paragraph 29 of this judgment, the residence of a person residing in the Member State of which he is a national cannot be made subject to conditions, Directive 2004/38, concerning the conditions governing the exercise of the right to move and reside freely within the territory of the Member States, cannot apply to a Union citizen who enjoys an unconditional right of residence due to the fact that he resides in the Member State of which he is a national.

35. Thirdly, it is apparent from Directive 2004/38, taken as a whole, that the residence to which it refers is linked to the exercise of the freedom of movement for persons.

36. Thus, first of all, Article 1(a) of that directive defines its subject by reference to the exercise of 'the' right 'of free movement and residence' within the territory of the Member States by Union citizens. Such a relationship between residence and free movement is also apparent both from the title of that directive and from the majority of its recitals, the second of which refers, moreover, exclusively to the free movement of persons.

37. Furthermore, the rights of residence referred to in Directive 2004/38, namely both the right of residence under Articles 6 and 7 and the permanent right of residence under Article 16, refer to the residence of a Union citizen either in 'another Member State' or in 'the host Member State' and therefore govern the legal situation of a Union citizen in a Member State of which he is not a national.

38. Lastly, although, as stated in paragraph 32 of this judgment, Article 3(1) of Directive 2004/38 designates as 'beneficiaries' of that directive all Union citizens who move to 'or' reside in a Member State, it is apparent from Article 22 that the territorial scope of the right of residence and the right of permanent residence referred to in that directive covers the whole territory of 'the host Member State', the latter being defined in Article 2(3) as the Member State to which a Union citizen 'moves' in order to exercise 'his/her' right of free movement and residence within the territory of the Member States.

39. Hence, in circumstances such as those of the main proceedings, in so far as the Union citizen concerned has never exercised his right of free movement and has always resided in a Member State of which he is a national, that citizen is not covered by the concept of 'beneficiary' for the purposes of Article 3(1) of Directive 2004/38, so that that directive is not applicable to him.

40. That finding cannot be influenced by the fact that the citizen concerned is also a national of a Member State other than that where he resides.

41. Indeed, the fact that a Union citizen is a national of more than one Member State does not mean that he has made use of his right of freedom of movement.

42. Lastly, it should also be noted that, since a Union citizen such as Mrs McCarthy is not covered by the concept of 'beneficiary' for the purposes of Article 3(1) of Directive 2004/38, her spouse is not covered by that concept either, given that the rights conferred by that directive on the family members of a beneficiary of that directive are not autonomous rights of those family members, but derived rights, acquired through their status as members of the beneficiary's family (see, in relation to instruments of European Union law prior to Directive 2004/38, Case C-243/91*Taghavi* [1992] ECR I-4401, paragraph 7, and *Eind*, paragraph 23).

43. It follows that Article 3(1) of Directive 2004/38 is to be interpreted as meaning that that directive is not applicable to a Union citizen who has never exercised his right of free movement, who has always resided in a Member State of which he is a national and who is also a national of another Member State.

The applicability of Article 21 TFEU

44. The second part of this question, as reformulated by the Court, concerns whether Article 21 TFEU is applicable to a Union citizen who has never exercised his right of free movement, who has always resided in a Member State of which he is a national and who is also a national of another Member State.

45. In that regard, it is settled case-law that the Treaty rules governing freedom of movement for persons and the measures adopted to implement them cannot be applied to situations which have no factor linking them with any of the situations governed by European Union law and which are confined in all relevant respects within a single Member State (see, to that effect, Case C-212/06 *Government of the French Community and Walloon Government* [2008] ECR I-1683, paragraph 33, and *Metock and Others*, paragraph 77).

46. On this point, it must be observed, however, that the situation of a Union citizen who, like Mrs McCarthy, has not made use of the right to freedom of movement

cannot, for that reason alone, be assimilated to a purely internal situation (see Case C-403/03 *Schempp* [2005] ECR I-6421, paragraph 22).

47. Indeed, the Court has stated several times that citizenship of the Union is intended to be the fundamental status of nationals of the Member States (see Case C-34/09 *Ruiz Zambrano* [2011] ECR I-0000, paragraph 41 and case-law cited). Furthermore, the Court has held that Article 20 TFEU precludes national measures which have the effect of depriving Union citizens of the genuine enjoyment of the substance of the rights conferred by virtue of that status (see *Ruiz Zambrano*, paragraph 42).

48. As a national of at least one Member State, a person such as Mrs McCarthy enjoys the status of a Union citizen under Article 20(1) TFEU and may therefore rely on the rights pertaining to that status, including against his Member State of origin, in particular the right conferred by Article 21 TFEU to move and reside freely within the territory of the Member States (see Case C-33/07 *Jipa* [2008] ECR I-5157, paragraph 17 and case-law cited).

49. However, no element of the situation of Mrs McCarthy, as described by the national court, indicates that the national measure at issue in the main proceedings has the effect of depriving her of the genuine enjoyment of the substance of the rights associated with her status as a Union citizen, or of impeding the exercise of her right to move and reside freely within the territory of the Member States, in accordance with Article 21 TFEU. Indeed, the failure by the authorities of the United Kingdom to take into account the Irish nationality of Mrs McCarthy for the purposes of granting her a right of residence in the United Kingdom in no way affects her in her right to move and reside freely within the territory of the Member States, or any other right conferred on her by virtue of her status as a Union citizen.

50. In that regard, by contrast with the case of *Ruiz Zambrano*, the national measure at issue in the main proceedings in the present case does not have the effect of obliging Mrs McCarthy to leave the territory of the European Union. Indeed, as is clear from paragraph 29 of the present judgment, Mrs McCarthy enjoys, under a principle of international law, an unconditional right of residence in the United Kingdom since she is a national of the United Kingdom.

51. The case in the main proceedings also differs from Case C-148/02 *García Avello* [2003] ECR I-11613. In that judgment, the Court held that the application of the law of one Member State to nationals of that Member State who were also nationals of another Member State had the effect that those Union citizens had different surnames under the two legal systems concerned, and that that situation was liable to cause serious inconvenience for them at both professional and private levels resulting from, inter alia, difficulties in benefiting, in one Member State of which

they are nationals, from the legal effects of diplomas or documents drawn up in the surname recognised in the other Member State of which they are also nationals.

52. As the Court noted in Case C-353/06 *Grunkin and Paul* [2008] ECR I-7639, in circumstances such as those examined in *Garcia Avello*, what mattered was not whether the discrepancy in surnames was the result of the dual nationality of the persons concerned, but the fact that that discrepancy was liable to cause serious inconvenience for the Union citizens concerned that constituted an obstacle to freedom of movement that could be justified only if it was based on objective considerations and was proportionate to the legitimate aim pursued (see, to that effect,*Grunkin et Paul*, paragraphs 23, 24 and 29).

53. Thus, in *Ruiz Zambrano* and *García Avello*, the national measure at issue had the effect of depriving Union citizens of the genuine enjoyment of the substance of the rights conferred by virtue of that status or of impeding the exercise of their right of free movement and residence within the territory of the Member States.

54. As stated in paragraph 49 of the present judgment, in the context of the main proceedings in this case, the fact that Mrs McCarthy, in addition to being a national of the United Kingdom, is also a national of Ireland does not mean that a Member State has applied measures that have the effect of depriving her of the genuine enjoyment of the substance of the rights conferred by virtue of her status as a Union citizen or of impeding the exercise of her right of free movement and residence within the territory of the Member States. Accordingly, in such a context, such a factor is not sufficient, in itself, for a finding that the situation of the person concerned is covered by Article 21 TFEU.

55. In those circumstances, the situation of a person such as Mrs McCarthy has no factor linking it with any of the situations governed by European Union law and the situation is confined in all relevant respects within a single Member State.

56. It follows that Article 21 TFEU is not applicable to a Union citizen who has never exercised his right of free movement, who has always resided in a Member State of which he is a national and who is also a national of another Member State, provided that the situation of that citizen does not include the application of measures by a Member State that would have the effect of depriving him of the genuine enjoyment of the substance of the rights conferred by virtue of his status as a Union citizen or of impeding the exercise of his right of free movement and residence within the territory of the Member States.

57. In the light of the foregoing, the answer to the first question is as follows:

   – Article 3(1) of Directive 2004/38 must be interpreted as meaning that that directive is not applicable to a Union citizen who has never exercised his right of free movement, who has always resided in a Member State of which he is a national and who is also a national of another Member State.

– Article 21 TFEU is not applicable to a Union citizen who has never exercised his right of free movement, who has always resided in a Member State of which he is a national and who is also a national of another Member State, provided that the situation of that citizen does not include the application of measures by a Member State that would have the effect of depriving him of the genuine enjoyment of the substance of the rights conferred by virtue of his status as a Union citizen or of impeding the exercise of his right of free movement and residence within the territory of the Member States.

The second question

58. In view of the answer to the first question referred by the national court, there is no need to answer the second question.

Costs

[Para. 59 omitted]

On those grounds,

THE COURT (Third Chamber),

hereby rules:

1. **Article 3(1) of Directive 2004/38/EC of the European Parliament and of the Council of 29 April 2004 on the right of citizens of the Union and their family members to move and reside freely within the territory of the Member States amending Regulation (EEC) No 1612/68 and repealing Directives 64/221/EEC, 68/360/EEC, 72/194/EEC, 73/148/EEC, 75/34/EEC, 75/35/EEC, 90/364/EEC, 90/365/EEC and 93/96/EEC, must be interpreted as meaning that that directive is not applicable to a Union citizen who has never exercised his right of free movement, who has always resided in a Member State of which he is a national and who is also a national of another Member State.**

2. **Article 21 TFEU is not applicable to a Union citizen who has never exercised his right of free movement, who has always resided in a Member State of which he is a national and who is also a national of another Member State, provided that the situation of that citizen does not include the application of measures by a Member State that would have the effect of depriving him of the genuine enjoyment of the substance of the rights con-**

ferred by virtue of his status as a Union citizen or of impeding the exercise of his right of free movement and residence within the territory of the Member States.

Comments and questions

The CJEU's decision in Case C-434/09 *McCarthy* [2011] ECR I-3375 is an important clarification of its decision in the *Zambrano* case printed above. The *Zambrano* case raised the question of whether the TFEU provisions on Union citizenship also apply to 'a purely internal situation', i.e. to situations in which the Union citizen in question has not exercised the right of free movement and where there is otherwise no cross-border element.

As in the *Zambrano* case, the *McCarthy* case concerned whether a third-country national could derive a right of residence from a Union citizen in a situation where that third -country national does not have a right of residence under national law. However, while the *Zambrano* case concerned a father's right to reside in a Member State as a consequence of his providing for his Union citizen children who were minors, and these minors would have had to leave the Member States where they were citizens (and leave the EU as a whole) if the father did not have a right of residence, the situation was significantly different in the *McCarthy* case. The *McCarthy* case concerned the right of a third-country national to reside in a Member State where they were married to a Union citizen. At no point had the Union citizen exercised the right of freedom of movement, and in principle there was no cross-border element in the case. However, the Union citizen had dual nationality – both British and Irish – which could have been relevant to the decision in the case.

First, the CJEU ruled that 'citizenship of the Union confers on each Union citizen a primary and individual right to move and reside freely within the territory of the Member States'. With particular regard to Directive 2004/38/EC on the right of citizens of the Union and their family members to move and reside freely within the territory of the Member States, the CJEU noted that it had already had occasion to point out that: 'it aims to facilitate the exercise of the primary and individual right to move and reside freely within the territory of the Member States that is conferred directly on Union citizens by the Treaty and that it aims in particular to strengthen that right'. At the same time, the CJEU noted that, according to international law, a Member State cannot refuse its own nationals the right of entry to and residence in its territory, nor can a Member State expel its own nationals from its territory or refuse their right to reside in that territory or make such right conditional.

Following these introductory remarks, the CJEU turned to the question of whether Article 3(1) of Directive 2004/38 can apply to a Union citizen who has never exercised their right of free movement, who has always resided in the same Member State where they are a national, while being a national of another Member State.

The CJEU first remarked that Directive 2004/38 aims to facilitate 'the exercise of the primary and individual right to move and reside freely within the territory of the Member States that is conferred directly on Union citizens by the Treaty', and not a Union citizen 'who enjoys an unconditional right of residence due to the fact that he resides in the Member State of which he is a national'. Moreover, the CJEU stated that, according to its title, the majority of its recitals and operative part of the Directive itself, 'taken as a whole, that the residence to which it refers is linked to the exercise of the freedom of movement for persons'. In other words, the Directive only governs 'the legal situation of a Union citizen in a Member State of which he is not a national'.

The fact that a Union citizen is a national of more than one Member State does not in itself mean that they have exercised their right to free movement and are thus covered by the Directive. And since Shirley McCarthy was not covered by the Directive's definition of a beneficiary of the Directive, neither she nor her husband could enjoy the rights which the Directive gives to 'beneficiaries'. Thus, the Directive did not apply to a Union citizen such as Shirley McCarthy, who had never exercised her right of free movement, who had always been resident in the same Member State of which she was a national, even though she was also a national of another Member State.

Having decided that Directive 2004/38 did not apply to the case, the CJEU then turned to the question of whether Article 21 TFEU was applicable to the facts of the case. The CJEU first noted that, even though it had long been accepted that in relation to the rules on freedom of movement of persons these rules do not apply when all the circumstances of a case exclusively relate to the territory of one Member State, this did not mean one could automatically reject the application of Article 21 TFEU to a situation where a Union citizen had not exercised their right to free movement. The CJEU thus seems to have made an important distinction between, on the one hand, the classic rules on freedom of movement and, on the other hand, the rules on Union citizenship. What are the key elements of the latter rules (see in particular paragraphs 47-49)?

The next question was whether the refusal of the British authorities to allow a residence permit to Shirley McCarthy's husband from a third country meant that she had been deprived of her 'genuine enjoyment of the substance of the rights associated with her status as a Union citizen', or whether the refusal impeded 'the exercise of her right to move and reside freely within the territory of the Member States, in accordance with Article 21 TFEU'. This was not the case, and this conclusion was not influenced by the fact that Shirley McCarthy had both Irish and British citizenship.

Consider whether the CJEU's decision in the *McCarthy* case is in line with its decision in the *Zambrano* case; see in particular paragraphs 50-54. Do you think that there is harmony between the results in the *Zambrano* case and the *McCarthy* case with regard to when the enforcement of a Member State's aliens law in relation to a Union citizen's family member has the effect of depriving Union citizens of 'the genuine enjoyment of the substance of the rights conferred by virtue of that status'?

When Shirley McCarthy's husband could not obtain a right to reside in the United Kingdom, the couple had either to move to another Member State and establish their family there in accordance with Directive 2004/38, (see the *Metlock* case printed above) or move to a third country (for example Jamaica) in order to unify their family. The CJEU's ruling must presumably be understood as meaning that it does not deprive Union citizens of the genuine enjoyment of the substance of the rights conferred by virtue of their status as Union citizens, or impede the exercise of their right of free movement and residence within the territory of the Member States (see paragraph 56).

At the end of 2011, the CJEU gave judgment in Case C-256/11 *Dereci* [2011] ECR I-11315. In this case the CJEU clarified the extent of Article 20 TFEU on Union citizenship. It was thus a clarification of its decisions in the *Zambrano* case and the *McCarthy* case, both printed above. The background to the case was five Austrian cases in which some third -country nationals wanted to move to reside with family members who were Union citizens resident in Austria. None of these Union citizens had exercised their right of free movement and they were not maintained by their family members who were the third-country nationals. However, the five cases could be distinguished from each other in that some of the applicants were lawfully resident in Austria, while others did not have lawful residence, and the family relations between the Union citizens and the third-country nationals differed.

In the *Zambrano* case and the *McCarthy* case, among others, the CJEU ruled that Article 20 TFEU means that Union citizens may not be deprived of the genuine enjoyment of the substance of the rights conferred by virtue of their status as Union citizens. In the *Dereci* case the CJEU had to decide whether the Austrian rejection of the family reunification between Austrian nationals (and Union citizens) on the one hand and third-country nationals on the other hand would effectively deprive the Union citizens of the rights conferred on them by virtue of their status as Union citizens.

The CJEU ruled that the rejection did not deprive the Union citizens of the substance of these rights. The CJEU noted that the substance of the rights conferred by virtue of Union citizen status refers to situations in which the Union citizen has to leave not only the territory of the Member State of which they are a national, but also the territory of the Union as a whole. The criterion of the substance of the rights is thus not fulfilled where it merely appears 'desirable to a national of a Member State, for economic reasons or in order to keep his family together in the territory of the Union, for the members of his family who do not have the nationality of a Member State to be able to reside with him in the territory of the Union'. On this basis, the CJEU concluded that the Union provisions on Union citizenship do not prevent a Member State refusing to issue residence permits to third-country nationals if the Union citizen who wishes to unite their family, but has never exercised their right of freedom of movement, and the refusal does not deprive the Union citizen of the rights conferred on them by virtue of their status as a Union citizen.

The decisions in the *McCarthy* and *Dereci* cases show that Union citizenship only bestows rights on Union citizens, and that third-country nationals cannot obtain rights under the rules on Union citizenship. In those cases where it might appear that third-country nationals obtain rights under these rules, these will always be derivative rights, in other words third-country nationals may be granted some rights (typically a right of residence) as a result of protecting a Union citizen's rights.

If one compares the *Zambrano* case with the *McCarthy* case (and the *Dereci* case), would it be reasonable to say that in the *Zambrano* case the CJEU seemed to assume that Union citizenship gives a positive right of residence in the EU, while in the *McCarthy* case the CJEU seems rather to have applied a negative right not to be dismissed from the EU's territory? Does it make any difference whether the CJEU adopts one or the other of these approaches – and if so, what? In the same context, consider whether the CJEU looks differently at parents' rights to unify their families in relation to children who are Union citizens (the *Zambrano* case), and the rights of Union citizens to live together as a family together with their third-country national spouses pursuant to Articles 20 and 1 TFEU.

JUDGMENT OF THE COURT (Second Chamber)
10 October 2013

Adzo Domenyo Alokpa, Jarel Moudoulou, Eja Moudoulou v Ministre du Travail, de l'Emploi et de l'Immigration. (Request for a preliminary ruling: Cour administrative – Luxembourg)

'Citizenship of the Union – Articles 20 TFEU and 21 TFEU – Directive 2004/38/EC – Right of residence of a third-country national who is a direct relative in the ascending line of Union citizens who are minor children – Union citizens born in a Member State other than that of which they are nationals and who have not made use of their right of freedom of movement – Fundamental rights'

Case C-86/12

Judgment

1. This request for a preliminary ruling concerns the interpretation of Articles 20 TFEU and 21 TFEU, and Directive 2004/38/EC of the European Parliament and of the Council of 29 April 2004 on the right of citizens of the Union and their family members to move and reside freely within the territory of the Member States amending Regulation (EEC) No 1612/68 and repealing Directives 64/221/EEC, 68/360/EEC, 72/194/EEC, 73/148/EEC, 75/34/EEC, 75/35/EEC, 90/364/EEC, 90/365/EEC and 93/96/EEC (OJ 2004 L 158, p. 77, and corrigenda OJ 2004 L 229, p. 35, and OJ 2005 L 197, p. 34).

2. The request was made in proceedings between Mrs Alokpa, her sons Jarel and Eja Moudoulou, and the Ministre du Travail, de l'Emploi et de l'Immigration (the Minister for Labour, Employment and Immigration) ('the Minister') concerning the Minister's decision refusing to grant Mrs Alokpa a right of residence in Luxembourg and ordering her to leave that Member State.

Legal context

European Union law

Directives 2003/86/EC and 2003/109/EC

3. According to Article 1 of Council Directive 2003/86/EC of 22 September 2003 on the right to family reunification (OJ 2003 L 251, p. 12), and Article 1(a) of Council Directive 2003/109/EC of 25 November 2003 concerning the status of third-country nationals who are long-term residents (OJ 2004 L 16, p. 44), the purpose of those directives is to determine, respectively, the conditions for the exercise of the right to

family reunification by third-country nationals residing lawfully in the territory of the Member States, and the terms for conferring and withdrawing long-term resident status granted by a Member State in relation to third-country nationals legally residing in its territory, and the rights pertaining thereto.

Directive 2004/38/EC

4. Under the heading 'Definitions', Article 2 of Directive 2004/38 states:

   'For the purpose of this Directive:

   1. "Union citizen" means any person having the nationality of a Member State;

   2. "family member" means:
      ...
      (d) the dependent direct relatives in the ascending line and those of the spouse or partner as defined in point (b);

   3. "host Member State" means the Member State to which a Union citizen moves in order to exercise his/her right of free movement and residence.'

5. Article 3 of Directive 2004/38, which is entitled 'Beneficiaries', provides in paragraph 1:

   'This Directive shall apply to all Union citizens who move to or reside in a Member State other than that of which they are a national, and to their family members as defined in point 2 of Article 2 who accompany or join them.'

6. Article 7 of that directive, entitled 'Right of residence for more than three months', is worded as follows:

   '1. All Union citizens shall have the right of residence on the territory of another Member State for a period of longer than three months if they:

      (a) are workers or self-employed persons in the host Member State; or
      (b) have sufficient resources for themselves and their family members not to become a burden on the social assistance system of the host Member State during their period of residence and have comprehensive sickness insurance cover in the host Member State; or
      (c) – are enrolled at a private or public establishment, accredited or financed by the host Member State on the basis of its legislation or administrative practice, for the principal purpose of following a course of study, including vocational training; and

– have comprehensive sickness insurance cover in the host Member State and assure the relevant national authority, by means of a declaration or by such equivalent means as they may choose, that they have sufficient resources for themselves and their family members not to become a burden on the social assistance system of the host Member State during their period of residence; or

(d) are family members accompanying or joining a Union citizen who satisfies the conditions referred to in points (a), (b) or (c).

2. The right of residence provided for in paragraph 1 shall extend to family members who are not nationals of a Member State, accompanying or joining the Union citizen in the host Member State, provided that such Union citizen satisfies the conditions referred to in paragraph 1(a), (b) or (c).

...'

Luxembourg law

7. The Law of 29 August 2008 on the freedom of movement of persons and on immigration (*Mémorial* A 2008, p. 2024, 'the Law on freedom of movement') is intended to transpose Directives 2003/86 and 2004/38 into Luxembourg law.

8. Under Article 6 of that law:

'1. Union citizens shall have the right of residence in the territory for a period of longer than three months provided they satisfy one of the following conditions:

(1) they work in an employed or self-employed capacity;
(2) they have sufficient resources for themselves and their family members as defined in Article 12 not to become a burden on the social assistance system and have sickness insurance cover;
(3) they are enrolled at a private or public establishment, accredited by the Grand-Duchy of Luxembourg in accordance with the legislative provisions and rules in force, for the principal purpose of following a course of study or, within that context, vocational training, while guaranteeing that they have sufficient resources for themselves and their family members not to become a burden on the social assistance system and have sickness insurance cover.

2. A Grand-Ducal Regulation shall specify the resources required at points 2 and 3 of paragraph (1) above, and the manner in which proof of those resources is to be furnished.

...'

9 Article 12 of that law provides:

‘1. “Family member” means:

...

(d) the dependent direct relatives in the ascending line of the Union citizen and the dependent direct relatives in the ascending line of the spouse or partner as defined in point (b).

2. The Minister may authorise any other family members, irrespective of their nationality, not falling under the definition in paragraph 1, to reside in the territory, provided they satisfy one of the following conditions:

(1) in the country from which they have come, they were dependants or members of the household of the Union citizen having the primary right of residence;
(2) serious health grounds strictly require the personal care of the family member by the Union citizen.

The application for entry or residence of family members referred to in the preceding subparagraph shall be subject to a detailed examination of their personal circumstances.

...’

10. Under Article 103 of that law:

‘Before taking a decision refusing residence, withdrawing or refusing to renew a residence permit or an expulsion decision regarding a third-country national, the Minister shall take account of considerations such as how long the individual concerned has resided in Luxembourg, his/her age, state of health, family and economic situation, social and cultural integration into the country and the extent of his/her links with the country of origin, except where his/her presence constitutes a threat to public policy or public security.

No expulsion decision, other than on imperative grounds of public security, may be taken in respect of a minor who is not accompanied by a legal representative, unless expulsion is in his/her best interests.’

The dispute in the main proceedings and the question referred for a preliminary ruling

11. On 21 November 2006, Mrs Alokpa, a citizen of Togo, applied to the Luxembourg authorities for international protection for the purposes of the Law of 5 May 2006 on the right of asylum and complimentary forms of protection (*Mémorial* A 2006,

p. 1402). That application was, however, rejected by those authorities and their decision was confirmed by the Luxembourg courts.

12. Subsequently, Mrs Alokpa applied to those authorities for discretionary leave to remain. Although, initially, that application was rejected, it was reconsidered and such discretionary leave was granted to Mrs Alokpa until 31 December 2008, as a result of the fact that she had given birth to twins on 17 August 2008, in Luxembourg, and that the latter required care due to their premature birth.

13. Mrs Alokpa's children were recognised, when the birth certificates were drawn up, by Mr Moudoulou, a French national. They are French nationals and were issued with French passports and national identity cards on 15 May and 4 June 2009 respectively.

14. In the meantime, an application for extension of her discretionary leave to remain made by Mrs Alokpa was rejected by the Luxembourg authorities, who, however, granted Mrs Alokpa a suspension of removal valid until 5 June 2010, which was not subsequently extended.

15. On 6 May 2010, Mrs Alokpa applied for a residence permit in accordance with the Law on free movement. In response to a request for further information from the Minister, Mrs Alokpa stated that she was unable to settle with her children in France, or reside with their father on the ground that she had no relations with the latter and that those children required follow-up medical treatment in Luxembourg as a result of their premature birth. By decision of 14 October 2010, the minister rejected that application.

16. According to that decision, first, since the right of residence of a Union citizen's family members is restricted to dependent relatives in the direct ascending line, Mrs Alokpa does not satisfy that condition. Secondly, Mrs Alokpa's children also fail to satisfy the conditions set out in Article 6(1) of the Law on free movement. Furthermore, that decision held that those children's follow-up medical treatment could easily be provided in France and that Mrs Alokpa also failed to satisfy the necessary conditions for eligibility for another category of residence permit referred to in that law.

17. Mrs Alokpa brought, in her own name and in that of her two children, an action for annulment of the decision of the Minister before the Tribunal administratif (Luxembourg) (Administrative Court, Luxembourg). By judgment of 21 September 2011, that court dismissed the action as unfounded. By application lodged on 31 October 2011, Mrs Alokpa brought an appeal against that judgment before the referring court.

18. That court held that it is not disputed that Mrs Alokpa's children never enjoyed a family life with their father, who limited himself to declaring their birth and to ena-

bling the issue of the French identity documents relating to them. Likewise, that court held that Mrs Alokpa and her children have in fact led a common family life in a hostel, following the children's extended stay in maternity care, and that the latter have not genuinely exercised their right to free movement.

19. In those circumstances, the Cour administrative decided to stay the proceedings and to refer the following question to the Court of Justice for a preliminary ruling:

'Is Article 20 TFEU – if necessary, read in conjunction with Articles 20, 21, 24, 33 and 34 of the Charter of Fundamental Rights [of the European Union], or with one or more of those provisions read separately or in conjunction – to be interpreted as precluding a Member State from refusing a third-country national, with sole responsibility for his or her minor children who are citizens of the European Union, residence in the Member State of residence of the children, where they have been living with that person since birth, without having that nationality, while refusing the third-country national a residence permit, or even a work permit?

Are such decisions to be regarded as being in the nature of decisions depriving those children, in their country of residence, in which they have lived since birth, of effective enjoyment of the substance of the rights attaching to the status of citizen of the European Union also in the situation where their other direct ascendant, with whom they have never shared family life, is resident in another Member State of the European Union, of which that person is a national?'

The question referred for a preliminary ruling

20. At the outset, it should be noted that, even though, formally, the referring court has limited its questions to the interpretation of Article 20 TFEU, such a situation does not prevent the Court from providing the referring court with all the elements of interpretation of European Union law which may be of assistance in adjudicating on the case before it, whether or not that court has specifically referred to them in the questions (see, to that effect, Case C-434/09 *McCarthy* [2011] ECR I-3375, paragraph 24 and the case-law cited).

21. Therefore, question referred by the national court must be construed as seeking to ascertain, in essence, whether, in a situation such as that at issue in the main proceedings, Articles 20 TFEU and 21 TFEU must be interpreted as meaning that they preclude a Member State from refusing to allow a third-country national to reside in its territory, where that third-country national has sole responsibility for her minor children who are citizens of the European Union, and who have resided with her in that Member State since their birth, without possessing the nationality of that Member State and having made use of their right to freedom of movement.

22. In that regard, it should be recalled that any rights conferred on third-country nationals by the Treaty provisions on Union citizenship are not autonomous rights of those nationals but rights derived from the exercise of freedom of movement by a Union citizen. The purpose and justification of those derived rights, in particular rights of entry and residence of family members of a Union citizen, are based on the fact that a refusal to allow them would be such as to interfere with freedom of movement by discouraging that citizen from exercising his rights of entry into and residence in the host Member State (see, to that effect, Case C-87/12 *Ymeraga and Ymeraga-Tafarshiku* [2013] ECR, paragraph 35 and the case-law cited).

23. Likewise, it must be pointed out that there are situations characterised by the fact that, although they are governed by legislation which falls *a priori* within the competence of the Member States, namely legislation on the right of entry and stay of third-country nationals outside the scope of provisions of secondary legislation which, under certain conditions, provide for the attribution of such a right, they none the less have an intrinsic connection with the freedom of movement of a Union citizen, which prevents the right of entry and residence being refused to those nationals in the Member State of residence of that citizen, in order not to interfere with that freedom (see *Ymeraga and Ymeraga-Tafarshiku*, paragraph 37).

24. In this case, it must be observed, in the first place, that Mrs Alokpa cannot be regarded as a beneficiary of Directive 2004/38, within the meaning of Article 3(1) thereof.

25. It is clear from the case-law of the Court that the status of 'dependent' family member of a Union citizen holding a right of residence is the result of a factual situation characterised by the fact that material support for the family member is provided by the holder of the right of residence, so that, when the converse situation occurs and the holder of the right of residence is dependent on a third-country national, the third-country national cannot rely on being a 'dependent' relative in the ascending line of that right-holder, within the meaning of Directive 2004/38, with a view to having the benefit of a right of residence in the host Member State (Case C-40/11 *Iida* [2012] ECR, paragraph 55).

26. In the present case, it is the holders of the right of residence, namely, Mrs Alokpa's two sons, who are effectively dependant on her, so that she cannot rely on being a relative in the ascending line dependant on them, within the meaning of Directive 2004/38.

27. However, in the context of a case such as that at issue in the main proceedings, in which a Union citizen was born in the host Member State and had not made use of the right to free movement, the Court has held that the expression 'have' sufficient resources in a provision similar to Article 7(1)(b) of Directive 2004/38 must be interpreted as meaning that it suffices that such resources are available to the Union

citizens, and that that provision lays down no requirement whatsoever as to their origin, since they could be provided, inter alia, by a national of a non-Member State, the parent of the citizens who are minor children at issue (see, to that effect, concerning European Union law instruments pre-dating that directive, Case C-200/02 *Zhu and Chen* [2004] ECR I-9925, paragraphs 28 and 30).

28. Consequently, it has been held that a refusal to allow a parent, whether a national of a Member State or of a third country, who is the carer of a minor child who is a Union citizen to reside with that child in the host Member State would deprive the child's right of residence of any useful effect, since enjoyment by a young child of a right of residence necessarily implies that the child is entitled to be accompanied by the person who is his primary carer and accordingly that the carer must be in a position to reside with the child in the host Member State for the duration of such residence (see *Zhu and Chen*, paragraph 45, and *Iida*, paragraph 69).

29. Thus, while Article 21 TFEU and Directive 2004/38 grant a right to reside in the host Member State to a minor child who is a national of another Member State and who satisfies the conditions of Article 7(1)(b) of that directive, the same provisions allow a parent who is that minor's primary carer to reside with the child in the host Member State (see, to that effect, *Zhu and Chen*, paragraphs 46 and 47).

30. In the present case, it is for the referring court to ascertain whether Mrs Alokpa's children satisfy the conditions set out in Article 7(1) of Directive 2004/38 and have, therefore, the right to reside in a host Member State on the basis of Article 21 TFEU. In particular, that court must determine whether those children have, on their own or through their mother, sufficient resources and comprehensive sickness insurance cover, within the meaning of Article 7(1)(b) of Directive 2004/38.

31. If the conditions set out in Article 7(1) of Directive 2004/38 are not satisfied, Article 21 TFEU must be interpreted as meaning that it does not preclude Mrs Alokpa from being refused a right of residence in Luxembourg.

32. Concerning, in the second place, Article 20 TFEU, the Court has held that there are very specific situations in which, despite the fact that the secondary law on the right of residence of third-country nationals does not apply and the Union citizen concerned has not made use of his freedom of movement, a right of residence cannot, exceptionally, without undermining the effectiveness of the Union citizenship that citizen enjoys, be refused to a third-country national who is a family member of his if, as a consequence of refusal, that citizen would be obliged in practice to leave the territory of the European Union altogether, thus denying him the genuine enjoyment of the substance of the rights conferred by virtue of the status of citizen of the European Union (see *Iida*, paragraph 71, and *Ymeraga and Ymeraga-Tafarshiku*, paragraph 36).

33. Therefore, if the referring court holds that Article 21 TFEU does not preclude Mrs Alokpa from being refused a right of residence in Luxembourg, that court must still determine whether such a right of residence may nevertheless be granted to her, exceptionally – if the effectiveness of the Union citizenship that her children enjoy is not to be undermined – in light of the fact that, as a consequence of such a refusal, those children would find themselves obliged in practice to leave the territory of the European Union altogether, thus denying them the genuine enjoyment of the substance of the rights conferred by virtue of that status.

34. In that regard, as the Advocate-General stated in points 55 and 56 of his Opinion, Mrs Alokpa, as the mother of Jarel and Eja Moudoulou and as sole carer of those children since their birth, could have the benefit of a derived right to reside in France.

35. It follows that, in principle, the refusal by the Luxembourg authorities to grant Mrs Alokpa a right of residence cannot result in her children being obliged to leave the territory of the European Union altogether. It is, however, for the referring court to determine whether, in the light of all of the facts of the main proceedings, that is in fact the case.

36. In the light of all of the foregoing considerations, the answer to the question referred is that, in a situation such as that at issue in the main proceedings, Articles 20 TFEU and 21 TFEU must be interpreted as meaning that they do not preclude a Member State from refusing to allow a third-country national to reside in its territory, where that third-country national has sole responsibility for her minor children who are citizens of the European Union, and who have resided with her in that Member State since their birth, without possessing the nationality of that Member State and making use of their right to freedom of movement, in so far as those Union citizens do not satisfy the conditions set out in Directive 2004/38 or such a refusal does not deprive those citizens of effective enjoyment of the substance of the rights conferred by virtue of the status of European Union citizenship, a matter which is to be determined by the referring court.

Costs

[Para. 37 omitted]

On those grounds,

THE COURT (Second Chamber)

hereby rules:

In a situation such as that at issue in the main proceedings, Articles 20 TFEU and 21 TFEU must be interpreted as meaning that they do not preclude a Member State from refusing to allow a third-country national to reside in its territory, where that third-country national has sole responsibility for her minor children who are citizens of the European Union, and who have resided with her in that Member State since their birth, without possessing the nationality of that Member State and making use of their right to freedom of movement, in so far as those Union citizens do not satisfy the conditions set out in Directive 2004/38/EC of the European Parliament and of the Council of 29 April 2004 on the right of citizens of the Union and their family members to move and reside freely within the territory of the Member States amending Regulation (EEC) No 1612/68 and repealing Directives 64/221/EEC, 68/360/EEC, 72/194/EEC, 73/148/EEC, 75/34/EEC, 75/35/EEC, 90/364/EEC, 90/365/EEC and 93/96/EEC, or such a refusal does not deprive those citizens of effective enjoyment of the substance of the rights conferred by virtue of the status of European Union citizenship, a matter which is to be determined by the referring court.

Comments and questions

In the *Zambrano* case from 2011, printed above, the CJEU ruled that a third-country national who cares for their children who are minors and Union citizens can derive a right to reside in the Member State of which the children are citizens pursuant to Article 20 TFEU, regardless of whether the children have exercised their right to freedom of movement. The CJEU reasoned that 'such a refusal would lead to a situation where those children, citizens of the Union, would have to leave the territory of the Union in order to accompany their parents. Similarly, if a work permit were not granted to such a person, he would risk not having sufficient resources to provide for himself and his family, which would also result in the children, citizens of the Union, having to leave the territory of the Union. In those circumstances, those citizens of the Union would, in fact, be unable to exercise the substance of the rights conferred on them by virtue of their status as citizens of the Union.' However, since giving its judgment in the *Zambrano* case the CJEU has restricted the scope of the judgment, emphasising that the case concerned an exceptional situation. The *Alokpa* case has many similarities with the *Zambrano* case, but as we shall see in the following there were also important differences between them.

Alokpa was not herself a Union citizen, but she had given birth to twins, both of whom had French citizenship because their father was French. However, Alokpa and her twins were resident in Luxembourg. As was natural, Alokpa cared for her two small sons; it was not the sons that cared for Alokpa. Thus Alokpa could not be regarded as a person entitled pursuant to Article 3(1) of the Free Movement Directive as she could not be regarded as being a family member who was 'cared for' by a Union citizen with a right of residence. Thus the key question was whether Alokpa could derive a right of residence from her two children and their Union citizenship pursuant to Article 7(1) (b) of the Free Movement Directive and Article 21 TFEU on Union citizenship and the right to freedom of movement. On this the CJEU commented that refusal to allow a parent, whether a national of a Member State or of a third country, who is the carer of a minor child who is a Union citizen to reside with that child in the host Member State would deprive the child's right of residence of any useful effect. A young child's exercise of their right of residence necessarily implies that the child is entitled to be accompanied by the person who is their primary carer. Accordingly the carer (typically the child's parent) must be allowed to reside with the child in the host Member State. By giving a right of residence in a host Member State to a minor who is a citizen of another Member State and who fulfils the conditions of Article 7(1)(b) of the Free Movement Directive, Article 21 TFEU and the Free Movement Directive must allow the parent who cares for such a child to take up residence with the child in the host Member State.

As for whether the conditions of Article 7(1)(b) were fulfilled, the CJEU left it to the referring court to decide. The CJEU thus followed a different line than that referred to by the Advocate General his Opinion in the case. The Advocate General had argued that even if 'the conditions laid down in Article 7(1)(b) of Directive 2004/38 are not satisfied, consideration could nevertheless be given to the possibility that the provisions of the Charter of Fundamental Rights, to which the national court makes reference, might result in those conditions being relaxed or even disregarded, in particular with a view to ensuring that account is taken of the child's best interests (Article 24 of the Charter) and respect for family life (Articles 7 and 33 of the Charter). Nevertheless, it appears difficult to envisage such a possibility, since this would mean disregarding the limits laid down by Article 21 TFEU on the right of citizens of the Union to move and reside freely within the territory of the Member States, and would therefore, in my opinion, result in the modification of the powers and tasks defined in the Treaties, in breach of Article 51(2) of the Charter.' Consider why the CJEU chose not to take up the question of the significance of the Charter? Do you find the argument of the Advocate General convincing, or is it possible to make a strong argument against his opinion?

If the conditions of Article 7(1)(b) of the Free Movement Directive were not fulfilled, so that Article 21 TFEU could not prevent the Luxembourg authorities from refusing Alokpa a right of residence, the question arose as to the relevance of the role of Article 20 TFEU. In this connection the CJEU referred to the fact that it had previously held that there are *very specific situations* in which, even though the secondary law on the right of residence of third-country nationals does not apply and the Union citizen concerned has not made use of their freedom of movement, in *exceptional* cases a right of residence cannot be refused to a third-country national who is a family member, without undermining the effectiveness of the Union citizenship if such refusal would mean that the Union citizen would effectively have to leave the EU altogether, thus denying them of the enjoyment of the rights conferred on Union citizens. These *very specific situations* arise when the rights of Union citizenship would otherwise be at risk if the refusal of a right of residence to a family member who is a third-country national effectively means that the Union citizen has to leave the EU. If no exception were made in these situations a Union citizen would be deprived of the effective enjoyment of the substance of the rights of Union citizens.

In the present case this meant that Alokpa, as mother to the two minor Union citizens, had a right to reside in the host Member State (Luxembourg) under Article 20 TFEU if a refusal of a right of residence would mean she would have to leave the EU and that effectively her twins would also have to leave the EU, despite their Union citizenship. However, without this being expressly stated in the judgment, the CJEU indirectly rejected the idea that there was such a special situation pursuant to Article 20 TFEU which could justify a right of residence in the host Member State. As French citizens Alokpa's children had an unconditional right of residence in France and, under the law as established in the *Zambrano* judgment, their mother could presumably derive a right to reside in France from her children's French citizenship. See paragraphs 34-35 of the *Alokpa* judgment.

What obligation did the CJEU impose on the Luxembourg authorities in paragraph 35? Consider in particular whether the comment, that in principle the refusal by the Luxembourg authorities to grant Mrs Alokpa a right of residence cannot result in her children being obliged to leave the territory of the European Union altogether, meant that the Luxembourg authorities had an obligation to contact the French immigration authorities to find out whether Alokpa would be allowed to reside in France if she and her children moved there? What would be the consequence if the French authorities allowed such residence?

To a large extent the Alokpa case is similar to the *Zambrano* case, but the two cases differ significantly in that Alokpa, who was a third-country national, and her children, who were French citizens, were resident in Luxembourg, and thus not resident in the Member State of which they were citizens. As we have seen above, the question was thus the extent to which the legal situation established in the *Zambrano* case could apply in the *Alokpa* case. As we have also seen, the CJEU denied that in these circumstances the *Zambrano* situation was directly applicable. However, Alokpa could derive a right from her children's Union citizenship, since she and her children could take up residence in the children's home Member State (France). At the same time the CJEU emphasised that, by refusing a right of residence to Alokpa, the host Member State (Luxembourg) must not be the cause of the children, as Union citizens, being forced to leave the EU territory altogether.

The scope of the *Alokpa* judgment is at the heart of a reference for a preliminary ruling from the English Court of Appeal in Case C-115/15 *NA*, which concerns a situation in which a Pakistani national is mother to two minors who are German citizens and is resident in the United Kingdom with the children, while the father to the two minors, who is a German citizen, has moved permanently to Pakistan. The mother and father were divorced after the German father had left the United Kingdom. Among other things, the Court of Appeal has asked whether a third country parent parent who cares for a child who is a minor and Union Citizen derives a right of residence in the host Member State according to Article 20 and 21 TFEU if the Union citizen would else have to accompany the parent if expelled from the host Member State. What do you expect the answers of the CJEU to be?

CHAPTER 4

Free Movement of Workers

JUDGMENT OF THE COURT
6 June 2000

Roman Angonese v Cassa di Risparmio di Bolzano SpA.
(Reference for a preliminary ruling: Pretore di Bolzano – Italy)

'Freedom of movement for persons – Access to employment – Certificate of bilingualism issued by a local authority – Article 48 of the EC Treaty (now, after amendment, Article 39 EC) – Council Regulation (EEC) No 1612/68'

Case C-281/98

Judgment

1. By order of 8 July 1998, received at the Court on 23 July 1998, the Pretura Circondariale di Bolzano referred to the Court for a preliminary ruling under Article 177 of the EC Treaty (now Article 234 EC) a question on the interpretation of Article 48 of the EC Treaty (now, after amendment, Article 39 EC) and of Articles 3(1) and 7(1) and (4) of Regulation (EEC) No 1612/68 of the Council of 15 October 1968 on freedom of movement for workers within the Community (Official Journal, English Special Edition 1968 (II), p. 475) (the Regulation)).

2. The question has been raised in the proceedings between Mr Angonese and the Cassa di Risparmio di Bolzano SpA (the Cassa di Risparmio) concerning a requirement imposed by the Cassa di Risparmio for admission to a recruitment competition.

Community law

3. Article 3(1) of the Regulation provides:

   Under this Regulation, provisions laid down by law, regulation or administrative action or administrative practices of a Member State shall not apply:

   – where they limit application for and offers of employment, or the right of foreign nationals to take up and pursue employment or subject these to conditions not applicable in respect of their own nationals; or
   – where, though applicable irrespective of nationality, their exclusive or principal aim or effect is to keep nationals of other Member States away from the employment offered.

   This provision shall not apply to conditions relating to linguistic knowledge required by reason of the nature of the post to be filled.

4. Article 7(1) and (4) of the Regulation provide:

   A worker who is a national of a Member State may not, in the territory of another Member State, be treated differently from national workers by reason of his nationality in respect of any conditions of employment and work, in particular as regards remuneration, dismissal, and should he become unemployed, reinstatement or re-employment.

   ...

   Any clause of a collective or individual agreement or of any other collective regulation concerning eligibility for employment, employment, remuneration and other conditions of work or dismissal shall be null and void in so far as it lays down or authorises discriminatory conditions in respect of workers who are nationals of the other Member States.

The main proceedings

5. Mr Angonese, an Italian national whose mother tongue is German and who is resident in the province of Bolzano, went to study in Austria between 1993 and 1997. In August 1997, in response to a notice published in the local Italian daily Dolomiten on 9 July 1997, he applied to take part in a competition for a post with a private banking undertaking in Bolzano, the Cassa di Risparmio.

6. One of the conditions for entry to the competition was possession of a type-B certificate of bilingualism (in Italian and German) (the Certificate), which used to be required in the province of Bolzano for access to the former carriera di concetto (managerial career) in the public service.

7. According to the file, the Certificate is issued by the public authorities of the province of Bolzano after an examination which is held only in that province. It is usual for residents of the province of Bolzano to obtain the Certificate as a matter of course for employment purposes. Obtaining the Certificate is viewed as an almost compulsory step as part of normal training.

8. The national court has found as a fact that, although Mr Angonese was not in possession of the Certificate, he was perfectly bilingual. With a view to gaining admission to the competition, he had submitted a certificate showing completion of his studies as a draughtsman and certificates attesting to his studies of languages (English, Slovene and Polish) at the Faculty of Philosophy at Vienna University and had stated that his professional experience included practising as a draughtsman and translating from Polish into Italian.

9. On 4 September 1997, the Cassa de Risparmio informed Mr Angonese that he could not be admitted to the competition because he had not produced the Certificate.

10. The Pretore di Bolzano draws attention to the fact that non-residents of Bolzano may have difficulty obtaining the Certificate in good time. He explains that, in the present case, applications to take part in the competition had to be submitted by 1 September 1997, just less than two months after publication of the competition notice. However, there is a minimum period of 30 days between the written tests and the oral tests organised for the purpose of awarding the Certificate and there are a limited number of examination sittings in any given year.

11. The requirement for the Certificate imposed by the Cassa de Risparmio was founded on Article 19 of the National Collective Agreement for Savings Banks of 19 December 1994 (the Collective Agreement), which provides:

    The institution has the right to decide whether the recruitment of staff referred to in paragraphs 1 and 2, subject in any event to Article 21 below, is to be by way of an internal competition on the basis of either qualifications and/or tests or in accordance with selection criteria specified by the institution.

    The institution must lay down as and when necessary the conditions and rules for internal competitions, must appoint selection panels and must lay down the selection criteria mentioned in the first paragraph ...

12. Although he has acknowledged the Cassa di Risparmio's right to select its future staff from persons who are perfectly bilingual, Mr Angonese has complained that the requirement to have and produce the Certificate is unlawful and contrary to the principle of freedom of movement for workers laid down in Article 48 of the Treaty.

13. Mr Angonese claims that the requirement should be declared void and that the Cassa di Risparmio should be ordered to compensate him for his loss of opportunity and to reimburse him the costs he has incurred in the proceedings.

14. According to the national court, the requirement to hold the Certificate in order to provide evidence of linguistic knowledge, may, contrary to Community law, penalise job candidates not resident in Bolzano and, in the present case, could have been prejudicial to Mr Angonese who had taken up residence in another Member State for the purpose of studying there. The national court takes the view, moreover, that, if the requirement in issue were held to be inherently contrary to Community law, it would be void under Italian law.

The question submitted for a preliminary ruling

15. In those circumstances, the Pretore di Bolzano decided to stay proceedings and to refer the following question to the Court:

    Is it compatible with Article 48(1), (2) and (3) of the EC Treaty and Articles 3(1) and 7(1) and (4) of Regulation (EEC) No 1612/68 to make the admission of candidates for a competition organised to fill posts in a company governed by private law conditional on possession of the official certificate attesting to knowledge of local languages issued exclusively by a public authority of a Member State at a single examination centre (namely, Bolzano), on completion of a procedure of considerable duration (to be precise, of not less than 30 days, on account of the minimum lapse of time envisaged between the written test and the oral test)?

16. Before examining the question put by the Pretore di Bolzano, it should be noted that observations have been submitted as to its relevance for resolution of the main proceedings and the Court's jurisdiction to answer it.

17. The Italian Government and the Cassa di Risparmio contend that, since Mr Angonese is regarded as having been resident in the province of Bolzano since his birth, the question is artificial and has no connection with Community law.

18. In that respect, it should be noted that the Court has consistently held that it is for the national courts alone, which are seised of a case and which must assume responsibility for the judgment to be given, to determine, having regard to the particular features of each case, both the need for a preliminary ruling in order to enable them to give their judgment and the relevance of the questions which they refer to the Court. A reference for a preliminary ruling from a national court may be rejected only if it is quite obvious that the interpretation of Community law sought by that court bears no relation to the actual nature of the case or the subject-matter of the main action (see, in particular, Case C-230/96 Cabour and Nord Distribution Automobile v Arnor [1998] ECR I-2055, paragraph 21).

19. Whether or not the reasoning of the order for a reference mentioned in paragraph 14 above is well founded, it is far from clear that the interpretation of Community law it seeks has no relation to the actual facts of the case or to the subject-matter of the main action.

20. In those circumstances, the question submitted must be answered.

21. The national court is asking essentially whether Article 48 of the EC Treaty and Articles 3 and 7 of the Regulation preclude an employer from requiring persons applying to take part in a recruitment competition to provide evidence of their linguistic

knowledge solely by means of one particular diploma, such as the Certificate, issued in a single province of a Member State.

22. As far as the effect of the Regulation is concerned, Article 3(1) is concerned only with provisions laid down by the laws, regulations or administrative action or administrative practices of Member States. Article 3(1) is not therefore relevant in determining the lawfulness of a requirement not based on such provisions or practices.

23. As regards Article 7 of the Regulation, the Cassa di Risparmio submits that the requirement to possess the Certificate does not arise under a collective agreement or an individual employment contract, and so the question whether it is lawful under that provision is not relevant.

24. Mr Angonese and the Commission contend, however, that Article 19 of the Collective Agreement allows banking undertakings to include discriminatory selection criteria, such as possession of the Certificate, and that it infringes Article 7(4) of the Regulation.

25. It should be noted that Article 19 of the Collective Agreement authorises the institutions concerned to lay down the conditions and rules for competitions, as well as the selection criteria.

26. Nevertheless, such a provision does not authorise the institutions concerned, either expressly or implicitly, to adopt discriminatory criteria in relation to workers who are nationals of other Member States, which would be incompatible with Article 7 of the Regulation.

27. It follows that such a provision does not in itself constitute an infringement of Article 7 of the Regulation and does not have any effect on the lawfulness, under the Regulation, of a requirement such as the one imposed by the Cassa di Risparmio.

28. In those circumstances, the question submitted falls to be examined solely in relation to Article 48 of the Treaty.

29. Under that provision, freedom of movement for workers within the Community entails the abolition of any discrimination based on nationality between workers of the Member States as regards employment, remuneration and other conditions of work and employment.

30. It should be noted at the outset that the principle of non-discrimination set out in Article 48 is drafted in general terms and is not specifically addressed to the Member States.

31. Thus, the Court has held that the prohibition of discrimination based on nationality applies not only to the actions of public authorities but also to rules of any other nature aimed at regulating in a collective manner gainful employment and the provision of services (see Case 36/74 Walrave v Union Cycliste Internationale [1974] ECR 1405, paragraph 17).

32. The Court has held that the abolition, as between Member States, of obstacles to freedom of movement for persons would be compromised if the abolition of State barriers could be neutralised by obstacles resulting from the exercise of their legal autonomy by associations or organisations not governed by public law (see Walrave, paragraph 18, and Case C-415/93 Union Royale Belge des Sociétés de Football Association and Others v Bosman and Others [1995] ECR I-4921, paragraph 83).

33. Since working conditions in the different Member States are governed sometimes by provisions laid down by law or regulation and sometimes by agreements and other acts concluded or adopted by private persons, limiting application of the prohibition of discrimination based on nationality to acts of a public authority risks creating inequality in its application (see Walrave, paragraph 19, and Bosman, paragraph 84).

34. The Court has also ruled that the fact that certain provisions of the Treaty are formally addressed to the Member States does not prevent rights from being conferred at the same time on any individual who has an interest in compliance with the obligations thus laid down (see Case 43/75 Defrenne v Sabena [1976] ECR 455, paragraph 31). The Court accordingly held, in relation to a provision of the Treaty which was mandatory in nature, that the prohibition of discrimination applied equally to all agreements intended to regulate paid labour collectively, as well as to contracts between individuals (see Defrenne, paragraph 39).

35. Such considerations must, a fortiori, be applicable to Article 48 of the Treaty, which lays down a fundamental freedom and which constitutes a specific application of the general prohibition of discrimination contained in Article 6 of the EC Treaty (now, after amendment, Article 12 EC). In that respect, like Article 119 of the EC Treaty (Articles 117 to 120 of the EC Treaty have been replaced by Articles 136 EC to 143 EC), it is designed to ensure that there is no discrimination on the labour market.

36. Consequently, the prohibition of discrimination on grounds of nationality laid down in Article 48 of the Treaty must be regarded as applying to private persons as well.

37. The next matter to be considered is whether a requirement imposed by an employer, such as the Cassa di Risparmio, which makes admission to a recruitment competi-

tion conditional on possession of one particular diploma, such as the Certificate, constitutes discrimination contrary to Article 48 of the Treaty.

38. According to the order for reference, the Cassa di Risparmio accepts only the Certificate as evidence of the requisite linguistic knowledge and the Certificate can be obtained only in one province of the Member State concerned.

39. Persons not resident in that province therefore have little chance of acquiring the Certificate and it will be difficult, or even impossible, for them to gain access to the employment in question.

40. Since the majority of residents of the province of Bolzano are Italian nationals, the obligation to obtain the requisite Certificate puts nationals of other Member States at a disadvantage by comparison with residents of the province.

41. That is so notwithstanding that the requirement in question affects Italian nationals resident in other parts of Italy as well as nationals of other Member States. In order for a measure to be treated as being discriminatory on grounds of nationality under the rules relating to the free movement of workers, it is not necessary for the measure to have the effect of putting at an advantage all the workers of one nationality or of putting at a disadvantage only workers who are nationals of other Member States, but not workers of the nationality in question.

42. A requirement, such as the one at issue in the main proceedings, making the right to take part in a recruitment competition conditional upon possession of a language diploma that may be obtained in only one province of a Member State and not allowing any other equivalent evidence could be justified only if it were based on objective factors unrelated to the nationality of the persons concerned and if it were in proportion to the aim legitimately pursued.

43. The Court has ruled that the principle of non-discrimination precludes any requirement that the linguistic knowledge in question must have been acquired within the national territory (see Case C-379/87 Groener v Minister for Education and the City of Dublin Vocational Educational Committee [1989] ECR 3967, paragraph 23).

44. So, even though requiring an applicant for a post to have a certain level of linguistic knowledge may be legitimate and possession of a diploma such as the Certificate may constitute a criterion for assessing that knowledge, the fact that it is impossible to submit proof of the required linguistic knowledge by any other means, in particular by equivalent qualifications obtained in other Member States, must be considered disproportionate in relation to the aim in view.

45. It follows that, where an employer makes a person's admission to a recruitment competition subject to a requirement to provide evidence of his linguistic know-

ledge exclusively by means of one particular diploma, such as the Certificate, issued only in one particular province of a Member State, that requirement constitutes discrimination on grounds of nationality contrary to Article 48 of the EC Treaty.

46. The reply to be given to the question submitted must therefore be that Article 48 of the Treaty precludes an employer from requiring persons applying to take part in a recruitment competition to provide evidence of their linguistic knowledge exclusively by means of one particular diploma issued only in one particular province of a Member State.

Costs

[Para. 47 omitted]

On those grounds,

THE COURT,

in answer to the question referred to it by the Pretura Circondariale di Bolzano by order of 8 July 1998, hereby rules:

> **Article 48 of the EC Treaty (now, after amendment, Article 39 EC) precludes an employer from requiring persons applying to take part in a recruitment competition to provide evidence of their linguistic knowledge exclusively by means of one particular diploma issued only in one particular province of a Member State.**

Comments and questions

In Case C-281/98 *Angonese* v *Cassa di Risparmio di Bolzano SpA* [2000] ECR I-4139, the CJEU had to consider the special linguistic conditions that applied in the Italian province of Bolzano. The case concerned the employment conditions of a *private employer* (Cassa di Risparmio di Bolzano, a savings bank). In order to take part in a selection process, candidates had to be in possession of a type-B certificate of bilingualism (in Italian and German). This certificate could only be issued by the public authorities of the province of Bolzano after an examination held only in that province. Angonese did not have such a certificate.

Since this was an employment condition laid down by a private employer, the question was whether the savings bank was obliged to comply with Regulation No 1612/68 on freedom of movement for workers within the Union, then in force, (now Regulation 492/2011) or with Article 39 TFEU (formerly Article 48 TEC). As for Regulation No 1612/68, the CJEU rejected the idea that this employment condition could be authorised by an Italian collective agreement for savings bank employees, and since the Regulation only applies to provisions laid down in collective agreements or by law, the Regulation could not have any effect on the lawfulness of a condition such as the one imposed by the savings bank.

The question referred for preliminary ruling should therefore only be dealt with under Article 45 TFEU, and the CJEU had to consider whether its provisions could bind private employers. It may seem surprising that the CJEU had not had the opportunity to express its views on this point prior to the *Angonese* case. The CJEU had indeed stated in a number of cases that the provisions of Article 39 do not only apply to the regulations issued by public authorities, but also to *other forms of rules whose purpose is to lay down collective conditions for employees and service providers*, see for example the Case 13/76 *Donà* [1976] ECR 1333, Case 36/74 *Walrave* [1974] ECR 1405, and Case C-415/93 *Bosman* [1995] ECR I-4921, printed below. Public bodies or private organisations which have been given delegated public law powers are also obliged to comply with the TFEU's provisions on freedom of movement, see for example Case 71/76 *Thieffry* v *Conseil de l'ordre des avocats à la cour de Paris* [1977] ECR 765, printed below in Chapter 5.

According to the *wording* of Article 45 TFEU, there is nothing to prevent private employers being covered by its provisions. The Article is not addressed to the Member States, and indeed Article 39(1) and (2) lay down a general prohibition of discrimination. Correspondingly, it can be argued that the *Dona, Walrave* and *Bosman* cases do not exclude the idea that private employers are covered by the provisions. Already in 1976 the prohibition in (now) Article 157 TFEU of discrimination on the grounds of sex was also held to apply to private employers; cf. Case 43/75 *Defrenne* v *Sabena* [1976] ECR 455.

In paragraphs 31-35 of the *Angonese* case the CJEU considered the arguments for why private employers should be bound by Article 45 TFEU, and it concluded, in paragraph 36, that Article 45 TFEU must be regarded as applying to private persons as well. Among other things it is argued in paragraph 33 that, in the *Bosman* case, the CJEU established that since working conditions are sometimes governed by provisions laid down by law or regulation and sometimes by agreements and other measures adopted by *private persons,* so the prohibition of discrimination in Article 45 TFEU is not limited to public legal acts. Do you agree that the *Bosman* case shows that the CJEU had previously considered provisions adopted by private individuals?

As is generally recognised, the CJEU had previously established that a private employer could base a claim against national authorities on Article 45 TFEU; cf. Case C-350/96 *Clean Car Autoservice GesmbH* v *Landeshauptmann von Wien* [1998] ECR I-2521, printed below. It can be argued, on this basis, that it is not so great a step from this to making private employers bound by the provisions. Rights and duties under the provision would thus go hand in hand. Nevertheless, the *Angonese* case does not contain a single reference to the *Clean Car Autoservice* case, which is somewhat surprising.

It has now been established in the *Angonese* case that Article 45 TFEU contains a *horizontal prohibition against discrimination.* It will thus be natural to assume that the judgment will apply widely to private individuals and undertakings in employment relations.

It is important to note that the horizontal prohibition under Article 45 TFEU is wider than mere discrimination on the grounds of nationality and indirect discrimination. In its more recent decisions the CJEU has held that Article 45 TFEU also contains a prohibition against non-discriminatory rules which nevertheless affect access to the labour market; see for example Case C-415/93 *Bosman*, printed below. Such restrictions are prohibited unless they can be justified to protect mandatory requirements or by the exemptions listed in Article 45(3) and (4) TFEU, and provided they are reasonable in relation to their purposes (the principle of proportionality).

A requirement that a candidate for employment should have a particular certificate of language proficiency, as in the *Angonese* case, is an example of a restriction covered by Article 45 TFEU. The requirement is only lawful if it is justified on objective grounds and is proportionate. This means that in future, private employers must be prepared to justify their arrangements, even though they may apply without distinction between the Member State's own nationals and foreign nationals, where the measures are restrictive, limiting or burdensome on migrant workers. Give examples of restrictions which private employers apply to their work forces.

The *Angonese* case contains a *second* notable element. According to the established practice of the CJEU, the TFEU provisions on freedom of movement apply to activities falling within the scope of the TFEU that do not concern *purely internal matters* of a Member State; see for example, Joined Cases C-64/96 and C-65/96 *Jacquet* [1997] ECR I-3171, printed below, and Joined Cases C-54/88 and others *Nino* [1990] ECR I-3537. The *Angonese* case concerned an Italian national who was resident in Bolzano in Italy, and who applied to take part in a selection process with a view to being employed by a savings bank in Bolzano. Thus, all the elements of the case were linked to Italy. The only cross-border element was that Roman Angonese had studied English, Polish and certain Slav languages for four years at Vienna University, though without having obtained his degree at the time when he applied to take part in the selection process.

Did these studies constitute a sufficient foreign element for Angonese to rely on the right of freedom of movement under Article 45 TFEU in his home Member State? Prior to the *Angonese* judgment, in cases where the CJEU had allowed Union citizens to base claims against their home Member State on the TFEU provisions on freedom of movement, the claimant had previously undertaken some relevant cross-border action. For example, the claimant had obtained some professional qualification in another country (Case C-19/92 *Kraus* v *Land Baden-Wuerttemberg* [1993] ECR I-1663, and Case C-61/89 *Bouchoucha* [1990] ECR I-3551), or had undertaken some economic activity, such as being an employee or trainee in some other Member State (Case C-370/90 *Singh* [1992] ECR I-4265). If, on the other hand, the cross-border activity merely consisted in the claimant having changed residence so that he or she now lived in another Member State, then prior to the *Angonese* case the CJEU had rejected the idea that Article 49 TFEU was applicable against the authorities of the claimant's home Member State. A change of residence alone did thus not constitute a sufficiently relevant cross-border activity; cf. Case C-112/91 *Werner* v *Finanzamt Aachen-Innenstadt* [1993] ECR I-429.

The question in the *Angonese* case was thus whether Angonese's language studies at Vienna University were a sufficiently relevant connection with the situation to which he sought to have the TFEU provisions on freedom of movement of workers applied. On the face of it, there does not seem to be any relevant connection between language studies in English, Polish and certain Slav languages, and an application for employment in a savings bank. This applies equally to the possession of a certificate of language proficiency in Italian and German which the savings bank required as a pre-condition for taking part in the selection process. In his Opinion, Advocate General Fennelly dismissed the idea that there was the necessary connection. The CJEU did not discuss the issue on more detail than the statement in paragraph 14 of the judgment that in the referral from the national court it was stated that if the requirement at issue were held to be inherently contrary to Union law, it would be void under Italian law. It is natural to assume that this was the reason why the CJEU allowed that Angonese's situation was covered by Article 45 TFEU without further discussion, so that Angonese could make use of the provision in his case against the savings bank before the Italian court. Not long after giving judgment in the *Angonese* case, the CJEU stated in paragraphs 22-23 in Case C-448/98 *Guimont* [2000] ECR I-10663, printed in Chapter 2, that it is for the national courts alone to determine whether a reference for a preliminary ruling is necessary. This means that, in principle, the CJEU can only reject a reference if the interpretation of Union law sought by the referring court bears no relation to the actual facts or subject-matter of the main action. In the *Guimont* case the CJEU added that a reference might be useful if national law required that persons or undertakings of the Member State should be given the same right under national law as they would have been able to derive from Union law if the situation had not had a purely internal character. On this point French law corresponds to Italian law.

How do you think that an English court would apply Union law in a case similar to the situation in the *Guimont* case? Is there a corresponding principle in English law that British nationals should not enjoy less protection than that which would otherwise be enjoyed by the nationals of other Member States?

The CJEU has since changed its view on the requirement that a cross-border event should relate to some commercial activity. Following the introduction of Union citizenship, under which Union citizens have a right to enter and to take up residence in other Member States, the CJEU is no longer concerned with whether or not the cross-border event is associated with some commercial activity. See, for example, Case C-456/12 *O*, printed in Chapter 3.

What are the consequences of the *Angonese* case as to who is bound by the other Treaty provisions on freedom of movement? The arguments which the CJEU puts forward in the *Angonese* case, that Article 45 TFEU should be binding on private individuals, can easily be applied to Articles 34, 49, 56 and 63 TFEU. These provisions are equally formulated in general terms and are not specifically addressed to the Member States. The CJEU has also used a broad Union law concept of the State in relation to these provisions. In other words, the fact that the provision applies to the State in a broad sense (government departments, regional and local government authorities), to bodies subject to public law and State-owned companies (such as The Royal Mint, British Nuclear Fuels Limited etc.) and to collective agreements (for example, provisions adopted by a bar association or by sport associations such as UEFA). Moreover, it is possible to talk of fundamental freedoms in relation to these provisions, and they are also a special expression of the general prohibition of discrimination on the grounds of nationality contained in Article 18 TFEU. In relation to Article 34 TFEU, the CJEU appears to have rejected such an interpretation of those on whom the provision is binding; cf. Case C-325/00 *Commission* v *Germany* (the *Markenqualität* case) [2002] ECR I-9977, and Case C-171/11 *Fra.bo*, Judgment of 12 July 2012, both printed in Chapter 2. It has not yet been made clear whether the other Treaty provisions on freedom of movement are now also binding on private individuals and private employers. With its decisions in Case C-438/05 *Viking Line* [2007] ECR I-10779 and Case C-341/05 *Laval* [2007] ECR I-11767 (reproduced below in Chapters 5 and 6 respectively), the CJEU has established that an individual trade union is capable of being subject to certain duties pursuant to Articles 49 and 56 TFEU.

JUDGMENT OF THE COURT
23 March 1982

D.M. Levin v Staatssecretaris van Justitie.
(Reference for a preliminary ruling from the Netherlands Raad van State)

'Right of residence'

Case 53/81

Judgment

1. By interlocutory judgment of 28 November 1980, received at the Court on 11 March 1981, the Raad van State [State Council] of the Netherlands referred to the Court for a preliminary ruling under Article 177 of the EEC Treaty three questions relating to the interpretation of Article 48 of the Treaty and of certain provisions of Community regulations and directives on the free movement of persons within the Community.

2. The appellant in the main proceedings, Mrs Levin, of British nationality and the wife of a national of a non-member country, applied for a permit to reside in the Netherlands. The permit was refused, on the basis of Netherlands legislation, on the ground, amongst others, that Mrs Levin was not engaged in a gainful occupation in the Netherlands and therefore could not be described as a favoured EEC citizin within the meaning of that legislation.

3. Mrs Levin applied to the Staatssecretaris van Justitie [Secretary of State for Justice] for the decision to be reconsidered. Her application was rejected and she appealed to the Raad van State claiming that in the meantime she had taken up an activity as an employed person in the Netherlands and that, in any event, she and her husband had property and income more than sufficient to support themselves, even without pursuing such an activity.

4. Since the Raad van State considered that the judgment to be given depended on the interpretation of Community law it referred the following three questions to the Court for a preliminary ruling:

   1. Should the concept of 'favoured EEC citizen', which in the Netherlands legislation is taken to mean a national of a Member State as described in Article 1 of Directive 64/221/EEC of the Council of the European Communities of 25 February 1964 and is used in that legislation to determine the category of persons to whom Article 48 of the Treaty establishing the European Economic Community, Regulation (EEC) No 1612/68 of 15 October 1968 and Directives

64/221/EEC of 25 February 1964 and 68/360/EEC of 15 October 1968 adopted by the Council of the European Communities in application of Article 48 apply, also be taken to mean a national of a Member State who in the territory of another Member State pursues an activity, whether paid or not as an employed person, or provides services to such a limited extent that in so doing he earns income which is less than that which in the last-mentioned Member State is considered as the minimum necessary to enable him to support himself?

2. In the answer to Question 1, should a distinction be drawn between, on the one hand, persons who apart from or in addition to their income derived from limited employment have other income (for example from property or from the employment of their spouses living with them who are not nationals of a Member State) as a result of which they have sufficient means of support as referred to in Question 1 and, on the other hand, persons who do not have such additional income at their disposal and yet for reasons of their own wish to make do with an income less than what is generally considered to be the minimum required?

3. Assuming that Question 1 is answered in the affirmative, can the right of such a worker to free admission into and establishment in the Member State in which he pursues or wishes to pursue an activity or provides or wishes to provide services to a limited extent still be relied upon if it is demonstrated or seems likely that his chief motive for residing in that Member State is for a purpose other than the pursuit of an activity or provision of services to a limited extent?

5. Although these questions, as worded, are concerned not only with freedom of movement for workers but also with freedom of establishment and freedom to provide services, it is apparent from the particulars of the dispute in the main procceedings that the national court really has in mind only the issue of freedom of movement for workers. The answers to be given should therefore be confined to those aspects which have a bearing on that freedom.

First and second questions

6. In its first and second questions, which should be considered together, the national court is essentially asking whether the provisions of Community law relating to freedom of movement for workers also cover a national of a Member State whose activity as an employed person in the territory of another Member State provides him with an income less than the minimum required for subsistence within the meaning of the legislation of the second Member State. In particular the court asks whether those provisions cover such a person where he either supplements his income from his activity as an employed person with other income so as to arrive at that minimum or is content with means of support which fall below it.

7. Under Article 48 of the Treaty freedom of movement for workers is to be secured within the Community. That freedom is to entail the abolition of any discrimination based on nationality between workers of the Member States as regards employment, remuneration and other conditions of work and is to include the right, subject to limitations justified on grounds of public policy, public security or public health, to accept offers of employment actually made, to move freely within the territory of Member States for this purpose, to stay in a Member State for the purpose of employment and to remain there after the termination of that employment.

8. That provision was implemented inter alia by Regulation (EEC) No 1612/68 of the Council of 15 October 1968 on freedom of movement for workers within the Community (Official Journal, English Special Edition 1968 (II), p. 475) and Council Directive 68/360/EEC of the same date on the abolition of restrictions on movement and residence within the Community for workers of the Member States and their families (Official Journal, English Special Edition 1968 (II), p. 485). Under Article 1 of Regulation (EEC) No 1612/68 any national of a Member State is, irrespective of his place of residence, to have the right to take up activity as an employed person, and to pursue such activity, within the territory of another Member State in accordance with the provisions laid down by law, regulation or administrative action governing the employment of nationals of that State.

9. Although the rights deriving from the principle of freedom of movement for workers and more particularly the right to enter and stay in the territory of a Member State are thus linked to the status of a worker or of a person pursuing an activity as an employed person or desirous of so doing, the terms worker and activity as an employed person are not expressly defined in any of the provisions on the subject. It is appropriate, therefore, in order to determine their meaning, to have recourse to the generally recognized principles of interpretation, beginning with the ordinary meaning to be attributed to those terms in their context and in the light of the objectives of the Treaty.

10. The Netherlands and Danish Governments have maintained that the provisions of Article 48 may only be relied upon by persons who receive a wage at least commensurate with the means of subsistence considered as necessary by the legislation of the Member State in which they work, or who work at least for the number of hours considered as usual in respect of full-time employment in the sector in question. In the absence of any provisions to that effect in Community legislation, it is suggested that it is necessary to have recourse to national criteria for the purpose of defining both the minimum wage and the minimum number of hours.

11. That argument cannot, however, be accepted. As the Court has already stated in its judgment of 19 March 1964 in Case 75/63 Hoekstra (née Unger) [1964] ECR 1977 the terms worker and activity as an employed person may not be defined by reference to the national laws of the Member States but have a Community meaning. If

that were not the case, the Community rules on freedom of movement for workers would be frustrated, as the meaning of those terms could be fixed and modified unilaterally, without any control by the Community institutions, by national laws which would thus be able to exclude at will certain categories of persons from the benefit of the Treaty.

12. Such would, in particular, be the case if the enjoyment of the rights conferred by the principle of freedom of movement for workers could be made subject to the criterion of what the legislation of the host State declares to be a minimum wage, so that the field of application ratione personae of the Community rules on this subject might vary from one Member State to another. The meaning and the scope of the terms worker and activity as an employed person should thus be clarified in the light of the principles of the legal order of the Community.

13. In this respect it must be stressed that these concepts define the field of application of one of the fundamental freedoms guaranteed by the Treaty and, as such, may not be interpreted restrictively.

14. In conformity with this view the recitals in the preamble to Regulation (EEC) No 1612/68 contain a general affirmation of the right of all workers in the Member States to pursue the activity of their choice within the Community, irrespective of whether they are permanent, seasonal or frontier workers or workers who pursue their activities for the purpose of providing services. Furthermore, although Article 4 of Directive 68/36/EEC grants the right of residence to workers upon the mere production of the document on the basis of which they entered the territory and of a confirmation of engagement from the employer or a certificate of employment, it does not subject this right to any condition relating to the kind of employment or to the amount of income derived from it.

15. An interpretation which reflects the full scope of these concepts is also in conformity with the objectives of the Treaty which include, according to Articles 2 and 3, the abolition, as between Member States, of obstacles to freedom of movement for persons, with the purpose inter alia of promoting throughout the Community a harmonious development of economic activities and a raising of the standard of living. Since part-time employment, although it may provide an income lower than what is considered to be the minimum required for subsistence, constitutes for a large number of persons an effective means of improving their living conditions, the effectiveness of Community law would be impaired and the achievement of the objectives of the Treaty would be jeopardized if the enjoyment of rights conferred by the principle of freedom of movement for workers were reserved solely to persons engaged in full-time employment and earning, as a result, a wage at least equivalent to the guaranteed minimum wage in the sector under consideration.

16. It follows that the concepts of worker and activity as an employed person must be interpreted as meaning that the rules relating to freedom of movement for workers also concern persons who pursue or wish to pursue an activity as an employed person on a part-time basis only and who, by virtue of that fact obtain or would obtain only remuneration lower than the minimum guaranteed remuneration in the sector under consideration. In this regard no distinction may be made between those who wish to make do with their income from such an activity and those who supplement that income with other income, whether the latter is derived from property or from the employment of a member of their family who accompanies them.

17. It should however be stated that whilst part-time employment is not excluded from the field of application of the rules on freedom of movement for workers, those rules cover only the pursuit of effective and genuine activities, to the exclusion of activities on such a small scale as to be regarded as purely marginal and ancillary. It follows both from the statement of the principle of freedom of movement for workers and from the place occupied by the rules relating to that principle in the system of the Treaty as a whole that those rules guarantee only the free movement of persons who pursue or are desirous of pursuing an economic activity.

18. The answer to be given to the first and second questions must therefore be that the provisions of Community law relating to freedom of movement for workers also cover a national of a Member State who pursues, within the territory of another Member State, an activity as an employed person which yields an income lower than that which, in the latter State, is considered as the minimum required for subsistence, whether that person supplements the income from his activity as an employed person with other income so as to arrive at that minimum or is satisfied with means of support lower than the said minimum, provided that he pursues an activity as an employed person which is effective and genuine.

Third question

19. The third question essentially seeks to ascertain whether the right to enter and reside in the territory of a Member State may be denied to a worker whose main objectives, pursued by means of his entry and residence, are different from that of the pursuit of an activity as an employed person as defined in the answer to the first and second questions.

20. Under Article 48 (3) of the Treaty the right to move freely within the territory of the Member States is conferred upon workers for the purpose of accepting offers of employment actually made. By virtue of the same provision workers enjoy the right to stay in one of the Member States for the purpose of employment there. Moreover, it is stated in the preamble to Regulation (EEC) No 1612/68 that freedom of movement for workers entails the right of workers to move freely within the Community in order to pursue activities as employed persons, whilst Article 2 of Di-

rective 68/360/EEC requires the Member States to grant workers the right to leave their territory in order to take up activities as employed persons or to pursue them in the territory of another Member State.

21. However, these formulations merely give expression to the requirement, which is inherent in the very principle of freedom of movement for workers, that the advantages which Community law confers in the name of that freedom may be relied upon only by persons who actually pursue or seriously wish to pursue activities as employed persons. They do not, however, mean that the enjoyment of this freedom may be made to depend upon the aims pursued by a national of a Member State in applying for entry upon and residence in the territory of another Member State, provided that he there pursues or wishes to pursue an activity which meets the criteria specified above, that is to say, an effective and genuine activity as an employed person.

22. Once this condition is satisfied, the motives which may have prompted the worker to seek employment in the Member State concerned are of no account and must not be taken into consideration.

23. The answer to be given to the third question put to the Court by the Raad van State must therefore be that the motives which may have prompted a worker of a Member State to seek employment in another Member State are of no account as regards his right to enter and reside in the territory of the latter State provided that he there pursues or wishes to pursue an effective and genuine activity.

Costs

[Para. 24 omitted]

On those grounds,

THE COURT

in answer to the questions referred to it by the Judicial Division of the Raad van State of the Netherlands by interlocutory judgment of 28 November 1980, hereby rules:

1. **The provisions of Community law relating to freedom of movement for workers also cover a national of a Member State who pursues, within the territory of another Member State, an activity as an employed person which yields an income lower than that which, in the latter State, is considered as the minimum required for subsistence, whether that person supplements the income from his activity as an employed person with other income so as to arrive at that minimum or is satisfied with means of sup-**

port lower than the said minimum, provided that he pursues an activity as an employed person which is effective and genuine.

2. **The motives which may have prompted a worker of a Member State to seek employment in another Member State are of no account as regards his right to enter and reside in the territory of the latter State provided that he pursues or wishes to pursue an effective and genuine activity.**

Comments and questions

Case 53/81 *Levin* v *Staatssecretaris van Justitie* [1982] ECR 1035, concerned a British national who was married to a national from a third country who sought a residence permit in the Netherlands. Mrs Levin had undertaken a small amount of part time work, and she and her husband supplemented their earned income with investment income. The earned income lay well below what could be regarded as a necessary income, as understood in Dutch law. The question was whether she could be regarded as a worker within the meaning of Article 45 TFEU (formerly Article 48 EEC Treaty).

In paragraph 9 of the judgment it was noted that the terms 'worker' and 'activity as an employed person' are not expressly defined in Article 345 TFEU or in Regulation No 1612/68 on freedom of movement for workers within the Union, then in force, (now Regulation No 492/2011). The CJEU therefore stated that in order to determine their meaning, it was appropriate 'to have recourse to the generally recognized principles of interpretation, beginning with the ordinary meaning to be attributed to those terms in their context and in the light of the objectives of the Treaty'. In paragraph 11 it was stated that the terms have a Union law meaning, so they cannot be defined by reference to the national laws of the Member States.

The CJEU accepted that part time work is also covered by the concept of 'activity as an employed person'. It was recognised in paragraph 15 that, for many people, part time work is an effective means of improving their living conditions. *The intended effect of Union law would not be achieved, and the realisation of the objectives of the Treaty would be jeopardised* if the exercise of rights under Article 45 TFEU were to be reserved to people in full-time employment. It was emphasised in paragraph 16 that 'no distinction may be made between those who wish to make do with their income from such an activity and those who supplement that income with other income, whether the latter is derived from property or from work carried out by a member of their family who accompanies them.'

It is only *effective and genuine* work activities which are covered by the freedom of movement of workers. However, the CJEU laid down a *de minimis* rule for what work is covered by the provisions in Article 45 TFEU. Activities which are on such a small scale as to be regarded as *purely marginal and ancillary* are not covered, see paragraph 17.

Do you think that the CJEU's decision interprets the provision too widely? Do you believe it is right to say, as the CJEU did in paragraph 15, that the objectives of the

TFEU would be endangered, if the exercise of rights conferred by the principle of freedom of movement for workers were reserved solely to persons engaged in full-time employment and in this way earning a wage at least equivalent to the guaranteed minimum wage in the sector in question. Which objectives do you think the CJEU is referring to? The Danish Government intervened in this case, arguing that the provisions of Article 45 TFEU should only be relied upon by those receiving a wage at least equal to the means of subsistence considered necessary in the Member State where they work. If not, there would be a danger that such people would have to supplement their income by social security benefits. Following the *Levin* case, what argument can a Member State use to deny social security benefits to a babysitter from another Member State who works for a family for two hours per week?

Barely five years after the Dutch Raad van State had referred its questions in the *Levin* case, the same court referred questions for preliminary rulings in Case 139/85 *Kempf* v *Staatssecretaris van Justitie* [1986] ECR 1741. In this case, Kempf, who was a German national, had moved to the Netherlands where he had part-time work as a music teacher, teaching 12 hours per week for a small wage. Kempf applied to be given social security benefits, which could be paid to people who had the status of a worker. He was given such benefits. Later, Kempf was unable to work because of illness, so he received further social benefits from the Dutch authorities. Shortly after arriving in the Netherlands, Kempf had sought a residence permit. This was refused, among other things on the ground that he had had recourse to public funds and was therefore 'manifestly unable to meet his needs out of the income received from his employment'. Kempf appealed against this refusal, and the case came before the Raad van State which referred the following question to the CJEU: 'Where a national of a Member State pursues within the territory of another Member State an activity which may in itself be regarded as effective and genuine work within the meaning of the CJEU's judgment in *Levin* v *Staatssecretaris van Justitie*, does the fact that he claims financial assistance payable out of the public funds of the latter Member State in order to supplement the income he receives from that activity exclude him from the provisions of [Union] law relating to freedom of movement for workers?' In its reasons for referring the question, the Raad van State expressly found that Kempf's work was not on such a small scale as to be purely a marginal and ancillary activity. The question which the CJEU had to address was whether a Member State can exclude a Union citizen who pursues an effective and genuine activity as a part-time employed person, from which he obtained payment which is lower than the minimum means of subsistence, and who wished to supplement his payment by other lawful means. The CJEU answered that: 'it is irrelevant whether those supplementary means of subsistence are derived from property or from the employment of a member of his family, as was the case in Levin, or whether, as in this instance, they are obtained from financial assistance drawn from the public funds of the member state in which he resides, provided that the effective and genuine nature of his work is established.'

In the *Kempf* case the CJEU also laid down, under reference to the *Levin* case, that the term 'worker' would not have a Union-wide definition if a worker were to lose his or her rights under the principle of freedom of movement of workers upon seeking public social benefits in accordance with the host Member State's laws. Do you agree with this?

In the *Kempf* case the CJEU made it clear that even a limited number of working hours per week can be sufficient for a person to qualify as a worker within the meaning of Article 45 TFEU. In the subsequent Case C-14/09 *Genc* [2010] ECR I-931, the CJEU took a significant further step. In the *Genc* case, Ms Genc had been working as a cleaner for only 5.5 hours per week at a very low hourly rate. This represented only 14% of the normal working time for a person who is employed full time, and thereby she earned only approximately 25% of the amount determined under the national law of the Member State to be necessary for subsistence. It was thus natural to ask whether this work was not on such a small scale as to be purely marginal and ancillary as to fall outside the concept of a 'worker' within the meaning of Article 45 TFEU.

Before the CJEU decided on this question, it first established that it is a characteristic of an employment relationship that a person has, for an extended period for and under the instruction of another, performed services of a certain economic value in return for remuneration. And the CJEU added that: 'Neither the origin of the funds from which the remuneration is paid nor the limited amount of that remuneration, nor indeed the fact that the person in question seeks to supplement that remuneration by other means of subsistence such as financial assistance drawn from the public funds of the State in which he resides, can have any consequence in regard to whether or not the person is a 'worker' for the purposes of European Union law'. The CJEU also stated that the two basic conditions for an employment relationship, namely subordination and the payment of remuneration in return for services rendered, were satisfied. What was decisive in this specific case for whether the person was a 'worker' within the meaning of Union law was whether the particularly low number of hours of work performed by the person concerned was capable of entitling her to the status of worker within the meaning of Union law.

Referring to its previous decisions, the CJEU noted that the fact that a worker's earnings do not cover all his needs cannot preclude him from being a member of the working population, and that employment which yields an income lower than the minimum required for subsistence or whose working hours do not normally exceed a very limited number of hours does not prevent that person being regarded as a worker within the meaning of Article 45 TFEU. However, the CJEU took an important step further and ruled that the condition that the work may not be on such a small scale as to be purely marginal and ancillary can be satisfied even where the hours worked are very limited if, following an overall assessment of the employment relationship, the activity may be considered to be real and genuine. Thus, in the specific case, it was 'necessary to take into account factors relating not only to the number of working hours and the level of remuneration but also to the right to 28 days of paid leave, to the continued payment of wages in the event of sickness, and to a contract of employment which is subject to the relevant collective agreement, in conjunction with the fact that her contractual relationship with the same undertaking has lasted for almost four years.' Consider whether, on the basis of the CJEU's judgment in the *Genc* case, it is possible to set a minimum threshold for when a person can be regarded as being a 'worker' within the meaning of Article 45 TFEU.

The CJEU has also had to consider whether the conditions for being considered a 'worker' can be fulfilled where the employer-employee relationship differs markedly from what is customary. This was the situation in Case 196/87 *Steymann* [1988] ECR 6159, which concerned a German national, Udo Steymann, who had gone to the Netherlands where he worked as a plumber. Not long after, he became a member of the Bhagwan Community, a religious community that carried on various commercial activities. By virtue of his membership of the Bhagwan Community, Steymann carried out plumbing tasks on the community's property, as well as performing general household work, and took part in the community's commercial activities. Regardless of the nature and extent of Steymann's activities, the religious community provided for all Steymann's material needs. When Steymann sought a residence permit, his application was rejected. When the case came before a Dutch court, the question of whether Steymann was a 'worker' was referred to the CJEU. The CJEU found that to the extent that Steymann's work, which was to secure the religious community's financial independence, was a significant part of his participation in the community, the community's provision for its members could be regarded as an indirect remuneration for his work. In this context, the CJEU not only required that there should be 'genuine and effective work', but also that Steymann's work should constitute an 'essential part' of ensuring that community's financial independence.

Assume that the religious community had not carried on any real commercial activity, but rather operated a farm in which all the produce was used to provide for the community (100% self-sufficient). Assume also that Steymann was a member of the community, in which he undertook both plumbing work and general housework. How should this situation be assessed?

Back in 1988, the CJEU gave its judgment in Case 39/86 *Lair* v *Universität Hannover* [1988] ECR 3161. From 1st January 1979, Lair who was a French national was employed as a banking officer in Germany, where she also resided. She lost her job on 30th June 1981, and in the following year she had periods of unemployment, received retraining and had short-term work, all while living in Germany. On 1st October 1984 she began studying Romance and Germanic literature at Hannover University. It was not disputed that this course would lead to a professional qualification. Lair applied to the German authorities for a 'maintenance and training grant' for the pursuit of her university studies. Her application was refused. Under German law she should have had lawful residence and paid employment in Germany for a period of altogether five years prior to the commencement of her course, in order to qualify for a grant. There was no equivalent requirement for German nationals, who were given grants only on the basis of aptitude and need.

First, the CJEU considered whether the general provision in (now) Article 18 TFEU on the prohibition of discrimination applied to Lair's situation. This would be the case if the grant which was the subject of the dispute fell within the scope of the TFEU. Grants which are intended to cover registration fees, tuition fees, and other fees charged for access to education are covered by the TFEU, while, in principle, maintenance grants fall outside the scope of the TFEU. The CJEU therefore found that at its then stage of development of Union law, the German rule did not infringe against the TFEU's general prohibition of discrimination.

The CJEU then considered whether Lair could base her claim on Article 7 of Regulation No 1612/68 on freedom of movement for workers within the Union, then in force (now Regulation 492/2011). First, the CJEU stated that maintenance and training grants awarded for university studies leading to a professional qualification constitute a 'social advantage' within the meaning of Article 7(2) of the Regulation. The next question was whether Lair, as a student, could claim some of the rights which were granted by the Regulation to 'workers'. The CJEU noted that a migrant worker is entitled to certain of these rights, even if the migrant worker is no longer in employment. As for support for university studies, there is the necessary connection between a person's status as a worker and maintenance and training grants awarded for university studies, but only if there is continuity between the study and the previous employment in the sense that there must be a relationship between the purpose of the studies and the previous occupational activity. However, such continuity cannot be required where a migrant worker has involuntarily become unemployed and is obliged by the conditions of the job market to undertake occupational retraining in another field. Finally, the CJEU stated that the host Member State cannot make the right to enjoy equivalent social advantages conditional on a minimum period of prior employment within its territory. The concept of a worker is a concept in Union law whose content cannot be determined by criteria laid down in national laws. However, the CJEU added that Member States are entitled to adopt measures which are intended to prevent abuse.

In paragraph 36 of the *Lair* judgment the CJEU states that *certain* rights linked to the status of workers continue to apply, even when they are no longer in an employment relationship. On this point, compare this case with Case C-85/96 *Sala* v *Freistaat Bayern* [1998] ECR I-2691. More recent cases have dealt with this in more detail. In Case C-302/98 *Sehrer* v *Bundesknappschaft* [2000] ECR I-4585, the CJEU held that a supplementary retirement pension, whose grant was dependent on the prior existence of an employment relationship which has come to an end, falls within this category of rights. The CJEU also stated that pension entitlement is intrinsically linked to the objective status of worker; cf. paragraph 30 of the judgment. However, this does not mean that a migrant worker who has, for example, been granted an invalidity pension by a different Member State than that in which he is now resident, and who thus receives a benefit linked to previous employment, should continue to have the status of a worker under Regulation No 1612/68, then in force, and Article 45 TFEU, purely on the basis of the payment of the pension. A person who is no longer in employment cannot thus acquire new rights which are not linked to his previous employment. In Case C-43/99 *Leclere and another* v *Caisse nationale des prestations familiales* [2001] ECR I-4265, a Belgian national had sought maternity, childbirth and child-raising allowances from the Luxembourg authorities. The applicant was resident in Belgium, but had previously been employed in Luxembourg as frontier worker and in this capacity he received an invalidity pension paid by the Luxembourg social security services. The CJEU found that a person receiving an invalidity pension, who is resident in a different Member State from that from where the pension is paid, is not a worker in the sense used in Regulation No 1612/68, then in force. Such a person therefore only has the rights which are linked to his status by virtue of his previous employment.

In paragraph 37 of the *Lair* case, the CJEU emphasised that, in respect of support for university education, a link between the status of worker and a grant awarded for maintenance and training, presupposes some continuity between the previous occupational activity and the course of study; cf. Article 7(2) of Regulation No 1612/68, then in force, in the sense that there must be a relationship between the purpose of the study and the previous occupational activity. However, this requirement does not apply if the worker has become involuntarily unemployed and needs to undertake occupational retraining. The CJEU's case law on maintaining the status of a 'worker' after the termination of an employment relationship has now been codified in Article 7(3) of Directive 2004/38 on the right of citizens of the Union and their family members to move and reside freely within the territory of the Member States.

What decision should the referring court come to on the question of to what extent Lair, as a former bank employee, ought to have a grant to support her studies in Romance and Germanic literature?

In the *Lair* case, the CJEU held that the disputed social benefit fell outside the scope of the then EC Treaty. The benefit nevertheless fell within the scope of Regulation No 1612/68 which was adopted under the authority of the EC Treaty. How can this be, compatible with the Union law principle of conferral of power as stated in Article 5 TEU and Article 7 TFEU?

Case C-357/89 *Raulin* v *Minister van Onderwijs en Wetenschappen* [1992] ECR I-1027, concerned a French national Raulin who went to the Netherlands where she took up residence without registering her residence and without obtaining a residence permit. She entered into an 'on-call contract' for a limited period under which she worked a total of 60 hours as a waitress at the start of the contract period. Before the end of the contract period, she began a full-time course of study at an educational institution in the Netherlands, and then applied for an educational grant from the Dutch Ministry of Education, partly to cover tuition fees and partly for maintenance. This application was refused on the grounds that she could not be treated in the same way as Dutch nationals as she did not have a residence permit. Raulin appealed against this decision, arguing primarily that she had the status of a worker on the basis of her 'on-call contract' and that she was therefore entitled to a grant to cover the costs of study and maintenance under Regulation No 1612/68, then in force. In the alternative, she argued that, because of the prohibition of discrimination on the grounds of nationality now in Article 18 TFEU, she was entitled to that part of the study grant which corresponded to the tuition fees.

In responding to the questions for preliminary rulings, the CJEU put forward a number of interpretative guidelines for assessing whether a worker performs effective and genuine activities: Is the work irregular or of limited duration, or must the worker remain available to work if called upon to do so by the employer?

Why did the CJEU merely give these interpretative guidelines, instead of deciding itself whether Raulin's 60 hours of work as a waitress for a limited period under an 'on-call contract' constituted effective and genuine activities, or whether it should merely be regarded as marginal and ancillary? What decision do you think the referring court ought to make when deciding whether or not Raulin should be regarded as a worker within the terms of Article 45 TFEU?

On the basis of the *Lair* judgment, consider whether Raulin was entitled to receive educational grants from the Dutch authorities under Article 7(2) of Regulation No 1612/68 if it could be shown that she had not been dismissed by the Dutch employer with whom she had agreed the 'on-call contract' referred to. In your answer, bear in mind the requirement for a link between the employment activity and the course of study followed. In this connection, see Article 7(3) of Directive 2004/38 on the right of citizens of the Union and their family members to move and reside freely within the territory of the Member States.

Finally, it should be noted that in the *Raulin* case the CJEU stated that a residence permit is evidence of the status of a national of another Member State, but it is not the permit which creates a right of residence, since these rights are derived from Union law. Therefore, the lack of a permit cannot affect the exercise of those rights.

In the subsequent Case C-413/01 *Franca Ninni-Orasche* v *Bundesminister für Wissenschaft, Verkehr und Kunst* [2003] ECR I-13187, the CJEU considered a referral for a preliminary ruling on the question of whether employment for a limited period of two and a half months as a waiter in a host Member State could give the person concerned the status of a worker within the meaning of Article 39, provided the activity performed was not purely marginal and ancillary. The question was relevant to whether the person, as a worker, was entitled to receive student support in connection with the pursuit of higher education in the host Member State. The CJEU left it to the referring court to examine the facts necessary to determine whether this was so in this case. The CJEU listed the following factors which the referring court could *not* include as relevant in its considerations; cf. paragraph 32:

- Whether the person concerned took up the job only some years after his entry into the host Member State,
- Whether the person concerned became eligible for entry to university in the host Member State shortly after the end of his short, fixed-term employment, by virtue of having completed his schooling in his country of origin, and
- Whether the person concerned attempted to find a new job in the period between the end of the short, fixed-term employment and the time when he took up his studies.

The CJEU also stated that a person is not necessarily voluntarily unemployed solely because their contract of employment, initially for a fixed term, has expired.

JUDGMENT OF THE COURT (Sixth Chamber)
7 May 1998

Clean Car Autoservice GesmbH v Landeshauptmann von Wien.
(Reference for a preliminary ruling: Verwaltungsgerichtshof – Austria)

'Freedom of movement for workers – National legislation requiring legal persons to appoint as manager a person residing in the country – Indirect discrimination'

Case C-350/96

Judgment

1. By order of 8 October 1996, received at the Court on 24 October 1996, the Verwaltungsgerichtshof (Administrative Court) referred to the Court for a preliminary ruling under Article 177 of the EC Treaty two questions on the interpretation of Article 48 of that Treaty and Articles 1 to 3 of Regulation (EEC) No 1612/68 of the Council of 15 October 1968 on freedom of movement for workers within the Community (OJ, English Special Edition 1968 (II), p. 475).

2. Those questions were raised in proceedings brought by Fortress Immobilien Entwicklungs GmbH, now Clean Car Autoservice GmbH ('Clean Car'), an Austrian company established in Vienna, against the Landeshauptmann von Wien (Prime Minister of Vienna *Land*), concerning the rejection of an application by Clean Car to register for a trade on the ground that it had appointed as manager a person who did not reside in Austria.

The Austrian legislation

3. Under Paragraph 9(1) of the Gewerbeordnung 1994 (the Austrian Trade Code, hereinafter 'the GewO 1994'), legal persons, commercial-law partnerships (whether general or limited) and registered civil partnerships (whether general or limited) may exercise a trade, provided that they have appointed a manager or tenant in accordance with Paragraphs 39 and 40 of the GewO 1994.

4. Paragraph 39 of the GewO 1994 provides as follows:

    1. The owner may for the exercise of his trade appoint a manager who is responsible to the owner for the proper exercise of the trade and to the authorities (Paragraph 333) for compliance with the provisions of the law on trades; he must appoint a manager if he is not resident in Austria.

2. The manager must satisfy the personal requirements prescribed for the exercise of the trade, be resident in Austria, and be in a position to act accordingly in the business. In the case of a trade for which the production of proof of qualification is prescribed, the manager of a legal person, to be appointed in accordance with Paragraph 9(1), must also:

    1) belong to the statutory representative organ of the legal person or
    2) be a worker employed in the business for at least half the normal weekly working hours and subject to full compulsory insurance in accordance with the provisions of social security law.

    The manager of an owner who is not resident in Austria, to be appointed under subparagraph 1 for the exercise of a trade for which the production of proof of qualifications is prescribed, must be a worker employed in the business for at least half the normal weekly working hours and subject to full compulsory insurance in accordance with the provisions of social security law. The provisions of Paragraph 39(2), in force until the coming into force of Federal law BGBl. No 29/1993, shall continue until 31 December 1998 to apply to persons who have been appointed as manager by 1 July 1993.

3. In cases where a manager must be appointed, the owner must make use of a manager who acts in the business accordingly.'

5. Pursuant to Paragraph 370(2) of the GewO 1994, where the appointment of a manager has been notified or approved, any fines regarding the conduct of a trade are to be imposed on that manager.

6. Paragraph 5(1) of the GewO 1994 provides that trades may be exercised on the basis of the application to register the trade in question, pursuant to Paragraph 339, when the general conditions and any specific conditions are fulfilled, subject to certain exceptions which are not relevant in the present case.

7. Under Paragraph 339(1) of the GewO 1994, any person wishing to exercise a trade, other than a trade for which authorisation is required and proof of competence other than a proficiency certificate must be produced, must apply for registration to the administrative authority of the district in which the establishment is situated.

8. Pursuant to Paragraph 340(1) of the GewO 1994, the district administrative authority examines the application for registration for a trade under Paragraph 339(1) to ensure that the statutory conditions for the exercise of the trade applied for are satisfied by the applicant at the location concerned. If they are not, the district administrative authority must, under Paragraph 340(7), make a finding to that effect by administrative decision and prohibit the exercise of the trade in question.

The main proceedings

9. On 13 June 1995, Clean Car applied to the Magistrat der Stadt Wien (Vienna City Council) to register for the trade of 'maintenance and care of motor vehicles (service station) excluding all artisanal activity'. When making that application, it stated that it had appointed Mr Rudolf Henssen, a German national residing in Berlin, as manager in accordance with the GewO 1994; it further indicated that Mr Henssen was actively seeking to rent accommodation in Austria and that the declaration relating to his residence there would be forwarded in due course.

10. By decision of 20 July 1995, the Magistrat der Stadt Wien found that the statutory prerequisites for the exercise of that trade were not satisfied and therefore prohibited it, on the ground that the manager must satisfy the personal conditions laid down for the exercise of the trade in question, must have a residence in Austria and must be in a position to act effectively as manager in the business, in accordance with Paragraph 39(2) of the GewO 1994.

11. On 10 August 1995, Clean Car lodged an administrative appeal against that decision with the Landeshauptmann von Wien, submitting that the person appointed as manager now had a residence in Austria and that, in any event, since the accession of the Republic of Austria to the European Union, residence anywhere in the European Union was sufficient to satisfy the statutory requirements.

12. By decision of 2 November 1995, the Landeshauptmann von Wien dismissed the appeal, principally on the ground that, because of the constitutive nature of the application to register a trade, the material factual and legal situation was that pertaining at the time the application was lodged, when the person appointed as manager did not yet have a residence in Austria.

13. On 21 December 1995, Clean Car brought proceedings before the Verwaltungsgerichtshof, submitting that the arguments based on Community law had been ignored in the decisions of both the Magistrat der Stadt Wien and the Landeshauptmann von Wien. Clean Car referred in particular to Articles 6 and 48 of the EC Treaty and submitted that the person whom it had appointed as manager was entitled, as an employee in its service and thus as a worker, to enjoy the right to freedom of movement established by Article 48.

14. Taking the view that, in order to reach a decision in the case, it must determine whether the Austrian legislation prohibiting the owner of a trade undertaking from appointing as manager an employee not resident in Austria is contrary to Community law as laid down in Article 48 of the Treaty and Articles 1 to 3 of Regulation No 1612/68, the Verwaltungsgerichtshof stayed proceedings and requested a preliminary ruling from the Court on the following questions:

'1. Are Article 48 of the EC Treaty and Articles 1 to 3 of Regulation No 1612/68 to be interpreted as meaning that employers in the host State also derive therefrom the right to employ workers who are nationals of another Member State without being bound by conditions which – even if they do not depend on nationality – are typically linked with nationality?

2. If employers of the host State have the right stated in Question 1: Are Article 48 of the EC Treaty and Articles 1 to 3 of Regulation No 1612/68 to be interpreted as meaning that a provision such as Paragraph 39(2) of the Gewerbeordnung 1994, under which the owner of a trade may appoint as a manager for trade law purposes only a person whose residence is in the host State (Austria), is consistent therewith?'

15. In its order for reference, the national court indicates that the first matter to be considered is whether the provisions of Community law concerning freedom of movement for workers, which are addressed primarily to workers as such, may also be relied upon by employers. If so, the question then arises whether those provisions preclude a rule such as that in Paragraph 39(2) of the GewO 1994, having regard in particular to the limitations envisaged in Article 48(3) of the Treaty and to the fact that, under Paragraph 370(2) of the GewO 1994, the manager is responsible, in the exercise of the trade, for compliance with the applicable statutory provisions.

The first question

16. By its first question, the national court seeks in substance to determine whether the rule of equal treatment in the context of freedom of movement for workers, enshrined in Article 48 of the Treaty and Articles 1 to 3 of Regulation No 1612/68, may also be relied upon by an employer in order to employ, in the Member State in which he is established, workers who are nationals of another Member State.

17. It should be borne in mind, first of all, that Articles 1 to 3 of Regulation No 1612/68 merely clarify and give effect to the rights already conferred by Article 48 of the Treaty (see, to that effect, Case C-419/92 *Scholz* v *Opera Universitaria di Cagliari* [1994] ECR I-505, paragraph 6).

18. Next, it must be noted that Article 48(1) states, in general terms, that freedom of movement for workers is to be secured within the Community. Under Article 48(2) and (3), such freedom of movement is to entail the abolition of any discrimination based on nationality between workers of the Member States as regards employment, remuneration and other conditions of work and employment, and to entail the right, subject to limitations justified on grounds of public policy, public security or public health, to accept offers of employment actually made, to move freely within the territory of Member States for that purpose, to stay in a Member State in order

to be employed there under the same conditions as nationals of that State and to remain there after such employment.

19. Whilst those rights are undoubtedly enjoyed by those directly referred to – namely, workers – there is nothing in the wording of Article 48 to indicate that they may not be relied upon by others, in particular employers.

20. It must further be noted that, in order to be truly effective, the right of workers to be engaged and employed without discrimination necessarily entails as a corollary the employer's entitlement to engage them in accordance with the rules governing freedom of movement for workers.

21. Those rules could easily be rendered nugatory if Member States could circumvent the prohibitions which they contain merely by imposing on employers requirements to be met by any worker whom they wish to employ which, if imposed directly on the worker, would constitute restrictions on the exercise of the right to freedom of movement to which that worker is entitled under Article 48 of the Treaty.

22. Finally, the above interpretation is corroborated both by Article 2 of Regulation No 1612/68 and by the Court's case-law.

23. It is made explicitly clear in Article 2 of Regulation No 1612/68 that any employer pursuing an activity in the territory of a Member State and any national of a Member State must be able to conclude and perform contracts of employment in accordance with the provisions in force laid down by law, regulation or administrative action, without any discrimination resulting therefrom.

24. It is, furthermore, clear from, in particular, the judgment in Case C-415/93 *Union Royale Belge des Sociétés de Football Association and Others* v *Bosman and Others* [1995] ECR I-4921, paragraphs 84 to 86, that justifications on grounds of public policy, public security or public health, as envisaged in Article 48(3) of the Treaty, may be relied upon not only by Member States in order to justify limitations on freedom of movement for workers under their laws, regulations or administrative provisions but also by individuals in order to justify such limitations under agreements or other measures adopted by persons governed by private law. Thus, if an employer may rely on a derogation under Article 48(3), he must also be able to rely on the same principles under, in particular, Article 48(1) and (2).

25. In the light of those considerations, the answer to the first question must be that the rule of equal treatment in the context of freedom of movement for workers, enshrined in Article 48 of the Treaty, may also be relied upon by an employer in order to employ, in the Member State in which he is established, workers who are nationals of another Member State.

The second question

26. By its second question, the national court wishes to ascertain, in substance, whether Article 48 of the Treaty precludes a Member State from providing that the owner of an undertaking exercising a trade on the territory of that State may not appoint as manager a person not resident there.

27. The Court has consistently held that the rules of equal treatment prohibit not only overt discrimination based on nationality but also all covert forms of discrimination which, by applying other distinguishing criteria, achieve in practice the same result (see, *inter alia,* Case C-266/95 *Merino García* v *Bundesanstalt für Arbeit* [1997] ECR I-3279, paragraph 33).

28. It is true that a provision such as Paragraph 39(2) of the GewO 1994 applies without regard to the nationality of the person to be appointed as manager.

29. However, as the Court has already held (see, *inter alia*, Case C-279/93 *Finanzamt Köln-Altstadt* v *Schumacker* [1995] ECR I-225, paragraph 28), national rules under which a distinction is drawn on the basis of residence are liable to operate mainly to the detriment of nationals of other Member States, as non-residents are in the majority of cases foreigners.

30. A requirement that nationals of the other Member States must reside in the State concerned in order to be appointed managers of undertakings exercising a trade is therefore such as to constitute indirect discrimination based on nationality, contrary to Article 48(2) of the Treaty.

31. It would be otherwise only if the imposition of such a residence requirement were based on objective considerations independent of the nationality of the employees concerned and proportionate to a legitimate aim pursued by the national law (see, to that effect, Case C-15/96 *Schöning-Kougebetopoulou* v *Freie und Hansestadt Hamburg* [1998] ECR I-47, paragraph 21).

32. In that context, as stated at paragraph 15 above, the national court has expressly referred in its order for reference to the fact that, under Paragraph 370(2) of the GewO 1994, the person appointed as manager is responsible for compliance with the applicable statutory provisions in the exercise of the trade concerned and fines may be imposed upon him.

33. In their written observations, the Landeshauptmann von Wien and the Austrian Government have explained that the residence requirement is intended to ensure that the manager can be served with notice of the fines which may be imposed upon him and that they can be enforced against him. The intention is also to ensure that the manager satisfies the other requirement imposed on him by Paragraph 39(2) of

the GewO 1994, namely that he must be in a position to act effectively as such in the business.

34. In that regard, the residence requirement must be held either to be inappropriate for ensuring that the aim pursued is achieved or to go beyond what is necessary for that purpose.

35. In the first place, the fact that the manager resides in the Member State in which the undertaking is established and exercises its trade does not itself necessarily ensure that he will be in a position to act effectively as manager in the business. A manager residing in the State but at a considerable distance from the place at which the undertaking exercises its trade should normally find it more difficult to act effectively in the business than a person whose place of residence, even if in another Member State, is at no great distance from that at which the undertaking exercises its trade.

36. Secondly, other less restrictive measures, such as serving notice of fines at the registered office of the undertaking employing the manager and ensuring that they will be paid by requiring a guarantee to be provided beforehand, would make it possible to ensure that the manager can be served with notice of any such fines imposed upon him and that they can be enforced against him.

37. Finally, it must be added, even such measures as those just indicated are not justified by the aims in question if the service of notice of fines imposed on a manager resident in another Member State and their enforcement against him are guaranteed by an international convention concluded between the Member State in which the undertaking exercises its trade and that in which the manager resides.

38. It must be concluded, therefore, that the residence requirement in question constitutes indirect discrimination.

39. As regards the justifications based on Article 48(3) of the Treaty, to which the national court has also referred, it must be observed that a general rule of the kind in issue in the main proceedings cannot be justified on any grounds of public security or public health.

40. As regards the justification on grounds of public policy, also envisaged in Article 48(3) of the Treaty, the Court has already held (Case 30/77 *R* v *Bouchereau* [1977] ECR 1999) that in so far as it may justify certain restrictions on the free movement of persons subject to Community law, recourse to the concept of public policy as used in that provision presupposes, in any event, the existence, in addition to the perturbation of the social order which any infringement of the law involves, of a genuine and sufficiently serious threat affecting one of the fundamental interests of society.

41. Here, however, it does not appear from the documents in the case that any such interest is liable to be affected if the owner of an undertaking is free to appoint, for the purpose of exercising that undertaking's trade, a manager who does not reside in the Member State concerned.

42. It is thus also impossible for a national provision such as that in issue in the main proceedings, which requires any worker appointed as manager for the exercise of a trade to reside in the State concerned, to be justified on grounds of public policy within the meaning of Article 48(3) of the Treaty.

43. In view of the foregoing considerations, the answer to the second question must be that Article 48 of the Treaty precludes a Member State from providing that the owner of an undertaking exercising a trade on the territory of that State may not appoint as manager a person not resident there.

Costs

[Para. 44 omitted]

On those grounds,

THE COURT (Sixth Chamber),

in answer to the questions referred to it by the Verwaltungsgerichtshof by order of 8 October 1996, hereby rules:

1. **The rule of equal treatment in the context of freedom of movement for workers, enshrined in Article 48 of the EC Treaty, may also be relied upon by an employer in order to employ, in the Member State in which he is established, workers who are nationals of another Member State.**

2. **Article 48 of the Treaty precludes a Member State from providing that the owner of an undertaking exercising a trade on the territory of that State may not appoint as manager a person not resident there.**

Comments and questions

The judgment in Case C-350/96 *Clean Car Autoservice GesmbH* v *Landeshauptmann von Wien* [1998] ECR I-2521, marked a watershed, even though its precedent value may be disputed on the grounds that the judgment was not given by the CJEU's Full Court. In its judgment, the CJEU ruled that *employers* can be covered by the scope of Article 45 TFEU (formerly Article 48 EEC Treaty), so that they can also rely on the terms of its provisions; cf. paragraph 19 of the judgment. However, it is not absolutely clear from the wording of Article 45 TFEU that employers can rely on it. Consider what principle of interpretation the CJEU used to arrive at this decision, and where is this expressed in the judgment?

In its judgment the CJEU argued that its interpretation of Article 45 TFEU was based on its own previous practice. It referred to its decision in Case C-415/93 *Union royale belge des sociétés de football association* v *Bosman* [1995] ECR I-4921, printed below, according to which sports organisations can rely on the public policy grounds referred to in Article 45(3) TFEU to justify restrictions resulting from agreements entered into between private individuals. However, this argument is presumably not absolute since in the *Bosman* case the CJEU itself argued that sports organisations such as FIFA and UEFA have regulatory powers over their members which correspond to the powers of a public authority so they are covered by the obligations in Article 45 TFEU. This means that these organisations have the same scope as Member States for relying on the public policy provisions in Article 45(3) TFEU. The reference to the *Bosman* case can therefore hardly be accepted as supporting the view that, since a private employer can in general rely on the exemptions in Article 45(3) TFEU, therefore a private employer can rely on the principles laid down in Article 45(1) and (2) TFEU.

In his Opinion in the case, the Advocate General argued that the CJEU should answer the first question to the effect that: 'employers in the host State derive from Article [45 TFEU] the directly effective right to employ workers who are nationals of another Member State without being bound by national rules which discriminate, directly or indirectly, on grounds of the nationality of the workers in question.' The Advocate General based this proposal on three different observations.

First, he noted that, although Article 45 TFEU is couched in terms of rights which are, of their nature, attributed to workers, the provision does not expressly identify any particular beneficiary of the rights. He argued that it would add greatly to the effectiveness of these rights and prohibitions if they could also be invoked by economic actors other than workers. He also pointed out that the freedom of movement of workers should not merely be seen in terms of workers' personal rights, since ultimately it serves an objective of general interest, provided for in Article 3(c) TEC on the establishment of an internal market characterised by the abolition, as between Member States, of obstacles to the free movement of persons.

Second, the Advocate General argued that it is also well established that Article 45 TFEU gives rise to rights which are directly effective before national courts.

Third, in his review of the practice of the CJEU, the Advocate General noted that: 'It would be strange if consumers had a directly effective [Union] law right to travel to other Member States to avail of tourist or other services, or to shop for goods, but employers did not have an equivalent right to travel to recruit workers in another Member State. It would also be illogical if an employer could not complain of discriminatory limitations of his ability to hire workers abroad, whereas a recruiting agency which he hired to do so could complain before the national courts about such restrictions on its freedom to provide services.' In order to bring freedom of movement for service providers and for workers into line, thus in accordance with this reasoning it was necessary to allow Article 45 TFEU to have direct effect in relation to employers.

To what extent do you find the arguments of the Advocate General reflected in the judgment of the CJEU?

In paragraph 30 of the judgment it was stated that the Austrian requirement that directors of a company must be resident in Austria constituted indirect discrimination based on nationality, contrary to Article 45(2) TFEU, since non-resident directors will most often be nationals of other Member States. The CJEU here used a *formal discrimination criterion*, since discrimination presupposed *direct and overt discrimination based on nationality*. Such discrimination can only be justified on the grounds referred to in Article 45(3) and (4) TFEU. On the other hand, if national rules apply regardless of nationality, but where in reality they adversely affect nationals of other Member States, this will be *indirect (or hidden) discrimination*; here nationals from other Member States are discriminated against, even if the discrimination is formally based on criteria other than nationality; cf. paragraph 27. Indirect discrimination is prohibited, unless it can be justified on objective grounds (the 'Rule of Reason' or the '*Cassis de Dijon*' doctrine), and is proportionate in relation to the lawful aims of the national law, see Case C-237/94 *O'Flynn* v *Adjudication Officer* [1996] ECR I-2617, printed below.

The CJEU dismissed the argument that the residential requirement was intended to ensure that the penalties to which a member of a board of directors may be subject should be fully enforceable against them and that the board of directors should be able to take part in the running of the business. Do you think this decision is reasonable?

The CJEU also dismissed the claim that considerations of public policy, as referred to in Article 458(3) TFEU, can justify the Austrian residence requirements, since a reference to public policy would presume a genuine and sufficiently serious threat affecting one of the fundamental interests of society; cf. paragraph 40 of the judgment.

Can a German employer rely on Article 45 TFEU in a case against the Danish authorities where the Danish law on the registration of cars means that a Danish national, who is resident in Denmark and works for a German company, and who is provided with a company car for use in working both in Germany and Denmark, may only drive the company car if it is registered in Denmark? See Case C-464/02 *Commission* v *Denmark* [2005] ECR I-7929 (the *Company cars* case), printed below.

JUDGMENT OF THE COURT (Grand Chamber)
7 September 2004

Michel Trojani v Centre public d'aide sociale de Bruxelles (CPAS).
(Reference for a preliminary ruling: Tribunal du travail de Bruxelles – Belgium)

'Freedom of movement of persons – Citizenship of the European Union – Right of residence – Directive 90/364/EEC – Limitations and conditions – Person working in a hostel in return for benefits in kind – Entitlement to social assistance benefits'

Case C-456/02

Judgment

1. This reference for a preliminary ruling concerns the interpretation of Articles 18 EC, 39 EC, 43 EC and 49 EC; Article 7(1) of Regulation (EEC) No 1612/68 of the Council of 15 October 1968 on freedom of movement for workers within the Community (OJ, English Special Edition 1968 (II), p. 475), as amended by Council Regulation (EEC) No 2434/92 of 27 July 1992 (OJ 1992 L 245, p. 1) ('Regulation No 1612/68'); and Council Directive 90/364/EEC of 28 June 1990 on the right of residence (OJ 1990 L 180, p. 26).

2. The reference was made in the course of proceedings between Mr Trojani and the Centre public d'aide sociale de Bruxelles ('the CPAS') concerning its refusal to grant him the minimum subsistence allowance ('the minimex').

Legal background

Community legislation

3. Under Article 18 EC:

'1. Every citizen of the Union shall have the right to move and reside freely within the territory of the Member States, subject to the limitations and conditions laid down in this Treaty and by the measures adopted to give it effect.

...'

4. Article 39(1) EC reads as follows:

'Freedom of movement for workers shall be secured within the Community.'

5. Under Article 39(3) EC, freedom of movement for workers 'shall entail the right, subject to limitations justified on grounds of public policy, public security or public health:

   ...

   (c) to stay in a Member State for the purpose of employment in accordance with the provisions governing the employment of nationals of that State laid down by law, regulation or administrative action;

   ...'

6. Article 1(1) of Directive 90/364 provides:

   'Member States shall grant the right of residence to nationals of Member States who do not enjoy this right under other provisions of Community law and to members of their families as defined in paragraph 2, provided that they themselves and the members of their families are covered by sickness insurance in respect of all risks in the host Member State and have sufficient resources to avoid becoming a burden on the social assistance system of the host Member State during their period of residence.'

National legislation

7. Article 1 of the Law of 7 August 1974 establishing the right to a minimum subsistence allowance (*Moniteur belge*, 18 September 1974, p. 11363) provides:

   '1. Any Belgian having reached the age of majority, who is actually resident in Belgium and who does not have adequate resources and is not able to obtain them either by his own efforts or by other means, is entitled to a minimum subsistence allowance.

   ...'

8. Under Article 1 of the Royal Decree of 27 March 1987 (*Moniteur belge*, 7 April 1987, p. 5086) extending the scope of the Law of 7 August 1974 establishing the right to a minimum subsistence allowance to persons not possessing Belgian nationality:

   'The scope of the Law of 7 August 1974 establishing the right to a minimum subsistence allowance is extended to the following persons:

   1. those to whom Regulation (EEC) No 1612/68 of the Council of the European Communities of 15 October 1968 on freedom of movement for workers within the Community applies;

   ...'

The main proceedings and the reference for a preliminary ruling

9. Mr Trojani is a French national who after a short stay in Belgium in 1972, during which he is said to have worked as a self-employed person in the sales sector, returned there in 2000. He resided, without being registered, first at a campsite in Blankenberge and then from December 2001 in Brussels. After a stay at the Jacques Brel youth hostel, he was given accommodation in a Salvation Army hostel from 8 January 2002, where in return for board and lodging and some pocket money he does various jobs for about 30 hours a week as part of a personal socio-occupational reintegration programme.

10. As he had no resources, he approached the CPAS with a view to obtaining the minimex, on the grounds that he had to pay EUR 400 a month to the hostel and should also be able to leave the hostel and live independently.

11. The CPAS's refusal, on the grounds that, first, Mr Trojani did not have Belgian nationality and, second, he could not benefit from the application of Regulation No 1612/68, was the subject of proceedings in the Tribunal du travail de Bruxelles (Labour Court, Brussels).

12. That court granted Mr Trojani the right to receive provisional financial assistance of EUR 300 from the CPAS. It also decided to stay the proceedings and refer the following questions to the Court for a preliminary ruling:

   '1. Can a citizen of the Union in the factual circumstances described in this judgment

   - who has temporary leave to reside,
   - does not have sufficient resources,
   - carries out work for the hostel to the extent of approximately 30 hours a week in the context of a personal reintegration programme,
   - and receives in return benefits in kind which cover his basic needs at the hostel itself claim a right of residence
   - as a worker within the meaning of Article 39 EC or Article 7(1) of Regulation No 1612/68,
   - or as a worker pursuing an activity as a self-employed person within the meaning of Article 43 EC,
   - or as a person providing a service, in view of the tasks he performs at the hostel, or as a person for whom services are intended, in view of the benefits in kind granted to him by that hostel, within the meaning of Article 49 EC,
   - or merely because he is taking part in a programme for his socio-occupational reintegration?

2. If not, can he rely directly on Article 18 EC, which guarantees the right to move and reside freely in the territory of another Member State of the Union, merely in his capacity as a European citizen?

   What then becomes of the conditions laid down by Directive 90/364 ... and/or the 'limitations and conditions' laid down in the EC Treaty, in particular the condition as to minimum resources which, if it were applied on entry to the host country, would deprive him of the very substance of the right of residence?

   If, on the other hand, the right of residence arises automatically on the basis of citizenship of the Union, could the host State subsequently refuse an application for the minimex or for social assistance (non-contributory benefits), curtailing his right of residence on the ground that he does not have sufficient resources, when those benefits are granted to nationals of the host country subject to conditions which Belgians too must satisfy (proof of their availability for work, proof that they are in need)?

   Must the host country comply with any other rules in order to avoid rendering meaningless the right of residence, such as a duty to assess the situation in the light of the fact that the application for the minimex or for social assistance is temporary, or to take into account the principle of proportionality (would the burden on the State in question be unreasonable)?'

The questions referred for a preliminary ruling

The first question

13. By its first question, the national court essentially asks whether a person in a situation such as that of the claimant in the main proceedings can claim a right of residence as a worker, a self-employed person or a provider or recipient of services, within the meaning of Articles 39 EC, 43 EC and 49 EC respectively.

14. In the context of freedom of movement for workers, it should be recalled that Article 39(3)(c) EC grants nationals of the Member States the right of residence in the territory of a Member State for the purpose of employment.

15. As the Court has held, the concept of 'worker' within the meaning of Article 39 EC has a specific Community meaning and must not be interpreted narrowly. Any person who pursues activities which are real and genuine, to the exclusion of activities on such a small scale as to be regarded as purely marginal and ancillary, must be regarded as a 'worker'. The essential feature of an employment relationship is, according to that case-law, that for a certain period of time a person performs services for and under the direction of another person in return for which he receives remu-

neration (see, in particular, Case 66/85 *Lawrie-Blum* [1986] ECR 2121, paragraphs 16 and 17, and Case C-138/02 *Collins* [2004] ECR I-0000, paragraph 26).

16. Moreover, neither the *sui generis* nature of the employment relationship under national law, nor the level of productivity of the person concerned, the origin of the funds from which the remuneration is paid or the limited amount of the remuneration can have any consequence in regard to whether or not the person is a worker for the purposes of Community law (see Case 53/81 *Levin* [1982] ECR 1035, paragraph 16; Case 344/87 *Bettray* [1989] ECR 1621, paragraphs 15 and 16; and Case C-188/00 *Kurz* [2002] ECR I-10691, paragraph 32).

17. With respect more particularly to establishing whether the condition of the pursuit of real and genuine activity for remuneration is satisfied, the national court must base its examination on objective criteria and make an overall assessment of all the circumstances of the case relating to the nature both of the activities concerned and of the employment relationship at issue (see Case C-413/01 *Ninni-Orasche* [2003] ECR I-0000, paragraph 27).

18. In this respect, the Court has held that activities cannot be regarded as a real and genuine economic activity if they constitute merely a means of rehabilitation or reintegration for the persons concerned (*Bettray*, paragraph 17).

19. However, that conclusion can be explained only by the particular characteristics of the case in question, which concerned the situation of a person who, by reason of his addiction to drugs, had been recruited on the basis of a national law intended to provide work for persons who, for an indefinite period, are unable, by reason of circumstances related to their situation, to work under normal conditions (see, to that effect, Case C-1/97 *Birden* [1998] ECR I-7747, paragraphs 30 and 31).

20. In the present case, as is apparent from the decision making the reference, Mr Trojani performs, for the Salvation Army and under its direction, various jobs for approximately 30 hours a week, as part of a personal reintegration programme, in return for which he receives benefits in kind and some pocket money.

21. Under the relevant provisions of the decree of the Commission communautaire française of 27 May 1999 on the grant of authorisation and subsidies to hostels (*Moniteur belge*, 18 June 1999, p. 23101), the Salvation Army has the task of receiving, accommodating and providing psycho-social assistance appropriate to the recipients in order to promote their autonomy, physical well-being and reintegration in society. For that purpose it must agree with each person concerned a personal reintegration programme setting out the objectives to be attained and the means to be employed to attain them.

22. Having established that the benefits in kind and money provided by the Salvation Army to Mr Trojani constitute the consideration for the services performed by him for and under the direction of the hostel, the national court has thereby established the existence of the constituent elements of any paid employment relationship, namely subordination and the payment of remuneration.

23. For the claimant in the main proceedings to have the status of worker, however, the national court, in the assessment of the facts which is within its exclusive jurisdiction, would have to establish that the paid activity in question is real and genuine.

24. The national court must in particular ascertain whether the services actually performed by Mr Trojani are capable of being regarded as forming part of the normal labour market. For that purpose, account may be taken of the status and practices of the hostel, the content of the social reintegration programme, and the nature and details of performance of the services.

25. On the question of the applicability of Articles 43 EC and 49 EC, it must be stated that, in the case at issue in the main proceedings, neither of those provisions of the EC Treaty may be relied on as a legal basis for a right of residence.

26. As may be seen from paragraph 20 above, Mr Trojani performs services on a continuing basis for and under the direction of the Salvation Army, in return for which he receives a remuneration.

27. Now, first, the freedom of establishment provided for in Articles 43 EC to 48 EC, includes only the right to take up and pursue all types of self-employed activity, to set up and manage undertakings, and to set up agencies, branches or subsidiaries (see, in particular, Case C-255/97 *Pfeiffer* [1999] ECR I-2835, paragraph 18, and Case C-79/01 *Payroll and Others* [2002] ECR I-8923, paragraph 24). Paid activities are therefore excluded.

28. Second, according to the settled case-law of the Court, an activity carried out on a permanent basis, or at least without a foreseeable limit to its duration, does not fall within the Community provisions concerning the provision of services (see Case 196/87 *Steymann* [1988] ECR 6159, paragraph 16, and Case C-215/01 *Schnitzer* [2003] I-0000, paragraphs 27 to 29).

29. In those circumstances, the answer to the first question must be that a person in a situation such as that of the claimant in the main proceedings, first, does not come under Articles 43 EC and 49 EC and, second, can claim a right of residence as a worker within the meaning of Article 39 EC only if the paid activity he carries out is real and genuine. It is for the national court to carry out the examinations of fact necessary to determine whether that is so in the case pending before it.

The second question

30. By its second question, the national court essentially asks whether, if the first question is answered in the negative, a person in the situation of the claimant in the main proceedings may, simply by virtue of being a citizen of the European Union, enjoy a right of residence in the host Member State by the direct application of Article 18 EC.

31. It must be recalled that the right to reside in the territory of the Member States is conferred directly on every citizen of the Union by Article 18(1) EC (see Case C-413/99 *Baumbast and R* [2002] ECR I-7091, paragraph 84). Mr Trojani therefore has the right to rely on that provision of the Treaty simply as a citizen of the Union.

32. That right is not unconditional, however. It is conferred subject to the limitations and conditions laid down by the Treaty and by the measures adopted to give it effect.

33. Among those limitations and conditions, it follows from Article 1 of Directive 90/364 that Member States can require of the nationals of a Member State who wish to enjoy the right to reside within their territory that they themselves and the members of their families be covered by sickness insurance in respect of all risks in the host Member State and have sufficient resources to avoid becoming a burden on the social assistance system of that State during their period of residence.

34. As the Court has previously held, those limitations and conditions must be applied in compliance with the limits imposed by Community law and in accordance with the general principles of that law, in particular the principle of proportionality (*Baumbast and R*, paragraph 91).

35. It follows from the judgment making the reference that a lack of resources was precisely the reason why Mr Trojani sought to receive a benefit such as the minimex.

36. In those circumstances, a citizen of the Union in a situation such as that of the claimant in the main proceedings does not derive from Article 18 EC the right to reside in the territory of a Member State of which he is not a national, for want of sufficient resources within the meaning of Directive 90/364. Contrary to the circumstances of the case of *Baumbast and R* (paragraph 92), there is no indication that, in a situation such as that at issue in the main proceedings, the failure to recognise that right would go beyond what is necessary to achieve the objective pursued by that directive.

37. However, it must be observed that, according to information put before the Court, Mr Trojani is lawfully resident in Belgium, as is attested by the residence permit

which has in the meantime been issued to him by the municipal authorities of Brussels.

38. It should be recalled here that it is for the Court to provide the national court with all those elements for the interpretation of Community law which may be of assistance in adjudicating on the case pending before it, whether or not that court has specifically referred to them in its questions (see inter alia, to that effect, Case C-241/89 *SARPP* [1990] ECR I-4695, paragraph 8; Case C-315/92 *Verband Sozialer Wettbewerb ('Clinique')* [1994] ECR I-317, paragraph 9; and Case C-87/97 *Consorzio per la tutela del formaggio Gorgonzola* [1999] ECR I-1301, paragraph 16).

39. In the context of the present case, it should be examined more particularly whether, despite the conclusion in paragraph 36 above, a citizen of the Union in a situation such as that of the claimant in the main proceedings may rely on Article 12 EC, under which, within the scope of application of the Treaty and without prejudice to any special provisions contained therein, all discrimination on grounds of nationality is prohibited.

40. In the present case, it must be stated that, while the Member States may make residence of a citizen of the Union who is not economically active conditional on his having sufficient resources, that does not mean that such a person cannot, during his lawful residence in the host Member State, benefit from the fundamental principle of equal treatment as laid down in Article 12 EC.

41. In that connection three points should be made.

42. First, as the Court has held, a social assistance benefit such as the minimex falls within the scope of the Treaty (see Case C-184/99 *Grzelczyk* [2001] ECR I-6193, in particular paragraph 46).

43. Second, with regard to such benefits, a citizen of the Union who is not economically active may rely on Article 12 EC where he has been lawfully resident in the host Member State for a certain time or possesses a residence permit.

44. Third, national legislation such as that at issue in the main proceedings, in so far as it does not grant the social assistance benefit to citizens of the European Union, non-nationals of the Member State, who reside there lawfully even though they satisfy the conditions required of nationals of that Member State, constitutes discrimination on grounds of nationality prohibited by Article 12 EC.

45. It should be added that it remains open to the host Member State to take the view that a national of another Member State who has recourse to social assistance no longer fulfils the conditions of his right of residence. In such a case the host Member State may, within the limits imposed by Community law, take a measure to re-

move him. However, recourse to the social assistance system by a citizen of the Union may not automatically entail such a measure (see, to that effect, *Grzelczyk*, paragraphs 42 and 43).

46. Consequently, the answer to the second question must be that a citizen of the Union who does not enjoy a right of residence in the host Member State under Articles 39 EC, 43 EC or 49 EC may, simply as a citizen of the Union, enjoy a right of residence there by direct application of Article 18(1) EC. The exercise of that right is subject to the limitations and conditions referred to in that provision, but the competent authorities must ensure that those limitations and conditions are applied in compliance with the general principles of Community law, in particular the principle of proportionality. However, once it is ascertained that a person in a situation such as that of the claimant in the main proceedings is in possession of a residence permit, he may rely on Article 12 EC in order to be granted a social assistance benefit such as the minimex.

Costs

[Para. 47 omitted]

On those grounds,

THE COURT (Grand Chamber)

hereby rules:

1. **A person in a situation such as that of the claimant in the main proceedings, first, does not come under Articles 43 EC and 49 EC and, second, can claim a right of residence as a worker within the meaning of Article 39 EC only if the paid activity he carries out is real and genuine. It is for the national court to carry out the examinations of fact necessary to determine whether that is so in the case pending before it.**

2. **A citizen of the European Union who does not enjoy a right of residence in the host Member State under Articles 39 EC, 43 EC or 49 EC may, simply as a citizen of the Union, enjoy a right of residence there by direct application of Article 18(1) EC. The exercise of that right is subject to the limitations and conditions referred to in that provision, but the competent authorities must ensure that those limitations and conditions are applied in compliance with the general principles of Community law, in particular the principle of proportionality. However, once it is ascertained that a person in a situation such as that of the claimant in the main proceedings is in possession of a residence permit, he may rely on Article 12 EC in order to be granted a social assistance benefit such as the minimex.**

Comments and questions

In 2000 Michel Trojani, a French citizen, moved to Belgium. He was homeless and so lived in a shelter for homeless people. He carried out various tasks in the shelter for about 30 hours per week, and in return he received lodging and pocket money. When after some time he applied to the Belgian authorities for a small social benefit, this was refused. The principal grounds for the refusal were that Michel Trojani was not a Belgian citizen and that he was not a worker.

In his Opinion, the Advocate General made a detailed review of the CJEU's practice with regard to the concept of a 'worker'. He found that each of the following four conditions should be satisfied:

- the activity must last for a certain period,
- there must be a relationship of subordination,
- the person carrying out the activities must be remunerated, and
- there must be real and genuine economic activity.

As for the first condition, he noted that in fact this would always be satisfied, unless the activity was of such minimal extent as to be characterised as purely marginal and ancillary.

The Advocate General did not spend much time on the condition that there should be a relationship of subordination. However, he remarked that in Case 196/87 *Udo Steymann* v *Staatssecretaris van Justitie* [1988] ECR 6159 (discussed in the comments on Case 53/81 *Levin* [1982] ECR 1035 above), it appeared that the CJEU had not considered whether there had been such a relationship of subordination at all.

As for the requirement that there should be remuneration for the work, the Advocate General noted that even people who receive minimal payment could be regarded as workers. Thus it was not necessary that the person in question should be able to care for him or herself. Nor is the person's productivity decisive. The only requirement is that the activity should not be completely insignificant.

Thereafter, what mattered was whether the fourth and last condition was met. The Advocate General found that the activities of Michel Trojani could not be regarded as real and genuine economic activity. Michel Trojani undertook cleaning and kitchen work, which the Advocate General compared with the kind of tasks which sometimes go with staying in a youth hostel. On this basis the Advocate General proposed that the CJEU should deny that Michel Trojani could be regarded as worker covered by Article 45 TFEU.

The CJEU was notably less categorical than the Advocate General in its reply to the question before it.

Since the referring national court had established that Michel Trojani received money and goods and services in kind for his work, and that he carried out his work in accordance with the instructions from the shelter, the CJEU could quickly decide that the first conditions were satisfied. Just as the Advocate General did, the CJEU therefore turned its attention to the fourth condition: the question of whether the work which

Michel Trojani carried out was a real and genuine economic activity covered by Article 45 TFEU.

The CJEU noted that there was not real and genuine economic activity where the persons involved were not able to work under normal conditions and were therefore in job training. In such cases these were merely a means of rehabilitation for the persons concerned, or a means for finding work, but did not constitute work itself. The work which Michel Trojani carried out for the shelter was arranged on an individual basis, so it was not possible to say anything general about whether there was a real and genuine economic activity. The referring court therefore has to decide whether or not there was such activity. In this connection it should, among other things, determine whether the tasks carried out by Michel Trojani would normally be regarded as belonging in the employment market.

Consider what the CJEU meant by the preceding statement.

Consider in general what circumstances would support the argument that Michel Trojani should be regarded as a worker in respect of receiving social support from the Belgian authorities, and what circumstances argue against this.

Note that in paragraph 43 of the judgment the CJEU held that a citizen of the Union who is not economically active may rely on the principle of equality in Article 18(1) TFEU where he has been lawfully resident in the host Member State for a certain time or possesses a residence permit (under national law.).

As stated above in Chapter 3 in the comments on Case C-333/13 *Dano*, following this judgment under the law today only in cases where a Union citizen is lawfully resident pursuant to the Free Movement Directive (Directive 2004/38) can a Union citizen claim equal treatment with regard to social assistance pursuant to Articles 18 and 21 TFEU. On this basis paragraphs 37-44 of the *Trojani* judgment must be regarded as having been overruled by the *Dano* judgment.

Consider whether Union citizens from other EU Member States who have been resident in Sweden for at least three months, and who are not in active employment, have a right to spend the night at Swedish hostels for homeless people on the same terms as Swedish citizens. The hostels are run either by municipal authorities or are mutually owned bodies which receive State support. In this connection, see Articles 6, 14(1) and 24(1) of Directive 2004/38 on the right of citizens of the Union and their family members to move and reside freely within the territory of the Member States.

JUDGMENT OF THE COURT (Third Chamber)
21 February 2013

L.N. v Styrelsen for Videregående Uddannelser og Uddannelsesstøtte. (Request for a preliminary ruling from the Ankenævnet for Statens Uddannelsesstøtte – Denmark)

'Citizenship of the Union – Freedom of movement for workers – Principle of equal treatment – Article 45(2) TFEU – Regulation (EEC) No 1612/68 – Article 7(2) – Directive 2004/38/EC – Article 24(1) and (2) – Derogation from the principle of equal treatment for maintenance aid for studies consisting in student grants or student loans – European Union citizen studying in a host Member State – Paid employment prior to and subsequent to the start of studies – Principal objective of the person concerned at the time of entry on the territory of the host Member State – Effect on his classification as worker and on his entitlement to student grants'

Case C-46/12

Judgment

1. This request for a preliminary ruling concerns the interpretation of Article 7(1)(c) and Article 24(2) of Directive 2004/38/EC of the European Parliament and of the Council of 29 April 2004 on the right of citizens of the Union and their family members to move and reside freely within the territory of the Member States amending Regulation (EEC) No 1612/68 and repealing Directives 64/221/EEC, 68/360/EEC, 72/194/EEC, 73/148/EEC, 75/34/EEC, 75/35/EEC, 90/364/EEC, 90/365/EEC and 93/96/EEC (OJ 2004 L 158, p. 77, corrigenda OJ 2004 L 229, p. 35 and OJ 2005 L 197, p. 34).

2. The request has been made in proceedings between Mr N. and the Styrelsen for Videregående Uddannelser og Uddannelsesstøtte (Danish Agency for Higher Education and Educational Support) ('the VUS') concerning the latter's refusal to grant him education assistance.

Legal context

European Union legislation

Regulation No (EEC) No 1612/68

3. Article 7 of Regulation (EEC) No 1612/68 of the Council of 15 October 1968 on freedom of movement for workers within the Community (OJ, English Special Edition 1968 (II), p. 475) provides:

'1. A worker who is a national of a Member State may not, in the territory of another Member State, be treated differently from national workers by reason of his nationality in respect of any conditions of employment and work, in particular as regards remuneration, dismissal, and should he become unemployed, reinstatement or re-employment.

2. He shall enjoy the same social and tax advantages as national workers.

...'

Directive 2004/38

4. Recitals 1, 3, 10, 20 and 21 in the preamble to Directive 2004/38 state:

(1) Citizenship of the Union confers on every citizen of the Union a primary and individual right to move and reside freely within the territory of the Member States, subject to the limitations and conditions laid down in the Treaty and to the measures adopted to give it effect.

...

(3) Union citizenship should be the fundamental status of nationals of the Member States when they exercise their right of free movement and residence. It is therefore necessary to codify and review the existing Community instruments dealing separately with workers, self-employed persons, as well as students and other inactive persons in order to simplify and strengthen the right of free movement and residence of all Union citizens.

...

(10) Persons exercising their right of residence should not, however, become an unreasonable burden on the social assistance system of the host Member State during an initial period of residence. Therefore, the right of residence for Union citizens and their family members for periods in excess of three months should be subject to conditions.

...

(20) In accordance with the prohibition of discrimination on grounds of nationality, all Union citizens and their family members residing in a Member State on the basis of this Directive should enjoy, in that Member State, equal treatment with nationals in areas covered by the Treaty, subject to such specific provisions as are expressly provided for in the Treaty and secondary law.

(21) However, it should be left to the host Member State to decide whether it will grant social assistance during the first three months of residence, or for a longer period in the case of job-seekers, to Union citizens other than those who are workers or self-employed persons or who retain that status or their

family members, or maintenance assistance for studies, including vocational training, prior to acquisition of the right of permanent residence, to these same persons.'

5. Article 3(1) of Directive 2004/38 provides that that directive is to apply to all Union citizens who move to or reside in a Member State other than that of which they are a national.

6. Article 7(1) and (3) of Directive 2004/38 is worded as follows:

'1. All Union citizens shall have the right of residence on the territory of another Member State for a period of longer than three months if they:
   (a) are workers or self-employed persons in the host Member State; or
   (b) have sufficient resources for themselves and their family members not to become a burden on the social assistance system of the host Member State during their period of residence and have comprehensive sickness insurance cover in the host Member State; or
   (c) – are enrolled at a private or public establishment, accredited or financed by the host Member State on the basis of its legislation or administrative practice, for the principal purpose of following a course of study, including vocational training; and
   – have comprehensive sickness insurance cover in the host Member State and assure the relevant national authority, by means of a declaration or by such equivalent means as they may choose, that they have sufficient resources for themselves and their family members not to become a burden on the social assistance system of the host Member State during their period of residence ...

...

3. For the purposes of paragraph 1(a), a Union citizen who is no longer a worker or self-employed person shall retain the status of worker or self-employed person in the following circumstances:

...

   (d) he/she embarks on vocational training. Unless he/she is involuntarily unemployed, the retention of the status of worker shall require the training to be related to the previous employment.'

7. Article 24 of Directive 2004/38, entitled 'Equal treatment', is worded as follows:

'1. Subject to such specific provisions as are expressly provided for in the Treaty and secondary law, all Union citizens residing on the basis of this Directive in the territory of the host Member State shall enjoy equal treatment with the nationals of that Member State within the scope of the Treaty. The benefit of this right shall be extended to family members who are not nationals of a Member State and who have the right of residence or permanent residence.

2. By way of derogation from paragraph 1, the host Member State shall not be obliged to confer entitlement to social assistance during the first three months of residence or, where appropriate, the longer period provided for in Article 14(4)(b), nor shall it be obliged, prior to acquisition of the right of permanent residence, to grant maintenance aid for studies, including vocational training, consisting in student grants or student loans to persons other than workers, self-employed persons, persons who retain such status and members of their families.'

Danish legislation

8. Paragraph 2a(2) and (4) of Consolidated Law No 661 of 29 June 2009 on the Students' Grants and Loans Scheme (Lovbekendtgørelse nr. 661 af 29. juni 2009 om statens uddannelsesstøtte) (*Folketingstidende* 2005/2006 L 95, Supplement A, p. 2854) is worded as follows:
   '...

   2. Applicants for courses of study who are EU or EEA [European Economic Area] citizens and their family members may receive education assistance for courses of study in Denmark and abroad under the conditions laid down in EU law and the EEA Agreement. EU citizens and EEA citizens who are not workers or self-employed persons in Denmark and their family members shall be entitled to education assistance only after five years' continuous residence in Denmark ...

   ...

   4. The Minister for Education may adopt rules governing non-Danish citizens' entitlement to [education assistance] for education in Denmark and abroad.'

9. Paragraph 2a(2) of Consolidated Law No 661 was implemented by paragraph 67 of Regulation No 455 of 8 June 2009 on State education assistance (Bekendtgørelse nr. 455 af 8. juni 2009 om statens uddannelsesstøtte). Paragraph 67 reads as follows:

   'An EU citizen who is a worker or self-employed person in Denmark under EU law may be granted assistance for education in Denmark or abroad on the same terms as a Danish citizen. A worker or self-employed person under [European Union] law shall also be deemed to include an EU citizen who was previously a worker or self-employed person in Denmark, where there is a substantive and temporal connection between the education and the previous work in Denmark, or an involuntarily unemployed person who, due to health reasons or structural causes on the labour market requires retraining for the purpose of employment in a field which does not have a substantive and temporal connection with the previous work in Denmark.'

10. Under paragraph 3 of Regulation No 474 of 12 May 2011 on residence in Denmark for non-Danish citizens covered by the European Union rules (EU residence law) (Bekendtgørelse nr. 474 af 12. maj 2011 om ophold i Danmark for udlændinge, der er omfattet af Den Europæiske Unions regler (EU-opholdsbekendtgørelsen)):

'1. An EU citizen who is a worker or self-employed person, including service provider, in Denmark, shall have a right of residence for more than the three months provided for in § 2(1) of the Aliens Act (udlændingeloven);

2. An EU citizen who was previously covered by subparagraph (1) but is no longer in active employment retains his or her status as worker or self-employed person,
(1) if the EU citizen is temporarily unemployed due to illness or accident;
(2) if the EU citizen is involuntarily unemployed after having been in paid employment or a self-employed person for over one year, duly recorded, and has registered at an employment office as a job-seeker;
(3) if the EU citizen is involuntarily unemployed after the expiry of a fixed-term employment contract of less than one year's duration, duly recorded, and has registered at an employment office as a job-seeker;
(4) if the EU citizen, in the course of the first 12 months has lost his or her employment involuntarily or is no longer a self-employed person, duly recorded, and has registered at an employment office as a job-seeker; or
(5) if the EU citizen either commences a course of vocational training connected to that person's previous employment or is involuntarily unemployed and commences any type of vocational training.

2. An EU citizen covered by subparagraph 2(3) or (4) shall retain his or her status as worker or self-employed person for six months.

3. An EU citizen who has entered the country to seek employment shall have a right of residence as a job-seeker for up to six months from the time of entering the country. After that time the person shall have a right of residence as a job-seeker in so far as it can be documented that that person is still seeking employment and has actual employment prospects.

...'

The dispute in the main proceedings and the question referred for a preliminary ruling

11. Mr N., a European Union citizen whose nationality is not indicated by the national court, entered Denmark on 6 June 2009.

12. On 10 June 2009 Mr N. was offered full-time employment in an international wholesale firm.

13. On 29 June 2009, the regional government administration issued a certificate of registration to him as a worker on the basis of paragraph 3 of Regulation No 474.

14. The case-file indicates that Mr N. had applied to the Copenhagen Business School ('CBS') before 15 March 2009, the deadline for applications, that is, before entering Danish territory.

15. On 10 August 2009, Mr N. filed an application for education assistance from September 2009 onwards.

16. On 10 September 2009, Mr N. began his studies at the CBS. Mr N. then resigned from his employment with the international wholesale firm, but then carried on other part-time employment.

17. On 27 October 2009, the VUS informed Mr N. that it had rejected his application for education assistance.

18. On 30 October 2009, Mr N. filed a complaint against that decision with the Ankenævnet for Statens Uddannelsesstøtte (Appeals Tribunal, the Danish Students' Grants and Loans Scheme), arguing that he had the status of 'worker' within the meaning of Article 45 TFEU and was entitled to education assistance.

19. On 7 December 2009, the VUS requested the regional government administration to inform it as to whether Mr N. satisfied the criteria for status as a worker within the meaning of Article 45 TFEU. First, in a letter of 11 December 2009, the government administration stated that Mr N. was deemed to be a worker for the period from 29 June to 10 September 2009. Then, by letter of 12 April 2010, it changed the basis for Mr N.'s residence from that of worker to that of student, on the ground that his principal objective in coming to Denmark was to pursue a course of study.

20. By letter of 28 September 2010, the VUS referred the case to the national court. In that letter, it indicated that, in the examination of the evidence in the case, account had to be taken of the fact that Mr N. had come to Denmark for the purpose of pursuing a course of study, since he had applied to the CBS before coming to Denmark

and had commenced his studies shortly thereafter. Consequently, in the VUS's view, Mr N. could not fulfil the requirements to be considered a worker.

21. On 31 August 2011 the national court contacted the VUS, asking for a review as to whether Mr N. came within the concept of 'worker' under EU law. At the same time that court requested the VUS to contact the regional public authorities for clarification on the same question. The VUS indicated that, in its view, there were no grounds to cast doubt on the regional public authorities' earlier decision on the basis for Mr N.'s residence.

22. The national court takes the view that Articles 7(1)(c) and 24(2) of Directive 2004/38 must be interpreted as meaning that a person considered to be a student is not entitled to a study grant even if he can also be classified as a 'worker'. It accords importance to the fact that Article 7(1)(c) of that directive defines a student as a person enrolled at a private or public establishment 'for the principal purpose of following a course of study'.

23. In those circumstances the Ankenævnet for Statens Uddannelsesstøtte (Appeals Tribunal, the Danish Students' Grants and Loans Scheme) decided to stay the proceedings and to refer the following question to the Court of Justice for a preliminary ruling:

'Does Article 7(1)(c), read in conjunction with Article 24(2) of the Directive 2004/38, mean that a Member State (host Member State), in the assessment of whether a person must be deemed to be a worker entitled to education assistance, may take account of the fact that the person entered the host Member State for the principal purpose of following a course of study, with the result that the host Member State is not obliged to grant education assistance aid for studies to that person (see aforementioned Article 24(2))?'

The question referred for a preliminary ruling

24. By its question, the national court asks, in essence, whether Articles 7(1)(c) and 24(2) of Directive 2004/38 must be interpreted as meaning that a European Union citizen who pursues a course of studies in a host Member State whilst at the same time being in employment may be refused maintenance aid for studies granted to the nationals of that Member State where he entered the territory of that State with the principal intention of pursuing a course of study.

25. it should be observed as a preliminary point that Article 20(1) TFEU confers on any person holding the nationality of a Member State the status of citizen of the Union.

26. Both students from Member States other than the host Member State who follow a course of study in that State and nationals of Member States having the status of

'worker' within the meaning of Article 45 TFEU have that status, provided that they hold the nationality of a Member State.

27. As the Court has held on numerous occasions, the status of citizen of the Union is destined to be the fundamental status of nationals of the Member States, enabling those among such nationals who find themselves in the same situation to receive, as regards the material scope of the FEU Treaty, the same treatment in law irrespective of their nationality, subject to such exceptions as are provided for in that regard (see, to that effect, Case C-184/99 *Grzelczyk* [2001] ECR I-6193, paragraph 31, and Case C-224/98 *D'Hoop* [2002] ECR I-6191, paragraph 28).

28. Every citizen of the Union may therefore rely on the prohibition of discrimination on grounds of nationality laid down in Article 18 TFEU, provided for in other Treaty provisions and in Article 24 of Directive 2004/38, in all situations falling within the scope *ratione materiae* of European Union law. Those situations include the exercise of the fundamental freedoms conferred by inter alia Article 45 TFEU and those relating to the exercise of the freedom conferred by Article 21 TFEU to move and reside within the territory of the Member States (see, inter alia, Case C-85/96*Martínez Sala* [1998] ECR I-2691, paragraph 63; *Grzelczyk*, paragraphs 32 and 33; Case C-209/03 *Bidar* [2005] ECR I-2119, paragraphs 32 and 33; and Case C-75/11 *Commission* v *Austria* [2012] ECR I-0000, paragraph 39).

29. There is no provision of the Treaty to suggest that when students who are citizens of the Union move to another Member State to study there, they lose the rights which the Treaty confers on citizens of the Union, including the rights conferred on those citizens when they are in employment in the host Member State (see, to that effect, *Grzelczyk*, paragraph 35, and *Bidar*, paragraph 34).

30. It follows that a citizen of the Union who is studying in a host Member State or is in employment in that State and holds the status of 'worker' within the meaning of Article 45 TFEU may rely on the right, enshrined in Articles 18 TFEU, 21 TFEU and/or 45 TFEU, to move and reside freely within the territory of the host Member State, without being subject to direct or indirect discrimination on grounds of his nationality.

31. Both the Danish and the Norwegian Governments contend, however, that Articles 7(1)(c) and 24(2) of Directive 2004/38, read together, must be interpreted as meaning that a citizen of the Union who studies full-time in a host Member State and who entered the territory of that Member State for that purpose may be refused maintenance aid for studies for the first five years he is resident in the country, even if he is in part-time employment alongside his studies.

32. It should be borne in mind in that regard that Article 24(2) of Directive 2004/38 provides that the host Member State is not obliged, prior to acquisition of the right

of permanent residence, to grant maintenance aid for studies, including vocational training, consisting in student grants or student loans to persons other than workers, self-employed persons, persons who retain such status and members of their families.

33. As a derogation from the principle of equal treatment provided for in Article 18 TFEU, of which Article 24(1) of Directive 2004/38 is merely a specific expression, Article 24(2) must, according to the Court's case-law, be interpreted narrowly and in accordance with the provisions of the Treaty, including those relating to citizenship of the Union and the free movement of workers (see, to that effect, Joined Cases C-22/08 and C-23/08 *Vatsouras and Koupatantze* [2009] ECR I-4585, paragraph 44, and Case C-75/11 *Commission* v *Austria*, paragraphs 54 and 56).

34. According to the information provided to the Court, the aid for which Mr N. applied is maintenance aid in the form of a study grant. It may therefore come within the derogation from the principle of equal treatment provided for in Article 24(2) of Directive 2004/38.

35. However, as is readily evident from the wording of that provision, that derogation may not be applied as against persons having acquired a right of permanent residence or to 'workers, self-employed persons, persons who retain such status and members of their families'.

36. Although Article 7(1)(c) of Directive 2004/38 does provide that a Union citizen is to have the right of residence on the territory of another Member State for a period of longer than three months if he is enrolled at a 'private or public establishment' within the meaning of that provision 'for the principal purpose of following a course of study', it does not however follow from that provision that a citizen of the Union who fulfils those conditions is thereby automatically precluded from having the status of 'worker' within the meaning of Article 45 TFEU.

37. The order for reference and the observations submitted to the Court indicate that Mr N. was in full-time employment from the time he arrived in the territory of the host Member State and that, once he began his studies, he was in part-time employment.

38. The case-file also indicates that he was refused maintenance aid for studies on the ground that he entered the territory of Denmark with the principal intention of following a course of study, the purpose of his residence in Denmark being, according to the competent national authorities, such as to preclude him from having the status of 'worker' within the meaning of Article 45 TFEU.

39. It is settled case-law, however, that the concept of 'worker' within the meaning of Article 45 TFEU has an autonomous meaning specific to European Union law and must not be interpreted narrowly (see, to that effect, inter alia Case 66/85 *Law-*

rie-Blum [1986] ECR 2121, paragraph 16; Case 197/86 *Brown* [1988] ECR 3205, paragraph 21; Case C-3/90 *Bernini* [1992] ECR I-1071, paragraph 14; and Case C-413/01 *Ninni-Orasche* [2003] ECR I-13187, paragraph 23).

40. Moreover, that concept must be defined in accordance with objective criteria which distinguish the employment relationship by reference to the rights and duties of the persons concerned. The essential feature of an employment relationship is that, for a certain period of time, a person performs services for and under the direction of another person, in return for which he receives remuneration (see *Lawrie-Blum*, paragraph 17; *Ninni-Orasche*, paragraph 24; and also *Vatsouras and Kouptantze*, paragraph 26).

41. The low level of or origin of the resources for that remuneration, the rather low productivity of the person concerned, or the fact that he works only a small number of hours per week do not preclude that person from being recognised as a 'worker' within the meaning of Article 45 TFEU (see, to that effect, *Lawrie-Blum*, paragraph 21; Case 344/87 *Bettray* [1989] ECR 1621, paragraph 15; and *Bernini*, paragraph 16).

42. In order to qualify as a 'worker', the person concerned must nevertheless pursue effective and genuine activities which are not on such a small scale as to be regarded as purely marginal and ancillary (see, inter alia, Case 53/81 *Levin* [1982] ECR 1035, paragraph 17, and *Vatsouras and Kouptantze*, paragraph 26 and the case-law cited).

43. In investigating whether a specific case involves effective and genuine employment, the national court must base itself on objective criteria and make a comprehensive assessment of all the circumstances of the case that have to do with the activities and the employment relationship concerned (*Ninni-Orasche*, paragraph 27).

44. It is for the national court to conduct an analysis of all the aspects which characterise an employment relationship for the purpose of determining whether the employment activities pursued by Mr N. before and after he began his studies were effective and genuine in nature and, therefore, such as to confer the status of worker on him. That court alone has direct knowledge of the facts of the main proceedings and the aspects characterising the employment relationship of the applicant in the main proceedings and is accordingly the best placed to make the necessary findings.

45. As there is nothing in the order for reference to cast doubt on the fact that the employment relationship between Mr N. and his employers had the features of an employment relationship as outlined in paragraph 40 above, it is for the national court to make sure inter alia that the employment activities of the applicant in the main

proceedings are not on such a small scale as to be regarded as purely marginal and ancillary.

46. As regards the argument put forward by the Danish and Norwegian Governments to the effect that the intention the applicant in the main proceedings had when he entered Danish territory to follow a course of study precludes him from having the status of 'worker' within the meaning of Article 45 TFEU, it should be remembered that, in order to assess whether employment is capable of conferring the status of worker within the meaning of Article 45 TFEU, factors relating to the conduct of the person concerned before and after the period of employment are not relevant in establishing the status of worker within the meaning of that article. Such factors are not in any way related to the objective criteria referred to in the case-law referred to in paragraph 40 of this judgment (*Ninni-Orasche*, paragraph 28).

47. It should be noted that the definition of the concept of 'worker' within the meaning of Article 45 TFEU expresses the requirement, which is inherent in the very principle of the free movement of workers, that the advantages conferred by European Union law under that freedom may be relied on only by people genuinely pursuing or genuinely wishing to pursue employment activities. It does not mean, however, that the enjoyment of that freedom may be made contingent on which objectives are being pursued by a national of a Member State in applying to enter the territory of a host Member State, provided that he pursues or wishes to pursue effective and genuine employment activities. Once that condition is satisfied, the motives which may have prompted a worker of a Member State to seek employment in another Member State are of no account and must not be taken into consideration (see, to that effect, *Levin*, paragraphs 21 and 22, and Case C-109/01 *Akrich* [2003] ECR I-9607, paragraph 55).

48. Should the national court decide that Mr N. must be considered a 'worker' within the meaning of Article 45 TFEU, it is clear that a refusal to grant that citizen of the Union maintenance aid for studies infringes his right to equal treatment which he enjoys in his capacity as worker.

49. Under Article 7(2) of Regulation No 1612/68, a citizen of the Union who has exercised his right of free movement of workers guaranteed by Article 45 TFEU enjoys, in the host Member State, the same social benefits as national workers.

50. Moreover, the Court has held previously that maintenance aid for studies constitutes a social advantage within the meaning of Article 7(2) of Regulation No 1612/68 (see Case 39/86 *Lair* [1988] ECR 3161, paragraphs 23 and 24, and *Bernini*, paragraph 23).

51. In the light of the foregoing, the answer to the question referred is that Articles 7(1)(c) and 24(2) of Directive 2004/38 must be interpreted as meaning that a

European Union citizen who pursues a course of studies in a host Member State whilst at the same time pursuing effective and genuine employment activities such as to confer on him the status of 'worker' within the meaning of Article 45 TFEU may not be refused maintenance aid for studies which is granted to the nationals of that Member State. It is for the national court to make the necessary findings of fact in order to ascertain whether the employment activities of the applicant in the main proceedings are sufficient to confer that status on him. The fact that the person entered the territory of the host Member State with the principal intention of pursuing a course of study is not relevant for determining whether he is a 'worker' within the meaning of Article 45 TFEU and, accordingly, whether he is entitled to that aid under the same terms as a national of the host Member State under Article 7(2) of Regulation No 1612/68.

Costs

[Para. 52 omitted]

On those grounds,

THE COURT (Third Chamber),

hereby rules:

Articles 7(1)(c) and 24(2) of Directive 2004/38/EC of the European Parliament and of the Council of 29 April 2004 on the right of citizens of the Union and their family members to move and reside freely within the territory of the Member States amending Regulation (EEC) No 1612/68 and repealing Directives 64/221/EEC, 68/360/EEC, 72/194/EEC, 73/148/EEC, 75/34/EEC, 75/35/EEC, 90/364/EEC, 90/365/EEC and 93/96/EEC must be interpreted as meaning that a European Union citizen who pursues a course of studies in a host Member State whilst at the same time pursuing effective and genuine employment activities such as to confer on him the status of 'worker' within the meaning of Article 45 TFEU may not be refused maintenance aid for studies which is granted to the nationals of that Member State. It is for the national court to make the necessary findings of fact in order to ascertain whether the employment activities of the applicant in the main proceedings are sufficient to confer that status on him. The fact that the person entered the territory of the host Member State with the principal intention of pursuing a course of study is not relevant for determining whether he is a 'worker' within the meaning of Article 45 TFEU and, accordingly, whether he is entitled to that aid under the same terms as a national of the host Member State under Article 7(2) of Regulation (EEC) No 1612/68 of the Council of 15 October 1968 on freedom of movement for workers within the Community.

Comments and questions

In recent years the CJEU has had to decide on the extent to which Union citizens who travel to another Member State with a view to pursuing a course of study have a right, under Union law, to receive student financial support on an equal footing with the host Member State's own nationals. This includes whether Union citizens have a right to receive student financial support for a course in another Member State without having to comply with a particular residence condition in the host Member State prior to beginning their studies. In this connection it is important to note the Union law distinction between economically active and non-economically active Union citizens; see e.g. Case C-158/07 Förster [2008] ECR I-8507, included in Chapter 3 above. Economically active Union citizens and their family members are entitled to treatment equal to that of the nationals of the Member State where they are economically active, while non-economically active citizens can be required to show greater real connection with the host Member State as a condition for receiving social benefits etc.

The L.N. case concerned a Union citizen, L.N., who sought to become a student at Copenhagen Business School. Having submitted his application and shortly prior to the start of his course, L.N. moved to Denmark, and immediately after arriving he started full-time work. The Danish authorities then certified him as a worker. L.N.'s full-time work ended when he began his studies, but he had paid part-time work in parallel with his studies. Immediately prior to the start of his course, while he was still in full-time employment, L.N. sought Danish student financial support. This was refused, as the Danish authorities pointed out that his principal purpose for coming to Denmark was to study and not to work. In the view of the Danish authorities, the fact that, after arriving in Denmark with a view to study, he had had a short period of full-time work did not mean that L.N. had become entitled to financial support on the same footing as other Union citizens who had come to Denmark to work and who had thereafter, as workers, sought to follow a course of study. Thus, L.N.'s application was refused. He appealed against the decision, and this led to a request being made to the CJEU for a preliminary ruling.

At the heart of the case was the interpretation of Article 7(1)(c) and Article 24(2) of Directive 2004/38 on the right of citizens of the Union and their family members to move and reside freely within the territory of the Member States, together with Article 45 TFEU on the free movement of workers. The main argument of the Danish Government in the case was that in Directive 2004/38, the Union legislator had expressly denied the right of a Union citizen to receive student support in the host Member State, pursuant to Union law, if the Union citizen's principal activity was to pursue a course of study, and this was so even if that person was simultaneously a 'worker' within the meaning of Union law. Seen from this perspective, what was crucial in this case was the relationship between the Union legislator on the one hand and the role of the CJEU on the other. However, the CJEU did not share the Danish Government's opinion in this respect.

The CJEU first stated that a Union citizen who studies in a host Member State, or who performs paid work in that State and has the status of a 'worker' within the meaning of Article 45 TFEU, can claim rights pursuant to Articles 18 and 21 TFEU and/or Article 45 TFEU to move and reside within the territory of the host Member State, without being subject to either direct or indirect discrimination on the grounds of nationality. There was nothing new in this.

Thereafter the CJEU turned to the main question in the case, namely the relationship between Article 7(1)(c) and Article 24(2) of Directive 2004/38 and Article 45 TFEU. The CJEU noted that Article 24(2) of Directive 2004/38 provides that the host Member State is not obliged, prior to acquisition of the right of permanent residence, to grant maintenance aid for studies, including vocational training, consisting in student grants or student loans to persons other than workers, self-employed persons, persons who retain such status and members of their families. Since this provision is an exception to the principle of equal treatment set out in Article 18 TFEU, it must be interpreted narrowly and in accordance with the provisions of the Treaty, including those relating to citizenship of the Union and the free movement of workers. The CJEU went on to state that it is clear that from the wording of that provision, that this derogation may not be applied as against persons having acquired a right of permanent residence or to 'workers, self-employed persons, persons who retain such status and members of their families'.

The CJEU then stated as follows:

> 'Although Article 7(1)(c) of Directive 2004/38 does provide that a Union citizen is to have the right of residence on the territory of another Member State for a period of longer than three months if he is enrolled at a 'private or public establishment' within the meaning of that provision 'for the principal purpose of following a course of study', it does not however follow from that provision that a citizen of the Union who fulfils those conditions is thereby automatically precluded from having the status of 'worker' within the meaning of Article 45 TFEU' (emphasis added).

The CJEU had regard for the fact that L.N. had part-time work alongside his full-time studies and, depending on the circumstances, the part-time work could mean that L.N. qualified as a 'worker' within the meaning of Article 45 TFEU. Thus, a Union citizen can claim entitlement to student support on equal terms with the nationals of the host Member State, if the Union citizen has part-time work alongside their studies which is of such an extent that the Union citizen qualifies as a 'worker'. As can be seen from the other judgments in this chapter, the requirements for qualifying as a worker are very modest.

Consider what importance the CJEU attached to the fact that L.N. had entered Denmark for the purpose of study with respect to his possibility of being categorised as a 'worker' and thus his entitlement to claim student support. See in particular paragraphs 46-47. Does the judgment mean that Union citizens who come to Denmark with a view to studying, and who thereafter take part-time work alongside their studies, have a right to Danish student support in line with the support given to Danish nationals?

How would you assess the situation where a Union citizen travels to Denmark, is accepted on a course at Copenhagen University, and parallel with their university studies have 20 hours of work per week until the final stage of their studies, whereupon they give up their job? Would such a person be entitled to student financial support in the final stage of their studies in Denmark? In this connection, see Case C-158/07 Förster [2008] ECR I-8507, included in Chapter 3 above, Article 7(1)(c) and Article 24(2) of Directive 2004/38.

JUDGMENT OF THE COURT (First Chamber)
19 June 2014

Jessy Saint Prix v Secretary of State for Work and Pensions, intervening party: AIRE Centre. (Request for a preliminary ruling from the Supreme Court of the United Kingdom)

'Reference for a preliminary ruling – Article 45 TFEU – Directive 2004/38/EC – Article 7 – 'Worker' – Union citizen who gave up work because of the physical constraints of the late stages of pregnancy and the aftermath of childbirth'

Case C-507/12

Judgment

1. This request for a preliminary ruling concerns the interpretation of 'worker' for the purposes of Article 45 TFEU and Article 7 of Directive 2004/38/EC of the European Parliament and of the Council of 29 April 2004 on the right of citizens of the Union and their family members to move and reside freely within the territory of the Member States amending Regulation (EEC) No 1612/68 and repealing Directives 64/221/EEC, 68/360/EEC, 72/194/EEC, 73/148/EEC, 75/34/EEC, 75/35/EEC, 90/364/EEC, 90/365/EEC and 93/96/EEC (OJ 2004 L 158, p. 77, and corrigenda OJ 2004 L 229, p. 35, and OJ 2005 L 197, p. 34).

2. The request has been made in the context of proceedings between Ms Saint Prix and the Secretary of State for Work and Pensions ('the Secretary of State') concerning the latter's refusal to grant income support to Ms Saint Prix.

Legal context

EU law

[Paras 3-13 omitted]

The dispute in the main proceedings and the questions referred for a preliminary ruling

14. Ms Saint Prix is a French national who entered the United Kingdom on 10 July 2006 where she worked, mainly as a teaching assistant, from 1 September 2006 until 1 August 2007. She then enrolled on a Post-Graduate Certificate in Education course at the University of London, the envisaged period of study being from 17 September 2007 until 27 June 2008.

15. During that period she became pregnant, with an expected date of confinement of 2 June 2008.

16. On 22 January 2008, hoping to find work in secondary schools, Ms Saint Prix registered with an employment agency and, on 1 February 2008, she withdrew from the course that she had been attending at the University of London. As no secondary school work was available, she took agency positions working in nursery schools. On 12 March 2008, when she was nearly six months pregnant, Ms Saint Prix stopped that work, however, on the grounds that the demands of caring for nursery school children had become too strenuous for her. She looked for a few days, without success, for work that was more suited to her pregnancy.

17. On 18 March 2008, that is, 11 weeks before her expected date of confinement, Ms Saint Prix made a claim for income support. As that claim was refused by the Secretary of State by decision of 4 May 2008, she brought an appeal before the First Tier Tribunal.

18. On 21 August 2008, namely three months after the premature birth of her child, Ms Saint Prix resumed work.

19. By decision of 4 September 2008, the First Tier Tribunal upheld her appeal. However, on 7 May 2010, the Upper Tribunal upheld the appeal brought by the Secretary of State against that decision. The Court of Appeal confirmed the decision of the Upper Tribunal and Ms Saint Prix then brought the matter before the referring court.

20. That court asks whether a pregnant woman who temporarily gives up work because of her pregnancy is to be considered a 'worker' for the purposes of the freedom of movement for workers as laid down in Article 45 TFEU and of the right of residence conferred by Article 7 of Directive 2004/38.

21. In that regard, the referring court states that neither Article 45 TFEU nor Article 7 of that directive defines 'worker'.

22. The referring court thus considers, in essence, that whereas, when adopting that directive, the EU legislature intended to codify the existing legislation and case-law, it nevertheless did not intend to exclude further development of the concept of 'worker' that takes into account situations not expressly considered when it was adopted. The Court may, therefore, taking into account special circumstances such as those characterising pregnancy and the immediate aftermath of childbirth, decide to extend this concept to pregnant women who give up work for a reasonable period.

23. In those circumstances the Supreme Court decided to stay the proceedings and to refer the following questions to the Court:

    '1. Is the right of residence conferred upon a "worker" in Article 7 of [Directive 2004/38] to be interpreted as applying only to those (i) in an existing employment relationship, (ii) (at least in some circumstances) seeking work, or (iii) covered by the extensions in Article 7(3) [of that directive], or is [Article 7 of that directive] to be interpreted as not precluding the recognition of further persons who remain "workers" for this purpose?

    2. (a) If the latter, does it extend to a woman who reasonably gives up work, or seeking work, because of the physical constraints of the late stages of pregnancy (and the aftermath of childbirth)?

       (b) If so, is she entitled to the benefit of the national law's definition of when it is reasonable for her to do so?'

Consideration of the questions referred

24. By its questions, which it is appropriate to consider together, the referring court asks, in essence, whether EU law, and in particular Article 45 TFEU and Article 7 of Directive 2004/38, are to be interpreted as meaning that a woman who gives up work, or seeking work, because of the physical constraints of the late stages of pregnancy and the aftermath of childbirth, retains the status of 'worker' within the meaning of those articles.

25. In order to answer those questions, it should be stated at the outset that it is apparent from recitals 3 and 4 in the preamble to that directive that the aim of the directive is to remedy the sector-by-sector piecemeal approach to the primary and individual right of Union citizens to move and reside freely within the territory of the Member States, in order to facilitate the exercise of that right by providing a single legislative act codifying and revising the instruments of EU law which preceded that directive (see, to that effect, *Ziolkowski* and *Szeja*, C-424/10 and C-425/10, EU:C:2011:866, paragraph 37).

26. In that regard, it is apparent from Article 1(a) of Directive 2004/38 that that directive is intended to set out the conditions governing the exercise of that right, which include, where residence is desired for a period of longer than three months, in particular the condition laid down in Article 7(1)(a) of that directive that Union citizens must be workers or self-employed persons in the host Member State (see, to that effect, *Brey*, C-140/12, EU:C:2013:565, paragraph 53 and the case-law cited).

27. Article 7(3) of Directive 2004/38 provides that, for the purposes of paragraph 7(1)(a) of that directive, a Union citizen who is no longer a worker or self-

employed person shall nevertheless retain the status of worker or self-employed person in specific cases, namely where he is temporarily unable to work as the result of an illness or accident, where, in certain situations, he is in involuntary unemployment, or where, under specified conditions, he embarks on vocational training.

28. However, Article 7(3) of Directive 2004/38 does not expressly envisage the case of a woman who is in a particular situation because of the physical constraints of the late stages of her pregnancy and the aftermath of childbirth.

29. In that regard, the Court has consistently held that pregnancy must be clearly distinguished from illness, in that pregnancy is not in any way comparable with a pathological condition (see to that effect, inter alia, *Webb*, C-32/93, EU:C:1994:300, paragraph 25 and the case-law cited).

30. It follows that a woman in the situation of Ms Saint Prix, who temporarily gives up work because of the late stages of her pregnancy and the aftermath of childbirth, cannot be regarded as a person temporarily unable to work as the result of an illness, in accordance with Article 7(3)(a) of Directive 2004/38.

31. However, it does not follow from either Article 7 of Directive 2004/38, considered as a whole, or from the other provisions of that directive, that, in such circumstances, a citizen of the Union who does not fulfil the conditions laid down in that article is, therefore, systematically deprived of the status of 'worker', within the meaning of Article 45 TFEU.

32. The codification, sought by the directive, of the instruments of EU law existing prior to that directive, which expressly seeks to facilitate the exercise of the rights of Union citizens to move and reside freely within the territory of the Member States, cannot, by itself, limit the scope of the concept of worker within the meaning of the FEU Treaty.

33. In that regard, it must be noted that, according to the settled case-law of the Court, the concept of 'worker', within the meaning of Article 45 TFEU, in so far as it defines the scope of a fundamental freedom provided for by the FEU Treaty, must be interpreted broadly (see, to that effect, *N.*, C-46/12, EU:C:2013:97, paragraph 39 and the case-law cited).

34. Accordingly, the Court has held that any national of a Member State, irrespective of his place of residence and of his nationality, who has exercised the right to freedom of movement for workers and who has been employed in a Member State other than that of his residence falls within the scope of Article 45 TFEU (see, inter alia, *Ritter-Coulais*, C-152/03, EU:C:2006:123, paragraph 31, and *Hartmann*, C-212/05, EU:C:2007:437, paragraph 17).

35. The Court has thus also held that, in the context of Article 45 TFEU, a person who, for a certain period of time, performs services for and under the direction of another person in return for which he receives remuneration must be considered to be a worker. Once the employment relationship has ended, the person concerned, as a rule, loses the status of worker, although that status may produce certain effects after the relationship has ended, and a person who is genuinely seeking work must also be classified as a worker (*Caves Krier Frères*, C-379/11, EU:C:2012:798, paragraph 26 and the case-law cited).

36. Consequently, and for the purposes of the present case, it must be pointed out that freedom of movement for workers entails the right for nationals of Member States to move freely within the territory of other Member States and to stay there for the purposes of seeking employment (see, inter alia, *Antonissen*, C-292/89, EU:C:1991:80, paragraph 13).

37. It follows that classification as a worker under Article 45 TFEU, and the rights deriving from such status, do not necessarily depend on the actual or continuing existence of an employment relationship (see, to that effect, *Lair*, 39/86, EU:C:1988:322, paragraphs 31 and 36).

38. In those circumstances, it cannot be argued, contrary to what the United Kingdom Government contends, that Article 7(3) of Directive 2004/38 lists exhaustively the circumstances in which a migrant worker who is no longer in an employment relationship may nevertheless continue to benefit from that status.

39. In the present case, it is clear from the order for reference, a finding not contested by the parties in the main proceeding, that Ms Saint Prix was employed in the territory of the United Kingdom before giving up work, less than three months before the birth of her child, because of the physical constraints of the late stages of pregnancy and the immediate aftermath of childbirth. She returned to work three months after the birth of her child, without having left the territory of that Member State during the period of interruption of her professional activity.

40. The fact that such constraints require a woman to give up work during the period needed for recovery does not, in principle, deprive her of the status of 'worker' within the meaning Article 45 TFEU.

41. The fact that she was not actually available on the employment market of the host Member State for a few months does not mean that she has ceased to belong to that market during that period, provided she returns to work or finds another job within a reasonable period after confinement (see, by analogy, *Orfanopoulos and Oliveri*, C-482/01 and C-493/01, EU:C:2004:262, paragraph 50).

42. In order to determine whether the period that has elapsed between childbirth and starting work again may be regarded as reasonable, the national court concerned should take account of all the specific circumstances of the case in the main proceedings and the applicable national rules on the duration of maternity leave, in accordance with Article 8 of Council Directive 92/85/EEC of 19 October 1992 on the introduction of measures to encourage improvements in the safety and health at work of pregnant workers and workers who have recently given birth or are breastfeeding (tenth individual Directive within the meaning of Article 16(1) of Directive 89/391/EEC) (OJ 1992 L 348, p. 1).

43. The approach adopted in paragraph 41 of the present judgment is consistent with the objective pursued by Article 45 TFEU of enabling a worker to move freely within the territory of the other Member States and to stay there for the purpose of employment (see *Uecker and Jacquet*, C-64/96 and C-65/96, EU:C:1997:285, paragraph 21).

44. As the Commission contends, a Union citizen would be deterred from exercising her right to freedom of movement if, in the event that she was pregnant in the host State and gave up work as a result, if only for a short period, she risked losing her status as a worker in that State.

45. Furthermore, it must be pointed out that EU law guarantees special protection for women in connection with maternity. In that regard, it should be noted that Article 16(3) of Directive 2004/38 provides, for the purpose of calculating the continuous period of five years of residence in the host Member State allowing Union citizens to acquire the right of permanent residence in that territory, that the continuity of that residence is not affected, inter alia, by an absence of a maximum of 12 consecutive months for important reasons such as pregnancy and childbirth.

46. If, by virtue of that protection, an absence for an important event such as pregnancy or childbirth does not affect the continuity of the five years of residence in the host Member State required for the granting of that right of residence, the physical constraints of the late stages of pregnancy and the immediate aftermath of childbirth, which require a woman to give up work temporarily, cannot, a fortiori, result in that woman losing her status as a worker.

47. In the light of all the foregoing considerations, the answer to the questions referred for a preliminary ruling by the referring court is that Article 45 TFEU must be interpreted as meaning that a woman who gives up work, or seeking work, because of the physical constraints of the late stages of pregnancy and the aftermath of childbirth retains the status of 'worker', within the meaning of that article, provided she returns to work or finds another job within a reasonable period after the birth of her child.

Costs

[Para. 48 omitted]

On those grounds,

THE COURT (First Chamber),

hereby rules:

> **Article 45 TFEU must be interpreted as meaning that a woman who gives up work, or seeking work, because of the physical constraints of the late stages of pregnancy and the aftermath of childbirth retains the status of 'worker', within the meaning of that article, provided she returns to work or finds another job within a reasonable period after the birth of her child.**

Comments and queries

Despite the fact that there is comprehensive case law from the CJEU on the concept of 'a 'worker', the term continues to give rise to new cases. The most important characteristic of an employment relationship is that a person, for a certain period of time, performs services for and under the direction of another person in return for which they receive remuneration. However, the CJEU has also established that, in order to be considered 'a 'worker', a person must have real and actual employment. Thus a person will not be considered to be a 'worker' if their employment is on such a small scale as to be regarded as purely marginal and ancillary.

In the *Saint Prix* case the question arose as to whether a Union citizen from another Member State could maintain her status as a migrant worker in the host Member State pursuant to Article 45 TFEU if she ceased to work or to seek work due to her physical limitations connected with her late stage of pregnancy and the after-effects of giving birth.

Article 7(3) of the Free Movement Directive (Directive 2004/38) lists the situations in which a Union citizen, who is no longer working, maintains their status as a worker. This is possible if the Union citizen is temporarily unable to work due to illness or an accident. However, the provision does not refer to pregnancy. Thus the question in the Saint Prix case was whether Article 7(3) of the Free Movement Directive should be considered as giving an exhaustive list of the situations in which a Union citizen who is no longer working can maintain their status as a worker, or whether there can be other situations than those referred to in which a Union citizen can retain their status as a 'worker'. In its reference for a preliminary ruling the United Kingdom Supreme Court stated, among other things, that it was of the view that even though the EU legislature intended to codify the existing legislation and case-law, it nevertheless did not intend to exclude further development of the concept of 'worker' to take into account situations not expressly considered when it was adopted.

In its judgment the CJEU started by finding that Article 7(3) of the Free Movement Directive states that, with a view to applying Article 7(1)(a) of the Directive, on the right of residence for more than three months of a Union citizen who has the status of a 'worker', a Union citizen who is no longer in employment retains their status as a worker in specific cases, namely where they are temporarily unable to work as the result of an illness or accident, where they are involuntarily unemployed, or where, under specified conditions, they embark on vocational training. Moreover, the CJEU found that Article 7(3) of the Free Movement Directive does not expressly cover the circumstances where a woman finds herself in a special situation as a result of physical limitations resulting from the late stages of pregnancy or the after-effects of giving birth. The CJEU has consistently held that pregnancy must be clearly distinguished from illness, in that pregnancy is not in any way comparable with a pathological condition. On the basis of these findings the CJEU established that a Union citizen who temporarily gives up work in the late stages of pregnancy or due to the after-effects of giving birth, cannot be regarded as a person temporarily unable to work as the result of an illness pursuant to Article 7(3)(a).

However, this did not prevent Jessy Saint Prix nevertheless being able to be regarded as a 'worker'. Thus the CJEU stated:

> 'However, it does not follow from either Article 7 of Directive 2004/38, considered as a whole, or from the other provisions of that Directive, that, in such circumstances, a citizen of the Union who does not fulfil the conditions laid down in that article is, therefore, systematically deprived of the status of 'worker', within the meaning of Article 45 TFEU. The codification, sought by the directive, of the instruments of EU law existing prior to that directive, which expressly seeks to facilitate the exercise of the rights of Union citizens to move and reside freely within the territory of the Member States, cannot, by itself, limit the scope of the concept of worker within the meaning of the [TFEU].'

The CJEU then reviewed its case law on the concept of a 'worker', according to which the qualification of a worker under Article 45 TFEU and the rights that follow from this status do not necessarily depend on the actual or continuing existence of an employment relationship. On this basis it could not be argued that Article 7(3) of the Free Movement exhaustively lists the circumstances under which a migrant worker who is no longer in employment can nevertheless be covered by the status of a 'worker'. In the view of the CJEU, the fact that physical limitations connected with the late stages of pregnancy and the after-effects of giving birth which compel a woman to stop doing paid work for a period, as necessary for her health, do not in principle deprive her of the status of a 'worker' pursuant to Article 45 TFEU. The CJEU also ruled that the fact that such a person has not been in the employment market of the host Member State for some months does not mean that she ceases to be linked to the employment market during this period, provided she resumes her job or takes up some other work within a reasonable period following the birth.

Finally, on the question of whether the period elapsing between childbirth and starting work again may be regarded as reasonable, the CJEU stated: 'the national court concerned should take account of all the specific circumstances of the case in the main proceedings and the applicable national rules on the duration of maternity leave, in accordance with Article 8 of Council Directive 92/85/EEC of 19 October 1992 on the introduction of measures to encourage improvements in the safety and health at work of pregnant workers and workers who have recently given birth or are breastfeeding'. It appeared from the judgment that in the United Kingdom the normal maternity leave was 26 weeks (11 weeks before birth and 15 weeks after).

Should the United Kingdom Supreme Court decide that the period between giving birth and the resumption of work was reasonable or unreasonable in the actual case if Jessy Saint Prix had sought income support from the British authorities 11 weeks before the expected birth and she resumed work three months after giving birth?

In the *Saint Prix* case the CJEU established that Article 7(3) does not contain an exhaustive list of the situations in which a Union citizen who is no longer in work or self-employed retains their status as a 'worker' or a self-employed person. Thus, the provision also covers cases where a female Union citizen stops working or seeking work because of their physical limitations connected with the later stages of pregnancy and the after-effects of giving birth, provided she resumes work or finds another job within a reasonable period after giving birth.

Do you find the judgment surprising? Is your answer to this question influenced by whether a strict legal approach is taken to Article 7(3) of the Free Movement Directive. Or whether a more equitable approach is applied, where there is regard for the Union law principle of non-discrimination on the ground of nationality, and the non-discrimination principle based on gender.

Are there possible situations, other than under Article 7(3) of the Free Movement Directive, where a Union citizen retains his or her status as a 'worker' so as to be treated equally with the citizens of the home Member State? In point 52 of his Opinion on the case, the Advocate General suggested that there should be limits to an expanded interpretation:

> 'it cannot be categorically ruled out that, in order to avoid "benefit tourism", more restraint may be warranted in the case of economically inactive Union citizens who have never established any link with the society of their host Member State by working and paying taxes there.'

JUDGMENT OF THE COURT (Grand Chamber)
15 September 2015

Jobcenter Berlin Neukölln v Nazifa Alimanovic, Sonita Alimanovic, Valentina Alimanovic, Valentino Alimanovic. (Request for a preliminary ruling: Bundessozialgericht – Germany)

Reference for a preliminary ruling – Freedom of movement for persons – Citizenship of the Union – Equal treatment – Directive 2004/38/EC – Article 24(2) – Social assistance – Regulation (EC) No 883/2004 – Articles 4 and 70 – Special non-contributory cash benefits – Member State nationals who are job-seekers and resident in a different Member State – Excluded – Retention of the status of 'worker''

Case C-67/14

Judgment

1. This request for a preliminary ruling concerns the interpretation of Articles 18 TFEU and 45(2) TFEU, of Articles 4 and 70 of Regulation (EC) No 883/2004 of the European Parliament and of the Council of 29 April 2004 on the coordination of social security systems (OJ 2004 L 166, p. 1, and corrigendum at OJ 2004 L 200, p. 1), as amended by Commission Regulation (EU) No 1244/2010 of 9 December 2010 (OJ 2010 L 338, p. 35) ('Regulation No 883/2004'), and of Article 24(2) of Directive 2004/38/EC of the European Parliament and of the Council of 29 April 2004 on the right of citizens of the Union and their family members to move and reside freely within the territory of the Member States, amending Regulation (EEC) No 1612/68 and repealing Directives 64/221/EEC, 68/360/EEC, 72/194/EEC, 73/148/EEC, 75/34/EEC, 75/35/EEC, 90/364/EEC, 90/365/EEC and 93/96/EEC (OJ 2004 L 158, p. 77).

2. The request has been made in proceedings between, on one hand, Jobcenter Berlin Neukölln (the Employment Centre, Berlin Neukölln) ('the Job Centre') and, on the other hand, Nazifa Alimanovic and her three children, Sonita, Valentina and Valentino Alimanovic (together 'the Alimanovic family'), concerning the withdrawal by that agency of benefits by the way of basic provision ('Grundsicherung') provided for under German law.

Legal context

International law

[Paras 3-24 omitted]

The dispute in the main proceedings and the questions referred for a preliminary ruling

25. Nazifa Alimanovic, born in 1966, and her children, Sonita, Valentina and Valentino, born in 1994, 1998 and 1999 respectively, are all Swedish nationals. Ms Alimanovic was born in Bosnia whereas her children were all born in Germany.

26. The request for a preliminary ruling states that the Alimanovic family left Germany in 1999 for Sweden and returned to Germany in June 2010, although neither their exact departure date nor the reason for that absence are stated.

27. On 1 July 2010, the members of the Alimanovic family were issued with a certificate attesting the right of permanent residence in accordance with Paragraph 5 of the Law on freedom of movement. After her return to Germany, Ms Alimanovic and her daughter Sonita, who were fit for work within the meaning of the German legislation, worked between June 2010 and May 2011 in temporary jobs lasting less than a year.

28. During the period from 1 December 2011 to 31 May 2012, Ms Alimanovic was paid family allowances for her children Valentina and Valentino and, like her daughter Sonita, basic provision under Book II, namely subsistence allowances for the long-term unemployed (known as 'Arbeitslosengeld II'), plus social allowances for beneficiaries unfit to work, those latter beneficiaries being her other two children, Valentina and Valentino (together, 'the benefits at issue').

29. For the purpose of granting the benefits at issue during that period, the Job Centre took the view that the exclusion applying to Union citizens seeking employment, set out in the second sentence of Paragraph 7(1), point 2, of Book II, was not applicable to the Alimanovic family in so far as, since the members of that family were Swedish nationals, that rule had to be disregarded under the principle of non-discrimination provided for in Article 1 of the Assistance Convention. In a judgment of 19 October 2010, the Federal Social Court had held that the obligation imposed on the Federal Republic of Germany under that provision, namely to grant, in the same way as to its own nationals, social assistance to the nationals of the other contracting parties who are lawfully present in any part of its territory and without sufficient resources, also covered the grant of a minimum subsistence income under Paragraph 19 et seq of Book II.

30. However, under the first sentence of Paragraph 48(1) of Book X of the Social Code, an administrative measure must be annulled with prospective effect when a significant change has occurred in the legal and factual circumstances which existed when that measure was adopted. In respect of the grant of benefits on the basis of Article 1 of the Assistance Convention, a change occurred in May 2012, as a result of the reservation issued by the German Government on 19 December 2011 with re-

gard to that convention. The Job Centre withdrew the decision on the grant of all the benefits at issue in respect of May 2012 on that basis.

31. On application by the Alimanovic family, the Social Court, Berlin, (Sozialgericht Berlin) annulled that decision and held, inter alia, that Ms Alimanovic and her daughter Sonita were entitled to the benefits at issue which applied to them, under, inter alia, Article 4 of Regulation No 883/2004, which prohibits any discrimination against Union citizens in relation to the nationals of the Member State concerned, read in conjunction with Article 70 of that regulation, which concerns special non-contributory cash benefits such as those at issue in the case before it.

32. In its appeal brought before the referring court, the Job Centre submits, in particular, that the benefits to cover subsistence costs under Book II constitute 'social assistance' within the meaning of Article 24(2) of Directive 2004/38 and, therefore, job-seekers may be refused the grant of such benefits.

33. The referring court states in particular that, according to the findings of the Social Court, Berlin, by which it is bound, Ms Alimanovic and her daughter Sonita could no longer rely on a right of residence as workers under Paragraph 2 of the Law on freedom of movement. Since June 2010, they had worked only in temporary jobs lasting less than a year and, since May 2011, they had been neither workers nor self-employed.

34. With reference to the judgment in *Vatsouras and Koupatantze* (C-22/08 and C-23/08, EU:C:2009:344), the referring court states that it follows from the second sentence of Paragraph 2(3) of the Law on freedom of movement, read in the light of Article 7(3)(c) of Directive 2004/38, that neither Ms Alimanovic nor her daughter Sonita still have the status of an employee or self-employed worker and that they must therefore be regarded as seeking employment within the meaning of Paragraph 2(2), point 1, of the Law on freedom of movement.

35. Ms Alimanovic and her daughter Sonita, among others, were thus precluded from claiming subsistence allowances for the long-term unemployed on the basis of Paragraph 7(1), second sentence, point 2, of Book II, which excludes both persons whose right of residence arises solely out of the search for employment and their family members from entitlement to the benefits provided for by that legislation.

36. The referring court therefore, first, raises the issue of whether that provision of Book II breaches the principle of equal treatment laid down in Article 4 of Regulation No 883/2004.

37. Secondly, that court raises the issue of whether that provision of Book II may be regarded as a valid transposition of Article 24(2) of Directive 2004/38 into domestic

law or, should that latter provision be held inapplicable, whether it infringes Article 45(2) TFEU, read in conjunction with Article 18 TFEU.

38. In those circumstances, the Bundessozialgericht (Federal Social Court) decided to stay the proceedings and to refer the following questions to the Court of Justice for a preliminary ruling:

‘1. Does the principle of equal treatment under Article 4 of Regulation [No 883/2004] – with the exception of the clause in Article 70(4) [thereof] excluding the provision of benefits outside the Member State of residence – apply also to the special non-contributory cash benefits referred to in Article 70(1) and (2) of Regulation [No 883/2004]?

2. If the first question is answered in the affirmative: may the principle of equal treatment laid down in Article 4 of Regulation [No 883/2004] be limited by provisions of national legislation implementing Article 24(2) of Directive 2004/38 that do not in any circumstances allow access to those benefits in the case in which the right of residence of the citizen of the Union in another Member State arises solely out of the search for employment and, if so, to what extent may that principle be so limited?

3. Does Article 45(2) TFEU, [read] in conjunction with Article 18 TFEU, preclude a provision of national law that does not in any circumstances allow the grant of a social benefit, intended to ensure subsistence and to facilitate access to the labour market, to citizens of the Union who, as job-seekers, may invoke the exercise of their right of free movement when they enjoy a right of residence arising solely out of the search for employment, irrespective of a link to the host Member State?’

39. By letter of 26 November 2014, the Court Registry sent the referring court the judgment in *Dano* (C-333/13, EU:C:2014:2358), requesting it to inform it whether, in the light of the first point in the operative part of that judgment, it still wished to refer the first question in the order for reference. By order of 11 February 2015, received at the Court Registry on 19 February 2015, the Federal Social Court decided that it would withdraw the first question referred.

Consideration of the questions referred

The classification of the benefits at issue

40. The file submitted to the Court states that the referring court is of the view that the rights of residence held by Ms Alimanovic and her daughter Sonita arise solely out of their status as job-seekers and that it is bound by the findings of fact made by the court of first instance in that regard.

41. By its second and third questions, the referring court asks the Court as to, in essence, the compatibility, first, with Article 24(2) of Directive 2004/38 and, secondly, with Articles 18 TFEU and 45(2) TFEU, of national legislation which excludes from entitlement to certain benefits nationals of other Member States who have the status of job-seekers, whereas those benefits are guaranteed to the nationals of the Member State concerned who are in the same situation.

42. Since the issue of whether the benefits at issue constitute 'social assistance' or measures intended to facilitate access to the labour market is determinative for the purposes of identifying the EU rule under which that compatibility falls to be assessed, it is necessary to classify them.

43. In this connection, it is sufficient to note that the referring court has itself characterised the benefits at issue as 'special non-contributory cash benefits' within the meaning of Article 70(2) of Regulation No 883/2004. It states in that regard that those benefits are intended to cover subsistence costs for persons who cannot cover those costs themselves and that they are not financed through contributions, but through tax revenue. Since those benefits are moreover mentioned in Annex X to Regulation No 883/2004, they meet the conditions in Article 70(2) thereof, even if they form part of a scheme which also provides for benefits to facilitate the search for employment.

44. That said, it should be added that, as is apparent from the Court's case-law, such benefits are also covered by the concept of 'social assistance' within the meaning of Article 24(2) of Directive 2004/38. That concept refers to all assistance schemes established by the public authorities, whether at national, regional or local level, to which recourse may be had by an individual who does not have resources sufficient to meet his own basic needs and those of his family and who by reason of that fact may, during his period of residence, become a burden on the public finances of the host Member State which could have consequences for the overall level of assistance which may be granted by that State (judgment in *Dano*, C-333/13, EU:C:2014:2358, paragraph 63).

45. However, in the present case it must be found that, as the Advocate General observed in point 72 of his Opinion, the predominant function of the benefits at issue in the main proceedings is in fact to cover the minimum subsistence costs necessary to lead a life in keeping with human dignity.

46. It follows from those considerations that those benefits cannot be characterised as benefits of a financial nature which are intended to facilitate access to the labour market of a Member State (see, to that effect, judgment in *Vatsouras and Koupatantze*, C-22/08 and C-23/08, EU:C:2009:344, paragraph 45) but, as the Advocate General observed in points 66 to 71 of his Opinion, must be regarded as 'social assistance' within the meaning of Article 24(2) of Directive 2004/38.

47. Consequently, there is no need to answer the third question referred.

The second question

48. By its second question, the referring court asks, in essence, whether Article 24 of Directive 2004/38 and Article 4 of Regulation No 883/2004 must be interpreted as precluding legislation of a Member State under which nationals of other Member States who are job-seekers in the host Member State are excluded from entitlement to certain 'special non-contributory cash benefits' within the meaning of Article 70(2) of Regulation No 883/2004, which also constitute 'social assistance' within the meaning of Article 24(2) of Directive 2004/38, although those benefits are granted to nationals of the Member State concerned who are in the same situation.

49. It must first be recalled in this connection that, so far as concerns access to social assistance, such as that at issue in the main proceedings, a Union citizen can claim equal treatment with nationals of the host Member State under Article 24(1) of Directive 2004/38 only if his residence in the territory of the host Member State complies with the conditions of Directive 2004/38 (judgment in *Dano*, C-333/13, EU:C:2014:2358, paragraph 69).

50. To accept that persons who do not have a right of residence under Directive 2004/38 may claim entitlement to social assistance under the same conditions as those applicable to nationals of the host Member State would run counter to an objective of the directive, set out in recital 10 in its preamble, namely preventing Union citizens who are nationals of other Member States from becoming an unreasonable burden on the social assistance system of the host Member State (judgment in *Dano*, C-333/13, EU:C:2014:2358, paragraph 74).

51. In order to determine whether social assistance, such as the benefits at issue in the main proceedings, may be refused on the basis of the derogation laid down in Article 24(2) of Directive 2004/38, it is therefore necessary to determine beforehand whether the principle of equal treatment referred to in Article 24(1) of that directive is applicable and, accordingly, whether the Union citizen concerned is lawfully resident on the territory of the host Member State.

52. Only two provisions of Directive 2004/38 may confer on job-seekers in the situation of Ms Alimanovic and her daughter Sonita a right of residence in the host Member State under that directive, namely Article 7(3)(c) and Article 14(4)(b) thereof.

53. In this connection, Article 7(3)(c) of Directive 2004/38 provides that if the worker is in duly recorded involuntary unemployment after completing a fixed-term employment contract of less than a year or after having become involuntarily unemployed during the first 12 months and has registered as a jobseeker with the relevant

employment office, he retains the status of worker for no less than six months. During that period, the Union citizen concerned retains his right of residence in the host Member State under Article 7 of Directive 2004/38 and may, consequently, rely on the principle of equal treatment, laid down in Article 24(1) of that directive.

54. The Court thus held, in the judgment in *Vatsouras and Koupatantze* (C-22/08 and C-23/08, EU:C:2009:344, paragraph 32), that Union citizens who have retained the status of workers on the basis of Article 7(3)(c) of Directive 2004/38 have the right to social assistance, such as the benefits at issue, during that period of at least six months.

55. However, as the Advocate General observes in point 41 of his Opinion, it is not disputed that Ms Alimanovic and her daughter Sonita, who retained the status of workers for at least six months after their last employment had ended, no longer enjoyed that status when they were refused entitlement to the benefits at issue.

56. As regards the question whether a right of residence under Directive 2004/38 might be established on the basis of Article 14(4)(b) thereof for Union citizens in the situation of Ms Alimanovic and her daughter Sonita, that provision stipulates that Union citizens who have entered the territory of the host Member State in order to seek employment may not be expelled for as long as they can provide evidence that they are continuing to seek employment and that they have a genuine chance of being engaged.

57. Although, according to the referring court, Ms Alimanovic and her daughter Sonita may rely on that provision to establish a right of residence even after the expiry of the period referred to in Article 7(3)(c) of Directive 2004/38, for a period, covered by Article 14(4)(b) thereof, which entitles them to equal treatment with the nationals of the host Member State so far as access to social assistance is concerned, it must nevertheless be observed that, in such a case, the host Member State may rely on the derogation in Article 24(2) of that directive in order not to grant that citizen the social assistance sought.

58. It follows from the express reference in Article 24(2) of Directive 2004/38 to Article 14(4)(b) thereof that the host Member State may refuse to grant any social assistance to a Union citizen whose right of residence is based solely on that latter provision.

59. It must be stated in this connection that, although the Court has held that Directive 2004/38 requires a Member State to take account of the individual situation of the person concerned before it adopts an expulsion measure or finds that the residence of that person is placing an unreasonable burden on its social assistance system (judgment in *Brey*, C-140/12, EU:C:2013:565, paragraphs 64, 69 and 78), no such

individual assessment is necessary in circumstances such as those at issue in the main proceedings.

60. Directive 2004/38, establishing a gradual system as regards the retention of the status of 'worker' which seeks to safeguard the right of residence and access to social assistance, itself takes into consideration various factors characterising the individual situation of each applicant for social assistance and, in particular, the duration of the exercise of any economic activity.

61. By enabling those concerned to know, without any ambiguity, what their rights and obligations are, the criterion referred to both in Paragraph 7(1) of Book II, read in conjunction with Paragraph 2(3) of the Law on freedom of movement, and in Article 7(3)(c) of Directive 2004/38, namely a period of six months after the cessation of employment during which the right to social assistance is retained, is consequently such as to guarantee a significant level of legal certainty and transparency in the context of the award of social assistance by way of basic provision, while complying with the principle of proportionality.

62. Moreover, as regards the individual assessment for the purposes of making an overall appraisal of the burden which the grant of a specific benefit would place on the national system of social assistance at issue in the main proceedings as a whole, it must be observed that the assistance awarded to a single applicant can scarcely be described as an 'unreasonable burden' for a Member State, within the meaning of Article 14(1) of Directive 2004/38. However, while an individual claim might not place the Member State concerned under an unreasonable burden, the accumulation of all the individual claims which would be submitted to it would be bound to do so.

63. Having regard to all the foregoing considerations, the answer to the second question is that Article 24 of Directive 2004/38 and Article 4 of Regulation No 883/2004 must be interpreted as not precluding legislation of a Member State under which nationals of other Member States who are in a situation such as that referred to in Article 14(4)(b) of that directive are excluded from entitlement to certain 'special non-contributory cash benefits' within the meaning of Article 70(2) of Regulation No 883/2004, which also constitute 'social assistance' within the meaning of Article 24(2) of Directive 2004/38, although those benefits are granted to nationals of the Member State concerned who are in the same situation.

Costs

[Para. 64 omitted]

On those grounds,

THE COURT (Grand Chamber),

hereby rules:

Article 24 of Directive 2004/38/EC of the European Parliament and of the Council of 29 April 2004 on the right of citizens of the Union and their family members to move and reside freely within the territory of the Member States, amending Regulation (EEC) No 1612/68 and repealing Directives 64/221/EEC, 68/360/EEC, 72/194/EEC, 73/148/EEC, 75/34/EEC, 75/35/EEC, 90/364/EEC, 90/365/EEC and 93/96/EEC and Article 4 of Regulation (EC) No 883/2004 of the European Parliament and of the Council of 29 April 2004 on the coordination of social security systems, as amended by Commission Regulation (EU) No 1244/2010 of 9 December 2010, must be interpreted as not precluding legislation of a Member State under which nationals of other Member States who are in a situation such as that referred to in Article 14(4)(b) of that directive are excluded from entitlement to certain 'special non-contributory cash benefits' within the meaning of Article 70(2) of Regulation No 883/2004, which also constitute 'social assistance' within the meaning of Article 24(2) of Directive 2004/38, although those benefits are granted to nationals of the Member State concerned who are in the same situation.

Comments and questions

In the *Dano* case, printed above in Chapter 3, the CJEU ruled that Union law does not grant a right to social assistance to Union citizens who exercise their right of freedom of movement without the intention of being economically active if they do not have sufficient resources to entitle them to claim a right of residence for more than three months pursuant to Article 7(1)(b) of the Free Movement Directive (Directive 2004/38). Thereby the CJEU largely dealt with those cases where a Union citizen takes up residence in another Member State with a view to obtaining social assistance in the host Member State, often referred to as 'welfare tourism'.

While the *Dano* case has been important in dealing with welfare tourism, the ruling did not deal with welfare tourism where a Union citizen takes up residence in another Member State and claims social assistance as a job-seeker. This was the situation in the *Alimanovic* case

This case concerned Nazifa Alimanovic and her three children, all of whom were Swedish citizens. In 2010 the family travelled from Sweden to Germany, where the mother and the oldest daughter had several temporary jobs or activities in employment schemes. This employment lasted less than a year. Thereafter the family was not economically active, and the family received benefits by the way of basic provision for half a year. After that the German authorities decided to stop paying assistance to the family, as it was considered that the mother and oldest daughter were not entitled to the assistance in their capacity as foreign job-seekers whose right of residence arose solely out of the search for employment. This also meant that the authorities ceased to pay assistance in respect of the family's other children.

When the case was brought before the German courts, the main question was whether the refusal by the German authorities to, pay (further) assistance was contrary to the Union law principle of equal treatment. The CJEU found that the purpose of the social assistance in question was to ensure the subsistence of those who were unable to obtain a minimum subsistence income. As in the *Dano* case, the payments should be regarded as 'social assistance'. The CJEU also noted that, in relation to such social assistance, a Union citizen could only claim a right to the same treatment as the citizens of the host Member State if their residence in the host Member State fulfilled the conditions of the Free Movement Directive.

In contrast to the *Dano* case, the *Alimanovic* case concerned job-seeking Union citizens. The CJEU ruled that, in this situation there are two possibilities for giving a Union citizen a right of residence:

1) If a Union citizen has exercised their right as a worker and becomes involuntary unemployed after having worked for less than 12 months, and if the Union citizen registers as a jobseeker with the relevant employment office, they retain the status of worker for no less than six months; see Article 7(3) of the Free Movement Directive. During this period, the Union citizen retains their right of residence in the host Member State and may rely on the principle of equal treatment and have a right to social assistance.

2) If a Union citizen has not yet worked in the host Member State, or when the six-month period comes to an end, a job-seeker cannot be expelled from the host Member State as long as it is shown that the Union citizen is still seeking work and has a genuine possibility of finding a job. However, in this situation the host Member State may refuse to pay social assistance; see Article 24(2) of the Free Movement Directive.

The requirement in the first category, that the Union citizen must register with the employment office, is important, as it provides evidence that the Union citizen is actively seeking work. It is by demanding that a Union citizen actively seek work that the host Member State can restrict welfare tourism.

The Alimanovic family fell within the first of these two categories. Based on the information given in the judgment, is it possible to decide whether the family was entitled to social assistance?

In its judgment of 4 June 2009 in Joined Cases C-22/08 and C-23/08 *Vatsouras* [2009] ECR I-4585, the CJEU had to decide whether the entitlement of two Greek jobseekers were entitled to German benefits by the way of basic provision, if they had not retained the status of an employee pursuant to Article 7(3) of the Free Movement Directive and were thus not covered by Article 24(1) TFEU, but by Article 24(2) TFEU. In this connection the CJEU stated as follows in paragraphs 40-43:

> 'nationals of the Member States seeking employment in another Member State who have established real links with the labour market of that State can rely on Article 39(2) EC [now Article 45(2) TFEU] in order to receive a benefit of a financial nature intended to facilitate access to the labour market ... It is for the competent national authorities and, where appropriate, the national courts not only to establish the existence of a real link with the labour market, but also to assess the constituent elements of that benefit, in particular its purposes and the conditions subject to which it is granted ... the objective of the benefit must be analysed according to its results and not according to its formal structure ... A condition such as that in Paragraph 7(1) of the SGB II [Book II of the German Code of Social Law], under which the person concerned must be capable of earning a living, could constitute an indication that the benefit is intended to facilitate access to employment.'

It should be noted that the *Vatsouras* judgment was not delivered by the CJEU's Grand Chamber, but by its lesser Third Chamber.

Does the *Alimanovic* decision overturns the *Vatsouras* decision, or is possible to reconcile the two decisions? The mother and oldest daughter of the Alimanovic family had worked for a little under 12 months. If they had instead had paid work for more than a year and had then become involuntarily unemployed, would they have retained their status as workers and the rights attached to this (i.e. would they have been entitled to the social assistance they sought)? In this respect, see Article 7(3)(b) of the Free Movement Directive.

The *Alimanovic* case is the latest in a long line of important cases. In 1991 the CJEU established that Article 45 TFEU covers the right of Union citizens to reside in another Member State with a view to seeking work there; see Case C-292/89 *Antonissen* [1991] ECR I-745. In the *Antonissen* case the CJEU ruled that Article 45(3) TFEU does not contain an exhaustive list of the rights of Union citizens in relation to the free movement of workers, and that this freedom includes the right of Union citizens to move to other Member States with a view to seeking work there. The question was then whether the duration of this right could be limited. The CJEU ruled that what was decisive was whether a job-seeker had reasonable time to become acquainted with job offers in the host Member State and to take the necessary steps to become employed. One important question was whether it was possible to establish a norm for this time limit. The CJEU acknowledged that, in principle, the British limit of six months appeared reasonable. However, it added that if, after the expiry of such a six-month period, a job-seeker could show that they continued to seek work and had a genuine chance of being employed,, the host Member State cannot expel them. In the subsequent *Collins* case the CJEU confirmed that a job-seeker has a right of residence for a limited period pursuant to Article 45 TFEU. Moreover, Article 14(4) of the Free Movement Directive expressly states that job-seekers and their family members may not be expelled as long as it can be shown that the job-seeker continues to seek work and had a genuine chance of being employed.

In 1980-81, Collins, who had dual Irish and American citizenship, had spent 10 months in the United Kingdom, where he had had various small jobs working in bars etc. He then left the United Kingdom and worked outside the EU. 17 years later, in

1998, Collins returned to the United Kingdom in order to seek work there. Immediately after his return he sought unemployment benefit, which the British authorities refused. The refusal was based on the fact that Collins could not be regarded as a worker in the United Kingdom. Collins appealed against the decision at several stages, and the case was eventually referred by the British Social Security Commissioner to the CJEU.

The CJEU first established that the concept of 'worker' has a specific meaning in Union law and must not be interpreted narrowly. A person is covered by the concept if he or she pursues activities which are real and genuine, unless the work is of such a small scale as to be regarded as purely marginal and ancillary. The CJEU also held that the essential feature of an employment relationship is that for a certain period a person performs services for and under the direction of another person in return for which he receives remuneration. It was not disputed that Collins did not satisfy these criteria as he was merely seeking work. The CJEU went on to state that persons, who do not satisfy these criteria, can claim the rights of workers. This applies where the person concerned has been a worker but is no longer in employment.

The work which Collins had carried out in 1980-81 presumably fulfilled the requirements for him to be regarded as a worker in the United Kingdom at that time. However, there was no close connection between his previous employment and his seeking work 17 years later. Consequently, he could not be regarded as being covered by the concept of a 'worker'. Collins should therefore be treated like any other Union citizen seeking work in another Member State. With regard to a right to work, he could only make a claim under the principle of equal treatment whereas he could not rely on Article 7(2) of Regulation No 1612/68, then in force (now Regulation 492/2011), on freedom of movement for workers within the Union. The latter ensured that citizens from one Member State who were workers in another Member State could claim social and tax benefits as domestic workers.

The CJEU did not go into greater detail on when the connection between a person's previous employment and the subsequent seeking for work is sufficiently strong for that person to be considered as being covered by the concept of a 'worker'. However it is natural to assume that weight can be given to three factors. First, there is the aspect of time. Second, there can be a connection between the previous work and the work which is now sought. And third, there can be other connecting factors. Consider whether a person should be regarded as a worker in the following situations:

- An Irish citizen has worked in Finland for a number of years as a taxi driver. He decides to travel around the world for two years, and then returns to Finland to seek new work as a taxi driver.
- An Irish citizen works as a bar tender in Finland for a short period. He then moves to Dublin, where he opens his own bar. At the same time he trains as an accountant. Seven years later he returns to Finland, where he seeks work as an accountant.
- An Irish citizen works as an unpaid trainee cook in Finland. After completing his training, he works for a short period in Finland, before moving to France, Denmark, Ireland, Spain and Italy, in order to improve his skills by working in some of the best

restaurants in these countries. Five years later he wants to work as a cook in Finland on a more permanent basis, and seeks work in the best restaurants in Helsinki.

It is interesting to note that, since the introduction of Union citizenship, the CJEU has changed its earlier view, that according to Article 45 TFEU people seeking work were entitled to financial support from the host Member State; see for example, Case 316/85 *Lebon* [1987] ECR 2811. In the *Collins* case the CJEU stated in paragraph 63:

> 'In view of the establishment of citizenship of the Union and the interpretation in the case-law of the right to equal treatment enjoyed by citizens of the Union, it is no longer possible to exclude from the scope of [Article 45(2) TFEU] – which expresses the fundamental principle of equal treatment, guaranteed by [Article 18 TFEU] – a benefit of a financial nature intended to facilitate access to employment in the labour market of a Member State.'

Union citizenship has thus been used by the CJEU for interpreting Article 45 TFEU extensively. It follows that, even though persons seeking work are not covered by the EU concept of a 'worker', such persons may invoke both Article 45 TFEU and, after the Collins judgment, Article 14(4)(b) of the Free Movement Directive (Directive 2004/38). Following the judgment in the *Alimanovic* case, in which the CJEU attached decisive weight to Article 24(2) of the Free Movement Directive, which derogates from the principle of equal treatment in the case of first-time job-seekers, whereby they are not characterised as migrant workers, the CJEU has effectively overruled paragraph 63 of the *Collins* judgment on this point. Nevertheless, the CJEU refrained from stating this explicitly.

JUDGMENT OF THE COURT (Third Chamber)
5 June 1997

Land Nordrhein-Westfalen v Kari Uecker and Vera Jacquet
v Land Nordrhein-Westfalen.
(Reference for a preliminary ruling: Landesarbeitsgericht Hamm – Germany)

'Freedom of movement for workers – Right of a spouse of a Community national who has the nationality of a non-member country to be employed – Situation purely internal to a Member State'

Joined Cases C-64/96 and C-65/96

Judgment

1. By orders of 26 January 1996 (Case C-64/96) and 1 March 1996 (Case C-65/96), received at the Court on 8 March 1996, the Landesarbeitsgericht (Higher Labour Court) Hamm referred to the Court for a preliminary ruling under Article 177 of the EC Treaty three questions, identical in the two cases, on the interpretation of Article 48(2) of the EC Treaty and Articles 7(1) and 11 of Regulation (EEC) No 1612/68 of the Council of 15 October 1968 on freedom of movement for workers within the Community (OJ, English Special Edition 1968 (II), p. 475).

2. Those questions were raised in two sets of proceedings in which Ms Uecker and Ms Jacquet are in dispute with the Land Nordrhein-Westfalen.

3. Ms Uecker, a Norwegian national, and Ms Jacquet, a Russian national, teach Norwegian and Russian respectively in German universities, are married to German nationals and live in Germany. It appears from the files in the main proceedings that their husbands exercise a professional or trade activity in Germany.

4. Ms Uecker and Ms Jacquet entered into contracts of employment with the Land Nordrhein-Westfalen on 24 September 1990 and on 14 March 1994 respectively to work as foreign-language assistants, in Ms Uecker's case at the University of Münster and in Ms Jacquet's case at the University of Bochum. For various reasons, and in particular in pursuance of Paragraph 57b(3) of the Hochschulrahmengesetz (Framework Law on Higher Education, hereinafter 'the HRG'), those contracts were for a limited period, expiring on 30 September 1994 in Ms Uecker's case and on 30 September 1996 in Ms Jacquet's.

5. Paragraph 57b(3) of the HRG provides:

   'An objective ground also exists for the engagement on a fixed-term contract of an instructor performing special duties who is a speaker of a foreign language where the instructor is mainly engaged to teach foreign languages (as a 'foreign language assistant').'

6. Ms Uecker and Ms Jacquet brought proceedings before the Arbeitsgericht (Labour Court) Münster and the Arbeitsgericht Bochum respectively. Ms Uecker sought a declaration that the clause limiting the duration of the contract was invalid and Ms Jacquet sought a finding that there was an employment relationship not limited in duration between the parties.

7. Referring to Case C-272/92 Spotti v Freistaat Bayern [1993] ECR I-5185, Ms Uecker submitted in support of her action that Paragraph 57b(3) of the HRG was incompatible with Article 28 of the Agreement on the European Economic Area of 2 May 1992, which entered into force on 1 January 1994 ('the EEA Agreement'), and Article 48(2) of the Treaty. The fact that her contract of employment was concluded before the EEA Agreement entered into force was, she argued, irrelevant since it had to be interpreted in accordance with the case-law of the Court of Justice.

8. Ms Jacquet also put forward the argument that, according to the case-law of the Court of Justice, Paragraph 57b(3) of the HRG is no longer applicable and further based her case on the right to equal treatment provided for in Article 11 of Regulation No 1612/68 and Article 7 of Regulation (EEC) No 1251/70 of the Commission of 29 June 1970 on the right of workers to remain in the territory of a Member State after having been employed in that State (OJ, English Special Edition 1970 (II), p. 402).

9. Ms Uecker's application was allowed by judgment of the Arbeitsgericht Münster of 23 September 1994, which also relied on Article 11 of Regulation No 1612/68. The Land Nordrhein-Westfalen appealed against that decision to the Landesarbeitsgericht Hamm.

10. Ms Jacquet's action, however, was dismissed by judgment of the Arbeitsgericht Bochum of 28 April 1995, on the basis of Paragraph 57b(3) of the HRG. Ms Jacquet appealed against that decision to the Landesarbeitsgericht Hamm.

11. The Landesarbeitsgericht Hamm states in its orders for reference that it does not share the view taken by the Oberverwaltungsgericht (Higher Administrative Court) Münster on 12 February 1990 (12 A 2363/87 NVwZ 1990, p. 889), that Article 11 of Regulation No 1612/68 does not apply where a foreign national not having the nationality of a Member State resides in a Member State with his or her spouse who

is a national of that State and who exercises a professional or trade activity there, since it presupposes that the national of a Member State exercises a professional or trade activity and lives with his or her spouse in a Member State other than his or her State of origin. The Landesarbeitsgericht Hamm does not accept the assumption, underlying that view, that a national of a Member State cannot rely on the provisions of Community law on freedom of movement against his or her own State because the legal relations between a Member State and its nationals are irrelevant to Community law.

12. It observes, moreover, that it is doubtful whether the fundamental principles of a Community moving towards European Union continue to permit a rule of national law incompatible with Article 48(2) of the EC Treaty still to be applied by a Member State against its own nationals.

13. Taking the view that its decision would be dependent on the interpretation of provisions of Community law, the Landesarbeitsgericht Hamm stayed proceedings and referred the following questions to the Court for a preliminary ruling:

‘1. May the spouse – not being a national of a Member State – of a national of that Member State in which the spouses live and in which the spouse who is a national is employed also rely on the right under Article 11 of Regulation (EEC) No 1612/68 of 15 October 1968 on freedom of movement for workers within the Community?

2. If Question 1 is answered in the affirmative:

Does that right of the spouse who is not a national of a Member State to ‘take up any activity as an employed person’ throughout the territory of the Member State concerned include the right, with respect to the conditions of employment and work, in particular with respect to the conditions for an effective temporal limitation of an employment relationship, to be treated by an employer in the Member State concerned in the same way as that employer would have to treat the spouse who is a national of the Member State?

3. If Question 2 is also answered in the affirmative:

Does Article 7(1) of the said Regulation (EEC) No 1612/68 in conjunction with Article 48(2) of the EEC Treaty confer on a worker in a Member State of which he is a national the right to the same treatment as is due to workers who are nationals of another Member State, and is a national provision which has been held by the Court of Justice to be inapplicable against the latter persons therefore also inapplicable against the relevant Member State's own nationals and their spouses who are not nationals of a Member State?’

14. By order of the President of the Court of 21 March 1996, these two cases were joined for the purposes of the written and oral procedure and of the judgment.

The first question

15. The national court's first question is, in substance, whether a national of a non-member country married to a worker having the nationality of a Member State can rely on the right conferred by Article 11 of Regulation No 1612/68 within that same Member State when the worker exercises a professional or trade activity there.

16. It has consistently been held that the Treaty rules governing freedom of movement and regulations adopted to implement them cannot be applied to cases which have no factor linking them with any of the situations governed by Community law and all elements of which are purely internal to a single Member State (Joined Cases 35/82 and 36/82 Morson and Jhanjan v State of the Netherlands [1982] ECR 3723, paragraph 16; Case 147/87 Zaoui v Cramif [1987] ECR 5511, paragraph 15; Case C-332/90 Steen v Deutsche Bundespost [1992] ECR I-341, paragraph 9; Case C-153/91 Petit v Office National des Pensions [1992] ECR I-4973, paragraph 8; and Case C-206/91 Koua Poirrez v Caisse d'Allocations Familiales [1992] ECR I-6685, paragraph 11).

17. Consequently, Community legislation regarding freedom of movement for workers cannot be applied to the situation of workers who have never exercised the right to freedom of movement within the Community.

18. According to the orders for reference, however, the husbands of Ms Uecker and Ms Jacquet are German nationals who reside and work in Germany and have never exercised the right to freedom of movement within the Community.

19. In those circumstances, a member of the family of a worker who is a national of a Member State cannot rely on Community law to challenge the validity of a limitation on the duration of his or her contract of employment within that same State when the worker in question has never exercised the right to freedom of movement within the Community.

20. The fact that the German version of Article 11 of Regulation No 1612/68, unlike other language versions (English, Danish, Spanish, Swedish and Finnish), does not mention that it concerns the spouse and dependent children of a national of a Member State pursuing an activity as an employed or self-employed person 'in the territory of another Member State' but merely refers to 'the territory of a Member State' cannot affect that conclusion.

21. To grant the spouse of a worker who is a national of a Member State the right to be employed in that State, in which the worker exercises a professional or trade activi-

ty, would not correspond to the objective of Article 48 of the Treaty which Regulation No 1612/68 seeks to implement, namely in particular that of enabling a worker to move freely within the territory of the other Member States and to stay there for the purpose of employment.

22. Finally, the national court asks whether the fundamental principles of a Community moving towards European Union still permit a rule of national law which is incompatible with Community law because it is in breach of Article 48(2) of the Treaty to continue to be applied by a Member State against its own nationals and their spouses from non-member countries.

23. In that regard, it must be noted that citizenship of the Union, established by Article 8 of the EC Treaty, is not intended to extend the scope ratione materiae of the Treaty also to internal situations which have no link with Community law. Furthermore, Article M of the Treaty on European Union provides that nothing in that Treaty is to affect the Treaties establishing the European Communities, subject to the provisions expressly amending those treaties. Any discrimination which nationals of a Member State may suffer under the law of that State fall within the scope of that law and must therefore be dealt with within the framework of the internal legal system of that State.

24. The answer to be given must therefore be that a national of a non-member country married to a worker having the nationality of a Member State cannot rely on the right conferred by Article 11 of Regulation No 1612/68 when that worker has never exercised the right to freedom of movement within the Community.

25. In view of the answer given to the first question, there is no need to answer the second and third questions, which were submitted only in the event of the first question being answered in the affirmative.

Costs

[Para. 26 omitted]

On those grounds,

THE COURT (Third Chamber),

in answer to the questions referred to it by the Landesarbeitsgericht Hamm by orders of 26 January and 1 March 1996, hereby rules:

A national of a non-member country married to a worker having the nationality of a Member State cannot rely on the right conferred by Article 11 of Regulation (EEC) No 1612/68 of the Council of 15 October 1968 on freedom of

movement for workers within the Community when that worker has never exercised the right to freedom of movement within the Community.

Comments and questions

If a case contains no elements of cross-border activities between Member States, the Treaty rules on freedom of movement of workers and freedom to provide services do not apply. This is expressed as follows in paragraph 16 of the judgment in Joined Cases C-64/96 and C-65/96 *Land Nordrhein-Westfalen* v *Uecker and Jacquet* v *Land Nordrhein-Westfalen* [1997] ECR I-3171 (the *Jacquet* case): 'It has consistently been held that the Treaty rules governing freedom of movement and regulations adopted to implement them cannot be applied to cases which have no factor linking them with any of the situations governed by [Union] law and all elements of which are *purely internal* to a single Member State' (emphasis added). This means that provisions on the freedom of movement for workers cannot be applied to workers who have never exercised the right to freedom of movement within the Union; cf. paragraph 17. Does this statement appear to be limited to the freedom of movement of persons, or does it apply to all four fundamental freedoms? Compare this point with Case C-448/98 *Guimont* [2000] ECR I-10663, printed in Chapter 2 above, and Case C-159/12 *Venturini*, printed in Chapter 5 below.

The spouses of both Jacquet (a Russian national) and Uecker (a Norwegian national) were both German nationals who were resident in and worked in Germany, but who had never exercised their right of freedom of movement in the EU. On this basis, neither Jacquet nor Uecker could rely on Article 45 (formerly Article 48 TEC), even though they were married to workers who were nationals of an EU Member State. Under what circumstances could they have relied on Article 45 TFEU in a case against the German authorities? In this case, would the appointment of a lecturer in a foreign language for a limited period be compatible with Article 45 TFEU?

Even though, in principle (see the *Zambrano* judgment printed in Chapter 3 above), Article 20 TFEU does not apply to purely internal matters, in paragraph 40 of Case C-212/06 *Government of Communauté française* [2008] ECR I-1683, the CJEU stated that 'interpretation of provisions of [Union] law might possibly be of use to the national court ... in particular if the law of the Member State concerned were to require every national of that State to be allowed to enjoy the same rights as those which a national of another Member State would derive from [Union] law in a situation considered to be comparable by that court'. See similarly paragraph 14 of the judgment in Case C-281/98 *Angonese* [2000] ECR I-4139, reproduced above. Case C-212/06 concerned the relationship between the provisions in the TFEU and a Flemish care insurance scheme, under which persons who were not resident in the Flemish region or in Brussels, but who were employed there, were not covered by the scheme. The CJEU ruled that such a scheme was in breach of Articles 45 and 49 TFEU 'in so far as such limitation affects nationals of other Member States or nationals of the Member State concerned who have made use of their right to freedom of movement within the European [Union].'

JUDGMENT OF THE COURT (Grand Chamber)
18 July 2007

Gertraud Hartmann v Freistaat Bayern. (Reference for a preliminary ruling from the Bundessozialgericht – Germany)

'Frontier worker – Regulation (EEC) No 1612/68 – Transfer of residence to another Member State – Non-working spouse – Child-raising allowance – Not granted to spouse – Social advantage – Residence condition'

Case C-212/05

Judgment

1. This reference for a preliminary ruling concerns the interpretation of Regulation (EEC) No 1612/68 of the Council of 15 October 1968 on freedom of movement for workers within the Community (OJ, English Special Edition 1968 (II), p. 475).

2. The reference was made in the course of proceedings between Ms Hartmann and Freistaat Bayern (Free State of Bavaria) concerning the latter's refusal to grant her child-raising allowance for her children.

Legal context

Community legislation

3. Article 7(1) and (2) of Regulation No 1612/68 reads as follows:

   '1. A worker who is a national of a Member State may not, in the territory of another Member State, be treated differently from national workers by reason of his nationality in respect of any conditions of employment and work, in particular as regards remuneration, dismissal, and should he become unemployed, reinstatement or re-employment;

   2. He shall enjoy the same social and tax advantages as national workers.'

National legislation

4. According to the order for reference, Paragraph 1(1) of the Bundeserziehungsgeldgesetz (Law on child-raising allowance and parental leave, 'the BErzGG'), in the version applicable at the material time, provides that any person permanently or ordinarily resident in Germany who has a dependent child in his household, looks af-

ter and brings up that child, and has no, or no full-time, employment can claim child-raising allowance.

5. In addition, under Paragraph 1(4) of the BErzGG, in the version applicable at the material time, nationals of the Member States of the European Union and frontier workers from countries having a common frontier with Germany are entitled to child-raising allowance, provided that they are engaged in more than minor employment in Germany.

6. Under Paragraph 1(7) of the BErzGG, in the amended version of 12 October 2000, the spouse resident in another Member State of a person working in the civil service or a public-law employment in Germany may receive child-raising allowance. However, under Paragraph 24(1) of the BErzGG, in the amended version of 12 October 2000, that provision does not apply for children born before 1 January 2001.

The main proceedings and the order for reference

7. Ms Hartmann is an Austrian national married since 1990 to a German national who previously lived in Germany. Since 1990 they have lived in Austria with their three children, who were born in March 1991, May 1993 and September 1997. The applicant's husband works in Germany as a civil servant (for Deutsche Bundespost from 1986, and for Deutsche Telekom AG since 1995).

8. By decisions of 25 September 1991, in the version of the decision of 7 January 1992 on her objection, and 20 September 1993, in the version of the decision of 26 January 1994 on her objection, the Free State of Bavaria refused to grant Ms Hartmann the child-raising allowance provided for by the BErzGG, in the version applicable at the material time, for her first two children.

9. By decisions of 10 and 23 June 1998, in the version of the decision of 7 September 1998 on her objection, Ms Hartmann's applications for review were rejected, as was her application for child-raising allowance for the first year of the life of her younger son. The grounds for the refusal to grant that child-raising allowance were that Ms Hartmann was not resident in Germany and did not work there.

10. After the Sozialgericht München (Social Court, Munich) had, by decision of 14 February 2001, dismissed the action brought by Ms Hartmann, she appealed against that decision to the Bayerisches Landessozialgericht (Bavarian Higher Social Court), which likewise dismissed her appeal by judgment of 1 July 2003. That court considered that under German law Ms Hartmann was not entitled to child-raising allowance, since she did not live in Germany. Nor could the allowance be granted her under Community law.

11. In that court's view, Council Regulation (EEC) No 1408/71 of 14 June 1971 on the application of social security schemes to employed persons, to self-employed persons and to members of their families moving within the Community, as amended and updated by Council Regulation (EEC) No 2001/83 of 2 June 1983 (OJ 1983 L 230, p. 6), as amended by Council Regulation (EEC) No 1249/92 of 30 April 1992 (OJ 1992 L 136, p. 28) ('Regulation No 1408/71'), was not applicable in this case because neither Ms Hartmann nor her husband fell within the scope of that regulation: Ms Hartmann was not employed, and her husband, as a civil servant, was not an 'employed person' within the meaning of point 1(C) ('Germany') of Annex I to Regulation No 1408/71.

12. The Bayerisches Landessozialgericht added that a right to child-raising allowance could not be based on Article 7(2) of Regulation No 1612/68 either, since Regulation No 1408/71 took precedence over that regulation.

13. Ms Hartmann thereupon appealed on a point of law to the Bundessozialgericht (Federal Social Court).

14. In those circumstances, the Bundessozialgericht decided to stay the proceedings and refer the following two questions to the Court for a preliminary ruling:

 '1. Is a German national who, while continuing his service as a post office official in Germany, moved his permanent residence from Germany to Austria in 1990 and has since then carried on his occupation as a frontier worker to be regarded as a migrant worker within the meaning of Regulation (EEC) No 1612/68 ... for periods between January 1994 and September 1998?

 2. If so:
 Does it constitute indirect discrimination within the meaning of Article 7(2) of Regulation No 1612/68 if the non-working spouse of the person mentioned in Question 1, who lives in Austria and is an Austrian national, was excluded from receiving German child-raising allowance in the period in question because she did not have either her permanent or ordinary residence in Germany?'

The questions referred for a preliminary ruling

Question 1

15. By its first question, the national court essentially asks whether a national of a Member State who, while maintaining his employment in that State, has transferred his residence to another Member State and has since then carried on his occupation as a frontier worker can claim the status of migrant worker for the purposes of Regulation No 1612/68.

16. The German Government, the United Kingdom Government and the Commission of the European Communities, in their written observations, and the Netherlands Government, at the hearing, submitted that only the movement of a person to another Member State for the purpose of carrying on an occupation should be regarded as an exercise of the right of freedom of movement for workers. A person such as Mr Hartmann, who never left his employment in the Member State of which he is a national and merely transferred his residence to the Member State of his spouse, could not therefore benefit from the Community provisions on freedom of movement for workers.

17. That argument must be considered in the light of the judgment in Case C-152/03 *Ritter-Coulais* [2006] ECR I-1711. In that case the Court, examining the position of the appellants in the main proceedings in the light of the principle of freedom of movement for workers set out in Article 48 of the EC Treaty (now, after amendment, Article 39 EC), observed in paragraphs 31 and 32 of the judgment that any national of a Member State, irrespective of his place of residence and his nationality, who has exercised the right to freedom of movement for workers and who has been employed in a Member State other than that of residence falls within the scope of that provision. It followed that the appellants in the main proceedings, who worked in a Member State other than that of their actual place of residence, fell within the scope of Article 48 of the Treaty.

18. In the present case, the situation which gave rise to the main proceedings is that of a person who, since the transfer of his residence, resides in one Member State and works in another Member State. That Mr Hartmann settled in Austria for reasons not connected with his employment does not justify refusing him the status of migrant worker which he acquired as from the time when, following the transfer of his residence to Austria, he made full use of his right to freedom of movement for workers by going to Germany to carry on an occupation there.

19. It follows that for the period from January 1994 to September 1998 the situation of a frontier worker such as Mr Hartmann falls within the scope of the provisions of the EC Treaty on freedom of movement for workers, and hence of Regulation No 1612/68.

20. Having regard to the above considerations, the answer to Question 1 must be that a national of a Member State who, while maintaining his employment in that State, has transferred his residence to another Member State and has since then carried on his occupation as a frontier worker can claim the status of migrant worker for the purposes of Regulation No 1612/68.

Question 2

21. By its second question, the national court essentially asks whether, in circumstances such as those at issue in the main proceedings, Article 7(2) of Regulation No 1612/68 precludes a migrant worker's non-working spouse, who lives in Austria and has the nationality of that Member State, from being refused child-raising allowance on the ground that she did not have his permanent or ordinary residence in Germany.

22. The Court has already held that German child-raising allowance constitutes a social advantage within the meaning of Article 7(2) of Regulation No 1612/68 (see Case C-85/96 *Martínez Sala* [1998] ECR I-2691, paragraph 26).

23. The German and United Kingdom Governments observed that it would be unfair to allow a frontier worker whose residence and workplace are in different Member States to enjoy the same social advantages in both Member States and to combine them. To avoid that risk, and in view of the fact that Regulation No 1612/68 does not contain any coordinating rules to avoid cumulation of benefits, the possibility of 'exporting' child-raising allowance to the frontier worker's Member State of residence could be excluded.

24. It should be noted that Mr Hartmann's status of frontier worker does not in any way prevent him from being able to claim the equal treatment prescribed by Article 7(2) of Regulation No 1612/68 in relation to the grant of social advantages. The Court has already held that frontier workers can rely on the provisions of Article 7 of Regulation No 1612/68 on the same basis as any other worker to whom that article applies. The fourth recital in the preamble to that regulation expressly states that the right of freedom of movement must be enjoyed 'without discrimination by permanent, seasonal and frontier workers and by those who pursue their activities for the purpose of providing services', and Article 7 of the regulation refers, without reservation, to a 'worker who is a national of a Member State' (Case C-57/96 *Meints* [1997] ECR I-6689, paragraph 50).

25. In the case at issue in the main proceedings, child-raising allowance is claimed by Ms Hartmann, who, as the spouse of a worker who falls within the scope of Regulation No 1612/68, is only an indirect beneficiary of the equal treatment granted to migrant workers by Article 7(2) of that regulation. Consequently, the benefit of German child-raising allowance can be extended to Ms Hartmann only if that allowance constitutes for her husband a 'social advantage' within the meaning of Article 7(2) of Regulation No 1612/68 (see, by analogy, Case C-3/90 *Bernini* [1992] ECR I-1071, paragraph 26).

26. That is the case here. A benefit such as German child-raising allowance, which enables one of the parents to devote himself or herself to the raising of a young child,

by meeting family expenses (see, to that effect, Joined Cases C-245/94 and C-312/94 *Hoever and Zachow* [1996] ECR I-4895, paragraphs 23 to 25), benefits the family as a whole, whichever parent it is who claims the allowance. The grant of such an allowance to a worker's spouse is capable of reducing that worker's obligation to contribute to family expenses, and therefore constitutes for him or her a 'social advantage' within the meaning of Article 7(2) of Regulation No 1612/68 (see, by analogy, *Bernini*, paragraph 25).

27. Article 7(2) of Regulation No 1612/68 provides that a migrant worker is to enjoy the same social and tax advantages in the host Member State as national workers. Since child-raising allowance is a 'social advantage' within the meaning of that provision, a migrant worker in a situation such as that of Mr Hartmann, and consequently his spouse, must, for the reasons stated in paragraphs 25 and 26 above, be able to enjoy it on the same basis as a national worker.

28. According to the documents before the Court, the German legislation makes the grant of child-raising allowance conditional principally on the recipients being resident on national territory. Since such a rule can lead to indirect discrimination against workers who do not live in Germany, the national court wonders whether the rule can be justified and whether it satisfies the criterion of proportionality.

29. It should be recalled that the equal treatment rule which appears both in Article 39 EC and in Article 7 of Regulation No 1612/68 prohibits not only overt discrimination on grounds of nationality but also all covert forms of discrimination which, by the application of other criteria of differentiation, lead in fact to the same result (*Meints*, paragraph 44).

30. Unless it is objectively justified and proportionate to the aim pursued, a provision of national law must be regarded as indirectly discriminatory if it is intrinsically liable to affect migrant workers more than national workers and if there is a consequent risk that it will place the former at a particular disadvantage (*Meints*, paragraph 45).

31. That is true of a residence condition such as that at issue in the main proceedings, which, as the national court points out, can naturally be more easily met by German workers or their spouses, who usually live in Germany, than by workers from other Member States or their spouses, who more often reside in another Member State (see, by analogy, Case C-337/97 *Meeusen* [1999] ECR I-3289, paragraphs 23 and 24).

32. As explained by the national court, German child-raising allowance constitutes an instrument of national family policy intended to encourage the birth-rate in that country. The primary purpose of the allowance is to allow parents to care for their children themselves by giving up or reducing their employment in order to concentrate on bringing up their children in the first years of their life.

33. The German Government adds essentially that child-raising allowance is granted in order to benefit persons who, by their choice of residence, have established a real link with German society. It says that, in that context, a residence condition such as that at issue in the main proceedings is justified.

34. Regardless of whether the aims pursued by the German legislation could justify a national rule based exclusively on the criterion of residence, it must be observed that, according to the information provided by the national court, the German legislature did not confine itself to a strict application of the residence condition for the grant of child-raising allowance but allowed exceptions under which frontier workers could also claim it.

35. It appears from the order for reference that, under Paragraph 1(4) of the BErzGG, in the version applicable at the material time, frontier workers who carry on an occupation in Germany but reside in another Member State can claim German child-raising allowance if they carry on an occupation of a more than minor extent.

36. Consequently, it is apparent that, under the German legislation in force at the material time, residence was not regarded as the only connecting link with the Member State concerned, and a substantial contribution to the national labour market also constituted a valid factor of integration into the society of that Member State.

37. In those circumstances, the allowance at issue in the main proceedings could not be refused to a couple such as Mr and Ms Hartmann who do not live in Germany, but one of whom works full-time in that State.

38. Having regard to the above considerations, the answer to Question 2 must be that, in circumstances such as those at issue in the main proceedings, Article 7(2) of Regulation No 1612/68 precludes the spouse of a migrant worker carrying on an occupation in one Member State, who does not work and is resident in another Member State, from being refused a social advantage with the characteristics of German child-raising allowance on the ground that he did not have his permanent or ordinary residence in the former State.

Costs

[Para. 39 omitted]

On those grounds,

THE COURT (Grand Chamber)

hereby rules:

1. **A national of a Member State who, while maintaining his employment in that State, has transferred his residence to another Member State and has since then carried on his occupation as a frontier worker can claim the status of migrant worker for the purposes of Regulation (EEC) No 1612/68 of the Council of 15 October 1968 on freedom of movement for workers within the Community.**

2. **In circumstances such as those at issue in the main proceedings, Article 7(2) of Regulation No 1612/68 precludes the spouse of a migrant worker carrying on an occupation in one Member State, who does not work and is resident in another Member State, from being refused a social advantage with the characteristics of German child-raising allowance on the ground that he did not have his permanent or ordinary residence in the former State.**

Comments and questions

In the Case C-112/91 *Werner* v *Finanzamt Aachen-Innenstadt* [1993] ECR I-429, the CJEU ruled that a German dentist who had obtained all his professional qualifications in Germany, had exclusively practiced his profession in Germany and was subject to German tax law but resident in the Netherlands, could not rely on Article 49 TFEU to challenge the tax burden imposed on him, which was greater than it would have been if he had been resident in Germany. The only point on which Hans Werner did not have connection with his country of origin was that he had his residence in a different Member State than that in which he practised his profession. On that occasion the CJEU ruled that the mere fact that Hans Werner resided in the Netherlands was not sufficient to establish that his business in Germany constituted a cross-border establishment, allowing him to rely on Article 49 TFEU. The '*Hans Werner* doctrine' has since been applied not only in relation to the Union rules on establishment, but also to the rules on freedom of movement of workers pursuant to Article 49 TFEU. Thus the fact that an employee moved to another Member State, while remaining employed in his original Member State did not mean that that person could rely on the rights of a migrant worker in relation to his original Member State.

However, in Case C-152/03 *Ritter-Coulais* [2006] ECR I-1711, the CJEU changed its practice so that once it is established that a person is resident in one Member State but employed in another, this is sufficient for Article 45 TFEU to be applicable in relation to the Member State where he is employed (in relation to the Member State where he is resident, Articles 21 and 45 TFEU equally apply). In this connection it is immaterial why the Union citizen has moved residence to another Member State. Somewhat surprisingly, the *Ritter-Coulais* decision was only given limited attention.

In the *Hartmann* case the CJEU again had referred to it the question of whether Article 45 TFEU applies in a situation where a national of one Member State moves his residence to another Member State, while continuing to be employed in the first Member State. In his Opinion, the Advocate General argued that a person should only be considered to be a migrant worker if that person moves to another Member State with the aim of seeking employment or being employed in that Member State. The Advocate General also argued that if an employee moves to another Member State for reasons that have nothing to do with seeking employment or being employed, the provisions on the free movement of workers should not apply. It was the Advocate General's view that a person who exercises the right to move freely to another Member State for non-economic reasons should be treated in accordance with the Treaty provisions on Union citizenship. In the Advocate General's view the decision in the *Ritter-Coulais* case was not fully in accordance with the system for the free movement of persons between the Member States laid down in the TFEU. The CJEU did not agree with its Advocate General. On the contrary, in paragraph 20 the CJEU laconically stated 'that a national of a Member State who, while maintaining his employment in that State, has transferred his residence to another Member State and has since then carried on his occupation as a frontier worker can claim the status of migrant worker for the purposes of Regulation No 1612/68 [then in force, now Regulation 492/2011].'

Consider the consequences of the CJEU's new practice in a situation where, for example, a Danish national moves to Malmø in Sweden but continues to work in Denmark. To what extent will they be able to rely on the Treaty provisions on the free movement of workers, including the right to the same social and tax advantages as migrant workers working and resident in Denmark?

JUDGMENT OF THE COURT (Grand Chamber)
12 March 2014

S. v Minister voor Immigratie, Integratie en Asiel, and Minister voor Immigratie, Integratie en Asiel v G. (Request for a preliminary ruling: Raad van State - Netherlands)

'Articles 20 TFEU, 21(1) TFEU and 45 TFEU – Directive 2004/38/EC – Right to move and reside freely within the territory of the Member States – Beneficiaries – Right of residence of a third-country national who is a family member of a Union citizen in the Member State of which that citizen is a national – Union citizen residing in the Member State of which he is a national – Professional activities – Regular travel to another Member State'

Case C-457/12

Judgment

1. This request for a preliminary ruling concerns the interpretation of Articles 20 TFEU, 21(1) TFEU and 45 TFEU and Directive 2004/38/EC of the European Parliament and of the Council of 29 April 2004 on the right of citizens of the Union and their family members to move and reside freely within the territory of the Member States amending Regulation (EEC) No 1612/68 and repealing Directives 64/221/EEC, 68/360/EEC, 72/194/EEC, 73/148/EEC, 75/34/EEC, 75/35/EEC, 90/364/EEC, 90/365/EEC and 93/96/EEC (OJ 2004 L 158, p. 77, and corrigenda at OJ 2004 L 229, p. 35, and OJ 2005 L 197, p. 34).

2. The request has been made in two sets of proceedings between the Minister voor Immigratie, Integratie en Asiel (Minister for Immigration, Integration and Asylum) ('the Minister'), on the one hand, and, respectively, Ms S. and Ms G., third-country nationals and family members of a European Union citizen of Netherlands nationality, on the other, concerning the Minister's refusal to grant them a certificate of lawful residence as a family member of a Union citizen in the Netherlands.

Legal context

[Paras 3-12 omitted]

The disputes in the main proceedings and the questions referred for a preliminary ruling

Ms S.'s situation

13. Ms S. is an Ukranian national. She claims to be entitled, under Union law, to a right of residence with her son-in-law ('sponsor S'), who is a Netherlands national. Ms S. stated, in the main proceedings, that she takes care of her grandson, the son of sponsor S.

14. Sponsor S resides in the Netherlands and, since 1 June 2002, has worked for an employer established in the Netherlands and spends 30% of his weekly working time on preparing and making business trips to Belgium. Sponsor S therefore travels to Belgium at least once a week.

15. By decision of 26 August 2009, the Staatssecretaris van Justitie (State Secretary of Justice) rejected Ms S.'s application for a residence document.

16. By decision of 16 November 2009, the Minister rejected Ms S.'s objection to that decision as unfounded.

17. By judgment of 25 June 2010, the Rechtbank 's-Gravenhage rejected the action brought by Ms S. against the decision of 16 November 2009 as unfounded.

18. Ms S. lodged an appeal against that judgment before the Raad van State.

Ms G.'s situation

19. Ms G., a Peruvian national, married a Netherlands national ('sponsor G') on 6 March 2009. Ms G. stated, in the main proceedings, that she and sponsor G have a daughter and that she is also the mother of a son who has been received into her and sponsor G's family.

20. Sponsor G lives in the Netherlands and, since 2003, has worked for an undertaking established in Belgium. He travels daily between the Netherlands and Belgium for his work.

21. By decision of 1 December 2009, the Staatssecretaris van Justitie rejected Ms G.'s application for a residence document. By decision of 12 July 2010, the Minister rejected Ms G.'s objection to that decision as unfounded.

22. By judgment of 28 June 2011, the Rechtbank 's-Gravenhage upheld the action brought by Ms G. against the decision of 12 July 2010, annulled that decision and

ordered the Minister to adopt a new decision taking into account the considerations set out in that judgment.

23. The Minister lodged an appeal against that judgment before the referring court.

The questions referred for a preliminary ruling

24. As Ms S. and Ms G. are family members of a Union citizen within the meaning of Article 2(2) of Directive 2004/38, the referring court is unsure whether that directive grants them a right of residence in the Member State of which the citizen is a national.

25. According to the referring court, it is conceivable that the term 'move to' within the meaning of Article 3(1) of Directive 2004/38 means travelling to and from, without moving to, a Member State other than the Member State of which the citizen is a national. Likewise, it is conceivable that the term 'join them' within the meaning of Article 3(1) of that directive could be construed to mean joining the Union citizen in the Member State of which he is a national.

26. However, the referring court states that other provisions of Directive 2004/38, in particular Article 6(1) and Article 7(1)(a) and (2), seem to rule out such an interpretation, in so far as they expressly mention 'another Member State' and 'the host Member State' as the Member State to which the right of residence applies. The judgment in Case C-434/09 *McCarthy* [2011] ECR I-3375 confirms that Articles 6 and 7 of that directive govern the legal situation of a Union citizen in a Member State of which he is not a national.

27. Next, the referring court points out that it is apparent from Case C-370/90 *Singh* [1992] ECR I-4265 and Case C-291/05 *Eind* [2007] ECR I-10719 that when a national of a Member State who has availed himself or herself of the right to freedom of movement returns to his or her State of origin, his or her spouse must enjoy at least the same rights of entry and residence as would be granted to him or her under Union law if the Union citizen chose to enter and reside in another Member State. However, the referring court expresses doubts as to whether that case-law may be applied to situations such as those at issue in the main proceedings. It states, in that regard, that the third-country nationals in question have not previously resided, on the basis of Union law, with their respective sponsors in a Member State other than the Member State of which those sponsors are nationals.

28. The referring court also refers to the judgment in Case C-60/00 *Carpenter* [2002] ECR I-6279 in which the Court held that Article 56 TFEU, read in the light of the fundamental right to respect for family life, may preclude a refusal, by the Member State of origin of a provider of services established in that Member State who provides services to recipients established in other Member States, of the right to reside

in its territory for that provider's spouse, who is a national of a third country. It also points out, however, that unlike the case which gave rise to the judgment in *Carpenter*, there is no question in the main proceedings of Union citizens providing cross-border services from the Member State of which they are nationals, but rather of workers who move to another Member State in the course of their professional activities.

29. Lastly, the referring court, with reference to Case C-34/09 *Ruiz Zambrano* [2011] ECR I-1177, and Case C-256/11 *Dereci and Others* [2011] ECR I-11315, asks whether, on the basis of Articles 20 TFEU and 21(1) TFEU, a right of residence could be granted to third-country nationals such as those in question in the main proceedings.

30. In those circumstances the Raad van State decided to stay the proceedings and to refer the following questions to the Court of Justice for a preliminary ruling:

'(1) Can a member, having third-country nationality, of the family of a Union citizen who lives in the Member State of which he is a national but who, in the course of his work for an employer established in that same Member State, travels to and from another Member State derive, in circumstances such as those of the present case [concerning Ms S.], a right of residence from Union law?

(2) Can a member, having third-country nationality, of the family of a Union citizen who lives in the Member State of which he is a national but who works in another Member State for an employer established in that other Member State derive, in circumstances such as those of the present case [concerning Ms G.], a right of residence from Union law?'

Consideration of the questions referred

Preliminary observations

31. The questions asked in the order for reference do not specify any particular provision that requires interpretation in order to enable the referring court to give judgment in the main proceedings. The questions just refer generally to Union law.

32. However, having regard to the information contained in the order for reference, as set out in paragraphs 24 to 29 above, the questions must be understood as asking, in essence, whether Directive 2004/38 and Articles 20 TFEU, 21(1) TFEU and 45 TFEU must be interpreted as precluding a refusal by a Member State to grant a right of residence to a third-country national who is a family member of a Union citizen within the meaning of Article 2(2) of Directive 2004/38 where that citizen is a national of and resides in that Member State but regularly travels to another Member State in the course of his professional activities.

Interpretation of Directive 2004/38

33. In accordance with settled case-law, the rights conferred by Directive 2004/38 on third-country nationals are not autonomous rights of those third-country nationals, but derived rights, acquired through their status as family members, as defined in Article 2(2) of that directive, of a Union citizen (see *McCarthy*, paragraph 42; *Dereci and Others*, paragraph 55; and Case C-87/12 *Ymeraga and Ymeraga-Tafarshiku* [2013] ECR, paragraph 31).

34. However, as is apparent from paragraphs 37 to 43 of the judgment delivered today in Case C-456/12 *O. and B.*, Directive 2004/38 grants an autonomous right of residence to a Union citizen and a derived right of residence to his family members only where that citizen exercises his right of freedom of movement by becoming established in a Member State other than the Member State of which he is a national. Directive 2004/38 does not therefore confer a derived right of residence on third-country nationals who are family members of a Union citizen in the Member State of which that citizen is a national.

35. It follows from the foregoing that Directive 2004/38 must be interpreted as not precluding the refusal by a Member State, in circumstances such as those in the main proceedings, to grant a derived right of residence to a third-country national who is a family member of a Union citizen residing in the Member State of which he is a national.

Interpretation of Article 45 TFEU

36. Next, the referring court asks whether the third-country national in each of the actions in the main proceedings may invoke a right of residence on the basis of Article 45 TFEU. The referring court cites, for that purpose, the judgment in *Carpenter*.

37. In that regard, it should be borne in mind that, in paragraph 46 of the judgment in *Carpenter*, the Court held that Article 56 TFEU, read in the light of the fundamental right to respect for family life, precludes, in circumstances such as those in the case which gave rise to that judgment, a refusal, by the Member State of origin of a provider of services established in that Member State who provides services to recipients established in other Member States, of the right to reside in its territory to that provider's spouse, who is a national of a third country.

38. With regard to the situations at issue in the main proceedings, it should be noted that the Union citizen, in the action concerning Ms G., works for a company established in a Member State other than the Member State in which he resides. The Union citizen, in the action concerning Ms S., regularly travels, in the course of his professional activities, to a Member State other than the Member State in which he

resides even though the company employing him is established in the Member State in which he resides.

39. Union citizens in comparable situations to sponsor S and sponsor G fall within the scope of Article 45 TFEU. Any Union citizen who, under an employment contract, works in a Member State other than that of their place of residence falls within the scope of Article 45 TFEU (see, to that effect, Case C-152/03 *Ritter-Coulais* [2006] ECR I-1711, paragraph 31; Case C-212/05 *Hartmann* [2007] ECR I-6303, paragraph 17; and Case C-202/11 *Las* [2013] ECR, paragraph 17).

40. Admittedly, the Court's interpretation of Article 56 TFEU in *Carpenter* is transposable to Article 45 TFEU. The effectiveness of the right to freedom of movement of workers may require that a derived right of residence be granted to a third-country national who is a family member of the worker – a Union citizen – in the Member State of which the latter is a national.

41. However, the purpose and justification of such a derived right of residence is based on the fact that a refusal to allow it would be such as to interfere with the exercise of fundamental freedoms guaranteed by the FEU Treaty (see, to that effect, Case C-40/11 *Iida* [2012] ECR, paragraph 68; *Ymeraga and Ymeraga-Tafarshiku*, paragraph 35; and Case C-86/12 *Alokpa and Others* [2013] ECR, paragraph 22).

42. It is therefore for the referring court to determine whether, in each of the situations at issue in the main proceedings, the grant of a derived right of residence to the third-country national in question who is a family member of a Union citizen is necessary to guarantee the citizen's effective exercise of the fundamental freedom guaranteed by Article 45 TFEU.

43. In that regard, the fact noted by the referring court that the third-country national in question takes care of the Union citizens' child may, as is apparent from the judgment in *Carpenter*, be a relevant factor to be taken into account by the referring court when examining whether the refusal to grant a right of residence to that third-country national may discourage the Union citizen from effectively exercising his rights under Article 45 TFEU. However, it must be noted that, although in the judgment in *Carpenter* the fact that the child in question was being taken care of by the third-country national who is a family member of a Union citizen was considered to be decisive, that child was, in that case, taken care of by the Union citizen's spouse. The mere fact that it might appear desirable that the child be cared for by the third-country national who is the direct relative in the ascending line of the Union citizen's spouse is not therefore sufficient in itself to constitute such a dissuasive effect.

44. In the light of the foregoing, Article 45 TFEU must be interpreted as conferring on a third-country national who is the family member of a Union citizen a derived right

of residence in the Member State of which that citizen is a national, where the citizen resides in that Member State but regularly travels to another Member State as a worker within the meaning of that provision, if the refusal to grant such a right of residence discourages the worker from effectively exercising his rights under Article 45 TFEU, which it is for the referring court to determine.

45. In those circumstances, it is no longer necessary to interpret Articles 20 TFEU and 21(1) TFEU. Those provisions, which set out generally the right of every citizen of the Union to move and reside freely within the territory of the Member States, find specific expression in Article 45 TFEU in relation to freedom of movement for workers (see Case C-233/12 *Gardella* [2013] ECR, paragraph 38 and the case-law cited).

46. In the light of all the foregoing, the answer to the questions referred is as follows:

- Directive 2004/38 must be interpreted as not precluding a refusal by a Member State to grant a right of residence to a third-country national who is a family member of a Union citizen where that citizen is a national of and resides in that Member State but regularly travels to another Member State in the course of his professional activities;
- Article 45 TFEU must be interpreted as conferring on a third-country national who is the family member of a Union citizen a derived right of residence in the Member State of which that citizen is a national, where the citizen resides in that Member State but regularly travels to another Member State as a worker within the meaning of that provision, if the refusal to grant such a right of residence discourages the worker from effectively exercising his rights under Article 45 TFEU, which it is for the referring court to determine.

Costs

[Para. 47 omitted]

On those grounds,

THE COURT (Grand Chamber),

hereby rules:

Directive 2004/38/EC of the European Parliament and of the Council of 29 April 2004 on the right of citizens of the Union and their family members to move and reside freely within the territory of the Member States amending Regulation (EEC) No 1612/68 and repealing Directives 64/221/EEC, 68/360/EEC, 72/194/EEC, 73/148/EEC, 75/34/EEC, 75/35/EEC, 90/364/EEC, 90/365/EEC and 93/96/EEC must be interpreted as not precluding a refusal by

a Member State to grant a right of residence to a third-country national who is a family member of a Union citizen where that citizen is a national of and resides in that Member State but regularly travels to another Member State in the course of his professional activities.
Article 45 TFEU must be interpreted as conferring on a third-country national who is the family member of a Union citizen a derived right of residence in the Member State of which that citizen is a national, where the citizen resides in that Member State but regularly travels to another Member State as a worker within the meaning of that provision, if the refusal to grant such a right of residence discourages the worker from effectively exercising his rights under Article 45 TFEU, which it is for the referring court to determine.

Comments and questions

The *S* case concerned whether a person from a third country can derive a right of residence in a Member State from a family member who is a Union citizen, if at no time the Union citizen and the third-country national family member have taken up residence in a Member State other than the Union citizen's home Member State. In this case the Union citizen had been resident together with the third-country national family member in the Union citizen's home Member State while the Union citizen had exercised the right to free movement of workers (which was the basis for one of the preliminary rulings) by undertaking business trips to another Member States, and in the case that was the subject of the other preliminary ruling, by working for an employer in another Member State.

The *S* case should be seen against the background of the CJEU's judgment in Case C-60/00 *Carpenter*, printed in Chapter 6 below. In the *Carpenter* case the CJEU ruled that, under Article 49 TFEU on the freedom to provide services, a Union citizen had a right to unite their family with a third-country national family member in their home State in a case where the Union citizen, who was resident in his home State, ran a business selling advertising space in medical and scientific journals to advertisers based in other Member States and offering various services to the editors of those journals. The CJEU attached weight to the fact that a large part of the services which the Union citizen provided in the *Carpenter* case were provided in the home State for persons who were established in other Member States, while other parts of his work were carried out in the Member States where the recipients of the services were established. In this connection, in paragraph 39 of the *Carpenter* judgment the CJEU stated:

> 'It is clear that the separation of Mr and Mrs Carpenter would be detrimental to their family life and, therefore, to the conditions under which Mr Carpenter exercises a fundamental freedom. That freedom could not be fully effective if Mr Carpenter were to be deterred from exercising it by obstacles raised in his country of origin to the entry and residence of his spouse.'

In principle there is nothing to prevent the CJEU applying its reasoning in the *Carpenter* case to a situation where a Union citizen is not a service provider but an employee. However, it was first in the *S* case that the CJEU had the opportunity to decide whether or not the reasoning in the *Carpenter* case also applicable to the free movement of workers pursuant to Article 45 TFEU. In the *S* case the CJEU had the opportunity to decide whether a Union citizen has a right to unite their family with a third-country national family member in their home State where a Union citizen was resident in their home State but worked for an employer in another Member State.

In the *S* case the CJEU ruled that Article 45 should be interpreted so as to give a Union citizen's third-country national family member a derived right of residence in the Union citizen's home State if the Union citizen is resident there, but regularly travels to another Member State as a worker within the meaning of Article 45 TFEU, if the refusal of such a right of residence would deter the Union citizen from exercising their right pursuant to this provision.

However, it is important to note that the CJEU has not established an absolute and unconditional right to family unification under Article 45 TFEU. On the contrary, paragraphs 41-43 of the judgment expressly draw attention to the following reservations (italics added):

> 41. However, the purpose and justification of such a derived right of residence is based on the fact that a refusal to allow it would be such as to interfere with the exercise of fundamental freedoms guaranteed by the FEU Treaty ...
>
> 42. It is therefore for the referring court to determine whether, in each of the situations at issue in the main proceedings, the grant of a derived right of residence to the thirdcountry national in question who is a family member of a Union citizen is *necessary* to guarantee the citizen's effective exercise of the fundamental freedom guaranteed by Article 45 TFEU.
>
> 43. In that regard, the fact noted by the referring court that the thirdcountry national in question takes care of the Union citizens' child may, as is apparent from the judgment in Carpenter, be a relevant factor to be taken into account by the referring court when examining whether the refusal to grant a right of residence to that thirdcountry national may *discourage* the Union citizen from effectively exercising his rights under Article 45 TFEU. However, it must be noted that, although in the judgment in Carpenter the fact that the child in question was being taken care of by the thirdcountry national who is a family member of a Union citizen was considered to be decisive, that child was, in that case, taken care of by the Union citizen's spouse. The mere fact that it might appear *desirable* that the child be cared for by the thirdcountry national who is the direct relative in the ascending line of the Union citizen's spouse *is not therefore sufficient in itself* to constitute such a dissuasive effect.

The *S* case is also important because, as something entirely new, the CJEU established that there is an employment situation covered by Article 45 TFEU when a Union citizen as part of his or her employment regularly travels to a Member State other than his or her State of residence, even though the Union citizen's employer is based in thei former's State of residence. It was thus surprising when in the S case the CJEU stated as follows in paragraph 39 of its judgment:

> 'Any Union citizen who, under an employment contract, works in a Member State other than that of their place of residence falls within the scope of Article 45 TFEU'.

Prior to the *S* case the Danish immigration authorities had refused a right of residence to a third-country national family member who was in a situation corresponding to that of S. Such cases were not considered as being covered by Union law, either as primary or secondary movement, and they were therefore dealt with under the national law on immigration.

What is the relevance of the *S* case for Danish citizens who live in Denmark but commute to work for an employer based in, for example, Germany or Sweden, if these Danish citizens want to unite their family with a third-country national family member pursuant to Article 45 TFEU?

What does the *S* case mean for a Dutch citizen's right to unite their family where, in connection with their work for a Dutch employer based in the Netherlands, the Dutch citizen regularly travels between the Netherlands and one or more other Member States in connection with their employment?

Consider whether the *S* judgment extends the former practice of the CJEU in relation to Article 45 TFEU, or whether it should be seen as a surprising, new and expanded interpretation of the scope of this provision in cases where the employer is established in the Member State where the Union citizen both works and is resident.

Obviously, depends on the facts of the case whether a Union citizen's works in his or her home Member State means that he or she and regularly travels to another Member State as part of his/her work. In the *S* case the Dutch citizen spent 30% of his time every week preparing business trips to Belgium, and travelled there at least once a week, leading the CJEU to consider that he was covered by Article 45 TFEU.

JUDGMENT OF THE COURT
15 December 1995

Union royale belge des sociétés de football association ASBL v Jean-Marc Bosman, Royal club liégeois SA v Jean-Marc Bosman and others and Union des associations européennes de football (UEFA) v Jean-Marc Bosman.
(Reference for a preliminary ruling: Cour d'appel de Liège – Belgium)

'Freedom of movement for workers – Competition rules applicable to undertakings – Professional footballers – Sporting rules on the transfer of players requiring the new club to pay a fee to the old club – Limitation of the number of players having the nationality of other Member States who may be fielded in a match'

Case C-415/93

Judgment

[Paras 1-67 omitted]

Interpretation of Article 48 of the Treaty with regard to the transfer rule

68. By its first question, the national court seeks in substance to ascertain whether Article 48 of the Treaty precludes the application of rules laid down by sporting associations, under which a professional footballer who is a national of one Member State may not, on the expiry of his contract with a club, be employed by a club of another Member State unless the latter club has paid to the former a transfer, training or development fee.

Application of Article 48 to rules laid down by sporting associations

69. It is first necessary to consider certain arguments which have been put forward on the question of the application of Article 48 to rules laid down by sporting associations.

70. URBSFA argued that only the major European clubs may be regarded as undertakings, whereas clubs such as RC Liège carry on an economic activity only to a negligible extent. Furthermore, the question submitted by the national court on the transfer rules does not concern the employment relationships between players and clubs but the business relationships between clubs and the consequences of freedom to affiliate to a sporting federation. Article 48 of the Treaty is accordingly not applicable to a case such as that in issue in the main proceedings.

71. UEFA argued, inter alia, that the Community authorities have always respected the autonomy of sport, that it is extremely difficult to distinguish between the economic and the sporting aspects of football and that a decision of the Court concerning the situation of professional players might call in question the organization of football as a whole. For that reason, even if Article 48 of the Treaty were to apply to professional players, a degree of flexibility would be essential because of the particular nature of the sport.

72. The German Government stressed, first, that in most cases a sport such as football is not an economic activity. It further submitted that sport in general has points of similarity with culture and pointed out that, under Article 128(1) of the EC Treaty, the Community must respect the national and regional diversity of the cultures of the Member States. Finally, referring to the freedom of association and autonomy enjoyed by sporting federations under national law, it concluded that, by virtue of the principle of subsidiarity, taken as a general principle, intervention by public, and particularly Community, authorities in this area must be confined to what is strictly necessary.

73. In response to those arguments, it is to be remembered that, having regard to the objectives of the Community, sport is subject to Community law only in so far as it constitutes an economic activity within the meaning of Article 2 of the Treaty (see Case 36/74 *Walrave* v *Union Cycliste Internationale* [1974] ECR 1405, paragraph 4). This applies to the activities of professional or semi-professional footballers, where they are in gainful employment or provide a remunerated service (see Case 13/76 *Donà* v *Mantero* [1976] ECR 1333, paragraph 12).

74. It is not necessary, for the purposes of the application of the Community provisions on freedom of movement for workers, for the employer to be an undertaking; all that is required is the existence of, or the intention to create, an employment relationship.

75. Application of Article 48 of the Treaty is not precluded by the fact that the transfer rules govern the business relationships between clubs rather than the employment relationships between clubs and players. The fact that the employing clubs must pay fees on recruiting a player from another club affects the players' opportunities for finding employment and the terms under which such employment is offered.

76. As regards the difficulty of severing the economic aspects from the sporting aspects of football, the Court has held (in Donà, cited above, paragraphs 14 and 15) that the provisions of Community law concerning freedom of movement of persons and of provision of services do not preclude rules or practices justified on non-economic grounds which relate to the particular nature and context of certain matches. It stressed, however, that such a restriction on the scope of the provisions in question

must remain limited to its proper objective. It cannot, therefore, be relied upon to exclude the whole of a sporting activity from the scope of the Treaty.

77. With regard to the possible consequences of this judgment on the organization of football as a whole, it has consistently been held that, although the practical consequences of any judicial decision must be weighed carefully, this cannot go so far as to diminish the objective character of the law and compromise its application on the ground of the possible repercussions of a judicial decision. At the very most, such repercussions might be taken into consideration when determining whether exceptionally to limit the temporal effect of a judgment (see, inter alia, Case C-163/90 *Administration des Douanes* v *Legros and Others* [1992] ECR I-4625, paragraph 30).

78. The argument based on points of alleged similarity between sport and culture cannot be accepted, since the question submitted by the national court does not relate to the conditions under which Community powers of limited extent, such as those based on Article 128(1), may be exercised but on the scope of the freedom of movement of workers guaranteed by Article 48, which is a fundamental freedom in the Community system (see, inter alia, Case C-19/92 *Kraus* v *Land Baden-Wuerttemberg* [1993] ECR I-1663, paragraph 16).

79. As regards the arguments based on the principle of freedom of association, it must be recognized that this principle, enshrined in Article 11 of the European Convention for the Protection of Human Rights and Fundamental Freedoms and resulting from the constitutional traditions common to the Member States, is one of the fundamental rights which, as the Court has consistently held and as is reaffirmed in the preamble to the Single European Act and in Article F(2) of the Treaty on European Union, are protected in the Community legal order.

80. However, the rules laid down by sporting associations to which the national court refers cannot be seen as necessary to ensure enjoyment of that freedom by those associations, by the clubs or by their players, nor can they be seen as an inevitable result thereof.

81. Finally, the principle of subsidiarity, as interpreted by the German Government to the effect that intervention by public authorities, and particularly Community authorities, in the area in question must be confined to what is strictly necessary, cannot lead to a situation in which the freedom of private associations to adopt sporting rules restricts the exercise of rights conferred on individuals by the Treaty.

82. Once the objections concerning the application of Article 48 of the Treaty to sporting activities such as those of professional footballers are out of the way, it is to be remembered that, as the Court held in paragraph 17 of its judgment in Walrave, cited above, Article 48 not only applies to the action of public authorities but extends

also to rules of any other nature aimed at regulating gainful employment in a collective manner.

83. The Court has held that the abolition as between Member States of obstacles to freedom of movement for persons and to freedom to provide services would be compromised if the abolition of State barriers could be neutralized by obstacles resulting from the exercise of their legal autonomy by associations or organizations not governed by public law (see Walrave, cited above, paragraph 18).

84. It has further observed that working conditions in the different Member States are governed sometimes by provisions laid down by law or regulation and sometimes by agreements and other acts concluded or adopted by private persons. Accordingly, if the scope of Article 48 of the Treaty were confined to acts of a public authority there would be a risk of creating inequality in its application (see Walrave, cited above, paragraph 19). That risk is all the more obvious in a case such as that in the main proceedings in this case in that, as has been stressed in paragraph 24 above, the transfer rules have been laid down by different bodies or in different ways in each Member State.

85. UEFA objects that such an interpretation makes Article 48 of the Treaty more restrictive in relation to individuals than in relation to Member States, which are alone in being able to rely on limitations justified on grounds of public policy, public security or public health.

86. That argument is based on a false premiss. There is nothing to preclude individuals from relying on justifications on grounds of public policy, public security or public health. Neither the scope nor the content of those grounds of justification is in any way affected by the public or private nature of the rules in question.

87. Article 48 of the Treaty therefore applies to rules laid down by sporting associations such as URBSFA, FIFA or UEFA, which determine the terms on which professional sportsmen can engage in gainful employment.

Whether the situation envisaged by the national court is of a purely internal nature

88. UEFA considers that the disputes pending before the national court concern a purely internal Belgian situation which falls outside the ambit of Article 48 of the Treaty. They concern a Belgian player whose transfer fell through because of the conduct of a Belgian club and a Belgian association.

89. It is true that, according to consistent case-law (see, inter alia, Case 175/78 Regina v Saunders [1979] ECR 1129, paragraph 11; Case 180/83 Moser v Land Baden-Wuerttemberg [1984] ECR 2539, paragraph 15; Case C-332/90 Steen v Deutsche Bundespost [1992] ECR I-341, paragraph 9; and Case C-19/92 Kraus, cited above,

paragraph 15), the provisions of the Treaty concerning the free movement of workers, and particularly Article 48, cannot be applied to situations which are wholly internal to a Member State, in other words where there is no factor connecting them to any of the situations envisaged by Community law.

90. However, it is clear from the findings of fact made by the national court that Mr Bosman had entered into a contract of employment with a club in another Member State with a view to exercising gainful employment in that State. By so doing, as he has rightly pointed out, he accepted an offer of employment actually made, within the meaning of Article 48(3)(a).

91. Since the situation in issue in the main proceedings cannot be classified as purely internal, the argument put forward by UEFA must be dismissed.

Existence of an obstacle to freedom of movement for workers

92. It is thus necessary to consider whether the transfer rules form an obstacle to freedom of movement for workers prohibited by Article 48 of the Treaty.

93. As the Court has repeatedly held, freedom of movement for workers is one of the fundamental principles of the Community and the Treaty provisions guaranteeing that freedom have had direct effect since the end of the transitional period.

94. The Court has also held that the provisions of the Treaty relating to freedom of movement for persons are intended to facilitate the pursuit by Community citizens of occupational activities of all kinds throughout the Community, and preclude measures which might place Community citizens at a disadvantage when they wish to pursue an economic activity in the territory of another Member State (see Case 143/87 Stanton v INASTI [1988] ECR 3877, paragraph 13, and Case C-370/90 The Queen v Immigration Appeal Tribunal and Surinder Singh [1992] ECR I-4265, paragraph 16).

95. In that context, nationals of Member States have in particular the right, which they derive directly from the Treaty, to leave their country of origin to enter the territory of another Member State and reside there in order there to pursue an economic activity (see, inter alia, Case C-363/89 Roux v Belgium [1991] ECR I-273, paragraph 9, and Singh, cited above, paragraph 17).

96. Provisions which preclude or deter a national of a Member State from leaving his country of origin in order to exercise his right to freedom of movement therefore constitute an obstacle to that freedom even if they apply without regard to the nationality of the workers concerned (see also Case C-10/90 *Masgio* v *Bundesknappschaft* [1991] ECR I-1119, paragraphs 18 and 19).

97. The Court has also stated, in Case 81/87 *The Queen* v *H.M. Treasury and Commissioners of Inland Revenue ex parte Daily Mail and General Trust plc* [1988] ECR 5483, paragraph 16, that even though the Treaty provisions relating to freedom of establishment are directed mainly to ensuring that foreign nationals and companies are treated in the host Member State in the same way as nationals of that State, they also prohibit the Member State of origin from hindering the establishment in another Member State of one of its nationals or of a company incorporated under its legislation which comes within the definition contained in Article 58. The rights guaranteed by Article 52 et seq. of the Treaty would be rendered meaningless if the Member State of origin could prohibit undertakings from leaving in order to establish themselves in another Member State. The same considerations apply, in relation to Article 48 of the Treaty, with regard to rules which impede the freedom of movement of nationals of one Member State wishing to engage in gainful employment in another Member State.

98. It is true that the transfer rules in issue in the main proceedings apply also to transfers of players between clubs belonging to different national associations within the same Member State and that similar rules govern transfers between clubs belonging to the same national association.

99. However, as has been pointed out by Mr Bosman, by the Danish Government and by the Advocate General in points 209 and 210 of his Opinion, those rules are likely to restrict the freedom of movement of players who wish to pursue their activity in another Member State by preventing or deterring them from leaving the clubs to which they belong even after the expiry of their contracts of employment with those clubs.

100. Since they provide that a professional footballer may not pursue his activity with a new club established in another Member State unless it has paid his former club a transfer fee agreed upon between the two clubs or determined in accordance with the regulations of the sporting associations, the said rules constitute an obstacle to freedom of movement for workers.

101. As the national court has rightly pointed out, that finding is not affected by the fact that the transfer rules adopted by UEFA in 1990 stipulate that the business relationship between the two clubs is to exert no influence on the activity of the player, who is to be free to play for his new club. The new club must still pay the fee in issue, under pain of penalties which may include its being struck off for debt, which prevents it just as effectively from signing up a player from a club in another Member State without paying that fee.

102. Nor is that conclusion negated by the case-law of the Court cited by URBSFA and UEFA, to the effect that Article 30 of the Treaty does not apply to measures which restrict or prohibit certain selling arrangements so long as they apply to all

relevant traders operating within the national territory and so long as they affect in the same manner, in law and in fact, the marketing of domestic products and of those from other Member States (see Joined Cases C-267/91 and C-268/91 *Keck and Mithouard* [1993] ECR I-6097, paragraph 16).

103. It is sufficient to note that, although the rules in issue in the main proceedings apply also to transfers between clubs belonging to different national associations within the same Member State and are similar to those governing transfers between clubs belonging to the same national association, they still directly affect players'access to the employment market in other Member States and are thus capable of impeding freedom of movement for workers. They cannot, thus, be deemed comparable to the rules on selling arrangements for goods which in Keck and Mithouard were held to fall outside the ambit of Article 30 of the Treaty (see also, with regard to freedom to provide services, Case C-384/93 *Alpine Investments* v *Minister van Financiën* [1995] ECR I-1141, paragraphs 36 to 38).

104. Consequently, the transfer rules constitute an obstacle to freedom of movement for workers prohibited in principle by Article 48 of the Treaty. It could only be otherwise if those rules pursued a legitimate aim compatible with the Treaty and were justified by pressing reasons of public interest. But even if that were so, application of those rules would still have to be such as to ensure achievement of the aim in question and not go beyond what is necessary for that purpose (see, inter alia, the judgment in Kraus, cited above, paragraph 32, and Case C-55/94 *Gebhard* [1995] ECR I-4165, paragraph 37).

Existence of justifications

105. First, URBSFA, UEFA and the French and Italian Governments have submitted that the transfer rules are justified by the need to maintain a financial and competitive balance between clubs and to support the search for talent and the training of young players.

106. In view of the considerable social importance of sporting activities and in particular football in the Community, the aims of maintaining a balance between clubs by preserving a certain degree of equality and uncertainty as to results and of encouraging the recruitment and training of young players must be accepted as legitimate.

107. As regards the first of those aims, Mr Bosman has rightly pointed out that the application of the transfer rules is not an adequate means of maintaining financial and competitive balance in the world of football. Those rules neither preclude the richest clubs from securing the services of the best players nor prevent the availability of financial resources from being a decisive factor in competitive sport, thus considerably altering the balance between clubs.

108. As regards the second aim, it must be accepted that the prospect of receiving transfer, development or training fees is indeed likely to encourage football clubs to seek new talent and train young players.

109. However, because it is impossible to predict the sporting future of young players with any certainty and because only a limited number of such players go on to play professionally, those fees are by nature contingent and uncertain and are in any event unrelated to the actual cost borne by clubs of training both future professional players and those who will never play professionally. The prospect of receiving such fees cannot, therefore, be either a decisive factor in encouraging recruitment and training of young players or an adequate means of financing such activities, particularly in the case of smaller clubs.

110. Furthermore, as the Advocate General has pointed out in point 226 et seq. of his Opinion, the same aims can be achieved at least as efficiently by other means which do not impede freedom of movement for workers.

111. It has also been argued that the transfer rules are necessary to safeguard the worldwide organization of football.

112. However, the present proceedings concern application of those rules within the Community and not the relations between the national associations of the Member States and those of non-member countries. In any event, application of different rules to transfers between clubs belonging to national associations within the Community and to transfers between such clubs and those affiliated to the national associations of non-member countries is unlikely to pose any particular difficulties. As is clear from paragraphs 22 and 23 above, the rules which have so far governed transfers within the national associations of certain Member States are different from those which apply at the international level.

113. Finally, the argument that the rules in question are necessary to compensate clubs for the expenses which they have had to incur in paying fees on recruiting their players cannot be accepted, since it seeks to justify the maintenance of obstacles to freedom of movement for workers simply on the ground that such obstacles were able to exist in the past.

114. The answer to the first question must therefore be that Article 48 of the Treaty precludes the application of rules laid down by sporting associations, under which a professional footballer who is a national of one Member State may not, on the expiry of his contract with a club, be employed by a club of another Member State unless the latter club has paid to the former club a transfer, training or development fee.

Interpretation of Article 48 of the Treaty with regard to the nationality clauses

115. By its second question, the national court seeks in substance to ascertain whether Article 48 of the Treaty precludes the application of rules laid down by sporting associations, under which, in matches in competitions which they organize, football clubs may field only a limited number of professional players who are nationals of other Member States.

Existence of an obstacle to freedom of movement for workers

116. As the Court has held in paragraph 87 above, Article 48 of the Treaty applies to rules laid down by sporting associations which determine the conditions under which professional sports players may engage in gainful employment. It must therefore be considered whether the nationality clauses constitute an obstacle to freedom of movement for workers, prohibited by Article 48.

117. Article 48(2) expressly provides that freedom of movement for workers entails the abolition of any discrimination based on nationality between workers of the Member States as regards employment, remuneration and conditions of work and employment.

118. That provision has been implemented, in particular, by Article 4 of Regulation (EEC) No 1612/68 of the Council of 15 October 1968 on freedom of movement for workers within the Community (OJ, English Special Edition, 1968(II), p. 475), under which provisions laid down by law, regulation or administrative action of the Member States which restrict by number or percentage the employment of foreign nationals in any undertaking, branch of activity or region, or at a national level, are not to apply to nationals of the other Member States.

119. The same principle applies to clauses contained in the regulations of sporting associations which restrict the right of nationals of other Member States to take part, as professional players, in football matches (see the judgment in Donà, cited above, paragraph 19).

120. The fact that those clauses concern not the employment of such players, on which there is no restriction, but the extent to which their clubs may field them in official matches is irrelevant. In so far as participation in such matches is the essential purpose of a professional player's activity, a rule which restricts that participation obviously also restricts the chances of employment of the player concerned.

Existence of justifications

121. The existence of an obstacle having thus been established, it must be considered whether that obstacle may be justified in the light of Article 48 of the Treaty.

122. URBSFA, UEFA and the German, French and Italian Governments argued that the nationality clauses are justified on non-economic grounds, concerning only the sport as such.

123. First, they argued, those clauses serve to maintain the traditional link between each club and its country, a factor of great importance in enabling the public to identify with its favourite team and ensuring that clubs taking part in international competitions effectively represent their countries.

124. Secondly, those clauses are necessary to create a sufficient pool of national players to provide the national teams with top players to field in all team positions.

125. Thirdly, they help to maintain a competitive balance between clubs by preventing the richest clubs from appropriating the services of the best players.

126. Finally, UEFA points out that the '3 + 2' rule was drawn up in collaboration with the Commission and must be revised regularly to remain in line with the development of Community policy.

127. It must be recalled that in paragraphs 14 and 15 of its judgment in Donà, cited above, the Court held that the Treaty provisions concerning freedom of movement for persons do not prevent the adoption of rules or practices excluding foreign players from certain matches for reasons which are not of an economic nature, which relate to the particular nature and context of such matches and are thus of sporting interest only, such as, for example, matches between national teams from different countries. It stressed, however, that restriction on the scope of the provisions in question must remain limited to its proper objective.

128. Here, the nationality clauses do not concern specific matches between teams representing their countries but apply to all official matches between clubs and thus to the essence of the activity of professional players.

129. In those circumstances, the nationality clauses cannot be deemed to be in accordance with Article 48 of the Treaty, otherwise that article would be deprived of its practical effect and the fundamental right of free access to employment which the Treaty confers individually on each worker in the Community rendered nugatory (on this last point, see Case 222/86 *Unectef* v *Heylens and Others* [1987] ECR 4097, paragraph 14).

130. None of the arguments put forward by the sporting associations and by the governments which have submitted observations detracts from that conclusion.

131. First, a football club's links with the Member State in which it is established cannot be regarded as any more inherent in its sporting activity than its links with its

locality, town, region or, in the case of the United Kingdom, the territory covered by each of the four associations. Even though national championships are played between clubs from different regions, towns or localities, there is no rule restricting the right of clubs to field players from other regions, towns or localities in such matches.

132. In international competitions, moreover, participation is limited to clubs which have achieved certain results in competition in their respective countries, without any particular significance being attached to the nationalities of their players.

133. Secondly, whilst national teams must be made up of players having the nationality of the relevant country, those players need not necessarily be registered to play for clubs in that country. Indeed, under the rules of the sporting associations, foreign players must be allowed by their clubs to play for their country's national team in certain matches.

134. Furthermore, although freedom of movement for workers, by opening up the employment market in one Member State to nationals of the other Member States, has the effect of reducing workers' chances of finding employment within the Member State of which they are nationals, it also, by the same token, offers them new prospects of employment in other Member States. Such considerations obviously apply also to professional footballers.

135. Thirdly, although it has been argued that the nationality clauses prevent the richest clubs from engaging the best foreign players, those clauses are not sufficient to achieve the aim of maintaining a competitive balance, since there are no rules limiting the possibility for such clubs to recruit the best national players, thus undermining that balance to just the same extent.

136. Finally, as regards the argument based on the Commission's participation in the drafting of the '3 + 2' rule, it must be pointed out that, except where such powers are expressly conferred upon it, the Commission may not give guarantees concerning the compatibility of specific practices with the Treaty (see also Joined Cases 142/80 and 143/80 Amministrazione delle Finanze dello Stato v Essevi and Salengo [1981] ECR 1413, paragraph 16). In no circumstances does it have the power to authorize practices which are contrary to the Treaty.

137. It follows from the foregoing that Article 48 of the Treaty precludes the application of rules laid down by sporting associations under which, in matches in competitions which they organize, football clubs may field only a limited number of professional players who are nationals of other Member States.

Interpretation of Articles 85 and 86 of the Treaty

138. Since both types of rule to which the national court's question refer are contrary to Article 48, it is not necessary to rule on the interpretation of Articles 85 and 86 of the Treaty.

The temporal effects of this judgment

[Paras 139-146 omitted]

Costs

[Para. 147 omitted]

On those grounds,

THE COURT,

in answer to the questions referred to it by the Cour d'Appel, Liège, by judgment of 1 October 1993, hereby rules:

1. **Article 48 of the EEC Treaty precludes the application of rules laid down by sporting associations, under which a professional footballer who is a national of one Member State may not, on the expiry of his contract with a club, be employed by a club of another Member State unless the latter club has paid to the former club a transfer, training or development fee.**

2. **Article 48 of the EEC Treaty precludes the application of rules laid down by sporting associations under which, in matches in competitions which they organize, football clubs may field only a limited number of professional players who are nationals of other Member States.**

3. **The direct effect of Article 48 of the EEC Treaty cannot be relied upon in support of claims relating to a fee in respect of transfer, training or development which has already been paid on, or is still payable under an obligation which arose before, the date of this judgment, except by those who have brought court proceedings or raised an equivalent claim under the applicable national law before that date.**

Comments and questions

Case C-415/93 *Union royale belge des sociétés de football association* v *Bosman* [1995] ECR I-4921, (the *Bosman* case) is listed under the heading of 'discriminatory restrictions' in this chapter because the CJEU had to decide whether the so-called 'nationality clauses' were compatible with Article 45 TFEU (formerly Article 48 EEC Treaty). The CJEU also had to consider the more interesting question of whether the transfer rules, which restricted the free movement of workers, were contrary to this Article.

Professional sport is subject to Union law; cf. paragraph 73 of the *Bosman* judgment, where references are made to previous decisions in cases concerning sport, Case 36/74 *Walrave* v *Union Cycliste Internationale* [1974] ECR 1405 and Case 13/76 *Donà* v *Mantero* [1976] ECR 1333. However, Union law does allow for rules or practices which are justified on non-economic grounds and which relate to the particular nature and context of certain matches; cf. paragraph 76. What do you think this entails? The Lisbon Treaty inserted Article 6(e) into the TFEU, whereby the Union is given competence to carry out actions to support, coordinate or supplement the actions of the Member States, including in the area of sport. The Union cannot legislate for, for example, amateur sport, but only adopt supplementary measures which must not entail harmonisation of Member States' laws or regulations; see Article 2(5) TFEU.

The CJEU held that the principle of freedom of association in Article 11 of the European Convention on Human Rights is protected in Union law, but that it cannot be assumed that transfer rules are necessary to enable football clubs to exercise their rights, nor can they be seen as an inevitable result of them; cf. paragraphs 79-80 of the judgment.

Who is subject to the provisions under Article 45 TFEU (formerly Article 48 EEC Treaty)? The State, in a broad sense, is bound by its provisions. This means that government ministries, public boards and directorates, regional and local government authorities, and wholly publicly owned companies are bound by Article 45 TFEU. The CJEU added that the terms of Article 39 do *not only apply to public authorities but also extend to rules of any other nature aimed at regulating gainful employment in a collective manner, including the exercise of their legal autonomy by associations or organisations not governed by public law*; cf. paragraphs 82-83. Transfer rules, as issued by sports bodies such as the Belgian Football Association, FIFA or UEFA, are thus covered by Article 39; cf. paragraph 87. This is a reflection of the particularly *broad concept of the State in Union law*; cf. also Case 249/81 *Commission* v *Ireland* [1982] ECR 4005; and Case 71/76 *Thieffry* v *Conseil de l'ordre des avocats à la cour de Paris* [1977] ECR 765, printed in Chapter 5. Furthermore, Article 45 TFEU now applies in principle to private individuals; cf. Case C-281/98 *Angonese* v *Cassa di Risparmio di Bolzano* [2000] ECR I-4139, printed above. In other words, Article 45 TFEU contains a horizontal prohibition of discrimination, so that private employers may not discriminate against employees from other Member States in connection with recruitment, wages, working conditions and so on. This also applies to indirect discrimination, for example, on the basis of linguistic or residential requirements. Consequently, private employers must be able to justify their conduct even when their policies do not formally discriminate between their own nationals and nationals of other Member States, if the result of their policies is more burdensome for foreign nationals.

The next question was whether the transfer rules could be regarded as a restriction on the free movement of workers. The question arose because the transfer rules applied whether the transfer was between two clubs in the same Member State, or to a club in another Member State. The transfer rules thus applied without distinction to different nationalities; in other words, there was neither direct nor indirect discrimination. However, the transfer rules did restrict a football player from changing club, so that in the view of the CJEU, the rules constituted an obstacle to freedom of movement for workers (a non-discriminatory regulation which affected access to the work market, i.e., a restriction); cf. paragraph 100.

The plaintiffs in the main case argued that the case should be covered by the *Keck* doctrine. In response to this the CJEU simply limited itself to observing that the transfer rules were subject to Article 45 TFEU, because they 'directly affect players' access to the employment market in other Member States'; cf. paragraph 103. The CJEU thus dismissed the idea that the *Keck* doctrine was applicable to this case. On that basis it seems clear that Article 45 TFEU covers all measures taken by organs which are covered by the Union law concept of a State body which can hinder or restrict *access* to the employment market in a Member State. What is the significance of this condition of *access*? What measures affect access to the employment market, regardless of the fact that they apply without distinction between nationals of the home State and nationals of another Member State? Will the *Keck* doctrine ever be applicable in Article 39 situations? The CJEU has also rejected the applicability of the *Keck* doctrine in Case C-176/96 *Lehtonen and another* v *Fédération royale belge des sociétés de basket-ball* [2000] ECR I-2681. This case involved the rules of a Belgian sports association which prevented Belgian basketball clubs from using players from other Member States in matches for the Belgian championship, if the transfer of the player in question had taken place after a given date. In paragraph 50 of the judgment, the CJEU stated that a rule which restricts the participation of a player obviously also restricts the chances of employment of the player concerned. Do you agree?

In 2007, nine ice hockey clubs in the Danish ice hockey league approached the Danish Ice Hockey Union with a view to limiting the number of foreign players who could be used in individual matches to ten per team for the coming season. However, it was not proposed to limit the number of foreign players who could be employed. The aim of the rule was to ensure the development of Danish players. Would such a rule be contrary to Union law? Would it make a difference if the rule only applied to players from Canada and Russia?

The EU has a number of association agreements with third countries, such as Turkey and Morocco, and it has comprehensive agreements with nearly 80 developing third countries, primarily in Africa. These agreements often contain provisions corresponding to Article 45 TFEU. Thus, in a case against the German Handball Federation, prior to Slovakia's admission to membership of the EU, a Slovak handball player could rely on Article 38 (prohibiting discrimination) of the association agreement between the EU and Slovakia where the Handball Federation gave the Slovak player a restricted right to play. According to the rules of the Handball Federation, as a national of a third country, the Slovak player could only obtain limited permission to play and the Handball Federation therefore decided to give the Slovak such a limited playing licence. Article 38 of the association agreement had immediate effect, and the CJEU held that the rules of the

Handball Federation contravened this provision. In other words, the CJEU's interpretation of Article 45(2) TFEU in the *Bosman* case, prohibiting nationality clauses, could be applied to Article 38 of the association agreement; cf. Case C-438/00 *Deutscher Handballbund eV* v *Kolpak* [2003] ECR I-4135.

Would a German national, employed by a Swedish company, be able to rely on the provisions of Article 45 TFEU against the Swedish tax authorities, by characterising the high Swedish tax rates as a restriction which is incompatible with Article 45 TFEU unless the tax rates can be justified? In this connection see Case C-190/98 *Volker Graf* v *Filzmoser Maschinenbau GmbH* [2000] ECR I-493, printed below, which concerned a German national, who had been employed by an Austrian company, but who resigned from his job in order to take up work in Germany. In connection with his resignation, Graf was not paid compensation on termination of employment since, under Austrian law, this compensation was only payable to those who were dismissed. Graf argued that the rule restricted his freedom of movement. Would it be possible to apply the *Keck* doctrine in Graf's situation?

JUDGMENT OF THE COURT (Fifth Chamber)
23 May 1996

John O'Flynn v Adjudication Officer.
(Reference for a preliminary ruling: Social Security Commissioner – United Kingdom)

'Social advantages for workers – Funeral payment'

Case C-237/94

Judgment

1. By order of 28 June 1994, received at the Court Registry on 22 August 1994, the Social Security Commissioner referred to the Court for a preliminary ruling under Article 177 of the EC Treaty three questions on the interpretation of Article 7 of Regulation (EEC) No 1612/68 of the Council of 15 October 1968 on freedom of movement for workers within the Community (OJ, English Special Edition 1968 (II), p. 475).

2. Those questions arose in proceedings between Mr O'Flynn and the Adjudication Officer concerning the refusal of a funeral payment under the Social Fund (Maternity and Funeral Expenses) Regulations 1987 (hereinafter 'the 1987 Regulations').

3. The funeral payment is a means-tested social benefit. It is intended to cover the costs incurred, by the claimant or a member of his family, described in the 1987 Regulations as 'the responsible member', on the occasion of a death in the family.

4. Under Regulation 7(1)(c) of the 1987 Regulations, a funeral payment is made only if 'the funeral takes place within the United Kingdom'. According to Regulation 3(1), ''funeral' means a burial or a cremation'.

5. Under Regulation 7(2) of the 1987 Regulations, the funeral payment is to be an amount sufficient to meet the essential expenses met by the responsible member. So it covers all the costs normally associated with burial or cremation at a place near the deceased's home, and if necessary the costs of transporting the body within the United Kingdom to that home. On the other hand, it does not cover the cost of transporting the coffin to a place of burial or cremation which is distant from the deceased's home. In that case the additional cost of transporting the coffin has to be met by the responsible member.

6. Mr O'Flynn is an Irish national resident in the United Kingdom as a former migrant worker. His son died in the United Kingdom on 25 August 1988. A religious ceremony was held in the United Kingdom but the burial took place in Ireland.

7. Mr O'Flynn applied for a funeral payment, which was refused on the ground that the burial had not taken place in the United Kingdom as required by Regulation 7(1)(c) of the 1987 Regulations.

8. Mr O'Flynn appealed against the refusal. His contention before the national tribunal was, inter alia, that Regulation 7(1)(c) of the 1987 Regulations indirectly discriminated against migrant workers and was in breach of Article 7(2) of Regulation No 1612/68, under which a worker from one Member State is to enjoy in the territory of the other Member States the same social and tax advantages as national workers. The parties disagreed on the criteria to be applied to determine whether a provision such as Article 7(1)(c) of the 1987 Regulations constitutes discrimination against migrant workers.

9. Mr O'Flynn submitted that the condition at issue, being a territorial condition, was by its nature indirectly discriminatory against migrant workers. He submitted, in the alternative, that the discriminatory character of the provision should in any event be taken to be established if it was shown that migrant workers were normally less likely to fulfil the condition at issue.

10. The respondent authorities submitted for their part that the condition was to be regarded as discriminatory only if it was shown that it was substantially more difficult for migrant workers than for national workers to satisfy it, having regard inter alia to their customs. For that it was necessary to show that the condition at issue was satisfied only by a substantially lower proportion of workers from all the other Member States than of national workers. In any event, a migrant worker could not rely on the discriminatory character of the condition at issue if the condition was not satisfied for reasons unconnected with that worker's nationality.

11. In those circumstances the Social Security Commissioner stayed proceedings and referred the following questions to the Court for a preliminary ruling:

'1. Is it compatible with the Community principle of non-discrimination on grounds of nationality for the purposes of Article 7 of Regulation No 1612/68 for the United Kingdom to make the payment of Social Fund funeral expenses subject to a territorial condition, namely that the funeral takes place in the United Kingdom?

2. Does the answer to Question 1 depend upon any of the following considerations:

(a) Is the test to be applied for determining the existence of indirect discrimination on grounds of nationality:

(i) whether nationals of other Member States acting reasonably and in the normal course of events are, by reason of the territorial condition, less likely to receive payments than are United Kingdom nationals (and, if so, must it be shown that, by reason of the condition, a substantially lower proportion of nationals of other Member States than of United Kingdom nationals is likely to receive payments); or

(ii) whether it is substantially more difficult in practice for nationals of other Member States to satisfy the condition; or

(iii) some other and, if so, what test?

(b) In each case is it sufficient to make a comparison between United Kingdom nationals and nationals of the specific Member State of which the claimant is a national, or is it necessary to make a comparison between United Kingdom nationals and nationals of all other Member States?

3. Is such a condition capable of amounting to unlawful discrimination on grounds of nationality, and/or is it open to a claimant to rely on such discrimination, in circumstances in which the claimant's failure to satisfy the condition was for reasons unrelated to nationality, i.e. on grounds of cost?'

12. The order for reference shows that the Social Security Commissioner wishes to know whether Article 7(2) of Regulation No 1612/68 precludes a provision, such as that in Regulation 7(1)(c) of the 1987 Regulations, which makes grant of a payment to cover funeral expenses incurred by a migrant worker subject to the condition that the funeral take place within the territory of the Member State whose legislation provides for that payment. Having regard to the arguments advanced before him, the Commissioner wishes to know in particular whether he should take account of the following factors: the proportion and nationality of the migrant workers who actually satisfy the condition at issue; how difficult it is in practice for migrant workers to satisfy that condition; and the reasons why a migrant worker fails to satisfy the condition at issue in a particular situation.

13. Those questions are closely linked and can be considered together.

14. The first point to note is that an allowance such as the funeral payment constitutes a 'social advantage' within the meaning of Article 7(2) of Regulation No 1612/68 and, in accordance with that provision, migrant workers must enjoy that advantage under the same conditions as national workers.

15. The United Kingdom says that the purpose of a funeral payment is to ensure, in the light of its civic responsibilities and in the interests of public health, the decent burial or cremation in the United Kingdom of all deceased persons. The allowance is granted in a non-discriminatory manner, being paid to migrant workers and national workers alike if the burial or cremation takes place within the United Kingdom, and

refused to migrant workers and national workers alike if the burial or cremation takes place outside the United Kingdom.

16. It is, however, to be noted that an allowance such as the funeral payment covers not only the necessary costs of the burial or cremation of the body but also all the costs incurred by the responsible member in order to ensure that the deceased receives a modest but decent funeral at a place near his home. The costs of transporting the coffin to a place of burial or cremation distant from that home are not covered by the payment.

17. The Court has consistently held that the equal treatment rule laid down in Article 48 of the Treaty and in Article 7 of Regulation No 1612/68 prohibits not only overt discrimination by reason of nationality but also all covert forms of discrimination which, by the application of other distinguishing criteria, lead in fact to the same result (see inter alia Case 152/73 Sotgiu v Deutsche Bundespost [1974] ECR 153, paragraph 11; Case C-27/91 URSSAF v Le Manoir [1991] ECR I-5531, paragraph 10; Case C-111/91 Commission v Luxembourg [1993] ECR I-817, paragraph 9; and Case C-419/92 Scholz v Opera Universitaria di Cagliari [1994] ECR I-505, paragraph 7).

18. Accordingly, conditions imposed by national law must be regarded as indirectly discriminatory where, although applicable irrespective of nationality, they affect essentially migrant workers (see Case 41/84 *Pinna* v *Caisse d'Allocations Familiales de la Savoie* [1986] ECR 1, paragraph 24; Case 33/88 *Allué and Another* v *Università degli Studi di Venezia* [1989] ECR 1591, paragraph 12; and Le Manoir, paragraph 11) or the great majority of those affected are migrant workers (see Case C-279/89 *Commission* v *United Kingdom* [1992] ECR I-5785, paragraph 42, and Case C-272/92 *Spotti* v *Freistaat Bayern* [1993] ECR I-5185, paragraph 18), where they are indistinctly applicable but can more easily be satisfied by national workers than by migrant workers (see Commission v Luxembourg, paragraph 10, and Case C-349/87 *Paraschi* v *Landesversicherungsanstalt Wuerttemberg* [1991] ECR I-4501, paragraph 23) or where there is a risk that they may operate to the particular detriment of migrant workers (see Case C-175/88 *Biehl* v *Administration des Contributions* [1990] ECR I-1779, paragraph 14, and Case C-204/90 *Bachmann* v *Belgium* [1992] ECR I-249, paragraph 9).

19. It is otherwise only if those provisions are justified by objective considerations independent of the nationality of the workers concerned, and if they are proportionate to the legitimate aim pursued by the national law (see, to that effect, Bachmann, paragraph 27; Commission v Luxembourg, paragraph 12; and Joined Cases C-259/91, C-331/91 and C-332/91 *Allué and Others* v *Università degli Studi di Venezia* [1993] ECR I-4309, paragraph 15).

20. It follows from all the foregoing case-law that, unless objectively justified and proportionate to its aim, a provision of national law must be regarded as indirectly discriminatory if it is intrinsically liable to affect migrant workers more than national workers and if there is a consequent risk that it will place the former at a particular disadvantage.

21. It is not necessary in this respect to find that the provision in question does in practice affect a substantially higher proportion of migrant workers. It is sufficient that it is liable to have such an effect. Further, the reasons why a migrant worker chooses to make use of his freedom of movement within the Community are not to be taken into account in assessing whether a national provision is discriminatory. The possibility of exercising so fundamental a freedom as the freedom of movement of persons cannot be limited by such considerations, which are purely subjective.

22. A migrant worker will, in his capacity as responsible member, incur costs of the same type as, and of comparable amount to, those incurred by a national worker. On the other hand, it is above all the migrant worker who may, on the death of a member of the family, have to arrange for burial in another Member State, in view of the links which the members of such a family generally maintain with their State of origin.

23. To make payment of any expenses incurred by a migrant worker in his capacity as responsible member subject to the condition that burial or cremation take place within the United Kingdom therefore constitutes indirect discrimination, unless it be objectively justified and proportionate to the aim pursued.

24. Although, as the United Kingdom submits, the Social Security Commissioner has not expressly raised the question of justification for the national provision at issue, his first question is, as the Advocate General observes at point 33 of his Opinion, a general one on the point as to whether such a provision is directly or indirectly discriminatory.

25. The Court therefore considers that, in order to give as complete and as useful a reply as possible to the national tribunal, it is necessary to examine that aspect of the problem.

26. As regards protection of public health, it suffices to note that that objective is also safeguarded if the body is transported outside the United Kingdom for burial or cremation in another Member State.

27. The United Kingdom has further put forward a justification based on the prohibitive cost and practical difficulties of paying the allowance if the burial or cremation takes place outside the United Kingdom.

28. However, in such a case, leaving aside the cost of transporting the coffin outside the United Kingdom, the expenses incurred within the United Kingdom by a migrant worker will be no different from those that would be incurred if burial or cremation were to take place within the United Kingdom. Checking those expenses would be no more difficult than if burial or cremation took place within the United Kingdom. The cost of transporting the coffin to a place distant from the deceased's home is not covered in any event.

29. With respect to the costs of burial or cremation in another Member State, there is nothing to prevent the United Kingdom from limiting the allowance to a lump sum or reasonable amount fixed by reference to the normal cost of a burial or cremation within the United Kingdom.

30. Consequently, the answer to the Social Security Commissioner's questions must be that Article 7(2) of Regulation No 1612/68 precludes a provision such as that in Regulation 7(1)(c) of the 1987 Regulations which makes grant of a payment to cover funeral expenses incurred by a migrant worker subject to the condition that burial or cremation take place within the territory of the Member State whose legislation provides for that payment.

Costs

[Para. 31 omitted]

On those grounds,

THE COURT (Fifth Chamber),

in answer to the questions referred to it by the Social Security Commissioner by order of 28 June 1994, hereby rules:

> **Article 7(2) of Regulation (EEC) No 1612/68 of the Council of 15 October 1968 on freedom of movement for workers within the Community precludes a provision such as that in Regulation 7(1)(c) of the Social Fund (Maternity and Funeral Expenses) Regulations 1987 which makes grant of a payment to cover funeral expenses incurred by a migrant worker subject to the condition that burial or cremation take place within the territory of the Member State whose legislation provides for that payment.**

Comments and questions

In paragraphs 18 and 19 of its judgment in Case C-237/94 *O'Flynn* v *Adjudication Officer* [1996] ECR I-2617, the CJEU undertook a 'textbook' review of its practice governing when conditions imposed by national law must be regarded as indirectly discriminatory. This is so where, although applicable irrespective of nationality, the conditions affect essentially migrant workers or the great majority of those affected are migrant workers, where the conditions are indistinctly applicable but can more easily be satisfied by national workers than by migrant workers or where there is a risk that the conditions may operate to the particular detriment of migrant workers Such provisions can only be justified by objective considerations and if they are proportionate to the legitimate aim pursued by the national law.

The CJEU stated that the rules on the allocation of a grant to cover funeral expenses constituted indirect discrimination; cf. paragraph 23. Why were these rules not justified?

Do you think it is realistic to suggest that the British rules on grants to cover funeral expenses had an effect on the freedom of movement of workers, so that these rules would have influenced the decision of workers whether or not to take up employment in the United Kingdom? If the case had not involved an examination of the grant on the basis of Regulation No 1612/68 (then in force, now Regulation 492/2011), but had merely been decided on the basis of the Treaty provision on the free movement of workers, would it have been possible to argue that the effect of the rules on this freedom was so uncertain and indirect that they could not be considered to be a restriction within the meaning of the TFEU (cf. for example, Case C-44/98 *BASF AG* v *Präsident des Deutschen Patentamts* [1999] ECR I-6269.

Were the rules on grants for funeral expenses covered by Article 7(2) of Regulation No 1612/68 (then in force) on freedom of movement for workers within the Union?

JUDGMENT OF THE COURT
27 January 2000

Volker Graf v Filzmoser Maschinenbau GmbH.
(Reference for a preliminary ruling: Oberlandesgericht Linz – Austria)

'Freedom of movement of workers – Compensation on termination of employment – Refusal where a worker terminates his contract of employment in order to take a job in another Member State'

Case C-190/98

Judgment

1. By order of 15 April 1998, received at the Court on 19 May 1998, the Oberlandesgericht Linz (Higher Regional Court, Linz) referred to the Court for a preliminary ruling under Article 177 of the EC Treaty (now Article 234 EC) a question on the interpretation of Article 48 of the EC Treaty (now, after amendment, Article 39 EC).

2. That question was raised in proceedings between Mr Graf, a German national, and Filzmoser Maschinenbau GmbH ('Filzmoser'), whose registered office is in Wels, Austria, concerning the latter's refusal to pay Mr Graf the compensation on termination of employment to which he claimed entitlement under Paragraph 23 of the Angestelltengesetz (Law on Employees; 'the AngG') when he terminated his contract of employment with Filzmoser in order to go and work in Germany.

National legislation

3. Paragraph 23 of the AngG provides:

   '1) If the employment relationship has continued uninterruptedly for three years, the employee shall be entitled to a compensation payment on termination of that relationship. That payment shall amount to twice the salary due to the employee for the last month's employment and after five years' service shall increase to three times, after ten years' service to four times, after 15 years' service to six times, after 20 years' service to nine times and after 25 years' service to 12 times the monthly salary. ...

   ...

7) Without prejudice to Paragraph 23a, there shall be no entitlement to compensation if the employee gives notice, leaves prematurely for no important reason or bears responsibility for his premature dismissal ...'

4. Paragraph 23a of the AngG has no bearing on the main proceedings.

The main proceedings

5. By letter of 29 February 1996, Mr Graf terminated the contract of employment which he had had with Filzmoser since 3 August 1992, in order to move to Germany and take up new employment in that country from 1 May 1996 with G. Siempelkamp GmbH & Co., whose registered office is in Düsseldorf.

6. Filzmoser refused, on the basis of Paragraph 23(7) of the AngG, to pay Mr Graf the compensation on termination of employment equal to two months' salary which he was claiming from it under Paragraph 23(1). Mr Graf thereupon brought proceedings against his former employer before the Landesgericht Wels (Regional Court, Wels) for payment of that compensation, contending in particular that Paragraph 23(7) of the AngG was contrary to Article 48 of the Treaty.

7. By judgment of 4 February 1998 the Landesgericht Wels dismissed Mr Graf's action, holding, in particular, that Paragraph 23(7) of the AngG was not discriminatory and did not constitute an obstacle prohibited by Article 48 of the Treaty since, first, it did not restrict cross-border mobility to a greater extent than mobility within Austria and, second, the loss of compensation on termination of employment equal to two months' salary was not such as to result in a perceptible restriction on freedom of movement for workers, as stated by the Court in Case C-415/93 *Union Royal Belge des Sociétés de Football Association and Others* v *Bosman and Others* [1995] ECR I-4921.

8. The Landesgericht also found that the provision at issue in the main proceedings served in particular to provide maintenance and temporary assistance and thus pursued legitimate social-policy objectives, so that it was in any event justified by overriding reasons in the public interest. In this connection, it observed in particular that, where an employer terminated a contract of employment, the employee found himself, through no fault of his own and very often to his complete surprise, in a situation where temporary assistance was needed, whereas an employee who voluntarily gave up his job by giving notice himself could plan for the resulting consequences.

9. Mr Graf appealed against the judgment of the Landesgericht Wels to the Oberlandesgericht Linz, before which he amplified the arguments already rejected at first instance with the submission that it could not be inferred from the judgment in Bosman, cited above, that a restriction on freedom of movement had to be 'percep-

tible' in order to be prohibited by Article 48 of the Treaty. He also disputed the validity of the social-policy grounds adopted by the Landesgericht to justify payment of compensation on loss of employment, at any rate so far as concerns the loss of compensation entitlement by virtue of Paragraph 23(7) of the AngG.

10. The Oberlandesgericht Linz found first of all that there was no case-law of the Court of Justice relating to a comparable set of facts, that while the arguments of the parties were irreconcilable they all appeared cogent at first sight, that the Landesgericht reached its decision only after careful and detailed assessment, and that in the most recent legal literature published in Austria the view had almost unanimously been taken that the loss of compensation on termination of employment when the employee himself gave notice was irreconcilable, or at least difficult to reconcile, with the principle of freedom of movement.

11. It then expressed doubts that social-policy objectives, however legitimate they might be, or overriding reasons in the public interest could, in view of the case-law of the Court of Justice on the principle of proportionality, justify an exclusion from entitlement to compensation on termination of employment as broad and general as that laid down in Paragraph 23(7) of the AngG. It held that the line of argument of the court at first instance was founded in that regard on incomplete and incorrect premisses. It was not evident that every termination of a contract by an employer took the employee by surprise and occurred through no fault of his own. Conversely, all sorts of circumstances relating to the undertaking, whether or not the employer was responsible for them, could equally prompt an employee who was long-serving and therefore entitled to a large amount of compensation on termination of employment to change jobs without him necessarily being at fault. Finally, there were terminations which were not decisively influenced by either the employee or the employer but were brought about by outside factors affecting one or other of the parties to the contract of employment.

12. The Oberlandesgericht Linz considered, finally, that the import of Bosman for labour law in general was no longer clear either, given in particular that in that case the Court had, on the one hand, accepted broad grounds of justification for restrictions, including non-economic grounds, but had, on the other, referred to the very general formulations used in Case C-10/90 *Masgio* v *Bundesknappschaft* [1991] ECR I-1119 and Case C-19/92 *Kraus* v *Land Baden-Württemberg* [1993] ECR I-1663. It therefore decided to stay proceedings and refer the following question to the Court for a preliminary ruling:

    'Does Article 48 of the EC Treaty preclude national provisions under which an employee who is a national of a Member State is not entitled to compensation on termination of his employment relationship simply because he himself gave notice terminating that relationship in order to take up employment in another Member State?'

Consideration of the question submitted

13. By its question, the national court essentially asks whether Article 48 of the Treaty precludes national provisions which deny a worker entitlement to compensation on termination of employment if he terminates his contract of employment himself in order to take up employment in another Member State, when those provisions grant him entitlement to such compensation if the contract ends without the termination being at his own initiative or attributable to him.

14. First, it must be borne in mind that Article 48(2) of the Treaty expressly provides that freedom of movement for workers is to entail the abolition of any discrimination based on nationality between workers of the Member States as regards employment, remuneration and other conditions of work and employment. In addition, according to the Court's case-law, the rule of equal treatment, laid down in Article 48, prohibits not only overt discrimination based on nationality but also all covert forms of discrimination which, by applying other distinguishing criteria, achieve in practice the same result (see, in particular, Case C-350/96 *Clean Car Autoservice* v *Landeshauptmann von Wien* [1998] ECR I-2521, paragraph 27).

15. Legislation such as that at issue in the main proceedings applies irrespective of the nationality of the worker concerned.

16. Moreover, legislation of that kind denies compensation on termination of employment to all workers who end their contract of employment themselves in order to take up employment with a new employer, regardless of whether the latter is established in the same Member State as the previous employer or in another Member State. In those circumstances, it cannot be maintained that such legislation affects migrant workers to a greater extent than national workers and that it might therefore place at a disadvantage the former in particular.

17. Furthermore, as the national court expressly stated in its order for reference, there is nothing on the file to indicate that such legislation operates to the disadvantage of a particular group of workers wishing to take up new employment in another Member State.

18. Second, it is clear from the Court's case-law, in particular from the judgment in Bosman, cited above, that Article 48 of the Treaty prohibits not only all discrimination, direct or indirect, based on nationality but also national rules which are applicable irrespective of the nationality of the workers concerned but impede their freedom of movement.

19. According to Mr Graf, the loss of compensation on termination of employment where the worker himself terminates the contract constitutes such an obstacle to freedom of movement for workers, comparable to the obstacle which was at issue

in Bosman. In his submission, it is largely immaterial in this connection whether the worker suffers a financial loss because he changes employer or the new employer is required to make a payment in order to take him on.

20. By contrast, the other parties who have submitted observations to the Court maintain that national legislation applicable irrespective of the nationality of the workers concerned which is liable to dissuade the latter from deciding to exercise their right to freedom of movement does not necessarily constitute an obstacle to freedom of movement for workers.

21. In that regard, the Court has held on numerous occasions that the Treaty provisions relating to freedom of movement for persons are intended to facilitate the pursuit by Community nationals of occupational activities of all kinds throughout the Community, and preclude measures which might place Community nationals at a disadvantage when they wish to pursue an economic activity in the territory of another Member State (see, in particular, Bosman, cited above, paragraph 94, and Case C-18/95 *Terhoeve* v *Inspecteur van de Belastingdienst Particulieren/Ondernemingen Buitenland* [1999] ECR I-345, paragraph 37).

22. Nationals of Member States have in particular the right, which they derive directly from the Treaty, to leave their country of origin to enter the territory of another Member State and reside there in order to pursue an economic activity (see, in particular, Bosman, paragraph 95, and Terhoeve, paragraph 38).

23. Provisions which, even if they are applicable without distinction, preclude or deter a national of a Member State from leaving his country of origin in order to exercise his right to freedom of movement therefore constitute an obstacle to that freedom. However, in order to be capable of constituting such an obstacle, they must affect access of workers to the labour market.

24. Legislation of the kind at issue in the main proceedings is not such as to preclude or deter a worker from ending his contract of employment in order to take a job with another employer, because the entitlement to compensation on termination of employment is not dependent on the worker's choosing whether or not to stay with his current employer but on a future and hypothetical event, namely the subsequent termination of his contract without such termination being at his own initiative or attributable to him.

25. Such an event is too uncertain and indirect a possibility for legislation to be capable of being regarded as liable to hinder freedom of movement for workers where it does not attach to termination of a contract of employment by the worker himself the same consequence as it attaches to termination which was not at his initiative or is not attributable to him (see to that effect, with regard to the free movement of goods, in particular Case C-69/88 *Krantz* v *Ontvanger der Directe Belastingen*

[1990] ECR I-583, paragraph 11, and Case C-44/98 *BASF* v *Präsident des Deutschen Patentamts* [1999] ECR I-6269, paragraphs 16 and 21).

26. In view of all the foregoing considerations, the answer to the question submitted must be that Article 48 of the Treaty does not preclude national provisions which deny a worker entitlement to compensation on termination of employment if he terminates his contract of employment himself in order to take up employment in another Member State, when those provisions grant him entitlement to such compensation if the contract ends without the termination being at his own initiative or attributable to him.

Costs

[Para. 27 omitted]

On those grounds,

THE COURT,

in answer to the question referred to it by the Oberlandesgericht Linz by order of 15 April 1998, hereby rules:

Article 48 of the EC Treaty (now, after amendment, Article 39 EC) does not preclude national provisions which deny a worker entitlement to compensation on termination of employment if he terminates his contract of employment himself in order to take up employment in another Member State, when those provisions grant him entitlement to such compensation if the contract ends without the termination being at his own initiative or attributable to him.

Comments and questions

In Case C-190/98 *Volker Graf* v *Filzmoser Maschinenbau GmbH* [2000] ECR I-493, the central question was hardly whether the Austrian provision had in fact contravened the (now) TFEU. Even though it appeared to be the almost unanimous view of writers in recent Austrian legal literature that the provision in question conflicted with the TFEU rules on the free movement of workers, it was relatively clear that it did not contravene the TFEU. The central question in the case, therefore, was why did it not contravene the TFEU?

Volker Graf was a German national who was employed by an Austrian company. Graf resigned from his job with a view to taking employment in Germany. Under Austrian law, an employee is entitled to receive compensation from his employer on termination of employment if the employment relationship has continued without interruption for three years. However, there is no entitlement to compensation if the employee himself gives notice, leaves prematurely for no important reason or bears responsibility for his premature dismissal. Graf himself wished to leave his job, so the Austrian employer refused to give him compensation, in accordance with the Austrian law. Graf then took his claim before the Austrian courts, where he argued that the provision constituted a restriction on the free movement of workers.

In paragraph 23 of the judgment the CJEU made some general comments on the scope of application of Article 45 TFEU (formerly Article 39 TEC). It stated that non-discriminatory provisions which preclude or deter a national of a Member State from leaving his country of origin in order to exercise his right to freedom of movement constitute an obstacle to freedom of movement. However, the CJEU added that '*in order to be capable of constituting such an obstacle, they must affect access of workers to the labour market*' (emphasis added). This latest sentence is a clear reference to the *Keck* doctrine, which should be understood in the light of the fact that the Commission, Denmark, Italy and the United Kingdom had all submitted arguments in the case, recommending that the criterion 'access to the market', which had first been established in Joined Cases C-267/91 and C-268/91 *Keck and Mithouard* [1993] ECR I-6097, printed in Chapter 2, should be applied to the employment market as well. It is difficult to interpret paragraph 23 other than as meaning that the *Keck* doctrine on 'access to the market' also applies to Article 45 TFEU. This means that at least the requirements as to language qualifications, examination certificates, conditions for payment and suchlike which concern *access* to the employment market fall within the scope of Article 45 TFEU. In the view of the CJEU, the conditions for carrying on an undertaking, such as the tax rules under which an employer can make a company car available to an employee (cf. Case C-464/02 *Commission* v *Denmark* [2005] ECR I-7929, printed below) can also affect the employer's access to the market for labour. There are corresponding ideas in several of the CJEU's other judgments. See, for example in relation to Article 63 TFEU, Case C-98/01 *Commission* v *United Kingdom* [2003] ECR I-4641, paragraph 47, cited in the comments on Case C-503/99 *Commission* v *Belgium* [2002] ECR I-4809 (the *Golden shares* case), printed in Chapter 7 below. This thinking occurs again in relation to Article 56 TFEU in Joined Cases C-544/03 and C-545/03 *Mobistar SA* v *Commune de Fléron* [2005] ECR I-7723, where it is stated in paragraph 31:

> 'By contrast, measures, the only effect of which is to create additional costs in respect of the service in question and which affect in the same way the provision of services between Member States and that within one Member State, do not fall within the scope of Article [56 TFEU].'

In paragraphs 24 and 25, the CJEU also held that the Austrian rule on loss of entitlement to compensation on termination of employment, when a worker leaves his employment on his own initiative, is too uncertain and indirect for the legislation to be regarded as liable to hinder freedom of movement for workers, as prohibited by Article 45 TFEU. The basis for the CJEU's reasoning seems to indicate that two different lines of argument were considered for rejecting the idea that the Austrian provisions were contrary to the TFEU. These were, on the one hand, the *Keck* doctrine, and on the other hand, the argument that the restrictive effect of the disputed rule was insufficiently certain and direct to be covered by the Treaty prohibition.

Either of these two grounds would have been enough to find that the Austrian provision did not contravene the (now) TFEU. The case can presumably be read in two different ways on this point. Either the CJEU referred to the K*eck* doctrine in paragraph 23, but refrained from deciding on that basis, whereas in paragraphs 24 and 25 it dealt with the question of whether the restriction was too uncertain and indirect to be covered by the Treaty prohibition. Or the judgment can be understood so that in paragraph 23 the CJEU referred to the *Keck* doctrine, whereupon in paragraph 24 it finds that the Austrian law is covered by the *Keck* doctrine, since its effects are too uncertain and indirect to affect a worker's access to the employment market. Why did the CJEU find it necessary to present two parallel and independent justifications? Was this and expression of disagreement within the CJEU?

In his Opinion, Advocate General Fennelly suggested that the answer to the question which had been referred by the Austrian court depended on the clarification of a number of factors, as follows:

1. the definition of a prohibited non-discriminatory restriction on the freedom of movement of workers,
2. whether its restrictive effects must be in some way conditional on the exercise of freedom of movement,
3. whether it must affect access to an economic activity or can also arise from regulation of its exercise,
4. whether its effect must be to prevent workers exercising their rights or simply to deter or hamper them in so doing,
5. whether its restrictive effects must be of a certain level of gravity or intensity,
6. whether its preventive or dissuasive effects must be direct or may be indirect, and
7. whether these burdensome effects must be certain or may be merely contingent.

What are the answers to these seven questions? Are all the answers laid down, directly or indirectly, in the *Graf* case?

JUDGMENT OF THE COURT (First Chamber)
15 September 2005

Commission of the European Communities v Kingdom of Denmark

'Failure of a Member State to fulfil obligations – Freedom of movement for workers – Motor vehicles – Making available to the employee by the employer – Vehicle registered in the Member State of the employer – Employee resident in another Member State – Taxation of the motor vehicle'

Case C-464/02

Judgment

1. By its application, the Commission of the European Communities seeks a declaration from the Court that:

   – in so far as its legislation and administrative practice do not allow employees who are employed in a neighbouring Member State and resident in Denmark to use for business or private purposes a company vehicle registered in that neighbouring Member State where the undertaking of their employer is established,
   – in so far as its legislation and administrative practice allow employees who are employed in another Member State of the European Union and resident in Denmark to use for business and/or private purposes a motor vehicle, in particular a company vehicle, which is registered in another Member State in which their employer has its registered office or principal establishment, only subject to the condition that the work in the foreign undertaking is their main employment and that tax is paid for that purpose, the Kingdom of Denmark has failed to fulfil its obligations under Articles 39 EC and 10 EC, and must be ordered to pay the costs of the present proceedings.

2. The Kingdom of Denmark contends that the action should be dismissed and the Commission ordered to pay the costs.

Law

Community legislation

[Paras 3-30 omitted]

The action

31. The Commission claims that both the original scheme and the amended scheme (together 'the Danish legislation') impede freedom of movement for workers, contrary to the provisions of Article 39 EC in conjunction with Article 10 EC, and cannot be justified by overriding reasons relating to the public interest.

The scope of Article 39 EC

Arguments of the parties

32. The Commission submits that the Danish legislation at issue falls within the scope of Article 39 EC on the ground that the provisions governing the pursuit of an occupational activity also affect access to the labour market.

33. The Danish Government, supported by the Finnish Government, counters that the Danish legislation falls outside the scope of Article 39 EC since it does not affect access to the labour market. The Danish Government takes the view that the legislation relates solely to conditions of employment. The principle according to which an employee resident in Denmark is not allowed to drive there freely in a company car registered abroad is not covered by Article 39 EC.

Findings of the Court

34. The provisions of the Treaty on freedom of movement for persons are intended to facilitate the pursuit by Community citizens of occupational activities of all kinds throughout the Community, and preclude measures which might place Community citizens at a disadvantage when they wish to pursue an economic activity in the territory of another Member State (Case C-415/93 *Bosman* [1995] ECR I-4921, paragraph 94; Case C-232/01 *Van Lent* [2003] ECR I-11525, paragraph 15; and Case C-387/01 *Weigel* [2004] ECR I-4981, paragraph 52).

35. Provisions which preclude or deter a national of a Member State from leaving his country of origin in order to exercise his right to freedom of movement therefore constitute an obstacle to that freedom even if they apply without regard to the nationality of the workers concerned (*Bosman*, paragraph 96).

36. However, in order to be capable of constituting such an obstacle, they must affect access of workers to the labour market (Case C-190/98 *Graf* [2000] ECR I-493, paragraph 23).

37. The manner in which an activity is pursued is liable also to affect access to that activity. Consequently, legislation which relates to the conditions in which an eco-

nomic activity is pursued may constitute an obstacle to freedom of movement within the meaning of that case-law.

38. It follows that the Danish legislation at issue in this case is not excluded from the outset from the scope of Article 39 EC.

The existence of restrictions on freedom of movement for workers

Arguments of the parties

39. The Commission submits that both the original scheme and the amended scheme are contrary to the freedom of movement for workers enshrined in Article 39 EC on the basis that they have the effect of hindering the right of employees to seek employment in another Member State and the freedom of employers in other Member States to take on employees resident in Denmark.

40. The original scheme prohibits Danish residents from driving in that country with company cars registered abroad. The obstacle resulting from the amended scheme consists in the requirement to obtain prior authorisation and the payment of a tax equivalent to the payment by instalment of the total amount of the registration tax. The Commission takes the view that, in the light of the Danish legislation, undertakings established in other Member States will refrain from employing employees resident in Denmark.

41. The Danish Government asserts that the Danish legislation does not constitute discrimination on grounds of nationality. The rules relating to company vehicles ensure equality between all residents in Denmark, irrespective of whether they are employed in that country or abroad. The rules on registration tax put Danish nationals or foreign nationals residing and working in Denmark and Danish nationals or foreign nationals residing in Denmark but working abroad on a level footing.

42. The Danish Government concedes that, in cases where a company vehicle forms part of the terms of employment, the Danish rules on registration tax, taken in isolation, might appear to be such as to encourage an employer to take on an employee from his own country rather than an employee resident in Denmark. However, it argues against such an isolated assessment, since the additional charges are not necessarily and always an obstacle to taking on an employee resident in Denmark. Where the company vehicle may be used for private purposes, that vehicle constitutes an element of the employee's remuneration. The employer may take account of the additional expense associated with such use when determining other recruitment conditions, in particular salary conditions. For an employer, the overall amount of expense that the future employee will necessitate is a relevant factor. That expense includes, for example, in addition to the salary in the narrow sense, employers' contributions to social security schemes.

43. According to the Finnish Government, the Danish tax system applicable to company vehicles registered abroad and made available to permanent Danish residents does not constitute an obstacle to freedom of movement for workers within the meaning of Article 39 EC. A vehicle which employees use freely is treated in the same way as an employee's personal vehicle. The vehicle is not used on a temporary basis, but on a permanent one.

44. The Commission replies to the argument claiming that there is no discrimination that there is clear discrimination against an employee resident in Denmark compared with an employee resident abroad who makes exactly the same use, in Denmark, of a company vehicle registered abroad. The Danish legislation is incompatible with Community law to the extent that it deters an employer from taking on an employee resident in Denmark to pursue occupational activities in that country with the aid of a company vehicle registered abroad, whereas employees in the same undertaking, resident abroad, are able to pursue their activities without difficulty. It is not a matter of conferring on residents in Denmark a tax position which is more advantageous than that conferred on their colleagues resident abroad. It is not relevant to compare a resident in Denmark employed by a Danish undertaking with a resident in Denmark employed by a foreign undertaking.

Findings of the Court

45. It is settled case-law that Article 39 EC prohibits not only all discrimination, direct or indirect, based on nationality, but also national rules which are applicable irrespective of the nationality of the workers concerned but impede their freedom of movement (*Graf*, paragraph 18, and *Weigel*, paragraphs 50 and 51).

46. It is clear that the original scheme, in so far as it remains applicable, could, on account of the obligation to register in Denmark a company car made available to the employee by an employer established in another Member State, deter such an employer from taking on an employee resident in Denmark for work which is not the employee's principal employment and, consequently, impede access to such employment by residents in Denmark.

47. As regards employees resident in Denmark who wish to pursue their principal employment in an undertaking established in another Member State, the amended scheme also impedes freedom of movement for those workers since it imposes additional costs in the form of a temporary registration tax.

48. In so far as the undertaking established in another Member State bears those costs without being compensated, it is deterred from taking on an employee resident in Denmark in respect of whom the costs are higher than those borne for an employee who does not reside in that State.

49. It is true, as the Danish Government asserts that the employer could attempt to adjust the salary of an employee resident in Denmark in order to offset the additional expense in question. In other words, he could try to pay to that employee a salary lower than that paid to an employee engaged in the same activity, but who resides in another Member State.

50. However, an employee resident in Denmark might already be deterred from seeking employment in another Member State faced with the prospect of receiving a salary lower than that of a comparable employee resident in that other Member State. As the Court ruled in paragraph 18 of Case 127/86 *Ledoux* [1988] ECR 3741, the fact that an employee is placed at a disadvantage in regard to working conditions compared to his colleagues residing in the country of their employer has a direct effect on the exercise of his right to freedom of movement within the Community.

51. As regards the Finnish Government's argument that, in the case of mixed-use company vehicles registered in another Member State and made available to permanent Danish residents, there is no obstacle to freedom of movement for workers on the basis that such a vehicle is treated in the same way as an employee's personal vehicle, that argument is based on a false premiss. An employee resident in Denmark, who is able to use a company vehicle not only for business purposes but also for private purposes, does not have the same freedom to use that vehicle as he might have with his private car, the use of which is not restricted by the requirements of his professional duties.

52. Consequently, it must be held that the Danish legislation, both in its original version and in its amended version, constitutes a restriction on freedom of movement for workers.

53. Such measures could be allowed only as a derogation expressly provided for by Article 39(3) EC or if they pursued a legitimate aim compatible with the Treaty and were justified by pressing reasons of public interest. But even if that were so, application of those measures would still have to be such as to ensure achievement of the aim in question and not go beyond what is necessary for that purpose (see, in particular, *Bosman* paragraph 104, and Case C-224/01 *Köbler* [2003] ECR I-10239, paragraph 77).

Justification of the restriction on freedom of movement for workers

Arguments of the parties

54. The Danish Government, supported by the Finnish Government, states that the Danish legislation is lawful and compatible with Community law and that the obligation to register is the natural corollary of the exercise of the powers of taxation. It is therefore lawful to adopt measures in order to ensure that registration tax is col-

lected, provided that those measures do not go beyond what is necessary and appropriate for that purpose.

55. The Danish Government asserts that any restrictive effect both of the original scheme and of the amended scheme is based on the need to ensure that the liability of Danish residents to registration tax is not circumvented. Without the rules, Danish residents might avoid paying the tax by setting up companies or branches in another Member State through which to acquire and use in Denmark vehicles registered in the other State.

56. As regards the amended scheme, the Danish Government submits that the requirement of prior authorisation to pay the tax in the form of a daily or quarterly tax is prompted by the need to undertake, in advance, an assessment as to whether the conditions relating to the application of the Danish legislation have been met, just as it is prompted by the need to be able to demonstrate that subsequently. The procedure for obtaining authorisation is relatively simple in so far as authorisation is automatically granted to any person requesting it who satisfies the conditions laid down.

57. As regards the obligation to pay a quarterly or daily tax as laid down by the amended scheme, the Danish Government asserts that, in Case C-451/99 *Cura Anlagen* [2002] ECR I-3193, the Court accepted that a consumption tax proportionate to the duration of the registration of the vehicle in the State where it is used is proportionate. The Danish Government adds that the Court's ruling that the consumption tax at issue in that case was unlawful appeared particularly to be prompted by the fact that the amount of the tax was not proportionate to the duration of that registration. The Danish Government concludes from those statements that its legislation on registration tax applicable to vehicles registered in another Member State is not incompatible with the Treaty provisions on freedom of movement for workers.

58. The Danish Government submits that the condition of 'principal employment', which must be satisfied for the amended scheme to apply, is proportionate. 'Principal employment' arises when the Danish resident is employed by a foreign undertaking in work equivalent to full-time employment or where he receives, from that employment, at least half his income.

59. That condition seeks to ensure that an employee benefiting from a company car is genuinely employed by the provider; a purely formal employment relationship is not sufficient. The condition is objective and easy to verify. The Danish Government adds that if the amended scheme were applicable to any Danish resident employed, whether full or part time, in another Member State, it would be much more difficult to guard against abuse. It considers that if that were the case the police would have to check every foreign-registered car driven in Denmark by a resident

of that State with a view to verifying that such drivers were genuinely employed, whether full or part time, in another Member State, which would be inappropriate.

60. The Commission disputes all justification. It objects to the Danish registration tax being classified as a lawful tax. It submits that the Danish legislation is not appropriate to ensuring the attainment of the objective of being able to verify efficiently that the vehicle is being used only lawfully.

61. According to the Commission, the prohibition on using a company vehicle registered abroad without taking into account whether the vehicle is being imported on a temporary basis, whether the vehicle has to be used both in Denmark and in the State where it is legally registered, and whether the vehicle is frequently driven back to the State in which it is registered, is neither appropriate, nor proportionate in the light of road safety. The general obligation to obtain prior authorisation to pay the tax in the form of a daily or quarterly tax brought in by the amended scheme is disproportionate. Such measures cannot be justified by the fight against tax evasion.

62. As regards the prior administrative procedure, the Commission disputes that it is a simple procedure.

Findings of the Court

– The original scheme

63. As regards the original scheme referred to in the first part of the claim, the Commission complains that the legislation and the administrative practice of the Kingdom of Denmark do not allow employees resident in Denmark and employed in a neighbouring Member State in work which is not their principal employment to use for business or private purposes a company vehicle registered in the neighbouring Member State where their employer's undertaking is established.

64. In that respect, it must be noted that, in the framework of Article 39 EC, a person who, for a certain period of time, performs services for and under the direction of another person in return for which he receives remuneration must be considered to be a worker. Any person who pursues activities which are real and genuine, to the exclusion of activities on such a small scale as to be regarded as purely marginal and ancillary, is entitled to freedom of movement as a worker (see, to that effect, Case 66/85 *Lawrie-Blum* [1986] ECR 2121, paragraphs 16 and 17, and Case C-138/02 *Collins* [2004] ECR I-2703, paragraph 26).

65. In order to justify the application of the original scheme to employees whose employment in the undertaking established in another Member State is not their principal employment, the Danish Government relies on the prevention of abuse.

66. It follows from the case-law, in particular from Case C-212/97 *Centros* [1999] ECR I-1459, paragraph 24, that a Member State is entitled to take measures designed to prevent certain of its nationals from attempting, under cover of the rights created by the Treaty, improperly to circumvent their national legislation or to prevent individuals from improperly or fraudulently taking advantage of provisions of Community law.

67. However, the fact that a worker resident in Denmark, who uses a company car of an employer established in another Member State, is employed in work in that State which is not his principal employment cannot form the basis for a general presumption of abuse.

68. To automatically deny such workers the possibility afforded by the amended scheme to use in Denmark, without registering with Danish registration plates, a company vehicle registered in another Member State, goes beyond what is necessary in order to avoid abuses.

69. Consequently, the Commission's action is well founded in so far as it concerns the original scheme.

– The amended scheme

70. As regards the amended scheme, referred to in the second part of the claim, the Commission complains that the authorisation granted to an employee resident in Denmark to use a vehicle registered in another Member State is subject, first, to the condition that the employment in the undertaking established in that other Member State is the principal employment of the worker – an issue which has been dealt with above – and, second, to payment of a tax.

71. The requirement of prior authorisation to pay that tax in the form of a daily or quarterly tax is not referred to in the Commission's head of claim. There is therefore no need to examine the complaints made in that respect.

72. It must also be observed that this case does not concern the normal operation of the registration tax, but its application to vehicles registered in another Member State by an owner established in that Member State.

73. The Court has ruled, in Case C-47/88 *Commission* v *Denmark* [1990] ECR I-4509 and Case C-383/01 *De Danske Bilimportører* [2003] ECR I-6065, paragraph 43, that a tax such as the Danish tax on the registration of new motor vehicles is not contrary to Articles 28 EC and 90 EC. However, that does not mean that the temporary registration tax does not restrict freedom of movement for workers contrary to Article 39 EC.

74. Subject to certain exceptions which are not relevant here, the taxation of motor vehicles has not been harmonised. Member States are therefore free to exercise their powers of taxation in that area, provided they do so in compliance with Community law (*Cura Anlagen*, paragraph 40).

75. For the purposes of determining the restrictions imposed by Article 39 EC on the power of the Kingdom of Denmark to levy a registration tax, it should be borne in mind that the *Cura Anlagen* case concerned only the situation created by a three-year leasing contract concluded by a company registered in Austria with a company registered in another Member State concerning a vehicle intended to be used essentially in Austria. In paragraph 35 of that judgment, the Court stated that hiring contracts made for short periods, such as the hiring of a replacement vehicle from a company established in another Member State were not therefore concerned.

76. Where the company vehicle is intended to be used essentially in Denmark on a permanent basis or where it is in fact used in that manner, the situation is comparable to that at issue in *Cura Anlagen.*

77. In those circumstances, it is open to the Kingdom of Denmark to impose a registration tax on a vehicle made available to an employee who resides there by a company established in another Member State.

78. In that situation, treating equally the use of a company car by the employees in question and other residents of the Kingdom of Denmark as regards the imposition of such a tax is legitimate and is sufficient to justify the restriction on freedom of movement for workers.

79. On the other hand, if the conditions set out in paragraph 76 above are not satisfied, the connection with Denmark of the company vehicle registered in another Member State is weaker, so that another justification for the restriction in question is necessary.

80. In that regard, it should be noted that the temporary registration tax cannot be justified on the basis that it seeks to prevent fiscal erosion. It is settled case-law that reduction in tax revenue cannot be regarded as an overriding reason in the public interest which may be relied on to justify a measure which is in principle contrary to a fundamental freedom (Case C-319/02 *Manninen* [2004] ECR I-7477 paragraph 49).

81. In so far as the Danish Government submits that the temporary tax registration system is justified by the aim of preventing tax avoidance through the use of a company vehicle registered in another Member State, it should be noted that the fact that an employer established in a Member State other than Denmark makes available to an employee resident in Denmark a vehicle for business purposes, or indeed for business and private purposes, cannot form the basis for a general presumption of

tax avoidance or tax evasion. Such a presumption cannot therefore justify a fiscal measure which prejudices the enjoyment of a fundamental freedom guaranteed by the Treaty.

82. Consequently, the Commission's action in relation to the amended scheme is in part well founded.

83. That finding is valid not only in respect of use of a company vehicle for business purposes but also in respect of use for private purposes that are incidental to the business use (see, to that effect, *Ledoux*, paragraph 18).

Article 10 EC

84. There are no grounds for holding that there has been a failure to fulfil the general obligations contained in Article 10 EC which is separate from the failures, previously noted, to fulfil the more specific Community obligations which the Kingdom of Denmark was bound to do under Article 39 EC.

85. Having regard to all of the foregoing considerations it must be held that, in so far as

- its legislation and administrative practice do not allow workers resident in Denmark and employed in another Member State in work which is not their principal employment to use for business or private purposes a company vehicle registered in that other Member State where the undertaking of their employer is established, and

- its legislation and administrative practice allow employees resident in Denmark and employed in another Member State to use for business purposes or business and private purposes a company vehicle registered in that other Member State in which their employer has its registered office or principal establishment, the vehicle neither being intended to be essentially used in Denmark on a permanent basis nor being actually so used, only subject to the condition that the employment with that employer is their main employment and that a tax is paid for that purpose, the Kingdom of Denmark has failed to fulfil its obligations under Article 39 EC, and the remainder of the action must be dismissed.

Costs

[Para. 86 omitted]

On those grounds,

THE COURT (First Chamber)

hereby:

1. **Declares that, in so far as**

- **its legislation and administrative practice do not allow workers resident in Denmark and employed in another Member State in work which is not their principal employment to use for business or private purposes a company vehicle registered in that other Member State where the undertaking of their employer is established, and**
- **its legislation and administrative practice allow employees resident in Denmark and employed in another Member State to use for business purposes or business and private purposes a company vehicle registered in that other Member State in which their employer has its registered office or principal establishment, the vehicle neither being intended to be essentially used in Denmark on a permanent basis nor being actually so used, only subject to the condition that the employment with that employer is their main employment and that a tax is paid for that purpose, the Kingdom of Denmark has failed to fulfil its obligations under Article 39 EC;**

[Paras 2-4 of the ruling omitted]

Comments and questions

Denmark has some very high registration taxes for cars. It is therefore attractive for residents in Denmark to drive cars that are registered in another country with lower taxes. In order to counter this, Denmark adopted rules that stated that residents in Denmark could only use cars registered in Denmark (so that tax was paid on the vehicle). There was one exception to this rule which was conditional on the vehicle being overwhelmingly used outside Denmark, and the exception did not allow a company car to be used for private purposes in Denmark. In relation to company cars, i.e. cars that employers makes available to employees in connection with their employment, Denmark introduced a rule whereby employees who were resident in Denmark, but whose main employment was with a foreign undertaking, could lawfully use a foreign registered company car. In order to qualify for this exception the employee had to use the car both in Denmark and in the country where the foreign undertaking was located. If a company car was covered by the exception it was not required to pay the full Danish registration tax. However, the exception to the Danish rules did not mean there was complete exemption from the tax, as the foreign undertaking had to pay Danish registration tax corresponding to the number of days the car was used in Denmark. Even if a car qualified for the exemption, an employee resident in Denmark who had been provided with a car could not use it for private purposes in Denmark.

It was the Commission's view that the Danish rule was contrary to Article 45 TFEU on the free movement of workers. Against this the Danish Government argued that Article 45 TFEU was not at all applicable to the circumstances. The Danish rule was non-discriminatory, and it only concerned conditions of work and thus did not restrict access to the employment market. Residents in Denmark who wished to seek work with an employer in Germany, for example, could freely do so, regardless of the rule.

The CJEU agreed that the Danish rule concerned the conditions of employment. But at the same time it pointed out that such conditions could constitute a restriction on freedom of movement. Therefore it could not be assumed that the case fell outside the scope of Article 45 TFEU. Consider which conditions for carrying on the business of an undertaking will not be covered by Article 45 TFEU. See Joined Cases C-544/03 and C-545/03 *Mobistar SA* v *Commune de Fléron* [2005] ECR I-7723, paragraph 31.

Thereafter it was necessary to consider whether the Danish rule in fact constituted a restriction on freedom of movement of workers. The Commission argued that the rule would inhibit undertakings located outside Denmark from employing people who were resident in Denmark. The Danish Government agreed that the Danish rule imposed an extra tax, as argued by the Commission. However, the Danish Government pointed out that there were many other similar taxes which were dependent on where the employee was resident. For example, this applied to requirements for the employer to contribute to social costs.

The CJEU held that the Danish rule constituted a restriction on the free movement of workers as it involved an extra cost for employers who wished to employ persons resident in Denmark. While the employer could compensate for this extra expense by giving a correspondingly lower salary, this difference in salary would discourage residents in Denmark from seeking such a job.

Consider the consequences of the CJEU's argument. Does it mean that there is in principle a restriction contrary to Article 45 TFEU whenever there is any form of extra cost which an employer must pay when taking on an employee who is resident in another Member State? In the Scandinavian countries social contributions are primarily paid via taxes, while in many other Member States they are paid directly by employers and employees. Would there be a restriction if an undertaking in Scandinavia wished to employ a person resident in a Member State where, in addition to the usual salary, the Scandinavian employer would have to pay a substantial amount to cover, for example, the new employee's health insurance? Would there be a restriction if an employee who is resident in one Member State, when employed by an undertaking in another Member State, had to pay tax in the Member State where they are resident, and this tax is higher than the tax in the Member State where the employer is located? The employee will have less income after tax than his or her colleagues who are resident in the Member State where the undertaking is located.

Does the CJEU require that, in assessing whether a restriction exists, it is necessary to look at the totality of costs associated with the employment of a person from another Member State, compared with the costs of employing a person resident in the Member State where the employer is located? Or does the CJEU require one to look at the individual elements which can give rise to costs? Do you think it would have changed the view of the CJEU if the Danish Government had been able to point to a number of costs associated with the use of company cars in Denmark's closest EU neighbours – Germany, Poland and Sweden – so that the total costs were the same in Germany, Poland, Sweden and Denmark?

How did the Danish Government justify the disputed rule (see paragraphs 55-56)? The Advocate General argued that the Danish rule did not pursue a lawful purpose which was compatible with the (now) TFEU and was justified by overriding reasons in the public interest. Did the CJEU agree with Denmark, or with the Commission and the Advocate General (see paragraphs 76-79 and 81-82)?

Subsequently in Joined Cases C-151/04 and C-152/04 *Criminal proceedings against Claude Nadin and others* [2005] ECR I-11203, the CJEU held that a corresponding principle applies in relation to the use of the company cars of self-employed persons.

There can be some confusion as to when a national rule can affect an employer's access to the labour market under Article 45 TFEU. For example, if a German married couple, resident in Germany, where each owns a BMW, obtain work in Denmark and move to Denmark bringing their cars as part of their household goods, should they pay the higher Danish car registration tax in order to use them? Is the imposition of the registration tax covered by Article 45 TFEU? See Case C-387/01 *Weigel and Weigel* v *Finanzlandesdirektion für Vorarlberg* [2004] ECR I-4981, where in paragraphs 53-55 the CJEU stated as follows on a related Austrian case:

'53. A rule such as that at issue in the main proceedings applies without regard to the nationality of the worker concerned to all those who register a car in Austria and, accordingly, it is applicable without distinction.

54. It is true that it is likely to have a negative bearing on the decision of migrant workers to exercise their right to freedom of movement.

55. However, the Treaty offers no guarantee to a worker that transferring his activities to a Member State other than the one in which he previously resided will be neutral as regards taxation. Given the disparities in the legislation of the Member States in this area, such a transfer may be to the worker's advantage in terms of indirect taxation or not, according to circumstance. It follows that, in principle, any disadvantage, by comparison with the situation in which the worker pursued his activities prior to the transfer, is not contrary to Article [45 TFEU] if that legislation does not place that worker at a disadvantage as compared with those who were already subject to it'.

JUDGMENT OF THE COURT (Second Chamber)
17 January 2008

Commission of the European Communities v Federal Republic of Germany. (Action under Article 226 EC for failure to fulfil obligations)

'Failure of a Member State to fulfil obligations – Articles 18 EC, 39 EC and 43 EC – National legislation – Conditions for the grant of a subsidy for the construction or purchase of a dwelling for personal occupation – Dwelling required to be situated in the territory of the Member State concerned'

Case C-152/05

Judgment

1. By its application the Commission of the European Communities requests the Court to declare that, by excluding in the first sentence of Paragraph 2(1) of the Law on subsidies for owner-occupied dwellings (Eigenheimzulagengesetz), in the version published in BGBl. 1997 I, p. 734, as amended by the ancillary budget law of 2004 (Haushaltsbegleitgesetz 2004, BGBl. 2003 I, p. 3076, 'the EigZulG'), real property in another Member State from eligibility for the subsidy for owner-occupied dwellings granted to persons liable to unlimited taxation on income, whether or not those persons are able to obtain a comparable subsidy in that other Member State, the Federal Republic of Germany has failed to fulfil its obligations under Articles 18 EC, 39 EC and 43 EC.

The German legislation

2. Paragraph 1 of the Law relating to income tax (Einkommensteuergesetz), in the version published in the BGBl. 2002 I, p. 4210 ('the EStG'), provides:

'(1) Natural persons having their domicile or habitual residence in Germany shall be liable to unlimited taxation of income ...

(2) The following shall also be liable to unlimited taxation of income: German nationals who
1. have neither their domicile nor their habitual residence in Germany and who
2. are linked by a contract of employment to a German legal person governed by public law and who therefore receive a salary from German public funds and the members of their households, possessing German nationality or not in receipt of income or only of income taxable in Germany alone. This shall apply exclusively to natural persons who, in the country in which they have

their domicile or habitual residence, are liable to income tax only to an extent equivalent to limited liability to tax.

(3) At their request, natural persons having neither their domicile nor habitual residence in Germany may also be liable to unlimited taxation of income insofar as they receive income arising in Germany ... This option applies only if at least 90% of their income during a calendar year is subject to German income tax or if their income not subject to German income tax is no more than EUR 6 136 a calendar year; this amount will be reviewed downward if that should be necessary and appropriate having regard to the situation in the State of residence. ...'

3. Paragraph 1 of the EigZulG provides that persons liable to unlimited taxation of income for the purpose of the EStG are entitled to that property subsidy.

4. By virtue of the first sentence of Paragraph 2(1) of the EigZulG, that subsidy is granted for the construction or purchase of a dwelling in an owner-occupied house in Germany or of an owner-occupied dwelling in Germany.

5. According to Paragraph 4 of that law, the right to the subsidy may be acquired only in calendar years in which the beneficiary uses the dwelling for his own occupation. Occupation of the dwelling free of charge by a member of the beneficiary's family also enables the grant of the subsidy.

Pre-litigation procedure

[Paras 6 and 7 omitted]

The action

Admissibility

[Paras 8-13 omitted]

Substance

14. A preliminary point to be noted here is that by letter of 4 January 2006 the Federal Republic of Germany informed the Court of the adoption on 22 December 2005 of the Law abolishing the subsidy for owner-occupied dwellings (Gesetz zur Abschaffung der Eigenheimzulage, BGBl. 2005 I, p. 76).

15. In this regard it is sufficient to observe that, according to settled case-law, the question whether a Member State has failed to fulfil its obligations must be determined by reference to the situation prevailing in the Member State at the end of the period laid down in the reasoned opinion and that the Court cannot take account of any subsequent changes (see, in particular, Case C-161/02 *Commission* v *France* [2003]

ECR I-6567, paragraph 6, and judgment of 18 July 2007 in Case C-26/07 *Commission* v *Greece*, not published in the ECR, paragraph 6). Since it is established that the law abolishing the subsidy was adopted after the expiry of that period, it is not to be taken into consideration in these proceedings.

16. It is settled case-law that, although direct taxation falls within their competence, the Member States must none the less exercise that competence consistently with Community law (Case C-446/03 *Marks & Spencer* [2005] ECR I-10837, paragraph 29; Case C-345/05 *Commission* v*Portugal* [2006] ECR I-10633, paragraph 10; and Case C-104/66 *Commission* v *Sweden* [2007] ECR I-671, paragraph 12).

17. It is therefore necessary to consider whether, as the Commission maintains, the EigZulG, in particular the first sentence of Paragraph 2(1) thereof, constitutes a restriction of the freedom of movement and freedom of establishment enshrined in Articles 18 EC, 39 EC and 43 EC.

18. Article 18 EC, which sets out in general terms the right of every citizen of the European Union to move and reside freely within the territory of the Member States, finds specific expression in Article 39 EC with regard to freedom of movement for workers and in Article 43 EC with regard to freedom of establishment (*Commission* v *Portugal*, paragraph 13; *Commission* v *Sweden*, paragraph 15; and Case C-318/05 *Commission* v *Germany* [2007] ECR I-0000, paragraph 35).

19. The first question for consideration is therefore whether a provision of national law, such as the first sentence of Paragraph 2(1) of the EigZulG, that makes the grant of the subsidy for owner-occupied dwellings, to which persons liable to unlimited taxation of income in Germany are entitled by virtue of Paragraph 1 of that law, subject to the condition that the dwellings built or purchased by those persons for their own occupation should be situated in Germany, is contrary to Articles 39 EC and 43 EC.

20. In this connection it is to be borne in mind that any national of a Member State, irrespective of his place of residence and his nationality, who has exercised the right to freedom of movement for workers or freedom of establishment and who has been employed in a Member State other than that of residence falls within the ambit of Article 39 EC or of Article 43 EC, as the case may be (Case C-152/03 *Ritter-Coulais* [2006] ECR I-1711, paragraph 31; Case C-470/04 *N* [2006] ECR I-7409, paragraph 28; and Case C-212/05 *Hartmann* [2007] ECR I-0000, paragraph 17).

21. What is more, the provisions of the Treaty on freedom of movement for persons are intended to facilitate the pursuit by Community nationals of occupational activities of all kinds throughout the European Community, and they preclude measures which might place those nationals at a disadvantage when they wish to pursue an economic activity in the territory of another Member State (Case C-464/02 *Commission* v *Denmark* [2005] ECR I-7929, paragraph 34; *Commission* v *Portugal*,

paragraph 15; *Commission* v *Sweden*, paragraph 17; and Case C-318/05 *Commission* v *Germany*, paragraph 114).

22. Provisions preventing or deterring a national of a Member State from leaving his country of origin in order to exercise his right to freedom of movement constitute an obstacle to that freedom, even if they apply without regard to the nationality of the workers concerned (*Commission* v *Denmark*, paragraph 35; *Commission* v *Portugal*, paragraph 16; *Commission* v *Sweden*, paragraph 18; and Case C-318/05 *Commission* v *Germany*, paragraph 115).

23. In this case, the first sentence of Paragraph 2(1) of the EigZulG places at a disadvantage persons liable in Germany to unlimited taxation of income who build or purchase a dwelling for their own occupation in the territory of another Member State. That provision does not allow such persons to receive the property subsidy, whereas persons are entitled to it who are in the same situation with regard to income tax and who, when building or purchasing a dwelling, decide to maintain or establish domicile in Germany.

24. In those circumstances, as Advocate General Bot observes in point 64 of his Opinion, that provision has a deterrent effect on persons liable to unlimited taxation on income in Germany who have the right to freedom of movement under Articles 39 EC and 43 EC and who wish to build or purchase a dwelling for their own occupation in another Member State.

25. It follows that, by reserving entitlement to the subsidy for owner-occupied dwellings to persons liable in Germany to unlimited taxation of income on condition that the dwelling built or purchased for their own occupation is situated in German territory, the first sentence of Paragraph 2(1) of the EigZulG is capable of impeding freedom of movement for workers and freedom of establishment, as guaranteed by Articles 39 EC and 43 EC.

26. According to well-established case-law, however, national measures which are liable to hinder or make less attractive the exercise of fundamental freedoms guaranteed by the Treaty may nevertheless be allowed provided that they pursue an objective in the public interest, are appropriate to ensuring the attainment of that objective and do not go beyond what is necessary to attain the objective pursued (*Commission* v *Portugal*, paragraph 24, and *Commission* v *Sweden*, paragraph 25).

27. In this case, the Federal Republic of Germany contends that the condition laid down in the first sentence of Paragraph 2(1) of the EigZulG is justified by the aim of encouraging the building of dwellings in its territory in order to ensure an adequate supply of housing. However, on any view that condition goes beyond what is necessary to attain the objective pursued.

28. In point of fact, the objective of satisfying demand for housing is just as easily attained if the person liable in Germany to unlimited taxation of income chooses to establish his residence in another Member State rather than in Germany (*Commission* v *Portugal*, paragraph 35).

29. It follows from the foregoing that the first sentence of Paragraph 2(1) of the EigZulG constitutes a restriction prohibited by Articles 39 EC and 43 EC and that the Commission's claim alleging that the Member State concerned had failed to fulfil its obligations under the Treaty is well founded.

30. Second, with regard to persons liable in Germany to unlimited taxation of income who are not economically active, the same conclusion applies, for the same reasons, to the complaint relating to Article 18 EC.

31. It must therefore be declared that, by excluding in the first sentence of Paragraph 2(1) of the EigZulG dwellings in another Member State from eligibility for the subsidy for owner-occupied dwellings granted to persons liable to unlimited taxation on income, the Federal Republic of Germany has failed to fulfil its obligations under Articles 18 EC, 39 EC and 43 EC.

Costs

[Para. 32 omitted]

On those grounds,

THE COURT (Second Chamber),

hereby:

1. **Declares that, by excluding in the first sentence of Paragraph 2(1) of the Law on subsidies for owner-occupied dwellings (Eigenheimzulagengesetz), in the version published in 1997, as amended by the ancillary budget law of 2004 (Haushaltsbegleitgesetz 2004) dwellings in another Member State from eligibility for the subsidy for owner-occupied dwellings granted to persons liable to unlimited taxation on income, the Federal Republic of Germany has failed to fulfil its obligations under Articles 18 EC, 39 EC and 43 EC;**

[Para. 2 of the ruling omitted]

Comments and questions

Case C-152/05 *Commission* v *Germany* [2008] ECR I-39, on subsidies for owner-occupied dwellings, concerned a provision in German law under which it was possible to obtain a subsidy for the construction of an owner-occupied dwelling in Germany, provided the owner was liable to tax in Germany and paid German income tax. However, with regard to the possibility of obtaining this subsidy, the provision was framed in such a way as to treat German nationals and non-nationals differently, even though they might be in a comparable situation with regard to tax, being fully liable to tax in Germany. There was thus different treatment which put non-nationals who were fully liable to tax in Germany in a less favourable position. It was the Commission's view that Germany had breached its obligations under Article 21 TFEU (formerly Article 18 TEC) on the rights of Union citizens to move and reside freely within the territory of the Member States, Article 45 TFEU (formerly Article 39 TEC) on the free movement of workers, and Article 49 TFEU (formerly Article 43 TEC) on the right of establishment, since the subsidy for the construction of owner-occupied dwellings was only given if the dwelling was situated in Germany.

It was the view of the German Government that the situation of non-nationals who worked in Germany and who were fully liable to tax in Germany, such as frontier workers, was not covered by Articles 45 and 49 TFEU. The Government referred to Case C-112/91 *Werner* v *Finanzamt Aachen-Innenstadt* [1993] ECR I-429, in which the CJEU had ruled that Article 49 TFEU did not apply to a situation of a national of a Member State who carried on their commercial activities in the territory of that Member State, derived all or nearly all of their income there, but was resident in another Member State. In other words, in the *Werner* case the CJEU had denied that moving residence to another Member State could in itself constitute a sufficiently relevant cross-border activity so that Article 49 TFEU could be relied on by the authorities of the home Member State.

It is clear from Case C-212/05 *Hartmann* [2007] ECR I-6303, printed above, that the CJEU has since abandoned this interpretation of Article 45 TFEU. In the case on subsidies for owner-occupied dwellings, the CJEU restated its more recent practice, while taking it a step further in paragraph 20 by extending it to cover Article 49 TFEU as well.

Moreover, the CJEU ruled that the fact that the German scheme for granting subsidies for owner-occupied dwellings put non-nationals who were fully liable to tax in Germany in a less favourable position, as the scheme could have a deterrent effect on those persons who might wish to construct or acquire a dwelling in another Member State with a view to living there. It was thus the view of the CJEU that the German scheme could constitute a hindrance to the free movement of workers and the right of establishment. The German Government sought to justify the scheme on the grounds that it was intended to increase the German housing stock. The CJEU rejected this argument; what argument did the CJEU use for doing so (see paragraphs 27-28)? The CJEU thus found that there was a prohibited restriction pursuant to Articles 45 and 49 TFEU.

On the same grounds, the CJEU found that the German scheme was also incompatible with Article 21 TFEU, on Union citizenship, as regards persons who were fully liable to tax in Germany but who were not actively employed.

JUDGMENT OF THE COURT (Fifth Chamber)
20 June 2013

Elodie Giersch, Benjamin Marco Stemper, Julien Taminiaux, Xavier Renaud Hodin, Joëlle Hodin v État du Grand-Duché de Luxembourg. (Request for a preliminary ruling from the tribunal administratif – Luxembourg)

'Freedom of movement for persons – Equal treatment – Social advantages – Regulation (EEC) No 1612/68 – Article 7(2) – Financial aid for higher education studies – Condition of residence in the Member State granting the assistance – Refusal to grant the aid to students, who are European Union citizens not residing in the Member State concerned, whose father or mother, a frontier worker, works in that Member State – Indirect discrimination – Justification – Objective of increasing the proportion of residents with a higher education degree – Whether appropriate – Proportionality'

Case C-20/12

Judgment

1. This request for a preliminary ruling concerns the interpretation of Article 7(2) of Council Regulation (EEC) No 1612/68 of 15 October 1968 on freedom of movement for workers within the Community (OJ, English Special Edition 1968(II), p. 475), as amended by Directive 2004/38/EC of the European Parliament and of the Council of 29 April 2004 (OJ 2004 L 158, p. 77 and corrigenda OJ 2004 L 229, p. 35 and OJ 2005 L 197, p. 34) ('Regulation No 1612/68').

2. The request has been made in proceedings between the ministre de l'Enseignement supérieur et de la Recherche luxembourgeois (Luxembourg Minister for Higher Education and Research) ('the Minister') and students who have requested financial aid from the State for higher education studies in order to pursue such studies in a Member State other than the Grand Duchy of Luxembourg.

3. In addition, the European Commission commenced, in April 2011, infringement proceedings against the Grand Duchy of Luxembourg, which remain at the pre-litigation stage. By reasoned opinion of 27 February 2012, the Commission requested that Member State to end discrimination against migrant workers and members of their families in relation to the grant of financial aid by the State for higher education studies, the grant of monthly assistance to young volunteers and the grant of so-called 'boni pour enfant' allowances.

[Paragraphs 4-32 omitted]

The question referred for a preliminary ruling

33. By its question, the referring court asks, in essence, whether Article 7(2) of Regulation No 1612/68 must be interpreted as precluding legislation of a Member State, such as that at issue in the main proceedings, which makes the grant of financial aid for higher education studies conditional on residence by the student and which differentiates between persons residing in the Member State concerned and those who, not being resident in that Member State, are children of frontier workers carrying out an activity in that Member State, with the aim of bringing about an increase in the proportion of residents who hold a higher education degree while avoiding an excessive financial burden which the grant of such aid to every student would entail.

The existence of discrimination

34. In that regard, it must be borne in mind that Article 45(2) TFEU expressly provides that freedom of movement for workers is to entail the abolition of any discrimination based on nationality between workers of the Member States as regards employment, remuneration and other conditions of work and employment.

35. Article 7(2) of Regulation No 1612/68 is the particular expression, in the specific area of the grant of social advantages, of the principle of equal treatment enshrined in Article 45(2) TFUE, and must be accorded the same interpretation as that provision (Case C-287/05 *Hendrix* [2007] ECR I-6909, paragraph 53).

36. Under Article 7(2) of Regulation No 1612/68, a worker who is a national of a Member State is to enjoy, in the territory of another Member State, the same social and tax advantages as national workers.

37. That provision equally benefits both migrant workers resident in a host Member State and frontier workers employed in that Member State while residing in another Member State (Case C-213/05 *Geven* [2007] ECR I-6347, paragraph 15, and Case C-542/09 *Commission* v *Netherlands* [2012] ECR I-0000, paragraph 33).

38. According to settled case-law, assistance granted for maintenance and education in order to pursue university studies evidenced by a professional qualification constitutes a social advantage within the meaning of Article 7(2) of Regulation No 1612/68 (Case 39/86 *Lair* [1988] ECR 3161, paragraph 24, and *Commission* v *Netherlands* paragraph 34).

39. The Court has also held that study finance granted by a Member State to the children of workers constitutes, for the migrant worker, a social advantage within the meaning of Article 7(2) of Regulation No 1612/68, where the worker continues to

support the child (*Bernini*, paragraphs 25 and 29; Case C-337/97 *Meussen* [1999] ECR I-3289, paragraph 19; and *Commission* v *Netherlands*, paragraph 35).

40. The members of a migrant worker's family are the indirect recipients of the equal treatment granted to the worker under Article 7(2) of Regulation No 1612/68. Since the grant of funding for studies to a child of a migrant worker constitutes a social advantage for the migrant worker, the child may himself rely on that provision in order to obtain that funding if, under national law, such funding is granted directly to the student (Case 316/85 *Lebon* [1987] ECR 2811, paragraphs 12 and 13; *Bernini* paragraph 26; and *Commission* v *Netherlands*, paragraph 48).

41. The Court has also consistently held that the equal treatment rule laid down both in Article 45 TFEU and in Article 7 of Regulation No 1612/68 prohibits not only overt discrimination by reason of nationality but also all covert forms of discrimination which, by the application of other distinguishing criteria, lead in fact to the same result (see Case C-57/96 *Meints* [1997] ECR I-6689, paragraph 44; C-147/03 *Commission* v *Austria* [2005] ECR I-5969, paragraph 41; Case C-269/07 *Commission* v *Germany* [2009] ECR I-7811, paragraph 53; and *Commission* v*Netherlands*, paragraph 37).

42. In the present case in the main proceedings, the referring court, when interpreting national law, considered the conditions of domicile and residence required by the amended Law of 22 June 2000 to be equivalent, with the result that the condition of residence applies equally to Luxembourg nationals and to nationals of other Member States.

43. Accordingly, the requirement, in relation to nationals of other Member States, that they reside in Luxembourg, does not amount to direct discrimination.

44. By contrast, in so far as it provides for a distinction based on residence, a measure such as that at issue in the main proceedings is liable to operate mainly to the detriment of nationals of others Member States, as non-residents are in the majority of cases foreign nationals (see, inter alia, Case C-224/97 *Ciola* [1999] ECR I-2517, paragraph 14; Case C-382/08 *Neukirchinger* [2011] ECR I-139, paragraph 34; and *Commission* v *Netherlands*, paragraph 38).

45. In that context, it is immaterial whether, in some circumstances, the contested measure affects, as well as nationals of other Member States, nationals of the Member State in question who are unable to meet such a criterion. In order for a measure to be treated as being indirectly discriminatory, it is not necessary for it to have the effect of placing all the nationals of the Member State in question at an advantage or of placing at a disadvantage only nationals of other Member States, but not nationals of the State in question (see, to that effect, Case C-388/0 *Commission* v *Italy*

[2003] ECR I-721, paragraph 14; *Commission* v *Netherlands*, paragraph 38; and Case C-172/11 *Erny* [2012] ECR I-0000, paragraph 41).

46. The difference in treatment which arises from a condition of residence being imposed on students who are the children of frontier workers thus constitutes indirect discrimination on the ground of nationality which is in principle prohibited, unless it is objectively justified. In order to be justified, it must be appropriate for securing the attainment of a legitimate objective and must not go beyond what is necessary to attain that objective (see, to that effect, Case C-73/08 *Bressol and Others* [2010] ECR I-2735, paragraphs 47 and 48, and *Commission* v *Netherlands*, paragraph 55).

The pursuit of a legitimate objective

47. In order to justify the different treatment of frontier workers concerning the grant of State financial aid for higher education studies, the Luxembourg Government relies on two arguments, one based on social considerations, the other on budgetary considerations, maintaining that they are inextricably linked.

48. The objective referred to as 'social' by that government aims to significantly increase the proportion of Luxembourg residents holding a higher education degree. That figure is, at 28%, considerably lower than the percentage of persons holding such a degree in States comparable to the Grand Duchy of Luxembourg, and the Luxembourg Government considers it necessary to achieve a figure of 66% of Luxembourg residents holding a higher education degree so as to satisfy the increasingly urgent need for Luxembourg to make the transition to a knowledge-based economy.

49. The Luxembourg Government asserts that the entitlement to State financial aid is confined to persons resident in Luxembourg because in its view only they have an attachment with Luxembourg society of such a kind as to justify the assumption that, having benefited from the possibility offered by the system of aid concerned in order to finance their studies – undertaken as the case may be abroad – they will return to Luxembourg in order to apply their knowledge for the benefit of that country's economic development.

50. According to that government, because of budgetary constraints it cannot be more generous towards non-resident students without putting the entire system of financial aid into question. The aim from a budgetary point of view is to prevent the unreasonable burden on State finances which would result from the extension of the grant of financial aid to those non-resident students, who are children of frontier workers.

51. As regards the justification based on the additional burden which would result from non-application of the residence requirement, it should be borne in mind that, alt-

hough budgetary considerations may underlie a Member State's choice of social policy and influence the nature or scope of the social protection measures which it wishes to adopt, they do not in themselves constitute an aim pursued by that policy and cannot therefore justify discrimination against migrant workers (see *Commission* v *Netherlands*, paragraph 57 and case-law cited).

52. To accept that budgetary considerations may justify a difference in treatment between migrant workers and national workers would imply that the application and the scope of a rule of European Union law as fundamental as the principle of non-discrimination on grounds of nationality might vary in time and place according to the state of the public finances of the Member States (see *Commission* v *Netherlands*, paragraph 58 and case-law cited).

53. With regard to the social objective, it should be pointed out that the promotion of higher education is an objective in the public interest, acknowledged at the level of the European Union, as stated inter alia by the Austrian and Luxembourg Governments.

54. Thus, in the Commission Communication of 3 March 2010 entitled 'Europe 2020: a strategy for smart, sustainable and inclusive growth' (COM(2010) 2020 final), increasing the share of the population aged 30-34 having completed tertiary education from 31% to at least 40% in 2020 is listed as one of the headline targets agreed at European Union level. That document encourages each Member State to adopt specific measures implementing those headline targets at national level.

55. In addition, in the context of its Conclusions of 12 May 2009 on a strategic framework for European cooperation in education and training ('ET 2020') (OJ 2009 C 119, p. 2), the Council of the European Union had already adopted that objective of increasing the number of persons with a higher education degree. In the Council Conclusions of 11 May 2010 on the social dimension of education and training (OJ 2010 C 135, p. 2), the Member States are called upon on, in relation to higher education, to develop policies aimed at increasing completion rates.

56. It follows that an action undertaken by a Member State in order to ensure that its resident population is highly educated and to promote the development of the economy pursues a legitimate objective which can justify indirect discrimination on grounds of nationality.

The appropriateness of the residence condition

57. The Luxembourg Government maintains that the rules to the effect that aid is reserved for persons residing in Luxembourg are appropriate for ensuring the attainment of the legitimate social objective of increasing the number of Luxembourg residents holding a higher education degree.

58. That government claims, in that regard, that it is probable that, after undertaking higher education studies abroad, the students concerned will return to their State of residence to live and work there. It considers that there is no particular reason why students who reside abroad – even if they are also the children of frontier workers carrying out an activity in Luxembourg – would make themselves available to the Luxembourg labour market after completing their studies or integrate themselves in Luxembourg society. That government considers that it is justified in restricting the grant of the aid at issue in the main proceedings to students resident in Luxembourg when they are about to undertake higher education, since they are already integrated in Luxembourg society and, after completing their studies, would be more than likely to make themselves available to the Luxembourg employment market.

59. The Luxembourg government adds that there is, in addition, a strong 'turnover rate' of persons carrying out a professional activity as a frontier worker, those persons working in that capacity for only a limited period, with the result that employment as a frontier worker cannot be regarded as an integration factor in the society of the State of employment similar to residence in that Member State and sufficient to exercise an influence on the choice of residence of the children of frontier workers, once their studies are over.

60. The applicants in the main proceedings dispute the appropriateness of the residence condition. Such a condition does not guarantee that the objective of increasing the number of persons resident in Luxembourg holding a higher education degree, so as to cover the needs of the Luxembourg employment market, will be attained. The grant of the aid in question only to students residing in Luxembourg when they make the application for financial aid will not result in their making themselves permanently available to the Luxembourg labour market after finishing their studies. Moreover, because the University of Luxembourg lacks a broad-based academic curriculum, a large number of those student residents will be inclined to pursue their studies outside Luxembourg and become integrated in the State where they are studying rather than in Luxembourg, thus benefiting from professional opportunities which go far beyond its territory.

61. Those applicants contend that, contrary to what is claimed by the Luxembourg government, non-resident students who are the children of frontier workers have specific reasons to make themselves available to the Luxembourg labour market when their studies are over. Thus, first, the fact that one of the parents of the student works in Luxembourg implies that there is a certain geographic proximity to Luxembourg territory of the household to which that student belongs. Second, because of the economic crisis severely affecting the Member States which border upon Luxembourg, the children of frontier workers will be inclined, once they have finished their studies, to look for stable employment, like that of their parents, who have been working in that Member State for a number of years.

62. According to the Commission, frontier workers not only have links with but are integrated in Luxembourg society because of their employment there. Since such a link exists, a condition of residence is neither necessary nor appropriate for ensuring that the children of such workers, whose studies would be financed by the financial aid at issue in the main proceedings, have a close link with the Member State which grants that aid.

63. In that regard, it should be noted that the Court has already held that migrant and frontier workers, since they have participated in the labour market of a Member State, have in principle created a sufficient link of integration with the society of that State, allowing them to benefit from the principle of equal treatment, as compared, respectively with national workers and resident workers. The link of integration arises, in particular, from the fact that, through the taxes which they pay in the host Member State by virtue of their employment there, migrant and frontier workers also contribute to the financing of the social policies of that State (see, to that effect, Case C-379/11 *Caves Krier Frères* [2012] ECR I-0000, paragraph 53).

64. However, it must be held that, with regard inter alia to frontier workers, the Court has allowed certain grounds of justification concerning legislation which distinguishes between residents and non-residents carrying out a professional activity in the State concerned, depending on the extent of their integration in the society of that Member State or their attachment to that State (see, to that effect, *Hartmann*, paragraphs 35 and 36; *Geven*, paragraph 26; and *Hendrix*, paragraphs 54 and 55).

65. In that regard, it must be noted that the frontier worker is not always integrated in the Member State of employment in the same way as a worker who is resident in that State.

66. In the cases at issue in the main proceedings, as stated by the Advocate General in point 59 of his Opinion, it must be examined whether the imposition of a condition of residence on the children of frontier workers by Luxembourg law in order to be entitled to receive financial aid for higher education studies could make it reasonably likely that the student will return to Luxembourg, after completing his or her studies, such a return being regarded by the Luxembourg Government as necessary in order to attain the legitimate objective pursued.

67. In that regard, admittedly, students who are resident in Luxembourg when they are about to embark on their higher education studies may be more likely than non-resident students to settle in Luxembourg and become integrated in the Luxembourg labour market after completing their studies, even if those studies were undertaken abroad.

68. It must therefore be held that the condition of residence provided for under the amended Law of 22 June 2000 is appropriate for attaining the objective of promot-

ing higher education and of significantly increasing the proportion of Luxembourg residents who hold a higher education degree.

69. It remains however necessary to determine whether that condition does not go beyond what is necessary to attain that objective.

The necessity of the residence condition

70. According to the Luxembourg Government, the adoption of a residence condition does not go beyond what is necessary in order to attain the objective sought. That condition is justified by budgetary reasons and is directly linked to the economic objective relied upon. Because of budgetary constraints, it is not possible to be more generous towards non-resident students without putting the whole system of financing in question. In addition, the adoption of another criterion for the grant of aid, that is, in particular, that based on the fact that one of the parents of the non-resident student is employed in Luxembourg, would run directly counter to the twin combined objectives of the rules governing the aid at issue in the main proceedings.

71. In that regard, it must be examined whether only a condition of prior residence can ensure with reasonable probability for the Luxembourg State that the recipients of that aid will return to settle in Luxembourg and make themselves available to the Luxembourg labour market in order to contribute to its economic development, or whether other criteria exist which would also ensure that probability without excluding all non-resident children of frontier workers.

72. The Court has already accepted that a condition of residence may be disproportionate if it is too exclusive in nature because it favours an element which is not necessarily representative of the real and effective degree of connection and excludes all other representative elements (see Joined Cases C-11/06 and C-12/06 *Morgan and Bucher* [2007] ECR I-9161, paragraph 46 and case-law cited, and Case C-503/09 *Stewart* [2011] ECR I-0000, paragraph 95 and case-law cited).

73. In paragraphs 86 and 87 of the judgment in *Commission* v *Netherlands*, the Court thus considered that the Member State had not convincingly explained why the objective pursued could not be attained, in a less restrictive fashion, either by a more flexible rule than the 'three out of six years' rule or by taking into account other elements which represent a similar degree of attachment, such as employment. It therefore held that, by requiring specific periods of residence in the territory of the Member State concerned, that rule favoured an element which is not necessarily the sole representative element of the actual degree of attachment between the party concerned and the Member State, and is too exclusive in nature. The 'three out of six years' rule thus went beyond what was necessary in order to attain the objective pursued.

74. The Luxembourg system of State financial aid for higher education studies excludes all non-residents from entitlement to that aid, an exclusion which concerns only non-resident students.

75. Consequently, the child of a migrant worker who resides with his parents in a Member State bordering upon the Grand Duchy of Luxembourg and who would like to study in Luxembourg is not entitled to receive State financial aid for higher education studies. In addition, even if their parents reside in Luxembourg, students who are not resident there when they make their application for aid are not entitled to receive that aid even if their parents continue to support them. Furthermore, the effect of the system of financial aid at issue in the main proceedings is to exclude the children of non-residents workers who have been working in Luxembourg for a significant period of time from receipt of that aid.

76. In that regard, it must be stated that the system of financial aid at issue in the main proceedings is too exclusive in nature. By requiring the student to reside in the territory of the Member State concerned, the law favours an element which is not necessarily the sole representative element of the actual degree of attachment between the party concerned and that Member State (see, to that effect, *Commission* v *Netherlands*, paragraph 86).

77. In particular, to the extent that State financial aid for higher education studies is intended to encourage the pursuit of such studies both in Luxembourg and in any other country, the existence of a reasonable probability that the recipients of that aid will return to settle in Luxembourg and make themselves available to the labour market of that Member State, in order to contribute to its economic development, may be established on the basis of elements other than a prior residence requirement in relation to the student concerned.

78. A sufficient attachment of the student in question with the Grand Duchy such as to make it possible to conclude that that probability exists may also be derived from the fact that that student resides alone or with his parents in a Member State which borders upon the Grand Duchy of Luxembourg and that, for a significant period of time, his parents have worked in Luxembourg and live near to that Member State.

79. With regard to the possibilities open to the Luxembourg legislature, it can be observed, in line with the Commission's submission at the hearing, that where the aid granted consists in, for example, a loan, a system of financing which made the grant of that loan, or even the outstanding balance thereof, or its non-reimbursement, conditional on the student who receives it returning to Luxembourg after his or her studies abroad in order to work and reside there, could attain the objective pursued, without adversely affecting the children of frontier workers. In addition, the risk of duplication with equivalent financial aid paid in the Member State in which the student resides, with or without his parents, could be avoided by taking that aid into

account in the grant of the aid paid by the State of the Grand Duchy of Luxembourg.

80. Above all, in order to avoid the risk of 'study grant forum shopping' referred to by all the governments which submitted observations to the Court, and to ensure that the frontier worker who is a taxpayer and who makes social security contributions in Luxembourg has a sufficient link with Luxembourg society, the financial aid could be made conditional on the frontier worker, the parent of the student who does not reside in Luxembourg, having worked in that Member State for a certain minimum period of time. In another context, Article 24(2) of Directive 2004/38 provides that, by derogation from Article 24(1) – according to which all Union citizens residing on the basis of that directive in the territory of the host Member State are to enjoy equal treatment with the nationals of that Member State – the host Member State is not to be obliged to grant maintenance aid for studies before the acquisition of a right of permanent residence which, under Article 16(1) of Directive 2004/38, is subject to a condition of residence of five years in the territory of the Member State concerned.

81. It should be noted that, in the cases in the main proceedings, such a risk can be ruled out in so far as it is common ground that Ms Giersch, Mr Stemper, Mr Taminiaux and Ms Hodin each has a mother or father who has been working in Luxembourg for 23 years, 32 years, 28 years and 23 years respectively.

82. Accordingly, a law such as that at issue in the main proceedings, which makes the grant of financial aid for higher education studies conditional on residence by the student and gives rise to a difference in treatment between residents and non-residents of that Member State who are the children of frontier workers carrying out an activity in that Member State, goes beyond what is necessary in order to attain the legitimate objective of increasing the proportion of the resident population with a higher education degree, so as to promote the development of the national economy.

83. It follows from all the above considerations that the answer to the question referred is that:

- Article 7(2) of Regulation No 1612/68 must be interpreted as precluding, in principle, legislation of a Member State such as that at issue in the main proceedings, which makes the grant of financial aid for higher education studies conditional upon residence by the student in that Member State and gives rise to a difference in treatment, amounting to indirect discrimination, between persons who reside in the Member State concerned and those who, not being residents of that Member State, are the children of frontier workers carrying out an activity in that Member State;

– While the objective of increasing the proportion of residents with a higher education degree in order to promote the development of the economy of that same Member State is a legitimate objective which can justify such a difference in treatment, and while a condition of residence, such as that provided for by the national legislation at issue in the main proceedings, is appropriate for ensuring the attainment of that objective, such a condition nevertheless goes beyond what is necessary in order to attain the objective pursued, to the extent that it precludes the taking into account of other elements potentially representative of the actual degree of attachment of the applicant for the financial aid with the society or with the labour market of the Member State concerned, such as the fact that one of the parents, who continues to support the student, is a frontier worker who has stable employment in that Member State and has already worked there for a significant period of time.

Costs

[Para. 84 omitted]

On those grounds,

THE COURT (Fifth Chamber),

hereby rules:

Article 7(2) of Council Regulation (EEC) No 1612/68 of 15 October 1968 on freedom of movement for workers within the Community, as amended by Directive 2004/38/EC of the European Parliament and of the Council of 29 April 2004, must be interpreted as precluding, in principle, legislation of a Member State such as that at issue in the main proceedings, which makes the grant of financial aid for higher education studies conditional upon residence by the student in that Member State and gives rise to a difference in treatment, amounting to indirect discrimination, between persons who reside in the Member State concerned and those who, not being residents of that Member State, are the children of frontier workers carrying out an activity in that Member State.
While the objective of increasing the proportion of residents with a higher education degree in order to promote the development of the economy of that same Member State is a legitimate objective which can justify such a difference in treatment and while a condition of residence, such as that provided for by the national legislation at issue in the main proceedings, is appropriate for ensuring the attainment of that objective, such a condition nevertheless goes beyond what is necessary in order to attain the objective pursued, to the extent that it precludes the taking into account of other elements potentially representative of the actual degree of attachment of the applicant for the financial

aid with the society or with the labour market of the Member State concerned, such as the fact that one of the parents, who continues to support the student, is a frontier worker who has stable employment in that Member State and has already worked there for a significant period of time.

Comments and questions

The CJEU judgment in Case C-20/12 *Giersch*, Judgement of 20 June 2013, is illustrative in many respects. First and foremost it shows how Union law challenges national welfare systems, where a Member State disburses benefits financed from taxes. In the *Giersch* case, Luxembourg was providing student support. Given its small size, Luxembourg does not have a fully developed university system. Luxembourgers who want to follow a longer-term higher education are to a large extent required to study outside the Grand Duchy. The Luxembourg State provided support for such studies, but it required that recipients of such aid should be resident in Luxembourg. Among other things, this prevented the children of frontier workers (living outside Luxembourg, but working there) from obtaining student support from Luxembourg. In practice this requirement deprived many from the entitlement to support, as can be seen from the fact that in academic year 2010/2011 alone, the referring Luxembourg court received more than 600 claims on obtaining the support. In other words, it was of significant financial importance whether Luxembourg could maintain the restriction of Union citizens' entitlement to receive student support for other Member States.

The question on which the referring Luxembourg court sought a preliminary ruling was whether the residence requirement was unlawful different treatment. In its answer, the CJEU found that the grant of student support to a child of a frontier worker was a social benefit for the worker. Since the Luxembourg legislation used a residence criterion, in the view of the CJEU it risked treating nationals of other Member States less favourably, since non-resident persons will more usually be nationals of other Member States. This different treatment, which followed from the residence requirement for student children of frontier workers, was thus indirect discrimination which was, in principle, prohibited unless it could be objectively justified. In connection with this, the CJEU noted that even if the different treatment could be justified, it should still satisfy the proportionality principle.

The CJEU went on to consider whether there was a lawful purpose behind the residence requirement. The Luxembourg Government put forward two arguments, one social and the other financial. The CJEU rejected the financial purpose, saying that although budgetary considerations may underlie a Member State's choice of social policy and influence the nature or scope of the social protection measures which it wishes to adopt, they do not in themselves constitute an aim pursued by that policy and cannot therefore justify discrimination against migrant workers. To accept that budgetary considerations may justify a difference in treatment between migrant workers and national workers would imply that the application and the scope of a rule of Union law as fundamental as the principle of non-discrimination on grounds of nationality might vary in time and place according to the state of the public finances of the Member States.

On the other hand, the CJEU accepted that the social objective was an overriding public interest. The objective of the Luxembourg student support was to increase the proportion of the resident population with a higher education degree so as to reach 40% by 2020, against only 28% in 2010. The CJEU stated that this goal was in accordance with an EU goal.

The residence requirement thus pursued a lawful purpose. But the question was whether it was also appropriate for achieving this lawful social objective. It was the view of the CJEU that the residence requirement was suitable for achieving the goal of promoting participation in higher education and of significantly increasing the number of residents in Luxembourg with a higher education degree. However, the CJEU considered that the condition of residence may be disproportionate if it is too exclusive in nature because it favours an element which is not necessarily representative of the real and effective degree of connection and excludes all other representative elements.

However, remarkably, the CJEU did not stop at declaring the Luxembourg student support incompatible with Union law. It went further by pointing to a number of possibilities which the Luxembourg legislator might use in future instead of a residence requirement for students. Which alternative possibilities did the CJEU suggest in this context (see paragraphs 79-80)? Has the CJEU previously permitted a Member State to lay down requirements for the duration of an employment relationship in the host Member State before an employee and their family members can obtain the same social benefits?

The statement in paragraph 80 of the *Giersch* judgment, which refers to the fact that the host Member State can demand that a frontier worker (i.e. a person who is resident in one Member State but works in another) must have worked in the granting Member State for five years as a condition for one of their family members receiving a student grant, to ensure that the frontier worker has a 'sufficient link' with the granting Member State, cannot be applied in general to migrant workers who are resident and working in the granting Member State. However, it is remarkable that the CJEU at all recognised that a condition for a 'sufficient link' may be imposed on economically active Union citizens who are frontier workers. On this, see Case C-212/05 *Hartmann*, printed above, and Case C-213/05 *Wendy Geven*, where the CJEU similarly recognised the requirement for a 'sufficient link' between the granting Member State and the frontier worker. Previously the CJEU only recognised such a requirement in relation to non-economically active persons and job-seekers; see e.g. Case C-138/02 *Collins*, which is referred to above in connection with the *Alimanovic* case.

CHAPTER 5

Freedom of Establishment

JUDGMENT OF THE COURT (Grand Chamber)
11 December 2007

International Transport Workers' Federation, Finnish Seamen's Union, v Viking Line ABP, OÜ Viking Line Eesti. (Reference for a preliminary ruling from the Court of Appeal (England and Wales) (Civil Division) – United Kingdom)

'Maritime transport – Right of establishment – Fundamental rights – Objectives of Community social policy – Collective action taken by a trade union organisation against a private undertaking – Collective agreement liable to deter an undertaking from registering a vessel under the flag of another Member State'

Case C-438/05

Judgment

1. This reference for a preliminary ruling concerns the interpretation first, of Article 43 EC, and secondly, of Council Regulation (EEC) No 4055/86 of 22 December 1986 applying the principle of freedom to provide services to maritime transport between Member States and between Member States and third countries (OJ 1986 L 378, p. 1).

2. The reference has been made in connection with a dispute between the International Transport Workers' Federation ('ITF') and the Finnish Seamen's Union (Suomen Merimies-Unioni ry, 'FSU'), on the one hand, and Viking Line ABP ('Viking') and its subsidiary OÜ Viking Line Eesti ('Viking Eesti'), on the other, concerning actual or threatened collective action liable to deter Viking from reflagging one of its vessels from the Finnish flag to that of another Member State.

Legal context

Community law

3. Article 1(1) of Regulation No 4055/86 provides:

'Freedom to provide maritime transport services between Member States and between Member States and third countries shall apply in respect of nationals of Member States who are established in a Member State other than that of the person for whom the services are intended.'

National law

4. According to the order for reference, Article 13 of the Finnish constitution, which confers on all individuals the freedom to form trade unions and freedom of association in order to safeguard other interests, has been interpreted as allowing trade unions to initiate collective action against companies in order to defend workers' interests.

5. In Finland, however, the right to strike is subject to certain limitations. Thus, according to Finland's Supreme Court, it may not be relied on, inter alia, where the strike is *contra bonos mores* or is prohibited under national law or under Community law.

The dispute in the main proceedings and questions referred

6. Viking, a company incorporated under Finnish law, is a large ferry operator. It operates seven vessels, including the *Rosella* which, under the Finnish flag, plies the route between Tallinn (Estonia) and Helsinki (Finland).

7. FSU is a Finnish union of seamen which has about 10 000 members. The crew of the *Rosella* are members of the FSU. FSU is affiliated to the ITF, which is an international federation of transport workers' unions with its headquarters in London (United Kingdom). The ITF groups together 600 unions in 140 different States.

8. According to the order for reference, one of the principal ITF policies is its 'Flag of Convenience' ('FOC') policy. The primary objectives of this policy are, on the one hand, to establish a genuine link between the flag of the ship and the nationality of the owner and, on the other, to protect and enhance the conditions of seafarers on FOC ships. ITF considers that a vessel is registered under a flag of convenience where the beneficial ownership and control of the vessel is found to lie in a State other than the State of the flag. In accordance with the ITF policy, only unions established in the State of beneficial ownership have the right to conclude collective agreements covering the vessel concerned. The FOC campaign is enforced by boycotts and other solidarity actions amongst workers.

9. So long as the *Rosella* is under the Finnish flag, Viking is obliged under Finnish law and the terms of a collective bargaining agreement to pay the crew wages at the same level as those applicable in Finland. Estonian crew wages are lower than Finnish crew wages. The *Rosella* was running at a loss as a result of direct competition from Estonian vessels operating on the same route with lower wage costs. As an alternative to selling the vessel, Viking sought in October 2003 to reflag it by registering it in either Estonia or Norway, in order to be able to enter into a new collective agreement with a trade union established in one of those States.

10. In accordance with Finnish law, Viking gave notice of its plans to the FSU and to the crew of the *Rosella*. During meetings between the parties, FSU made clear that it was opposed to those plans.

11. On 4 November 2003, FSU sent an email to ITF which referred to the plan to reflag the *Rosella*. The email further stated that 'the *Rosella* was beneficially owned in Finland and that FSU therefore kept the right to negotiate with Viking'. FSU asked ITF to pass this information on to all affiliated unions and to request them not to enter into negotiations with Viking.

12. On 6 November 2003, ITF sent a circular ('the ITF circular') to its affiliates asking them to refrain from entering into negotiations with Viking or Viking Eesti. The affiliates were expected to follow this recommendation because of the principle of solidarity between trade unions and the sanctions which they could face if they failed to comply with that circular.

13. The manning agreement for the *Rosella* expired on 17 November 2003 and therefore FSU was, as from that date, no longer under an obligation of industrial peace under Finnish law. Consequently, it gave notice of a strike requiring Viking, on the one hand, to increase the manning on the *Rosella* by eight and, on the other, to give up its plans to reflag the *Rosella*.

14. Viking conceded the extra eight crew but refused to give up its plans to reflag.

15. FSU was still not prepared, however, to agree to a renewal of the manning agreement and, by letter of 18 November 2003, it indicated that it would only accept such renewal on two conditions: first, that Viking, regardless of a possible change of the *Rosella*'s flag, gave an undertaking that it would continue to follow Finnish law, the collective bargaining agreement, the general agreement and the manning agreement on the Rosella and, second, that the possible change of flag would not lead to any laying-off of employees on any Finnish flag vessel belonging to Viking, or to changes to the terms and conditions of employment without the consent of the employees. In press statements FSU justified its position by the need to protect Finnish jobs.

16. On 17 November 2003, Viking started legal proceedings before the employment tribunal (Finland) for a declaration that, contrary to the view of the FSU, the manning agreement remained binding on the parties. On the basis of its view that the manning agreement was at an end, FSU gave notice, in accordance with Finnish law on industrial dispute mediation that it intended to commence strike action in relation to the *Rosella* on 2 December 2003.

17. On 24 November 2003, Viking learnt of the existence of the ITF circular. The following day it brought proceedings before the Court of First Instance of Helsinki

(Finland) to restrain the planned strike action. A preparatory hearing date was set for 2 December 2003.

18. According to the referring court, FSU was fully aware of the fact that its principal demand, that in the event of reflagging the crew should continue to be employed on the conditions laid down by Finnish law and the applicable collective agreement, would render reflagging pointless, since the whole purpose of such reflagging was to enable Viking to reduce its wage costs. Furthermore, a consequence of reflagging the *Rosella* to Estonia would be that Viking would, at least as regards the *Rosella*, no longer be able to claim State aid which the Finnish Government granted to Finnish flag vessels.

19. In the course of conciliation proceedings, Viking gave an undertaking, at an initial stage, that the reflagging would not involve any redundancies. Since FSU nevertheless refused to defer the strike, Viking put an end to the dispute on 2 December 2003 by accepting the trade union's demands and discontinuing judicial proceedings. Furthermore, it undertook not to commence reflagging prior to 28 February 2005.

20. On 1 May 2004, the Republic of Estonia became a member of the European Union.

21. Since the *Rosella* continued to run at a loss, Viking pursued its intention to reflag the vessel to Estonia. Because the ITF circular remained in force, on account of the fact that the ITF had never withdrawn it, the request to affiliated unions from the ITF in relation to the *Rosella* consequently remained in effect.

22. On 18 August 2004, Viking brought an action before the High Court of Justice of England and Wales, Queen's Bench Division (Commercial Court) (United Kingdom), requesting it to declare that the action taken by ITF and FSU was contrary to Article 43 EC, to order the withdrawal of the ITF circular and to order FSU not to infringe the rights which Viking enjoys under Community law.

23. By decision of 16 June 2005, that court granted the form of order sought by Viking, on the grounds that the actual and threatened collective action by the ITF and FSU imposed restrictions on freedom of establishment contrary to Article 43 EC and, in the alternative, constituted unlawful restrictions on freedom of movement for workers and freedom to provide services under Articles 39 EC and 49 EC.

24. On 30 June 2005, ITF and FSU brought an appeal against that decision before the referring court. In support of their appeal they claimed, inter alia, that the right of trade unions to take collective action to preserve jobs is a fundamental right recognised by Title XI of the EC Treaty and, in particular, Article 136 EC, the first paragraph of which provides that '[t]he Community and the Member States, having in mind fundamental social rights such as those set out in the European Social Charter

signed at Turin on 18 October 1961 and in the 1989 Community Charter of the Fundamental Social Rights of Workers, shall have as their objectives the promotion of employment, improved living and working conditions, so as to make possible their harmonisation while the improvement is being maintained, proper social protection, dialogue between management and labour, the development of human resources with a view to lasting high employment and the combating of exclusion'.

25. It was argued that the reference to the European Social Charter and the Community Charter of the Fundamental Social Rights of Workers incorporated a reference to the right to strike recognised by those legal instruments. Consequently, the trade unions had the right to take collective action against an employer established in a Member State to seek to persuade him not to move part or all of his undertaking to another Member State.

26. The question therefore arises whether the Treaty intends to prohibit trade union action where it is aimed at preventing an employer from exercising his right of establishment for economic reasons. By analogy with the Court's rulings regarding Title VI of the Treaty (Case C-67/96 *Albany* [1999] ECR I-5751; Joined Cases C-180/98 to C-184/98 *Pavlov and Others* [2000] ECR I-6451; and Case C-222/98 *Van der Woude* [2000] ECR I-7111), it is argued that Title III of the Treaty and the articles relating to free movement of persons and of services do not apply to 'genuine trade union activities'.

27. In those circumstances, since it considered that the outcome of the case before it depended on the interpretation of Community law, the Court of Appeal (England and Wales) (Civil Division) decided to stay proceedings and refer the following questions to the Court for a preliminary ruling:

'*Scope of the free movement provisions*

(1) Where a trade union or association of trade unions takes collective action against a private undertaking so as to require that undertaking to enter into a collective bargaining agreement with a trade union in a particular Member State which has the effect of making it pointless for that undertaking to re-flag a vessel in another Member State, does that action fall outside the scope of Article 43 EC and/or Regulation No 4055/86 by virtue of the EC's social policy including, inter alia, Title XI of the EC Treaty and, in particular, by analogy with the Court's reasoning in ... *Albany* (paragraphs 52 to 64)?

Horizontal direct effect

(2) Do Article 43 EC and/or Regulation No 4055/86 have horizontal direct effect so as to confer rights on a private undertaking which may be relied on against

another private party and, in particular, a trade union or association of trade unions in respect of collective action by that union or association of unions?

Existence of restrictions on free movement

(3) Where a trade union or association of trade unions takes collective action against a private undertaking so as to require that undertaking to enter into a collective bargaining agreement with a trade union in a particular Member State, which has the effect of making it pointless for that undertaking to re-flag a vessel in another Member State, does that action constitute a restriction for the purposes of Article 43 EC and/or Regulation No 4055/86?

(4) Is a policy of an association of trade unions which provides that vessels should be flagged in the registry of the country in which the beneficial ownership and control of the vessel is situated so that the trade unions in the country of beneficial ownership of a vessel have the right to conclude collective bargaining agreements in respect of that vessel, a directly discriminatory, indirectly discriminatory or non-discriminatory restriction under Article 43 EC or Regulation No 4055/86?

(5) In determining whether collective action by a trade union or association of trade unions is a directly discriminatory, indirectly discriminatory or non-discriminatory restriction under Article 43 EC or Regulation No 4055/86, is the subjective intention of the union taking the action relevant or must the national court determine the issue solely by reference to the objective effects of that action?

Establishment/services

(6) Where a parent company is established in Member State A and intends to undertake an act of establishment by reflagging a vessel to Member State B to be operated by an existing wholly owned subsidiary in Member State B which is subject to the direction and control of the parent company:

(a) is threatened or actual collective action by a trade union or association of trade unions which would seek to render the above a pointless exercise capable of constituting a restriction on the parent company's right of establishment under Article 43, and

(b) after reflagging of the vessel, is the subsidiary entitled to rely on Regulation No 4055/86 in respect of the provision of services by it from Member State B to Member State A?

Justification

Direct discrimination

(7) If collective action by a trade union or association of trade unions is a directly discriminatory restriction under Article 43 EC or Regulation No 4055/86, can it, in principle, be justified on the basis of the public policy exception set out in Article 46 EC on the basis that:
  (a) the taking of collective action (including strike action) is a fundamental right protected by Community law; and/or
  (b) the protection of workers?

The policy of [ITF]: objective justification

(8) Does the application of a policy of an association of trade unions which provides that vessels should be flagged in the registry of the country in which the beneficial ownership and control of the vessel is situated so that the trade unions in the country of beneficial ownership of a vessel have the right to conclude collective bargaining agreements in respect of that vessel, strike a fair balance between the fundamental social right to take collective action and the freedom to establish and provide services, and is it objectively justified, appropriate, proportionate and in conformity with the principle of mutual recognition?

FSU's actions: objective justification

(9) Where:
  – a parent company in Member State A owns a vessel flagged in Member State A and provides ferry services between Member State A and Member State B using that vessel;
  – the parent company wishes to re-flag the vessel to Member State B to apply terms and conditions of employment which are lower than in Member State A;
  – the parent company in Member State A wholly owns a subsidiary in Member State B and that subsidiary is subject to its direction and control;
  – it is intended that the subsidiary will operate the vessel once it has been re-flagged in Member State B with a crew recruited in Member State B covered by a collective bargaining agreement negotiated with an ITF affiliated trade union in Member State B;
  – the vessel will remain beneficially owned by the parent company and be bareboat chartered to the subsidiary;
  – the vessel will continue to provide ferry services between Member State A and Member State B on a daily basis;
  – a trade union established in Member State A takes collective action so as to require the parent and/or subsidiary to enter into a collective bargaining

agreement with it which will apply terms and conditions acceptable to the union in Member State A to the crew of the vessel even after reflagging and which has the effect of making it pointless for the parent to re-flag the vessel to Member State B,

does that collective action strike a fair balance between the fundamental social right to take collective action and the freedom to establish and provide services and is it objectively justified, appropriate, proportionate and in conformity with the principle of mutual recognition?

(10) Would it make any difference to the answer to [Question] 9 if the parent company provided an undertaking to a court on behalf of itself and all the companies within the same group that they will not by reason of the reflagging terminate the employment of any person employed by them (which undertaking did not require the renewal of short term employment contracts or prevent the redeployment of any employee on equivalent terms and conditions)?'

The questions referred

Preliminary observations

28. It must be borne in mind that, in accordance with settled case-law, in the context of the cooperation between the Court and the national courts provided for in Article 234 EC, it is solely for the national court before which a dispute has been brought, and which must assume responsibility for the subsequent judicial decision, to determine in the light of the particular circumstances of the case both the need for a preliminary ruling in order to enable it to deliver judgment and the relevance of the questions which it submits to the Court. However, the Court has regarded itself as not having jurisdiction to give a preliminary ruling on a question submitted by a national court where it is quite obvious, inter alia, that the interpretation of Community law sought by that court bears no relation to the actual facts of the main action or its purpose or where the problem is hypothetical (see Case C-415/93 *Bosman* [1995] ECR I-4921 and Case C-350/03 *Schulte* [2005] ECR I-9215, paragraph 43).

29. In the present case, the reference for a preliminary ruling concerns the interpretation, first, of provisions of the Treaty on freedom of establishment, and secondly, of Regulation No 4055/86 applying the principle of freedom to provide services to maritime transport.

30. However, since the question on freedom to provide services can arise only after the reflagging of the *Rosella* envisaged by Viking, and since, on the date on which the questions were referred to the Court, the vessel had not yet been re-flagged, the reference for a preliminary ruling is hypothetical and thus inadmissible in so far as it relates to the interpretation of Regulation No 4055/86.

31. In those circumstances, the questions referred by the national court can be answered only in so far as they concern the interpretation of Article 43 EC.

The first question

32. By its first question, the national court is essentially asking whether Article 43 EC must be interpreted as meaning that collective action initiated by a trade union or a group of trade unions against an undertaking in order to induce that undertaking to enter into a collective agreement, the terms of which are liable to deter it from exercising freedom of establishment, falls outside the scope of that article.

33. In this regard, it must be borne in mind that, according to settled case-law, Articles 39 EC, 43 EC and 49 EC do not apply only to the actions of public authorities but extend also to rules of any other nature aimed at regulating in a collective manner gainful employment, self-employment and the provision of services (see Case 36/74 *Walrave and Koch* [1974] ECR 1405, paragraph 17; Case 13/76 *Donà* [1976] ECR 1333, paragraph 17; *Bosman*, paragraph 82; Joined Cases C-51/96 and C-191/97 *Deliège* [2000] ECR I-2549, paragraph 47; Case C-281/98 *Angonese* [2000] ECR I-4139, paragraph 31; and Case C-309/99 *Wouters and Others* [2002] ECR I-1577, paragraph 120).

34. Since working conditions in the different Member States are governed sometimes by provisions laid down by law or regulation and sometimes by collective agreements and other acts concluded or adopted by private persons, limiting application of the prohibitions laid down by these articles to acts of a public authority would risk creating inequality in its application (see, by analogy, *Walrave and Koch*, paragraph 19; *Bosman*, paragraph 84; and *Angonese*, paragraph 33).

35. In the present case, it must be stated, first, that the organisation of collective action by trade unions must be regarded as covered by the legal autonomy which those organisations, which are not public law entities, enjoy pursuant to the trade union rights accorded to them, inter alia, by national law.

36. Secondly, as FSU and ITF submit, collective action such as that at issue in the main proceedings, which may be the trade unions' last resort to ensure the success of their claim to regulate the work of Viking's employees collectively, must be considered to be inextricably linked to the collective agreement the conclusion of which FSU is seeking.

37. It follows that collective action such as that described in the first question referred by the national court falls, in principle, within the scope of Article 43 EC.

38. This view is not called into question by the various arguments put forward by FSU, ITF and certain Member States which submitted observations to the Court to support the position contrary to that set out in the previous paragraph.

39. First of all, the Danish Government submits that the right of association, the right to strike and the right to impose lock-outs fall outside the scope of the fundamental freedom laid down in Article 43 EC since, in accordance with Article 137(5) EC, as amended by the Treaty of Nice, the Community does not have competence to regulate those rights.

40. In that respect it is sufficient to point out that, even if, in the areas which fall outside the scope of the Community's competence, the Member States are still free, in principle, to lay down the conditions governing the existence and exercise of the rights in question, the fact remains that, when exercising that competence, the Member States must nevertheless comply with Community law (see, by analogy, in relation to social security, Case C-120/95 *Decker* [1998] ECR I-1831, paragraphs 22 and 23, and Case C-158/96 *Kohll* [1998] ECR I-1931, paragraphs 18 and 19; in relation to direct taxation, Case C-334/02 *Commission* v *France* [2004] ECR I-2229, paragraph 21, and Case C-446/03 *Marks & Spencer* [2005] ECR I-10837, paragraph 29).

41. Consequently, the fact that Article 137 EC does not apply to the right to strike or to the right to impose lock-outs is not such as to exclude collective action such as that at issue in the main proceedings from the application of Article 43 EC.

42. Next, according to the observations of the Danish and Swedish Governments, the right to take collective action, including the right to strike, constitutes a fundamental right which, as such, falls outside the scope of Article 43 EC.

43. In that regard, it must be recalled that the right to take collective action, including the right to strike, is recognised both by various international instruments which the Member States have signed or cooperated in, such as the European Social Charter, signed at Turin on 18 October 1961 – to which, moreover, express reference is made in Article 136 EC – and Convention No 87 concerning Freedom of Association and Protection of the Right to Organise, adopted on 9 July 1948 by the International Labour Organisation – and by instruments developed by those Member States at Community level or in the context of the European Union, such as the Community Charter of the Fundamental Social Rights of Workers adopted at the meeting of the European Council held in Strasbourg on 9 December 1989, which is also referred to in Article 136 EC, and the Charter of Fundamental Rights of the European Union proclaimed in Nice on 7 December 2000 (OJ 2000 C 364, p. 1).

44. Although the right to take collective action, including the right to strike, must therefore be recognised as a fundamental right which forms an integral part of the gene-

ral principles of Community law the observance of which the Court ensures, the exercise of that right may none the less be subject to certain restrictions. As is reaffirmed by Article 28 of the Charter of Fundamental Rights of the European Union, those rights are to be protected in accordance with Community law and national law and practices. In addition, as is apparent from paragraph 5 of this judgment, under Finnish law the right to strike may not be relied on, in particular, where the strike is *contra bonos mores* or is prohibited under national law or Community law.

45. In that regard, the Court has already held that the protection of fundamental rights is a legitimate interest which, in principle, justifies a restriction of the obligations imposed by Community law, even under a fundamental freedom guaranteed by the Treaty, such as the free movement of goods (see Case C-112/00 *Schmidberger* [2003] ECR I-5659, paragraph 74) or freedom to provide services (see Case C-36/02 *Omega* [2004] ECR I-9609, paragraph 35).

46. However, in *Schmidberger* and *Omega*, the Court held that the exercise of the fundamental rights at issue, that is, freedom of expression and freedom of assembly and respect for human dignity, respectively, does not fall outside the scope of the provisions of the Treaty and considered that such exercise must be reconciled with the requirements relating to rights protected under the Treaty and in accordance with the principle of proportionality (see, to that effect, *Schmidberger*, paragraph 77, and *Omega*, paragraph 36).

47. It follows from the foregoing that the fundamental nature of the right to take collective action is not such as to render Article 43 EC inapplicable to the collective action at issue in the main proceedings.

48. Finally, FSU and ITF submit that the Court's reasoning in *Albany* must be applied by analogy to the case in the main proceedings, since certain restrictions on freedom of establishment and freedom to provide services are inherent in collective action taken in the context of collective negotiations.

49. In that regard, it should be noted that in paragraph 59 of *Albany*, having found that certain restrictions of competition are inherent in collective agreements between organisations representing employers and workers, the Court nevertheless held that the social policy objectives pursued by such agreements would be seriously undermined if management and labour were subject to Article 85(1) of the EC Treaty (now, Article 81(1) EC) when seeking jointly to adopt measures to improve conditions of work and employment.

50. The Court inferred from this, in paragraph 60 of *Albany*, that agreements concluded in the context of collective negotiations between management and labour in pursuit of such objectives must, by virtue of their nature and purpose, be regarded as falling outside the scope of Article 85(1) of the Treaty.

51. The Court must point out, however, that that reasoning cannot be applied in the context of the fundamental freedoms set out in Title III of the Treaty.

52. Contrary to the claims of FSU and ITF, it cannot be considered that it is inherent in the very exercise of trade union rights and the right to take collective action that those fundamental freedoms will be prejudiced to a certain degree.

53. Furthermore, the fact that an agreement or an activity are excluded from the scope of the provisions of the Treaty on competition does not mean that that agreement or activity also falls outside the scope of the Treaty provisions on the free movement of persons or services since those two sets of provisions are to be applied in different circumstances (see, to that effect, Case C-519/04 P *Meca-Medina and Majcen* v *Commission* [2006] ECR I-6991).

54. Finally, the Court has held that the terms of collective agreements are not excluded from the scope of the Treaty provisions on freedom of movement for persons (Case C-15/96 *Schöning-Kougebetopoulou* [1998] ECR I-47; Case C-35/97 *Commission* v *France* [1998] ECR I-5325; and Case C-400/02 *Merida* [2004] ECR I-8471).

55. In the light of the foregoing, the answer to the first question must be that Article 43 EC is to be interpreted as meaning that, in principle, collective action initiated by a trade union or a group of trade unions against an undertaking in order to induce that undertaking to enter into a collective agreement, the terms of which are liable to deter it from exercising freedom of establishment, is not excluded from the scope of that article.

The second question

56. By that question, the referring court is asking in essence whether Article 43 EC is such as to confer rights on a private undertaking which may be relied on against a trade union or an association of trade unions.

57. In order to answer that question, the Court would point out that it is clear from its case-law that the abolition, as between Member States, of obstacles to freedom of movement for persons and freedom to provide services would be compromised if the abolition of State barriers could be neutralised by obstacles resulting from the exercise, by associations or organisations not governed by public law, of their legal autonomy (*Walrave and Koch*, paragraph 18; *Bosman*, paragraph 83; *Deliège*, paragraph 47; *Angonese*, paragraph 32; and *Wouters and Others*, paragraph 120).

58. Moreover, the Court has ruled, first, that the fact that certain provisions of the Treaty are formally addressed to the Member States does not prevent rights from being conferred at the same time on any individual who has an interest in compliance with the obligations thus laid down, and, second, that the prohibition on prejudicing a

fundamental freedom laid down in a provision of the Treaty that is mandatory in nature, applies in particular to all agreements intended to regulate paid labour collectively (see, to that effect, Case 43/75 *Defrenne* [1976] ECR 455, paragraphs 31 and 39).

59. Such considerations must also apply to Article 43 EC which lays down a fundamental freedom.

60. In the present case, it must be borne in mind that, as is apparent from paragraphs 35 and 36 of the present judgment, the collective action taken by FSU and ITF is aimed at the conclusion of an agreement which is meant to regulate the work of Viking's employees collectively, and, that those two trade unions are organisations which are not public law entities but exercise the legal autonomy conferred on them, inter alia, by national law.

61. It follows that Article 43 EC must be interpreted as meaning that, in circumstances such as those in the main proceedings, it may be relied on by a private undertaking against a trade union or an association of trade unions.

62. This interpretation is also supported by the case-law on the Treaty provisions on the free movement of goods, from which it is apparent that restrictions may be the result of actions by individuals or groups of such individuals rather than caused by the State (see Case C-265/95 *Commission* v *France* [1997] ECR I-6959, paragraph 30, and *Schmidberger*, paragraphs 57 and 62).

63. The interpretation set out in paragraph 61 of the present judgment is also not called into question by the fact that the restriction at issue in the proceedings before the national court stems from the exercise of a right conferred by Finnish national law, such as, in this case, the right to take collective action, including the right to strike.

64. It must be added that, contrary to the claims, in particular, of ITF, it does not follow from the case-law of the Court referred to in paragraph 57 of the present judgment that that interpretation applies only to quasi-public organisations or to associations exercising a regulatory task and having quasi-legislative powers.

65. There is no indication in that case-law that could validly support the view that it applies only to associations or to organisations exercising a regulatory task or having quasi-legislative powers. Furthermore, it must be pointed out that, in exercising their autonomous power, pursuant to their trade union rights, to negotiate with employers or professional organisations the conditions of employment and pay of workers, trade unions participate in the drawing up of agreements seeking to regulate paid work collectively.

66. In the light of those considerations, the answer to the second question must be that Article 43 EC is capable of conferring rights on a private undertaking which may be relied on against a trade union or an association of trade unions.

The third to tenth questions

67. By those questions, which can be examined together, the national court is essentially asking the Court of Justice whether collective action such as that at issue in the main proceedings constitutes a restriction within the meaning of Article 43 EC and, if so, to what extent such a restriction may be justified.

The existence of restrictions

68. The Court must first point out, as it has done on numerous occasions, that freedom of establishment constitutes one of the fundamental principles of the Community and that the provisions of the Treaty guaranteeing that freedom have been directly applicable since the end of the transitional period. Those provisions secure the right of establishment in another Member State not merely for Community nationals but also for the companies or firms referred to in Article 48 EC (Case 81/87 *Daily Mail and General Trust* [1988] ECR 5483, paragraph 15).

69. Furthermore, the Court has considered that, even though the provisions of the Treaty concerning freedom of establishment are directed mainly to ensuring that foreign nationals and companies are treated in the host Member State in the same way as nationals of that State, they also prohibit the Member State of origin from hindering the establishment in another Member State of one of its nationals or of a company incorporated under its legislation which also comes within the definition contained in Article 48 EC. The rights guaranteed by Articles 43 EC to 48 EC would be rendered meaningless if the Member State of origin could prohibit undertakings from leaving in order to establish themselves in another Member State (*Daily Mail and General Trust*, paragraph 16).

70. Secondly, according to the settled case-law of the Court, the definition of establishment within the meaning of those articles of the Treaty involves the actual pursuit of an economic activity through a fixed establishment in another Member State for an indefinite period and registration of a vessel cannot be separated from the exercise of the freedom of establishment where the vessel serves as a vehicle for the pursuit of an economic activity that includes fixed establishment in the State of registration (Case C-221/89 *Factortame and Others* [1991] ECR I-3905, paragraphs 20 to 22).

71. The Court concluded from this that the conditions laid down for the registration of vessels must not form an obstacle to freedom of establishment within the meaning of Articles 43 EC to 48 EC (*Factortame and Others*, paragraph 23).

72. In the present case, first, it cannot be disputed that collective action such as that envisaged by FSU has the effect of making less attractive, or even pointless, as the national court has pointed out, Viking's exercise of its right to freedom of establishment, inasmuch as such action prevents both Viking and its subsidiary, Viking Eesti, from enjoying the same treatment in the host Member State as other economic operators established in that State.

73. Secondly, collective action taken in order to implement ITF's policy of combating the use of flags of convenience, which seeks, primarily, as is apparent from ITF's observations, to prevent shipowners from registering their vessels in a State other than that of which the beneficial owners of those vessels are nationals, must be considered to be at least liable to restrict Viking's exercise of its right of freedom of establishment.

74. It follows that collective action such as that at issue in the main proceedings constitutes a restriction on freedom of establishment within the meaning of Article 43 EC.

Justification of the restrictions

75. It is apparent from the case-law of the Court that a restriction on freedom of establishment can be accepted only if it pursues a legitimate aim compatible with the Treaty and is justified by overriding reasons of public interest. But even if that were the case, it would still have to be suitable for securing the attainment of the objective pursued and must not go beyond what is necessary in order to attain it (see, inter alia, Case C-55/94 *Gebhard* [1995] ECR I-4165, paragraph 37, and *Bosman*, paragraph 104).

76. ITF, supported, in particular, by the German Government, Ireland and the Finnish Government, maintains that the restrictions at issue in the main proceedings are justified since they are necessary to ensure the protection of a fundamental right recognised under Community law and their objective is to protect the rights of workers, which constitutes an overriding reason of public interest.

77. In that regard, it must be observed that the right to take collective action for the protection of workers is a legitimate interest which, in principle, justifies a restriction of one of the fundamental freedoms guaranteed by the Treaty (see, to that effect, *Schmidberger*, paragraph 74) and that the protection of workers is one of the overriding reasons of public interest recognised by the Court (see, inter alia, Joined Cases C-369/96 and C-376/96 *Arblade and Others* [1999] ECR I-8453, paragraph 36; Case C-165/98 *Mazzoleni and ISA* [2001] ECR I-2189, paragraph 27; and Joined Cases C-49/98, C-50/98, C-52/98 to C-54/98 and C-68/98 to C-71/98 *Finalarte and Others* [2001] ECR I-7831, paragraph 33).

78. It must be added that, according to Article 3(1)(c) and (j) EC, the activities of the Community are to include not only an 'internal market characterised by the abolition, as between Member States, of obstacles to the free movement of goods, persons, services and capital', but also 'a policy in the social sphere'. Article 2 EC states that the Community is to have as its task, inter alia, the promotion of 'a harmonious, balanced and sustainable development of economic activities' and 'a high level of employment and of social protection'.

79. Since the Community has thus not only an economic but also a social purpose, the rights under the provisions of the Treaty on the free movement of goods, persons, services and capital must be balanced against the objectives pursued by social policy, which include, as is clear from the first paragraph of Article 136 EC, inter alia, improved living and working conditions, so as to make possible their harmonisation while improvement is being maintained, proper social protection and dialogue between management and labour.

80. In the present case, it is for the national court to ascertain whether the objectives pursued by FSU and ITF by means of the collective action which they initiated concerned the protection of workers.

81. First, as regards the collective action taken by FSU, even if that action – aimed at protecting the jobs and conditions of employment of the members of that union liable to be adversely affected by the reflagging of the *Rosella* – could reasonably be considered to fall, at first sight, within the objective of protecting workers, such a view would no longer be tenable if it were established that the jobs or conditions of employment at issue were not jeopardised or under serious threat.

82. This would be the case, in particular, if it transpired that the undertaking referred to by the national court in its 10th question was, from a legal point of view, as binding as the terms of a collective agreement and if it was of such a nature as to provide a guarantee to the workers that the statutory provisions would be complied with and the terms of the collective agreement governing their working relationship maintained.

83. In so far as the exact legal scope to be attributed to an undertaking such as that referred to in the 10th question is not clear from the order for reference, it is for the national court to determine whether the jobs or conditions of employment of that trade union's members who are liable to be affected by the reflagging of the *Rosella* were jeopardised or under serious threat.

84. If, following that examination, the national court came to the conclusion that, in the case before it, the jobs or conditions of employment of the FSU's members liable to be adversely affected by the reflagging of the *Rosella* are in fact jeopardised or under serious threat, it would then have to ascertain whether the collective action initi-

ated by FSU is suitable for ensuring the achievement of the objective pursued and does not go beyond what is necessary to attain that objective.

85. In that regard, it must be pointed out that, even if it is ultimately for the national court, which has sole jurisdiction to assess the facts and interpret the national legislation, to determine whether and to what extent such collective action meets those requirements, the Court of Justice, which is called on to provide answers of use to the national court, may provide guidance, based on the file in the main proceedings and on the written and oral observations which have been submitted to it, in order to enable the national court to give judgment in the particular case before it.

86. As regards the appropriateness of the action taken by FSU for attaining the objectives pursued in the case in the main proceedings, it should be borne in mind that it is common ground that collective action, like collective negotiations and collective agreements, may, in the particular circumstances of a case, be one of the main ways in which trade unions protect the interests of their members (European Court of Human Rights, *Syndicat national de la police belge* v *Belgium*, of 27 October 1975, Series A, No 19, and *Wilson, National Union of Journalists and Others* v *United Kingdom* of 2 July 2002, 2002-V, § 44).

87. As regards the question of whether or not the collective action at issue in the main proceedings goes beyond what is necessary to achieve the objective pursued, it is for the national court to examine, in particular, on the one hand, whether, under the national rules and collective agreement law applicable to that action, FSU did not have other means at its disposal which were less restrictive of freedom of establishment in order to bring to a successful conclusion the collective negotiations entered into with Viking, and, on the other, whether that trade union had exhausted those means before initiating such action.

88. Secondly, in relation to the collective action seeking to ensure the implementation of the policy in question pursued by ITF, it must be emphasised that, to the extent that that policy results in shipowners being prevented from registering their vessels in a State other than that of which the beneficial owners of those vessels are nationals, the restrictions on freedom of establishment resulting from such action cannot be objectively justified. Nevertheless, as the national court points out, the objective of that policy is also to protect and improve seafarers' terms and conditions of employment.

89. However, as is apparent from the file submitted to the Court, in the context of its policy of combating the use of flags of convenience, ITF is required, when asked by one of its members, to initiate solidarity action against the beneficial owner of a vessel which is registered in a State other than that of which that owner is a national, irrespective of whether or not that owner's exercise of its right of freedom of establishment is liable to have a harmful effect on the work or conditions of em-

ployment of its employees. Therefore, as Viking argued during the hearing without being contradicted by ITF in that regard, the policy of reserving the right of collective negotiations to trade unions of the State of which the beneficial owner of a vessel is a national is also applicable where the vessel is registered in a State which guarantees workers a higher level of social protection than they would enjoy in the first State.

90. In the light of those considerations, the answer to the third to tenth questions must be that Article 43 EC is to be interpreted to the effect that collective action such as that at issue in the main proceedings, which seeks to induce an undertaking whose registered office is in a given Member State to enter into a collective work agreement with a trade union established in that State and to apply the terms set out in that agreement to the employees of a subsidiary of that undertaking established in another Member State, constitutes a restriction within the meaning of that article. That restriction may, in principle, be justified by an overriding reason of public interest, such as the protection of workers, provided that it is established that the restriction is suitable for ensuring the attainment of the legitimate objective pursued and does not go beyond what is necessary to achieve that objective.

Costs

[Para. 91 omitted]

On those grounds,

THE COURT (Grand Chamber)

hereby rules:

1. **Article 43 EC is to be interpreted as meaning that, in principle, collective action initiated by a trade union or a group of trade unions against a private undertaking in order to induce that undertaking to enter into a collective agreement, the terms of which are liable to deter it from exercising freedom of establishment, is not excluded from the scope of that article.**

2. **Article 43 EC is capable of conferring rights on a private undertaking which may be relied on against a trade union or an association of trade unions.**

3. **Article 43 EC is to be interpreted to the effect that collective action such as that at issue in the main proceedings, which seeks to induce a private undertaking whose registered office is in a given Member State to enter into a collective work agreement with a trade union established in that State and to apply the terms set out in that agreement to the employees of a subsidi-**

ary of that undertaking established in another Member State, constitutes a restriction within the meaning of that article.

That restriction may, in principle, be justified by an overriding reason of public interest, such as the protection of workers, provided that it is established that the restriction is suitable for ensuring the attainment of the legitimate objective pursued and does not go beyond what is necessary to achieve that objective.

Comments and questions

Like the decision in Case C-341/05 *Laval* [2007] ECR I-11767, reproduced below in Chapter 6, the CJEU's decision in the *Viking Line* case has wide-ranging significance, not least for the Nordic Member States, where the two sides of industry play a central role in the regulation of labour market conditions.

The facts in the *Viking Line* case were that a Finnish shipping company, Viking Line, operated a number of ferries, including the ship *Rosella* which sailed under the Finnish flag between the Estonian capital Tallinn and the Finnish capital Helsinki. As long as the ship sailed under the Finnish flag, Viking Line had to pay its crew in accordance with the collective agreement entered into with the Finnish Seamen's Union. This meant that the wages followed the Finnish wage levels. In 2003, before Estonia joined the EU, Viking Line tried to re-flag the *Rosella* to Estonia. 'Flagging out' the ship would have meant that Viking Line would not have been obliged to pay wages in accordance with the Finnish collective agreement, so that wage costs could have been reduced substantially. The Finnish Seamen's Union reacted by threatening to strike, which caused Viking Line to give up its plan to flag out, at least for the time being.

On 1 May 2004 Estonia joined the EU. Viking Line still wanted to flag out the Rosella to Estonia, and the shipping company therefore brought an action against the Finnish Seamen's Union and the International Transport Workers' Federation, claiming that their measures for collective action were in breach of Article 49 TFEU (formerly Article 43 TEC) on the right of establishment. A key question in this connection was whether Article 49 TFEU only applies to the actions of public authorities or whether it also extends to collective agreements.

Referring to the considerable number of cases in which questions have been referred on the application of the TFEU's provisions on free movement to collective agreements, the CJEU pointed out that working conditions in the different Member States are sometimes governed by provisions laid down by law or regulation and sometimes by collective agreements and other acts concluded or adopted by private persons. Limiting the application of the prohibition in Article 49 TFEU to acts of a public authority would therefore risk creating inequality in its application. Collective agreements thus also fall within the scope of the provision.

However, there was a further question as to whether Article 49 TFEU also applied to the collective actions taken by trade unions, for example in the event of a strike or a lock-out. In this connection, the CJEU expressly recognised that trade unions are not public law entities, but at the same time it emphasised that collective action is necessarily linked to collective agreements. On this basis the CJEU concluded that the collective action of a trade union is covered by Article 49 TFEU.

The Danish and Swedish Governments, in particular, argued before the CJEU that the right to take collective action is a fundamental right and, as such, it falls outside the scope of Article 49 TFEU. The CJEU rejected this argument. The right to take collective action, including the right to strike, is recognised as a fundamental right under Union law. However, such collective action falls within the scope of the TFEU, so that the exercise of this right must be compatible with the requirements associated with the other rights protected under the TFEU, such as the principle of proportionality. Thus, collective action taken by a trade union to induce a private undertaking to enter into a collective agreement falls within the scope of Article 49 TFEU. Consequently, such collective action constitutes a restriction within the meaning of Article 49 TFEU, and it will only be lawful under Union law if it is justified by an overriding reason of public interest, and if it is in accordance with the principle of proportionality.

In his Opinion, the Advocate General clearly drew attention to the fact that the application of the (now) TFEU provisions on free movement were not limited to the acts of State authorities but also apply to a private action that, 'by virtue of its general effect on the holders of rights to freedom of movement, is capable of restricting them from exercising those rights, by raising an obstacle that they cannot reasonably circumvent.' If one follows the Opinion of the Advocate General, then specific employment law measures that are not part of an overall coordinated policy, and which do not therefore have general effect, will not be covered by the prohibition in Article 49 TFEU. Conversely, measures that are part of a coordinated policy, with a view to restricting freedom of establishment, could be covered. To what extent did the CJEU follow the Advocate General's distinction, and to what extent did it reject it?

In the *Viking Line* case the CJEU held that the protection of workers constitutes an overriding public interest. Are there cases where collective action is not aimed at protecting workers? If there is no such case, does the CJEU's decision merely mean that in reality trade unions can take collective action as long as they fulfil the requirements of the principle of proportionality?

JUDGMENT OF THE COURT
30 November 1995

Reinhard Gebhard v Consiglio dell'Ordine degli Avvocati e Procuratori di Milano.
(Reference to the Court by the Consiglio Nazionale Forense (Italy) for a preliminary ruling)

'Directive 77/249/EEC – Freedom to provide services – Lawyers – Possibility of opening chambers – Articles 52 and 59 of the EC Treaty'

Case C-55/94

Judgment

1. By order of 16 December 1993, received at the Court on 8 February 1994, the Consiglio Nazionale Forense (National Council of the Bar) referred to the Court for a preliminary ruling under Article 177 of the EC Treaty two questions on the interpretation of Council Directive 77/249/EEC of 22 March 1977 to facilitate the effective exercise by lawyers of freedom to provide services (OJ 1977 L 78, p. 17).

2. The questions have been raised in the course of disciplinary proceedings opened by the Consiglio dell'Ordine degli Avvocati e Procuratori di Milano (Council of the Order of Advocates and Procurators of Milan, hereinafter 'the Milan Bar Council') against Mr Gebhard, who is accused of contravening his obligations under Law No 31 of 9 February 1982 on freedom for lawyers who are nationals of a Member State of the European Community to provide services (GURI No 42 of 12 February 1982) on the ground that he pursued a professional activity in Italy on a permanent basis in chambers set up by himself whilst using the title *avvocato*.

3. According to the case-file and information provided in answer to the written questions put by the Court, Mr Gebhard, a German national, has been authorized to practise as a *Rechtsanwalt* in Germany since 3 August 1977. He is a member of the Bar of Stuttgart, where he is an 'independent collaborator' in a set of chambers (*Bürogemeinschaft*) although he does not have chambers of his own in Germany.

4. Mr Gebhard has resided since March 1978 in Italy, where he lives with his wife, an Italian national, and his three children. His income is taxed entirely in Italy, his country of residence.

5. Mr Gebhard has pursued a professional activity in Italy since 1 March 1978, initially as a collaborator (*con un rapporto di libera collaborazione*) in a set of chambers of lawyers practising in association in Milan, and subsequently, from 1 January 1980 until the beginning of 1989, as an associate member (*associato*) of those

chambers. No criticism has been made of him in relation to his activities in those chambers.

6. On 30 July 1989, Mr Gebhard opened his own chambers in Milan in which Italian *avvocati* and *procuratori* work in collaboration with him. In response to a written question from the Court, Mr Gebhard stated that he instructed them from time to time to act in judicial proceedings involving Italian clients in Italy.

7. Mr Gebhard avers that his activity in Italy is essentially non-contentious, assisting and representing German-speakers (65% of his turnover) and representing Italian-speakers in Germany and Austria (30% of his turnover). The remaining 5% is accounted for by assistance to Italian practitioners whose clients are faced with problems of German law.

8. A number of Italian practitioners, including the Italian *avvocati* with whom Mr Gebhard was associated until 1989, lodged a complaint with the Milan Bar Council. They complained of his use of the title *avvocato* on the letterhead of notepaper which he used for professional purposes, of his having appeared using the title *avvocato* directly before the Pretura and the Tribunale di Milano and of his having practised professionally from 'Studio Legale Gebhard'.

9. The Milan Bar Council prohibited Mr Gebhard from using the title *avvocato*. Thereafter, on 19 September 1991, it decided to open disciplinary proceedings against him on the ground that he had contravened his obligations under Law No 31/82 by pursuing a professional activity in Italy on a permanent basis in chambers set up by himself whilst using the title *avvocato*.

10. On 14 October 1991 Mr Gebhard applied to the Milan Bar Council to be entered on the role of members of the Bar. His application was based on Council Directive 89/48/EEC of 21 December 1988 on a general system for the recognition of higher-education diplomas awarded on completion of professional education and training of at least three years' duration (OJ 1989 L 19, p. 16) and on his having completed a ten-year training period in Italy. It does not appear that the Bar Council has taken any formal decision on that application.

11. The disciplinary proceedings opened on 19 September 1991 were completed by a decision of 30 December 1992 by which the Milan Bar Council imposed on Mr Gebhard the sanction of suspension from pursuing his professional activity (*sospensione dell'esercizio dell'attività professionale*) for six months.

12. Mr Gebhard appealed against that decision to the Consiglio Nazionale Forense, making it clear, however, that he was also appealing against the implied rejection of his application to be entered on the roll. In particular, he argued in his appeal that

Directive 77/249 entitled him to pursue his professional activities from his own chambers in Milan.

13. Directive 77/249 applies to the activities of lawyers pursued by way of provision of services. It states that a lawyer providing services is to adopt the professional title used in the Member State from which he comes, expressed in the language or one of the languages of that State, with an indication of the professional organization by which he is authorized to practise or the court of law before which he is entitled to practise pursuant to the laws of that State (Article 3).

14. The directive draws a distinction between (a) activities relating to the representation of a client in legal proceedings or before public authorities and (b) all other activities.

15. In pursuing activities relating to representation, the lawyer must observe the rules of professional conduct of the host Member State, without prejudice to his obligations in the Member State from which he comes (Article 4(2)). As far as the pursuit of all other activities is concerned, the lawyer remains subject to the conditions and rules of professional conduct of the Member State from which he comes, without pre-judice to respect for the rules, whatever their source, which govern the profession in the host Member State, especially those concerning the incomepatibility of the exercise of the activities of a lawyer with the exercise of other activities in that State, professional secrecy, relations with other lawyers, the prohibition on the same lawyer acting for parties with mutually conflicting interests, and secrecy (Article 4(4)).

16. Article 4(1) of Directive 77/249 provides that 'Activities relating to the representation of a client in legal proceedings or before public authorities shall be pursued in each host Member State under the conditions laid down for lawyers established in that State, with the exception of any conditions requiring residence, or registration with a professional organization, in that State.'

17. Directive 77/249 was implemented in Italy by Law No 31/82, Article 2 of which provides as follows: '[Nationals of Member States authorized to practise as lawyers in the Member State from which they come] shall be permitted to pursue lawyers' professional activities on a temporary basis (*con carattere di temporaneità*) in contentious and non-contentious matters in accordance with the detailed rules laid down in this title. For the purpose of the pursuit of the professional activities referred to in the preceding paragraph, the establishment on the territory of the Republic either of chambers or of a principal or branch office is not permitted.'

18. In those circumstances, the Consiglio Nazionale Forense stayed the proceedings and referred questions to the Court for a preliminary ruling:

(a) as to whether Article 2 of Law No 31 of 9 February 1982 on freedom for lawyers who are nationals of the Member States of the European Community to provide services (enacted in implementation of Council Directive 77/249/EEC of 22 March 1977) which prohibits 'the establishment on the territory of the Republic either of chambers or of a principal or branch office', is compatible with the rules laid down by that directive, given that in the directive there is no reference to the fact that the possibility of opening an office could be interpreted as reflecting a practitioner's intention to carry on his activities, not on a temporary or occasional basis, but on a regular basis;

(b) as to the criteria to be applied in assessing whether activities are of a temporary nature, with respect to the continuous and repetitive nature of the services provided by lawyers practising under the system referred to in the abovementioned directive of 22 March 1977.'

19. In view of the wording of the preliminary questions, it should be remembered that the Court has consistently held that it does not have jurisdiction to rule on the compatibility of a national measure with Community law. However, the Court is competent to provide the national court with all criteria for the interpretation of Community law which may enable it to determine the issue of compatibility for the purposes of the decision in the case before it (see in particular Case C-63/94 *Groupement National des Négociants en Pommes de Terre de Belgique (Belgapom)* [1995] ECR I-2467, paragraph 7).

20. The situation of a Community national who moves to another Member State of the Community in order there to pursue an economic activity is governed by the chapter of the Treaty on the free movement of workers, or the chapter on the right of establishment or the chapter on services, these being mutually exclusive.

21. Since the questions referred are concerned essentially with the concepts of 'establishment' and 'provision of services', the chapter on workers can be disregarded as having no bearing on those questions.

22. The provisions of the chapter on services are subordinate to those of the chapter on the right of establishment in so far, first, as the wording of the first paragraph of Article 59 assumes that the provider and the recipient of the service concerned are 'established' in two different Member States and, second, as the first paragraph of Article 60 specifies that the provisions relating to services apply only if those relating to the right of establishment do not apply. It is therefore necessary to consider the scope of the concept of 'establishment'.

23. The right of establishment, provided for in Articles 52 to 58 of the Treaty, is granted both to legal persons within the meaning of Article 58 and to natural persons who are nationals of a Member State of the Community. Subject to the exceptions and conditions laid down, it allows all types of self-employed activity to be taken

up and pursued on the territory of any other Member State, undertakings to be formed and operated, and agencies, branches or subsidiaries to be set up.

24. It follows that a person may be established, within the meaning of the Treaty, in more than one Member State – in particular, in the case of companies, through the setting-up of agencies, branches or subsidiaries (Article 52) and, as the Court has held, in the case of members of the professions, by establishing a second professional base (see Case 107/83 *Ordre des Avocats au Barreau de Paris* v *Klopp* [1984] ECR 2971, paragraph 19).

25. The concept of establishment within the meaning of the Treaty is therefore a very broad one, allowing a Community national to participate, on a stable and continuous basis, in the economic life of a Member State other than his State of origin and to profit therefrom, so contributing to economic and social interpenetration within the Community in the sphere of activities as self-employed persons (see, to this effect, Case 2/74 *Reyners* v *Belgium* [1974] ECR 631, paragraph 21).

26. In contrast, where the provider of services moves to another Member State, the provisions of the chapter on services, in particular the third paragraph of Article 60, envisage that he is to pursue his activity there on a temporary basis.

27. As the Advocate General has pointed out, the temporary nature of the activities in question has to be determined in the light, not only of the duration of the provision of the service, but also of its regularity, periodicity or continuity. The fact that the provision of services is temporary does not mean that the provider of services within the meaning of the Treaty may not equip himself with some form of infrastructure in the host Member State (including an office, chambers or consulting rooms) in so far as such infrastructure is necessary for the purposes of performing the services in question.

28. However, that situation is to be distinguished from that of Mr Gebhard who, as a national of a Member State, pursues a professional activity on a stable and continuous basis in another Member State where he holds himself out from an established professional base to, amongst others, nationals of that State. Such a national comes under the provisions of the chapter relating to the right of establishment and not those of the chapter relating to services.

29. The Milan Bar Council has argued that a person such as Mr Gebhard cannot be regarded for the purposes of the Treaty as being 'established' in a Member State – in his case, Italy – unless he belongs to the professional body of that State or, at least, pursues his activity in collaboration or in association with persons belonging to that body.

30. That argument cannot be accepted.

31. The provisions relating to the right of establishment cover the taking-up and pursuit of activities (see, in particular, the judgment in *Reyners*, paragraphs 46 and 47). Membership of a professional body may be a condition of taking up and pursuit of particular activities. It cannot itself be constitutive of establishment.

32. It follows that the question whether it is possible for a national of a Member State to exercise his right of establishment and the conditions for exercise of that right must be determined in the light of the activities which he intends to pursue on the territory of the host Member State.

33. Under the terms of the second paragraph of Article 52, freedom of establishment is to be exercised under the conditions laid down for its own nationals by the law of the country where establishment is effected.

34. In the event that the specific activities in question are not subject to any rules in the host State, so that a national of that Member State does not have to have any specific qualification in order to pursue them, a national of any other Member State is entitled to establish himself on the territory of the first State and pursue those activities there.

35. However, the taking-up and pursuit of certain self-employed activities may be conditional on complying with certain provisions laid down by law, regulation or administrative action justified by the general good, such as rules relating to organization, qualifications, professional ethics, supervision and liability (see Case C-71/76 *Thieffry* v *Conseil de l'Ordre des Avocats à la Cour de Paris* [1977] ECR 765, paragraph 12). Such provisions may stipulate in particular that pursuit of a particular activity is restricted to holders of a diploma, certificate or other evidence of formal qualifications, to persons belonging to a professional body or to persons subject to particular rules or supervision, as the case may be. They may also lay down the conditions for the use of professional titles, such as *avvocato*.

36. Where the taking-up or pursuit of a specific activity is subject to such conditions in the host Member State, a national of another Member State intending to pursue that activity must in principle comply with them. It is for this reason that Article 57 provides that the Council is to issue directives, such as Directive 89/48, for the mutual recognition of diplomas, certificates and other evidence of formal qualifications or, as the case may be, for the coordination of national provisions concerning the taking-up and pursuit of activities as self-employed persons.

37. It follows, however, from the Court's case-law that national measures liable to hinder or make less attractive the exercise of fundamental freedoms guaranteed by the Treaty must fulfil four conditions: they must be applied in a non-discriminatory manner; they must be justified by imperative requirements in the general interest; they must be suitable for securing the attainment of the objective which they pur-

sue; and they must not go beyond what is necessary in order to attain it (see Case C-19/92 *Kraus* v *Land Baden-Württemberg* [1993] ECR I-1663, paragraph 32).

38. Likewise, in applying their national provisions, Member States may not ignore the knowledge and qualifications already acquired by the person concerned in another Member State (see Case C-340/89 *Vlassopoulou* v *Ministerium für Justiz, Bundes- und Europaangelegenheiten Baden-Württemberg* [1991] ECR I-2357, paragraph 15). Consequently, they must take account of the equivalence of diplomas (see the judgment in *Thieffry*, paragraphs 19 and 27) and, if necessary, proceed to a comparison of the knowledge and qualifications required by their national rules and those of the person concerned (see the judgment in *Vlassopoulou*, paragraph 16).

39. Accordingly, it should be stated in reply to the questions from the Consiglio Nazionale Forense that:

- the temporary nature of the provision of services, envisaged in the third paragraph of Article 60 of the EC Treaty, is to be determined in the light of its duration, regularity, periodicity and continuity;
- the provider of services, within the meaning of the Treaty, may equip himself in the host Member State with the infrastructure necessary for the purposes of performing the services in question;
- a national of a Member State who pursues a professional activity on a stable and continuous basis in another Member State where he holds himself out from an established professional base to, amongst others, nationals of that State comes under the provisions of the chapter relating to the right of establishment and not those of the chapter relating to services;
- the possibility for a national of a Member State to exercise his right of establishment, and the conditions for his exercise of that right, must be determined in the light of the activities which he intends to pursue on the territory of the host Member State;
- where the taking-up of a specific activity is not subject to any rules in the host State, a national of any other Member State will be entitled to establish himself on the territory of the first State and pursue that activity there. On the other hand, where the taking-up or the pursuit of a specific activity is subject to certain conditions in the host Member State, a national of another Member State intending to pursue that activity must in principle comply with them;
- however, national measures liable to hinder or make less attractive the exercise of fundamental freedoms guaranteed by the Treaty must fulfil four conditions: they must be applied in a non-discriminatory manner; they must be justified by imperative requirements in the general interest; they must be suitable for securing the attainment of the objective which they pursue; and they must not go beyond what is necessary in order to attain it;

- likewise, Member States must take account of the equivalence of diplomas and, if necessary, proceed to a comparison of the knowledge and qualifications required by their national rules and those of the person concerned.

Costs

[Para. 40 omitted]

On those grounds,

THE COURT

in answer to the questions referred to it by the Consiglio Nazionale Forense, by order of 16 December 1993, hereby rules:

1. **The temporary nature of the provision of services, envisaged in the third paragraph of Article 60 of the EC Treaty, is to be determined in the light of its duration, regularity, periodicity and continuity.**

2. **The provider of services, within the meaning of the Treaty, may equip himself in the host Member State with the infrastructure necessary for the purposes of performing the services in question.**

3. **A national of a Member State who pursues a professional activity on a stable and continuous basis in another Member State where he holds himself out from an established professional base to, amongst others, nationals of that State comes under the provisions of the chapter relating to the right of establishment and not those of the chapter relating to services.**

4. **The possibility for a national of a Member State to exercise his right of establishment, and the conditions for the exercise of that right, must be determined in the light of the activities which he intends to pursue on the territory of the host Member State.**

5. **Where the taking-up of a specific activity is not subject to any rules in the host State, a national of any other Member State will be entitled to establish himself on the territory of the first State and pursue that activity there. On the other hand, where the taking-up or the pursuit of a specific activity is subject to certain conditions in the host Member State, a national of another Member State intending to pursue that activity must in principle comply with them.**

6. **National measures liable to hinder or make less attractive the exercise of fundamental freedoms guaranteed by the Treaty must fulfil four con-**

ditions: they must be applied in a non-discriminatory manner; they must be justified by imperative requirements in the general interest; they must be suitable for securing the attainment of the objective which they pursue; and they must not go beyond what is necessary in order to attain it.

7. **Member States must take account of the equivalence of diplomas and, if necessary, proceed to a comparison of the knowledge and qualifications required by their national rules and those of the person concerned.**

Comments and questions

In paragraph 25 of Case C-55/94 *Gebhard* v *Consiglio dell'Ordine degli Avvocati e Procuratori di Milano* [1995] ECR I-4165, the CJEU stated that the concept of 'establishment' is very broad, allowing a national of a Member State to participate, on a stable and continuous basis, in the economic life of a Member State other than his State of origin and to profit therefrom, in carrying on an independent commercial undertaking. This contrasts with when a provider of services moves to another Member State for a commercial purpose, and it is envisaged that the service provider will pursue an activity there on a temporary basis; cf. paragraph 26.

Article 49 TFEU (formerly Article 52 TEC) covers both discriminatory and restrictive national measures; cf. paragraphs 37 and 39 (sixth indent) of the judgment. Consider in more detail what is meant by the CJEU's statement in these same paragraphs that: 'national measures liable to hinder or make less attractive the exercise of fundamental freedoms guaranteed by the Treaty must fulfil four conditions' (the *Gebhard* test). Is this a general statement which applies to all four freedoms in the TFEU, or should this statement perhaps be limited to the TFEU provisions on the freedom of movement of persons? Compare this with paragraph 16 in Joined Cases C-64/96 and C-65/96 *Land Nordrhein-Westfalen* v *Uecker and Jacquet* v *Land Nordrhein-Westfalen* [1997] ECR I-3171, printed in Chapter 4.

Is a German architect covered by Article 49 TFEU if, for five weeks of the year, he prepares architectural drawings for German customers in a house in France, while maintaining his main architectural studio in Germany, and if he has his income from fees for work carried out in France taxed in France? Would the prohibition by a Member State of the remuneration of sight accounts constitute a restriction on the right of establishment, contrary to Article 49 TFEU? In this respect see Case C-442/02 *CaixaBank France* v *Ministère de l'Économie, des Finances et de l'Industrie* [2004] ECR I-8961, printed below. Consider whether one can apply the *de minimis* rule to Article 49 TFEU, as the CJEU did in Case 53/81 *Levin* v *Staatssecretaris van Justitie* [1982] ECR 1035 in relation to Article 45 TFEU (formerly Article 48 TEC), so that the scope of the rules on the free movement of workers only covers actual and effective employment, to the exclusion work which is of such a small scale as to be considered only marginal and ancillary. In Case C-170/05 *Denkavit* v *Ministre de l'Économie, des Finances et de l'Industrie* [2006] ECR I-11949, the CJEU seems to have refused to apply the *de minimis* rule to Article 49 TFEU. In paragraph 50 of the judgment the CJEU stated: 'A restriction on freedom of establishment is prohibited by Article 43 EC, even if it is of limited scope or minor importance'. This judgment was not given by the Full Court so its precedent value is limited.

A residence requirement for the establishment of an undertaking can constitute a restriction on the right of establishment. In Case C-370/05 *Criminal proceedings against Uwe Kay Festersen* [2007] ECR I-1129, the CJEU considered such a residence requirement. See the commentary on this case in Chapter 7 below.

According to the CJEU's most recent decisions, the requirement for authorisation to carry on a particular form of business must be regarded as a restriction, even if the requirement applies without distinction on the basis of nationality. See further in Case C-169/07 *Hartlauer* [2009] ECR I-1721, printed below.

JUDGMENT OF THE COURT
9 March 1999

Centros Ltd v Erhvervs- og Selskabsstyrelsen.
(Reference to the Court by the Højesteret (Denmark) for a preliminary ruling)

'Freedom of establishment – Establishment of a branch by a company not carrying on any actual business – Circumvention of national law – Refusal to register'

Case C-212/97

Judgment

1. By order of 3 June 1997, received at the Court on 5 June 1997 the Højesteret referred to the Court for a preliminary ruling under Article 177 of the EC Treaty a question on the interpretation of Articles 52, 56 and 58 of the Treaty.

2. That question was raised in proceedings between Centros Ltd, a private limited company registered on 18 May 1992 in England and Wales, and Erhvervs- og Selskabsstyrelsen (the Trade and Companies Board, 'the Board') which comes under the Danish Department of Trade, concerning that authority's refusal to register a branch of Centros in Denmark.

3. It is clear from the documents in the main proceedings that Centros has never traded since its formation. Since United Kingdom law imposes no requirement on limited liability companies as to the provision for and the paying-up of a minimum share capital, Centros's share capital, which amounts to GBP 100, has been neither paid up nor made available to the company. It is divided into two shares held by Mr and Mrs Bryde, Danish nationals residing in Denmark. Mrs Bryde is the director of Centros, whose registered office is situated in the United Kingdom, at the home of a friend of Mr Bryde.

4. Under Danish law, Centros, as a 'private limited company', is regarded as a foreign limited liability company. The rules governing the registration of branches ('filialer') of such companies are laid down by the Anpartsselskabslov (Law on private limited companies).

5. In particular, Article 117 of the Law provides:

   '1. Private limited companies and foreign companies having a similar legal form which are established in one Member State of the European Communities may do business in Denmark through a branch.'

6. During the summer of 1992, Mrs Bryde requested the Board to register a branch of Centros in Denmark.

7. The Board refused that registration on the grounds, *inter alia*, that Centros, which does not trade in the United Kingdom, was in fact seeking to establish in Denmark, not a branch, but a principal establishment, by circumventing the national rules concerning, in particular, the paying-up of minimum capital fixed at DKK 200 000 by Law No 886 of 21 December 1991.

8. Centros brought an action before the Østre Landsret against the refusal of the Board to effect that registration.

9. The Østre Landsret upheld the arguments of the Board in a judgment of 8 September 1995, whereupon Centros appealed to the Højesteret.

10. In those proceedings, Centros maintains that it satisfies the conditions imposed by the law on private limited companies relating to the registration of a branch of a foreign company. Since it was lawfully formed in the United Kingdom, it is entitled to set up a branch in Denmark pursuant to Article 52, read in conjunction with Article 58, of the Treaty.

11. According to Centros the fact that it has never traded since its formation in the United Kingdom has no bearing on its right to freedom of establishment. In its judgment in Case 79/85 *Segers* v *Bedrijfsvereniging voor Bank- en Verzekeringswegen, Groothandel en Vrije Beroepen* [1986] ECR 2375, the Court ruled that Articles 52 and 58 of the Treaty prohibited the competent authorities of a Member State from excluding the director of a company from a national sickness insurance scheme solely on the ground that the company had its registered office in another Member State, even though it did not conduct any business there.

12. The Board submits that its refusal to grant registration is not contrary to Articles 52 and 58 of the Treaty since the establishment of a branch in Denmark would seem to be a way of avoiding the national rules on the provision for and the paying-up of minimum share capital. Furthermore, its refusal to register is justified by the need to protect private or public creditors and other contracting parties and also by the need to endeavour to prevent fraudulent insolvencies.

13. In those circumstances, the Højesteret has decided to stay proceedings and to refer the following question to the Court for a preliminary ruling:

   'Is it compatible with Article 52 of the EC Treaty, in conjunction with Articles 56 and 58 thereof, to refuse registration of a branch of a company which has its registered office in another Member State and has been lawfully founded with company capital of GBP 100 (approximately DKK 1 000) and exists in conformity with the legislation of that Member State, where the company does not itself carry on any business but it is desired to set up the branch in order to carry on the entire business in the country in which the branch is established, and where, instead of incorporating a company in the latter Member State, that procedure must be regarded as having been employed in order to avoid paying up company capital of not less than DKK 200 000 (at present DKR 125 000)?'

14. By its question, the national court is in substance asking whether it is contrary to Articles 52 and 58 of the Treaty for a Member State to refuse to register a branch of a company formed in accordance with the legislation of another Member State in which it has its registered office but where it does not carry on any business when the purpose of the branch is to enable the company concerned to carry on its entire business in the State in which that branch is to be set up, while avoiding the formation of a company in that State, thus evading application of the rules governing the formation of companies which are, in that State, more restrictive so far as minimum paid-up share capital is concerned.

15. As a preliminary point, it should be made clear that the Board does not in any way deny that a joint stock or private limited company with its registered office in another Member State may carry on business in Denmark through a branch. It therefore agrees, as a general rule, to register in Denmark a branch of a company formed in accordance with the law of another Member State. In particular, it has added that, if Centros had conducted any business in England and Wales, the Board would have agreed to register its branch in Denmark.

16. According to the Danish Government, Article 52 of the Treaty is not applicable in the case in the main proceedings, since the situation is purely internal to Denmark. Mr and Mrs Bryde, Danish nationals, have formed a company in the United Kingdom which does not carry on any actual business there with the sole purpose of carrying on business in Denmark through a branch and thus of avoiding application of Danish legislation on the formation of private limited companies. It considers that in such circumstances the formation by nationals of one Member State of a company in another Member State does not amount to a relevant external element in the light of Community law and, in particular, freedom of establishment.

17. In this respect, it should be noted that a situation in which a company formed in accordance with the law of a Member State in which it has its registered office desires to set up a branch in another Member State falls within the scope of Community law. In that regard, it is immaterial that the company was formed in the first Member State only for the purpose of establishing itself in the second, where its main, or indeed entire, business is to be conducted (see, to this effect, *Segers* paragraph 16).

18. That Mrs and Mrs Bryde formed the company Centros in the United Kingdom for the purpose of avoiding Danish legislation requiring that a minimum amount of

share capital be paid up has not been denied either in the written observations or at the hearing. That does not, however, mean that the formation by that British company of a branch in Denmark is not covered by freedom of establishment for the purposes of Article 52 and 58 of the Treaty. The question of the application of those articles of the Treaty is different from the question whether or not a Member State may adopt measures in order to prevent attempts by certain of its nationals to evade domestic legislation by having recourse to the possibilities offered by the Treaty.

19. As to the question whether, as Mr and Mrs Bryde claim, the refusal to register in Denmark a branch of their company formed in accordance with the law of another Member State in which its has its registered office constitutes an obstacle to freedom of establishment, it must be borne in mind that that freedom, conferred by Article 52 of the Treaty on Community nationals, includes the right for them to take up and pursue activities as self-employed persons and to set up and manage undertakings under the same conditions as are laid down by the law of the Member State of establishment for its own nationals. Furthermore, under Article 58 of the Treaty companies or firms formed in accordance with the law of a Member State and having their registered office, central administration or principal place of business within the Community are to be treated in the same way as natural persons who are nationals of Member States.

20. The immediate consequence of this is that those companies are entitled to carry on their business in another Member State through an agency, branch or subsidiary. The location of their registered office, central administration or principal place of business serves as the connecting factor with the legal system of a particular State in the same way as does nationality in the case of a natural person (see, to that effect, *Segers*, paragraph 13, Case 270/83 *Commission* v *France* [1986] ECR 273, paragraph 18, Case C-330/91 *Commerzbank* [1993] ECR I-4017, paragraph 13, and Case C-264/96 *ICI* [1998] I-4695, paragraph 20).

21. Where it is the practice of a Member State, in certain circumstances, to refuse to register a branch of a company having its registered office in another Member State, the result is that companies formed in accordance with the law of that other Member State are prevented from exercising the freedom of establishment conferred on them by Articles 52 and 58 of the Treaty.

22. Consequently, that practice constitutes an obstacle to the exercise of the freedoms guaranteed by those provisions.

23. According to the Danish authorities, however, Mr and Mrs Bryde cannot rely on those provisions, since the sole purpose of the company formation which they have in mind is to circumvent the application of the national law governing formation of private limited companies and therefore constitutes abuse of the freedom of estab-

lishment. In their submission, the Kingdom of Denmark is therefore entitled to take steps to prevent such abuse by refusing to register the branch.

24. It is true that according to the case-law of the Court a Member State is entitled to take measures designed to prevent certain of its nationals from attempting, under cover of the rights created by the Treaty, improperly to circumvent their national legislation or to prevent individuals from improperly or fraudulently taking advantage of provisions of Community law (see, in particular, regarding freedom to supply services, Case 33/74 *Van Binsbergen* v *Bedrijfsvereniging Metaalnijverheid* [1974] ECR 1299, paragraph 13, Case C-148/91 *Veronica Omroep Organisatie* v *Commissariaat voor de Media* [1993] ECR I-487, paragraph 12, and Case C-23/93 *TV 10* v *Commissariaat voor de Media* [1994] ECR I-4795, paragraph 21; regarding freedom of establishment, Case 115/78 *Knoors* [1979] ECR 399, paragraph 25, and Case C-61/89 *Bouchoucha* [1990] ECR I-3551, paragraph 14; regarding the free movement of goods, Case 229/83 *Leclerc and Others* v *'Au Blé Vert' and Others* [1985] ECR 1, paragraph 27; regarding social security, Case C-206/94 *Brennet* v *Paletta* [1996] ECR I-2357, '*Paletta II*', paragraph 24; regarding freedom of movement for workers, Case 39/86 *Lair* v *Universität Hannover* [1988] ECR 3161, paragraph 43; regarding the common agricultural policy, Case C-8/92 *General Milk Products* v *Hauptzollamt Hamburg-Jonas* [1993] ECR I-779, paragraph 21, and regarding company law, Case C-367/96 *Kefalas and Others* v *Greece* [1988] ECR I-2843, paragraph 20).

25. However, although, in such circumstances, the national courts may, case by case, take account – on the basis of objective evidence – of abuse or fraudulent conduct on the part of the persons concerned in order, where appropriate, to deny them the benefit of the provisions of Community law on which they seek to rely, they must nevertheless assess such conduct in the light of the objectives pursued by those provisions (*Paletta II*, paragraph 25).

26. In the present case, the provisions of national law, application of which the parties concerned have sought to avoid, are rules governing the formation of companies and not rules concerning the carrying on of certain trades, professions or businesses. The provisions of the Treaty on freedom of establishment are intended specifically to enable companies formed in accordance with the law of a Member State and having their registered office, central administration or principal place of business within the Community to pursue activities in other Member States through an agency, branch or subsidiary.

27. That being so, the fact that a national of a Member State who wishes to set up a company chooses to form it in the Member State whose rules of company law seem to him the least restrictive and to set up branches in other Member States cannot, in itself, constitute an abuse of the right of establishment. The right to form a company in accordance with the law of a Member State and to set up branches in other

Member States is inherent in the exercise, in a single market, of the freedom of establishment guaranteed by the Treaty.

28. In this connection, the fact that company law is not completely harmonised in the Community is of little consequence. Moreover, it is always open to the Council, on the basis of the powers conferred upon it by Article 54(3)(g) of the EC Treaty, to achieve complete harmonisation.

29. In addition, it is clear from paragraph 16 of *Segers* that the fact that a company does not conduct any business in the Member State in which it has its registered office and pursues its activities only in the Member State where its branch is established is not sufficient to prove the existence of abuse or fraudulent conduct which would entitle the latter Member State to deny that company the benefit of the provisions of Community law relating to the right of establishment.

30. Accordingly, the refusal of a Member State to register a branch of a company formed in accordance with the law of another Member State in which it has its registered office on the grounds that the branch is intended to enable the company to carry on all its economic activity in the host State, with the result that the secondary establishment escapes national rules on the provision for and the paying-up of a minimum capital, is incompatible with Articles 52 and 58 of the Treaty, in so far as it prevents any exercise of the right freely to set up a secondary establishment which Articles 52 and 58 are specifically intended to guarantee.

31. The final question to be considered is whether the national practice in question might not be justified for the reasons put forward by the Danish authorities.

32. Referring both to Article 56 of the Treaty and to the case-law of the Court on imperative requirements in the general interest, the Board argues that the requirement that private limited companies provide for and pay up a minimum share capital pursues a dual objective: first, to reinforce the financial soundness of those companies in order to protect public creditors against the risk of seeing the public debts owing to them become irrecoverable since, unlike private creditors, they cannot secure those debts by means of guarantees and, second, and more generally, to protect all creditors, whether public or private, by anticipating the risk of fraudulent bankruptcy due to the insolvency of companies whose initial capitalisation was inadequate.

33. The Board adds that there is no less restrictive means of attaining this dual objective. The other way of protecting creditors, namely by introducing rules making it possible for shareholders to incur personal liability, under certain conditions, would be more restrictive than the requirement to provide for and pay up a minimum share capital.

34. It should be observed, first, that the reasons put forward do not fall within the ambit of Article 56 of the Treaty. Next, it should be borne in mind that, according to the Court's case-law, national measures liable to hinder or make less attractive the exercise of fundamental freedoms guaranteed by the Treaty must fulfil four conditions: they must be applied in a non-discriminatory manner; they must be justified by imperative requirements in the general interest; they must be suitable for securing the attainment of the objective which they pursue; and they must not go beyond what is necessary in order to attain it (see Case C-19/92 *Kraus* v *Land Baden-Württemberg* [1993] ECR I-1663, paragraph 32, and Case C-55/94 *Gebhard* v *Consiglio dell'Ordine degli Avvocati e Procuratori di Milano* [1995] ECR I-4165, paragraph 37).

35. Those conditions are not fulfilled in the case in the main proceedings. First, the practice in question is not such as to attain the objective of protecting creditors which it purports to pursue since, if the company concerned had conducted business in the United Kingdom, its branch would have been registered in Denmark, even though Danish creditors might have been equally exposed to risk.

36. Since the company concerned in the main proceedings holds itself out as a company governed by the law of England and Wales and not as a company governed by Danish law, its creditors are on notice that it is covered by laws different from those which govern the formation of private limited companies in Denmark and they can refer to certain rules of Community law which protect them, such as the Fourth Council Directive 78/660/EEC of 25 July 1978 based on Article 54(3)(g) of the Treaty on the annual accounts of certain types of companies (OJ 1978 L 222, p. 11), and the Eleventh Council Directive 89/666/EEC of 21 December 1989 concerning disclosure requirements in respect of branches opened in a Member State by certain types of company governed by the law of another State (OJ 1989 L 395, p. 36).

37. Second, contrary to the arguments of the Danish authorities, it is possible to adopt measures which are less restrictive, or which interfere less with fundamental freedoms, by, for example, making it possible in law for public creditors to obtain the necessary guarantees.

38. Lastly, the fact that a Member State may not refuse to register a branch of a company formed in accordance with the law of another Member State in which it has its registered office does not preclude that first State from adopting any appropriate measure for preventing or penalising fraud, either in relation to the company itself, if need be in cooperation with the Member State in which it was formed, or in relation to its members, where it has been established that they are in fact attempting, by means of the formation of the company, to evade their obligations towards private or public creditors established on the territory of a Member State concerned. In any event, combating fraud cannot justify a practice of refusing to register a branch of a company which has its registered office in another Member State.

39. The answer to the question referred must therefore be that it is contrary to Articles 52 and 58 of the Treaty for a Member State to refuse to register a branch of a company formed in accordance with the law of another Member State in which it has its registered office but in which it conducts no business where the branch is intended to enable the company in question to carry on its entire business in the State in which that branch is to be created, while avoiding the need to form a company there, thus evading application of the rules governing the formation of companies which, in that State, are more restrictive as regards the paying up of a minimum share capital. That interpretation does not, however, prevent the authorities of the Member State concerned from adopting any appropriate measure for preventing or penalising fraud, either in relation to the company itself, if need be in cooperation with the Member State in which it was formed, or in relation to its members, where it has been established that they are in fact attempting, by means of the formation of a company, to evade their obligations towards private or public creditors established in the territory of the Member State concerned.

Costs

[Para. 40 omitted]

On those grounds,

THE COURT,

in answer to the question referred to it by the Højesteret by order of 3 June 1997, hereby rules:

It is contrary to Articles 52 and 58 of the EC Treaty for a Member State to refuse to register a branch of a company formed in accordance with the law of another Member State in which it has its registered office but in which it conducts no business where the branch is intended to enable the company in question to carry on its entire business in the State in which that branch is to be created, while avoiding the need to form a company there, thus evading application of the rules governing the formation of companies which, in that State, are more restrictive as regards the paying up of a minimum share capital. That interpretation does not, however, prevent the authorities of the Member State concerned from adopting any appropriate measure for preventing or penalising fraud, either in relation to the company itself, if need be in cooperation with the Member State in which it was formed, or in relation to its members, where it has been established that they are in fact attempting, by means of the formation of a company, to evade their obligations towards private or public creditors established in the territory of the Member State concerned.

Comments and questions

In Case C-212/97 *Centros Ltd* v *Erhvervs- og Selskabsstyrelsen* [1999] ECR I-1459, the CJEU overruled the decision of the Danish Commerce and Companies Agency which refused to register a branch of an English private limited company, where it was clear that the 'set-up' was intended to circumvent the Danish minimum capital requirements for limited companies. The CJEU stated that under the (now) TFEU rules on freedom of establishment, the refusal to register a branch of a company which has been lawfully established in another Member State could only be upheld either if the reasons for so doing fall within the ambit of (now) Article 52 TFEU which was not the situation in this case, or where the rules

(1) are applied in a non-discriminatory manner,
(2) are justified by imperative requirements in the general interest,
(3) are appropriate for attaining the objective which they pursue, and
(4) do not go beyond what is necessary in order to attain the objective (see paragraph 34).

The CJEU dismissed the idea that these four concurrent conditions were satisfied. The aim of the practice of the Danish Commerce and Companies Agency was to combat the risk of fraudulent bankruptcy due to the insolvency of companies whose initial capitalisation was inadequate (see paragraph 32). However, the CJEU dismissed the idea that this practice was well suited for this purpose, pointing out that the Commerce and Companies Agency would have registered the branch if the company had conducted business in the United Kingdom, even though Danish creditors could have been equally exposed to risk (see paragraph 35).

Another argument put forward by the Commerce and Companies Agency was that the Danish State should protect public creditors against the risk of seeing the public debts owing to them become irrecoverable since, unlike private creditors, it cannot itself choose whether or not to give credit to undertakings. The State is thus an obligatory creditor. The Agency argued that there was a need for a minimum capital requirement in order to protect the interests of the State. What was the response of the CJEU to this (see in particular paragraph 37)?

The *Centros* case concerns freedom of establishment. Is there the same freedom of establishment for trust funds? What difference will it make if the trust fund is a not-for-profit fund?

One interesting aspect of the *Centros* case is the rejection by the CJEU of the idea of applying the '*Binsbergen* doctrine' to Centros Ltd. This doctrine is reviewed in paragraph 24 of the *Centros* judgment. The essence of the *Binsbergen* doctrine is that a Member State is entitled to take measures to prevent its nationals from putting themselves in a situation which is governed by Union law, for example where the four freedoms apply, *merely* in order to circumvent the requirements which the Member State imposes on undertakings established in the Member State. The doctrine thus hinders the rules on freedom of movement being used merely to create a better legal position. In this respect see Case 33/74 *van Binsbergen* v *Bestuur van de Bedrijfsvereniging voor de Metaalnijverheid* [1974] ECR 1299, printed in Chapter 6. The reason why the CJEU refused to regard the behaviour of Mr and Mrs Bryde in the *Centros* case as improper or fraudulent was presumably because they had *solely* wanted to avoid the stricter Danish requirements for share capital in connection with *setting up* a private limited company. There was no suggestion that the couple wanted to avoid the Danish rules on carrying on some specific commercial undertaking. In this respect the *Centros* case is distinguished from the *TV 10* case, in which a media company tried to avoid being subject to the Dutch rules on television broadcasts. This difference is reflected in paragraph 26 of the *Centros* judgment, where it is stated that 'the provisions of national law, application of which the parties concerned have sought to avoid, are rules governing the *formation* of companies and *not* rules concerning the *carrying on* of certain trades, professions or businesses' (emphasis added). Mr and Mrs Bryde had merely exercised the right, under (now) Article 49 TFEU, to choose where it was most advantageous to form a company. There was therefore no improper conduct; cf. paragraph 27, in which the CJEU stated: 'The right to form a company in accordance with the law of a Member State and to set up branches in other Member States is inherent in the exercise, in a single market, of the freedom of establishment guaranteed by the Treaty.' In other words, the rules on establishment give those setting up a company freedom of choice as to which Member State's laws they wish the company to be formed under. These laws can normally be relied on by the company so formed, even where the only link with the Member State is that it is where the company is incorporated.

Consider whether the CJEU would have arrived at a different conclusion if Mr and Mrs Bryde had intended to avoid the Danish rules on employee representation.

In Case C-210/06 *Cartesio* [2008] ECR I-9641, a Hungarian court referred a question for preliminary ruling on whether a company could rely on Articles 49 and 54 TFEU with regard to being able to transfer its company seat to another Member State, even though this might be contrary to the law of the original Member State. In the case in question, the Cartesio company wanted to transfer its seat from Hungary to Italy, while remaining a Hungarian company, i.e. without changing what national law were to apply to the company. The Hungarian authorities had rejected this application on the ground that this was contrary to Hungarian law.

The CJEU answered the question by saying that, as long as the area of the law in question had not been harmonised, a Member State has the power to define both the connecting factors required of a company to be considered established under that Member State's laws and thus capable of enjoying the right of establishment under the TFEU, and the Member State has the power to define those connecting factors that are required if the company is to be able subsequently to maintain that status. The CJEU also stated that this power includes the possibility for a Member State not to permit a company governed by its law to retain that status if the company intends to reorganise itself by moving its seat to the territory of another Member State, thereby breaking the connecting factors required under the national law of the Member State of incorporation.

Normally a company's real seat is situated in the Member State where it is registered, and there is no conflict between real seat state criteria and incorporation state criteria. However, where the real seat state and incorporation state are not the same, there can be significant problems. Assume, for example, that a company is formed in the United Kingdom which follows the incorporation state doctrine. The company's head office is later moved to Germany, which follows the real seat doctrine. In the United Kingdom the company will still be regarded as a properly constituted legal person. In Germany, under the real seat doctrine, the company will be required to comply with the German law in order to be recognised as a legal person. This means that the company will have to be re-incorporated in Germany. If this requirement is not satisfied, the company's existence will not be recognised in Germany – it will thus not have the capacity to act there. It was precisely this situation which arose in Case C-208/00 *Überseering BV* v *Nordic Construction Company Baumanagement* [2002] ECR I-9919. Überseering was a company formed under the laws of the Netherlands, and it moved its real seat, apparently without intending to do so, from the Netherlands to Germany, since all its shares were sold to some Germans. Under German law the company's legal capacity should be judged according to the laws of the place where it has its real seat, which in this case, according to German law, meant Germany. In order to have legal capacity in Germany, the company had to be re-incorporated in Germany, and this re-incorporation had not taken place. The question was whether this rule contravened the provision on the freedom of establishment, and if so, whether it could be justified.

The CJEU made it clear that: where a company which is validly incorporated in Member State 'A', in which it has its registered office, is deemed under the law of a Member State 'B' to have moved its actual centre of administration to Member State B, following the transfer of all its shares to nationals of that State residing there, the rules which Member State B applies to that company do not, as Union law now stands, fall outside the scope of Union rules on freedom of establishment. Überseering could therefore rely on the right of freedom of establishment to oppose the German refusal to accept that the company had capacity as a legal person and capacity to act.

The CJEU also held that Überseering, as a company lawfully formed in the Netherlands, where it had its registered domicile, was entitled to exercise freedom of establishment in Germany, under Articles 49 and 54 TFEU, as a company formed under Dutch law. This was not altered by the fact that after its formation the whole of the company's share capital had been acquired by German nationals resident in Germany, since this had not led to the company losing its status as a legal person under Dutch law. The CJEU added that the very existence of the company was inextricably bound up in its character as a company under Dutch law, since a company only existed by virtue of the national laws which determined its formation and functioning. The requirement for the company to be re-incorporated in Germany was therefore tantamount to a denial of the right of establishment.

The German authorities had argued that, to the extent that the German requirements constituted a restriction on freedom of establishment, this was based on legitimate considerations. The CJEU acknowledged that it was possible that overriding reasons of public policy, such as protecting the interests of creditors, minority shareholders, employees and even of the tax authorities may, in some circumstances and subject to certain conditions, justify restrictions on freedom of establishment. However, such objectives cannot justify denying legal capacity and thus the capacity to be a party to legal proceedings to a company properly incorporated in another Member State in which it has its registered office. The CJEU repeated that such a measure is tantamount to an outright negation of the freedom of establishment conferred on companies by Articles 49 and 54 TFEU.

Both the *Centros* and the *Überseering* cases concerned companies formed in accordance with the law of Member States which followed the incorporation state doctrine, but where the companies' real seats were in other Member States. The question is whether the real links to a Member State affect that Member State's capacity to require compliance with its mandatory rules by a company whose existence is based on the laws of another Member State.

It has been argued that the *Centros* and *Überseering* decisions are the final reckoning for the real seat doctrine. Do you agree with this view? Consider if it makes a difference whether the situation concerns two Member States which both apply the incorporation state doctrine or two Member States which both apply the real seat doctrine, or whether the situation concerns a company which is incorporated in a Member State which applies the real seat doctrine, but where the company has its real seat in a Member State which applies the incorporation state doctrine – or vice versa, or a situation in which a company is either incorporated in or has its real seat in a non-Member State.

Did the CJEU in the *Centros* and *Überseering* cases take a view as to whether the disputed measures could be characterised as discriminatory? Do you think that these were directly discriminatory measures?

Both the United Kingdom and the Netherlands apply the incorporation state doctrine. However, the Netherlands has a special law on 'formally foreign companies', i.e., companies which have been incorporated under the laws of another state, but which carry on virtually all their activities in the Netherlands, without having any substantive connection with the state of incorporation. This law lays down requirements on the disclosure of information, liability, minimum capital and special accounting requirements. In Case C-167/01 *Kamer van Koophandel en Fabrieken voor Amsterdam* v *Inspire Art Ltd* [2003] ECR I-10155, the CJEU decided that it was contrary to the rules on freedom of establishment that the Dutch authorities required compliance with Dutch company law by a company incorporated in the United Kingdom, but which carried on all its activities in the Netherlands. As in the *Centros* case, the CJEU stated that the reason for choosing to set up a company in a particular Member State was not relevant to the application of the rules on freedom of establishment, except in the case of fraud; cf. paragraph 95 of the judgment.

JUDGMENT OF THE COURT
1 February 2001

Criminal proceedings against Dennis Mac Quen and others. (Reference for a preliminary ruling: Tribunal de premièère instance de Bruxelles – Belgium)

'Interpretation of Article 5 of the EC Treaty (now Article 10 EC) and of Articles 30, 52 and 59 of the EC Treaty (now, after amendment, Articles 28 EC, 43 EC and 49 EC) – National legislation prohibiting opticians from carrying out certain optical examinations – National legislation restricting the marketing of equipment for carrying out certain optical examinations which are reserved exclusively for ophthalmologists'

Case C-108/96

Judgment

1. By judgment of 27 March 1996, received at the Court on 3 April 1996, the Tribunal de Premièère Instance de Bruxelles (Court of First Instance, Brussels) referred to the Court for a preliminary ruling under Article 177 of the EC Treaty (now Article 234 EC) two questions on the interpretation of Article 5 of the EC Treaty (now Article 10 EC) and of Articles 30, 52 and 59 of the EC Treaty (now, after amendment, Articles 28 EC, 43 EC and 49 EC).

2. Those questions have arisen in criminal proceedings brought against Ms Godts, Mr Mac Quen, Mr Antoun and Mr Pouton, and Grandvision Belgium SA (Grandvision), in its capacity as employer of the four accused, for having unlawfully performed one or more acts relating to the practice of medicine.

The legal framework

3. The applicable provisions of national law are to be found in the Royal Decree of 30 October 1964 (Moniteur Belge (Belgian Official Journal) of 24 December 1964, p. 13274), establishing the conditions governing the exercise of the profession of optician and spectacle-maker in skilled-trade undertakings, small and medium-size businesses and small-scale industries, as amended by the Royal Decrees of 16 September 1966, 14 January 1975, 3 October 1978 and 2 March 1988 (Moniteur Belge of 17 March 1988, p. 3812), and in Royal Decree No 78 of 10 November 1967 on the exercise of medical, nursing and paramedical professions and on the medical committees dealing with the prevention of the unlawful practice of medicine (Moniteur Belge of 14 November 1967, p. 11881).

4. Article 2(1) of the Royal Decree of 30 October 1964 provides:

   The profession of optician shall, for the purposes of the present Decree, consist in the habitual and independent exercise of one or more of the following activities:
   (a) the offering to the public, sale, maintenance and repair of optical articles designed to correct and/or compensate vision;
   (a) a the trial, adaptation, sale and maintenance of artificial eyes;
   (b) the making-up of prescriptions issued by ophthalmologists for the purpose of correcting vision.

5. Article 2(1), first subparagraph, of Royal Decree No 78 provides:

   No person may operate as a medical practitioner unless he or she holds the statutory qualification of medical doctor, surgeon or obstetrician obtained in accordance with the legislation on the conferment of academic titles and the syllabus for university examinations, unless that person has been lawfully exempted from that requirement and also satisfies the conditions laid down by Article 7(1) or (2).

6. The second subparagraph of Article 2(1) of Royal Decree No 78 provides:

   The unlawful practice of medicine shall consist in the habitual performance, by a person who does not satisfy all of the requisite conditions under the first subparagraph of the present paragraph, of any act involving, or stated to involve, in regard to a human being, an examination of that person's state of health, detection of disease and deficiencies, establishment of a diagnosis, introduction or administration of treatment for a pathological state, whether physical or mental, real or imaginary, or vaccination.

7. By judgment of 28 June 1989 (Cass., 28 June 1989, Pas. 1989 I-1182), the Belgian Cour de Cassation (Court of Cassation) ruled that account had to be taken of the provisions of Royal Decree No 78 in construing Article 2(1) of the Royal Decree of 30 October 1964.

8. The Cour de Cassation ruled in that judgment that, while opticians who are not medical doctors are authorised to perform acts designed to correct defects of a purely optical nature, whether or not they use equipment or instruments for that purpose, they are none the less prohibited from examining the state of vision of their clients otherwise than by using a method under which the patient alone determines the sight defects from which he suffers, inter alia on the basis of printed scales which may be incorporated in a control instrument and which the patient himself corrects by choosing, as the optician proposes, the lenses which satisfy him. The optician is obliged to advise his client to consult an ophthalmologist if the indications thus obtained leave any doubt as to the nature of the defect which has been established.

The facts of the main proceedings and the questions submitted for preliminary ruling

9. According to the case-file, Grandvision is a limited-liability company with its registered office in Brussels. Grandvision belongs to a group of companies marketing products and services in the field of optics. It is controlled by Vision Express UK Ltd, a company established under English law. Mr Mac Quen was the managing director of Vision Express UK before acting, from November 1990 to July 1991, as general manager of Vision Express Belgium SA. Mr Pouton succeeded him in this capacity from July 1991 to 1993.

10. Shortly after being established, Vision Express Belgium SA distributed in Belgium advertisements for a variety of eyesight examinations conducted in its shops, including, inter alia, computer tonometry intended to test for internal hypertension of the eye, general retinoscopy designed to examine the state of the retina, as well as a measurement of the field of vision using state-of-the-art equipment and biomicroscopy to check the state of your cornea, your conjunctiva, eyelids and tear ducts .... It appears that these advertisements were a verbatim translation of Vision Express UK Ltd's advertisements in the United Kingdom.

11. On the basis of those advertisements, the Union Professionnelle Belge des Médecins Spécialistes en Ophtalmologie et Chirurgie Oculaire (Belgian Association of Ophthalmologists and Eye Surgeons) (UPBMO) lodged a complaint in September 1991 against Grandvision alleging unlawful practice of medicine and use of misleading advertising, and appeared as the civil plaintiff in the criminal proceedings subsequently instituted.

12. At the conclusion of the criminal investigation, proceedings against Mr Mac Quen and Mr Pouton, together with Mr Antoun, an optician, Ms Godts, a secretary, and Grandvision which, as the employer of the four accused, was civilly liable were instituted before the Tribunal de Premièère Instance de Bruxelles, sitting in criminal matters.

13. Since it was unsure whether the Belgian legislation referred to in paragraphs 3 to 6 of the present judgment, as construed by the Cour de Cassation, was consistent with Community law, the Tribunal de Premièère Instance de Bruxelles decided to stay proceedings and to refer the following questions to the Court for a preliminary ruling:

    1. Is a prohibition, arising from the interpretation or the application of a provision of national law, restraining opticians in other Member States from offering within a Member State, for the correction of purely optical defects, services consisting of an objective eyesight examination, that is to say otherwise than by using a method by which the client himself determines the eyesight defects and

sees to the correction to be made, compatible with Articles 5, 52 and 59 of the EC Treaty?

2. Are obstacles within a Member State to the marketing of equipment which enables an objective eyesight examination to be carried out with a view to correcting purely optical defects, such as, for example, an autorefractor, arising from the ban imposed by national law on opticians established in other Member States preventing them from offering, within that Member State, services consisting of an objective eyesight examination, that is to say a non-subjective examination, for the correction of purely optical defects, compatible with Article 30 of the EC Treaty?

14. UPBMO appealed against that decision. The President of the Court of Justice therefore decided, by order of 28 June 1996, to stay proceedings. After the Belgian Cour de Cassation, on appeal from a judgment of the Cour d'Appel de Bruxelles (Brussels Court of Appeal), confirmed, by judgment of 12 May 1999, that the appeal brought before it by UPBMO had been withdrawn, the proceedings before the Court of Justice resumed on 11 June 1999.

Preliminary observations

15. UPBMO submits that the dispute in the main proceedings concerns a purely internal situation which has no connection with Community law. It argues that the situation of Grandvision, being a company established under Belgian law and operating in Belgium, does not come within the scope of Community law.

16. In this regard, it is clear from the observations submitted to the Court and from the details provided at the hearing that Grandvision is a limited-liability company which was established under Belgian law in 1990 under the name Vision Express Belgium SA by the Netherlands company VE Holdings BV. As a subsidiary of Vision Express UK Ltd, a company governed by English law, it belongs to a group of companies established in various Member States which markets products and services in the optics sector. The legal position of such a company comes within the scope of Community law pursuant to the provisions of Article 52 of the Treaty.

17. Grandvision contends that the Belgian authorities disagree as to the interpretation of the national legislation cited in paragraph 3 of the present judgment. More particularly, it argues that the interpretation adopted by the Cour de Cassation, which would prohibit opticians who are not qualified medical doctors from conducting objective eyesight examinations and reserve this type of examination to ophthalmologists, is not shared by other Belgian courts, so that it is not established that opticians are necessarily prohibited from conducting such examinations in Belgium.

18. As to that, where there are actual or apparent differences in analysis between the administrative or judicial authorities of a Member State regarding the proper construction of national legislation, particularly in respect of its exact scope, it is not for the Court to rule on which interpretation is in accordance, or most in accordance, with Community law. On the other hand, the Court is required to interpret Community law with regard to a factual and legal situation such as that described by the referring court, in order to provide that court with such guidance as will assist it in resolving the dispute before it.

The questions submitted for preliminary ruling

19. By its questions, the national court is in substance asking whether Articles 5, 30, 52 and 59 of the Treaty preclude the competent authorities of a Member State from interpreting the national law governing the practice of medicine in such a way that, within the context of the correction of purely optical defects, the objective examination of a client's eyesight, that is to say, an examination which does not use a method under which the client alone determines the optical defects from which he is suffering, is reserved to ophthalmologists, to the exclusion, in particular, of opticians who are not qualified medical doctors.

20. Since the main proceedings do not involve a supply of services provided by Grandvision or its employees to recipients established in other Member States and do not relate to the obligations of Member States within the meaning of Article 5 of the Treaty, it is unnecessary to consider whether the prohibition in issue in the main proceedings (the prohibition under challenge) is or is not in accordance with Articles 5 and 59 of the Treaty.

21. So far as Article 30 of the Treaty is concerned, even assuming the prohibition under challenge to be restrictive of the free movement of goods, those restrictive effects would be the unavoidable consequence of that prohibition. To the extent that the prohibition might be justified, its effects would have to be accepted for the purposes of Article 30 of the Treaty.

22. With regard to Article 52 of the Treaty, it is to be observed at the outset that the question whether an objective examination of eyesight is an activity reserved to ophthalmologists is not regulated by Council Directives 75/362/EEC and 75/363/EEC of 16 June 1975 concerning, respectively, the mutual recognition of diplomas, certificates and other evidence of formal qualifications in medicine, including measures to facilitate the effective exercise of the right of establishment and freedom to provide services, and the coordination of provisions laid down by law, regulation or administrative action in respect of activities of doctors (OJ 1975 L 167, p. 1 and p. 14), nor is it regulated by Council Directive 93/16/EEC of 5 April 1993 to facilitate the free movement of doctors and the mutual recognition of their diplomas, certificates and other evidence of formal qualifications (OJ 1993 L 165,

p. 1), which repealed the two directives first mentioned. Furthermore, it is common ground that the activity of optician is not the subject of any specific Community legislation.

23. UPBMO submits that, in those circumstances, Member States are entitled to reserve certain eyesight examinations to those persons who are best qualified, that is to say, ophthalmologists. In paragraph 12 of its judgment in Case C-61/89 *Bouchoucha* [1990] ECR I-3551, the Court recognised that, in the absence of Community legislation governing the paramedical activity at issue in that case, each Member State is free to regulate the exercise of that activity within its territory, on condition only that it does not discriminate between its own nationals and those of the other Member States. The same considerations must, UPBMO submits, obtain in the main proceedings here.

24. While it is true that, in the absence of harmonisation of the activities at issue in the main proceedings, Member States remain, in principle, competent to define the exercise of those activities, they must none the less, when exercising their powers in this area, respect the basic freedoms guaranteed by the Treaty (see Joined Cases C-193/97 and C-194/97 *De Castro Freitas and Escallier* [1998] ECR I-6747, paragraph 23, and judgment of 3 October 2000 in Case C-58/98 *Corsten* [2000] ECR I-7919, paragraph 31).

25. The second paragraph of Article 52 of the Treaty provides that freedom of establishment is to be exercised under the conditions which the legislation of the country of establishment lays down for its own nationals. It follows that, where the taking-up or pursuit of a specific activity is subject to such conditions in the host Member State, a national of another Member State intending to pursue that activity must in principle comply with those conditions (Case C-55/94 *Gebhard* [1995] ECR I-4165, paragraph 36).

26. According to the Court's case-law, however, national measures liable to hinder or make less attractive the exercise of fundamental freedoms guaranteed by the Treaty can be justified only if they fulfil four conditions: they must be applied in a non-discriminatory manner; they must be justified by overriding reasons based on the general interest; they must be suitable for securing the attainment of the objective which they pursue; and they must not go beyond what is necessary in order to attain that objective (see, in particular, judgments in Case C-19/92 *Kraus* [1993] ECR I-1663, paragraph 32, in *Gebhard*, cited above, paragraph 37, and, most recently, of 4 July 2000 in Case C-424/97 *Haim* [2000] ECR I-5123, paragraph 57).

27. In that regard, first of all, the prohibition under challenge applies irrespective of the nationality and Member State of establishment of those to whom it is addressed.

28. Next, with regard to the question whether there are overriding reasons based on the general interest which may justify the restriction on freedom of establishment resulting from the prohibition under challenge, it must be remembered that the protection of public health is one of the reasons which may, under Article 56(1) of the EC Treaty (now, after amendment, Article 46(1) EC), justify restrictions resulting from special treatment for foreign nationals. Protection of public health is therefore, in principle, also capable of justifying national measures which apply indiscriminately, such as those in this case.

29. The importance of protecting public health is also emphasised by the fact that Article 3(o) of the EC Treaty (now, after amendment, Article 3(1)(p) EC) provides that the activities of the Community are to include, as provided in the Treaty and in accordance with the timetable set out therein, a contribution to the attainment of a high level of health protection.

30. The choice of a Member State to reserve to a category of professionals holding specific qualifications, such as ophthalmologists, the right to carry out objective eyesight examinations on their patients using sophisticated instruments that make it possible to assess internal eye pressure, determine the field of vision or analyse the condition of the retina, may be regarded as an appropriate means by which to ensure attainment of a high level of health protection.

31. That being so, it is necessary to consider whether the prohibition under challenge is necessary and proportionate to secure the objective of attaining a high level of health protection.

32. While it acknowledges the importance of public health, Grandvision denies that the mere fact that ophthalmologists have higher professional qualifications than opticians is such as to justify objective examinations of purely optical defects being reserved to them. It has not, Grandvision submits, been established that the use of those instruments by opticians involves a risk to public health, particularly bearing in mind the fact that the activities at issue in the main proceedings are lawful in other Member States even when carried out by opticians who are not qualified medical doctors.

33. It should be borne in mind in this regard that the fact that one Member State imposes less strict rules than another Member State does not mean that the latter's rules are disproportionate and hence incompatible with Community law (Case C-384/93 *Alpine Investments* [1995] ECR I-1141, paragraph 51, and Case C-3/95 *Reisebüüro Broede* [1996] ECR I-6511, paragraph 42).

34. The mere fact that a Member State has chosen a system of protection different from that adopted by another Member State cannot affect the appraisal as to the need for

and proportionality of the provisions adopted (Case C-67/98 *Zenatti* [1999] ECR I-7289, paragraph 34).

35. It must, however, be pointed out that the prohibition under challenge, which is relied on in the main proceedings as the basis for criminal charges, is not expressly provided for by any legislative provision of national law but follows rather from the interpretation which the Belgian Cour de Cassation gave in 1989 to a number of relevant national provisions with a view to attaining a high level of protection of public health. It appears that that interpretation is based on an assessment of the risks to public health which might result if opticians were authorised to carry out certain eyesight examinations.

36. An assessment of this kind is liable to change with the passage of time, particularly as a result of technical and scientific progress. It is significant in this regard that the Bundesverfassungsgericht (Federal Constitutional Court) (Germany) concluded, in its decision of 7 August 2000 (1 BvR 254/99), that the risks which might follow from authorising opticians to carry out certain examinations of their clients' eyesight, such as tonometry and computerised perimetry, are not such as to preclude them from conducting those examinations.

37. It is for the national court to assess, in the light of the Treaty requirements relating to freedom of establishment and the demands of legal certainty and the protection of public health, whether the interpretation of domestic law adopted by the competent national authorities in that regard remains a valid basis for the prosecutions brought in the case in the main proceedings.

38. The answer to the questions submitted for a preliminary ruling must therefore be that, as Community law stands at present, Article 52 of the Treaty does not preclude the competent authorities of a Member State from interpreting the national law governing the practice of medicine in such a way that, within the context of the correction of purely optical defects, the objective examination of a client's eyesight, that is to say, an examination which does not use a method under which the client alone determines the optical defects from which he is suffering, is reserved, for reasons relating to the protection of public health, to a category of professionals holding specific qualifications, such as ophthalmologists, to the exclusion, in particular, of opticians who are not qualified medical doctors. It is for the national court to assess, in the light of the Treaty requirements relating to freedom of establishment and the demands of legal certainty and the protection of public health, whether the interpretation of domestic law adopted by the competent national authorities in that regard remains a valid basis for the prosecutions brought in the case in the main proceedings.

Costs

[Para. 39 omitted]

On those grounds,

THE COURT (Fifth Chamber),

in answer to the questions referred to it by the Tribunal de Premièère Instance de Bruxelles by judgment of 27 March 1996, hereby rules:

> **As Community law stands at present, Article 52 of the EC Treaty (now, after amendment, Article 43 EC) does not preclude the competent authorities of a Member State from interpreting the national law governing the practice of medicine in such a way that, within the context of the correction of purely optical defects, the objective examination of a client's eyesight, that is to say, an examination which does not use a method under which the client alone determines the optical defects from which he is suffering, is reserved, for reasons relating to the protection of public health, to a category of professionals holding specific qualifications, such as ophthalmologists, to the exclusion, in particular, of opticians who are not qualified medical doctors. It is for the national court to assess, in the light of the Treaty requirements relating to freedom of establishment and the demands of legal certainty and the protection of public health, whether the interpretation of domestic law adopted by the competent national authorities in that regard remains a valid basis for the prosecutions brought in the case in the main proceedings.**

Comments and questions

Judgment in Case C-108/96 *Mac Quen and others* [2001] ECR I-837, was given by a chamber of three judges, which limits its precedent value. Nevertheless, the judgment contains an interesting statement of when a purely internal situation will be found to exist, and it is a fine example of how the CJEU examines whether a national law contravenes the (now) TFEU provisions on freedom of movement.

Vision Express was an English company providing optician's services. It was active in a number of Member States via subsidiary companies. In Belgium it operated via a subsidiary company Grandvision, which was incorporated under Belgian law. In the United Kingdom the company was free to provide a number of advanced services, whereas in Belgium these services could only be provided by a qualified ophthalmologist.

The first question to be considered by the CJEU was whether the case concerned a purely internal situation, which was not subject to the relevant Treaty provisions. In his Opinion, the Advocate General had limited himself to simply observing: 'it is clear from the findings of the national court ... that the case before it involves sufficient trans-frontier elements. The Court therefore has jurisdiction to rule on the two questions referred to it.' The CJEU itself was less laconic. It stated that '[a]s a subsidiary of Vision Express UK Ltd, a company governed by English law, [Grandvision] belongs to a group of companies established in various Member States which markets products and services in the optics sector. The legal position of such a company comes within the scope of Union law pursuant to the provisions of Article [49 TFEU]'; see paragraph 16 of the judgment. Does this statement mean, in effect, that the TFEU rules on freedom of establishment will always apply in cases which involve a subsidiary which has a parent company in another Member State? Do you find the CJEU's definition of a 'purely internal situation' reasonable?

Having established that the case was subject to the Treaty provisions on freedom of establishment, in paragraph 20 the CJEU dismissed the idea that the case was subject to the rules on the freedom to provide services. The CJEU justified this view on the grounds that the case did not concern the provision of services to recipients established in other Member States. The Advocate General reached the same conclusion, but on the different grounds that Grandvision's activities were not carried out temporarily in Belgium. The Advocate General also pointed out that the TFEU provisions in the chapter on services are subordinate to those of the chapter on the right of establishment. Why did the CJEU not follow the view of the Advocate General? Do you agree that the case concerned the right of establishment (pursuant to Article 57 TFEU) and not the freedom to provide services?

To the extent that the case concerned the right of establishment, consider whether the disputed prohibition prevented the establishment of optician's businesses in Belgium, or whether the prohibition was more concerned with the requirements for carrying on business as an optician? On this basis, consider whether it could be argued that the prohibition ought to be covered by a rule similar to the *Keck* doctrine, or whether the effects of the prohibition should be considered as being too uncertain and indirect for the prohibition to be regarded as being a restriction on the right of establishment.

The Belgian rules requiring that certain eye examinations should only be undertaken by an ophthalmologist meant that the instruments used for the examinations could not be sold to opticians. However, in paragraph 21 the CJEU dismissed the idea that the case fell under the TFEU rules on the freedom of movement of goods. How did it justify this decision?

In considering whether the disputed prohibition was lawful under the terms of Article 49 TFEU, the CJEU found that the prohibition applied irrespective of the nationality and Member State of establishment of those to whom it was addressed. Next, the CJEU found that the prohibition was intended to protect public health, which is a lawful objective. Finally, the CJEU held the prohibition was proportionate to the objective of public health protection. In this respect the CJEU rejected the idea that it was significant that, in other Member States, opticians are permitted to carry out examinations which, in Belgium, are reserved to a category of professionals holding specific qualifications. The CJEU added that it is for the referring national court to make a careful assessment of whether the prohibition is necessary and reasonable in relation to its purposes. In assessing this, the national court should not merely rely on previous assessments, such as previous court decisions, but must assess the question in the light of such technical and scientific progress as may have taken place in this area.

What decision do you think the referring national court ought to come to?

Would the decision have been different if there had been existing harmonisation of Union law on the conduct of opticians' business, which gave the Member States the possibility of allowing, but did not require them to allow, opticians to perform the services which were the subject of this dispute?

The question of when there is a 'purely internal situation' is well illustrated by two judgments, both of which were given by the CJEU's First Chamber on 3 October 1990. These were Joined Cases C-54/88, C-91/88 and C-14/89 *Nino* [1990] ECR I-3537 and Case C-61/89 *Bouchoucha* [1990] ECR I-3551. Both cases concerned the right to carry on paramedical activities. However, all the facts of the *Nino* case related to only one Member State. Thus in paragraph 10 of its judgment the CJEU stated:

> 'It is apparent from the documents before the Court that all the accused are Italian nationals who qualified as biotherapists and pranotherapists while residing in Italy and who have been charged under Article 348 of the Italian Penal Code as a result of treatment administered solely within the territory of that Member State. All these factors demonstrate that the main proceedings concern situations which are purely internal to a Member State.'

In paragraph 11 the CJEU went on to state that: 'the absence of any element going beyond a purely national setting in a given case means, in matters of freedom of establishment, that the provisions of [Union] law are not applicable to such a situation.' Compare this with paragraphs 16 and 17 of Joined Cases C-64/96 and C-65/96 *Jacquet* [1997] ECR I-3171, printed in Chapter 4. It is clear from both the *Nino* and the *Jacquet* cases that the provisions of neither Article 45 nor Article 49 TFEU are applicable to a case where there is no relevant cross-border activity, regardless of whether the national rules in question in fact constitute discrimination or a restriction. In contrast to this, see Case C-281/98 *Angonese* [2000] ECR I-4139, printed above in Chapter 4.

In contrast to the *Nino* case, the *Bouchoucha* involved the exercise of the right to free movement by M. Bouchoucha who had acquired a vocational qualification in another Member State than his native France. Thus the case did not concern a 'purely internal situation', so the CJEU had to consider whether (now) Article 49 TFEU applied. The CJEU found, if indirectly, that Bouchoucha could rely on Article 49 TFEU. However, Article 49 TFEU did not prevent a Member State reserving the practice of a paramedical activity, such as osteopathy, exclusively to persons holding the qualification of doctor of medicine. At the relevant date there was no Union harmonisation of what is covered by the qualification of doctor of medicine, and this meant that France could maintain a requirement for such a qualification.

However, the CJEU has modified its practice since the *Nino* case. Thus the CJEU now accepts references for preliminary rulings relating to Article 49 TFEU for substantive hearing, even if all the elements of the case are linked to only one Member State. This will be the case if the CJEU finds it possible that the disputed provisions of national law will have cross-border effects; see for example Joined Cases C-159/12 to C-161/12 *Venturini*, printed below.

JUDGMENT OF THE COURT (Fourth Chamber)
5 December 2013

Alessandra Venturini and others v ASL Varese, Ministero della Salute, Regione Lombardia, Comune di Saronno, Agenzia Italiana del Farmaco (AIFA) and others (Request for a preliminary ruling: Tribunale amministrativo regionale per la Lombardia – Italy)

'Freedom of establishment – Article 49 TFEU – Public health – National legislation prohibiting para-pharmacies from selling prescription-only medicinal products the cost of which is borne by the patient'

Joined Cases C-159/12 to C-161/12

Judgment

1. These requests for a preliminary ruling concern the interpretation of Article 49 TFEU.

2. The requests have been made in proceedings between Ms Venturini (Case C-159/12), Ms Gramegna (Case C-160/12) and Ms Muzzio (Case C-161/12), who are three qualified pharmacists, registered with the Milan Order of Pharmacists and owners of business premises ('para-pharmacies'), and the Aziende Sanitarie Locali (ASL) (local health authorities), namely the Varese ASL (Case C-159/12), the Lodi ASL (Case C-160/12), and the Pavia ASL (Case C-161/12), the Ministero della Salute, the Regione Lombardia, the Comune di Saronno (Case C-159/12), the Comune di Sant'Angelo Lodigiano (Case C-160/12) and the Comune de Bereguardo (Case C-161/12), and the Agenzia Italiana del Farmaco (AIFA), concerning a prohibition on para-pharmacies selling prescription-only medicinal products which are not chargeable to the Servizio sanitorio nazionale (SSN) ('national health service') and are entirely paid for by the purchaser.

Legal context

European Union law

3. Recital 26 of the preamble to Directive 2005/36/EC of the European Parliament and of the Council of 7 September 2005 on the recognition of professional qualifications (OJ 2005 L 255, p. 22), states:

'This Directive does not coordinate all the conditions for access to activities in the field of pharmacy and the pursuit of these activities. In particular, the geographical distribution of pharmacies and the monopoly for dispensing medicines should remain a matter for the Member States. This Directive leaves unchanged the legislative, regulatory and administrative provisions of the Member States forbidding companies from pursuing certain pharmacists' activities or subjecting the pursuit of such activities to certain conditions.'

Italian law

4. Law No 468 of 22 May 1913 defined the provision of pharmaceutical services as 'a primary State activity' which could be engaged in only by municipal pharmacies or by private pharmacies operating under government licence.

5. In order to ensure a proper distribution of dispensing pharmacies throughout the national territory and to prevent them from becoming concentrated solely in commercially more desirable areas, an administrative instrument for controlling supply was established, the 'pianta organica' ('the grid') which provides that the distribution of those dispensing pharmacies, in the territory, is to be subject to quotas considered to be suitable to respond to the demand from people concerned in order to ensure each such dispensing pharmacy a market share and to meet the requirements for medicinal products throughout the national territory.

6. Essentially, subsequent legislative developments have perpetuated that model.

7. Accordingly, in the words of Article 1(1), (2) and (7) of Law No 475 on rules on the provision of pharmaceutical services (legge n. 475 – Norme concernenti il servizio farmaceutico) of 2 April 1968 (GURI No 107, 27 April 1968, p. 2638), as amended by Law No 362 on rules governing the reorganisation of the pharmaceutical sector (legge n. 362 – Norme di riordino del settore farmaceutico) of 8 November 1991 (GURI No 269, 16 November 1991, p. 3):

'1. Authorisation to open and operate a dispensing pharmacy shall be issued by the competent authority for the area concerned.

2. The number of authorisations to be issued for each municipality shall be determined in such a manner that there is one pharmacy for every 5 000 inhabitants in municipalities with a population of up to 12 500 inhabitants and one pharmacy for every 4 000 inhabitants in all other municipalities.

...

7. Any new dispensing pharmacy must be situated at a distance of at least 200 metres from other such pharmacies and must in any case be located in such a manner as to meet the requirements of the local inhabitants.'

8. Article 122 of a Royal Decree, No 1265 of 27 July 1934, had reserved the sale of medicinal products exclusively to pharmacies.

9. Law No 537 of 24 December 1993 later re-categorised medicinal products on the basis of the following classes, namely Class A for essential medicinal products and medicinal products for chronic diseases, Class B for medicinal products other than those falling into Class A and of significant therapeutic value, Class C for medicinal products other than those falling within Class A or Class B. Under Article 8(14) of Law No 537 of 24 December 1993, the cost of medicinal products falling within Class A or Class B is wholly to be borne by the national health service, whereas the cost of medicinal products in Class C is wholly to be borne by the customer.

10. Subsequently, Article 85(1) of Law No 388 of 23 December 2000 abolished Class B, while Article 1 of Law No 311 of 30 December 2004 created a new category of medicinal products – Class C(a) – to cover medicinal products for which a prescription is not required and which, unlike products falling within the other categories, may be publicly advertised. As in the case of Class C medicinal products, the cost of Class C(a) medicinal products is to be borne by the customer.

11. Decree-Law No 223 of 4 July 2006, converted into Law No 248 of 4 August 2006, allowed the opening of para-pharmacies, by means of which their owners were authorised to sell medicinal products falling within the scope of Class C(a). More recently, Decree-Law No 201 of 6 December 2011, converted into Law No 214 of 22 December 2011, further extended the number of medicinal products that can be sold by para-pharmacies, so that they can now offer to the public some of the Class C medicinal products for which no prescription is required.

The disputes in the main proceedings and the question referred

12. The applicants in the main proceedings each submitted a request to the competent ASL, as well as to the municipalities concerned, the Ministero della Salute and the Agenzia Italiana del Farmaco, for authorisation to sell to the public prescription-only medicinal products for human use but the cost of which is wholly borne by the customer, as well medicinal products for veterinary use for which a prescription is also required and the cost of which is also wholly borne by the customer.

13, On 17 August 2011 the competent ASLs rejected the requests of the applicants in the main proceedings on the ground that, on the basis of the domestic legislation in force, such medicinal products could be sold only in pharmacies. Similar refusals were given by the Ministry of Health on 16 and 18 August 2011.

14. The applicants in the main proceedings brought an action against those decisions before the Tribunale amministrativo regionale per la Lombardia, claiming that the legislation on which those decisions were based was incompatible with European Union law ('EU law'), in that it provides that the sale in para-pharmacies of prescription-only Class C medicinal products, the cost of which is however not borne by the national health service, is prohibited.

15. In those circumstances, the Tribunale amministrativo regionale per la Lombardia decided to stay the proceedings and to refer the following question, which is identically worded in Cases C-159/12 to C-161/12, to the Court of Justice for a preliminary ruling:

    'Do the principles of freedom of establishment, non-discrimination and the preservation of competition under Article 49 et seq TFEU preclude national legislation which does not allow a pharmacist, who is qualified and registered with the appropriate professional body but does not own a pharmacy in the grid, also to offer for retail sale, in the para-pharmacy owned by that pharmacist, medicinal products for which a prescription in the form of a 'ricetta bianca' is required – that is to say, medicinal products the cost of which is borne not by the national health service but wholly by the purchaser – and which also establishes in that sector a prohibition on the sale of certain categories of pharmaceutical products, as well as a quota in relation to the number of commercial outlets which may be established in the national territory?'

16. By order of the President of the Court of 27 April 2012, Cases C-159/12 to C-161/12 were joined for the purposes of the written and oral procedures and of the judgment.

Consideration of the question referred for a preliminary ruling

Preliminary observations

17. It should be noted that in the question submitted by it for a preliminary ruling the national court referred not only to freedom of establishment, but also to the principle of non-discrimination and to the preservation of competition.

18. In that regard, in relation to, first, the principle of non-discrimination, it must be borne in mind that the Court has consistently held that that principle is intended to apply independently only to situations governed by EU law for which the FEU Treaty lays down no specific prohibition of discrimination. In the field of freedom of establishment, the principle of the prohibition of discrimination is given specific expression in Article 49 TFEU (see, in particular, Case C-193/94 *Skanavi and Chryssanthakopoulos* [1996] ECR I-929, paragraphs 20 and 21; Case C-251/98 *Baars* [2000] ECR I-2787, paragraphs 23 and 24; and Case C-384/08 *Attanasio Group* [2010] ECR I-2055, paragraph 37).

19, Therefore, in the present case, it is necessary to take account of the principle of non-discrimination in the context of Article 49 TFEU.

20. Secondly, it should be recalled that the need to provide an interpretation of EU law which will be of use to the national court requires that the national court define the

factual and legal context of its questions or, at the very least, that it explain the factual circumstances on which those questions are based. Those requirements are of particular importance in the area of competition, where the factual and legal situations are often complex (see, inter alia, *Attanasio Group*, paragraph 32, and Joined Cases C-357/10 to C-359/10 *Duomo Gpa and Others* [2012] ECR, paragraph 22).

21. In the present case, the orders for reference do not provide the Court with the factual and legal information necessary for it to determine the conditions under which State measures such as those at issue in the main proceedings might fall within the scope of the Treaty provisions on competition. In particular, those orders do not provide any indication of the specific rules of competition which require interpretation nor do they provide an explanation of the connection made between those rules and the disputes in the main proceedings or their subject-matter.

22. In those circumstances, there is no need to examine the question referred in the light of preservation of competition.

23. It follows from all the foregoing that the question referred by the national court should be understood as asking, in essence, whether Article 49 TFEU must be interpreted as precluding legislation, such as that at issue in the main proceedings, which does not allow a pharmacist, who is qualified and registered with the professional body but does not own a pharmacy in the grid, also to offer for retail sale, in the para-pharmacy owned by that pharmacist, prescription-only medicinal products the cost of which is borne not by the national health service but wholly by the purchaser.

Admissibility

24. Federpharma – Federazione Nazionale Unitaria dei Titolari di Farmacia Italiani disputes the admissibility of the requests for a preliminary ruling on the ground that the disputes in the main proceedings contain no cross-border elements. The present case is, in essence, identical to that which gave rise to the judgment in Case C-393/08 *Sbarigia* [2010] ECR I-6337, in which the Court considered that the exercise of the right of establishment was clearly not at issue, and, therefore, dismissed the request for a preliminary ruling as being inadmissible.

25. In that regard, the Court has consistently held that, while national legislation such as that at issue in the main proceedings – which applies indiscriminately to Italian nationals and to nationals of other Member States – is, generally, capable of falling within the scope of the provisions relating to the fundamental freedoms established by the Treaty only to the extent that it applies to situations connected with trade between the Member States, it is far from inconceivable that nationals established in Member States other than the Italian Republic have been or are interested in operating para-pharmacies in that latter Member State (see, to that effect, Joined Cases

C-570/07 and C-571/07 *Blanco Pérez and Chao Gómez* [2010] ECR I-4629, paragraph 40 and the case-law cited).

26. Admittedly, although it is apparent from the orders for reference that the applicants in the main proceedings are of Italian nationality and that all the factual aspects of the main proceedings are limited to one Member State, nevertheless the legislation at issue in the main proceedings is capable of producing effects which are not confined to that Member State.

27. Moreover, the cases in the main proceedings differ from that which gave rise to the judgment in *Sbarigia*, which concerned a decision on the possible grant of an exemption in relation to the opening hours of a particular pharmacy, and, as a result, there was nothing to indicate how such a decision might affect economic operators coming from other Member States.

28. Moreover, even in a purely internal situation such as that at issue in the main proceedings, where all the factors are confined within a single Member State, a response could nevertheless be useful for the referring court, in particular if its national law were to require it to grant to an Italian national the same rights as those which a national of another Member State would derive from EU law in the same situation (see *Blanco Pérez and Chao Gómez*, paragraph 39 and the case-law cited).

29. In those circumstances, the requests for a preliminary ruling must be held to be admissible.

Substance

[Paras 30-67 omitted]

On those grounds,

THE COURT (Fourth Chamber),

hereby rules:

Article 49 TFEU must be interpreted as not precluding national legislation, such as that at issue in the main proceedings, which does not allow a pharmacist, who is qualified and registered with the professional body but does not own a pharmacy in the grid, also to offer for retail sale, in the para-pharmacy owned by that pharmacist, prescription-only medicinal products the cost of which is borne not by the national health service but wholly by the purchaser.

Comments and questions

In principle, the Union law rules on freedom of movement only apply where there is a cross-border element. This means that where all the elements of a case are linked to a sole Member State, the Treaty rules on freedom of movement do not apply; the situation will be considered to be purely internal to that Member State. If a case before a national court concerns matters that are purely internal to that Member State, the CJEU will normally decline to give a preliminary ruling that stems from that national case.

This stance the CJEU, however modifies in three situations:

The *first* modification applies where all the elements of the case that has been referred to it for a preliminary ruling are only connected with one Member State, but where it is possible that the disputed provisions of national law can have a cross-border effect. Thus, it is the ability of the disputed national provisions to produce cross-border effects with regards to the freedom of movement that can form the basis for a matter not being regarded as purely internal.

The *second* modification concerns situations where under the law of a Member State there is a principle that the citizens of this Member State should not be put in a less advantageous position under national law than the citizens of other countries. Thus, for example, if a Member State's own citizen is accused of having infringed some national rules and the citizen claims that the national rules would be contrary to Union law if they had had a cross-border effect, the CJEU will normally be willing to decide the question if it is referred for a preliminary ruling. The reason for this is that a national court required to decide on a purely internal matter needs to know how the question would be decided if the accused were a citizen of another Member State, so that any more favourable treatment offered under EU law should also be allowed the Member State's own citizen in accordance with the just-mentioned principle.

The *third* modification concerns cases where a Member State has adopted national legislation modelled on Union legislation, for example where a Member State implements an EU directive in national law and where a Member State finds it appropriate to give the directive's rules wider scope than required by the directive itself. It often makes better sense for Member States and their citizens to have a single set of rules (i.e. the directive's rules) governing a given area, rather than having two different sets of rules governing the same area (i.e. both the directive's rules and national rules). Similarly, several Member States have 'copied' the EU competition rules into their national laws. If a situation subsequently arises where a national court needs to interpret the rules of a directive, but where the facts of the case are not formally covered by the directive, the national court will nevertheless be able to refer questions for a preliminary ruling on the interpretation of the directive – and may more or less always expect that the CJEU will give a preliminary ruling.

There was no cross-border element in the *Venturini* case. The case concerned an Italian prohibition of 'para-pharmacies' being able to sell prescription medicines, the cost of which is partly covered from public funds. All the parties involved were Italian, and on the face of it no elements could be said to have a cross-border effect. It was therefore disputed that the CJEU could admit the case and give a preliminary ruling, on the ground that the disputes in the main proceedings contained no cross-border elements.

The CJEU dismissed the objections. *First*, it stated that the disputed rule was such that it was possible that it could have a cross-border effect. More specifically, the CJEU said that it was quite conceivable that nationals established in Member States other than Italy could be interested in operating para-pharmacies in Italy, and this would give the rules a cross-border element. *Second*, the CJEU stated that: 'a response could nevertheless be useful for the referring court, in particular if its national law were to require it to grant to an Italian national the same rights as those which a national of another Member State would derive from EU law in the same situation'. In other words, the CJEU ruled that both the first and the second of the three modifications referred to above applied in the *Venturini* case.

Try to construct a case on establishment in an EU Member State in which there are no cross-border elements and where none of the three modifications is applicable.

JUDGMENT OF THE COURT
21 June 1974
Jean Reyners v The Belgian State.
(Reference for a preliminary ruling: Conseil d'Etat – Belgium)

'Right of establishment'

Case 2/74

Judgment

1. By judgment dated 21 December 1973, filed at the Registry on 9 January 1974, the Conseil d'Etat of Belgium raised two questions under Article 177 of the EEC Treaty on the interpretation of Articles 52 and 55 of the EEC Treaty relating to the right of establishment in relation to the practice of the profession of avocat.

2. These questions had been raised in the context of an action brought by a Dutch national, the holder of the legal diploma giving the right to take up the profession of avocat in Belgium, who has been excluded from that profession by reason of his nationality as a result of the Royal Decree of 24 August 1972 relating to the title and exercise of the profession of avocat (Moniteur Belge 1970, p. 9060).

On the interpretation of Article 52 of the EEC Treaty

3. The Conseil d'Etat inquires whether Article 52 of the EEC Treaty is, since the end of the transitional period, a 'directly applicable provision' despite the absence of directives as prescribed by Articles 54 (2) and 57 (1) of the Treaty.

4. The Belgian and Irish Governments have argued, for reasons largely in agreement, that Article 52 does not have such an effect.

5. Taken in the context of the Chapter on the right of establishment, to which reference is expressly made by the wording 'within the framework of the provisions set out below', this Article, in view of the complexity of the subject, is said to constitute only the expression of a simple principle, the implementation of which is necessarily subject to a set of complementary provisions, both Community and national, provided for by Articles 54 and 57.

6. The form chosen by the Treaty for these implementing acts – the establishment of a 'general programme', implemented in turn by a set of directives – confirms, it is argued, that Article 52 does not have a direct effect.

7. It is not for the courts to exercise a discretionary power reserved to the legislative institutions of the Community and the Member States.

8. This argument is supported in substance by the British and Luxembourg Governments, as well as by the Ordre national des avocats de Belgique, the intervening party in the main action.

9. The plaintiff in the main action, for his part, states that all that is in question in his case is a discrimination based on nationality by reason of the fact that he is subject to conditions of admission to the profession of avocat which are not applicable to Belgian nationals.

10. In this respect (he submits) Article 52 is a clear and complete provision, capable of producing a direct effect.

[Paras 11-32 omitted]

On the interpretation of Article 55 of the EEC Treaty

33. The Conseil d'Etat has also requested a definition of what is meant in the first paragraph of Article 55 by 'activities which in that State are connected, even occasionally, with the exercise of official authority'.

34. More precisely, the question is whether, within a profession such as that of avocat, only those activities inherent in this profession which are connected with the exercise of official authority are excepted from the application of the Chapter on the right of establishment, or whether the whole of this profession is excepted by reason of the fact that it comprises activities connected with the exercise of this authority.

35. The Luxembourg Government and the Ordre national des avocats de Belgique consider that the whole profession of avocat is exonerated from the rules in the Treaty on the right of establishment by the fact that it is connected organically with the functioning of the public service of the administration of justice.

36. This situation (it is argued) results both from the legal organization of the Bar, involving a set of strict conditions for admission and discipline, and from the functions performed by the avocat in the context of judicial procedure where his participation is largely obligatory.

37. These activities, which make the advocate an indispensable auxiliary of the administration of justice, form a coherent whole, the parts of which cannot be separated.

38. The plaintiff in the main action, for his part, contends that at most only certain activities of the profession of avocat are connected with the exercise of official au-

thority and that they alone therefore come within the exception created by Article 55 to the principle of free establishment.

39. The German, Belgian, British, Irish and Dutch Governments, as well as the Commission, regard the exception contained in Article 55 as limited to those activities alone within the various professions concerned which are actually connected with the exercise of official authority, subject to their being separable from the normal practice of the profession.

40. Differences exist, however, between the Governments referred to as regards the nature of the activities which are thus excepted from the principle of the freedom of establishment, taking into account the different organization of the professions corresponding to that of avocat from one Member State to another.

41. The German Government in particular considers that by reason of the compulsory connection of the Rechtsanwalt with certain judicial processes, especially as regards criminal or public law, there are such close connexions between the profession of Rechtsanwalt and the exercise of judicial authority that large sectors of this profession, at least, should be excepted from freedom of establishment.

42. Under the terms of the first paragraph of Article 55 the provisions of the Chapter on the right of establishment shall not apply 'so far as any given member State is concerned, to activities which in that State are connected, even occasionally, with the exercise of official authority'.

43. Having regard to the fundamental character of freedom of establishment and the rule on equal treatment with nationals in the system of the Treaty, the exceptions allowed by the first paragraph of Article 55 cannot be given a scope which would exceed the objective for which this exemption clause was inserted.

44. The first paragraph of Article 55 must enable Member States to exclude non-nationals from taking up functions involving the exercise of official authority which are connected with one of the activities of self-employed persons provided for in Article 52.

45. This need is fully satisfied when the exclusion of nationals is limited to those activities which, taken on their own, constitute a direct and specific connexion with the exercise of official authority.

46. An extension of the exception allowed by Article 55 to a whole profession would be possible only in cases where such activities were linked with that profession in such a way that freedom of establishment would result in imposing on the Member State concerned the obligation to allow the exercise, even occasionally, by non-nationals of functions appertaining to official authority.

47. This extension is on the other hand not possible when, within the framework of an independent profession, the activities connected with the exercise of official authority are separable from the professional activity in question taken as a whole.

48. In the absence of any directive issued under Article 57 for the purpose of harmonizing the national provisions relating, in particular, to professions such as that of avocat, the practice of such professions remains governed by the law of the various Member States.

49. The possible application of the restrictions on freedom of establishment provided for by the first paragraph of Article 55 must therefore be considered separately in connexion with each Member State having regard to the national provisions applicable to the organization and the practice of this profession.

50. This consideration must however take into account the Community character of the limits imposed by Article 55 on the exceptions permitted to the principle of freedom of establishment in order to avoid the effectiveness of the Treaty being defeated by unilateral provisions of Member States.

51. Professional activities involving contacts, even regular and organic, with the courts, including even compulsory cooperation in their functioning, do not constitute, as such, connexion with the exercise of official authority.

52. The most typical activities of the profession of avocat, in particular, such as consultation and legal assistance and also representation and the defence of parties in court, even when the intervention or assistance of the avocat is compulsory or is a legal monopoly, cannot be considered as connected with the exercise of official authority.

53. The exercise of these activities leaves the discretion of judicial authority and the free exercise of judicial power intact.

54. It is therefore right to reply to the question raised that the exception to freedom of establishment provided for by the first paragraph of Article 55 must be restricted to those of the activities referred to in Article 52 which in themselves involve a direct and specific connexion with the exercise of official authority.

55. In any case it is not possible to give this description, in the context of a profession such as that of avocat, to activities such as consultation and legal assistance or the representation and defence of parties in court, even if the performance of these activities is compulsory or there is a legal monopoly in respect of it.

Costs

[Paras 56-57 omitted]

On those grounds,

THE COURT

in answer to the questions referred to it by the Conseil d'Etat of Belgium, section d'administration, IIIe Chambre, by judgment dated 21 December 1973, hereby rules:

1. **Since the end of the transitional period Article 52 of the Treaty is a directly applicable provision, despite the absence, in a particular sphere, of the directives prescribed by Articles 54 (2) and 57 (1) of the Treaty.**

2. **The exception to freedom of establishment provided for by the first paragraph of Article 55 must be restricted to those of the activities referred to in Article 52 which in themselves involve a direct and specific connexion with the exercise of official authority; it is not possible to give this description, in the context of a profession such as that of avocat, to activities such as consultation and legal assistance or the representation and defence of parties in court, even if the performance of these activities is compulsory or there is a legal monopoly in respect of it.**

Comments and questions

In Case 2/74 *Reyners* v *Belgium* [1974] ECR 631, the CJEU was requested to give its view on the meaning of the term 'official authority', as used in Article 51 TFEU (formerly Article 55 EEC Treaty). The CJEU stated that, since Article 51 TFEU lays down exceptions to the principle of freedom of establishment, it should be interpreted narrowly, so that the term 'official authority' should be limited to such activities as have a direct and specific connection with the exercise of official authority; cf. paragraph 45. A Member State could therefore only extend the exception to a whole profession where the exercise of official authority was linked to that profession in such a way that freedom of establishment would result in imposing on that Member State the obligation to allow the exercise of official authority by non-nationals; cf. paragraphs 46 and 47 (the proportionality principle). This means that a Member State cannot reserve the profession of advocate in its entirety for its own nationals.

In Case C-114/97 *Commission* v *Spain* [1998] ECR I-6717, the CJEU had to consider a Spanish law which made the grant of authorisation to carry on private security activities conditional, among other things, on the security staff being Spanish nationals. In this connection, the Spanish government argued that private security activities involved the exercise of official authority within the meaning of Article 51 TFEU, since the aim was the maintenance of public security. Do you think that the CJEU accepted the Spanish argument that this case concerned official authority so as to justify the requirement of Spanish nationality?

In the United Kingdom, jails are operated not just by the State but also by private undertakings such as G4S. Would the United Kingdom be able to require that private undertakings that wish to operate British jails commercially must be British-owned, by reference to the fact that the operation of jails constitutes the exercise of a public authority, and that the United Kingdom has merely delegated the authority to selected private undertakings?

JUDGMENT OF THE COURT (Fifth Chamber)
8 June 1999

C.P.M. Meeusen v Hoofddirectie van de Informatie Beheer Groep.
(Reference for a preliminary ruling: Commissie van Beroep Studiefinanciering – Netherlands)

'Regulation (EEC) No 1612/68 – Free movement of persons – Concept of 'worker' – Freedom of establishment – Study finance – Discrimination on the ground of nationality – Residence requirement'

Case C-337/97

Judgment

1. By order of 26 September 1997, received at the Court on 29 September 1997, the Commissie van Beroep Studiefinanciering (Study Finance Tribunal) referred to the Court for a preliminary ruling under Article 177 of the EC Treaty (now Article 234 EC) several questions on the interpretation of Articles 48 and 52 of the EC Treaty (now, after amendment, Articles 39 EC and 43 EC) and of Article 7 of Regulation (EEC) No 1612/68 of the Council of 15 October 1968 on freedom of movement for workers within the Community (OJ, English Special Edition 1968 (II), p. 475).

2. Those questions were raised in proceedings between Miss Meeusen, the plaintiff in the main proceedings, and the Hoofddirectie van de Informatie Beheer Groep (governing board of the information management group, the 'IBG'), the defendant in the main proceedings, relating to an application for a study grant made by Miss Meeusen under the Wet op de Studiefinanciering (Law on the financing of studies, 'the WSF') when she registered at the Provincial Higher Technical Institute for Chemistry, Antwerp, an institution of higher education.

3. Article 7 of Regulation No 1612/68 provides:

'1. A worker who is a national of a Member State may not, in the territory of another Member State, be treated differently from national workers by reason of his nationality in respect of any conditions of employment and work ...

2. He shall enjoy the same social and tax advantages as national workers.'

4. Under Article 7 of the WSF, that Law applies to:

'(a) students who possess Netherlands nationality;

(b) students who do not possess Netherlands nationality but are resident in the Netherlands and are treated as Netherlands nationals in respect of the financing of studies under provisions in agreements with other States or in a decision of an organisation in public international law which is binding on the Netherlands;

(c) ...'

5. The finance provided for in the WSF is granted directly to students aged 18 and over. It consists of a basic grant, the level of which is independent of the parents' income, and a supplementary grant, the level of which varies according to parental income.

6. Under Article 9(1) of the WSF, only studies pursued in a Netherlands institution give rise to an entitlement to study finance. Article 9(3) provides, however, for an exception to that rule in the case of certain foreign institutions which are treated as Netherlands institutions for the purpose of applying the WSF. It is common ground that the Provincial Higher Technical Institute for Chemistry, Antwerp, is covered by that exception.

7. It is clear from the order for reference that Miss Meeusen, of Belgian nationality and residing at the material time in Belgium, began her studies in August 1993 at the Provincial Higher Technical Institute for Chemistry, Antwerp. Her father and mother are both of Belgian nationality and resident in Belgium. Her father is the director and sole shareholder of a company established in the Netherlands. Her mother is employed by that company for two days a week. The national court takes the view that her activity is effective and genuine.

8. On 14 October 1993, Miss Meeusen applied to the IBG for study finance under the WSF.

9. Finance was initially granted to Miss Meeusen, who obtained a basic grant for the period from November 1993 to March 1994, but her application was later rejected by a decision of 2 October 1994, by which she was also required to refund the sums already received. A complaint against that refusal of finance was also dismissed by decision of the IBG of 12 January 1995.

10. After her complaint was dismissed, Miss Meeusen brought proceedings before the Commissie van Beroep Studiefinanciering. Before that tribunal, she claimed that the right to study finance could not be made subject to the requirement that the child live or be resident in the territory of the Member State where his parents are employed, any more than it could be related to nationality. In its defence, the IBG contended that the applicant's parents could not be regarded as migrant workers within the meaning of Article 48 of the Treaty, since they do not live in the Netherlands.

For a person to be classified as a migrant worker he would have to have the status of an employee and have established his residence in the host country. As for frontier workers, to which the preamble to Regulation No 1612/68 refers, these are persons working in the immediate proximity of a border.

11. In those circumstances the national court decided to stay proceedings and refer the following questions to the Court for a preliminary ruling:

'1. (a) Does a situation such as that in the present case, in which the plaintiff's mother is employed by the limited company of which her husband is the director and sole shareholder, preclude her from being regarded as a migrant worker within the meaning of Article 48 of the EC Treaty and of Regulation (EEC) No 1612/68?

If question 1(a) is answered in the negative:

(b) In the Bernini judgment (Case C-3/90 Bernini v Minister van Onderwijs en Wetenschappen [1992] ECR I-1071) the Court ruled that study finance awarded by a Member State to children of workers constitutes a social advantage to a migrant worker, as provided for in Article 7(2) of Regulation (EEC) No 1612/68, where the worker continues to support the child. In such a case the child may rely on Article 7(2) in order to obtain study finance under the same conditions as are applicable to children of national workers, and in particular without any further requirement as to place of residence.

Does this rule equally apply if the migrant worker must be regarded as a frontier worker?

(c) Does the rule of law in Bernini, as stated in question 1(b) above, also apply if the child of a migrant worker, as in the present case, has never lived in the Netherlands?

2. Must Article 52 of the EC Treaty be interpreted in such a way that the safeguard provided for under the rule laid down in Bernini, as mentioned above in question 1(b), also applies to the child of a national of a Member State who pursues activities in another Member State as a self-employed person? To what extent is it also decisive in that connection that the child has never been resident in the Netherlands and that the parent is not resident in the country in which the activity as a self-employed person is pursued?'

Question 1(a)

12. By this question the national court seeks to ascertain, in substance, whether the fact that a person is related by marriage to the director and sole shareholder of the com-

pany for which he pursues his activity precludes that person from being classified as a 'worker' within the meaning of Article 48 of the Treaty and of Regulation No 1612/68.

13. The Court has consistently held that the concept of 'worker', within the meaning of the abovementioned provisions, has a specific Community meaning and must not be interpreted narrowly. Any person who pursues activities which are effective and genuine, to the exclusion of activities on such a small scale as to be regarded as purely marginal and ancillary, must be regarded as a 'worker'. The essential feature of an employment relationship is, according to that case-law, that for a certain period of time a person performs services for and under the direction of another person in return for which he receives remuneration (see, in particular, Case 66/85 *Lawrie-Blum* v *Land Baden-Wüürttemberg* [1986] ECR 2121, paragraphs 16 and 17; and Case C-85/96 *Martíínez Sala* v *Freistaat Bayern* [1998] ECR I-2691, paragraph 32).

14. The fact that that person is related by marriage to the director and sole owner of the undertaking is not, of itself, such as to affect that classification.

15. The Court did indeed hold, in Case C-107/94 *Asscher* v *Staatssecretaris van Financiëën* [1996] ECR I-3089, paragraph 26, that the director of a company of which he is the sole shareholder is not carrying out his activity in the context of a relationship of subordination, and so he is not to be regarded as a 'worker' within the meaning of Article 48 of the Treaty. However, that result cannot be automatically transposed to his spouse. The personal and property relations between spouses which result from marriage do not rule out the existence, in the context of the organisation of an undertaking, of a relationship of subordination characteristic of an employment relationship.

16. The existence of a relationship of subordination is a matter which it is for the national court to verify.

17. The answer to question 1(a) must therefore be that the fact that a person is related by marriage to the director and sole shareholder of the company for which he pursues an effective and genuine activity does not preclude that person from being classified as a 'worker' within the meaning of Article 48 of the Treaty and of Regulation No 1612/68, so long as he pursues his activity in the context of a relationship of subordination.

Question 1(b) and (c)

18. By these questions, which it is appropriate to examine together, the national court seeks to ascertain, in substance, whether the dependent child of a national of one Member State who pursues an activity as an employed person in another Member

State while maintaining his residence in the State of which he is a national can rely on Article 7(2) of Regulation No 1612/68 in order to obtain study finance under the same conditions as are applicable to children of nationals of the State of employment, and in particular without any further requirement as to the child's place of residence.

19. As is clear from Bernini, paragraph 25, study finance awarded by a Member State to children of workers constitutes for a migrant worker a social advantage within the meaning of Article 7(2) of Regulation No 1612/68 where the worker continues to support the child.

20. The Netherlands and German Governments submit that that rule cannot be extended to cover the case of a frontier worker. The equality of treatment provided for in Article 7(2) of Regulation No 1612/68 aims, as is evident from the fifth recital in its preamble, only to facilitate the mobility of workers and the integration of the migrant worker and his family in the host State. The granting by the host State, for the child of a worker resident with his family in another Member State, of finance for the pursuit of studies abroad does not come within that context. A residence requirement, as imposed by the national legislation at issue in the main proceedings, is thus objectively justified and proportionate to the objective pursued by Regulation No 1612/68.

21. As the Court held in Case C-57/96 *Meints* v *Minister van Landbouw, Natuurbeheer en Visserij* [1997] ECR I-6689, paragraph 50, that argument disregards the wording of Regulation No 1612/68. It is expressly stated in the fourth recital in the preamble to that regulation that the right of free movement must be enjoyed 'without discrimination by permanent, seasonal and frontier workers and by those who pursue their activities for the purpose of providing services' and Article 7 of the Regulation refers, without reservation, to a 'worker who is a national of a Member State'. The Court deduced from that and ruled, in Meints, that a Member State may not make the grant of a social advantage within the meaning of Article 7 of the Regulation dependent on the condition that the beneficiaries be resident within its territory.

22. It should also be added that the Court has consistently held that the principle of equal treatment laid down in Article 7 of Regulation No 1612/68 is also intended to prevent discrimination to the detriment of descendants dependent on the worker (see Case 94/84 *ONEM* v *Deak* [1985] ECR 1873, paragraph 22). Those descendants can thus rely on Article 7(2) in order to obtain study finance under the same conditions as are applicable to children of national workers (Bernini, paragraph 28).

23. It follows that, in a situation where national legislation, such as that in point in the main proceedings, does not impose any residence requirement on the children of national workers for the financing of their studies, such a requirement must be re-

garded as discriminatory if it is imposed on the children of workers who are nationals of other Member States.

24. Such a requirement would operate to the detriment of, in particular, migrant workers who, by definition, are resident in a Member State where, as a general rule, the members of their family are also resident.

25. In the light of the foregoing, the answer to the questions referred must be that the dependent child of a national of one Member State who pursues an activity as an employed person in another Member State while maintaining his residence in the State of which he is a national can rely on Article 7(2) of Regulation No 1612/68 in order to obtain study finance under the same conditions as are applicable to children of nationals of the State of employment, and in particular without any further requirement as to the child's place of residence.

The second question

26. By this question, the national court seeks to ascertain, in substance, whether the dependent child of a national of one Member State who pursues an activity as a self-employed person in another Member State while maintaining his residence in the State of which he is a national can obtain study finance under the same conditions as are applicable to children of nationals of the State of establishment, and in particular without any further requirement as to the child's place of residence.

27. In that regard, it should be observed that Article 52 of the Treaty confers on nationals of one Member State who wish to pursue activities as self-employed persons in another Member State the benefit of the same treatment as the host State's own nationals and prohibits any discrimination based on nationality which hinders the taking up or pursuit of such activities. As the Court held in Case C-111/91 *Commission* v *Luxembourg* [1993] ECR I-817, paragraph 17, that prohibition covers not only specific rules on the pursuit of occupational activities, but also, as emerges from the General Programme for the abolition of restrictions on the freedom of establishment (OJ, English Special Edition, Second Series (IX), p. 7), any measure which, pursuant to any provision laid down by law, regulation or administrative action in a Member State, or as the result of the application of such a provision, or of administrative practices, hinders nationals of other Member States in their pursuit of activities as self-employed persons by treating nationals of other Member States differently from nationals of the country concerned.

28. That prohibition thus applies to the imposition of a residence requirement in respect of the grant of a social advantage where it has been established that that requirement is discriminatory in nature (Commission v Luxembourg, cited above, paragraph 18).

29. The principle of equal treatment thus laid down is also intended to prevent discrimination to the detriment of descendants who are dependent on a self-employed worker. It precludes, therefore, the imposition of a residence requirement such as that provided for in the national legislation concerned which, as stated in paragraph 23 of this judgment, must be regarded as discriminatory.

30. In the light of the foregoing, the answer to the second question must be that the dependent child of a national of one Member State who pursues an activity as a self-employed person in another Member State while maintaining his residence in the State of which he is a national can obtain study finance under the same conditions as are applicable to children of nationals of the State of establishment, and in particular without any further requirement as to the child's place of residence.

Costs

[Para. 31 omitted]

On those grounds,

THE COURT (Fifth Chamber),

in answer to the questions referred to it by the Commissie van Beroep Studiefinanciering by order of 26 September 1997, hereby rules:

1. **The fact that a person is related by marriage to the director and sole shareholder of the company for which he pursues an effective and genuine activity does not preclude that person from being classified as a 'worker' within the meaning of Article 48 of the EC Treaty (now, after amendment, Article 39 EC) and of Regulation (EEC) No 1612/68 of the Council of 15 October 1968 on freedom of movement for workers within the Community, so long as he pursues his activity in the context of a relationship of subordination;**

2. **The dependent child of a national of one Member State who pursues an activity as an employed person in another Member State while maintaining his residence in the State of which he is a national can rely on Article 7(2) of Regulation No 1612/68 in order to obtain study finance under the same conditions as are applicable to children of nationals of the State of employment, and in particular without any further requirement as to the child's place of residence;**

3. **The dependent child of a national of one Member State who pursues an activity as a self-employed person in another Member State while maintaining his residence in the State of which he is a national can obtain study fi-**

nance under the same conditions as are applicable to children of nationals of the State of establishment, and in particular without any further requirement as to the child's place of residence.

Comments and questions

In Case C-337/97 *Meeusen* v *Hoofddirectie van de Informatie Beheer Groep* [1999] ECR I-3289, the CJEU considered the concept of a 'worker' and examined the legal consequences of being a 'frontier worker'. The CJEU also examined the social advantages which can come from exercising the right of freedom of establishment. The case is dealt with in this chapter dealing with freedom of establishment, rather than in the Chapter 5 on the free movement of workers, because, to a certain extent, the judgment may be viewed as a parallel application of Regulation No 1612/68 (then in force, now Regulation 492/2011) on freedom of movement for workers within the Union, meaning that the rights granted by the Regulation to employees were also granted to self-employed persons. Only, in the case of self-employed persons were the rights formally derived from Article 49 TFEU (formerly Article 52 TEC).

The facts of the *Meeusen* case were that a Belgian national, Chantal Meeusen, who lived in Belgium with her Belgian parents, wanted to study chemistry at a Belgian educational institution. Chantal Meeusen's father was the sole owner and managing director of Inpechem Inspectors BV, a company based in the Dutch city of Rotterdam. Among the company's approximately 20 employees was Chantal Meeusen's mother, who worked for the company for two days per week. Chantal Meeusen's parents paid tax to the Dutch state, and were covered by the social security system of the Netherlands.

Chantal Meeusen applied for an educational grant from the Dutch state for her chemistry studies in Belgium. The Dutch authorities refused her application on the basis that she was neither a Dutch national, nor was resident in the Netherlands. Thereupon Chantal Meeusen sued the Dutch authorities. The Dutch court decided to seek the advice of the CJEU.

First, the CJEU established that the fact that a person is married to the director and sole owner of an undertaking for which he or she performs work does not, in itself, prevent that person being characterised as a 'worker' in the sense used in (now) Article 45 TFEU and Regulation No 1612/68. The essential feature of an employment relationship under these provisions is that, for a certain period of time, a person performs services for and under the direction of another person in return for remuneration. It was therefore a requirement that Chantal Meeusen's mother's work in the company had been carried out in a relationship of subordination characteristic of an employment relationship.

It appeared from the case that Chantal Meeusen's mother worked for the Dutch company for two days per week, but it was not clear whether this work was actually performed at the company's premises in the Netherlands, or whether there was perhaps 'remote' work, so that the work was actually carried out in Belgium. Was it important to the decision of the CJEU where the work was in fact performed? Would Chantal

Meeusen's father, as director of his wholly owned company, be covered by the TFEU concept of a 'worker'? The Commission proposed that the property arrangements between Mr and Mrs Meeusen were significant (whether they held their property severally or jointly). The Commission believed that if Mr and Mrs Meeusen held their property jointly, then Mrs Meeusen could not be regarded as an employee, since she would effectively be subordinate to herself (together with her husband). However, Advocate General La Pergola rejected this distinction and argued that the property rights which the married couple would have if they were to be divorced should not be decisive, as the question of joint ownership or individual ownership would only become relevant after a divorce. According to the Advocate General, the only thing that mattered was whether Mrs Meeusen was in fact in a subordinate relationship in respect of her work.

The CJEU stated that educational grants which Member States give to the children of workers constitute a social advantage within the terms of Regulation No 1612/68, provided that the worker continues to support the child. This social advantage is payable to permanent workers, seasonal workers, workers who pursue their activities for the purpose of providing services, and frontier workers; cf. paragraph 21 of the judgment. A Member State may not make the grant of a social advantage dependent on the beneficiaries being resident within its territory. Furthermore, the CJEU stated that if a Member State does not impose any residence requirement on the children of its national workers for the financing of their studies, such a requirement must be regarded as discriminatory if it is imposed on the children of workers who are nationals of other Member States. Compare this with the CJEU's ruling in paragraph 80 of the *Giersch* case, printed in Chapter 4 above.

What is of particular interest in the *Meeusen* case is that the CJEU appeared to make a parallel application of Regulation No 1612/68, so that social rights secured to *workers* were also to some extent also secured under Article 49 TFEU to *self-employed persons* who have taken advantage of the TFEU provisions on freedom of establishment. The CJEU thus held that under Article 49 TFEU, a child who is supported by a person who is a national of one Member State, while carrying on business as a self-employed person in another Member State, but who continues to be resident in the Member State of which he is a national, can obtain an educational grant on the same conditions as apply to children of nationals of the Member State in which the business of the self-employed persons is established. The CJEU added that this does not imply any residential requirement for the child. Even though the CJEU characterised the restriction as discriminatory (cf. paragraphs 23 and 28 of the judgment), there is no basis for assuming that the CJEU requires there to be actual discrimination on the grounds of nationality. This is supported by the fact that in paragraph 28 there is a reference to Case C-111/91 *Commission* v *Luxembourg* [1993] ECR I-817, which concerned indirect discrimination.

JUDGMENT OF THE COURT

28 April 1977Jean Thieffry v Conseil de l'ordre des avocats à la Cour de Paris.

(Preliminary ruling requested by the Cour d'Appel of Paris – France)

'Freedom of establishment for advocates'

Case 71/76

Decision

1. By order of 13 July 1976, lodged at the Court Registry on 19 July 1976, the Cour d'Appel, Paris, put to the Court, under Article 177 of the EEC Treaty, a question concerning the interpretation of Article 57 of the Treaty, which relates to the mutual recognition of evidence of professional qualifications for the purposes of access to activities as self-employed persons, with regard in particular to admission to exercise the profession of advocate.

2. The case before the Cour d'Appel concerns the admission to the Ordre des Avocats auprès de la Cour de Paris (the Paris Bar) of a Belgian advocate, who is the holder of a Belgian diploma of Doctor of Laws which has been recognized by a French university as equivalent to the French licenciate's degree in law, and who subsequently obtained the 'Certificat d'Aptitude à la Profession d'Avocat (qualifying certificate for the profession of advocate), having sat and passed that examination, in accordance with French legislation.

3. The appellant in the main action applied for admission to the Paris Bar, but by an order of 9 March 1976 the Conseil de l'Ordre (Bar Council) rejected his application on the ground that the person concerned offers no French diploma evidencing a licentiate's degree or a doctor's degree.

4. It appears from the wording of that decision that the application for admission was refused solely by reason of the fact that, although the person concerned had obtained university recognition of the equivalence of his basic diploma and furthermore had acquired the Certificat d'Aptitude à la Profession d'Avocat, that was not enough for him to be treated in the same way as a holder of the diploma of the licentiate's degree or doctor's degree within the meaning of French legislation.

5. According to the Conseil de l'Ordre, although the effect of the Treaty is to abolish any discrimination on grounds of nationality in this field, the equivalence of diplomas does not follow automatically from the application of its provisions, since such equivalence can result only from directives concerning recognition adopted pursuant to Article 57 of the Treaty, which do not yet exist for the profession of advocate.

6. The person concerned appealed to the Cour d'Appel against the order of the Conseil de l'Ordre and the Cour d'Appel put to the Court a question in the following terms:

   When a national of one Member State desirious of exercising the profession of advocate in another Member State has obtained a diploma in his country of origin which has been recognized as an equivalent qualification by the university authority of the country of establishment and which has enabled him to sit in the latter country the advocate's professional qualifying examinations – which he has passed – does the act of demanding the national diploma prescribed by the law of the country of establishment constitute, in the absence of the directives provided for in Article 57 (1) and (2) of the Treaty of Rome, an obstacle to the attainment of the objective of the Community provisions in question?

7. Under Article 3 of the Treaty, the activities of the Community include, inter alia, the abolition of obstacles to freedom of movement for persons and services.

8. With a view to attaining this objective, the first paragraph of Article 52 provides that restrictions on the freedom of establishment of nationals of a Member State in the territory of another Member State shall be abolished by progressive stages in the course of the transitional period.

9. Under the second paragraph of the same article, freedom of establishment includes the right to take up activities as self-employed persons, under the conditions laid down for its own nationals by the law of the country where such establishment is effected.

10. Article 53 emphasizes the irreversible nature of the liberalization achieved in this regard at any given time, by providing that Member States shall not introduce any new restrictions on the right of establishment in their territories of nationals of other Member States.

11. With a view to making it easier for persons to take up and pursue activities as self-employed persons, Article 57 assigns to the Council the duty of issuing directives concerning, first, the mutual recognition of diplomas, and secondly, the coordination of the provisions laid down by law or administrative action in Member States concerning the taking up and pursuit of activities as self-employed persons.

12. That article is therefore directed towards reconciling freedom of establishment with the application of national professional rules justified by the general good, in particular rules relating to organization, qualifications, professional ethics, supervision and liability, provided that such application is effected without discrimination.

13. In the General Programme for the abolition of restrictions on freedom of establishment, adopted on 18 December 1961 pursuant to Article 54 of the Treaty, the

Council proposed to eliminate not only overt discrimination, but also any form of disguised discrimination, by designating in Title III (B) as restrictions which are to be eliminated, 'Any requirements imposed, pursuant to any provision laid down by law, regulation or administrative action or in consequence of any administrative practice, in respect of the taking up or pursuit of an activity as a self-employed person where, although applicable irrespective of nationality, their effect is exclusively or principally to hinder the taking up or pursuit of such activity by foreign nationals (OJ, English Special Edition, Second Series, IX, p. 8).

14. In the context of the abolition of restrictions on freedom of establishment, that programme provides useful guidance for the implementation of the relevant provisions of the Treaty.

15. It follows from the provisions cited taken as a whole that freedom of establishment, subject to observance of professional rules justified by the general good, is one of the objectives of the Treaty.

16. In so far as Community law makes no special provision, these objectives may be attained by measures enacted by the Member States, which under Article 5 of the Treaty are bound to take all appropriate measures, whether general or particular, to ensure fulfilment of the obligations arising out of this Treaty or resulting from action taken by the institutions of the Community, and to abstain from any measure which could jeopardize the attainment of the objectives of this Treaty.

17. Consequently, if the freedom of establishment provided for by Article 52 can be ensured in a Member State either under the provisions of the laws and regulations in force, or by virtue of the practices of the public service or of professional bodies, a person subject to Community law cannot be denied the practical benefit of that freedom solely by virtue of the fact that, for a particular profession, the directives provided for by Article 57 of the Treaty have not yet been adopted.

18. Since the practical enjoyment of freedom of establishment can thus in certain circumstances depend upon national practice or legislation, it is incumbent upon the competent public authorities – including legally recognized professional bodies – to ensure that such practice or legislation is applied in accordance with the objective defined by the provisions of the Treaty relating to freedom of establishment.

19. In particular, there is an unjustified restriction on that freedom where, in a Member State, admission to a particular profession is refused to a person covered by the Treaty who holds a diploma which has been recognized as an equivalent qualification by the competent authority of the country of establishment and who furthermore has fulfilled the specific conditions regarding professional training in force in that country, solely by reason of the fact that the person concerned does not possess

the national diploma corresponding to the diploma which he holds and which has been recognized as an equivalent qualification.

20. The national court specifically referred to the effect of a recognition of equivalence by the university authority of the country of establishment, and in the course of the proceedings the question has been raised whether a distinction should be drawn, as regards the equivalence of diplomas, between university recognition, granted with a view to permitting the pursuit of certain studies, and a recognition having civil effect, granted with a view to permitting the pursuit of a professional activity.

21. It emerges from the information supplied in this connexion by the Commission and the governments which took part in the proceedings that the distinction between the academic effect and the civil effect of the recognition of foreign diplomas is acknowledged, in various forms, in the legislation and practice of several Member States.

22. Since this distinction falls within the ambit of the national law of the different States, it is for the national authorities to assess the consequences thereof, taking account, however, of the objectives of Community law.

23. In this connexion it is important that, in each Member State, the recognition of evidence of a professional qualification for the purposes of establishment may be accepted to the full extent compatible with the observance of the professional requirements mentioned above.

24. Consequently, it is for the competent national authorities, taking account of the requirements of Community law set out above, to make such assessments of the facts as will enable them to judge whether a recognition granted by a university authority can, in addition to its academic effect, constitute valid evidence of a professional qualification.

25. The fact that a national legislation provides for recognition of equivalence only for university purposes does not of itself justify the refusal to recognize such equivalence as evidence of a professional qualification.

26. This is particularly so when a diploma recognized for university purposes is supplemented by a professional qualifying certificate obtained according to the legislation of the country of establishment.

27. In these circumstances, the answer to the question referred to the Court should be that when a national of one Member State desirous of exercising a professional activity such as the profession of advocate in another Member State has obtained a diploma in his country of origin which has been recognized as an equivalent qualification by the competent authority under the legislation of the country of establish-

ment and which has thus enabled him to sit and pass the special qualifying examination for the profession in question, the act of demanding the national diploma prescribed by the legislation of the country of establishment constitutes, even in the absence of the directives provided for in Article 57, a restriction incompatible with the freedom of establishment guaranteed by Article 52 of the Treaty.

Costs

[Paras 28-29 omitted]

On those grounds,

THE COURT

in answer to the question referred to it by the Court D'Appel, Paris, by a judgment delivered in chambers on 13 July 1976, Hereby rules:

> **When a national of one Member State desirous of exercising a professional activity such as the profession of advocate in another Member State has obtained a diploma in his country of origin which has been recognized as an equivalent qualification by the competent authority under the legislation of the country of establishment and which has thus enabled him to sit and pass the special qualifying examination for the profession in question, the act of demanding the national diploma prescribed by the legislation of the country of establishment constitutes, even in the absence of the directives provided for in article 57, a restriction incompatible with the freedom of establishment guaranteed by article 52 of the Treaty.**

Comments and questions

According to the wording of (now) Article 49, second paragraph, TFEU the provision only contains a prohibition against discrimination (the principle of equal treatment). However, already by 1977, in Case 71/76 *Thieffry* v *Conseil de l'ordre des avocats à la cour de Paris* [1977] ECR 765, the CJEU interpreted Article 49 TFEU as covering not only overt discrimination, but also any form of disguised discrimination, i.e., measures which, although applicable irrespective of nationality, effectively restrict primarily foreign nationals. The requirement that an advocate should possess a French professional diploma applied regardless of nationality. Note that the CJEU made use of Article 4(3) TEU (formerly Article 5 EEC Treaty) on the principle of loyalty, to achieve its result. The CJEU often uses the principle of loyalty to arrive at its more 'progressive' decisions, see for example Joined Cases C-46/93 and C-48/93 *Brasserie du Pêcheur SA* v *Germany and R* v *Secretary of State for Transport, ex parte: Factortame Ltd and others* [1996] ECR I-1029, in Chapter 1.

Did the decision of the Paris Bar affect Thieffry's ability (i.e., his 'access') to carry on his profession as an advocate in Paris?

Note that the CJEU held that the decision of a private professional organisation (the Paris Bar) was subject to the provisions of Article 49 TFEU; cf. paragraph 18 of the judgment. Compare this with Case C-415/93 *Bosman* [1995] ECR I-4921, printed in Chapter 4.

It appears from paragraphs 16-19 of the judgment that, even though the national requirements for practising a profession have not been harmonised at Union level, the Member States are required to take into account exam qualifications from other Member States when assessing whether a Union citizen already satisfies the national requirements for practising a profession. Do you find the decision of the CJEU reasonable? Subsequently the European Parliament and the Council adopted Directive 2005/36 on the recognition of professional qualifications. This Directive had to be implemented by October 2007. It replaced, among others, Directive 89/48 on a general system for the recognition of higher-education diplomas awarded on completion of professional education and training of at least three years' duration. Recital 11 of Directive 2005/36 states that a host Member State:

> 'in which a profession is regulated must take account of the qualifications obtained in another Member State and assess whether they correspond to those which it requires. The general system for recognition, however, does not prevent a Member State from making any person pursuing a profession on its territory subject to specific requirements due to the application of professional rules justified by the general public interest. Rules of this kind relate, for example, to organisation of the profession, professional standards, including those concerning ethics, and supervision and liability. Lastly, this Directive is not intended to interfere with Member States' legitimate interest in preventing any of their citizens from evading enforcement of the national law relating to professions.'

To what extent does Recital 11 of Directive 2005/36 merely correspond to what followed from Article 49 TFEU, as this provision was interpreted by the CJEU in the *Thieffry* case, and to what extent does Recital 11 go beyond the CJEU's interpretation?

JUDGMENT OF THE COURT
12 February 1987

Commission of the European Communities v Kingdom of Belgium

'Failure of a State to fulfil its obligations – Infringement of Article 52 – Right of establishment in relation to clinical biology laboratories'

Case 221/85

Judgment

1. By an application lodged at the Court Registry on 20 June 1985, the Commission of the European Communities brought an action under Article 169 of the EEC Treaty for a declaration that the Kingdom of Belgium has failed to fulfil its obligations under Article 52 of the EEC Treaty by providing that services in the field of clinical biology carried out in laboratories operated by a legal person governed by private law whose members, partners or directors are not all natural persons authorized to carry out medical analyses may not be reimbursed under the social security scheme.

2. Reference is made to the Report for the Hearing for the Belgian legislation on services in the field of clinical biology, the background to the application and the arguments of the parties, which are mentioned or discussed hereinafter only in so far as is necessary for the reasoning of the Court.

3. The Commission considers that Belgian Royal Decree No. 143 of 30 December 1982, laying down the conditions which a laboratory must satisfy in order for clinical biology services to qualify for reimbursement from the sickness insurance scheme, is incompatible with Article 52 of the Treaty.

4. Where a laboratory is operated for profit by a legal person, the decree requires that all its members, partners and directors should be doctors or pharmacist. As a result it is impossible for companies established in another Member State to set up secondary establishments, especially subsidiary companies, in Belgium.

5. Furthermore, the Commission maintains that the restrictions on the right of establishment prohibited by Article 52 of the Treaty are not confined to discriminatory measures but include measures which apply to both nationals and foreigners without distinction where they constitute an unjustified constraint for the latter.

6. The Commission adds that the abovementioned conditions which laboratories must satisfy under Decree No. 143 are not necessary to prevent excessive recourse to clinical biology services. On the one hand, the danger of excessive recourse to ana-

lyses is in general attributable principally to the prescribing doctor, since an analysis requested by him can hardly be refused by the laboratory. Secondly, if there is any collusion, Article 9 of Royal Decree No. 143 provides for the possibility of penalizing the operator of the laboratory, whether or not he is a person entitled to carry out analyses.

7. The Belgian Government considers that it has exclusive power to lay down rules governing the activity in question and such rules are compatible with Community law in so far as they do not discriminate against nationals of other Member States and companies assimilated to them by virtue of Article 58 of the EEC Treaty.

8. It also contends that the contested royal decree pursues a purpose which is in the public interest, namely the prevention of excessive recourse to clinical biology services which, the Belgian Government believes, might result from collusion between prescribing doctors and laboratories. That is why the law provides for clinical biology services to be reimbursed only if the laboratory in question is operated by a doctor or pharmacist or, where it is operated for profit by a legal person, only if its members, partners or directors are doctors or pharmacists. Those professions are subject to disciplinary rules laid down by the respective governing bodies, the effectiveness of which has been demonstrated in practice, in particular as regards the prevention of prescription abuses. The possibility of criminal sanctions, such as those provided for in Article 9 of the royal decree, is insufficient.

9. In the first place it must be stressed that under the second paragraph of Article 52 of the EEC Treaty freedom of establishment includes the right to take up and pursue activities as self-employed persons under the conditions laid down by the legislation of the country of establishment for its own nationals. It is clear from that provision and its context that, provided that such equality of treatment is respected, each Member State is, in the absence of Community rules in this area, free to lay down rules for its own territory governing the activities of laboratories providing clinical biology services.

10. Secondly, the Court has already observed, in particular in its judgment of 28 January 1986 in Case 270/83 *Commission* v *French Republic* [1986] ECR 273, that Article 52 is intended to ensure that all nationals of Member States who establish themselves in another Member State, even if that establishment is only secondary, for the purpose of pursuing activities there as a self-employed person receive the same treatment as nationals of that State and it prohibits, at a restriction on freedom of establishment, any discrimination on grounds of nationality.

11. It must be stated that Belgian law does not prevent doctors or pharmacists who are nationals of other Member States from establishing themselves in Belgium and operating there a laboratory to carry out clinical analyses qualifying for reimbursement under the social security system. The legislation therefore applies without dis-

tinction to Belgian nationals and those of other Member States, and its provisions and objectives do not permit the conclusion that it was adopted for discriminatory purposes or that it produces discriminatory effects.

12. In the light of the foregoing considerations, it must be concluded that the Belgian State, by adopting Royal Decree No. 143 of 30 December 1982, has not failed to fulfil its obligations under Article 52 of the EEC Treaty and the application must be dismissed.

Costs

[Para. 13 omitted]

On those grounds,

THE COURT

hereby:

(1) Dismisses the application;

[Para. 2 of the ruling omitted]

Comments and questions

Case 221/85 *Commission* v *Belgium* (*Clinical Biology Services*) [1987] ECR 719, concerned Belgian social security law, under which payments for clinical biological examinations undertaken by laboratories was only reimbursed under the social security scheme if all the members, partners and directors of the laboratory were natural persons authorised to carry out medical analyses. It was the view of the Commission that this was incompatible with Article 49 TFEU (formerly Article 52 EEC Treaty). This was so because the provision was not confined to discriminatory measures but also included measures which applied without distinction between the Member State's own nationals and foreign nationals, but which, in the view of the Commission, nevertheless constituted an unjustified constraint on foreign nationals; cf. paragraph 5 of the judgment. While the Belgian law applied without regard to nationality, it nevertheless restricted laboratory companies in other Member States from setting up subsidiary companies to run laboratories in Belgium, since its owners and members of the board of directors must all be doctors or pharmacists in order to obtain approval from the public authorities to carry out examinations.

The CJEU rejected the arguments of the Commission, since it held that Member States were *only* required to respect the *principle of equal treatment* under Article 49 TFEU; cf. paragraph 9. It therefore held that Article 49 TFEU merely requires that undertakings from other Member States should receive the same treatment as nationals of the host State; cf. paragraph 10. Since the Belgian law did not contain any discrimination, with regard to the establishment and conduct of a laboratory business in Belgium, it did not fall foul of Article 49 TFEU. However, in reality, the CJEU had already established in 1977 that Article 49 TFEU also covers national rules that restrict access to the market (see Case 71/76 *Thieffry* v *Conseil de l'ordre des avocats à la cour de Paris* [1977] ECR 765, above). Today, Article 49 TFEU certainly covers all national restrictions which affect the right of establishment, see Case C-55/94 *Gebhard* v *Consiglio dell'Ordine degli Avvocati e Procuratori di Milano* [1995] ECR I-4165, printed above.

In Case C-531/06 *Commission* v *Italy* [2009] ECR I-4103, the CJEU had to consider Italian legislation restricting the right to operate a pharmacy to pharmacists alone. The CJEU found that there was a restriction pursuant to Article 49 TFEU, 'because it allows only pharmacists to operate pharmacies, denying other economic operators access to this self-employed activity'; see paragraph 45. However, the CJEU ruled that the legislation was justified by regard for protection of public health, that it was appropriate for this purpose, and that it did not go beyond what was necessary for this purpose.

In its judgment in Case C-424/97 *Haim* v *Kassenzahnärztliche Vereinigung Nordrhein* [2000] ECR I-5123, the CJEU considered whether it was in accordance with Article 49 TFEU that a dentist, who was a national of a different Member State than that in which he had established his practice, was only eligible for appointment as a dental practitioner under a social security scheme if he had sufficient knowledge of the language of the host State. The CJEU also considered whether such a language requirement fell within the scope of Article 49 TFEU. What do you think the CJEU decided?

When the Danish telecommunications company TDC wanted to offer a cheap mobile telephony service in the United Kingdom, it chose to sell its services via the internet under the name 'Easy Mobile'. However, it appeared that customers in the United Kingdom were protected by a rule that, within six months after making a credit payment on the internet, they could rescind their payment. This caused considerable problems for Easy Mobile, since a customer would usually long since have exhausted their credit account for connection time when the six months were up. If a customer cancelled a payment, Easy Mobile had to show in each case that the payment had in fact been used on mobile connection services, and this would not be worthwhile for the small amounts relating to each customer. Thus the rule constituted a very real barrier to access to the British market for internet sales of mobile telephony services. Was the British rule a restriction which was subject to the TFEU rules on freedom of establishment?

JUDGMENT OF THE COURT
16 June 1992

Commission of the European Communities v Grand Duchy of Luxembourg

'Failure of a Member State to fulfil its obligations – Freedom of establishment – Access to the professions of doctor, dentist and veterinary surgeon'

Case C-351/90

Judgment

1. By application lodged at the Court Registry on 28 November 1990, the Commission of the European Communities brought an action under Article 169 of the EEC Treaty for a declaration that, by not providing that the rule laid down in its legislation to the effect that persons exercising the professions of doctor, dentist or veterinary surgeon must have a single practice does not prevent nationals of Member States established in another Member State or working there as employed persons who wish to establish themselves in Luxembourg or work there as employed persons from maintaining their practice or continuing to be employed in a Member State other than Luxembourg, the Grand Duchy of Luxembourg had failed to fulfil its obligations under Articles 48 and 52 of the EEC Treaty.

2. The legislation at issue is contained in the Law of 29 April 1983 concerning the exercise of the professions of medicine, dentistry and veterinary medicine (Gazette A – No 31 of 10 May 1983, p. 746, hereinafter referred to as 'the Law'). Article 16 of the Law provides that a doctor or dentist may not have more than one surgery. Article 29 contains a similar provision for veterinary surgeons, in so far as it provides that they may have only one place of establishment.

3. However, the second sentence of Article 16 of the Law provides that: '... a doctor or dentist established in Luxembourg may be authorized by the Minister of Health, on the advice of the College of Physicians, to have a second surgery in the country for regular consultations, on condition that the surgery is in a region where there is no doctor practising the same discipline or no dentist, and where medical cover for the region is insufficient.'

4. Articles 2(2) and 9 of the Law allow a doctor or dentist established in another Member State to practise in Luxembourg as a substitute for a doctor or dentist who is established there. According to Article 22(2) of the Law, the same applies to veterinary surgeons.

5. Finally, Articles 4, 11 and 25 of the Law authorize doctors, dentists or veterinary surgeons who are nationals of a Member State of the Community and who are established in another Member State to provide services in Luxembourg.

6. By a letter dated 19 April 1989, the Commission drew to the attention of the Luxembourg authorities the question whether the single-practice rule, imposed on doctors, dentists and veterinary surgeons by the Law, was compatible with Community law.

7. Having received no reply to that letter, on 21 November 1989 the Commission issued a reasoned opinion in accordance with Article 169 of the EEC Treaty, requesting the Luxembourg Government to adopt the measures necessary for compliance with its obligations within two months of notification.

8. By a letter dated 29 January 1990, the Luxembourg Government challenged the terms of the reasoned opinion, pleading that the Law is neither ambiguous nor discriminatory as regards the nationals of Member States having an establishment in a Member State other than Luxembourg. Considering this line of argument to be unsatisfactory, the Commission brought this action.

9. Reference is made to the Report for the Hearing for a fuller account of the facts of the case, the procedure and the pleas and arguments of the parties, which are mentioned or discussed hereinafter only in so far as is necessary for the reasoning of the Court.

10. It must be stated first of all that the so-called single-practice rule for the medical, dental and veterinary professions has the effect of restricting the freedom of movement of workers and the right of establishment which are guaranteed by Articles 48 and 52 of the Treaty.

11. It should be borne in mind that it is settled case-law (see, for example, the judgment in Case 107/83 *Ordre des Avocats au Barreau de Paris* v *Klopp* [1984] ECR 2971, paragraph 19; the judgment in Case 143/87 *Stanton and SA Belge d'Assurances L'Etoile 1905* v *Inasti* [1988] ECR 3877, paragraph 11 and the judgment in Joined Cases 154 and 155/87 *Rijksinstituut voor de Sociale Verzekering der Zelfstandigen* v *Wolf and NV Microtherm Europe and Others* [1988] ECR 3897, paragraph 11; the judgment in Case 106/91 *Ramrath*, not yet published in the ECR, paragraph 20), that the right of establishment entails the freedom to set up and maintain, subject to observance of the professional rules of conduct, more than one place of work within the Community.

12. Those considerations are equally valid where an employee or an independent practitioner, established in one Member State, wishes to practise his profession in another Member State, irrespective of the question whether he intends to practise as an em-

ployee or as an independent practitioner (see paragraph 12 of the judgments in the abovementioned Cases 143/87 and 154 and 155/87 and paragraphs 25 and 26 of the abovementioned judgment in Case 106/91).

13. As the Court acknowledged in its judgment in Case 96/85 *Commission* v *France* [1986] ECR 1475, at paragraph 10, as far as the medical and dental professions are concerned, the professional rules that must be observed are in particular those inspired by concern to protect the health of individuals as efficiently and fully as possible. The rules governing practice of the veterinary profession must be regarded as meeting the same health objective.

14. It is apparent, however, from that judgment that those rules, in so far as they have the effect of restricting in particular the right of establishment and the freedom of movement of workers, are compatible with the Treaty only if the restrictions which they entail are actually justified in view of the general obligations inherent in the proper practice of the professions in question and apply to nationals of that State and to the nationals of other Member States alike. In this connection, the Court has found that such was not the case where the restrictions were liable to create discrimination against practitioners established in other Member States or raise obstacles to access to the profession which go beyond what is necessary in order to achieve the intended objectives.

15. In this regard, it must be observed first of all that the single-practice rule, which, according to the Luxembourg Government is essential to continuity of care, is applied more strictly to doctors and dentists practising in other Member States than to those practising in Luxembourg. The second sentence of Article 16 of the Law permits derogation from the single-practice rule only for persons practising in Luxembourg.

16. On this point, the Luxembourg Government contends that in special cases that derogation may be extended by ministerial decision to persons established in other Member States.

17. This argument cannot be accepted. First of all, Article 16 of the Law refers only to practitioners established in Luxembourg. Secondly, observance of the principles of equality of treatment cannot depend on the unilateral will of national authorities.

18. It must therefore be observed that, although the objective legal position is clear, in the sense that Articles 48 and 52 of the Treaty are directly applicable in the territory of Member States, the maintenance of Article 16 of the Law in question still gives rise to an ambiguous situation by keeping the entitled persons concerned in a state of uncertainty as to the possibilities open to them to rely on Community law (see the judgment in Case 167/73 *Commission* v *France* [1974] ECR 359, at paragraph 41).

19. It must be observed next that a general rule prohibiting practitioners established in another Member State or employed there from carrying on their practice from an establishment in Luxembourg is unduly restrictive.

20. In this respect, the Luxembourg Government contends that the single-practice rule is objectively justified on the grounds of public health and public policy, and also on the grounds of the general interest. It states that a medical contract is a contract intuitu personae, requiring the continuous presence of the practitioner at his surgery or place of employment in order to ensure that care is permanently available, and states that the emergency service would be disrupted if practitioners with more than one place of work helped to provide it.

21. This argument cannot be accepted either.

22. First, it is not essential for a practitioner, whether general practitioner, dentist or veterinary surgeon, or even a medical specialist (see the judgment in Case 96/85 *Commission* v *France* [1986] ECR 1475, at paragraph 13, cited above), to be close to the patient or client all the time. Moreover, the practitioner's permanent availability is not necessarily guaranteed by the single-practice rule when, for example, the practitioner is travelling, or practises part-time or belongs to a group practice. Secondly, the permanent availability of care and the efficient organization of the emergency service may be achieved in less restrictive ways, such as by requiring minimum attendance or having arrangements for providing replacements.

23. From these considerations it is apparent that the prohibition in question is too absolute and general in nature for it to be justified by the need to have care permanently available.

24. It must therefore be declared that by preventing doctors, dentists and veterinary surgeons established in another Member State or working there as employed persons from establishing themselves in Luxembourg or holding employment there while maintaining their practice or employment in that other Member State, the Grand Duchy of Luxembourg has failed to fulfil its obligations under Articles 48 and 52 of the EEC Treaty.

Costs

[Para. 25 omitted]

On those grounds,

THE COURT

hereby rules:

1. **By preventing medical practitioners, dentists and veterinary surgeons established in another Member State or working there as employed persons from establishing themselves in Luxembourg or holding employment there while maintaining their practice or employment in that other Member State, the Grand Duchy of Luxembourg has failed to fulfil its obligations under Articles 48 and 52 of the EEC Treaty;**

[Para. 2 of the ruling omitted]

Comments and questions

This case, on Luxembourg's prohibition of secondary establishments by doctors, dentists and veterinary surgeons, is a classic example of the CJEU's approach to restrictions on freedom of establishment. The Luxembourg legislation did not contain an absolute prohibition, as in special circumstances the minister responsible had the possibility of granting a dispensation to people who had established businesses in Luxembourg, and the Luxembourg Government argued that this possibility of granting a dispensation could also be used by those who had established businesses in other Member States.

Even if the prohibition applied equally to both domestic and foreign citizens, it affected business people in other Member States considerably more severely than business people in Luxembourg. A doctor who had established a practice in Luxembourg had access to the Luxembourg market for health services by virtue of his or her establishment in Luxembourg, while a doctor established in, for example, Belgium was effectively excluded from the market because he or she could not establish a branch in Luxembourg. This was incompatible with Article 49 TFEU (formerly Article 52 EEC Treaty), which contains a specific right to set up branches.

The Luxembourg Government's argument that the minister responsible could give dispensation from the prohibition on secondary establishments was rejected by the CJEU. First, the CJEU pointed out that the legislation itself only stated that dispensation could be given to businesses that were already established in Luxembourg. A doctor established in another Member State would thus not be able to know of the possibility of getting a dispensation. Second, the right to a dispensation meant that the Luxembourg authorities could take a unilateral decision on whether permission should be given to establish a branch. The CJEU remarked that the exercise of the right to establish a branch pursuant to the TFEU could not be made subject to the unilateral decision of a national authority.

Would the CJEU have reached a different conclusion if the Luxembourg legislation had expressly stated that the minister responsible could also allow doctors etc. established in other Member States to set up branches in Luxembourg? Is it relevant to the answer whether the legislation listed the factors which the minister must take into account when making such a decision?

In paragraph 14 of the judgment the CJEU introduced 'rule of reason' thinking (the *Cassis de Dijon* doctrine which related to the free movement of goods) to Article 49 TFEU, and rejected the argument that the Luxembourg legislation was compatible with Article 49 TFEU by applying the principle of proportionality. When assessing proportionality the CJEU considers, first, whether the rules are suitable for achieving the claimed lawful purpose. Next, it considers whether the rules are necessary, in other words, whether they are the least restrictive method for achieving that purpose. Luxembourg argued that the prohibition of secondary establishment was 'justified on the grounds of public health and public policy, and also on the grounds of the general interest'. This is undoubtedly a lawful purpose. However, the question is whether it is the real purpose of the Luxembourg prohibition. The CJEU refrained from expressing a view on this. Instead it found that the Luxembourg prohibition was not a suitable method for achieving the claimed (lawful) purpose, as well as finding that the prohibition was not the least restrictive method. Thus the prohibition was contrary to the principle of proportionality.

The Luxembourg law precluded *access* to making secondary establishments in Luxembourg. On this point, compare the case with, on the one hand, Case C-212/97 *Centros* [1999] ECR I-1459, printed above, and, on the other hand, Case 221/85 *Commission* v *Belgium* (the *Clinical Biology Services Case*) [1987] ECR 719 printed above.

JUDGMENT OF THE COURT
31 March 1993

Dieter Kraus v Land Baden-Württemberg.
(Reference for a preliminary ruling by the Verwaltungsgericht Stuttgart
– Federal Republic of Germany)

'Use of a post-graduate academic title – Legislation of a Member State requiring authorization for the use of academic titles awarded in another Member State'

Case C-19/92

Judgment

1. By order of 19 December 1991, received at the Court on 24 January 1992, the Verwaltungsgericht Stuttgart (Administrative Court, Stuttgart), Federal Republic of Germany, referred to the Court for a preliminary ruling under Article 177 of the EEC Treaty a question on the interpretation of Article 48 of the Treaty, with a view to determining the compatibility with Community law of legislation of a Member State requiring prior authorization for the use by one of its nationals, on its territory, of a postgraduate academic title awarded in another Member State.

2. This question was raised in proceedings between Mr Dieter Kraus, a German national, and the *Land* Baden-Württemberg, represented by the Ministry of Sciences and Arts, concerning the refusal of the Ministry to accept that the use of the postgraduate academic title awarded to Mr Kraus in the United Kingdom was not subject to the rules on prior authorization established by German legislation.

3. The documents before the Court show that the German Law of 7 June 1939 relating to the use of academic titles (Reichsgesetzblatt 1939 I, p. 985) provides that persons holding academic diplomas awarded by a German higher education establishment may use those titles on German territory without special authorization to do so.

4. In contrast, German nationals who have obtained an academic title in a foreign establishment of higher education must, in order to be able to use it in the Federal Republic of Germany, apply for authorization from the competent ministry of the relevant *Land*. The requirement of individual authorization also applies to non-nationals, including Community nationals, with the exception of persons staying in the Federal Republic of Germany, either on official mission or on a temporary basis, for a period not exceeding three months, and for a non-professional purpose. In those cases it is sufficient for such persons to have been authorized to use their academic titles under the law of their country of origin.

5. The authorization in question may be granted in the form of a general authorization for academic titles awarded by certain foreign establishments. The German *Länder*, which have competence in this matter, have however made use of this possibility only with respect to titles awarded by French and Netherlands higher education establishments.

6. The application for authorization to use academic titles in the Federal Republic of Germany must be made on a special form, to which a number of documents must be attached. In the *Land* Baden-Württemberg the applicant must also pay an administrative fee of DM 130.

7. Under the German Criminal Code it is an offence punishable by a term of imprisonment not exceeding one year or by a fine to use without authorization academic titles awarded abroad.

8. Mr Kraus studied law in the Federal Republic of Germany and in 1986 he passed the first State examination in law. In 1988 he obtained the university degree of 'Master of Laws (LL.M)' following postgraduate study at the University of Edinburgh (United Kingdom). After temporary employment as an assistant at the University of Tübingen (Federal Republic of Germany), he underwent various periods of professional training in the *Land* Baden-Württemberg with a view to taking the second State examination in law.

9. In 1989 Mr Kraus sent a copy of his degree certificate from the University of Edinburgh to the Ministry of Sciences and Arts of the *Land* Baden-Württemberg, requesting confirmation that, having done so, there was nothing further to prevent him from using his title in the Federal Republic of Germany.

10. The Ministry replied that his request could be allowed only if he made formal application for the authorization prescribed for the purpose by German law, using the appropriate form and attaching to it a certified copy of the diploma in question. Mr Kraus subsequently sent a certified copy of his Edinburgh degree, but refused to submit a formal application for authorization on the ground that the requirement for such an authorization prior to the use of an academic title awarded in another Member State constituted an obstacle to the free movement of persons and also discrimination, both prohibited by the EEC Treaty, since no such authorization was required for the use of a diploma awarded by a German establishment.

11. Mr Kraus then brought the matter before the Verwaltungsgericht Stuttgart, which referred to the Court the following question for a preliminary ruling: 'Is it contrary to Article 48 of the EEC Treaty – or to any other provision of Community law which may afford an answer to the point at issue – for a Member State of the European Community to require its nationals to obtain authorization from the State before using, in its territory, in their original form, academic titles acquired through

postgraduate studies in another Member State which do not provide access to a profession but which are advantageous for the exercise of that profession, and to threaten to punish use of the academic title without the aforementioned authorization?'

12. Reference is made to the Report of the hearing for a fuller account of the facts in the main case, the procedure before the Court and the observations submitted to the Court, which are mentioned as discussed hereinafter only in so far as is necessary for the reasoning of the Court.

13. The documents before the Court show that the point of the question put by the national court is to ascertain whether on their proper construction Articles 48 and 52 of the Treaty preclude a Member State from prohibiting one of its own nationals who holds a postgraduate academic title awarded in another Member State from using that title on its territory unless he has obtained administrative authorization to do so.

14. In order to answer that question, it is necessary first to consider whether Community law applies in such a situation.

15. Although the provisions in the Treaty relating to freedom of movement for persons do not apply to situations which are purely internal to a Member State, the Court has already held that Article 52 of the Treaty may not be interpreted in such a way as to exclude from the benefit of Community law the nationals of a given Member State when, owing to the fact that they have lawfully resided on the territory of another Member State and have there acquired a vocational qualification which is recognized under Community law, they are, with regard to their State of origin, in a situation which may be assimilated to that of any other persons enjoying the rights and liberties guaranteed by the Treaty (see judgments in Case 115/78 *Knoors* v *Staatssecretaris voor Economische Zaken* [1979] ECR 399, paragraph 24, and in Case 61/89 *Bouchoucha* [1990] ECR I-3551, paragraph 13).

16. The same reasoning must be followed as regards Article 48 of the Treaty. In its judgment in *Knoors*, cited above (paragraph 20), the Court held that freedom of movement for workers and the right of establishment guaranteed by Article 48 and 52 of the Treaty were fundamental rights in the Community system, and would not be fully realized if the Member States were able to refuse to grant the benefit of the provisions of Community law to those of their nationals who had taken advantage of its provisions to acquire vocational qualifications in a Member State other than that of which they were nationals.

17. The same consideration applies where a national of a Member State has obtained in another Member State a university qualification which supplements his basic education and training and of which he intends to make use after he returns to his country of origin.

18. Although a postgraduate academic title is not usually a prerequisite for access to a profession, either as an employee or on or on a self-employed basis, the possession of such a title nevertheless constitutes, for the person entitled to make use of it, an advantage for the purpose both of gaining entry to such a profession and of prospering in it.

19. Accordingly, in so far as it constitutes proof of possession of an additional professional qualification and thereby confirms its holder's fitness for a particular post, and also, as the case may be, his command of the language of the country where it was awarded, a university diploma of the kind in point in the main proceedings is by its nature such as to improve its holder's chances of appointment as compared with those of other candidates who are unable to make use of any qualification supplementary to the basic education and training required for the post in question.

20. In some cases possession of a postgraduate academic title obtained in another State may even be a prerequisite for access to certain professions, where those professions require specific knowledge such as that evidenced by the diploma in question. That may be so in the case of a postgraduate diploma in law required, for example, for access to an academic career in the fields of international or comparative law.

21. Furthermore, the holder of a diploma such as that in question in the main proceedings may find himself in an advantageous position in the pursuit of his professional activity in so far, as through possession of that diploma, he can obtain higher remuneration or more rapid advancement or, in the course of his career, access to certain specific posts reserved to persons with particularly high qualifications.

22. Similarly, the possibility of using academic titles awarded abroad and supplementing national diplomas required for access to a profession greatly facilitates establishment as an independent practitioner and, in any event, the pursuit of a corresponding professional activity.

23. It follows that the situation of a Community national who holds a postgraduate academic title which, obtained in another Member State, facilitates access to a profession or, at least, the pursuit of an economic activity, is governed by Community law, even as regards the relations between that national and the Member State whose nationality he possesses.

24. However, although the question put to the Court thus falls within the scope of application of the Treaty, it is not governed, as Community law stands at present, by any specific legislation.

25. Council Directive 89/48/EEC of 21 December 1988, relating to a general system of recognition of higher education diplomas awarded on completion of professional education and training of at least three years' duration (OJ 1989 L 19, p. 16) does

not cover an academic title such as that in point before the national court, which was awarded on completion of studies of only one year's duration.

26. In contrast, Council Directive 92/51/EEC on a second general system for the recognition of professional education and training to supplement Directive 89/48/EEC (OJ 1992 L 209, p. 25) extends the system of recognition to diplomas evidencing completion of studies of at least one year's duration. That directive, however, was adopted after the occurrence of the circumstances giving rise to the main proceedings and the period prescribed for its transposition into national law has not yet expired.

27. In the absence of harmonization of the conditions under which a person holding a postgraduate academic title may make use of it in Member States other than the one in which it was awarded, the Member States remain, as a matter of principle, competent to lay down the detailed rules governing the use of such a title on their territory.

28. On that point, it must however be stressed that Community law sets limits to the exercise of those powers by the Member States in so far as provisions of national law adopted in that connection must not constitute an obstacle to the effective exercise of the fundamental freedoms guaranteed by Articles 48 and 52 of the Treaty (see, to that effect, the judgment in Case 222/86 *UNECTEF* v *Heylens and Others* [1987] ECR 4097, paragraph 11).

29. The Court has confirmed that Articles 48 and 52 of the Treaty implement the fundamental principle contained in Article 3c of the Treaty in which it is stated that, for the purposes set out in Article 2, the activities of the Community are to include the abolition, as between Member States, of obstacles to freedom of movement for persons (see, in particular, judgments in Case 118/75 *Watson and Belmann* [1976] ECR 1185, paragraph 16; in *Heylens*, cited above, paragraph 8 and in Case C-370/90 *The Queen, ex parte Secretary of State for the Home Department* v *Immigration Appeal Tribunal and Surinder Singh* [1992] ECR I-4265).

30. In stating that freedom of movement for workers and freedom of establishment are to be secured by the end of the transitional period, Articles 48 and 52 lay down a precise obligation of result. The performance of that obligation was to be facilitated by but not to be made dependent upon the implementation of Community measures. The fact that such measures have not yet been adopted does not authorize a Member State to deny to a person subject to Community law the practical benefit of the freedoms guaranteed by the Treaty.

31. Furthermore, Member States are required, in conformity with Article 5 of the Treaty, to take all appropriate measures, whether general or particular, to ensure fulfil-

ment of the obligations arising out of the Treaty and to abstain from any measures which could jeopardize the attainment of the objectives of the Treaty.

32. Consequently, Articles 48 and 52 preclude any national measure governing the conditions under which an academic title obtained in another Member State may be used, where that measure, even though it is applicable without discrimination on grounds of nationality, is liable to hamper or to render less attractive the exercise by Community nationals, including those of the Member State which enacted the measure, of fundamental freedoms guaranteed by the Treaty. The situation would be different only if such a measure pursued a legitimate objective compatible with the Treaty and was justified by pressing reasons of public interest (see to that effect, judgment in Case 71/76 *Thieffry* v *Conseil de l'Ordre des Avocats à la Cour de Paris* [1977] ECR 765, paragraphs 12 and 15). It would however also be necessary in such a case for application of the national rules in question to be appropriate for ensuring attainment of the objective they pursue and not to go beyond what is necessary for that purpose (see judgment in Case C-106/91 *Ramrath* v *Ministre de la Justice* [1992] ECR I-3351, paragraphs 29 and 30).

33. It should be noted that, as the *Land* Baden-Württemberg has pointed out in its observations, national legislation such as that described by the national court is designed to protect the public against misleading use of academic titles awarded outside the territory of the Member State concerned.

34. Community law does not preclude a Member State from adopting, in the absence of harmonization, measures designed to prevent the opportunities created under the Treaty from being abused in a manner contrary to the legitimate interests of the State (see the judgment in *Knoors*, cited above, paragraph 25).

35. The need to protect a public which will not necessarily be alerted to abuse of academic titles which have not been awarded according to the rules laid down in the country in which the holder of the title intends to make use of it constitutes a legitimate interest such as to justify a restriction, by the Member State in question, of the fundamental freedoms guaranteed by the Treaty.

36. It follows that the fact that a Member State establishes a procedure for the issue of administrative authorizations, to be obtained prior to using postgraduate academic titles awarded in another State, and prescribes criminal penalties for non-compliance with that procedure is not, in itself, incompatible with the requirements of Community law.

37. However, in order to satisfy the requirements laid down by Community law with respect to the observance of the principle of proportionality, national rules of that kind must fulfil certain conditions.

38. Thus, the authorization procedure must in the first place be intended solely to verify whether the postgraduate academic title obtained in another Member State was properly awarded, following a course of studies which was actually completed, in an establishment of higher education which was competent to award it.

39. Next, the authorization procedure must be easy of access to interested parties, and should not, in particular, be dependent on the payment of excessive administration fees.

40. Moreover, verification of the academic title, referred to in paragraph 38 of this judgment, must be carried out by the national authorities in accordance with a procedure which is in conformity with the requirements of Community law as regards the effective protection of the fundamental rights conferred by the Treaty on Community nationals. It follows that any refusal of authorization by the competent national authority must be capable of being subject to judicial proceedings in which its legality under Community law can be reviewed and that the person concerned must be able to ascertain the reasons for the decision taken with respect to him (see judgment in *Heylens*, cited above, paragraphs 14 to 17, and judgment in Case 340/89 *Vlassopoulou* v *Ministerium für Justiz, Bundes-und Europaangelegenheiten Baden-Württemburg* [1991] ECR I-2357, paragraph 22).

41. Finally, whilst the national authorities are entitled to prescribe penalties for non-compliance with the authorization procedure, the penalties imposed should not exceed what appears proportionate to the offence committed. It is for the national court to determine whether the penalties laid down for that purpose in the rules of the Member State concerned are not so severe as to impede the exercise of the fundamental freedoms guaranteed by the Treaty (see judgment in Case 8/77 *Sagulo and Others* [1977] ECR 1495, paragraphs 12 and 13).

42. It follows that the answer to the question put by the national court must be that Articles 48 and 52 of the Treaty must be interpreted as meaning that they do not preclude a Member State from prohibiting one of its own nationals, who holds a postgraduate academic title awarded in another Member State, from using that title on its territory without having obtained an administrative authorization for that purpose, provided that the authorization procedure is intended solely to verify whether the postgraduate academic title was properly awarded, that the procedure is easily accessible and does not call for the payment of excessive administrative fees, that any refusal of authorization is capable of being subject to proceedings, that the person concerned is able to ascertain the reasons for the decision and that the penalties prescribed for non-compliance with the authorization procedure are not disproportionate to the gravity of the offence.

Costs

[Para. 43 omitted]

On those grounds,

THE COURT,

in answer to the question referred to it by the Verwaltungsgericht Stuttgart, by order of 19 December 1991, hereby rules:

> **Articles 48 and 52 of the Treaty must be interpreted as meaning that they do not preclude a Member State from prohibiting one of its own nationals, who holds a postgraduate academic title awarded in another Member State, from using that title on its territory without having obtained an administrative authorization for that purpose, provided that the authorization procedure is intended solely to verify whether the postgraduate academic title was properly awarded, that the procedure is easily accessible and does not call for the payment of excessive administrative fees, that any refusal of authorization is capable of being subject to judicial proceedings, that the person concerned is able to ascertain the reasons for the decision and that the penalties prescribed for non-compliance with the authorization procedure are not disproportionate to the gravity of the offence.**

Comments and questions

Dieter Kraus was a young German lawyer who had received an LL.M. degree in the United Kingdom. He wanted to make use of this academic qualification in connection with his professional work. The German rules provided that German academic qualifications could be used without prior permission. Other academic qualifications could only be used with prior permission, and in the case of *Dieter Kraus* the German authorities refused his application for permission to make use of his LL.M. degree.

The CJEU held that the German rule was covered by Article 45 TFEU (formerly Article 48 EEC Treaty) and Article 49 TFEU (formerly Article 52 EEC Treaty). Why was a rule on the use of an academic qualification covered by these provisions? Was the German rule direct discrimination, indirect discrimination, or a non-discriminatory restriction? In your opinion, did the German law affect access to employment in Germany? Compare this point with Case 221/85 *Commission* v *Belgium* (the *Clinical Biology Services Case*) [1987] ECR 719. What legitimate interests did the CJEU find could justify the restrictions in the German law, and are these interests mentioned in the TFEU?

The CJEU held that it was not, in itself, incompatible with the requirements of Union law that German law required prior authorisation to be obtained before an advocate could use, among others, the academic title LL.M; cf. paragraph 36 of the judgment.

After the CJEU had given judgment, the referring German court found in favour of Land Baden-Württemberg which had denied Dieter Kraus the right to make use of his LL.M. degree. Is it in accordance with the ruling of the CJEU that Dieter Kraus did not have his claim upheld in the substantive case? See in particular paragraphs 38-40.

This case did not concern a situation which was 'purely internal to a Member State', since Dieter Kraus had obtained his LL.M. degree in another Member State. Compare this with Joined Cases C-54/88 and others *Nino and others* [1990] ECR I-3537, which is referred to in the comments on Case C-108/96 *MacQuen* [2001] ECR I-837, printed above.

Note that in paragraphs 25-30 of the *Dieter Kraus* case, the CJEU seemed to treat the TFEU as a kind of 'framework law' which is to be 'filled out' with secondary law (typically by directives) before rights can be derived from it. However, in paragraphs 38-41 the CJEU derives clear and detailed rules directly from the Treaty provisions. What is the basis for this seeming paradox?

In some Member States accountancy firms are prohibited from also acting as law firms. Does this give rise to questions in relation to Article 49 TFEU if it can be argued that this requirement is justified by the need to protect lawyers' duty of confidentiality, also in relation to public authorities, which is in contrast to the position of auditors who are normally legally bound to give public authorities information about the internal circumstances of their clients? See Case C-309/99 Wouters [2002] ECR I-1577.

JUDGMENT OF THE COURT
8 July 1999

Société Baxter, B. Braun Médical SA, Société Fresenius France and Laboratoires Bristol-Myers-Squibb SA v Premier Ministre, Ministère du Travail et des Affaires sociales, Ministère de l'Economie et des Finances and Ministère de l'Agriculture, de la Pêche et de l'Alimentation. (Reference for a preliminary ruling: Conseil d'État – France)

'Internal taxation – Tax deduction – Expenditure on research – Proprietary medicinal products'

Case C-254/97

Judgment

1. By decision of 28 March 1997, received at the Court on 14 July 1997, the Conseil d'État (Council of State) referred to the Court for a preliminary ruling under Article 177 of the EC Treaty (now Article 234 EC) three questions on the interpretation of Articles 52 of the EC Treaty (now, after amendment, Article 43 EC), 58 of the EC Treaty (now Article 48 EC), 92 and 95 of the EC Treaty (now, after amendment, Articles 87 EC and 90 EC).

2. Those questions have been raised in actions brought before the Conseil d'État by Société Baxter ('Baxter') and other companies exploiting proprietary medicinal products by which they seek annulment, on the ground of ultra vires, of Article 12 of Ordonnance No 96-51 du 24 janvier 1996 relative aux mesures urgentes tendant au rétablissement de l'équilibre financier de la sécurité sociale (Order of 24 January 1996 on urgent measures for restoring financial stability in the social security system) (Journal Officiel de la République Française of 25 January 1996, p. 1230), for infringement of, in particular, Articles 52, 58, 93(3) of the EC Treaty (now Article 88(3) EC) and 95 of the same treaty.

3. Article 12 of that Order subjects undertakings exploiting one or more proprietary medicinal products in France to three special levies. In particular, that provision imposes on such undertakings a special levy whose basis of assessment consists of the pre-tax turnover achieved in France between 1 January 1995 and 31 December 1995 in reimbursable proprietary medicinal products and medicinal products approved for use by public authorities, after deduction of the costs accounted for during the same period corresponding to expenditure on scientific and technical research carried out in France.

4. Baxter and the other applicants in the main proceedings, which are subsidiaries of parent companies established in other Member States, argued before the Conseil

d'État that the mechanism for deducting expenditure on scientific and technical research from the amount of special levy payable caused discrimination between French laboratories carrying out research mainly in France and foreign laboratories which have their principal research units outside France.

5. Since it considered that that argument raised serious questions concerning the interpretation of Community law, the Conseil d'État decided to stay proceedings and to refer the following questions to the Court for a preliminary ruling:

   '1. Do Articles 52 and 58 of the Treaty of 25 March 1957 establishing the European Community preclude domestic legislation, enacted in 1996, which for that year imposes a special levy, the rate of which is to be fixed between 1.5% and 2%, on the pre-tax turnover achieved in the State of taxation between 1 January 1995 and 31 December 1995 by undertakings exploiting proprietary medicinal products, in reimburseable proprietary medicinal products and medicinal products approved for use by public authorities, and under which costs accounted for during that same period only in respect of expenditure on research carried out in the State of taxation may be deducted from the taxable amount?

   2. Does Article 95 of the Treaty establishing the European Community preclude such legislation?

   3. In the event that either of the previous two questions is answered in the negative, is the deduction which is allowed for expenditure on research carried out in the State of taxation to be considered aid within the meaning of Article 92 of the Treaty establishing the European Community?'

The first question

6. By its first question, the national court is asking whether Articles 52 and 58 of the Treaty preclude a Member State's legislation under which undertakings established in that State and exploiting proprietary medicinal products there are charged a special levy on their pre-tax turnover in certain of those proprietary medicinal products during the last tax year before the enactment of that legislation and are allowed to deduct from the amount payable only expenditure incurred during the same tax year on research carried out in the levying State, when it applies to Community undertakings operating in that State through a secondary place of business.

7. According to the applicants in the main proceedings and the Commission, that levy, in allowing only expenditure on research carried out in France to be deducted, is such as to put the secondary places of business established on French territory of pharmaceutical companies whose headquarters are located in another Member State at a disadvantage in relation to pharmaceutical undertakings whose principal places of business are located in France, by virtue of the fact that, in the majority of cases,

research units are located in the same Member State as the undertaking's principal place of business. Such a result is, it is claimed, contrary to Articles 52 and 58 of the Treaty.

8. The French Government submits that, in areas such as the pharmaceutical industry, where it is common for a research laboratory having its principal place of business in France to become a secondary place of business of an undertaking having its headquarters in another Member State or, conversely, for such a secondary place of business to be taken over by an undertaking having its headquarters in France, the place where the research expenditure of the pharmaceutical laboratories is incurred will then be independent of the location of their headquarters, central administration or principal place of business. According to the French Government, since the levy in question is exceptional and unique, and since it is based on past activities, it would be contrary to Articles 52 and 58 of the Treaty only if it appeared, taking account of the economic data for the year of reference, that, in fact, generally and by its very nature, it puts undertakings having their headquarters, central administration or principal place of business in a Member State other than that in which the levy is charged at a disadvantage in relation to undertakings for which those places are located in the levying Member State.

9. It should be observed first of all that the freedom of establishment conferred by Article 52 of the Treaty on the nationals of a Member State, giving them the right to take up activities as self-employed persons and pursue them on the same conditions as those laid down by the law of the Member State of establishment for its own nationals, comprises, pursuant to Article 58 of the Treaty, for companies constituted in accordance with the law of a Member State and having their registered office, central administration or principal place of business within the Community, the right to carry on business in the Member State concerned through a branch, agency or subsidiary (see Case C-1/93 *Halliburton Services* v *Staatssecretaris van Financiën* [1994] ECR I-1137, paragraph 14).

10. Next, it follows from the case-law of the Court (see Case C-330/91 *The Queen* v *Inland Revenue Commissioners, ex parte Commerzbank* [1993] ECR I-4017, paragraph 14) that the rules regarding equality of treatment prohibit not only overt discrimination by reason of nationality or, in the case of a company, its seat, but all covert forms of discrimination which, by the application of other criteria of differentiation, lead in fact to the same result.

11. Finally, it must also be borne in mind that, as the Court has repeatedly stated (see, in particular, Halliburton Services, paragraph 16), since the end of the transitional period Article 52 of the Treaty has been directly applicable notwithstanding the absence, in a particular area, of the directives provided for in Articles 54(2) and 57(1) of the EC Treaty (now, after amendment, Articles 44(1) EC and 47(1) EC).

12. The point at issue in the main proceedings is the possibility for taxable persons to deduct expenditure on research carried out in France during 1995 from the turnover liable to the special levy. It is alleged, in substance, that that allowance, even if it does not create direct discrimination against undertakings having their principal place of business in other Member States and operating in France through a secondary place of business, none the less puts those undertakings at a disadvantage by virtue of the fact that they generally carry out their research activities outside France, while undertakings established in that Member State generally carry out their research activities there.

13. In that regard, it should be observed that, although there certainly exist French undertakings which incur research expenditure outside France and foreign undertakings which incur such expenditure within that Member State, it remains the case that the tax allowance in question seems likely to work more particularly to the detriment of undertakings having their principal place of business in other Member States and operating in France through secondary places of business. It is, typically, those undertakings which, in most cases, have developed their research activity outside the territory of the Member State levying the tax.

14. That finding is not affected by the fact that the special levy in question was, as the French Government submits, exceptional in nature and based on activities relating to an earlier tax year.

15. In those circumstances, the question is whether, in the light of the provisions of the Treaty on freedom of establishment, there is any justification for the unequal treatment found in paragraph 13 above

16. In that regard, the French Government submits that the special levy made it possible to tax one of the factors which had contributed to the financial imbalance in the social security system, which was the sale of proprietary medicinal products, and that it allowed a factor contributing to the reduction of expenditure on health, namely expenditure on research relating to proprietary medicinal products, to be deducted. In that context, the restriction of the deductibility of research costs to expenditure relating only to research carried out in the levying Member State was, it submits, essential so that the tax authorities of that State could ascertain the nature and genuineness of the research expenditure incurred.

17. The Commission and, in substance, the applicants in the main proceedings claim that the information in the accounts of parent companies which have their seat in another Member State, prepared pursuant to the Fourth Council Directive (78/660/EEC) of 25 July 1978 based on Article 54(3)(g) of the Treaty on the annual accounts of certain types of companies (OJ 1978 L 222, p. 11) and the Seventh Council Directive (83/349/EEC) of 13 June 1983 based on Article 54(3)(g) of the Treaty on consolidated accounts (OJ 1983 L 193, p. 1), constitute a basis from

which the tax authorities can proceed in their supervision of research expenditure. The Commission also points out that, as far as the specific needs of fiscal supervision are concerned, the competent authorities have the power to require production of supplementary information, subject to the principle of proportionality.

18. The Court has repeatedly held that effectiveness of fiscal supervision constitutes an overriding requirement of general interest capable of justifying a restriction on the exercise of fundamental freedoms guaranteed by the Treaty (see, inter alia, Case C-250/95 *Futura Participations and Singer* v *Administration des Contributions* [1997] ECR I-2471, paragraph 31). A Member State may therefore apply measures which enable the amount of costs deductible in that State as research expenditure to be ascertained clearly and precisely.

19. However, national legislation which absolutely prevents the taxpayer from submitting evidence that expenditure relating to research carried out in other Member States has actually been incurred cannot be justified in the name of effectiveness of fiscal supervision.

20. The taxpayer should not be excluded a priori from providing relevant documentary evidence enabling the tax authorities of the Member State imposing the levy to ascertain, clearly and precisely, the nature and genuineness of the research expenditure incurred in other Member States.

21. Consequently, the answer to be given to the first question must be that Articles 52 and 58 of the Treaty preclude a Member State's legislation under which undertakings established in that State and exploiting proprietary medicinal products there are charged a special levy on their pre-tax turnover in certain of those proprietary medicinal products during the last tax year before the enactment of that legislation and are allowed to deduct from the amount payable only expenditure incurred during the same tax year on research carried out in the levying State, when it applies to Community undertakings operating in that State through a secondary place of business.

Second and third questions

22. In the light of the answer given to the first question, it is not necessary to answer the second and third questions.

Costs

[Para. 23 omitted]

On those grounds,

THE COURT,

in answer to the questions referred to it by the Conseil d'État by decision of 28 March 1997, hereby rules:

> **Articles 52 of the EC Treaty (now, after amendment, Article 43 EC) and 58 of the EC Treaty (now Article 48 EC) preclude a Member State's legislation under which undertakings established in that State and exploiting proprietary medicinal products there are charged a special levy on their pre-tax turnover in certain of those proprietary medicinal products during the last tax year before the enactment of that legislation and are allowed to deduct from the amount payable only expenditure incurred during the same tax year on research carried out in the levying State, when it applies to Community undertakings operating in that State through a secondary place of business.**

Comments and questions

Case C-254/97 *Société Baxter and others* v *Premier Ministre of France and others* [1999] ECR I-4809, concerned four pharmaceutical companies with their head offices outside France, but with French subsidiaries. In January 1996 the French Government issued an Executive Order with urgent measures for restoring financial stability in the social security system. Among other things, the Order laid down that producers of medicines should pay a special levy based on their pre-tax turnover in France in 1995. In calculating this turnover, producers could deduct expenditure on scientific and technical research carried out in France. Did this rule infringe the TFEU provisions on freedom of establishment?

In principle, direct taxes do not fall within the competence of the Union. On the other hand, Article 4(3) TEU states that Member States shall refrain from any measure which could jeopardise the attainment of the Union's objectives. This means, among other things, that they cannot, without due justification, issue tax rules which restrict freedom of movement.

In the *Baxter* case, the tax rule was not based on the nationality of the pharmaceutical companies, so it was clear that the rule was not directly discriminatory. However, the question was whether the rule constituted a restriction. The CJEU noted in paragraphs 12 and 13 that pharmaceutical companies generally carry out their research at their principal place of business. The consequence was that French companies typically carried out their research in France, while foreign companies usually only had a marketing company in France, without research activities. This meant that the tax allowance could seldom be used by foreign producers to the same extent as by French producers. The disputed rule would thus be detrimental to foreign producers and constitute a restriction (cf. paragraph 13).

However, the French Government argued that the special levy in question was an exceptional and unique single tax based on past activities. It was therefore impossible that the rule could have hindered undertakings from setting up in France, so it could not be argued that the rule restricted the right of establishment. The CJEU merely stated that this fact did not affect its finding. What arguments can it be assumed the CJEU used to arrive at this decision? Consider, in particular, whether the freedom of establishment itself only concerns *access* to establish an undertaking, or whether the CJEU can be assumed to give further protection, so that it covers a period which extends beyond the phase where an undertaking is established, so as also to cover national rules affecting the *exercise* of a given form of undertaking? It has been said that the *Baxter* judgment gives very wide protection to subsidiaries, and that the concept of a restriction has been stretched quite far. Do you agree with this?

By reference to paragraph 16 of the judgment in Case 81/87 *Daily Mail and General Trust* [1988] ECR 5483, the Advocate General argued that freedom of establishment should not be assumed merely to be the right to establish oneself in a given Member State, but also the right to leave one Member State with a view to establishing oneself in another Member State. This right to leave a Member State to exercise the right of establishment within the Union applies both to natural and legal persons. The Advocate General was of the opinion that the French tax rule could constitute a restriction on that right, in that it could deter French undertakings from moving or from starting research activities outside France. Would such an interpretation of the freedom of establishment mean that any positive measure for undertakings in a Member State could constitute a restriction on freedom of movement?

The French Government had argued that the restriction of tax allowances to the costs of research carried out in France was necessary to enable the French tax authorities to control the nature and the genuineness of the research costs for which a company might wish to claim a tax allowance. The CJEU accepted that consideration for the effectiveness of fiscal supervision can constitute an overriding requirement of general interest capable of justifying a restriction on the exercise of fundamental freedoms guaranteed by the TFEU. However, the CJEU held that in this case the disputed rule could not justify such a consideration. Why did the CJEU come to this conclusion (see in particular paragraph 19)?

In recent years the CJEU has had the opportunity to consider the compatibility of a number of national taxation laws with Article 49 TFEU. The results have often been that the taxation laws have been found to be contrary to this provision. See, for example, Case C-170/05 *Denkavit* v *Ministre de l'Économie, des Finances et de l'Industrie* [2006] ECR I-11949, where the CJEU held that it was contrary to Article 49 TFEU for French tax legislation to withhold tax paid on dividends from a domestic subsidiary company to a foreign parent company, while dividends from a domestic subsidiary company paid to a domestic parent company were almost totally exempt from such tax.

JUDGMENT OF THE COURT (Grand Chamber)
5 October 2004

Caixa-Bank France v Ministère de l'Économie, des Finances et de l'Industrie.
(Reference for a preliminary ruling from the Conseil d'État – France)

'Freedom of establishment – Credit institutions – National legislation prohibiting the payment of remuneration on sight accounts'

Case C-442/02

Judgment

1. This reference for a preliminary ruling concerns the interpretation of Article 43 EC.

The national legal background

2. Under Article L. 312-3 of the Code monétaire et financier (Monetary and Financial Code), in the version applicable in the present case:

   'Notwithstanding any provisions to the contrary, it shall be prohibited for any credit establishment which receives funds from the public for sight accounts or accounts for less than five years, by any means whatever, to pay remuneration on those funds exceeding that fixed by regulation of the Committee for Banking and Financial Regulation or the minister responsible for the economy.'

3. Regulation No 86-13 of the Comité de la réglementation bancaire et financière (Committee for Banking and Financial Regulation), approved by decree of the Ministre de l'Économie et des Finances (Minister for Economic and Financial Affairs), of 14 May 1986 (JORF, 15 May 1986, p. 6330), prohibits the payment of remuneration on sight accounts.

4. That prohibition applies to accounts in euros opened by residents of France, whatever their nationality.

The main proceedings and the questions referred for a preliminary ruling

5. From 18 February 2002 Caixa-Bank France ('Caixa-Bank'), a company governed by French law with its seat in France which is a subsidiary of Caixa Holding, a company governed by Spanish law with its seat in Spain which holds the Caixa group's holdings in the credit institutions established under that name in Spain and in other countries of the European Union, marketed in France a sight account remunerated at the rate of 2% per annum on balances of at least EUR 1 500. By decision

of the Committee for Banking and Financial Regulation of 16 April 2002, Caixa-Bank was prohibited from concluding new contracts with residents of France relating to remunerated sight accounts in euros and ordered to rescind the clauses in existing contracts which provided for the remuneration of such accounts.

6. Caixa-Bank appealed against that decision to the Conseil d'État, which decided to stay the proceedings and refer the following questions to the Court for a preliminary ruling:

   '1. As Directive 2000/12/EC of the European Parliament and of the Council of 20 March 2000 is silent on the point, does the prohibition by a Member State of banking institutions duly established in its territory from remunerating sight accounts and other repayable funds constitute an obstacle to freedom of establishment?

   2. If the answer to the first question is in the affirmative, what kind of reasons of the public interest might in an appropriate case be relied on to justify such an obstacle?'

The questions referred for a preliminary ruling

7. It should be noted, as a preliminary point, that Directive 2000/12/EC of the European Parliament and of the Council of 20 March 2000 relating to the taking up and pursuit of the business of credit institutions (OJ 2000 L 126, p. 1) is not applicable in a case such as that at issue in the main proceedings, in particular because that directive does not refer to restrictions on the establishment of companies which, like Caixa-Bank, make use of freedom of establishment in a Member State as subsidiaries of credit institutions established in other Member States.

8. By its questions the national court essentially asks whether Article 43 EC precludes legislation of a Member State which prohibits a credit institution which is a subsidiary of a company from another Member State from remunerating sight accounts in euros opened by residents of the former Member State.

9. The freedom of establishment provided for in Article 43 EC, read in conjunction with Article 48 EC, is conferred both on natural persons who are nationals of a Member State and on legal persons within the meaning of Article 48 EC. Subject to the exceptions and conditions specified, it includes the right to take up and pursue all types of self-employed activity in the territory of any other Member State, to set up and manage undertakings, and to set up agencies, branches or subsidiaries (see, inter alia, Case C-255/97 *Pfeiffer* [1999] ECR I-2835, paragraph 18).

10. The legal position of a company such as Caixa-Bank falls within the scope of Community law by virtue of the provisions of Article 43 EC.

11. Article 43 EC requires the elimination of restrictions on the freedom of establishment. All measures which prohibit, impede or render less attractive the exercise of that freedom must be regarded as such restrictions (see, inter alia, Case C-55/94 *Gebhard* [1995] ECR I-4165, paragraph 37, Case C-108/96 *Mac Quen and Others* [2001] ECR I-837, paragraph 26, and Case C-79/01 *Payroll and Others* [2002] ECR I-8923, paragraph 26).

12. A prohibition on the remuneration of sight accounts such as that laid down by the French legislation constitutes, for companies from Member States other than the French Republic, a serious obstacle to the pursuit of their activities via a subsidiary in the latter Member State, affecting their access to the market. That prohibition is therefore to be regarded as a restriction within the meaning of Article 43 EC.

13. That prohibition hinders credit institutions which are subsidiaries of foreign companies in raising capital from the public, by depriving them of the possibility of competing more effectively, by paying remuneration on sight accounts, with the credit institutions traditionally established in the Member State of establishment, which have an extensive network of branches and therefore greater opportunities than those subsidiaries for raising capital from the public.

14. Where credit institutions which are subsidiaries of foreign companies seek to enter the market of a Member State, competing by means of the rate of remuneration paid on sight accounts constitutes one of the most effective methods to that end. Access to the market by those establishments is thus made more difficult by such a prohibition.

15. While the French Government asserted at the hearing that there are forms of account comparable to sight accounts, such as 15-day accounts, which are not covered by the prohibition of remuneration and have helped credit institutions such as Caixa-Bank to compete with French credit institutions in raising funds from the public and increasing their market share in France, the Government conceded, however, that those accounts, unlike sight accounts, do not allow the use of bank cards or cheques. The prohibition at issue therefore entails a hindrance for credit institutions such as Caixa-Bank in their activity of raising capital from the public, which the existence of other forms of account with remunerated deposits cannot remedy.

16. The restriction on the pursuit and development of the activities of those subsidiaries resulting from the prohibition at issue is all the greater in that it is common ground that the taking of deposits from the public and the granting of credits represent the basic activities of credit institutions (see, to that effect, inter alia Article 1(1) of and Annex I to Directive 2000/12).

17. It is clear from settled case-law that where, as in the case at issue in the main proceedings, such a measure applies to any person or undertaking carrying on an acti-

vity in the territory of the host Member State, it may be justified where it serves overriding requirements relating to the public interest, is suitable for securing the attainment of the objective it pursues and does not go beyond what is necessary in order to attain it (see, inter alia, Case C-424/97 *Haim* [2000] ECR I-5123, paragraph 57, *Mac Quen*, paragraph 26, and Case C-439/99 *Commission* v *Italy* [2002] ECR I-305, paragraph 23).

18. It must therefore be examined whether the grounds put forward by the French Government meet those criteria.

19. To justify the restriction on freedom of establishment resulting from the prohibition at issue, the French Government prayed in aid both the protection of consumers and the encouragement of medium and long-term saving.

20. It submits, first, that the prohibition at issue in the main proceedings is necessary for maintaining the provision of basic banking services without charge. Introducing remuneration for sight accounts would substantially increase the operating costs of banks, which, to recover those costs, would increase charges and introduce charges for the various banking services currently provided free, in particular the issuing of cheques.

21. It must be observed, however, that while the protection of consumers is among the overriding requirements that can justify restrictions on a fundamental freedom guaranteed by the EC Treaty, the prohibition at issue in the main proceedings, even supposing that it ultimately presents certain benefits for the consumer, constitutes a measure which goes beyond what is necessary to attain that objective.

22. Even supposing that removing the prohibition of paying remuneration on sight accounts necessarily entails for consumers an increase in the cost of basic banking services or a charge for cheques, the possibility might be envisaged inter alia of allowing consumers to choose between an unremunerated sight account with certain basic banking services remaining free of charge and a remunerated sight account with the credit institution being able to make charges for banking services previously provided free, such as the issuing of cheques.

23. As regards, next, the French authorities' concern to encourage long-term saving, it must be observed that, while the prohibition of remuneration on sight accounts is indeed suitable for encouraging medium and long-term saving, it nevertheless remains a measure which goes beyond what is necessary to attain that objective.

24. In the light of the above considerations, the answer to the questions referred for a preliminary ruling must be that Article 43 EC precludes legislation of a Member State which prohibits a credit institution which is a subsidiary of a company from

another Member State from remunerating sight accounts in euros opened by residents of the former Member State.

Costs

[Para. 25 omitted]

On those grounds,

THE COURT (Grand Chamber),

rules as follows:

Article 43 EC precludes legislation of a Member State which prohibits a credit institution which is a subsidiary of a company from another Member State from remunerating sight accounts in euros opened by residents of the former Member State.

Comments and questions

France did not allow the remuneration of sight accounts, i.e. accounts in which the money was not bound up for a given period, in other words like normal current accounts. The prohibition applied without distinction to all banks in France, and this meant that there was neither direct nor indirect discrimination against banks from other Member States.

In his Opinion, Advocate General Tizzano reviewed the practice of the CJEU in determining when there is a restriction. In this connection he reviewed the decision in the *Keck* case and the subsequent practice, and on this basis concluded, in paragraph 76 of his Opinion, that: 'as regards the freedom of establishment, national rules of a Member State regulating the pursuit of economic activities constitute restrictions contrary to the Treaty if they are such as to place the operator exercising that freedom in conditions of law or of fact that are worse than those of an operator established in the said State or if, by reason of their objective *or* effects, they directly affect access to the market', (emphasis added). The Advocate General believed that in the case in question there was a restriction which was contrary to Article 49 TFEU (formerly Article 43 TEC).

The CJEU also concluded that the French prohibition was contrary to Article 49 TFEU. Its reasoning was very similar to that of the Advocate General. The CJEU thus argued in paragraph 11 of the judgment that 'All measures which prohibit, impede or render less attractive the exercise of that freedom must be regarded as such restrictions'. The possibility of offering competitive interest rates on sight accounts was one of the most effective ways of breaking into the banking market of a Member State. Therefore, the prohibition on paying remuneration on sight accounts meant that it would be harder for foreign banks to break into the French market, and this restriction on access to the market constituted a restriction according to the CJEU's definition.

What was the market concerned in the *CaixaBank France* case? Did the French rule mean that there was a restriction on CaixaBank's access to this market? Or did the rule mean that CaixaBank had access to the relevant market, but was merely prevented from using a particular marketing tool (interest payment on credit balances) for persuading customers to switch to CaixaBank?

In Case C-405/98 *Gourmet International* [2001] ECR I-1795, printed in Chapter 2 above, an undertaking was to a certain extent prevented from advertising for alcoholic drinks. Consider whether the fact that an undertaking is prevented from using important competitive parameters is comparable with the denial of an undertaking's possibility of advertising its goods or services. In this connection, see Case C-464/02 *Commission* v *Denmark* [2005] ECR I-7929 (the *Company car* case), in Chapter 4 above.

On the basis of the CJEU's arguments it must be assumed that there will be a restriction where a Member State issues rules which mean that undertakings are prevented from using a method which would otherwise have been suitable for competing on the market. Consider whether the following circumstances would constitute a restriction:

- A Member State has a requirement that accountants may not enter into financial partnerships where other than auditing services are provided – for example general business consultancy or legal services.
- A Member State has a requirement that retail shops in urban areas may not be larger than 450 square metres.
- A Member State has a requirement that lottery tickets may not be sold during the period from 17.00 on Fridays until 08.00 on Mondays or on public holidays.
- A Member State has a requirement that rental cars must use fuels in which at least 10% must be biofuel. This type of fuel is more expensive to produce than normal petrol, so car rental firms will be prevented from competing by using cheaper fuels.

In his Opinion, the Advocate General was aware that if there were considered to be a restriction every time a national rule in a non-harmonised area meant that some undertaking would be less profitable, the consequence would be that the Member State which had the strictest rules would automatically create a restriction on freedom of establishment by those from other Member States; cf. paragraph 45 of the Opinion. Does the CJEU provide any guidelines to ensure that the situation described does not arise?

After having decided that there was a restriction, the CJEU had to decide whether the restriction pursued a lawful purpose, and whether the restriction was proportional.

What was the purpose of the prohibition on paying remuneration on sight accounts, according to the French Government? Was this a lawful purpose?

In assessing whether a restriction is proportional it must first be considered whether the measure is suitable for achieving the lawful purpose. Next, it must be considered whether the measure is necessary, in other words, that it is the least restrictive means for achieving the purpose. And finally it must be considered whether there is *absolute proportionality* between the restrictive effect of the measure and the lawful purpose pursued.

These conditions are cumulative. Thus, if one of the conditions is not satisfied, there is no need to consider whether the succeeding conditions are satisfied. What did the CJEU decide on the compliance with the principle of proportionality in this case (see paragraphs 21-23)?

The practice of the CJEU, under which the Member States' regulation of commerce is covered by the concept of a restriction in Article 49 TFEU, means that the Member States must be able to justify their regulation of commerce on the grounds of overriding reasons of public interest, and the Member States must be able to show that an individual measure is proportional. However, one may question whether a regulation of commerce that applies without discrimination and which cannot be said to affect foreign undertakings more than domestic undertakings ought to be covered by Article 49 TFEU. In Case C-400/08 *Commission* v *Spain* [2011] ECR I-1915, the Commission brought an action against Spain because the town planning laws in the Spanish region of Catalonia do not allow shopping centres to be more than 2,500 square metres. This regulation affected the Carrefour supermarket chain which operates larger centres in France and which wished to operate a shopping centre in Catalonia of an equivalent size. But should it be possible, on the basis of Article 49 TFEU, to lay down requirements for the regulation of the market structure in a Member State? Do you think it is reasonable that it is up to the CJEU to decide such questions? What do you think the CJEU decided in this case?

See also Case C-518/06 *Commission* v *Italy* [2009] ECR I-3491, which is included in Chapter 6.

On the basis of the above it could be natural to conclude that national measures that regulate the market structures of a Member State generally, such as a prohibition against banks paying interest on deposits in current accounts or an obligation for insurance companies to provide third party insurance for motor vehicles, is only covered by the concept of a restriction in Article 49 TFEU *if* access to the market is *directly* and *actually* affected (as opposed to merely affecting access indirectly and potentially). In this connection, see the comments of the CJEU in Case C-531/06 *Commission* v *Italy* [2009] ECR I-4103, on the Italian regulation of the pharmacy sector, according to which the right to run a pharmacy business was reserved to pharmacists, so that other economic operators were prevented from establishing pharmacies in Italy. The CJEU ruled that this regulation constituted a hindrance contrary to Articles 49 and 63 TFEU, preventing investors from other Member States, who were not pharmacists, buying shares in Italian pharmacies that were organised in the form of limited companies. However, the CJEU found that the regulation was based on considerations for protecting public health, that it was appropriate for this purpose, and that it did not go further than was necessary.

JUDGMENT OF THE COURT (Grand Chamber)
10 March 2009

Hartlauer Handelsgesellschaft mbH v Wiener Landesregierung, Oberösterreichische Landesregierung. (Reference for a preliminary ruling from the Verwaltungsgerichtshof – Austria)

'Freedom of establishment – Social security – National health system financed by the State – System of benefits in kind – System of reimbursement of costs paid by the person insured – Authorisation to set up a private outpatient dental clinic – Criterion of assessment of the need to set up a health institution – Objective of maintaining a balanced high-quality medical or hospital service open to all – Objective of preventing a risk of serious harm to the financial balance of the social security system – Consistency – Proportionality'

Case C-169/07

Judgment

1. This reference for a preliminary ruling concerns the interpretation of Articles 43 EC and 48 EC.

2. The reference was made in the course of proceedings between Hartlauer Handelsgesellschaft mbH ('Hartlauer') and the Wiener Landesregierung (Government of the Province of Vienna) and between Hartlauer and the Oberösterreichische Landesregierung (Government of the Province of Upper Austria) concerning those governments' decisions to refuse Hartlauer authorisation to set up and operate independent outpatient dental clinics.

[Paragraphs 3-17 omitted]

The main proceedings and the order for reference

18. By decision of 29 August 2001 the Wiener Landesregierung rejected the application by Hartlauer, a company established in Germany, for authorisation to set up a private health institution in the form of a outpatient dental clinic in the 21st District of Vienna. The Wiener Landesregierung based its decision on Paragraph 4 of the Wr. KAG and a report produced by an official medical expert. According to the report, dental care was adequately ensured in Vienna by public and private non-profit-making health institutions and other contractual practitioners offering comparable services. That assessment had been carried out on the basis of the ratio of the number of inhabitants to the number of dental practitioners, which was 2 207 inhabitants per practitioner. On the basis of the expert's findings, the Wiener

Landesregierung concluded that the health institution whose establishment was sought would not have the effect of substantially accelerating, intensifying or improving the provision of dental medical care for patients resident in Vienna, so that there was no need for the institution.

19. On similar grounds, the Oberösterreichische Landesregierung by decision of 20 September 2006 rejected Hartlauer's application for authorisation to set up a outpatient dental clinic in Wels. The application was examined on the basis of the waiting time for appointments with the providers of services mentioned in Paragraph 5(2) of the Oö. KAG, including the outpatient departments of the health institutions concerned.

20. Hartlauer brought proceedings against those decisions before the Verwaltungsgerichtshof (Administrative Court), which joined the two cases.

21. The Verwaltungsgerichtshof is uncertain as to the compatibility with Article 43 EC of the national legislation on the definition of needs in connection with the setting up of health institutions, and the effect on that compatibility of the fact that, when assessing those needs, Paragraph 5(2) of the Oö. KAG now requires account also to be taken of the care offered by the outpatient departments of certain health institutions, with the consequence of making access to the market in question by a new candidate even more difficult.

22. In those circumstances the Verwaltungsgerichtshof decided to stay the proceedings and refer the following questions to the Court for a preliminary ruling:

'1. Does Article 43 EC (in conjunction with Article 48 EC) preclude the application of national legislation under which authorisation is required to set up a private health institution in the operational form of an independent outpatient clinic for dental medicine (outpatient dental clinic) and authorisation is to be refused if, according to the stated purpose of the institution and the services proposed to be offered, having regard to the existing provision of care by established doctors contracted to sickness funds, establishments owned by sickness funds and establishments contracted to sickness funds and by established dentists (Dentisten) contracted to sickness funds, there is no need for the planned outpatient dental clinic?

2. Is the answer to Question 1 any different if the existing provision of care by outpatient departments of public, private non-profit-making and other health institutions contracted to sickness funds is also to be included in the examination as to need?'

The questions referred for a preliminary ruling

Admissibility

[Paras 23-27 omitted]

Question 1

28. By this question the national court asks essentially whether Articles 43 EC and 48 EC preclude national legislation such as that at issue in the main proceedings under which authorisation is necessary for setting up a private health institution in the form of an independent outpatient dental clinic, and authorisation must be refused if there is no need for that outpatient clinic, having regard to the care already offered by contractual practitioners.

Preliminary observations

29. First, it should be recalled that it is clear, both from the case-law of the Court and from Article 152(5) EC, that Community law does not detract from the power of the Member States to organise their social security systems and to adopt, in particular, provisions intended to govern the organisation and delivery of health services and medical care. In exercising that power, however, the Member States must comply with Community law, in particular the provisions of the Treaty on the freedoms of movement, including freedom of establishment. Those provisions prohibit the Member States from introducing or maintaining unjustified restrictions on the exercise of those freedoms in the healthcare sector (see, to that effect, Case 238/82 *Duphar and Others* [1984] ECR 523, paragraph 16; Case C-372/04 *Watts* [2006] ECR I-4325, paragraphs 92 and 146; and Case C-141/07 *Commission* v *Germany* [2008] ECR I-0000, paragraphs 22 and 23).

30. In accordance with settled case-law, when assessing whether that obligation has been complied with, account must be taken of the fact that a Member State has the power to determine the level of protection which it wishes to afford to public health and the way in which that level is to be achieved. Since the level of protection may vary from one Member State to the other, Member States must be allowed discretion (*Commission* v *Germany*, paragraph 51 and the case-law cited).

31. Second, it must be pointed out that the main proceedings relate to the rule that an authorisation based on the criterion of the needs of the population is required simply to set up an independent outpatient dental clinic, regardless of whether that institution is likely subsequently to conclude a contract with a social security institution which would enable it to provide medical services in the context of the system of benefits in kind. In this respect, Hartlauer asserts that it intends to provide care ser-

vices within the system of reimbursement of the costs paid by the person insured, and does not wish to obtain the status of a contractual establishment.

32. It must therefore be examined whether that requirement constitutes a restriction within the meaning of Article 43 EC and, if so, whether such a restriction may be justified.

Existence of a restriction of freedom of establishment

33. According to settled case-law, Article 43 EC precludes any national measure which, even though it is applicable without discrimination on grounds of nationality, is liable to hinder or render less attractive the exercise by Community nationals of the freedom of establishment that is guaranteed by the Treaty (see, inter alia, Case C-299/02 *Commission* v *Netherlands* [2004] ECR I-9761, paragraph 15, and Case C-140/03 *Commission* v *Greece* [2005] ECR I-3177, paragraph 27).

34. A national rule under which the establishment of an undertaking from another Member State is subject to the issue of a prior authorisation constitutes a restriction within the meaning of Article 43 EC, since it is capable of hindering the exercise by that undertaking of freedom of establishment by preventing it from freely carrying on its activities through a fixed place of business.

35. First, that undertaking may have to bear the additional administrative and financial costs involved in any grant of such an authorisation. Second, the national legislation reserves the pursuit of self-employed activity to certain economic operators who satisfy predetermined requirements, compliance with which is a condition for the issue of that authorisation (see, in relation to the freedom to provide services, Case C-76/90 *Säger* [1991] ECR I-4221, paragraph 14, and Case C-168/04 *Commission* v *Austria* [2006] ECR I-9041, paragraph 40).

36. Moreover, the Court has already held that national legislation under which the pursuit of an activity is subject to a condition linked to the economic or social need for that activity constitutes a restriction in that it tends to limit the number of providers of services (see, to that effect, Case C-63/99 *Gloszczuk* [2001] ECR I-6369, paragraph 59, and Case C-255/04 *Commission* v *France* [2006] ECR I-5251, paragraph 29).

37. In the main proceedings, the national legislation makes the setting up of a health institution such as an independent outpatient dental clinic subject to the issue of a prior administrative authorisation. It further provides that authorisation can be granted only if 'there is a need' to set up a new institution, having regard to the care already available, inter alia from contractual practitioners.

38. That legislation deters or even prevents undertakings from other Member States from pursuing their activities on the territory of the Republic of Austria through a health institution designed as a fixed place of business. In the present case, its application had the effect of depriving Hartlauer altogether of access to the market in dental care in Austria.

39. Consequently, the legislation constitutes a restriction of freedom of establishment within the meaning of Article 43 EC, notwithstanding the alleged absence of discrimination on grounds of the nationality of the persons concerned.

40. In those circumstances, it must be examined whether the provisions at issue can be objectively justified.

Justification of the restriction of freedom of establishment

41. The Oberösterreichische Landesregierung and the Austrian and Norwegian Governments submit that the requirement of a prior authorisation for the setting up of an independent outpatient dental clinic is justified on grounds of the protection of public health. The system ensures a medical service of high quality, balanced and accessible to all, and ensures the financial balance of the social security system in that in enables social security institutions to control expenditure by adapting it to planned needs.

42. They submit that such a requirement is indispensable for maintaining the bases of the medical system established by the Austrian legislature, which chose to give priority to a system of benefits in kind and to the provision of medical care for the population by establishments financed from public funds. Care was thus to be provided primarily by contractual practitioners. An uncontrolled expansion of services on offer by the establishment of new independent outpatient dental clinics would have harmful consequences for the economic situation of those practitioners, and therefore also for the access of patients to the medical services provided by them throughout national territory, since such clinics would to some extent displace them from the market.

43. The Austrian Government further submits that those restrictions are necessary because, in the public health sector, the ordinary laws of the market apply only to a very limited extent and failures of the market are frequent. In particular, the sector is not governed by the law of supply and demand. Demand is induced by supply, so that an increase in supply does not produce a fall in prices or a division of the same volume of services among several providers of services, but an increase in the volume of supplies at constant prices. Uncontrolled growth in the number of providers of medical services would thus impose uncontrollable burdens on the social security institutions. They would not have any possibility of taking corrective action by means of a policy on contracts, since even if they did not offer contracts to the new

service providers they would be obliged, in the context of the system of reimbursement of costs paid by the person insured, to spend sums substantially the same as those spent in the context of the system of benefits in kind. The result would be an immediate endangering of the financial capacities of the social security system.

44. On this point, it must be recalled that a restriction of freedom of establishment, applicable without discrimination on grounds of nationality, may be justified by overriding reasons in the general interest, provided that it is appropriate for ensuring attainment of the objective pursued and does not go beyond what is necessary for attaining that objective (*Commission* v *Greece*, paragraph 34 and the case-law cited).

45. In the present case, it is common ground that the system of prior authorisation at issue in the main proceedings applies without discrimination on grounds of nationality.

46. Moreover, the protection of public health is one of the overriding reasons in the general interest which can, under Article 46(1) EC, justify restrictions of freedom of establishment.

47. It follows from the case-law that two objectives may, more precisely, be covered by that derogation in so far as they contribute to achieving a high level of protection of health, namely the objective of maintaining a balanced high-quality medical or hospital service open to all and the objective of preventing the risk of serious harm to the financial balance of the social security system (see, to that effect, *Watts*, paragraphs 103 and 104 and the case-law cited).

48. As regards the first of those objectives, Article 46 EC allows the Member States, in particular, to restrict the freedom to provide medical and hospital services in so far as the maintenance of treatment capacity or medical competence on national territory is essential for the public health, and even the survival, of the population (see, to that effect, Case C-385/99 *Müller-Fauré and van Riet* [2003] ECR I-4509, paragraph 67, and *Watts*, paragraph 105).

49. As regards the second of those objectives, it should be noted that the planning of medical services, of which the requirement that authorisation is needed for the setting up of a new health institution is a corollary, is intended to control costs and to prevent, as far as possible, any wastage of financial, technical and human resources, since the medical care sector generates considerable costs and must satisfy increasing needs, while the financial resources which may be made available for healthcare are not unlimited, whatever the mode of funding applied (see, with regard to hospital care in the context of the freedom to provide services, *Müller-Fauré and van Riet*, paragraph 80, and *Watts*, paragraph 109).

50. Consequently, it must be ascertained whether the restrictions at issue in the main proceedings are appropriate for ensuring attainment of the objectives of maintaining a balanced high-quality medical service open to all and preventing the risk of serious harm to the financial balance of the social security system.

51. It cannot be excluded from the outset that, as the Court has already ruled with respect to hospitals (Case C-157/99 *Smits and Peerbooms* [2001] ECR I-5473, paragraphs 76 to 80, and *Watts*, paragraphs 108 to 110), establishments providing outpatient care such as doctors' surgeries and outpatient clinics may also be the subject of planning.

52. Planning which requires prior authorisation for setting up new providers of services may prove indispensable for filling in possible gaps in access to outpatient care and for avoiding the duplication of structures, so as to ensure medical care which is adapted to the needs of the population, covers the entire territory and takes account of geographically isolated or otherwise disadvantaged regions.

53. From that point of view, it is permissible for a Member State to organise medical care in such a way that it gives priority to a system of benefits in kind, so that all patients have easy access, throughout national territory, to the services of contractual practitioners.

54. In the present case, however, two series of considerations prevent the legislation in question from being accepted as appropriate for ensuring attainment of the above objectives.

55. First, it must be recalled that national legislation is appropriate for ensuring attainment of the objective pursued only if it genuinely reflects a concern to attain it in a consistent and systematic manner (see, to that effect, Joined Cases C-338/04, C-359/04 and C-360/04 *Placanica and Others* [2007] ECR I-1891, paragraphs 53 and 58, and Case C-500/06 *Corporación Dermoestética* [2008] ECR I-0000, paragraphs 39 and 40).

56. However, it follows from Paragraph 3(1) and (2) of the KAG and Paragraph 3(1) and (2) of the KAKuG, which were implemented by Paragraph 4 of the Wr. KAG and Paragraph 5 of the Oö. KAG, that a prior authorisation based on an assessment of the needs of the market is required for setting up and operating new independent outpatient dental clinics, whatever their size, and that the setting up of new group practices, by contrast, is not subject to any system of authorisation, regardless of their size.

57. Yet it appears from the order for reference that the premises and equipment of group practices and those of outpatient dental clinics may have comparable features and that in many cases the patient will not notice any difference between them.

58. Moreover, group practices generally offer the same medical services as outpatient dental clinics and are subject to the same market conditions.

59. Similarly, group practices and outpatient dental clinics may have comparable numbers of practitioners. It is true that the practitioners who provide medical services within group practices have the status of personally liable partner and are authorised to practice independently as dental practitioners, whereas the practitioners in an outpatient clinic have the status of employee. However, the documents before the Court do not show that that circumstance has any definite effect on the nature or volume of the services provided.

60. Since those two categories of providers of services may have comparable features and a comparable number of practitioners and provide medical services of equivalent volume, they may therefore have a similar impact on the market in medical services, and are thus liable to affect in an equivalent manner the economic situation of contractual practitioners in certain geographical areas and, in consequence, the attainment of the planning objectives pursued by the competent authorities.

61. That inconsistency also affects the attainment of the objective of preventing a risk of serious harm to the financial balance of the national social security system. Even supposing that the uncontrolled establishment of independent outpatient dental clinics may lead to a considerable increase in the volume of medical services at constant prices to be paid for by that system, the Austrian Government has not put forward anything capable of explaining why the establishment of those clinics but not of group practices could have such an effect.

62. Moreover, the provision of dental care in those independent outpatient clinics is liable to prove more rational, in view of the way they are organised, the fact of having several practitioners, and the use in common of medical installations and equipment, which enable them to reduce their operating costs. They will thus be able to provide medical services in conditions that are less costly than those, in particular, of independent practitioners who do not have such opportunities. The provision of care services by those institutions may have the consequence of more efficient use of the public funds allocated to the statutory health insurance system.

63. In those circumstances, it must be concluded that the national legislation at issue in the main proceedings does not pursue the stated objectives in a consistent and systematic manner, since it does not make the setting up of group practices subject to a system of prior authorisation, as is the case with new outpatient dental clinics.

64. Second, it follows from settled case-law that a prior administrative authorisation scheme cannot render legitimate discretionary conduct on the part of the national authorities which is liable to negate the effectiveness of provisions of Community law, in particular those relating to a fundamental freedom such as that at issue in the

main proceedings. Therefore, if a prior administrative authorisation scheme is to be justified even though it derogates from a fundamental freedom, it must be based on objective, non-discriminatory criteria known in advance, in such a way as adequately to circumscribe the exercise of the national authorities' discretion (see, to that effect, inter alia, Case C-205/99 *Analir and Others* [2001] ECR I-1271, paragraphs 37 and 38, and *Müller-Fauré and van Riet*, paragraphs 84 and 85).

65. In the main proceedings, the provisions concerned make the issue of authorisation to set up a new outpatient dental clinic subject to a single condition, namely the existence of a need for the services offered by the new institution. That condition follows from Paragraph 3(2) of the KAG and Paragraph 3(2) of the KAKuG and was taken up by the legislation of the provinces concerned, in Paragraph 4 of the Wr. KAG and Paragraph 5 of the Oö. KAG.

66. It is apparent from the documents submitted to the Court that in practice different criteria are used, depending on the province, to ascertain whether that condition is satisfied.

67. Thus in the province of Vienna, the existence of a need is assessed on the basis of the number of patients per dental practitioner in the area covered. In the province of Upper Austria, the assessment is based on the waiting time for an appointment with a dental practitioner.

68. However, as regards the province of Vienna, it is clear that the number of patients in question is not fixed or brought in advance to the notice of the persons concerned in any way.

69. In the province of Upper Austria, the relevant assessment is made on the basis of the answers given by practitioners practising in the catchment area of the independent outpatient dental clinic intended to be set up, even though they are potential direct competitors of that clinic. Such a method is liable to affect the objectivity and impartiality of the treatment of the application for authorisation.

70. In those circumstances, it must be concluded that the system of prior administrative authorisation at issue in the main proceedings is not based on a condition capable of adequately circumscribing the exercise by the national authorities of their discretion.

71. It follows from all the foregoing that the national legislation at issue in the main proceedings is not appropriate for ensuring attainment of the objectives of maintaining a balanced high-quality medical service open to all and preventing the risk of serious harm to the financial balance of the social security system.

72. Consequently, the answer to Question 1 is that Articles 43 EC and 48 EC preclude national legislation such as that at issue in the main proceedings under which authorisation is necessary for the setting up of a private health institution in the form of an independent outpatient dental clinic, and authorisation must be refused if there is no need for that outpatient clinic, having regard to the care already offered by contractual practitioners, where that legislation does not also subject group practices to such a system and is not based on a condition capable of adequately circumscribing the exercise by the national authorities of their discretion.

Question 2

73. In view of the answer to Question 1, there is no need to answer Question 2.

Costs

[Para. 74 omitted]

On those grounds,

THE COURT (Grand Chamber),

hereby rules:

> **Articles 43 EC and 48 EC preclude national legislation such as that at issue in the main proceedings under which authorisation is necessary for the setting up of a private health institution in the form of an independent outpatient dental clinic, and authorisation must be refused if there is no need for that outpatient clinic, having regard to the care already offered by contractual practitioners, where that legislation does not also subject group practices to such a system and is not based on a condition capable of adequately circumscribing the exercise by the national authorities of their discretion.**

Comments and questions

In Case C-169/07 *Hartlauer* [2009] ECR I-1721, the CJEU had to consider the relationship between, on the one hand, Article 49 TFEU (formerly Article 43 TEC) and, on the other hand, the Austrian requirement for prior authorisation for setting up a new outpatient dental clinic. The Austrian Government argued that this requirement was based on concern for the protection of public health. The problem in this case was that the setting up of new group practices was not subject to any system of authorisation, regardless of their size. Thus the Austrian legislation did not pursue the stated objective 'in a consistent and systematic manner'. On this basis the CJEU ruled that the legislation in question was not appropriate for protecting public health, and thus did not comply with the proportionality principle. In addition, different provincial governments in Austria made differing assessments of whether there was a need to set up new sole practitioner outpatient dental clinics. Even though the individual Member States are free to organise their health services, the *Hartlauer* case shows that, to the extent that the regulation of commercial activities is covered by Article 49 TFEU, Member States must be able to establish that their arrangements are in the overriding public interest and that they comply with the proportionality principle. Consider whether it would be compatible with Article 49 TFEU for a national legislator to lay down a requirement for owners of newly constructed windmills to offer a 20% share of the ownership of such windmills to the neighbours to the windmills, with a view to encouraging those neighbours' more ready acceptance of their construction. The CJEU has further developed the requirement for proportionality so that it requires that a national measure must be consistent and systematic. Thus, it is not sufficient for a national measure to be 'appropriate' and 'necessary' (i.e. not going beyond what is necessary).

JUDGMENT OF THE COURT (Grand Chamber)
29 March 2011

European Commission v Italian Republic. (Action under Article 226 EC for failure to fulfil obligations, brought on 19 December 2008)

'Failure of a Member State to fulfil obligations – Articles 43 EC and 49 EC – Lawyers – Obligation to comply with maximum fee tariffs – Obstacle to market access – No obstacle'

Case C-565/08

Judgment

1. By its application, the Commission of the European Communities asks the Court to declare that, by maintaining provisions which oblige lawyers to comply with maximum tariffs, the Italian Republic has failed to fulfil its obligations under Articles 43 EC and 49 EC.

[Paras 2-40 omitted]

Findings of the Court

41. At the outset, it must be stated that it is evident from all of the contested provisions that the maximum tariffs applicable to lawyers' fees are legally binding rules in so far as they are prescribed by legislation.

42. Even if it were accepted that lawyers and their clients are in practice free to agree contractually on the lawyer's remuneration, on an hourly basis or on the basis of the outcome of the proceedings, as the Italian Republic contends, the fact remains that the maximum tariffs remain mandatory if there is no agreement between lawyers and their clients.

43. Furthermore, the Commission correctly took the view that the existence of derogations allowing the maximum limits on the amount of fees to be exceeded, under certain conditions, by up to twice or four times that amount, or even more, confirms that the maximum fee tariffs apply as a general rule.

44. Consequently, the Italian Republic's argument that, in its legal order, there is no obligation on lawyers to comply with the maximum tariffs for the calculation of their fees cannot be accepted.

45. Next, as regards the existence of restrictions on the freedom of establishment and on the freedom to provide services referred to in Articles 43 EC and 49 EC respectively, it is settled case-law that measures which prohibit, impede or render less attractive the exercise of such freedoms constitute such restrictions (see, to that effect, Case C-439/99 *Commission* v *Italy* [2002] ECR I-305, paragraph 22; Case C-442/02 *CaixaBank France* [2004] ECR I-8961, paragraph 11; Case C-451/03 *Servizi Ausiliari Dottori Commercialisti* [2006] ECR I-2941, paragraph 31; and Case C-330/07 *Jobra* [2008] ECR I-9099, paragraph 19).

46. In particular, the concept of restriction covers measures taken by a Member State which, although applicable without distinction, affect access to the market for economic operators from other Member States (see, inter alia, *CaixaBank France*, paragraph 12, and Case C-518/06*Commission* v *Italy* [2009] ECR I-3491, paragraph 64).

47. In the present case, it is common ground that the contested provisions apply without distinction to all lawyers providing services on Italian territory.

48. However, the Commission takes the view that those provisions constitute a restriction within the meaning of the abovementioned articles in that they are liable to subject lawyers established in Member States other than the Italian Republic, who provide services in Italy, to additional costs resulting from the application of the Italian system of fees, as well as to a reduction in profit margins and therefore a loss of competitiveness.

49. In this regard, it must be borne in mind at the outset that rules of a Member State do not constitute a restriction within the meaning of the EC Treaty solely by virtue of the fact that other Member States apply less strict, or more commercially favourable, rules to providers of similar services established in their territory (see Case C-518/06 *Commission* v *Italy*, paragraph 63 and the case-law cited).

50. The existence of a restriction within the meaning of the Treaty cannot therefore be inferred from the mere fact that lawyers established in Member States other than the Italian Republic must become accustomed to the rules applicable in that latter Member State for the calculation of their fees for services provided in Italy.

51. By contrast, such a restriction exists, in particular, if those lawyers are deprived of the opportunity of gaining access to the market of the host Member State under conditions of normal and effective competition (see, to that effect, *CaixaBank France*, paragraphs 13 and 14; Joined Cases C-94/04 and C-202/04 *Cipolla and Others* [2006] ECR I-11421, paragraph 59; and Case C-384/08 *Attanasio Group* [2010] ECR I-0000, paragraph 45).

52. The Commission has not, however, demonstrated that the contested provisions have such an object or effect.

53. The Commission has not succeeded in demonstrating that the system at issue was established in a manner which adversely affects access to the Italian market for the services in question under conditions of normal and effective competition. It must be noted, in that regard, that the Italian system of fees is characterised by a flexibility which appears to allow proper remuneration for all types of services provided by lawyers. Thus, in cases which are particularly important, complex or difficult, the fees may be increased by up to twice the maximum tariffs applicable by default, and, for cases which are exceptionally important, by up to four times those limits or even more where there is a clear lack of proportionality, in view of the circumstances of the individual case, between the services of the lawyer and the maximum tariffs. It is also open to lawyers, in numerous situations, to conclude a special agreement with their clients to fix the amount of the fees.

54. Since it has therefore not established that the contested provisions impede the access of lawyers from other Member States to the Italian market at issue, the Commission's argument that there is a restriction within the meaning of Articles 43 EC and 49 EC cannot be upheld.

55. The action must accordingly be dismissed.

Costs

[Para. 56 omitted]

On those grounds,

THE COURT (Grand Chamber),

hereby:

1. Dismisses the action;

[Para. 2 of the ruling omitted].

Comments and questions

According to the settled case-law of the CJEU, measures which prohibit, impede or render less attractive the exercise of freedoms of movement constitute restrictions. On the other hand it is far from always clear when there is such a restriction. In Case C-442/02 *CaixaBank France* [2004] ECR I-8961, printed above, the CJEU ruled that a prohibition of credit institutions paying interest on sight accounts was a restriction, as such a measure would deprive credit institutions from other Member States of a competitive parameter. But does the same apply to a Member State's rule that advocates must comply with maximum tariffs for the calculation of their fees? One could argue that such an arrangement would mean that advocates from other Member States who are able to command high fees will be discouraged from entering that Member State's market.

In the Italian case on maximum tariffs for advocates, the Commission brought proceedings against Italy for breach of the TFEU, as it was the Commission's view that the obligatory Italian maximum tariffs for the calculation of lawyers' fees was contrary to Articles 49 and 56 TFEU. The Commission believed that such maximum tariffs could dissuade advocates from other Member States from setting up in Italy or from providing services to clients in Italy. From this point of view the maximum tariffs constitute both a restriction on the right of establishment and on the freedom to provide services. In other words, the Commission argued that the disputed provisions constituted a hindrance to access to the Italian market for the provision of legal services by advocates based in other Member States. To what extent do you believe that this view is in line with the CJEU's more recent decisions in relation to restrictions?

The CJEU rejected the Commission's arguments and found in favour of Italy. The CJEU found that it had not been proved that the Italian measures would prevent advocates from other Member States having access to the Italian market. Read paragraphs 49-53 of the judgment, where the CJEU explains when a restriction that is contrary to the TFEU rules on freedom of movement exists. Is this definition in line with the CJEU's previous decisions, or does it break new ground? To what extent is the CJEU's conclusion based on the issue of the burden of proof and to what extent on the concept of a 'restriction'? Is the result in the case on maximum tariffs for advocates in line with the result in the *CaixaBank* case printed above?

JUDGMENT OF THE COURT (Fourth Chamber)
26 September 2013

Ottica New Line di Accardi Vincenzo v Comune di Campobello di Mazara, intervener: Fotottica Media Visione di Luppino Natale Fabrizio e. C. s.n.c. (Request for a preliminary ruling: Consiglio di Giustizia Amministrativa per la Regione Siciliana - Italy)

'Articles 49 TFEU and 56 TFEU – Freedom of establishment – Public health – Opticians – Regional legislation making the establishment of new opticians' shops subject to authorisation – Demographic and geographical limitations – Justification – Appropriateness for attaining the objective pursued – Coherency – Proportionality'

Case C-539/11

Judgment

1. This request for a preliminary ruling concerns the interpretation of Articles 49 TFEU and 56 TFEU.

2. The request has been made in proceedings between Ottica New Line di Accardi Vincenzo ('Ottica New Line') and the Comune di Campobello di Mazara (Italy) concerning the latter's decision to authorise Fotottica Media Visione di Luppino Natale Fabrizio e. C. s.n.c. ('Fotottica') to carry out the activity of optician, on a permanent basis, in the territory of that municipality.

Legal context

European Union law

3. According to recital 22 in the preamble to Directive 2006/123/EC of the European Parliament and of the Council of 12 December 2006 on services in the internal market (OJ 2006 L 376, p. 36):

'The exclusion of healthcare from the scope of this Directive should cover healthcare and pharmaceutical services provided by health professionals to patients to assess, maintain or restore their state of health where those activities are reserved to a regulated health profession in the Member State in which the services are provided.'

4. Article 1(1) of Directive 2006/123 provides:

'This Directive establishes general provisions facilitating the exercise of the freedom of establishment for service providers and the free movement of services, while maintaining a high quality of services.'

5. Article 2(2)(f) of the directive provides:

'This Directive shall not apply to the following activities:

...

(f) healthcare services whether or not they are provided via healthcare facilities, and regardless of the ways in which they are organised and financed at national level or whether they are public or private.'

6. Article 15(2) of the directive comes under Chapter III thereof concerning freedom of establishment for service providers. Pursuant to that article, Member States are to examine whether their legal system makes access to a service activity or the exercise of it subject to compliance with quantitative or territorial restrictions, in particular in the form of limits fixed according to population or of a minimum geographical distance between providers. Article 15(3) states that Member States are to verify that such requirements satisfy the conditions of non-discrimination, necessity and proportionality.

Italian law

7. Under Article 1 of Regional Law No 12 ('Rules governing the activity of optician and amendment to Regional Law No 28 of 22 February 1999') (legge regionale n. 12 'Disciplina dell'esercizio dell'attività di ottico e modifica alla legge regionale 22 febbraio 1999, n. 28') of 9 July 2004 (*Gazzetta ufficiale della Regione Siciliana* No 30 of 16 July 2004; 'Regional Law No 12/2004'):

'1 For the purposes of the grant of authorisation by the relevant municipal authority to exercise the activity of optician, in addition to entry in the appropriate special register provided for under Article 71 of Regional Law No 25 of 1 September 1993, account shall be taken of the ratio of inhabitants to opticians' shops, in order to secure a rational distribution of supply throughout the territory. That ratio shall be established on the basis of one optician's shop per 8 000 residents. The distance between one optician's shop and another may be no less than 300 metres. The above limits shall not apply to premises which transfer from rented to owner-occupied premises or which are compelled to transfer as a result of eviction or other reasons of *force majeure*. Authorisations granted before the entry into force of this law shall not be affected.

2. Where the existence of territorial needs has been substantiated, the competent municipal authority shall, in derogation from paragraph 1, issue the relevant authorisation or transfer an existing authorisation, after obtaining the mandatory

opinion of the provincial committee of the Chamber of Commerce, referred to in Article 8 of the regulation implementing Article 71 of Regional Law No 25 of 1 September 1993, enacted by Presidential Decree No 64 of 1 June 1995.

3. In municipalities in which the number of inhabitants does not exceed 8 000, the competent municipal authority may, without obtaining the opinion of the committee referred to in paragraph 2, grant a maximum of two authorisations. Applications processed prior to the entry into force of this law shall not be affected.'

The dispute in the main proceedings and the questions referred for a preliminary ruling

8. By decision of 18 December 2009, the comune di Campobello di Mazara authorised Fotottica to establish an optician's shop in its territory.

9. It is not disputed that that decision was issued in breach of Article 1(1) of Regional Law No 12/2004, since that establishment did not comply the limits relating to population density and on distance between opticians' shops laid down in that provision.

10. Ottica New Line contested that decision before the Tribunale amministrativo regionale per la Sicilia. By decision of 18 March 2010, that court ruled out the application of Article 1(1) of Regional Law No 12/2004, holding that it was incompatible with European Union law, and dismissed Ottica New Line's action.

11. Ottica New Line appealed against the decision of the Tribunale amministrativo regionale per la Sicilia before the referring court. The latter is uncertain as to whether it is possible to transpose the principles arising from the Court of Justice's judgment in Joined Cases C-570/07 and C-571/07 *Blanco Pérez and Chao Gómez* [2010] ECR I-4629 to applications to establish an optician's shop. In that judgment, the Court of Justice concluded that European Union law does not preclude, in principle, national legislation which makes the establishment of new pharmacies conditional upon limits based on population density and on distance between pharmacies, in so far as such limits are likely to result in an even distribution of pharmacies throughout the national territory, so as to ensure that the population as a whole has adequate access to pharmaceutical services and, as a consequence, to improve the reliability and the quality of the provision of medicinal products to the public.

12. According to the referring court, the profession of optician, even more so than that of pharmacist, is indisputably subject to commercial considerations. However, it considers that the existence of an analogous healthcare interest in introducing and maintaining a particular system for the territorial distribution of opticians' shops cannot be entirely excluded. In that regard, the referring court draws attention to the

potential danger that, without any form of regulation, opticians' shops would end up converging on localities which are regarded as being the most profitable, with the result that other, less attractive localities would suffer a shortfall in numbers of opticians.

13. In those circumstances, the Consiglio di Giustizia Amministrativa per la Regione Siciliana decided to stay the proceedings and to refer the following questions to the Court of Justice for a preliminary ruling:

'(1) Must European Union law on the freedom of establishment and the freedom to provide services be interpreted as meaning that a provision of national law (in the present case, Article 1 of [Regional Law No 12/2004] under which the establishment of opticians' [shops] in the territory of a Member State (in the present case, in a part of that territory) is subject to restrictions based on population density and the distance between [such shops] – restrictions which, in theory, constitute an infringement of those fundamental freedoms – reflects an overriding reason relating to the public interest, linked to the need to protect human health?

(2) If the answer to Question (1) is in the affirmative, then, under European Union law, must the restrictions based on population density (one [establishment] for every 8 000 residents) and on distance (300 metres between one [optician's shop] and the next), laid down by [Regional Law No 12/2004] for the establishment of opticians' [shops] in the regional territory, be regarded as appropriate for the purposes of attaining the objective reflecting the abovementioned overriding reason relating to the public interest?

(3) If the answer to Question (1) is in the affirmative, then, under European Union law, are the restrictions based on population density (one [establishment] for every 8 000 residents) and on distance (300 metres between one [optician's shop] and the next), laid down by [Regional Law No 12/2004] for the establishment of opticians' [shops] in the regional territory, proportionate – that is to say, not excessive – for the purposes of attaining the objective reflecting the abovementioned overriding reason relating to the public interest?'

Consideration of the questions referred

14. By its questions, which need to be examined together, the referring court asks, in essence, whether European Union law precludes regional legislation, such as that at issue in the main proceedings, which limits the grant of authorisation for the establishment of a new optician's shop in providing that:

- in each geographical area, only one optician's shop may be established, in principle, for every 8 000 residents, and

– each new optician's shop must, in principle, be a minimum distance of 300 metres from an existing optician's shop.

Preliminary observations

15. First of all, the Court notes that, although the referring court makes reference, in its questions, to both European Union rules on the freedom to provide services and those on the freedom of establishment, the legislation at issue must be assessed in the light only of the rules on the freedom of establishment.

16. The legislation at issue in the main proceedings governs only the conditions for establishing an optician's shop in a part of Italian territory, with a view to a stable and continuous participation of such professionals in the economic life of that Member State. In those circumstances, the provisions concerning the freedom to supply services, which apply only if those relating to the freedom of establishment do not apply, are not relevant (see, by analogy, Case C-384/08 *Attanasio Group* [2010] ECR I-2055, paragraph 39 and the case-law cited).

17. Secondly, the Court notes that Directive 2006/123 is not applicable in the present case, even though it governs the freedom of establishment of providers from other Member States and it is alluded to by the referring court.

18. It is apparent from Article 2(2)(f) of Directive 2006/123, read in the light of recital 22 in the preamble thereto, that the directive does not apply to healthcare services provided by health professionals to patients to assess, maintain or restore their state of health where those activities are reserved to a regulated health profession in the Member State in which the services are provided.

19. First, the Court has already held that the intervention of opticians was likely to limit certain health risks and thus ensures the protection of public health (see, to that effect, Case C-108/09 *Ker-Optika* [2010] ECR I-2213, paragraph 64).

20. Second, the referring court points out that the opticians at issue in the main proceedings not only supply, check and adjust devices to correct sight defects, but may also themselves correct sight defects by using corrective visual devices or acting to prevent eye problems. As noted by the Advocate General in points 20 and 21 of his Opinion, an optician who is authorised to conduct eye tests, to measure visual acuity, to define and check the ocular correction needed, to detect eye problems and to treat defects of vision using corrective optical devices, to advise customers in that regard and to refer them to an ophthalmic specialist is exercising an activity encompassed by the protection of public health. By contrast, opticians who carry out technical activities, such as assembling frames and repairing spectacles, and who sell products which do not, strictly speaking, form part of the treatment of visual

problems, such as non-prescription sunglasses or spectacle care products, exercise a commercial activity which is not associated with the protection of public health.

21. Moreover, the referring court points out that the activity of optician is a regulated profession in Italy.

22. In those circumstances, pursuant to Article 2(2)(f) of Directive 2006/123, the activities of the opticians at issue in the main proceedings are excluded from the scope of that directive.

23. Accordingly, the restrictions at issue in the main proceedings need to be examined only with regard to their compatibility with the TFEU and, more specifically, with Article 49 thereof.

24. Third, the Court notes that, in accordance with Article 168(7) TFEU, as interpreted in its case-law, European Union law does not detract from the power of the Member States to adopt provisions aimed at organising their health services. In exercising that power, however, the Member States must comply with European Union law, in particular the provisions of the TFEU on the freedom of establishment, which prohibit the Member States from introducing or maintaining unjustified restrictions on the exercise of that freedom in the healthcare sector (see, to that effect, Joined Cases C-171/07 and C-172/07*Apothekerkammer des Saarlandes and Others* [2009] ECR I-4171, paragraph 18, and *Blanco Pérez and Chao Gómez*, paragraph 43).

Whether there is a restriction on the freedom of establishment

25. It is settled case-law that any national measure which, albeit applicable without discrimination on grounds of nationality, is liable to hinder or render less attractive the exercise by European Union nationals of the freedom of establishment guaranteed by the Treaty constitutes a restriction within the meaning of Article 49 TFEU (Case C-140/03 *Commission* v *Greece* [2005] ECR I-3177, paragraph 27, and*Blanco Pérez and Chao Gómez*, paragraph 53).

26. A national rule which makes the establishment of a service provider from another Member State conditional upon the issue of prior authorisation falls within that category, since it is capable of hindering the exercise by that service provider of the freedom of establishment by preventing it from freely pursuing its activities through a fixed place of business. First, that service provider may have to bear the additional administrative and financial costs involved in any grant of such an authorisation. Second, the prior authorisation system excludes from the pursuit of self-employed activity economic operators who do not satisfy predetermined requirements, compliance with which is a condition for the issue of that authorisation (Case C-169/07 *Hartlauer* [2009] ECR I-1721, paragraphs 34 and 35, and *Blanco Pérez and Chao Gómez*, paragraph 54).

27. Moreover, national legislation constitutes a restriction where it makes the pursuit of an activity subject to a condition which is linked to the economic or social needs for that activity, since it tends to limit the number of service providers (*Hartlauer*, paragraph 36, and *Blanco Pérez and Chao Gómez*, paragraph 55).

28. In so far as concerns the dispute in the main proceedings, the Court notes, firstly, that Regional Law No 12/2004 makes the establishment of new opticians' shops subject to prior administrative authorisation.

29. Secondly, that legislation takes account of the ratio between population density and the number of opticians' shops, with a view to distributing supply throughout the given territory in a rational manner. In authorising the establishment of only a limited number of opticians' shops in a given territory, that legislation thus restricts the access of opticians to their economic activity in that territory.

30. Thirdly, the legislation at issue in the main proceedings is capable of preventing opticians from freely choosing where to exercise their independent activity, in so far as those seeking to establish shops are required to observe a minimum distance of 300 metres from existing opticians' shops.

31. The effect of such rules is thus to hinder and render less attractive the exercise by opticians from other Member States of their activities in Italian territory through a fixed place of business.

32. Consequently, regional legislation such as that at issue in the main proceedings amounts to a restriction on the freedom of establishment within the meaning of Article 49 TFEU.

Justification for the restriction on the freedom of establishment

33. It is settled case-law that restrictions on the freedom of establishment which are applicable without discrimination on grounds of nationality may be justified by overriding reasons relating to the general interest, provided that the restrictions are appropriate for securing attainment of the objective pursued and do not go beyond what is necessary for attaining that objective (*Hartlauer*, paragraph 44, and*Apothekerkammer des Saarlandes and Others*, paragraph 25).

34. In that regard, it is clear form Article 52(1) TFEU that restrictions on the freedom of establishment may be justified by the general objective of the protection of public health (see, to that effect, *Hartlauer*, paragraph 46, and *Apothekerkammer des Saarlandes and Others*, paragraph 27).

35. It is also apparent from the Court's case-law that that general objective may seek, more specifically, to ensure even distribution of healthcare providers throughout the

national territory (see, to that effect,*Blanco Pérez and Chao Gómez*, paragraphs 64, 70 and 78).

36. In pursuing such an objective, the establishment of service providers, such as pharmacies, may be subject to planning. That may include prior authorisation for the establishment of a pharmacy, where that planning proves indispensable for filling in possible gaps in access to public health services and for avoiding the duplication of structures, so as to ensure the provision of public health care which is adapted to the needs of the population, which covers the entire territory and which takes account of geographically isolated or otherwise disadvantaged regions (see, to that effect, *Blanco Pérez and Chao Gómez*, paragraph 70).

37. Those principles appear to be transposable to the establishment of opticians' shops, in so far as, as noted in paragraph 20 above, the opticians at issue in the main proceedings provide services aimed at assessing, maintaining or restoring the state of health of patients, with the result that those services are encompassed by the protection of public health.

38. The legislation at issue in the main proceedings introduces planning measures concerning the establishment of opticians' shops throughout the territory of the Region of Sicily. It contains two main rules, namely (i) that only one optician's shop may be established per 8 000 residents, and (ii) that there must be a minimum distance of 300 metres between opticians' shops.

39. It is not disputed, first of all, that Regional Law No 12/2004 does not discriminate on grounds of nationality.

40. Next, in so far as concerns the rule that only one optician's shop may be established per 8 000 residents, the Court has already held that national authorities may adopt measures to avoid the risk of healthcare providers converging on localities in the territory concerned which are considered to be attractive. Thus, national authorities may opt, in the light of that risk, for legislation which provides that only one service provider may be established for a given population density, since such a rule seeks to encourage such service providers to establish premises in parts of the national territory where access to healthcare is lacking (see, to that effect, *Blanco Pérez and Chao Gómez*, paragraphs 72 to 77).

41. In those circumstances, the rule that only one optician's shop may be established for a given number of residents is likely to facilitate the even distribution of opticians' shops throughout the territory concerned and thus ensure that the entire population has appropriate access to the services offered by them.

42. Finally, as regards the rule imposing a minimum distance between two opticians' shops, it is apparent from the Court's case-law that, together with the rule referred

to in the preceding paragraph, this requirement leads members of the public to be more confident that they have a access to a healthcare provider nearby and thus also contributes to a better protection of public health in the territory concerned (see, to that effect, *Blanco Pérez and Chao Gómez*, paragraphs 81 and 82).

43. The Court points out, however, that it is not indispensable, as a general rule, for customers to obtain optical products quickly, and even less indispensable that they obtain them immediately. It follows that the need for rapid access to those products is less great than is inherently the case for the provision of many medicinal products, with the result that the interest in having an optician's shop close by is not as acute as is the case with the distribution of medicinal products.

44. None the less, the Court notes that it is for the Member States to decide on the degree of protection which they wish to afford to public health and on the way in which that protection is to be achieved. Since the level may vary from one Member State to another, Member States should be allowed a margin of discretion (see, to that effect, *Apothekerkammer des Saarlandes and Others*, paragraph 19, and *Blanco Pérez and Chao Gómez*, paragraph 44).

45. In exercising that margin of discretion, it is permissible for the Member States to organise the planning of opticians' shops in a way comparable to that provided for the distribution of pharmacies, notwithstanding the differences which exist between the two types of healthcare service.

46. In those circumstances, it must be found that legislation such as that at issue in the main proceedings is, in principle, appropriate for securing attainment of the general objective pursued of protecting public health and, in particular, the objectives of ensuring even distribution of opticians' shops throughout the national territory and ensuring rapid access to such establishments.

47. None the less, it is also necessary that the way in which Regional Law No 12/2004 pursues those objectives is coherent. According to the Court's case-law, the national legislation as a whole and the various relevant rules are appropriate for ensuring attainment of the objective relied upon only if they genuinely reflect a concern to attain that objective in a consistent and systematic manner (see, to that effect, *Hartlauer*, paragraph 55, and *Apothekerkammer des Saarlandes and Others*, paragraph 42).

48. In that regard, it is ultimately for the national court, which has sole jurisdiction to assess the facts and interpret the national legislation, to determine whether and to what extent Regional Law No 12/2004 satisfies those conditions (see, to that effect, Case 171/88 *Rinner-Kühn* [1989] ECR 2743, paragraph 15, and Joined Cases C-4/02 and C-5/02 *Schönheit and Becker* [2003] ECR I-12575, paragraphs 82 and 83).

49. However, the Court of Justice, which is called on to provide answers of use to the national court, may provide guidance based on the documents relating to the main proceedings and on the written and oral observations which have been submitted to it, in order to enable the national court to give judgment (Case C-187/00 *Kutz-Bauer* [2003] ECR I-2741, paragraph 52, and *Schönheit and Becker*, paragraph 83).

50. To that end, the Court points out, first of all, that Article 1(1) to (3) of Regional Law No 12/2004 lays down conditions which differ for municipalities with fewer than 8 000 residents and those with more than that number. It is not inconceivable that the municipalities which fall within the first category are largely free to authorise the establishment of two opticians' shops in their territory, whereas those in the second category can grant such authorisation only if 'the existence of territorial needs has been substantiated' and if those municipalities have gained the prior and mandatory opinion of a committee.

51. Such legislation risks bringing about unequal access to the establishment of opticians' shops in the various areas of the region concerned. In particular, as pointed out by the Advocate General in point 82 of his Opinion, in municipalities with populations of between 8 000 and 16 000 – of which there are many, according to the referring court – legislation of that nature could excessively restrict such access.

52. The risk of unequal access to the establishment of opticians' shops is accentuated, moreover, by the fact alluded to in the decision to refer that the municipal authorities have significant discretion since the requirement that 'the existence of territorial needs be substantiated' is not further regulated.

53. In addition, the competent authorities may authorise the establishment of an additional optician's shop only after receiving a mandatory opinion from a committee of the Chamber of Commerce which is made up, according to the information submitted to the Court, of representatives of opticians active on the market, namely direct competitors of those seeking establishment.

54. In those circumstances, Regional Law No 12/2004 risks, as of its implementation, failing to ensure an even distribution of opticians' shops throughout the entire territory concerned and, consequently, an equal level of protection of public health throughout that territory.

55. That regional law also gives rise to similar issues in relation to municipalities with fewer than 8 000 residents. It cannot be ruled out that, in those municipalities, the competent authorities enjoy quasi unlimited powers when authorising – or not – the establishment of a second optician's shop. There is thus no guarantee, in that respect, that a second optician's shop would be authorised, even if, in the present case, the requirements of the protection of public health were to deem it necessary.

56. None the less, since the Court cannot, a priori, neither presume nor exclude that the risks referred to above related to the implementation of Regional Law No 12/2004 would materialise, it is for the national court to examine, using specific statistical data or other means, whether the competent authorities use appropriately, in accordance with transparent and objective criteria, the powers made available under the legislation, with a view to attaining, in a coherent and systematic manner, the objectives pursued relating to the protection of public health throughout the territory concerned.

57. Having regard to the foregoing, the answer to the questions referred is that Article 49 TFEU must be interpreted as not precluding regional legislation, such as that at issue in the main proceedings, which imposes restrictions on the grant of authorisation for the establishment of a new optician's shop, by providing that:

    – in each geographical area, only one optician's shop may be established, in principle, for every 8 000 residents, and

    – each new optician's shop must, in principle, be a minimum distance of 300 metres from an existing optician's shop,

    provided that the competent authorities use appropriately, in accordance with transparent and objective criteria, the powers made available under the legislation concerned, with a view to attaining, in a coherent and systematic manner, the objectives pursued by that legislation relating to the protection of public health throughout the given territory, which is a matter for the national court to assess.

Costs

[Para. 58 omitted]

On those grounds,

THE COURT (Fourth Chamber),

hereby rules:

Article 49 TFEU must be interpreted as not precluding regional legislation, such as that at issue in the main proceedings, which imposes restrictions on the grant of authorisation for the establishment of a new optician's shop, by providing that:
- **in each geographical area, only one optician's shop may be established, in principle, for every 8 000 residents, and**
- **each new optician's shop must, in principle, be a minimum distance of 300 metres from an existing optician's shop,**

provided that the competent authorities use appropriately, in accordance with transparent and objective criteria, the powers made available under the legislation concerned, with a view to attaining, in a coherent and systematic manner, the objectives pursued by that legislation relating to the protection of public health throughout the given territory, which is a matter for the national court to assess.

Comments and question

With a view to ensuring rational distribution of opticians' shops in Sicily, a regional law provided that the establishment of new opticians' shops required prior authorisation from the authorities. To obtain such authorisation two conditions had to be fulfilled: (1) there should be no more than one optician's shop per 8,000 inhabitants; and (2) there should be at least 300 metres between opticians' shops. The authorities could derogate from these requirements in special circumstances.

When, in 2009, a Sicilian municipal authority gave permission to open an optician's shop in contravention of the law, competing opticians challenged the decision before the national courts. The case was referred to the CJEU for a preliminary ruling.

The referring Italian court referred to the Union law provisons on both freedom to provide services and freedom of establishment. However, the CJEU ruled that, since the rules on freedom of establishment applied to the case, and since freedom to provide services is subordinate to the rules on freedom of establishment, the case should only be assessed under the rules on freedom of establishment.

The Sicilian law prevented opticians from deciding for themselves where to conduct their business. Thus, the Sicilian law made it less attractive for opticians from other Member States to do their business in Italy. While, in principle, the regional law gave neither a direct nor an indirect advantage to Sicilian opticians, the law nevertheless constituted a restriction on access to the market for opticians.

The question was whether the restriction could be justified by an overriding reason relating to the public interest, linked to the need to protect human health. The CJEU ruled that restrictions on freedom of establishment could be justified by the public interest in protecting human health. These general aims could be achieved by ensuring a balanced distribution of health services in the national territory, and it was possible to make service provision, such as the establishment of pharmacies, subject to planning in order to pursue such a goal. For example, such planning could mean that prior authorisation must be given for establishing a pharmacy, if such a system were necessary to ensure effective cover of the needs of the population, covering the whole of the relevant territory and having regard for geographically isolated or otherwise disadvantaged areas.

The CJEU found that, to the extent that the services of opticians fall within the scope of the protection of public health, these principles could apply to the establishment of opticians' shops. As the CJEU found that the services of opticians consist of assessing, maintaining and restoring their patients' health, the provisions of the Sicilian regional law, whereby an optician's shop could only be established in relation to a certain number of inhabitants, could promote a balanced distribution of such shops in the area concerned. Thus, the provision could ensure appropriate access to the services of opticians for the whole population.

As for the requirement that there must be at least 300 metres between opticians' shops, the CJEU found that this contributed to the public being more confident of having access to a healthcare provider nearby, and thus to the better protection of public health in the area concerned. However, the CJEU was aware that it is not generally essential for customers to obtain optical products quickly, and there is inherently less need for rapid access to optical products than to many medicinal products, so the need to have an optician's shop close by is not as acute as is the case of pharmacies. On this basis the CJEU decided that it was for the Member State to decide how far to extend the protection of public health and how this goal is to be achieved. The CJEU recognised that this could vary from one Member State to another, so the Member States must have some discretion in the matter.

To this extent the CJEU accepted the Sicilian regional law. However, it added that the way in which the Sicilian law pursued its objective must be coherent. In the view of the CJEU there was a risk that the Sicilian law could lead to unequal access to establish opticians' shops in the region concerned. In particular the CJEU pointed out that the municipal authorities had considerable discretion when giving authorisation and that representatives for the opticians who were already in the market appeared to have the possibility of participating in decisions on whether new (competing) opticians should be given access to the market.

While the CJEU accepted the Sicilian law in general, it made its acceptance conditional on the competent authorities using the powers made available under the legislation appropriately and in accordance with transparent and objective criteria, with a view to attaining the objectives pursued by the legislation relating to the protection of public health coherently and systematically.

How do you believe the decision in the main case that gave rise to the reference for a preliminary ruling was decided? Do you find the CJEU's decision on the Sicilian regional legislation to be 'mild' or 'strict'?

Would it be reasonable to interpret the judgment as meaning that, based on the quite broad TFEU rules on freedom of establishment, the CJEU lays down administrative law rules with which the Sicilian authorities are required to comply?

CHAPTER 6

Free Movement of Services

JUDGMENT OF THE COURT (Grand Chamber)
18 December 2007

Laval un Partneri Ltd v Svenska Byggnadsarbetareförbundet, Svenska Byggnadsarbetareförbundets avd. 1, Byggettan, Svenska Elektrikerförbundet.
(Reference for a preliminary ruling from the Arbetsdomstolen – Sweden)

'Freedom to provide services – Directive 96/71/EC – Posting of workers in the construction industry – National legislation laying down terms and conditions of employment covering the matters referred to in Article 3(1), first subparagraph, (a) to (g), save for minimum rates of pay – Collective agreement for the building sector the terms of which lay down more favourable conditions or relate to other matters – Possibility for trade unions to attempt, by way of collective action, to force undertakings established in other Member States to negotiate on a case-by-case basis in order to determine the rates of pay for workers and to sign the collective agreement for the building sector'

Case C-341/05

Judgment

1. This reference for a preliminary ruling concerns the interpretation of Articles 12 EC and 49 EC and Directive 96/71/EC of the European Parliament and of the Council of 16 December 1996 concerning the posting of workers in the framework of the provision of services (OJ 1997 L 18, p. 1).

2. The reference was made in the context of proceedings between Laval un Partneri Ltd ('Laval'), a company incorporated under Latvian law and having its registered office in Riga (Latvia), on the one hand, and Svenska Byggnadsarbetareförbundet (Swedish building and public works trade union, 'Byggnads'), Svenska Byggnadsarbetareförbundet avdelning 1, Byggettan (local branch No 1 of that trade union, 'Byggettan') and Svenska Elektrikerförbundet (Swedish electricians' trade union, 'Elektrikerna'), on the other, brought by Laval for the purposes of obtaining, first, a declaration that the collective action by Byggnads and Byggettan affecting all Laval's worksites and the Elektrikerna sympathy action consisting of blockading all electrical work being carried out is unlawful, second, an order that such action should cease, and, third, an order that the trade unions pay compensation for the loss suffered by Laval.

Legal context

Community law

3. Recitals 6, 13, 17 and 22 in the preamble to Directive 96/71 state:

'... the transnationalisation of the employment relationship raises problems with regard to the legislation applicable to the employment relationship; ... it is in the interests of the parties to lay down the terms and conditions governing the employment relationship envisaged;

... the laws of the Member States must be coordinated in order to lay down a nucleus of mandatory rules for minimum protection to be observed in the host country by employers who post workers to perform temporary work in the territory of a Member State where the services are provided; ... such coordination can be achieved only by means of Community law;

... the mandatory rules for minimum protection in force in the host country must not prevent the application of terms and conditions of employment which are more favourable to workers;

... this Directive is without prejudice to the law of the Member States concerning collective action to defend the interests of trades and professions'.

4. Article 1 of Directive 96/71 provides:

'1. This Directive shall apply to undertakings established in a Member State which, in the framework of the transnational provision of services, post workers, in accordance with paragraph 3, to the territory of a Member State.

...

3. This Directive shall apply to the extent that the undertakings referred to in paragraph 1 take one of the following transnational measures:

(a) ...

or

(b) post workers to an establishment or to an undertaking owned by the group in the territory of a Member State, provided there is an employment relationship between the undertaking making the posting and the worker during the period of posting

...'

5. Article 3 of that directive provides:

'Terms and conditions of employment

1. Member States shall ensure that, whatever the law applicable to the employment relationship, the undertakings referred to in Article 1(1) guarantee workers posted to their territory the terms and conditions of employment covering the following matters which, in the Member State where the work is carried out, are laid down:

   – by law, regulation or administrative provision,

   and/or

   – by collective agreements or arbitration awards which have been declared universally applicable within the meaning of paragraph 8, in so far as they concern the activities referred to in the Annex:

     (a) maximum work periods and minimum rest periods;
     (b) minimum paid annual holidays;
     (c) the minimum rates of pay, including overtime rates; this point does not apply to supplementary occupational retirement pension schemes;
     (d) the conditions of hiring-out of workers, in particular the supply of workers by temporary employment undertakings;
     (e) health, safety and hygiene at work;
     (f) protective measures with regard to the terms and conditions of employment of pregnant women or women who have recently given birth, of children and of young people;
     (g) equality of treatment between men and women and other provisions on non-discrimination.

   For the purposes of this directive, the concept of minimum rates of pay referred to in paragraph 1(c) is defined by the national law and/or practice of the Member State to whose territory the worker is posted.

...

7. Paragraphs 1 to 6 shall not prevent application of terms and conditions of employment which are more favourable to workers.

   Allowances specific to the posting shall be considered to be part of the minimum wage, unless they are paid in reimbursement of expenditure actually incurred on account of the posting, such as expenditure on travel, board and lodging.

8. 'Collective agreements or arbitration awards which have been declared universally applicable' means collective agreements or arbitration awards which must be observed by all undertakings in the geographical area and in the profession or industry concerned.

   In the absence of a system for declaring collective agreements or arbitration awards to be of universal application within the meaning of the first subparagraph, Member States may, if they so decide, base themselves on:

   – collective agreements or arbitration awards which are generally applicable to all similar undertakings in the geographical area and in the profession or industry concerned,

   and/or

   – collective agreements which have been concluded by the most representative employers' and labour organisations at national level and which are applied throughout national territory,

   provided that their application to the undertakings referred to in Article 1(1) ensures equality of treatment on matters listed in the first subparagraph of paragraph 1 of this Article between those undertakings and the other undertakings referred to in this subparagraph which are in a similar position.

   Equality of treatment, within the meaning of this Article, shall be deemed to exist where national undertakings in a similar position:

   – are subject, in the place in question or in the sector concerned, to the same obligations as posting undertakings as regards the matters listed in the first subparagraph of paragraph 1, and
   – are required to fulfil such obligations with the same effects.

...

10. This Directive shall not preclude the application by Member States, in compliance with the Treaty, to national undertakings and to the undertakings of other States, on a basis of equality of treatment, of:

   – terms and conditions of employment on matters other than those referred to in the first subparagraph of paragraph 1 in the case of public policy provisions;
   – terms and conditions of employment laid down in the collective agreements or arbitration awards within the meaning of paragraph 8 and concerning activities other than those referred to in the Annex.'

6. According to Article 4 of Directive 96/71:

'Cooperation on information

1. For the purposes of implementing this directive, Member States shall, in accordance with national legislation and/or practice, designate one or more liaison offices or one or more competent national bodies.

2. Member States shall make provision for cooperation between the public authorities which, in accordance with national legislation, are responsible for monitoring the terms and conditions of employment referred to in Article 3. Such cooperation shall in particular consist in replying to reasoned requests from those authorities for information on the transnational hiring-out of workers, including manifest abuses or possible cases of unlawful transnational activities.

The Commission and the public authorities referred to in the first subparagraph shall cooperate closely in order to examine any difficulties which might arise in the application of Article 3(10).

Mutual administrative assistance shall be provided free of charge.

3. Each Member State shall take the appropriate measures to make the information on the terms and conditions of employment referred to in Article 3 generally available.

4. Each Member State shall notify the other Member States and the Commission of the liaison offices and/or competent bodies referred to in paragraph 1.'

National law

The transposition of Directive 96/71

7. It is apparent from the Court's file that Sweden does not have a system for declaring collective agreements universally applicable, and, in order to avoid the creation of discriminatory situations, Swedish law does not require foreign undertakings to apply Swedish collective agreements, since not all Swedish employers are bound by a collective agreement.

8. Directive 96/71 was transposed in Sweden by the Law on the posting of workers (lag om utstationering av arbetstagare (1999:678) ('Law on the posting of workers')). According to the procedural documents, terms and conditions of employment applicable to posted workers in relation to Article 3(1), first subparagraph, (a), (b) and (d) to (g) of Directive 96/71 are laid down by law within the meaning of the first indent of the first subparagraph of Article 3(1) of the directive. The Swedish

legislation does not provide, however, for minimum rates of pay as referred to in the Article 3(1), first subparagraph, (c).

9. It is clear from the file that the liaison office (Arbetsmiljöverket, 'the liaison office'), set up in accordance with Article 4(1) of Directive 96/71, is responsible, inter alia, for informing interested persons of the existence of collective agreements that may be applicable in the event of workers being posted to Sweden and for referring such interested persons to the parties to the collective agreement for further information.

The right to take collective action

10. Chapter 2 of the Swedish Basic Law (Regeringsformen) sets out the freedoms and fundamental rights enjoyed by citizens. Under Article 17 thereof, workers' associations, employers and employers' associations have the right to take collective action, unless otherwise provided by law or agreement.

11. The Law on workers' participation in decisions (Medbestämmandelagen, 'the MBL') of 10 June 1976 lays down rules applicable to the right of association and of negotiation, collective agreements, mediation of collective labour disputes and the obligation of social peace, and contains provisions restricting the right of trade unions to take collective action.

12. It is apparent from Article 41 of the MBL that there is a mandatory social truce between employers and workers bound by a collective agreement and it is prohibited, inter alia, to take collective action with the aim of obtaining amendments to the agreement. However, collective action is authorised where management and labour have not entered into a collective agreement between themselves.

13. Article 42 of the MBL provides:

    'Employers' or workers' associations shall not be entitled to organise or encourage illegal collective action in any way whatsoever. Nor shall they be entitled to participate in any illegal collective action, by providing support or in any other way. An association which is itself bound by a collective agreement shall also, in the event of collective action which its members are preparing to take or are taking, seek to prevent such action or help to bring it to an end.

    If any illegal collective action is taken, third parties shall be prohibited from participating in it.

    The provisions of the first two sentences of the first paragraph shall apply only if an association takes collective action by reason of terms and conditions of employment falling directly within the scope of the present Law'.

14. As the case-law on the first paragraph of Article 42 of the MBL, it is prohibited to take collective action with the aim of having a collective agreement between other parties set aside or amended. In the '*Britannia*' judgment (1989, No 120), the Arbetsdomstolen held that that prohibition extends to collective action taken in Sweden in order to have a collective agreement concluded between foreign parties in a workplace abroad set aside or amended, if such collective action is prohibited by the foreign legislation applicable to the signatories to that collective agreement.

15. By the 'Lex Britannia', which entered into force on 1 July 1991, the legislature sought to reduce the scope of the principle expounded in the *Britannia* judgment. The Lex Britannia consists of three provisions inserted into the MBL, namely Articles 25a, 31a and the third paragraph of Article 42.

16. It is apparent from the explanations provided by the national court that, since the introduction of the third paragraph of Article 42 of the MBL, collective action against a foreign employer carrying out temporary activities in Sweden is no longer prohibited where, considered as a whole, the particular situation suggests that the link with that Member State is too tenuous for the MBL to be deemed to apply directly to the terms and conditions of employment in question.

The collective agreement for the building sector

17. Byggnads is a trade union which groups together workers in the construction sector in Sweden. According to Byggnads' observations, in 2006, it comprised 31 local sections, including Byggettan, and had a membership of 128 000, 95 000 being of working age. Its membership included carpenters and builders, masons, parquet layers, workers in the construction and road sector, and plumbers. Around 87% of building sector workers were affiliated to that trade union.

18. A collective agreement was entered into between, on the one hand, Byggnads, in its capacity as the central organisation representing building workers, and the central organisation for employers in the construction sector (Sveriges Byggindustrier) ('the collective agreement for the building sector').

19. The collective agreement for the building sector contains specific rules relating to working time and annual leave, matters in which collective agreements may depart from the legislative provisions. In addition, the agreement includes provisions relating to temporary unemployment and waiting time, reimbursement of travelling expenses and subsistence allowances, employment protection, training leave and training.

20. Being a party to the collective agreement for the building sector also requires the undertakings concerned to accept a number of pecuniary obligations. Thus, they are required to pay to Byggettan a sum equal to 1.5% of total gross wages for the purposes of the pay review which that section of the trade union carries out, and to the

insurance company, FORA, sums representing first, 0.8% of total gross wages for the purposes of a charge 'Tilläggsören' [penny supplement] or 'special building supplement', and, second, a further 5.9% for the purposes of a number of insurance premiums.

21. The 'tilläggsören' or 'special building supplement' is intended to finance group life insurance contracts, contingency contracts and insurance contracts covering accidents occurring outside working hours, the research fund for Swedish building undertakings (Svenska Byggbranschens Utvecklingsfond), the Galaxen organisation, managed by employers and which has as its objective the adaptation of work places for persons with reduced mobility and the re-training of such persons, the promotion of training development in building trades and administrative and management costs.

22. The various insurance contracts proposed by FORA guarantee workers supplementary retirement insurance, payment of health benefits, unemployment benefits, compensation for accidents at work, and financial assistance for survivors in the event of the death of the worker.

23. After signing the collective agreement for the building sector, employers, including those who post workers to Sweden, are, in principle, bound by all the terms of that agreement, although some of those rules are applicable on a case-by-case basis according to, in essence, the nature of the site and the way in which the work is carried out.

Determination of wages

24. It is apparent from the observations of the Swedish Government that, in Sweden, employees' remuneration is decided on by management and labour by way of collective negotiation. Generally, collective agreements do not provide for a minimum wage as such. The lowest level of pay appearing in numerous collective agreements is aimed at employees without qualifications or work experience, which means that, as a general rule, it concerns only a very small number of persons. As regards other employees, their pay is determined by way of negotiations conducted at the place of work, having regard to the qualifications of the particular employee and the tasks performed by the latter.

25. According to the observations submitted in this case by the three defendant trade unions, in the collective agreement for the building sector, performance-related pay follows the usual model of remuneration in the construction sector. The rules on performance-related pay require new pay agreements to be concluded in respect of each construction project. It is open to the employers and the local branch of the trade union, however, to agree on the application of an hourly wage in respect of a specific site. No system of monthly wages is applicable to the type of workers concerned in the main proceedings.

26. According to those trade unions, negotiations on pay are conducted in the context of a social truce which must follow the conclusion of a collective agreement. The agreement on pay is concluded, in principle, at local level between the trade union and the employer. If management and labour fail to reach an agreement at this level, negotiations on pay are centralised, at which point Byggnads acts as the principal party on the side of the employees. If management and labour still do not reach an agreement in such negotiations, the basic wage is then determined according to the 'fall-back clause'. According to those trade unions, the 'fall-back' wage, which in fact represents only a negotiating mechanism of last resort, and does not constitute a minimum wage, amounted to SEK 109 approximately (EUR 12) per hour for the second half of 2004.

The dispute in the main proceedings

27. It is apparent from the order of reference that Laval is a company incorporated under Latvian law, whose registered office is in Riga. Between May and December 2004, it posted around 35 workers to Sweden to work on building sites operated by L&P Baltic Bygg AB ('Baltic'), a company incorporated under Swedish law whose entire share capital was held by Laval until the end of 2003, inter alia, for the purposes of the construction of school premises in Vaxholm.

28. Laval, which had signed, on 14 September and 20 October 2004, in Latvia, collective agreements with the Latvian building sector's trade union, was not bound by any collective agreement entered into with Byggnads, Byggettan or Elektrikerna, none of whose members were employed by Laval. Around 65% of the Latvian workers concerned were members of the building workers' trade union in their State of origin.

29. It is clear from the file that, in June 2004, contacts were established between Byggettan, on the one hand, and Baltic and Laval, on the other, and negotiations were begun with a view to Laval's signing the collective agreement for the building sector. Laval asked for wages and other terms and conditions of employment to be defined in parallel with the negotiations, so that the level of pay and terms and conditions of employment would already be fixed by the time that agreement was signed. Byggettan agreed to this request, even though, generally, the negotiation of a collective agreement needs to have been completed before discussions on wages and other terms and conditions of employment are entered into in the framework of the mandatory social truce. Byggettan refused to allow the introduction of a system of monthly wages, but did agree to Laval's proposal on the principle of an hourly wage.

30. According to the order for reference, during the negotiations held on 15 September 2004, Byggettan had demanded that Laval, first, sign the collective agreement for the building sector in respect of the Vaxholm site, and secondly, guarantee that the posted workers would receive an hourly wage of SEK 145 (approximately

EUR 16). That hourly wage was based on statistics on wages for the Stockholm (Sweden) region for the first quarter of 2004, relating to professionally-qualified builders and carpenters. Byggettan declared that it was prepared to take collective action forthwith in the event that Laval failed to agree to this.

31. According to the documents on the file, during the procedure before the Arbedstomstolen, Laval stated that it would pay its workers a monthly wage of SEK 13 600 (approximately EUR 1 500), which would be supplemented by benefits in kind in respect of meals, accommodation and travel amounting to SEK 6 000 (approximately EUR 660) per month.

32. If the collective agreement for the building sector had been signed, Laval would have been bound, in principle, by all its terms, including those relating to the pecuniary obligations to Byggettan and FORA set out in paragraph 20 of this judgment. A proposal to subscribe to insurance contracts with FORA was made to Laval by way of a declaration form sent to it in December 2004.

33. Since those negotiations were not successful, Byggettan requested Byggnads to take measures to initiate the collective action against Laval announced at the meeting of 15 September 2004. Notice was given in October 2004.

34. Blockading ('blockad') of the Vaxholm building site began on 2 November 2004. The blockading consisted, inter alia, of preventing the delivery of goods onto the site, placing pickets and prohibiting Latvian workers and vehicles from entering the site. Laval asked the police for assistance but they explained that since the collective action was lawful under national law they were not allowed to intervene or to remove physical obstacles blocking access to the site.

35. At the end of November 2004, Laval spoke to the liaison office referred to in paragraph 9 above in order to obtain information on the terms and conditions of employment which it had to apply in Sweden, on whether or not there was a minimum wage and on the nature of any contributions which it had to pay. By letter of 2 December 2004, the liaison office's head of legal affairs informed Laval that it was required to apply the provisions to which the law on the posting of workers refers, that it was for management and labour to agree on wage issues, that the minimum requirements under the collective agreements also applied to foreign posted workers, and that, if a foreign employer was having to pay double contributions, the matter could be brought before the courts. In order to ascertain what provisions under the agreements were applicable, Laval had to speak to management and labour in the sector concerned.

36. At the mediation meeting arranged on 1 December 2005 and at the conciliation hearing held before the Arbetsdomstolen on 20 December 2005, Laval was requested by Byggettan to sign the collective agreement for the building sector before the

issue of wages was dealt with. If Laval had accepted that proposal, the collective action would have ceased immediately, and the social truce, which would have allowed negotiations on wages to begin, would have come into effect. Laval, however, refused to sign the agreement, since it was not possible for it to know in advance what conditions would be imposed on it in relation to wages.

37. In December 2004, the collective action directed against Laval intensified. On 3 December 2004, Elektrikerna initiated sympathy action. That measure had the effect of preventing Swedish undertakings belonging to the organisation of electricians' employers from providing services to Laval. At Christmas, the workers posted by Laval went back to Latvia and did not return to the site in question.

38. In January 2005, other trade unions announced sympathy actions, consisting of a boycott of all Laval's sites in Sweden, with the result that the undertaking was no longer able to carry out its activities in that Member State. In February 2005, the town of Vaxholm requested that the contract between it and Baltic be terminated, and on 24 March 2005 the latter was declared bankrupt.

The questions referred

39. On 7 December 2004, Laval commenced proceedings before the Arbetsdomstolen against Byggnads, Byggettan and Elektrikerna, seeking a declaration that both the blockading and the sympathy action affecting all its worksites were illegal and an order that such action should cease. It also sought an order that the trade unions pay compensation for the damage suffered. By decision of 22 December 2004, the national court dismissed Laval's application for an interim order that the collective action should be brought to an end.

40. Since it wished to ascertain whether Articles 12 EC and 49 EC and Directive 96/71 preclude trade unions from attempting, by means of collective action, to force a foreign undertaking which posts workers to Sweden to apply a Swedish collective agreement, the Arbetsdomstolen decided on 29 April 2005 to make a reference to the Court of Justice for a preliminary ruling. In its order for reference, of 15 September 2005, the national court refers the following questions for a preliminary ruling:

'(1) Is it compatible with rules of the EC Treaty on the freedom to provide services and the prohibition of any discrimination on the grounds of nationality and with the provisions of Directive 96/71/EC ... for trade unions to attempt, by means of collective action in the form of a blockade ('blockad'), to force a foreign provider of services to sign a collective agreement in the host country in respect of terms and conditions of employment, such as that described in the decision of the Arbetsdomstolen [of 29 April 2005 (collective agreement for the building sector)], if the situation in the host country is such that the legislation to implement Directive 96/71 has no express provisions concerning the application of terms and conditions of employment in collective agreements?

(2) The [MBL] prohibits a trade union from taking collective action with the intention of circumventing a collective agreement concluded by other parties. That prohibition applies, however, pursuant to a special provision contained in part of the law known as the 'Lex Britannia', only where a trade union takes collective action in relation to conditions of work to which the [MBL] is directly applicable, which means in practice that the prohibition is not applicable to collective action against a foreign undertaking which is temporarily active in Sweden and which brings its own workforce. Do the rules of the EC Treaty on the freedom to provide services and the prohibition of discrimination on grounds of nationality and the provisions of Directive 96/71 preclude application of the latter rule – which, together with other parts of the Lex Britannia, mean in practice that Swedish collective agreements become applicable and take precedence over foreign collective agreements already concluded – to collective action in the form of a blockade taken by Swedish trade unions against a foreign temporary provider of services in Sweden?'

41. By order of the President of the Court of Justice of 15 November 2005, the application for a ruling to be given in this case under the accelerated procedure provided for in the first paragraph of Article 104a of the Rules of Procedure was dismissed.

Admissibility

[Paras 42-50 omitted]

The first question

51. By its first question, the national court is asking whether it is compatible with rules of the EC Treaty on the freedom to provide services and the prohibition of any discrimination on the grounds of nationality and with the provisions of Directive 96/71/EC, for trade unions to attempt, by means of collective action in the form of a blockade, to force a foreign provider of services to sign a collective agreement in the host country in respect of terms and conditions of employment, such as the collective agreement for the building sector, if the situation in the host country is characterised by the fact that the legislation to implement that directive has no express provision concerning the application of terms and conditions of employment in collective agreements.

52. It is clear from the order of reference that the collective action initiated by Byggnads and Byggettan was motivated by Laval's refusal to guarantee its workers posted in Sweden the hourly wage demanded by those trade unions, even though that Member State does not provide for minimum rates of pay, and Laval's refusal to

sign the collective agreement for the building sector, some terms of which lay down, in relation to certain matters referred to in Article 3(1), first subparagraph, (a) to (g) of Directive 96/71, more favourable conditions than those resulting from the relevant legislative provisions, while other terms relate to matters not referred to in that article.

53. Accordingly, the national court's first question must be understood as asking, in essence, whether Articles 12 EC and 49 EC, and Directive 96/71, are to be interpreted as precluding a trade union, in a Member State in which the terms and conditions of employment concerning the matters referred to in Article 3(1), first subparagraph, (a) to (g) of that directive, save for minimum rates of pay, are contained in legislative provisions, from attempting, by means of collective action in the form of blockading sites such as that at issue in the main proceedings, to force a provider of services established in another Member State to enter into negotiations with it on the rates of pay for posted workers, and to sign a collective agreement, the terms of which lay down, as regards some of those matters, more favourable conditions than those resulting from the relevant legislative provisions, while other terms relate to matters not referred to in Article 3 of the directive.

The relevant provisions of Community law

54. In order to ascertain the provisions of Community law applicable to a case such as that in the main proceedings, it must be noted that, according to the settled case-law of the Court, Article 12 EC, which lays down the general principle of the prohibition of discrimination on grounds of nationality, applies independently only to situations governed by Community law for which the Treaty lays down no specific prohibition of discrimination (see Case C-100/01 *Oteiza Olazabal* [2002] ECR I-10981, paragraph 25, and Case C-387/01 *Weigel* [2004] ECR I-4981, paragraph 57).

55. So far as the freedom to provide services is concerned, that principle was given specific expression and effect by Article 49 EC (Case C-22/98 *Becu and Others* [1999] ECR I-5665, paragraph 32, and Case C-55/98 *Vestergaard* [1999] ECR I-7641, paragraph 17). It is for that reason unnecessary to rule on Article 12 EC.

56. As regards the temporary posting of workers to another Member State so that they can carry out construction work or public works in the context of services provided by their employer, it is clear from the settled case-law of the Court that Articles 49 EC and 50 EC preclude a Member State from prohibiting a person providing services established in another Member State from moving freely on its territory with all his staff and also preclude that Member State from making the movement of staff in question subject to more restrictive conditions. To impose such conditions on the person providing services established in another Member State discriminates against that person in relation to his competitors established in the host country who are able to use their own staff without restrictions, and moreover affects his ability

to provide the service (Case C-113/89 *Rush Portuguesa* [1990] ECR I-1417, paragraph 12).

57. Conversely, Community law does not preclude Member States from applying their legislation, or collective labour agreements entered into by management and labour relating to minimum wages, to any person who is employed, even temporarily, within their territory, no matter in which country the employer is established (see, in particular, Joined Cases 62/81 and 63/81 *Seco and Desquenne & Giral* [1982] ECR 223, paragraph 14, and Case C-164/99 *Portugaia Construções* [2002] ECR I-787, paragraph 21). The application of such rules must, however, be appropriate for securing the attainment of the objective which they pursue, that is, the protection of posted workers, and must not go beyond what is necessary in order to attain that objective (see, to that effect, inter alia, Joined Cases C-369/96 and C-376/96 *Arblade and Others* [1999] ECR I-8453, paragraph 35 and Case C-341/02 *Commission* v *Germany* [2005] ECR I-2733, paragraph 24).

58. In that context, the Community legislature adopted Directive 96/71, with a view, as is clear from recital 6 in the preamble to that directive, to laying down, in the interests of the employers and their personnel, the terms and conditions governing the employment relationship where an undertaking established in one Member State posts workers on a temporary basis to the territory of another Member State for the purposes of providing a service.

59. It follows from recital 13 to Directive 96/71 that the laws of the Member States must be coordinated in order to lay down a nucleus of mandatory rules for minimum protection to be observed in the host country by employers who post workers there.

60. Nevertheless, Directive 96/71 did not harmonise the material content of those mandatory rules for minimum protection. That content may accordingly be freely defined by the Member States, in compliance with the Treaty and the general principles of Community law (Case C-490/04 *Commission* v *Germany* [2007] ECR I-0000, paragraph19).

61. Consequently, since the facts at issue in the main proceedings, as described in the order of reference, occurred in 2004, that is to say, on a date subsequent to the expiry of the period allowed to the Member States for transposing Directive 96/71, that date being fixed for 16 December 1999, and since those facts fall within the scope of that directive, the first question must be examined with regard to the provisions of that directive interpreted in the light of Article 49 EC (Case C-60/03 *Wolff & Müller* [2004] ECR I-9553, paragraphs 25 to 27 and 45), and, where appropriate, with regard to the latter provision itself.

The possibilities available to the Member States for determining the terms and conditions of employment applicable to posted workers, including minimum rates of pay

62. In the context of the procedure established by Article 234 EC providing for cooperation between national courts and the Court of Justice, and in order to provide the national court with an answer which will be of use to it and enable it to determine the case before it (C-334/95 *Krüger* [1997] ECR I-4517, paragraph 22; C-88/99 *Roquette Frères* [2000] ECR I-10465, paragraph 18, and Joined Cases C-393/04 and C-41/05 *Air Liquide Industries Belgium* [2006] ECR I-5293, paragraph 23), it is appropriate to examine the possibilities available to the Member States for determining the terms and conditions of employment covering the matters referred to in Article 3(1), first subparagraph, (a) to (g), including minimum rates of pay, which undertakings are to guarantee workers they post in the framework of the transnational provision of services.

63. It is clear from both the order for reference and the observations submitted in the course of the present proceedings that underlying the dispute is, first, as regards the determination of the terms and conditions of the employment of posted workers relating to those matters, the fact that minimum rates of pay constitute the only term of employment which, in Sweden, is not laid down in accordance with one of the means provided for in Directive 96/71 and, second, the requirement imposed on Laval to negotiate with trade unions in order to ascertain the wages to be paid to its workers and to sign the collective agreement for the building sector.

64. According to the first and second indents of the first subparagraph of Article 3(1) of Directive 96/71, the terms and conditions of employment covering the matters referred to in (a) to (g) thereof are established, in relation to the transnational provision of services in the construction sector, either by law, regulation or administrative provision, or by collective agreements or arbitration awards which have been declared universally applicable. Collective agreements and arbitration awards for the purposes of that provision are those which must be observed by all undertakings in the geographical area and in the profession or industry concerned.

65. The second subparagraph of Article 3(8) of Directive 96/71 also gives Member States the possibility, in the absence of a system for declaring collective agreements or arbitration awards to be of universal application, to base themselves on those which are generally applicable to all similar undertakings in the industry concerned or those which have been concluded by the most representative employers' and labour organisations at national level and which are applied throughout the national territory.

66. It is clear from the wording of that provision that recourse to the latter possibility requires, first, that the Member State must so decide, and second, that the application of collective agreements to undertakings which post workers should guarantee equality of treatment in the matters listed in Article 3(1), first subparagraph, (a) to

(g) of Directive 96/71 between the latter undertakings and national undertakings in the profession or industry concerned which are in a similar position. Equality of treatment, within the meaning of Article 3(8) of the directive, is deemed to exist where national undertakings are subject to the same obligations, as regards those matters, as posting undertakings, and where each are required to fulfil such obligations with the same effects.

67. It is common ground that, in Sweden, the terms and conditions of employment covering the matters listed in Article 3(1), first subparagraph, (a) to (g) of Directive 96/71, save for minimum rates of pay, have been laid down by law. It is also not disputed that the collective agreements have not been declared universally applicable, and that that Member State has not made use of the possibility provided for in the second subparagraph of Article 3(8) of that directive.

68. It must be noted, in this respect, that since the purpose of Directive 96/71 is not to harmonise systems for establishing terms and conditions of employment in the Member States, the latter are free to choose a system at the national level which is not expressly mentioned among those provided for in that directive, provided that it does not hinder the provision of services between the Member States.

69. It is clear from the file that the national authorities in Sweden have entrusted management and labour with the task of setting, by way of collective negotiations, the wage rates which national undertakings are to pay their workers and that, as regards undertakings in the construction sector, such a system requires negotiation on a case-by-case basis, at the place of work, having regard to the qualifications and tasks of the employees concerned.

70. As regards the requirements as to pay which can be imposed on foreign service providers, it should be recalled that the first subparagraph of Article 3(1) of Directive 96/71 relates only to minimum rates of pay. Therefore, that provision cannot be relied on to justify an obligation on such service providers to comply with rates of pay such as those which the trade unions seek in this case to impose in the framework of the Swedish system, which do not constitute minimum wages and are not, moreover, laid down in accordance with the means set out in that regard in Article 3(1) and (8) of the directive.

71. It must therefore be concluded at this stage that a Member State in which the minimum rates of pay are not determined in accordance with one of the means provided for in Article 3(1) and (8) of Directive 96/71 is not entitled, pursuant to that directive, to impose on undertakings established in other Member States, in the framework of the transnational provision of services, negotiation at the place of work, on a case-by-case basis, having regard to the qualifications and tasks of the employees, so that the undertakings concerned may ascertain the wages which they are to pay their posted workers.

72. It is necessary to assess further, the obligations on undertakings established in another Member State which stem from such a system for determining wages with regard to Article 49 EC.

Matters which may be covered by the terms and conditions of work applicable to posted workers

73. In order to ensure that the nucleus of mandatory rules for minimum protection are observed, the first subparagraph of Article 3(1) of Directive 96/71 provides that Member States are to ensure that, whatever the law applicable to the employment relationship, in the framework of the transnational provision of services, undertakings guarantee workers posted to their territory the terms and conditions of employment covering the matters listed in that provision, namely: maximum work periods and minimum rest periods; minimum paid annual holidays; the minimum rates of pay, including overtime rates; the conditions of hiring-out of workers, in particular the supply of workers by temporary employment undertakings; health, safety and hygiene at work; protective measures with regard to the terms and conditions of employment of pregnant women or women who have recently given birth, of children and of young people; and equality of treatment between men and women and other provisions on non-discrimination.

74. That provision seeks, first, to ensure a climate of fair competition between national undertakings and undertakings which provide services transnationally, in so far as it requires the latter to afford their workers, as regards a limited list of matters, the terms and conditions of employment laid down in the host Member State by law, regulation or administrative provision or by collective agreements or arbitration awards within the meaning of Article 3(8) of Directive 96/71, which constitute mandatory rules for minimum protection.

75. That provision thus prevents a situation arising in which, by applying to their workers the terms and conditions of employment in force in the Member State of origin as regards those matters, undertakings established in other Member States would compete unfairly against undertakings of the host Member State in the framework of the transnational provision of services, if the level of social protection in the host Member State is higher.

76. Secondly, that provision seeks to ensure that posted workers will have the rules of the Member States for minimum protection as regards the terms and conditions of employment relating to those matters applied to them while they work on a temporary basis in the territory of that Member State.

77. The consequence of affording such minimum protection – if the level of protection resulting from the terms and conditions of employment granted to posted workers in the Member State of origin, as regards the matters referred to in Article 3(1), first

subparagraph, (a) to (g) of Directive 96/71, is lower than the level of minimum protection afforded in the host Member State – is to enable those workers to enjoy better terms and conditions of employment in the host Member State.

78. However, in the case in the main proceedings, it is apparent from paragraph 19 of this judgment that, in respect of some of the matters referred to in Article 3(1), first subparagraph, (a) to (g) of Directive 96/71, in particular as regards working time and annual leave, certain terms of the collective agreement for the building sector depart from the provisions of Swedish law which lay down the terms and conditions of employment applicable to posted workers, by establishing more favourable terms.

79. It is true that Article 3(7) of Directive 96/71 provides that paragraphs 1 to 6 are not to prevent application of terms and conditions of employment which are more favourable to workers. In addition, according to recital 17, the mandatory rules for minimum protection in force in the host country must not prevent the application of such terms and conditions.

80. Nevertheless, Article 3(7) of Directive 96/71 cannot be interpreted as allowing the host Member State to make the provision of services in its territory conditional on the observance of terms and conditions of employment which go beyond the mandatory rules for minimum protection. As regards the matters referred to in Article 3(1), first subparagraph, (a) to (g), Directive 96/71 expressly lays down the degree of protection for workers of undertakings established in other Member States who are posted to the territory of the host Member State which the latter State is entitled to require those undertakings to observe. Moreover, such an interpretation would amount to depriving the directive of its effectiveness.

81. Therefore – without prejudice to the right of undertakings established in other Member States to sign of their own accord a collective labour agreement in the host Member State, in particular in the context of a commitment made to their own posted staff, the terms of which might be more favourable – the level of protection which must be guaranteed to workers posted to the territory of the host Member State is limited, in principle, to that provided for in Article 3(1), first subparagraph, (a) to (g) of Directive 96/71, unless, pursuant to the law or collective agreements in the Member State of origin, those workers already enjoy more favourable terms and conditions of employment as regards the matters referred to in that provision.

82. Moreover, it must be pointed out that, pursuant to the first indent of Article 3(10) of Directive 96/71, Member States may apply terms and conditions of employment on matters other than those specifically referred to in Article 3(1), first subparagraph, (a) to (g), in compliance with the Treaty and, in the case of public policy provisions, on a basis of equality of treatment, to national undertakings and to the undertakings of other Member States.

83. In the main proceedings, certain terms of the collective agreement for the building sector relate to matters which are not specifically referred to in Article 3(1), first subparagraph, (a) to (g) of Directive 96/71. In that regard, it follows from paragraph 20 of this judgment that signing that collective agreement entails undertakings accepting pecuniary obligations such as those requiring them to pay to Byggettan a sum equal to 1.5% of total gross wages for the purposes of the pay review which that section trade union carries out, and to the insurance company, FORA, first, 0.8% of total gross wages for the purposes of a charge called the 'special building supplement', and, second, a further 5.9% for the purposes of a number of insurance premiums.

84. It is common ground, however, that those obligations were imposed without the national authorities' having had recourse to Article 3(10) of Directive 96/71. The terms of the collective agreement for the building sector in question were in fact established through negotiation between management and labour; not being bodies governed by public law, they cannot avail themselves of that provision by citing grounds of public policy in order to maintain that collective action such as that at issue in the main proceedings complies with Community law.

85. It is also necessary to assess from the point of view of Article 49 EC the collective action taken by the trade unions in the case in the main proceedings, both in so far as it seeks to force a service provider established in another Member State to enter into negotiations on the wages to be paid to posted workers and in so far as it seeks to force that service provider to sign a collective agreement the terms of which lay down, as regards some of the matters referred to in Article 3(1), first subparagraph, (a) to (g) of Directive 96/71, more favourable conditions than those stemming from the relevant legislative provisions, while other terms cover matters not referred to in that provision.

Assessment of the collective action at issue in the case in the main proceedings from the point of view of Article 49 EC

86. As regards use of the means available to the trade unions to bring pressure to bear on the relevant parties to sign a collective agreement and to enter into negotiations on pay, the defendants in the main proceedings and the Danish and Swedish Governments submit that the right to take collective action in the context of negotiations with an employer falls outside the scope of Article 49 EC, since, pursuant to Article 137(5) EC, as amended by the Treaty of Nice, the Community has no power to regulate that right.

87. In this regard, it suffices to point out that, even though, in the areas in which the Community does not have competence, the Member States remain, in principle, free to lay down the conditions for the existence and exercise of the rights at issue, they must nevertheless exercise that competence consistently with Community law

(see, by analogy, as regards social security, Case C-120/95 *Decker* [1998] ECR I-1831, paragraphs 22 and 23, and Case C-158/96 *Kohll* [1998] ECR I-1931, paragraphs 18 and 19; as regards direct taxation, Case C-334/02 *Commission* v *France* [2004] ECR I-2229, paragraph 21, and Case C-446/03 *Marks & Spencer* [2005] ECR I-10837, paragraph 29).

88. Therefore, the fact that Article 137 EC does not apply to the right to strike or to the right to impose lock-outs is not such as to exclude collective action such as that at issue in the main proceedings from the domain of freedom to provide services.

89. According to the observations of the Danish and Swedish Governments, the right to take collective action constitutes a fundamental right which, as such, falls outside the scope of Article 49 EC and Directive 96/71.

90. In that regard, it must be recalled that the right to take collective action is recognised both by various international instruments which the Member States have signed or cooperated in, such as the European Social Charter, signed at Turin on 18 October 1961 – to which, moreover, express reference is made in Article 136 EC – and Convention No 87 of the International Labour Organisation concerning Freedom of Association and Protection of the Right to Organise of 9 July 1948 – and by instruments developed by those Member States at Community level or in the context of the European Union, such as the Community Charter of the Fundamental Social Rights of Workers adopted at the meeting of the European Council held in Strasbourg on 9 December 1989, which is also referred to in Article 136 EC, and the Charter of Fundamental Rights of the European Union proclaimed in Nice on 7 December 2000 (OJ 2000 C 364, p. 1).

91. Although the right to take collective action must therefore be recognised as a fundamental right which forms an integral part of the general principles of Community law the observance of which the Court ensures, the exercise of that right may none the less be subject to certain restrictions. As is reaffirmed by Article 28 of the Charter of Fundamental Rights of the European Union, it is to be protected in accordance with Community law and national law and practices.

92. Although it is true, as the Swedish Government points out, that the right to take collective action enjoys constitutional protection in Sweden, as in other Member States, nevertheless as is clear from paragraph 10 of this judgment, under the Swedish constitution, that right – which, in that Member State, covers the blockading of worksites – may be exercised unless otherwise provided by law or agreement.

93. In that regard, the Court has already held that the protection of fundamental rights is a legitimate interest which, in principle, justifies a restriction of the obligations imposed by Community law, even under a fundamental freedom guaranteed by the Treaty, such as the free movement of goods (see Case C-112/00 *Schmidberger*

[2003] ECR I-5659, paragraph 74) or freedom to provide services (see Case C-36/02 *Omega* [2004] ECR I-9609, paragraph 35).

94. As the Court held, in *Schmidberger* and *Omega*, the exercise of the fundamental rights at issue, that is, freedom of expression and freedom of assembly and respect for human dignity, respectively, does not fall outside the scope of the provisions of the Treaty. Such exercise must be reconciled with the requirements relating to rights protected under the Treaty and in accordance with the principle of proportionality (see, to that effect, *Schmidberger*, paragraph 77, and *Omega*, paragraph 36).

95. It follows from the foregoing that the fundamental nature of the right to take collective action is not such as to render Community law inapplicable to such action, taken against an undertaking established in another Member State which posts workers in the framework of the transnational provision of services.

96. It must therefore be examined whether the fact that a Member State's trade unions may take collective action in the circumstances described above constitutes a restriction on the freedom to provide services, and, if so, whether it can be justified.

97. It should be noted that, in so far as it seeks to abolish restrictions on the freedom to provide services stemming from the fact that the service provider is established in a Member State other than that in which the service is to be provided, Article 49 EC became directly applicable in the legal orders of the Member States on expiry of the transitional period and confers on individuals rights which are enforceable by them and which the national courts must protect (see, inter alia, Case 33/74 *Van Binsbergen* [1974] ECR 1299, paragraph 26; Case 13/76 *Donà* [1976] ECR 1333, paragraph 20; Case 206/84 *Commission* v *Ireland* [1986] ECR 3817, paragraph 16; and Case C-208/05 *ITC* [2007] ECR I-181, paragraph 67).

98. Furthermore, compliance with Article 49 EC is also required in the case of rules which are not public in nature but which are designed to regulate, collectively, the provision of services. The abolition, as between Member States, of obstacles to the freedom to provide services would be compromised if the abolition of State barriers could be neutralised by obstacles resulting from the exercise of their legal autonomy by associations or organisations not governed by public law (see Case 36/74 *Walrave and Koch* [1974] ECR 1405, paragraphs 17 and 18; Case C-415/93 *Bosman* [1995] ECR I-4921, paragraphs 83 and 84, and Case C-309/99 *Wouters and Others* [2002] ECR I-1577, paragraph 120).

99. In the case in the main proceedings, it must be pointed out that the right of trade unions of a Member State to take collective action by which undertakings established in other Member States may be forced to sign the collective agreement for the building sector – certain terms of which depart from the legislative provisions and establish more favourable terms and conditions of employment as regards the mat-

ters referred to in Article 3(1), first subparagraph, (a) to (g) of Directive 96/71 and others relate to matters not referred to in that provision – is liable to make it less attractive, or more difficult, for such undertakings to carry out construction work in Sweden, and therefore constitutes a restriction on the freedom to provide services within the meaning of Article 49 EC.

100. The same is all the more true of the fact that, in order to ascertain the minimum wage rates to be paid to their posted workers, those undertakings may be forced, by way of collective action, into negotiations with the trade unions of unspecified duration at the place at which the services in question are to be provided.

101. It is clear from the case-law of the Court that, since the freedom to provide services is one of the fundamental principles of the Community (see, inter alia, Case 220/83 *Commission* v *France* [1986] ECR 3663, paragraph 17, and Case 252/83 *Commission* v *Denmark* [1986] ECR 3713, paragraph 17), a restriction on that freedom is warranted only if it pursues a legitimate objective compatible with the Treaty and is justified by overriding reasons of public interest; if that is the case, it must be suitable for securing the attainment of the objective which it pursues and not go beyond what is necessary in order to attain it (Case C-398/95 *SETTG* [1997] ECR I-3091, paragraph 21; Case C-451/03 *Servizi Ausiliari Dottori Commercialisti* [2006] ECR I-2941, paragraph 37, and Case C-94/04 *Cipolla* [2006] ECR I-11421, paragraph 61).

102. The Swedish Government and the defendant trade unions in the main proceedings submit that the restrictions in question are justified, since they are necessary to ensure the protection of a fundamental right recognised by Community law and have as their objective the protection of workers, which constitutes an overriding reason of public interest.

103. In that regard, it must be pointed out that the right to take collective action for the protection of the workers of the host State against possible social dumping may constitute an overriding reason of public interest within the meaning of the case--law of the Court which, in principle, justifies a restriction of one of the fundamental freedoms guaranteed by the Treaty (see, to that effect, Joined Cases C-369/96 and C-376/96 *Arblade and Others* [1999] ECR I-8453, paragraph 36; Case C-165/98 *Mazzoleni and ISA* [2001] ECR I-2189, paragraph 27; Joined Cases C-49/98, C-50/98, C-52/98 to C-54/98 and C-68/98 to C-71/98 *Finalarte and Others* [2001] ECR I-7831, paragraph 33, and Case C-438/05 *International Transport Workers' Federation and Finnish Seamen's Union* [2007] ECR I-0000, paragraph 77).

104. It should be added that, according to Article 3(1)(c) and (j) EC, the activities of the Community are to include not only an 'internal market characterised by the abolition, as between Member States, of obstacles to the free movement of goods, per-

sons, services and capital', but also 'a policy in the social sphere'. Article 2 EC states that the Community is to have as its task, inter alia, the promotion of 'a harmonious, balanced and sustainable development of economic activities' and 'a high level of employment and of social protection'.

105. Since the Community has thus not only an economic but also a social purpose, the rights under the provisions of the EC Treaty on the free movement of goods, persons, services and capital must be balanced against the objectives pursued by social policy, which include, as is clear from the first paragraph of Article 136 EC, inter alia, improved living and working conditions, so as to make possible their harmonisation while improvement is being maintained, proper social protection and dialogue between management and labour.

106. In the case in the main proceedings, Byggnads and Byggettan contend that the objective of the blockade carried out against Laval was the protection of workers.

107. In that regard, it must be observed that, in principle, blockading action by a trade union of the host Member State which is aimed at ensuring that workers posted in the framework of a transnational provision of services have their terms and conditions of employment fixed at a certain level, falls within the objective of protecting workers.

108. However, as regards the specific obligations, linked to signature of the collective agreement for the building sector, which the trade unions seek to impose on undertakings established in other Member States by way of collective action such as that at issue in the case in the main proceedings, the obstacle which that collective action forms cannot be justified with regard to such an objective. In addition to what is set out in paragraphs 81 and 83 of the present judgment, with regard to workers posted in the framework of a transnational provision of services, their employer is required, as a result of the coordination achieved by Directive 96/71, to observe a nucleus of mandatory rules for minimum protection in the host Member State.

109. Finally, as regards the negotiations on pay which the trade unions seek to impose, by way of collective action such as that at issue in the main proceedings, on undertakings, established in another Member State which post workers temporarily to their territory, it must be emphasised that Community law certainly does not prohibit Member States from requiring such undertakings to comply with their rules on minimum pay by appropriate means (see *Seco and Desquenne & Giral*, paragraph 14; *Rush Portuguesa*, paragraph 18, and *Arblade and Others*, paragraph 41).

110. However, collective action such as that at issue in the main proceedings cannot be justified in the light of the public interest objective referred to in paragraph 102 of the present judgment, where the negotiations on pay, which that action seeks to require an undertaking established in another Member State to enter into, form

part of a national context characterised by a lack of provisions, of any kind, which are sufficiently precise and accessible that they do not render it impossible or excessively difficult in practice for such an undertaking to determine the obligations with which it is required to comply as regards minimum pay (see, to that effect, *Arblade and Others*, paragraph 43).

111. In the light of the foregoing, the answer to the first question must be that Article 49 EC and Directive 96/71 are to be interpreted as precluding a trade union, in a Member State in which the terms and conditions of employment covering the matters referred to in Article 3(1), first subparagraph, (a) to (g) of that directive are contained in legislative provisions, save for minimum rates of pay, from attempting, by means of collective action in the form of a blockade ('blockad') of sites such as that at issue in the main proceedings, to force a provider of services established in another Member State to enter into negotiations with it on the rates of pay for posted workers and to sign a collective agreement the terms of which lay down, as regards some of those matters, more favourable conditions than those resulting from the relevant legislative provisions, while other terms relate to matters not referred to in Article 3 of the directive.

The second question

Costs

[Paragraphs 112-121 omitted]

On those grounds,

THE COURT (Grand Chamber)

hereby rules:

1. **Article 49 EC and Article 3 of Directive 96/71/EC of the European Parliament and of the Council of 16 December 1996 concerning the posting of workers in the framework of the provision of services are to be interpreted as precluding a trade union, in a Member State in which the terms and conditions of employment covering the matters referred to in Article 3(1), first subparagraph, (a) to (g) of that directive are contained in legislative provisions, save for minimum rates of pay, from attempting, by means of collective action in the form of a blockade ('blockad') of sites such as that at issue in the main proceedings, to force a provider of services established in another Member State to enter into negotiations with it on the rates of pay for posted workers and to sign a collective agreement the terms of which lay down, as regards some of those matters, more favourable condi-**

tions than those resulting from the relevant legislative provisions, while other terms relate to matters not referred to in Article 3 of the directive.

2. **Where there is a prohibition in a Member State against trade unions undertaking collective action with the aim of having a collective agreement between other parties set aside or amended, Articles 49 EC and 50 EC preclude that prohibition from being subject to the condition that such action must relate to terms and conditions of employment to which the national law applies directly.**

Comments and questions

Within just one week in December 2007, the CJEU delivered two judgments that had been awaited with particular interest – not least by trade unions in the Nordic countries. First came the decision in Case C-438/05 *Viking Line* [2007] ECR I-10779, which is reproduced above in Chapter 5. In that case the CJEU ruled that (now) Article 49 TFEU, on freedom of establishment, applies to collective agreements entered into by private persons, and that collective action initiated by private persons is subject to the Treaty rules. Next, the CJEU delivered judgment in the *Laval* case, in which the central question was whether a private undertaking could rely on Article 56 TFEU (formerly Article 49 TEC), on the freedom to provide services, against a (private) trade union that used collective action, among other things in order to persuade the service provider to enter into a collective agreement. As in the *Viking Line* case, the CJEU answered this in the affirmative.

Would the circumstances be covered by Article 56 TFEU if, for example, a theme park such as Disneyland outside Paris decided to discriminate between French and non-French visitors so that visitors who paid with British pounds should pay a higher price than visitors who paid with euro?

However, the *Laval* case is not just interesting with reference to the question of which persons can be subject to the provisions of Article 56 TFEU. As appears from the judgment, the starting point for the dispute was that the Latvian company Laval un Partneri had secured a contract for some construction work on a school in the Swedish town of Vaxholm. With a view to fulfilling this contract, in 2004 Laval had posted a number of Latvian employees to Sweden. The construction work was carried out by Laval's Swedish subsidiary, L&P Baltic Bygg AB. Not long after the posting of the Latvian workers, Laval and Baltic Bygg entered into negotiations with Svenska Byggnadsarbejtareförbundet, the Swedish trade union for building and construction workers, on the payment of the posted employees and on Laval's signing up for the Swedish collective agreement for the construction industry. These negotiations stalled in the autumn of 2004. On the other hand, at this point Laval entered into a collective agreement with the Latvian trade union for construction workers, of which 65% of the posted employees were members.

After the negotiations had stalled, Byggnadsarbejtareförbundet initiated collective action in the form of picketing all Laval's construction sites in Sweden. The Swedish electrician's union took sympathy action, so that all electricians were prevented from providing services to Laval. None of the trade unions concerned had members employed by Laval. When the interruption of work had lasted some time, Baltic Bygg was declared bankrupt and the Latvian workers went back to Latvia. Laval commenced proceedings before the *Arbetsdomstolen* (the Labour Court), seeking a declaration that the collective action had been illegal and seeking compensation for the damage suffered. The Labour Court then asked the CJEU to rule on whether Union law prevented the disputed collective action.

Just as in the *Viking Line* case, so in the *Laval* case the CJEU confirmed that the right to take collective action is a fundamental right, but that its exercise can be subject to certain restrictions. This applies whenever an undertaking established in another Member State posts workers in the context of the cross-border provision of services.

The CJEU also held that the Swedish trade unions' right to take collective action against Laval, so that Laval was forced into endless negotiations in order to know the minimum wages the company should pay (paragraph 100), and so that the unions tried to force Laval to enter into a collective agreement whose provisions went further than the minimum protection guaranteed by Directive 96/71/EC (paragraph 99) concerning the posting of workers in the framework of the provision of services, could constitute a restriction on the freedom to provide services. Consider whether, in this respect, the CJEU has effectively laid down that any collective negotiation where a trade union seeks to obtain conditions for posted workers from another Member State that are better than the minimum protection provided by the Directive on the posting of workers, would constitute a restriction under Article 56 TFEU. If the answer to this is in the affirmative, does this mean that a trade union can only enter such negotiations under a threat of collective action if the trade union can show that the negotiations pursue a legitimate purpose, and if the proportionality principle is complied with? Does the CJEU express itself on whether a trade union's desire to protect workers in the host Member State against possible social dumping can be a lawful purpose (an overriding public interest)? Can picketing, such as that in the *Laval* case, which was aimed at guaranteeing for workers, who were posted as part of the cross-border provision of services, working and employment conditions of a certain level, be covered by the (lawful) aim of protecting workers? In answering this last question, is it relevant that Directive 96/71/EC concerning the posting of workers in the framework of the provision of services laid down some mandatory rules for minimum protection in the host Member State?

In relation to the use of collective action to ensure that service providers from other Member States comply with their provisions on minimum wages, the CJEU has ruled that this does not, in itself, conflict with Union law. However, it added that such action cannot be justified by reference to the overriding public interest to protect workers when the wage negotiations which the collective action is intended to support form part of a national context characterised by a lack of provisions which are sufficiently precise and accessible as to make it impossible or excessively difficult in practice for an undertaking to determine the obligations with which it is required to comply as regards minimum pay. What does the CJEU mean by this in the actual case?

Finally, the CJEU deals with the special Swedish *lex Britannica*, which in reality means there is discrimination between domestic and foreign service providers. Here the CJEU stated that national rules which fail to take into account, irrespective of their content, collective agreements to which undertakings that post workers to Sweden are already bound in the Member State where they are established, give rise to discrimination against such undertakings, in so far as they are treated under those national rules in the same way as national undertakings which have not concluded a collective agreement. Since this is direct discrimination, the Swedish legislation can only be justified by the concerns that are expressly stated in the TFEU, i.e. public policy, public security or public health. The CJEU found that none of these considerations was present in the *Laval* case. Consider whether a Member State can require that an undertaking that posts foreign workers must:

- Only post employees who have a written contract of employment,
- Comply with national provisions on part-time work and short-term contracts (in addition to any corresponding provisions in the home Member State),
- Apply the host Member State's rules on the automatic indexing of wages,
- Acknowledge that provisions, including those in collective agreements, that are generally applicable are mandatory provisions of public policy in the host Member State,
- Not work on Sundays and public holidays or on the national day of the host Member State,
- Have a maximum working day of six hours if the work concerned has been classified by the host Member State as being dangerous and requiring a high level of concentration,
- Ensure that the posted workers have suitable safety training, to the extent that they are to undertake tasks that can be dangerous for themselves or others, and
- Notify a public authority in the host Member State, prior to providing the service, that there is to be the provision of the service, where the service is to be provided, and the nature and extent of the service.

Consider whether it was in accordance with Article 56 TFEU for Frank Jensen, the Lord Mayor of Copenhagen, to encourage employees of the muncipality not to buy flight tickets from Ryanair on the ground that, in the Lord Mayor's view, Ryanair did not pay its employees properly. Take account of the facts that Ryanair had not entered into a collective agreement in Denmark, even though it claimed to have a 'base' in the country and even though the Danish transport workers' union had tried and failed to enter into an agreement in connection with a strike.

In Case C-577/10 *Commission* v *Belgium*, judgment of 19 December 2012, the Commission had brought proceedings against Belgium for breach of the Treaty because, according to the Commission, Belgium had breached Article 56 TFEU on the freedom to provide services since it required self-employed service providers without employees to make a declaration prior to carrying on their activities in Belgium. The obligation to make a declaration had been introduced within the framework of a more comprehensive project under the name of 'Limosa', the acronym of 'Landenoverschrijdend Informatiesysteem ten behoeve van Migratieonderzoek bij de Sociale Administratie' (cross-border information system for the investigation of migration by the social security administration; 'the Limosa system'). That project sought to create an electronic one-stop-shop for all formalities related to employment in Belgium. The information gathered via the Limosa declaration was intended to feed a central register and to be made accessible, for purposes of statistics and monitoring, in particular to the Belgian federal and regional inspection services, by means of a common IT platform.

It was the Commission's view that the Belgian measure was a discriminatory restriction on the freedom to provide services, since the obligation to make a Limosa declaration only applied to self-employed service providers based in a Member State other than Belgium. It was also the Commission's view that the Belgian measure in any case was neither justified by nor proportionate with regard to the public interest, as Belgium claimed in support of its measure. Moreover, it was the Commission's view that it was possible to claim justification with regard to combating fraud and protecting employees, but that the measures which had the purpose of ensuring compliance with requirements that were justified by such considerations must not make the freedom to provide services illusory. According to the Commission this was the situation in the case in question.

In its decision, the CJEU began by noting that the obligation to make a declaration meant that self-employed persons who resided or were established in a Member State other than Belgium were required to register by creating an account and then, before each supply of services on Belgian territory, to provide the Belgian authorities with a certain amount of information such as the date, duration and place of the service to be supplied, its nature and the identity of the legal or natural person receiving it. That information had to be provided on a form. Failure to comply with these formalities was subject to criminal penalties.

The CJEU found that the formalities required by the obligation to make a declaration could make it more difficult for self-employed service providers based in another Member State to provide services in Belgium. The obligation to make a declaration thus constituted a hindrance to freedom to provide services. The CJEU then considered whether the declaration requirement at issue could be justified, given that the cross-border supply of services by self-employed workers had not then been harmonised at European Union level. In contrast to the Commission, the CJEU found that the Limosa system was not discriminatory. The CJEU noted that, in the light of the necessary checks and the absence of harmonisation of national laws in the field of employment and labour, in order to ensure the protection of the overriding requirements in the public interest relied on by Belgium, self-employed service providers established in a Member State other than Belgium who travelled temporarily to Belgium to supply services there were in a position objectively different from that of self-employed service providers permanently established on Belgian territory. The CJEU also noted that it had previously held that: 'as regards the ability of the authorities of the Member State in whose territory services are supplied to check that the rules intended to ensure that the rights conferred by national law on workers in its territory are followed, there are, clearly, objective differences between businesses established in the Member State where the services are supplied and those established in other Member States posting workers to the first Member State to supply services there ... The fact that self-employed service providers established in Belgium are not subject to strictly equivalent requirements, in particular as regards the information to be provided, to those following from the declaration requirement at issue for self-employed service providers established in another Member State may thus be attributed to objective differences between those two categories of self-employed service providers.'

The CJEU then turned to the question of whether the Belgian Limosa system satisfied the principle of proportionality. Here it was the view of the CJEU that the Belgian system went beyond what was necessary to ensure the protection of the overriding requirements in the public interest claimed by Belgium and recognised by the CJEU. Consequently, the Limosa system did not satisfy the principle of proportionality.

Thus, even though the CJEU accepted that an arrangement corresponding to the Limosa system was not discriminatory, and even though the CJEU recognised that the Limosa system was justified in part by the objective of preventing unfair competition, which includes a social security dimension connected with the protection of workers and consumers and the prevention of social dumping, such a measure would only comply with Union law if the Member State were able to show that the measure satisfied the principle of proportionality.

JUDGMENT OF THE COURT
28 April 1998

Raymond Kohll v Union des caisses de maladie.
(Reference for a preliminary ruling: Cour de cassation – Grand Duchy of Luxemburg)

'Freedom to provide services – Reimbursement of medical expenses incurred in another Member State – Prior authorisation of the competent institution – Public health – Dental treatment'

Case C-158/96

Judgment

1. By judgment of 25 April 1996, received at the Court on 9 May 1996, the Luxembourg Cour de Cassation (Court of Cassation) referred to the Court for a preliminary ruling under Article 177 of the EC Treaty two questions on the interpretation of Articles 59 and 60 of that Treaty.

2. Those questions arose in proceedings between Mr Kohll, a Luxembourg national, and the Union des Caisses de Maladie (hereinafter 'UCM'), with which he is insured, concerning a request by a doctor established in Luxembourg for authorisation for his daughter, who is a minor, to receive treatment from an orthodontist established in Trier (Germany).

3. By decision of 7 February 1994 following a negative opinion of the social security medical supervisors, the request was rejected on the grounds that the proposed treatment was not urgent and that it could be provided in Luxembourg. That decision was confirmed on 27 April 1994 by a decision of the UCM board.

4. Mr Kohll appealed against that dècision to the Conseil Arbitral des Assurances Sociales (Social Insurance Arbitration Council), arguing that the provisions relied on were contrary to Article 59 of the Treaty. The appeal was dismissed by decision of 6 October 1994.

5. Mr Kohll appealed against the latter decision to the Conseil Supérieur des Assurances Sociales (Higher Social Insurance Council), which by judgment of 17 July 1995 upheld the contested decision on the ground that Article 20 of the Luxembourg Codes des Assurances Sociales (Social Insurance Code) and Articles 25 and 27 of the UCM statutes were consistent with Council Regulation (EEC) No 1408/71 of 14 June 1971 on the application of social security schemes to employed persons, to self-employed persons and to members of their families moving within the

Community (see the version amended and updated by Council Regulation (EC) No 118/97 of 2 December 1996, OJ 1997 L 28, p. 1).

6. It appears from Article 20(1) of the Code des Assurances Sociales, as amended by the Law of 27 July 1992, which entered into force on 1 January 1994, that with the exception of emergency treatment received in the event of illness or accident abroad, insured persons may be treated abroad or approach a treatment centre or centre providing ancillary facilities abroad only after obtaining the prior authorisation of the competent social security institution.

7. The terms and conditions for granting authorisation are laid down by Articles 25 to 27 of the UCM statutes, in the version which entered into force on 1 January 1995. Article 25 prescribes in particular that authorisation may not be given for services which are not reimbursable under the national rules. Article 26 states that the cost of duly authorised treatment is to be reimbursed in accordance with the tariffs applicable to persons insured under the social security system of the State in which the treatment is provided. Under Article 27, finally, authorisation will be granted only after a medical assessment and on production of a written request from a doctor established in Luxembourg indicating the doctor or hospital centre recommended and the facts and criteria which make it impossible for the treatment in question to be carried out in Luxembourg.

8. Article 22 of Regulation No 1408/71 provides in particular:

 '1. An employed or self-employed person who satisfies the conditions of the legislation of the competent State for entitlement to benefits, taking account where appropriate of the provisions of Article 18, and:

 ...

 (c) who is authorised by the competent institution to go to the territory of another Member State to receive there the treatment appropriate to his condition, shall be entitled:

 (i) to benefits in kind provided on behalf of the competent institution by the institution of the place of stay or residence in accordance with the provisions of the legislation which it administers, as though he were insured with it; the length of the period during which benefits are provided shall be governed, however, by the legislation of the competent State;

 (ii) to cash benefits provided by the competent institution in accordance with the provisions of the legislation which it administers. However, by agreement between the competent institution and the institution of the place of stay or residence, such benefits may be provided by the latter institution on behalf of the former, in accordance with the provisions of the legislation of the competent State.

2. ...

The authorisation required under paragraph 1(c) may not be refused where the treatment in question is among the benefits provided for by the legislation of the Member State on whose territory the person concerned resides and where he cannot be given such treatment within the time normally necessary for obtaining the treatment in question in the Member State of residence taking account of his current state of health and the probable course of the disease.

3. The provisions of paragraphs 1 and 2 shall apply by analogy to members of the family of an employed or self-employed person.

...'

9. Mr Kohll appealed against the judgment of the Conseil Supérieur des Assurances Sociales, arguing in particular that it had considered only whether the national rules were consistent with Regulation No 1408/71, and not whether they were consistent with Articles 59 and 60 of the Treaty.

10. Since it considered that that argument raised a question concerning the interpretation of Community law, the Cour de Cassation stayed the proceedings and referred the following two questions to the Court for a preliminary ruling:

'1. Are Articles 59 and 60 of the Treaty establishing the EEC to be interpreted as precluding rules under which reimbursement of the cost of benefits is subject to authorisation by the insured person's social security institution if the benefits are provided in a Member State other than the State in which that person resides?

2. Is the answer to Question 1 any different if the aim of the rules is to maintain a balanced medical and hospital service accessible to everyone in a given region?'

11. By those questions, which should be taken together, the national court essentially asks whether Articles 59 and 60 of the Treaty preclude the application of social security rules such as those at issue in the main proceedings.

12. Mr Kohll submits that Articles 59 and 60 of the Treaty preclude such national rules which make reimbursement, in accordance with the scale of the Member State of insurance, of the cost of dental treatment provided by an orthodontist

established in another Member State subject to authorisation by the insured person's social security institution.

13. UCM and the Luxembourg, Greek and United Kingdom Governments contend that those provisions are not applicable, or, in the alternative, do not preclude the rules in question from being maintained. The German, French and Austrian Governments agree with the alternative submission.

14. The Commission submits that the rules constitute a barrier to the freedom to provide services but may be justified, under certain conditions, by overriding reasons relating to the general interest.

15. Having regard to the observations submitted, the questions to be considered concern first the application of the principle of freedom of movement in the field of social security, then the effect of Regulation No 1408/71, and finally the application of the provisions on freedom to provide services.

Application of the fundamental principle of freedom of movement in the field of social security

16. The Luxembourg, Greek and United Kingdom Governments submit that the rules at issue in the main proceedings do not fall within the scope of the Community provisions on freedom to provide services, in that they concern social security, and so should be examined solely from the point of view of Article 22 of Regulation No 1408/71.

17. It must be observed, first of all, that, according to settled case-law, Community law does not detract from the powers of the Member States to organise their social security systems (Case 238/82 *Duphar and Others* v *Netherlands* [1984] ECR 523, paragraph 16, and Case C-70/95 *Sodemare and Others* v *Regione Lombardia* [1997] ECR I-3395, paragraph 27).

18. In the absence of harmonisation at Community level, it is therefore for the legislation of each Member State to determine, first, the conditions concerning the right or duty to be insured with a social security scheme (Case 110/79 *Coonan* v *Insurance Officer* [1980] ECR 1445, paragraph 12, and Case C-349/87 *Paraschi* v *Landesversicherungsanstalt Württemberg* [1991] ECR I-4501, paragraph 15) and, second, the conditions for entitlement to benefits (Joined Cases C-4/95 and C-5/95 *Stöber and Piosa Pereira* v *Bundesanstalt für Arbeit* [1997] ECR I-511, paragraph 36).

19. As the Advocate General observes in points 17 to 25 of his Opinion, the Member States must nevertheless comply with Community law when exercising those powers.

20. The Court has held that the special nature of certain services does not remove them from the ambit of the fundamental principle of freedom of movement (Case 279/80 *Webb* [1981] ECR 3305, paragraph 10).

21. Consequently, the fact that the national rules at issue in the main proceedings fall within the sphere of social security cannot exclude the application of Articles 59 and 60 of the Treaty.

Effect of Regulation No 1408/71

22. UCM and the Luxembourg Government submit that Article 22 of Regulation No 1408/71 lays down the principle that prior authorisation is required for any treatment in another Member State. To challenge the national provisions relating to reimbursement of the cost of services obtained abroad amounts to calling into question the validity of the corresponding provision in Regulation No 1408/71.

23. In the proceedings before the Court, Mr Kohll submitted that he sought reimbursement by UCM of the amount he would have been entitled to if the treatment had been carried out by the only specialist established in Luxembourg at the material time.

24. On that point, UCM considers that the principle that a person is subject to one social security tariff only would indeed be complied with if the Luxembourg tariff were applied, but claims that Regulation No 1408/71 would compel it to reimburse expenditure according to the tariffs in force in the State in which the service was provided.

25. It must be stated that the fact that a national measure may be consistent with a provision of secondary legislation, in this case Article 22 of Regulation No 1408/71, does not have the effect of removing that measure from the scope of the provisions of the Treaty.

26. Moreover, as the Advocate General observes in points 55 and 57 of his Opinion, Article 22(1) of Regulation No 1408/71 is intended to allow an insured person, authorised by the competent institution to go to another Member State to receive there treatment appropriate to his condition, to receive sickness benefits in kind, on account of the competent institution but in accordance with the provisions of the legislation of the State in which the services are provided, in particular where the need for the transfer arises because of the state of health of the person concerned, without that person incurring additional expenditure.

27. On the other hand, Article 22 of Regulation No 1408/71, interpreted in the light of its purpose, is not intended to regulate and hence does not in any way prevent the reimbursement by Member States, at the tariffs in force in the competent State, of

costs incurred in connection with treatment provided in another Member State, even without prior authorisation.

28. Consequently, the Court must examine the compatibility of national rules such as those at issue in the main proceedings with the Treaty provisions on freedom to provide services.

Application of the provisions on freedom to provide services

29. The dispute before the national court concerns treatment provided by an orthodontist established in another Member State, outside any hospital infrastructure. That service, provided for remuneration, must be regarded as a service within the meaning of Article 60 of the Treaty, which expressly refers to activities of the professions.

30. It must therefore be examined whether rules such as those at issue in the main proceedings constitute a restriction on freedom to provide services, and if so, whether they may be objectively justified.

Restrictive effects of the rules at issue

31. Mr Kohll and the Commission submit that the fact that reimbursement of the cost of medical services, in accordance with the legislation of the State of insurance, is subject to prior authorisation by the institution of that State where the services are provided in another Member State constitutes a restriction on freedom to provide services within the meaning of Articles 59 and 60 of the Treaty.

32. The Member States which have submitted observations consider, on the contrary, that the rules at issue do not have as their purpose or effect to restrict freedom to provide services, but merely lay down the conditions for the reimbursement of medical expenses.

33. It should be noted that, according to the Court's case-law, Article 59 of the Treaty precludes the application of any national rules which have the effect of making the provision of services between Member States more difficult than the provision of services purely within one Member State (Case C-381/93 *Commission* v *France* [1994] ECR I-5145, paragraph 17).

34. While the national rules at issue in the main proceedings do not deprive insured persons of the possibility of approaching a provider of services established in another Member State, they do nevertheless make reimbursement of the costs incurred in that Member State subject to prior authorisation, and deny such reimbursement to insured persons who have not obtained that authorisation. Costs incurred in the State of insurance are not, however, subject to that authorisation.

35. Consequently, such rules deter insured persons from approaching providers of medical services established in another Member State and constitute, for them and their patients, a barrier to freedom to provide services (see Joined Cases 286/82 and 26/83 *Luisi and Carbone* v *Ministero del Tesoro* [1984] ECR 377, paragraph 16, and Case C-204/90 *Bachmann* v *Belgium* [1992] ECR I-249, paragraph 31).

36. The Court must therefore examine whether a measure of the kind at issue in this case may be objectively justified.

Justification of the rules at issue

37. UCM and the Governments of the Member States which have submitted observations submit that freedom to provide services is not absolute and that reasons connected with the control of health expenditure must be taken into consideration. The requirement of prior authorisation constitutes the only effective and least restrictive means of controlling expenditure on health and balancing the budget of the social security system.

38. According to UCM, the Luxembourg Government and the Commission, the risk of upsetting the financial balance of the social security scheme, which aims to ensure a balanced medical and hospital service available to all its insured, constitutes an overriding reason in the general interest capable of justifying restrictions on freedom to provide services.

39. The Commission adds that the refusal of the national authorities to grant prior authorisation must be justified by a genuine and actual risk of upsetting the financial balance of the social security scheme.

40. On the latter point, Mr Kohll submits that the financial burden on the budget of the Luxembourg social security institution is the same whether he approaches a Luxembourg orthodontist or one established in another Member State, since he asked for medical expenses to be reimbursed at the rate applied in Luxembourg. The rules at issue therefore cannot be justified by the need to control health expenditure.

41. It must be recalled that aims of a purely economic nature cannot justify a barrier to the fundamental principle of freedom to provide services (see, to that effect, Case C-398/95 *SETTG* v *Ypourgos Ergasias* [1997] ECR I-3091, paragraph 23). However, it cannot be excluded that the risk of seriously undermining the financial balance of the social security system may constitute an overriding reason in the general interest capable of justifying a barrier of that kind.

42. But, contrary to the submissions of UCM and the Luxembourg Government, it is clear that reimbursement of the costs of dental treatment provided in other Member

States in accordance with the tariff of the State of insurance has no significant effect on the financing of the social security system.

43. The Luxembourg Government also relies on grounds based on the protection of public health, arguing, first, that the rules at issue are necessary to guarantee the quality of medical services, which in the case of persons going to another Member State can be ascertained only at the time of the request for authorisation, and, second, that the Luxembourg sickness insurance system aims to provide a balanced medical and hospital service open to all insured persons.

44. Mr Kohll submits, on the other hand, that there is no scientific reason to conclude that treatment provided in Luxembourg is more effective, now that the pursuit of the medical professions is the subject of mutual recognition between Member States. He further submits that the reference to a balanced medical and hospital sector open to all must above all be categorised as an economic aim intended to protect UCM's financial resources.

45. It should be noted, first of all, that under Articles 56 and 66 of the EC Treaty Member States may limit freedom to provide services on grounds of public health.

46. However, that does not permit them to exclude the public health sector, as a sector of economic activity and from the point of view of freedom to provide services, from the application of the fundamental principle of freedom of movement (see Case 131/85 *Gül* v *Regierungspräsident Düsseldorf* [1986] ECR 1573, paragraph 17).

47. The conditions for taking up and pursuing the profession of doctor and dentist have been the subject of several coordinating or harmonising directives (see Council Directive 78/686/EEC of 25 July 1978 concerning the mutual recognition of diplomas, certificates and other evidence of the formal qualifications of practitioners of dentistry, including measures to facilitate the effective exercise of the right of establishment and freedom to provide services (OJ 1978 L 233, p. 1); Council Directive 78/687/EEC of 25 July 1978 concerning the coordination of provisions laid down by law, regulation or administrative action in respect of the activities of dental practitioners (OJ 1978 L 233, p. 10); and Council Directive 93/16/EEC of 5 April 1993 to facilitate the free movement of doctors and the mutual recognition of their diplomas, certificates and other evidence of formal qualifications (OJ 1993 L 165, p. 1)).

48. It follows that doctors and dentists established in other Member States must be afforded all guarantees equivalent to those accorded to doctors and dentists established on national territory, for the purposes of freedom to provide services.

49. Consequently, rules such as those applicable in the main proceedings cannot be justified on grounds of public health in order to protect the quality of medical services provided in other Member States.

50. As to the objective of maintaining a balanced medical and hospital service open to all, that objective, although intrinsically linked to the method of financing the social security system, may also fall within the derogations on grounds of public health under Article 56 of the Treaty, in so far as it contributes to the attainment of a high level of health protection.

51. Article 56 of the Treaty permits Member States to restrict the freedom to provide medical and hospital services in so far as the maintenance of a treatment facility or medical service on national territory is essential for the public health and even the survival of the population (see, with respect to public security within the meaning of Article 36 of the Treaty, Case 72/83 *Campus Oil* v *Minister for Industry and Energy* [1984] ECR 2727, paragraphs 33 to 36).

52. However, neither UCM nor the Governments of the Member States which have submitted observations have shown that the rules at issue were necessary to provide a balanced medical and hospital service accessible to all. None of those who have submitted observations has argued that the rules were indispensable for the maintenance of an essential treatment facility or medical service on national territory.

53. The conclusion must therefore be drawn that the rules at issue in the main proceedings are not justified on grounds of public health.

54. In those circumstances, the answer must be that Articles 59 and 60 of the Treaty preclude national rules under which reimbursement, in accordance with the scale of the State of insurance, of the cost of dental treatment provided by an orthodontist established in another Member State is subject to authorisation by the insured person's social security institution.

Costs

[Para. 55 omitted]

On those grounds,

THE COURT,

in answer to the questions referred to it by the Luxembourg Cour de Cassation by judgment of 25 April 1996, hereby rules:

> **Articles 59 and 60 of the EC Treaty preclude national rules under which reimbursement, in accordance with the scale of the State of insurance, of the cost of dental treatment provided by an orthodontist established in another Member State is subject to authorisation by the insured person's social security institution.**

Comments and questions

Case C-158/96 *Kohll* v *Union des caisses de maladie* [1998] ECR I-1931, concerned medical treatment which had been provided outside any hospital system by an orthodontist established in another Member State. The CJEU found that the treatment, provided for remuneration, must be regarded as a service within the meaning of Article 57 TFEU (formerly Article 60 TEC), which expressly refers to activities of the professions; cf. paragraph 29 of the judgment. What is the significance of this statement? Do hospitals fall outside the scope of Article 56 TFEU (formerly Article 59 TEC)? See also judgment of the CJEU in Case C-385/99 *Müller-Fauré* v *Onderlinge Waarborgmaatschappij OZ Zorgverzekeringen* [2003] ECR I-4509, printed below.

The problem in the *Kohll* case was that the Luxembourg law only required prior authorisation for approval of medical expenses if the provision of the medical service took place in another Member State. The CJEU held that the law did not deprive insured persons of the possibility of approaching a provider of services or goods established in another Member State, but the fact that reimbursement was conditional upon the person obtaining prior approval nevertheless deterred insured persons from approaching such providers. Did a restriction exist, in the view of the CJEU?

Presumably the *Kohll* case is significant for access to medical services abroad where the following three conditions are fulfilled: (1) The provision of medical services is provided for commercial profit, (2) the patient pays a substantial proportion of the cost, and (3) fixed reimbursement is made according to a fixed tariff.

Against the background of the *Kohll* judgment, consider whether the following situations can be assumed to fall within the scope of the rules on freedom of movement:

(a) The medical service is provided in the public hospital sector so the patient does *not* pay when receiving the service.
(b) The medical service is provided at a private hospital upon referral from a public authority, and the public authority pays for the service in full.
(c) The medical service is provided at a private hospital or clinic, which is run for commercial profit, and where the patient pays a substantial proportion of the cost.
(d) The patient is free to choose whether the medical service is provided in the public or the private sector, and the national social security scheme pays an amount according to a fixed tariff upon the patient receiving the medical service.

In point 31 of his Opinion in Case C-147/03 *Commission* v *Austria* [2005] ECR I-5969 (printed above in Chapter 1), Advocate General Jacobs stated, as regards the CJEU's decision in the *Kohll* case: 'by accepting aims of a purely economic nature as possible justifications, *Kohll* and *Vanbraekel* represent a departure from the orthodox approach of the CJEU that such aims may not justify a restriction of the fundamental freedoms guaranteed by the Treaty'. Do you agree that the *Kohll* judgment should be interpreted in this way (see in particular paragraph 41)? See also paragraphs 72-73 in Case C-385/99 *Müller-Fauré* v *Onderlinge Waarborgmaatschappij* [2003] ECR I-4509, printed below. In the *Kohll* case the CJEU held that consideration for public health could not justify the Luxembourg measure; cf. paragraph 46. However, the CJEU acknowledged that the arrangements for financing the social security scheme were justified 'in so far as the maintenance of a treatment facility or medical service on national territory is essential for the public health and even the survival of the population'; cf. paragraphs 50-51. The CJEU thus accepted a wide interpretation of (now) Article 62 TFEU, wider than that suggested by the Advocate General. However, neither the Luxembourg Government nor the other parties in the case argued that the disputed measure was necessary for establishing a stable service of doctors and hospitals to which all had access. For this reason the CJEU dismissed the idea that the measure could be regarded as being based on public health considerations. Could a Finnish national choose to be treated at, for example, a Swedish hospital and then require the Finnish authorities to cover all the costs of his treatment, since the Finnish health insurance scheme makes free hospital treatment available in Finland?

The implications of the *Kohll* judgment have since been given in more detail in Case C-157/99 *Geraets-Smits* v *Stichting Ziekenfonds VGZ* [2001] ECR I-5473; Case C-368/98 *Vanbraekel and Others* v *Alliance nationale des mutualités chrétiennes* [2001] ECR I-5363; and Case C-385/99 *Müller-Fauré* v *Onderlinge Waarborgmaatschappij OZ Zorgverzekeringen* [2003] ECR I-4509 (this last has already been referred to and is printed below).

The *Kohll* decision has the remarkable consequence that, where a patient has received prior authorisation from the social security institution of the State of insurance to receive hospital treatment in another Member State, the patient will receive full cover for the costs of the hospital treatment, in accordance with (then applicable) Regulation No 1408/71 (now Regulation 883/04). On the other hand, if the patient has not received prior authorisation, then under Union law only partial reimbursement can be claimed, and only to the extent that national law provides for contributions to medical services, including hospital treatment; this follows from Article 49; cf. the *Kohll* case. A patient will thus be covered differently depending on whether a claim may be based on (then applicable) Regulation 1408/71 (now Regulation 883/04) or on Article 56 TFEU.

On the same day that judgment was given in the *Kohll* case, judgment was also given in Case C-120/95 *Decker* v *Caisse de maladie des employés privés* [1998] ECR I-1831. Nicolas Decker, a Luxembourg national, had bought a pair of spectacles in Belgium on the prescription of an ophthalmologist in Luxembourg. He subsequently requested his Luxembourg social security fund to reimburse him for the cost of the spectacles, but the fund refused his request on the ground that they had been purchased abroad without its prior authorisation. The *Decker* case is a parallel to the *Kohll* case, except that it concerned the provision of goods instead of the provision of a service.

The CJEU decided the *Decker* case in the same way as it decided the *Kohll* case. Thus, it held that the Luxembourg requirement for prior authorisation constituted a restriction on the free movement of goods, because it encouraged those with social security cover to buy their spectacles and other products in Luxembourg rather than in other Member States. The Luxembourg Government submitted that the rules were necessary for 'the control of the health expenditure which must necessarily be taken into consideration', and were justified on this basis. The CJEU accepted that it was possible that the risk of seriously undermining the financial balance of the social security system may constitute an overriding reason in the public interest capable of justifying a barrier of that kind. However, in the case before the CJEU, the social security fund paid a flat rate for the cost of spectacles and corrective lenses, so the CJEU found it clear that this payment had no effect on the financial balance of the social security system. The CJEU added that there had been harmonisation of the conditions for taking up and pursuing the profession of an optician, which meant that the purchase of a pair of spectacles from an optician established in another Member State provided guarantees equivalent to those afforded on the sale of spectacles by an optician established in the national territory. Since, in this case, the spectacles had been purchased on a prescription from an ophthalmologist, the protection of public health was ensured. On this basis the CJEU concluded that the Luxembourg rules were contrary to Articles 34 and 36 TFEU.

JUDGMENT OF THE COURT
13 May 2003

V.G. Müller-Fauré v Onderlinge Waarborgmaatschappij OZ Zorgverzekeringen UA and E.E.M. van Riet v Onderlinge Waarborgmaatschappij ZAO Zorgverzekeringen. (Reference for a preliminary ruling: Centrale Raad van Beroep – Netherlands)

'Freedom to provide services – Articles 59 of the EC Treaty (now, after amendment, Article 49 EC) and 60 of the EC Treaty (now Article 50 EC) – Sickness insurance – System providing benefits in kind – System of agreements – Medical costs incurred in another Member State – Prior authorisation – Criteria – Justification'

Case C-385/99

Judgment

1. By order of 6 October 1999, received at the Court on 11 October 1999, the Centrale Raad van Beroep (Higher Social Security Court) referred to the Court for a preliminary ruling under Article 234 EC three questions on the interpretation of Article 59 of the EC Treaty (now, after amendment, Article 49 EC) and Article 60 of the EC Treaty (now Article 50 EC).

2. Those questions have been raised in two sets of proceedings between Ms Müller-Fauré and Onderlinge Waarborgmaatschappij OZ Zorgverzekeringen UA (mutual sickness insurance fund; 'the Zwijndrecht Fund'), established in Zwijndrecht (Netherlands), and between Ms Van Riet and Onderlinge Waarborgmaatschappij ZAO Zorgverzekeringen ('the Amsterdam Fund'), established in Amsterdam (Netherlands), concerning the reimbursement of medical costs incurred in Germany and Belgium respectively.

National legal framework

3. In the Netherlands, the sickness insurance scheme is based inter alia on the Ziekenfondswet (Law on Sickness Funds) of 15 October 1964 (Staatsblad 1964, No 392), which has been subsequently amended ('the ZFW'), and on the Algemene Wet Bijzondere Ziektekosten (Law on general insurance for special sickness costs) of 14 December 1967 (Staatsblad 1967, No 617), which has also been subsequently amended, ('the AWBZ'). Both the ZFW and the AWBZ establish a system of benefits in kind under which an insured person is entitled not to reimbursement of costs incurred for medical treatment but to free treatment. Both laws are based on a system of agreements between sickness funds and providers of health care.

4. Under Articles 2 to 4 of the ZFW, workers whose annual income does not exceed an amount determined by that law, persons treated as such and persons in receipt of social benefits, as well as dependent members of their families living with them in the same household, are compulsorily and automatically insured under that law.

5. Article 5(1) of the ZFW provides that any person coming within its scope who wishes to claim entitlement under that law must be affiliated to a sickness fund operating in the municipality in which he resides.

6. Article 8 of the ZFW provides:

 ‘1. An insured person shall be entitled to benefits in the form of necessary medical care, provided that he is not entitled to such care under the Algemene Wet Bijzondere Ziektekosten ... Sickness funds shall ensure that any insured person registered with them is able to rely on that right.

 2. The nature, content and extent of the benefits shall be defined by or pursuant to a Royal Decree, it being understood that they shall in any event include medical assistance, the extent of which remains to be defined, and also the care and treatment provided in categories of institutions to be defined. Furthermore, the grant of a benefit may be conditional on a financial contribution by the insured person; this contribution need not be the same for all insured persons.

 ...’

7. The Verstrekkingenbesluit Ziekenfondsverzedering (Decree on sickness insurance benefits in kind) of 4 January 1966, (Staatsblad 1966, No 3), which has been subsequently amended (‘the Verstrekkingenbesluit’), implements Article 8(2) of the ZFW.

8. The Verstrekkingenbesluit thus determines entitlement to benefits and the extent of such benefits for various categories of care, including in particular the categories ‘medical and surgical assistance’ and ‘in-patient hospital care’.

9. The principal features of the system of agreements put in place by the ZFW are as follows.

10. Article 44(1) of the ZFW provides that the sickness funds are to ‘enter into agreements with persons and establishments offering one or more forms of care, as referred to in the Royal Decree adopted to implement Article 8’.

11. Article 44(3) of the ZFW provides that such agreements are to include as a minimum provisions concerning the nature and extent of the parties’ mutual obligations and rights, the categories of care to be provided, the quality and effectiveness of the

care provided, supervision of compliance with the terms of the agreement, including supervision of the benefits provided or to be provided and the accuracy of the amounts charged for those benefits, and also an obligation to communicate the information necessary for that supervision.

12. The sickness funds are free to enter into agreements with any care provider, subject to a twofold reservation. First, under Article 47 of the ZFW, every sickness fund 'is required to enter into an agreement ... with any establishment in the region in which it operates or which the population of that region regularly attends'. Second, agreements can be entered into only with establishments which are duly authorised to provide the care in question or with persons lawfully authorised to do so.

13. Article 8a of the ZFW provides:

    '1. An establishment providing services such as those referred to in Article 8 must be authorised to do so.

    2. A Royal Decree may provide that an establishment belonging to a category to be defined by Royal Decree is to be regarded as authorised for the purposes of this Law. ...'

14. Under Article 8c(a) of the ZFW approval of an establishment operating a hospital facility must be refused if that establishment does not meet the requirements of the Wet ziekenhuisvoorzieningen (Law on hospital facilities) on distribution and needs. That law, its implementing directives (in particular the directive based on Article 3 of the law, Nederlandse Staatscourant 1987, No 248) and also the district plans determine in greater detail national needs in relation to various categories of hospitals and their distribution between the various health regions within the Netherlands.

15. As regards the specific exercise of the right to benefits, Article 9 of the ZFW provides:

    '1. Save as provided for in the Royal Decree referred to in Article 8, an insured person wishing to claim entitlement to a benefit shall apply to a person or an establishment with whom or with which the sickness fund with which he is registered has entered into an agreement for that purpose, subject to the provisions of paragraph 4.

    The insured person may choose from among the persons and establishments mentioned in paragraph 1, subject to the provisions of paragraph 5 and the provisions regarding conveyance by ambulance, as laid down in the Wet ambulancevervoer ((Law on conveyance by ambulance), Staatsblad 1971, No 369).

    3. [repealed]

4. A sickness fund may, by way of derogation from paragraphs 1 and 2 hereof, authorise an insured person, for the purpose of claiming entitlement to a benefit, to apply to another person or establishment in the Netherlands where this is necessary for his health care. The Minister may determine the cases and circumstances in which an insured person may be granted authorisation, in claiming entitlement to a benefit, to apply to a person or an establishment outside the Netherlands.

...'

16. The Minister exercised the powers conferred on him by the final sentence of Article 9(4) of the ZFW in adopting the Regeling hulp in het buitenland ziekenfondsverzekering (Regulation on care provided abroad under the sickness insurance rules) of 30 June 1988, (Nederlandse Staatscourant 1988, No 123; 'the Rhbz'). Article 1 of the Rhbz provides:

    'A sickness fund may authorise an insured person claiming entitlement to a benefit to apply to a person or establishment outside the Netherlands in those cases in which the sickness fund has determined that such action is necessary for the health care of the insured person.'

17. In the event of an insured person obtaining authorisation to apply to a provider established outside the Netherlands, the cost of any treatment is wholly assumed by the sickness fund to which the person is affiliated.

18. The Centrale Raad van Beroep explains that, according to its established case-law, applications for authorisation to undergo medical treatment abroad funded under the ZFW must be submitted to the insured person's sickness fund and the latter must, except in exceptional circumstances such as an emergency, have given its prior agreement to the provision of treatment, failing which it will not be possible to obtain reimbursement of the cost of the treatment.

19. Furthermore, as regards the condition laid down in Article 9(4) of the ZFW and Article 1 of the Rhbz that the insured's treatment abroad must be medically necessary, it appears from the documents before the Court that the fund takes account, in practice, of the methods of treatment available in the Netherlands and ascertains whether appropriate treatment can be provided there without undue delay.

The main proceedings

The Müller-Fauré case

20. While on holiday in Germany, Ms Müller-Fauré underwent dental treatment involving the fitting of six crowns and a fixed prosthesis on the upper jaw. The treatment

was provided between 20 October and 18 November 1994 without recourse to any hospital facilities.

21. When she returned from her holiday, she applied to the Zwijndrecht Fund for reimbursement of the costs of the treatment, which amounted to a total of DEM 7 444.59. By letter of 12 May 1995 the Fund refused reimbursement on the basis of the opinion of its advisory dental officer.

22. Ms Müller-Fauré sought the opinion of the Ziekenfonsraad, which is responsible for supervising the management and administration of sickness funds and which, on 16 February 1996, confirmed the Zwijndrecht Fund's decision on the ground that insured persons are entitled only to treatment itself and not to reimbursement of any related costs, except in exceptional circumstances which did not exist in this case.

23. Ms Müller-Fauré then brought an action before the Arrondissementsrechtbank te Rotterdam (District Court, Rotterdam) (Netherlands). By judgment of 21 August 1997, that court upheld the Fund's decision, having also found that the case entailed no exceptional circumstances such as to justify reimbursement of the costs, given, in particular, the scale of the treatment and the fact that it extended over several weeks.

24. The Centrale Raad van Beroep points out that in any event only a limited part of the treatment received by Ms Müller-Fauré is covered by the Verstrekkingenbesluit and is therefore eligible for reimbursement. Furthermore, it finds that Ms Müller-Fauré voluntarily sought treatment from a dentist established in Germany while she was on holiday there because she lacked confidence in dental practitioners in the Netherlands. Such circumstances cannot, according to the case-law of the court concerned, provide grounds under the national legislation for reimbursement in respect of medical treatment undergone abroad without authorisation from the insured person's fund.

The Van Riet case

25. Ms Van Riet had been suffering from pain in her right wrist since 1985. On 5 April 1993, the doctor treating her requested that the Amsterdam Fund's medical adviser should grant authorisation for his patient to have an arthroscopy performed in Deurne hospital (Belgium) where that examination could be carried out much sooner than in the Netherlands. The Fund rejected that request by letters of 24 June and 5 July 1993 on the ground that the test could also be performed in the Netherlands.

26. In the meantime, Ms Van Riet had already had the arthroscopy carried out at Deurne hospital in May 1993 and, following that examination, the decision was taken to carry out an ulnar reduction to relieve the patient's pain. Care before and after the treatment, and the treatment itself, were provided in Belgium, partly in hospital and

partly elsewhere. The Amsterdam Fund refused to reimburse the cost of the care, which amounted to a total of BEF 93 782. That decision was confirmed by the Ziekenfondsraad on the ground that there was no emergency nor any medical necessity such as to justify Ms Van Riet receiving treatment in Belgium, since appropriate treatment was available in the Netherlands within a reasonable period. The competent Arrondissementsrechtbank rejected as unfounded Ms Van Riet's action against the decision for the same reasons as the Amsterdam Fund.

27. The Centrale Raad van Beroep, before which the applicant in the main proceedings brought an appeal, states that, although it is not disputed that most of the treatment given to Ms Van Riet is indeed covered by the Verstrekkingenbesluit, the treatment was provided in Belgium without prior authorisation and without it being established that Ms Van Riet could not reasonably wait, for medical or other reasons, until the Amsterdam Fund had taken a decision on her application. Furthermore, in that court's view, the time which Ms Van Riet would have had to wait for the arthroscopy in the Netherlands was not unreasonable. The documents before the Court show that the waiting time was about six months.

28. The referring court submits that, in this instance, the conditions for application of Article 22(1)(a) of Regulation (EEC) No 1408/71 of the Council of 14 June 1971 on the application of social security schemes to employed persons, to self-employed persons and to members of their families moving within the Community, as amended and updated by Council Regulation (EC) No 118/97 of 2 December 1996 (OJ 1997 L 28, p. 1; 'Regulation No 1408/71'), were not met, since neither Ms Müller-Fauré's nor Ms Van Riet's state of health necessitated immediate treatment during a stay in the territory of another Member State. Furthermore, nor has it been established, in conformity with Article 22(1)(c) and (2), second paragraph, of that regulation that the treatment concerned could not, account being taken of the state of health of the applicants in the main actions, be given in the Netherlands within the time 'normally necessary', a fact which would have obliged the sickness funds to authorise treatment in another Member State.

29. The national court none the less raises a question as to the compatibility of the decisions refusing reimbursement with Articles 59 and 60 of the Treaty in the light of the judgment in Case C-158/96 Kohll [1998] ECR I-1931. It notes that the national provisions at issue do not of themselves prevent insured persons from applying to a service provider established in another Member State but impose a precondition that the sickness insurance fund of which the insured persons are members must have entered into an agreement with that provider, something which, as a rule, is not the case. In the absence of such an agreement, reimbursement of costs incurred in another Member State is subject to prior authorisation, which is not granted unless 'it is necessary for [the insured person's] health care', which in general is the case only where the contracted care providers cannot offer all the appropriate care. The obligation to obtain prior authorisation therefore works to the advantage of

contracted medical care providers – which are virtually always from the Netherlands – and to the detriment of care providers from other Member States. The referring court adds that the administrative powers of the Netherlands authorities do not extend to care providers established in other Member States, which may hinder the conclusion of agreements with those providers.

30. If it were found that the authorisation required by Article 9(4) of the ZFW impedes the freedom to provide services, the Centrale Raad van Beroep seeks to ascertain whether the requirement is justified.

31. In that connection, the referring court draws attention to the characteristics of the Netherlands sickness insurance scheme. In essence, unlike 'reimbursement' schemes, the scheme guarantees that benefits in kind will be provided. In the submission of the defendants in the main actions, the financial balance of the scheme could be jeopardised if it were possible for insured persons to obtain reimbursement, without prior authorisation, of the costs of care provided in another Member State. The national court refers in that regard to national measures taken to control the costs of hospital care, in particular the rules laid down in the Wet ziekenhuisvoorzieningen concerning the planning and geographical distribution of care, and those in the ZFW limiting reimbursement to care provided by authorised hospitals.

The questions referred for a preliminary ruling

32. Those were the circumstances in which the Centrale Raad van Beroep decided to stay proceedings and refer the following questions to the Court for a preliminary ruling:

'1. Are Articles 59 and 60 of the EC Treaty ... to be interpreted as meaning that in principle a provision such as Article 9(4) of the Ziekenfondswet, read in conjunction with Article 1 of the Regeling hulp in het buitenland ziekenfondsverzekerig, is incompatible therewith in so far as it stipulates that in order to assert his entitlement to benefits a person insured with a sickness insurance fund requires the prior authorisation of that fund to seek treatment from a person or establishment outside the Netherlands with whom or which the sickness insurance fund has not concluded an agreement?

2. If so, do the objectives of the Netherlands system of benefits in kind referred to above constitute an overriding reason in the general interest capable of justifying a restriction on the fundamental principle of freedom to provide services?

3. Does the question whether the treatment as a whole or only a proportion thereof involved hospital care affect the answers to these questions?'

33. By letter of 12 July 2001, the Court Registry asked the referring court whether it wished to maintain its reference for a preliminary ruling in the light of the judgment delivered on that date in Case C-157/99 Smits and Peerbooms [2001] ECR I-5473.

34. By letter of 25 October 2001, the referring court informed the Court that it was maintaining the reference since Smits and Peerbooms did not specifically deal with the attributes of the Netherlands sickness insurance scheme, which is a benefits-in-kind scheme based on agreements. It also asked the Court to explain the import of paragraph 103 of the judgment, which states:

   '... the condition concerning the necessity of the treatment, laid down by the rules at issue in the main proceedings, can be justified under Article 59 of the Treaty, provided that the condition is construed to the effect that authorisation to receive treatment in another Member State may be refused on that ground only if the same or equally effective treatment [for the patient] can be obtained without undue delay from an establishment with which the insured person's sickness insurance fund has contractual arrangements.'

35. More specifically, the referring court asks the Court what is meant by 'without undue delay' and, in particular, whether that condition must be assessed on a strictly medical basis, regardless of the waiting time for the treatment sought.

36. By letter of 6 March 2002, the Court Registry requested the parties to the main actions, the Member States and the Commission to submit any observations which they might have on the conclusions to be drawn from the judgment in Smits and Peerbooms in the light of the questions raised by the Centrale Raad van Beroep.

The first question

37. By its first question, the national court is essentially asking whether Articles 59 and 60 of the Treaty are to be interpreted as precluding legislation of a Member State, such as the legislation at issue in the main proceedings, which makes assumption of the costs of care provided in another Member State, by a person or an establishment with whom or which the insured person's sickness fund has not concluded an agreement, conditional upon prior authorisation by the fund.

38. It should be borne in mind, as a preliminary point, that it is settled case-law that medical activities fall within the scope of Article 60 of the Treaty, there being no need to distinguish in that regard between care provided in a hospital environment and care provided outside such an environment (see, most recently, Smits and Peerbooms, paragraph 53).

39. The Court also found, in paragraphs 54 and 55 of Smits and Peerbooms, that the fact that the applicable rules are social security rules and, more specifically, pro-

vide, as regards sickness insurance, for benefits in kind rather than reimbursement does not mean that the medical treatment in question falls outside the scope of the freedom to provide services guaranteed by the EC Treaty. Indeed, in the disputes before the national court, the treatment provided in a Member State other than that in which the persons concerned were insured resulted in direct payment by the patient to the doctor providing the service or the establishment in which the care was provided.

40. Since medical services fall within the ambit of freedom to provide services for the purposes of Articles 59 and 60 of the Treaty, it is necessary to determine whether the legislation at issue in the main actions introduces restrictions on that freedom in making assumption of the costs of care provided in a Member State other than that in which the insured person's sickness fund is established, by a person or establishment which has not concluded an agreement with that fund, conditional upon prior authorisation by the fund.

41. In that regard the Court has already held, in paragraph 62 of the judgment in Smits and Peerbooms, that while the ZFW does not deprive insured persons of the possibility of using a service provider established in a Member State other than that in which the sickness fund covering the insured is situated, it does nevertheless make reimbursement of the costs thus incurred subject to prior authorisation, which may be given, as the referring court points out, only where provision of the care at issue, irrespective of whether it involves a hospital, is a medical necessity.

42. Since the requirement of medical necessity is in practice satisfied only where adequate treatment cannot be obtained without undue delay from a contracted doctor or hospital in the Member State in which the person is insured, this requirement by its very nature is liable severely to limit the circumstances in which such authorisation will be issued (Smits and Peerbooms, paragraph 64).

43. Admittedly, it is open to the Netherlands sickness insurance funds to enter into agreements with hospital establishments outside the Netherlands. In such a case no prior authorisation would be required in order for the cost of treatment provided by such establishments to be assumed under the ZFW. However, with the exception of hospitals situated in regions adjoining the Netherlands, it seems unlikely that a significant number of hospitals in other Member States would ever enter into agreements with those sickness insurance funds, given that their prospects of admitting patients insured by those funds remain uncertain and limited (Smits and Peerbooms, paragraphs 65 and 66).

44. The Court has therefore already held that rules such as those at issue in the main proceedings deter, or even prevent, insured persons from applying to providers of medical services established in Member States other than that of the insurance fund

and constitute, both for insured persons and service providers, a barrier to freedom to provide services (Smits and Peerbooms, paragraph 69).

45. However, before coming to a decision on whether Articles 59 and 60 of the Treaty preclude rules such as those at issue in the main actions, it is appropriate to determine whether those rules can be objectively justified, which is the subject of the second question.

The second and third questions

46. By its second and third questions, which it is appropriate to examine together, the referring court is asking whether legislation such as that at issue in the main proceedings, which has restrictive effects on freedom to provide services, can be justified by the actual particular features of the national sickness insurance scheme, which provides not for reimbursement of costs incurred but essentially for benefits in kind and is based on a system of agreements intended both to ensure the quality of the care and to control the costs thereof. It also wishes to know whether the fact that the treatment at issue is provided in whole or in part in a hospital environment has any effect in that regard.

The arguments submitted to the Court

47. In the submission of the Netherlands Government and the Zwijndrecht Fund, the authorisation required by Article 9(4) of the ZFW is an integral part of the Netherlands sickness insurance scheme. Sickness cover by way of benefits in kind, as provided by that scheme, necessitates the prior conclusion, between the fund and care providers, of agreements dealing with the volume, quality, effectiveness and costs of health care in order, first, to allow for needs-based planning and expenditure control and, second, to ensure that a high-quality medical service is provided, that benefits are comparable and thus that insured persons are treated equally. A system of agreements of that kind is in the main advantageous to the insured.

48. In those circumstances, insured persons must apply to contracted care providers alone or, if they none the less wish to be treated by a non-contracted doctor or establishment established in the Netherlands or abroad, obtain prior authorisation from the sickness insurance scheme to which they belong.

49. The Netherlands Government and the Zwijndrecht Fund add that, if there were no requirement for prior authorisation, it would never be in the interest of care providers to participate in the system of agreements by becoming subject to contractual clauses dealing with the availability, volume, quality, effectiveness and cost of services, with the result that the authorities managing the sickness insurance scheme would be unable to make any needs-related plans by adjusting expenditure to needs and to ensure that a high-quality medical service was open to all. The system of

agreements would thus lose its raison d'être as a means of managing health care, which would prejudice the sovereign power of the Member States, recognised by the Court's case-law, to organise their social security systems. The Netherlands Government explains in that connection that there are waiting lists because of the limited financial resources available for health-care cover and that this gives rise to a need to quantify the benefits to be provided and to make them subject to priorities which must be strictly observed.

50. Furthermore, the Netherlands sickness funds cannot be forced to conclude agreements with a greater number of care providers than is necessary to meet the needs of people living in the Netherlands. The Netherlands Government points out that it is specifically to meet those needs that most of the agreements are entered into with care providers established in the Netherlands since demand from the insured is clearly greatest within the national territory.

51. Finally, as regards the way in which it is appropriate to determine whether 'the same or equally effective treatment can be obtained without undue delay', in the words of paragraph 103 of Smits and Peerbooms, the Zwijndrecht Fund submits that the mere fact of a person being on a waiting list does not mean that such treatment is not available. If it were to adopt a different interpretation, the Court would significantly extend the conditions in which benefits are awarded, which are a matter of national competence. Moreover, it would cast uncertainty over all attempted planning and rationalisation in the health-care sector aimed at avoiding overcapacity, supply-side imbalance, wastage and loss.

52. The Netherlands Government argues, in that regard, that it is quite apparent from paragraph 103 of Smits and Peerbooms that the period within which medical treatment is necessary is to be determined by reference to the patient's medical condition and history. It is the national court's responsibility to ascertain whether the treatment is available within that period, which amounts to a factual assessment.

53. The Danish, German, Spanish, Irish, Italian, Swedish and United Kingdom Governments, together with the Icelandic and Norwegian Governments, generally endorse the foregoing observations.

54. In particular, the Spanish Government maintains that any distinction between treatment provided by a practitioner and treatment provided in a hospital is unnecessary where a sickness insurance scheme provides exclusively benefits in kind. If an insured person is given health care or purchases a medicinal product in a Member State other than that in which his insurance fund is established, the duties and taxes paid by providers or suppliers are not paid into the budget of the Member State of affiliation, which adversely affects one of the sources of financing of social security in that State.

55. The Irish and United Kingdom Governments submit that if insured persons were entitled to go to a Member State other than that in which they are insured in order to receive treatment there, there would be adverse consequences for the setting of priorities for medical treatment and the management of waiting lists, which are significant aspects of the organisation of sickness insurance. In that regard, the United Kingdom Government points out that the finite financial resources allocated to the National Health Service ('the NHS') are managed by local health authorities which establish timetables based on clinical judgments and medically determined priorities for different treatments. Patients do not have the right to demand a certain timetable for their hospital treatment. It follows that if patients could shorten their waiting time by obtaining, without prior authorisation, medical treatment in other Member States for which the competent fund was none the less obliged to assume the cost, the financial balance of the system would be threatened and the resources available for more urgent treatment would be severely depleted, thereby placing at risk its ability to provide adequate levels of health care.

56. The United Kingdom Government adds that if hospital services were to be liberalised, its own hospitals would be unable to predict either the loss of demand that would follow from recourse being had to hospital treatment in other Member States or the increase in demand that would follow from persons insured in those other States being able to seek hospital treatment in the United Kingdom. Those effects of liberalisation would not necessarily offset each other and the impact would be different for every hospital in the United Kingdom.

57. As regards the criteria by which it should be ascertained whether treatment which is the same or equally effective for the patient could be obtained without undue delay in the Member State in which the person is insured, the United Kingdom Government, like the Swedish Government, refers to Article 22(2), second paragraph, of Regulation No 1408/71, in conjunction with Article 22(1)(c), from which it is apparent that the person concerned may not be refused the authorisation required to go to the territory of another Member State to receive there the treatment where, taking account of his current state of health and the probable course of the disease, he cannot be given the treatment within the time normally necessary in the Member State of residence. There is also a reference to the way in which those provisions were interpreted in paragraph 10 of the judgment in Case 182/78 Pierik [1979] ECR 1977.

58. In that regard the United Kingdom Government draws attention to the fact that in practice authorisation for treatment in another Member State is generally given in the United Kingdom when there is a delay for treatment beyond the maximum waiting times. National waiting lists take account of the different needs of different categories of patients and permit the best possible allocation of hospital resources. The lists are flexible so that if a patient's condition suddenly deteriorates, he can be moved up the waiting list and treated more quickly. To compel the competent authorities to authorise treatment abroad in circumstances other than where there is a

delay beyond the normal waiting time and to pass the cost on to the NHS would have damaging consequences for its management and financial viability.

59. In any event, the United Kingdom Government points to the specific characteristics of the NHS and asks the Court to uphold the principle that health care provided under such a national sickness insurance scheme does not fall within the scope of Article 60 of the Treaty and that the NHS, which is a non-profit-making body, is not a service provider for the purposes of the Treaty.

60. The Danish Government argues that there would be a risk of excessive consumption of medical services if patients had unrestricted access to free medical care in Member States other than that in which the insured's sickness insurance fund is established and also a risk, in the event of numerous journeys abroad for medical purposes, of it not being possible to maintain the competence of doctors established in national territories at an adequate level as regards unusual and complex diseases.

61. The Belgian Government submits that the specific nature of the Netherlands scheme, in providing not for reimbursement of costs incurred but for benefits in kind, does not amount per se to a general-interest reason justifying a restriction on freedom to provide services. It submits that it is appropriate to draw a distinction between services supplied elsewhere than in a hospital and those supplied in a hospital.

62. In the first case, there is no justification for any restriction on freedom to provide services, as can be seen from the judgment in Kohll. However, in the second case, there are sound reasons, linked to protecting the financial balance of the social security system and to maintaining a balanced medical and hospital service open to all, which justify requiring prior authorisation when services are to be provided in a hospital environment in a Member State other than that in which the insured's sickness insurance fund is established. Furthermore, in the absence of prior authorisation, the Member States with waiting lists for hospital treatment might have a tendency to send their nationals abroad for treatment instead of investing in their own infrastructure, thereby thwarting the other Member States' attempted hospital-related planning.

63. The Commission distinguishes between care provided in a surgery, which it places on the same footing as out-patient treatment within a hospital environment, and hospital treatment as such. As regards the first category, the analysis in the judgments in Case C-120/95 Decker [1998] ECR I-1831 and Kohll should be upheld, by regarding the requirement for prior authorisation as incompatible with Community law, except in the case of certain services, dental work in particular, which are extremely costly and specialised. As to the second category of care, provided in a hospital environment, reference should be made to the analysis in the judgment in Smits and Peerbooms, and whilst it should be recognised that the requirement for

prior authorisation is justified by planning needs, refusal of authorisation should none the less be subject to the limits set by the Court in that judgment.

64. As to the interpretation of the words 'without undue delay' employed in paragraph 103 of the judgment in Smits and Peerbooms, the Commission submits that only the patient's medical condition should be taken into account, as is clear from paragraph 104 of the judgment.

65. Finally, the Norwegian Government argues that the conditions on which benefits are granted and the periods within which they can be given are a matter solely for national legislation. Community law cannot confer on patients the right to receive, in a Member State other than that in which the persons concerned are insured, health care to which they are not entitled in their own Member State. Nor can it entitle them to receive treatment within a shorter time-limit than that provided for by national legislation. If it did so, it would prejudice the Member State's power to organise their social security systems and would go beyond the scope of the Treaty provisions on freedom to provide services.

Findings of the Court

66. It is clear from the documents before the Court that the reasons put forward to justify the requirement for prior authorisation where sickness insurance is to cover benefits provided in a Member State other than that in which the person concerned is insured, whether within a hospital environment or not, are linked (i) to the protection of public health inasmuch as the system of agreements is intended to ensure that there is a high-quality, balanced medical and hospital service open to all, (ii) to the financial balance of the social security system in that a system of that kind also permits the managing authorities to control expenditure by adjusting it to projected requirements, according to preestablished priorities, and (iii) to the essential characteristics of the sickness insurance scheme in the Netherlands, which provides benefits in kind.

The risk that the protection of public health may be adversely affected

67. It is apparent from the Court's case-law that the objective of maintaining a high-quality, balanced medical and hospital service open to all, may fall within one of the derogations provided for in Article 56 of the EC Treaty (now, after amendment, Article 46 EC), in so far as it contributes to the attainment of a high level of health protection (Kohll, paragraph 50, and Smits and Peerbooms, paragraph 73). In particular, that Treaty provision permits Member States to restrict the freedom to provide medical and hospital services in so far as the maintenance of treatment capacity or medical competence on national territory is essential for public health, and even the survival of the population (Kohll, paragraph 51, and Smits and Peerbooms, paragraph 74).

68. However, it is settled case-law that it is necessary, where justification is based on an exception laid down by the Treaty or indeed on an overriding general-interest reason, to ensure that the measures taken in that respect do not exceed what is objectively necessary for that purpose and that the same result cannot be achieved by less restrictive rules (see Case 205/84 Commission v Germany [1986] ECR 3755, paragraphs 27 and 29; Case C-180/89 Commission v Italy [1991] ECR I-709, paragraphs 17 and 18; Case C-106/91 Ramrath [1992] ECR I-3351, paragraphs 30 and 31, and Smits and Peerbooms, paragraph 75).

69. In this instance the arguments put forward to justify the requirement for prior authorisation seek to establish that, if it were open to patients to get treatment in a Member State other than that in which they are insured, without prior authorisation to that effect, the competent State could no longer guarantee that in its territory there would be a high-quality, balanced medical and hospital service open to all and hence a high level of public health protection.

70. As to the Danish Government's argument that the actual competence of practitioners, working in surgeries or in a hospital environment, would be undermined because of numerous journeys abroad for medical purposes, the Court finds that no specific evidence has been adduced in support of this argument.

71. The objective of maintaining a balanced medical and hospital service open to all is inextricably linked to the way in which the social security system is financed and to the control of expenditure, which are dealt with below. The risk of seriously undermining the financial balance of the social security system

72. It must be recalled, at the outset, that, according to the Court's case-law, aims of a purely economic nature cannot justify a barrier to the fundamental principle of freedom to provide services (see, to that effect, Case C-398/95 SETTG [1997] ECR I-3091, paragraph 23, and Kohll, paragraph 41).

73. However, in so far as, in particular, it could have consequences for the overall level of public-health protection, the risk of seriously undermining the financial balance of the social security system may also constitute per se an overriding general-interest reason capable of justifying a barrier of that kind (Kohll, paragraph 41, and Smits and Peerbooms, paragraph 72).

74. It is self-evident that assuming the cost of one isolated case of treatment, carried out in a Member State other than that in which a particular person is insured with a sickness fund, can never make any significant impact on the financing of the social security system. Thus an overall approach must necessarily be adopted in relation to the consequences of freedom to provide health-related services.

75. In that regard, the distinction between hospital services and non-hospital services may sometimes prove difficult to draw. In particular, certain services provided in a hospital environment but also capable of being provided by a practitioner in his surgery or in a health centre could for that reason be placed on the same footing as non-hospital services. However, in the main actions, the fact that the care at issue is partly hospital treatment and partly non-hospital treatment has not given rise to disagreement between the parties to the main proceedings or on the part of the Member States which have submitted observations under Article 23 of the EC Statute of the Court of Justice or the Commission.

Hospital services

76. As regards hospital services, such as those provided to Ms Van Riet in Deurne hospital, the Court, in paragraphs 76 to 80 of the judgment in Smits and Peerbooms, made the following findings.

77. It is well known that the number of hospitals, their geographical distribution, the way in which they are organised and the facilities with which they are provided, and even the nature of the medical services which they are able to offer, are all matters for which planning must be possible.

78. As may be seen, in particular, from the system of agreements involved in the main actions, this kind of planning generally meets a variety of concerns.

79. For one thing, it seeks to achieve the aim of ensuring that there is sufficient and permanent accessibility to a balanced range of high-quality hospital treatment in the State concerned.

80. For another thing, it assists in meeting a desire to control costs and to prevent, as far as possible, any wastage of financial, technical and human resources. Such wastage would be all the more damaging because it is generally recognised that the hospital care sector generates considerable costs and must satisfy increasing needs, while the financial resources which may be made available for health care are not unlimited, whatever the mode of funding applied.

81. In those circumstances, a requirement that the assumption of costs, under a national social security system, of hospital treatment provided in a Member State other than that of affiliation must be subject to prior authorisation appears to be a measure which is both necessary and reasonable.

82. As regards specifically the system set up by the ZFW, the Court clearly acknowledged that, if insured persons were at liberty, regardless of the circumstances, to use the services of hospitals with which their sickness insurance fund had no agreement, whether those hospitals were situated in the Netherlands or in another Mem-

ber State, all the planning which goes into the system of agreements in an effort to guarantee a rationalised, stable, balanced and accessible supply of hospital services would be jeopardised at a stroke (Smits and Peerbooms, paragraph 81).

83. Although Community law does not therefore in principle preclude a system of prior authorisation for this category of services, the conditions attached to the grant of such authorisation must none the less be justified in the light of the overriding considerations mentioned above and must satisfy the requirement of proportionality referred to in paragraph 68 above.

84. It likewise follows from settled case-law that a scheme of prior administrative authorisation cannot legitimise discretionary decisions taken by the national authorities, which are liable to negate the effectiveness of provisions of Community law, in particular those relating to a fundamental freedom such as that at issue in the main proceedings (see Joined Cases C-358/93 and C-416/93 Bordessa and Others [1995] ECR I-361, paragraph 25; Joined Cases C-163/94, C-165/94 and C-250/94 Sanz de Lera and Others [1995] ECR I-4821, paragraphs 23 to 28, and Case C-205/99 Analir and Others [2001] ECR I-1271, paragraph 37).

85. Thus, in order for a prior administrative authorisation scheme to be justified even though it derogates from a fundamental freedom of that kind, it must be based on objective, non-discriminatory criteria which are known in advance, in such a way as to circumscribe the exercise of the national authorities' discretion, so that it is not used arbitrarily (Analir and Others, paragraph 38). Such a prior administrative authorisation scheme must likewise be based on a procedural system which is easily accessible and capable of ensuring that a request for authorisation will be dealt with objectively and impartially within a reasonable time and refusals to grant authorisation must also be capable of being challenged in judicial or quasi-judicial proceedings (Smits and Peerbooms, paragraph 90).

86. In the main actions, the disputes do not concern the actual cover provided by the Netherlands sickness insurance scheme for the medical and hospital treatment with which Ms Müller-Fauré and Ms Van Riet were provided. In those actions, what is disputed is whether it was a medical necessity for them to have the treatment at issue in Germany and Belgium respectively, rather than in the Netherlands. In that regard, in paragraphs 99 to 107 of Smits and Peerbooms, the Court also ruled on that condition concerning the necessity of the proposed treatment, to which the grant of authorisation is subject.

87. As the national court states, it follows from the wording of Article 9(4) of the ZFW and Article 1 of the Rhbz that in principle that condition applies irrespective of whether the request for authorisation relates to treatment in an establishment located in the Netherlands with which the insured person's sickness insurance fund has no agreement or in an establishment located in another Member State.

88. As regards hospital treatment carried out outside the Netherlands, the national court states that the condition concerning the necessity of the treatment is in practice interpreted as meaning that such treatment is not to be authorised unless it appears that appropriate treatment cannot be provided without undue delay in the Netherlands. The Netherlands Government explains that if Article 9(4) of the ZFW is read in conjunction with Article 1 of the Rhbz, authorisation must be refused solely where the care required by the insured person's state of health is available from contracted care providers.

89. The condition concerning the necessity of the treatment, laid down by the legislation at issue in the main proceedings, can be justified under Article 59 of the Treaty, provided that the condition is construed to the effect that authorisation to receive treatment in another Member State may be refused on that ground only if treatment which is the same or equally effective for the patient can be obtained without undue delay from an establishment with which the insured person's sickness insurance fund has an agreement (Smits and Peerbooms, paragraph 103).

90. In order to determine whether treatment which is equally effective for the patient can be obtained without undue delay in an establishment having an agreement with the insured person's fund, the national authorities are required to have regard to all the circumstances of each specific case and to take due account not only of the patient's medical condition at the time when authorisation is sought and, where appropriate, of the degree of pain or the nature of the patient's disability which might, for example, make it impossible or extremely difficult for him to carry out a professional activity, but also of his medical history (see, to that effect, Smits and Peerbooms, paragraph 104).

91. The Court also stated, at paragraphs 105 and 106 of Smits and Peerbooms, that:

- thus construed, the condition concerning the necessity of treatment can allow an adequate, balanced and permanent supply of high-quality hospital treatment to be maintained on the national territory and the financial stability of the sickness insurance system to be assured;
- were large numbers of insured persons to decide to be treated in other Member States even when the hospitals having agreements with their sickness insurance funds offer adequate identical or equivalent treatment, the consequent outflow of patients would be liable to put at risk the very principle of having agreements with hospitals and, consequently, undermine all the planning and rationalisation carried out in this vital sector in an effort to avoid the phenomena of hospital overcapacity, imbalance in the supply of hospital medical care and logistical and financial wastage.

92. However, a refusal to grant prior authorisation which is based not on fear of wastage resulting from hospital overcapacity but solely on the ground that there are

waiting lists on national territory for the hospital treatment concerned, without account being taken of the specific circumstances attaching to the patient's medical condition, cannot amount to a properly justified restriction on freedom to provide services. It is not clear from the arguments submitted to the Court that such waiting times are necessary, apart from considerations of a purely economic nature which cannot as such justify a restriction on the fundamental principle of freedom to provide services, for the purpose of safeguarding the protection of public health. On the contrary, a waiting time which is too long or abnormal would be more likely to restrict access to balanced, high-quality hospital care.

Non-hospital services

93. As regards non-hospital medical services such as those supplied to Ms Müller-Fauré and, in part, to Ms Van Riet, no specific evidence has been produced to the Court, not even by the Zwijndrecht and Amsterdam Funds or the Netherlands Government, to support the assertion that, were insured persons at liberty to go without prior authorisation to Member States other than those in which their sickness funds are established in order to obtain those services from a non-contracted provider, that would be likely seriously to undermine the financial balance of the Netherlands social security system.

94. It is true that removal of the condition that there should be a system of agreements in respect of services supplied abroad adversely affects the ways in which health-care expenditure may be controlled in the Member State of affiliation.

95. However, the documents before the Court do not indicate that removal of the requirement for prior authorisation for that type of care would give rise to patients travelling to other countries in such large numbers, despite linguistic barriers, geographic distance, the cost of staying abroad and lack of information about the kind of care provided there, that the financial balance of the Netherlands social security system would be seriously upset and that, as a result, the overall level of public-health protection would be jeopardised – which might constitute proper justification for a barrier to the fundamental principle of freedom to provide services.

96. Furthermore, care is generally provided near to the place where the patient resides, in a cultural environment which is familiar to him and which allows him to build up a relationship of trust with the doctor treating him. If emergencies are disregarded, the most obvious cases of patients travelling abroad are in border areas or where specific conditions are to be treated. Furthermore, it is specifically in those areas or in respect of those conditions that the Netherlands sickness funds tend to set up a system of agreements with foreign doctors, as the observations submitted to the Court reveal.

97. Those various factors seem likely to limit any financial impact on the Netherlands social security system of removal of the requirement for prior authorisation in respect of care provided in foreign practitioners' surgeries.

98. In any event, it should be borne in mind that it is for the Member States alone to determine the extent of the sickness cover available to insured persons, so that, when the insured go without prior authorisation to a Member State other than that in which their sickness fund is established to receive treatment there, they can claim reimbursement of the cost of the treatment given to them only within the limits of the cover provided by the sickness insurance scheme in the Member State of affiliation.

The argument based on the essential characteristics of the Netherlands sickness insurance scheme

99. The Zwijndrecht Fund and the Netherlands, Spanish and Norwegian Governments have drawn attention to the fact that Member States are free to set up the social security system of their choice. In this instance, in the absence of prior authorisation, insured persons could apply freely to non-contracted care providers with the result that the existence of the Netherlands system of benefits in kind, the operation of which is in essence dependent upon the system of agreements, would be jeopardised. Furthermore, the Netherlands authorities would be obliged to introduce mechanisms for reimbursement into their method of organising access to health care since, instead of receiving free health services on national territory, the insured would have to advance the sums needed to pay for the services received and wait for some time before being reimbursed. Thus, Member States would be obliged to abandon the principles and underlying logic of their sickness insurance schemes.

100. In that regard it follows from settled case-law that Community law does not detract from the power of the Member States to organise their social security systems (see, in particular, Case 238/82 Duphar and Others [1984] ECR 523, paragraph 16, and Case C-70/95 Sodemare and Others [1997] ECR I-3395, paragraph 27). Therefore, in the absence of harmonisation at Community level, it is for the legislation of each Member State to determine the conditions on which social security benefits are granted (see, in particular, Case 110/79 Coonan [1980] ECR 1445, paragraph 12; Case C-349/87 Paraschi [1991] ECR I-4501, paragraph 15, and Joined Cases C-4/95 and C-5/95 Stöber and Piosa Pereira [1997] ECR I-511, paragraph 36). However, it is nevertheless the case that the Member States must comply with Community law when exercising that power (Decker, paragraph 23, and Kohll, paragraph 19).

101. Two preliminary observations must be made on this point.

102. First, achievement of the fundamental freedoms guaranteed by the Treaty inevitably requires Member States to make some adjustments to their national systems of social security. It does not follow that this would undermine their sovereign powers in this field. It is sufficient in this regard to look to the adjustments which they have had to make to their social security legislation in order to comply with Regulation No 1408/71, in particular with the conditions laid down in Article 69 thereof regarding the payment of unemployment benefit to workers residing in the territory of other Member States when no national system provided for the grant of such benefits to unemployed persons registered with an employment agency in another Member State.

103. Second, as has already been made clear in paragraph 39 above, a medical service does not cease to be a provision of services because it is paid for by a national health service or by a system providing benefits in kind. The Court has, in particular, held that a medical service provided in one Member State and paid for by the patient cannot cease to fall within the scope of the freedom to provide services guaranteed by the Treaty merely because reimbursement of the costs of the treatment involved is applied for under another Member State's sickness insurance legislation which is essentially of the type which provides for benefits in kind (Smits and Peerbooms, paragraph 55). The requirement for prior authorisation where a person is subsequently to be reimbursed for the costs of that treatment is precisely what constitutes, as has already been stated in paragraph 44 above, the barrier to freedom to provide services, that is to say, to a patient's ability to go to the medical service provider of his choice in a Member State other than that of affiliation. There is thus no need, from the perspective of freedom to provide services, to draw a distinction by reference to whether the patient pays the costs incurred and subsequently applies for reimbursement thereof or whether the sickness fund or the national budget pays the provider directly.

104. It is in the light of those observations that it is appropriate to determine whether removal of the requirement for sickness insurance funds to grant prior authorisation for non-hospital health care provided in a Member State other than that of affiliation, is such as to call in question the essential characteristics of the system of access to health care in the Netherlands.

105. First, when applying Regulation No 1408/71, those Member States which have established a system providing benefits in kind, or even a national health service, must provide mechanisms for ex post facto reimbursement in respect of care provided in a Member State other than the competent State. That is the case, for example, where it has not been possible to complete the formalities during the relevant person's stay in that State (see Article 34 of Regulation (EEC) No 574/72 of the Council of 21 March 1972 fixing the procedure for implementing Regulation No 1408/71) or where the competent State has authorised access to treatment abroad in accordance with Article 22(1)(c) of Regulation No 1408/71.

106. Second, as has already been stated in paragraph 98 above, insured persons who go without prior authorisation to a Member State other than the one in which their sickness fund is established to receive treatment there can claim reimbursement of the cost of the treatment received only within the limits of the cover provided by the sickness insurance scheme of the Member State of affiliation. Thus, in the present case, it is apparent from the documents before the Court that, in relation to the EUR 3 806.35 paid by Ms Müller-Fauré to a provider established in Germany, the Zwijndrecht Fund would in any event, given the extent of the insurance cover provided by the Fund, contribute only up to a maximum amount of EUR 221.03. Likewise, the conditions on which benefits are granted, in so far as they are neither discriminatory nor an obstacle to freedom of movement of persons, remain enforceable where treatment is provided in a Member State other than that of affiliation. That is particularly so in the case of the requirement that a general practitioner should be consulted prior to consulting a specialist.

107. Third, nothing precludes a competent Member State with a benefits in kind system from fixing the amounts of reimbursement which patients who have received care in another Member State can claim, provided that those amounts are based on objective, non-discriminatory and transparent criteria.

108. Consequently, the evidence and arguments submitted to the Court do not show that removal of the requirement that sickness insurance funds grant prior authorisation to their insured to enable them to receive health care, in particular other than in a hospital, provided in a Member State other than that of affiliation would undermine the essential characteristics of the Netherlands sickness insurance scheme.

109. In the light of all the foregoing considerations, the answer to the questions must be that:

- Articles 59 and 60 of the Treaty must be interpreted as not precluding legislation of a Member State, such as that at issue in the main proceedings, which (i) makes the assumption of the costs of hospital care provided in a Member State other than that in which the insured person's sickness fund is established, by a provider with which that fund has not concluded an agreement, conditional upon prior authorisation by the fund and (ii) makes the grant of that authorisation subject to the condition that such action is necessary for the insured person's health care. However, authorisation may be refused on that ground only if treatment which is the same or equally effective for the patient can be obtained without undue delay in an establishment which has concluded an agreement with the fund;
- by contrast, Articles 59 and 60 of the Treaty do preclude the same legislation in so far as it makes the assumption of the costs of non-hospital care provided in another Member State by a person or establishment with whom or which

> the insured person's sickness fund has not concluded an agreement conditional upon prior authorisation by the fund, even when the national legislation concerned sets up a system of benefits in kind under which insured persons are entitled not to reimbursement of costs incurred for medical treatment, but to the treatment itself which is provided free of charge.

Costs

[Para. 110 omitted]

On those grounds,

THE COURT,

in answer to the questions referred to it by the Centrale Raad van Beroep by order of 6 October 1999, hereby rules:

- **Article 59 of the EC Treaty (now, after amendment, Article 49 EC) and Article 60 of the EC Treaty (now Article 50 EC) must be interpreted as not precluding legislation of a Member State, such as that at issue in the main proceedings, which (i) makes the assumption of the costs of hospital care provided in a Member State other than that in which the insured person's sickness fund is established, by a provider with which that fund has not concluded an agreement, conditional upon prior authorisation by the fund and (ii) makes the grant of that authorisation subject to the condition that such action is necessary for the insured person's health care. However, authorisation may be refused on that ground only if treatment which is the same or equally effective for the patient can be obtained without undue delay in an establishment which has concluded an agreement with the fund;**

- **by contrast, Articles 59 and 60 of the Treaty do preclude the same legislation in so far as it makes the assumption of the costs of non-hospital care provided in another Member State by a person or establishment with whom or which the insured person's sickness fund has not concluded an agreement conditional upon prior authorisation by the fund, even when the national legislation concerned sets up a system of benefits in kind under which insured persons are entitled not to reimbursement of costs incurred for medical treatment, but to the treatment itself which is provided free of charge.**

Comments and questions

In a number of recent cases the CJEU has held that the provision of services by hospitals is covered by the TFEU's provisions on the freedom to provide services. This means that Member States can only restrict the freedom to provide hospital services if the restriction can be justified and if the principle of proportionality is complied with.

Already in Case C-157/99 *Geraets-Smits* v *Stichting Ziekenfonds VGZ and Peerbooms* v *Stichting CZ Groep Zorgverzekeringen* [2001] ECR I-5473, which is repeatedly referred to in Case C-385/99 *Müller-Fauré* v *Onderlinge Waarborgmaatschappij OZ Zorgverzekeringen* [2003] ECR I-4509, the CJEU stated in paragraph 82 that it is compatible with Article 56 TFEU (formerly Article 49 TEC) for a Member State's rules to make it conditional for treatment at a hospital in a second Member State at the expense of the first Member State to have prior authorisation from the authorities of the first Member State. This requirement for prior authorisation is justified with regard to planning the number of hospitals, their geographical distribution, the mode of their organisation and their equipment etc. The CJEU thus recognised that the medical services provided in a hospital take place within an infrastructure with distinct characteristics; cf. paragraph 76 of the judgment. In the *Geraets-Smits* and *Peerbooms* case the CJEU also stated that the requirement for prior authorisation was both 'necessary and reasonable'; cf. paragraph 80. Prior authorisation would only be incompatible with Article 56 TFEU if it were not proportionate. The CJEU stated that it would not be proportionate if the Dutch authorities only gave authorisation for treatment abroad if the proposed medical or surgical treatment could be regarded as 'normal' in the Netherlands medical circles. The national authorities should thus not only assess the treatment from a purely national point of view, but should also take into account what treatment has been tested and approved by medical science at an *international* level; cf. paragraph 94 in the judgment of the *Geraets-Smits* and *Peerbooms* case. The CJEU equally stated that it would also not be proportionate to refuse prior authorisation if a hospital in the state of origin could not provide treatment within a reasonable time. However, it was emphasised that Union law does not require a Member State to extend the list of medical services paid for by its social insurance system: the fact that a particular type of medical treatment is covered or not covered by the sickness insurance schemes of other Member States is irrelevant in this regard; cf. paragraph 87.

In the *Müller-Fauré* case the CJEU followed up and expanded on its decision in the *Geraets-Smits* case. In the *Müller-Fauré* case, two Dutch people had bought various health services from a German dentist and a Belgian hospital, respectively. They had applied to their sickness insurance funds for partial refunds of their expenses. However, under Netherlands rules such a refund required either that the supplier of the health services had entered into an agreement with the sickness insurance funds, or that the patients should have obtained prior authorisation from the sickness insurance funds. Neither of these alternative conditions had been met in this case, and since there were no other circumstances in the case which justified the reimbursement under Dutch law, the applications were refused.

In its judgment the CJEU confirmed that both hospital services and non-hospital medical services were covered by the TFEU rules on the freedom to provide services. The Dutch rules were in particular based on considerations for ensuring a stable medical and hospital service open to all. Furthermore, this was justified by the need to protect against the serious risk that disturbance to the financial balance of the social security system could affect the overall level of protection of public health. The CJEU held that these considerations concerned the protection of public health so that, in principle, the Dutch rules pursued a lawful purpose. The CJEU then considered whether the lawful purpose was proportionate in its consequences for the freedom to provide services.

In assessing this proportionality, the CJEU distinguished between 'hospital services' and 'non-hospital services'. In relation to hospital services, the CJEU recognised that there is a special need for planning which may justify the Dutch requirement for prior authorisation, if the costs of care are to be paid for treatment provided at a hospital which has not entered into an agreement with the sickness insurance fund in question. However, the CJEU added that such requirement for prior authorisation can only be acceptable if the conditions for granting prior authorisation are justified and proportionate, and if the requirement for prior authorisation is not used to justify arbitrary conduct by the national authorities.

As for non-hospital services, the CJEU held that it was unlikely that the removal of the Dutch requirement for prior authorisation would lead to Dutch patients seeking treatment abroad in such large numbers that it would lead to a serious disturbance of the financial stability of the Dutch sickness insurance scheme. The CJEU also stated that the national authorities could attach conditions for the provision of services in a Member State other than that in which the patient is a member of a sickness insurance fund, provided that such conditions are neither an expression of discriminatory treatment, nor constitute a restriction on the free movement of persons. Where, in his home State, a patient receives a service (treatment) without having to pay for it, the national authorities can set limits on how much patients treated in other Member States can claim to have reimbursed. This is on condition that such amounts are laid down on the basis of objective, non-discriminatory and transparent criteria. However, the CJEU held that there could not be a general requirement for members of a sickness insurance fund to obtain prior authorisation in order to receive health services in another Member State.

How does the CJEU define hospital services and non-hospital services (see paragraph 75 in particular)? The CJEU accepts that the risk of seriously undermining the financial balance of the social security system may be an overriding public interest capable of justifying some protective measure; cf. paragraph 73. However, in paragraph 72, the CJEU states that aims of a purely economic nature cannot justify a barrier to the fundamental principle of freedom to provide services. How does the CJEU reconcile these two statements?

Can there be a general requirement that patients must consult a general practitioner before consulting a specialist? Would the answer to this be different if this requirement only applied to specialists who were not authorised specialists in the Member State in question?

In paragraph 103, the CJEU stated that there is 'no need, from the perspective of freedom to provide services, to draw a distinction by reference to whether the patient pays the costs incurred and subsequently applies for reimbursement thereof or whether the sickness fund or the national budget pays the provider directly'. Consider the concept of services in relation to education offered at public universities. Studying at a Danish university is free. Does a course at a Danish university constitute a service within the meaning of Article 57 TFEU? On this, see Case C-281/06 *Jundt* [2007] ECR I-12231, printed immediately below.

JUDGMENT OF THE COURT (Third Chamber)
18 December 2007

Hans-Dieter Jundt and, Hedwig Jundt v Finanzamt Offenburg. (Reference for a preliminary ruling from the Bundesfinanzhof – Germany)

'Freedom to provide services – Secondary teaching activity – Concept of 'remuneration' – Allowances for professional expenses – Legislation concerning tax exemption – Conditions – Remuneration paid by a national university'

Case C-281/06

Judgment

1. This request for a preliminary ruling concerns the interpretation of Article 59 of the EEC Treaty (which became Article 59 of the EC Treaty and is now, following amendment, Article 49 EC) and Article 128 of the EEC Treaty (which became, after amendment, Article 126 of the EC Treaty and is now Article 149 EC).

2. The request has been made in proceedings between Mr and Mrs Jundt, who are resident in Germany, and the Finanzamt (Tax Office) Offenburg with regard to the latter's refusal to take into account, as revenue exempt from income tax for the tax assessment year 1991, expense allowances received in respect of teaching carried out on a spare-time basis at a university established in another Member State, on the ground that the national income tax legislation reserved the application of the exemption in question to remuneration emanating from German public-law bodies.

National legal framework

3. The first sentence of Paragraph 1(1) of the Law on Income Tax (Einkommensteuergesetz; EStG'), in the version applicable at the time of the facts in the main proceedings, provides that natural persons who are permanently or normally resident in Germany are subject to unlimited taxation on their income.

4. Under Paragraph 2(2) of the EStG, income is constituted either by profit or by the surplus of revenue over professional expenses.

5. Paragraph 3(26) of the EStG, which appears in the section of that Law dealing with 'exempt revenue', states as follows:

'The following are exempt from tax:

...

26. expense allowances for secondary activities as training supervisor, instructor or educator or for comparable secondary activities, for secondary artistic activities or for second jobs caring for the elderly, ill or handicapped persons for or on behalf of a national public-law legal person or a body falling within Paragraph 5(1)(9) of the Law on Corporation Tax (Körperschaftssteuergesetz; 'KStG') and which is for the promotion of the public good or of charitable or ecclesiastical purposes (Paragraphs 52 to 54 of the Tax Code (Abgabenordnung)). Revenue not exceeding a total of DM 2 400 per annum received in respect of the activities referred to in the first sentence shall be treated as expense allowances ...'

The main proceedings and the questions referred for a preliminary ruling

6. Mr and Mrs Jundt are subject to joint assessment for income tax purposes in Germany. Working principally as a lawyer in Germany, where he resides, in 1991 Mr Jundt taught a 16-hour course at the University of Strasbourg for which he received the sum of FRF 5 760 (gross) (corresponding to DEM 1 612).

7. The Finanzamt Offenburg charged income tax on that gross amount in its tax assessment notice for 1991.

8. Mr and Mrs Jundt have submitted that that amount should be exempted from income tax under Paragraph 3(26) of the EStG. They are of the view that it is contrary to Community law to restrict the application of that exemption to remuneration paid by German bodies established under public law.

9. Their objection against the decision of the Finanzamt Offenburg and their appeal to the Finanzgericht having failed, Mr and Mrs Jundt appealed on a point of law ('Revision') to the Bundesfinanzhof.

10. The Bundesfinanzhof points out that Mr Jundt could have benefited from the exemption provided for under Paragraph 3(26) of the EStG if he had carried out his activity in a German university, a legal person established under public law, and not in a university of another Member State. In order to determine whether or not such legislation is compatible with the provisions of Community law on the freedom to provide services, it considers it necessary to refer three questions for a preliminary ruling.

11. First, it raises the question whether a secondary activity as a teacher for a university falls within the scope of the provisions on the freedom to provide services inasmuch as it is not certain that the sums eligible for exemption under Paragraph 3(26) of the EStG constitute actual remuneration. According to that provision, the exempted revenue has the character of an 'expense allowance', which seems to imply

a simple reimbursement of the expenses connected with the performance of the activity in question.

12. Second, the Bundesfinanzhof raises the question whether, if that is the case, the restriction on the freedom to provide services resulting from Paragraph 3(26) of the EStG can be justified. It is of the opinion that there may be a legitimate interest in confining the tax concession to activities carried out for or on behalf of German legal persons established under public law.

13. According to the Bundesfinanzhof, it is possible that such justification is to be found in the cohesion of the tax system, as acknowledged by the Court in Case C-204/90 *Bachmann* [1992] ECR I-249 and Case C-300/90 *Commission* v *Belgium* [1992] ECR I-305. It takes the view that, in the main proceedings, there is a direct link between the teaching activity on behalf of a German legal person established under public law and the exemption from income tax. That tax concession is granted only by reason of the fact that the taxpayer provides, on a quasi-honorary basis, a specific service for the community which levies the tax and thus relieves it of certain tasks. If the taxpayer did not provide that service, the tax authorities would in theory have to increase the tax in order to finance the higher teaching costs which would result. According to the Bundesfinanzhof, Paragraph 3(26) of the EStG is based on a reciprocal relationship between the waiver of tax and the provision of a service in return.

14. Finally, as regards the teaching activities, the Bundesfinanzhof raises the question whether legislation such as that in issue in the main proceedings is not an element of the freedom explicitly left to the Member States by the EC Treaty to assume responsibility for the organisation of their education systems. According to it, that freedom comprises not only the duty to provide for the financing of the national education system, but also the possibility to confine the fiscal measures designed to promote education to 'national' activities, and it therefore inclines to the view that the freedom to provide services has not been infringed. Its third question concerns the effect of Article 126 of the EC Treaty on a finding that the restriction on the freedom to provide services was unjustified.

15. In those circumstances, the Bundesfinanzhof decided to stay the proceedings and to refer the following questions to the Court for a preliminary ruling:

'(1) Is Article 59 of the EC Treaty ... to be interpreted as including within its scope also part-time teaching activity for or on behalf of a public-law legal person (a university) where only an expense allowance is paid for that activity, as being an activity in a quasi-honorary capacity?

(2) If the first question is answered in the affirmative, is the restriction on freedom to provide services whereby allowances are taxed favourably only if

they are paid by national public-law legal persons (here, Paragraph 3(26) of the EStG) justified by the fact that the State tax concession applies only where the activity is for the benefit of a national public-law legal person?

(3) If the second question is answered in the negative, is Article 126 of the EC Treaty ... to be interpreted as meaning that a provision of tax law designed to help supplement the organisation of the education system (such as, here, Paragraph 3(26) of the EstG) is lawful in the light of the fact that the Member States continue to have responsibility in that regard?'

The questions referred for a preliminary ruling

[Paras 16-20 omitted]

The first question

21. By its first question, the national court asks essentially whether a teaching activity carried out by a taxpayer of one Member State for a legal person established under public law in another Member State, in this case a university, comes within the scope of Article 49 EC even if it is carried out on a secondary basis and in a quasi-honorary capacity.

Observations submitted to the Court

22. Mr and Mrs Jundt, the German Government and the Commission take the view that secondary activities as a teacher at a university constitute a provision of services for the purposes of Article 50 EC, that is to say, an economic activity normally performed for remuneration.

23. Mr and Mrs Jundt point out that Paragraph 3(26) of the EStG itself defines 'expense allowances' as 'revenue' and that, in the current version of that provision, the reference is no longer to 'expense allowances', but to 'revenue for secondary professional activities'.

24. According to the German Government, the scope of Article 49 EC also covers activities carried out on a secondary and quasi-honorary basis as a teacher for or on behalf of a legal person established under public law such as a university, in return for an expense allowance. Those economic activities, it argues, have the particular feature of being intended not to make profits but merely to offset expenditure incurred.

25. The Commission notes that the doubts entertained by the Bundesfinanzhof as to the existence of remuneration are based on the use by the provision of national law in question of the expression 'expense allowance', which suggests a payment not ex-

ceeding the amount of expenses incurred and the absence of profit. According to the Commission, a payment does not lose its character as 'remuneration' for the sole reason that it does not allow a profit to be made. For there to be an economic activity, the terms of Article 50 EC require only the payment of remuneration and not the existence of a profit.

26. The Commission submits that, in any event, the main proceedings and the legislation at issue in those proceedings do not concern remuneration which is limited to covering actual expenses incurred. Had the payment made by the University of Strasbourg been limited to covering the expenses borne by Mr Jundt for the purpose of performing his teaching activities successfully, he would not have relied on Paragraph 3(26) of the EStG to apply for exemption of the sums received since the application of the ordinary rules of the EStG would already have resulted in his activity not being taxed.

27. According to the Commission, Paragraph 3(26) of the EStG grants a tax concession to the taxpayer precisely in the case where revenue exceeds expenses and the taxpayer is therefore left with net revenue, that is to say, a 'profit'.

Reply of the Court

28. In order to determine whether an activity such as that at issue in the main proceedings comes within the scope of Article 49 EC, it should be recalled, first, that according to the first paragraph of Article 50 EC the concept of 'services' means 'services ... normally provided for remuneration' (Case C-355/00 *Freskot* [2003] ECR I-5263, paragraph 54).

29. In that regard, it has already been held that, for the purposes of that latter provision, the essential characteristic of remuneration lies in the fact that it constitutes consideration for the service in question (see, inter alia, Case 263/86 *Humbel* [1988] ECR 5365, paragraph 17; Case C-422/01 *Skandia and Ramstedt* [2003] ECR I-6817, paragraph 23; Case C-76/05 *Schwarz and Gootjes-Schwarz* [2007] ECR I-0000, paragraph 38; and Case C-318/05 *Commission* v *Germany* [2007] ECR I-0000, paragraph 67).

30. Second, the Court has excluded from the concept of 'services' within the meaning of Article 50 EC courses provided by certain establishments forming part of a system of public education and financed, entirely or mainly, by public funds (see, to that effect,*Humbel*, paragraph 18, and Case C-109/92 *Wirth* [1993] ECR I-6447, paragraphs 15 and 16). The Court has thus stated that, by establishing and maintaining such a system of public education, normally financed from the public purse and not by pupils or their parents, the State does not intend to become involved in activities for remuneration, but carries out its task towards its population in the social, cultural and educational fields (see *Schwarz and Gootjes-Schwarz*, paragraph 39).

31. The main proceedings in the present case, however, do not relate to the teaching activity of the universities themselves, financed by public funds. On the contrary, the present case and the national legislation in question concern services provided on a secondary basis by natural persons called upon by universities to help them fulfil their mission. Payment for those services may constitute remuneration on the part of the university concerned.

32. As the Advocate General noted in point 12 of his Opinion, the decisive factor which brings an activity within the ambit of the Treaty provisions on the freedom to provide services is its economic character, that is to say, the activity must not be provided for nothing.

33. By contrast, contrary to the view which the national court appears to take, there is no need in that regard for the person providing the service to be seeking to make a profit (see, inter alia, C-157/99 *Smits and Peerbooms* [2001] ECR I-5473, paragraphs 50 and 52).

34. Consequently, the main proceedings, in the same way as Paragraph 3(26) of the EStG, concern services provided for 'remuneration'. The sum received by Mr Jundt from the university for his teaching activity constitutes remuneration for the purposes of Article 50 EC, that is to say, consideration for the service provided by him, even if it is assumed that that activity was carried out on a quasi-honorary basis.

35. Finally, the fact that the teaching activity is carried out on behalf of a university, a legal person established under public law, does not have the effect of removing the service provided from the scope of Article 49 EC.

36. The national court expresses some doubts in that regard, questioning whether the services carried out for or on behalf of an institution established under public law and capable of coming within the scope of Article 45 EC – which must also be taken into consideration in the framework of the free provision of services – can constitute a provision of services. According to the national court, those services are to be considered as 'semi-public' and fall within the sphere of State activity under public law.

37. While, under the first paragraph of Article 45 EC, in conjunction with Article 50 EC, the freedom to provide services does not extend to activities connected in a Member State, even occasionally, with the exercise of official authority, that derogation must, however, be restricted to activities which in themselves are directly and specifically connected with the exercise of official authority (Case 2/74*Reyners* [1974] ECR 631, paragraph 45; Case C-283/99 *Commission* v *Italy* [2001] ECR I-4363, paragraph 20; and Case C-451/03*Servizi Ausiliari Dottori Commercialisti* [2006] ECR I-2941, paragraph 46).

38. It follows from the Court's case-law concerning Article 39(4) EC that university teaching activities, being activities of civil society, do not fall within the scope of that derogation (see, to that effect, Case 33/88 *Allué and Coonan* [1989] ECR 1591, paragraph 7, and Case C-290/94 *Commission* v *Greece* [1996] ECR I-3285, paragraph 34).

39. The answer to the first question referred must therefore be that a teaching activity carried out by a taxpayer of one Member State for a legal person established under public law, in the present case a university, situated in another Member State comes within the scope of Article 49 EC, even if it is carried out on a secondary basis and in a quasi-honorary capacity.

The second question

[Paras 40-73 omitted]

The third question

[Paras 74-89 omitted]

Costs

[Para. 90 omitted]

On those grounds,

THE COURT (Third Chamber),

hereby rules:

1. **A teaching activity carried out by a taxpayer of one Member State for a legal person established under public law, in the present case a university, situated in another Member State comes within the scope of Article 49 EC, even if it is carried out on a secondary basis and in a quasi-honorary capacity.**

2. **The restriction on the freedom to provide services constituted by the fact that national legislation confines the application of an exemption from income tax to remuneration paid by universities, that is to say, public-law legal persons, established on national territory, in return for teaching activities carried out on a secondary basis, and refuses to apply that exemption where that remuneration is paid by a university established in another Member State, is not justified by overriding reasons relating to the public interest.**

3. **The fact that the Member States are themselves competent to organise their respective education systems is not such as to render compatible with Community law national legislation which confines the benefit of a tax exemption to taxpayers carrying out activities for or on behalf of national public universities.**

Comments and questions

In strictly formal terms, Article 56 TFEU (formerly Article 49 TEC), on freedom to provide services, is a 'reserve' provision that only applies where the other freedoms do not apply; see Article 57 TFEU. However, in practice the provision ranks alongside the other freedoms, so that the classification of a service is important:

- In the case of the repair of a washing machine, where some bolts are replaced, this is a 'service', even though the service includes the supply of new bolts (goods);
- In the case of the purchase of a washing machine, when the seller connects the water and electricity, this is a provision of goods, even though the installation is a service.

Where one aspect cannot be regarded as having priority over the other the CJEU has been willing to apply the rules on the freedom to provide services and the rules on the free movement of goods simultaneously; see Case C-390/99 *Canal Satélite Digital* [2002] ECR I-607.

The rules on the provision of services do not apply to an undertaking that is carried on permanently, or at least without a specific time-limit; see e.g. Case C-456/02 *Trojani* [2004] ECR I-7573, paragraph 28, printed above in Chapter 4.

The scope of the TFEU provisions on freedom to provide services has been at issue in a number of cases. What has often been a key issue in many of these cases has been what constitutes a 'service', or who can derive rights in a situation when there is a provision of services. In the *Jundt* case the question was whether a German national's teaching at a French university for a small fee qualified as a service when in Germany such activities were widely regarded as being of a quasi-honorary nature. The starting point for the CJEU's answer to this question was whether there was a Union law interpretation which should be laid down by the CJEU and which should not vary from Member State to Member State. First, the CJEU noted that the concept of 'services' pursuant to Article 57(1) TFEU (formerly Article 50(1) TEC) means 'services ... normally provided for remuneration'. In other words, the payment must be the financial consideration for the service in question.

With particular regard to teaching, there is not the provision of a service within the meaning of the TFEU if the teaching is offered in courses provided by certain establishments forming part of a system of public education and financed, entirely or mainly, by public funds. This applies to the teaching which educational institutions provide to students. However, in the *Jundt* case, there was the provision of a service (in the form of teaching) by an outside party to the University of Strasbourg which in turn was responsible for providing this service to the students. In the relationship between the University of Strasbourg and its students there was thus not the provision of a service, but in the relationship between Hr Jundt and the University of Strasbourg there was the provision of a service.

At the same time, the CJEU noted that it was not a condition that the person providing the service (in this case Herr Jundt) should be seeking to make a profit from the provision of the service. Even if there is merely an 'expense allowance' whereby the teacher only receives payment covering the costs connected with the provision of the service in question, the condition of payment for the service will have been fulfilled.

The referring German court had also asked whether Herr Jundt's teaching at the University of Strasbourg could be considered as being covered by the Treaty-based right of freedom to provide services on a significantly different basis. Article 62 in conjunction with Article 51 TFEU (formerly Article 55 in conjunction with Article 45 TEC) states that the Treaty provisions on freedom to provide services do not apply, in so far as any given Member State is concerned, to activities which in that State are connected, even occasionally, with the exercise of official authority. However, the CJEU rejected this argument, stating that university teaching is not covered by the exception. What activities could be covered by this exception – for example, do you think a guest lecturer at a military academy would be excluded from the scope of Article 56 TFEU?

Another case that illustrates the limits to the scope of the rules on the provision of services is Case 186/87 *Cowan* [1989] ECR 195, which concerned a British tourist in Paris who was a victim of an assault. Since it was not possible to determine who had carried out the assault, Cowan sought compensation from the French State in accordance with French law. However, French law only gave a right of compensation to French nationals and to a limited category of nationals from other Member States. Consequently Cowan's application was refused. When the question of whether this refusal was contrary to Union law came before the CJEU, it ruled that the Union rules prohibiting discrimination apply to recipients of services as regards protection from assault and the right to obtain compensation provided for by national law when an assault materialises. Thus the French law must not be applied so as to discriminate against those who are entitled to equal treatment pursuant to Union law, nor might there be a restriction on the fundamental rights guaranteed in Union law. Consider whether a German national who takes a day trip to Strasbourg, which is just on the French side of the Franco-German border, and eats lunch there would be considered a recipient of services.

In Case C-17/00 *De Coster* [2001] ECR I-9445, the Région de Bruxelles-Capitale (the Belgian capital region) had introduced a tax on satellite dishes for the reception of television signals transmitted by satellite. In contrast, television broadcasts via cable were not subject to a corresponding tax. It could be argued that most of the television broadcasts transmitted from other Member States could only be received by using satellite dishes. On the other hand, radio and television stations located in Belgium had unrestricted access to broadcast via cable in Belgium. Is a television broadcast a service? If so, was the Région de Bruxelles-Capitale obliged to comply with Article 56 TFEU?

Was the tax discriminatory? It was said that the tax was raised in order to protect the urban environment, and Région de Bruxelles-Capitale argued that the erection of many large satellite dishes could visually impair the urban environment. Do you believe that the CJEU found the tax was necessary for the pursuit of this goal?

In Case C-20/92 *Hubbard* [1993] ECR I-3777, the CJEU had to decide on a dispute in which Mr Hubbard, an English solicitor acting in the capacity of an executor under English law, sought an order from a German court vesting in him property located in Germany forming part of the testator's estate. The defendant thereupon demanded security for costs relating to the court proceedings, which was a requirement that did not apply to German citizens. Hubbard argued that this would be contrary to Union law and the question was referred to the CJEU. The CJEU ruled that where a service is provided by a member of a profession and therefore, as referred to in Article 57 TFEU, is normally provided for remuneration, the principle of equal treatment laid down in Article 56 TFEU applies. In this connection it was not relevant that the service provider (the solicitor) and the recipient of services (the heir) were resident in the same Member State. What was relevant was that the service (the conduct of litigation in Germany) was provided in another Member State than that in which the service provider was established.

The demand for the provision of security for costs from foreign plaintiffs constituted discrimination pursuant to Article 56 TFEU. The fact that the litigation proceeded from an inheritance case (at that time, inheritance law was outside the scope of Union competence) did not alter the right to have Union law applied. The CJEU has subsequently ruled that: 'national legislative provisions which fall within the scope of application of the Treaty are, by reason of their effects on intra-[Union] trade in goods and services, necessarily subject to the general principle of non-discrimination laid down by the first paragraph of [Article 18(1) TFEU], without there being any need to connect them with the specific provisions of [Articles 34, 36, 56 and 62 TFEU]'; cf. paragraph 16 in Case C-323/95 *Hayes* [1997] ECR I-1711. The CJEU has also ruled that Articles 18 and 49 TFEU prohibit a demand for the provision of security for the costs of proceedings in connection with a case brought by a Union citizen concerning the legal status of a shareholder in a company; see Case C-122/96 *Saldanha* [1997] ECR I-5325.

JUDGMENT OF THE COURT
11 July 2002

Mary Carpenter v Secretary of State for the Home Department.
(Reference for a preliminary ruling: Immigration Appeal Tribunal – United Kingdom)

'Freedom to provide services – Article 49 EC – Directive 73/148/EEC – National of a Member State established in that State and providing services to persons established in other Member States – Right of residence in that State of a spouse who is a national of a third country'

Case C-60/00

Judgment

1. By order of 16 December 1999, received at the Court on 21 February 2000, the Immigration Appeal Tribunal referred to the Court for a preliminary ruling under Article 234 EC a question on the interpretation of Article 49 EC and Council Directive 73/148/EEC of 21 May 1973 on the abolition of restrictions on movement and residence within the Community for nationals of Member States with regard to establishment and the provision of services (OJ 1973 L 172, p. 14, hereinafter 'the Directive').

2. The question was raised in proceedings between Mrs Carpenter, a national of the Philippines, and the Secretary of State for the Home Department (hereinafter 'the Secretary of State') concerning her right to reside in the United Kingdom.

Legislative framework

Community legislation

3. The first paragraph of Article 49 EC provides:

   'Within the framework of the provisions set out below, restrictions on freedom to provide services within the Community shall be prohibited in respect of nationals of Member States who are established in a State of the Community other than that of the person for whom the services are intended.'

4. The first recital of the preamble to the Directive states as follows:

   'Whereas freedom of movement of persons as provided for in the Treaty and the General Programmes for the abolition of restrictions on freedom of establishment and on freedom to provide services entails the abolition of restrictions on movement and residence within the Community for nationals of Member States wishing to establish themselves or to provide services within the territory of another Member State'.

5. Article 1(1) of the Directive provides:

   'The Member States shall, acting as provided in this Directive, abolish restrictions on the movement and residence of:

   (a) nationals of a Member State who are established or who wish to establish themselves in another Member State in order to pursue activities as self-employed persons, or who wish to provide services in that State;
   (b) nationals of Member States wishing to go to another Member State as recipients of services;
   (c) the spouse and the children under 21 years of age of such nationals, irrespective of their nationality;
   (d) the relatives in the ascending and descending lines of such nationals and of the spouse of such nationals, which relatives are dependent on them, irrespective of their nationality.'

6. The first subparagraph of Article 4(2) of the Directive provides:

   'The right of residence for persons providing and receiving services shall be of equal duration with the period during which the services are provided.'

United Kingdom legislation

7. In terms of the Immigration Act 1971 and the 1994 United Kingdom Immigration Rules (House of Commons Paper 395, hereinafter 'the Immigration Rules'), a person who is not a British citizen may not, as a general rule, enter or remain in the United Kingdom unless he has obtained permission to do so. Such permission is called respectively 'leave to enter' and 'leave to remain'.

8. Section 7(1) of the Immigration Act 1988 provides:

   'A person shall not under the [Immigration Act 1971] require leave to enter or remain in the United Kingdom in any case in which he is entitled to do so by virtue of an enforceable Community right or of any provision made under section 2(2) of the European Communities Act 1972.'

9. Paragraph 281 of the Immigration Rules lists the requirements for leave to enter the United Kingdom as the spouse of a person present and settled in the United Kingdom. Paragraph 281(vi) states that the applicant must hold a valid United Kingdom entry clearance for entry as a spouse. However, a person present in the United

Kingdom with leave to enter or remain in another capacity may switch into the spouse category if he or she satisfies the requirements of paragraph 284 of the Immigration Rules.

10. Paragraph 284 of the Immigration Rules lays down the requirements for an extension of stay in the United Kingdom as the spouse of a person present and settled in the United Kingdom. Paragraph 284(i) provides that the applicant must have limited leave to remain in the United Kingdom (this would include leave to enter) and Paragraph 284(iv) states that the applicant must not have remained in breach of the immigration laws.

11. Section 3(5)(a) of the Immigration Act 1971 lays down the general rules relating to deportation from the United Kingdom. It provides:

    'A person who is not a British Citizen shall be liable to deportation from the United Kingdom –

    (a) if, having only a limited leave to enter or remain, he does not observe a condition attached to the leave or remains beyond the time limited by the leave ...'.

12. As regards, more particularly, the deportation of spouses of UK nationals, the Secretary of State is required, under paragraph 364 of the Immigration Rules, to consider the particular circumstances of each case before deciding whether or not to order deportation. However, a published policy concession, DP 3/96, sets out the circumstances in which the Secretary of State will normally grant leave to remain to spouses who are liable to deportation or who are in the United Kingdom illegally. Paragraph 5 of the concession states that, as a general rule, deportation action should not normally be initiated where the person concerned has a genuine and subsisting marriage with someone settled in the United Kingdom and the couple have lived together in the United Kingdom continuously since their marriage for at least two years before the commencement of enforcement action, and it is unreasonable to expect the settled spouse to accompany his/her spouse on removal.

The dispute in the main proceedings

13. Mrs Carpenter, a national of the Philippines, was given leave to enter the United Kingdom as a visitor on 18 September 1994 for six months. She overstayed that leave and failed to apply for any extension of her stay. On 22 May 1996 she married Peter Carpenter, a United Kingdom national.

14. It appears from the order for reference that Mr Carpenter runs a business selling advertising space in medical and scientific journals and offering various administrative and publishing services to the editors of those journals. The business is established in the UK, where the publishers of the journals for which he sells advertising

space are based. A significant proportion of the business is conducted with advertisers established in other Member States of the European Community. Mr Carpenter travels to other Member States for the purpose of his business.

15. On 15 July 1996 Mrs Carpenter applied to the Secretary of State for leave to remain in the UK as the spouse of a national of that Member State. Her application was refused by a decision of the Secretary of State of 21 July 1997.

16. The Secretary of State also decided to make a deportation order against Mrs Carpenter removing her to the Philippines. Under that decision it is open to Mrs Carpenter to leave the United Kingdom voluntarily. If she does not do so, the Secretary of State will sign the deportation order and Mrs Carpenter will have to obtain its revocation before she can seek leave to enter the United Kingdom as the spouse of a UK citizen.

17. Mrs Carpenter appealed against the decision to make a deportation order to an Immigration Adjudicator (United Kingdom), arguing that the Secretary of State was not entitled to deport her because she was entitled to a right to remain in the United Kingdom under Community law. She maintained that since her husband's business required him to travel around in other Member States, providing and receiving services, he could do so more easily as she was looking after his children from his first marriage, so that her deportation would restrict her husband's right to provide and receive services.

18. The Immigration Adjudicator was satisfied that Mrs Carpenter's marriage was genuine and that she played an important part in the upbringing of her stepchildren. He also accepted that she could be indirectly responsible for the increased success of her husband's business and that her husband was a provider of services for the purposes of Community law. According to the Immigration Adjudicator, Mr Carpenter has the right to travel to other Member States to provide services and to be accompanied for that purpose by his spouse. However, while he is resident in the United Kingdom, he cannot be considered to be exercising any freedom of movement within the meaning of Community law. The Immigration Adjudicator therefore dismissed Mrs Carpenter's appeal by decision of 10 June 1998.

19. On Mrs Carpenter's appeal to the Immigration Appeal Tribunal, it considered that the issue of Community law raised by the proceedings before it was whether it was contrary to Community law and, in particular, Article 49 EC and/or the Directive, for the Secretary of State to refuse to grant a right of residence to, and to decide to deport Mrs Carpenter where, first, Mr Carpenter was exercising his freedom to provide services in other Member States, and second, the childcare and homemaking performed by Mrs Carpenter might indirectly assist and facilitate Mr Carpenter's exercise of his rights under Article 49 EC, by providing him with economic assistance which permitted him to spend greater time on his business.

20. Since it considered that the case turned on the interpretation of Community law, the Immigration Appeal Tribunal decided to stay proceedings and refer the following question to the Court of Justice for a preliminary ruling:

'In circumstances where:

(a) a national of a Member State, who is established in that Member State and who provides services to persons in other Member States; and
(b) has a spouse who is not a national of a Member State; can the non-national spouse rely on
(i) Article 49 EC and/or
(ii) Council Directive 73/148/EEC of 21 May 1973 on the abolition of restrictions on movement and residence within the Community for nationals of Member States with regard to establishment and the provision of services, to provide the non-national spouse with the right to reside with his or her spouse in his or her spouse's Member State of origin? Is the answer to the question referred different if the non-national spouse indirectly assists the national of a Member State in carrying on the provision of services in other Member States by carrying out childcare?'

The question referred

Observations submitted to the Court

21. Mrs Carpenter admits that she has no right of her own to reside in any Member State but claims that her rights derive from those enjoyed by Mr Carpenter to provide services and to travel within the European Union. Her husband is entitled to carry on his business throughout the internal market without being subjected to unlawful restrictions. Her deportation would require Mr Carpenter to go to live with her in the Philippines or separate the members of the family unit if he remained in the United Kingdom. In both cases Mr Carpenter's business would be affected. Moreover it cannot be maintained that the restriction on the freedom to provide services, to which Mr Carpenter would be subjected if his spouse was deported, would be a purely internal matter, since he provides services throughout the internal market.

22. According to the United Kingdom Government the provisions of the Directive mean, for example, that a UK national wishing to provide services in another Member State is entitled to reside in that State for the period during which the services are provided, and that his or her spouse would be entitled to reside there for the same period. Those provisions do not, however, give any right of residence in the United Kingdom to UK nationals, who have such a right in any event under United Kingdom law, or to their spouses. The Court has confirmed that interpretation in its judgment in Case C-370/90 Singh [1992] ECR I-4265, paragraphs 17 and 18.

23. The United Kingdom Government points out that, in its judgment in Case C-107/94 Asscher [1996] ECR I-3089, the Court considered the question whether a national of a Member State pursuing an activity as a self-employed person in another Member State, in which he resides, may rely on Article 52 of the EC Treaty (now, after amendment, Article 43 EC) against his Member State of origin, on whose territory he pursues another activity as a self-employed person. The Court held, at paragraph 32 of that judgment, that, although the provisions of the Treaty relating to freedom of establishment cannot be applied to situations which are purely internal to a Member State, the scope of Article 52 of the Treaty nevertheless cannot be interpreted in such a way as to exclude a given Member State's own nationals from the benefit of Community law where by reason of their conduct they are, with regard to their Member State of origin, in a situation which may be regarded as equivalent to that of any other person enjoying the rights and liberties guaranteed by the Treaty.

24. However, since Mr Carpenter has not exercised his right to freedom of movement, his spouse cannot rely on Singh or Asscher, cited above. Therefore, a person in Mrs Carpenter's position is not entitled to derive from Community law any right to enter or remain in the United Kingdom.

25. According to the Commission, the situation of Mrs Carpenter must be clearly distinguished from that of a spouse of a national of a Member State who has exercised his right to freedom of movement and has left his Member State of origin and moved to another Member State in order to become established or to work there.

26. In that case the spouse, whatever his or her nationality, would undoubtedly be covered by Community law, and would be entitled to establish himself or herself, with the Community national in the host Member State, since otherwise that national might be deterred from exercising his or her right to freedom of movement. Also, as the Court held at paragraph 23 of its judgment in Singh, cited above, when that Community national returns to his or her country of origin, his or her spouse must enjoy at least the same rights of entry and residence as would be granted to him or her under Community law, if his or her spouse chose to enter and reside in another Member State.

27. On the other hand, the principle expressed in paragraph 23 of the judgment in Singh, cited above, cannot be applied to a situation such as that in issue in the main proceedings, in which a national of a Member State has never sought to establish himself with his spouse in another Member State but merely provides services from his State of origin. The Commission submits that such a situation is rather to be classified as an internal situation within the meaning of the judgment in Joined Cases 35/82 and 36/82 Morson and Jhanjan [1982] ECR 3723, so that Mrs Carpenter's right to remain in the United Kingdom, if it exists, depends exclusively on United Kingdom law.

Findings of the Court

28. It is to be noted, at the outset, that the provisions of the Treaty relating to the freedom to provide services, and the rules adopted for their implementation, are not applicable to situations which do not present any link to any of the situations envisaged by Community law (see, to that effect, among others, Case C-97/98 Jägerskiöld [1999] ECR I-7319, paragraphs 42 to 45).

29. As is apparent from paragraph 14 of this judgment, a significant proportion of Mr Carpenter's business consists of providing services, for remuneration, to advertisers established in other Member States. Such services come within the meaning of 'services' in Article 49 EC both in so far as the provider travels for that purpose to the Member State of the recipient and in so far as he provides cross-border services without leaving the Member State in which he is established (see, in respect of 'cold-calling', Case C-384/93 Alpine Investments [1995] ECR I-1141, paragraphs 15 and 20 to 22).

30. Mr Carpenter is therefore availing himself of the right freely to provide services guaranteed by Article 49 EC. Moreover, as the Court has frequently held, that right may be relied on by a provider as against the State in which he is established if the services are provided for persons established in another Member State (see, among others, Alpine Investments, cited above, paragraph 30).

31. With regard to the right of establishment and the freedom to provide services, the Directive aims to abolish restrictions on the movement and residence of nationals of Member States within the Community.

32. It follows both from the objective of the Directive and the wording of Article 1(1)(a) and (b) thereof, that it applies to cases where nationals of Member States leave their Member State of origin and move to another Member State in order to establish themselves there, or to provide services in that State, or to receive services there.

33. That interpretation is borne out, in particular, by Article 2(1) of the Directive, whereby 'Member States shall grant the persons referred to in Article 1 the right to leave their territory'; Article 3(1), whereby 'Member States shall grant to the persons referred to in Article 1 the right to enter their territory merely on production of a valid identity card or passport'; Article 4(1), whereby '[e]ach Member State shall grant the right of permanent residence to nationals of other Member States who establish themselves within its territory'; and Article 4(2) of the Directive, whereby, '[t]he right of residence for persons providing and receiving services shall be of equal duration with the period during which the services are provided'.

34. It is true that Article 1(1)(c) of the Directive extends to the spouses of the Member States' nationals referred to in subparagraphs (a) and (b) of that article the right to enter and reside in another Member State, irrespective of their nationality. But, in so far as the Directive aims to facilitate the exercise by Member States' nationals of freedom of establishment and freedom to provide services, the rights were accorded to their spouses so that they can accompany them when they exercise, in the circumstances provided for by the Directive, the rights which they derive from the Treaty by moving to or residing in a Member State other than their Member State of origin.

35. Therefore, it follows from both its objectives and its content that the Directive governs the conditions under which a national of a Member State, and the other persons covered by Article 1(1)(c) and (d), may leave that national's Member State of origin and enter and reside in another Member State, for one of the purposes set out in Article 1(1)(a) and (b), for a period specified in Article 4(1) or (2).

36. Since the Directive does not govern the right of residence of members of the family of a provider of services in his Member State of origin, the answer to the question referred to the Court therefore depends on whether, in circumstances such as those in the main proceedings, a right of residence in favour of the spouse may be inferred from the principles or other rules of Community law.

37. As has been held in paragraphs 29 and 30 of this judgment, Mr Carpenter is exercising the right freely to provide services guaranteed by Article 49 EC. The services provided by Mr Carpenter make up a significant proportion of his business, which is carried on both within his Member State of origin for the benefit of persons established in other Member States, and within those States.

38. In that context it should be remembered that the Community legislature has recognised the importance of ensuring the protection of the family life of nationals of the Member States in order to eliminate obstacles to the exercise of the fundamental freedoms guaranteed by the Treaty, as is particularly apparent from the provisions of the Council regulations and directives on the freedom of movement of employed and self-employed workers within the Community (see, for example, Article 10 of Council Regulation (EEC) No 1612/68 of 15 October 1968 on freedom of movement for workers within the Community (OJ, English Special Edition 1968 (II), p. 475); Articles 1 and 4 of Council Directive 68/360/EEC of 15 October 1968 on the abolition of restrictions on movement and residence within the Community for workers of Member States and their families (OJ, English Special Edition 1968 (II), p. 485), and Articles 1(1)(c) and 4 of the Directive).

39. It is clear that the separation of Mr and Mrs Carpenter would be detrimental to their family life and, therefore, to the conditions under which Mr Carpenter exercises a fundamental freedom. That freedom could not be fully effective if Mr Carpenter

were to be deterred from exercising it by obstacles raised in his country of origin to the entry and residence of his spouse (see, to that effect, Singh, cited above, paragraph 23).

40. A Member State may invoke reasons of public interest to justify a national measure which is likely to obstruct the exercise of the freedom to provide services only if that measure is compatible with the fundamental rights whose observance the Court ensures (see, to that effect, Case C-260/89 ERT [1991] ECR I-2925, paragraph 43, and Case C-368/95 Familiapress [1997] ECR I-3689, paragraph 24).

41. The decision to deport Mrs Carpenter constitutes an interference with the exercise by Mr Carpenter of his right to respect for his family life within the meaning of Article 8 of the Convention for the Protection of Human Rights and Fundamental Freedoms, signed at Rome on 4 November 1950 (hereinafter 'the Convention'), which is among the fundamental rights which, according to the Court's settled case-law, restated by the Preamble to the Single European Act and by Article 6(2) EU, are protected in Community law.

42. Even though no right of an alien to enter or to reside in a particular country is as such guaranteed by the Convention, the removal of a person from a country where close members of his family are living may amount to an infringement of the right to respect for family life as guaranteed by Article 8(1) of the Convention. Such an interference will infringe the Convention if it does not meet the requirements of paragraph 2 of that article, that is unless it is 'in accordance with the law', motivated by one or more of the legitimate aims under that paragraph and 'necessary in a democratic society', that is to say justified by a pressing social need and, in particular, proportionate to the legitimate aim pursued (see, in particular, Boultif v Switzerland, no. 54273/00, §§ 39, 41 and 46, ECHR 2001-IX).

43. A decision to deport Mrs Carpenter, taken in circumstances such as those in the main proceedings, does not strike a fair balance between the competing interests, that is, on the one hand, the right of Mr Carpenter to respect for his family life, and, on the other hand, the maintenance of public order and public safety.

44. Although, in the main proceedings, Mr Carpenter's spouse has infringed the immigration laws of the United Kingdom by not leaving the country prior to the expiry of her leave to remain as a visitor, her conduct, since her arrival in the United Kingdom in September 1994, has not been the subject of any other complaint that could give cause to fear that she might in the future constitute a danger to public order or public safety. Moreover, it is clear that Mr and Mrs Carpenter's marriage, which was celebrated in the United Kingdom in 1996, is genuine and that Mrs Carpenter continues to lead a true family life there, in particular by looking after her husband's children from a previous marriage.

45. In those circumstances, the decision to deport Mrs Carpenter constitutes an infringement which is not proportionate to the objective pursued.

46. In view of all the foregoing, the answer to the question referred to the Court is that Article 49 EC, read in the light of the fundamental right to respect for family life, is to be interpreted as precluding, in circumstances such as those in the main proceedings, a refusal, by the Member State of origin of a provider of services established in that Member State who provides services to recipients established in other Member States, of the right to reside in its territory to that provider's spouse, who is a national of a third country.

Costs

[Para. 47 omitted]

On those grounds,

THE COURT,

in answer to the question referred to it by the Immigration Appeal Tribunal by order of 16 December 1999, hereby rules:

> **Article 49 EC, read in the light of the fundamental right to respect for family life, is to be interpreted as precluding, in circumstances such as those in the main proceedings, a refusal, by the Member State of origin of a provider of services established in that Member State who provides services to recipients established in other Member States, of the right to reside in its territory to that provider's spouse, who is a national of a third country.**

Comments and questions

In Case C-60/00 *Carpenter* v *Home Secretary* [2002] ECR I-6279, Mrs Carpenter, who was a Philippine national, was to be deported from the United Kingdom where she did not have a residence permit. With a view to avoiding deportation, Mrs Carpenter argued that her right to residence was derived from the rights exercised by her British husband in providing services and travelling in other Member States. She argued that her husband had a right to carry on his business throughout the internal market without being subject to unlawful restrictions. Her deportation would either require Mr Carpenter to live with her in the Philippines or separate the members of the family unit if he remained in the United Kingdom. In both cases Mr Carpenter's business would be affected. Mrs Carpenter also argued that it could not be said that the restriction on the freedom to provide services, to which her husband would be subjected if she were deported, would be a purely internal matter, since he provided services throughout the internal market.

The CJEU agreed that Mrs Carpenter's husband's business was covered by the (now) TFEU provisions on freedom to provide services. However, this did not mean that Mrs Carpenter could derive a right of residence from this. Under Directive 73/148, on the abolition of restrictions on movement and residence within the Union for nationals of Member States with regard to establishment and the provision of services, spouses of Union citizens, regardless of nationality, have a right to accompany their spouses to another Member State, when that Union citizen exercises their rights under the rules on freedom to provide services; i.e. Union citizens' spouses only had a derived right to freedom of movement. Directive 73/148, which has since been repealed and replaced by Directive 2004/38, did not govern the right of residence of spouses of service providers in their home Member State. The CJEU therefore considered whether, in the case before it, it was possible to derive a right of residence for spouses on the basis of Union law principles or other Union laws. In this context the CJEU emphasised that Union legislator recognised the importance of ensuring the protection of the family life of nationals of the Member States and eliminating obstacles to the exercise of the fundamental freedoms guaranteed by the TFEU. It was clear that the separation of Mr and Mrs Carpenter would be detrimental to their family life and thus to the conditions under which Mr Carpenter exercised the fundamental freedom to provide cross-border services.

In other words, the deportation of Mrs Carpenter would restrict Mr Carpenter's scope for providing services in other Member States. However, the United Kingdom argued that the deportation was justified on the grounds of public order or public safety. There is no doubt that public order or public safety are lawful considerations. However, the measures to attain these must be proportionate. The CJEU held that the deportation of Mrs Carpenter did not represent a reasonable balance between Mr Carpenter's right to respect for his family life within the meaning of Article 8 of the Convention for the Protection of Human Rights and Fundamental Freedoms on the one hand, and consideration for public order or public safety on the other hand. In other words, the deportation of Mrs Carpenter infringed Mr Carpenter's Treaty-based rights to provide services to other Member States.

To what extent do you think the decision in the *Carpenter* case falls within the natural scope of the TFEU provisions on freedom to provide services? Note that in the case the CJEU considered the right to family life within the meaning of Article 8 of the Convention for the Protection of Human Rights. Do you think it is natural to involve a fundamental human right, such as the right to family life, in the interpretation of TFEU rules on the freedom to provide services? Do you agree, in principle, that the deportation of a national of a third state, who does not have a right of residence in a Member State, but who is married to a Union citizen who is resident in his own State, can conflict with that Union citizen's right of freedom to provide services? To what extent do you think this judgment accords with the practice of the CJEU in other decisions on the provision of services, and to what extent do you find this judgment reflects 'judicial activism'?

In other cases the CJEU has also allowed a Union citizen, who is resident in his State of origin, the right to rely on the TFEU rules on freedom of movement in cases against his State of origin. Among other things, the CJEU has allowed nationals of third countries, who are married to such Union citizens, to claim a right of residence to be derived from Union law when the Union citizen has exercised his or her right of freedom of movement. See, for example Case C-109/01 *Home Secretary* v *Akrich* [2003] ECR I-9607, printed above in Chapter 3. Consider whether the *Carpenter* case is in line with the CJEU's more recent decisions on secondary movement, including Case C-457/12 *S*, printed in Chapter 4 above, or whether the *Carpenter* decision differs from this practice.

JUDGMENT OF THE COURT (First Chamber)
22 December 2010

Omalet NV v Rijksdienst voor Sociale Zekerheid. (Reference for a preliminary ruling from the Arbeidshof te Brussel – Belgium)

'Freedom to provide services – Article 49 EC – Contractor established in a Member State – Recourse to contracting partners established in the same Member State – Purely internal situation – Inadmissibility of the reference for a preliminary ruling'

Case C-245/09

Judgment

1. This reference for a preliminary ruling concerns the applicability and interpretation of Article 49 EC.

2. The reference has been made in the course of proceedings between Omalet NV ('Omalet') and the Rijksdienst voor Sociale Zekerheid (National Social Security Office) ('the Rijksdienst') concerning, firstly, Omalet's joint and several liability, in its capacity as principal contractor, for part of the social security debts of an unregistered subcontractor established in Belgium, and, secondly, Omalet's obligation to withhold payments to that subcontractor.

Legal context

3. Article 30a of the Law of 27 June 1969 revising the Decree-Law of 28 December 1944 on social security for workers, in the version applicable at the material time in the main proceedings ('the Law of 1969'), stated as follows:
'...

   3. A principal who, for work covered by paragraph (1), has recourse to a contractor who is unregistered at the time the contract is concluded, shall be jointly and severally liable for the payment of that contractor's social security debts.

   A contractor who, for work covered by paragraph (1), has recourse to a subcontractor who is unregistered at the time the contract is concluded, shall be jointly and severally liable for the payment of that subcontractor's social security debts.

   ...

Joint and several liability shall be limited to 50% of the total price, excluding value added tax, of the work commissioned from an unregistered contractor or subcontractor.

...

4. A principal who pays a contractor who is unregistered at the time of payment for all or part of the cost of work covered by paragraph (1) must, at the time of payment, withhold 15% of the sum invoiced, excluding value added tax, and pay that amount to [the Rijksdienst], in accordance with the detailed rules laid down by the King.

   A contractor who pays a subcontractor for all or part of the cost of work covered by paragraph (1) must, at the time of payment, withhold 35% of the sum invoiced, excluding value added tax, and pay that amount to [the Rijksdienst], in accordance with the detailed rules laid down by the King.

   The contractor is, however, excused from the obligation to withhold and pay laid down in the previous subparagraph, if, at the time of payment, in accordance with the detailed rules laid down by the King, the subcontractor does not owe debts to [the Rijksdienst] or to a subsistence fund or has obtained for the sums due deadlines for payment, without legal proceedings or by a judicial decision with the authority of res judicata, and strictly adheres to those deadlines and is registered as a contractor. To that end, [the Rijksdienst] shall create a database accessible to the public, which has the weight of evidence for the application of this subparagraph.

   Where a contractor is an employer not established in Belgium, who does not have any social security debts in Belgium and all of whose employees are in the possession of a valid posting certificate, the withholding provisions in this paragraph are not applicable to the payment owed to that contractor'.

The dispute in the main proceedings and the questions referred for a preliminary ruling

4. Omalet, in its capacity as a project developer, had recourse to a subcontractor established but unregistered in Belgium. The subcontractor drew up two invoices, the first on 2 April 2003 for a sum of EUR 4 136.10, and the second on 29 April 2003 for a sum of EUR 4 493.69. Both invoices were paid.

5. The subcontractor was declared insolvent on 25 September 2003 and at that time owed EUR 57 593.87 to the Rijksdienst. Pursuant to Article 30a(3) of the Law of 1969, the Rijksdienst sought payment from Omalet of the sum of EUR 4 314.90 on the basis that it was jointly and severally liable for the social security debts of the subcontractor, limited to 50% of the total price of the work. Pursuant to Article

30a(4) of that law, payment of a further sum of EUR 6 040.85 was sought on the ground that Omalet had failed to make the deduction required under that article.

6. Having failed to reach an amicable settlement, the Rijksdienst, by summons issued on 25 April 2007, requested Omalet to appear before the Arbeidsrechtbank te Brussel (Brussels Labour Court). By a ruling of 25 April 2008, that court held that the Rijksdienst's claim was well founded and ordered Omalet to pay the sum of EUR 10 355.75, together with statutory late payment interest from 1 February 2006 and interest relating to the judicial proceedings.

7. By an application of 23 May 2008, Omalet appealed against that ruling before the Arbeidshof te Brussel (Brussels Higher Labour Court), claiming, inter alia, that Article 30a of the Law of 1969 was incompatible with Articles 49 EC and 50 EC.

8. In those circumstances, the Arbeidshof te Brussel decided to stay the proceedings and refer the following questions to the Court for a preliminary ruling:

   (1) Must a national court apply Article 49 EC to a dispute between [the Rijksdienst] and a principal contractor established in Belgium, where judgment is sought against that principal contractor pursuant to Article 30a(3) of [the Law of 1969] (in the version applicable prior to the amendment of that article by Article 55 of the Programme Law of 27 April 2007) as being jointly and severally liable for a portion of the debts of a subcontractor who is unregistered and established in Belgium, or where judgment is sought against that principal contractor because he has not complied with the withholding obligation laid down by Article 30(4) of the Law of 1969?

   (2) In the alternative, is Article 49 EC incompatible with a rule such as that laid down by Article 30a(3) and (4) of [the Law of 1969] (in the version applicable prior to the amendment of that article by Article 55 of the Programme Law of 27 April 2007)?

The Court's jurisdiction

9. The reference for a preliminary ruling concerns the interpretation of the provisions of the EC Treaty relating to the freedom to provide services in a situation in which, as the referring court itself points out, all of the facts of the dispute in the main proceedings are confined within a single Member State.

10. In those circumstances, the Court must assess whether it has jurisdiction to rule on the interpretation of those provisions (see, to that effect, Case C-380/05 *Centro Europa 7* [2008] ECR I-349, paragraph 64, and Case C-384/08 *Attanasio Group* [2010] ECR I-0000, paragraph 22).

11. The Court has declined jurisdiction where it was obvious that the provision of European Union law referred to the Court for interpretation was incapable of applying (Case C-567/07 *Woningstichting Sint Servatius* [2009] ECR I-9021, paragraph 43).

12. It is settled case-law that the Treaty provisions relating to the freedom to provide services do not apply to situations where all the relevant facts are confined within a single Member State (see, inter alia, Case C-108/98 *RI.SAN* [1999] ECR I-5219, paragraph 23, and Case C-97/98 *Jägerskiöld* [1999] ECR I-7319, paragraph 42).

13. In the present case, it is clear from the case-file submitted to the Court that all the facts relating to the dispute in the main proceedings are indeed confined within a single Member State, in that both the principal contractor and the subcontractor are established in Belgium and all of the facts took place within that Member State.

14. It is therefore clear that the dispute in the main proceedings does not present any link to the situations envisaged by Article 49 EC, and so that provision does not apply.

15. It is true that, according to the Court's case-law, even in such a purely internal situation, the Court's answer may nevertheless be useful to the referring court, in particular if its national law required it to grant the same rights to a national of a given Member State as those which a national of another Member State in the same situation would derive from European Union law (see, inter alia, Case C-448/98 *Guimont* [2000] ECR I-10663, paragraph 23; Case C-451/03 *Servizi Ausiliari Dottori Commercialisti* [2006] ECR I-2941, paragraph 29; Joined Cases C-94/04 and C-202/04 *Cipolla and Others* [2006] ECR I-11421, paragraph 30; and Joined Cases C-570/07 and C-571/07 *Blanco Pérez and Chao Gómez* [2010] ECR I-0000, paragraph 36).

16. However, that does not apply in the present case. In its reference for a preliminary ruling, the referring court itself cited a judgment of the Grondwettelijk Hof (Constitutional Court) in which that court found that Article 49 EC did not apply where the case pending before the court was situated entirely within the domestic legal system. In answer to the question of whether Article 30a(1) of the Law of 1969 was incompatible with the principles of equality and non-discrimination enshrined by the Belgian Constitution in that it envisaged different treatment as between, on the one hand, principals and developers established in Belgium and having recourse to foreign contracting parties unregistered in Belgium, who can rely on Articles 49 and 50 EC, and, on the other, those having recourse to service providers established in Belgium, who cannot rely on those provisions, that court found that situations relating exclusively to the domestic legal system could not be compared with those falling within the jurisdiction of European Union law.

17. Consequently, it does not appear from the reference for a preliminary ruling that, in circumstances such as those of the dispute in the main proceedings, the referring court has a duty to grant undertakings established in Belgium the same rights that undertakings established in other Member States in the same situation would derive from European Union law.

18. Accordingly, in circumstances such as those of the dispute in the main proceedings, where all of the facts are confined within the Member State in question, the Court does not have jurisdiction to answer the questions referred for a preliminary ruling by the Arbeidshof te Brussel.

19. Therefore, the request for a preliminary ruling submitted by the Arbeidshof te Brussel must be regarded as inadmissible.

Costs

[Para. 20 omitted]

On those grounds,

THE COURT (First Chamber),

hereby rules:

> **The reference for a preliminary ruling from the Arbeidshof te Brussel (Belgium), made by decision of 25 June 2009, is inadmissible.**

Comments and questions

According to the established practice of the CJEU, the TFEU provisions on free movement do not generally apply where all the elements of a case exclusively relate to the territory of a single Member State. In such cases there is a 'purely internal situation'. However, the CJEU has not always been consistent in its practice, as in some circumstances it has nevertheless applied the provisions on freedom of movement to cases in which the cross-border element has been very slight, if indeed it has existed at all. See, for example, the *Carpenter* case printed above.

Some Advocates General have encouraged the CJEU to abandon the requirement for there to be a cross-border element and to apply the Treaty provisions on freedom of movement even to cases where there is a purely internal situation. It can be seen from the judgment in the *Omalet* case that the CJEU was not yet ready to take such a significant step. However, see now the *Venturini* case printed above in Chapter 5.

In the *Omalet* case the CJEU had to decide whether Article 56 TFEU on the freedom to provide services could apply in a case in which there were no cross-border elements.

The case concerned a Belgian principal contractor who had entered into an agreement under Belgian law with a subcontractor established in Belgium for carrying out building works in Belgium. The Belgian principal contractor wanted to challenge Belgian legislation on the principal contractor's joint and several liability and obligation to withhold payments to subcontractors in relation to that contractor's social security debts.

As can be seen from the judgment, the CJEU started by noting that: 'The reference for a preliminary ruling concerns the interpretation of the provisions of the [TFEU] relating to the freedom to provide services in a situation in which, as the referring court itself points out, all of the facts of the dispute in the main proceedings are confined within a single Member State. In those circumstances, the Court must assess whether it has jurisdiction to rule on the interpretation of those provisions'. And in connection with this, the CJEU remarked that: 'The Court has declined jurisdiction where it was obvious that the provision of European Union law referred to the Court for interpretation was incapable of applying'. The CJEU then stated: 'It is settled case-law that the Treaty provisions relating to the freedom to provide services do not apply to situations where all the relevant facts are confined within a single Member State'.

The CJEU then ruled that: 'In the present case, it is clear from the case-file submitted to the Court that all the facts relating to the dispute in the main proceedings are indeed confined within a single Member State, in that both the principal contractor and the subcontractor are established in Belgium and all of the facts took place within that Member State'. Thus, the CJEU concluded that the case contained no elements linking it to Article 56 TFEU, and that this provision therefore did not apply.

The CJEU went on to remark that, under special circumstances, it is competent to give preliminary rulings on the interpretation of the Treaty provisions even when there is a purely internal situation. When is this possible (see in particular, paragraph 15)?

JUDGMENT OF THE COURT (Fifth Chamber)
4 May 1993Discriminatory barriers

Federación de Distribuidores Cinematográficos v Estado Español et
Unión de Productores de Cine y Televisión.
(Reference for a preliminary ruling: Tribunal Supremo – Spain)

'National rules intended to promote the distribution of national films'

Case C-17/92

Judgment

1. By order of 12 December 1991, which was received at the Court Registry on 22 January 1992, the Tribunal Supremo, Sala Tercera de lo Contencioso-Administrativo (Supreme Court, Third Chamber for Contentious Administrative Proceedings, hereinafter 'the Tribunal Supremo') referred to the Court for a preliminary ruling under Article 177 of the EEC Treaty a question on the interpretation of the provisions of the Treaty for the purpose of determining the compatibility with Community law of national rules making the grant of licences to dub films from third countries with a view to their distribution in Spain in a version dubbed into one of the official languages of Spain, subject to a prior contractual undertaking by the distributor applying for the licence to distribute a Spanish film.

2. That question was raised in the course of administrative proceedings brought by the Federación de Distribuidores Cinematográficos (hereinafter 'Fedicine'), an association governed by Spanish law, for the annulment of the sole article of the Real Decreto Legislativo 1257/1986 of 13 June 1986, issued so as to adapt the Law of 27 April 1946 and the Law 3/1980 of 10 January 1980 to the rules of Community law in pursuance of the enabling legislation contained in the Enabling Law of 27 December 1986 (*Boletin Oficial del Estado* No 153 of 27 June 1986, p. 23427) (hereinafter 'the Decree-Law').

3. That sole article, which came into force on 1 July 1986, is worded as follows:

   '1. Legally constituted distribution undertakings may freely distribute films produced in the Community.

   2. The said undertakings shall also be entitled to a maximum of four licences for dubbing films originating in third countries into one of the official languages of Spain for each Spanish film for which they show that they have concluded a distribution contract in the following circumstances:

(a) the first licence shall be granted when the Instituto de Cinematografía y de las Artes Audiovisuales (Cinema and Audiovisual Arts Institute) has been informed of the commencement of filming of a Spanish film for which the distributor applying for the licence has previously signed a contract. That licence shall be automatically cancelled if the film is not presented for approval within 200 days following the commencement of filming. The Instituto de la Cinematografía y de las Artes Audiovisuales may extend that period where the persons concerned show good cause;

(b) the second, third and fourth licences shall be granted upon its being demonstrated that the said film has realized gross takings of PTA 30, 60 and 100 million respectively.

3. The distribution in dubbed version of a film originating in a third country shall require the prior grant of a licence for that purpose.'

4. Fedicine claimed before the national court that the Decree-Law was a protectionist, restrictive and discriminatory measure contrary to Articles 30 to 36, 59 and 92 of the EEC Treaty, to Council Directive 63/607/EEC of 15 October 1963 implementing in respect of the film industry the provisions of the General Programme for the abolition of restrictions on freedom to provide services (OJ, English Special Edition 1963-1964, p. 52) (hereinafter 'the General Programme'), to the Second Council Directive 65/264/EEC of 13 May 1965 implementing in respect of the film industry the provisions of the General Programme for the abolition of restrictions on freedom of establishment and freedom to provide services (OJ, English Special Edition 1965-1966, p. 62) (hereinafter 'the Second Directive') and to the General Agreement on Tariffs and Trade (GATT).

5. The Tribunal Supremo took the view that, as a problem concerning the interpretation of Community law had been raised before it and as it was sitting in first and last instance, it was obliged to refer a question to the Court for a preliminary ruling.

6. The question was worded as follows: 'Is a measure making the grant of licences to dub films from non-member countries, with a view to their distribution in Spain in a version dubbed into one of the official languages of Spain, subject to a prior contractual undertaking by the distributor applying for the licence to distribute a Spanish film compatible with Community law?'.

7. Reference is made to the Report of the Judge-Rapporteur for a fuller account of the facts, the procedure and the written observations of the parties, which are mentioned or discussed hereinafter only in so far as is necessary for the reasoning of the Court.

8. It is appropriate to point out at the outset that in the context of Article 177 of the EEC Treaty the Court has no jurisdiction to decide either as to the interpretation of the provisions of national laws or regulations or their conformity with Community law. It may however supply the national court with a ruling on the interpretation of Community law to enable that court to resolve the legal problem before it. It may be seen from the file that, by the question referred to the Court, the national court seeks to ascertain whether the rules of the Treaty on the freedom to provide services and the free movement of goods must be interpreted as precluding national rules which reserve the grant of licences for dubbing films from third countries into one of the official national languages to distributors who undertake to distribute national films.

The applicable provisions of Community law

9. First it is appropriate to determine which provisions of the Treaty relate to the distribution of films.

10. It follows from the judgment in Case 262/81 *Coditel* v *Ciné-Vog Films* ([1982] ECR 3381, paragraph 11) that the exploitation of films in a cinema or on television implies that the author may make any public projection of the work subject to his authorization and that the commercial exploitation of films by such means, which involves the grant of performing licences, is an activity which comes under the freedom to provide services.

11. That service is in particular one which producers of films provide to distributors by allowing them to make copies of their films and to organize public performances by means of such copies. When the producers and distributors are not established in one and the same Member State, that service is of a trans-frontier nature. Finally, since it is common ground that the distributors pay back to the producers a part of their box-office takings, that service is also provided for remuneration within the meaning of Article 60 of the Treaty.

12. It follows that the problems raised by the national court must be considered from the angle of Article 59 of the Treaty.

The freedom to provide services

13. As regards Article 59, the Court has consistently held (see, in particular, the judgments in Case C-288/89 *Collectieve Antennevoorziening Gouda* [1991] ECR I-4007, paragraph 10, and in Case C-353/89 *Commission* v *Netherlands* [1991] ECR I-4069, paragraph 14) that freedom to provide services entails in particular the abolition of any discrimination against the person providing services on account of his nationality or the fact that he is established in a Member State other than that in which the service is to be provided.

14. In that respect it should be pointed out that, by linking the grant of licences for dubbing films from third countries to the filming and distribution of Spanish films, the Decree-Law is granting an advantage to the producers of such films in comparison with producers established in other Member States who wish to distribute their films in Spain.

15. It appears from the information furnished by the Commission that Spanish public preference as regards the cinema is to a very large extent for films from third countries, in particular those from the United States of America when they are dubbed into one of the official languages of Spain. However, the Decree-Law links the grant of licences for dubbing such films to the obligation to distribute a Spanish film. It thus accords preferential treatment to the producers of national films in comparison with producers established in other Member States, since the former have a guarantee that their films will be distributed and that they will receive the corresponding receipts, whereas the latter are dependent solely on the choice of the Spanish distributors. That obligation therefore has the effect of protecting undertakings producing Spanish films and by the same token places undertakings of the same type established in other Member States at a disadvantage. Since the producers of films from other Member States are thus deprived of the advantage granted to the producers of Spanish films, that restriction is of a discriminatory nature.

16. As the Court has stated in its judgments in Case 352/85 *Bond van Adverteerders* v *Netherlands State* ([1988] ECR 2085, paragraphs 32 to 34) and in *Collectieve Antennevoorziening Gouda* (paragraph 10) and *Commission* v *Netherlands* (paragraph 15), previously cited, national rules which are not applicable to services without distinction whatever their origin are compatible with Community law only if they can be brought within the scope of an express derogation such as Article 56 of the Treaty, to which Article 66 refers. It may also be seen from those judgments that objectives of an economic nature cannot constitute grounds of public policy within the meaning of that article.

17. There is no doubt that the Decree-Law pursues such an economic objective since by seeking to guarantee the distribution of a large number of national films it succeeds in ensuring sufficient receipts for the producers of such films.

18. However, the Spanish Government has contended that the Decree-Law pursued a cultural aim, namely that of protecting the national film industry.

19. That argument cannot be upheld.

20. Apart from the fact that cultural policy is not one of the justifications set out in Article 56, it is important to note that the Decree-Law promotes the distribution of national films whatever their content or quality.

21. In those circumstances, the link between the grant of licences for dubbing films from third countries and the distribution of national films pursues an objective of a purely economic nature which does not constitute a ground of public policy within the meaning of Article 56 of the Treaty.

22. The answer to the national court's question must therefore be that the provisions of the Treaty concerning freedom to provide services must be interpreted as precluding national rules which reserve the grant of licences for dubbing films from third countries into one of the official national languages to distributors who undertake to distribute national films.

Costs

[Para. 23 omitted]

On those grounds,

THE COURT (Fifth Chamber),

in answer to the question referred to it by the Tribunal Supremo by order of 12 December 1991, hereby rules:

> **The provisions of the Treaty concerning freedom to provide services must be interpreted as precluding national rules which reserve the grant of licences for dubbing films from third countries into one of the official national languages to distributors who undertake to distribute national films.**

Comments and questions

Discrimination in relation to the provision of services can be seen from three different angles:

- From the point of view of the nationality of the service provider,
- From the point of view of where the service is performed, and
- From the point of view of the nationality of the receiver of the service.

Case C-55/98 *Skatteministeriet* v *Vestergaard* [1999] ECR I-7641, printed below, and Case C-158/96 *Kohll* v *Union des caisses de maladie* [1998] ECR I-1931, printed above, are examples of cases where emphasis was put on where the service was provided, and they can therefore be seen as expressions of discrimination. Case C-204/90 *Bachmann* v *Belgium* [1992] ECR I-249, printed below, can both be seen as emphasising where the business of the service provider (an insurance company) was established, so that on this basis there was direct discrimination, or it can be seen as meaning that the disputed tax deduction rule will disadvantage migratory workers, without expressly having regard to their nationality, so that there is indirect discrimination. In this connection it is interesting to note that the CJEU allows the protection of overriding reasons in the general interest to justify measures which can also be regarded as directly discriminatory; cf. for example the *Bachmann* case.

In Case C-17/92 *Federación de Distribuidores Cinematográficos* v *Estado Español et Unión de Productores de Cine y Televisión* (the *Cinematográficos* case) [1993] ECR I-2239, the Spanish law, which was challenged, made a distinction between Spanish films and films from third countries. Attention was expressly paid to the origin of films so that, according to its own wording, the law was directly discriminatory on this point. This meant that the Spanish Government could only justify the provisions if they could be brought within the scope of an express derogation such as Article 52 TFEU (formerly Article 56 EEC Treaty), as referred to by Article 62 TFEU (formerly Article 66 EEC Treaty),; cf. paragraph 16. Would it have made a difference if instead the Spanish law had sought to achieve its aims by distinguishing between, on the one hand, films made in another Member State in one of Spain's official languages, and, on the other hand, films made in other languages? Note that the CJEU re-iterated that objectives of an economic nature cannot constitute grounds of public policy within the meaning of Article 52 TFEU. Is this interpretation of Article 52 TFEU justified? Can there be conceivable situations in which this interpretation ought to be varied? The Spanish Government sought to justify the measure on the basis of consideration for 'cultural policy'. Why did the CJEU dismiss this argument?

In his Opinion, Advocate General Van Gerven argued that, at the relevant time, the roll of film, on which a cinematographic work is recorded, undoubtedly constitutes a 'good'. In this connection he referred to the judgment of the CJEU in Joined Cases 60 and 61/84 *Cinéthèque SA and others* v *Fédération nationale des cinémas français* [1985] ECR 2605, in which the manufacture of video-cassettes was not regarded as the provision of a service, but as the production of goods. The Advocate General also noted that, for the import of a film to a Member State, it was (then) necessary for at least one physical copy of it to be imported. Nevertheless, the Advocate General concluded that a cinematographic work is bound by the rules on the provision of services. He referred to the fact that the core business of exploiting a cinematographic work does not consist of trading in rolls of film, but rather the transfer of the right to present public performances in a given geographical market. Consider whether the hiring out of video films and the sale of video films respectively are covered by the rules on goods or services.

The Norwegian Film Institute undertook to pay DKK 2 million towards the production of the Danish television series *1864*. However, among other things this support was conditional on a minimum number of Norwegians being involved in the project. When the Danish producer of the series decided to replace the Norwegian composer, the Norwegian Film Institute's offer of support was withdrawn. Norway is not a member of the EU, but many of the EU rules on freedom of movement apply in Norway by virtue of Norway's membership of the European Economic Area (EEA). Do the conditions for the financial support from Norway give rise to problems, assuming that the situation is covered by the same rules as apply within the EU?

JUDGMENT OF THE COURT (Second Chamber)
29 April 1999

Erich Ciola v Land Vorarlberg.
(Reference for a preliminary ruling: Verwaltungsgerichtshof – Austria)

'Free movement of services – Restriction – Moorings –
Restriction for boat-owners resident in another Member State'

Case C-224/97

Judgment

1. By order of 26 May 1997, received at the Court Registry on 16 June 1997, the Verwaltungsgerichtshof (Administrative Court) referred to the Court for a preliminary ruling under Article 177 of the EC Treaty two questions on the interpretation of Articles 59 to 66 in conjunction with Article 5 of the EC Treaty and Article 2 of the Act concerning the conditions of accession of the Republic of Austria, the Republic of Finland and the Kingdom of Sweden and the adjustments to the Treaties on which the European Union is founded (OJ 1994 C 241, p. 21, and OJ 1995 L 1, p. 1, hereinafter 'the Act of Accession').

2. Those questions were raised in proceedings brought by Mr Ciola against fines imposed on him for exceeding the maximum quota of moorings on the shore of Lake Constance reserved for boats whose owners are resident abroad.

3. Mr Ciola is the manager *inter alia* of ABC-Boots-Charter GmbH. In 1990 that company leased certain land on the shore of Lake Constance. It obtained permission to establish 200 moorings for pleasure boats there.

4. At the company's request, the Bezirkshauptmannschaft Bregenz (the administrative authority of first instance of the *Land* of Vorarlberg) addressed to it on 9 August 1990 an individual administrative decision (*Bescheid*), point 2 of which stated:

   'With effect from 1 January 1996 a maximum of 60 boats whose owners are resident abroad may be accommodated in the harbour. Until that time the proportion of boats owned by persons resident abroad is to be progressively reduced. No new allocation of moorings to boat-owners resident abroad or extension of expired rental contracts with such owners is permitted until the maximum foreigner quota has been reached ...'.

5. Under the first sentence of Paragraph 4(1) of the Landschaftsschutzgesetz (Countryside Protection Law) of the *Land* of Vorarlberg, any alteration to the landscape in

lake areas and in a 500-metre-wide strip of shore adjacent thereto, calculated at mean water level, is prohibited.

6. However, Paragraph 4(2) allows the administrative authority to authorise exceptions to that prohibition if there is a guarantee that such alterations will not harm the interests of landscape protection, in particular that they will not obstruct views of the lake, or if the alterations are necessary for reasons of public safety.

7. By decision of 10 July 1996 the Unabhängiger Verwaltungssenat (Independent Administrative Senate) of the *Land* of Vorarlberg found Mr Ciola, in his capacity as manager of the aforesaid company, guilty of renting two moorings to boat-owners who were resident abroad, namely in the Principality of Liechtenstein and the Federal Republic of Germany, even though the maximum quota of 60 moorings reserved for foreigners had already been exceeded.

8. Consequently, as Mr Ciola had failed to comply with the conditions of point 2 of the administrative decision of 9 August 1990 and had therefore committed an administrative offence within the meaning of Paragraph 34(1)(f) of the Landschaftsschutzgesetz, he was fined ATS 75 000 for each of the two offences.

9. Since it considered that Mr Ciola's appeal against the fines raised questions concerning the interpretation of Community law, the Verwaltungsgerichtshof stayed proceedings and referred the following two questions to the Court:

   '1. Are the provisions concerning the freedom to provide services to be interpreted as precluding a Member State from prohibiting the operator of a boat harbour, on pain of criminal prosecution, from renting more than a specific quota of moorings to boat-owners who are resident in another Member State?

   2. Does Community law, in particular the provisions concerning the freedom to provide services in conjunction with Article 5 of the EC Treaty and Article 2 of the Act concerning the conditions of accession of the Republic of Austria, the Republic of Finland and the Kingdom of Sweden and the adjustments to the Treaties on which the European Union is founded (OJ 1994 C 241, p. 21; OJ 1995 L 1, p. 1), give the provider of the services referred to in Question 1 above, who is resident in Austria, the right to assert that the prohibition issued in the terms set out in Question 1 by a specific individual administrative decision (*Bescheid*) adopted in 1990 should not be applied in decisions of the Austrian courts and administrative authorities adopted after 1 January 1995?'

Question 1

10. By its first question, the national court essentially asks whether the Treaty provisions on freedom to provide services are to be interpreted as precluding a Member

State from establishing a maximum quota of moorings which may be rented to boat-owners resident in another Member State.

11. It should be observed at the outset that, as the national court has pointed out, first, the right freely to provide services may be relied on by an undertaking as against the State in which it is established if the services are provided for persons established in another Member State (Case C-70/95 *Sodemare and Others* v *Regione Lombardia* [1997] ECR I-3395, paragraph 37) and, second, in accordance with Joined Cases 286/82 and 26/83 *Luisi and Carbone* v *Ministero del Tesoro* [1984] ECR 377, paragraph 16, and Case 186/87 *Cowan* v *Trésor Public* [1989] ECR 195, paragraph 15, that right includes the freedom for recipients of services to go to another Member State in order to receive a service there, without being obstructed by restrictions.

12. Consequently, Articles 59 to 66 of the Treaty apply to a service such as that which the company of which Mr Ciola is manager provides, by means of a contract for the rental of a mooring, to a boat-owner resident in another Member State who receives and enjoys the service in a Member State other than that in which he resides.

13. In those circumstances, a restriction on moorings of the kind at issue in the main proceedings infringes the prohibition under the first paragraph of Article 59 of the Treaty of all discrimination, even indirect, with regard to providers of services.

14. While the restriction of the number of moorings which may be allocated to non-resident boat-owners is not based on their nationality, and so may not be regarded as direct discrimination, it does, however, use as the distinguishing criterion their place of residence. It is settled case-law that national rules under which a distinction is drawn on the basis of residence are liable to operate mainly to the detriment of nationals of other Member States, as non-residents are in the majority of cases foreigners (see Case C-350/96 *Clean Car Autoservice* v *Landeshauptmann von Wien* [1998] ECR I-2521, paragraph 29).

15. To justify imposing a quota on moorings reserved for nationals of other Member States on mandatory grounds in the general interest, the *Land* of Vorarlberg relied at the hearing on the need to reserve access to the moorings for local boat-owners, as there is a risk of such moorings being monopolised by persons resident in other Member States and willing to pay higher rental charges. Because of the limitation of the total number of moorings available, for reasons concerning protection of the environment, lifting the quota would increase the pressure on the authorities of the *Land* of Vorarlberg.

16. National rules which are not applicable to services without distinction whatever the place of residence of the recipient, and which are therefore discriminatory, are compatible with Community law only if they can be brought within the scope of an

express derogation, such as Article 56 of the EC Treaty (see Case 352/85 *Bond van Adverteerders and Others* v *Netherlands State* [1988] ECR 2085, paragraph 32); however, economic aims cannot constitute grounds of public policy within the meaning of that provision (Case C-288/89 *Collectieve Antennevoorziening Gouda* v *Commissariaat voor de Media* [1991] ECR I-4007, paragraph 11).

17. Since the *Land* of Vorarlberg has justified the imposition of a quota on moorings for non-resident owners not on grounds of public policy, public security or public health, but for economic reasons for the benefit of local owners, Article 56 of the Treaty cannot be applied; in those circumstances, it must be ascertained whether the existence of an exception in the Act of Accession authorised the *Land* of Vorarlberg to take measures such as the quota at issue in the main proceedings in order to limit the influx of boat-owners from other Member States.

18. On this point, it suffices to note that Article 70 of the Act of Accession lays down an express derogation, for a limited time, only for existing legislation regarding secondary residences.

19. Consequently, the establishment by a Member State of a maximum quota for moorings which may be rented to boat-owners resident in another Member State is contrary to the principle of freedom to provide services.

20. The answer to Question 1 must therefore be that Article 59 of the Treaty is to be interpreted as precluding a Member State from prohibiting the manager of a boat harbour, on pain of prosecution, from renting moorings in excess of a specified quota to boat-owners who are resident in other Member States.

Question 2

[Paras 21-34 omitted]

Costs

[Para. 35 omitted]

On those grounds,

THE COURT (Second Chamber),

in answer to the questions referred to it by the Verwaltungsgerichtshof by order of 26 May 1997, hereby rules:

1. **Article 59 of the EC Treaty must be interpreted as precluding a Member State from prohibiting the manager of a boat harbour, on pain of prosecu-**

tion, from renting moorings in excess of a specified quota to boat-owners who are resident in other Member States.

2. **A prohibition which is contrary to the freedom to provide services, laid down before the accession of a Member State to the European Union not by a general abstract rule but by a specific individual administrative decision that has become final, must be disregarded when assessing the validity of a fine imposed for failure to comply with that prohibition after the date of accession.**

Comments and questions

Case C-224/97 *Ciola* v *Land Vorarlberg* [1999] ECR I-2517, concerned Mr Ciola who as the manager of a marina obtained a permit to establish a number of moorings on Bodensee in Austria. A condition attached to this permit was that no more than 60 of the 200 moorings could be rented out to persons who were resident outside Austria. Ciola contravened this condition and was fined. In proceedings brought by Mr Ciola against fines imposed on him, the question whether the condition complied with Union law was referred to the CJEU. In this book the *Ciola* case is dealt with in the chapter dealing with service provision under the heading of 'Discrimination'. Do you agree with this categorisation?

The CJEU itself noted, in paragraph 14 of the judgment, that this was not a hindrance based on the nationality of the receivers of the service, so it could not be regarded as direct discrimination. However, in paragraph 16 the CJEU concluded that the Austrian authority's requirement that the moorings should be allocated according to residence was itself discriminatory. The CJEU also stated that such a discrimination could be compatible with Union law only if it could be brought within the scope of an express Treaty derogation. Since the disputed rule could not be brought within the scope of a derogation, (and since there was no provision in the Austrian Accession Treaty which could justify such a restriction), the CJEU found that the condition contravened the TFEU.

The CJEU's decision was closely in line with the arguments put forward by the Advocate General in his Opinion (in particular paragraphs 23 and 24 of the Opinion). The Advocate General himself substantially based his proposals on the decision in Case C-288/89 *Stichting Collectieve Antennevoorziening Gouda and others* v *Commissariaat voor de Media* [1991] ECR I-4007, (the *Gouda* case) in which the CJEU stated in paragraph 10 of the judgment 'that Article [56 TFEU] entails, in the first place, the abolition of any discrimination against a person providing services on account of his nationality or the fact that he is established in a Member State other than the one in which the service is provided.' In paragraph 10 of the *Gouda* case, the CJEU defined direct discrimination as being different treatment on the grounds of *the nationality of natural persons* or *the place of establishment of legal persons*. In the *Ciola* case the Advocate General, and subsequently the CJEU, apparently re-interpreted this requirement in relation to the place of establishment of legal persons as a 'residential requirement' for natural persons, so such a residence requirement was regarded as constituting direct discrimination. This must be considered as mistaken in relation to the CJEU's usual practice. Compare this with Case C-350/96 *Clean Car Autoservice* [1998] ECR I-2521, printed in Chapter 4, where the CJEU considered a residence requirement to be a restriction.

The *Ciola* case is included in this book to show that even the CJEU can make mistakes in distinguishing between discrimination and restriction. The case concerned a restriction (indirect discrimination) which was treated by the CJEU as direct discrimination. Note that the CJEU only consisted of a Chamber of three judges, which is the smallest number of judges who can decide a case.

Ciola was an Austrian national who was manager of a company set up in Austria to rent out moorings on Bodensee in Austria. The case therefore gave rise to the question as to whether it concerned a purely internal situation, so that Ciola should be denied the opportunity of relying on Article 56 TFEU (formerly Article 49 TEC) in challenging the decision of the Austrian administration. In paragraph 11 of the judgment the CJEU dismissed this idea, stating that under Article 56 TFEU, 'the right freely to provide services may be relied on by an undertaking as against the State in which it is established if the services are provided for persons established in another Member State.'

Finally, it should be noted that Mr Ciola claimed that there was discriminatory treatment which was not directed at him, but rather against the customers for his services.

Consider whether a campaign, wholly or partly financed by the Polish State, that is aimed at reducing energy consumption in order to tackle climate change, would be contrary to the freedom to provide services if, among its 13 specific measures, it contained the following: 'Do without a flight to Southern Europe and holiday in Poland instead'?

JUDGMENT OF THE COURT (Grand Chamber)
30 January 2007

Commission of the European Communities v Kingdom of Denmark

'Failure of a Member State to fulfil obligations – Freedom of movement for workers – Freedom to provide services – Free movement of capital – Freedom of establishment – Income tax – Pensions – Policy taken out with a pension institution in another Member State – Tax legislation – Limitation on the deductibility or exemption from taxable income of contributions paid into a pension scheme – Overriding reasons in the public interest – Effectiveness of supervision of taxation – Cohesion of the tax system – Symmetry of the tax system – Double taxation convention'

Case C-150/04

Judgment

1. By its application, the Commission of the European Communities seeks a declaration by the Court that, by introducing and maintaining in force a system for life assurance and pensions under which tax deductions and tax exemptions for payments are granted only for payments under contracts entered into with pension institutions established in Denmark, whereas no such tax relief is granted for payments made under contracts entered into with pension institutions established in other Member States ('the contested legislation'), the Kingdom of Denmark has failed to fulfil its obligations under Articles 39 EC, 43 EC, 49 EC and 56 EC.

Legal context

Community legislation

[Paras 2-27 omitted]

Pre-litigation procedure

28. In its letters of formal notice of 5 April 1991 and 31 July 1992 and its supplementary letter of formal notice of 11 April 2000, the Commission drew the attention of the Danish authorities to the incompatibility of certain national provisions, concerning the deductibility or exemption of contributions to pension schemes at the time of the calculation of taxable income, with Articles 39 EC, 43 EC, 49 EC and 56 EC.

29. Following the responses of the Danish Government of 12 March and 22 December 1992 and 29 June 2000, and, after having heard the arguments of the Danish authorities at the meetings on 4 November 1997 and 14 January 2000, the Commission

sent that government a reasoned opinion on 5 February 2003 claiming that, by retaining the contested legislation, the Kingdom of Denmark had failed to fulfil its obligations under those articles.

30. On 15 April 2003, in its response to the Commission's reasoned opinion, the Danish Government acknowledged that the legislation was liable to constitute an obstacle to freedom to provide services, freedom of movement for workers and freedom of establishment, but claimed that it would not constitute an obstacle to free movement of capital.

31. The Danish Government takes the view, however, that the restrictions on those freedoms are justified by overriding reasons in the public interest and the need to maintain the cohesion of the national tax system. According to that government, the national provisions on the taxation of pensions are symmetrical because a direct connection exists between the deductibility or exemption of contributions and the taxation of benefits provided.

32. Taking the view that the explanations provided by the Kingdom of Denmark in response to the reasoned opinion were not satisfactory, the Commission decided to bring the present action.

33. By order of the President of the Court of 19 November 2004, the Kingdom of Sweden was granted leave to intervene in support of the Kingdom of Denmark.

The action

The obstacles to the freedoms

34. It should be noted, at the outset, that, although direct taxation falls within their competence, Member States must none the less exercise that competence consistently with Community law (see, in particular, Case C-80/94 *Wielockx* [1995] ECR I-2493, paragraph 16; Case C-35/98 *Verkooijen* [2000] ECR I-4071, paragraph 32; and Case C-422/01 *Skandia and Ramstedt* [2003] ECR I-6817, paragraph 25).

35. It is necessary to consider whether the contested legislation is, as the Commission argues, an obstacle to freedom to provide services, freedom of movement for workers, free movement of capital and freedom of establishment. The Danish Government disputes only the existence of an obstacle to free movement of capital.

36. According to that government, the contested legislation places no direct restriction on cross-border capital transactions paid to or by foreign pension institutions. There are merely indirect limitations arising from the obstacles which that legislation may

constitute to freedom to provide services, freedom of movement for workers and freedom of establishment.

37. In that regard, first, it should be noted that the provision of insurance constitutes a service within the meaning of Article 50 EC and that Article 49 EC precludes the application of any national legislation which, without objective justification, impedes a provider of services from actually exercising the freedom to provide them (see, to that effect, Case C-118/96 *Safir* [1998] ECR I-1897, paragraph 22; Case C-136/00 *Danner* [2002] ECR I-8147, paragraphs 25 to 27; and *Skandia and Ramstedt*, paragraphs 22 to 24).

38. With reference to the single market and in order to permit the achievement of its objectives, Article 49 EC also precludes the application of any national rules which have the effect of making the provision of services between Member States more difficult than the provision of services purely within one Member State (see *Safir*, paragraph 23).

39. In the present case, in order for pension institutions established in other Member States to offer their services on the Danish market with the same tax advantages as those offered by pension institutions established in Denmark, they must have a branch office or a permanent establishment in that Member State.

40. With regard to Article 49 EC, two categories of situation in which such a requirement is liable to have a dissuasive effect must be distinguished. In the first, service providers are dissuaded from establishing themselves in Denmark because of the costs involved. Such a situation constitutes, of itself, a denial of that freedom (see, to that effect, Case C-496/01 *Commission* v *France* [2004] ECR I-2351, paragraph 65, and Case C-439/99 *Commission* v *Italy* [2002] ECR I-305, paragraph 30). In the second, the recipients of those services are dissuaded from becoming members of a pension scheme with a pension institution established in another Member State, in view of the important role played, at the time when a pension insurance contract is taken out, by the possibility of obtaining tax relief under that head (see *Danner*, paragraph 31).

41. Secondly, with regard to freedom of movement for workers, salaried workers who have carried on an occupation in a Member State other than the Kingdom of Denmark and who are subsequently employed, or seek employment, in the latter Member State will normally have concluded their pension and life assurance contracts or invalidity and sickness insurance contracts with insurers established in the first State. It follows that there is a risk that the provisions in question may operate to the particular detriment of these workers who are, as a general rule, nationals of other Member States (see, to that effect, Case C-204/90 *Bachmann* [1992] ECR I-249, paragraph 9, and Case C-300/90 *Commission* v *Belgium* [1992] ECR I-305, paragraph 7).

42. In the present case, the grant of a right to deduct or exempt contributions, provided that the pension scheme is taken out with a pension institution established in Denmark, is, because of the efforts and costs which it entails, liable to dissuade the insured person from transferring his place of residence to Denmark and, therefore, constitutes an obstacle to freedom of movement for workers.

43. Thirdly, for the same reasons as above, the view must be taken that the contested legislation also constitutes an obstacle to the freedom of establishment in Denmark of self-employed workers who are nationals of another Member State.

44. By not granting any right to deduct or exempt contributions paid to pension institutions established in other Member States, the contested legislation is liable to dissuade self-employed workers from establishing themselves in Denmark.

45. Having regard to the foregoing, it must be held that the contested legislation constitutes an obstacle to freedom to provide services, freedom of movement for workers and freedom of establishment.

46. According to well-established case-law, however, national measures which are liable to hinder the exercise of fundamental freedoms guaranteed by the EC Treaty or make them less attractive may nevertheless be allowed if they pursue a legitimate objective in the public interest, are appropriate to ensuring the attainment of that objective, and do not go beyond what is necessary to attain it (Case C-470/04 *N* [2006] ECR I-0000, paragraph 40).

47. Consequently, it is necessary to consider whether the obstacles found may be justified by overriding reasons in the public interest, on the one hand, as argued by the Danish Government, with the aim of maintaining the cohesion of the national tax system and, on the other, as argued by the Swedish Government, with the aim of ensuring the effectiveness of fiscal supervision and, as was argued in particular at the hearing, with that of preventing the risk of tax avoidance.

The justifications put forward

With regard to the effectiveness of supervision of the taxation and the prevention of tax avoidance

– *Arguments of the parties*

48. According to the Commission, other grounds in Directive 77/799, such as the requirement incumbent on the taxpayer to supply the proof required to assess whether the conditions for deductibility or exemption of contributions are met, are sufficient to ensure effective supervision of the taxation. That directive, like Council Directive 76/308/EEC of 15 March 1976 on mutual assistance for the recovery of claims re-

sulting from operations forming part of the system of financing the European Agricultural Guidance and Guarantee Fund, and of the agricultural levies and customs duties (OJ 1976 L 73, p. 18), as amended by Council Directive 2001/44/EC of 15 June 2001 (OJ 2001 L 175, p. 17), guarantees the recovery of income tax in other Member States.

49. At the hearing, the Danish Government submitted that although the scope of Directive 76/308, as amended by Directive 2001/44, was extended in 2001 to cover direct taxes, no new obligation is imposed on foreign pension institutions to retain the tax due from taxpayers resident in the Member State in question. Accordingly the conditions on the basis of which the Court delivered the judgment in *Bachmann* remain valid.

50. According to the Swedish Government, the effectiveness of Directive 77/799 is limited by the fact that it is the national laws of the Member States which determine what information they may hold and are required to furnish pursuant to that directive. In particular, as is clear from Article 8 of the Directive, a Member State is not obliged to furnish information which it has been asked to provide where it is prevented by its laws or administrative practices from carrying out enquiries or from collecting or using such information for its own purposes or where it relies on legislation on confidentiality.

– *Findings of the Court*

51. The Court has held that the prevention of tax avoidance (see Case C-264/96 *ICI* [1998] ECR I-4695, paragraph 26; Joined Cases C-397/98 and C-410/98 *Metallgesellschaft and Others* [2001] ECR I-1727, paragraph 57; and Case C-315/02 *Lenz* [2004] ECR I-7063, paragraph 27) and the effectiveness of fiscal supervision (see, Case C-436/00 *X and Y* [2002] ECR I-10829, paragraph 51, and Case C-334/02 *Commission* v *France* [2004] ECR I-2229, paragraphs 31 and 32) constitute overriding requirements of general interest capable of justifying legislation which restricts the exercise of fundamental freedoms guaranteed by the Treaty (see, to that effect, Case C-386/04 *Centro di Musicologia Walter Stauffer* [2006] ECR I-0000, paragraph 32).

52. In that connection, it should be recalled that Council Directive 77/799 enables a Member State to obtain from the competent authorities of another Member State all the information enabling it to determine the correct amount of income tax (see Case C-55/98 *Vestergaard* [1999] ECR I-7641, paragraph 26), or all the information it considers necessary to ascertain the correct amount of income tax payable by a taxpayer according to the legislation which it applies (see, to that effect, *Wielockx*, paragraph 26).

53. In the present case, the Danish authorities are in a position to check whether contributions have actually been paid by a taxpayer to an institution established in another Member State. Pursuant to Paragraph 11C(1) and (3) of Codified Law No 726 on supervision of the taxation (Bekendtgørelse af skattekontrolloven), of 13 August 2001 (*Lovtidende* 2001 A, p. 4620), persons who are members of a pension scheme abroad and who are fully taxable in Denmark are required to inform the tax administration thereof.

54. The fact that Article 8(1) of the Directive imposes no obligation on the tax authorities of Member States to collaborate where the conditions laid down in that provision are met cannot justify the lack of deductibility or exemption of contributions paid to pension schemes. There is nothing to prevent the Danish tax authorities from demanding from the person involved such proof as they consider necessary and, where appropriate, from refusing to allow deduction or exemption where such proof is not forthcoming (see, to that effect, *Bachmann*, paragraphs 18 and 20, and Case 300/90 *Commission* v *Belgium*, paragraphs 11 and 13).

55. It follows that the difficulties connected with the exchange of information in view of Directive 77/799, insofar as the latter does not permit effective verification of whether foreign pension schemes meet the conditions to which the contested legislation makes deductibility or exemption subject, do not justify the obstacles set out in paragraph 45 of the present judgment.

56. Clearly, too, the effectiveness of the supervision of the taxation of pensions paid to insured persons resident in Denmark may be ensured by means less restrictive on the freedom to provide services than the contested legislation, in particular by an obligation on taxpayers to provide documentary evidence when applying for a deduction or exemption.

57. It should be pointed out that, before receiving a pension provided by a scheme managed by a foreign pension institution, the taxpayer will normally have applied for deduction or exemption of the contributions relating thereto. The application for deduction or exemption and the documentary evidence provided by taxpayers at the time such applications are made will constitute in that regard a valuable source of information about the pensions which will be paid to taxpayers at a later stage.

58. Furthermore, it must be noted that the mere fact that a taxpayer makes contributions to a pension scheme taken out with an institution established outside Denmark cannot form the basis for a general presumption of tax avoidance or justify a fiscal measure which prejudices the enjoyment of a fundamental freedom guaranteed by the Treaty (see, to that effect, Case C-478/98 *Commission* v *Belgium* [2000] ECR I-7587, paragraph 45, and Case C-334/02 *Commission* v *France*, paragraph 27).

59. In the light of all the foregoing, the obstacles resulting from the contested legislation cannot be justified by the effectiveness of the supervision of taxation and the prevention of tax avoidance.

The cohesion of the tax system

– *Arguments of the parties*

60. With regard to the existence of the cohesion of the tax system, the Commission takes the view that that cohesion is maintained if two conditions are met. On the one hand, there should be a direct connection between deduction or exemption of contributions and taxation of benefits and, on the other, the contested legislation should provide for the possibility of granting deductibility or exemption of contributions paid to a pension scheme in another Member State except where the State of residence cannot tax the benefits provided by that scheme.

61. According to the Danish Government, as long as the contested legislation excludes taxation of benefits provided if the contributions were not deductible or exempt, it would be compatible with the Treaty to limit or exclude the possibility of deducting or exempting contributions paid to pension institutions established in other Member States. The Danish rules are symmetrical in that they do not tax benefits provided where they do not grant the right to deduct or exempt contributions paid, but tax those contributions where they do grant the right to deduct or exempt them. The cohesion of the tax system is also ensured at the level of a single taxpayer.

62. With regard to the need to ensure the cohesion of the tax system, the Commission takes the view that all pension schemes taken out with pension institutions established in other Member States should enjoy the same tax advantages as those taken out in Denmark. It is pertinent to take into account the need to ensure the cohesion of the tax system only in the event that the Kingdom of Denmark did not have the right to tax the benefits provided. The Commission adds that that Member State would lose the right to tax such benefits provided to the insured person resident in its territory, whether the pension scheme was taken out on its territory or abroad, only if that insured person transferred his residence to another Member State.

63. According to the Danish Government, the uncertainty surrounding the receipt of tax paid on benefits provided by foreign pension institutions is the determining factor justifying the need to ensure the cohesion of the tax system. On the transfer of residence of an insured person, the authorities in the Member State in question do not know at the time when contributions are being made whether the insured person will emigrate and it is also unknown, therefore, whether, pursuant to a double taxation convention, tax will be paid not in the Member State in which the contributions were made and in respect of which deductions or exemptions were granted, but in the new State of residence.

64. The Swedish Government states that the cohesion of the tax system requires that the tax authorities accept deductibility or exemption of contributions to pension schemes from taxable income only if they are certain that the capital paid by the pension institution on maturity of the pension scheme will actually be taxed.

– *Findings of the Court*

[Paras 65-69 omitted]

70. With regard to the justification of the cohesion of the tax system, it is established that the need to preserve such cohesion requires the existence of a direct link between a tax advantage and a corresponding disadvantage (see Case 300/90 *Commission* v *Belgium*, paragraph 14; Case C-484/93 *Svensson and Gustavsson* [1995] ECR I-3955, paragraph 18; *ICI*, paragraph 29; *Vestergaard*, paragraph 24; Case C-478/98 *Commission* v *Belgium*, paragraph 35; and *X and Y*, paragraph 52).

71. In that regard, the factor liable adversely to affect the cohesion of the Danish tax system is to be found in the fact that the transfer of the residence of the person concerned occurs between the time of payment of contributions to a pension scheme and that of payment of the corresponding benefits, and less in the fact that the pension institution is in another Member State.

72. When a Danish resident, having become a member of a pension scheme with an institution established in Denmark, receives tax advantages on the contributions paid into that scheme, then, before benefits fall to be paid, transfers his residence to another Member State, the Kingdom of Denmark is deprived of the power to tax the benefits corresponding to the contributions deducted or exempted, at least where it has concluded with the Member State to which the person concerned has transferred his residence a double taxation convention based on the OECD Convention. However, in such a case, that result is not due to the fact that the pension institution is established abroad.

73. Conversely, there is nothing to prevent the Kingdom of Denmark from exercising its power of taxation over the benefits paid by a pension institution established in another Member State to a taxpayer still resident in Denmark when that payment is made, as a counterbalance to the contributions which it allowed to be deducted or exempted. It is only in the case where, before benefits fall to be paid, that taxpayer transferred his residence to a Member State other than the Kingdom of Denmark that it might encounter difficulties in taxing the benefits paid and where, therefore, the cohesion of the Danish tax system with regard to the taxation of private pensions would be adversely affected.

74. It follows that, by refusing in general to grant a tax advantage in respect of contributions paid to a pension institution established in another Member State, the con-

tested legislation cannot be justified by the need to guarantee the cohesion of the tax system.

75. It follows from the foregoing that the contested legislation cannot be justified either by considerations of the effectiveness of the supervision of taxation and the prevention of tax avoidance or by the need to ensure cohesion of the tax system.

76. Since the provisions of the Treaty on freedom to provide services, free movement for workers and freedom of establishment preclude the contested legislation, it is not necessary to consider that legislation separately in the light of Article 56 EC on free movement of capital (see, to that effect, Case C-345/05 *Commission* v *Portugal* [2006] ECR I-0000, paragraph 45).

77. Consequently, it must be held that, by introducing and maintaining in force a system for life assurance and pensions under which tax deductions and tax exemptions for payments are granted only for payments under contracts entered into with pension institutions established in Denmark, whereas no such tax relief is granted for payments made under contracts entered into with pension institutions established in other Member States, the Kingdom of Denmark has failed to fulfil its obligations under Articles 39 EC, 43 EC and 49 EC.

Costs

[Para. 78 omitted]

On those grounds,

THE COURT (Grand Chamber)

hereby:

1. **Declares that, by introducing and maintaining in force a system for life assurance and pensions under which tax deductions and tax exemptions for payments are granted only for payments under contracts entered into with pension institutions established in Denmark, whereas no such tax relief is granted for payments made under contracts entered into with pension institutions established in other Member States, the Kingdom of Denmark has failed to fulfil its obligations under Articles 39 EC, 43 EC and 49 EC;**

[Paras 2 and 3 of the ruling omitted]

Comments and questions

The CJEU's judgment in the Danish case on the taxation of pensions concerned the legality of the Danish rules on taxation of contributions paid into pension schemes and payments paid out by pension schemes. The principle behind the Danish scheme was very simple. When an employee paid part of his wages into a pensions savings scheme, that part of his wages was not taxed. On the other hand, when the employee later retired and received payments from the pension scheme, the recipient of these payments was taxed. In other words the system amounted to a postponement of tax until pensionable age. This had two important advantages for employees. First, most employees can expect a reduction of income when they retire. A fall in income will normally mean that income tax is paid at a lower rate. Thus paying into a pension scheme with postponed taxation will normally lead to a reduction in tax. At the same time the postponement of taxation will mean that more is paid into the pension account, so there is more money which can accumulate.

For the Danish system to hang together it was important that the tax deductions on contributions should be matched by tax assessments when payments were later made from the pension fund. For this reason Denmark only allowed tax deductions to be made on pension contributions made to pension schemes held with a pensions institute based in Denmark. Such a restriction constituted a restriction on the free provision of services, the free movement of workers and freedom of establishment. How could the measures restrict the free provisions of services, free movement of workers and freedom of establishment, respectively? In Article 57 TFEU (formerly Article 50 TEC) the freedom to provide services is expressly allowed 'in so far as they are not governed by the provisions relating to freedom of movement for goods, capital and persons'. How does this coincide with the CJEU's statement in paragraph 45? What kind of restriction was there (direct discrimination etc.)?

The Commission argued that the Danish rules also constituted a restriction on the free movement of capital. Against this Denmark argued that the measures did not involve any direct restriction on cross-border transactions with capital that was paid into or out of foreign financial institutions. In its judgment the CJEU only considered that the Danish rules were a restriction on the free provision of services and free movement of persons (workers and establishment), but not to free movement of capital. How did the CJEU justify this? Compare this with the Advocate General's treatment of the question in points 49-53 of his Opinion.

It was clear that the key question was not whether the Danish rules constituted a restriction. There was agreement that they did. The key question was whether the measures were justified. In this connection the Danish Government put special emphasis on the CJEU's 1992 judgment in the *Bachmann* case.

In Case C-204/90 *Hanns-Martin Bachmann* v *Belgium* [1992] ECR I-249, the CJEU acknowledged that the 'need to safeguard the cohesion of the tax system' could justify a national tax arrangement which, according to the practice of the CJEU, constituted a restriction (indirect discrimination) on the free movement of workers, Article 45 TFEU. The *Bachmann* case concerned Belgian legislation under which only premiums paid to insurance companies in Belgium for, among others, voluntary pensions and life insurance could be deducted from taxable income. The case was thus very similar to the Danish case on the taxation of pensions. The coherence of the tax system required that, if Belgium were to recognise the right to make tax deductions for insurance premiums which were paid in another Member State, it could tax payments later paid out by the insurance companies when the insured event occurred. Furthermore, the CJEU held that the Belgian measures satisfied the proportionality principle.

That the 'need to safeguard the cohesion of the tax system' was a lawful purpose for a Member State was confirmed in Case C-35/98 *Staatssecretaris van Financiën* v *Verkooijen* [2000] ECR I-4071. This case concerned a Netherlands tax rule according to which it was possible to obtain tax exemption for dividends paid on shares of a company based in another Member State than the Netherlands. In paragraph 58 of the judgment the CJEU stated that: 'No such direct link exists in this case between the grant to shareholders residing in the Netherlands of income tax exemption in respect of dividends received and taxation of the profits of companies with their seat in another Member State. They are two separate taxes levied on different taxpayers.' Thus, in the *Verkooijen* case the CJEU established that consideration for the 'need to safeguard the cohesion of the tax system' required there to be a direct link between the two forms of taxation. Loss of tax revenue can thus not be regarded as an overriding public interest which can justify a national rule which is in conflict with a fundamental freedom.

The CJEU has also considered the need to safeguard the cohesion of the tax system in subsequent cases. These include Case C-136/00 *Rolf Dieter Danner* [2002] ECR I-8147 and Case C-422/01 *Försäkringsaktiebolaget Skandia and Ola Ramstedt* v *Riksskatteverket* [2003] ECR I-6817 which both concerned pension schemes. Here too the CJEU rejected the claim that the disputed restrictions could be justified because of the need to safeguard the cohesion of the tax system. Some commentators have interpreted these two cases as indicating that the CJEU will no longer consider it possible to justify a restriction on such grounds. However, this is probably not correct. Rather it appears more correct to seek the reason for the CJEU's rejection of the argument that the need to safeguard the cohesion of the tax system justified the disputed restrictions in the Finnish and Swedish cases in the fact that there was no direct link between the right to make a tax deduction for the insurance premiums paid in and the taxation of the pensions paid out.

In the Finnish *Danner* case, the pensions paid by foreign institutions to persons who were resident in Finland were taxed without regard to whether or not the premiums previously paid in could have been deducted from the pensioner's taxable income. By contrast, premiums paid to pension schemes that were either based in Finland or had a fixed place of business there could be deducted from taxable income at the date of payment, with the effect that the pension was taxed when it was paid out. This discriminatory measure only applied to voluntary pension schemes, as payments to compulsory schemes were fully deductible from taxable income, regardless of whether they were Finnish or foreign schemes. On this basis the CJEU held that the Finnish tax measure was contrary to Article 56 TFEU.

The *Ola Ramstedt* case concerned the Swedish tax system. As with the Finnish system there was a lack of symmetry between the right to make a deduction from taxable income when paying premiums in and the later taxation of pensions paid out. In paragraphs 34-37 of the *Ramstedt* case, the CJEU rejected the argument that there was a direct link between the right to make tax deductions for premiums paid in and the obligation to pay tax on the amounts paid out by the insurance companies. The CJEU stated as follows:

> '35. In the Swedish system, an employer who has taken out an insurance policy with an insurer established in another Member State has to wait until pension benefits are paid to his employee to enjoy the right to deduct. There is no compensatory measure to offset the disadvantage he suffers compared with an employer who takes out comparable insurance with a company established in Sweden.
>
> 36. However, in both situations, the employee who is the beneficiary is liable to tax at the same time and in the same way.
>
> 37. Moreover, the argument of the Swedish and Danish Governments that the insurance premium is, essentially, a part of the employee's remuneration does not explain why it can be deducted immediately [where] the employer takes out the occupational insurance with an insurer established in Sweden while deduction is deferred where it is taken out with an insurer established in another Member State.'

Thus, according to the *Ramstedt* case, the CJEU has very strict requirements for there to be a link between tax deductions for premiums paid in, on the one hand, and the taxation of pensions paid out, on the other hand. If these strict requirements are not satisfied, the tax rules will be regarded as being incompatible with Article 56 TFEU.

Returning to the CJEU's decision in the Danish case on the taxation of pensions, it is natural to ask whether in this case the CJEU entirely rejected the argument that the Member States could claim the need to safeguard the cohesion of the tax system as justifying measures which constituted a restriction on freedom of movement. Or did the CJEU accept the principle that a restriction could be justified by this consideration, even though in the actual case it denied that the Danish measures in general could be justified in this way? In this connection see paragraphs 72-74.

JUDGMENT OF THE COURT (Sixth Chamber)
28 October 1999

Skatteministeriet v Bent Vestergaard.
(Reference for a preliminary ruling: Højesteret – Denmark)

'Freedom to provide services – Income tax – Taxable income – Deduction of expenses for professional training courses – Distinction according to the location of the courses'

Case C-55/98

Judgment

1. By order of 18 February 1998, received at the Court on 24 February 1998, the Højesteret (Supreme Court), Denmark, referred to the Court for a preliminary ruling under Article 177 of the EC Treaty (now Article 234 EC) two questions on the interpretation of Articles 6 and 59 of the EC Treaty (now, after amendment, Articles 12 EC and 49 EC).

2. The questions have been raised in proceedings between the Danish Skatteministeriet (Ministry of Fiscal Affairs) and Mr Vestergaard concerning the refusal of the Ministry to allow expenses incurred by Mr Vestergaard in taking part in professional training courses held abroad to be deducted as operating costs from the taxable income of the company Bent Vestergaard A/S, of which Mr Vestergaard is the sole shareholder.

Danish law

3. In Denmark, Article 4 of the Statsskatteloven (State Law Tax) No 149 of 10 April 1922 (hereinafter 'the 1922 Law') provides that income, in the form of money or goods evaluable in money, is liable to tax.

4. Article 6 of the 1922 Law provides:

'1) The following are to be deducted from taxable income:

(a) operating costs, that is expenses which, during the course of the year, have been incurred with a view to acquiring, ensuring or maintaining income, including ordinary depreciation;

...

2) The fiscal income is taxable irrespective of the manner in which it is used, whether it is for personal or family purposes, the purchase of services, benefits

or leisure, to increase assets, improve property, extend a business or a company, for savings or funds of the same type, for gifts or in any other way.'

5. The operating costs which are deductible under Article 6(1)(a) of the 1922 Law are defined by administrative practice and case-law. Thus, the guidelines produced by the Danish Ministry of Fiscal Affairs for the 1988 tax year stated:

   'Expenditure relating to participation in professional courses is deductible in the case of courses intended to maintain and update the professional knowledge and training of participants ...

   In the case where a professional conference or course is transferred to a foreign country (generally ordinary tourist resorts), this will have the effect of setting aside the right to deduct, unless the travel destination/course location can as such be treated as justified on professional grounds.'

6. In the guidelines covering tax years after the year in question in the main proceedings, such as 1996, the following statement also appears:

   'It is thus presumed that the holding of the course in a foreign tourist resort involves such a significant tourism element that the course expenditure cannot be regarded as constituting deductible operating costs.'

7. The file shows that this statement was added as a result of judgments of the Vestre Landsret (Western Regional Court) of 17 April 1984 and 8 October 1984, published in the Tidsskrift for Skatteret 1984, Nos 238 and 471 respectively, which were subsequently upheld by the Højesteret in a judgment of 19 October 1994, published in the Ugeskrift for Retsvæsen 1994, p. 970. In its order for reference, the national court states in this regard:

   'When a course is held in an ordinary tourist resort abroad, and this location cannot be justified as such on professional grounds, there is a presumption that the course involves such a significant tourism element that the course expenditure cannot be regarded as constituting deductible operating costs.

   This presumption can be rebutted through information concerning, in particular, the content and duration of the course in relation to the duration of the stay ...

   When the course is held in an ordinary tourist resort in Denmark, this presumption does not exist.

   There is no case-law, whether in the form of judicial rulings or decisions taken by administrative authorities, to the effect that the right to deduct in connection with the participation in courses held in Denmark should be set aside on the grounds that a course was held in an ordinary tourist resort.'

The facts and the main proceedings

8. Mr Vestergaard is a certified auditor and employed by the company Bent Vestergaard A/S which is an auditing company, of which he is the sole shareholder.

9. From 3 to 10 October 1988 Mr Vestergaard attended a tax training course on the island of Crete. It was organised solely for Danish participants by a firm of Danish auditors in conjunction with a travel agency. Out of the seven days spent in Greece, three whole days and two half days were devoted to the course.

10. The costs relating to Mr Vestergaard's participation in the course, his travel and accommodation, amounting to DKK 5 516, were paid by the company Bent Vestergaard A/S. Mr Vestergaard's wife accompanied him on the trip and at the hotel, for which she paid a sum of DKK 3 700 privately.

11. By decision of 29 June 1993, the Landsskatteretten (National Tax Tribunal) decided that the expenses relating to Mr Vestergaard's participation in the course on Crete should be treated as a salary bonus paid to him as sole shareholder in the company Bent Vestergaard A/S and could not therefore be deducted from his taxable income under Article 6(1)(a) of the 1922 Law.

12. Mr Vestergaard instituted proceedings against this decision before the Vestre Landsret (Western Regional Court), which, by judgment of 3 May 1995, found that he had succeeded in overturning the presumption that the course had such a significant tourism element that the costs could not be regarded as deductible operating costs and that, consequently, the tax administration was wrong in treating the costs of the course as a salary bonus for Mr Vestergaard.

13. The Skatteministeriet appealed against the judgment of the Vestre Landsret to the Højesteret. When a new argument, that the taxation of the course fees in question as a salary bonus was incompatible with Articles 6 and 59 of the Treaty, was raised by Mr Vestergaard before the national court, it decided to stay proceedings and to submit the following two questions to the Court for a preliminary ruling:

'1) Is it in accordance with Articles 6 and 59 of the EC Treaty for Danish case-law (see the judgment of the Højesteret of 19 October 1994, published in the Ugeskrift for Retsvæsen 1994, p. 970) to apply a presumption that, in cases in which a course is held in an ordinary tourist resort outside Denmark, and the course location cannot, as such, be justified on professional grounds, the course involves such a significant tourism element that the costs relating to the course cannot be treated as constituting deductible operating costs?

2) If the answer is in the negative, can the position in domestic tax law, as described above ..., be justified by reference to the case-law of the Court of Justice, in particular Case C-204/90 *Bachmann* v *Belgium* and Case C-250/95 *Futura Participations and Singer* v *Administration des Contributions*?'

The questions referred for a preliminary ruling

14. By its two questions, which can be examined together, the national court asks essentially whether Articles 6 and 59 of the Treaty preclude rules of a Member State which, for the purposes of determining taxable income, presume that professional training courses held in ordinary tourist resorts located in other Member States involve such a significant tourism element that the costs involved in taking part in those courses cannot be treated as deductible operating costs, while such a presumption does not exist for training courses held in ordinary tourist resorts located within the territory of that Member State.

15. It must be observed first of all that, although, as Community law stands at present, direct taxation does not as such fall within the purview of the Community, the powers retained by the Member States must nevertheless be exercised consistently with Community law (see, in particular, Case C-118/96 *Safir* [1998] ECR I-1897, at paragraph 21).

16. Secondly, according to settled case-law, the first paragraph of Article 6 of the Treaty, which lays down the general principle of the prohibition of discrimination on grounds of nationality, applies independently only to situations governed by Community law in respect of which the Treaty lays down no specific rule against discrimination (see, in particular, Case C-22/98 *Becu and Others* [1999] ECR I-5665, at paragraph 32).

17. With regard to freedom to provide services, this principle is given specific expression and effect by Article 59 of the Treaty. There is therefore no need to rule on the interpretation of Article 6 of the Treaty.

18. Thirdly, it is important to point out that in order for services such as those in question in the main proceedings, namely the organisation of professional training courses, to fall within the scope of Article 59 of the Treaty, it is sufficient for them to be provided to nationals of a Member State on the territory of another Member State, irrespective of the place of establishment of the provider or recipient of the services.

19. Article 59 of the Treaty applies not only where a person providing a service and the recipient are established in different Member States, but also whenever a provider of services offers those services in a Member State other than the one in which he is established (see Case C-381/93 *Commission* v *France* [1994] ECR I-5145, at para-

graph 14), wherever the recipients of those services may be established (see Case C-398/95 *SETTG* [1997] ECR I-3091, at paragraph 8).

20. In addition, the right to exercise freedom to provide services includes the freedom for the recipients of services to go to another Member State in order to receive a service there, without being obstructed by restrictions (see, in particular, Case C-224/97 *Ciola* [1999] ECR I-2517, at paragraph 11).

21. As regards the question whether the rules of a Member State, such as at issue in the main proceedings, contains a restriction prohibited under Article 59 of the Treaty, it must be observed that, by making the right to deduct costs relating to participation in professional training courses held in an ordinary tourist resort abroad conditional upon the rebuttal, by the taxpayer, of a presumption that such courses involve such a significant tourism element that the costs cannot be treated as deductible operating costs, while such a presumption does not exist for courses held in ordinary tourist resorts located in the said Member State, those rules subject the provision of services constituted by the organisation of professional courses to different tax arrangements depending on whether the services are provided in other Member States or in the Member State concerned.

22. Rules of a Member State which, like those in question in the main proceedings, make it more difficult to deduct costs relating to participation in professional training courses organised abroad than to deduct costs relating to such courses organised in that Member State involve a difference in treatment, based on the place where the service is provided, prohibited by Article 59 of the Treaty.

23. Such a difference in treatment is not justified by the need to preserve the cohesion of a tax system nor by the effectiveness of fiscal supervision, which, in the judgments in, respectively, *Bachmann* (Case C-204/90 [1992] ECR I-249) and *Futura Participations and Singer* (Case C-250/95 [1997] ECR I-2471), mentioned by the referring court, have been recognised as capable of justifying the regulations and thus restricting the fundamental freedoms guaranteed by the Treaty.

24. In the cases which led to the judgment in Bachmann, cited above, and to the judgment delivered on the same day in Case C-300/90 *Commission* v *Belgium* [1992] ECR I-305, there was a direct link between the deductibility of contributions and the taxation of sums payable by insurers under pension and life assurance contracts, and that link had to be maintained to preserve the cohesion of the tax system in question (see C-484/93 *Svensson and Gustavsson* [1995] ECR I-3955, at paragraph 18; Case C-107/94 *Asscher* [1996] ECR I-3089, at paragraph 58, and Case C-264/96 *ICI* [1998] ECR I-4695, at paragraph 29). In the present case, as the Advocate General observes in paragraph 39 of his Opinion, there is no such direct link between any taxation and the deductibility of costs relating to participation in professional training courses.

25. Furthermore, while a Member State may, in the interests of the effectiveness of fiscal supervision, apply measures which allow the amount of costs deductible in that State as operating costs to be ascertained clearly and precisely, and in particular those incurred in taking part in professional training courses (see Futura Participations and Singer, cited above, at paragraph 31, and Case C-254/97 *Baxter and Others* [1999] ECR I-4809, at paragraph 18), it cannot however provide any justification for that Member State to make the deduction subject to different conditions according to whether the courses take place in that State or in another Member State.

26. In that regard, it should be remembered that Council Directive 77/799/EEC of 19 December 1977 concerning mutual assistance by the competent authorities of the Member States in the field of direct taxation (OJ 1977 L 336, p. 15) can be invoked by a Member State in order to obtain from the competent authorities of another Member State all the information enabling it to ascertain the correct amount of income tax. In addition, there is nothing to prevent the tax authorities concerned from requiring the taxpayer himself to produce the proof which they consider necessary to assess whether or not the deduction requested should be allowed (see *Bachmann and Commission* v *Belgium*, cited above, at respectively paragraphs 18 and 20 and paragraphs 11 and 13).

27. The Skatteministeriet argues that the exchange of information between national tax authorities provided for by Directive 77/799 is not sufficient to enable them to resolve problems which, like those in the instant case, would require an assessment, in particular, of the nature of the training in question and its duration in relation to the duration of the stay, having regard to the rules and case-law of the Member State to which those authorities belong.

28. However, it should be emphasised that the information which Directive 77/799 allows the competent authorities of a Member State to request is in fact all the information which appears to them to be necessary to ascertain the correct amount of revenue tax payable by a taxpayer in relation to the legislation which they have to apply themselves (see, to this effect, Futura Participations and Singer, at paragraph 41) and that the directive does not in any way affect the competence of those authorities to assess in particular whether the conditions to which that legislation subjects the deduction of certain costs are fulfilled.

29. The answer to be given to the questions submitted must therefore be that Article 59 of the Treaty precludes a Member State from having rules which, for the purposes of determining taxable income, presume that professional training courses held in ordinary tourist resorts located in other Member States involve such a significant tourism element that the costs of taking part in those courses cannot be treated as deductible operating costs, while such a presumption does not exist in the case of professional training courses held in ordinary tourist resorts located within the territory of that Member State.

Costs

[Para. 30 omitted]

On those grounds,

THE COURT (Sixth Chamber),

in answer to the questions referred to it by the Højesteret by judgment of 18 February 1998, hereby rules:

> **Article 59 of the EC Treaty (now, after amendment, Article 49 EC) precludes a Member State from having rules which, for the purposes of determining taxable income, presume that professional training courses held in ordinary tourist resorts located in other Member States involve such a significant tourism element that the costs of taking part in those courses cannot be treated as deductible operating costs, while such a presumption does not exist in the case of professional training courses held in ordinary tourist resorts located within the territory of that Member State.**

Comments and questions

In Case C-55/98 *Skatteministeriet* v *Vestergaard* [1999] ECR I-7641, the Danish Supreme Court asked the CJEU to clarify whether it was compatible with Article 56 TFEU (formerly Article 59 TEC) that the tax authorities applied a rebuttable presumption by which professional training courses held abroad in ordinary tourist resorts were considered as predominantly made for tourist purposes so that the expenses could not be deducted from taxable income. In contrast there was no corresponding presumption with regard to courses held in Denmark.

Both the CJEU and the Advocate General stated that 'although, as [Union] law stands at present, direct taxation does not as such fall within the purview of the [Union], the powers retained by the Member States must nevertheless be exercised consistently with [Union] law.' The question was whether the presumption in the Danish tax rule was contrary to the prohibition on restrictions in Article 56 TFEU.

The Netherlands Government made a submission in favour of the position of the Danish Ministry of Taxation. Among other things, the Dutch argued that the presumption was merely a slight intensification of the burden of proof upon taxpayers who want to obtain tax deductions. In other words, there was merely an insignificant effect which should be disregarded. The CJEU did not express a view on this argument in its judgment. However, it is the well-established practice of the CJEU that even the slightest restriction on the freedom of movement of goods, workers, services or capital is unlawful. What matters is not whether the restriction is significant or insignificant, but whether there is a restriction at all.

The Danish Ministry of Taxation argued that its presumption did not lead to unequal treatment in practice, since the tax advantages and possibilities for making tax deductions were in principle the same, whether the training course was held in Denmark or in another Member State. The only difference was that the actual assessment in respect of courses held abroad was made on the rebuttable presumption that they were not deductible. However, the CJEU did not agree that this presumption did not constitute a restriction on the freedom to provide services. It thus held that the rule made it more difficult to obtain tax deductions for professional courses held in other Member States than for courses held in Denmark. This meant that there was a difference based on the location of the courses. Such a difference is contrary to Article 56 TFEU.

The CJEU also stated that the Danish presumption could not be justified by the need to preserve fiscal cohesion or by the need for effective fiscal supervision. How did the CJEU justify this finding? Will it be possible, following this decision, for the Danish tax authorities to undertake proper control of tax deductions for professional training courses held at a tourist resort in another Member State? If so, how?

In his Opinion, the Advocate General came to the same conclusion as the CJEU. In his grounds for believing that the presumption of the Danish tax authorities constituted discrimination, he argued, first, that owing to the presumption of non-deductibility, in order to obtain a deduction, taxpayers must undergo more onerous procedures. Secondly, given that the granting of the deduction was subject to more restrictive assessment criteria, it was therefore less likely that it would be granted. Also, the possibility of a refusal of deduction has a considerable influence on taxpayers' choices. The Advocate General referred to the decisions of the CJEU in Case C-118/96 *Safir* v *Skattemyndigheten i Dalarnas Län* [1998] ECR I-1897 and in Case C-158/96 *Kohll* v *Union des caisses de maladie* [1998] ECR I-1931, printed above. In the *Safir* case it was held that the mere fact that administrative procedures relating to a given service make it more onerous, must be assumed to be capable of deterring a potential recipient of a service from buying it. The *Kohll* case concerned a requirement for prior authorisation for obtaining medical treatment from a health service provider in another Member State, while the same requirement did not apply if the service was provided in the home Member State. Here, the CJEU pointed out that such a rule would deter patients from obtaining such services from providers in other Member States, so it constituted a restriction on the freedom to provide services.

In his Opinion, the Advocate General discussed (paragraph 30) whether the measure should be categorised as direct discrimination or a restriction. However, he refrained from answering the question since his view was that the measure was contrary to the Treaty regardless of the answer. What do you think the right answer is, and what did the CJEU say?

In the *Vestergaard* case the disputed rule had merely been created by administrative practice and the practice of the courts and it was therefore necessary to change this practice. If there had been a legislative provision, then under Union law the Member State must formally repeal the unlawful measure, otherwise the infringement of the TFEU will not be brought to an end. The CJEU has held that there is an infringement of the TFEU if a Member State maintains a legislative provision whose wording is contrary to the TFEU, regardless of the fact that, in practice, the law is administered in accordance with the TFEU. Otherwise people will get the wrong impression by reading the relevant legislative text, making it conceivable that they will refrain from asserting their Treaty-based rights. See the decisions of the CJEU in Case 159/78 *Commission* v *Italy* [1979] ECR 3247, paragraphs 21-23, and Case C-80/92 *Commission* v *Belgium* [1994] ECR I-1019, paragraphs 18-20. Likewise, the mere fact that the authorities of a Member State can grant exemptions or vary a legislative measure whose wording is contrary to the TFEU (so that through the use of the exemption/exception the legal provision is applied in such a way that, in the specific case, there is no breach of the TFEU), does not mean that the measure in question becomes lawful. This will be so, even if the authorities exercise their powers to grant exemptions liberally. See the decisions of the CJEU in Case C-221/89 *R* v *Secretary of State for Transport, ex parte Factortame* (the *Factortame II* case) [1991] ECR I-3905, paragraph 38, and in Case 27/80 *Fietje* [1980] ECR 3839, paragraph 14.

Note also that the *Vestergaard* case was decided by three judges, the minimum number of judges who are capable of making judgments at the CJEU. This indicates that the CJEU in general regarded the case as being relatively straightforward.

JUDGMENT OF THE COURT (Grand Chamber)
8 September 2009

Liga Portuguesa de Futebol Profissional, Bwin International Ltd, formerly Baw International Ltd, v Departamento de Jogos da Santa Casa da Misericórdia de Lisboa. (Reference for a preliminary ruling from the Tribunal de Pequena Instância Criminal do Porto – Portugal)

'Reference for a preliminary ruling – Article 49 EC – Restrictions on the freedom to provide services – Offer of games of chance via the internet'

Case C-42/07

Judgment

1. This reference for a preliminary ruling concerns the interpretation of Articles 43 EC, 49 EC and 56 EC.

2. The reference has been made in the course of proceedings between, on the one hand, the Liga Portuguesa de Futebol Profissional ('the Liga') and Bwin International Ltd ('Bwin'), formerly Baw International Ltd, and, on the other, the Departamento de Jogos da Santa Casa da Misericórdia de Lisboa ('Santa Casa') concerning fines imposed on the Liga and Bwin by the directors of Santa Casa on the ground that they had infringed the Portuguese legislation governing the provision of certain games of chance via the internet.

Legal framework

The regulation of games of chance in Portugal

3. In Portugal games of chance are, in principle, prohibited. However, the State has reserved the right to authorise, in accordance with the system which it deems most appropriate, the operation of one or more games directly, through a State body or a body controlled directly by the State, or to grant the right to operate such games to private entities, whether profit-making or not, by calls for tender conducted in accordance with the Code of Administrative Procedure.

4. Games of chance in the form of lotteries, lotto games and sports betting are known in Portugal as games of a social nature ('jogos sociais') and the operation of such games is systematically entrusted to Santa Casa.

5. Each type of game of chance organised by Santa Casa is instituted separately by a decree-law and the entire organisation and operation of the various games offered

by it, including the amount of stakes, the system for awarding prizes, the frequency of draws, the specific percentage of each prize, methods of collecting stakes, the method of selecting authorised distributors, and the methods and periods for payment of prizes, are covered by government regulation.

6. The first type of game in question was the national lottery (Lotaria Nacional), which was established by a royal edict of 18 November 1783, and a concession was awarded to Santa Casa, the concession being renewed regularly thereafter. Today that lottery consists in the monthly drawing of numbers by lot.

7. Following a number of legislative developments, Santa Casa acquired the right to organise other games of chance based on the drawing of numbers by lot or on sporting events. This led to the introduction of two games involving betting on football matches called 'Totobola' and 'Totogolo', respectively enabling participants to bet on the result (win, draw or loss) and the number of goals scored by the teams. There are also two lotto games, namely Totoloto, in which six numbers are chosen from a total of 49, and EuroMillions, a type of European lotto. Players of Totobola or Totoloto may also take part in a game called 'Joker', which consists in the drawing of a single number by lot. Lastly, there is also the Lotaria Instantânea, an instant game with a scratch card, commonly called 'raspadinha'.

The provision of games of a social nature via the internet

8. In 2003 the legal framework governing lotteries, lotto games and sports betting was adapted in order to take account of technical developments enabling games to be offered by electronic means, in particular the internet. Those measures feature in Decree-Law No 282/2003 of 8 November 2003 (*Diário da República* I, series A, No 259, 8 November 2003). They seek essentially, first, to license Santa Casa to distribute its products by electronic means and, secondly, to extend Santa Casa's exclusive right of operation to include games offered by electronic means, in particular the internet, thereby prohibiting all other operators from using those means.

9. Article 2 of Decree-Law No 282/2003 confers on Santa Casa, through its Departamento de Jogos (Gaming Department), exclusive rights for the operation by electronic means of the games in question and for any other game the operation of which may be entrusted to Santa Casa, and states that that system covers all of the national territory, and includes, in particular, the internet.

10. Under Article 11(1) of Decree-Law No 282/2003 the following are classed as administrative offences:

'(a) the promotion, organisation or operation by electronic means of games [the operation of which has been entrusted to Santa Casa], in contravention of the exclusive rights granted by Article 2 [of the present Decree-Law], and also the issue, distribution or sale of virtual tickets and the advertisement of the related draws, whether they take place within national territory or not;

(b) the promotion, organisation or operation by electronic means of lotteries or other draws similar to those of the Lotaria Nacional or the Lotaria Instantânea, in contravention of the exclusive rights granted by Article 2, and also the issue, distribution or sale of virtual tickets and the advertisement of the related draws, whether they take place within national territory or not;

...'.

11. Article 12(1) of Decree-Law No 282/2003 sets the maximum and minimum fines for the administrative offences laid down in, inter alia, Article 11(1)(a) and (b) of that Decree-Law. For legal persons, the fine is to be not less than EUR 2 000 or more than three times the total amount deemed to have been collected from organising the game in question, provided that the triple figure is greater than EUR 2 000 but does not exceed a maximum of EUR 44 890.

The organisation and activities of Santa Casa

12. The activities of Santa Casa were, at the material time, regulated by Decree-Law No 322/91 of 26 August 1991 adopting the statutes of Santa Casa da Misericórdia de Lisboa (*Diário da República* I, series A, No 195, 26 August 1991), as amended by Decree-Law No 469/99 of 6 November 1999 (*Diário da República* I, series A, No 259, 6 November 1999) ('Decree-Law No 322/91').

13. The preamble to Decree-Law No 322/91 emphasises the importance of the various aspects of Santa Casa – historical, social, cultural and economic – and concludes that the Government must pay 'specific and continuous attention in order to prevent negligence and failures ... while nevertheless granting [Santa Casa] the broadest possible autonomy in the management and operation of games of a social nature'.

14. Under Article 1(1) of its statutes, Santa Casa is a 'legal person in the public administrative interest'. The administrative organs of Santa Casa consist, by virtue of Article 12(1) of its statutes, of a director and a board of management. Pursuant to Article 13 of those statutes, the director is appointed by decree of the Prime Minister, the other members of Santa Casa's board of management being appointed by decree of the members of the Government under whose supervision Santa Casa falls.

15. Under Article 20(1) of its statutes, Santa Casa has been given specific tasks in the areas of protection of the family, mothers and children, help for unprotected minors at risk, assistance for old people, social situations of serious deprivation, and primary and specialised health care.

16. The earnings generated by the operation of games of chance are allocated between Santa Casa and other public-interest institutions or institutions involved in social projects. Those other public-interest institutions include associations of voluntary fire crews, private social solidarity institutions, establishments for the safety and rehabilitation of handicapped persons, and the cultural development fund.

17. The operation of games of chance falls within the responsibilities of the Gaming Department of Santa Casa. That department is governed by regulations adopted, as in the case of Santa Casa's statutes, by Decree-Law No 322/91, and it has its own administrative and control organs.

18. In accordance with Article 5 of the regulations governing the Gaming Department, the administrative organ of that department consists of the director of Santa Casa, who is the ex officio chairman, and two deputy directors appointed by joint decree of the Minister for Employment and Solidarity and the Minister for Health. Pursuant to Articles 8, 12 and 16 of the regulations of the Gaming Department, the majority of the members of the committees in charge of games, draws and complaints are representatives of the public authorities, that is to say, the General Tax Inspectorate and the District Government in Lisbon. Accordingly, the chairman of the complaints committee, who has a casting vote, is a judge appointed by decree of the Minister for Justice. Two of the three members of that committee are appointed by decree of the chief tax inspector and decree of the chief administrative officer (prefect) of the District of Lisbon respectively, while the third member of the committee is appointed by the director of Santa Casa.

19. The Gaming Department has the powers of an administrative authority to open, institute and prosecute proceedings concerning offences involving the illegal operation of games of chance in relation to which Santa Casa has the exclusive rights, and to investigate such offences. Decree-Law No 282/2003 confers upon the directors of the Gaming Department, inter alia, the necessary administrative powers to impose fines as provided for under Article 12(1) of that Decree-Law.

The actions in the main proceedings and the question referred for a preliminary ruling

20. Bwin is an on-line gambling undertaking which has its registered office in Gibraltar. It offers games of chance on an internet site.

21. Bwin has no establishment in Portugal. Its servers for the on-line service are in Gibraltar and Austria. All bets are placed directly by the consumer on Bwin's internet site or by some other means of direct communication. Stakes on that site are paid by credit card in particular, but also by other means of electronic payment. The value of any winnings is credited to the gambling account opened for the gambler by

Bwin. The gambler may use that money in order to gamble or ask for it to be transferred to his bank account.

22. Bwin offers a wide range of on-line games of chance covering sports betting, casino games, such as roulette and poker, and games based on drawing numbers by lot which are similar to the Totoloto operated by Santa Casa.

23. Betting is on the results of football matches and other sporting events. The different games offered include bets on the result (win, draw or loss) of football matches in the Portuguese championship equivalent to the Totobola and Totogolo games operated exclusively by Santa Casa. Bwin also offers on-line betting in real time, in which the odds are variable and change as the sporting event in question unfolds. Information such as the match score, the time elapsed, yellow and red cards given, and so on, are displayed in real time on the Bwin internet site, thus enabling gamblers to place bets interactively as the sporting event unfolds.

24. The order for reference states that the Liga is a private-law legal person with the structure of a non-profit-making association, made up of all the clubs taking part in football competitions at professional level in Portugal. It organises, inter alia, the football competition corresponding to the national First Division and is responsible for the commercial operation of that competition.

25. The Liga and Bwin stated in the observations which they submitted to the Court that a sponsorship agreement, concluded by them on 18 August 2005 for four playing seasons starting in 2005/2006, made Bwin the main institutional sponsor of the First Football Division in Portugal. Under the terms of that agreement, the First Division, previously known as the 'Super Liga', changed its name first to the Liga betandwin.com, and then subsequently to the Bwin Liga. In addition, the Bwin logos were displayed on the sports kit worn by the players and affixed around the stadiums of the First Division clubs. The Liga's internet site also included references and a link allowing access to Bwin's internet site, making it possible for consumers in Portugal and other States to use the gambling services thus offered to them.

26. Subsequently, in exercising the powers conferred on them by Decree-Law No 282/2003, the directors of the Gaming Department of Santa Casa adopted decisions imposing fines of EUR 75 000 and EUR 74 500 respectively on the Liga and Bwin in respect of the administrative offences referred to in Article 11(1)(a) and (b) of that Decree-Law. Those sums represent the aggregated amounts of two fines imposed on each of the Liga and Bwin for promoting, organising and operating, via the internet, games of a social nature reserved to Santa Casa or such similar games, and also for advertising such gambling.

27. The Liga and Bwin brought actions before the national court for annulment of those decisions, invoking, inter alia, the relevant Community rules and case-law.

28. In those circumstances, the Tribunal de Pequena Instância Criminal do Porto (Local Criminal Court, Oporto) (Portugal) decided to stay the proceedings and to refer the following question to the Court for a preliminary ruling:

'[Do] the exclusive rights granted to Santa Casa, when relied on against [Bwin], that is to say, against a provider of services established in another Member State in which it lawfully provides similar services, which has no physical establishment in Portugal, [constitute] an impediment to the free provision of services, in breach of the principles of freedom to provide services, freedom of establishment and the free movement of payments enshrined in Articles 49, 43 and 56 of the EC Treaty [?]

[Is it] contrary to Community law, in particular to the abovementioned principles, for rules of domestic law such as those at issue in the main proceedings first to grant exclusive rights in favour of a single body for the operation of lotteries and off-course betting and then to extend those exclusive rights to 'the entire national territory, including ... the internet'[?]'

The application to have the oral procedure reopened

[Paras 29-35 omitted]

The admissibility of the reference for a preliminary ruling

[Paras 36-43 omitted]

The question referred for a preliminary ruling

44. By its question, the national court seeks a ruling from the Court on the interpretation of Articles 43 EC, 49 EC and 56 EC.

The applicability of Articles 43 EC and 56 EC

45. In so far as the question referred by the national court refers not only to Article 49 EC but also to Articles 43 EC and 56 EC, it should be made clear from the outset that it is not apparent, in the light of the information in the file, that those last two articles might be applicable to the dispute in the main proceedings.

46. As to whether Article 43 EC is applicable, it is common ground that Bwin carries on its activities in Portugal exclusively via the internet, without resorting to intermediaries in Portugal and thus without having established a principal place of business or secondary establishment in that State. Similarly, it is not apparent from the file that Bwin had any intention to establish itself in Portugal. Consequently, there is nothing to suggest that the Treaty provisions on freedom of establishment might be applicable to the dispute in the main proceedings.

47. As to whether Article 56 EC is applicable, it must be noted that any restrictive effects which the national legislation at issue in the main proceedings might have on the free movement of capital and payments would be no more than the inevitable consequence of any restrictions on the freedom to provide services. Where a national measure relates to several fundamental freedoms at the same time, the Court will in principle examine the measure in relation to only one of those freedoms if it appears, in the circumstances of the case, that the other freedoms are entirely secondary in relation to the first and may be considered together with it (see, to that effect, Case C-452/04 *Fidium Finanz* [2006] ECR I-9521, paragraph 34 and case-law cited).

48. In those circumstances, the question referred by the national court must be answered in the light of Article 49 EC alone.

The scope of the question referred for a preliminary ruling

49. The dispute in the main proceedings concerns the marketing in Portugal of a number of games of chance played on an electronic medium, namely the internet. Bwin, a private operator established in another Member State, offers games of chance in Portugal exclusively via the internet, and the administrative offences laid down in Article 11(1)(a) and (b) of Decree-Law No 282/2003, of which the Liga and Bwin are accused in the main proceedings, concern exclusively conduct in relation to games of chance organised by electronic means.

50. The question referred by the national court must therefore be construed as asking in essence whether Article 49 EC precludes legislation of a Member State, such as that at issue in the main proceedings, which prohibits operators, such as Bwin, which are established in other Member States, in which they lawfully provide similar services, from offering games of chance via the internet within the territory of that first Member State.

The existence of restrictions on the freedom to provide services

51. Article 49 EC requires the abolition of all restrictions on the freedom to provide services, even if those restrictions apply without distinction to national providers of services and to those from other Member States, when they are liable to prohibit, impede or render less advantageous the activities of a service provider established in another Member State where it lawfully provides similar services (see, to that effect, Case C-76/90 *Säger* [1991] ECR I-4221, paragraph 12, and Case C-58/98 *Corsten* [2000] ECR I-7919, paragraph 33). Moreover, the freedom to provide services is for the benefit of both providers and recipients of services (see, to that effect, Joined Cases 286/82 and 26/83 *Luisi and Carbone* [1984] ECR 377, paragraph 16).

52. It is accepted that the legislation of a Member State which prohibits providers such as Bwin, established in other Member States, from offering via the internet services in the territory of that first Member State constitutes a restriction on the freedom to provide services enshrined in Article 49 EC (see, to that effect, Case C-243/01 *Gambelli and Others* [2003] ECR I-13031, paragraph 54).

53. Such legislation also imposes a restriction on the freedom of the residents of the Member State concerned to enjoy, via the internet, services which are offered in other Member States.

54. Consequently, as indeed the Portuguese Government expressly concedes, the legislation at issue in the main proceedings gives rise to a restriction of the freedom to provide services enshrined in Article 49 EC.

The justification of the restriction of the freedom to provide services

55. It is necessary to consider to what extent the restriction at issue in the main proceedings may be allowed as a derogation expressly provided for by Articles 45 EC and 46 EC, applicable in this area by virtue of Article 55 EC, or justified, in accordance with the case-law of the Court, by overriding reasons in the public interest.

56. Article 46(1) EC allows restrictions justified on grounds of public policy, public security or public health. In addition, a certain number of overriding reasons in the public interest have been recognised by case-law, such as the objectives of consumer protection and the prevention of both fraud and incitement to squander money on gambling, as well as the general need to preserve public order (see, to that effect, *Placanica and Others*, paragraph 46 and case-law cited).

57. In that context, as most of the Member States which submitted observations to the Court have noted, the legislation on games of chance is one of the areas in which there are significant moral, religious and cultural differences between the Member States. In the absence of Community harmonisation in the field, it is for each Member State to determine in those areas, in accordance with its own scale of values, what is required in order to ensure that the interests in question are protected (see, inter alia, Case 34/79 *Henn and Darby* [1979] ECR 3795, paragraph 15; Case C-275/92 *Schindler* [1994] ECR I-1039, paragraph 32; Case C-268/99 *Jany and Others* [2001] ECR I-8615, paragraphs 56 and 60, and *Placanica and Others*, paragraph 47).

58. The mere fact that a Member State has opted for a system of protection which differs from that adopted by another Member State cannot affect the assessment of the need for, and proportionality of, the provisions enacted to that end. Those provisions must be assessed solely by reference to the objectives pursued by the competent authorities of the Member State concerned and the degree of protection which

they seek to ensure (Case C-124/97 *Läärä and Others* [1999] ECR I-6067, paragraph 36, and Case C-67/98 *Zenatti* [1999] ECR I-7289, paragraph 34).

59. The Member States are therefore free to set the objectives of their policy on betting and gambling and, where appropriate, to define in detail the level of protection sought. However, the restrictive measures that they impose must satisfy the conditions laid down in the case-law of the Court as regards their proportionality (*Placanica and Others*, paragraph 48).

60. In the present case, it is thus necessary to examine in particular whether the restriction of the provision of games of chance via the internet, imposed by the national legislation at issue in the main proceedings, is suitable for achieving the objective or objectives invoked by the Member State concerned, and whether it does not go beyond what is necessary in order to achieve those objectives. In any event, those restrictions must be applied without discrimination (see, to that effect, *Placanica and Others*, paragraph 49).

61. In that context, it must be recalled that national legislation is appropriate for ensuring attainment of the objective pursued only if it genuinely reflects a concern to attain it in a consistent and systematic manner (Case C-169/07 *Hartlauer* [2009] ECR I-0000, paragraph 55).

62. The Portuguese Government and Santa Casa submit that the main objective pursued by the national legislation is the fight against crime, more specifically the protection of consumers of games of chance against fraud on the part of operators.

63. In that connection, it should be noted that the fight against crime may constitute an overriding reason in the public interest that is capable of justifying restrictions in respect of operators authorised to offer services in the games-of-chance sector. Games of chance involve a high risk of crime or fraud, given the scale of the earnings and the potential winnings on offer to gamblers.

64. The Court has also recognised that limited authorisation of games on an exclusive basis has the advantage of confining the operation of gambling within controlled channels and of preventing the risk of fraud or crime in the context of such operation (see *Läärä and Others*, paragraph 37, and *Zenatti*, paragraph 35).

65. The Portuguese Government submits that the grant of exclusive rights to Santa Casa to organise games of chance ensures that the system will function in a secure and controlled way. First, Santa Casa's long existence, spanning more than five centuries, is evidence of that body's reliability. Second, the Portuguese Government points out that Santa Casa operates under its strict control. The legal framework for games of chance, Santa Casa's statutes and government involvement in appointing the members of its administrative organs enable the State to exercise an effective

power of supervision over Santa Casa. That system, based on legislation and Santa Casa's statutes, provides the State with sufficient guarantees that the rules for ensuring fairness in the games of chance organised by Santa Casa will be observed.

66. In that regard, it is apparent from the national legal framework, set out in paragraphs 12 to 19 of the present judgment, that the organisation and functioning of Santa Casa are governed by considerations and requirements relating to the pursuit of objectives in the public interest. The Gaming Department of Santa Casa has been given the powers of an administrative authority to open, institute and prosecute proceedings involving offences of illegal operation of games of chance in relation to which Santa Casa has the exclusive rights.

67. In that connection, it must be acknowledged that the grant of exclusive rights to operate games of chance via the internet to a single operator, such as Santa Casa, which is subject to strict control by the public authorities, may, in circumstances such as those in the main proceedings, confine the operation of gambling within controlled channels and be regarded as appropriate for the purpose of protecting consumers against fraud on the part of operators.

68. As to whether the system in dispute in the main proceedings is necessary, the Portuguese Government submits that the authorities of a Member State do not, in relation to operators having their seat outside the national territory and using the internet to offer their services, have the same means of control at their disposal as those which they have in relation to an operator such as Santa Casa.

69. In that regard, it should be noted that the sector involving games of chance offered via the internet has not been the subject of Community harmonisation. A Member State is therefore entitled to take the view that the mere fact that an operator such as Bwin lawfully offers services in that sector via the internet in another Member State, in which it is established and where it is in principle already subject to statutory conditions and controls on the part of the competent authorities in that State, cannot be regarded as amounting to a sufficient assurance that national consumers will be protected against the risks of fraud and crime, in the light of the difficulties liable to be encountered in such a context by the authorities of the Member State of establishment in assessing the professional qualities and integrity of operators.

70. In addition, because of the lack of direct contact between consumer and operator, games of chance accessible via the internet involve different and more substantial risks of fraud by operators against consumers compared with the traditional markets for such games.

71. Moreover, the possibility cannot be ruled out that an operator which sponsors some of the sporting competitions on which it accepts bets and some of the teams taking

part in those competitions may be in a position to influence their outcome directly or indirectly, and thus increase its profits.

72. It follows that, in the light of the specific features associated with the provision of games of chance via the internet, the restriction at issue in the main proceedings may be regarded as justified by the objective of combating fraud and crime.

73. Consequently, the answer to the question referred is that Article 49 EC does not preclude legislation of a Member State, such as that at issue in the main proceedings, which prohibits operators such as Bwin, which are established in other Member States, in which they lawfully provide similar services, from offering games of chance via the internet within the territory of that Member State.

Costs

[Para. 74 omitted]

On those grounds,

THE COURT (Grand Chamber)

hereby rules:

> **Article 49 EC does not preclude legislation of a Member State, such as that at issue in the main proceedings, which prohibits operators such as Bwin International Ltd, which are established in other Member States, in which they lawfully provide similar services, from offering games of chance via the internet within the territory of that Member State.**

Comments and questions

In the *Liga Portuguesa* case the CJEU had to decide whether it was compatible with Article 56 TFEU (formerly Article 49 TEC) on the freedom to provide services, that a Member State which had arranged its gambling laws in such a way that there was a general prohibition of operators offering games of chance, including games of chance established in other Member States, while at the same time that Member State had granted an undertaking the exclusive right to operate such games of chance in the State in question.

The Portuguese prohibition meant that operators offering games of chance which were located in other Member States were prevented from selling their services in Portugal via the internet. Bwin was one of the operators of games of chance affected by the Portuguese prohibition. Bwin operated on-line gaming and was based in Gibraltar. Bwin offered such games of chance on a website but did not have a place of business in

Portugal. Bwin's servers for its on-line games were located in Gibraltar and Austria. An agreement to take part in one of Bwin's games of chance was entered into by consumers directly on the company's website or via other means of direct communication.

Bwin entered into a sponsorship and marketing agreement with Liga Portuguesa de Futebol Profissional, an association made up of all the clubs taking part in football competitions at professional level in Portugal which was responsible for the commercial operation of those competitions. However, Liga Portuguesa and Bwin's advertising for and offering of games of chance on the internet breached the Portuguese gambling laws, and they were fined. When Liga Portuguesa and Bwin challenged the decision to impose a fine before a Portuguese court, the question of the compatibility of the Portuguese legislation with the Union rules on freedom to provide services was referred to the CJEU.

As in many other Member States, in Portugal a single undertaking had been granted the exclusive right to offer games of chance in the Member State's territory. This included games offered via electronic media such as the internet. In Portugal, where this exclusive right had been granted to an undertaking called Santa Casa, this exclusive right was effectively protected by the Portuguese legislation which also prohibited operators from other Member States advertising their services in Portugal. The same legislation also allocated to Santa Casa a number of social tasks in Portugal. The earnings generated by the operation of games of chance were allocated between Santa Casa and other public-interest institutions or institutions involved in social projects. In other words, there was a significant social element associated with the grant of Santa Casa's exclusive right in the area of games of chance.

Before it could consider the case in more detail, the CJEU had first to determine on which of the fundamental freedoms it should base its assessment of the case. Should it be on the basis of the right of establishment, freedom of movement of capital or freedom to provide services? The CJEU found that the case should be assessed solely on the basis of the right to provide services. What was the reason for this – and why did the CJEU not apply several freedoms in parallel in the case (see in particular paragraphs 46-47)?

In its judgment the CJEU stated that the Portuguese prohibition of offering games of chance in Portuguese territory via the internet constituted a restriction on the provision of services. The prohibition was also a restriction on persons resident in Portugal using services offered in other Member States.

The question then became whether the Portuguese legislation could be justified on the grounds referred to in Articles 51, 52 and 62 TFEU (formerly Articles 45, 46 and 55 TEC), or the grounds of the overriding public interest recognised in the case law of the CJEU. In this connection the CJEU noted that: 'the legislation on games of chance is one of the areas in which there are significant moral, religious and cultural differences between the Member States. In the absence of [Union] harmonisation in the field, it is for each Member State to determine in those areas, in accordance with its own scale of values, what is required in order to ensure that the interests in question are protected'. But the CJEU added that: 'The mere fact that a Member State has opted for a system of protection which differs from that adopted by another Member State cannot affect the assessment of the need for, and proportionality of, the provisions enacted to that end. Those provisions must be assessed solely by reference to the objectives pursued by the competent authorities of the Member State concerned and the degree of protection which they seek to ensure'. Member States are thus free to determine the goals of their policies in the area of games of chance and the level of protection desired. In other words, there can be differences in the levels of protection between Member States, so the fact that one Member State has more restrictive measures than other Member States does not in itself mean that the more restrictive measures are in breach of Union law.

In the course of the case, both the Portuguese Government and Santa Casa had stated that the main purpose of the Portuguese legislation on games of chance was to combat crime, in particular to protect the users of games of chance from fraud committed by undertakings that arrange games of chance. The CJEU agreed that this was a lawful purpose. However, it is not enough that national legislation that constitutes a restriction should pursue a lawful purpose. The restrictive effects of the legislation must also be proportionate to the lawful purpose pursued. In particular this means that the national legislation must be *suitable* for achieving the objective or objectives invoked by the Member State concerned, and that it may not go beyond what is *necessary* in order to achieve those objectives. In this connection it should be noted that the CJEU will only regard national legislation as being appropriate for ensuring attainment of the objective pursued if it genuinely reflects a concern to attain it in a *consistent and systematic manner*.

What did the CJEU decide with regard to whether the legislation complied with the proportionality principle – and in particular on the question of necessity (see paragraphs 60-72)?

In its decision in the *Liga Portguesa* case the CJEU appears to have assumed that there is a real risk of fraud and criminality unless games of chance are operated by some public body. For this reason the Member States are not obliged to mutually recognise operators of games of chance that are lawfully conducted in another Member State. Consider whether it would have been possible to argue that a distinction should be made between large operators of games of chance such as Bwin, which are dependent on customers' trust in them, and smaller operators of games of chance where fraudulent activity will not have the same effect on the possibilities of carrying on the business?

JUDGMENT OF THE COURT (Grand Chamber)
28 April 2009

Commission of the European Communities v Italian Republic, supported by Republic of Finland. (Action under Article 226 EC for failure to fulfil obligations)

'Failure of a Member State to fulfil obligations – Third-party liability motor insurance – Articles 43 EC and 49 EC – Directive 92/49/EEC – National legislation imposing an obligation to contract on insurance undertakings – Restriction on the freedom of establishment and on the freedom to provide services – Social protection for victims of road traffic accidents – Proportionality – Insurance undertakings' freedom to set rates – Principle of supervision by the home Member State'

Case C-518/06

Judgment

1. By its action, the Commission of the European Communities requests the Court to declare that:

   – by implementing and maintaining legislation pursuant to which premiums for insurance against civil liability in respect of the use of motor vehicles (third-party liability motor insurance) must be calculated on the basis of specific parameters, and by making such premiums subject to controls *ex post facto*, the Italian Republic has failed to fulfil its obligations under Articles 6, 29 and 39 of Council Directive 92/49/EEC of 18 June 1992 on the coordination of laws, regulations and administrative provisions relating to direct insurance other than life assurance and amending Directives 73/239/EEC and 88/357/EEC (third non-life insurance Directive) (OJ 1992 L 228, p. 1);

   – by controlling the detailed rules in accordance with which insurance undertakings which have their head office in another Member State, but which pursue their business in Italy by virtue of the freedom of establishment or the freedom to provide services, calculate their insurance premiums, and by imposing in particular on such undertakings penalties for breach of the national rules concerning the calculation of insurance premiums, the Italian Republic has failed to fulfil its obligations under Article 9 of Directive 92/49, and

   – by maintaining an obligation to provide coverage for third-party motor vehicle liability insurance, incumbent on insurance undertakings, including those which have their head office in another Member State, but which pursue their business in Italy by virtue of the freedom of establishment or the freedom to provide services, the Italian Republic has failed to fulfil its obligations under Articles 43 EC and 49 EC.

Legal context

[Paragraphs 2-27 omitted]

Pre-litigation procedure

[Paras 28-38 omitted]

Procedure before the Court

[Paras 39-41 omitted]

The action

42. In its reply, the Commission indicated that the principal infringement of Community law alleged against the Italian Republic is the incompatibility of the obligation to contract with Articles 43 EC and 49 EC. That complaint, therefore, falls to be examined first of all.

The complaint alleging infringement of Articles 43 EC and 49 EC by reason of the obligation to contract

Arguments of the parties

43. The Commission claims that the obligation to contract, which is imposed on all insurance undertakings operating in the field of third-party liability motor insurance and in relation to all vehicle owners, and, likewise, the possibility offered to the ISVAP of imposing penalties in the event of infringement of that obligation, are incompatible with Articles 43 EC and 49 EC.

44. That obligation dissuades insurance undertakings established in other Member States from establishing themselves or offering services in Italy, thus hindering access to the Italian market. In particular, those undertakings are prevented from freely determining the insurance services they offer and the recipients of those services. Thus, they are required to bear costs that are excessive in relation to their commercial strategy. Those costs are even more significant for undertakings which intend solely to operate in Italy occasionally.

45. The restrictive effect of the obligation to contract is comparable to the restrictive effect found by the Court in *CaixaBank France*.

46. The Commission argues, next, that the obligation to contract is unjustified and disproportionate to the objective pursued.

47. As regards the objective, cited by the Italian Republic, of protecting vehicle owners, the Commission acknowledges that the obligation to contract contributes to guaranteeing that a vehicle owner will find an insurance undertaking prepared to issue a third-party liability motor insurance policy. However, the obligation to contract goes beyond what is necessary to attain the objective of consumer protection, since it is imposed on insurance undertakings in respect of all vehicle owners throughout Italian territory, whereas the Italian Republic has referred to difficulties in finding an insurance undertaking prepared to issue a third-party liability motor insurance policy for a specific geographical area and category of persons, that is to say, the south of Italy and new drivers.

48. In relation to the other objective cited by the Italian Republic, which consists of guaranteeing appropriate compensation for victims of road traffic accidents, the Commission takes the view that that is already achieved by the obligation imposed on vehicle owners – following transposition of Article 3 of Directive 72/166 – to take out a third-party liability motor insurance policy, and the existence in each Member State of a guarantee fund pursuant to Directive 84/5.

49. Lastly, the Commission notes that other Member States have less restrictive systems for obtaining the same results as the Italian legislation is claimed to be pursuing. It refers, in that regard, to the Bureau central de tarification (Central Rates Office) established both in Belgium and in France, the Consorcio de Compensación de Seguros (Insurance Compensation Consortium) established in Spain, the consortium of major insurance undertakings established in the Netherlands, and the mutual insurance system established in Portugal.

50. The Italian Republic points out that third-party liability motor insurance, while being a private form of insurance, has a social purpose, in particular the need to ensure that victims of road traffic accidents receive compensation. That is the reason why an obligation was introduced for vehicle owners to take out insurance in order to compensate third parties.

51. By choosing to impose that obligation to contract both on insurance undertakings and motor vehicle users, the Italian Republic wished to offer maximum protection to, on the one hand, policyholders, in their capacity as consumers, against discrimination in relation to access to insurance and use of public highways and, on the other, the victims of road traffic accidents.

52. According to the Italian Republic, those objectives should not be frustrated by the commercial freedom of undertakings. It considers that, if the Court were to accept the Commission's reasoning, third-party liability motor insurance would become

insurance based solely on market logic and would lose, to a large extent, its social character.

53. The Italian Republic points out, next, that the obligation to contract has no dissuasive effect on insurance undertakings established in a Member State other than the Italian Republic which wish to penetrate the Italian market.

54. In the event that the Court were, nevertheless, to hold that the obligation to contract restricts the freedom of establishment and the freedom to provide services, the Italian Republic contends that that obligation is appropriate to achieve the abovementioned objectives of consumer protection and protection for victims of road traffic accidents.

55. The obligation to contract is, furthermore, compatible with the principle of proportionality. Contrary to what the Commission claims, it would be neither practical nor lawful to limit the obligation to contract to certain areas of Italian territory or to certain types of consumer. To limit the obligation to certain categories of consumers would raise discrimination issues, while a geographical limitation of that obligation would encourage insurance undertakings not to operate in those areas subject to the obligation to insure.

56. As regards, lastly, alternative mechanisms established in other Member States, the Italian Republic points out that, in the absence of harmonised rules on the means of implementing the obligation to insure motor vehicles in respect of third-party liability, each Member State remains free to choose the solution which best suits the national social situation. It is, moreover, precisely because of the differences between the various national situations that the Community legislature was not able to lay down rules on harmonisation in that regard.

57. The Republic of Finland argues that, irrespective of whether the obligation to contract restricts the freedom of establishment and the freedom to provide services, it is in any event justified.

58. In that regard, it contends that there is a close link between third-party liability motor insurance and social security, on account of the reimbursement of hospital and recuperation costs for victims of road traffic accidents and costs relating to loss of earnings suffered by those victims.

59. According to the Republic of Finland, the obligation to contract is necessary for and proportionate to the attainment of the objectives pursued. It is, for consumers, the most straightforward means of fulfilling their legal obligation.

Findings of the Court

– The existence of a restriction on the freedom of establishment and the freedom to provide services

60. It is not in dispute that the obligation to contract applies without distinction to all undertakings providing third-party liability motor insurance on Italian territory.

61. The Commission takes the view, nevertheless, that that obligation, in so far as it reduces the ability of insurance undertakings to implement their strategic market choices independently, hinders, in Italy, the establishment of and provision of services by undertakings having their head office in another Member State.

62. It is settled case-law that the term 'restriction' within the meaning of Articles 43 EC and 49 EC covers all measures which prohibit, impede or render less attractive the freedom of establishment or the freedom to provide services (*CaixaBank France*, paragraph 11; Case C-465/05 *Commission* v *Italy* [2007] ECR I-11091, paragraph 17; and Case C-389/05 *Commission* v *France* [2008] ECR I-1057, paragraph 52).

63. As regards the question of the circumstances in which a measure applicable without distinction, such as the obligation to contract at issue in the present case, may come within that concept, it should be borne in mind that rules of a Member State do not constitute a restriction within the meaning of the EC Treaty solely by virtue of the fact that other Member States apply less strict, or more commercially favourable, rules to providers of similar services established in their territory (see, to that effect, Case C-384/93 *Alpine Investments* [1995] ECR I-1141, paragraph 27, and Case C-403/03 *Schempp* [2005] ECR I-6421, paragraph 45).

64. By contrast, the concept of restriction covers measures taken by a Member State which, although applicable without distinction, affect access to the market for undertakings from other Member States and thereby hinder intra-Community trade (see, to that effect, *Alpine Investments*, paragraphs 35 and 38, and *CaixaBank France*, paragraph 12).

65. In the present case, it is common ground that the obligation to contract does not have any repercussions for the acceptance by the Italian authorities of the administrative authorisation, referred to in paragraph 13 of this judgment, which insurance undertakings having their head office in a Member State other than the Italian Republic obtain in the Member State in which they have their head office. It therefore leaves intact the right of access to the Italian market as regards third-party liability motor insurance resulting from that authorisation.

66. Nevertheless, the imposition by a Member State of an obligation to contract such as that at issue constitutes a substantial interference in the freedom to contract which economic operators, in principle, enjoy.

67. In a sector like that of insurance, such a measure affects the relevant operators' access to the market, in particular where it subjects insurance undertakings not only to an obligation to cover any risks which are proposed to them, but also to requirements to moderate premium rates.

68. Inasmuch as it obliges insurance undertakings which enter the Italian market to accept every potential customer, that obligation to contract is likely to lead, in terms of organisation and investment, to significant additional costs for such undertakings.

69. If they wish to enter the Italian market under conditions which comply with Italian legislation, such undertakings will be required to re-think their business policy and strategy, inter alia, by considerably expanding the range of insurance services offered.

70. Inasmuch as it involves changes and costs on such a scale for those undertakings, the obligation to contract renders access to the Italian market less attractive and, if they obtain access to that market, reduces the ability of the undertakings concerned to compete effectively, from the outset, against undertakings traditionally established in Italy (see, to that effect, *CaixaBank France*, paragraphs 13 and 14).

71. Therefore, the obligation to contract restricts the freedom of establishment and the freedom to provide services.

– Justification for the restriction

72. A restriction on the freedom of establishment and the freedom to provide services may be justified where it serves overriding requirements relating to the public interest, is suitable for securing the attainment of the objective which it pursues and does not go beyond what is necessary in order to attain it (see, inter alia, Joined Cases C-94/04 and C-202/04 *Cipolla and Others* [2006] ECR I-11421, paragraph 61; Case C-250/06 *United Pan-Europe Communications Belgium and Others* [2007] ECR I-11135, paragraph 39; and Case C-212/06 *Government of the French Community and Walloon Government* [2008] ECR I-1683, paragraph 55).

73. In order to justify the obligation to contract, the Italian Republic has cited a number of objectives, including the social protection for victims of road traffic accidents.

74. That social protection objective, which amounts, essentially, to ensuring that such victims will be adequately compensated, can be taken into account as an overriding requirement relating to the public interest.

75. As is clear from the Community legislation cited in paragraphs 3 to 12 of this judgment, and as the Italian Republic and the Republic of Finland have pointed out, the very purpose of compulsory third-party liability motor insurance is to guarantee compensation for victims of road traffic accidents.

76. Under that same legislation, such compensation is to be principally financed on the basis of contracts underwritten by insurance undertakings, while the guarantee fund set up in each Member State has only a subsidiary role in compensating victims of road traffic accidents, namely in cases where the accident was caused by a vehicle in respect of which the insurance requirement has not been met.

77. Article 3 of Directive 72/166 accordingly requires the Member States to take all appropriate measures to ensure that their citizens comply with the obligation to take out third-party liability motor insurance.

78. Clearly, one of the ways in which Member States may fulfil that obligation imposed by Article 3 of Directive 72/166 is to ensure that every owner of a vehicle is able to take out such insurance for a premium which is not excessive.

79. In that regard, the Commission's argument that the objective of social protection for victims of road traffic accidents is, in any event, achieved by the existence in each Member State of a guarantee fund cannot be accepted.

80. Admittedly, the existence of the guarantee fund ensures that the victims of accidents caused by vehicles in respect of which the insurance requirement has not been met will be compensated. It is therefore not in dispute that, even in the absence of an obligation to contract such as that introduced by the Italian Republic, every victim of a road traffic accident will receive compensation.

81. However, as has been pointed out in paragraph 76 of this judgment, it is also apparent from the Community legislation that the existence of an individual contract for third-party liability motor insurance, and the possibility of invoking that insurance contract directly against the insurance undertaking, constitutes the principal basis for the protection of victims of road traffic accidents. In those circumstances, Member States cannot be criticised for taking initiatives aimed at preventing the owners of vehicles from being unable to meet the requirement to take out third-party liability motor insurance.

82. It follows from the foregoing that the obligation to contract at issue in the present case is apt to contribute to implementing the Community legislation relating to the

obligation, for every vehicle owner, to take out third-party liability motor insurance and, therefore, to the attainment of the objective of that legislation, which is to guarantee adequate compensation for victims of road traffic accidents.

83. As regards whether the obligation to contract as it is in force in the Italian Republic goes beyond what is necessary to achieve the objective of social protection for victims of road traffic accidents, it must be borne in mind, first of all, that it is not essential, with regard to the proportionality criterion, that a restrictive measure laid down by the authorities of a Member State should correspond to a view shared by all the Member States concerning the means of protecting the legitimate interest at issue.

84. The situation relating to road traffic, and to the relevant public interest objectives in that area, varies from one Member State to another. Consequently, Member States must be recognised as having some discretion in that area. Whilst it is true that it is for a Member State which relies on an imperative requirement to justify a restriction within the meaning of the EC Treaty to demonstrate that its rules are appropriate and necessary to attain the legitimate objective being pursued, that burden of proof cannot be so extensive as to require the Member State to prove, positively, that no other conceivable measure could enable that objective to be attained under the same conditions (Case C-110/05 *Commission* v *Italy* [2009] ECR I-0000, paragraphs 65 and 66).

85. Therefore, the fact that some Member States have chosen to establish a system different from that introduced by the Italian Republic to ensure that every vehicle owner is able to take out third-party liability motor insurance for a premium that is not excessive does not indicate that the obligation to contract goes beyond what is necessary to attain the objectives pursued. The explanations given by the Commission concerning the systems in place in a number of Member States other than the Italian Republic do not, moreover, enable the conclusion to be drawn that those systems are, ultimately, less restrictive and more advantageous for insurance undertakings than the obligation to contract introduced by the Italian legislature.

86. It is appropriate, next, to consider the Commission's argument that it is disproportionate to impose on insurance undertakings an obligation to contract vis-à-vis all potential customers and throughout Italian territory.

87. On that point, the Italian Republic contended, without being challenged by the Commission, that, in the southern part of its territory, there are difficult circumstances which require corrective measures on the part of the public authorities in order that third-party liability motor insurance can be provided under conditions which are acceptable both for policyholders and insurance undertakings.

88. It appears, inter alia, that the number of road traffic accidents declared to insurance undertakings is particularly high in certain areas in the south of Italy. That situation has led to a considerable increase in the financial risks incurred by those undertakings in that region.

89 In those circumstances, the Italian Republic could consider that it was appropriate to impose on all undertakings operating in its territory an obligation to contract vis-à-vis all vehicle owners domiciled in Italy, in order to avoid those undertakings withdrawing from the southern part of Italian territory and thereby depriving vehicle owners domiciled there of the possibility of taking out third-party liability motor insurance, which is nevertheless compulsory.

90. It follows, moreover, from Article 11(1a) of Law No 990/69 and from Article 35(1) of the Code of Private Insurance that in taking that measure the Italian Republic did not prohibit insurance undertakings from applying premium rates differentiated on the basis of past statistics on the average cost of the risk within categories of insured that have been sufficiently broadly defined.

91. In particular, it is not in dispute that the obligation to insure does not prevent insurance undertakings from calculating a higher premium for a policyholder domiciled in an area characterised by a significant number of accidents than for a policyholder domiciled in an area where the risk is not so high.

92. Furthermore, it is not inconceivable that an obligation to contract limited to only the southern part of Italian territory would give rise, as the Italian Republic has claimed, to a questionable legal situation, inasmuch as vehicle owners domiciled in other regions of Italy could complain of unequal treatment if, in a region in which there was no such obligation to contract, they experienced difficulties in finding an insurance undertaking prepared to enter into a contract for third-party liability motor insurance with them.

93. It follows from all of the foregoing that the obligation to contract is appropriate to ensure the achievement of the objective which it pursues and does not go beyond what it necessary to attain it.

94. It follows that the complaint alleging breach of Articles 43 EC and 49 EC must be rejected.

[Paras 95-121 omitted]

Costs

[Paras 122 and 123 omitted]

On those grounds,

THE COURT (Grand Chamber),

hereby:

1. **Dismisses the action;**

[Para. 2 of the ruling omitted]

Comments and questions

In the case on Italian third-party motor vehicle liability insurance, the Commission was of the view that Italy had breached Articles 49 and 56 TFEU (formerly Articles 43 and 49 TEC) by maintaining an obligation to provide coverage for third-party motor vehicle liability insurance, incumbent on insurance undertakings, including those which have their head office in another Member State, but which pursue their business in Italy by virtue of the freedom of establishment or the freedom to provide services. The Commission found that such an obligation, that was imposed on all insurance companies which offered compulsory insurance in Italy, was incompatible with the provisions referred to because the obligation to enter into such contracts would dissuade insurance undertakings established in other Member States from establishing themselves or offering services in Italy. Those undertakings were prevented from freely determining the insurance services they offered and the recipients of those services. In other words, in the view of the Commission the obligation to contract hindered access to the Italian market.

The CJEU agreed with the Commission that the obligation to contract was a restriction. It was clear that the obligation applied without distinction to all companies that offered third-party motor vehicle liability insurance in Italy, but the obligation nevertheless was a significant interference in the freedom to contract which economic operators, in principle, enjoy. The CJEU thus ruled that: 'In a sector like that of insurance, such a measure *affects the relevant operators' access to the market*, in particular where it subjects insurance undertakings not only to an obligation to cover any risks which are proposed to them, but also to requirements to moderate premium rates. Inasmuch as it obliges insurance undertakings which enter the Italian market to accept every potential customer, that obligation to contract is likely to lead, in terms of organisation and investment, to significant additional costs for such undertakings' (emphasis added). By making access to the Italian market less interesting and by limiting the possibilities for foreign insurance companies to compete effectively with insurers traditionally based in Italy, the obligation to contract constituted a restriction on the right of establishment and on freedom to provide services.

After having thus established that the Italian legislation constituted a restriction, the CJEU had to consider whether this restriction was lawful. The overall purpose of the insurance measure was to ensure that those who suffered injury from a motor vehicle accident could obtain compensation. The CJEU said that this was a lawful purpose. However, there was the further question of whether the obligation to contract was suitable and necessary for achieving this purpose. The CJEU ruled that it was. How did the CJEU argue that both the suitability and the necessity requirements had been fulfilled (see in particular paragraphs 75-93)?

Note that the CJEU remarked with regard to the proportionality principle that the burden of proof cannot be so extensive as to require the Member State to prove, positively, that no other conceivable measure could enable the invoked objective to be attained under the same conditions; see paragraph 84 of the judgment, where there is a reference to paragraphs 65 and 66 in Case C-110/05 *Commission* v *Italy* [2009] ECR I-519, (the *motorcycle trailers* case printed in Chapter 2).

Compare the judgment in this case on third-party motor vehicle liability insurance with Case C-565/08 *Commission* v *Italy* (the *maximum tariffs for advocates* case) in Chapter 5. Why did the CJEU reach different conclusions in its assessment of whether the Italian legislation affected 'access to the market'?

JUDGMENT OF THE COURT (First Chamber)
19 June 2014

Strojírny Prostějov, a.s., ACO Industries Tábor s.r.o. v Odvolací finanční ředitelství.
(Requests for a preliminary ruling: Krajský soud v Ostravě and the Nejvyšší správní soud - Czech Republic)

'Freedom to provide services – Temporary employment agency – Secondment of workers by an agency established in another Member State – Restriction – Undertaking using the workforce – Tax on the income of those workers withheld at source – Obligation – Payment to national budget – Obligation – Situation of workers seconded by a national agency – Absence of such obligations'

Joined Cases C-53/13 and C-80/13

Judgment

1. These requests for a preliminary ruling concern the interpretation of Articles 18 TFEU, 45 TFEU, 49 TFEU and 56 TFEU.

2. The requests have been made in proceedings between Strojírny Prostějov, a.s. ('Strojírny Prostějov') and Odvolací finanční ředitelství (Tax Appeals Directorate) and between ACO Industries Tábor s.r.o. ('ACO Industries Tábor') and Odvolací finanční ředitelství, concerning the tax treatment to which those two undertakings were subject.

Legal context

[Paras 3-21 omitted]

Consideration of the questions referred

The question referred in Case C-53/13 and the first and third questions referred in Case C-80/13

22. By the question in Case C-53/13 and by the first and third questions in Case C-80/13, which it is appropriate to consider together, the referring courts ask, in essence, whether Articles 18 TFEU, 45 TFEU, 49 TFEU, 56 TFEU or 57 TFEU preclude legislation, such as that at issue in the main proceedings, under which companies established in one Member State using workers employed and seconded by temporary employment agencies established in another Member State, but operating in the first State through a branch, are obliged to withhold tax and to pay to the first State an advance payment on the income tax due by those workers, whereas the

same obligation is not laid down for companies established in the first State which use the services of temporary employment agencies established in that State.

Preliminary observations

23. In order to reply to those questions, it must be noted at the outset that, as EU law stands at present, although direct taxation does not as such fall within the purview of the European Union, the powers retained by the Member States must nevertheless be exercised consistently with EU law (see FKP Scorpio Konzertproduktionen, C-290/04, EU:C:2006:630, paragraph 30 and the case-law cited).

24. Furthermore, as regards the question whether national legislation falls within the scope of one or other of the freedoms of movement laid down by the Treaties, it is clear from well-established case-law that the purpose of the legislation concerned must be taken into consideration (see, inter alia, Test Claimants in the FII Group Litigation, C-35/11, EU:C:2012:707, paragraph 90, and Cadbury Schweppes and Cadbury Schweppes Overseas, C-196/04, EU:C:2006:544, paragraphs 31 to 33).

25. In this case, the Czech legislation imposes on Czech undertakings wishing to avail themselves of the intermediary services of a temporary employment agency not established in the Czech Republic an obligation to withhold the income tax payable by the workers seconded for their benefit by that agency, whereas the same obligation is not imposed on Czech undertakings wishing to avail themselves of the intermediary services of a temporary employment agency established in the Czech Republic.

26. According to settled case-law, Article 56 TFEU confers rights not only on the provider of services but also on the recipient of those services (see, inter alia, Luisi and Carbone, 286/82 and 26/83, EU:C:1984:35, paragraph 10; FKP Scorpio Konzertproduktionen, EU:C:2006:630, paragraph 32; and X, C-498/10, EU:C:2012:635, paragraph 23).

27. Consequently, the legislation at issue in the main proceedings is covered by the freedom to provide services.

28. It is true that, as the European Commission claims, such legislation is also liable to affect the freedom of establishment of temporary employment agencies wishing to provide their services in the Czech Republic while maintaining their seat in another Member State, particularly because, in this case, the agencies concerned carried out their activities in the Czech Republic through a branch.

29. The same is true as regards the freedom movement of workers, given that the legislation concerns detailed rules for the collection of income tax which are imposed on Czech undertakings to which those workers have been seconded in the context of a

contractual relationship with the agencies of which they are employees, which is liable indirectly to affect their chance of exercising their freedom of movement.

30. However, notwithstanding the possible restrictive effects of that legislation on freedom of establishment and the free movement of workers, such effects are an unavoidable consequence of any restriction on the freedom to provide services and do not justify, in any event, an independent examination of that legislation in the light of Articles 45 TFEU and 49 TFEU (see, to that effect, Omega, C-36/02, EU:C:2004:614, paragraph 27, and Cadbury Schweppes and Cadbury Schweppes Overseas, EU:C:2006:544, paragraph 33).

31. Finally, in those circumstances, there is also no need to proceed to an interpretation of Article 18 TFEU.

32. That provision applies independently only to situations governed by EU law for which the FEU Treaty lays down no specific rules of non-discrimination. In relation to the freedom to provide services, the principle of non-discrimination was implemented by Articles 56 TFEU to 62 TFEU (see, by analogy, Attanasio Group, C-384/08, EU:C:2010:133, paragraph 37, and Schulz-Delzers and Schulz, C-240/10, EU:C:2011:591, paragraph 29).

33. The Czech legislation at issue in the main proceedings must therefore be examined in the light of Article 56 TFEU.

Restriction on the freedom to provide services

34. In order to determine whether the legislation at issue in the main proceedings is consistent with the freedom to provide services, it should be recalled that, according to the Court's case-law, Article 56 TFEU requires the abolition of any restriction on that fundamental freedom imposed on the ground that the person providing a service is established in a Member State other than the one in which the service is provided (see Commission v Germany, 205/84, EU:C:1986:463, paragraph 25; Commission v Italy, C-180/89, EU:C:1991:78, paragraph 15; FKP Scorpio Konzertproduktionen, EU:C:2006:630, paragraph 31; and X, EU:C:2012:635, paragraph 21).

35. Restrictions on the freedom to provide services are national measures which prohibit, impede or render less attractive the exercise of that freedom (X, EU:C:2012:635, paragraph 22 and the case-law cited).

36. Furthermore, as was noted in paragraph 26 above, Article 56 TFEU confers rights not only on the provider of services but also on their recipient.

37. It is clear that, in the present case, the obligation to withhold an advance payment on the income tax of workers supplied by temporary employment agencies not established in the Czech Republic and to pay that advance payment to the Czech State is inevitably imposed on the recipients of the services provided by those agencies and entails an additional administrative burden which is not required for the recipients of the same services provided by a resident service provider. Consequently, such an obligation is liable to render cross-border services less attractive for those recipients than services provided by resident service providers, and consequently to deter those recipients from having recourse to service providers resident in other Member States (see, to that effect, FKP Scorpio Konzertproduktionen, EU:C:2006:630, paragraph 33; Commission v Belgium, C-433/04, EU:C:2006:702, paragraphs 30 to 32; and X, EU:C:2012:635, paragraph 28).

38. The Danish Government, relying on Truck Center (C-282/07, EU:C:2008:762, paragraphs 49 to 51), maintains that the situation of agencies established in the Czech Republic is objectively different from that of agencies established outside the Czech Republic and that, consequently, the restriction on the freedom to provide services at issue is not discriminatory.

39. In this respect, however, it is sufficient to note that the provider and the recipient of the services are two distinct legal entities, each with its own interests and each entitled to claim the benefit of the freedom to provide services if their rights are infringed (X, EU:C:2012:635, paragraph 27).

40. In this case, the difference in treatment established by the legislation at issue in the main proceedings affects the right of recipients of services freely to choose cross-border services. In addition, in so far as those recipients reside in the Czech Republic, those who decide to have recourse to the services of resident agencies find themselves in a situation comparable to those who prefer the services of a non-resident agency.

41. It follows that legislation such as that at issue in the main proceedings constitutes a restriction on freedom to provide services, prohibited in principle by Article 56 TFEU.

42. That conclusion cannot challenged by the argument of the Czech Government that the effects of the legislation at issue are negligible, given that, according to settled case-law, a restriction on a fundamental freedom is prohibited by the Treaty even if it is of limited scope or minor importance (Commission v France, C-34/98, EU:C:2000:84, paragraph 49, and X, EU:C:2012:635, paragraph 30).

Justification of a restriction on the freedom to provide services

43. As regards the possibility of justifying such a restriction, none of the interested parties which have submitted observations before the Court or the referring courts consider that that restriction may be justified for reasons of public policy, public security or public health.

44. However, according to settled case-law of the Court, where national legislation falling within an area which has not been harmonised at EU level is applicable without distinction to all persons and undertakings operating in the territory of the Member State concerned, it may, notwithstanding its restrictive effect on the freedom to provide services, be justified where it meets overriding requirements in the public interest in so far as that interest is not already safeguarded by the rules to which the service provider is subject in the Member State in which he is established and in so far as it is appropriate for securing the attainment of the objective which it pursues and does not go beyond what is necessary in order to attain it (see, inter alia, Säger, C-76/90, EU:C:1991:331, paragraph 15, and Commission v Belgium EU:C:2006:702, paragraph 33).

45. Both the Nejvyšší správní soud, in its request, and the Czech Government, during the hearing, in essence considered that the Czech legislation at issue in the main proceeding is justified in the light of the need to ensure the effective collection of income tax. In this respect, the Government claimed, inter alia, that withholding tax constitutes a very efficient way of recovering tax since it allows the tax administration to acquaint itself with relevant information about the person liable without delay.

46. It should be noted, in that respect, that the Court has already recognised that the need to ensure the effective collection of income tax may constitute an overriding reason in the public interest capable of justifying a restriction on the freedom to provide services (FKP Scorpio Konzertproduktionen, EU:C:2006:630, paragraph 35, and X, EU:C:2012:635, paragraph 39).

47. In particular, the Court even stated that the procedure of retention at source is a legitimate and appropriate means of ensuring the tax treatment of the income of a person established outside the State of taxation and ensuring that the income concerned does not escape taxation in the State of residence and the State where the services are provided (FKP Scorpio Konzertproduktionen, EU:C:2006:630, paragraph 36, and X, EU:C:2012:635, paragraph 39).

48. However, that conclusion was based, both in FKP Scorpio Konzertproduktionen (EU:C:2006:630) and in X (EU:C:2012:635), on the fact that the service providers at issue in those cases provided occasional services in a Member State other than that in which they were established, and remained there for only a short period of time (see, in particular, X, EU:C:2012:635, paragraph 42).

49. As the Advocate General noted at point 70 of his Opinion, it is clear that, in this case, it cannot be claimed that the temporary employment agencies at issue in the main proceedings provide their services in the Czech Republic only on an occasional basis, given that they acted through a branch registered in the commercial register of the Czech Republic.

50. In those circumstances, even though, as the Czech Government states, a branch, under Czech law, does not have legal personality and cannot therefore be obliged to pay taxes under Czech law, the fact remains that such a branch provides the service provider with a physical presence in the territory of the host Member State and performs certain administrative tasks on behalf of the temporary employment agency concerned such as signing contracts.

51. In this respect, not only can it not be excluded that the Czech tax authorities recover the tax due from that branch and that therefore that branch carries out the withholding at issue, but it is also apparent from the documents before the Court in Case C-80/13 that, in this case, the advance payments on the salaries of the employees concerned were in fact made by the branch of the Slovak temporary employment agency.

52. Furthermore, the imposition on the resident recipients of those services, instead of on the Czech branch of the agencies resident in other Member States, of the administrative burden linked to the withholding tax on income payable by the seconded workers does not appear to be simpler or more efficient from the point of view of the service providers or from the point of view of the Czech administration. Since the branch of the temporary employment agency of which the workers are employees has the necessary information concerning the income of those workers more easily available to it, the administrative burden connected to the withholding operation would be less onerous for that branch than for the recipient of the services.

53. It follows that, accordingly, the national legislation at issue in the main proceedings is not appropriate to ensure the effective collection of income tax.

54. The Odvolací finanční ředitelství adds that the legislation may nevertheless be justified by the need to prevent tax evasion and avoidance. Furthermore, according to the Czech Government, the arrangements for administrative co-operation in the field of taxation are not sufficiently effective to prevent potential tax avoidance. The experience of the tax authorities shows that there have been numerous cases of tax evasion and avoidance in connection with the international hiring of workers.

55. It is true that the Court has held on several occasions that the prevention of tax avoidance and the need for effective fiscal supervision may be relied on to justify restrictions on the exercise of the fundamental freedoms guaranteed by the Treaty

(see Baxter and Others, C-254/97, EU:C:1999:368, paragraph 18, and Commission v Belgium EU:C:2006:702, paragraph 35).

56. However, the Court has also stated that a general presumption of tax avoidance or evasion based on the fact that a service provider is based in another Member State is not sufficient to justify a fiscal measure which compromises the objectives of the Treaty (see, to that effect, Centro di Musicologia Walter Stauffer, C-386/04, EU:C:2006:568, paragraph 61; Commission v Belgium, EU:C:2006:702, paragraph 35; and Commission v Spain, C-153/08, EU:C:2009:618, paragraph 39).

57. First, the contentions of the Czech Republic concerning numerous cases of tax evasion and avoidance in connection with the international hiring of workers are vague, inter alia concerning the specific situation of temporary employment agencies established in other Member States with a branch registered in the Czech Republic.

58. Secondly, the fact that the branch concerned in Case C-80/13 is responsible for the administrative tasks which enable the withholding tax at issue in the main proceedings to be deducted and paid make it possible to doubt the validity of such a general presumption.

59. In those circumstances, the application of the withholding tax at issue in the main proceedings cannot be justified as being necessary for the prevention of tax evasion and avoidance.

60. In the light of the foregoing, the answer to the question in Case C-53/13 and to the first and third questions in Case C-80/13 is that Article 56 TFEU precludes legislation, such as that at issue in the main proceedings, under which companies established in one Member State using workers employed and seconded by temporary employment agencies established in another Member State, but operating in the first Member State through a branch, are obliged to withhold tax and to pay to the first Member State an advance payment on the income tax due by those workers, whereas the same obligation is not imposed on companies established in the first Member State which use the services of temporary employment agencies established in that Member State.

Second question in Case C-80/13

61. By its second question in Case C-80/13 the referring court asks, in essence, whether Article 56 TFEU precludes legislation, such as that at issue in the main proceedings, under which, where the amount invoiced by the temporary employment agency resident in another Member State contains both the salary of the seconded workers and the intermediation fee, the basis of assessment for calculating that advance payment is set at at least 60% of that amount, without it being possible for the taxa-

ble person to show that the salary actually received by the workers is less than 60% of that amount.

62. It must be stated that, in so far as the procedure for calculating the withholding tax at question is closely linked to the obligation to carry out that withholding operation and, as is apparent from the order for reference in Case C-80/13, applies only where the recipient of the services at issue is called on to carry out that withholding operation, in the light of the answer given to the question in Case C-53/13 and to the first and third questions in Case C-80/13, there is no need to reply to that question.

Costs

[Para. 63 omitted]

On those grounds,

THE COURT (First Chamber,)

hereby rules:

Article 56 TFEU precludes legislation, such as that at issue in the main proceedings, under which companies established in one Member State using workers employed and seconded by temporary employment agencies established in another Member State, but operating in the first Member State through a branch, are obliged to withhold tax and to pay to the first Member State an advance payment on the income tax due by those workers, whereas the same obligation is not imposed on companies established in the first Member State which use the services of temporary employment agencies established in that Member State.

Comments and questions

The *Prostějov* case concerned the compatibility of Czech tax law with Union law. Under the Czech law a Czech resident (the recipient of services) was required to withhold and pay tax on income payable by the workers whose labour they had used. The labour had been made available by an employment bureau based in another Member State. However, if the Czech resident had instead hired labour from an employment bureau based in the Czech Republic, the obligation to withhold and pay tax would fall on the Czech employment bureau and the recipient of the sevices would not have to fulfil this obligation.

The case concerned two Czech undertakings, Strojírny Prostějov and ACO Industries Tábor, which had used the services of an employment bureau which was based in Slovakia but which conducted business in the Czech Republic through a branch which was listed in the Czech commercial register. As recipients of services for a limited period, these two undertakings had used labour provided by employees of the employment bureau.

The CJEU started by establishing that the Czech law should only be assessed in relation to Article 56 TFEU, on the freedom to provide services. Thus the CJEU rejected the Commission's argument that the disputed legislation should be assessed in relation to Article 45 TFEU, on the free movement of workers, and Article 49 on freedom of establishment. Why did the CJEU choose to focus on Article 56 rather than the other two freedoms?

Having ruled that the case should be judged under the rules on freedom to provide services, the CJEU turned to the question of whether there was a restriction on this freedom. In this connection the CJEU reviewed its settled case law on the concept of a restriction, which covers national measures that prohibit, impede or render less attractive the exercise of the freedom to provide services. The CJEU also confirmed that Article 56 TFEU concerns not only the rights of the service provider, but also the rights of the service recipient. The CJEU found that there was a restriction covered by Article 56 TFEU, since the obligation to withhold advance payments of the income tax of workers supplied by temporary employment bureaus established outside the Czech Republic and to pay that advance payment to the Czech State inevitably imposed a burden on the recipients of the services and was an additional administrative burden which was not imposed on recipients of the same services provided by a resident service provider. Such an obligation may make cross-border services less attractive for recipients of service from foreign service providers than services provided by domestic service providers. This will deter service users using the services of providers resident in other Member States.

Denmark intervened in the proceedings before the CJEU, and argued that the situation of agencies established in the Czech Republic is objectively different from that of agencies established outside the Czech Republic with regard to the conditions for withholding and collecting tax. Denmark argued that a Member State cannot withhold and collect tax from foreign service providers and their foreign employees. In relation to these foreign service providers and their foreign employees the Member State acts in its capacity as withholding tax at source and cooperates independently with the tax authorities in the other Member State where the service provider is established. The CJEU dismissed the Danish Government's arguments; see paragraphs 39-41. What were the CJEU's reasons? Do you agree with the CJEU or do you find is reasonable to criticis the ruling?

Since the CJEU had found that the Czech system constituted a restriction, it had to decide whether this restriction could be justified on the ground of overriding requirements in the public interest. According to the referring court and the submission of the Czech Government, the Czech legislation was based on the need to ensure the effective collection of income tax. The CJEU accepted this consideration, noting 'that the Court has already recognised that the need to ensure the effective collection of income tax may constitute an overriding reason in the public interest capable of justifying a restriction on the freedom to provide services ... In particular, the Court even stated that the procedure of retention at source is a legitimate and appropriate means of ensuring the tax treatment of the income of a person established outside the State of taxation and ensuring that the income concerned does not escape taxation in the State of residence and the State where the services are provided.' In connection with this, the CJEU emphasised that its acceptance was based on the fact that 'the service providers at issue in those cases provided occasional services in a Member State other than that in which they were established, and remained there for only a short period of time.'

However, in the case before it, it could not reasonably be argued that that the employment bureau in the case provided 'occasional services' in the Czech Republic. The bureau operated through a branch that was listed in the Czech commercial register. In relation to this the CJEU stated:

> 'In those circumstances, even though, as the Czech Government states, a branch, under Czech law, does not have legal personality and cannot therefore be obliged to pay taxes under Czech law, the fact remains that such a branch provides the service provider with a physical presence in the territory of the host Member State and performs certain administrative tasks on behalf of the temporary employment agency concerned such as signing contracts. In this respect, not only can it not be excluded that the Czech tax authorities recover the tax due from that branch and that therefore that branch carries out the withholding at issue, but it is also apparent from the documents before the Court in Case C-80/13 that, in this case, the advance payments on the salaries of the employees concerned were in fact made by the branch of the Slovak temporary employment agency. Furthermore, the imposition on the resident recipients of those services, instead of on the Czech branch of the agencies resident in other Member States, of the administrative burden linked to the withholding tax on income payable by the seconded workers does not appear to be simpler or more efficient from the point of view of the service providers or from the point of view of the Czech administration. Since the branch of the temporary employment agency of which the workers are employees has the necessary information concerning the income of those workers more easily available to it, the administrative burden connected to the withholding operation would be less onerous for that branch than for the recipient of the services.'

In these circumstances the CJEU concluded that the Czech legislation was not designed to ensure the effective collection of income tax. In other words, the CJEU found that the Czech legislation in the case did not fulfil the requirements of Article 56 TFEU in a proportionate manner.

JUDGMENT OF THE COURT
4 October 1991

The Society for the Protection of Unborn Children Ireland Ltd v Stephen Grogan and others. (Reference for a preliminary ruling: High Court – Ireland)

'Freedom to provide services – Prohibition on the distribution of information on clinics carrying out voluntary terminations of pregnancy in other Member States'

Case C-159/90

Judgment

1. By order dated 5 March 1990, which was received at the Court on 23 May 1990, the High Court of Ireland referred to the Court for a preliminary ruling under Article 177 of the EEC Treaty three questions on the interpretation of Community law, in particular Article 60 of the EEC Treaty.

2. The questions arose in proceedings brought by the Society for the Protection of Unborn Children Ireland Ltd ('SPUC') against Stephen Grogan and fourteen other officers of students associations in connection with the distribution in Ireland of specific information relating to the identity and location of clinics in another Member State where medical termination of pregnancy is carried out.

3. Abortion has always been prohibited in Ireland, first of all at common law, then by statute. The relevant provisions at present in force are Sections 58 and 59 of the Offences Against the Person Act 1861, as reaffirmed in the Health (Family Planning) Act 1979.

4. In 1983 a constitutional amendment approved by referendum inserted in Article 40, Section 3, of the Irish Constitution a third subsection worded as follows: 'The State acknowledges the right to life of the unborn and, with due regard to the equal right to life of the mother, guarantees in its laws to respect, and, as far as practicable, by its laws to defend and vindicate that right.'

5. According to the Irish courts (High Court, judgment of 19 December 1986, and Supreme Court, judgment of 16 March 1988, The Attorney General (at the relation of the Society for the Protection of Unborn Children Ireland Ltd) v Open Door Counselling Ltd and Dublin Wellwoman Centre Ltd [1988] Irish Reports 593), to assist pregnant women in Ireland to travel abroad to obtain abortions, inter alia by informing them of the identity and location of a specific clinic or clinics where abortions are performed and how to contact such clinics, is prohibited under Article 40.3.3 of the Irish Constitution.

6. SPUC, the plaintiff in the main proceedings, is a company incorporated under Irish law whose purpose is to prevent the decriminalization of abortion and to affirm, defend and promote human life from the moment of conception. In 1989/90 Stephen Grogan and the other defendants in the main proceedings were officers of students associations which issued certain publications for students. Those publications contained information about the availability of legal abortion in the United Kingdom, the identity and location of a number of abortion clinics in that country and how to contact them. It is undisputed that the students associations had no links with clinics in another Member State.

7. In September 1989 SPUC requested the defendants, in their capacity as officers of their respective associations, to undertake not to publish information of the kind described above during the academic year 1989/90. The defendants did not reply, and SPUC then brought proceedings in the High Court for a declaration that the distribution of such information was unlawful and for an injunction restraining its distribution.

8. By a judgment of 11 October 1989 the High Court decided to refer certain questions to the Court of Justice for a preliminary ruling under Article 177 of the EEC Treaty before ruling on the injunction applied for by the plaintiff. An appeal was brought against that judgment and, on 19 December 1989, the Supreme Court granted the injunction applied for but did not overturn the High Court's decision to refer questions to the Court of Justice for a preliminary ruling. Moreover, each of the parties was given leave to apply to the High Court in order to vary the decision of the Supreme Court in the light of the preliminary ruling to be given by the Court of Justice.

9. As it had already indicated in its judgment of 11 October 1989, the High Court considered that the case raised problems of interpretation of Community law; it therefore stayed the proceedings and referred the following questions to the Court of Justice for a preliminary ruling:

   '1. Does the organized activity or process of carrying out an abortion or the medical termination of pregnancy come within the definition of 'services' provided for in Article 60 of the Treaty establishing the European Economic Community?

   2. In the absence of any measures providing for the approximation of the laws of Member States concerning the organized activity or process of carrying out an abortion or the medical termination of pregnancy, can a Member State prohibit the distribution of specific information about the identity, location and means of communication with a specified clinic or clinics in another Member State where abortions are performed?

3. Is there a right at Community law in a person in Member State A to distribute specific information about the identity, location and means of communication with a specified clinic or clinics in Member State B where abortions are performed, where the provision of abortion is prohibited under both the Constitution and the criminal law of Member State A but is lawful under certain conditions in Member State B?'

10. Reference is made to the Report for the Hearing for a fuller account of the facts of the case, the course of the procedure and the written observations submitted to the Court, which are mentioned or discussed hereinafter only in so far as is necessary for the reasoning of the Court.

Jurisdiction of the Court

[Paras 11-15 omitted]

First question

16. In its first question, the national court essentially seeks to establish whether medical termination of pregnancy, performed in accordance with the law of the State where it is carried out, constitutes a service within the meaning of Article 60 of the EEC Treaty.

17. According to the first paragraph of that provision, services are to be considered to be 'services' within the meaning of the Treaty where they are normally provided for remuneration, in so far as they are not governed by the provisions relating to freedom of movement for goods, capital or persons. Indent (d) of the second paragraph of Article 60 expressly states that activities of the professions fall within the definition of services.

18. It must be held that termination of pregnancy, as lawfully practised in several Member States, is a medical activity which is normally provided for remuneration and may be carried out as part of a professional activity. In any event, the Court has already held in the judgment in Luisi and Carbone (Joined Cases 286/82 and 26/83 Luisi and Carbone v Ministero del Tesoro [1984] ECR 377, paragraph 16) that medical activities fall within the scope of Article 60 of the Treaty.

19. SPUC, however, maintains that the provision of abortion cannot be regarded as being a service, on the grounds that it is grossly immoral and involves the destruction of the life of a human being, namely the unborn child.

20. Whatever the merits of those arguments on the moral plane, they cannot influence the answer to the national court's first question. It is not for the Court to substitute

its assessment for that of the legislature in those Member States where the activities in question are practised legally.

21. Consequently, the answer to the national court's first question must be that medical termination of pregnancy, performed in accordance with the law of the State in which it is carried out, constitutes a service within the meaning of Article 60 of the Treaty.

Second and third questions

22. Having regard to the facts of the case, it must be considered that, in its second and third questions, the national court seeks essentially to establish whether it is contrary to Community law for a Member State in which medical termination of pregnancy is forbidden to prohibit students associations from distributing information about the identity and location of clinics in another Member State where medical termination of pregnancy is lawfully carried out and the means of communicating with those clinics, where the clinics in question have no involvement in the distribution of the said information.

23. Although the national court's questions refer to Community law in general, the Court takes the view that its attention should be focused on the provisions of Article 59 et seq. of the EEC Treaty, which deal with the freedom to provide services, and the argument concerning human rights, which has been treated extensively in the observations submitted to the Court.

24. As regards, first, the provisions of Article 59 of the Treaty, which prohibit any restriction on the freedom to supply services, it is apparent from the facts of the case that the link between the activity of the students associations of which Mr Grogan and the other defendants are officers and medical terminations of pregnancies carried out in clinics in another Member State is too tenuous for the prohibition on the distribution of information to be capable of being regarded as a restriction within the meaning of Article 59 of the Treaty.

25. The situation in which students associations distributing the information at issue in the main proceedings are not in cooperation with the clinics whose addresses they publish can be distinguished from the situation which gave rise to the judgment in GB-INNO-BM (Case C-362/88 GB-INNO-BM v Confédération du Commerce Luxembourgeois [1990] I-667), in which the Court held that a prohibition on the distribution of advertising was capable of constituting a barrier to the free movement of goods and therefore had to be examined in the light of Articles 30, 31 and 36 of the EEC Treaty.

26. The information to which the national court's questions refer is not distributed on behalf of an economic operator established in another Member State. On the contra-

ry, the information constitutes a manifestation of freedom of expression and of the freedom to impart and receive information which is independent of the economic activity carried on by clinics established in another Member State.

27. It follows that, in any event, a prohibition on the distribution of information in circumstances such as those which are the subject of the main proceedings cannot be regarded as a restriction within the meaning of Article 59 of the Treaty.

28. Secondly, it is necessary to consider the argument of the defendants in the main proceedings to the effect that the prohibition in question, inasmuch as it is based on a constitutional amendment approved in 1983, is contrary to Article 62 of the EEC Treaty, which provides that Member States are not to introduce any new restrictions on the freedom to provide services in fact attained at the date when the Treaty entered into force.

29. It is sufficient to observe, as far as that argument is concerned, that Article 62, which is complementary to Article 59, cannot prohibit restrictions which do not fall within the scope of Article 59.

30. Thirdly and lastly, the defendants in the main proceedings maintain that a prohibition such as the one at issue is in breach of fundamental rights, especially of freedom of expression and the freedom to receive and impart information, enshrined in particular in Article 10(1) of the European Convention on Human Rights.

31. According to, inter alia, the judgment of 18 June 1991 in Elliniki Radiophonia Tileorasi (Case C-260/89 *Elliniki Radiophonia Tileorasi* v *Dimotiki Etairia Pliroforissis* [1991] ECR I-2951, paragraph 42), where national legislation falls within the field of application of Community law the Court, when requested to give a preliminary ruling, must provide the national court with all the elements of interpretation which are necessary in order to enable it to assess the compatibility of that legislation with the fundamental rights – as laid down in particular in the European Convention on Human Rights – the observance of which the Court ensures. However, the Court has no such jurisdiction with regard to national legislation lying outside the scope of Community law. In view of the facts of the case and of the conclusions which the Court has reached above with regard to the scope of Articles 59 and 62 of the Treaty, that would appear to be true of the prohibition at issue before the national court.

32. The reply to the national court's second and third questions must therefore be that it is not contrary to Community law for a Member State in which medical termination of pregnancy is forbidden to prohibit students associations from distributing information about the identity and location of clinics in another Member State where voluntary termination of pregnancy is lawfully carried out and the means of com-

municating with those clinics, where the clinics in question have no involvement in the distribution of the said information.

Costs

[Para. 33 omitted]

On those grounds,

THE COURT,

in reply to the questions submitted to it by the High Court of Ireland, by order of 5 March 1990, hereby rules:

1. **Medical termination of pregnancy, performed in accordance with the law of the State in which it is carried out, constitutes a service within the meaning of Article 60 of the Treaty;**

2. **It is not contrary to Community law for a Member State in which medical termination of pregnancy is forbidden to prohibit students associations from distributing information about the identity and location of clinics in another Member State where voluntary termination of pregnancy is lawfully carried out and the means of communicating with those clinics, where the clinics in question have no involvement in the distribution of the said information.**

Comments and questions

Abortions, undertaken at medical clinics for payment, are a service; cf. paragraph 18 of Case C-159/90 *The Society for the Protection of Unborn Children Ireland Ltd (SPUC)* v *Grogan and others* [1991] ECR I-4685. It was SPUC's view that abortions could not be regarded as a service, since they involve an immoral action. The CJEU rejected this argument, stating that it is 'not for the Court to substitute its assessment for that of the legislature in those Member States where the activities in question are practised legally'; cf. paragraph 20.

At the date of the judgment (1991), the view of the CJEU was that advertisements for services were unquestionably protected under Article 56 TFEU (formerly Article 59 EEC Treaty) to the same extent as the services for which they advertised. This can be seen from the CJEU's reference to Case C-362/88 *GB-INNO-BM* v *Confédération du commerce luxembourgeois* [1990] ECR I-667, at paragraph 25 of the judgment, which concerned Article 34 TFEU (formerly Article 30 EEC Treaty). In the *Grogan* case it appeared, however, that student organisations did not distribute advertising on behalf of abortion clinics. On this basis the CJEU found that the connection between the work of the student organisations and the abortions which took place at clinics in another Member State was too tenuous for a prohibition against the dissemination of information to be regarded as a restriction within the meaning of Article 56 TFEU; cf. paragraph 24 of the judgment. There was therefore no restriction contrary to this provision.

Advertising is certainly covered by the protection of freedom of expression, as laid down in Article 10 of the European Convention for the Protection of Human Rights and Fundamental Freedoms, and thus the European Court of Human Rights (ECHR) has subsequently held that the Irish prohibition on the dissemination of advertisements for abortion services at clinics in the United Kingdom was incompatible with the right to make and to receive free expression; cf. ECHR 246 *Open Door*. The CJEU has repeatedly held that Union law must respect the European Convention on Human Rights, and the CJEU considers that it has a duty to ensure that Union law complies with the Convention. However, the CJEU does *not* have such powers with regard to national laws on matters which do not fall within the scope of Union law; cf. paragraph 31. Would it have affected the outcome of the case if a business agreement had been entered into between Grogan and the British clinics, under which Grogan should place advertisements in student newspapers etc.? Could the Irish prohibition have been justified on public policy grounds; cf. Article 62 TFEU (formerly Article 66 EEC Treaty)? In this connection, refer to Protocol 35 to the TEU and the TFEU, under which 'nothing in these Treaties shall affect the application in Ireland of Article 40.3.3 of the Constitution of Ireland' (which recognises the right to life of unborn children).

Under the CJEU's *Keck* doctrine, non-discriminatory national rules on advertising for goods fall outside the scope of Article 34 TFEU. The question is whether this practice is transferable to Article 56 TFEU. The answer seems to be equivocal. On the one hand, in Joined Cases C-51/96 and C-191/97 *Deliège* v *Ligue francophone de judo* [2000] ECR I-2549, the CJEU considered that non-discriminatory rules for selection to international sports competitions, which do not regulate access to the market for service provision, fall outside the scope of Article 56 TFEU. This case is discussed below in the commentary on Case C-384/93 *Alpine Investments* [1995] ECR I-1141. On the other hand, the CJEU has held that non-discriminatory national rules on marketing and on television advertising for certain services fall within the scope of Article 56 TFEU, and, in this respect, the CJEU has rejected the transference of the *Keck* doctrine to Article 56 TFEU. On this point, see Case C-384/93 *Alpine Investments BV* v *Minister van Financiën* [1995] ECR I-1141, printed below, and Joined Cases C-34/95 and others *Konsument-ombudsmannen* v *De Agostini (Svenska) Förlag and TV-Shop* [1997] ECR I-3843.

JUDGMENT OF THE COURT
10 May 1995

Alpine Investments BV v Minister van Financiën.
(Reference for a preliminary ruling: College van Beroep voor het Bedrijfsleven – Netherlands)

'Freedom to provide services – Article 59 of the EEC Treaty – Prohibition of cold calling by telephone for financial services'

Case C-384/93

Judgment

1. By order of 28 April 1993, received at the Court on 6 August 1993, the College van Beroep voor het Bedrijfsleven (Administrative Court for Trade and Industry; hereinafter 'the Administrative Court') referred to the Court for a preliminary ruling under Article 177 of the EEC Treaty several questions on the interpretation of Article 59 of the Treaty.

2. Those questions were raised in proceedings brought by Alpine Investments BV challenging the restriction imposed on it by the Netherlands Ministry of Finance prohibiting it from contacting individuals by telephone without their prior consent in writing in order to offer them various financial services (a practice known as 'cold calling').

3. Alpine Investments BV, the applicant in the main proceedings (hereinafter 'Alpine Investments'), is a company incorporated under Netherlands law and established in the Netherlands which specializes in commodities futures.

4. The parties to a commodities futures contract undertake to buy or sell a specified quantity of a commodity of a given quality at a price and date fixed at the time the contract is concluded. They do not, however, intend actually to take delivery of or to deliver the commodity but contract solely in the hope of profiting from price fluctuations between the time the contract is concluded and the month of delivery. This can be done by entering into a mirror-image transaction on the futures market before the beginning of the month of delivery.

5. Alpine Investments offers three types of service in relation to commodities futures contracts: portfolio management, investment advice and the transmission of clients' orders to brokers operating on commodities futures markets both within and outside the Community. It has clients not only in the Netherlands but also in Belgium,

France and the United Kingdom. It is not however established anywhere outside the Netherlands.

6. At the time of the events which gave rise to the main proceedings, financial services were governed in the Netherlands by the Wet Effectenhandel (Law on Securities Transactions) of 30 October 1985. Article 6(1) of that law prohibited a person from acting as an intermediary in securities transactions without a licence. Article 8(1) empowered the Minister for Finance to grant an exemption from that prohibition in special circumstances. However, Article 8(2) provided that the exemption could 'be subject to restrictions and conditions with a view to preventing undesirable developments in securities trading'.

7. On 6 September 1991 the Minister for Finance, respondent in the main proceedings, granted Alpine Investments an exemption permitting it to place orders with a specified broker, Merrill Lynch Inc. The exemption required Alpine Investments to comply with any rules which might be issued by the Minister for Finance in the near future regarding its contacts with potential clients.

8. On 1 October 1991 the Minister for Finance decided to impose a general prohibition on financial intermediaries who offered investments in off-market commodities futures from cold calling potential clients.

9. According to the Netherlands Government, that decision was taken following numerous complaints received during 1991 by the Minister for Finance from investors who had made unfortunate investments in that sector. Since some of those complaints came from investors established in other Member States, he extended the prohibition to offers of services made to other Member States from the Netherlands, with a view to preserving the reputation of the Netherlands financial sector.

10. Those are the circumstances in which the Minister for Finance on 12 November 1991 prohibited Alpine Investments from contacting potential clients by telephone or in person unless those clients had first expressly authorized it in writing to contact them in such a manner.

11. Alpine Investments raised an administrative objection against the Minister's decision prohibiting it from cold calling. Subsequently, the exemption having been replaced on 14 January 1992 by another exemption allowing it to place orders with another broker, Rodham & Renshaw Inc., an exemption which also included the prohibition of cold calling, it raised a new administrative objection on 13 February 1992.

12. By decision of 29 April 1992, the Minster for Finance rejected Alpine Investment's administrative objection. On 26 May 1992 Alpine Investments appealed to the Administrative Court.

13. Alpine Investments pleaded in particular that the prohibition of cold calling was incompatible with Article 59 of the Treaty in so far as it concerned potential clients established in Member States other than the Netherlands. The Administrative Court referred several questions on the interpretation of that provision to the Court of Justice:

    '1) Must Article 59 of the EEC Treaty be interpreted as meaning that it also covers services which the provider offers by telephone from the Member State of his establishment to (potential) clients established in another Member State and therefore also provides from that Member State?

    2) Does Article 59 also apply to the provisions and/or restrictions which in the Member State of establishment of the provider of services govern the lawful exercise of the occupation or business concerned but do not apply – in any event not in the same way and to the same extent – to the exercise of that occupation or business in the Member State of establishment of (potential) recipients of the service in question and for that reason may constitute for the provider of services when offering his services to (potential) clients established in another Member State hindrances that do not apply to providers of similar services established in that other Member State?

    If the answer to the second question is yes:

    3) (a) Can the concern to protect consumers and safeguard the reputation of the Netherlands securities trading sector which underlies a provision aimed at combating undesirable developments in the securities trading sector be regarded as imperative reasons of public interest justifying a hindrance such as that referred to in question (2)?

    (b) Is a proviso in an exemption banning cold calling to be regarded as objectively necessary to protect the aforementioned concern and as proportionate to the objective pursued?'

14. It should be noted as a preliminary point that, were it applicable to transactions on commodities futures markets, Council Directive 93/22/EEC of 10 May 1993 on investment services in the securities field (OJ 1993 L 141, p. 27) post-dates the events which gave rise to the main proceedings. Furthermore, Council Directive 85/577/EEC of 20 December 1985 concerning the protection of consumers in respect of contracts negotiated away from business premises (OJ 1985 L 372, p. 31) applies neither to contracts concluded by telephone nor to contracts for securities (Article 3(2)(e)).

15. The questions referred to the Court must therefore be examined solely in the light of the Treaty provisions on the freedom to provide services. It is common ground that,

since they were provided for remuneration, the services provided by Alpine Investments are services covered by Article 60 of the EEC Treaty.

16. The national court's first and second questions essentially ask whether the prohibition of cold calling falls within the scope of Article 59 of the Treaty. If so, its third question asks whether that prohibition may none the less be justified.

The first question

17. There are two aspects to the national court's first question.

18. First, it asks whether the fact that the services in question are just offers without, as yet, an identifiable recipient of the service precludes application of Article 59 of the Treaty.

19. The freedom to provide services would become illusory if national rules were at liberty to restrict offers of services. The prior existence of an identifiable recipient cannot therefore be a condition for application of the provisions on the freedom to provide services.

20. The second aspect of the question is whether Article 59 covers services which the provider offers by telephone to persons established in another Member State and which he provides without moving from the Member State in which he is established.

21. In this case, the offers of services are made by a provider established in one Member State to a potential recipient established in another Member State. It follows from the express terms of Article 59 that there is therefore a provision of services within the meaning of that provision.

22. The answer to the first question is therefore that, on a proper construction, Article 59 of the EEC Treaty covers services which the provider offers by telephone to potential recipients established in other Member States and provides without moving from the Member State in which he is established.

The second question

23. The national court's second question asks whether rules of a Member State which prohibit providers of services established in its territory from making unsolicited telephone calls to potential clients established in other Member States in order to offer their services constitute a restriction on freedom to provide services within the meaning of Article 59 of the Treaty.

24. The preliminary observation should be made that the prohibition at issue applies to the offer of cross-border services.

25. In order to reply to the national court's question, three points must be examined in turn.

26. First, it must be determined whether the prohibition against telephoning potential clients in another Member State without their prior consent can constitute a restriction on freedom to provide services. The national court draws the Court's attention to the fact that providers established in the Member States where the potential recipients reside are not necessarily subject to the same prohibition or in any event not on the same terms.

27. A prohibition such as that at issue in the main proceedings does not constitute a restriction on freedom to provide services within the meaning of Article 59 solely by virtue of the fact that other Member States apply less strict rules to providers of similar services established in their territory (see the judgment in Case C-379/92 Peralta [1994] ECR I-3453, paragraph 48).

28. However, such a prohibition deprives the operators concerned of a rapid and direct technique for marketing and for contacting potential clients in other Member States. It can therefore constitute a restriction on the freedom to provide cross-border services.

29. Secondly, it must be considered whether that conclusion may be affected by the fact that the prohibition at issue is imposed by the Member State in which the provider is established and not by the Member State in which the potential recipient is established.

30. The first paragraph of Article 59 of the Treaty prohibits restrictions on freedom to provide services within the Community in general. Consequently, that provision covers not only restrictions laid down by the State of destination but also those laid down by the State of origin. As the Court has frequently held, the right freely to provide services may be relied on by an undertaking as against the State in which it is established if the services are provided for persons established in another Member State (see Case C-18/93 *Corsica Ferries Italia* v *Corpo dei Piloti del Porto di Genova* [1994] ECR I-1783, paragraph 30; Peralta, cited above, paragraph 40, and Case C-381/93 Commission v France [1994] ECR I-5145, paragraph 14).

31. It follows that the prohibition of cold calling does not fall outside the scope of Article 59 of the Treaty simply because it is imposed by the State in which the provider of services is established.

32. Finally, certain arguments adduced by the Netherlands Government and the United Kingdom must be considered.

33. They submit that the prohibition at issue falls outside the scope of Article 59 of the Treaty because it is a generally applicable measure, it is not discriminatory and neither its object nor its effect is to put the national market at an advantage over providers of services from other Member States. Since it affects only the way in which the services are offered, it is analogous to the non-discriminatory measures governing selling arrangements which, according to the decision in Joined Cases C-267 and 268/91 *Keck and Mithouard* [1993] ECR I-6097, paragraph 16, do not fall within the scope of Article 30 of the Treaty.

34. Those arguments cannot be accepted.

35. Although a prohibition such as the one at issue in the main proceedings is general and non-discriminatory and neither its object nor its effect is to put the national market at an advantage over providers of services from other Member States, it can none the less, as has been held above (see paragraph 28), constitute a restriction on the freedom to provide cross-border services.

36. Such a prohibition is not analogous to the legislation concerning selling arrangements held in *Keck and Mithouard* to fall outside the scope of Article 30 of the Treaty.

37. According to that judgment, the application to products from other Member States of national provisions restricting or prohibiting, within the Member State of importation, certain selling arrangements is not such as to hinder trade between Member States so long as, first, those provisions apply to all relevant traders operating within the national territory and, secondly, they affect in the same manner, in law and in fact, the marketing of domestic products and of those from other Member States. The reason is that the application of such provisions is not such as to prevent access by the latter to the market of the Member State of importation or to impede such access more than it impedes access by domestic products.

38. A prohibition such as that at issue is imposed by the Member State in which the provider of services is established and affects not only offers made by him to addressees who are established in that State or move there in order to receive services but also offers made to potential recipients in another Member State. It therefore directly affects access to the market in services in the other Member States and is thus capable of hindering intra-Community trade in services.

39. The answer to the second question is therefore that rules of a Member State which prohibit providers of services established in its territory from making unsolicited telephone calls to potential clients established in other Member States in order to of-

fer their services constitute a restriction on freedom to provide services within the meaning of Article 59 of the Treaty.

The third question

40. The national court's third question asks whether imperative reasons of public interest justify the prohibition of cold calling and whether that prohibition must be considered to be objectively necessary and proportionate to the objective pursued.

41. The Netherlands Government argues that the prohibition of cold calling in off-market commodities futures trading seeks both to safeguard the reputation of the Netherlands financial markets and to protect the investing public.

42. Financial markets play an important role in the financing of economic operators and, given the speculative nature and the complexity of commodities futures contracts, the smooth operation of financial markets is largely contingent on the confidence they inspire in investors. That confidence depends in particular on the existence of professional regulations serving to ensure the competence and trustworthiness of the financial intermediaries on whom investors are particularly reliant.

43. Although the protection of consumers in the other Member States is not, as such, a matter for the Netherlands authorities, the nature and extent of that protection does none the less have a direct effect on the good reputation of Netherlands financial services.

44. Maintaining the good reputation of the national financial sector may therefore constitute an imperative reason of public interest capable of justifying restrictions on the freedom to provide financial services.

45. As for the proportionality of the restriction at issue, it is settled case-law that requirements imposed on the providers of services must be appropriate to ensure achievement of the intended aim and must not go beyond that which is necessary in order to achieve that objective (see Case C-288/89 Collectieve Antennevoorziening Gouda and Others v Commissariat voor de Media [1991] ECR I-4007, paragraph 15).

46. As the Netherlands Government has justifiably submitted, in the case of cold calling the individual, generally caught unawares, is in a position neither to ascertain the risks inherent in the type of transactions offered to him nor to compare the quality and price of the caller's services with competitors' offers. Since the commodities futures market is highly speculative and barely comprehensible for non-expert investors, it was necessary to protect them from the most aggressive selling techniques.

47. Alpine Investments argues however that the Netherlands Government's prohibition of cold calling is not necessary because the Member State of the provider of services should rely on the controls imposed by the Member State of the recipient.

48. That argument must be rejected. The Member State from which the telephone call is made is best placed to regulate cold calling. Even if the receiving State wishes to prohibit cold calling or to make it subject to certain conditions, it is not in a position to prevent or control telephone calls from another Member State without the cooperation of the competent authorities of that State.

49. Consequently, the prohibition of cold calling by the Member State from which the telephone call is made, with a view to protecting investor confidence in the financial markets of that State, cannot be considered to be inappropriate to achieve the objective of securing the integrity of those markets.

50. Alpine Investments also argues that a general prohibition of telephone canvassing of potential clients is not necessary for the achievement of the objectives pursued by the Netherlands authorities. Requiring broking firms to tape-record unsolicited telephone calls made by them would suffice to protect consumers effectively. Such rules have moreover been adopted in the United Kingdom by the Securities and Futures Authority.

51. That point of view cannot be accepted. As the Advocate General correctly states in point 88 of his Opinion, the fact that one Member State imposes less strict rules than another Member State does not mean that the latter's rules are disproportionate and hence incompatible with Community law.

52. Alpine Investments argues finally that, since it is of a general nature, the prohibition of cold calling does not take into account the conduct of individual undertakings and accordingly imposes an unnecessary burden on undertakings which have never been the subject of complaints by consumers.

53. That argument must also be rejected. Limiting the prohibition of cold calling to certain undertakings because of their past conduct might not be sufficient to achieve the objective of restoring and maintaining investor confidence in the national securities markets in general.

54. In any event, the rules at issue are limited in scope. First, they prohibit only the contacting of potential clients by telephone or in person without their prior agreement in writing, while other techniques for making contact are still permitted. Next, the measure affects relations with potential clients but not with existing clients who may still give their written agreement to further calls. Finally, the prohibition of unsolicited telephone calls is limited to the sector in which abuses have been found, namely the commodities futures market.

55. In the light of the above, the prohibition of cold calling does not appear disproportionate to the objective which it pursues.

56. The answer to the third question is therefore that Article 59 does not preclude national rules which, in order to protect investor confidence in national financial markets, prohibit the practice of making unsolicited telephone calls to potential clients resident in other Member States to offer them services linked to investment in commodities futures.

Costs

[Para. 57 omitted]

On those grounds,

THE COURT,

in answer to the questions referred to it by the College van Beroep voor het Bedrijfsleven by order of 28 April 1993, hereby rules:

1. **On a proper construction, Article 59 of the EEC Treaty covers services which the provider offers by telephone to potential recipients established in other Member States and provides without moving from the Member State in which he is established.**

2. **Rules of a Member State which prohibit providers of services established in its territory from making unsolicited telephone calls to potential clients established in other Member States in order to offer their services constitute a restriction on freedom to provide services within the meaning of Article 59 of the Treaty.**

3. **Article 59 does not preclude national rules which, in order to protect investor confidence in national financial markets, prohibit the practice of making unsolicited telephone calls to potential clients resident in other Member States to offer them services linked to investment in commodities futures.**

Comments and questions

Case C-384/93 *Alpine Investments BV* v *Minister van Financiën* [1995] ECR I-1141, concerned Dutch marketing rules under which there was a prohibition on the sale of certain forms of financial services by means of telephone cold-calling. The prohibition applied both to calls made within the Netherlands and calls made abroad, so that this was a cross-border regulation. By way of introduction, the CJEU stated that Article 56 TFEU (formerly Article 59 EEC Treaty) applies to cases where a service provider offers services to potential customers and is not restricted to the supply of services to already identified recipients of services; cf. paragraphs 18 and 19. Next, the CJEU held that the Dutch rule did not constitute a restriction on the freedom to provide services within the meaning of Article 56 TFEU solely by virtue of the fact that other Member States apply less strict rules to providers of similar services established in their territory; cf. paragraph 27.

The CJEU regarded the Dutch rule as a restriction, since it deprived undertakings of the possibility of making rapid and direct sales contact with potential customers in other Member States, and is thus capable of being a restriction; cf. paragraph 28. Compare this with Case 249/81 *Commission* v *Ireland* (the *Buy Irish* case) [1982] ECR 4005, printed in Chapter 2. Furthermore, the CJEU held that Article 56 TFEU not only covers restrictions laid down by the Member State where the services are received, but also those laid down by the Member State from which they are provided; cf. paragraph 30.

It was the view of both the Netherlands Government and the British Government that the Dutch rule did not fall within the scope of Article 56 TFEU, since it was a general measure which applied to all services, regardless of nationality, and which did not have the effect of giving the domestic market an advantage in relation to service providers from other Member States, since the prohibition only concerned the method by which the services were offered. The prohibition ought therefore to be considered as comparable to the national measures covered by the *Keck* doctrine. The CJEU dismissed this argument. It held that that the prohibition did constitute a restriction on the freedom to provide cross-border services, so that it was not analogous to 'selling arrangements' referred to in the *Keck* case; cf. paragraphs 35-36. Presumably this was because the CJEU took the view that the Dutch rule in the *Alpine Investments* case concerned *access* to foreign markets.

Does this case mean that the CJEU has generally refused to interpret the *Keck* doctrine as applying to service provision under Article 56 TFEU, so that non-discriminatory marketing rules are effectively always covered by Article 56 TFEU?

It has still not been entirely clarified whether the *Keck* doctrine, which applies to goods, is also applicable to the area of service provision (see the similar Case C-483/12 *Pelckmans*, judgment of 8 May 2014, printed below). The idea behind such application is that the Treaty rules on service provision determine the norms for the Member States' legislation on non-discrimination with regard to the requirements as to the qualifications etc. of service providers. This corresponds to the requirements relating to goods that are clearly covered by Article 34 TFEU. A requirement as to the qualifications etc. of a service provider who is already established in another Member State would undoubtedly be an obstacle to the freedom to provide services. But what about the non-discriminatory marketing rules in a broad sense which, under the *Keck* doctrine, fall outside the scope of Article 34 TFEU? Do rules on *when* a service can be provided, *who* can provide the service, and under *what conditions* a service can be provided etc. fall outside the scope of Article 56 TFEU?

In Joined Cases C-51/96 and C-191/97 *Deliège* [2000] ECR I-2549, the CJEU had to consider whether Article 56 TFEU was applicable to some non-discriminatory selection rules laid down by the Belgian Judo Federation for individual participation in international judo competitions.

The CJEU rejected the argument that Article 56 TFEU was applicable, stating in paragraph 61 that:

> 'in contrast to the rules applicable to the *Bosman* case, the selection rules at issue in the main proceedings do not determine the conditions governing access to the labour market by professional sportsmen and do not contain nationality clauses limiting the number of nationals of other Member States who may participate in a competition.'

The CJEU went on to state in paragraph 64 that:

> 'although selection rules like those at issue in the main proceedings inevitably have the effect of limiting the number of participants in a tournament, such a limitation is inherent in the conduct of an international high-level sports event, which necessarily involves certain selection rules or criteria being adopted. *Such rules may not therefore in themselves be regarded as constituting a restriction on the freedom to provide services* prohibited by Article [56 TFEU]' (emphasis added).

Paragraph 61 of the judgment can be understood as an acknowledgement that the CJEU, to a certain extent, accepts a *Keck* doctrine in relation to Article 56 TFEU. Non-discriminatory rules that affect a service provider but which do not lay down conditions for a service provider's access to the market are not a restriction, and are therefore outside the scope of Article 56 TFEU.

In the same way, the CJEU's statement in paragraph 31 of Joined Cases C-544/03 and C-545/03 *Mobistar* [2005] ECR I-7723 seems to echo the *Keck* doctrine. See paragraph 31 of this case which is quoted in the commentary on Case C-190/98 *Volker Graf* [2000] ECR I-493, in Chapter 4 above.

As opposed to this, the CJEU has rejected the application of the *Keck* doctrine in cases concerning national requirements for the marketing of a specific service. In this situation Article 56 TFEU applies. Such national requirements are therefore only compatible with Article 56 TFEU if they protect overriding public interests, and if they are necessary for and appropriate to the protection of that public interest. See also Joined Cases C-34/95 and others *TV-Shop* [1997] ECR I-3843. The rationale for applying Article 56 TFEU in these cases on national regulation of the marketing of a service is presumably that such national rules affect the access of foreign service providers to the national market. For example, a Croatian dentist established in Croatia would presumably have difficulty in obtaining Slovenian patients if Slovenian regulations prohibited the advertising of dentists' services.

Consider whether it would be contrary to the freedom to provide services if a Member State prohibited law firms with more than 100 employees keeping their offices open for making or receiving client communications at the weekends and on public holidays, and on ordinary working days from 5 o'clock in the evening until 9 o'clock in the morning. Would your assessment be different if the regulations applied to all law firms, regardless of size? Would your assessment be different if, instead of law firms, the regulations affected hairdressing salons or news bureaus? Also, consider whether a requirement that taxi services in London may only be provided by using the well-known London black cab, and not by other vehicle, will fulfil the requirement that a measure may only relate to 'certain selling arrangements'.

While *Keck* thinking is reflected in the *Deliège* case, the CJEU did not include the *Keck* doctrine in its assessment of whether the prohibition in the *TV-Shop* case was a restriction on freedom to provide services. This is because a prohibition on the broadcasting of television advertisements would mean that the service provider was wholly prevented from providing its services (i.e. the broadcasting of advertisements). In other words there would be no access to the market at all.

It must be assumed that, under normal circumstances, a Member State cannot claim protection of interests which are outside its territory. This means, for example, that Germany would not be able to prohibit the import of certain goods by reference to the interests of environmental protection or animal welfare in the Member State where the goods are produced. This policy is reflected in paragraph 43 of the judgment in the *Alpine Investments* case, where it is stated that 'the protection of consumers in the other Member States is not, as such, a matter for the Netherlands authorities'. Nevertheless, the Dutch prohibition of telephone cold-calling was justified by the need to protect the good reputation of the Dutch financial sector. This consideration directly concerned the Dutch national territory as opposed to the protection of foreign consumers.

Could Spain prohibit the import of aerosol containers, containing propellants which break down the ozone layer, without infringing Article 34 TFEU? Could Spain, without infringing Article 34 TFEU, prohibit the import and production in Spain of pelts from dogs and cats, by claiming that it is contrary to Spanish animal welfare ethics to breed dogs and cats for their fur, since these animals are pets and are part of so many Spanish families?

JUDGMENT OF THE COURT (First Chamber)
8 May 2014

Pelckmans Turnhout NV v Walter Van Gastel Balen NV, Walter Van Gastel NV, Walter Van Gastel Lifestyle NV, Walter Van Gastel Schoten NV, intervening parties: Ministerraad. (Request for a preliminary ruling: Grondwettelijk Hof - Belgium)

'Reference for a preliminary ruling – Charter of Fundamental Rights of the European Union – Principles of equality and non-discrimination – Implementation of EU law – Scope of application of EU law – None – Lack of jurisdiction of the Court'

Case C-483/12

Judgment

1. This request for a preliminary ruling concerns the interpretation of Articles 6(3) TEU and 20 and 21 of the Charter of Fundamental Rights of the European Union ('the Charter'), read in the light of Articles 15 and 16 of the Charter and Articles 34 TFEU to 36 TFEU, 56 TFEU and 57 TFEU.

2. The request has been made in proceedings between Pelckmans Turnhout NV ('Pelckmans') and Walter Van Gastel Balen NV, Walter Van Gastel NV, Walter Van Gastel Lifestyle NV and Walter Van Gastel Schoten NV, all companies which run garden centres.

Belgian legal context

[Paras 3-13 omitted]

Jurisdiction of the Court

14. By its question, the referring court asks, in essence, whether the principles of equality and non-discrimination, laid down in Articles 20 and 21 of the Charter, read in the light of Articles 15 and 16 of the Charter and Articles 34 TFEU to 36 TFEU, 56 TFEU and 57 TFEU, must be interpreted as precluding national legislation such as the LHO which, subject to a few exceptions, prohibits traders from opening their establishments seven days a week by imposing a requirement of one day of rest per week.

15. The German Government and the European Commission take the view that the Court of Justice has no jurisdiction to answer that question because there is nothing in the order for reference establishing that the subject-matter of the main proceedings has any connection with EU law.

16. In that regard, it should be borne in mind that, under Article 94(c) of the Rules of Procedure of the Court of Justice, a request for a preliminary ruling must contain a statement of the reasons which prompted the referring court or tribunal to inquire about the interpretation or validity of certain provisions of EU law, and the connection between those provisions and the national legislation applicable to the main proceedings. That statement of reasons, like the summary of the relevant findings of fact required under Article 94(a) of those Rules, must be of such a kind as to enable the Court to ascertain, not only whether the request for a preliminary ruling is admissible, but also whether it has jurisdiction to answer the question referred.

17. It should also be remembered that the Charter's field of application so far as concerns action of the Member States is defined in Article 51(1) thereof, according to which the provisions of the Charter are addressed to the Member States only when they are implementing EU law (Case C-617/10 *Åkerberg Fransson* EU:C:2013:105, paragraph 17).

18. That provision confirms the Court's settled case-law, according to which the fundamental rights guaranteed in the legal order of the European Union are applicable in all situations governed by EU law, but not outside such situations (see *Åkerberg Fransson* EU:C:2013:105, paragraph 19 and the case-law cited).

19. That definition of the field of application of the fundamental rights of the European Union is borne out by the explanations relating to Article 51 of the Charter, which, in accordance with the third subparagraph of Article 6(1) TEU and Article 52(7) of the Charter, have to be taken into consideration for the purpose of interpreting it. According to those explanations, 'the requirement to respect fundamental rights defined in the context of the Union is only binding on the Member States when they act in the scope of Union law' (*Åkerberg Fransson* EU:C:2013:105, paragraph 20).

20. It follows that, where a legal situation does not come within the scope of EU law, the Court does not have jurisdiction to rule on it and any provisions of the Charter relied upon cannot, of themselves, form the basis for such jurisdiction (see, to that effect, the order in Case C-466/11 *Currà and Others* EU:C:2012:465, paragraph 26, and *Åkerberg Fransson* EU:C:2013:105, paragraph 22).

21. These considerations correspond to those underlying Article 6(1) TEU, according to which the provisions of the Charter are not to extend in any way the competences of the European Union as defined in the Treaties. Likewise, the Charter, pursuant to Article 51(2) thereof, does not extend the field of application of EU law beyond the powers of the European Union or establish any new power or task for the European Union, or modify powers and tasks as defined in the Treaties (see Case C-400/10 PPU *McB.* EU:C:2010:582, paragraph 51; Case C-256/11 *Dereci and Others* EU:C:2011:734, paragraph 71; and *Åkerberg Fransson* EU:C:2013:105, paragraph 23).

22. There is nothing specific in the order for reference demonstrating that the legal situation at issue in the main proceedings comes within the scope of EU law.

23. Like the written observations submitted to the Court, that order contains nothing which establishes a connection between the facts of those proceedings and the Treaty provisions referred to by the referring court.

24. In any event, as regards the application of Articles 34 TFEU to 36 TFEU governing the free movement of goods, referred to by that court, it must be borne in mind, as this Court has observed on a number of occasions, that those provisions do not apply to national rules concerning the closure of shops that are enforceable against all economic operators pursuing activities within the national territory and that affect, in the same way, in law and in fact, the sale of domestic products and of products from other Member States (see, inter alia, Joined Cases C-69/93 and C-258/93 *Punto Casa and PPV* EU:C:1994:226, paragraph 15, and Joined Cases C-418/93 to C-421/93, C-460/93 to C-462/93, C-464/93, C-9/94 to C-11/94, C-14/94, C-15/94, C-23/94, C-24/94 and C-332/94 *Semeraro Casa Uno and Others* EU:C:1996:242, paragraph 28).

25. Similarly, as regards Articles 56 TFEU and 57 TFEU governing the freedom to provide series, also referred to by the referring court, suffice it to state that the legislation in question is applicable to all traders exercising their activity on national territory; that its purpose is not to regulate the conditions concerning the establishment of the undertakings concerned; and that any restrictive effects which it might have on freedom of establishment are too uncertain and indirect for the obligation laid down to be regarded as being capable of hindering that freedom (see, by analogy, *Semeraro Casa Uno and Others* EU:C:1996:242, paragraph 32).

26. It follows from all the foregoing that it has not been established that the Court has jurisdiction to interpret the provisions of the Charter referred to by the referring court.

27. In those circumstances, the Court has no jurisdiction to answer the question referred by the Grondwettelijk Hof.

Costs

[Para. 28 omitted]

On those grounds,

THE COURT (First Chamber),

hereby rules:

The Court of Justice of the European Union has no jurisdiction to answer the question referred by the Grondwettelijk Hof (Belgium).

Comments and questions

Whether the CJEU's decision in the *Pelckmans Turnhout* case is described as 'odd' or whether it is merely 'remarkable' is a matter of choice, but the judgment was certainly unusual. Thus, in the end the CJEU found that it did not have jurisdiction to give a preliminary ruling on the questions referred by the Belgian Constitutional Court. And this decision is – apparently –taken after the CJEU has applied the *Keck* doctrine on the free movement of services.

The *Pelckmans Turnhout* case concerned Belgian legislation on commercial opening hours. Among other things the CJEU found that Articles 34-36 TFEU, on the free movement of goods, and Articles 56 and 57 TFEU, on the free movement of services, did not apply to the facts of the case. In this connection, in relation to both of these freedoms the CJEU applied an approach that was in essence modelled on the *Keck* doctrine (Joined Cases C-267/91 and C-268/91 *Keck* [1993] ECR I-6097, printed in Chapter 2). In the *Keck* doctrine the CJEU established an assumption that national rules on specific forms of sale (i.e. marketing in a broad sense) fall outside the scope of Article 34 TFEU if the provisions:

(1) Apply to all commercial undertakings that operate in the domestic market; and

(2) Both in law and in fact affect the sales of domestically produced goods and goods from other Member States in the same way.

In the legal literature there is still a debate about whether it is possible to apply the Keck doctrine to the free movement of services pursuant to Article 56 TFEU. In several cases the CJEU has declined to apply the *Keck* doctrine to a national rule that governs the marketing of services.

The *Pelckmans Turnhout* case concerned national rules on 'sales' as traditionally understood. The case concerned Belgian legislation from 2006 on opening hours in commerce, crafts and services. The legislation included the following provision:

> 'Access of consumers to a unit of an establishment, the direct sale of goods and services to consumers and home deliveries shall be prohibited during an uninterrupted period of twenty-four hours beginning on Sunday at 05.00 or at 13.00 and finishing at the same time on the following day.'

Under the legislation a trader or service provider could chose a weekly closing day other than Sunday. However, the provision did not apply to categories of places selling specific forms of goods or services.

After a Belgian undertaking had infringed the obligation to have a weekly closing day, a dispute had arisen which ended up before the Belgian courts. This led the Belgian Constitutional Court to refer the following preliminary questions to the CJEU:

> 'Must the principle of equality, which is enshrined in Article 6(3) [TEU] and in Articles 20 and 21 of the Charter ..., in conjunction with Articles 15 and 16 of [the] Charter and Articles 34 to 36, 56 and 57 [TFEU], be interpreted as precluding rules such as those contained in Articles 8, 9, 16 and 17 of the [the Law of 10 November 2006 on opening hours in commerce, crafts and services], in so far as the obligation contained in those articles that a weekly closing day be provided for:
>
> – does not apply to traders established in railway stations or in units of establishment of public transport companies, to sales in airports and port areas open to international travel or to sales in petrol stations or units of establishment located in motorway areas, but does apply to traders established in other locations,
> – does not apply to traders engaged in the sale of goods such as newspapers, magazines, tobacco products and smoking accessories, telephone cards and National Lottery products, the sale of audiovisual media and video games and the sale of ice cream, but does apply to traders who offer other goods for sale,
> – applies only to the retail trade, namely to undertakings which are engaged in sales to consumers, whilst it does not apply to other traders,
> – entails, at least for traders who carry out their activity by means of a physical sales point and who are in direct contact with consumers, a significantly larger restriction than for traders who carry out their activity via an online shop or possibly via other forms of distance selling?'

On the question of the interpretation of the Charter of Fundamental Rights of the European Union, the CJEU denied that the Charter was applicable. Having ruled on the applicability of the Charter to the case, the CJEU then considered whether Articles 34-36 TFEU were applicable. The CJEU rejected their applicability on the following ground:

> 'In any event, as regards the application of Articles 34 TFEU to 36 TFEU governing the free movement of goods, referred to by that court, it must be borne in mind, as this Court has observed on a number of occasions, that those provisions do not apply to *national rules concerning the closure of shops that are enforceable against all economic operators pursuing activities within the national territory and that affect, in the same way, in law and in fact, the sale of domestic products and of products from other Member States*'. [Emphasis added]

It can be seen that the CJEU clearly based its decision on the *Keck* doctrine summarised above.

The CJEU likewise denied that Articles 56 and 57 TFEU applied in the case, on the following grounds:

> 'Similarly, as regards Articles 56 TFEU and 57 TFEU governing the freedom to provide series, also referred to by the referring court, suffice it to state that the legislation in question is *applicable to all traders exercising their activity on national territory*; that *its purpose is not to regulate the conditions concerning the establishment of the undertakings concerned*; and that any restrictive effects which it might have on freedom of establishment are too uncertain and indirect for the obligation laid down to be regarded as being capable of hindering that freedom'. [Emphasis added]

As can be seen from the parts of the judgment highlighted in italics, it seems that here too the CJEU relied on the *Keck* doctrine in ruling that the TFEU provisions on the freedom movement of services did not apply to the case before it. However, the CJEU did not merely rely on the *Keck* doctrine; it also justified its rejection of the applicability of Articles 56 and 57 on the fact that: 'any restrictive effects which it might have on freedom of establishment are too uncertain and indirect for the obligation laid down to be regarded as being capable of hindering that freedom'. Over the years the CJEU has used this justification on several occasions to deny that national rules have conflicted with Union law, and this 'too uncertain and indirect' reason could only have justified the rejection of the applicability of Articles 56 and 57 TFEU.

In other words, the CJEU used two parallel justifications for finding that the Belgian legislation did not infringe the Treaty provisions on freedom to provide services. While it is natural to interpret the judgment as acknowledging that the *Keck* doctrine also applies to the free movement of services, one should nevertheless be careful not to draw too firm conclusions. Thus it is not impossible that the framing of the judgment is itself a sign that there was disagreement among the judges about allowing the full parallel application of the *Keck* doctrine to the provision of services.

Consider, first, whether a possible interpretation of the CJEU's reasoning could be that the CJEU acknowledges that the *Keck* doctrine (as originally set out in paragraph 17 of the *Keck* case) in reality covers over the fact that its two cumulative conditions are 'too uncertain and indirect for the obligation laid down to be regarded as being capable of hindering that freedom'. Such an understanding of the judgment would mean that the Keck doctrine should merely be seen as a tool for clarifying whether a national marketing rule is of such a nature as to constitute a material hindrance to the free movement. If this is the case, consider, second, why the CJEU did not use the same formulation when rejecting under the *Keck* doctrine that the Belgian legislation constituted a hindrance to the free movement of goods.

JUDGMENT OF THE COURT
3 December 1974

Johannes Henricus Maria van Binsbergen v Bestuur van de Bedrijfsvereniging voor de Metaalnijverheid.
(Reference for a preliminary ruling: Centrale Raad van Beroep – Netherlands)

'Freedom to provide services'

Case 33/74

Judgment

1. By order of 18 April 1974, lodged at the Registry of the Court on 15 May, the Centrale Raad van Beroep put to the Court, under Article 177 of the EEC Treaty, questions relating to the interpretation of Articles 59 and 60 of the Treaty establishing the European Economic Community concerning freedom to provide services within the Community.

2. These questions arose incidentally, during the course of an action before the said court, and are concerned with the admission before that court of the person whom the appellant in the main action chose to act as his legal representative.

3. It appears from the file that the appellant had entrusted the defence of his interests to a legal representative of Netherlands nationality entitled to act for parties before courts and tribunals where representation by an advocaat is not obligatory.

4. Since this legal representative had, during the course of the proceedings, transferred his residence from the Netherlands to Belgium, his capacity to represent the party in question before the Centrale Raad van Beroep was contested on the basis of a provision of Netherlands law under which only persons established in the Netherlands may act as legal representatives before that court.

5. In support of his claim the person concerned invoked the provisions of the Treaty relating to freedom to provide services within the Community, and the Centrale Raad van Beroep referred to the Court two questions relating to the interpretation of Articles 59 and 60 of the Treaty.

The actual scope of Articles 59 and 60

6. The Court is requested to interpret Articles 59 and 60 in relation to a provision of national law whereby only persons established in the territory of the State concerned are entitled to act as legal representatives before certain courts or tribunals.

7. Article 59, the first paragraph of which is the only provision in question in this connexion, provides that: 'Within the framework of the provisions set out below, restrictions on freedom to provide services within the Community shall be progressively abolished during the transitional period in respect of nationals of Member States who are established in a State of the Community other than that of the person for whom the services are intended'.

8. Having defined the concept 'services' within the meaning of the Treaty in its first and second paragraphs, Article 60 lays down in the third paragraph that, without prejudice to the provisions of the chapter relating to the right of establishment, the person providing a service may, in order to provide that service, temporarily pursue his activity in the State where the service is provided, under the same conditions as are imposed by that State on its own nationals.

9. The question put by the national court therefore seeks to determine whether the requirement that legal representatives be permanently established within the territory of the State where the service is to be provided can be reconciled with the prohibition, under Articles 59 and 60, on all restrictions on freedom to provide services within the Community.

10. The restrictions to be abolished pursuant to Articles 59 and 60 include all requirements imposed on the person providing the service by reason in particular of his nationality or of the fact that he does not habitually reside in the State where the service is provided, which do not apply to persons established within the national territory or which may prevent or otherwise obstruct the activities of the person providing the service.

11. In particular, a requirement that the person providing the service must be habitually resident within the territory of the State where the service is to be provided may, according to the circumstances, have the result of depriving Article 59 of all useful effect, in view of the fact that the precise object of that Article is to abolish restrictions on freedom to provide services imposed on persons who are not established in the State where the service is to be provided.

12. However, taking into account the particular nature of the services to be provided, specific requirements imposed on the person providing the service cannot be considered incompatible with the Treaty where they have as their purpose the application of professional rules justified by the general good – in particular rules relating to organization, qualifications, professional ethics, supervision and liability – which are binding upon any person established in the State in which the service is provided, where the person providing the service would escape from the ambit of those rules being established in another Member State.

13. Likewise, a Member State cannot be denied the right to take measures to prevent the exercise by a person providing services whose activity is entirely or principally directed towards its territory of the freedom guaranteed by Article 59 for the purpose of avoiding the professional rules of conduct which would be applicable to him if he were established within that State; such a situation may be subject to judicial control under the provisions of the chapter relating to the right of establishment and not of that on the provision of services.

14. In accordance with these principles, the requirement that persons whose functions are to assist the administration of justice must be permanently established for professional purposes within the jurisdiction of certain courts or tribunals cannot be considered incompatible with the provisions of Articles 59 and 60, where such requirement is objectively justified by the need to ensure observance of professional rules of conduct connected, in particular, with the administration of justice and with respect for professional ethics.

15. That cannot, however, be the case when the provision of certain services in a Member State is not subject to any sort of qualification or professional regulation and when the requirement of habitual residence is fixed by reference to the territory of the State in question.

16. In relation to a professional activity the exercise of which is similarly unrestricted within the territory of a particular Member State, the requirement of residence within that State constitutes a restriction which is incompatible with Articles 59 and 60 of the Treaty if the administration of justice can satisfactorily be ensured by measures which are less restrictive, such as the choosing of an address for service.

17. It must therefore be stated in reply to the question put to the Court that the first paragraph of Article 59 and the third paragraph of Article 60 of the EEC Treaty must be interpreted as meaning that the national law of a Member State cannot, by imposing a requirement as to habitual residence within that State, deny persons established in another Member State the right to provide services, where the provision of services is not subject to any special condition under the national law applicable.

The question of the direct applicability of Articles 59 and 60

18. The Court is also asked whether the first paragraph of Article 59 and the third paragraph of Article 60 of the EEC Treaty are directly applicable and create individual rights which national courts must protect.

19. This question must be resolved with reference to the whole of the chapter relating to services, taking account, moreover, of the provisions relating to the right of establishment to which reference is made in Article 66.

20. With a view to the progressive abolition during the transitional period of the restrictions referred to in Article 59, Article 63 has provided for the drawing up of a 'general programme' – laid down by Council Decision of 18 December 1961 (1962, p. 32) – to be implemented by a series of directives.

21. Within the scheme of the chapter relating to the provision of services, these directives are intended to accomplish different functions, the first being to abolish, during the transitional period, restrictions on freedom to provide services, the second being to introduce into the law of Member States a set of provisions intended to facilitate the effective exercise of this freedom, in particular by the mutual recognition of professional qualifications and the coordination of laws with regard to the pursuit of activities as self-employed persons.

22. These directives also have the task of resolving the specific problems resulting from the fact that where the person providing the service is not established, on a habitual basis, in the State where the service is performed he may not be fully subject to the professional rules of conduct in force in that State.

23. As regards the phased implementation of the chapter relating to services, Article 59, interpreted in the light of the general provisions of Article 8 (7) of the Treaty, expresses the intention to abolish restrictions on freedom to provide services by the end of the transitional period, the latest date for the entry into force of all the rules laid down by the Treaty.

24. The provisions of Article 59, the application of which was to be prepared by directives issued during the transitional period, therefore became unconditional on the expiry of that period.

25. The provisions of that article abolish all discrimination against the person providing the service by reason of his nationality or the fact that he is established in a Member State other than that in which the service is to be provided.

26. Therefore, as regards at least the specific requirement of nationality or of residence, Articles 59 and 60 impose a well-defined obligation, the fulfilment of which by the Member States cannot be delayed or jeopardized by the absence of provisions which were to be adopted in pursuance of powers conferred under Articles 63 and 66.

27. Accordingly, the reply should be that the first paragraph of Article 59 and the third paragraph of Article 60 have direct effect and may therefore be relied on before national courts, at least in so far as they seek to abolish any discrimination against a person providing a service by reason of his nationality or of the fact that he resides in a Member State other than that in which the service is to be provided.

Costs

[Paras 28-29 omitted]

On those grounds,

THE COURT

in answer to the questions referred to it by the Centrale Raad van Beroep by order of 18 April 1974, hereby rules:

1. **The first paragraph of Article 59 and the third paragraph of Article 60 of the EEC Treaty must be interpreted as meaning that the national law of a Member State cannot, by imposing a requirement as to habitual residence within that State, deny persons established in another Member State the right to provide services, where the provision of services is not subject to any special condition under the national law applicable;**

2. **The first paragraph of Article 59 and the third paragraph of Article 60 have direct effect and may therefore be relied on before national courts, at least in so far as they seek to abolish any discrimination against a person providing a service by reason of his nationality or of the fact that he resides in a Member State other than that in which the service is to be provided.**

Comments and questions

In Case 33/74 *van Binsbergen* v *Bestuur van de Bedrijfsvereniging voor de Metaalnijverheid* [1974] ECR 1299, for the first time the CJEU held, in paragraph 10, that Article 56 TFEU (formerly Article 59 EEC Treaty) not only contained a prohibition against discrimination, but also against restrictions. It expressly stated that Article 56 TFEU not only covers conditions based on a person's nationality, but also conditions that a person should habitually reside in the Member State in question, or conditions which may prevent or otherwise obstruct the activities of the person providing the service. Since the contested Dutch law required a person acting as a legal representative, in an action before a court where representation by an advocate was not obligatory, to be resident in the Netherlands, there was a restriction. The CJEU also extended the scope of Article 56 TFEU, by including a 'Rule of reason' in paragraph 12 of its judgment. The CJEU dismissed the argument that the Dutch law complied with Article 56 TFEU. This could not be the case when the provision of certain services in a Member State is not subject to any sort of qualification or professional regulation, apart from the residence requirement; cf. paragraph 15. The CJEU then pointed out that the administration of justice could be satisfactorily ensured by less restrictive measures, such as requiring the legal representative to have an address for service in the Netherlands.

In paragraph 13 of its judgment the CJEU laid down what has come to be known as the '*Binsbergen* doctrine', that even if, as a point of departure, a service provider shall only be subject to regulation in his home State, this does not exclude the host State's right to lay down conditions as to the content of the services provided, if they are entirely or principally directed towards the host State's territory, and if the service provider intends to avoid laws which would be applicable to him if he were established within that state; cf. paragraph 13. How do you interpret this ruling? Is such a service provider who tries to circumvent the laws of the receiving Member State covered by Article 56 TFEU, or is it, in the view of the CJEU, a purely internal matter? According to the CJEU's recent practice the doctrine in the *van Binsbergen* case on avoidance can only be applied against a Union citizen if the national legislation which the Union citizen wishes to avoid can be justified on the grounds of overriding public interest and satisfies the requirements for proportionality. Compare this with Case C-61/89 *Bouchoucha* [1990] ECR I-3551, in Chapter 5. Look too at the commentary on Case C-212/97 *Centros* [1999] ECR I-1459, also in Chapter 5.

Finally, the CJEU established for the first time that Articles 56 and 57 TFEU (formerly Articles 59 and 60 EEC Treaty) have direct effect; cf. paragraph 27.

CHAPTER 7

Free Movement of Capital

JUDGMENT OF THE COURT
23 February 1995

Criminal proceedings against Aldo Bordessa and Vicente Marí Mellado and Concepción Barbero Maestre.
(References for a preliminary ruling: Audiencia Nacional – Spain)

'Directive 88/361/EEC – Authorization for the transfer of money in the form of banknotes'

Joined Cases C-358/93 and C-416/93

Judgment

1. By order of 19 June 1993, received at the Court on 16 July 1993 and registered under number C-358/93, and by order of 20 September 1993, received at the Court on 7 October 1993 and registered under number C-416/93, the Audiencia Nacional (National High Court) referred to the Court for a preliminary ruling under Article 177 of the EEC Treaty four questions on the interpretation of Articles 30 and 59 of the EEC Treaty, and Articles 1 and 4 of Council Directive 88/361/EEC of 24 June 1988 for the implementation of Article 67 of the Treaty (OJ 1988 L 178, p. 5, hereinafter 'the Directive').

2. Those questions were raised in two sets of criminal proceedings. On 10 November 1992 Aldo Bordessa (Case C-358/93), an Italian national residing in Italy, arrived at the customs post of La Junquera, Gerona (Spain) travelling towards France. When his car was inspected, banknotes worth approximately PTA 50 million were discovered in it, concealed in different places. Since Mr Bordessa did not possess the authorization required under Spanish law for the export of such a sum, he was arrested and the money confiscated. On 19 November 1992, Marí Mellado and Barbero Maestre (Case C-416/93), a married couple of Spanish nationality residing in Spain, crossed the frontier at the same customs post. In the course of an inspection carried out inside France, the French authorities subsequently discovered banknotes worth a total of PTA 38 million in their car. Since no application had been made to the Spanish authorities for authorization to export that amount, criminal proceedings were initiated before the Spanish courts.

3. Under Article 4(1) of Royal Decree 1816 of 20 December 1991 on economic transactions with other countries, the export of such items as coins, banknotes and bank cheques payable to the bearer, made out in pesetas or in foreign currencies, is subject to a prior declaration when the amount is in excess of PTA 1 million per person and per journey and subject to prior administrative authorization when the amount is in excess of PTA 5 million per person and per journey.

4. That decree was amended by Royal Decree 42 of 15 January 1993 which, according to the national court, constitutes no more than a technical improvement.

5. The national court considers that it is necessary to determine the validity and effect of that provision in the light of Community law before making a finding on a criminal offence under Law No 40 of 10 December 1979 on the regulations governing exchange control, as amended by Organic Law No 10 of 16 August 1983. Accordingly it stayed proceedings and submitted the following questions to the Court for a preliminary ruling:

   '1) Does Article 30 of the EEC Treaty preclude rules of a Member State which require a person leaving national territory bearing coins, banknotes or bearer cheques to make a prior declaration if the amount is in excess of PTA 1 million and to obtain prior administrative authorization if the amount exceeds PTA 5 million, where non-compliance with those requirements entails criminal penalties which may include detention?

   2) Does Article 59 of the EEC Treaty preclude rules such as those described in Question 1?

   3) Are rules such as those described in the previous questions compatible with Articles 1 and 4 of Directive 88/361/EEC?

   4) If Question 3 is answered in the negative, do the rules in Article 1 in conjunction with Article 4 of Directive 88/361/EEC meet the necessary conditions in order for them to be relied on as against the Spanish State before national courts and to render inapplicable national rules which conflict with them?'

6. By order of the President of 13 June 1994 the two cases were joined, in accordance with Article 43 of the Rules of Procedure, for the purposes of the oral procedure and the final judgment.

7. It should first be observed that Article 1(1) of the Directive requires Member States to abolish restrictions on movements of capital taking place between persons resident in Member States. However, as indeed the national court pointed out, the Kingdom of Spain was authorized under Article 6(2) of the Directive temporarily to continue to apply restrictions to the capital movements listed in Annex IV, subject to the conditions and time-limits laid down therein. Among the transactions mentioned in Annex IV, List IV specifies *inter alia* the physical import and export of financial assets – means of payment, the liberalization of which the Kingdom of Spain was permitted to defer until 31 December 1992.

8. Since the facts which gave rise to the two cases occurred before that date, the French and Portuguese Governments have expressed doubts regarding the applicability of the Directive to those facts.

9. It is clear nevertheless from the order for reference that the national court considered it necessary to seek a ruling from the Court of Justice on the interpretation of Articles 1 and 4 of the Directive on the ground that, if appropriate, it would apply the principle recognized in its domestic law of the retroactive effect of the more favourable criminal provision. It would therefore refrain from applying domestic law in so far as it conflicted with Community law. That was moreover confirmed at the hearing by the parties to the main proceedings.

10. Consequently it is necessary to answer the questions submitted since it is for the national court to determine both the need for a preliminary ruling in order to enable it to deliver judgment and the relevance of the questions which it submits to the Court (see the judgment in Case C-30/93 *AC-ATEL Electronics Vertriebs GmbH* v *Hauptzollamt München-Mitte* [1994] ECR I-2305).

Questions 1 and 2

11. By its first two questions, the national court wishes to know whether Articles 30 and 59 of the Treaty preclude rules which, as in the present case, make the export of coins, banknotes or bearer cheques conditional upon a prior declaration or administrative authorization and make that requirement subject to criminal penalties.

12. As regards Article 30 of the Treaty in particular, it should first be pointed out that, according to settled case-law, under the system of the Treaty means of payment are not to be regarded as goods falling within the purview of Articles 30 to 37 of the Treaty (see Case 7/78 *Regina* v *Thompson and Others* [1978] ECR 2247, paragraph 25).

13. It is also clear from the system of the Treaty that the physical transfer of assets falls not under Articles 30 and 59 but under Article 67 and the directive implementing that provision.

14. Even if it were established that such a transfer constituted a payment connected with trade in goods or services, the transaction would be governed not by Articles 30 and 59 but by Article 106 of the Treaty.

15. Consequently it should be stated in reply to the first two questions that rules which make the export of coins, banknotes or bearer cheques conditional upon a prior declaration or administrative authorization and which make that requirement subject to criminal penalties do not fall within the scope of Articles 30 and 59 of the Treaty.

Question 3

16. By its third question, the national court is essentially asking whether Articles 1 and 4 of the Directive preclude national legislation from making the export of coins, banknotes or bearer cheques conditional on a prior declaration or authorization.

17. It should first be noted that the Directive brought about the full liberalization of capital movements, for which purpose Article 1 required Member States to abolish restrictions on movements of capital taking place between persons resident in Member States.

18. Under the first paragraph of Article 4 of the Directive, Member States may 'take all requisite measures to prevent infringements of their laws and regulations, *inter alia* in the field of taxation and prudential supervision of financial institutions, or to lay down procedures for the declaration of capital movements for purposes of administrative or statistical information'.

19. The effectiveness of tax controls and the fight against illegal activities, such as tax evasion, money laundering, drug trafficking and terrorism, have been invoked as aims justifying the rules at issue.

20. It must therefore be examined whether Member States, in pursuing those aims, are taking measures which fall under the first paragraph of Article 4 of the Directive and consequently concern interests which those States are entitled to protect.

21. The first paragraph of Article 4 of the Directive expressly refers to the requisite measures to prevent infringements of the laws and regulations of Member States, '*inter alia*' in the field of taxation and the prudential supervision of financial institutions. It follows that other measures are also permitted in so far as they are designed to prevent illegal activities of comparable seriousness, such as money laundering, drug trafficking or terrorism.

22. That interpretation is confirmed moreover by the insertion in the Treaty establishing the European Community of Article 73d, paragraph (1)(b) of which essentially reproduces the first paragraph of Article 4 of the Directive but also provides that Member States have the right to take measures which are justified on grounds of public policy or public security.

23. It is in the light of those considerations that it should be determined whether the requirement laid down by the authorities of a Member State of a prior declaration or authorization for the transfer of coins, banknotes or bearer cheques is to be regarded as a requisite measure within the meaning of the first paragraph of Article 4 of the Directive.

24. As the Advocate General pointed out at point 17 of his Opinion, authorization has the effect of suspending currency exports and makes them conditional in each case upon the consent of the administrative authorities, which must be sought by means of a special application.

25. A requirement of that nature would cause the exercise of the free movement of capital to be subject to the discretion of the administrative authorities and thus be such as to render that freedom illusory (see Joined Cases 286/82 and 26/83 *Luisi and Carbone* v *Ministero del Tesoro* [1984] ECR 377, paragraph 34). It might have the effect of impeding capital movements carried out in accordance with Community law, contrary to the second paragraph of Article 4 of the Directive.

26. Pursuant to that provision, the application of the measures and procedures referred to in the first paragraph 'may not have the effect of impeding capital movements carried out in accordance with Community law'.

27. A prior declaration, on the other hand, may be one of the requisite measures which Member States are permitted to take since, unlike prior authorization, it does not entail suspension of the transaction in question but does still allow the national authorities to exercise effective supervision in order to prevent infringements of their laws and regulations.

28. However, the Spanish Government defended the need for prior authorization, claiming that it was only by virtue of such a system that non-compliance could be classified as criminal and hence criminal penalties imposed. Failure to meet that requirement could also lead to confiscation of the capital sums involved in the crime.

29. That view must, however, be rejected.

30. The Spanish Government has failed to provide sufficient proof that it is impossible to attach criminal penalties to the failure to make a prior declaration.

31. Consequently, it should be stated in reply to the third question that Articles 1 and 4 of the Directive preclude the export of coins, banknotes or bearer cheques being made conditional on prior authorization but do not by contrast preclude transactions of that nature being made conditional on a prior declaration.

Question 4

32. By its fourth question, the national court is asking whether the provisions of Article 1 in conjunction with Article 4 of the Directive have direct effect.

33. The requirement under Article 1 of the Directive for Member States to abolish all restrictions on movements of capital is precise and unconditional and does not require a specific implementing measure.

34. Application of the proviso in Article 4 of the Directive is amenable to review by the courts, and hence the fact that a Member State may avail itself of that possibility does not prevent Article 1 of the Directive, which enshrines the principle of the free movement of capital, from conferring rights on individuals which they may rely on before the courts and which the national courts must uphold.

35. Consequently, the reply to the national court's fourth question should be that Article 1 in conjunction with Article 4 of the Directive may be relied on before national courts and render inapplicable national rules which conflict with those provisions.

Costs

[Para. 36 omitted]

On those grounds,

THE COURT,

in answer to the questions referred to it by the Juzgado Central de lo Penal de la Audiencia Nacional, by order of 19 June 1993 (Case C-358/93) and by order of 20 September 1993 (Case C-416/93), hereby rules:

1. **Rules which make the export of coins, banknotes or bearer cheques conditional upon a prior declaration or an administrative authorization and make that requirement subject to criminal penalties do not fall within the scope of Articles 30 and 59 of the Treaty.**

2. **Articles 1 and 4 of Council Directive 88/361/EEC of 24 June 1988 for the implementation of Article 67 of the Treaty preclude the export of coins, banknotes or bearer cheques being made conditional on prior authorization but do not by contrast preclude a transaction of that nature being made conditional on a prior declaration.**

3. **Article 1 in conjunction with Article 4 of Directive 88/361/EEC may be relied on before national courts and render inapplicable national rules which conflict with those provisions.**

Comments and questions

According to paragraph 21 of the judgment in Joined Cases 286/82 and 26/83 *Luisi and Carbone* v *Ministero del Tesoro* [1984] ECR 377, capital movements are defined as 'financial operations essentially concerned with the investment of the funds in question rather than remuneration for a service.' Articles 63 et seq. TFEU were inserted by the Maastricht Treaty, and from 1 January 1994 replaced the capital provisions in Articles 67-73 in the earlier EEC Treaty and thereby introduced a thorough liberalisation of capital movements between the Member States themselves, and between the Member States and third countries.

In Joined Cases C-358/93 and C-416/93 *Bordessa and others* [1995] ECR I-361, the CJEU established that an actual transfer of capital assets does not belong under Articles 34, 56 and 63 TFEU and the directive implementing that provision; cf. paragraph 13. This is in line with paragraph 34 in Case C-204/90 *Bachmann* v *Belgium* [1992] ECR I-249.

The CJEU found that the then Spanish law which required prior permission for the export of Spanish currency was not compatible with Directive 88/361. How should the Spanish law have been framed in order to comply with Union law?

Consider whether the following would be covered by the rules on the freedom of movement of capital:

1. The sale of a collection of 2,000 year old Roman coins.
2. The sale of bonds issued by the Swedish State in euro, Swedish crowns and US dollars respectively.
3. The sale of mint Danish postage stamps from the 19th century, which have a much higher value than their nominal value, even though they can still be legally used on mail.

Is there a capital movement within the terms of Article 63 TFEU if a shareholder receives dividends from a company which is based in another Member State? See paragraphs 29-30 in Case C-35/98 *Staatssecretaris van Financiën* v *Verkooijen* [2000] ECR I-4071.

In the judgment in Joined Cases C-163/94, C-165/94 and C-250/94 *Sanz de Lera* [1995] ECR I-4821 which, like the *Bordessa* case, concerned the Spanish legislation then in force on the transfer of currency abroad, the CJEU ruled that Article 63 TFEU has direct effect, since the provision contains a clear and unconditional prohibition which did not require implementing measures. Thus, the provision creates rights for private persons which they can enforce through the courts and which national courts must protect. The provision can thus be relied upon before the National courts so that National rules that create obstacles to the free movement of capital cannot be enforced and must be set aside.

Among other things, the *Sanz de Lera* case dealt with a criminal prosecution of a Turkish citizen who, without obtaining prior permission from the Spanish authorities, wanted to transfer a large amount of the then Spanish currency to Turkey. In contrast to the other Treaty-based freedoms, Article 63 TFEU covers both movements between Member States and movements between a Member State and a third country, and third country citizens can also rely on the provision.

Prior to the entry into force of the Maastricht Treaty, and thereby Article 63 TFEU, the right to the free movement of capital was pursuant to Council Directive 88/361/EEC of 24 June 1988 for the implementation of Article 67 of the EEC Treaty (the Liberalisation of capital movements Directive). Even though this Directive is no longer legally binding, the CJEU considers that the Annex to the Directive, on the nomenclature of capital movements, has persuasive value for assessing whether a specific capital movement should be regarded as being covered by Article 63 TFEU. See, for example, Case C-222/97 *Trummer and Mayer* [1999] ECR I-1661, paragraph 21. In the *Trummer and Mayer* case the CJEU had to decide whether a mortgage on real property should be regarded as a capital movement covered by Article 63 TFEU. The CJEU confirmed that it was and referred, among other things, to the fact that a mortgage is covered by the Annex to the Directive relating to 'sureties, other guarantees and rights of pledge'. Investment in real property is accordingly a capital movement covered by Article 63 TFEU; see for example Case C-302/97 *Konle* [1999] ECR I-3099.

The significance of the nomenclature laid down in Directive 88/361/EEC is also made clear in Case C-318/07 *Hein Persche* [2009] ECR I-359. Here the CJEU had to consider whether a German citizen's gifts in kind, including bed linen, towels and zimmer frames to an old peoples' home were covered by the term 'capital movement'. In deciding this question, the CJEU noted that, according to the nomenclature in Directive 88/361/EEC, gifts and endowments were 'Personal capital movements'. The giving of bed linen etc. was therefore regarded as being covered by Article 63 TFEU.

JUDGMENT OF THE COURT (Second Chamber)
17 January 2008

Theodor Jäger v Finanzamt Kusel-Landstuhl. (Reference for a preliminary ruling from the Bundesfinanzhof – Germany)

'Free movement of capital – Articles 73b and 73d of the EC Treaty (now Articles 56 EC and 58 EC) – Inheritance tax – Valuation of assets forming part of the estate – Agricultural and forestry assets in another Member State – Less favourable method of valuation of assets and calculation of the tax payable'

Case C-256/06

Judgment

1. This reference for a preliminary ruling relates to the interpretation of Articles 73b and 73d of the EC Treaty (now Articles 56 EC and 58 EC respectively).

2. The reference has been made in proceedings between Mr Jäger and the Finanzamt (Tax Office) Kusel-Landstuhl ('the Finanzamt') concerning the calculation of the inheritance tax payable in respect of an inheritance consisting of assets situated in Germany and property in the form of agricultural land and forestry situated in France and, in particular, the rules on the valuation of those assets.

Legal framework

Community legislation

3. Annex I to Council Directive 88/361/EEC of 24 June 1988 for the implementation of Article 67 of the Treaty [Article repealed by the Treaty of Amsterdam] (OJ 1988 L 178, p. 5), entitled 'Nomenclature of the capital movements referred to in Article 1 of the Directive', includes 13 categories of capital movements.

4. The 11th of those categories, relating to 'Personal capital movements', includes a heading entitled 'Inheritances and legacies'.

National legislation
Application of inheritance tax to assets situated in another Member State

5. Under the first point of Paragraph 2(1) of the Law on inheritance and gift tax (Erbschaftsteuer- und Schenkungsteuergesetz), in the version published in BGBl. 1997 I, p. 378 ('the ErbStG'), the entire estate of a person domiciled in Germany is sub-

ject to inheritance tax on the date on which liability to the tax arises. Assets situated outside Germany are also subject to that tax.

6. Paragraph 21 of the ErbStG governs, for the purposes of calculating the inheritance tax in Germany, the offsetting of inheritance tax paid in another State in the absence of a double-taxation agreement. The first sentence of Paragraph 21(1) provides:

   'Where the foreign property of acquirors is subject, in a foreign country, to a foreign tax corresponding to German inheritance tax, the foreign tax set and payable by the acquiror, paid and not eligible for reduction, shall, in the cases referred to in the first point of Paragraph 2(1) and, in so far as the provisions of a double-taxation agreement do not apply, be offset, if an application is made for that purpose, against the German inheritance tax in so far as the foreign assets are also subject to German inheritance tax.'

7. The second sentence of Paragraph 21(1) states:

   'If the property transferred consists only partly of foreign property, the portion of the German inheritance tax corresponding to that property must be determined in such a way that the inheritance tax arising in respect of the total amount of the taxable property, including foreign taxable property, is divided up proportionally between the foreign taxable property and the total amount of taxable property.'

Rules for valuation of agricultural and forestry assets

8. Under Paragraph 12(6) of the ErbStG, read in conjunction with Paragraphs 9 and 31 of the Law on Valuation (Bewertungsgesetz, BGBl. 1991 I, p. 230; 'the BewG'), property consisting of agricultural land and forestry situated outside Germany is to be valued according to its fair market value. Under Paragraph 9(2) of the BewG, that value is defined as the price at which those assets could be sold in the ordinary course of business.

9. By contrast, under Paragraph 12(3) of the ErbStG property consisting of agricultural land and forestry situated in Germany is to be valued under a special procedure laid down in Paragraphs 140 to 144 of the BewG. The valuations carried out in accordance with that procedure amount, on average, to only 10% of the current market value of the assets in question.

10. Those provisions of the BeWG, which were inserted into that Law by point 36 of Paragraph 1 of the 1997 Annual Tax Law (Jahressteuergesetz 1997, BGBl. 1996 I, p. 2049) of 20 December 1996, enable the entire domestic holding of agricultural land and forestry to be valued under a simplified procedure for calculating the value of yield which has recourse to standardised values for the different types of holdings and is based, in particular, on the average constant yields of profit-making

holdings in Germany on 1 January 1996. In the alternative, and on request, the BewG provides for a valuation under the procedure based on individual income.

Rules for calculating the inheritance tax on agricultural land and forestry assets

11. The first point of Paragraph 13a(1) of the ErbStG provides, in respect of the acquisition by inheritance of agricultural land and forestry situated in Germany, for 'tax-free amounts in relation to specific objects' of DEM 500 000 on the value of that property, which is added to the personal tax-free amount of DEM 400 000 granted under Paragraph 16 of that Law.

12. Further, under Paragraph 13a(2) of the ErbStG, the remaining value of that property, after deduction of the tax-free amount granted in relation to those objects, is to be taken into account, for the purposes of calculating the tax, in the form of a 'valuation at a reduced rate' of only 60%.

13. Paragraph 13a(4) of the ErbStG provides that the tax-free amount granted in relation to those objects and the valuation at a reduced rate do not apply to agricultural land and forestry situated outside Germany.

The dispute in the main proceedings and the question referred for a preliminary ruling

14. Mr Jäger, who is resident in France, is the sole heir of his mother, who died in 1998 and was last living in Germany.

15. In addition to assets in Germany, the estate contained land in France used for agriculture and forestry. Mr Jäger's father, who himself died in 1994, had acquired one part of that property in August 1988 and subsequently acquired plots forming the other part of that property in January 1990.

16. Since it had been valued in France as having a fair market value of FRF 5 444 666 (DEM 1 618 152), that land was subject to inheritance tax in that Member State of FRF 1 192 148 (DEM 354 306).

17. By decision of 3 January 2000, the Finanzamt calculated the inheritance tax payable by Mr Jäger.

18. That tax was calculated on a net estate of DEM 1 737 167, including the land situated in France, totalling DEM 1 618 152, being its fair market value, and assets in Germany, valued at DEM 119 015. After deduction of the personal tax-free amount of DEM 400 000, the taxable amount was rounded down to DEM 1 337 100. On the basis of that amount, the Finanzamt set the tax at DEM 254 049.

19. On application by Mr Jäger brought under the second sentence of Paragraph 21(1) of the ErbStG, the Finanzamt offset against that latter amount DEM 236 644 in respect of the inheritance tax already paid in France.

20. On the basis of those factors, in its abovementioned decision of 3 January 2000, the Finanzamt set the inheritance tax payable by Mr Jäger at DEM 17 405.

21. Mr Jäger entered an objection against the Finanzamt's decision and brought an action before the Finanzgericht. As the objection and action were both unsuccessful, he then appealed on a point of law to the Bundesfinanzhof. Taking the view that, at least since the judgment of the Court of Justice in Case C-364/01 *Barbier* [2003] ECR I-15013, it was doubtful whether the provisions of German law, to the extent to which they differentiate according to the place in which the assets included in the estate or a part thereof are located, are reconcilable with the principle of the free movement of capital, the Bundesfinanzhof decided to stay the proceedings and refer the following question to the Court for a preliminary ruling:

'Is it compatible with Article 73b(1) of the Treaty establishing the European Community (now Article 56(1) EC) that for inheritance tax purposes:

(a) assets (held abroad) consisting of agricultural land and forestry situated in another Member State are valued in accordance with their fair market value (current market value), whereas a special valuation procedure exists for domestic assets consisting of agricultural land and forestry, the results of which amount on average to only 10% of their fair market value, and

(b) assessment of the acquisition of domestic assets consisting of agricultural land and forestry is excluded up to a special tax-free amount and the remaining value is assessed merely at 60%,

if, in the case of an heir inheriting an estate made up of both domestic assets and foreign assets consisting of agricultural land and forestry, this results in a situation whereby, as a result of the fact that the assets consisting of agricultural land and forestry are situated abroad, the acquisition of the domestic assets is subject to higher inheritance tax than would be applicable if the assets consisting of agricultural land and forestry were also domestic assets?'

The question referred

22. By its question, the Bundesfinanzhof asks, essentially, whether Article 73b(1) of the Treaty precludes legislation of a Member State, such as that at issue in the main proceedings, which, for the purposes of calculating the tax on an inheritance consisting of assets situated in the territory of that State and agricultural land and forestry situated in another Member State,

- provides that account be taken of the fair market value of the assets situated in that other Member State, whereas a special valuation procedure exists for identical domestic assets, the results of which amount on average to only 10% of the fair market value of those assets, and
- reserves application of a tax-free amount to domestic agricultural land and forestry in relation to those assets and takes account of their remaining value in the amount of only 60% thereof.

23. First of all, it must be noted that, although direct taxation falls within their competence, the Member States must none the less exercise that competence consistently with Community law (see, inter alia, Case C-319/02 *Manninen* [2004] ECR I-7477, paragraph 19; Case C-386/04 *Centro di Musicologia Walter Stauffer* [2006] ECR I-8203, paragraph 15; and Case C-347/04 *Rewe Zentralfinanz* [2007] ECR I-2647, paragraph 21).

24. It must also be observed that the EC Treaty does not define the term 'movement of capital'. However, it is settled case-law that, inasmuch as Article 73b of the Treaty substantially reproduced the content of Article 1 of Directive 88/361, and even if the latter was adopted on the basis of Articles 69 and 70(1) of the EEC Treaty (Articles 67 to 73 of the EEC Treaty were replaced by Articles 73b to 73g of the EC Treaty, now Articles 56 EC to 60 EC), the nomenclature relating to capital movements annexed thereto retains the same indicative value as before for the purposes of defining the term 'movement of capital' (see, inter alia, Case C-513/03 *van Hilten-van der Heijden* [2006] ECR I-1957, paragraph 39, and Case C-452/04 *Fidium Finanz* [2006] ECR I-9521, paragraph 41).

25. In that regard, the Court, noting in particular that inheritances involving a transfer to one or more persons of assets left by the deceased fall within heading XI of Annex I to Directive 88/361, entitled 'Personal capital movements', held in paragraph 42 of the judgment in *van Hilten-van der Heijden* that an inheritance is a movement of capital within the meaning of Article 73b of the Treaty (see also, to that effect, *Barbier*, paragraph 58), except in cases where its constituent elements are confined within a single Member State.

26. However, a situation in which a person resident in Germany at the time of his death leaves to another person resident in France assets situated in those two Member States and covered jointly by a calculation of inheritance tax in Germany is certainly not a purely domestic situation, as the Commission of the European Communities has correctly pointed out.

27. Consequently, the inheritance here at issue in the main proceedings constitutes a movement of capital within the meaning of Article 73b(1) of the Treaty.

28. It is thus necessary to examine, first, whether, as maintained by Mr Jäger and the Commission, a national provision such as that at issue in the main proceedings amounts to a restriction on the movement of capital.

29. The German Government submits that the national legislation at issue in the main proceedings does not amount to a restriction on the movement of capital. First, it submits that, since the assets situated in France were acquired initially by the father of Mr Jäger before 1 June 1990, the date by which Directive 88/361 had to be transposed into national law, the rights deriving from that directive or from the Treaty could not be relied on directly by the purchaser of the assets concerned. Secondly, according to the German Government, such a purchaser cannot be deterred by the effects of legislation such as that at issue in the main proceedings, which does not in any way affect the person in question but, at the very most, his heirs. For that reason, the effects of such legislation are too indirect to be capable of constituting a restriction on the movement of capital.

30. In that respect, according to the case-law of the Court, national provisions which determine the value of immovable property for the purposes of calculating the amount of tax due when it is acquired through inheritance may not only be such as to discourage the purchase of immovable property situated in the Member State concerned and the transfer of financial ownership of such property to another person by a resident of another Member State, but may also have the effect of reducing the value of the inheritance of a resident of a Member State other than that in which that property is situated (see to that effect, *Barbier*, paragraph 62).

31. Furthermore, as regards inheritances, the case-law has confirmed that the measures prohibited by Article 73b(1) of the Treaty as being restrictions on the movement of capital include those the effect of which is to reduce the value of the inheritance of a resident of a State other than the Member State in which the assets concerned are situated and which taxes the inheritance of those assets (*van Hilten-van der Heijden*, cited above, paragraph 44).

32. In the present case, the national provisions in issue in the main proceedings, in so far as they result in an inheritance consisting of agricultural land and forestry situated in another Member State being subject, in Germany, to inheritance tax that is higher than that which would be payable if the assets inherited were situated exclusively within the territory of that Member State, have the effect of restricting the movement of capital by reducing the value of an inheritance consisting of such an asset situated outside Germany.

33. That conclusion cannot be called into question by the arguments put forward by the German Government, noted in paragraph 29 of this judgment, since they are irrelevant in the light of the criteria arising from the case-law cited in paragraphs 30 and 31 of this judgment. In the present case, the effects of the national legislation in is-

sue in the main proceedings on the value of the inheritance occurred after 1 June 1990 and are manifestly not too indirect to be capable of constituting a restriction on the movement of capital.

34. The same is true of the German Government's argument that there cannot be a restriction resulting from a reduction in the value of the inheritance, since the effect of legislation such as that at issue in the main proceedings is merely the unavoidable consequence of the coexistence of national tax systems. That circumstance is irrelevant in the light of the criteria resulting from the case-law cited in paragraphs 30 and 31 of this judgment. Indeed, in any event it is clear that the reduction in the value of the estate flows solely from the application of the German legislation at issue.

35. It follows that the fact that the grant of tax advantages in relation to inheritance tax is made subject to the condition that the asset acquired by inheritance be situated in the national territory constitutes a restriction on the free movement of capital prohibited, in principle, by Article 73b(1) of the Treaty.

36. Next, it is necessary to examine whether the restriction on the free movement of capital thus determined may be justified having regard to the provisions of the Treaty.

37. In that respect, it should be noted that, under Article 73d(1)(a) of the Treaty, '... Article 73b shall be without prejudice to the right of Member States ... to apply the relevant provisions of their tax law which distinguish between taxpayers who are not in the same situation with regard to ... the place where their capital is invested'.

38. According to the Finanzamt and the German Government, under that provision the Federal Republic of Germany is entitled to reserve the benefit of assessment under the special procedure solely to assets situated within its territory. The Finanzamt adds that Paragraph 31 of the BewG is justified by Article 73d(1)(a) of the Treaty, read in the light of Declaration No 7 annexed to the Final Act of the Treaty on European Union, since the set of rules for the valuation of assets situated abroad, at issue in the main proceedings, existed at the end of 1993, within the terms of that declaration.

39. Without the need to rule on whether those rules for the valuation of assets situated abroad existed on 31 December 1993, it should be noted that in the judgment in Case C-35/98 *Verkooijen* [2000] ECR I-4071, the Court was required to address arguments based on Article 73d(1)(a) of the Treaty, although the facts in the main proceedings in that case occurred before that provision came into force. It stated that, before the entry into force of Article 73d(1)(a) of the Treaty, national tax provisions of the kind to which that article refers, in so far as they establish certain distinctions, could be compatible with Community law provided that they applied to situations which were not objectively comparable (paragraph 43).

40. That stated, Article 73d(1)(a) of the Treaty, in so far as it is a derogation from the fundamental principle of the free movement of capital, must be interpreted strictly. That provision cannot therefore be interpreted as meaning that all tax legislation which draws a distinction between taxpayers based on their place of residence or the Member State in which they invest their capital is automatically compatible with the Treaty.

41. The derogation provided for in Article 73d(1)(a) of the Treaty is itself, as the German Government observed, limited by Article 73d(3) of the Treaty, which provides that the national provisions referred to in paragraph 1 of that article 'shall not constitute a means of arbitrary discrimination or a disguised restriction on the free movement of capital and payments as defined in Article 73b' (see *Verkooijen*, paragraph 44, and *Manninen*, paragraph 28). Moreover, in order to be justified, the difference in treatment between the agricultural land and forestry assets situated in Germany and those situated in the other Member States must not go beyond what is necessary to achieve the objective pursued by the legislation at issue.

42. A distinction must therefore be made between the unequal treatment permitted under Article 73d(1)(a) of the Treaty and arbitrary discrimination prohibited under Article 73d(3). According to the case-law, in order for national tax legislation such as that at issue in the main proceedings, which, for the purposes of calculating inheritance tax, distinguishes between assets situated in another Member State and those situated in Germany, to be considered compatible with the provisions of the Treaty on the free movement of capital, the difference in treatment must concern situations which are not objectively comparable or be justified by overriding reasons in the general interest (see *Verkooijen*, paragraph 43, *Manninen*, paragraph 29, and Case C-443/06 *Hollmann* [2007] ECR I-0000, paragraph 45).

43. In that respect, it must be stated, first, that the difference in the amount of tax paid according to whether the inheritance consists only of agricultural land and forestry situated in Germany or consists also of such an asset situated in another Member State cannot be justified on the ground that it concerns situations which are not objectively comparable.

44. The calculation of the tax is, under the national legislation at issue in the main proceedings, directly linked to the value of the assets included in the estate, with the result that there is objectively no difference in situation such as to justify unequal tax treatment so far as concerns the level of inheritance tax payable in relation to, respectively, an asset situated in Germany and an asset situated in another Member State. A situation such as that of Mr Jäger is therefore comparable to that of any other heir whose inheritance consists only of agricultural land and forestry situated in Germany bequeathed by a person domiciled in that State.

45. Accordingly, it is, finally, necessary to examine whether the restriction on the movement of capital resulting from legislation such as that at issue in the main proceedings may be objectively justified by an overriding reason in the general interest.

46. The German Government submits that there is an overriding reason in the general interest which justifies that legislation.

47. First of all, it points out that that legislation is designed to compensate for the specific costs involved in maintaining the social role fulfilled by agricultural land and forestry holdings. That legislation makes it possible to prevent, first, the heir to an agricultural company from being forced to sell or relinquish it in order to be able to pay the inheritance tax and, secondly, the break-up of agricultural land and forestry holdings guaranteeing productivity and jobs and also required to comply with their obligations under the national legal order.

48. In the view of the German Government, that overriding reason in the general interest could be considered the same as, indeed, the need to safeguard the coherence of the tax system. There is, it argues, a direct link between the specific obligations resulting from the subordination of those holdings to the general interest and the particular kind of valuation applied to those holdings in inheritance matters.

49. The Finanzamt and the German Government also submit that the legislation at issue in the main proceedings is justified by the fact that the German authorities are not obliged to take account of the existence of a comparable general interest in other Member States. That is the case since the specific obligations and costs associated with agricultural land and forestry in Germany do not necessarily weigh in the same manner on similar assets situated in other Member States. In that respect, the Finanzamt adds that, even if comparable obligations and costs were imposed in other Member States on those kinds of assets, the Federal Republic of Germany would not be required to ensure compensation in respect of them.

50. It is, admittedly, conceivable that objectives connected with the carrying on of the activities of agricultural and forestry holdings and preservation of jobs in the latter in cases of inheritance may in themselves, in certain circumstances and under certain conditions, be in the public interest and capable of justifying restrictions on the free movement of capital (see, to that effect, Case C-370/05 *Festersen* [2007] ECR I-1129, paragraph 28).

51. However, with regard to the arguments put forward by the Finanzamt and the German Government, these have been unable to demonstrate a need to refuse the benefit of a favourable assessment and other tax advantages to any heir who acquires by inheritance an agricultural or forestry holding which is not situated within German territory (see, to that effect, with regard to a tax advantage limited to research carried out in the Member State concerned, Case C-39/04 *Laboratoires Fournier*

[2005] ECR I-2057, paragraph 23, and, with regard to an exemption from inheritance tax reserved to certain undertakings preserving jobs in the territory of the Member State concerned, Case C-464/05 *Geurts and Vogten* [2007] ECR I-0000, paragraph 27).

52. It should be noted that, in the case in the main proceedings, with regard to the objective of preventing the tax burden from jeopardising the continuation of the activities of agricultural and forestry holdings, and thereby the preservation of the social role of those holdings, there is no evidence in the present case to support a finding that the holdings established in other Member States are not in a comparable situation to that of holdings established in Germany.

53. Finally, in order to justify the national legislation at issue in the main proceedings, the German Government refers to practical difficulties which preclude the transposition of the assessment criteria provided for by the legislation at issue in the main proceedings to agricultural land and forestry assets situated in other Member States. It explains that that assessment procedure is based on standardised values of yield for the different types of holdings concerned and that those values have been derived from statistical documents compiled by the German authorities. Similar data are not available in respect of agricultural land and forestry assets situated in other Member States.

54. In that regard, it should be noted that, while it may indeed prove difficult for national authorities to apply the assessment procedure provided for in Paragraphs 140 to 144 of the BewG to agricultural land and forestry situated in another Member State, that difficulty cannot justify a categorical refusal to grant the tax advantage in question since the taxpayers concerned could be asked themselves to supply the authorities with the data which they consider necessary to ensure application of that procedure in such a way that it is adapted to holdings in other Member States.

55. It should be added that any disadvantages encountered in determining the value of assets situated in the territory of another Member State under a special national procedure cannot, in any event, be sufficient to justify restrictions on the free movement of capital such as those arising under the legislation at issue in the main proceedings, which, apart from that assessment procedure, also reserves application of two other tax advantages to assets situated within German territory (see, to that effect, Case C-334/02 *Commission* v *France* [2004] ECR I-2229, paragraph 29).

56. It must therefore be concluded that, as it has not been established that the national legislation at issue in the main proceedings is justified by overriding reasons in the general interest, Article 73b(1) of the Treaty precludes such legislation.

57. In those circumstances, the answer to the question referred must be that Article 73b(1) of the Treaty, read in conjunction with Article 73d thereof, must be inter-

preted as precluding legislation of a Member State which, for the purposes of calculating the tax on an inheritance consisting of assets situated in that State and agricultural land and forestry situated in another Member State,

- provides that account be taken of the fair market value of the assets situated in that other Member State, whereas a special valuation procedure exists for identical domestic assets, the results of which amount on average to only 10% of that fair market value, and
- reserves application of a tax-free amount to domestic agricultural land and forestry in relation to those assets and takes account of their remaining value in the amount of only 60% thereof.

Costs

[Para. 58 omitted]

On those grounds,

THE COURT (Second Chamber)

hereby rules:

Article 73b(1) of the EC Treaty (now Article 56(1) EC), read in conjunction with Article 73d of the EC Treaty (now Article 58 EC), must be interpreted as precluding legislation of a Member State which, for the purposes of calculating the tax on an inheritance consisting of assets situated in that State and agricultural land and forestry situated in another Member State,

- **provides that account be taken of the fair market value of the assets in that other Member State, whereas a special valuation procedure exists for identical domestic assets, the results of which amount on average to only 10% of that fair market value, and**

- **reserves application of a tax-free amount to domestic agricultural land and forestry in relation to those assets and takes account of their remaining value in the amount of only 60% thereof.**

Comments and questions

In the *Jäger* case the CJEU ruled that it is not compatible with Article 63 TFEU (formerly Article 56 TEC) on the free movement of capital for the inheritors of real property which is situated in another Member State to be subject to higher inheritance tax, due to differing methods for valuation, than inheritors of real property situated in the home

Member State. Thus, the CJEU recognises that tax advantages apply in relation to circumstances outside the national territory to which Union law is relevant.

In the *Jäger* case, the mother of Theodor Jäger, a German citizen, had died. At the time of her death Jäger's mother had been resident in Germany while Theodor Jäger himself was resident in France. His mother left various assets that were located in Germany as well as land and forestry property in France. According to the German rules on the calculation of inheritance tax, the land and forestry property in France should be included in the estate at their commercial value. However, if the property had been situated in Germany, it would have been valued at 10% of its commercial value. Furthermore, in contrast to assets located abroad, only 60% of the value of German land and forestry undertakings was included in the estate.

The first question which the CJEU had to settle was whether an inheritance (and inheritance tax) is a capital movement covered by Article 63 TFEU. A 'capital movement' is not defined in the TFEU, but the CJEU has consistently considered that the nomenclature of capital movements in the Annex to Council Directive 88/361/EEC on the liberalisation of capital movements is persuasive for the definition of the term 'capital movement'. On the basis of this nomenclature, the CJEU was able to determine that an inheritance that is not limited to a single Member State is covered by the concept of a capital movement in Article 63 TFEU.

The next question was whether the German inheritance tax rules constituted a restriction on the free movement of capital. In answering this question, the CJEU repeated, word for word, the statement in its judgment in Case C-513/03 *Van Hilten-van der Heijden* [2006] ECR I-1957, namely that the prohibition in Article 63 TFEU includes restrictions 'the effect of which is to reduce the value of the inheritance of a resident of a State other than the Member State in which the assets concerned are situated and which taxes the inheritance of those assets'. The intention of the CJEU was clearly to establish that the situation in the *Jäger* case was covered by the prohibition in Article 63 TFEU, even though the facts of the case did not appear to fit the statement (Jäger was resident in the same State as that in which the assets were located).

The German inheritance tax rules reduced the value of that part of Jäger's inheritance that was located outside Germany, so that the rules restricted the free movement of capital. The tax advantages which the German rules gave for assets located in Germany constituted a restriction within the meaning of Article 63 TFEU.

The nest question was whether the German inheritance tax rules could be justified by reference to Article 65(1)(a) TFEU (formerly Article 58(1)(a) TEC), according to which the provisions of Article 63 TFEU are without prejudice to the right of Member States to apply the relevant provisions of their tax law which distinguish between taxpayers who are not in the same situation with regard to their place of residence or with regard to the place where their capital is invested. Since Article 65(1)(a) TFEU is an exception to the basic principle of the free movement of capital, it must be interpreted restrictively. It is therefore not possible to interpret it as saying that any tax regulations that distinguish between taxpayers depending on where they are resident or the Member State where they have invested their capital is automatically incompatible with the TFEU. Indeed, according to Article 65(3) TFEU, the measures referred to in Article 65(1) TFEU do not constitute a means of arbitrary discrimination or a disguised restriction on the free movement of capital.

The CJEU noted, first, that there was no objective difference that could justify the different tax treatment with regard to the amount of the inheritance tax that should be paid in relation to assets located in Germany and assets located in another Member State. Theodor Jäger's situation could thus be compared with the situation of any other heirs whose inheritance consisted of land and forestry property situated in Germany, and who inherit from a person who was resident in the same Member State. Even though the purpose pursued by the German regulations, namely to increase the possibility of the carrying on of agricultural and forestry undertakings and maintaining workplaces in them in connection with inheritance, could in principle in certain circumstances and subject to certain conditions be a public interest which could justify restrictions on the free movement of capital, this did not apply in the *Jäger* case. In fact, the restriction could only be lawful if Germany could show that it was necessary to restrict the advantageous valuation of agricultural and forestry undertakings so as to only apply to those situated in Germany. Germany had not shown evidence to support this. The CJEU also pointed to several other circumstances that militated against the acceptability of the German regulations. Which?

In the *Jäger* case the CJEU was able to determine that the disputed German inheritance tax regulations could not be justified on the grounds of overriding public interest, so they were incompatible with Article 63 TFEU. Consider whether, following this case, a Member State is prevented from maintaining inheritance tax rules that mean that an heir who is resident in another Member State is in a less advantageous position than heirs resident in the Member State where the testator was resident at the time of his death – and that this applies regardless of where the assets of the estate are situated.

The CJEU has confirmed its decision in the *Jäger* case in Case C-11/07 *Eckelkamp* [2008] ECR I-6845 and Case C-43/07 *Arens-Sikken* [2008] ECR I-6887. In the latter case, which had substantial similarities to the *Jäger* case, there was also a dispute about the tax connected with the inheritance of property. The Netherlands, where the estate was situated, levied an inheritance tax. At the time of her death, the testator was resident in Italy. Under Dutch law, inheritance tax was calculated differently, depending on whether the testator was resident in the Netherlands or not, so that the calculation of tax was less advantageous to the heirs if the testator was resident outside the Netherlands. The CJEU determined that the situation in the *Arens-Sikken* case should be dealt with in the same way as the situation in the *Jäger* case. In this connection the CJEU commented that the Netherlands could not rely on the fact that Italy might allow the heirs a tax advantage to offset their loss in the Netherlands. It is clear from these cases that Member States cannot arrange their inheritance tax rules so that, merely because the testator or the heirs are resident in another Member State, higher inheritance tax is payable than would be payable if they were resident in the same Member State.

However, it is not every case where inheritance tax is increased because more than one Member State is involved that is covered by the prohibition on restrictions on the free movement of capital. Case C-67/08 *Block* [2009] ECR I-883 concerned a woman who was resident in Germany who inherited from another person who was also resident in Germany. However, most of the inheritance consisted of assets invested in Spain. In accordance with Spanish law, the Spanish authorities claimed payment of inheritance tax on that part of the property that was situated in Spain. In accordance with German law the German authorities claimed inheritance tax on the whole inheritance, including that part which had also been subjected to tax by the Spanish authorities. The heir argued that this double taxation was in breach of the Treaty rules on the free movement of capital. The CJEU rejected this. At the then stage of the development of Union law, the Member States enjoyed a certain autonomy in this area provided they complied with Union law, and they were not obliged to adapt their own tax systems to the tax systems of the other Member States in order to eliminate double taxation. Provided Union law is complied with, it is not an obstacle to double taxation that it arises from two Member States exercising their powers of taxation in parallel. The Member States have thus maintained their fiscal sovereignty in this area; see paragraph 31 of the judgment.

Furthermore, the CJEU referred to its settled case law, to the effect that the TFEU offers no guarantee to a citizen of the Union that transferring his residence to a Member State other than that in which he previously resided will be neutral as regards taxation. Given the disparities in the tax legislation of the Member States, such a transfer may be to the citizen's advantage or not, according to circumstances; see paragraph 35 of the judgment.

On the basis of the decision in the *Jäger* case, consider the following: If the German tax authorities allow owners of holiday homes in Germany to deduct from their taxable income payments to workmen for repairs, extensions etc. to the holiday homes, does this mean that this right to make a tax deduction should be extended to cover repairs etc. carried out on holiday homes in other Member States, such as Austria, in cases where the owner of the holiday home is fully taxable in Germany?

JUDGMENT OF THE COURT
4 June 2002

Commission of the European Communities v Kingdom of Belgium

'Failure by a Member State to fulfil its obligations – Articles 52 of the EC Treaty (now, after amendment, Article 43 EC) and 73b of the EC Treaty (now Article 56 EC) – Rights attaching to the 'golden shares held by the Kingdom of Belgium in Société nationale de transport par canalisations SA and in Société de distribution du gaz SA'

Case C-503/99

Judgment

1. By application received at the Court Registry on 22 December 1999, the Commission of the European Communities brought an action under Article 226 EC for a declaration that, by maintaining in force

   – the provisions of the Royal Decree of 10 June 1994 vesting in the State a 'golden share' in Société nationale de transport par canalisations (Moniteur belge of 28 June 1994, p. 17333, hereinafter 'the Royal Decree of 10 June 1994'), which carries the following rights:
   (a) advance notice of any transfer, use as security or change in the intended destination of the company's system of lines and conduits which are used or are capable of being used as major infrastructures for the domestic conveyance of energy products must be given to the Minister responsible, who shall be entitled to oppose such operations if he considers that they adversely affect the national interest in the energy sector;
   (b) the Minister may appoint two representatives of the Federal Government to the board of directors of the company. Those representatives may propose to the Minister the annulment of any decision of the board of directors which they regard as contrary to the guidelines for the country's energy policy, including the Government's objectives concerning the country's energy supply;

   – the provisions of the Royal Decree of 16 June 1994 vesting in the State a 'golden share' in Distrigaz (Moniteur belge of 28 June 1994, p. 17347, hereinafter 'the Royal Decree of 16 June 1994'), which carries the following rights:
   (a) advance notice of any transfer, use as security or change in the company's strategic assets must be given to the Minister responsible, who shall be entitled to oppose such operations if he considers that they adversely affect the national interest in the energy sector;

(b) the Minister may appoint two representatives of the Federal Government to the board of directors of the company. Those representatives may propose to the Minister the annulment of any decision of the board of directors or of the management committee which they regard as contrary to the guidelines for the country's energy policy, and by failing to lay down precise, objective and permanent criteria for approval of, or opposition to, the operations referred to above, the Kingdom of Belgium has failed to comply with its obligations under Articles 52 of the EC Treaty (now, after amendment, Article 43 EC) and 73b of the EC Treaty (now Article 56 EC).

2. By applications received at the Court Registry on 22 and 27 June 2000 respectively, the Kingdom of Denmark and the United Kingdom of Great Britain and Northern Ireland sought leave to intervene in the case in support of the form of order sought by the Kingdom of Belgium. By orders of the President of the Court of 12 and 13 July 2000 respectively, those Member States were granted leave to intervene. By letter of 2 October 2001, the Kingdom of Denmark withdrew its intervention.

[Paras 3-35 omitted]

Findings of the Court

Article 73b of the Treaty

36. It must be recalled at the outset that Article 73b(1) of the Treaty gives effect to free movement of capital between Member States and between Member States and third countries. To that end it provides, within the framework of the provisions of the chapter headed 'Capital and payments', that all restrictions on the movement of capital between Member States and between Member States and third countries are prohibited.

37. Although the Treaty does not define the terms 'movements of capital' and 'payments', it is settled case-law that Directive 88/361, together with the nomenclature annexed to it, may be used for the purposes of defining what constitutes a capital movement (Case C-222/97 *Trummer and Mayer* [1999] ECR I-1661, paragraphs 20 and 21).

38. Points I and III in the nomenclature set out in Annex I to Directive 88/361, and the explanatory notes appearing in that annex, indicate that direct investment in the form of participation in an undertaking by means of a shareholding or the acquisition of securities on the capital market constitute capital movements within the meaning of Article 73b of the Treaty. The explanatory notes state that direct investment is characterised, in particular, by the possibility of participating effectively in the management of a company or in its control.

39. In the light of those considerations, it is necessary to consider whether the rules vesting in the Kingdom of Belgium 'golden shares' in SNTC and Distrigaz, entitling that Member State to oppose, first, any transfer, use as security or change in the intended destination of lines and conduits or of certain other strategic assets and, second, certain management decisions regarded as contrary to the guidelines for the country's energy policy, constitute a restriction on the movement of capital between Member States.

40. The Belgian Government does not deny, in principle, that the restrictions to which the legislation in issue gives rise fall within the scope of the free movement of capital.

41. The United Kingdom Government likewise concedes, at least partially, that the Belgian legislation is restrictive in nature.

42. Consequently, it is necessary to consider whether, and in what circumstances, the legislation in issue may be justified.

43. As is also apparent from the 1997 Communication, it is undeniable that, depending on the circumstances, certain concerns may justify the retention by Member States of a degree of influence within undertakings that were initially public and subsequently privatised, where those undertakings are active in fields involving the provision of services in the public interest or strategic services (see today's judgments in Case C-367/98 Commission v Portugal, not yet published in the European Court Reports, paragraph 47, and Case C-503/99 Commission v Belgium, not yet published in the European Court Reports, paragraph 43).

44. However, those concerns cannot entitle Member States to plead their own systems of property ownership, referred to in Article 222 of the Treaty, by way of justification for obstacles, resulting from privileges attaching to their position as shareholder in a privatised undertaking, to the exercise of the freedoms provided for by the Treaty. As is apparent from the Court's case-law (Case C-302/97 Konle [1999] ECR I-3099, paragraph 38), that article does not have the effect of exempting the Member States' systems of property ownership from the fundamental rules of the Treaty.

45. The free movement of capital, as a fundamental principle of the Treaty, may be restricted only by national rules which are justified by reasons referred to in Article 73d(1) of the Treaty or by overriding requirements of the general interest and which are applicable to all persons and undertakings pursuing an activity in the territory of the host Member State. Furthermore, in order to be so justified, the national legislation must be suitable for securing the objective which it pursues and must not go beyond what is necessary in order to attain it, so as to accord with the principle of proportionality (see, to that effect, Joined Cases C-163/94, C-165/94 and C-250/94

Sanz de Lera and Others [1995] ECR I-4821, paragraph 23, and Case C-54/99 *glise de scientologie* [2000] ECR I-1335, paragraph 18).

46. In the present case, the objective pursued by the legislation at issue, namely the safeguarding of energy supplies in the event of a crisis, falls undeniably within the ambit of a legitimate public interest. Indeed, the Court has previously recognised that the public-security considerations which may justify an obstacle to the free movement of goods include the objective of ensuring a minimum supply of petroleum products at all times (Campus Oil, cited above, paragraphs 34 and 35). The same reasoning applies to obstacles to the free movement of capital, inasmuch as public security is also one of the grounds of justification referred to in Article 73d(1)(b) of the Treaty.

47. However, the Court has also held that the requirements of public security, as a derogation from the fundamental principle of free movement of capital, must be interpreted strictly, so that their scope cannot be determined unilaterally by each Member State without any control by the Community institutions. Thus, public security may be relied on only if there is a genuine and sufficiently serious threat to a fundamental interest of society (see, in particular, glise de scientologie, cited above, paragraph 17).

48. It is necessary, therefore, to ascertain whether the legislation in issue enables the Member State concerned to ensure a minimum level of energy supplies in the event of a genuine and serious threat, and whether or not it goes beyond what is necessary for that purpose.

49. First of all, it should be noted that the regime in issue is one of opposition. It is predicated on the principle of respect for the decision-making autonomy of the undertaking concerned, inasmuch as, in each individual case, the exercise of control by the minister responsible requires an initiative on the part of the Government authorities. No prior approval is required. Moreover, in order for that power of opposition to be exercised, the public authorities are obliged to adhere to strict time-limits.

50. Next, the regime is limited to certain decisions concerning the strategic assets of the companies in question, including in particular the energy supply networks, and to such specific management decisions relating to those assets as may be called in question in any given case.

51. Lastly, the Minister may intervene pursuant to Articles 3 and 4 of the Royal Decrees of 10 and 16 June 1994 only where there is a threat that the objectives of the energy policy may be compromised. Furthermore, as the Belgian Government has expressly stated in its written pleadings and at the hearing, without being contradicted on the point by the Commission, any such intervention must be supported by a

formal statement of reasons and may be the subject of an effective review by the courts.

52. The scheme therefore makes it possible to guarantee, on the basis of objective criteria which are subject to judicial review, the effective availability of the lines and conduits providing the main infrastructures for the domestic conveyance of energy products, as well as other infrastructures for the domestic conveyance and storage of gas, including unloading and cross-border facilities. Thus, it enables the Member State concerned to intervene with a view to ensuring, in a given situation, compliance with the public service obligations incumbent on SNTC and Distrigaz, whilst at the same time observing the requirements of legal certainty.

53. The Commission has not shown that less restrictive measures could have been taken to attain the objective pursued. There is no certainty that planning designed to encourage natural gas undertakings to conclude long-term supply contracts, to diversify their sources of supply or to operate a system of licences would be enough, on its own, to permit a rapid reaction in any particular situation. Moreover, the introduction of rules precisely defining the standards required of undertakings in the sector concerned, as proposed by the Commission, would appear to be even more restrictive than a right of opposition limited to specific situations.

54. As to the Commission's arguments concerning the gas directive, suffice it to note that the time-limit for transposition of that directive did not expire until 10 August 2000. Consequently, the Community framework which, according to the Commission, the directive is intended to establish as regards the exercise by Member States of powers in relation to the public service obligations imposed on undertakings in the sector concerned cannot in any event affect the present action, since the reasoned opinions were dated 18 December 1998 and the application was lodged on 22 December 1999.

55. The legislation in issue is therefore justified by the objective of guaranteeing energy supplies in the event of a crisis.

56. In those circumstances, there is no need to consider the alternative plea put forward by the Belgian Government, alleging the existence of a principle derived from Article 90(2) of the Treaty.

57. Accordingly, the Commission's application must be dismissed in so far as it concerns Article 73b of the Treaty.

Article 52 of the Treaty

58. The Commission also seeks a declaration of failure to comply with Article 52 of the Treaty, namely the Treaty rules regarding freedom of establishment, in so far as they concern undertakings.

59. It should be noted in that regard that Article 56 of the Treaty, like Article 73d, provides for a ground of justification based on public security. Thus, even if it were assumed that the power of a Member State to oppose any transfer, use as security or change in the intended use of certain assets of an existing undertaking, or certain management decisions taken by that undertaking, may constitute a restriction on freedom of establishment, such a restriction would be justified for the reasons set out in paragraphs 43 to 55 of this judgment.

60. It follows that the Commission's application must also be dismissed in so far as it concerns Article 52 of the Treaty.

Costs

[Para. 61 omitted]

On those grounds,

THE COURT

hereby:

1. **Dismisses the application;**

[Paras 2 and 3 of the ruling omitted]

Comments and questions

It has traditionally been assumed that certain functions which are important to society should be undertaken by bodies which are under public ownership and control. These functions have typically been related to infrastructure. Classic examples of this are transport (roads, railways, airports and harbours), energy (the generation and distribution of electricity, oil and gas), water and communications (post and telecommunications). This traditional view has changed somewhat in recent years, however, and in many Member States there has been complete or partial privatisation of a number of nationalised industries. Nevertheless, there is still little doubt that utility companies still play an important role in society so that Member States have a significant interest in their conduct. This significant interest is often reflected in the state retaining certain special rights over newly privatised companies. Thereby Member States try to ensure that the companies continue to perform their role in society satisfactorily. A Member State can secure these special rights in several ways. One of these is to grant special rights to one or more shares which the Member State retains. Such a share is known as a 'golden share'.

However, the Commission was not happy with the restrictions which member States imposed on privatised companies. It was the Commission's view that where a Member State had laid down measures involving discrimination against investors from other Member States, these were a breach of the TFEU provisions on the freedom of movement of capital and the freedom of establishment. If the measures were not discriminatory, the Commission considered that they constituted a restriction, so that they were only permitted if they were justified by some overriding reasons in the general interest and if they were proportionate. See, for example, Communication of the Commission on Certain legal aspects concerning intra-EU investment, (OJ 1997 C 220/15).

Case C-503/99 *Commission* v *Belgium* [2002] ECR I-4809, (the *Golden Shares* case) was one of the first cases on this issue which the Commission brought before the CJEU. Belgium had partially privatised two undertakings which, among other things, were responsible for part of the country's energy distribution. With a view to ensuring the stability of Belgian energy supply, the state arranged to retain certain special rights over each of the undertakings. The Commission was of the view that these rights constituted a hindrance on direct investment in the two companies, amounting to a hindrance on the freedom of movement of capital. Since the Commission did not believe this restriction was justified, it brought a case against Belgium before the CJEU.

The Belgian Government did not dispute that the restrictions caused by the disputed rules did, in principle, fall within the scope of the freedom of movement of capital. However, the Government contended that the rules were an effective method of ensuring a legitimate purpose, which was the security of energy supplies, and that this was accomplished in the least intrusive way. In other words, the Government claimed that the conditions of the proportionality principle were satisfied. The CJEU agreed with the Belgian Government on this point.

Under Article 345 TFEU, the Treaty 'shall in no way prejudice the rules in Member States governing the system of property ownership.' According to this, a Member State is not obliged to privatise publicly owned undertakings. This means that the Commission cannot, on the basis of Article 63 TFEU on the freedom of movement of capital, require that external investors shall be given the opportunity too buy shares in a publicly owned company. However, if a Member State chooses to privatise a publicly owned company, giving external investors the possibility of buying shares in it, a Member State's retention of special rights over the undertaking in question will constitute a restriction on the freedom of movement of capital. Such restrictions are only permitted if they pursue a lawful purpose and are proportionate, as stated above. Do you think it is reasonable that a Member State, which partially opens up a publicly owned company to investment by the general public, should be subject to stricter requirements than a Member State which does not allow any investment by the general public in publicly owned undertakings?

The Commission had disputed the Belgian rules, both on the basis of the rules on the freedom of movement of capital in Article 63 TFEU and the rules on freedom of establishment in Article 49 TFEU (former Article 52 TEC). The CJEU assessed the case on the basis of the rules on freedom of movement of capital in paragraphs 36-57 of the judgment, and on the basis of the rules on freedom of establishment in paragraphs 58-60. How did the Belgian rules affect the freedom of establishment? Is there a difference in the CJEU's assessment of the case, depending on whether it is judged on the basis of Article 49 TFEU or on the basis of Article 63 TFEU?

It is worth noting that in two later 'golden share' cases (Case C-98/01 *Commission* v *The United Kingdom* [2003] ECR I-4641, paragraph 47, and Case C-463/00 *Commission* v *Spain* [2003] ECR I-4581, paragraph 61) the CJEU has held:

> 'although the relevant restrictions on investment operations apply without distinction to both residents and non-residents, it must none the less be held that they affect the position of a person acquiring a shareholding as such and are thus liable to deter investors from other Member States from making such investments and, consequently, affect access to the market.'

The CJEU has hereby clearly established that the principle of freedom of access to the market, developed in relation to the freedom of movement of goods, also applies to the freedom of movement of capital.

JUDGMENT OF THE COURT (Third Chamber)
26 April 2012

Staatssecretaris van Financiën v L.A.C. van Putten (C-578/10), P. Mook (C-579/10), G. Frank (C-580/10). (References for a preliminary from the Hoge Raad der Nederlanden – Netherlands)

'Articles 18 EC and 56 EC – Motor vehicles – Use in a Member State of a borrowed private motor vehicle which is registered in another Member State – Taxation of that vehicle in the first Member State on its first use on the national road network'

Joined Cases C-578/10 to C-580/10

Judgment

1. This reference for a preliminary ruling concerns the interpretation of Articles 18 EC and 56 EC.

2. The references were made in the course of proceedings brought by the Staatssecretaris van Financiën (Secretary of State for Finance, 'the Staatssecretaris') against Mrs van Putten, Mr Mook and Mrs Frank respectively concerning tax assessment notices sent to them in relation to their failure to pay the tax on cars and motorcycles ('vehicle tax') when briefly using such vehicles made available to them free of charge by natural persons resident in other Member States.

Legal context

European Union law

3. Article 1(1) of Council Directive 88/361/EEC of 24 June 1988 for the implementation of Article 67 of the Treaty (OJ 1988 L 178, p. 5) provides:

   'Without prejudice to the following provisions, Member States shall abolish restrictions on movements of capital taking place between persons resident in Member States. To facilitate application of this Directive, capital movements shall be classified in accordance with the Nomenclature in Annex I.'

4. The capital movements referred to in Annex I to Directive 88/361 encompass, under heading XI of that Annex, personal capital movements, which include loans, gifts and inheritances.

National law

5. Article 1(1) of the Netherlands Law on tax on cars and motorcycles (Wet op de belasting van personenauto's en motorrijwielen 1992, Stb. 1992, No 709, 'the 1992 Law') provides that vehicle tax is to be levied on such private motor vehicles.

6. Under Article 1(2) and (5) of the 1992 Law, vehicle tax is due on registration of the vehicle in the Netherlands vehicle register. However, when a car or motorcycle which is not registered in the Netherlands is made available to a natural or legal person residing or established in the Netherlands, the tax is due on first use of that motor vehicle on the road network in the Netherlands within the meaning of that law.

7. Article 5(2) of the 1992 Law provides that, in the case of unregistered cars or motorcycles, the person liable for vehicle tax is the person who has the motor vehicle at his disposal.

8. Under Article 9(1) of the 1992 Law, the rate of that tax for a car amounts to 45.2% of the net list price of the vehicle, subject to the reductions and surcharges referred to in that article. That price is the sale price recommended by the manufacturer or importer to the dealer, less value added tax.

9. For new cars, the net list price is that which applied at the beginning of the day on which a registration number was issued in respect of the car in the Netherlands. For used cars, the net list price is that which applied when the car was first used, whether in or outside the Netherlands.

10. On first use on the road network in the Netherlands of a car or motorcycle not registered in the Netherlands which is at the disposal of a natural person resident or a legal person established in the Netherlands, the national legislation at issue in the main proceedings provides for the application of the net list price for used cars for the purposes of payment of vehicle tax.

11. In charging vehicle tax on used cars, account is taken of the length of time for which the vehicle has been used and is reduced by a certain percentage. Until 1 February 2007, vehicle tax was chargeable as a one-off payment without any possibility of a refund even if, after a certain length of time, the car ceased to be used on the road network in the Netherlands.

The actions in the main proceedings and the questions referred for a preliminary ruling

12. Mrs van Putten and Mr Mook are Dutch nationals. Mrs Frank is a German national. They were all resident in the Netherlands at the time of the facts at issue in the main proceedings.

13. In the course of checks, officers of the Belastingdienst (tax authority) established that the defendants in the main proceedings were using cars registered in other Member States on the road network in the Netherlands without having paid vehicle tax. Accordingly, they were advised that, on a subsequent check they might be issued with an assessment notice for the payment of that tax.

14. On a subsequent check the defendants in the main proceedings were stopped and found to be in the same situation again.

15. Assessment notices were therefore sent to them, amounting to EUR 5955 for Mrs van Putten, EUR 1859 for Mr Mook and EUR 6709 for Mrs Frank. The Belastingdienst rejected the appeal by the persons concerned. It took the view that the defendants in the main proceedings had used their vehicle within the meaning of Article 1(5) of the 1992 Law, so that, on that first use, vehicle tax was due at the rate and on the full basis of assessment referred to in Article 9 of that law. Moreover, as the notices pre-dated 1 February 2007, the tax was collected from the defendants in the main proceedings without the length of use of those vehicles having been taken into account.

16. As the actions brought by each of the defendants in the main proceedings were held to be unfounded, they appealed to the Gerechtshof te 's-Hertogenbosch (Court of appeal, 's-Hertogenbosch). That court upheld their claims and, accordingly, annulled the decisions of the Belastingdienst and the assessment notices. According to that court those notices constituted an unjustified obstacle to the right to move and reside freely within the territory of a Member State set out in Article 18 EC.

17. The Staatssecretaris brought an appeal before the referring court against the decision of the Gerechtshof te 's-Hertogenbosch in each of the cases. Essentially, it held that all the relevant aspects of the situations at issue in the main proceedings occurred within a single Member State, the Netherlands, so that the case does not fall within the scope of Article 18 EC.

18. The referring court points out that the Court of Justice has already had occasion to rule on the compatibility of vehicle tax with European Union law, but in connection with situations in which the principles relied on are freedom of movement for workers, freedom of establishment or freedom to provide services.

19. However, the disputes in the main proceedings concern natural persons resident in the Netherlands who used, in the Netherlands and for private purposes, a car registered in another Member State which was made available for no consideration by natural persons resident in that other Member State who were family members or friends.

20. In those circumstances, the Hoge Raad der Nederlanden (Supreme Court of the Netherlands) decided to stay the proceedings in all three cases and to refer the following questions to the Court of Justice for a preliminary ruling:

    In Case C-578/10:

    'In the light of Article 18 EC (now Article 21 TFEU), does Community law govern a situation in which a Member State levies a tax on the first use on the road network in its territory of a vehicle which is registered in another Member State, has been borrowed from a resident of that other Member State and has been driven by a resident of the first Member State in the territory of that Member State?'

    In Case C-579/10:

    'In the light of Article 18 EC (now Article 21 TFEU), does Community law govern a situation in which a Member State levies a tax on the first use on the road network in its territory of a vehicle which is registered in another Member State, has been borrowed from a resident of that other Member State and has been driven for private purposes by a resident of the first Member State between those two Member States?'

    In Case C-580/10:

    'In the light of Article 18 EC (now Article 21 TFEU), does Community law govern a situation in which a Member State levies a tax on the first use on the road network in its territory of a vehicle which is registered in another Member State, has been borrowed from a resident of that other Member State and has been driven for private purposes in the territory of the first Member State by a person who is a resident of that Member State but a national of the other Member State?'

21. By order of the President of the Court of 1 February 2011, Cases C-578/10 to C-580/10 were joined for the purposes of the written and oral procedure and the judgment.

The questions referred for a preliminary ruling

Preliminary observations

22. By its questions, which should be considered together, the referring court essentially asks whether, in the light of Article 18 EC, European Union law covers a situation in which a Member State levies a tax on the first use on the national road network of a motor vehicle by one of its residents, which has been driven either only on national territory or on that territory and that of another Member State, where that vehicle, which is registered in another Member State, has been loaned by a resident of the latter State.

23. In that regard, even though, formally, the national court has limited its questions to the interpretation of Article 18 EC, that does not prevent the Court from providing the national court with all the elements of interpretation of Community law which may be of assistance in adjudicating on the case before it, whether or not that court has specifically referred to them in the questions (see, to that effect, Case C-251/06 *ING. AUER* [2007] ECR I-9689, paragraph 38 and the case-law cited).

24. The questions referred must be resolved in the light of all the provisions of the Treaty and of secondary legislation which may be relevant to the problem (see Case 137/84 *Mutsch* [1985] ECR 2681, paragraph 10).

25. Moreover, it must be observed that, according to the referring court, the full amount of the tax at issue in the main proceedings was charged to the defendants without any account being taken of the actual duration of the use of the motor vehicles on the road network in the Netherlands and without the defendants having been able to invoke any right to exemption from or reimbursement of that tax.

26. Therefore, the questions referred must be understood as seeking to know whether European Union law must be interpreted as meaning that it precludes legislation of a Member State which requires its residents who have borrowed a car registered in another Member States from a resident of that State, to pay in full, on first use of that vehicle on the national road network, a tax normally due on registration of a vehicle in the first Member State, without any account being taken of the duration of the use of that vehicle on that road network and without the persons concerned being able to invoke any right to exemption or reimbursement.

Free movement of capital

27. As regards the provisions of European Union law which may be applicable to the circumstances of the cases in the main proceedings, it must be observed that, in those cases, the charging of tax is the result, not of the fact that the defendants in the main proceedings have exercised their right to freedom of movement, but of the

fact that, as residents, they have used a car registered in another Member State and loaned to them on the road network in the Netherlands.

28. With regard to a loan agreed between citizens residing in different Member States, the scope of Article 56 EC must first be considered. In that connection, it is settled case-law that, in the absence of a definition in the Treaty of 'movement of capital' for the purposes of Article 56(1) EC, the nomenclature annexed to Council Directive 88/361/EEC has indicative value, even though that directive was adopted on the basis of Articles 69 and 70(1) of the EEC Treaty (Articles 67 to 73 of the EEC Treaty were replaced by Articles 73B to 73G of the EC Treaty, now Articles 56 EC to 60 EC), subject to the qualification, contained in the introduction to the nomenclature, that the list set out there does not define exhaustively the concept of movements of capital (see, inter alia, Case C-318/07 *Persche* [2009] ECR I-359, paragraph 24 and the case-law cited; Case C-182/08 *Glaxo Wellcome* [2009] ECR I-8591, paragraph 39; Case C-35/08 *Busley and Cibrian Fernandez* [2009] ECR I-9807, paragraph 17, and Case C-25/10 *Missionswerk Werner Heukelbach* [2011] ECR I-0000, paragraph 15).

29. Thus, the Court has held that inheritances and gifts, which fall under heading XI of Annex I to Directive 88/361, entitled 'Personal Capital Movements', constitute movements of capital within the meaning of Article 63 TFEU, except in cases where their constituent elements are confined within a single Member State (see Case C-450/09 *Schröder* [2011] ECR I-0000, paragraph 26 and the case-law cited). The same applies to 'loans' which fall within the same heading of Annex I to that directive.

30. In situations such as those at issue in the main proceedings it is common ground that the constituent elements of the legal relationship between the owner of the motor vehicle and the user of that vehicle are not confined to a single Member State even though the national provision at issue is addressed only to the residents of the Netherlands. Vehicle tax must be paid by the residents of that Member State who use a motor vehicle on the national road network, even though the use is of short duration and in the context of a loan, free of charge, between those residents and residents of other Member States of vehicles also registered in other Member States.

31. In addition it must be verified whether the legal relationship at issue in each of the cases in the main proceedings, in other words the loan of a motor vehicle free of charge for cross-border use, can be deemed to be a movement of capital within the meaning of Article 56 EC and, in particular, a loan falling within heading XI of Annex I to Directive 88/361.

32. In that regard, it must first be held that 'loans' fall under that heading, without determining whether those loans are for consideration or free of charge or what their particular purpose is.

33. Next, as regards gifts, the Court has already had occasion to hold that, in order to determine whether the tax treatment by a Member State of certain transactions is covered by the provisions on the free movement of capital, there is no need to distinguish between transactions effected in money and those effected in kind (see *Persche*, paragraph 26).

34. Finally, it is apparent from the inclusion of inheritances and legacies under heading XI of Annex I to Directive 88/361 that the fact that a transaction is free of charge does not, in itself, prevent it being deemed a movement of capital within the meaning of Article 56 EC.

35. In addition, the loan of a motor vehicle for use free of charge constitutes a benefit which represents a specific economic value, corresponding to the cost of use of a hire car of the same type and for the same period.

36. It follows that, as the Advocate General pointed out in point 31 of her Opinion, the cross-border lending of a vehicle free of charge constitutes a capital movement within the meaning of Article 56 EC.

Whether there is any restriction on the free movement of capital and the possible justification for such restriction

37. First of all, it should be noted that, apart from certain exceptions not relevant to the main proceedings, taxation of motor vehicles has not been harmonised at European Union level. The Member States are thus free to exercise their powers of taxation in that area provided that they do so in compliance with European Union law (see Case C-451/99 *Cura Anlagen* [2002] ECR I-3193, paragraph 40; Case C-464/02 *Commission* v *Denmark* [2005] ECR I-7929, paragraph 74; Joined Cases C-151/04 and C-152/04 *Nadin and Nadin-Lux* [2005] ECR I-11203, paragraph 40; Case C-232/03 *Commission* v *Finland*, judgment of 23 February 2006, paragraph 46; order in Case C-242/05 *van de Coevering* [2006] ECR I-5843, paragraph 23; order of 22 May 2008 in Case C-42/08 *Ilhan*, paragraph 17, and order in Case C-364/08 *Vandermeir* [2008] ECR I-8087, paragraph 22).

38. Pursuant to the 1992 Law, vehicle tax is due in respect of cars or motorcycles not registered in the Netherlands which are made available to a person resident in that Member State from the moment of their first use on the road network in the Netherlands. The person liable to the tax is the person who actually has the vehicle at his disposal.

39. As the essential element of a loan is the option of using the goods loaned, it must be observed that the national legislation at issue in the main proceedings, by requiring residents of the Netherlands to pay a tax on first use of a vehicle registered in another Member State on the road network in the Netherlands, including where that vehicle was loaned free of charge by a resident of another Member State, results in the taxation of cross-border loans free of charge of motor vehicles.

40. On the other hand, loans of a motor vehicle for use free of charge are not subject to that tax where the vehicle is registered in the Netherlands. Such a difference, or at least apparent difference, in treatment according to the State in which the loaned vehicle is registered is, therefore, liable to make such cross border capital movements less attractive, by dissuading residents of the Netherlands from accepting loans offered by residents of another Member State of a vehicle registered in that State. Measures taken by a Member State which are liable to dissuade its residents from obtaining loans or making investments in other Member States constitute restrictions on movements of capital within the meaning of that provision (see Case C-478/98 *Commission* v *Belgium* [2000] ECR I-7587, paragraph 18 and the case-law cited).

41. Such national legislation therefore constitutes a restriction on the free movement of capital for the purposes of Article 56(1) EC.

42. However, the question whether there is actually such a difference of treatment must be examined and, if there is, whether it is none the less compatible with the provisions of the Treaty concerning free movement of capital.

43. According to the case-law of the Court the principle of non-discrimination, whether it has its basis in Article 12 EC or Articles 39 EC, 43 EC or 56 EC, requires that comparable situations must not be treated differently and that different situations must not be treated in the same way (see, to that effect, Case C-155/09 *Commission* v *Greece* [2011] ECR I-0000, paragraph 68 and the case-law cited).

44. Accordingly, it must first be considered whether, in circumstances such as those of the disputes in the main proceedings, the situation of a resident of the Netherlands who uses on the road network in the Netherlands a vehicle registered in that Member State made available to him free of charge is objectively comparable to that of a resident of the Netherlands who uses, on the same conditions, a vehicle registered in another Member State. Even if such a situation is comparable, it must be examined, secondly, whether they were treated equally or, if they were treated differently, whether the difference was justified by an overriding reason in the general interest and, finally, whether the measure at issue is consistent with the principle of proportionality.

45. In that connection, while it is true that the owners of vehicles registered in the Netherlands have already paid vehicle tax when the vehicle was entered on the vehicle register in the Netherlands, the fact none the less remains that, as a rule, those vehicles are intended to be used essentially in that Member State on a permanent basis or that they are, in fact, used in that way.

46. The Court has already held that a Member State may impose a registration tax on a motor vehicle registered in another Member State where that vehicle is intended to be used essentially in the first Member State on a permanent basis or where it is, in fact, used in that manner (see, to that effect, *Cura Anlagen*, paragraph 42; *Commission* v *Denmark*, paragraphs 75 to 78; *Nadin and Nadin-Lux*, paragraph 41; and *Commission* v *Finland*, paragraph 47, and the orders in *van de Coevering*, paragraph 24, and *Vandermeir*, paragraph 32).

47. However, if those conditions are not satisfied, the connection with one Member State of the vehicle registered in another Member State is weaker, so that another justification for the restriction in question is necessary (see *Commission* v *Denmark*, paragraph 79;*Commission* v *Finland*, paragraph 48; and orders in *van de Coevering*, paragraph 26, and *Vandermeir*, paragraph 33).

48. According to the order for reference the defendants in the main proceedings had to pay the full amount of the vehicle tax, as the amount was calculated without any account being taken of the duration of the use of the vehicles concerned and without the users of those vehicles having been able to invoke any right to exemption or reimbursement. However, it is not apparent from the documents submitted to the Court that those vehicles are intended to be used essentially in the Netherlands on a permanent basis or that they are, in fact, used in that way.

49. It is therefore the task of the national court to assess the duration of the loans at issue in the main proceedings and how the loaned vehicles have in fact been used (see the order in *van de Coevering*, paragraph 25).

50. Thus, if the vehicles at issue in the main proceedings, which are not registered in the Netherlands, are intended to be used essentially in the Netherlands on a permanent basis or if they are, in fact, used in that way, there is not actually a difference in the treatment of a person who resides in the Netherlands and uses such a vehicle free of charge and a person who uses a vehicle registered in that Member State on the same conditions, since the latter vehicle, which is also intended to be used essentially in the Netherlands on a permanent basis, was already subject to vehicle tax on its first registration in the Netherlands.

51. In those circumstances, the charging of vehicle tax on first use on the road network in the Netherlands of vehicles which are not registered in the Netherlands, is justified in the same way as the tax due on the registration of the vehicle in the Nether-

lands, mentioned in paragraph 46 of the present judgment, is, provided that the tax takes account, as appears to be required by the 1992 Law, of the depreciation of the vehicle at the time of that first use.

52. On the other hand, as is apparent from paragraph 47 of the present judgment, if the vehicles at issue in the main proceedings were not intended to be used essentially in the Netherlands on a permanent basis or were not, in fact, used in that way, there would be a difference in treatment between the two categories of persons mentioned in paragraph 50 of the present judgment and the charging of the tax concerned would not be justified. In such circumstances, the connection of those vehicles with the Netherlands would be insufficient to justify the charging of a tax normally due on registration of a vehicle in the Netherlands.

53. Even if such a difference in treatment might, in some circumstances, be justified by an overriding reason in the general interest, it is also necessary for the tax to comply with the principle of proportionality (see, to that effect, the order in *van de Coevering*, paragraph 27 and the case-law cited).

54. Since, on the one hand, it is not apparent from the order for reference that, in the disputes in the main proceedings, it has been established that the vehicles in question are intended to be used essentially in the Netherlands on a permanent basis or that they are, in fact, used in that way and, on the other hand, neither the referring court nor the Netherlands Government has put forward other overriding reasons in the general interest to justify the restriction at issue, it must be held that Article 56 EC must be interpreted as meaning that it precludes legislation of a Member State which requires residents who have borrowed a vehicle registered in another Member State from a resident of that State to pay, on first use of that vehicle on the national road network, the full amount of a tax normally due on registration of a vehicle in the first Member State, without taking account of the duration of the use of that vehicle on that road network and without that person being able to invoke a right to exemption or reimbursement where that vehicle is neither intended to be used essentially in the first Member State on a permanent basis nor, in fact, used in that way.

55. Since the cases in the main proceedings fall within the scope of Article 56 EC, it is not necessary to rule on the interpretation of Article 18 EC.

56. In the light of the foregoing, the answer to the questions referred is that Article 56 EC must be interpreted as meaning that it precludes legislation of a Member State which requires residents who have borrowed a vehicle registered in another Member State from a resident of that State to pay, on first use of that vehicle on the national road network, the full amount of a tax normally due on registration of a vehicle in the first Member State, without taking account of the duration of the use of that vehicle on that road network and without that person being able to invoke a

right to exemption or reimbursement where that vehicle is neither intended to be used essentially in the first Member State on a permanent basis nor, in fact, used in that way.

Costs

[Para. 57 omitted]

On those grounds,

THE COURT (Third Chamber),

hereby rules:

Article 56 EC must be interpreted as meaning that it precludes legislation of a Member State which requires residents who have borrowed a vehicle registered in another Member State from a resident of that State to pay, on first use of that vehicle on the national road network, the full amount of a tax normally due on registration of a vehicle in the first Member State, without taking account of the duration of the use of that vehicle on that road network and without that person being able to invoke a right to exemption or reimbursement where that vehicle is neither intended to be used essentially in the first Member State on a permanent basis nor, in fact, used in that way.

Comments and questions

In the *van Putten* case a Dutch court had to consider the imposition of a tax on motor vehicles in three cases in which Union citizens (two Dutchmen and one German) resident in the Netherlands had used the vehicles in the Netherlands but where the vehicles had been lent to them by a family member or friend who was resident in another Member State – where the vehicles were registered and where tax had been paid on the vehicles. The Dutch court thought that the imposition of the tax could conflict with the right of Union citizens to move freely in the territories of the Member States, and thus it referred the question to the CJEU for a preliminary ruling.

However, the CJEU took a very different approach to the question. Its starting point was that when something is lent from a Union citizen who is resident in one Member State to a Union citizen who is resident in another Member State, in principle this is a matter that is regulated by the Treaty rules on the free movement of capital. The CJEU based this approach on the nomenclature contained in Annex I to Directive 88/361. Even though this (old) Directive was adopted on the basis of Articles 69 and 70(1) of the EEC Treaty (Articles 67-73 of the EEC Treaty have been replaced, and the relevant provisions are now to be found in Articles 63-66 TFEU), the CJEU still finds the nomenclature a valid guideline for determining whether a matter is covered by the rules on capital movements, even though the nomenclature is not regarded as being exhaustive in this respect. According to the nomenclature, a 'loan' is covered, whether or not it is made for consideration. The CJEU also remarked that 'in order to determine whether the tax treatment by a Member State of certain transactions is covered by the provisions on the free movement of capital, there is no need to distinguish between transactions effected in money and those effected in kind'. The CJEU also noted that the loan of a motor vehicle for use free of charge constitutes a benefit which represents a specific economic value, corresponding to the cost of use of a hire car of the same type and for the same period. On this basis the CJEU concluded that the cross-border lending of a vehicle free of charge constituted a capital movement within the meaning of Article 63 TFEU.

Since it was established that the situation should be assessed pursuant to the Treaty-based freedom of movement of capital, it was then necessary to clarify whether the Dutch imposition of a tax constituted a hindrance to this freedom. The CJEU found that it was a hindrance. On what did it place special emphasis in this regard?

Since there was a hindrance to the free movement of capital, the Dutch demand for tax could only be lawful if the Dutch authorities could substantiate that the tax pursued a lawful purpose, and that there was proportionality between the purpose pursued and the restriction on free movement caused by the tax. In its decision, the CJEU let it be understood that the proportionality principle had not been satisfied. To what did the CJEU attach particular weight in this respect?

Consider whether a German national who is permanently resident in Denmark can claim that the Union rules on the free movement of capital mean that he is lawfully entitled to drive a German-registered car in Denmark, even though Danish tax has not been paid on the vehicle, on the basis that the German national has had the car lent to him. Is it relevant whether the use of the car is for permanent or short-term use? Is it relevant whether the car is lent to the German national by a family member or by a company which is 100% owned by the German national himself? Is it relevant that, in calculating the tax, the Danish authorities have taken account of the amount of the use of the car (the duration of the loan)? See also the judgment in Case C-464/02 Commission v Denmark (the Company car case) [2005] ECR I-7929, printed in Chapter 4 above.

JUDGMENT OF THE COURT (Sixth Chamber)
5 March 2002

Hans Reisch and Others v Bürgermeister der Landeshauptstadt Salzburg and Grundverkehrsbeauftragter des Landes Salzburg and Anton Lassacher and Others v Grundverkehrsbeauftragter des Landes Salzburg and Grundverkehrslandeskommission des Landes Salzburg.
(References for a preliminary ruling: Unabhängiger Verwaltungssenat Salzburg – Austria)

'Free movement of capital – Article 56 EC – Prior notification and authorisation procedure for the acquisition of building plots – Absence of purely internal situation'

Joined Cases C-515/99, C-519/99 to C-524/99 and C-526/99 to C-540/99

Judgment

1. By 22 orders dated 22 December 1999, received at the Court on 30 December 1999, the Unabhängiger Verwaltungssenat Salzburg (Independent Administrative Chamber, Salzburg) referred to the Court for a preliminary ruling under Article 234 EC two questions on the interpretation of Articles 56 EC to 60 EC.

2. In Cases C-515/99 and C-527/99 to C-540/99, a first question was raised in the course of actions brought against decisions of the Bürgermeister der Landeshauptstadt Salzburg (Mayor of Salzburg) imposing fines for late notification, as provided for in the Salzburger Grundverkehrsgesetz 1997 (Salzburg Land Transfer Law, Salzburg LGBl. No 11/97, hereinafter 'the SGVG'), to the Grundverkehrsbeauftragter des Landes Salzburg (land transfer agent of the Land of Salzburg, responsible for receiving the notification from acquirers of title in immovable property, hereinafter 'the Grundverkehrsbeauftragter').

3. In Cases C-519/99 to C-524/99 and C-526/99, a second question arose in the course of appeals against decisions of the Grundverkehrslandeskommission des Landes Salzburg (Land Transfer Commission of the Land of Salzburg, hereinafter 'the Grundverkehrslandeskommission') adopted pursuant to the SGVG, opposing the acquisition of building plots or authorising such acquisition only subject to provision of security.

The legal background

Community law

4. Article 56(1) EC provides:

   'Within the framework of the provisions set out in this chapter, all restrictions on the movement of capital between Member States and between Member States and third countries shall be prohibited.'

National legislation

5. Under Austrian law, ownership of immovable property is acquired by means of an entry in the land register confirmed by the Grundbuchsgericht (Land Registry Court), which is required to determine whether authorisation is necessary for the transfer and, if so, whether that authorisation has been granted.

6. In the Land of Salzburg, Paragraph 12 of the SGVG provides that certain legal transactions relating to building plots, such as the transfer of ownership or the grant of a right to build, are permissible only where the acquirer of title submits a declaration stating, first, that he is an Austrian national, or a national of another Member State exercising one of the freedoms guaranteed by the EC Treaty or the Agreement on the European Economic Area. The acquirer of title must, secondly, declare that the land will be used as his principal residence or to meet a commercial need. Use of the land as a secondary residence is possible only if the land was already used for that purpose before 1 March 1993 or if it is located in an area in which secondary residences are permitted.

7. On the basis of the declaration referred to in the preceding paragraph, the Grundverkehrsbeauftragter issues confirmation. He may only refuse to do so if there are grounds for suspecting that the property will not be used for the purpose stated in the declaration or if the acquisition is inconsistent with the aims of the SGVG. In that case the Grundverkehrsbeauftragter refers the acquirer of title to the Grundverkehrslandeskommission, which may authorise the transfer after ascertaining that the same substantive criteria relating to prohibition of use as a secondary residence have been met.

8. In the absence of confirmation from the Grundverkehrsbeauftragter or authorisation from the Grundverkehrslandeskommission no land may be acquired in the Land of Salzburg.

9. Paragraph 19 of the SGVG requires the acquirer of title to use the land in accordance with the declaration referred to in Paragraph 12 of the SGVG. Paragraph 19 also enables the Grundverkehrslandeskommission to attach conditions and require-

ments to its authorisation in order to ensure that the acquirer of title uses the land for the stated purpose, in particular by requiring security in an amount not exceeding the purchase price or the value of the land.

10. Paragraph 36 of the SGVG lays down the time-limits within which the acquirer of title must lodge the declaration of acquisition.

11. Under Paragraph 42 of the SGVG the Grundverkehrsbeauftragter may bring before the national court an action for annulment of the property transaction where this is intended to circumvent the application of the SGVG.

12. Paragraph 43 of the SGVG provides for fines of up to ATS 500 000 and sentences of imprisonment of up to six weeks, inter alia where the acquirer of title has failed to submit the necessary declaration or to apply for the necessary authorisation, or if he uses the land for an unauthorised purpose.

The main proceedings and the questions referred for a preliminary ruling

13. In Cases C-515/99 and C-527/99 to C-540/99 the Mayor of Salzburg imposed a fine on each of the applicants for failure to notify to the Grundverkehrsbeauftragter within the period laid down by Paragraph 36 of the SGVG a legal transaction relating to the acquisition of building plots. They appealed against those decisions to the Unabhängiger Verwaltungssenat Salzburg.

14. In Cases C-519/99 to C-522/99 and C-526/99, the Grundverkehrslandeskommission did not grant at first instance the authorisation necessary for the sale of building plots, and the acquirers of title appealed against the corresponding decisions to the Unabhängiger Verwaltungssenat Salzburg.

15. In Cases C-523/99 and C-524/99, the Grundverkehrslandeskommission granted authorisation to acquire building plots but required that security be provided pursuant to Paragraph 19(3) of the SGVG. The acquirers of title appealed against the corresponding decisions to the Unabhängiger Verwaltungssenat Salzburg.

16. In the light of the judgment in Case C-302/97 *Konle* [1999] ECR I-3099, which concerned the legislation of the Land of Tyrol on land transactions, the referring court was concerned with the issue whether the requirement of prior notification/authorisation in respect of the acquisition of building plots and the criminal sanctions attaching to failure to fulfil that requirement were compatible with the fundamental freedoms of the Treaty.

17. Accordingly, the Unabhängiger Verwaltungssenat Salzburg referred to the Court for a preliminary ruling the following questions:

In Cases C-515/99 and C-527/99 to C-540/99:

'Are the provisions of Article 56 EC et seq. to be interpreted as precluding the application of Paragraphs 12, 36 and 43 of the SGVG 1997 in the version published in LGBl. No 11/99, whereby any person who wishes to acquire a building plot in the federal Land of Salzburg must comply with a notification or authorisation procedure in respect of the acquisition of that plot, with the consequence that one of the fundamental freedoms of the acquirer of title as guaranteed by the laws of the European Union has been infringed in this case?'

In Cases C-519/99 to C-524/99 and C-526/99:

'Are the provisions of Article 56 EC et seq. to be interpreted as precluding the application of Paragraphs 12 to 14 of the SGVG 1997 in the version published in LGBl. No 11/99, whereby any person who wishes to acquire a building plot in the federal Land of Salzburg must comply with a notification or authorisation procedure in respect of the acquisition of that plot, with the consequence that one of the fundamental freedoms of the acquirer of title as guaranteed by the laws of the European Union has been infringed in this case?'

18. Cases C-515/99 and C-527/99 to C-540/99 were joined for the purposes of the written and oral procedure and of the judgment by order of the President of the Court of Justice of 24 February 2000. Cases C-519/99 to C-524/99 and C-526/99 were also joined for the purposes of the written and oral procedure and of the judgment by order of the President of the Court of Justice of 24 February 2000.

19. For the purposes of the present judgment, it is appropriate to order the joinder of all those cases.

The questions referred for a preliminary ruling

Admissibility

20. GWP Gewerbeparkentwicklung GmbH submits, first, that the question referred for a preliminary ruling in Cases C-519/99 to C-524/99 and C-526/99 is inadmissible since it does not concern the interpretation of the Treaty, but the interpretation or assessment of the validity of the provisions of the SGVG, which are matters for the national court alone.

21. Secondly, it considers that the main proceedings to which it is a party, which concern only the conditions for the acquisition by an Austrian company of land in Austria pursuant to the SGVG, have no connection with Community law and relate to a purely internal situation, thereby making the reference for a preliminary ruling inadmissible.

22. It will be recalled in respect of the first submission that, although the Court has no jurisdiction under Article 234 EC to apply a rule of Community law to a particular case and thus to judge a provision of national law by reference to such a rule it may, in the framework of the judicial cooperation provided for by that article and on the basis of the material presented to it, provide the national court with an interpretation of Community law which may be useful to it in assessing the effects of that provision (Case 20/87 *Gauchard* [1987] ECR 4879, paragraph 5).

23. In the main proceedings, the referring court asks the Court to interpret Treaty provisions solely for the purposes of determining whether those provisions are capable of affecting the effects of national rules which the referring court is required to apply. It cannot therefore be maintained that the purpose of the question referred for a preliminary ruling in each of the cases is anything other than the interpretation of provisions of the Treaty.

24. As for the second submission, it is apparent from the documents in the case file, and it is not, moreover, in dispute, that all the facts in the main proceedings are confined to a single Member State. National legislation such as the SGVG, which applies without distinction to Austrian nationals and to nationals of Member States of the European Communities, may generally fall within the scope of the provisions on the fundamental freedoms established by the Treaty only to the extent that it applies to situations related to intra-Community trade (see, to that effect, Case 286/81 *Oosthoek's Uitgeversmaatschappij* [1982] ECR 4575, paragraph 9, and Case 98/86 *Mathot* [1987] ECR 809, paragraphs 8 and 9).

25. However, that finding does not mean that there is no need to reply to the questions referred to the Court for a preliminary ruling in this case. In principle, it is for the national courts alone to determine, having regard to the particular features of each case, both the need for a preliminary ruling in order to enable them to give their judgment and the relevance of the questions which they refer to the Court (see Case C-448/98 *Guimont* [2000] ECR I-10663, paragraph 22). A reference for a preliminary ruling from a national court may be rejected by the Court only if it is quite obvious that the interpretation of Community law sought by that court bears no relation to the actual nature of the case or the subject-matter of the main action (see Case C-281/98 *Angonese* [2000] ECR I-4139, paragraph 18).

26. In this case, it is not obvious that the interpretation of Community law requested is not necessary for the referring court. Such a reply might be useful to it if its national law were to require that an Austrian national must be allowed to enjoy the same rights as those which a national of another Member State would derive from Community law in the same situation (Guimont, cited above, paragraph 23).

27. Accordingly, it is necessary to consider whether the provisions of the Treaty, interpretation of which is sought, preclude the application of national legislation such as

that in issue in the main proceedings to the extent that it is applied to persons resident in other Member States.

Substance

28. It should be stated, as a preliminary point, that national legislation which regulates the acquisition of land for the purposes of prohibiting, in the interests of regional planning, the establishment of secondary residences in certain areas must comply with the provisions of the Treaty on the free movement of capital (Konle, cited above, paragraph 22).

29. First, as is apparent from Article 44(2)(e) EC, the right to acquire, use or dispose of immovable property on the territory of another Member State, which is the corollary of freedom of establishment (Case 305/87 Commission v Greece [1989] ECR 1461, paragraph 22), generates capital movements when it is exercised.

30. Secondly, as is clear from the nomenclature of capital movements set out in Annex I to Council Directive 88/361/EEC of 24 June 1988 for the implementation of Article 67 of the Treaty (repealed by the Treaty of Amsterdam) (OJ 1988 L 178, p. 5), capital movements include investments in real estate on the territory of a Member State by non-residents. That nomenclature still has the same indicative value for the purposes of defining the notion of capital movements (see Case C-222/97 *Trummer and Mayer* [1999] ECR I-1661, paragraph 21, and Case C-464/98 *Stefan* [2001] ECR I-173, paragraph 5).

31. It is therefore necessary, as the referring court requests the Court to do, to determine the scope of the national measures in issue in the main proceedings in the light of Articles 56 EC to 60 EC.

32. It is not in dispute that those measures, by laying down a procedure of prior notification/authorisation for the acquisition of immovable property, restrict, by their very purpose, the free movement of capital (see, to that effect, Konle, cited above, paragraph 39).

33. Such restrictions may nevertheless be permitted if the national rules pursue, in a non-discriminatory way, an objective in the public interest and if they observe the principle of proportionality, that is if the same result could not be achieved by other less restrictive measures.

34. As regards the first requirement, it is apparent from paragraph 40 of the Konle judgment, cited above, that restrictions on the establishment of secondary residences in a specific geographical area, which a Member State imposes in order to maintain, for regional planning purposes, a permanent population and an economic activity independent of the tourist sector, may be regarded as contributing to an objec-

tive in the public interest. That finding can only be strengthened by the other concerns which may underly those same measures, such as protection of the environment. Moreover, it is apparent from the provisions of the SGVG that they do not discriminate between Austrian acquirers of title and persons resident in other Member States who exercise the freedoms guaranteed by the Treaty.

35. As regards the second requirement, the Court held, in paragraphs 44 to 48 of the Konle judgment, cited above, that a requirement of declaration prior to the purchase of building plots, coupled with the possibility of penalties for breach of the agreed declaration, for regional planning purposes, did comply with Community law. The procedure laid down by the SGVG is essentially declaratory in principle.

36. As the Austrian Government points out, it is only where the Grundverkehrsbeauftragter considers that there are grounds for believing that the property is not being used lawfully that he must refer the acquirer of title to the Grundverkehrslandeskommission for the transaction to be submitted to the authorisation procedure. That minimum requirement of prior notification has the advantage, unlike supervision procedures which are applied only a posteriori, of providing the acquirer of title with an element of legal certainty. Furthermore, it may be thought that prior examination is better suited to preventing certain damage, which is reparable only with difficulty, caused by hastily completed building projects. Thus, the formality of prior notification may be regarded as a step which is additional to the criminal sanctions and the action for annulment of the sale which the administrative authorities may bring before the national court. In those circumstances, this first aspect of the procedure instituted by the SGVG may be regarded as compatible with Community law.

37. As regards the procedure of prior authorisation before the Grundverkehrslandskommission, by contrast, the Court has already held that restrictions on the free movement of capital resulting from the requirement of prior authorisation were able to be eliminated by means of an appropriate notification system without thereby detracting from the effective pursuit of the aims of those rules (see Joined Cases C-358/93 and C-416/93 *Bordessa and Others* [1995] ECR I-361, paragraph 27, and Joined Cases C-163/94, C-165/94 and C-250/94 *Sanz de Lera and Others* [1995] ECR I-4821, paragraphs 26 and 27).

38. In the main proceedings, given the opportunity for supervision which the prior notification scheme affords to the public authority, the existence of criminal sanctions and a specific action for annulment which may be brought before the national court should the project carried out fail to comply with the initial declaration, the prior authorisation procedure, which the Grundverkehrsbeauftragter alone may initiate on the basis of mere presumptions, cannot be regarded as a measure which is strictly indispensable to prevent infringements of the legislation in issue in the main proceedings in respect of secondary residences. This is all the more so given that the

competent authorities may make the grant of prior authorisation subject to requirements on which the SGVG does not impose any substantive restriction, and require the acquirer of title to provide security up to the value of the property.

39. The provisions of the SGVG relating to the prior authorisation procedure before the Grundverkehrslandeskommission therefore go beyond both that which is necessary to achieve the chosen regional planning objective and the measures which Member States are entitled to take, as set out in Article 58(1)(b) EC, to prevent infringements of their laws and regulations.

40. Accordingly, the reply to the referring court should be that Articles 56 EC to 60 EC:

- do not preclude a prior notification procedure such as that laid down by the scheme for the acquisition of land established by the SGVG;
- preclude a prior authorisation procedure such as that laid down by that scheme.

Costs

[Para. 41 omitted]

On those grounds,

THE COURT (Sixth Chamber),

in answer to the questions referred to it by the Unabhängiger Verwaltungssenat Salzburg, by orders of 22 December 1999, hereby rules:

Articles 56 EC to 60 EC:

- **do not preclude a prior notification procedure such as that laid down by the scheme for the acquisition of land established by the Salzburger Grundverkehrsgesetz 1997;**
- **preclude a prior authorisation procedure such as that laid down by that scheme.**

Comments and questions

Joined Cases C-515/99 and others *Reisch and others* v *Bürgermeister der Landeshauptstadt Salzburg and others* [2002] ECR I-2157, concerned a local Austrian rule that land could only be purchased if the purchaser had either previously obtained a declaration (attestation) or in certain cases permission from the authorities. Infringement of this rule was subject to criminal sanctions. A number of Austrian nationals had either failed to obtain the necessary permission or had had their applications rejected. In other words, a number of Austrian nationals had come into conflict with the Austrian rules which governed the purchase of land in Austria. It was not disputed that all the main elements of the case were linked to one Member State, Austria. This prompted the question whether the CJEU should refuse to respond to the request for a preliminary ruling, on the grounds that the case lacked a necessary cross-border element. However, the CJEU chose to answer the question referred. It stated that, in principle, it is for the national courts alone to assess whether a preliminary ruling is necessary for them to give judgment, just as it is a matter for the national courts to decide on the relevance of the questions which they refer to the CJEU. Only if it is quite obvious that the interpretation of Union law sought by a referring court bears no relation to the actual nature of the case or the subject-matter of the main action will a reference from a national court for a preliminary ruling be rejected by the CJEU.

In paragraph 26 of the judgment, the CJEU referred to Case C-448/98 *Guimont* [2000] ECR I-10663, see Chapter 2, as an example of a case in which a national court needed a preliminary ruling, even though all the elements in the case were linked to one Member State. In the *Guimont* case, the legislation in the Member State in question (France) provided that the parties involved could not be placed in a worse position under purely national law than they would have been if the case had been judged under Union law. In the *Guimont* case it was therefore important to clarify what the position of the parties would have been under Union law.

In his Opinion on the *Reisch* case, Advocate General Geelhoed referred to the fact that the Austrian constitutional court had established that a principle similar to that in France also applied in Austria. In the *Reisch* case, did the CJEU seek to clarify whether the Advocate General's submission was correct? Would it be correct to explain the CJEU's decision in the *Reisch* case by saying that it effectively leaves it to the national courts to decide whether it is necessary to make a reference for a preliminary ruling, even in case where there is a purely internal situation, so that the CJEU will only refuse to give a ruling where the interpretation of Union law is so obviously irrelevant to the main case?

There can be doubt as to whether some given circumstances should be dealt with under Article 49, 56 or 63 TFEU. In Case C-208/00 *Überseering BV* v *Nordic Construction Company Baumanagement* [2002] ECR I-9919, referred to in the commentary on the *Centros* case in Chapter 5, the CJEU stated, in paragraph 77, that:

> 'it must be borne in mind that as a general rule the acquisition by one or more natural persons residing in a Member State of shares in a company incorporated and established in another Member State is covered by the [TFEU] provisions on the free movement of capital, provided that the shareholding does not confer on those natural persons definite influence over the company's decisions and does not allow them to determine its activities. By contrast, where the acquisition involves all the shares in a company having its registered office in another Member State and the shareholding confers a definite influence over the company's decisions and allows the sharehold-

ers to determine its activities, it is the [TFEU] provisions on freedom of establishment which apply'

As it appears from this, what was important in the decision was whether the acquisition of shares in the company involved obtaining a definite influence over the company. If this was the case, it would be a matter falling within the scope of Article 49 TFEU. If the acquisition did not give definite influence, the case would be dealt with as a matter of capital movement, under Article 63 TFEU.

As for the specific question in the *Reisch* case, the CJEU reasoned that the case concerned freedom of movement of capital. However, the Advocate General thought it was more correct to regard it as a case on the provision of services. Which view do you think is more correct, that of the CJEU or that of the Advocate General?

Having settled that the case concerned freedom of movement of capital, the CJEU made a classic review of the topic. First, it noted that national measures such as the Austrian rules, must respect the TFEU provisions on freedom of movement of capital. Then it noted that, by introducing a procedure for purchasers to submit a declaration or to obtain a permit before acquiring land, by their very purpose such measures restrict the movement of capital. However, such restrictions can be justified if they serve an overriding objective in the general interest, without being discriminating, and if they comply with the principle of proportionality. The CJEU found that the Austrian rules did pursue such an overriding objective in the general interest. It also found that the Austrian requirement for a purchaser to have prior permission was not proportionate. Why did the CJEU find that this requirement was not proportionate?

Note that, in principle, the TFEU rules on the free movement of capital only apply to Member State measures. Thus, the CJEU has not yet had referred to it the question of whether the rules on the free movement of capital are also binding on private undertakings, as is the case with the TFEU rules on the free movement of workers; see Case C-281/98 *Angonese* [2000] ECR I-4139, which is reproduced in Chapter 4 above.

The disputed rules were issued by the Salzburg regional authority. Why did the TFEU rules apply in the *Reisch* case?

The *Reisch* case together with Joined Cases C-358/93 and C-416/93 *Bordessa and others* [1995] ECR I-361 printed below, and other cases on the freedom of movement of capital show that, as a point of departure, the CJEU does not accept national measures, such as a licensing procedure, which hinder capital transactions themselves. On the other hand, Article 63 TFEU does not preclude requirements for reporting or for making declarations etc., where a transaction can take place without hindrance, but where subsequently the public authorities can step in, to control transactions on the basis of the information received.

Would it be incompatible with Article 63 TFEU for a Member State's legislation to allow undertakings to demand payment of a special fee for the use of foreign credit cards in a situation where there was a prohibition on demanding a corresponding fee for the use of credit cards issued in the Member State in question?

JUDGMENT OF THE COURT (Third Chamber)
25 January 2007

Criminal proceedings against Uwe Kay Festersen.
(Reference for a preliminary ruling from the Vestre Landsret – Denmark)

'Freedom of establishment – Free movement of capital – Articles 43 EC and 56 EC – Restrictions on the acquisition of agricultural property – Requirement that the acquirer take up fixed residence on the agricultural property'

Case C-370/05

Judgment

1. This reference for a preliminary ruling concerns the interpretation of Articles 43 EC and 56 EC.

2. The reference was made in the context of criminal proceedings brought against Mr Festersen for breach of the obligation to take up fixed residence on the agricultural property which he had acquired on the territory of the municipality of Bov in southern Jutland (Denmark).

National law

3. Under Paragraph 2 of the Danish Law on agriculture (landbrugsloven), in the version resulting from Codified Law No 598 (lovbekendtgørelse nr. 598) of 15 July 1999 ('the Law on agriculture'):

   '1. Agricultural properties shall be subject to an agricultural-use obligation under the provisions of this Law.

   2. 'Agricultural property' shall mean property which is registered as such in the land register.

   ...'

4. Paragraph 4(6) of the Law on agriculture provides:

   'When an agricultural property is divided up or otherwise reduced to a surface area of less than 2 hectares, the agricultural-use obligation shall no longer be applicable unless the owner wishes it still to apply. ...'

5. Under Paragraph 7 of that law:

'1. An agricultural property shall be maintained as an independent business and provided with an appropriate residential building from which the land shall be farmed by the residents, subject to Paragraph 8(4) and (6), Paragraph 9(1) and (2) and Paragraph 10.

2. The property shall be farmed properly having regard to the opportunities for commercial exploitation, the livestock health requirements, nature and the environment.

...'

6. Paragraph 16 of that law states:

'1. Title to an agricultural property which is situated in an agricultural zone and has an area exceeding 30 hectares may be acquired if:

...

(4) the acquirer takes up fixed residence on the property within six months after acquisition,

(5) the acquirer farms the property himself

...

2. Title to an agricultural property which has an area not exceeding 30 hectares may be acquired if the acquirer fulfils the requirements of subparagraph 1(1) to (4).

...'

7. Under Paragraph 18 of the Law on agriculture:

'1. Without prejudice to the cases covered by Paragraphs 16, 17 and 17a, title to an agricultural property in an agricultural zone may be acquired only with the authorisation of the Minister for Food, Agriculture and Fisheries.

...

4. The Minister may authorise the acquisition of an agricultural property, if:

(1) the acquisition is for the purposes of a use within the meaning of Paragraph 4(1)(1) and it is expected that the property will be used for the relevant purpose in the near future;

(2) the acquisition is for business purposes relating to a non-agricultural use which is otherwise to be regarded as desirable taking into account the general interests of society;

(3) the acquisition is for particular purposes, including use for scientific, training, general social, health or general recreational purposes;

(4) the acquisition is in connection with the creation of water meadows, the restoration of the environment or similar circumstances, or

(5) other special circumstances mitigate in its favour.

...'

8. Paragraph 27(2) of the Law on agriculture states:

'Where an application for authorisation to acquire or lease agricultural land is not submitted in due time, the competent minister may impose on the owner an order to dispose of the property within a period of a minimum of six months and a maximum of one year or impose on the tenant or lessee an order to cease use within a similar period. The same applies where authorisation is refused or lapses or the conditions placed on authorisation are not satisfied ...'

9. Paragraph 33 of that law provides:

'1. A fine shall be imposed on any person who:

...

(3) fails to comply with an order under Paragraph 8(5) and (7), Paragraph 9(5) or Paragraph 27.

...'

10. Under Paragraph 62 of Circular No 26 of 22 February 2000 relating to the Law on agriculture:

'Authorisation under Paragraph 18 of the Law [on agriculture] for the acquisition of agricultural property with an exemption from the residence requirement for an indefinite period may be granted only in exceptional cases (see Paragraph 16(1)(4) of the Law on agriculture). This applies for example in cases where due to the characteristics of the site it is physically impossible to fulfil the residence requirement for a large part of the year. The provision must be applied restrictively.'

11. According to Paragraph 4(1) of Decree No 627 of 26 July 1999 relating to training and residence requirements in connection with the Law on agriculture (bekendtgørelse nr. 627 af 26 juli 1999 om uddannelseskrav og bopælskrav m.v. i henhold til landbrugsloven), the requirement of fixed residence on an agricultural property presupposes that the person lives in a settled and continuous manner on that property and that he spends the night there, except in the event of special circumstances of fixed duration. That person must be listed in the local authority's population register

as residing at the property in such a way that it constitutes his principal residence for tax purposes.

12. Paragraph 4(2) of that decree provides that the acquirer must fulfil the residence requirement for eight years from the acquisition of an agricultural property.

The main proceedings and the questions referred for a preliminary ruling

13. Mr Festersen, a German national, acquired, in 1998, a property in southern Jutland which, according to the land register, is designated an agricultural property. It consists of two plots: one of an area of 0.24 hectares situated in an urban zone with buildings on it and the other, a piece of meadow land, of an area of 3.29 hectares situated in an agricultural zone.

14. Since Mr Festersen did not satisfy the requirement that residence be taken up on that property, the Agricultural Committee for Southern Jutland gave him notice to put his situation in order by ordering him, on 8 September 2000, to dispose of the property within six months, unless he had placed the ownership on a legal footing beforehand by acquiring an exemption from the agricultural-use obligation or by fulfilling the residence requirement.

15. On 16 July 2001 that committee gave Mr Festersen a new period of six months within which to dispose of the property, unless he took the necessary measures before that period expired, either to reduce the area of the property to under 2 hectares and at the same time seek an exemption from the agricultural-use obligation or to take up residence on the property.

16. On 18 August 2003, Mr Festersen was ordered by the District Court of Gråsten to pay a fine of DKK 5 000 on account of infringement of Paragraphs 33(1)(3) and 27(2) of the Law on agriculture, in that he had failed to comply with the order of the Agricultural Committee for Southern Jutland. He was also ordered to pay a penalty payment of DKK 5 000 for each month of delay if he failed to comply with that order by 1 December 2003.

17. Mr Festersen, who took up residence at the property on 12 June 2003, has been listed in the population register of the municipality of Bov as resident at that address since 12 September 2003.

18. He brought an appeal against his conviction before the Vestre Landsret (Western Regional Court) and claimed that it should be set aside. The prosecuting authorities contended that the judgment at first instance should be upheld.

19. Mr Festersen and the prosecuting authorities disagreed as to whether the residence requirement under the Law on agriculture was compatible with the principles of the

freedom of establishment and the free movement of capital as enshrined in Articles 43 EC and 56 EC.

20. Those were the circumstances in which the Vestre Landsret decided to stay the proceedings and to refer the following questions to the Court for a preliminary ruling:

    '1. Do Article 43 EC and Article 56 EC preclude a Member State from laying down as a condition for acquiring an agricultural property the requirement that the acquirer take up fixed residence on that property?

    2. Does it matter, as regards the answer to Question 1, that the property cannot constitute a self-sustaining unit and that the property's residential building is situated in an urban zone?'

The questions referred

The first question

21. By its first question the national court is effectively asking whether the provisions of the EC Treaty concerning the right of establishment (Article 43 EC) and the free movement of capital (Article 56 EC) preclude national legislation such as that at issue in the main proceedings from laying down as a condition for acquiring an agricultural property the requirement that the acquirer take up his fixed residence on that property.

22. It should be recalled at the outset that the right to acquire, use or dispose of immovable property on the territory of another Member State, which is the corollary of freedom of establishment, as is apparent from Article 44(2)(e) EC (Case 305/87 *Commission* v *Greece* [1989] ECR 1461, paragraph 22), generates capital movements when it is exercised (Joined Cases C-515/99, C-519/99 to C-524/99 and C-526/99 to C-540/99 *Reisch and Others* [2002] ECR I-2157, paragraph 29).

23. As is clear from the nomenclature of capital movements set out in Annex I to Council Directive 88/361/EEC of 24 June 1988 for the implementation of Article 67 of the Treaty (article repealed by the Treaty of Amsterdam) (OJ 1988 L 178, p. 5), capital movements include investments in real estate on the territory of a Member State by non-residents. That nomenclature still has the same indicative value for the purposes of defining the notion of capital movements (see Case C-222/97 *Trummer and Mayer* [1999] ECR I-1661, paragraph 21; Case C-464/98 *Stefan* [2001] ECR I-173, paragraph 5; *Reisch and Others*, paragraph 30; and Case C-386/04 *Centro di Musicologia Walter Stauffer* [2006] ECR I-0000, paragraph 22).

24. It must thus be examined whether national legislation such as that at issue in the main proceedings constitutes a restriction on capital movements. In that regard, it follows from settled case-law that the measures prohibited by Article 56(1) EC, as restrictions on the movement of capital, include those which are likely to discourage non-residents from making investments in a Member State or to discourage that Member State's residents to do so in other States (see, to that effect, Case C-513/03 *Van Hilten-van der Heijden* [2006] ECR I-1957, paragraph 44).

25. Although the Danish legislation on agriculture does not discriminate between Danish nationals and nationals of the other Member States of the European Union or the European Economic Area the fact nevertheless remains that the residence requirement which it imposes and which may be waived only with the authorisation of the minister responsible for agriculture restricts the free movement of capital.

26. Such a measure may nevertheless be permitted provided that it pursues an objective in the public interest, that it is applied in a non-discriminatory way and that it respects the principle of proportionality, that is to say that it is appropriate for ensuring that the aim pursued is achieved and does not go beyond what is necessary for that purpose (Case C-302/97 *Konle* [1999] ECR I-3099, paragraph 40; *Reisch and Others*, paragraph 33; and Case C-452/01 *Ospelt and Schlössle Weissenberg* [2003] ECR I-9743, paragraph 34).

27. As regards the condition relating to the pursuance of an objective in the public interest, the Danish Government submits that the national legislation seeks, first, to preserve the farming of agricultural land by means of owner-occupancy, which constitutes one of the traditional forms of farming in Denmark, and to ensure that agricultural property be occupied and farmed predominantly by the owners, second, as a town and country planning measure, to preserve a permanent agricultural community and, third, to encourage a reasonable use of the available land by resisting pressure on land.

28. Such objectives are themselves in the public interest and are capable of justifying restrictions to the free movement of capital (see, to that effect, *Konle*, paragraph 40; *Reisch and Others*, paragraph 34; and *Ospelt and Schlössle Weissenberg*, paragraphs 38 and 39). In addition, as the Danish Government and the Commission of the European Communities maintain, those objectives are consistent with those of the common agricultural policy which, under Article 33(1)(b) EC, aims 'to ensure a fair standard of living for the agricultural community' in the working-out of which, according to Article 33(2)(a), account must be taken 'of the particular nature of agricultural activity, which results from the social structure of agriculture and from structural and natural disparities between the various agricultural regions' (see, to that effect, *Ospelt and Schlössle Weissenberg*, paragraph 40).

29. As regards the condition of proportionality, it is necessary to check whether the requirement that the acquirer take up his fixed residence on the agricultural property acquired constitutes, as submitted by the Danish and Norwegian Governments, an appropriate and necessary measure for the attainment of the objectives mentioned in paragraph 27 above.

30. As regards whether the national measure at issue in the main proceedings is appropriate, it must be observed that it contains only a residence requirement and is not coupled, for an acquirer of an agricultural property of less than 30 hectares, with a requirement to farm the property personally. Such a measure thus does not appear, in itself, to ensure the attainment of the alleged objective seeking to preserve the traditional form of farming by owner-occupiers.

31. It is true that, as regards the second aim assigned to the Law on agriculture, the residence requirement is likely to contribute, by definition, to preserving an agricultural community and it can be met even further by farmers who, in accordance with one of the general objectives of the Law on agriculture seeking to encourage the owner-occupancy form of farming, personally farm their own land.

32. However, in the light of the phenomena of both reduction of the number of farms and regrouping of farms, as is apparent from the written observations lodged before the Court, and which were not challenged at the hearing, the objective of preserving an agricultural community cannot be met where the acquisition is made by a farmer who is already resident on another farm. In such a situation, the residence requirement does not guarantee the attainment of that objective, and thus it does not appear that that requirement is, in actual fact, appropriate, in itself, for the purpose of attaining such an objective.

33. In relation to the third aim which the Law on agriculture seeks to attain, it must be found that the residence requirement can reduce the number of potential acquirers of agricultural property and, consequently, it is capable of reducing the pressure on that land. It can therefore be accepted that national legislation containing such a requirement, which seeks to avoid the acquisition of agricultural land for purely speculative reasons, and which is thus likely to facilitate the preferential appropriation of that land by persons wishing to farm it does pursue a public interest objective in a Member State in which agricultural land is, and this is not challenged, a limited natural resource.

34. It is thus necessary to ascertain whether the residence requirement constitutes a measure which does not go beyond what is necessary to attain such an objective.

35. In such an assessment account must be taken of the fact that that requirement restricts not only the free movement of capital but also the right of the acquirer to choose his place of residence freely, a right which he is, however, guaranteed by

Article 2(1) of Protocol No 4 to the Convention for the Protection of Human Rights and Fundamental Freedoms, signed in Rome on 4 November 1950 ('the ECHR').

36. Article 6(2) EU states that 'the Union shall respect fundamental rights, as guaranteed by the [ECHR] and as they result from the constitutional traditions common to the Member States, as general principles of Community law' (Case C-540/03 *Parliament* v *Council* [2006] ECR I-0000, paragraph 36).

37. Given that the residence requirement thus adversely affects a fundamental right guaranteed by the ECHR, it therefore turns out to be particularly restrictive. The question thus arises whether other measures less restrictive than that requirement could have been adopted.

38. In that regard, the Danish Government submits that the requirement in question cannot be replaced by less restrictive measures which would be equally effective in preventing prices of agricultural land intended for production from being affected by an application motivated only by the desire to make investments to the detriment of professional farmers.

39. Although that government submits that the only solution remaining for maintaining prices at the desired level is State regulation of those prices, it does not state, however, in what way such a measure would be more restrictive than the residence requirement adopted. Nor did it justify in what way another measure, mentioned in the file, of incentives to lease residences acquired on agricultural property would prove to be more restrictive than that requirement. In the Danish Government's observations there was also no mention or evaluation of other measures capable, in some circumstances, of being less detrimental to the free movement of capital, such as provisions for higher tax on resale of land occurring shortly after acquisition, or even the requirement of a substantial minimum duration for leases of agricultural land.

40. Thus, none of the above enables the Court to find that the residence requirement is necessary to meet the objective sought.

41. Even supposing that that requirement is recognised as a measure necessary for meeting the objective sought on the ground that it would produce, by itself, positive effects on the property market (in the light of the constraints involved in any change of residence which in turn discourage property speculation), it must be pointed out that by coupling that requirement with a condition that residence be maintained for at least eight years, such an additional condition clearly goes beyond that which could be regarded as necessary, in particular as it implies a long-term suspension of the exercise of the fundamental freedom to choose one's place of residence.

42. It is true that, as submitted by the Danish Government, Paragraph 18 of the Law on agriculture enables the Minister for Food, Agriculture and Fisheries to authorise the acquisition of agricultural land with an indefinite exemption from the residence requirement. However, according to Circular No 26, the exercise of that power is strictly limited to 'exceptional cases' and must be 'applied restrictively'.

43. In addition, in providing only one example of such cases, that circular does not inform potential acquirers about the specific and objective situations in which a derogation from the residence requirement will be granted or refused. Such vagueness does not enable individuals to become familiar with the extent of their rights and obligations resulting from Article 56 EC, so that a system of that nature must be regarded as being contrary to the principle of legal certainty (see, to that effect, Case C-483/99 *Commission* v *France* [2002] ECR I-4781, paragraph 50, and Case C-463/00 *Commission* v *Spain* [2003] ECR I-4581, paragraphs 74 and 75). In any event, it does not appear that that system has taken into account the situation of citizens of the Union who are not resident in Denmark in order to avoid discriminatory application.

44. Accordingly, the residence requirement, particularly since it is coupled in this case with a condition that residence be maintained for eight years, to which the acquisition of agricultural properties of less than 30 hectares is made subject by the national legislation at issue in the main proceedings does not appear to be a measure which is proportionate to the objective pursued and therefore constitutes a restriction to the free movement of capital which is incompatible with Article 56 EC.

45. The Danish Government must be considered still to be claiming that the residence requirement at issue in the main proceedings must also fall within the derogation laid down in Protocol No 16 annexed to the Treaty, according to which 'notwithstanding the provisions of this Treaty, Denmark may maintain the existing legislation on the acquisition of second homes'.

46. It must however be found, in that regard, that the requirement to take up residence on the agricultural property acquired applies irrespective of whether the residence at issue is a principal or second home. Protocol No 16 cannot, therefore, effectively be relied on to justify such a requirement.

47. In the light of all the foregoing, there is no need to examine the questions concerning the interpretation of Article 43 EC.

48. The answer to the first question must therefore be that Article 56 EC precludes national legislation such as that at issue in the main proceedings from laying down as a condition for acquiring an agricultural property the requirement that the acquirer take up fixed residence on that property

The second question

49. By its second question the national court is effectively asking whether the interpretation of Article 56 EC required by the first question would be different where the agricultural property acquired did not constitute a viable farm and the residential building was situated in an urban zone.

50. It results from the answer to the first question that Article 56 EC precludes the residence requirement at issue, irrespective of particular circumstances relating to individual characteristics of the agricultural land concerned. Circumstances of that nature, such as those raised by the national court in its second question, are therefore irrelevant for the interpretation of that article.

51. Consequently, the answer to the second question must be that that interpretation of Article 56 EC would not be different where the agricultural property acquired did not constitute a viable farm and the residential building was situated in an urban zone.

Costs

[Para. 52 omitted]

On those grounds,

THE COURT (Third Chamber)

hereby rules:

1. **Article 56 EC precludes national legislation such as that at issue in the main proceedings from laying down as a condition for acquiring an agricultural property the requirement that the acquirer take up fixed residence on that property.**

2. **That interpretation of Article 56 EC would not be different where the agricultural property acquired did not constitute a viable farm and the residential building was situated in an urban zone.**

Comments and questions

The CJEU's judgment in Case C-370/05 *Criminal proceedings against Uwe Kay Festersen* [2007] ECR 1-1129, is a good example of the application of the proportionality principle. The case concerned a Danish requirement that a person acquiring agricultural land should live on the property for eight years. The referring national court asked for a preliminary ruling on whether the residence requirement constituted a restriction on freedom of establishment or to the free movement of capital. The CJEU considered the question solely on the basis of Article 63 TFEU (formerly Article 56 TEC). Why did the CJEU apply the rules of the free movement of capital, and not Article 49 TFEU?

The residence requirement applied, regardless of the nationality of the person acquiring the land, so there was not direct discrimination. However, the question was whether the Danish rule was a restriction. The CJEU stated that restrictions on the free movement of capital include measures 'which are likely to discourage non-residents from making investments in a Member State or to discourage that Member State's residents to do so in other States'. It was therefore a restriction to link a residence requirement to the acquisition of agricultural land.

Having established that there was a restriction, the CJEU had to consider whether the residence requirement was imposed in pursuit of a lawful purpose and whether the proportionality requirements were satisfied. The Danish Government referred to three factors which, in its opinion, each legitimised the residence requirement. First, the residence requirement served to maintain owner-occupation of agricultural land in Denmark, in other words that the owner of the land carries out the agricultural activities on it. Second, the residence requirement ensured that there was still a permanent population in rural districts. The requirement for land owners to live on their land should thus diminish the decline of the rural population. Finally, the requirement should promote the rational use of available land and reduce the pressure on land use. The argument here was that the residence requirement would reduce the pressure on the market for agricultural land, which in turn would reduce the risk that agricultural land would be acquired for purely speculative purposes. The residence requirement should thus help ensure that agricultural land should primarily be acquired by persons who wanted to use it for agricultural purposes.

The CJEU acknowledged that all three purposes served the public interest which could, in principle, justify a restriction on the free movement of capital. The next question was whether these three purposes satisfied the proportionality principle.

The proportionality principle requires, first, that the disputed measure is suitable for achieving the lawful purpose pursued. Second, the measure must be necessary in the sense that it must be the least restrictive for achieving the lawful purpose pursued. Third, the means must not be disproportionate in relation to the purpose.

Of the three purposes which the Danish Government put forward, the CJEU rejected the first two, because according to the CJEU they did not satisfy the requirement that the means used should be suitable for achieving the ends. Do you agree that the residence requirement is not a suitable means for achieving the end of owner-occupation and of limiting the depopulation of rural districts?

As for the aim that agricultural land should not be acquired for purely speculative purposes, the CJEU found that the residence requirement was a suitable measure. It was therefore necessary to consider whether the residence requirement was a measure which did not go beyond what was necessary for achieving its aims. In this connection the CJEU noted that the residence requirement not only restricted the free movement of capital, but also restricted the acquirer's right freely to choose where to live. This right, which is protected by the European Convention on Human Rights (ECHR), is a fundamental right in Union law. What role did this play in the CJEU's assessment of whether the residence requirement was in accordance with Article 63 TFEU on the free movement of capital?

The Danish Government argued that it was not possible to achieve the goal of ensuring that agricultural land should not be acquired for purely speculative purposes by using other less restrictive methods. The CJEU did not reject this in principle, but remarked that the stated end could have been achieved by several other means, and the Danish Government had not shown that these other means were more restrictive than the requirement that the acquirer should take up permanent residence on the agricultural land. Strictly speaking the CJEU did not reject the argument that the residence requirement could be a proportionate means, but it did not find that Denmark had sufficiently proved this in the actual case.

Consider whether the judgment means that Denmark is forced to repeal the residence requirement. Or would Denmark be able to maintain the residence requirement as long as in future it does not have to be the new owner but others, for example a tenant, who satisfies the residence requirement for eight years? If the judgment means that the residence requirement must be seen as unconditionally contrary to Union law, can the Danish authorities nevertheless maintain the requirement with regard to Danish citizens? Or would Danish citizens also be able to rely on the judgment in support of their right to acquire agricultural land without having a duty to reside on the property acquired?

It is notable that in paragraph 37 of the judgment, the CJEU stated that the residence requirement is contrary to Article 2(1) of Protocol No 4 of the ECHR, on the right freely to choose one's place of residence. This can hardly be right. First, it can be debated whether a residence requirement relating to a property which a person has freely chosen to buy, is covered by the provision at all. Second, it can be objected that even if a residence requirement does fall within the scope of this provision, the provision does not lay down absolute rights. Thus, according to the established practice of the European Court of Human Rights, a restriction of this right can be justified by overriding public interests, if the restriction is proportionate. By stating that the residence requirement is contrary to this provision the CJEU must necessarily have assumed that this requirement is 'particularly restrictive'. This statement is somewhat surprising, since if the residence requirement is contrary to the ECHR, it is also contrary to Union law, see for example Case C-112/00 *Eugen Schmidberger, Internationale Transporte und Planzüge* v *Austria* [2003] ECR I-5659, which is referred to above in the Comments and questions on Case C-265/95 *Commission* v *France* [1997] ECR I-6959 (the *Strawberries* case). Nevertheless, in paragraphs 38 *et seq.* of the *Festersen* case, the CJEU examined whether the residence requirement satisfied the proportionality principle. Do you agree with this legal method?

Chronological Table of Cases
of the European Court of Justice and the Court of First Instance

(In order of date when judgment was delivered)

1994

1995

1996

1997

2001

2002

2013

2014

2015

2016

Pending

Alphabetical Table of Cases of the European Court of Justice and the Court of First Instance

CS, Case C-304/14 563